11. Format for Bank Reconciliation:

Cash balance according to bank statement		$xxx
Add: Additions by company not on bank statement	$xx	
Bank errors	xx	xx
		$xxx
Deduct: Deductions by company not on bank statement	$xx	
Bank errors	xx	xx
Adjusted balance		$xxx
Cash balance according to company's records		$xxx
Add: Additions by bank not recorded by company ..	$xx	
Company errors..	xx	xx
		$xxx
Deduct: Deductions by bank not recorded by company..	$xx	
Company errors..	xx	xx
Adjusted balance		$xxx

12. Inventory Costing Methods:

1. First-in, First-out (FIFO)
2. Last-in, First-out (LIFO)
3. Average Cost

13. Interest Computations:

$$\text{Interest} = \text{Face Amount (or Principal)} \times \text{Rate} \times \text{Time}$$

14. Methods of Determining Annual Depreciation:

$$\text{STRAIGHT-LINE:} \ \frac{\text{Cost} - \text{Estimated Residual Value}}{\text{Estimated Life}}$$

DOUBLE-DECLINING-BALANCE: Rate* $\times$ Book Value at Beginning of Period

*Rate is commonly twice the straight-line rate (1 ÷ Estimated Life).

15. Adjustments to Net Income (Loss) Using the Indirect Method

	Increase (Decrease)
Net income (loss)	$ XXX
Adjustments to reconcile net income to net cash flow from operating activities:	
Depreciation of fixed assets	XXX
Amortization of intangible assets	XXX
Losses on disposal of assets	XXX
Gains on disposal of assets	(XXX)
Changes in current operating assets and liabilities:	
Increases in noncash current operating assets	(XXX)
Decreases in noncash current operating assets	XXX
Increases in current operating liabilities	XXX
Decreases in current operating liabilities	(XXX)
Net cash flow from operating activities	$ XXX
	or
	$(XXX)

16. Contribution Margin Ratio $= \dfrac{\text{Sales} - \text{Variable Costs}}{\text{Sales}}$

17. Break-Even Sales (Units) $= \dfrac{\text{Fixed Costs}}{\text{Unit Contribution Margin}}$

18. Sales (Units) $= \dfrac{\text{Fixed Costs} + \text{Target Profit}}{\text{Unit Contribution Margin}}$

19. Margin of Safety $= \dfrac{\text{Sales} - \text{Sales at Break-Even Point}}{\text{Sales}}$

20. Operating Leverage $= \dfrac{\text{Contribution Margin}}{\text{Income from Operations}}$

21. Variances

$$\begin{array}{l}\text{Direct Materials} \\ \text{Price Variance}\end{array} = \left(\begin{array}{l}\text{Actual Price} - \\ \text{Standard Price}\end{array}\right) \times \text{Actual Quantity}$$

$$\begin{array}{l}\text{Direct Materials} \\ \text{Quantity Variance}\end{array} = \left(\begin{array}{l}\text{Actual Quantity} - \\ \text{Standard Quantity}\end{array}\right) \times \begin{array}{l}\text{Standard} \\ \text{Price}\end{array}$$

$$\begin{array}{l}\text{Direct Labor} \\ \text{Rate Variance}\end{array} = \left(\begin{array}{l}\text{Actual Rate per Hour} - \\ \text{Standard Rate per Hour}\end{array}\right) \times \text{Actual Hours}$$

$$\begin{array}{l}\text{Direct Labor} \\ \text{Time Variance}\end{array} = \left(\begin{array}{l}\text{Actual Direct Labor Hours} - \\ \text{Standard Direct Labor Hours}\end{array}\right) \times \begin{array}{l}\text{Standard Rate} \\ \text{per Hour}\end{array}$$

$$\begin{array}{l}\text{Variable Factory} \\ \text{Overhead Controllable} \\ \text{Variance}\end{array} = \begin{array}{l}\text{Actual Variable} \\ \text{Factory} \\ \text{Overhead}\end{array} - \begin{array}{l}\text{Budgeted Variable} \\ \text{Factory Overhead}\end{array}$$

$$\begin{array}{l}\text{Fixed Factory} \\ \text{Overhead} \\ \text{Volume} \\ \text{Variance}\end{array} = \left(\begin{array}{l}\text{Standard Hours} \\ \text{for 100\% of} \\ \text{Normal} \\ \text{Capacity}\end{array} - \begin{array}{l}\text{Standard} \\ \text{Hours for} \\ \text{Actual Units} \\ \text{Produced}\end{array}\right) \times \begin{array}{l}\text{Fixed Factory} \\ \text{Overhead} \\ \text{Rate}\end{array}$$

22. Rate of Return on Investment (ROI) $= \dfrac{\text{Income from Operations}}{\text{Invested Assets}}$

Alternative ROI Computation:

$$\text{ROI} = \frac{\text{Income from Operations}}{\text{Sales}} \times \frac{\text{Sales}}{\text{Invested Assets}}$$

23. Capital Investment Analysis Methods:

1. Methods That Ignore Present Values:
   A. Average Rate of Return Method
   B. Cash Payback Method
2. Methods That Use Present Values:
   A. Net Present Value Method
   B. Internal Rate of Return Method

24. Average Rate of Return $= \dfrac{\text{Estimated Average Annual Income}}{\text{Average Investment}}$

25. Present Value Index $= \dfrac{\text{Total Present Value of Net Cash Flow}}{\text{Amount to Be Invested}}$

26. Present Value Factor for an Annuity of $1 $= \dfrac{\text{Amount to Be Invested}}{\text{Equal Annual Net Cash Flows}}$

WARREN REEVE DUCHAC

FINANCIAL ACCOUNTING

12e

Carl S. Warren
Professor Emeritus of Accounting
University of Georgia, Athens

James M. Reeve
Professor Emeritus of Accounting
University of Tennessee, Knoxville

Jonathan E. Duchac
Professor of Accounting
Wake Forest University

SOUTH-WESTERN
CENGAGE Learning

Australia • Brazil • Japan • Korea • Mexico • Singapore • Spain • United Kingdom • United States

Financial Accounting 12e

Carl S. Warren
James M. Reeve
Jonathan E. Duchac

Vice President of Editorial, Business: Jack W. Calhoun

Editor-in-Chief: Rob Dewey

Executive Editor: Sharon Oblinger

Developmental Editor: Tracy Newman

Editorial Assistant: Courtney Doyle

Marketing Coordinator: Nicki Parsons

Sr. Marketing Manager: Kristen Hurd

Sr. Marketing Communications Manager: Libby Shipp

Sr. Content Project Manager: Cliff Kallemeyn

Sr. Media Editor: Scott Fidler

Media Editor: Jessica Robbe

Frontlist Buyer, Manufacturing: Doug Wilke

Sr. Art Director: Stacy Shirley

Sr. Rights Acquisitions Acct. Manager: Mardell Glinski Schultz

Photo Manager: Tom Hill

ExamView® is a registered trademark of eInstruction Corp. Windows is a registered trademark of the Microsoft Corporation used herein under license. Macintosh and Power Macintosh are registered trademarks of Apple Computer, Inc. used herein under license. © 2008 Cengage Learning. All Rights Reserved.

Cengage Learning WebTutor™ is a trademark of Cengage Learning.

Library of Congress Control Number: 2010937504

Student Edition ISBN-10: 0-538-47851-9
Student Edition ISBN-13: 978-0-538-47851-9

South-Western Cengage Learning
5191 Natorp Boulevard
Mason, OH 45040
USA

Cengage Learning products are represented in Canada by Nelson Education, Ltd.

For your course and learning solutions, visit www.cengage.com
Purchase any of our products at your local college store or at our preferred online store **www.ichapters.com**

Printed in Canada
1 2 3 4 5 6 15 14 13 12 11 10

Carl S. Warren

Dr. Carl S. Warren is Professor Emeritus of Accounting at the University of Georgia, Athens. Dr. Warren has taught classes at the University of Georgia, University of Iowa, Michigan State University, and University of Chicago. Professor Warren focused his teaching efforts on principles of accounting and auditing. He received his Ph.D. from Michigan State University and his B.B.A. and M.A. from the University of Iowa. During his career, Dr. Warren published numerous articles in professional journals, including *The Accounting Review, Journal of Accounting Research, Journal of Accountancy, The CPA Journal,* and *Auditing: A Journal of Practice & Theory.* Dr. Warren has served on numerous committees of the American Accounting Association, the American Institute of Certified Public Accountants, and the Institute of Internal Auditors. He has also consulted with numerous companies and public accounting firms. Warren's outside interests include playing handball, golfing, skiing, backpacking, and fly-fishing.

James M. Reeve

Dr. James M. Reeve is Professor Emeritus of Accounting and Information Management at the University of Tennessee. Professor Reeve taught on the accounting faculty for 25 years, after graduating with his Ph.D. from Oklahoma State University. His teaching effort focused on undergraduate accounting principles and graduate education in the Master of Accountancy and Senior Executive MBA programs. Beyond this, Professor Reeve is also very active in the Supply Chain Certification program, which is a major executive education and research effort of the College. His research interests are varied and include work in managerial accounting, supply chain management, lean manufacturing, and information management. He has published over 40 articles in academic and professional journals, including the *Journal of Cost Management, Journal of Management Accounting Research, Accounting Review, Management Accounting Quarterly, Supply Chain Management Review,* and *Accounting Horizons.* He has consulted or provided training around the world for a wide variety of organizations, including Boeing, Procter & Gamble, Norfolk Southern, Hershey Foods, Coca-Cola, and Sony. When not writing books, Professor Reeve plays golf and is involved in faith-based activities.

Jonathan Duchac

Dr. Jonathan Duchac is the Merrill Lynch and Co. Professor of Accounting and Director of the Program in Enterprise Risk Management at Wake Forest University. He earned his Ph.D. in accounting from the University of Georgia and currently teaches introductory and advanced courses in financial accounting. Dr. Duchac has received a number of awards during his career, including the Wake Forest University Outstanding Graduate Professor Award, the T.B. Rose Award for Instructional Innovation, and the University of Georgia Outstanding Teaching Assistant Award. In addition to his teaching responsibilities, Dr. Duchac has served as Accounting Advisor to Merrill Lynch Equity Research, where he worked with research analysts in reviewing and evaluating the financial reporting practices of public companies. He has testified before the U.S. House of Representatives, the Financial Accounting Standards Board, and the Securities and Exchange Commission; and has worked with a number of major public companies on financial reporting and accounting policy issues. In addition to his professional interests, Dr. Duchac is the Treasurer of The Special Children's School of Winston-Salem; a private, nonprofit developmental day school serving children with special needs. Dr. Duchac is an avid long-distance runner, mountain biker, and snow skier. His recent events include the Grandfather Mountain Marathon, the Black Mountain Marathon, the Shut-In Ridge Trail run, and NO MAAM (Nocturnal Overnight Mountain Bike Assault on Mount Mitchell).

A History of Success

For nearly **85** years, *Accounting* has been used effectively to teach generations of businessmen and women. The text has been used by millions of business students. For many, this book provides the only exposure to accounting principles that they will ever receive. As the most successful business textbook of all time, it continues to introduce students to accounting through a variety of time-tested ways.

The previous edition, 23e, started a new journey into learning more about the changing needs of accounting students through a variety of new and innovative research and development methods. Our Blue Sky Workshops brought accounting faculty from all over the country into our book development process in a very direct and creative way. Many of the features and themes present in this text are a result of the collaboration and countless conversations we have had with accounting instructors over the last several years. 24e continues to build on this philosophy and strives to be reflective of the suggestions and feedback we receive from instructors and students on an ongoing basis. We are very happy with the results, and think you will be pleased with the improvements we have made to the text.

The original author of *Accounting*, James McKinsey, could not have imagined the success and influence this text has enjoyed or that his original vision would continue to lead the market into the twenty-first century. As the current authors, we appreciate the responsibility of protecting and enhancing this vision, while continuing to refine it to meet the changing needs of students and instructors. Always in touch with a tradition of excellence but never satisfied with yesterday's success, this edition enthusiastically embraces a changing environment and continues to proudly lead the way. We sincerely thank our many colleagues who have helped to make it happen.

Carl S. Warren

Jonathan Duchac

"The teaching of accounting is no longer designed to train professional accountants only. With the growing complexity of business and the constantly increasing difficulty of the problems of management, it has become essential that everyone who aspires to a position of responsibility should have a knowledge of the fundamental principles of accounting."

—James O. McKinsey, Author, first edition, 1929

Textbooks continue to play an invaluable role in the teaching and learning environments. Continuing our focus from previous editions, we reached out to accounting instructors in an effort to improve the textbook presentation. Our research informed us of the need to remain current in the areas of emerging topics/trends and to continue to look for ways to make the book more accessible to students. The results of this collaboration with hundreds of accounting instructors are reflected in the following major improvements made to the 24th edition:

International Financial Reporting Standards (IFRS)

IFRS is on the minds of many accounting educators of today. While the future is still unclear, our research indicates a growing need to provide more basic awareness of these standards within the text. We have incorporated some elements of IFRS throughout the text as appropriate to provide this level of awareness, being careful not to encroach upon the core GAAP principles that remain the hallmark focus of the book. These elements include icons that have been placed throughout the financial chapters which point to specific IFRS-related content, outlined with more detail in Appendix D. This table outlines the IFRS impact on the accounting concept.

International Connection

International Connection features highlight IFRS topics from a real-world perspective and appear in Chapters 1, 4, 7, 10, 13, and 16.

International Connection

IFRS FOR STATEMENT OF CASH FLOWS

The statement of cash flows is required under International Financial Reporting Standards (IFRS). The statement of cash flows under IFRS is similar to that reported under U.S. GAAP in that the statement has separate sections for operating, investing, and financing activities. Like U.S. GAAP, IFRS also allow the use of either the indirect or direct method of reporting cash flows from operating activities. IFRS differ from U.S. GAAP in some minor areas, including:

- Interest paid can be reported as either an operating or a financing activity, while interest received can be reported as either an operating or an investing activity. In contrast, U.S. GAAP reports interest paid or received as an operating activity.
- Dividends paid can be reported as either an operating or a financing activity, while dividends received can be reported as either an operating or an investing activity. In contrast, U.S. GAAP reports dividends paid as a financing activity and dividends received as an operating activity.
- Cash flows to pay taxes are reported as a separate line in the operating activities, in contrast to U.S. GAAP, which does not require a separate line disclosure.

* IFRS are further discussed and illustrated on pages 716-716G and in Appendix D.

Mornin' Joe International

Our authors have prepared statements for Mornin' Joe under IFRS guidelines as a basis for comparison with U.S.-prepared statements. This allows students to see how financial reporting differs under IFRS.

IFRS Training Video and IFRS PowerPoint Presentation

A training video with the voice of our distinguished author, Jim Reeve, will walk an instructor through the nuances of this complex topic. A PowerPoint deck, based on the training video, will allow instructors to customize the presentation for delivery to their students.

The Accounting Equation

A new format has been implemented in Chapter 2 for analyzing transactions. This new format includes the following elements: (1) transaction description, (2) analysis, (3) journal entry, and (4) accounting equation impact. This will help students understand that a transaction ultimately affects the accounting equation—*Assets = Liabilities + Owner's Equity.*

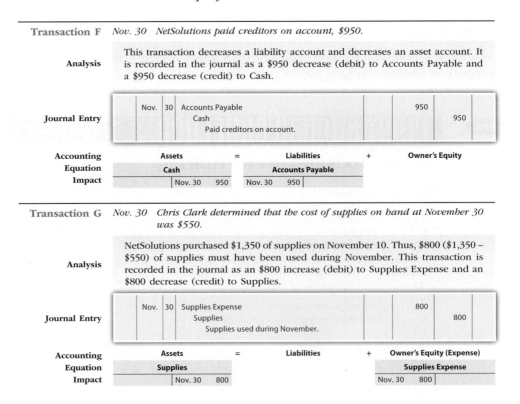

Transaction F	Nov. 30 NetSolutions paid creditors on account, $950.
Analysis	This transaction decreases a liability account and decreases an asset account. It is recorded in the journal as a $950 decrease (debit) to Accounts Payable and a $950 decrease (credit) to Cash.

Journal Entry

Nov.	30	Accounts Payable	950	
		Cash		950
		Paid creditors on account.		

Accounting Equation Impact

Assets	=	Liabilities	+	Owner's Equity
Cash		Accounts Payable		
Nov. 30 950		Nov. 30 950		

Transaction G	Nov. 30 Chris Clark determined that the cost of supplies on hand at November 30 was $550.
Analysis	NetSolutions purchased $1,350 of supplies on November 10. Thus, $800 ($1,350 – $550) of supplies must have been used during November. This transaction is recorded in the journal as an $800 increase (debit) to Supplies Expense and an $800 decrease (credit) to Supplies.

Journal Entry

Nov.	30	Supplies Expense	800	
		Supplies		800
		Supplies used during November.		

Accounting Equation Impact

Assets	=	Liabilities	+	Owner's Equity (Expense)
Supplies				Supplies Expense
Nov. 30 800				Nov. 30 800

Financial Analysis and Interpretation

New Financial Analysis and Interpretation learning objectives have been added to the financial chapters and where appropriate, linked to real-world situations. FAI encourages students to go deeper into the material to analyze accounting information and improve critical thinking skills.

Updated At a Glance

Students prepare for homework and tests by referring to our end-of-chapter grid which outlines learning objectives, linking concept coverage to specific examples. Through our updated At a Glance, students can review the chapter's learning objectives and key learning outcomes. In addition, all the *Example Exercises* and *Practice Exercises* have been indexed so that each learning objective and key outcomes can be viewed.

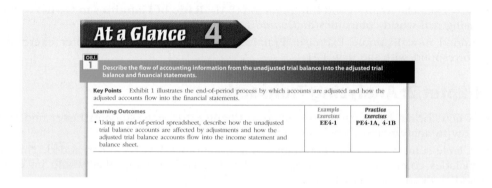

End-of-Chapter Exercises and Problems

All of our end-of-chapter materials have been updated, using new data, company names, and real-world data.

Test Bank

With the assistance of over fifteen distinguished professors, we completely revamped our test bank. We created more multiple choice, matching, and problem type questions.

Excel Templates

Our Excel templates have been enhanced to allow professors to turn off the "instant feedback" asterisks. Based on the file provided to them, students can complete the spreadsheet and email the file to their instructor. The instructor can then input a code that will automatically grade the student's work. These Excel templates complement end-of-chapter problems. They are located on the companion website (URL) and also within CengageNOW.

Chapter-by-Chapter Enhancements

The following specific content changes can be found in *Financial Accounting, 12e.*

Chapter 1: Introduction to Accounting and Business

- *Google* replaces *Starbucks* in the chapter opening example.
- Proprietorships, partnerships, corporations, and limited liability companies (LLC) are now discussed with the business entity concept.
- Added an International Connection feature to introduce students to IFRS.
- New Financial Analysis and Interpretation (FAI): **Ratio of Liabilities to Owner's Equity** using real-world companies *McDonald's* and *Google.*
- Added new Example Exercise, Practice Exercise, and end-of-chapter exercises to correspond with the new FAI.

Chapter 2: Analyzing Transactions

- A new format has been implemented in Chapter 2 to help students better understand how to analyze and record transactions.
- A table summarizing common transaction terminology has also been added. This table includes common transaction terms and the related accounts that would be debited and credited in a journal entry.
- New Financial Analysis and Interpretation: **Horizontal Analysis** using a fictitious company, *J. Holmes, Attorney at Law,* and a real-world company, *Apple, Inc.*
- Added new Example Exercise, Practice Exercise, and end-of-chapter exercises to correspond with the new FAI.

Chapter 3: The Adjusting Process

- The *Accounting Equation Impact* feature described in Chapter 2 is also used in Chapter 3 to describe and illustrate adjusting entries.
- New chapter opener features *Rhapsody,* an Internet-based music service.
- New Financial Analysis and Interpretation: **Vertical Analysis** continuing with fictitious company, *J. Holmes, Attorney at Law,* and adding a real-world company, *RealNetworks, Inc.*

Chapter 4: Completing the Accounting Cycle

- The Flow of Accounting Information exhibit at the beginning of the chapter has been revised to show the flow of accounting data from the adjusted trial balance directly into the income statement, statement of owner's equity, and balance sheet.
- New Financial Analysis and Interpretation: **Working Capital and Current Ratio** using *Electronic Arts, Inc.* and *Take-Two Interactive Software, Inc.*
- Added new Example Exercise, Practice Exercise, and end-of-chapter exercises to correspond with the new FAI.

Chapter 5: Accounting Systems

- An illustration of a computerized accounting system was updated using the screen shots from Quickbooks® Pro 2010 edition.
- Streamlined discussion of special journals.
- Removed discussion of "Manual Accounting Systems."
- Added a Business Connection feature.

- New Financial Analysis and Interpretation: **Segment Analysis** using real-world company *Intuit, Inc.*
- Added new Example Exercise and Practice Exercise to correspond with the new FAI.

Chapter 6: Accounting for Merchandising Businesses

- The computation of cost of merchandise sold (under the periodic inventory system) has been moved from the beginning of the chapter to an end-of-chapter appendix.
- A new section has been added that summarizes the effects of merchandise transactions on the merchandise inventory account. This is illustrated using a T account for merchandise inventory.
- Moved coverage of "Accounting Systems for Merchandisers" to our online site (www .cengage.com/accounting/warren).
- New Financial Analysis and Interpretation: **Ratio of Net Sales to Assets** using real-world company *Dollar Tree, Inc.*
- Added new Example Exercise and Practice Exercise to correspond with the new FAI.

Chapter 7: Inventories

- New Financial Analysis and Interpretation: **Inventory Turnover and Number of Days, Sales in Inventory** using real-world companies *Best Buy* and *Zales.*
- Added new Example Exercise and Practice Exercise to correspond with the new FAI.

Chapter 8: Sarbanes-Oxley, Internal Control, and Cash

- Updated chapter graphic for better clarity and snapshot comprehension.
- New Financial Analysis and Interpretation: **Ratio of Cash to Monthly Cash Expenses** using real-world company *Evergreen Solar, Inc.*
- Added new Example Exercise and Practice Exercise to correspond with the new FAI.

Chapter 9: Receivables

- New Financial Analysis and Interpretation: **Accounts Receivable Turnover and Number of Days' Sales in Receivables** using real-world company *FedEx.*
- Added new Example Exercise and Practice Exercise to correspond with the new FAI.

Chapter 10: Fixed Assets and Intangible Assets

- Updated many chapter graphics for better clarity and snapshot comprehension.
- New Financial Analysis and Interpretation: **Fixed Asset Turnover Ratio** using real-world company *Starbucks Corporation.*
- Added new Example Exercise and Practice Exercise to correspond with the new FAI.

Chapter 11: Current Liabilities and Payroll

- The example of *Starbucks Corporation* on long-term debt has been replaced by *P.F. Chang's.*
- Updated Wage Bracket Withholding table, based on data from the *2010 Publication 15.*
- Removed discussion of social security cap on withholding (above $100,000).

Chapter-by-Chapter Enhancements

- Updated Business Connection feature to cover *General Motors* and its pension problems.
- New Financial Analysis and Interpretation: **Quick Ratio** using real-world company *TechSolutions, Inc.*
- Added new Example Exercise and Practice Exercise to correspond with the new FAI.

Chapter 12: Accounting for Partnerships and Limited Liability Companies

- *Razor* replaces *AgentBlaze LLC* as the chapter opening example.
- Updated Business Connection feature to Kristen Hall, founding member of the country music group *Sugarland* and her lawsuit.
- New Financial Analysis and Interpretation: **Revenue per Employee** showing *McDonald's* and *Starbucks* to understand evaluation within an industry.
- Added new Example Exercise and Practice Exercise to correspond with the new FAI.
- Eliminated the section on "Errors in Liquidation" to reduce minor redundancy.

Chapter 13: Corporations: Organization, Stock Transactions, and Dividends

- New Financial Analysis and Interpretation: On website they say **JPMorgan Chase & Co. Earnings per Share** using *Hasbro, Bank of America Corporation*, and *J.P. Morgan Chase & Co.*
- Added new Example Exercise and Practice Exercise to correspond with the new FAI.

Chapter 14: Long-Term Liabilities: Bonds and Notes

- Updated Business Connection feature on U.S. government debt.
- Updated Business Connection feature to cover *General Motors* bonds.
- Added an Integrity, Objectivity, and Ethics feature to discuss "Liar's Loans."
- New Financial Analysis and Interpretation: **Number of Times Interest Charges Are Earned** using *Under Armour, Inc.*
- Added new Example Exercise and Practice Exercise to correspond with the new FAI.

Chapter 15: Investments and Fair Value Accounting

- Added an Integrity, Objectivity, and Ethics box titled *"Loan Loss Woes"* on mortgage loans called "sub-prime" and "Alt-A" loans.
- Updated Business Connection feature to "Apple's Entrance to Streaming Music."
- Revised "Value and Reporting Investments" to simplify the reading process.
- New Financial Analysis and Interpretation: **Dividend Yield** using *News Corporation*.
- Added new Example Exercise and Practice Exercise to correspond with the new FAI.
- Moved "Accounting for Held-to-Maturity Investments" appendix to www.cengage.com/accounting/warren.

Mornin' Joe

- To expand students' understanding of financial statement preparation outside the United States, the authors took our unique company example, *Mornin' Joe,* and show how it goes international after Chapter 15. They prepared a set of financial statements following IFRS guidelines. To aid in learning, callout features pinpoint the differences between U.S. GAAP and IFRS.

Chapter 16: Statement of Cash Flows

- Updated Business Connection feature to "Cash Crunch!" featuring *Chrysler Group LLC*.
- New Financial Analysis and Interpretation: **Free Cash Flow** using *Research in Motion, Inc.*, maker of BlackBerry® smartphones.
- Added new Example Exercise and Practice Exercise to correspond with the new FAI.

Chapter 17: Financial Statement Analysis

- Real-world financial statement analysis problem uses data from the *Nike, Inc.* 2010 10-K. A portion of Nike's 10-K is located in Appendix C.
- Updated Integrity, Objectivity, and Ethics feature discusses "Chief Financial Officer Bonuses."
- Updated Integrity, Objectivity, and Ethics feature to "Buy Low, Sell High."

Hallmark Features of Financial Accounting, 12e

Financial Accounting, 12e, is unparalleled in pedagogical innovation. Our constant dialogue with accounting faculty continues to affect how we refine and improve the text to meet the needs of today's students. Our goal is to provide a logical framework and pedagogical system that caters to how students of today study and learn.

Clear Objectives and Key Learning Outcomes   To guide students, the authors provide clear chapter objectives and important learning outcomes. All the chapter materials relate back to these key points and outcomes, which keeps students focused on the most important topics and concepts in order to succeed in the course.

Example Exercises   Example Exercises reinforce concepts and procedures in a bold, new way. Like a teacher in the classroom, students follow the authors' example to see how to complete accounting applications as they are presented in the text. This feature also provides a list of Practice Exercises that parallel the Example Exercises so students get the practice they need. In addition, the Practice Exercises include references to the chapter Example Exercises so that students can easily cross-reference when completing homework.

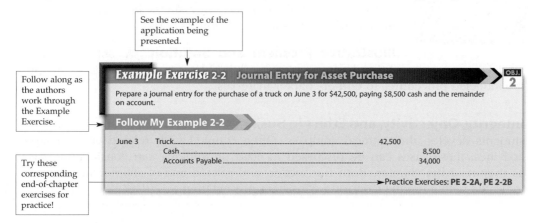

"At a Glance" Chapter Summary   At the end of each chapter, the "At a Glance" summary grid ties everything together and helps students stay on track.

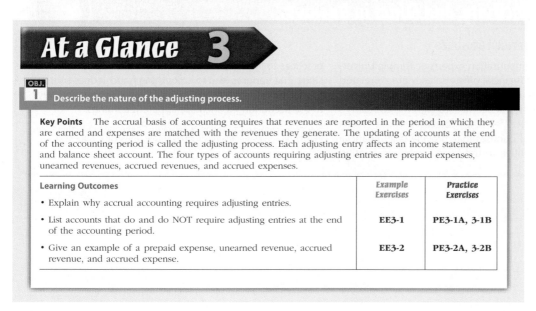

Hallmark Features of Financial Accounting, 12e

Real-World Chapter Openers Building on the strengths of past editions, these openers continue to relate the accounting and business concepts in the chapter to students' lives. These openers employ examples of real companies and provide invaluable insight into real practice. Several of the openers created especially for this edition focus on interesting companies such as Rhapsody, Razor, E.W. Scripps Company, a diverse media concern, and Facebook.

Continuing Case Study Students follow a fictitious company, **NetSolutions**, throughout Chapters 1–6, which demonstrates a variety of transactions. The continuity of using the same company facilitates student learning especially for Chapters 1–4, which cover the accounting cycle. Also, using the same company allows students to follow the transition of the company from a service business in Chapters 1–4 to a merchandising business in Chapters 5 and 6.

Illustrative Problem and Solution A solved problem models one or more of the chapter's assignment problems so that students can apply the modeled procedures to end-of-chapter materials.

Integrity, Objectivity, and Ethics in Business In each chapter, these cases help students develop their ethical compass. Often coupled with related end-of-chapter activities, these cases can be discussed in class or students can consider the cases as they read the chapter. Both the section and related end-of-chapter materials are indicated with a unique icon for a consistent presentation.

Integrity, Objectivity, and Ethics in Business

CHIEF FINANCIAL OFFICER BONUSES

A recent study by compensation experts at Temple University found that chief financial officer salaries are correlated with the complexity of a company's operations, but chief financial officer bonuses are correlated with the company's ability to meet analysts' earnings forecasts. These results suggest that financial bonuses may provide chief financial officers with an incentive to use questionable accounting practices to improve earnings. While the study doesn't conclude that bonuses lead to accounting fraud, it does suggest that bonuses give chief financial officers a reason to find ways to use accounting to increase apparent earnings.

Source: E. Jelesiewicz, "Today's CFO: More Challenge but Higher Compensation," *News Communications* (Temple University, August 2009).

Business Connection and Comprehensive Real-World Notes Students get a close-up look at how accounting operates in the marketplace through a variety of *Business Connection* boxed features.

BusinessConnection

AVATAR: THE MOST EXPENSIVE MOVIE EVER MADE (AND THE MOST SUCCESSFUL)

Prior to the release of the blockbuster *Avatar* in December 2009, many were skeptical if the movie's huge $500 million investment would pay off. After all, just to break even the movie would have to perform as one of the top 50 movies of all time. To provide a return that was double the investment, the movie would have to crack the top ten. Many thought this was a tall order, even though James Cameron, the force

behind this movie, already had the number one grossing movie of all time: *Titanic*, at $1.8 billion in worldwide box office revenues. Could he do it again? That was the question.

So, how did the film do? Only eight weeks after its release, Avatar had become the number one grossing film of all time, with over $2.2 billion in worldwide box office revenue. Executives at Fox anticipated that the profit might double after the film was released on DVD in the summer of 2010. Needless to say, James Cameron, 20th Century Fox, and other investors are very pleased with their return on this investment.

Sources: Michael Cieply, "A Movie's Budget Pops from the Screen," *New York Times*, November 8, 2009; "Bulk of Avatar Profit Still to Come," *The Age*, February 3, 2010.

Market Leading End-of-Chapter Material Students need to practice accounting so that they can understand and use it. To give students the greatest possible advantage in the real world, *Financial Accounting, 12e*, goes beyond presenting theory and procedure with comprehensive, time-tested, end-of-chapter material.

Online Solutions

South-Western, a division of Cengage Learning, offers a vast array of online solutions to suit your course needs. Choose the product that best meets your classroom needs and course goals. Please check with your Cengage representative for more details or for ordering information.

CengageNow

CengageNOW is a powerful course management and online homework tool that provides robust instructor control and customization to optimize the student learning experience and meet desired outcomes. CengageNOW offers:

- Auto-graded homework (static and algorithmic varieties), test bank, Personalized Study Plan, and eBook are all in one resource.
- Easy-to-use course management options offer flexibility and continuity from one semester to another.
- Different levels of feedback and engaging student resources guide students through material and solidify learning.
- The most robust and flexible assignment options in the industry.
- "Smart Entry" helps eliminate common data entry errors and prevents students from guessing their way through the homework.
- The ability to analyze student work from the gradebook and generate reports on learning outcomes. Each problem is tagged in the Solutions Manual and CengageNOW to AICPA, IMA, AACSB, and ACBSP outcomes so you can measure student performance.

CengageNOW Upgrades:

- Our General Ledger Software is now being offered in a new online format. Your students can solve selected end-of-chapter assignments in a format that emulates commercial general ledger software.
- For a complete list of CengageNOW upgrades, refer to page 6 in the brochure in front of the Instructor Edition.
- New Design: CengageNOW has been redesigned to enhance your experience.

For a CengageNOW demo, visit: www.cengage.com/community/warren

Aplia

Aplia is a premier online homework product that successfully engages students and maximizes the amount of effort they put forth, creating more efficient learners. Aplia's advantages are:

- In addition to static and algorithmic end-of-chapter homework, Aplia offers an **extra problem set** to give you more options!
- Students can receive **unique**, **detailed feedback** and the full solution after each attempt on homework.
- "**Grade It Now**" maximizes student effort on each attempt and ensures students do their own work. Students have three attempts. Each attempt produces an algorithmic variety. The final score is an average of the three attempts.
- "**Smart Entry**" helps eliminate common data entry errors and prevents students from guessing their way through the homework.

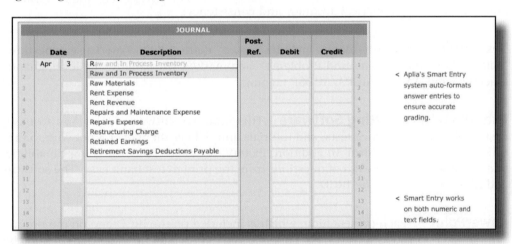

Aplia Upgrades:

- Increased Instructor Control: Instructors now have more options in how they assign materials from the question banks.
- ApliaText: Interactive ApliaText allows students to use eBooks in a new way. This unique flip-book also includes a Chapter Recap that helps students craft their own personal study guide.

For an Aplia demo, visit: www.cengage.com/community/warren

WebTutor™

WebTutor™ on Blackboard® and WebCT®—Improve student grades with online review and test preparation tools in an easy-to-use course cartridge.

   Visit www.cengage.com/webtutor for more information.

When it comes to supporting instructors, South-Western is unsurpassed. *Financial Accounting, 12e*, continues the tradition with powerful print and digital ancillaries aimed at facilitating greater course successes.

Instructor's Manual The Instructor's Manual includes: Brief Synopsis, List of Objectives, Key Terms, Ideas for Class Discussion, Lecture Aids, Demonstration Problems, Group Learning Activities, Exercises and Problems for Reinforcement, and Internet Activities. Suggested Approaches incorporate many modern teaching initiatives, including active learning, collaborative learning, critical thinking, and writing across the curriculum.

Solutions Manual The Solutions Manual contains answers to all exercises, problems, and activities in the text. The solutions are author-written and verified multiple times for numerical accuracy and consistency.

Test Bank The Test Bank includes more than 2,800 True/False questions, Multiple-Choice questions, and Problems, each marked with a difficulty level, chapter objective, and AASCB/AICPA/ACBSP tagging.

ExamView® Pro Testing Software This intuitive software allows you to easily customize exams, practice tests, and tutorials and deliver them over a network, on the Internet, or in printed form. In addition, ExamView comes with searching capabilities that make sorting the wealth of questions from the printed test bank easy. The software and files are found on the IRCD.

PowerPoint® Each presentation, which is included on the IRCD and on the product support site, enhances lectures and simplifies class preparation. Each chapter contains objectives followed by a thorough outline of the chapter that easily provides an entire lecture model. Also, exhibits from the chapter, such as the new Example Exercises, have been recreated as colorful PowerPoint slides to create a powerful, customizable tool.

Instructor Excel® Templates These templates provide the solutions for the problems that have Enhanced Excel® templates for students. Through these files, instructors can see the solutions in the same format as the students. All problems with accompanying templates are marked in the book with an icon and are listed in the information grid in the solutions manual. These templates are available for download on www.cengage.com/accounting/warren or on the IRCD.

Instructor's Resource CD The Instructor's Resource CD includes the PowerPoint® Presentations, Instructor's Manual, Solutions Manual, Test Bank, ExamView®, General Ledger Inspector, and Excel® Template Solutions.

For the Student

Students come to accounting with a variety of learning needs. *Financial Accounting, 12e*, offers a broad range of supplements in both printed form and easy-to-use technology. We continue to refine our entire supplement package around the comments instructors have provided about their courses and teaching needs.

Study Guide   This author-written guide provides students Quiz and Test Hints, Matching questions, Fill-in-the-Blank questions (Parts A & B), Multiple-Choice questions, True/False questions, Exercises, and Problems for each chapter.

Working Papers for Exercises and Problems   The traditional working papers include problem-specific forms for preparing solutions for Exercises, A & B Problems, the Continuing Problem, and the Comprehensive Problems from the textbook. These forms, with preprinted headings, provide a structure for the problems, which helps students get started and saves them time.

Blank Working Papers   These Working Papers are available for completing exercises and problems either from the text or prepared by the instructor. They have no preprinted headings. A guide at the front of the Working Papers tells students which form they will need for each problem and are available online in a .pdf, printable format.

Enhanced Excel® Templates   These templates are provided for selected long or complicated end-of-chapter problems and provide assistance to the student as they set up and work the problem. Certain cells are coded to display a red asterisk when an incorrect answer is entered, which helps students stay on track. Selected problems that can be solved using these templates are designated by an icon.

General Ledger Software   The CLGL software is now being offered in a new online format. Students can solve selected end-of-chapter assignments in a format that emulates commercial general ledger software. Students make entries into the general journal or special journals, track the posting of the entries to the general ledger, and create financial statements or reports. This gives students important exposure to commercial accounting software, yet in a manner that is more forgiving of student errors. Assignments are automatically graded online.

Product Support Web Site www.cengage.com/accounting/warren   This site provides students with a wealth of introductory accounting resources, including quizzing and supplement downloads and access to the Enhanced Excel® Templates.

Acknowledgments

Many of the enhancements made to *Financial Accounting, 12e,* are a direct result of countless conversations we've had with principles of accounting professors and students over the past several years. We want to take this opportunity to thank them for their perspectives and feedback on textbook use. *12e* represents our finest edition yet!

The following instructors are members of our Blue Sky editorial board, whose helpful comments and feedback continue to have a profound impact on the presentation and core themes of this text:

Rick Andrews
Sinclair Community College

Mia Breen
De Anza Community College

Anne M. Cardozo
Broward College

James Cieslak
Cuyahoga Community College

Rebecca A. Foote
Middle Tennessee State University

Gloria Grayless
Sam Houston State University

Robert Gronstal
Metropolitan Community College

Curtis Gustafson
South Dakota State University

Lynn P. Hedge
NHTI—Concord's Community College

Audrey Hunter
Broward College

Phillip Imel
Northern Virginia Community College—Annandale Campus

Christopher Kwak
De Anza College

Bruce W. McClain
Cleveland State University

Jenny Resnick
Santa Monica College

Lawrence A. Roman
Cuyahoga Community College

Robert Smolin
Citrus College

Robert C. Urell
Irvine Valley College

The following students attended our Blue Sky session, providing insights into the life of an accounting student:

Stacy Appleton
Northern Kentucky University

Danny Bradford
Xavier University

Steve Busey
Xavier University

Brandon Butcher
Xavier University

Suzanne Buzek
Xavier University

Jenny Daugherty
Northern Kentucky University

Richard Farmer
Sinclair Community College

Bobby Freking
Xavier University

Steve Latos
Xavier University

Cristi Liska
Northern Kentucky University

Mallory Malinoski
Xavier University

Clare McGrath
Xavier University

Hecia Mpanga
Xavier University

Jessica Nichols
Northern Kentucky University

Oscar Ochieng
Northern Kentucky University

Rick Riva
Sinclair Community College

Max Roberts
Sinclair Community College

Anthony Saxon
Xavier University

The following individuals took the time to participate in surveys, online sessions, content reviews, and test bank revisions:

Bridget Anakwe
Delaware State University

Julia L. Angel
North Arkansas College

Leah Arrington
Northwest Mississippi Community College

Donna T. Ascenzi
Bryant and Stratton College—Syracuse Campus

Ed Bagley
Darton College

James Baker
Harford Community College

Lisa Cooley Banks
University of Michigan

LuAnn Bean
Florida Institute of Technology

Judy Beebe
Western Oregon University

Brenda J. Bindschatel
Green River Community College

Eric D. Bostwick
The University of West Florida

Bryan C. Bouchard
Southern New Hampshire University

Thomas M. Branton
Alvin Community College

Celestino Caicoya
Miami Dade College

John Callister
Cornell University

Deborah Chabaud
Louisiana Technical College

Marilyn G. Ciolino
Delgado Community College

Earl Clay
Cape Cod Community College

Lisa M. Cole
Johnson County Community College

Cori Oliver Crews
Waycross College

Julie Daigle
Ft. Range Community College

Julie Dailey
Central Virginia Community College

John M. Daugherty
Pitt Community College

Becky Davis
East Mississippi Community College

Ginger Dennis
West Georgia Technical College

Scott A. Elza
Wisconsin Indianhead Technical College

Patricia Feller
Nashville State Community College

Mike Foland
Southwestern Illinois College—Belleville

Brenda S. Fowler
Alamance Community College

Jeanne Gerard
Franklin Pierce University

Christopher Gilbert
East Los Angeles College, Montery Park, CA

Mark S. Gleason
Metropolitan State University, St. Paul, Minnesota

Marina Grau
Houston Community College

Judith Grenkowicz
Kirtland Community College

Vicki Greshik
Jamestown College

Lillian S. Grose
Our Lady of Holy Cross College

Denise T. Guest
Germanna Community College

Bruce J. Gunning
Kent State University at East Liverpool

Rosie Hale
Southwest Tennessee Community College

Sara Harris
Arapahoe Community College

Matthew P. Helinski
Northeast Lakeview College

Wanda Hudson
Alabama Southern Community College

Todd A. Jensen
Sierra College

Paul T. Johnson
Mississippi Gulf Coast Community College

Mary Kline
Black Hawk College

Jan Kraft
Northwest College

David W. Krug
Johnson County Community College

Cathy Xanthaky Larson
Middlesex Community College

Brenda G. Lauer
Northeastern Junior College

Ted Lewis
Marshalltown Community College

Marion Loiola
SUNY—Orange County Community College

Ming Lu
Santa Monica College

Don Lucy
Indian River State College

Debbie Luna
El Paso Community College

Anna L. Lusher
Slippery Rock University

Kirk Lynch
Sandhills Community College

Bridgette Mahan
Harold Washington College

Irene Meares
Western New Mexico University

James B. Meir
Cleveland State Community College

John L. Miller
Metropolitan Community College

Peter Moloney
Cerritos College

Janet Morrow
East Central Community College

Pamela G. Needham
Northeast Mississippi Community College

Jeannie M. Neil
Orange Coast College, Costa Mesa, CA

Carolyn Nelson
Coffeyville Community College

Joseph Malino Nicassio
Westmoreland County Community College

Robert L. Osborne
Ohio Dominican University

Scott Paxton
North Idaho College

Ronald Pearson
Bay College

Rachel Pernia
Essex County College

Erick Pifer
Lake Michigan College

Marianne G. Pindar
Lackawanna College

Kenneth J. Plucinski
State University of New York at Fredonia

Debbie Porter
Tidewater Community College

Shirley J. Powell
Arkansas State University—Beebe

Eric M. Primuth
Cuyahoga Community College

Michael Prindle
Grand View University

Rita Pritchett
Brevard Community College

Judy Ramsay
San Jacinto College—North

Patrick Reihing
Nassau Community College

Richard Rickel
South Mountain Community College

Patricia G. Roshto
University of Louisiana—Monroe

Martin Sabo
Community College of Denver

Tracy M. Schmeltzer
Wayne Community College

Dennis C. Shea
Southern New Hampshire University

Acknowledgments

Robert W. Smith (retired)
formerly of Briarcliffe College—Patchogue, NY Campus

Kimberly D. Smith
County College of Morris

Richard Snapp
Olympic College— Bremerton

John L. Stancil
Florida Southern College

Barry Stephens
Bemidji State University

Jeff Strawser
Sam Houston State University

Stacie A. Surowiec
Harford Community College

Eric H. Sussman
UCLA Anderson Graduate School of Management

Bill Talbot
Montgomery College

Kenneth J. Tax
Farmingdale State College (SUNY)

Ronald Tidd
Central Washington University

Erol C. Tucker, Jr.
The Victoria College

Henry Velarde
Malcolm X College

Angela Waits
Gadsden State Community College

Dale Walker
Arkansas State University

Shunda Ware
Atlanta Technical College

Cheryl C. Willingham
Wisconsin Indianhead Technical College

Patrick B. Wilson
Tennessee Board of Regents

Jay E. Wright
New River Community College

The following instructors created content for the supplements that accompany the text:

LuAnn Bean
Florida Institute of Technology

Gary Bower
Community College of Rhode Island

Doug Cloud
Pepperdine University

Ana Cruz & Blanca Ortega
Miami Dade College

Kurt Fredricks
Valencia Community College

Lori Grady
Bucks County Community College

Jose Luis Hortensi
Miami Dade College

Christine Jonick
Gainesville State College

Patti Lopez
Valencia Community College

Don Lucy
Indian River State College

Tracie Nobles
Austin Community College

Craig Pence
Highland Community College

Alice Sineath
Forsyth Technical Community College

Janice Stoudemire
Midlands Technical College

Brief Contents

Contents

Practice Set: Glorious Garden Lawn Service
This set is a service business operated as a proprietorship. It includes a narrative of transactions and
instructions for an optional solution with no debits
and credits. This set can be solved manually or with
the General Ledger software.

> **Practice Set: Pumping Iron**
> This set is a merchandising business operated as a proprietorship. It includes business documents, and it can be solved manually or with the General Ledger software.

> **Practice Set: Lucy's Doggie Care**
> This set includes payroll transactions for a merchandising business operated as a proprietorship. It includes business documents, and it can be solved manually or with the General Ledger software.

> **Practice Set: Art by Design**
> This set is a service and merchandising business operated as a corporation. It includes narrative for six months of transactions, which are to be recorded in a general journal. The set can be solved manually or with the General Ledger software.

> **Practice Set: Digital Revolution Services**
> This set is a departmentalized merchandising business operated as a corporation. It includes a narrative of transactions, which are to be recorded in special journals. The set can be solved manually or with the General Ledger software.

WARREN REEVE DUCHAC

FINANCIAL ACCOUNTING

12e

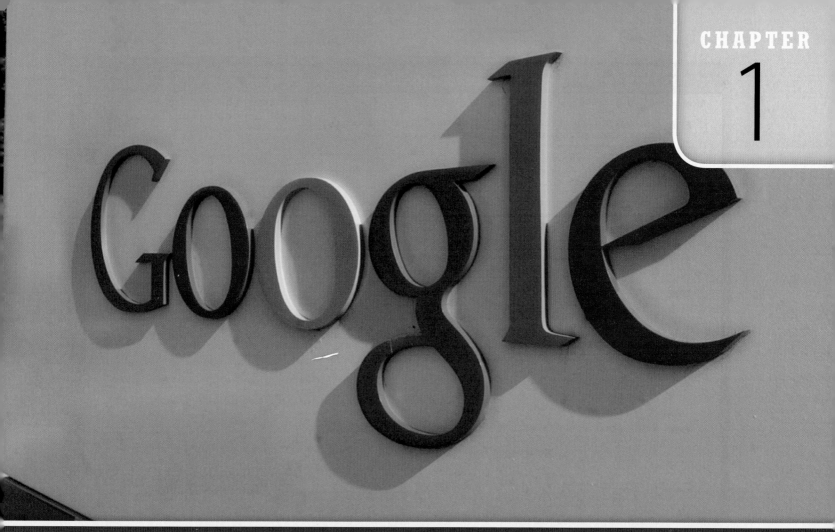
© AP Photo/Paul Sakuma

Introduction to Accounting and Business

Google™

When two teams pair up for a game of football, there is often a lot of noise. The band plays, the fans cheer, and fireworks light up the scoreboard. Obviously, the fans are committed and care about the outcome of the game. Just like fans at a football game, the owners of a business want their business to "win" against their competitors in the marketplace. While having your football team win can be a source of pride, winning in the marketplace goes beyond pride and has many tangible benefits. Companies that are winners are better able to serve customers, provide good jobs for employees, and make money for their owners.

One such successful company is **Google**, one of the most visible companies on the Internet. Many of us cannot visit the Web without using Google to

power a search. As one writer said, "Google is the closest thing the Web has to an ultimate answer machine." And yet, Google is a free tool—no one asks for your credit card when you use Google's search tools.

Do you think Google has been a successful company? Does it make money? How would you know? Accounting helps to answer these questions. Google's accounting information tells us that Google is a successful company that makes a lot of money, but not from you and me. Google makes its money from advertisers.

This textbook introduces you to accounting, the language of business. Chapter 1 begins by discussing what a business is, how it operates, and the role that accounting plays.

Learning Objectives

After studying this chapter, you should be able to:

OBJ. 1 Describe the nature of a business, the role of accounting, and ethics in business.

Nature of Business and Accounting

A **business**[1] is an organization in which basic resources (inputs), such as materials and labor, are assembled and processed to provide goods or services (outputs) to customers. Businesses come in all sizes, from a local coffee house to Starbucks, which sells over $10 billion of coffee and related products each year.

The objective of most businesses is to earn a **profit**. Profit is the difference between the amounts received from customers for goods or services and the amounts paid for the inputs used to provide the goods or services. This text focuses on businesses operating to earn a profit. However, many of the same concepts and principles also apply to not-for-profit organizations such as hospitals, churches, and government agencies.

Types of Businesses

Three types of businesses operated for profit include service, merchandising, and manufacturing businesses.

Each type of business and some examples are described below.

Service businesses provide services rather than products to customers.

    Delta Air Lines (transportation services)
    The Walt Disney Company (entertainment services)

Merchandising businesses sell products they purchase from other businesses to customers.

    Wal-Mart (general merchandise)
    Amazon.com (Internet books, music, videos)

Manufacturing businesses change basic inputs into products that are sold to customers.

    Ford Motor Co. (cars, trucks, vans)
    Dell Inc. (personal computers)

1 A complete glossary of terms appears at the end of the text.

The Role of Accounting in Business

The role of accounting in business is to provide information for managers to use in operating the business. In addition, accounting provides information to other users in assessing the economic performance and condition of the business.

Thus, **accounting** can be defined as an information system that provides reports to users about the economic activities and condition of a business. You may think of accounting as the "language of business." This is because accounting is the means by which businesses' financial information is communicated to users.

The process by which accounting provides information to users is as follows:

1. Identify users.
2. Assess users' information needs.
3. Design the accounting information system to meet users' needs.
4. Record economic data about business activities and events.
5. Prepare accounting reports for users.

As illustrated in Exhibit 1, users of accounting information can be divided into two groups: internal users and external users.

Note:
Accounting is an information system that provides reports to users about the economic activities and condition of a business.

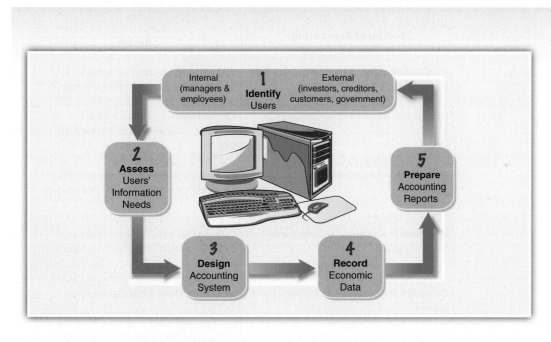

EXHIBIT 1

Accounting as an Information System

Internal users of accounting information include managers and employees. These users are directly involved in managing and operating the business. The area of accounting that provides internal users with information is called **managerial accounting** or **management accounting**.

The objective of managerial accounting is to provide relevant and timely information for managers' and employees' decision-making needs. Often times, such information is sensitive and is not distributed outside the business. Examples of sensitive information might include information about customers, prices, and plans to expand the business. Managerial accountants employed by a business are employed in **private accounting**.

External users of accounting information include investors, creditors, customers, and the government. These users are not directly involved in managing and operating the business. The area of accounting that provides external users with information is called **financial accounting**.

The objective of financial accounting is to provide relevant and timely information for the decision-making needs of users outside of the business. For example, financial reports on the operations and condition of the business are useful for banks and other creditors in deciding whether to lend money to the business. **General-purpose financial statements** are one type of financial accounting report that is distributed to external users. The term *general-purpose* refers to the wide range of decision-making needs that these reports are designed to serve. Later in this chapter, general-purpose financial statements are described and illustrated.

Role of Ethics in Accounting and Business

The objective of accounting is to provide relevant, timely information for user decision making. Accountants must behave in an ethical manner so that the information they provide users will be trustworthy and, thus, useful for decision making. Managers and employees must also behave in an ethical manner in managing and operating a business. Otherwise, no one will be willing to invest in or loan money to the business.

Ethics are moral principles that guide the conduct of individuals. Unfortunately, business managers and accountants sometimes behave in an unethical manner. A number of managers of the companies listed in Exhibit 2 engaged in accounting or

EXHIBIT 2   **Accounting and Business Frauds**

Company	Nature of Accounting or Business Fraud	Result
American International Group, Inc. (AIG)	Used sham accounting transactions to inflate performance.	CEO resigned. Executives criminally convicted. AIG paid $126 million in fines.
Computer Associates International, Inc.	Fraudulently inflated its financial results.	CEO and senior executives indicted. Five executives pled guilty. $225 million fine.
Enron	Fraudulently inflated its financial results.	Bankrupcty. Senior executives criminally convicted. Over $60 billion in stock market losses.
Fannie Mae	Improperly shifted financial performance between periods.	CEO and CFO fired. Company made a $9 billion correction to previously reported earnings.
HealthSouth	Overstated performance by $4 billion in false entries.	Senior executives criminally convicted.
Qwest Communications International, Inc.	Improperly recognized $3 billion in false receipts.	CEO and six other executives criminally convicted of "massive financial fraud." $250 million SEC fine.
Satyam Computer Services	Significantly inflated assets and earnings.	Chairman and founder is in jail; investors lost billions.
Terex	Recorded profit prematurely and inflated profits.	Company paid $8 million to Securities and Exchange Commission in settlement.
Tyco International, Ltd.	Failed to disclose secret loans to executives that were subsequently forgiven.	CEO forced to resign and subjected to frozen asset order and criminally convicted.
United Rental	Inflated profits to meet earnings forecasts and analysts expectations.	Vice chairman and chief financial officer indicted for conspiracy, securities fraud, and insider trading.
Xerox Corporation	Recognized $3 billion in revenue prior to when it should have been.	$10 million fine to SEC. Six executives forced to pay $22 million.

business fraud. These ethical violations led to fines, firings, and lawsuits. In some cases, managers were criminally prosecuted, convicted, and sent to prison.

What went wrong for the managers and companies listed in Exhibit 2? The answer normally involved one or both of the following two factors:

Failure of Individual Character. An ethical manager and accountant is honest and fair. However, managers and accountants often face pressures from supervisors to meet company and investor expectations. In many of the cases in Exhibit 2, managers and accountants justified small ethical violations to avoid such pressures. However, these small violations became big violations as the company's financial problems became worse.

Culture of Greed and Ethical Indifference. By their behavior and attitude, senior managers set the company culture. In most of the companies listed in Exhibit 2, the senior managers created a culture of greed and indifference to the truth.

As a result of the accounting and business frauds shown in Exhibit 2, Congress passed new laws to monitor the behavior of accounting and business. For example, the Sarbanes-Oxley Act of 2002 (SOX) was enacted. SOX established a new oversight body for the accounting profession called the Public Company Accounting Oversight Board (PCAOB). In addition, SOX established standards for independence, corporate responsibility, and disclosure.

How does one behave ethically when faced with financial or other types of pressure? Guidelines for behaving ethically are shown in Exhibit 3.[2]

EXHIBIT 3

Guidelines for Ethical Conduct

1. Identify an ethical decision by using your personal ethical standards of honesty and fairness.
2. Identify the consequences of the decision and its effect on others.
3. Consider your obligations and responsibilities to those that will be affected by your decision.
4. Make a decision that is ethical and fair to those affected by it.

Integrity, Objectivity, and Ethics in Business

BERNIE MADOFF

In June 2009, Bernard L. "Bernie" Madoff was sentenced to 150 years in prison for defrauding thousands of investors in one of the biggest frauds in American history. Madoff's fraud started several decades earlier when he began a "Ponzi scheme" in his investment management firm, Bernard L. Madoff Securities LLC.

In a Ponzi scheme, the investment manager uses funds received from new investors to pay a return to existing investors, rather than basing investment returns on the fund's actual performance. As long as the investment manager is able to attract new investors, he or she will have new funds to pay existing investors and continue the fraud. While most Ponzi schemes collapse quickly when the investment manager runs out of new investors, Madoff's reputation, popularity, and personal contacts provided a steady stream of investors which allowed the fraud to survive for decades.

Opportunities for Accountants

Numerous career opportunities are available for students majoring in accounting. Currently, the demand for accountants exceeds the number of new graduates entering the job market. This is partly due to the increased regulation of business caused by the accounting and business frauds shown in Exhibit 2. Also, more and

2 Many companies have ethical standards of conduct for managers and employees. In addition, the Institute of Management Accountants and the American Institute of Certified Public Accountants have professional codes of conduct.

more businesses have come to recognize the importance and value of accounting information.

As indicated earlier, accountants employed by a business are employed in private accounting. Private accountants have a variety of possible career options within a company. Some of these career options are shown in Exhibit 4 along with their starting salaries. Accountants who provide audit services, called auditors, verify the accuracy of financial records, accounts, and systems. As shown in Exhibit 4, several private accounting careers have certification options.

Accountants and their staff who provide services on a fee basis are said to be employed in **public accounting**. In public accounting, an accountant may practice as an individual or as a member of a public accounting firm. Public accountants who have met a state's education, experience, and examination requirements may become **Certified Public Accountants (CPAs)**. CPAs generally perform general accounting,

EXHIBIT 4 **Accounting Career Paths and Salaries**

Accounting Career Track	Description	Career Options	Annual Starting Salaries[1]	Certification
Private Accounting	Accountants employed by companies, government, and not-for-profit entities.	Bookkeeper	$36,125	
		Payroll clerk	$34,875	Certified Payroll Professional (CPP)
		General accountant	$42,000	
		Budget analyst	$44,375	
		Cost accountant	$43,750	Certified Management Accountant (CMA)
		Internal auditor	$48,250	Certified Internal Auditor (CIA)
		Information technology auditor	$56,500	Certified Information Systems Auditor (CISA)
Public Accounting	Accountants employed individually or within a public accounting firm in tax or audit services.	Local firms	$45,063	Certified Public Accountant (CPA)
		National firms	$54,250	Certified Public Accountant (CPA)

Source: Robert Half 2010 Salary Guide (Finance and Accounting), Robert Half International, Inc.
[1]Mean salaries of a reported range. Private accounting salaries are reported for large companies. Salaries may vary by region.

audit, or tax services. As can be seen in Exhibit 4, CPAs have slightly better starting salaries than private accountants. Career statistics indicate, however, that these salary differences tend to disappear over time.

Because all functions within a business use accounting information, experience in private or public accounting provides a solid foundation for a career. Many positions in industry and in government agencies are held by individuals with accounting backgrounds.

OBJ. 2 Summarize the development of accounting principles and relate them to practice.

Generally Accepted Accounting Principles

If a company's management could record and report financial data as it saw fit, comparisons among companies would be difficult, if not impossible. Thus, financial accountants follow **generally accepted accounting principles (GAAP)** in preparing reports. These reports allow investors and other users to compare one company to another.

Accounting principles and concepts develop from research, accepted accounting practices, and pronouncements of regulators. Within the United States, the **Financial Accounting Standards Board (FASB)** has the primary responsibility for developing accounting principles. The FASB publishes *Statements of Financial Accounting Standards* as well as *Interpretations* of these Standards. In addition, the **Securities and Exchange Commission (SEC),** an agency of the U.S. government, has authority over the accounting and financial disclosures for companies whose shares of ownership (stock) are traded and sold to the public. The SEC normally accepts the accounting principles set forth by the FASB. However, the SEC may issue *Staff Accounting Bulletins* on accounting matters that may not have been addressed by the FASB.

Many countries outside the United States use generally accepted accounting principles adopted by the **International Accounting Standards Board (IASB)**. The IASB issues *International Financial Reporting Standards (IFRSs)*. Significant differences currently exist between FASB and IASB accounting principles. However, the FASB and IASB are working together to reduce and eliminate these differences into a single set of accounting principles. Such a set of worldwide accounting principles would help facilitate investment and business in an increasingly global economy.

See Appendix D for more information

In this chapter and text, accounting principles and concepts are emphasized. It is by this emphasis on the "why" as well as the "how" that you will gain an understanding of accounting.

InternationalConnection

INTERNATIONAL FINANCIAL REPORTING STANDARDS (IFRS)

IFRS are considered to be more "principles-based" than U.S. GAAP, which is considered to be more "rules-based." For example, U.S. GAAP consists of approximately 17,000 pages, which includes numerous industry-specific accounting rules. In contrast, IFRS allow more judgment in deciding how business transactions are recorded. Many believe that the strong regulatory and litigation environment in the United States is the cause for the more rules-based GAAP approach. Regardless, IFRS and GAAP share more in common than differences.*

*Differences between U.S. GAAP and IFRS are further discussed and illustrated in Appendix D.

Business Entity Concept

The **business entity concept** limits the economic data in an accounting system to data related directly to the activities of the business. In other words, the business is viewed as an entity separate from its owners, creditors, or other businesses. For example, the accountant for a business with one owner would record the activities of the business only and would not record the personal activities, property, or debts of the owner.

Note:
Under the business entity concept, the activities of a business are recorded separately from the activities of its owners, creditors, or other businesses.

A business entity may take the form of a proprietorship, partnership, corporation, or limited liability company (LLC). Each of these forms and their major characteristics are listed below.

Form of Business Entity	Characteristics
Proprietorship is owned by one individual.	• 70% of business entities in the United States.
	• Easy and cheap to organize.
	• Resources are limited to those of the owner.
	• Used by small businesses.
Partnership is owned by two or more individuals.	• 10% of business organizations in the United States (combined with limited liability companies).
	• Combines the skills and resources of more than one person.

(continued)

Form of Business Entity	Characteristics
Corporation is organized under state or federal statutes as a separate legal taxable entity.	• Generates 90% of business revenues. • 20% of the business organizations in the United States. • Ownership is divided into shares called stock. • Can obtain large amounts of resources by issuing stock. • Used by large businesses.
Limited liability company (LLC) combines the attributes of a partnership and a corporation.	• 10% of business organizations in the United States (combined with partnerships). • Often used as an alternative to a partnership. • Has tax and legal liability advantages for owners.

The three types of businesses discussed earlier—service, merchandising, and manufacturing—may be organized as proprietorships, partnerships, corporations, or limited liability companies. Because of the large amount of resources required to operate a manufacturing business, most manufacturing businesses such as Ford Motor Company are corporations. Most large retailers such as Wal-Mart and Home Depot are also corporations.

The Cost Concept

Under the **cost concept**, amounts are initially recorded in the accounting records at their cost or purchase price. To illustrate, assume that Aaron Publishers purchased the following building on February 20, 2010, for $150,000:

Price listed by seller on January 1, 2010	$160,000
Aaron Publishers' initial offer to buy on January 31, 2010	140,000
Purchase price on February 20, 2010	150,000
Estimated selling price on December 31, 2012	220,000
Assessed value for property taxes, December 31, 2012	190,000

Under the cost concept, Aaron Publishers records the purchase of the building on February 20, 2010, at the purchase price of $150,000. The other amounts listed above have no effect on the accounting records.

The fact that the building has an estimated selling price of $220,000 on December 31, 2012, indicates that the building has increased in value. However, to use the $220,000 in the accounting records would be to record an illusory or unrealized profit. If Aaron Publishers sells the building on January 9, 2014, for $240,000, a profit of $90,000 ($240,000 − $150,000) is then realized and recorded. The new owner would record $240,000 as its cost of the building.

The cost concept also involves the objectivity and unit of measure concepts. The **objectivity concept** requires that the amounts recorded in the accounting records be based on objective evidence. In exchanges between a buyer and a seller, both try to get the best price. Only the final agreed-upon amount is objective enough to be recorded in the accounting records. If amounts in the accounting records were constantly being revised upward or downward based on offers, appraisals, and opinions, accounting reports could become unstable and unreliable.

The **unit of measure concept** requires that economic data be recorded in dollars. Money is a common unit of measurement for reporting financial data and reports.

Example Exercise 1-1   Cost Concept   OBJ. 2

On August 25, Gallatin Repair Service extended an offer of $125,000 for land that had been priced for sale at $150,000. On September 3, Gallatin Repair Service accepted the seller's counteroffer of $137,000. On October 20, the land was assessed at a value of $98,000 for property tax purposes. On December 4, Gallatin Repair Service was offered $160,000 for the land by a national retail chain. At what value should the land be recorded in Gallatin Repair Service's records?

Follow My Example 1-1

$137,000. Under the cost concept, the land should be recorded at the cost to Gallatin Repair Service.

Practice Exercises: **PE 1-1A, PE 1-1B**

The Accounting Equation

The resources owned by a business are its **assets**. Examples of assets include cash, land, buildings, and equipment. The rights or claims to the assets are divided into two types: (1) the rights of creditors and (2) the rights of owners. The rights of creditors are the debts of the business and are called **liabilities**. The rights of the owners are called **owner's equity**. The following equation shows the relationship among assets, liabilities, and owner's equity:

OBJ. 3 State the accounting equation and define each element of the equation.

Assets = Liabilities + Owner's Equity

This equation is called the **accounting equation**. Liabilities usually are shown before owner's equity in the accounting equation because creditors have first rights to the assets.

Given any two amounts, the accounting equation may be solved for the third unknown amount. To illustrate, if the assets owned by a business amount to $100,000 and the liabilities amount to $30,000, the owner's equity is equal to $70,000, as shown below.

Assets – Liabilities   =   Owner's Equity

$100,000 – $30,000   = $70,000

Example Exercise 1-2   Accounting Equation   **OBJ. 3**

John Joos is the owner and operator of You're A Star, a motivational consulting business. At the end of its accounting period, December 31, 2011, You're A Star has assets of $800,000 and liabilities of $350,000. Using the accounting equation, determine the following amounts:

a. Owner's equity, as of December 31, 2011.
b. Owner's equity, as of December 31, 2012, assuming that assets increased by $130,000 and liabilities decreased by $25,000 during 2012.

Follow My Example 1-2

a.   Assets = Liabilities + Owner's Equity
         $800,000 = $350,000 + Owner's Equity
      Owner's Equity = $450,000
b. First, determine the change in Owner's Equity during 2012 as follows:
            Assets = Liabilities + Owner's Equity
         $130,000 = –$25,000 + Owner's Equity
      Owner's Equity = $155,000

Next, add the change in Owner's Equity on December 31, 2011, to arrive at Owner's Equity on December 31, 2012, as shown below.
Owner's Equity on December 31, 2012 = $605,000 = $450,000 + $155,000

Practice Exercises: **PE 1-2A, PE 1-2B**

Business Transactions and the Accounting Equation

OBJ. 4 Describe and illustrate how business transactions can be recorded in terms of the resulting change in the elements of the accounting equation.

Paying a monthly telephone bill of $168 affects a business's financial condition because it now has less cash on hand. Such an economic event or condition that directly changes an entity's financial condition or its results of operations is a **business transaction**. For example, purchasing land for $50,000 is a business transaction. In contrast, a change in a business's credit rating does not directly affect cash or any other asset, liability, or owner's equity amount.

BusinessConnection

THE ACCOUNTING EQUATION

The accounting equation serves as the basic foundation for the accounting systems of all companies. From the smallest business, such as the local convenience store, to the

largest business, such as Ford Motor Company, companies use the accounting equation. Some examples taken from recent financial reports of well-known companies are shown below.

Company	Assets*	=	Liabilities	+	Owner's Equity
The Coca-Cola Company	$ 40,519	=	$20,047	+	$20,472
Dell, Inc.	26,500	=	22,229	+	4,271
eBay, Inc.	15,593	=	4,509	+	11,084
Google	31,768	=	3,529	+	28,239
McDonald's	28,462	=	15,079	+	13,383
Microsoft Corporation	77,888	=	38,330	+	39,558
Southwest Airlines Co.	14,308	=	9,355	+	4,953
Wal-Mart	163,429	=	98,144	+	65,285

*Amounts are shown in millions of dollars.

Note:
All business transactions can be stated in terms of changes in the elements of the accounting equation.

All business transactions can be stated in terms of changes in the elements of the accounting equation. How business transactions affect the accounting equation can be illustrated by using some typical transactions. As a basis for illustration, a business organized by Chris Clark is used.

Assume that on November 1, 2011, Chris Clark begins a business that will be known as NetSolutions. The first phase of Chris's business plan is to operate NetSolutions as a service business assisting individuals and small businesses in developing Web pages and installing computer software. Chris expects this initial phase of the business to last one to two years. During this period, Chris plans on gathering information on the software and hardware needs of customers. During the second phase of the business plan, Chris plans to expand NetSolutions into a personalized retailer of software and hardware for individuals and small businesses.

Each transaction during NetSolutions' first month of operations is described in the following paragraphs. The effect of each transaction on the accounting equation is then shown.

Transaction A Nov. 1, 2011 Chris Clark deposited $25,000 in a bank account in the name of NetSolutions.

This transaction increases the asset cash (on the left side of the equation) by $25,000. To balance the equation, the owner's equity (on the right side of the equation) increases by the same amount. The equity of the owner is identified using the owner's name and "Capital," such as "Chris Clark, Capital."

The effect of this transaction on NetSolutions' accounting equation is shown below.

Assets	=	Owner's Equity
Cash	=	Chris Clark, Capital
a. 25,000		25,000

Since Chris Clark is the sole owner, NetSolutions is a proprietorship. Also, the accounting equation shown above is only for the business, NetSolutions. Under the business entity concept, Chris Clark's personal assets, such as a home or personal bank account, and personal liabilities are excluded from the equation.

Nov. 5, 2011   NetSolutions paid $20,000 for the purchase of land as a future building site.   **Transaction B**

The land is located in a business park with access to transportation facilities. Chris Clark plans to rent office space and equipment during the first phase of the business plan. During the second phase, Chris plans to build an office and a warehouse on the land.

The purchase of the land changes the makeup of the assets, but it does not change the total assets. The items in the equation prior to this transaction and the effect of the transaction are shown below. The new amounts are called *balances*.

	Assets		=	**Owner's Equity**
	Cash	+ Land	=	Chris Clark, Capital
Bal.	25,000			25,000
b.	−20,000	+20,000		
Bal.	5,000	20,000		25,000

Nov. 10, 2011   NetSolutions purchased supplies for $1,350 and agreed to pay the supplier in the near future.   **Transaction C**

You have probably used a credit card to buy clothing or other merchandise. In this type of transaction, you received clothing for a promise to pay your credit card bill in the future. That is, you received an asset and incurred a liability to pay a future bill. Net-Solutions entered into a similar transaction by purchasing supplies for $1,350 and agreeing to pay the supplier in the near future. This type of transaction is called a purchase *on account* and is often described as follows: *Purchased supplies on account, $1,350.*

The liability created by a purchase on account is called an **account payable**. Items such as supplies that will be used in the business in the future are called **prepaid expenses**, which are assets. Thus, the effect of this transaction is to increase assets (Supplies) and liabilities (Accounts Payable) by $1,350, as follows:

	Assets			=	**Liabilities + Owner's Equity**	
					Accounts	+ Chris Clark,
	Cash	+ Supplies +	Land	=	Payable	Capital
Bal.	5,000		20,000			25,000
c.		+1,350			+1,350	
Bal.	5,000	1,350	20,000		1,350	25,000

Nov. 18, 2011   NetSolutions received cash of $7,500 for providing services to customers.   **Transaction D**

You may have earned money by painting houses or mowing lawns. If so, you received money for rendering services to a customer. Likewise, a business earns money by selling goods or services to its customers. This amount is called **revenue**.

During its first month of operations, NetSolutions received cash of $7,500 for providing services to customers. The receipt of cash increases NetSolutions' assets and also increases Chris Clark's equity in the business. The revenues of $7,500 are recorded in a Fees Earned column to the right of Chris Clark, Capital. The effect of this transaction is to increase Cash and Fees Earned by $7,500, as shown at the top of the next page.

	Assets			=	Liabilities +		Owner's Equity	
					Accounts	Chris Clark,		Fees
	Cash	+ Supplies +	Land	=	Payable	+ Capital	+	Earned
Bal.	5,000	1,350	20,000		1,350	25,000		
d.	+7,500							+7,500
Bal.	12,500	1,350	20,000		1,350	25,000		7,500

Different terms are used for the various types of revenues. As illustrated above, revenue from providing services is recorded as **fees earned**. Revenue from the sale of merchandise is recorded as **sales**. Other examples of revenue include rent, which is recorded as **rent revenue**, and interest, which is recorded as **interest revenue**.

Instead of receiving cash at the time services are provided or goods are sold, a business may accept payment at a later date. Such revenues are described as *fees earned on account* or *sales on account*. For example, if NetSolutions had provided services on account instead of for cash, transaction (d) would have been described as follows: *Fees earned on account, $7,500.*

In such cases, the firm has an **account receivable**, which is a claim against the customer. An account receivable is an asset, and the revenue is earned and recorded as if cash had been received. When customers pay their accounts, Cash increases and Accounts Receivable decreases.

Transaction E   *Nov. 30, 2011   NetSolutions paid the following expenses during the month: wages, $2,125; rent, $800; utilities, $450; and miscellaneous, $275.*

During the month, NetSolutions spent cash or used up other assets in earning revenue. Assets used in this process of earning revenue are called **expenses**. Expenses include supplies used and payments for employee wages, utilities, and other services.

NetSolutions paid the following expenses during the month: wages, $2,125; rent, $800; utilities, $450; and miscellaneous, $275. Miscellaneous expenses include small amounts paid for such items as postage, coffee, and newspapers. The effect of expenses is the opposite of revenues in that expenses reduce assets and owner's equity. Like fees earned, the expenses are recorded in columns to the right of Chris Clark, Capital. However, since expenses reduce owner's equity, the expenses are entered as negative amounts. The effect of this transaction is shown below.

	Assets			=	Liabilities +		Owner's Equity				
					Accounts	Chris Clark,	Fees	Wages	Rent	Utilities	Misc.
	Cash	+ Supplies +	Land	=	Payable	+ Capital	+ Earned –	Exp. –	Exp. –	Exp. –	Exp.
Bal.	12,500	1,350	20,000		1,350	25,000	7,500				
e.	–3,650							–2,125	–800	–450	–275
Bal.	8,850	1,350	20,000		1,350	25,000	7,500	–2,125	–800	–450	–275

Businesses usually record each revenue and expense transaction as it occurs. However, to simplify, NetSolutions' revenues and expenses are summarized for the month in transactions (d) and (e).

Transaction F   *Nov. 30, 2011   NetSolutions paid creditors on account, $950.*

When you pay your monthly credit card bill, you decrease the cash in your checking account and decrease the amount you owe to the credit card company. Likewise, when NetSolutions pays $950 to creditors during the month, it reduces assets and liabilities, as shown at the top of the next page.

Assets			=	Liabilities +		Owner's Equity				
				Accounts	Chris Clark,	Fees	Wages	Rent	Utilities	Misc.
Cash	+ Supplies +	Land	=	Payable +	Capital	+ Earned −	Exp. −	Exp. −	Exp. −	Exp.
Bal. 8,850	1,350	20,000		1,350	25,000	7,500	−2,125	−800	−450	−275
f. −950				−950						
Bal. 7,900	1,350	20,000		400	25,000	7,500	−2,125	−800	−450	−275

Paying an amount on account is different from paying an expense. The paying of an expense reduces owner's equity, as illustrated in transaction (e). Paying an amount on account reduces the amount owed on a liability.

Nov. 30, 2011 *Chris Clark determined that the cost of supplies on hand at the end of the month was $550.*   **Transaction G**

The cost of the supplies on hand (not yet used) at the end of the month is $550. Thus, $800 ($1,350 − $550) of supplies must have been used during the month. This decrease in supplies is recorded as an expense, as shown below.

Assets			=	Liabilities +		Owner's Equity					
				Accounts	Chris Clark,	Fees	Wages	Rent	Supplies	Utilities	Misc.
Cash	+ Supplies +	Land		Payable +	Capital	+ Earned −	Exp. −	Exp. −	Exp. −	Exp. −	Exp.
Bal. 7,900	1,350	20,000	=	400	25,000	7,500	−2,125	−800		−450	−275
g.	−800								−800		
Bal. 7,900	550	20,000		400	25,000	7,500	−2,125	−800	−800	−450	−275

Nov. 30, 2011 *Chris Clark withdrew $2,000 from NetSolutions for personal use.*   **Transaction H**

At the end of the month, Chris Clark withdrew $2,000 in cash from the business for personal use. This transaction is the opposite of an investment in the business by the owner. Withdrawals by the owner should not be confused with expenses. Withdrawals *do not* represent assets or services used in the process of earning revenues. Instead, withdrawals are a distribution of capital to the owner. Owner withdrawals are identified by the owner's name and *Drawing*. For example, Chris Clark's withdrawal is identified as Chris Clark, Drawing. Like expenses, withdrawals are recorded in a column to the right of Chris Clark, Capital. The effect of the $2,000 withdrawal is as follows:

Assets			=	Liabilities +		Owner's Equity						
				Accounts	Chris Clark,	Chris Clark,	Fees	Wages	Rent	Supplies	Utilities	Misc.
Cash +	Supp. +	Land	=	Payable +	Capital −	Drawing +	Earned −	Exp. −	Exp. −	Exp. −	Exp. −	Exp.
Bal. 7,900	550	20,000		400	25,000		7,500	−2,125	−800	−800	−450	−275
h. −2,000						−2,000						
Bal. 5,900	550	20,000		400	25,000	−2,000	7,500	−2,125	−800	−800	−450	−275

Summary The transactions of NetSolutions are summarized at the top of the next page. Each transaction is identified by letter, and the balance of each accounting equation element is shown after every transaction.

You should note the following:

1. The effect of every transaction *is an increase or a decrease in one or more of the accounting equation elements.*
2. The two sides of the accounting equation are *always equal.*
3. The owner's equity is *increased by amounts invested by the owner and is decreased by withdrawals by the owner.* In addition, the owner's equity is *increased by revenues and is decreased by expenses.*

	Assets			=	Liabilities +		Owner's Equity														
					Accounts		Chris Clark,		Chris Clark,		Fees		Wages		Rent		Supplies		Utilities		Misc.
	Cash	+ Supp. +	Land	=	Payable	+	Capital	−	Drawing	+	Earned −		Exp. −		Exp. −		Exp. −		Exp. −		Exp.
a.	+25,000						+25,000														
b.	−20,000		+20,000																		
Bal.	5,000		20,000				25,000														
c.		+1,350			+1,350																
Bal.	5,000	+1,350	20,000		+1,350		25,000														
d.	+7,500										+7,500										
Bal.	12,500	1,350	20,000		1,350		25,000				7,500										
e.	−3,650												−2,125		−800				−450		−275
Bal.	8,850	1,350	20,000		1,350		25,000				7,500		−2,125		−800				−450		−275
f.	−950				−950																
Bal.	7,900	1,350	20,000		400		25,000				7,500		−2,125		−800				−450		−275
g.		−800																−800			
Bal.	7,900	550	20,000		400		25,000				7,500		−2,125		−800		−800		−450		−275
h.	−2,000									−2,000											
Bal.	5,900	550	20,000		400		25,000		−2,000		7,500		−2,125		−800		−800		−450		−275

The four types of transactions affecting owner's equity are illustrated in Exhibit 5.

EXHIBIT 5

Types of Transactions Affecting Owner's Equity

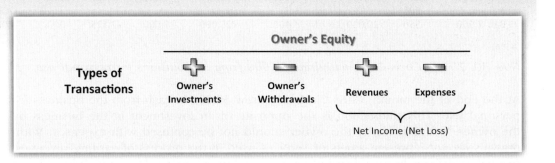

Example Exercise 1-3   Transactions   **OBJ. 4**

Salvo Delivery Service is owned and operated by Joel Salvo. The following selected transactions were completed by Salvo Delivery Service during February:

1. Received cash from owner as additional investment, $35,000.
2. Paid creditors on account, $1,800.
3. Billed customers for delivery services on account, $11,250.
4. Received cash from customers on account, $6,740.
5. Paid cash to owner for personal use, $1,000.

Indicate the effect of each transaction on the accounting equation elements (Assets, Liabilities, Owner's Equity, Drawing, Revenue, and Expense). Also, indicate the specific item within the accounting equation element that is affected. To illustrate, the answer to (1) is shown below.

(1) Asset (Cash) increases by $35,000; Owner's Equity (Joel Salvo, Capital) increases by $35,000.

Follow My Example 1-3

(2) Asset (Cash) decreases by $1,800; Liability (Accounts Payable) decreases by $1,800.
(3) Asset (Accounts Receivable) increases by $11,250; Revenue (Delivery Service Fees) increases by $11,250.
(4) Asset (Cash) increases by $6,740; Asset (Accounts Receivable) decreases by $6,740.
(5) Asset (Cash) decreases by $1,000; Drawing (Joel Salvo, Drawing) increases by $1,000.

Practice Exercises: **PE 1-3A, PE 1-3B**

Financial Statements

OBJ.
5   Describe the financial statements of a proprietorship and explain how they interrelate.

After transactions have been recorded and summarized, reports are prepared for users. The accounting reports providing this information are called **financial statements**. The primary financial statements of a proprietorship are the income statement, the statement of owner's equity, the balance sheet, and the statement of cash flows. The order that the financial statements are prepared and the nature of each statement is described as follows.

Order Prepared	Financial Statement	Description of Statement
1.	Income statement	A summary of the revenue and expenses *for a specific period of time*, such as a month or a year.
2.	Statement of owner's equity	A summary of the changes in the owner's equity that have occurred *during a specific period of time*, such as a month or a year.
3.	Balance sheet	A list of the assets, liabilities, and owner's equity *as of a specific date*, usually at the close of the last day of a month or a year.
4.	Statement of cash flows	A summary of the cash receipts and cash payments for a *specific period of time*, such as a month or a year.

The four financial statements and their interrelationships are illustrated in Exhibit 6, on page 17. The data for the statements are taken from the summary of transactions of NetSolutions on page 14.

All financial statements are identified by the name of the business, the title of the statement, and the *date* or *period of time*. The data presented in the income statement, the statement of owner's equity, and the statement of cash flows are for a period of time. The data presented in the balance sheet are for a specific date.

Income Statement

The income statement reports the revenues and expenses for a period of time, based on the **matching concept**. This concept is applied by *matching* the expenses incurred during a period with the revenue that those expenses generated. The excess of the revenue over the expenses is called **net income**, net profit, or **earnings**. If the expenses exceed the revenue, the excess is a **net loss**.

The revenue and expenses for NetSolutions were shown in the equation as separate increases and decreases. Net income for a period increases the owner's equity (capital) for the period. A net loss decreases the owner's equity (capital) for the period.

The revenue, expenses, and the net income of $3,050 for NetSolutions are reported in the income statement in Exhibit 6, on page 17. The order in which the expenses are listed in the income statement varies among businesses. Most businesses list expenses in order of size, beginning with the larger items. Miscellaneous expense is usually shown as the last item, regardless of the amount.

Note:
When revenues exceed expenses, it is referred to as *net income, net profits,* or *earnings*. When expenses exceed revenues, it is referred to as *net loss*.

Example Exercise 1-4   Income Statement

OBJ.
5

The revenues and expenses of Chickadee Travel Service for the year ended April 30, 2012, are listed below.

Fees earned	$263,200
Miscellaneous expense	12,950
Office expense	63,000
Wages expense	131,700

Prepare an income statement for the current year ended April 30, 2012.

(Continued)

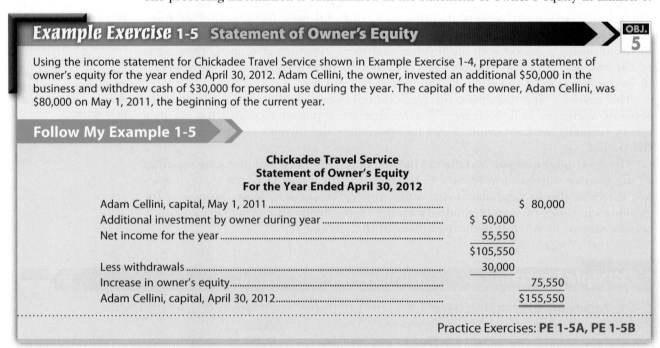

Chickadee Travel Service
Income Statement
For the Year Ended April 30, 2012

Fees earned		$263,200
Expenses:		
Wages expense	$131,700	
Office expense	63,000	
Miscellaneous expense	12,950	
Total expenses		207,650
Net income		$ 55,550

Practice Exercises: **PE 1-4A, PE 1-4B**

Statement of Owner's Equity

The statement of owner's equity reports the changes in the owner's equity for a period of time. It is prepared *after* the income statement because the net income or net loss for the period must be reported in this statement. Similarly, it is prepared *before* the balance sheet, since the amount of owner's equity at the end of the period must be reported on the balance sheet. Because of this, the statement of owner's equity is often viewed as the connecting link between the income statement and balance sheet.

Three types of transactions affected owner's equity of NetSolutions during November:

1. the original investment of $25,000,
2. the revenue and expenses that resulted in net income of $3,050 for the month, and
3. a withdrawal of $2,000 by the owner.

The preceding information is summarized in the statement of owner's equity in Exhibit 6.

Example Exercise 1-5   Statement of Owner's Equity   **OBJ. 5**

Using the income statement for Chickadee Travel Service shown in Example Exercise 1-4, prepare a statement of owner's equity for the year ended April 30, 2012. Adam Cellini, the owner, invested an additional $50,000 in the business and withdrew cash of $30,000 for personal use during the year. The capital of the owner, Adam Cellini, was $80,000 on May 1, 2011, the beginning of the current year.

Follow My Example 1-5

Chickadee Travel Service
Statement of Owner's Equity
For the Year Ended April 30, 2012

Adam Cellini, capital, May 1, 2011		$ 80,000
Additional investment by owner during year	$ 50,000	
Net income for the year	55,550	
	$105,550	
Less withdrawals	30,000	
Increase in owner's equity		75,550
Adam Cellini, capital, April 30, 2012		$155,550

Practice Exercises: **PE 1-5A, PE 1-5B**

Balance Sheet

The balance sheet in Exhibit 6 reports the amounts of NetSolutions' assets, liabilities, and owner's equity as of November 30, 2011. The asset and liability amounts are taken from the last line of the summary of transactions on page 14. Chris Clark, Capital

EXHIBIT 6

Financial Statements for NetSolutions

NetSolutions
Income Statement
For the Month Ended November 30, 2011

Fees earned		$7,500
Expenses:		
Wages expense	$2,125	
Rent expense	800	
Supplies expense	800	
Utilities expense	450	
Miscellaneous expense	275	
Total expense		4,450
Net income		$3,050

NetSolutions
Statement of Owner's Equity
For the Month Ended November 30 2011

Chris Clark, capital, November 1, 2011		$ 0
Investment on November 1, 2011	$25,000	
Net income for November	3,050	
	$28,050	
Less withdrawals	2,000	
Increase in owner's equity		26,050
Chris Clark, capital, November 30, 2011		$26,050

NetSolutions
Balance Sheet
November 30, 2011

Assets		Liabilities	
Cash	$ 5,900	Accounts payable	$ 400
Supplies	550	**Owner's Equity**	
Land	20,000	Chris Clark, capital	26,050
Total assets	$26,450	Total liabilities and owner's equity	$26,450

NetSolutions
Statement of Cash Flows
For the Month Ended November 30, 2011

Cash flows from operating activities:		
Cash received from customers	$ 7,500	
Deduct cash payments for expenses and payments to creditors	4,600	
Net cash flow from operating activities		$ 2,900
Cash flows from investing activities:		
Cash payments for purchase of land		(20,000)
Cash flows from financing activities:		
Cash received as owner's investment	$25,000	
Deduct cash withdrawal by owner	2,000	
Net cash flow from financing activities		23,000
Net cash flow and November 30, 2011, cash balance		$ 5,900

as of November 30, 2011, is taken from the statement of owner's equity. The form of balance sheet shown in Exhibit 6 is called the **account form**. This is because it resembles the basic format of the accounting equation, with assets on the left side and the liabilities and owner's equity sections on the right side.[3]

The assets section of the balance sheet presents assets in the order that they will be converted into cash or used in operations. Cash is presented first, followed by receivables, supplies, prepaid insurance, and other assets. The assets of a more permanent nature are shown next, such as land, buildings, and equipment.

In the liabilities section of the balance sheet in Exhibit 6, accounts payable is the only liability. When there are two or more liabilities, each should be listed and the total amount of liabilities presented as follows:

Liabilities		
Accounts payable	$12,900	
Wages payable	2,570	
Total liabilities		$15,470

Example Exercise 1-6 Balance Sheet OBJ. 5

Using the following data for Chickadee Travel Service as well as the statement of owner's equity shown in Example Exercise 1-5, prepare a balance sheet as of April 30, 2012.

Accounts receivable	$31,350
Accounts payable	12,200
Cash	53,050
Land	80,000
Supplies	3,350

Follow My Example 1-6

Chickadee Travel Service
Balance Sheet
April 30, 2012

Assets		**Liabilities**	
Cash....................................	$ 53,050	Accounts payable............................	$ 12,200
Accounts receivable	31,350		
Supplies..............................	3,350	**Owner's Equity**	
Land.................................	80,000	Adam Cellini, capital........................	155,550
Total assets...........................	$167,750	Total liabilities and owner's equity	$167,750

Practice Exercises: **PE 1-6A, PE 1-6B**

Statement of Cash Flows

The statement of cash flows consists of the following three sections, as shown in Exhibit 6:

1. operating activities,
2. investing activities, and
3. financing activities.

Each of these sections is briefly described below.

Cash Flows from Operating Activities This section reports a summary of cash receipts and cash payments from operations. The net cash flow from operating activities normally differs from the amount of net income for the period. In Exhibit 6, NetSolutions

3 An alternative form of balance sheet, called the *report form*, is illustrated in Chapter 6. It presents the liabilities and owner's equity sections below the assets section.

reported net cash flows from operating activities of $2,900 and net income of $3,050. This difference occurs because revenues and expenses may not be recorded at the same time that cash is received from customers or paid to creditors.

Cash Flows from Investing Activities This section reports the cash transactions for the acquisition and sale of relatively permanent assets. Exhibit 6 reports that NetSolutions paid $20,000 for the purchase of land during November.

Cash Flows from Financing Activities This section reports the cash transactions related to cash investments by the owner, borrowings, and withdrawals by the owner. Exhibit 6 shows that Chris Clark invested $25,000 in the business and withdrew $2,000 during November.

Preparing the statement of cash flows requires that each of the November cash transactions for NetSolutions be classified as an operating, investing, or financing activity. Using the summary of transactions shown on page 14, the November cash transactions for NetSolutions are classified as follows:

Transaction	Amount	Cash Flow Activity
a.	$25,000	Financing (Investment by Chris Clark)
b.	−20,000	Investing (Purchase of land)
d.	7,500	Operating (Fees earned)
e.	−3,650	Operating (Payment of expenses)
f.	−950	Operating (Payment of account payable)
h.	−2,000	Financing (Withdrawal by Chris Clark)

Transactions (c) and (g) are not listed above since they did not involve a cash receipt or payment. In addition, the payment of accounts payable in transaction (f) is classified as an operating activity since the account payable arose from the purchase of supplies, which are used in operations. Using the preceding classifications of November cash transactions, the statement of cash flows is prepared as shown in Exhibit 6.[4]

The ending cash balance shown on the statement of cash flows is also reported on the balance sheet as of the end of the period. To illustrate, the ending cash of $5,900 reported on the November statement of cash flows in Exhibit 6 is also reported as the amount of cash on hand in the November 30, 2011, balance sheet.

Since November is NetSolutions' first period of operations, the net cash flow for November and the November 30, 2011, cash balance are the same amount, $5,900, as shown in Exhibit 6. In later periods, NetSolutions will report in its statement of cash flows a beginning cash balance, an increase or a decrease in cash for the period, and an ending cash balance. For example, assume that for December NetSolutions has a decrease in cash of $3,835. The last three lines of NetSolutions' statement of cash flows for December would be as follows:

Decrease in cash	$3,835
Cash as of December 1, 2011	5,900
Cash as of December 31, 2011	$2,065

Example Exercise 1-7   Statement of Cash Flows

OBJ. 5

A summary of cash flows for Chickadee Travel Service for the year ended April 30, 2012, is shown below.

Cash receipts:

Cash received from customers	$251,000
Cash received from additional investment of owner	50,000

Cash payments:

Cash paid for expenses	210,000
Cash paid for land	80,000
Cash paid to owner for personal use	30,000

The cash balance as of May 1, 2011, was $72,050. Prepare a statement of cash flows for Chickadee Travel Service for the year ended April 30, 2012.

(Continued)

4 This method of preparing the statement of cash flows is called the "direct method." This method and the indirect method are discussed further in Chapter 16.

Follow My Example 1-7

Chickadee Travel Service
Statement of Cash Flows
For the Year Ended April 30, 2012

Cash flows from operating activities:		
Cash received from customers	$251,000	
Deduct cash payments for expenses	210,000	
Net cash flows from operating activities.....................		$ 41,000
Cash flows from investing activities:		
Cash payments for purchase of land		(80,000)
Cash flows from financing activities:		
Cash received from owner as investment....................	$ 50,000	
Deduct cash withdrawals by owner	30,000	
Net cash flows from financing activities		20,000
Net decrease in cash during year		$(19,000)
Cash as of May 1, 2011		72,050
Cash as of April 30, 2012		$ 53,050

Practice Exercises: **PE 1-7A, PE 1-7B**

Interrelationships Among Financial Statements

Financial statements are prepared in the order of the income statement, statement of owner's equity, balance sheet, and statement of cash flows. This order is important because the financial statements are interrelated. These interrelationships for NetSolutions are shown in Exhibit 6 and are described below.[5]

Financial Statements	Interrelationship	NetSolutions Example (Exhibit 6)
Income Statement *and* Statement of Owner's Equity	Net income or net loss reported on the income statement is also reported on the statement of owner's equity as either an addition (net income) to or deduction (net loss) from the beginning owner's equity and any additional investments by the owner during the period.	NetSolutions' net income of $3,050 for November is added to Chris Clark's investment of $25,000 in the statement of owner's equity.
Statement of Owner's Equity *and* Balance Sheet	Owner's capital at the end of the period reported on the statement of owner's equity is also reported on the balance sheet as owner's capital.	Chris Clark, Capital of $26,050 as of November 30, 2011, on the statement of owner's equity also appears on the November 30, 2011, balance sheet as Chris Clark, Capital.
Balance Sheet *and* Statement of Cash Flows	The cash reported on the balance sheet is also reported as the end-of-period cash on the statement of cash flows.	Cash of $5,900 reported on the balance sheet as of November 30, 2011, is also reported on the November statement of cash flows as the end-of-period cash.

The preceding interrelationships are important in analyzing financial statements and the impact of transactions on a business. In addition, these interrelationships serve as a check on whether the financial statements are prepared correctly. For example, if the ending cash on the statement of cash flows doesn't agree with the balance sheet cash, then an error has occurred.

5 Depending on the method of preparing the cash flows from operating activities section of the statement of cash flows, net income (or net loss) may also appear on the statement of cash flows. This interrelationship or method of preparing the statement of cash flows, called the "indirect method," is described and illustrated in Chapter 16.

Financial Analysis and Interpretation: Ratio of Liabilities to Owner's Equity

FAI

OBJ. 6 Describe and illustrate the use of the ratio of liabilities to owner's equity in evaluating a company's financial condition.

The basic financial statements illustrated in this chapter are useful to bankers, creditors, owners, and others in analyzing and interpreting the financial performance and condition of a company. Throughout this text, various tools and techniques that are often used to analyze and interpret a company's financial performance and condition are described and illustrated. The first such tool that is discussed is useful in analyzing the ability of a company to pay its creditors.

The relationship between liabilities and owner's equity, expressed as a **ratio of liabilities to owner's equity**, is computed as follows:

$$\text{Ratio of Liabilities to Owner's Equity} = \frac{\text{Total Liabilities}}{\text{Total Owner's Equity (or Total Stockholders' Equity)}}$$

NetSolutions' ratio of liabilities to owner's equity at the end of November is 0.015, as computed below.

$$\text{Ratio of Liabilities to Owner's Equity} = \frac{\$400}{\$26,050} = 0.015$$

Corporations refer to total owner's equity as total stockholders' equity. Thus, total stockholders' equity is substituted for total owner's equity when computing this ratio.

To illustrate, balance sheet data (in millions) for Google Inc. and McDonald's Corporation are shown below.

	Dec. 31, 2009	Dec. 31, 2008
Google Inc.		
Total liabilities	$ 3,529	$ 2,646
Total stockholders' equity	28,239	22,690
McDonald's Corporation		
Total liabilities	$15,079	$14,112
Total stockholders' equity	13,383	15,280

The ratio of liabilities to stockholders' equity as of December 31, 2009 and 2008 for Google and McDonald's is computed below.

	Dec. 31, 2009	Dec. 31, 2008
Google Inc.		
Total liabilities	$ 3,529	$ 2,646
Total stockholders' equity	28,239	22,690
Ratio of liabilities to stockholders' equity	0.12	0.12
	($3,529/$28,239)	($2,646/$22,690)
McDonald's Corporation		
Total liabilities	$15,079	$14,112
Total stockholders' equity	13,383	15,280
Ratio of liabilities to stockholders' equity	1.13	0.92
	($15,079/$13,383)	($14,112/$15,280)

The rights of creditors to a business's assets come before the rights of the owners or stockholders. Thus, the lower the ratio of liabilities to owner's equity, the better able the company is to withstand poor business conditions and pay its obligations to creditors.

Google is unusual in that it has a very low amount of liabilities; thus, its ratio of liabilities to stockholders' equity of 0.12 is small. In contrast, McDonald's has more liabilities; its ratio of liabilities to stockholders' equity is 1.13 and 0.92 on December 31, 2009 and 2008, respectively. Since McDonald's ratio of liabilities to stockholders' equity increased slightly from 2008 to 2009, its creditors are slightly more at risk on December 31, 2009, as compared to December 31, 2008. Also, McDonald's creditors are more at risk than are Google's creditors. The creditors of both companies are, however, well protected against the risk of nonpayment.

Example Exercise 1-8   Ratio of Liabilities to Owner's Equity

OBJ. 6

The following data were taken from Hawthorne Company's balance sheet:

	Dec. 31, 2012	Dec. 31, 2011
Total liabilities	$120,000	$105,000
Total owner's equity	80,000	75,000

a. Compute the ratio of liabilities to owner's equity.
b. Has the creditors' risk increased or decreased from December 31, 2011, to December 31, 2012?

Follow My Example 1-8

a.

	Dec. 31, 2012	Dec. 31, 2011
Total liabilities	$120,000	$105,000
Total owner's equity	80,000	75,000
Ratio of liabilities to owner's equity	1.50	1.40
	($120,000/$80,000)	($105,000/$75,000)

b. Increased

Practice Exercises: **PE 1-8A, PE 1-8B**

At a Glance   1

OBJ. 1   Describe the nature of a business, the role of accounting, and ethics in business.

Key Points   A business provides goods or services (outputs) to customers with the objective of earning a profit. Three types of businesses include service, merchandising, and manufacturing businesses.

Accounting is an information system that provides reports to users about the economic activities and condition of a business.

Ethics are moral principles that guide the conduct of individuals. Good ethical conduct depends on individual character and firm culture.

Accountants are engaged in private accounting or public accounting.

Learning Outcomes	Example Exercises	Practice Exercises
• Distinguish among service, merchandising, and manufacturing businesses.		
• Describe the role of accounting in business and explain why accounting is called the "language of business."		
• Define ethics and list the two factors affecting ethical conduct.		
• Describe what private and public accounting means.		

OBJ.
2 | Summarize the development of accounting principles and relate them to practice.

Key Points   Generally accepted accounting principles (GAAP) are used in preparing financial statements. Accounting principles and concepts develop from research, practice, and pronouncements of authoritative bodies.

The business entity concept views the business as an entity separate from its owners, creditors, or other businesses. Businesses may be organized as proprietorships, partnerships, corporations, and limited liability companies. The cost concept requires that purchases of a business be recorded in terms of actual cost. The objectivity concept requires that the accounting records and reports be based on objective evidence. The unit of measure concept requires that economic data be recorded in dollars.

Learning Outcomes	Example Exercises	Practice Exercises
• Explain what is meant by generally accepted accounting principles.		
• Describe how generally accepted accounting principles are developed.		
• Describe and give an example of what is meant by the business entity concept.		
• Describe the characteristics of a proprietorship, partnership, corporation, and limited liability company.		
• Describe and give an example of what is meant by the cost concept.	**EE1-1**	**PE1-1A, 1-1B**
• Describe and give an example of what is meant by the objectivity concept.		
• Describe and give an example of what is meant by the unit of measure concept.		

OBJ.
3 | State the accounting equation and define each element of the equation.

Key Points   The resources owned by a business and the rights or claims to these resources may be stated in the form of an equation, as follows:

Assets = Liabilities + Owner's Equity

Learning Outcomes	Example Exercises	Practice Exercises
• State the accounting equation.		
• Define assets, liabilities, and owner's equity.		
• Given two elements of the accounting equation, solve for the third element.	**EE1-2**	**PE1-2A, 1-2B**

OBJ.
4 | Describe and illustrate how business transactions can be recorded in terms of the resulting change in the elements of the accounting equation.

Key Points   All business transactions can be stated in terms of the change in one or more of the three elements of the accounting equation.

Learning Outcomes	Example Exercises	Practice Exercises
• Define a business transaction.		
• Using the accounting equation as a framework, record transactions.	**EE1-3**	**PE1-3A, 1-3B**

Describe the financial statements of a proprietorship and explain how they interrelate.

Key Points The primary financial statements of a proprietorship are the income statement, the statement of owner's equity, the balance sheet, and the statement of cash flows. The income statement reports a period's net income or net loss, which is also reported on the statement of owner's equity. The ending owner's capital reported on the statement of owner's equity is also reported on the balance sheet. The ending cash balance is reported on the balance sheet and the statement of cash flows.

Learning Outcomes	Example Exercises	Practice Exercises
• List and describe the financial statements of a proprietorship.		
• Prepare an income statement.	EE1-4	PE1-4A, 1-4B
• Prepare a statement of owner's equity.	EE1-5	PE1-5A, 1-5B
• Prepare a balance sheet.	EE1-6	PE1-6A, 1-6B
• Prepare a statement of cash flows.	EE1-7	PE1-7A, 1-7B
• Explain how the financial statements of a proprietorship are interrelated.		

Describe and illustrate the use of the ratio of liabilities to owner's equity in evaluating a company's financial condition.

Key Points A ratio useful in analyzing the ability of a business to pay its creditors is the ratio of liabilities to owner's (stockholders') equity. The lower the ratio of liabilities to owner's equity, the better able the company is to withstand poor business conditions and pay its obligations to creditors.

Learning Outcomes	Example Exercises	Practice Exercises
• Describe the usefulness of the ratio of liabilities to owner's (stockholders') equity.		
• Compute the ratio of liabilities to owner's (stockholders') equity.	EE1-8	PE1-8A, 1-8B

Key Terms

account form (18)
account payable (11)
account receivable (12)
accounting (3)
accounting equation (9)
assets (9)
balance sheet (15)
business (2)
business entity concept (7)
business transaction (9)
Certified Public Accountant (CPA) (6)
corporation (8)

cost concept (8)
earnings (15)
ethics (4)
expenses (12)
fees earned (12)
financial accounting (3)
Financial Accounting Standards Board (FASB) (7)
financial statements (15)
general-purpose financial statements (4)
generally accepted accounting principles (GAAP) (6)

income statement (15)
interest revenue (12)
International Accounting Standards Board (IASB) (7)
liabilities (9)
limited liability company (LLC) (8)
management (or managerial) accounting (3)
manufacturing business (2)
matching concept (15)
merchandising business (2)
net income (or net profit) (15)

net loss (15)

objectivity concept (8)

owner's equity (9)

partnership (7)

prepaid expenses (11)

private accounting (3)

profit (2)

proprietorship (7)

public accounting (6)

ratio of liabilities to owner's
(stockholders') equity (21)

rent revenue (12)

revenue (11)

sales (12)

Securities and Exchange
Commission (SEC) (7)

service business (2)

statement of cash flows (15)

statement of owner's
equity (15)

unit of measure concept (8)

Illustrative Problem

Cecil Jameson, Attorney-at-Law, is a proprietorship owned and operated by Cecil Jameson. On July 1, 2011, Cecil Jameson, Attorney-at-Law, has the following assets and liabilities: cash, $1,000; accounts receivable, $3,200; supplies, $850; land, $10,000; accounts payable, $1,530. Office space and office equipment are currently being rented, pending the construction of an office complex on land purchased last year. Business transactions during July are summarized as follows:

a. Received cash from clients for services, $3,928.

b. Paid creditors on account, $1,055.

c. Received cash from Cecil Jameson as an additional investment, $3,700.

d. Paid office rent for the month, $1,200.

e. Charged clients for legal services on account, $2,025.

f. Purchased supplies on account, $245.

g. Received cash from clients on account, $3,000.

h. Received invoice for paralegal services from Legal Aid Inc. for July (to be paid on August 10), $1,635.

i. Paid the following: wages expense, $850; answering service expense, $250; utilities expense, $325; and miscellaneous expense, $75.

j. Determined that the cost of supplies on hand was $980; therefore, the cost of supplies used during the month was $115.

k. Jameson withdrew $1,000 in cash from the business for personal use.

Instructions

1. Determine the amount of owner's equity (Cecil Jameson's capital) as of July 1, 2011.

2. State the assets, liabilities, and owner's equity as of July 1 in equation form similar to that shown in this chapter. In tabular form below the equation, indicate the increases and decreases resulting from each transaction and the new balances after each transaction.

3. Prepare an income statement for July, a statement of owner's equity for July, and a balance sheet as of July 31, 2011.

4. (Optional). Prepare a statement of cash flows for July.

Solution

1.

$$\text{Assets} - \text{Liabilities} = \text{Owner's Equity (Cecil Jameson, capital)}$$
$$(\$1,000 + \$3,200 + \$850 + \$10,000) - \$1,530 = \text{Owner's Equity (Cecil Jameson, capital)}$$
$$\$15,050 - \$1,530 = \text{Owner's Equity (Cecil Jameson, capital)}$$
$$\$13,520 = \text{Owner's Equity (Cecil Jameson, capital)}$$

2.

	Assets			=	Liabilities +		Owner's Equity								
	Cash +	Accts. Rec. +	Supp. +	Land =	Accts. Pay. +	Cecil Jameson, Capital –	Cecil Jameson, Drawing +	Fees Earned –	Paralegal Exp. –	Rent Exp. –	Wages Exp. –	Utilities Exp. –	Answering Service Exp. –	Supp Exp. –	Misc. Exp.
Bal.	1,000	3,200	850	10,000	1,530	13,520									
a.	+3,928							3,928							
Bal.	4,928	3,200	850	10,000	1,530	13,520		3,928							
b.	–1,055				–1,055										
Bal.	3,873	3,200	850	10,000	475	13,520		3,928							
c.	+3,700					+3,700									
Bal.	7,573	3,200	850	10,000	475	17,220		3,928							
d.	–1,200									–1,200					
Bal.	6,373	3,200	850	10,000	475	17,220		3,928		–1,200					
e.		+2,025						+2,025							
Bal.	6,373	5,225	850	10,000	475	17,220		5,953		–1,200					
f.			+245		+245										
Bal.	6,373	5,225	1,095	10,000	720	17,220		5,953		–1,200					
g.	+3,000	–3,000													
Bal.	9,373	2,225	1,095	10,000	720	17,220		5,953		–1,200					
h.					+1,635				–1,635						
Bal.	9,373	2,225	1,095	10,000	2,355	17,220		5,953	–1,635	–1,200					
i.	–1,500										–850	–325	–250		–75
Bal.	7,873	2,225	1,095	10,000	2,355	17,220		5,953	–1,635	–1,200	–850	–325	–250		–75
j.			–115											–115	
Bal.	7,873	2,225	980	10,000	2,355	17,220		5,953	–1,635	–1,200	–850	–325	–250	–115	–75
k.	–1,000						–1,000								
Bal.	6,873	2,225	980	10,000	2,355	17,220	–1,000	5,953	–1,635	–1,200	–850	–325	–250	–115	–75

3.

Cecil Jameson, Attorney-at-Law
Income Statement
For the Month Ended July 31, 2011

Fees earned..		$5,953
Expenses:		
Paralegal expense..	$1,635	
Rent expense	1,200	
Wages expense	850	
Utilities expense	325	
Answering service expense	250	
Supplies expense	115	
Miscellaneous expense	75	
Total expenses...		4,450
Net income		$1,503

Cecil Jameson, Attorney-at-Law
Statement of Owner's Equity
For the Month Ended July 31, 2011

Cecil Jameson, capital, July 1, 2011		$13,520
Additional investment by owner......................................	$3,700	
Net income for the month	1,503	
	$5,203	
Less withdrawals..	1,000	
Increase in owner's equity		4,203
Cecil Jameson, capital, July 31, 2011		$17,723

(continued)

Cecil Jameson, Attorney-at-Law
Balance Sheet
July 31, 2011

Assets		Liabilities	
Cash	$ 6,873	Accounts payable	$ 2,355
Accounts receivable	2,225	**Owner's Equity**	
Supplies	980	Cecil Jameson, capital	17,723
Land	10,000	Total liabilities and owner's	
Total assets	$20,078	equity	$20,078

4. Optional.

Cecil Jameson, Attorney-at-Law
Statement of Cash Flows
For the Month Ended July 31, 2011

Cash flows from operating activities:		
Cash received from customers	$6,928*	
Deduct cash payments for operating expenses	3,755**	
Net cash flows from operating activities		$3,173
Cash flows from investing activities		—
Cash flows from financing activities:		
Cash received from owner as investment	$3,700	
Deduct cash withdrawals by owner	1,000	
Net cash flows from financing activities		2,700
Net increase in cash during year		$5,873
Cash as of July 1, 2011		1,000
Cash as of July 31, 2011		$6,873

*$6,928 = $3,928 + $3,000
**$3,755 = $1,055 + $1,200 + $1,500

Discussion Questions

1. Name some users of accounting information.

2. What is the role of accounting in business?

3. Why are most large companies like Microsoft, PepsiCo, Caterpillar, and AutoZone organized as corporations?

4. Murray Stoltz is the owner of Ontime Delivery Service. Recently, Murray paid interest of $3,200 on a personal loan of $60,000 that he used to begin the business. Should Ontime Delivery Service record the interest payment? Explain.

5. On October 3, A2Z Repair Service extended an offer of $75,000 for land that had been priced for sale at $90,000. On November 23, A2Z Repair Service accepted the seller's counteroffer of $82,000. Describe how A2Z Repair Service should record the land.

6. a. Land with an assessed value of $400,000 for property tax purposes is acquired by a business for $525,000. Ten years later, the plot of land has an assessed value of $700,000 and the business receives an offer of $1,000,000 for it. Should the monetary amount assigned to the land in the business records now be increased?

   b. Assuming that the land acquired in (a) was sold for $1,000,000, how would the various elements of the accounting equation be affected?

7. Describe the difference between an account receivable and an account payable.

8. A business had revenues of $430,000 and operating expenses of $615,000. Did the business (a) incur a net loss or (b) realize net income?

9. A business had revenues of $825,000 and operating expenses of $708,000. Did the business (a) incur a net loss or (b) realize net income?

10. What particular item of financial or operating data appears on both the income statement and the statement of owner's equity? What item appears on both the balance sheet and the statement of owner's equity? What item appears on both the balance sheet and the statement of cash flows?

Practice Exercises

Learning Objectives	Example Exercises	
OBJ. 2	EE 1-1 *p. 8*	**PE 1-1A Cost concept**

On June 10, Easy Repair Service extended an offer of $95,000 for land that had been priced for sale at $118,500. On August 2, Easy Repair Service accepted the seller's counteroffer of $105,000. On August 27, the land was assessed at a value of $80,000 for property tax purposes. On April 1, Easy Repair Service was offered $125,000 for the land by a national retail chain. At what value should the land be recorded in Easy Repair Service's records?

OBJ. 2	EE 1-1 *p. 8*	**PE 1-1B Cost concept**

On February 7, AAA Repair Service extended an offer of $50,000 for land that had been priced for sale at $65,000. On February 21, AAA Repair Service accepted the seller's counteroffer of $57,500. On April 30, the land was assessed at a value of $40,000 for property tax purposes. On August 30, AAA Repair Service was offered $90,000 for the land by a national retail chain. At what value should the land be recorded in AAA Repair Service's records?

OBJ. 3	EE 1-2 *p. 9*	**PE 1-2A Accounting equation**

Shannon Cook is the owner and operator of Galaxy LLC, a motivational consulting business. At the end of its accounting period, December 31, 2011, Galaxy has assets of $800,000 and liabilities of $450,000. Using the accounting equation, determine the following amounts:

a. Owner's equity, as of December 31, 2011.

b. Owner's equity, as of December 31, 2012, assuming that assets increased by $175,000 and liabilities decreased by $60,000 during 2012.

OBJ. 3	EE 1-2 *p. 9*	**PE 1-2B Accounting equation**

Jan Petri is the owner and operator of You're the One, a motivational consulting business. At the end of its accounting period, December 31, 2011, You're the One has assets of $575,000 and liabilities of $125,000. Using the accounting equation, determine the following amounts:

a. Owner's equity, as of December 31, 2011.

b. Owner's equity, as of December 31, 2012, assuming that assets increased by $85,000 and liabilities increased by $30,000 during 2012.

OBJ. 4	EE 1-3 *p. 14*	**PE 1-3A Transactions**

Queens Delivery Service is owned and operated by Lisa Dewar. The following selected transactions were completed by Queens Delivery Service during June:

1. Received cash from owner as additional investment, $18,000.

2. Paid creditors on account, $1,800.

3. Billed customers for delivery services on account, $12,500.

4. Received cash from customers on account, $6,900.

5. Paid cash to owner for personal use, $4,000.

Indicate the effect of each transaction on the accounting equation elements (Assets, Liabilities, Owner's Equity, Drawing, Revenue, and Expense). Also, indicate the specific item within the accounting equation element that is affected. To illustrate, the answer to (1) is shown below.

(1) Asset (Cash) increases by $18,000; Owner's Equity (Lisa Dewar, Capital) increases by $18,000.

OBJ. 4   EE 1-3 *p. 14*   **PE 1-3B**   **Transactions**

Motorcross Delivery Service is owned and operated by Jim Smith. The following selected transactions were completed by Motorcross Delivery Service during February:

1. Received cash from owner as additional investment, $30,000.
2. Paid advertising expense, $1,200.
3. Purchased supplies on account, $450.
4. Billed customers for delivery services on account, $7,500.
5. Received cash from customers on account, $4,900.

Indicate the effect of each transaction on the accounting equation elements (Assets, Liabilities, Owner's Equity, Drawing, Revenue, and Expense). Also, indicate the specific item within the accounting equation element that is affected. To illustrate, the answer to (1) is shown below.

(1) Asset (Cash) increases by $30,000; Owner's Equity (Jim Smith, Capital) increases by $30,000.

OBJ. 5   EE 1-4 *p. 16*   **PE 1-4A**   **Income statement**

The revenues and expenses of Dynasty Travel Service for the year ended June 30, 2012, are listed below.

Fees earned	$950,000
Office expense	222,000
Miscellaneous expense	16,000
Wages expense	478,000

Prepare an income statement for the current year ended June 30, 2012.

OBJ. 5   EE 1-4 *p. 16*   **PE 1-4B**   **Income statement**

The revenues and expenses of Escape Travel Service for the year ended November 30, 2012, are listed below.

Fees earned	$942,500
Office expense	391,625
Miscellaneous expense	15,875
Wages expense	562,500

Prepare an income statement for the current year ended November 30, 2012.

OBJ. 5   EE 1-5 *p. 16*   **PE 1-5A**   **Statement of owner's equity**

Using the income statement for Dynasty Travel Service shown in Practice Exercise 1-4A, prepare a statement of owner's equity for the current year ended June 30, 2012. Nancy Coleman, the owner, invested an additional $60,000 in the business during the year and withdrew cash of $36,000 for personal use. Nancy Coleman, capital as of July 1, 2011, was $250,000.

OBJ. 5   EE 1-5 *p. 16*   **PE 1-5B**   **Statement of owner's equity**

Using the income statement for Escape Travel Service shown in Practice Exercise 1-4B, prepare a statement of owner's equity for the current year ended November 30, 2012. Brett Daniels, the owner, invested an additional $45,000 in the business during the year and withdrew cash of $25,000 for personal use. Brett Daniels, capital as of December 1, 2011, was $475,000.

OBJ. 5   EE 1-6 *p. 18*   **PE 1-6A**   **Balance sheet**

Using the following data for Dynasty Travel Service as well as the statement of owner's equity shown in Practice Exercise 1-5A, prepare a balance sheet as of June 30, 2012.

Accounts receivable	$ 64,000
Accounts payable	24,000
Cash	156,000
Land	300,000
Supplies	12,000

OBJ. 5 EE 1-6 *p. 18* **PE 1-6B   Balance sheet**

Using the following data for Escape Travel Service as well as the statement of owner's equity shown in Practice Exercise 1-5B, prepare a balance sheet as of November 30, 2012.

Accounts receivable	$ 94,375
Accounts payable	52,500
Cash	56,750
Land	362,500
Supplies	6,375

OBJ. 5 EE 1-7 *p. 20* **PE 1-7A   Statement of cash flows**

A summary of cash flows for Dynasty Travel Service for the year ended June 30, 2012, is shown below.

Cash receipts:	
Cash received from customers	$920,000
Cash received from additional investment of owner	60,000
Cash payments:	
Cash paid for operating expenses	710,000
Cash paid for land	208,000
Cash paid to owner for personal use	36,000

The cash balance as of July 1, 2011, was $130,000.

Prepare a statement of cash flows for Dynasty Travel Service for the year ended June 30, 2012.

OBJ. 5 EE 1-7 *p. 20* **PE 1-7B   Statement of cash flows**

A summary of cash flows for Escape Travel Service for the year ended November 30, 2012, is shown below.

Cash receipts:	
Cash received from customers	$875,000
Cash received from additional investment of owner	45,000
Cash payments:	
Cash paid for operating expenses	912,500
Cash paid for land	67,500
Cash paid to owner for personal use	25,000

The cash balance as of December 1, 2011, was $141,750.

Prepare a statement of cash flows for Escape Travel Service for the year ended November 30, 2012.

OBJ. 6 EE 1-8 *p. 22* **PE 1-8A   Ratio of liabilities to owner's equity**

FAI

The following data were taken from White Company's balance sheet:

	Dec. 31, 2012	Dec. 31, 2011
Total liabilities	$375,000	$287,500
Total owner's equity	300,000	250,000

a. Compute the ratio of liabilities to owner's equity.

b. Has the creditor's risk increased or decreased from December 31, 2011 to December 31, 2012?

OBJ. 6   EE 1-8 *p. 22*   **PE 1-8B   Ratio of liabilities to owner's equity**

The following data were taken from Stone Company's balance sheet:

	Dec. 31, 2012	Dec. 31, 2011
Total liabilities	$340,000	$300,000
Total owner's equity	500,000	400,000

a. Compute the ratio of liabilities to owner's equity.

b. Has the creditor's risk increased or decreased from December 31, 2011 to December 31, 2012?

Exercises

OBJ. 1

EX 1-1   Types of businesses

The following is a list of well-known companies.

1. H&R Block
2. eBay Inc.
3. Wal-Mart Stores, Inc.
4. Ford Motor Company
5. Citigroup
6. Boeing
7. SunTrust
8. Alcoa Inc.
9. Procter & Gamble
10. FedEx
11. Gap Inc.
12. Hilton Hospitality, Inc.
13. CVS
14. Caterpillar
15. The Dow Chemical Company

a. Indicate whether each of these companies is primarily a service, merchandise, or manufacturing business. If you are unfamiliar with the company, use the Internet to locate the company's home page or use the finance Web site of Yahoo (http://finance.yahoo.com).

b. For which of the preceding companies is the accounting equation relevant?

OBJ. 1

EX 1-2   Professional ethics

A fertilizer manufacturing company wants to relocate to Jones County. A report from a fired researcher at the company indicates the company's product is releasing toxic by-products. The company suppressed that report. A later report commissioned by the company shows there is no problem with the fertilizer.

➤ Should the company's chief executive officer reveal the content of the unfavorable report in discussions with Jones County representatives? Discuss.

OBJ. 2

EX 1-3   Business entity concept

Rocky Mountain Sports sells hunting and fishing equipment and provides guided hunting and fishing trips. Rocky Mountain Sports is owned and operated by Mike Weber, a well-known sports enthusiast and hunter. Mike's wife, Susan, owns and operates Madison Boutique, a women's clothing store. Mike and Susan have established a trust fund to finance their children's college education. The trust fund is maintained by National Bank in the name of the children, Kerri and Kyle.

a. For each of the following transactions, identify which of the entities listed should record the transaction in its records.

Entities	
R	Rocky Mountain Sports
B	National Bank Trust Fund
M	Madison Boutique
X	None of the above

1. Susan authorized the trust fund to purchase mutual fund shares.

2. Susan purchased two dozen spring dresses from a Chicago designer for a special spring sale.

3. Mike paid a breeder's fee for an English springer spaniel to be used as a hunting guide dog.

4. Susan deposited a $3,000 personal check in the trust fund at National Bank.

5. Mike paid a local doctor for his annual physical, which was required by the workmen's compensation insurance policy carried by Rocky Mountain Sports.

6. Mike received a cash advance from customers for a guided hunting trip.

7. Susan paid her dues to the YWCA.

8. Susan donated several dresses from inventory for a local charity auction for the benefit of a women's abuse shelter.

9. Mike paid for dinner and a movie to celebrate their fifteenth wedding anniversary.

10. Mike paid for an advertisement in a hunters' magazine.

b. What is a business transaction?

OBJ. 3

✔ Starbucks, $3,046

EX 1-4   Accounting equation

The total assets and total liabilities of Peat's Coffee & Tea Inc. and Starbucks Corporation are shown below.

	Peat's Coffee & Tea (in millions)	Starbucks (in millions)
Assets	$176	$5,577
Liabilities	32	2,531

Determine the owners' equity of each company.

OBJ. 3

✔ Dollar Tree, $1,253

EX 1-5   Accounting equation

The total assets and total liabilities of Dollar Tree Inc. and Target Corporation are shown below.

	Dollar Tree (in millions)	Target Corporation (in millions)
Assets	$2,036	$44,106
Liabilities	783	30,394

Determine the owners' equity of each company.

OBJ. 3

✔ a. 600,000

EX 1-6   Accounting equation

Determine the missing amount for each of the following:

	Assets	=	Liabilities	+	Owner's Equity
a.	×	=	$150,000	+	$450,000
b.	$275,000	=	×	+	50,000
c.	615,000	=	190,000	+	×

OBJ. 3, 4

✔ b. $530,000

EX 1-7   Accounting equation

Todd Olson is the owner and operator of Alpha, a motivational consulting business. At the end of its accounting period, December 31, 2011, Alpha has assets of $800,000 and liabilities of $350,000. Using the accounting equation and considering each case independently, determine the following amounts:

a. Todd Olson, capital, as of December 31, 2011.

b. Todd Olson, capital, as of December 31, 2012, assuming that assets increased by $150,000 and liabilities increased by $70,000 during 2012.

c. Todd Olson, capital, as of December 31, 2012, assuming that assets decreased by $60,000 and liabilities increased by $20,000 during 2012.

d. Todd Olson, capital, as of December 31, 2012, assuming that assets increased by $100,000 and liabilities decreased by $40,000 during 2012.

e. Net income (or net loss) during 2012, assuming that as of December 31, 2012, assets were $975,000, liabilities were $400,000, and there were no additional investments or withdrawals.

OBJ. 3

EX 1-8 Asset, liability, owner's equity items

Indicate whether each of the following is identified with (1) an asset, (2) a liability, or (3) owner's equity:

a. cash

b. wages expense

c. accounts payable

d. fees earned

e. supplies

f. land

OBJ. 4

EX 1-9 Effect of transactions on accounting equation

Describe how the following business transactions affect the three elements of the accounting equation.

a. Invested cash in business.

b. Purchased supplies for cash.

c. Purchased supplies on account.

d. Received cash for services performed.

e. Paid for utilities used in the business.

OBJ. 4

✔ a. (1) increase
$250,000

EX 1-10 Effect of transactions on accounting equation

a. A vacant lot acquired for $100,000 is sold for $350,000 in cash. What is the effect of the sale on the total amount of the seller's (1) assets, (2) liabilities, and (3) owner's equity?

b. Assume that the seller owes $75,000 on a loan for the land. After receiving the $350,000 cash in (a), the seller pays the $75,000 owed. What is the effect of the payment on the total amount of the seller's (1) assets, (2) liabilities, and (3) owner's equity?

c. Is it true that a transaction always affects at least two elements (Assets, Liabilities, or Owner's Equity) of the accounting equation? Explain.

OBJ. 4

EX 1-11 Effect of transactions on owner's equity

Indicate whether each of the following types of transactions will either (a) increase owner's equity or (b) decrease owner's equity:

1. owner's investments

2. revenues

3. expenses

4. owner's withdrawals

OBJ. 4

EX 1-12 Transactions

The following selected transactions were completed by Speedy Delivery Service during October:

1. Received cash from owner as additional investment, $30,000.

2. Purchased supplies for cash, $1,500.

3. Paid rent for October, $4,000.

4. Paid advertising expense, $2,500.

5. Received cash for providing delivery services, $18,750.

6. Billed customers for delivery services on account, $41,500.

7. Paid creditors on account, $6,000.

8. Received cash from customers on account, $26,200.

9. Determined that the cost of supplies on hand was $250; therefore, $1,250 of supplies had been used during the month.

10. Paid cash to owner for personal use, $2,000.

Indicate the effect of each transaction on the accounting equation by listing the numbers identifying the transactions, (1) through (10), in a column, and inserting at the right of each number the appropriate letter from the following list:

a. Increase in an asset, decrease in another asset.

b. Increase in an asset, increase in a liability.

c. Increase in an asset, increase in owner's equity.

d. Decrease in an asset, decrease in a liability.

e. Decrease in an asset, decrease in owner's equity.

OBJ. 4

✔ d. $13,200

EX 1-13   Nature of transactions

Jeremy Zabel operates his own catering service. Summary financial data for February are presented in equation form as follows. Each line designated by a number indicates the effect of a transaction on the equation. Each increase and decrease in owner's equity, except transaction (5), affects net income.

	Cash	+ Supplies +	Land	=	Accounts Payable +	Jeremy Zabel, Capital	Jeremy Zabel, Drawing +	Fees Earned	– Expenses
Bal.	25,000	2,000	75,000		12,000	90,000			
1.	+29,000							29,000	
2.	–20,000		+20,000						
3.	–14,000								–14,000
4.		+1,000			+1,000				
5.	– 2,000						–2,000		
6.	– 7,000				–7,000				
7.		–1800							–1,800
Bal.	11,000	1,200	95,000		6,000	90,000	–2,000	29,000	–15,800

(Header spanning: **Assests** over Cash + Supplies + Land; **= Liabilities +** over Accounts Payable; **Owner's Equity** over Jeremy Zabel Capital, Jeremy Zabel Drawing, Fees Earned, Expenses)

a. Describe each transaction.

b. What is the amount of net decrease in cash during the month?

c. What is the amount of net increase in owner's equity during the month?

d. What is the amount of the net income for the month?

e. How much of the net income for the month was retained in the business?

OBJ. 5

EX 1-14   Net income and owner's withdrawals

The income statement of a proprietorship for the month of December indicates a net income of $120,000. During the same period, the owner withdrew $130,000 in cash from the business for personal use.

➤ Would it be correct to say that the business incurred a net loss of $10,000 during the month? Discuss.

OBJ. 5

✔ Leo: Net income, $60,000

EX 1-15   Net income and owner's equity for four businesses

Four different proprietorships, Aries, Gemini, Leo, and Pisces, show the same balance sheet data at the beginning and end of a year. These data, exclusive of the amount of owner's equity, are summarized as follows:

	Total Assets	Total Liabilities
Beginning of the year	$400,000	$100,000
End of the year	750,000	300,000

On the basis of the above data and the following additional information for the year, determine the net income (or loss) of each company for the year. (*Hint:* First determine the amount of increase or decrease in owner's equity during the year.)

Aries: The owner had made no additional investments in the business and had made no withdrawals from the business.

Gemini: The owner had made no additional investments in the business but had withdrawn $40,000.

Leo: The owner had made an additional investment of $90,000 but had made no withdrawals.

Pisces: The owner had made an additional investment of $90,000 and had withdrawn $40,000.

OBJ. 5

EX 1-16 Balance sheet items

From the following list of selected items taken from the records of Hoosier Appliance Service as of a specific date, identify those that would appear on the balance sheet:

1. Accounts Receivable
2. Cash
3. Fees Earned
4. Land
5. Patsy Adkins, Capital

6. Supplies
7. Supplies Expense
8. Utilities Expense
9. Wages Expense
10. Wages Payable

OBJ. 5

EX 1-17 Income statement items

Based on the data presented in Exercise 1-16, identify those items that would appear on the income statement.

OBJ. 5

✔ Penny Beall, capital, June 30, 2012: $482,000

EX 1-18 Statement of owner's equity

Financial information related to Lost Trail Company, a proprietorship, for the month ended June 30, 2012, is as follows:

Net income for June	$125,000
Penny Beall's withdrawals during June	18,000
Penny Beall's capital, June 1, 2012	375,000

a. Prepare a statement of owner's equity for the month ended June 30, 2012.

b. Why is the statement of owner's equity prepared before the June 30, 2012, balance sheet?

OBJ. 5

✔ Net income: $449,000

EX 1-19 Income statement

Universal Services was organized on October 1, 2012. A summary of the revenue and expense transactions for October follows:

Fees earned	$800,000
Wages expense	270,000
Rent expense	60,000
Supplies expense	9,000
Miscellaneous expense	12,000

Prepare an income statement for the month ended October 31.

OBJ. 5

✔ (a) $45,000

EX 1-20 Missing amounts from balance sheet and income statement data

One item is omitted in each of the following summaries of balance sheet and income statement data for the following four different proprietorships:

	Aquarius	Libra	Scorpio	Taurus
Beginning of the year:				
Assets	$300,000	$500,000	$100,000	(d)
Liabilities	120,000	260,000	76,000	$120,000
End of the year:				
Assets	420,000	700,000	90,000	248,000
Liabilities	110,000	220,000	80,000	136,000
During the year:				
Additional investment in the business	(a)	100,000	10,000	40,000
Withdrawals from the business	25,000	32,000	(c)	60,000
Revenue	190,000	(b)	115,000	112,000
Expenses	80,000	128,000	122,500	128,000

Determine the missing amounts, identifying them by letter. (*Hint:* First determine the amount of increase or decrease in owner's equity during the year.)

EX 1-21   Balance sheets, net income

Financial information related to the proprietorship of Lady Interiors for July and August 2012 is as follows:

	July 31, 2012	August 31, 2012
Accounts payable	$ 90,000	$100,000
Accounts receivable	200,000	240,000
Garth Jacobs, capital	?	?
Cash	80,000	95,000
Supplies	20,000	15,000

a. Prepare balance sheets for Lady Interiors as of July 31 and August 31, 2012.

b. Determine the amount of net income for August, assuming that the owner made no additional investments or withdrawals during the month.

c. Determine the amount of net income for August, assuming that the owner made no additional investments but withdrew $35,000 during the month.

EX 1-22   Financial statements

Each of the following items is shown in the financial statements of ExxonMobil Corporation.

1. Accounts payable
2. Cash equivalents
3. Crude oil inventory
4. Equipment
5. Exploration expenses
6. Income taxes payable
7. Investments
8. Long-term debt
9. Marketable securities
10. Notes and loans payable
11. Notes receivable
12. Operating expenses
13. Prepaid taxes
14. Sales
15. Selling expenses

a. Identify the financial statement (balance sheet or income statement) in which each item would appear.

b. Can an item appear on more than one financial statement?

c. Is the accounting equation relevant for ExxonMobil Corporation?

EX 1-23   Statement of cash flows

Indicate whether each of the following activities would be reported on the statement of cash flows as (a) an operating activity, (b) an investing activity, or (c) a financing activity:

1. Cash received from fees earned.
2. Cash paid for expenses.
3. Cash paid for land.
4. Cash received as an additional investment by owner.

EX 1-24   Statement of cash flows

A summary of cash flows for Absolute Consulting Group for the year ended July 31, 2012, is shown below.

Cash receipts:	
Cash received from customers	$187,500
Cash received from additional investment of owner	40,000
Cash payments:	
Cash paid for operating expenses	127,350
Cash paid for land	30,000
Cash paid to owner for personal use	5,000

The cash balance as of August 1, 2011, was $27,100.

Prepare a statement of cash flows for Absolute Consulting Group for the year ended July 31, 2012.

OBJ. 5

✔ Correct amount of total assets is $88,200.

EX 1-25 Financial statements

Empire Realty, organized May 1, 2012, is owned and operated by Bertram Mitchell. How many errors can you find in the following statements for Empire Realty, prepared after its first month of operations?

Empire Realty
Income Statement
May 31, 2012

Sales commissions		$233,550
Expenses:		
Office salaries expense	$145,800	
Rent expense...	49,500	
Automobile expense...	11,250	
Miscellaneous expense...	3,600	
Supplies expense	1,350	
Total expenses		211,500
Net income		$ 67,050

Bertram Mitchell
Statement of Owner's Equity
May 31, 2011

Bertram Mitchell, capital, May 1, 2012...	$ 46,800
Less withdrawals during May..	9,000
	$ 37,800
Additional investment during May..	11,250
	$ 49,050
Net income for May	67,050
Bertram Mitchell, capital, May 31, 2012	$ 116,100

Balance Sheet
For the Month Ended May 31, 2012

Assets		Liabilities	
Cash	$14,850	Accounts receivable	$ 64,350
Accounts payable	17,100	Supplies................................	9,000
		Owner's Equity	
		Bertram Mitchell, capital.................	116,100
Total assets	$31,950	Total liabilities and owner's equity........	$189,450

OBJ. 6

EX 1-26 Ratio of liabilities to stockholders' equity

The Home Depot, Inc., is the world's largest home improvement retailer and one of the largest retailers in the United States based on net sales volume. The Home Depot operates over 2,000 Home Depot® stores that sell a wide assortment of building materials and home improvement and lawn and garden products.

The Home Depot reported the following balance sheet data (in millions):

	Feb. 1, 2009	Feb. 3, 2008
Total assets	$41,164	$44,324
Total stockholders' equity	17,777	17,714

a. Determine the total liabilities as of February 1, 2009, and February 3, 2008.

b. Determine the ratio of liabilities to stockholders' equity for 2009 and 2008. Round to two decimal places.

c. What conclusions regarding the margin of protection to the creditors can you draw from (b)?

OBJ. 6

EX 1-27 Ratio of liabilities to stockholders' equity

Lowe's, a major competitor of The Home Depot in the home improvement business, operates over 1,600 stores. For the years ending January 30, 2009, and February 1, 2008, Lowe's reported the following balance sheet data (in millions):

	Jan. 30, 2009	Feb. 1, 2008
Total assets	$32,686	$30,869
Total liabilities	14,631	14,771

a. Determine the total stockholders' equity as of January 30, 2009, and February 1, 2008.

b. Determine the ratio of liabilities to stockholders' equity for 2009 and 2008. Round to two decimal places.

c. What conclusions regarding the margin of protection to the creditors can you draw from (b)?

d. Using the balance sheet data for The Home Depot in Exercise 1-26, how does the ratio of liabilities to stockholders' equity of Lowe's compare to that of The Home Depot?

Problems Series A

OBJ. 4

✔ Cash bal. at end of September: $37,700

PR 1-1A   Transactions

On September 1 of the current year, Maria Edsall established a business to manage rental property. She completed the following transactions during September:

a. Opened a business bank account with a deposit of $40,000 from personal funds.

b. Purchased supplies (pens, file folders, and copy paper) on account, $2,200.

c. Received cash from fees earned for managing rental property, $6,000.

d. Paid rent on office and equipment for the month, $2,700.

e. Paid creditors on account, $1,000.

f. Billed customers for fees earned for managing rental property, $5,000.

g. Paid automobile expenses (including rental charges) for month, $600, and miscellaneous expenses, $300.

h. Paid office salaries, $1,900.

i. Determined that the cost of supplies on hand was $1,300; therefore, the cost of supplies used was $900.

j. Withdrew cash for personal use, $1,800.

Instructions

1. Indicate the effect of each transaction and the balances after each transaction, using the following tabular headings:

Assets			= Liabilities +		Owner's Equity							
Cash +	Accounts Receivable +	Supplies =	Accounts Payable +	Maria Edsall, Capital −	Maria Edsall, Drawing +	Fees Earned −	Rent Expense −	Salaries Expense −	Supplies Expense −	Auto Expense −	Misc. Expense

2. ➤ Briefly explain why the owner's investment and revenues increased owner's equity, while withdrawals and expenses decreased owner's equity.

3. Determine the net income for September.

4. How much did September's transactions increase or decrease Maria Edsall's capital?

OBJ. 5

✔ 1. Net income: $40,000

PR 1-2A   Financial statements

Following are the amounts of the assets and liabilities of New World Travel Agency at December 31, 2012, the end of the current year, and its revenue and expenses for the year. The capital of Kris Taber, owner, was $120,000 on January 1, 2012, the beginning of the current year. During the current year, Kris withdrew $10,000.

Accounts payable	$ 25,000	Rent expense	$45,000
Accounts receivable	60,000	Supplies	5,000
Cash	110,000	Supplies expense	3,000
Fees earned	200,000	Utilities expense	18,000
Miscellaneous expense	4,000	Wages expense	90,000

Instructions

1. Prepare an income statement for the current year ended December 31, 2012.

2. Prepare a statement of owner's equity for the current year ended December 31, 2012.

(*Continued*)

3. Prepare a balance sheet as of December 31, 2012.

4. What item appears on both the statement of owner's equity and the balance sheet?

OBJ. 5

✔ 1. Net income: $26,400

PR 1-3A   Financial statements

Heidi Fritz established Freedom Financial Services on March 1, 2012. Freedom Financial Services offers financial planning advice to its clients. The effect of each transaction and the balances after each transaction for March are shown below.

	Assets			= Liabilities +			Owner's Equity					
	Cash	+ Accounts Receivable	+ Supplies =	Accounts Payable	+ Heidi Fritz, Capital	– Heidi Fritz, Drawing +	Fees Earned	– Salaries Expense	– Rent Expense	– Auto Expense	– Supplies Expense	– Misco. Expense
a.	+45,000				+45,000							
b.			+6,540	+6,540								
Bal.	45,000		6,540	6,540	45,000							
c.	–1,800			–1,800								
Bal.	43,200		6,540	4,740	45,000							
d.	+84,000						+84,000					
Bal.	127,200		6,540	4,740	45,000		84,000					
e.	–22,500								–22,500			
Bal.	104,700		6,540	4,740	45,000		84,000		–22,500			
f.	–17,100									–13,500		–3,600
Bal.	87,600		6,540	4,740	45,000		84,000		–22,500	–13,500		–3,600
g.	–48,000							–48,000				
Bal.	39,600		6,540	4,740	45,000		84,000	–48,000	–22,500	–13,500		–3,600
h.			–4,500								–4,500	
Bal.	39,600		2,040	4,740	45,000		84,000	–48,000	–22,500	–13,500	–4,500	–3,600
i.		+34,500					+34,500					
Bal.	39,600	34,500	2,040	4,740	45,000		118,500	–48,000	–22,500	–13,500	–4,500	–3,600
j.	–15,000					–15,000						
Bal.	24,600	34,500	2,040	4,740	45,000	–15,000	118,500	–48,000	–22,500	–13,500	–4,500	–3,600

Instructions

1. Prepare an income statement for the month ended March 31, 2012.

2. Prepare a statement of owner's equity for the month ended March 31, 2012.

3. Prepare a balance sheet as of March 31, 2012.

4. (Optional). Prepare a statement of cash flows for the month ending March 31, 2012.

OBJ. 4, 5

✔ 2. Net income: $12,150

PR 1-4A   Transactions; financial statements

On January 1, 2012, Carlton Myers established Vista Realty. Carlton completed the following transactions during the month of January:

a. Opened a business bank account with a deposit of $25,000 from personal funds.

b. Purchased supplies (pens, file folders, paper, etc.) on account, $2,500.

c. Paid creditor on account, $1,600.

d. Earned sales commissions, receiving cash, $25,500.

e. Paid rent on office and equipment for the month, $5,000.

f. Withdrew cash for personal use, $8,000.

g. Paid automobile expenses (including rental charge) for month, $2,500, and miscellaneous expenses, $1,200.

h. Paid office salaries, $3,000.

i. Determined that the cost of supplies on hand was $850; therefore, the cost of supplies used was $1,650.

Instructions

1. Indicate the effect of each transaction and the balances after each transaction, using the following tabular headings:

Assets	= Liabilities +			Owner's Equity						
		Carlton	Carlton			Office				
	Accounts	Myers	Myers,	Sales	Rent	Salaries	Auto	Supplies	Misc.
Cash + Supplies =	Payable +	Capital	– Drawing +	Commissions	– Expense	– Expense	– Expense	– Expense	– Expense

2. Prepare an income statement for January, a statement of owner's equity for January, and a balance sheet as of January 31.

OBJ. 4, 5

✔ 3. Net income: $14,900

PR 1-5A   Transactions; financial statements

Kean Dry Cleaners is owned and operated by Wally Lowman. A building and equipment are currently being rented, pending expansion to new facilities. The actual work of dry cleaning is done by another company at wholesale rates. The assets and the liabilities of the business on March 1, 2012, are as follows: Cash, $15,000; Accounts Receivable, $31,000; Supplies, $3,000; Land, $36,000; Accounts Payable, $13,000. Business transactions during March are summarized as follows:

a. Wally Lowman invested additional cash in the business with a deposit of $28,000 in the business bank account.

b. Paid $14,000 for the purchase of land as a future building site.

c. Received cash from cash customers for dry cleaning revenue, $17,000.

d. Paid rent for the month, $5,000.

e. Purchased supplies on account, $2,500.

f. Paid creditors on account, $12,800.

g. Charged customers for dry cleaning revenue on account, $34,000.

h. Received monthly invoice for dry cleaning expense for March (to be paid on April 10), $13,500.

i. Paid the following: wages expense, $7,500; truck expense, $2,500; utilities expense, $1,300; miscellaneous expense, $2,700.

j. Received cash from customers on account, $28,000.

k. Determined that the cost of supplies on hand was $1,900; therefore, the cost of supplies used during the month was $3,600.

l. Withdrew $8,000 cash for personal use.

Instructions

1. Determine the amount of Wally Lowman's capital as of March 1 of the current year.

2. State the assets, liabilities, and owner's equity as of March 1 in equation form similar to that shown in this chapter. In tabular form below the equation, indicate increases and decreases resulting from each transaction and the new balances after each transaction.

3. Prepare an income statement for March, a statement of owner's equity for March, and a balance sheet as of March 31.

4. (Optional). Prepare a statement of cash flows for March.

OBJ. 5

✔ k. $300,000

PR 1-6A   Missing amounts from financial statements

The financial statements at the end of Alpine Realty's first month of operations are as follows:

Alpine Realty
Income Statement
For the Month Ended June 30, 2012

Fees earned..		$ (a)
Expenses:		
Wages expense..	$120,000	
Rent expense..	40,000	
Supplies expense..	(b)	
Utilities expense..	8,000	
Miscellaneous expense.......................................	10,000	
Total expenses...		190,000
Net income...		$110,000

Alpine Realty
Statement of Owner's Equity
For the Month Ended June 30, 2012

Aaron Gilbert, capital, June 1, 2012		$ (c)
Investment on June 1, 2012...	$150,000	
Net income for June...	(d)	
	$ (e)	
Less withdrawals..	50,000	
Increase in owner's equity		(f)
Aaron Gilbert, capital, June 30, 2012................................		$ (g)

Alpine Realty
Balance Sheet
June 30, 2012

Assets		Liabilities	
Cash	$ 185,000	Accounts payable	$40,000
Supplies.......................	5,000	**Owner's Equity**	
Land	60,000	Aaron Gilbert, capital............	(i)
Total assets	$ (h)	Total liabilities and owner's equity	$ (j)

Alpine Realty
Statement of Cash Flows
For the Month Ended June 30, 2012

Cash flows from operating activities:		
Cash received from customers......................................	$ (k)	
Deduct cash payments for expenses and payments to creditors.....	155,000	
Net cash flow from operating activities		$ (l)
Cash flows from investing activities:		
Cash payments for acquisition of land		(m)
Cash flows from financing activities:		
Cash received as owner's investment	$ (n)	
Deduct cash withdrawal by owner.................................	(o)	
Net cash flow from financing activities............................		(p)
Net cash flow and June 30, 2012, cash balance		$ (q)

Instructions

By analyzing the interrelationships among the four financial statements, determine the proper amounts for (a) through (q).

Problems Series B

OBJ. 4

✔ Cash bal. at end of January: $73,500

PR 1-1B   Transactions

Cody Macedo established an insurance agency on January 1 of the current year and completed the following transactions during January:

a. Opened a business bank account with a deposit of $75,000 from personal funds.

b. Purchased supplies on account, $3,000.

c. Paid creditors on account, $1,000.

d. Received cash from fees earned on insurance commissions, $11,800.

e. Paid rent on office and equipment for the month, $4,000.

f. Paid automobile expenses for month, $600, and miscellaneous expenses, $200.

g. Paid office salaries, $2,500.

h. Determined that the cost of supplies on hand was $1,900; therefore, the cost of supplies used was $1,100.

i. Billed insurance companies for sales commissions earned, $12,500.

j. Withdrew cash for personal use, $5,000.

Instructions

1. Indicate the effect of each transaction and the balances after each transaction, using the following tabular headings:

Assets			= Liabilities +					Owner's Equity					
				Cody Macedo,	Cody Macedo,	Fees	Rent	Salaries	Supplies	Auto	Misc.		
Cash +	Receivable +	Supplies =	Payable +	Capital −	Drawing +	Earned −	Expense −	Expense −	Expense −	Expense −	Expense		

2. ➤ Briefly explain why the owner's investment and revenues increased owner's equity, while withdrawals and expenses decreased owner's equity.

3. Determine the net income for January.

4. How much did January's transactions increase or decrease Cody Macedo's capital?

OBJ. 5

✔ 1. Net income:
$80,000

PR 1-2B   Financial statements

The amounts of the assets and liabilities of St. Simon Travel Service at June 30, 2012, the end of the current year, and its revenue and expenses for the year are listed below. The capital of Gwen Perez, owner, was $150,000 at July 1, 2011, the beginning of the current year, and the owner withdrew $30,000 during the current year.

Accounts payable	$ 25,000	Supplies	$ 12,000
Accounts receivable	90,000	Supplies expense	10,000
Cash	123,000	Taxes expense	8,000
Fees earned	500,000	Utilities expense	36,000
Miscellaneous expense	11,000	Wages expense	280,000
Rent expense	75,000		

Instructions

1. Prepare an income statement for the current year ended June 30, 2012.

2. Prepare a statement of owner's equity for the current year ended June 30, 2012.

3. Prepare a balance sheet as of June 30, 2012.

4. What item appears on both the income statement and statement of owner's equity?

OBJ. 5

✔ 1. Net income:
$91,900

PR 1-3B   Financial statements

Rory Kalur established Computers 4 Less on February 1, 2012. The effect of each transaction and the balances after each transaction for February are shown below.

	Assets			= Liabilities +		Owner's Equity							
	Cash +	Accounts Receivable +	Supplies =	Accounts Payable +	Rory Kalur, Capital −	Rory Kalur, Drawing +	Fees Earned −	Salaries Expense −	Rent Expense −	Auto Expense −	Supplies Expense −	Misc. Expense	
a.	+120,000				+120,000								
b.			+10,400	+10,400									
Bal.	120,000		10,400	10,400	120,000								
c.	+118,000						+118,000						
Bal.	238,000		10,400	10,400	120,000		118,000						
d.	−32,000								−32,000				
Bal.	206,000		10,400	10,400	120,000		118,000		−32,000				
e.	−5,000			−5,000									
Bal.	201,000		10,400	5,400	120,000		118,000		−32,000				
f.		+83,000					+83,000						
Bal.	201,000	83,000	10,400	5,400	120,000		201,000		−32,000				
g.	−23,000									−15,500		−7,500	
Bal.	178,000	83,000	10,400	5,400	120,000		201,000		−32,000	−15,500		−7,500	
h.	−48,000							−48,000					
Bal.	130,000	83,000	10,400	5,400	120,000		201,000	−48,000	−32,000	−15,500		−7,500	
i.			−6,100								−6,100		
Bal.	130,000	83,000	4,300	5,400	120,000		201,000	−48,000	−32,000	−15,500	−6,100	−7,500	
j.	−30,000					−30,000							
Bal.	100,000	83,000	4,300	5,400	120,000	−30,000	201,000	−48,000	−32,000	−15,500	−6,100	−7,500	

Instructions

1. Prepare an income statement for the month ended February 29, 2012.

2. Prepare a statement of owner's equity for the month ended February 29, 2012.

3. Prepare a balance sheet as of February 29, 2012.

4. (Optional). Prepare a statement of cash flows for the month ending February 29, 2012.

OBJ. 4, 5

✔ 2. Net income:
$9,300

PR 1-4B   Transactions; financial statements

On June 1, 2012, Lindsey Brown established Equity Realty. Lindsey completed the following transactions during the month of June:

a. Opened a business bank account with a deposit of $15,000 from personal funds.

b. Paid rent on office and equipment for the month, $4,000.

c. Paid automobile expenses (including rental charge) for month, $1,200, and miscellaneous expenses, $800.

d. Purchased supplies (pens, file folders, and copy paper) on account, $1,000.

e. Earned sales commissions, receiving cash, $18,500.

f. Paid creditor on account, $600.

g. Paid office salaries, $2,500.

h. Withdrew cash for personal use, $5,000.

i. Determined that the cost of supplies on hand was $300; therefore, the cost of supplies used was $700.

Instructions

1. Indicate the effect of each transaction and the balances after each transaction, using the following tabular headings:

Assets		= Liabilities +				Owner's Equity					
			Lindsey	Lindsey			Office				
		Accounts	Brown,	Brown,	Sales	Rent	Salaries	Auto	Supplies	Misc.	
Cash + Supplies	=	Payable +	Capital –	Drawing +	Commissions –	Expense –	Expense –	Expense –	Expense –	Expense	

2. Prepare an income statement for June, a statement of owner's equity for June, and a balance sheet as of June 30.

OBJ. 4, 5

✔ 3. Net income:
$3,700

PR 1-5B   Transactions; financial statements

Anny's Dry Cleaners is owned and operated by Anny Brum. A building and equipment are currently being rented, pending expansion to new facilities. The actual work of dry cleaning is done by another company at wholesale rates. The assets and the liabilities of the business on June 1, 2012, are as follows: Cash, $25,000; Accounts Receivable, $30,000; Supplies, $5,000; Land, $50,000; Accounts Payable, $18,000. Business transactions during June are summarized as follows:

a. Anny Brum invested additional cash in the business with a deposit of $15,000 in the business bank account.

b. Purchased land for use as a parking lot, paying cash of $20,000.

c. Paid rent for the month, $3,000.

d. Charged customers for dry cleaning revenue on account, $22,000.

e. Paid creditors on account, $13,000.

f. Purchased supplies on account, $1,000.

g. Received cash from cash customers for dry cleaning revenue, $28,000.

h. Received cash from customers on account, $27,000.

i. Received monthly invoice for dry cleaning expense for June (to be paid on July 10), $21,500.

j. Paid the following: wages expense, $14,000; truck expense, $2,100; utilities expense, $1,800; miscellaneous expense, $1,300.

k. Determined that the cost of supplies on hand was $3,400; therefore, the cost of supplies used during the month was $2,600.

l. Withdrew $1,000 for personal use.

Instructions

1. Determine the amount of Anny Brum's capital as of June 1.

2. State the assets, liabilities, and owner's equity as of June 1 in equation form similar to that shown in this chapter. In tabular form below the equation, indicate increases and decreases resulting from each transaction and the new balances after each transaction.

3. Prepare an income statement for June, a statement of owner's equity for June, and a balance sheet as of June 30.

4. (Optional) Prepare a statement of cash flows for June.

OBJ. 5

✔ i. $130,000

PR 1-6B Missing amounts from financial statements

The financial statements at the end of Cyber Realty's first month of operations are shown below.

Cyber Realty
Income Statement
For the Month Ended October 31, 2012

Fees earned...		$250,000
Expenses:		
Wages expense..	$ (a)	
Rent expense..	30,000	
Supplies expense...	11,000	
Utilities expense..	9,000	
Miscellaneous expense......................................	3,000	
Total expenses		180,000
Net income		$ (b)

Cyber Realty
Statement of Owner's Equity
For the Month Ended October 31, 2012

Kendra Garcia, capital, October 1, 2012		$ (c)
Investment on October 1, 2012..	$ (d)	
Net income for October..	(e)	
	$ (f)	
Less withdrawals	(g)	
Increase in owner's equity		(h)
Kendra Garcia, capital, October 31, 2012		$ (i)

Cyber Realty
Balance Sheet
October 31, 2012

Assets		Liabilities	
Cash	$77,000	Accounts payable	$ 30,000
Supplies............................	8,000	**Owner's Equity**	
Land	(j)	Kendra Garcia, capital	(l)
Total assets	$ (k)	Total liabilities and owner's equity.......	$ (m)

Cyber Realty
Statement of Cash Flows
For the Month Ended October 31, 2012

Cash flows from operating activities:		
Cash received from customers..	$ (n)	
Deduct cash payments for expenses and payments to creditors..........	158,000	
Net cash flow from operating activities................................		$ (o)
Cash flows from investing activities:		
Cash payments for acquisition of land.................................		(75,000)
Cash flows from financing activities:		
Cash received as owner's investment...................................	$100,000	
Deduct cash withdrawal by owner	40,000	
Net cash flow from financing activities		(p)
Net cash flow and October 31, 2012, cash balance		$ (q)

Instructions

By analyzing the interrelationships among the four financial statements, determine the proper amounts for (a) through (q).

Continuing Problem

✔ 2. Net income:
   $1,980

Pat Sharpe enjoys listening to all types of music and owns countless CDs. Over the years, Pat has gained a local reputation for knowledge of music from classical to rap and the ability to put together sets of recordings that appeal to all ages.

During the last several months, Pat served as a guest disc jockey on a local radio station. In addition, Pat has entertained at several friends' parties as the host deejay.

On June 1, 2012, Pat established a proprietorship known as PS Music. Using an extensive collection of music MP3 files, Pat will serve as a disc jockey on a fee basis for weddings, college parties, and other events. During June, Pat entered into the following transactions:

June 1. Deposited $5,000 in a checking account in the name of PS Music.
2. Received $3,600 from a local radio station for serving as the guest disc jockey for June.
2. Agreed to share office space with a local real estate agency, Downtown Realty. PS Music will pay one-fourth of the rent. In addition, PS Music agreed to pay a portion of the salary of the receptionist and to pay one-fourth of the utilities. Paid $750 for the rent of the office.
4. Purchased supplies from City Office Supply Co. for $350. Agreed to pay $100 within 10 days and the remainder by July 5, 2012.
6. Paid $450 to a local radio station to advertise the services of PS Music twice daily for two weeks.
8. Paid $700 to a local electronics store for renting digital recording equipment.
12. Paid $350 (music expense) to Cool Music for the use of its current music demos to make various music sets.
13. Paid City Office Supply Co. $100 on account.
16. Received $500 from a dentist for providing two music sets for the dentist to play for her patients.
22. Served as disc jockey for a wedding party. The father of the bride agreed to pay $1,250 the 1st of July.
25. Received $400 for serving as the disc jockey for a cancer charity ball hosted by the local hospital.
29. Paid $240 (music expense) to Galaxy Music for the use of its library of music demos.
30. Received $900 for serving as PS disc jockey for a local club's monthly dance.
30. Paid Downtown Realty $400 for PS Music's share of the receptionist's salary for June.
30. Paid Downtown Realty $300 for PS Music's share of the utilities for June.
30. Determined that the cost of supplies on hand is $170. Therefore, the cost of supplies used during the month was $180.
30. Paid for miscellaneous expenses, $300.
30. Paid $1,000 royalties (music expense) to National Music Clearing for use of various artists' music during the month.
30. Withdrew $500 of cash from PS Music for personal use.

Instructions

1. Indicate the effect of each transaction and the balances after each transaction, using the following tabular headings:

Assets			=	Liabilities +					Owner's Equity							
					Pat	Pat			Office	Equipment						
Accts.				Accounts	Sharpe,	Sharpe,	Fees	Music	Rent	Rent	Advertising	Wages	Utilities	Supplies	Misc.	
Cash +	Rec. +	Supplies =		Payable +	Capital –	Drawing +	Earned –	Exp. –	Exp. –	Exp. –	Exp. –	Exp. –	Exp. –	Exp. –	Exp.	

2. Prepare an income statement for PS Music for the month ended June 30, 2012.

3. Prepare a statement of owner's equity for PS Music for the month ended June 30, 2012.

4. Prepare a balance sheet for PS Music as of June 30, 2012.

Cases & Projects

CP 1-1   Ethics and professional conduct in business
Group Project

Vince Hunt, president of Sabre Enterprises, applied for a $200,000 loan from First National Bank. The bank requested financial statements from Sabre Enterprises as a basis for granting the loan. Vince has told his accountant to provide the bank with a balance sheet. Vince has decided to omit the other financial statements because there was a net loss during the past year.

In groups of three or four, discuss the following questions:

1. Is Vince behaving in a professional manner by omitting some of the financial statements?

2. a. What types of information about their businesses would owners be willing to provide bankers? What types of information would owners not be willing to provide?

    b. What types of information about a business would bankers want before extending a loan?

    c. What common interests are shared by bankers and business owners?

CP 1-2   Net income

On July 1, 2011, Dr. Heather Dewitt established Life Medical, a medical practice organized as a proprietorship. The following conversation occurred the following January between Dr. Dewitt and a former medical school classmate, Dr. Naomi Kennedy, at an American Medical Association convention in Boston.

Dr. Kennedy: Heather, good to see you again. Why didn't you call when you were in Chicago? We could have had dinner together.

Dr. Dewitt: Actually, I never made it to Chicago this year. My husband and kids went up to our Vail condo twice, but I got stuck in Fort Lauderdale. I opened a new consulting practice this July and haven't had any time for myself since.

Dr. Kennedy: I heard about it . . . Life . . . something . . . right?

Dr. Dewitt: Yes, Life Medical. My husband chose the name.

Dr. Kennedy: I've thought about doing something like that. Are you making any money? I mean, is it worth your time?

Dr. Dewitt: You wouldn't believe it. I started by opening a bank account with $40,000, and my December bank statement has a balance of $90,000. Not bad for six months—all pure profit.

Dr. Kennedy: Maybe I'll try it in Chicago! Let's have breakfast together tomorrow and you can fill me in on the details.

➤ Comment on Dr. Dewitt's statement that the difference between the opening bank balance ($40,000) and the December statement balance ($90,000) is pure profit.

CP 1-3   Transactions and financial statements

Jan Martinelli, a junior in college, has been seeking ways to earn extra spending money. As an active sports enthusiast, Jan plays tennis regularly at the Naples Tennis Club, where her family has a membership. The president of the club recently approached Jan with the proposal that she manage the club's tennis courts. Jan's primary duty would be to supervise the operation of the club's four indoor and 10 outdoor courts, including court reservations.

In return for her services, the club would pay Jan $300 per week, plus Jan could keep whatever she earned from lessons and the fees from the use of the ball machine. The club and Jan agreed to a one-month trial, after which both would consider an arrangement for the remaining two years of Jan's college career. On this basis, Jan organized Topspin. During April 2012, Jan managed the tennis courts and entered into the following transactions:

a. Opened a business account by depositing $1,000.

b. Paid $300 for tennis supplies (practice tennis balls, etc.).

c. Paid $200 for the rental of video equipment to be used in offering lessons during April.

d. Arranged for the rental of two ball machines during April for $250. Paid $100 in advance, with the remaining $150 due May 1.

e. Received $1,600 for lessons given during April.

f. Received $500 in fees from the use of the ball machines during April.

g. Paid $800 for salaries of part-time employees who answered the telephone and took reservations while Jan was giving lessons.

h. Paid $225 for miscellaneous expenses.

i. Received $1,200 from the club for managing the tennis courts during April.

j. Determined that the cost of supplies on hand at the end of the month totaled $180; therefore, the cost of supplies used was $120.

k. Withdrew $250 for personal use on April 30.

As a friend and accounting student, you have been asked by Jan to aid her in assessing the venture.

1. Indicate the effect of each transaction and the balances after each transaction, using the following tabular headings:

Assets	=	Liabilities	+			Owner's Equity				
				Jan	Jan					
		Accounts		Martinelli,	Martinelli,	Service	Salary	Rent	Supplies	Misc.
Cash + Supplies	=	Payable	+	Capital	– Drawing	+ Revenue	– Expense	– Expense	– Expense	– Expense

2. Prepare an income statement for April.

3. Prepare a statement of owner's equity for April.

4. Prepare a balance sheet as of April 30.

5. a. Assume that Jan Martinelli could earn $9 per hour working 30 hours a week as a waitress. Evaluate which of the two alternatives, working as a waitress or operating Topspin, would provide Jan with the most income per month.

    b. ➤ Discuss any other factors that you believe Jan should consider before discussing a long-term arrangement with the Naples Tennis Club.

Internet Project

CP 1-4 Certification requirements for accountants

By satisfying certain specific requirements, accountants may become certified as public accountants (CPAs), management accountants (CMAs), or internal auditors (CIAs). Find the certification requirements for one of these accounting groups by accessing the appropriate Internet site listed below.

Site	Description
http://www.ais-cpa.com	This site lists the address and/or Internet link for each state's board of accountancy. Find your state's requirements.
http://www.imanet.org	This site lists the requirements for becoming a CMA.
http://www.theiia.org	This site lists the requirements for becoming a CIA.

CP 1-5 Cash flows

Amazon.com, an Internet retailer, was incorporated and began operation in the mid-90s. On the statement of cash flows, would you expect Amazon.com's net cash flows from operating, investing, and financing activities to be positive or negative for its first three years of operations? Use the following format for your answers, and briefly explain your logic.

	First Year	Second Year	Third Year
Net cash flows from operating activities	negative		
Net cash flows from investing activities			
Net cash flows from financing activities			

CP 1-6 Financial analysis of Enron Corporation

The now defunct Enron Corporation, once headquartered in Houston, Texas, provided products and services for natural gas, electricity, and communications to wholesale and retail customers. Enron's operations were conducted through a variety of subsidiaries and affiliates that involved transporting gas through pipelines, transmitting electricity, and managing energy commodities. The following data was taken from Enron's financial statements:

	In millions
Total revenues	$100,789
Total costs and expenses	98,836
Operating income	1,953
Net income	979
Total assets	65,503
Total liabilities	54,033
Total owners' equity	11,470
Net cash flows from operating activities	4,779
Net cash flows from investing activities	(4,264)
Net cash flows from financing activities	571
Net increase in cash	1,086

The market price of Enron's stock was approximately $83 per share when the prior financial statement data was taken. Before it went bankrupt, Enron's stock sold for $0.22 per share.

━━━━▶ Review the preceding financial statement data and search the Internet for articles on Enron Corporation. Briefly explain why Enron's stock dropped so dramatically.

© AP Photo/Paul Sakuma

Analyzing Transactions

Apple, Inc. ™

Everyday it seems like we get an incredible amount of incoming e-mail messages; you get them from your friends, relatives, subscribed e-mail lists, and even spammers! But how do you organize all of these messages? You might create folders to sort messages by sender, topic, or project. Perhaps you use keyword search utilities. You might even use filters/rules to automatically delete spam or send messages from your best friend to a special folder. In any case, you are organizing information so that it is simple to retrieve and allows you to understand, respond, or refer to the messages.

In the same way that you organize your e-mail, companies develop an organized method for processing, recording, and summarizing financial transactions. For example, **Apple, Inc.**, has a huge volume of financial transactions, resulting from sales of its innovative computers, digital media

(iTunes), iPods, iPhones, and iPads. When Apple sells an iPad, a customer has the option of paying with credit card, a debit or check card, an Apple gift card, a financing arrangement, or cash. In order to analyze only the information related to Apple's cash transactions, the company must record or summarize all these similar sales using a single category or "cash" account. Similarly, Apple will record credit card payments for iPads and sales from financing arrangements in different accounts (records).

While Chapter 1 uses the accounting equation (Assets = Liabilities + Owner's Equity) to analyze and record financial transactions, this chapter presents more practical and efficient recording methods that most companies use. In addition, this chapter discusses possible accounting errors that may occur, along with methods to detect and correct them.

OBJ. 1 Describe the characteristics of an account and a chart of accounts.

Using Accounts to Record Transactions

In Chapter 1, the November transactions for NetSolutions were recorded using the accounting equation format shown in Exhibit 1. However, this format is not efficient or practical for companies that have to record thousands or millions of transactions daily. As a result, accounting systems are designed to show the increases and decreases in each accounting equation element as a separate record. This record is called an **account**.

To illustrate, the Cash column of Exhibit 1 records the increases and decreases in cash. Likewise, the other columns in Exhibit 1 record the increases and decreases in the other accounting equation elements. Each of these columns can be organized into a separate account.

An account, in its simplest form, has three parts.

1. A title, which is the name of the accounting equation element recorded in the account.
2. A space for recording increases in the amount of the element.
3. A space for recording decreases in the amount of the element.

The account form presented below is called a **T account** because it resembles the letter T. The left side of the account is called the *debit* side, and the right side is called the *credit* side.[1]

Title
Left side	Right side
debit	*credit*

1 The terms *debit* and *credit* are derived from the Latin *debere* and *credere*.

EXHIBIT 1   **NetSolutions November Transactions**

	Assets			=	Liabilities +		Owner's Equity							
	Cash	+ Supp. +	Land	=	Accounts Payable	+	Chris Clark, Capital	Chris Clark, − Drawing	Fees + Earned −	Wages Exp. −	Rent Exp. −	Supplies Exp. −	Utilities Exp. −	Misc. Exp.
a.	+25,000						+25,000							
b.	−20,000		+20,000											
Bal.	5,000		20,000				25,000							
c.		+1,350			+1,350									
Bal.	5,000	1,350	20,000		1,350		25,000							
d.	+7,500								+7,500					
Bal.	12,500	1,350	20,000		1,350		25,000		7,500					
e.	−3,650									−2,125	−800		−450	−275
Bal.	8,850	1,350	20,000		1,350		25,000		7,500	−2,125	−800		−450	−275
f.	−950				−950									
Bal.	7,900	1,350	20,000		400		25,000		7,500	−2,125	−800		−450	−275
g.		−800										−800		
Bal.	7,900	550	20,000		400		25,000		7,500	−2,125	−800	−800	−450	−275
h.	−2,000							−2,000						
Bal.	5,900	550	20,000		400		25,000	−2,000	7,500	−2,125	−800	−800	−450	−275

The amounts shown in the Cash column of Exhibit 1 would be recorded in a cash account as follows:

Note: Amounts entered on the left side of an account are debits, and amounts entered on the right side of an account are credits.

Cash

Debit Side of Account	(a)	25,000	(b)	20,000
	(d)	7,500	(e)	3,650
			(f)	950
			(h)	2,000
	Balance	5,900		

Credit Side of Account

Balance of account ───┘

Recording transactions in accounts must follow certain rules. For example, increases in assets are recorded on the **debit** (left side) of an account. Likewise, decreases in assets are recorded on the **credit** (right side) of an account. The excess of the debits of an asset account over its credits is the **balance of the account**.

To illustrate, the receipt (increase in Cash) of $25,000 in transaction (a) is entered on the debit (left) side of the cash account shown above. The letter or date of the transaction is also entered into the account. This is done so if any questions later arise related to the entry, the entry can be traced back to the underlying transaction data. In contrast, the payment (decrease in Cash) of $20,000 to purchase land in transaction (b) is entered on the credit (right) side of the account.

The balance of the cash account of $5,900 is the excess of the debits over the credits as shown below.

Debits ($25,000 + $7,500)	$32,500
Less credits ($20,000 + $3,650 + $950 + $2,000)	26,600
Balance of Cash as of November 30, 2011	$ 5,900

The balance of the cash account is inserted in the account, in the Debit column. In this way, the balance is identified as a debit balance.[2] This balance represents NetSolutions' cash on hand as of November 30, 2011. This balance of $5,900 is reported on the November 30, 2011, balance sheet for NetSolutions as shown in Exhibit 6 of Chapter 1.

2 The totals of the debit and credit columns may be shown separately in an account. When this is done, these amounts should be identified in some way so that they are not mistaken for entries or the ending balance of the account.

In an actual accounting system, a more formal account form replaces the T account. Later in this chapter, a four-column account is illustrated. The T account, however, is a simple way to illustrate the effects of transactions on accounts and financial statements. For this reason, T accounts are often used in business to explain transactions.

Each of the columns in Exhibit 1 can be converted into an account form in a similar manner as was done for the Cash column of Exhibit 1. However, as mentioned earlier, recording increases and decreases in accounts must follow certain rules. These rules are discussed after the chart of accounts is described.

Chart of Accounts

A group of accounts for a business entity is called a **ledger**. A list of the accounts in the ledger is called a **chart of accounts**. The accounts are normally listed in the order in which they appear in the financial statements. The balance sheet accounts are listed first, in the order of assets, liabilities, and owner's equity. The income statement accounts are then listed in the order of revenues and expenses.

Assets are resources owned by the business entity. These resources can be physical items, such as cash and supplies, or intangibles that have value. Examples of intangible assets include patent rights, copyrights, and trademarks. Assets also include accounts receivable, prepaid expenses (such as insurance), buildings, equipment, and land.

Liabilities are debts owed to outsiders (creditors). Liabilities are often identified on the balance sheet by titles that include *payable*. Examples of liabilities include accounts payable, notes payable, and wages payable. Cash received before services are delivered creates a liability to perform the services. These future service commitments are called *unearned revenues*. Examples of unearned revenues include magazine subscriptions received by a publisher and tuition received at the beginning of a term by a college.

Owner's equity is the owner's right to the assets of the business after all liabilities have been paid. For a proprietorship, the owner's equity is represented by the balance of the owner's **capital account**. A **drawing** account represents the amount of withdrawals made by the owner.

Revenues are increases in owner's equity as a result of selling services or products to customers. Examples of revenues include fees earned, fares earned, commissions revenue, and rent revenue.

Expenses result from using up assets or consuming services in the process of generating revenues. Examples of expenses include wages expense, rent expense, utilities expense, supplies expense, and miscellaneous expense.

A chart of accounts should meet the needs of a company's managers and other users of its financial statements. The accounts within the chart of accounts are numbered for use as references. A numbering system is normally used, so that new accounts can be added without affecting other account numbers.

Exhibit 2 is NetSolutions' chart of accounts that is used in this chapter. Additional accounts will be introduced in later chapters. In Exhibit 2, each account number has two digits. The first digit indicates the major account group of the ledger in which the account is located. Accounts beginning with 1 represent assets; 2, liabilities; 3, owner's equity; 4, revenue; and 5, expenses. The second digit indicates the location of the account within its group.

Procter & Gamble's account numbers have over 30 digits to reflect P&G's many different operations and regions.

EXHIBIT 2

Chart of Accounts for NetSolutions

Balance Sheet Accounts	**Income Statement Accounts**
1. Assets	**4. Revenue**
11 Cash	41 Fees Earned
12 Accounts Receivable	**5. Expenses**
14 Supplies	51 Wages Expense
15 Prepaid Insurance	52 Rent Expense
17 Land	54 Utilities Expense
18 Office Equipment	55 Supplies Expense
2. Liabilities	59 Miscellaneous Expense
21 Accounts Payable	
23 Unearned Rent	
3. Owner's Equity	
31 Chris Clark, Capital	
32 Chris Clark, Drawing	

Each of the columns in Exhibit 1 has been assigned an account number in the chart of accounts shown in Exhibit 2. In addition, Accounts Receivable, Prepaid Insurance, Office Equipment, and Unearned Rent have been added. These accounts will be used in recording NetSolutions' December transactions.

Double-Entry Accounting System

OBJ. 2 Describe and illustrate journalizing transactions using the double-entry accounting system.

All businesses use what is called the **double-entry accounting system**. This system is based on the accounting equation and requires:

1. Every business transaction to be recorded in at least two accounts.
2. The total debits recorded for each transaction to be equal to the total credits recorded.

The double-entry accounting system also has specific **rules of debit and credit** for recording transactions in the accounts.

Balance Sheet Accounts

The debit and credit rules for balance sheet accounts are as follows:

		Balance Sheet Accounts			
ASSETS		**LIABILITIES**		**OWNER'S EQUITY**	
Asset Accounts	=	**Liability Accounts**	+	**Owner's Equity Accounts**	
Debit for increases (+)	Credit for decreases (–)	Debit for decreases (–)	Credit for increases (+)	Debit for decreases (–)	Credit for increases (+)

Income Statement Accounts

The debit and credit rules for income statement accounts are based on their relationship with owner's equity. As shown on page 55, owner's equity accounts are increased by credits. Since revenues increase owner's equity, revenue accounts are increased by credits and decreased by debits. Since owner's equity accounts are decreased by debits, expense accounts are increased by debits and decreased by credits. Thus, the rules of debit and credit for revenue and expense accounts are as follows:

Income Statement Accounts			
Revenue Accounts		**Expense Accounts**	
Debit for decreases (–)	Credit for increases (+)	Debit for increases (+)	Credit for decreases (–)

Owner Withdrawals

The debit and credit rules for recording owner withdrawals are based on the effect of owner withdrawals on owner's equity. Since owner's withdrawals decrease owner's equity, the owner's drawing account is increased by debits. Likewise, the owner's drawing account is decreased by credits. Thus, the rules of debit and credit for the owner's drawing account are as follows:

Drawing Account	
Debit for increases (+)	Credit for decreases (–)

Normal Balances

The sum of the increases in an account is usually equal to or greater than the sum of the decreases in the account. Thus, the **normal balance of an account** is either a debit or credit depending on whether increases in the account are recorded as debits or credits. For example, since asset accounts are increased with debits, asset accounts normally have debit balances. Likewise, liability accounts normally have credit balances.

The rules of debit and credit and the normal balances of the various types of accounts are summarized in Exhibit 3. Debits and credits are sometimes abbreviated as Dr. for debit and Cr. for credit.

When an account normally having a debit balance has a credit balance, or vice versa, an error may have occurred or an unusual situation may exist. For example, a credit balance in the office equipment account could result only from an error. This

---

Example Exercise 2-1 Rules of Debit and Credit and Normal Balances OBJ. 2

State for each account whether it is likely to have (a) debit entries only, (b) credit entries only, or (c) both debit and credit entries. Also, indicate its normal balance.

1. Amber Saunders, Drawing
2. Accounts Payable
3. Cash

4. Fees Earned
5. Supplies
6. Utilities Expense

Follow My Example 2-1

1. Debit entries only; normal debit balance
2. Debit and credit entries; normal credit balance
3. Debit and credit entries; normal debit balance

4. Credit entries only; normal credit balance
5. Debit and credit entries; normal debit balance
6. Debit entries only; normal debit balance

Practice Exercises: **PE 2-1A, PE 2-1B**

EXHIBIT 3   **Rules of Debit and Credit, Normal Balances of Accounts**

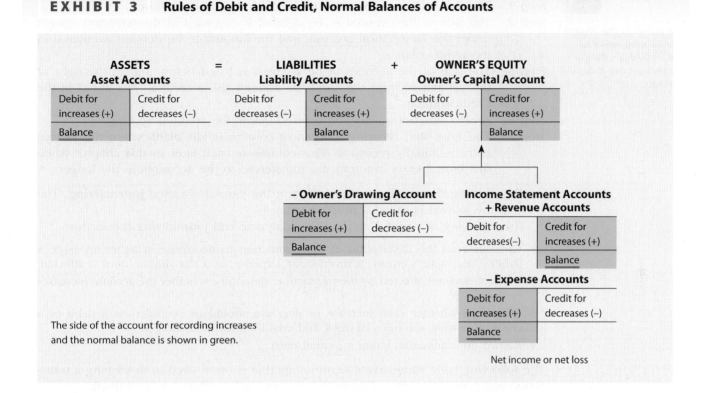

is because a business cannot have more decreases than increases of office equipment. On the other hand, a debit balance in an accounts payable account could result from an overpayment.

Journalizing

Using the rules of debit and credit, transactions are initially entered in a record called a **journal**. In this way, the journal serves as a record of when transactions occurred and were recorded. To illustrate, the November transactions of NetSolutions from Chapter 1 are used.

Nov. 1   Chris Clark deposited $25,000 in a bank account in the name of NetSolutions.   **Transaction A**

This transaction increases an asset account and increases an owner's equity account. It is recorded in the journal as an increase (debit) to Cash and an increase (credit) to Chris Clark, Capital.   **Analysis**

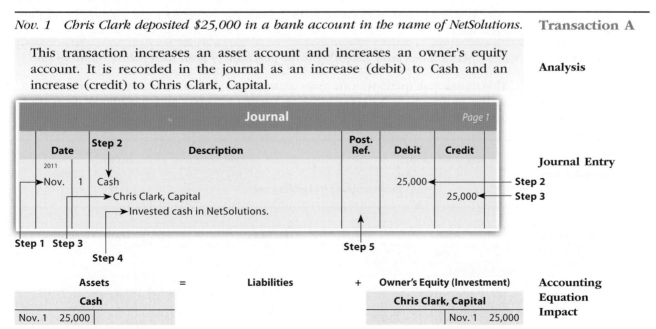

A journal can be thought of as being similar to an individual's diary of significant day-to-day life events.

The transaction is recorded in the journal using the following steps:

Step 1. The date of the transaction is entered in the Date column.

Step 2. The title of the account to be debited is recorded at the left-hand margin under the Description column, and the amount to be debited is entered in the Debit column.

Step 3. The title of the account to be credited is listed below and to the right of the debited account title, and the amount to be credited is entered in the Credit column.

Step 4. A brief description may be entered below the credited account.

Step 5. The Post. Ref. (Posting Reference) column is left blank when the journal entry is initially recorded. This column is used later in this chapter when the journal entry amounts are transferred to the accounts in the ledger.

The process of recording a transaction in the journal is called **journalizing**. The entry in the journal is called a **journal entry**.

The following is a useful method for analyzing and journalizing transactions:

1. Carefully read the description of the transaction to determine whether an asset, a liability, an owner's equity, a revenue, an expense, or a drawing account is affected.

2. For each account affected by the transaction, determine whether the account increases or decreases.

3. Determine whether each increase or decrease should be recorded as a debit or a credit, following the rules of debit and credit shown in Exhibit 3.

4. Record the transaction using a journal entry.

The following table summarizes terminology that is often used in describing a transaction along with the related accounts that would be debited and credited.

| | Journal Entry Account | |
Common transaction terminology	Debit	Credit
Received cash for services provided	Cash	Fees Earned
Services provided on account	Accounts Receivable	Fees Earned
Received cash on account	Cash	Accounts Receivable
Purchased on account	Asset Account	Accounts Payable
Paid on account	Accounts Payable	Cash
Paid cash	Asset or Expense Account	Cash
Owner investments	Cash and/or other assets	(Owner's Name), Capital
Owner withdrawals	(Owner's Name), Drawing	Cash

The remaining transactions of NetSolutions for November are analyzed and journalized next.

Transaction B *Nov. 5 NetSolutions paid $20,000 for the purchase of land as a future building site.*

Analysis This transaction increases one asset account and decreases another. It is recorded in the journal as a $20,000 increase (debit) to Land and a $20,000 decrease (credit) to Cash.

Journal Entry

Nov.	5	Land		20,000	
		Cash			20,000
		Purchased land for building site.			

Accounting Equation Impact

Assets	=	Liabilities	+	Owner's Equity

Land	
Nov. 5	20,000

Cash	
	Nov. 5 20,000

Nov. 10   NetSolutions purchased supplies on account for $1,350.   **Transaction C**

This transaction increases an asset account and increases a liability account. It
is recorded in the journal as a $1,350 increase (debit) to Supplies and a $1,350   **Analysis**
increase (credit) to Accounts Payable.

Nov.	10	Supplies		1,350	
		Accounts Payable			1,350
		Purchased supplies on account.			

Journal Entry

Assets	=	Liabilities	+	Owner's Equity
Supplies		**Accounts Payable**		
Nov. 10 1,350		Nov. 10 1,350		

Accounting Equation Impact

Nov. 18   NetSolutions received cash of $7,500 from customers for services provided.   **Transaction D**

This transaction increases an asset account and increases a revenue account.
It is recorded in the journal as a $7,500 increase (debit) to Cash and a $7,500   **Analysis**
increase (credit) to Fees Earned.

Nov.	18	Cash		7,500	
		Fees Earned			7,500
		Received fees from customers.			

Journal Entry

Assets	=	Liabilities	+	Owner's Equity (Revenue)
Cash				**Fees Earned**
Nov. 18 7,500				Nov. 18 7,500

Accounting Equation Impact

Nov. 30   NetSolutions incurred the following expenses: wages, $2,125; rent, $800;   **Transaction E**
utilities, $450; and miscellaneous, $275.

This transaction increases various expense accounts and decreases an asset
(Cash) account. You should note that regardless of the number of accounts, *the
sum of the debits is always equal to the sum of the credits in a journal entry.* It is
recorded in the journal with increases (debits) to the expense accounts (Wages   **Analysis**
Expense, $2,125; Rent Expense, $800; Utilities Expense, $450; and Miscellaneous
Expense, $275) and a decrease (credit) to Cash, $3,650.

Nov.	30	Wages Expense		2,125	
		Rent Expense		800	
		Utilities Expense		450	
		Miscellaneous Expense		275	
		Cash			3,650
		Paid expenses.			

Journal Entry

Assets	=	Liabilities	+	Owner's Equity (Expense)
Cash				**Wages Expense**
	Nov. 30 3,650			Nov. 30 2,125

Accounting Equation Impact

	Rent Expense
	Nov. 30 800

	Utilities Expense
	Nov. 30 450

	Miscellaneous Expense
	Nov. 30 275

Transaction F   *Nov. 30*   *NetSolutions paid creditors on account, $950.*

Analysis

This transaction decreases a liability account and decreases an asset account. It is recorded in the journal as a $950 decrease (debit) to Accounts Payable and a $950 decrease (credit) to Cash.

Journal Entry

Nov.	30	Accounts Payable		950	
		Cash			950
		Paid creditors on account.			

Accounting Equation Impact

Assets	=	Liabilities	+	Owner's Equity
Cash		**Accounts Payable**		
Nov. 30 950		Nov. 30 950		

Transaction G   *Nov. 30*   *Chris Clark determined that the cost of supplies on hand at November 30 was $550.*

Analysis

NetSolutions purchased $1,350 of supplies on November 10. Thus, $800 ($1,350 − $550) of supplies must have been used during November. This transaction is recorded in the journal as an $800 increase (debit) to Supplies Expense and an $800 decrease (credit) to Supplies.

Journal Entry

Nov.	30	Supplies Expense		800	
		Supplies			800
		Supplies used during November.			

Accounting Equation Impact

Assets	=	Liabilities	+	Owner's Equity (Expense)
Supplies				**Supplies Expense**
Nov. 30 800				Nov. 30 800

Transaction H   *Nov. 30*   *Chris Clark withdrew $2,000 from NetSolutions for personal use.*

Analysis

This transaction decreases assets and owner's equity. This transaction is recorded in the journal as a $2,000 increase (debit) to Chris Clark, Drawing and a $2,000 decrease (credit) to Cash.

Journal Entry

	Journal				Page 2
Date	**Description**		**Post. Ref.**	**Debit**	**Credit**
2011 Nov. 30	Chris Clark, Drawing			2,000	
	Cash				2,000
	Chris Clark withdrew cash for personal use.				

Accounting Equation Impact

Assets	=	Liabilities	+	Owner's Equity (Drawing)
Cash				**Chris Clark, Drawing**
Nov. 30 2,000				Nov. 30 2,000

Integrity, Objectivity, and Ethics in Business

WILL JOURNALIZING PREVENT FRAUD?

While journalizing transactions reduces the possibility of fraud, it by no means eliminates it. For example, embezzlement can be hidden within the double-entry bookkeeping system by creating fictitious suppliers to whom checks are issued.

Example Exercise 2-2   **Journal Entry for Asset Purchase**   OBJ. 2

Prepare a journal entry for the purchase of a truck on June 3 for $42,500, paying $8,500 cash and the remainder on account.

Follow My Example 2-2

June 3	Truck..	42,500	
	Cash		8,500
	Accounts Payable...		34,000

Practice Exercises: **PE 2-2A, PE 2-2B**

Posting Journal Entries to Accounts

OBJ. 3   Describe and illustrate the journalizing and posting of transactions to accounts.

As illustrated, a transaction is first recorded in a journal. Periodically, the journal entries are transferred to the accounts in the ledger. The process of transferring the debits and credits from the journal entries to the accounts is called **posting**.

The December transactions of NetSolutions are used to illustrate posting from the journal to the ledger. By using the December transactions, an additional review of analyzing and journalizing transactions is provided.

Dec. 1   NetSolutions paid a premium of $2,400 for an insurance policy for liability, theft, and fire. The policy covers a one-year period.   **Transaction**

Advance payments of expenses, such as for insurance premiums, are called prepaid expenses. Prepaid expenses are assets. For NetSolutions, the asset purchased is insurance protection for 12 months. This transaction is recorded as a $2,400 increase (debit) to Prepaid Insurance and a $2,400 decrease (credit) to Cash.   **Analysis**

Dec.	1	Prepaid Insurance	15	2,400	
		Cash	11		2,400
		Paid premium on one-year policy.			

Journal Entry

Assets	=	Liabilities	+	Owner's Equity

Cash   11

| Dec. 1 | 2,400 |

Accounting Equation Impact

Prepaid Insurance   15

| Dec. 1 | 2,400 | |

The posting of the preceding December 1 transaction is shown in Exhibit 4. Notice that the T account form is not used in Exhibit 4. In practice, the T account is usually replaced with a standard account form similar to that shown in Exhibit 4.

The debits and credits for each journal entry are posted to the accounts in the order in which they occur in the journal. To illustrate, the debit portion of the December 1 journal entry is posted to the prepaid account in Exhibit 4 using the following four steps:

Step 1.   The date (Dec. 1) of the journal entry is entered in the Date column of Prepaid Insurance.

EXHIBIT 4   **Diagram of the Recording and Posting of a Debit and a Credit**

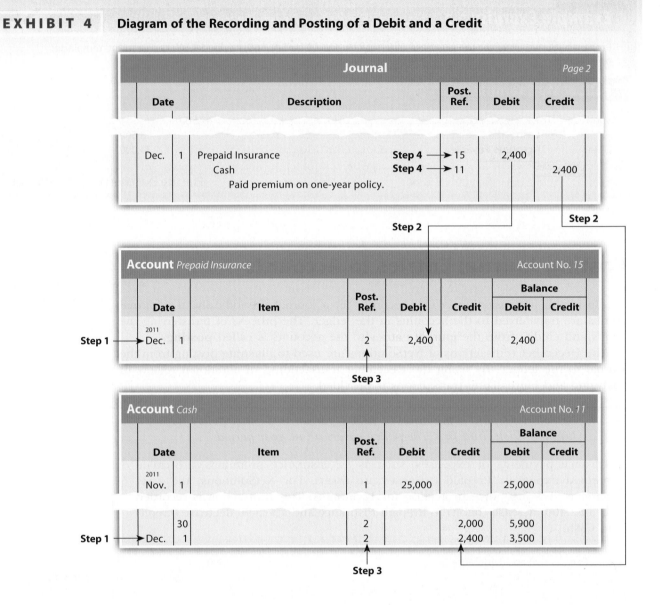

Step 2.   The amount (2,400) is entered into the Debit column of Prepaid Insurance.

Step 3.   The journal page number (2) is entered in the Posting Reference (Post. Ref.) column of Prepaid Insurance.

Step 4.   The account number (15) is entered in the Posting Reference (Post. Ref.) column in the journal.

As shown in Exhibit 4, the credit portion of the December 1 journal entry is posted to the cash account in a similar manner.

The remaining December transactions for NetSolutions are analyzed and journalized in the following paragraphs. These transactions are posted to the ledger in Exhibit 5 on pages 69–70. To simplify, some of the December transactions are stated in summary form. For example, cash received for services is normally recorded on a daily basis. However, only summary totals are recorded at the middle and end of the month for NetSolutions.

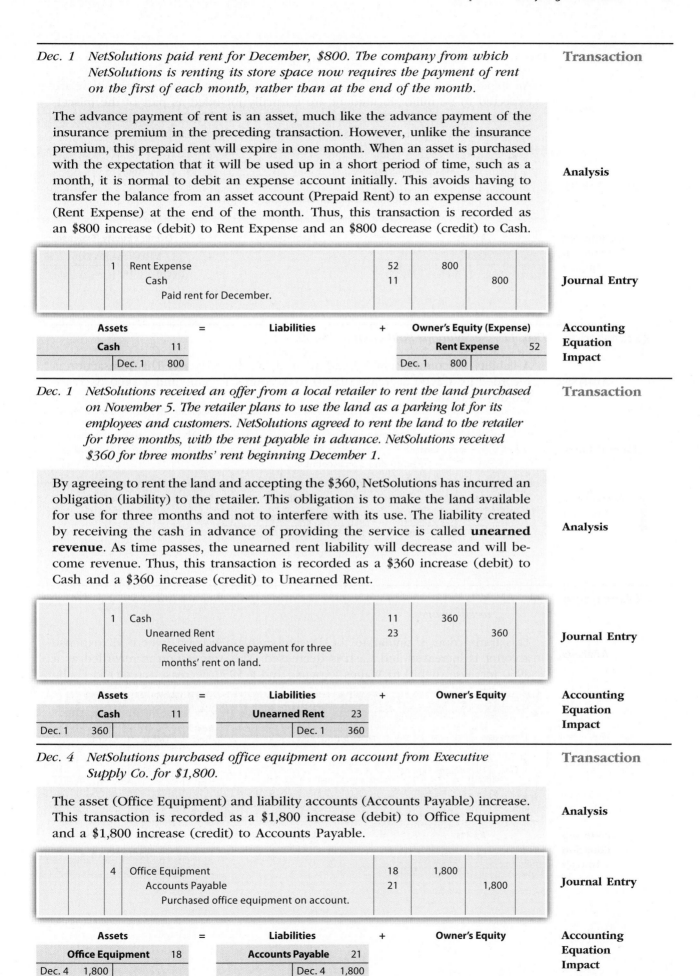

Dec. 1 NetSolutions paid rent for December, $800. The company from which NetSolutions is renting its store space now requires the payment of rent on the first of each month, rather than at the end of the month.

Transaction

The advance payment of rent is an asset, much like the advance payment of the insurance premium in the preceding transaction. However, unlike the insurance premium, this prepaid rent will expire in one month. When an asset is purchased with the expectation that it will be used up in a short period of time, such as a month, it is normal to debit an expense account initially. This avoids having to transfer the balance from an asset account (Prepaid Rent) to an expense account (Rent Expense) at the end of the month. Thus, this transaction is recorded as an $800 increase (debit) to Rent Expense and an $800 decrease (credit) to Cash.

Analysis

	1	Rent Expense	52	800	
		Cash	11		800
		Paid rent for December.			

Journal Entry

Assets	=	Liabilities	+	Owner's Equity (Expense)
Cash 11				**Rent Expense** 52
Dec. 1 800				Dec. 1 800

Accounting Equation Impact

Dec. 1 NetSolutions received an offer from a local retailer to rent the land purchased on November 5. The retailer plans to use the land as a parking lot for its employees and customers. NetSolutions agreed to rent the land to the retailer for three months, with the rent payable in advance. NetSolutions received $360 for three months' rent beginning December 1.

Transaction

By agreeing to rent the land and accepting the $360, NetSolutions has incurred an obligation (liability) to the retailer. This obligation is to make the land available for use for three months and not to interfere with its use. The liability created by receiving the cash in advance of providing the service is called **unearned revenue**. As time passes, the unearned rent liability will decrease and will become revenue. Thus, this transaction is recorded as a $360 increase (debit) to Cash and a $360 increase (credit) to Unearned Rent.

Analysis

	1	Cash	11	360	
		Unearned Rent	23		360
		Received advance payment for three months' rent on land.			

Journal Entry

Assets	=	Liabilities	+	Owner's Equity
Cash 11		**Unearned Rent** 23		
Dec. 1 360		Dec. 1 360		

Accounting Equation Impact

Dec. 4 NetSolutions purchased office equipment on account from Executive Supply Co. for $1,800.

Transaction

The asset (Office Equipment) and liability accounts (Accounts Payable) increase. This transaction is recorded as a $1,800 increase (debit) to Office Equipment and a $1,800 increase (credit) to Accounts Payable.

Analysis

	4	Office Equipment	18	1,800	
		Accounts Payable	21		1,800
		Purchased office equipment on account.			

Journal Entry

Assets	=	Liabilities	+	Owner's Equity
Office Equipment 18		**Accounts Payable** 21		
Dec. 4 1,800		Dec. 4 1,800		

Accounting Equation Impact

Transaction   *Dec. 6*   *NetSolutions paid $180 for a newspaper advertisement.*

Analysis   An expense increases and an asset (Cash) decreases. Expense items that are expected to be minor in amount are normally included as part of the miscellaneous expense. This transaction is recorded as a $180 increase (debit) to Miscellaneous Expense and a $180 decrease (credit) to Cash.

Journal Entry

	6	Miscellaneous Expense	59	180	
		Cash	11		180
		Paid for newspaper advertisement.			

Accounting Equation Impact

Assets	=	Liabilities	+	Owner's Equity (Expense)
Cash 11				**Miscellaneous Exp.** 59
Dec. 6 180				Dec. 6 180

Transaction   *Dec. 11*   *NetSolutions paid creditors $400.*

Analysis   A liability (Accounts Payable) and an asset (Cash) decrease. This transaction is recorded as a $400 decrease (debit) to Accounts Payable and a $400 decrease (credit) to Cash.

Journal Entry

	11	Accounts Payable	21	400	
		Cash	11		400
		Paid creditors on account.			

Accounting Equation Impact

Assets	=	Liabilities	+	Owner's Equity
Cash 11		**Accounts Payable** 21		
Dec. 11 400		Dec. 11 400		

Transaction   *Dec. 13*   *NetSolutions paid a receptionist and a part-time assistant $950 for two weeks' wages.*

Analysis   This transaction is similar to the December 6 transaction, where an expense account is increased and Cash is decreased. This transaction is recorded as a $950 increase (debit) to Wages Expense and a $950 decrease (credit) to Cash.

Journal Entry

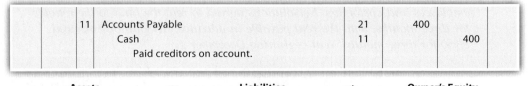

		Journal			Page 3
Date		**Description**	**Post. Ref.**	**Debit**	**Credit**
2011					
Dec.	13	Wages Expense	51	950	
		Cash	11		950
		Paid two weeks' wages.			

Accounting Equation Impact

Assets	=	Liabilities	+	Owner's Equity (Expense)
Cash 11				**Wages Expense** 51
Dec. 13 950				Dec. 13 950

BusinessConnection

COMPUTERIZED ACCOUNTING SYSTEMS

Computerized accounting systems are widely used by even the smallest of companies. These systems simplify the record keeping process in that transactions are recorded in electronic forms. Forms used to bill customers for services provided are often completed using drop down menus that list services that are normally provided to customers. An auto-complete entry feature may also be used to fill in

customer names. For example, type "ca" to display customers with names beginning with "Ca" (Caban, Cahill, Carey, and Caswell). And, to simplify data entry, entries are automatically posted to the ledger accounts when the electronic form is completed.

One popular accounting software package used by small- to medium-sized businesses is QuickBooks®. Some examples of using QuickBooks to record accounting transactions are illustrated and discussed in Chapter 5.

Dec. 16 NetSolutions received $3,100 from fees earned for the first half of December.

Transaction

An asset account (Cash) and a revenue account (Fees Earned) increase. This transaction is recorded as a $3,100 increase (debit) to Cash and a $3,100 increase (credit) to Fees Earned.

Analysis

	16	Cash	11	3,100	
		Fees Earned	41		3,100
		Received fees from customers.			

Journal Entry

Assets	=	Liabilities	+	Owner's Equity (Revenue)
Cash 11				**Fees Earned** 41
Dec. 16 3,100				Dec. 16 3,100

Accounting Equation Impact

Dec. 16 Fees earned on account totaled $1,750 for the first half of December.

Transaction

When a business agrees that a customer may pay for services provided at a later date, an **account receivable** is created. An account receivable is a claim against the customer. An account receivable is an asset, and the revenue is earned even though no cash has been received. Thus, this transaction is recorded as a $1,750 increase (debit) to Accounts Receivable and a $1,750 increase (credit) to Fees Earned.

Analysis

	16	Accounts Receivable	12	1,750	
		Fees Earned	41		1,750
		Fees earned on account.			

Journal Entry

Assets	=	Liabilities	+	Owner's Equity (Revenue)
Accounts Receivable 12				**Fees Earned** 41
Dec. 16 1,750				Dec. 16 1,750

Accounting Equation Impact

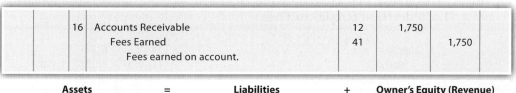

Example Exercise 2-3   Journal Entry for Fees Earned

OBJ. 3

Prepare a journal entry on August 7 for the fees earned on account, $115,000.

Follow My Example 2-3

Aug. 7	Accounts Receivable..	115,000	
	Fees Earned..		115,000

Practice Exercises: **PE 2-3A, PE 2-3B**

Transaction   *Dec. 20*   *NetSolutions paid $900 to Executive Supply Co. on the $1,800 debt owed from the December 4 transaction.*

Analysis   This is similar to the transaction of December 11. This transaction is recorded as a $900 decrease (debit) to Accounts Payable and a $900 decrease (credit) to Cash.

Journal Entry

	20	Accounts Payable	21	900	
		Cash	11		900
		Paid creditors on account.			

Accounting Equation Impact

Assets		=	Liabilities		+	Owner's Equity

Cash	11		**Accounts Payable**	21
	Dec. 20	900	Dec. 20	900	

Transaction   *Dec. 21*   *NetSolutions received $650 from customers in payment of their accounts.*

Analysis   When customers pay amounts owed for services they have previously received, one asset increases and another asset decreases. This transaction is recorded as a $650 increase (debit) to Cash and a $650 decrease (credit) to Accounts Receivable.

Journal Entry

	21	Cash	11	650	
		Accounts Receivable	12		650
		Received cash from customers on account.			

Accounting Equation Impact

Assets		=	Liabilities		+	Owner's Equity

Cash	11
Dec. 21	650

Accounts Receivable	12
	Dec. 21	650

Transaction   *Dec. 23*   *NetSolutions paid $1,450 for supplies.*

Analysis   One asset account (Supplies) increases and another asset account (Cash) decreases. This transaction is recorded as a $1,450 increase (debit) to Supplies and a $1,450 decrease (credit) to Cash.

Journal Entry

	23	Supplies	14	1,450	
		Cash	11		1,450
		Purchased supplies.			

Accounting Equation Impact

Assets		=	Liabilities		+	Owner's Equity

Cash	11
	Dec. 23	1,450

Supplies	14
Dec. 23	1,450

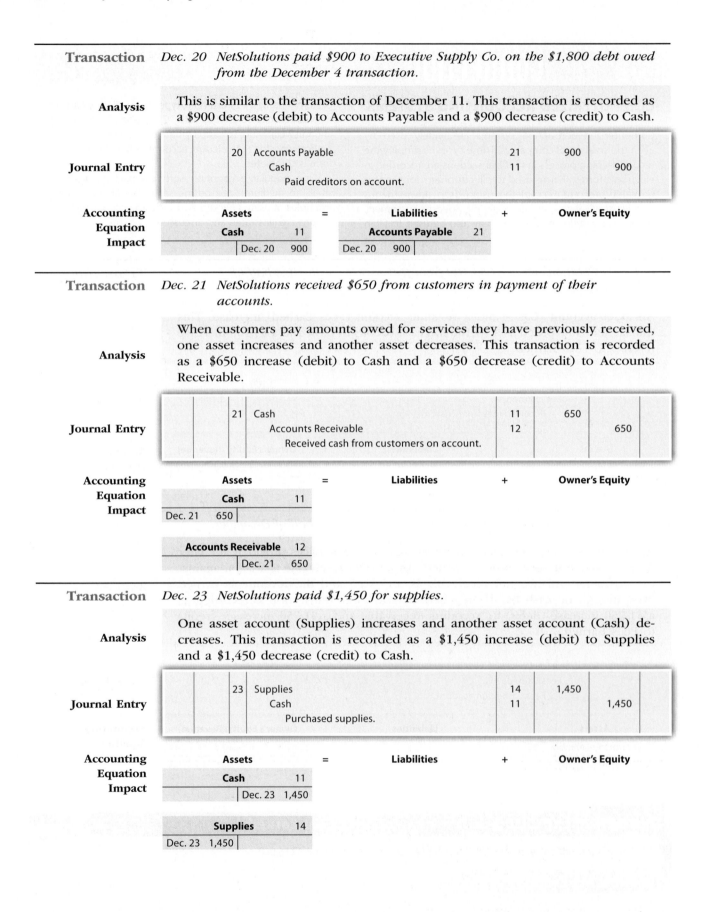

Dec. 27 NetSolutions paid the receptionist and the part-time assistant $1,200 for two weeks' wages.

Transaction

This transaction is similar to the transaction of December 13. This transaction is recorded as a $950 increase (debit) to Wages Expense and a $950 decrease (credit) to Cash.

Analysis

	27	Wages Expense		51	1,200	
		Cash		11		1,200
		Paid two weeks' wages.				

Journal Entry

Assets	=	Liabilities	+	Owner's Equity (Expense)
Cash 11				**Wages Expense** 51
Dec. 27 1,200				Dec. 27 1,200

Accounting Equation Impact

Dec. 31 NetSolutions paid its $310 telephone bill for the month.

Transaction

This is similar to the transaction of December 6. This transaction is recorded as a $310 increase (debit) to Utilities Expense and a $310 decrease (credit) to Cash.

Analysis

	31	Utilities Expense		54	310	
		Cash		11		310
		Paid telephone bill.				

Journal Entry

Assets	=	Liabilities	+	Owner's Equity (Expense)
Cash 11				**Utilities Expense** 54
Dec. 31 310				Dec. 31 310

Accounting Equation Impact

Dec. 31 NetSolutions paid its $225 electric bill for the month.

Transaction

This is similar to the preceding transaction. This transaction is recorded as a $225 increase (debit) to Utilities Expense and a $225 decrease (credit) to Cash.

Analysis

Journal					Page 4
Date	Description	Post. Ref.	Debit	Credit	
2011					
Dec. 31	Utilities Expense	54	225		
	Cash	11		225	
	Paid electric bill.				

Journal Entry

Assets	=	Liabilities	+	Owner's Equity (Expense)
Cash 11				**Utilities Expense** 54
Dec. 31 225				Dec. 31 225

Accounting Equation Impact

Dec. 31 NetSolutions received $2,870 from fees earned for the second half of December.

Transaction

This is similar to the transaction of December 16. This transaction is recorded as a $2,870 increase (debit) to Cash and a $2,870 increase (credit) to Fees Earned.

Analysis

	31	Cash		11	2,870	
		Fees Earned		41		2,870
		Received fees from customers.				

Journal Entry

Assets	=	Liabilities	+	Owner's Equity (Revenue)
Cash 11				**Fees Earned** 41
Dec. 31 2,870				Dec. 31 2,870

Accounting Equation Impact

Transaction   *Dec. 31   Fees earned on account totaled $1,120 for the second half of December.*

Analysis   This is similar to the transaction of December 16. This transaction is recorded as a $1,120 increase (debit) to Accounts Receivable and a $1,120 increase (credit) to Fees Earned.

Journal Entry

	31	Accounts Receivable	12	1,120	
		Fees Earned	41		1,120
		Fees earned on account.			

Accounting Equation Impact

Assets	=	Liabilities	+	Owner's Equity (Revenue)
Accounts Receivable 12				**Fees Earned** 41
Dec. 31 1,120				Dec. 31 1,120

Transaction   *Dec. 31   Chris Clark withdrew $2,000 for personal use.*

Analysis   This transaction decreases owner's equity and assets. This transaction is recorded as a $2,000 increase (debit) to Chris Clark, Drawing and a $2,000 decrease (credit) to Cash.

Journal Entry

	31	Chris Clark, Drawing	32	2,000	
		Cash	11		2,000
		Chris Clark withdrew cash for personal use.			

Accounting Equation Impact

Assets	=	Liabilities	+	Owner's Equity (Drawing)
Cash 11				**Chris Clark, Drawing** 32
Dec. 31 2,000				Dec. 31 2,000

Example Exercise 2-4   Journal Entry for Owner's Withdrawal

OBJ. 3

Prepare a journal entry on December 29 for the payment of $12,000 to the owner of Smartstaff Consulting Services, Dominique Walsh, for personal use.

Follow My Example 2-4

| Dec. 29 | Dominique Walsh, Drawing... | 12,000 | |
| | Cash .... | | 12,000 |

Practice Exercises: **PE 2-4A, PE 2-4B**

Example Exercise 2-5   Missing Amount from an Account

OBJ. 3

On March 1, the cash account balance was $22,350. During March, cash receipts totaled $241,880 and the March 31 balance was $19,125. Determine the cash payments made during March.

Follow My Example 2-5

Using the following T account, solve for the amount of cash payments (indicated by ? below).

	Cash		
Mar. 1 Bal.	22,350	?	Cash payments
Cash receipts	241,880		
Mar. 31 Bal.	19,125		

$19,125 = $22,350 + $241,880 − Cash payments
Cash payments = $22,350 + $241,880 − $19,125 = $245,105

Practice Exercises: **PE 2-5A, PE 2-5B**

Exhibit 5 shows the ledger for NetSolutions after the transactions for both November and December have been posted.

EXHIBIT 5   Ledger NetSolutions

Ledger

Account Cash — Account No. 11

Date	Item	Post. Ref.	Debit	Credit	Balance Debit	Balance Credit
2011						
Nov. 1		1	25,000		25,000	
5		1		20,000	5,000	
18		1	7,500		12,500	
30		1		3,650	8,850	
30		1		950	7,900	
30		2		2,000	5,900	
Dec. 1		2		2,400	3,500	
1		2		800	2,700	
1		2	360		3,060	
6		2		180	2,880	
11		2		400	2,480	
13		3		950	1,530	
16		3	3,100		4,630	
20		3		900	3,730	
21		3	650		4,380	
23		3		1,450	2,930	
27		3		1,200	1,730	
31		3		310	1,420	
31		4		225	1,195	
31		4	2,870		4,065	
31		4		2,000	2,065	

Account Accounts Receivable — Account No. 12

Date	Item	Post. Ref.	Debit	Credit	Balance Debit	Balance Credit
2011						
Dec. 16		3	1,750		1,750	
21		3		650	1,100	
31		4	1,120		2,220	

Account Supplies — Account No. 14

Date	Item	Post. Ref.	Debit	Credit	Balance Debit	Balance Credit
2011						
Nov. 10		1	1,350		1,350	
30		1		800	550	
Dec. 23		3	1,450		2,000	

Account Prepaid Insurance — Account No. 15

Date	Item	Post. Ref.	Debit	Credit	Balance Debit	Balance Credit
2011						
Dec. 1		2	2,400		2,400	

Account Land — Account No. 17

Date	Item	Post. Ref.	Debit	Credit	Balance Debit	Balance Credit
2011						
Nov. 5		1	20,000		20,000	

Account Office Equipment — Account No. 18

Date	Item	Post. Ref.	Debit	Credit	Balance Debit	Balance Credit
2011						
Dec. 4		2	1,800		1,800	

Account Accounts Payable — Account No. 21

Date	Item	Post. Ref.	Debit	Credit	Balance Debit	Balance Credit
2011						
Nov. 10		1		1,350		1,350
30		1	950			400
Dec. 4		2		1,800		2,200
11		2	400			1,800
20		3	900			900

Account Unearned Rent — Account No. 23

Date	Item	Post. Ref.	Debit	Credit	Balance Debit	Balance Credit
2011						
Dec. 1		2		360		360

Account Chris Clark, Capital — Account No. 31

Date	Item	Post. Ref.	Debit	Credit	Balance Debit	Balance Credit
2011						
Nov. 1		1		25,000		25,000

Account Chris Clark, Drawing — Account No. 32

Date	Item	Post. Ref.	Debit	Credit	Balance Debit	Balance Credit
2011						
Nov. 30		2	2,000		2,000	
Dec. 31		4	2,000		4,000	

(continued)

EXHIBIT 5 Ledger NetSolutions *(concluded)*

Account *Fees Earned*   Account No. *41*

Date	Item	Post. Ref.	Debit	Credit	Balance Debit	Balance Credit
2011						
Nov. 18		1		7,500		7,500
Dec. 16		3		3,100		10,600
16		3		1,750		12,350
31		4		2,870		15,220
31		4		1,120		16,340

Account *Wages Expense*   Account No. *51*

Date	Item	Post. Ref.	Debit	Credit	Balance Debit	Balance Credit
2011						
Nov. 30		1	2,125		2,125	
Dec. 13		3	950		3,075	
27		3	1,200		4,275	

Account *Rent Expense*   Account No. *52*

Date	Item	Post. Ref.	Debit	Credit	Balance Debit	Balance Credit
2011						
Nov. 30		1	800		800	
Dec. 1		2	800		1,600	

Account *Utilities Expense*   Account No. *54*

Date	Item	Post. Ref.	Debit	Credit	Balance Debit	Balance Credit
2011						
Nov. 30		1	450		450	
Dec. 31		3	310		760	
31		4	225		985	

Account *Supplies Expense*   Account No. *55*

Date	Item	Post. Ref.	Debit	Credit	Balance Debit	Balance Credit
2011						
Nov. 30		1	800		800	

Account *Miscellaneous Expense*   Account No. *59*

Date	Item	Post. Ref.	Debit	Credit	Balance Debit	Balance Credit
2011						
Nov. 30		1	275		275	
Dec. 6		2	180		455	

OBJ. 4 Prepare an unadjusted trial balance and explain how it can be used to discover errors.

Trial Balance

Errors may occur in posting debits and credits from the journal to the ledger. One way to detect such errors is by preparing a **trial balance**. Double-entry accounting requires that debits must always equal credits. The trial balance verifies this equality. The steps in preparing a trial balance are as follows:

Step 1. List the name of the company, the title of the trial balance, and the date the trial balance is prepared.
Step 2. List the accounts from the ledger and enter their debit or credit balance in the Debit or Credit column of the trial balance.
Step 3. Total the Debit and Credit columns of the trial balance.
Step 4. Verify that the total of the Debit column equals the total of the Credit column.

The trial balance for NetSolutions as of December 31, 2011, is shown in Exhibit 6. The account balances in Exhibit 6 are taken from the ledger shown in Exhibit 5. Before a trial balance is prepared, each account balance in the ledger must be determined. When the standard account form is used as in Exhibit 5, the balance of each account appears in the balance column on the same line as the last posting to the account.

EXHIBIT 6

Trial Balance

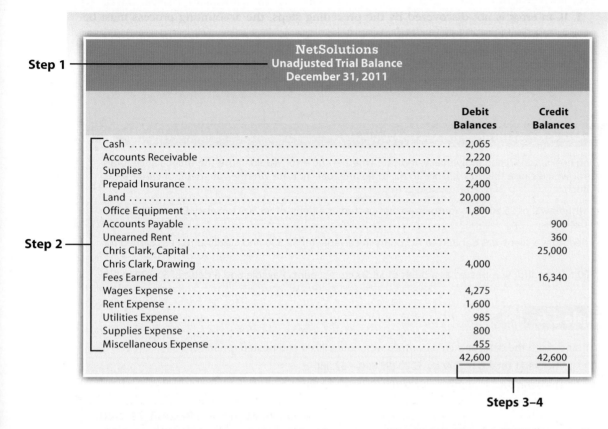

Step 1

Step 2

Steps 3–4

NetSolutions Unadjusted Trial Balance December 31, 2011		
	Debit Balances	**Credit Balances**
Cash	2,065	
Accounts Receivable	2,220	
Supplies	2,000	
Prepaid Insurance	2,400	
Land	20,000	
Office Equipment	1,800	
Accounts Payable		900
Unearned Rent		360
Chris Clark, Capital		25,000
Chris Clark, Drawing	4,000	
Fees Earned		16,340
Wages Expense	4,275	
Rent Expense	1,600	
Utilities Expense	985	
Supplies Expense	800	
Miscellaneous Expense	455	
	42,600	42,600

The trial balance shown in Exhibit 6 is titled an **unadjusted trial balance**. This is to distinguish it from other trial balances that will be prepared in later chapters. These other trial balances include an adjusted trial balance and a post-closing trial balance.[3]

Errors Affecting the Trial Balance

If the trial balance totals are not equal, an error has occurred. In this case, the error must be found and corrected. A method useful in discovering errors is as follows:

1. If the difference between the Debit and Credit column totals is 10, 100, or 1,000, an error in addition may have occurred. In this case, re-add the trial balance column totals. If the error still exists, recompute the account balances.

2. If the difference between the Debit and Credit column totals can be evenly divisible by 2, the error may be due to the entering of a debit balance as a credit balance, or vice versa. In this case, review the trial balance for account balances of one-half the difference that may have been entered in the wrong column. For example, if the Debit column total is $20,640 and the Credit column total is $20,236, the difference of $404 ($20,640 − $20,236) may be due to a credit account balance of $202 that was entered as a debit account balance.

3. If the difference between the Debit and Credit column totals is evenly divisible by 9, trace the account balances back to the ledger to see if an account balance was incorrectly copied from the ledger. Two common types of copying errors are transpositions and slides. A **transposition** occurs when the order of the digits is copied incorrectly, such as writing $542 as $452 or $524. In a **slide**, the entire number is copied incorrectly one or more spaces to the right or the left, such as writing $542.00 as $54.20 or $5,420.00. In both cases, the resulting error will be evenly divisible by 9.

4. If the difference between the Debit and Credit column totals is not evenly divisible by 2 or 9, review the ledger to see if an account balance in the amount of the error has been omitted from the trial balance. If the error is not discovered, review the journal postings to see if a posting of a debit or credit may have been omitted.

3 The adjusted trial balance is discussed in Chapter 3, and the post-closing trial balance is discussed in Chapter 4.

5. If an error is not discovered by the preceding steps, the accounting process must be retraced, beginning with the last journal entry.

The trial balance does not provide complete proof of the accuracy of the ledger. It indicates only that the debits and the credits are equal. This proof is of value, however, because errors often affect the equality of debits and credits.

Example Exercise 2-6   Trial Balance Errors

OBJ. 4

For each of the following errors, considered individually, indicate whether the error would cause the trial balance totals to be unequal. If the error would cause the trial balance totals to be unequal, indicate whether the debit or credit total is higher and by how much.

a. Payment of a cash withdrawal of $5,600 was journalized and posted as a debit of $6,500 to Salary Expense and a credit of $6,500 to Cash.

b. A fee of $2,850 earned from a client was debited to Accounts Receivable for $2,580 and credited to Fees Earned for $2,850.

c. A payment of $3,500 to a creditor was posted as a debit of $3,500 to Accounts Payable and a debit of $3,500 to Cash.

Follow My Example 2-6

a. The totals are equal since both the debit and credit entries were journalized and posted for $6,500..

b. The totals are unequal. The credit total is higher by $270 ($2,850 − $2,580).

c. The totals are unequal. The debit total is higher by $7,000 ($3,500 + $3,500).

Practice Exercises: **PE 2-6A, PE 2-6B**

Errors Not Affecting the Trial Balance

An error may occur that does not cause the trial balance totals to be unequal. Such an error may be discovered when preparing the trial balance or may be indicated by an unusual account balance. For example, a credit balance in the supplies account indicates an error has occurred. This is because a business cannot have "negative" supplies. When such errors are discovered, they should be corrected. If the error has already been journalized and posted to the ledger, a **correcting journal entry** is normally prepared.

To illustrate, assume that on May 5 a $12,500 purchase of office equipment on account was incorrectly journalized and posted as a debit to Supplies and a credit to Accounts Payable for $12,500. This posting of the incorrect entry is shown in the following T accounts:

Incorrect:

Supplies		Accounts Payable	
12,500			12,500

Before making a correcting journal entry, it is best to determine the debit(s) and credit(s) that should have been recorded. These are shown in the following T accounts:

Correct:

Office Equipment		Accounts Payable	
12,500			12,500

Comparing the two sets of T accounts shows that the incorrect debit to Supplies may be corrected by debiting Office Equipment for $12,500 and crediting Supplies for $12,500. The following correcting journal entry is then journalized and posted:

Entry to Correct Error:

May	31	Office Equipment	18	12,500	
		Supplies	14		12,500
		To correct erroneous debit			
		to Supplies on May 5. See invoice			
		from Bell Office Equipment Co.			

Example Exercise 2-7   Correcting Entries

OBJ. 4

The following errors took place in journalizing and posting transactions:
a. A withdrawal of $6,000 by Cheri Ramey, owner of the business, was recorded as a debit to Office Salaries Expense and a credit to Cash.
b. Utilities Expense of $4,500 paid for the current month was recorded as a debit to Miscellaneous Expense and a credit to Accounts Payable.
Journalize the entries to correct the errors. Omit explanations.

Follow My Example 2-7

a. Cheri Ramey, Drawing 6,000
    Office Salaries Expense... 6,000

b. Accounts Payable... 4,500
    Miscellaneous Expense... 4,500

    Utilities Expense 4,500
    Cash.. 4,500

Note: The first entry in (b) reverses the incorrect entry, and the second entry records the correct entry. These two entries could also be combined into one entry; however, preparing two entries will make it easier for someone later to understand what had happened and why the entries were necessary.

Practice Exercises: **PE 2-7A, PE 2-7B**

Financial Analysis and Interpretation: Horizontal Analysis

A single item in a financial statement, such as net income, is often useful in interpreting the financial performance of a company. However, a comparison with prior periods often makes the financial information even more useful. For example, comparing net income of the current period with the net income with the prior period will indicate whether the company's operating performance has improved.

In **horizontal analysis**, the amount of each item on a current financial statement is compared with the same item on an earlier statement. The increase or decrease in the *amount* of the item is computed together with the *percent* of increase or decrease. When two statements are being compared, the earlier statement is used as the base for computing the amount and the percent of change.

OBJ. 5 Describe and illustrate the use of horizontal analysis in evaluating a company's performance and financial condition.

To illustrate, the horizontal analysis of two income statements for J. Holmes, Attorney-at-Law, is shown below.

J. Holmes, Attorney-at-Law
Income Statements
For the Years Ended December 31

	2012	2011	Increase (Decrease) Amount	Percent
Fees earned	$187,500	$150,000	$37,500	25.0%*
Operating expenses:				
Wages expense	$ 60,000	$ 45,000	$15,000	33.3
Rent expense	15,000	12,000	3,000	25.0
Utilities expense	12,500	9,000	3,500	38.9
Supplies expense	2,700	3,000	(300)	(10.0)
Miscellaneous expense	2,300	1,800	500	27.8
Total operating expenses	$ 92,500	$ 70,800	$21,700	30.6
Net income	$ 95,000	$ 79,200	$15,800	19.9

*$37,500 ÷ $150,000

The horizontal analysis for J. Holmes, Attorney-at-Law, indicates both favorable and unfavorable trends. The increase in fees earned is a favorable trend, as is the decrease in supplies expense. Unfavorable trends include the increase in wages expense, utilities expense, and miscellaneous expense. These expenses increased the same as or faster than the increase in revenues, with total operating expenses increasing by 30.6%. Overall, net income increased by $15,800, or 19.9%, a favorable trend.

The significance of the various increases and decreases in the revenue and expense items should be investigated to see if operations could be further improved. For example, the increase in utilities expense of 38.9% was the result of renting additional office space for use by a part-time law student in performing paralegal services. This explains the increase in rent expense of 25% and the increase in wages expense of 33.3%. The increase in revenues of 25% reflects the fees generated by the new paralegal.

The preceding example illustrates how horizontal analysis can be useful in interpreting and analyzing the income statement. Horizontal analyses can also be performed for the balance sheet, the statement of owner's equity, and the statement of cash flows.

To illustrate, horizontal analysis for Apple Inc.'s 2009 and 2008 statements of cash flows (in millions) is shown below.

Apple Inc.
Statements of Cash Flows
For the Years Ended

	Sept. 26, 2009	Sept. 27, 2008	Increase (Decrease) Amount	Percent
Cash flows from operating activities	$10,159	$ 9,596	$ 563	5.9%
Cash flows used for investing activities	(17,434)	(8,189)	(9,245)	(112.9)
Cash flows from financing activities	663	1,116	(453)	(40.6)
Net increase (decrease) in cash	$ (6,612)	$ 2,523	$(9,135)	(362.1)
Beginning of the year balance of cash	11,875	9,352	2,523	27.0
End of the year balance of cash	$ 5,263	$11,875	$(6,612)	(55.7)

The horizontal analysis of cash flows for Apple Inc. indicates an increase in cash flows from operating activities of 5.9%, which is a favorable trend. At the same time, Apple increased the cash used in its investing activities by over 112.9% and decreased the cash it received from financing activities by 40.6%. Overall, Apple had a 362.1% decrease in cash for the year, which decreased the end of the year cash balance by 55.7%. In contrast, in the prior year Apple increased its ending cash balance, which is the beginning cash balance of the current year, by 27%.

Example Exercise 2-8   Horizontal Analysis

Two income statements for McCorkle Company are shown below.

McCorkle Company
Income Statements
For the Years Ended December 31

	2012	2011
Fees earned	$210,000	$175,000
Operating expenses	172,500	150,000
Net income	$ 37,500	$ 25,000

Prepare a horizontal analysis of McCorkle Company's income statements.

Follow My Example 2-8

McCorkle Company
Income Statements
For the Years Ended December 31

	2012	2011	Increase (Decrease) Amount	Increase (Decrease) Percent
Fees earned	$210,000	$175,000	$35,000	20%
Operating expenses	172,500	150,000	22,500	15
Net income	$ 37,500	$ 25,000	$12,500	50

Practice Exercises: **PE 2-8A, PE 2-8B**

At a Glance 2

Describe the characteristics of an account and a chart of accounts.

Key Points   The simplest form of an account, a T account, has three parts: (1) a title, which is the name of the item recorded in the account; (2) a left side, called the debit side; and (3) a right side, called the credit side. Periodically, the debits in an account are added, the credits in the account are added, and the balance of the account is determined.

The system of accounts that make up a ledger is called a chart of accounts.

Learning Outcomes	Example Exercises	Practice Exercises
• Record transactions in T accounts.		
• Determine the balance of a T account.		
• Prepare a chart of accounts for a proprietorship.		

OBJ. 2 Describe and illustrate journalizing transactions using the double-entry accounting system.

Key Points Transactions are initially entered in a record called a journal. The rules of debit and credit for recording increases or decreases in accounts are shown in Exhibit 3. Each transaction is recorded so that the sum of the debits is always equal to the sum of the credits. The normal balance of an account is indicated by the side of the account (debit or credit) that receives the increases.

Learning Outcomes	Example Exercises	Practice Exercises
• Indicate the normal balance of an account.	EE2-1	PE2-1A, 2-1B
• Journalize transactions using the rules of debit and credit.	EE2-2	PE2-2A, 2-2B

OBJ. 3 Describe and illustrate the journalizing and posting of transactions to accounts.

Key Points Transactions are journalized and posted to the ledger using the rules of debit and credit. The debits and credits for each journal entry are posted to the accounts in the order in which they occur in the journal.

Learning Outcomes	Example Exercises	Practice Exercises
• Journalize transactions using the rules of debit and credit.	EE2-3	PE2-3A, 2-3B
• Given other account data, determine the missing amount of an account entry.	EE2-4	PE2-4A, 2-4B
	EE2-5	PE2-5A, 2-5B
• Post journal entries to a standard account.		
• Post journal entries to a T account.		

OBJ. 4 Prepare an unadjusted trial balance and explain how it can be used to discover errors.

Key Points A trial balance is prepared by listing the accounts from the ledger and their balances. The totals of the Debit column and Credit column of the trial balance must be equal. If the two totals are not equal, an error has occurred. Errors may occur even though the trial balance totals are equal. Such errors may require a correcting journal entry.

Learning Outcomes	Example Exercises	Practice Exercises
• Prepare an unadjusted trial balance.		
• Discover errors that cause unequal totals in the trial balance.	EE2-6	PE2-6A, 2-6B
• Prepare correcting journal entries for various errors.	EE2-7	PE2-7A, 2-7B

OBJ. 5 Describe and illustrate the use of horizontal analysis in evaluating a company's performance and financial condition.

Key Points   In horizontal analysis, the amount of each item on a current financial statement is compared with the same item on an earlier statement. The increase or decrease in the *amount* of the item is computed together with the *percent* of increase or decrease. When two statements are being compared, the earlier statement is used as the base for computing the amount and the percent of change.

Learning Outcomes	Example Exercises	Practice Exercises
• Describe horizontal analysis.		
• Prepare a horizontal analysis report of a financial statement.	EE2-8	PE2-8A, 2-8B

Key Terms

account (52)	drawing (54)	posting (61)
account receivable (65)	expenses (55)	revenues (54)
assets (54)	horizontal analysis (73)	rules of debit and credit (55)
balance of the account (53)	journal (57)	slide (71)
capital account (54)	journal entry (58)	T account (52)
chart of accounts (54)	journalizing (58)	transposition (71)
correcting journal entry (72)	ledger (54)	trial balance (70)
credit (53)	liabilities (54)	unadjusted trial balance (71)
debit (53)	normal balance of an account (56)	unearned revenue (63)
double-entry accounting system (55)	owner's equity (54)	

Illustrative Problem

J. F. Outz, M.D., has been practicing as a cardiologist for three years. During April 2011, Outz completed the following transactions in her practice of cardiology:

Apr. 1. Paid office rent for April, $800.

   3. Purchased equipment on account, $2,100.

   5. Received cash on account from patients, $3,150.

   8. Purchased X-ray film and other supplies on account, $245.

   9. One of the items of equipment purchased on April 3 was defective. It was returned with the permission of the supplier, who agreed to reduce the account for the amount charged for the item, $325.

  12. Paid cash to creditors on account, $1,250.

Apr. 17. Paid cash for renewal of a six-month property insurance policy, $370.

20. Discovered that the balances of the cash account and the accounts payable account as of April 1 were overstated by $200. A payment of that amount to a creditor in March had not been recorded. Journalize the $200 payment as of April 20.

24. Paid cash for laboratory analysis, $545.

27. Paid cash from business bank account for personal and family expenses, $1,250.

30. Recorded the cash received in payment of services (on a cash basis) to patients during April, $1,720.

30. Paid salaries of receptionist and nurses, $1,725.

30. Paid various utility expenses, $360.

30. Recorded fees charged to patients on account for services performed in April, $5,145.

30. Paid miscellaneous expenses, $132.

Outz's account titles, numbers, and balances as of April 1 (all normal balances) are listed as follows: Cash, 11, $4,123; Accounts Receivable, 12, $6,725; Supplies, 13, $290; Prepaid Insurance, 14, $465; Equipment, 18, $19,745; Accounts Payable, 22, $765; J. F. Outz, Capital, 31, $30,583; J. F. Outz, Drawing, 32, $0; Professional Fees, 41, $0; Salary Expense, 51, $0; Rent Expense, 53, $0; Laboratory Expense, 55, $0; Utilities Expense, 56, $0; Miscellaneous Expense, 59, $0.

Instructions

1. Open a ledger of standard four-column accounts for Dr. Outz as of April 1. Enter the balances in the appropriate balance columns and place a check mark (✓) in the Posting Reference column. (*Hint:* Verify the equality of the debit and credit balances in the ledger before proceeding with the next instruction.)

2. Journalize each transaction in a two-column journal.

3. Post the journal to the ledger, extending the month-end balances to the appropriate balance columns after each posting.

4. Prepare an unadjusted trial balance as of April 30.

Solution 1., 2., and 3.

Journal				Page *27*

Date	Description	Post. Ref.	Debit	Credit
2011				
Apr. 1	Rent Expense	53	800	
	Cash	11		800
	Paid office rent for April.			
3	Equipment	18	2,100	
	Accounts Payable	22		2,100
	Purchased equipment on account.			
5	Cash	11	3,150	
	Accounts Receivable	12		3,150
	Received cash on account.			
8	Supplies	13	245	
	Accounts Payable	22		245
	Purchased supplies.			
9	Accounts Payable	22	325	
	Equipment	18		325
	Returned defective equipment.			
12	Accounts Payable	22	1,250	
	Cash	11		1,250
	Paid creditors on account.			
17	Prepaid Insurance	14	370	
	Cash	11		370
	Renewed six-month property policy.			
20	Accounts Payable	22	200	
	Cash	11		200
	Recorded March payment to creditor.			

Journal				Page *28*

Date	Description	Post. Ref.	Debit	Credit
2011				
Apr. 24	Laboratory Expense	55	545	
	Cash	11		545
	Paid for laboratory analysis.			
27	J. F. Outz, Drawing	32	1,250	
	Cash	11		1,250
	J. F. Outz withdrew cash for personal use.			
30	Cash	11	1,720	
	Professional Fees	41		1,720
	Received fees from patients.			
30	Salary Expense	51	1,725	
	Cash	11		1,725
	Paid salaries.			
30	Utilities Expense	56	360	
	Cash	11		360
	Paid utilities.			
30	Accounts Receivable	12	5,145	
	Professional Fees	41		5,145
	Recorded fees earned on account.			
30	Miscellaneous Expense	59	132	
	Cash	11		132
	Paid expenses.			

Account *Cash*   Account No. *11*

Date	Item	Post. Ref.	Debit	Credit	Balance Debit	Balance Credit
2011						
Apr. 1	Balance	✓			4,123	
1		27		800	3,323	
5		27	3,150		6,473	
12		27		1,250	5,223	
17		27		370	4,853	
20		27		200	4,653	
24		28		545	4,108	
27		28		1,250	2,858	
30		28	1,720		4,578	
30		28		1,725	2,853	
30		28		360	2,493	
30		28		132	2,361	

Account *Accounts Receivable*   Account No. *12*

Date	Item	Post. Ref.	Debit	Credit	Balance Debit	Balance Credit
2011						
Apr. 1	Balance	✓			6,725	
5		27		3,150	3,575	
30		28	5,145		8,720	

Account *Supplies*   Account No. *13*

Date	Item	Post. Ref.	Debit	Credit	Balance Debit	Balance Credit
2011						
Apr. 1	Balance	✓			290	
8		27	245		535	

Account *Prepaid Insurance* — Account No. 14

Date	Item	Post. Ref.	Debit	Credit	Balance Debit	Balance Credit
2011						
Apr. 1	Balance	✓			465	
17		27	370		835	

Account *Equipment* — Account No. 18

Date	Item	Post. Ref.	Debit	Credit	Balance Debit	Balance Credit
2011						
Apr. 1	Balance	✓			19,745	
3		27	2,100		21,845	
9		27		325	21,520	

Account *Accounts Payable* — Account No. 22

Date	Item	Post. Ref.	Debit	Credit	Balance Debit	Balance Credit
2011						
Apr. 1	Balance	✓				765
3		27		2,100		2,865
8		27		245		3,110
9		27	325			2,785
12		27	1,250			1,535
20		27	200			1,335

Account *J. F. Outz, Capital* — Account No. 31

Date	Item	Post. Ref.	Debit	Credit	Balance Debit	Balance Credit
2011						
Apr. 1	Balance	✓				30,583

Account *J. F. Qutz, Drawing* — Account No. 32

Date	Item	Post. Ref.	Debit	Credit	Balance Debit	Balance Credit
2011						
Apr. 27		28	1,250		1,250	

Account *Professional Fees* — Account No. 41

Date	Item	Post. Ref.	Debit	Credit	Balance Debit	Balance Credit
2011						
Apr. 30		28		1,720		1,720
30		28		5,145		6,865

Account *Salary Expense* — Account No. 51

Date	Item	Post. Ref.	Debit	Credit	Balance Debit	Balance Credit
2011						
Apr. 30		28	1,725		1,725	

Account *Rent Expense* — Account No. 53

Date	Item	Post. Ref.	Debit	Credit	Balance Debit	Balance Credit
2011						
Apr. 1		27	800		800	

Account *Laboratory Expense* — Account No. 55

Date	Item	Post. Ref.	Debit	Credit	Balance Debit	Balance Credit
2011						
Apr. 24		28	545		545	

Account *Utilities Expanse* — Account No. 56

Date	Item	Post. Ref.	Debit	Credit	Balance Debit	Balance Credit
2011						
Apr. 30		28	360		360	

Account *Miscellaneous Expense* — Account No. 59

Date	Item	Post. Ref.	Debit	Credit	Balance Debit	Balance Credit
2011						
Apr. 30		28	132		132	

4.

J. F. Outz, M.D. Unadjusted Trial Balance April 30, 2011	Debit Balances	Credit Balances
Cash	2,361	
Accounts Receivable	8,720	
Supplies	535	
Prepaid Insurance	835	
Equipment	21,520	
Accounts Payable		1,335
J. F. Outz, Capital		30,583
J. F. Outz, Drawing	1,250	
Professional Fees		6,865
Salary Expense	1,725	
Rent Expense	800	
Laboratory Expense	545	
Utilities Expense	360	
Miscellaneous Expense	132	
	38,783	38,783

Discussion Questions

1. What is the difference between an account and a ledger?

2. Do the terms *debit* and *credit* signify increase or decrease or can they signify either? Explain.

3. Weir Company adheres to a policy of depositing all cash receipts in a bank account and making all payments by check. The cash account as of December 31 has a credit balance of $3,190, and there is no undeposited cash on hand. (a) Assuming no errors occurred during journalizing or posting, what caused this unusual balance? (b) Is the $3,190 credit balance in the cash account an asset, a liability, owner's equity, a revenue, or an expense?

4. Resource Services Company performed services in February for a specific customer, for a fee of $11,250. Payment was received the following March. (a) Was the revenue earned in February or March? (b) What accounts should be debited and credited in (1) February and (2) March?

5. If the two totals of a trial balance are equal, does it mean that there are no errors in the accounting records? Explain.

6. Assume that a trial balance is prepared with an account balance of $21,740 listed as $2,174 and an account balance of $4,500 listed as $5,400. Identify the transposition and the slide.

7. Assume that when a purchase of supplies of $3,100 for cash was recorded, both the debit and the credit were journalized and posted as $1,300. (a) Would this error cause the trial balance to be out of balance? (b) Would the trial balance be out of balance if the $3,100 entry had been journalized correctly but the credit to Cash had been posted as $1,300?

8. Assume that Timberline Consulting erroneously recorded the payment of $9,000 of owner withdrawals as a debit to Salary Expense. (a) How would this error affect the equality of the trial balance? (b) How would this error affect the income statement, statement of owner's equity, and balance sheet?

9. Assume that Western Realty Co. borrowed $200,000 from Mountain First Bank and Trust. In recording the transaction, Western erroneously recorded the receipt as a debit to Cash, $200,000, and a credit to Fees Earned, $200,000. (a) How would this error affect the equality of the trial balance? (b) How would this error affect the income statement, statement of owner's equity, and balance sheet?

10. Checking accounts are the most common form of deposits for banks. Assume that Village Storage has a checking account at Camino Savings Bank. What type of account (asset, liability, owner's equity, revenue, expense, drawing) does the account balance of $8,750 represent from the viewpoint of (a) Village Storage and (b) Camino Savings Bank?

Practice Exercises

Learning Objectives	Example Exercises	
OBJ. 2	EE 2-1 *p. 56*	**PE 2-1A Rules of debit and credit and normal balances**

State for each account whether it is likely to have (a) debit entries only, (b) credit entries only, or (c) both debit and credit entries. Also, indicate its normal balance.

1. Accounts Receivable
2. Commissions Earned
3. Notes Payable
4. Paul Howe, Capital
5. Rent Revenue
6. Wages Expense

OBJ. 2	EE 2-1 *p. 56*	**PE 2-1B Rules of debit and credit and normal balances**

State for each account whether it is likely to have (a) debit entries only, (b) credit entries only, or (c) both debit and credit entries. Also, indicate its normal balance.

1. Accounts Payable
2. Cash
3. Malissa Wahl, Drawing
4. Miscellaneous Expense
5. Insurance Expense
6. Fees Earned

OBJ. 2	EE 2-2 *p. 61*	**PE 2-2A Journal entry for asset purchase**

Prepare a journal entry for the purchase of office equipment on March 4 for $27,150, paying $5,000 cash and the remainder on account.

OBJ. 2	EE 2-2 *p. 61*	**PE 2-2B Journal entry for asset purchase**

Prepare a journal entry for the purchase of office supplies on August 7 for $4,000, paying $1,000 cash and the remainder on account.

OBJ. 3	EE 2-3 *p. 65*	**PE 2-3A Journal entry for fees earned**

Prepare a journal entry on September 6 for fees earned on account, $8,000.

OBJ. 3	EE 2-3 *p. 65*	**PE 2-3B Journal entry for fees earned**

Prepare a journal entry on May 29 for cash received for services rendered, $5,000.

OBJ. 3	EE 2-4 *p. 68*	**PE 2-4A Journal entry for owner's withdrawal**

Prepare a journal entry on December 22 for the withdrawal of $10,000 by Jason Von Pentz for personal use.

OBJ. 3	EE 2-4 *p. 68*	**PE 2-4B Journal entry for owner's withdrawal**

Prepare a journal entry on February 3 for the withdrawal of $7,500 by Allene Collette for personal use.

Learning Objectives	Example Exercises	
OBJ. 3	EE 2-5 *p. 68*	**PE 2-5A Missing amount from an account**

On June 1, the cash account balance was $17,200. During June, cash payments totaled $178,300, and the June 30 balance was $23,900. Determine the cash receipts during June.

OBJ. 3   EE 2-5 *p. 68*   **PE 2-5B Missing amount from an account**

On October 1, the supplies account balance was $900. During October, supplies of $2,750 were purchased, and $1,025 of supplies were on hand as of October 31. Determine supplies expense for October.

OBJ. 4   EE 2-6 *p. 72*   **PE 2-6A Trial balance errors**

For each of the following errors, considered individually, indicate whether the error would cause the trial balance totals to be unequal. If the error would cause the trial balance totals to be unequal, indicate whether the debit or credit total is higher and by how much.

a. The payment of an insurance premium of $4,800 for a two-year policy was debited to Prepaid Insurance for $4,800 and credited to Cash for $8,400.

b. A payment of $318 on account was debited to Accounts Payable for $381 and credited to Cash for $381.

c. A purchase of supplies on account for $1,200 was debited to Supplies for $1,200 and debited to Accounts Payable for $1,200.

OBJ. 4   EE 2-6 *p. 72*   **PE 2-6B Trial balance errors**

For each of the following errors, considered individually, indicate whether the error would cause the trial balance totals to be unequal. If the error would cause the trial balance totals to be unequal, indicate whether the debit or credit total is higher and by how much.

a. The payment of cash for the purchase of office equipment of $15,000 was debited to Land for $15,000 and credited to Cash for $15,000.

b. The payment of $5,200 on account was debited to Accounts Payable for $520 and credited to Cash for $5,200.

c. The receipt of cash on account of $1,270 was recorded as a debit to Cash for $1,720 and a credit to Accounts Receivable for $1,270.

OBJ. 4   EE 2-7 *p. 73*   **PE 2-7A Correcting entries**

The following errors took place in journalizing and posting transactions:

a. Advertising expense of $2,700 paid for the current month was recorded as a debit to Miscellaneous Expense and a credit to Advertising Expense.

b. The payment of $3,950 from a customer on account was recorded as a debit to Cash and a credit to Accounts Payable.

Journalize the entries to correct the errors. Omit explanations.

OBJ. 4   EE 2-7 *p. 73*   **PE 2-7B Correcting entries**

The following errors took place in journalizing and posting transactions:

a. The receipt of $5,800 for services rendered was recorded as a debit to Accounts Receivable and a credit to Fees Earned.

b. The purchase of supplies of $1,800 on account was recorded as a debit to Office Equipment and a credit to Supplies.

Journalize the entries to correct the errors. Omit explanations.

OBJ. 5   EE 2-8 *p. 75*   **PE 2-8A Horizontal analysis**

Two income statements for Boyer Company are shown on the following page.

Learning   *Example*
Objectives   *Exercises*

Boyer Company Income Statements For Years Ended December 31		
	2012	**2011**
Fees earned	$315,000	$300,000
Operating expenses	176,400	180,000
Net income	$138,600	$120,000

Prepare a horizontal analysis of Boyer Company's income statements.

OBJ. 5   EE 2-8 *p. 75*   **PE 2-8B   Horizontal analysis**

Two income statements for Hitt Company are shown below.

Hitt Company Income Statements For Years Ended December 31		
	2012	**2011**
Fees earned	$937,500	$750,000
Operating expenses	612,500	500,000
Net income	$325.000	$250,000

Prepare a horizontal analysis of Hitt Company's income statements.

Exercises

OBJ. 1

EX 2-1   Chart of accounts

The following accounts appeared in recent financial statements of Continental Airlines:

Accounts Payable	Flight Equipment
Air Traffic Liability	Landing Fees (Expense)
Aircraft Fuel Expense	Passenger Revenue
Cargo and Mail Revenue	Purchase Deposits for Flight Equipment
Commissions (Expense)	Spare Parts and Supplies

Identify each account as either a balance sheet account or an income statement account. For each balance sheet account, identify it as an asset, a liability, or owner's equity. For each income statement account, identify it as a revenue or an expense.

OBJ. 1

EX 2-2   Chart of accounts

Innerscape Interiors is owned and operated by Jean Cartier, an interior decorator. In the ledger of Innerscape Interiors, the first digit of the account number indicates its major account classification (1—assets, 2—liabilities, 3—owner's equity, 4—revenues, 5—expenses). The second digit of the account number indicates the specific account within each of the preceding major account classifications.

Match each account number with its most likely account in the list below. The account numbers are 11, 12, 13, 21, 31, 32, 41, 51, 52, and 53.

Accounts Payable	Jean Cartier, Drawing
Accounts Receivable	Land
Cash	Miscellaneous Expense
Fees Earned	Supplies Expense
Jean Cartier, Capital	Wages Expense

OBJ. 1

EX 2-3   Chart of accounts

Alpha School is a newly organized business that teaches people how to inspire and influence others. The list of accounts to be opened in the general ledger is as follows:

Accounts Payable	Miscellaneous Expense
Accounts Receivable	Prepaid Insurance
Cash	Rent Expense
Equipment	Supplies
Fees Earned	Supplies Expense
Jan Pulver, Capital	Unearned Rent
Jan Pulver, Drawing	Wages Expense

List the accounts in the order in which they should appear in the ledger of Alpha School and assign account numbers. Each account number is to have two digits: the first digit is to indicate the major classification (1 for assets, etc.), and the second digit is to identify the specific account within each major classification (11 for Cash, etc.).

OBJ. 1,2

EX 2-4   Rules of debit and credit

The following table summarizes the rules of debit and credit. For each of the items (a) through (l), indicate whether the proper answer is a debit or a credit.

	Increase	Decrease	Normal Balance
Balance sheet accounts:			
Asset	(a)	Credit	(b)
Liability	Credit	(c)	(d)
Owner's equity:			
Capital	Credit	(e)	(f)
Drawing	(g)	(h)	(i)
Income statement accounts:			
Revenue	Credit	(j)	(k)
Expense	(l)	Credit	Debit

OBJ. 2

EX 2-5   Normal entries for accounts

During the month, Iris Labs Co. has a substantial number of transactions affecting each of the following accounts. State for each account whether it is likely to have (a) debit entries only, (b) credit entries only, or (c) both debit and credit entries.

1. Accounts Payable
2. Accounts Receivable
3. Cash
4. Fees Earned

5. Insurance Expense
6. Nicki Swanson, Drawing
7. Utilities Expense

OBJ. 1,2

EX 2-6   Normal balances of accounts

Identify each of the following accounts of Advanced Services Co. as asset, liability, owner's equity, revenue, or expense, and state in each case whether the normal balance is a debit or a credit.

a. Accounts Payable
b. Accounts Receivable
c. Barbara Mallary, Capital
d. Barbara Mallary, Drawing
e. Cash

f. Fees Earned
g. Office Equipment
h. Rent Expense
i. Supplies
j. Wages Expense

OBJ. 2

EX 2-7   Transactions

Chalet Co. has the following accounts in its ledger: Cash; Accounts Receivable; Supplies; Office Equipment; Accounts Payable; Andee Freese, Capital; Andee Freese, Drawing; Fees Earned; Rent Expense; Advertising Expense; Utilities Expense; Miscellaneous Expense.

Journalize the following selected transactions for October 2012 in a two-column journal. Journal entry explanations may be omitted.

Oct. 1. Paid rent for the month, $2,000.

2. Paid advertising expense, $900.

5. Paid cash for supplies, $1,300.

6. Purchased office equipment on account, $16,000.

10. Received cash from customers on account, $6,700.

15. Paid creditor on account, $1,200.

27. Paid cash for repairs to office equipment, $600.

30. Paid telephone bill for the month, $180.

31. Fees earned and billed to customers for the month, $26,800.

31. Paid electricity bill for the month, $400.

31. Withdrew cash for personal use, $3,000.

OBJ. 2,3

EX 2-8   Journalizing and posting

On February 3, 2012, Wilco Co. purchased $3,250 of supplies on account. In Wilco Co.'s chart of accounts, the supplies account is No. 15, and the accounts payable account is No. 21.

a. Journalize the February 3, 2012, transaction on page 19 of Wilco Co.'s two-column journal. Include an explanation of the entry.

b. Prepare a four-column account for Supplies. Enter a debit balance of $975 as of February 1, 2012. Place a check mark (✓) in the Posting Reference column.

c. Prepare a four-column account for Accounts Payable. Enter a credit balance of $13,150 as of February 1, 2012. Place a check mark (✓) in the Posting Reference column.

d. Post the February 3, 2012, transaction to the accounts.

e. Do the rules of debit and credit apply to all companies?

OBJ. 2,3

EX 2-9   Transactions and T accounts

The following selected transactions were completed during August of the current year:

1. Billed customers for fees earned, $35,700.

2. Purchased supplies on account, $2,000.

3. Received cash from customers on account, $26,150.

4. Paid creditors on account, $800.

a. Journalize the above transactions in a two-column journal, using the appropriate number to identify the transactions. Journal entry explanations may be omitted.

b. Post the entries prepared in (a) to the following T accounts: Cash, Supplies, Accounts Receivable, Accounts Payable, Fees Earned. To the left of each amount posted in the accounts, place the appropriate number to identify the transactions.

c. Assume that the unadjusted trial balance on August 31 shows a credit balance for Accounts Receivable. Does this credit balance mean an error has occurred?

OBJ. 1,2,3

EX 2-10   Cash account balance

During the month, Lathers Co. received $400,000 in cash and paid out $290,000 in cash.

a. Do the data indicate that Lathers Co. had net income of $110,000 during the month? Explain.

b. If the balance of the cash account is $185,000 at the end of the month, what was the cash balance at the beginning of the month?

OBJ. 1,2,3

✔ c. $284,175

EX 2-11   Account balances

a. During October, $90,000 was paid to creditors on account, and purchases on account were $125,000. Assuming the October 31 balance of Accounts Payable was $40,000, determine the account balance on October 1.

b. On May 1, the accounts receivable account balance was $25,000. During May, $240,000 was collected from customers on account. Assuming the May 31 balance was $36,000, determine the fees billed to customers on account during May.

c. On November 1, the cash account balance was $18,275. During November, cash receipts totaled $279,100 and the November 30 balance was $13,200. Determine the cash payments made during November.

OBJ. 1,2

EX 2-12 Capital account balance

As of January 1, Brenda Cikan, Capital, had a credit balance of $125,000. During the year, withdrawals totaled $7,000, and the business incurred a net loss of $130,000.

a. Compute the balance of Brenda Cikan, Capital, as of the end of the year.

b. Assuming that there have been no recording errors, will the balance sheet prepared at December 31 balance? Explain.

OBJ. 1,2

EX 2-13 Identifying transactions

Southwest Tours Co. is a travel agency. The nine transactions recorded by Southwest Tours during May 2012, its first month of operations, are indicated in the following T accounts:

Cash							
(1)	40,000	(2)	2,000
(7)	10,000	(3)	3,600
		(4)	2,700
		(6)	9,000
		(9)	4,000

Equipment	
(3)	18,000

Mickey O'Dell, Drawing	
(9)	4,000

Accounts Receivable			
(5)	18,500	(7)	10,000

Accounts Payable			
(6)	9,000	(3)	14,400

Service Revenue	
(5)	18,500

Supplies			
(2)	2,000	(8)	1,050

Mickey O'Dell, Capital	
(1)	40,000

Operating Expenses	
(4)	2,700
(8)	1,050

Indicate for each debit and each credit: (a) whether an asset, liability, owner's equity, drawing, revenue, or expense account was affected and (b) whether the account was increased (+) or decreased (–). Present your answers in the following form, with transaction (1) given as an example:

	Account Debited		Account Credited	
Transaction	Type	Effect	Type	Effect
(1)	asset	+	owner's equity	+

OBJ. 1,2

EX 2-14 Journal entries

Based upon the T accounts in Exercise 2-13, prepare the nine journal entries from which the postings were made. Journal entry explanations may be omitted.

OBJ. 4

EX 2-15 Trial balance

Based upon the data presented in Exercise 2-13, (a) prepare an unadjusted trial balance, listing the accounts in their proper order. (b) Based upon the unadjusted trial balance, determine the net income or net loss.

✔ Total Debit column: $63,900

OBJ. 4

✔ Total of Credit column: $491,400

EX 2-16 Trial balance

The accounts in the ledger of Diva Co. as of July 31, 2012, are listed in alphabetical order as follows. All accounts have normal balances. The balance of the cash account has been intentionally omitted.

Accounts Payable	$ 28,000	Notes Payable	$ 50,000
Accounts Receivable	40,000	Prepaid Insurance	6,400
Cash	?	Rent Expense	36,000
Cheryl Sievert, Capital	49,900	Supplies	4,000
Cheryl Sievert, Drawing	25,000	Supplies Expense	9,000
Fees Earned	350,000	Unearned Rent	13,500
Insurance Expense	6,000	Utilities Expense	18,000
Land	125,000	Wages Expense	195,000
Miscellaneous Expense	12,000		

Prepare an unadjusted trial balance, listing the accounts in their normal order and inserting the missing figure for cash.

OBJ. 4

EX 2-17 Effect of errors on trial balance

Indicate which of the following errors, each considered individually, would cause the trial balance totals to be unequal:

a. A fee of $15,000 earned and due from a client was not debited to Accounts Receivable or credited to a revenue account, because the cash had not been received.

b. A receipt of $6,000 from an account receivable was journalized and posted as a debit of $6,000 to Cash and a credit of $6,000 to Fees Earned.

c. A payment of $1,200 to a creditor was posted as a debit of $1,200 to Accounts Payable and a debit of $1,200 to Cash.

d. A payment of $10,000 for equipment purchased was posted as a debit of $1,000 to Equipment and a credit of $1,000 to Cash.

e. Payment of a cash withdrawal of $10,000 was journalized and posted as a debit of $1,000 to Salary Expense and a credit of $10,000 to Cash.

Indicate which of the preceding errors would require a correcting entry.

OBJ. 4

✔ Total of Credit column: $225,000

EX 2-18 Errors in trial balance

The following preliminary unadjusted trial balance of Seats-For-You Co., a sports ticket agency, does not balance:

Seats-For-You Co.
Unadjusted Trial Balance
March 31, 2012

	Debit Balances	Credit Balances
Cash	98,000	
Accounts Receivable..	17,800	
Prepaid Insurance		9,000
Equipment..	7,500	
Accounts Payable		16,500
Unearned Rent..		11,600
Gina Ness, Capital	81,700	
Gina Ness, Drawing...	13,000	
Service Revenue		125,000
Wages Expense		60,000
Advertising Expense..	11,300	
Miscellaneous Expense		15,400
	229,300	237,500

When the ledger and other records are reviewed, you discover the following: (1) the debits and credits in the cash account total $98,000 and $82,500, respectively; (2) a billing of $8,000 to a customer on account was not posted to the accounts receivable account; (3) a payment of $3,600 made to a creditor on account was not posted to the accounts payable account; (4) the balance of the unearned rent account is $5,400; (5) the correct balance of the equipment account is $75,000; and (6) each account has a normal balance.
    Prepare a corrected unadjusted trial balance.

OBJ. 4

EX 2-19 Effect of errors on trial balance

The following errors occurred in posting from a two-column journal:

1. A credit of $7,150 to Accounts Payable was not posted.
2. An entry debiting Accounts Receivable and crediting Fees Earned for $11,000 was not posted.
3. A debit of $1,000 to Accounts Payable was posted as a credit.
4. A debit of $800 to Supplies was posted twice.
5. A debit of $900 to Cash was posted to Miscellaneous Expense.
6. A credit of $360 to Cash was posted as $630.
7. A debit of $9,420 to Wages Expense was posted as $9,240.

Considering each case individually (i.e., assuming that no other errors had occurred), indicate: (a) by "yes" or "no" whether the trial balance would be out of balance; (b) if answer to (a) is "yes," the amount by which the trial balance totals would differ; and (c) whether the Debit or Credit column of the trial balance would have the larger total. Answers should be presented in the following form, with error (1) given as an example:

	(a)	(b)	(c)
Error	Out of Balance	Difference	Larger Total
1.	yes	$7,150	debit

OBJ. 4

✔ Total of Credit
column: $750,000

EX 2-20 Errors in trial balance

Identify the errors in the following trial balance. All accounts have normal balances.

Bluefin Co.
Unadjusted Trial Balance
For the Month Ending August 31, 2012

	Debit Balances	Credit Balances
Cash	45,000	
Accounts Receivable..		98,400
Prepaid Insurance	21,600	
Equipment...	300,000	
Accounts Payable	11,100	
Salaries Payable..		7,500
Ken Frye, Capital		259,200
Ken Frye, Drawing..		36,000
Service Revenue		472,200
Salary Expense..	196,860	
Advertising Expense..		43,200
Miscellaneous Expense	8,940	
	916,500	916,500

OBJ. 4

EX 2-21 Entries to correct errors

The following errors took place in journalizing and posting transactions:

a. Rent of $12,500 paid for the current month was recorded as a debit to Rent Expense and a credit to Prepaid Rent.
b. A withdrawal of $7,500 by Trent Benedict, owner of the business, was recorded as a debit to Wages Expense and a credit to Cash.

Journalize the entries to correct the errors. Omit explanations.

OBJ. 4

EX 2-22 Entries to correct errors

The following errors took place in journalizing and posting transactions:

a. Cash of $12,975 received on account was recorded as a debit to Fees Earned and a credit to Cash.
b. A $3,200 purchase of supplies for cash was recorded as a debit to Supplies Expense and a credit to Accounts Payable.

Journalize the entries to correct the errors. Omit explanations.

OBJ. 5

EX 2-23   Horizontal analysis of income statement

The following data (in millions) is taken from the financial statements of Target Corporation.

	2009	2008
Net sales (revenues)	$64,948	$63,367
Total operating expenses	60,546	58,095

a. For Target Corporation, comparing 2009 with 2008, determine the amount of change in millions and the percent of change for:

   1. Net sales (revenues)

   2. Total operating expenses

b. ▬▬▬▶What conclusions can you draw from your analysis of the net sales and the total operating expenses?

OBJ. 5

EX 2-24   Horizontal analysis of income statement

The following data were adapted from the financial statements of Kmart Corporation, prior to its filing for bankruptcy:

	In millions	
For years ending January 31	2000	1999
Sales	$ 37,028	$ 35,925
Cost of sales (expense)	(29,658)	(28,111)
Selling, general, and administrative expenses	(7,415)	(6,514)
Operating income (loss)	$ (45)	$ 1,300

a. Prepare a horizontal analysis for the income statement showing the amount and percent of change in each of the following:

   1. Sales

   2. Cost of sales

   3. Selling, general, and administrative expenses

   4. Operating income (loss)

b. Comment on the results of your horizontal analysis in part (a).

Problems Series A

OBJ. 1,2,3,4

✔ 3. Total of Debit column: $78,350

PR 2-1A   Entries into T accounts and trial balance

Leila Durkin, an architect, opened an office on May 1, 2012. During the month, she completed the following transactions connected with her professional practice:

a. Transferred cash from a personal bank account to an account to be used for the business, $30,000.

b. Paid May rent for office and workroom, $3,500.

c. Purchased used automobile for $25,000, paying $5,000 cash and giving a note payable for the remainder.

d. Purchased office and computer equipment on account, $9,000.

e. Paid cash for supplies, $1,200.

f. Paid cash for annual insurance policies, $2,400.

g. Received cash from client for plans delivered, $8,150.

h. Paid cash for miscellaneous expenses, $300.

i. Paid cash to creditors on account, $2,500.

j. Paid installment due on note payable, $400.

k. Received invoice for blueprint service, due in June, $1,200.

l. Recorded fee earned on plans delivered, payment to be received in June, $12,900.

m. Paid salary of assistant, $1,800.

n. Paid gas, oil, and repairs on automobile for May, $600.

Instructions

1. Record the above transactions directly in the following T accounts, without journalizing: Cash; Accounts Receivable; Supplies; Prepaid Insurance; Automobiles; Equipment; Notes Payable; Accounts Payable; Leila Durkin, Capital; Professional Fees; Rent Expense; Salary Expense; Blueprint Expense; Automobile Expense; Miscellaneous Expense. To the left of the amount entered in the accounts, place the appropriate letter to identify the transaction.

2. Determine account balances of the T accounts. Accounts containing a single entry only (such as Prepaid Insurance) do not need a balance.

3. Prepare an unadjusted trial balance for Leila Durkin, Architect, as of May 31, 2012.

4. Determine the net income or net loss for May.

OBJ. 1,2,3,4

✔ 4. c. $8,550

PR 2-2A   Journal entries and trial balance

On October 1, 2012, Faith Schultz established Heavenly Realty, which completed the following transactions during the month:

a. Faith Schultz transferred cash from a personal bank account to an account to be used for the business, $20,000.

b. Paid rent on office and equipment for the month, $3,750.

c. Purchased supplies on account, $1,100.

d. Paid creditor on account, $400.

e. Earned sales commissions, receiving cash, $16,750.

f. Paid automobile expenses (including rental charge) for month, $1,000, and miscellaneous expenses, $700.

g. Paid office salaries, $2,150.

h. Determined that the cost of supplies used was $600.

i. Withdrew cash for personal use, $1,000.

Instructions

1. Journalize entries for transactions (a) through (i), using the following account titles: Cash; Supplies; Accounts Payable; Faith Schultz, Capital; Faith Schultz, Drawing; Sales Commissions; Rent Expense; Office Salaries Expense; Automobile Expense; Supplies Expense; Miscellaneous Expense. Explanations may be omitted.

2. Prepare T accounts, using the account titles in (1). Post the journal entries to these accounts, placing the appropriate letter to the left of each amount to identify the transactions. Determine the account balances, after all posting is complete. Accounts containing only a single entry do not need a balance.

3. Prepare an unadjusted trial balance as of October 31, 2012.

4. Determine the following:

   a. Amount of total revenue recorded in the ledger.

   b. Amount of total expenses recorded in the ledger.

   c. Amount of net income for October.

5. Determine the increase or decrease in owner's equity for October.

OBJ. 1,2,3,4

✔ 3. Total of Credit column: $66,500

PR 2-3A   Journal entries and trial balance

On April 1, 2012, Kathleen Alvarez established an interior decorating business, Intrex Designs. During the month, Kathleen completed the following transactions related to the business:

Apr.   1. Kathleen transferred cash from a personal bank account to an account to be used for the business, $17,000.

2. Paid rent for period of April 2 to end of month, $3,400.

6. Purchased office equipment on account, $10,000.

8. Purchased a used truck for $21,000, paying $2,000 cash and giving a note payable for the remainder.

10. Purchased supplies for cash, $1,800.

12. Received cash for job completed, $13,000.

Apr. 15. Paid annual premiums on property and casualty insurance, $1,800.

23. Recorded jobs completed on account and sent invoices to customers, $9,000.

24. Received an invoice for truck expenses, to be paid in April, $1,000.

Enter the following transactions on Page 2 of the two-column journal.

29. Paid utilities expense, $1,500.

29. Paid miscellaneous expenses, $750.

30. Received cash from customers on account, $7,800.

30. Paid wages of employees, $4,000.

30. Paid creditor a portion of the amount owed for equipment purchased on April 6, $2,500.

30. Withdrew cash for personal use, $2,000.

Instructions

1. Journalize each transaction in a two-column journal beginning on Page 1, referring to the following chart of accounts in selecting the accounts to be debited and credited. (Do not insert the account numbers in the journal at this time.) Explanations may be omitted.

11 Cash	31 Kathleen Alvarez, Capital
12 Accounts Receivable	32 Kathleen Alvarez, Drawing
13 Supplies	41 Fees Earned
14 Prepaid Insurance	51 Wages Expense
16 Equipment	53 Rent Expense
18 Truck	54 Utilities Expense
21 Notes Payable	55 Truck Expense
22 Accounts Payable	59 Miscellaneous Expense

2. Post the journal to a ledger of four-column accounts, inserting appropriate posting references as each item is posted. Extend the balances to the appropriate balance columns after each transaction is posted.

3. Prepare an unadjusted trial balance for Intrex Designs as of April 30, 2012.

4. Determine the excess of revenues over expenses for April.

5. Can you think of any reason why the amount determined in (4) might not be the net income for April?

OBJ. 1,2,3,4

✔ 4. Total of Debit column: $259,600

PR 2-4A   Journal entries and trial balance

Utopia Realty acts as an agent in buying, selling, renting, and managing real estate. The unadjusted trial balance on October 31, 2012, is shown below.

Utopia Realty
Unadjusted Trial Balance
October 31, 2012

		Debit Balances	Credit Balances
11	Cash..	13,150	
12	Accounts Receivable...	30,750	
13	Prepaid Insurance..	1,500	
14	Office Supplies	900	
16	Land..	—	
21	Accounts Payable..		7,000
22	Unearned Rent		—
23	Notes Payable		—
31	Ian Rogstad, Capital...		23,000
32	Ian Rogstad, Drawing	1,000	
41	Fees Earned		120,000
51	Salary and Commission Expense	74,100	
52	Rent Expense..	15,000	
53	Advertising Expense	8,900	
54	Automobile Expense...	2,750	
59	Miscellaneous Expense......................................	1,950	
		150,000	150,000

The following business transactions were completed by Utopia Realty during November 2012:

Nov. 1. Paid rent on office for month, $5,000.

2. Purchased office supplies on account, $1,300.

5. Paid annual insurance premiums, $3,600.

10. Received cash from clients on account, $25,000.

15. Purchased land for a future building site for $90,000, paying $10,000 in cash and giving a note payable for the remainder.

17. Paid creditors on account, $4,500.

20. Returned a portion of the office supplies purchased on November 2, receiving full credit for their cost, $200.

23. Paid advertising expense, $2,000.

Enter the following transactions on Page 19 of the two-column journal.

27. Discovered an error in computing a commission; received cash from the salesperson for the overpayment, $1,000.

28. Paid automobile expense (including rental charges for an automobile), $1,500.

29. Paid miscellaneous expenses, $450.

30. Recorded revenue earned and billed to clients during the month, $30,000.

30. Paid salaries and commissions for the month, $7,500.

30. Withdrew cash for personal use, $1,000.

30. Rented land purchased on November 15 to local merchants association for use as a parking lot in December and January, during a street rebuilding program; received advance payment of $3,000.

Instructions

1. Record the November 1, 2010, balance of each account in the appropriate balance column of a four-column account, write *Balance* in the item section, and place a check mark (✓) in the Posting Reference column.

2. Journalize the transactions for November in a two-column journal beginning on Page 18. Journal entry explanations may be omitted.

3. Post to the ledger, extending the account balance to the appropriate balance column after each posting.

4. Prepare an unadjusted trial balance of the ledger as of November 30, 2012.

5. Assume that the November 30 transaction for salaries and commissions should have been $5,700. (a) Why did the unadjusted trial balance in (4) balance? (b) Journalize the correcting entry. (c) Is this error a transposition or slide?

OBJ. 4

✔ 7. Total of Debit column: $43,338.10

PR 2-5A   Errors in trial balance

If the working papers correlating with this textbook are not used, omit Problem 2-5A.

The following records of A-Aall Electronic Repair are presented in the working papers:

- Journal containing entries for the period May 1–31.

- Ledger to which the May entries have been posted.

- Preliminary trial balance as of May 31, which does not balance.

Locate the errors, supply the information requested, and prepare a corrected trial balance according to the following instructions. The balances recorded in the accounts as of May 1 and the entries in the journal are correctly stated. If it is necessary to correct any posted amounts in the ledger, a line should be drawn through the erroneous figure and the correct amount inserted above. Corrections or notations may be inserted on the preliminary trial balance in any manner desired. It is not necessary to complete all of the instructions if equal trial balance totals can be obtained earlier. However, the requirements of instructions (6) and (7) should be completed in any event.

Instructions

1. Verify the totals of the preliminary trial balance, inserting the correct amounts in the schedule provided in the working papers.

(Continued)

2. Compute the difference between the trial balance totals.

3. Compare the listings in the trial balance with the balances appearing in the ledger, and list the errors in the space provided in the working papers.

4. Verify the accuracy of the balance of each account in the ledger, and list the errors in the space provided in the working papers.

5. Trace the postings in the ledger back to the journal, using small check marks to identify items traced. Correct any amounts in the ledger that may be necessitated by errors in posting, and list the errors in the space provided in the working papers.

6. Journalize as of May 31 the payment of $100 for advertising expense. The bill had been paid on May 31 but was inadvertently omitted from the journal. Post to the ledger. (Revise any amounts necessitated by posting this entry.)

7. Prepare a new unadjusted trial balance.

OBJ. 4

✔ 1. Total of Debit column: $1,400,000

PR 2-6A   Corrected trial balance

Imperial Carpet has the following unadjusted trial balance as of March 31, 2012.

Imperial Carpet
Unadjusted Trial Balance
March 31, 2012

	Debit Balances	Credit Balances
Cash	38,200	
Accounts Receivable...	81,000	
Supplies	16,690	
Prepaid Insurance	3,600	
Equipment..	392,000	
Notes Payable...		200,000
Accounts Payable		54,000
Leonardo Pepin, Capital..		254,300
Leonardo Pepin, Drawing	116,000	
Fees Earned..		858,900
Wages Expense	490,000	
Rent Expense	112,600	
Advertising Expense..	50,400	
Miscellaneous Expense	10,200	
	1,310,690	508,300

The debit and credit totals are not equal as a result of the following errors:

a. The balance of cash was understated by $12,000.

b. A cash receipt of $13,900 was posted as a debit to Cash of $19,300.

c. A debit of $15,000 to Accounts Receivable was not posted.

d. A return of $90 of defective supplies was erroneously posted as a $900 credit to Supplies.

e. An insurance policy acquired at a cost of $2,500 was posted as a credit to Prepaid Insurance.

f. The balance of Notes Payable was understated by $35,200.

g. A credit of $7,600 in Accounts Payable was overlooked when determining the balance of the account.

h. A debit of $10,000 for a withdrawal by the owner was posted as a credit to Leonardo Pepin, Capital.

i. The balance of $116,200 in Rent Expense was entered as $112,600 in the trial balance.

j. Gas, Electricity, and Water Expense, with a balance of $48,300 was omitted from the trial balance.

Instructions

1. Prepare a corrected unadjusted trial balance as of March 31, 2012.

2. ▬▬▬▶ Does the fact that the unadjusted trial balance in (1) is balanced mean that there are no errors in the accounts? Explain.

Problems Series B

OBJ. 1,2,3

✔ 3. Total of Debit
column: $74,700

PR 2-1B Entries into T accounts and trial balance

April Layton, an architect, opened an office on June 1, 2012. During the month, she completed the following transactions connected with her professional practice:

a. Transferred cash from a personal bank account to an account to be used for the business, $25,000.

b. Purchased used automobile for $24,000, paying $5,000 cash and giving a note payable for the remainder.

c. Paid June rent for office and workroom, $2,000.

d. Paid cash for supplies, $1,450.

e. Purchased office and computer equipment on account, $8,000.

f. Paid cash for annual insurance policies on automobile and equipment, $3,600.

g. Received cash from a client for plans delivered, $10,500.

h. Paid cash to creditors on account, $1,750.

i. Paid cash for miscellaneous expenses, $600.

j. Received invoice for blueprint service, due in July, $1,500.

k. Recorded fee earned on plans delivered, payment to be received in July, $12,800.

l. Paid salary of assistant, $1,600.

m. Paid cash for miscellaneous expenses, $200.

n. Paid installment due on note payable, $350.

o. Paid gas, oil, and repairs on automobile for June, $550.

Instructions

1. Record the above transactions directly in the following T accounts, without journalizing: Cash; Accounts Receivable; Supplies; Prepaid Insurance; Automobiles; Equipment; Notes Payable; Accounts Payable; April Layton, Capital; Professional Fees; Rent Expense; Salary Expense; Blueprint Expense; Automobile Expense; Miscellaneous Expense. To the left of each amount entered in the accounts, place the appropriate letter to identify the transaction.

2. Determine account balances of the T accounts. Accounts containing a single entry only (such as Prepaid Insurance) do not need a balance.

3. Prepare an unadjusted trial balance for April Layton, Architect, as of June 30, 2012.

4. Determine the net income or net loss for June.

OBJ. 1,2,3,4

✔ 4. c. $5,500

PR 2-2B Journal entries and trial balance

On March 1, 2012, Mitch Quade established Marine Realty, which completed the following transactions during the month:

a. Mitch Quade transferred cash from a personal bank account to an account to be used for the business, $18,000.

b. Purchased supplies on account, $1,200.

c. Earned sales commissions, receiving cash, $14,000.

d. Paid rent on office and equipment for the month, $3,000.

e. Paid creditor on account, $750.

f. Withdrew cash for personal use, $2,000.

g. Paid automobile expenses (including rental charge) for month, $1,500, and miscellaneous expenses, $400.

h. Paid office salaries, $2,800.

i. Determined that the cost of supplies used was $800.

Instructions

1. Journalize entries for transactions (a) through (i), using the following account titles: Cash; Supplies; Accounts Payable; Mitch Quade, Capital; Mitch Quade, Drawing; Sales Commissions; Rent Expense; Office Salaries Expense; Automobile Expense; Supplies Expense; Miscellaneous Expense. Journal entry explanations may be omitted.

(Continued)

2. Prepare T accounts, using the account titles in (1). Post the journal entries to these accounts, placing the appropriate letter to the left of each amount to identify the transactions. Determine the account balances, after all posting is complete. Accounts containing only a single entry do not need a balance.

3. Prepare an unadjusted trial balance as of March 31, 2012.

4. Determine the following:

    a. Amount of total revenue recorded in the ledger.

    b. Amount of total expenses recorded in the ledger.

    c. Amount of net income for March.

5. Determine the increase or decrease in owner's equity for March

---

OBJ. 1,2,3,4

✔ 3. Total of Credit
column: $64,500

PR 2-3B   Journal entries and trial balance

On July 1, 2012, Kim Wheeler established an interior decorating business, Aztec Designs. During the month, Kim completed the following transactions related to the business:

July   1. Kim transferred cash from a personal bank account to an account to be used for the business, $21,000.

       4. Paid rent for period of July 4 to end of month, $2,750.

       10. Purchased a used truck for $18,000, paying $4,000 cash and giving a note payable for the remainder.

       13. Purchased equipment on account, $9,000.

       14. Purchased supplies for cash, $1,500.

       15. Paid annual premiums on property and casualty insurance, $3,600.

       15. Received cash for job completed, $12,000.

Enter the following transactions on Page 2 of the two-column journal.

       21. Paid creditor a portion of the amount owed for equipment purchased on July 13, $2,000.

       24. Recorded jobs completed on account and sent invoices to customers, $9,800.

       26. Received an invoice for truck expenses, to be paid in August, $700.

       27. Paid utilities expense, $1,000.

       27. Paid miscellaneous expenses, $300.

       29. Received cash from customers on account, $4,600.

       30. Paid wages of employees, $2,800.

       31. Withdrew cash for personal use, $2,500.

Instructions

1. Journalize each transaction in a two-column journal beginning on Page 1, referring to the following chart of accounts in selecting the accounts to be debited and credited. (Do not insert the account numbers in the journal at this time.) Journal entry explanations may be omitted.

11 Cash	31 Kim Wheeler, Capital
12 Accounts Receivable	32 Kim Wheeler, Drawing
13 Supplies	41 Fees Earned
14 Prepaid Insurance	51 Wages Expense
16 Equipment	53 Rent Expense
18 Truck	54 Utilities Expense
21 Notes Payable	55 Truck Expense
22 Accounts Payable	59 Miscellaneous Expense

2. Post the journal to a ledger of four-column accounts, inserting appropriate posting references as each item is posted. Extend the balances to the appropriate balance columns after each transaction is posted.

3. Prepare an unadjusted trial balance for Aztec Designs as of July 31, 2012.

4. Determine the excess of revenues over expenses for July.

5. Can you think of any reason why the amount determined in (4) might not be the net income for July?

OBJ. 1,2,3,4

✔ 4. Total of Debit
column: $575,400

PR 2-4B Journal entries and trial balance

Prime Time Realty acts as an agent in buying, selling, renting, and managing real estate. The unadjusted trial balance on July 31, 2012, is shown below.

Prime Time Realty
Unadjusted Trial Balance
July 31, 2012

		Debit Balances	Credit Balances
11	Cash..	30,000	
12	Accounts Receivable....................................	57,200	
13	Prepaid Insurance.......................................	7,200	
14	Office Supplies..	1,600	
16	Land...	—	
21	Accounts Payable.......................................		12,000
22	Unearned Rent..		—
23	Notes Payable...		—
31	Sandy Ulrich, Capital...................................		50,000
32	Sandy Ulrich, Drawing..................................	25,600	
41	Fees Earned..		338,000
51	Salary and Commission Expense......................	220,000	
52	Rent Expense..	28,000	
53	Advertising Expense....................................	18,400	
54	Automobile Expense....................................	9,000	
59	Miscellaneous Expense.................................	3,000	
		400,000	400,000

The following business transactions were completed by Prime Time Realty during August 2012:

Aug. 1. Purchased office supplies on account, $1,800.

2. Paid rent on office for month, $5,000.

3. Received cash from clients on account, $40,000.

5. Paid annual insurance premiums, $6,000.

9. Returned a portion of the office supplies purchased on August 1, receiving full credit for their cost, $400.

17. Paid advertising expense, $5,500.

23. Paid creditors on account, $7,000

Enter the following transactions on Page 19 of the two-column journal.

29. Paid miscellaneous expenses, $500.

30. Paid automobile expense (including rental charges for an automobile), $2,500.

31. Discovered an error in computing a commission; received cash from the salesperson for the overpayment, $8,000.

31. Paid salaries and commissions for the month, $18,000.

31. Recorded revenue earned and billed to clients during the month, $112,000.

31. Purchased land for a future building site for $75,000, paying $10,000 in cash and giving a note payable for the remainder.

31. Withdrew cash for personal use, $12,000.

31. Rented land purchased on August 31 to a local university for use as a parking lot during football season (September, October, and November); received advance payment of $4,000.

Instructions

1. Record the August 1 balance of each account in the appropriate balance column of a four-column account, write *Balance* in the item section, and place a check mark (✓) in the Posting Reference column.

2. Journalize the transactions for August in a two-column journal beginning on Page 18. Journal entry explanations may be omitted.

3. Post to the ledger, extending the account balance to the appropriate balance column after each posting.

(Continued)

4. Prepare an unadjusted trial balance of the ledger as of August 31, 2012.

5. Assume that the August 31 transaction for Sandy Ulrich's cash withdrawal should have been $1,200. (a) Why did the unadjusted trial balance in (4) balance? (b) Journalize the correcting entry. (c) Is this error a transposition or slide?

OBJ. 4

✔ 7. Total of Credit column: $43,338.10

PR 2-5B   Errors in trial balance

If the working papers correlating with this textbook are not used, omit Problem 2-5B.

The following records of A-Aall Electronic Repair are presented in the working papers:

- Journal containing entries for the period May 1–31.
- Ledger to which the May entries have been posted.
- Preliminary trial balance as of May 31, which does not balance.

Locate the errors, supply the information requested, and prepare a corrected trial balance according to the following instructions. The balances recorded in the accounts as of May 1 and the entries in the journal are correctly stated. If it is necessary to correct any posted amounts in the ledger, a line should be drawn through the erroneous figure and the correct amount inserted above. Corrections or notations may be inserted on the preliminary trial balance in any manner desired. It is not necessary to complete all of the instructions if equal trial balance totals can be obtained earlier. However, the requirements of instructions (6) and (7) should be completed in any event.

Instructions

1. Verify the totals of the preliminary trial balance, inserting the correct amounts in the schedule provided in the working papers.

2. Compute the difference between the trial balance totals.

3. Compare the listings in the trial balance with the balances appearing in the ledger, and list the errors in the space provided in the working papers.

4. Verify the accuracy of the balance of each account in the ledger, and list the errors in the space provided in the working papers.

5. Trace the postings in the ledger back to the journal, using small check marks to identify items traced. Correct any amounts in the ledger that may be necessitated by errors in posting, and list the errors in the space provided in the working papers.

6. Journalize as of May 31 the payment of $275 for gas and electricity. The bill had been paid on May 31 but was inadvertently omitted from the journal. Post to the ledger. (Revise any amounts necessitated by posting this entry.)

7. Prepare a new unadjusted trial balance.

OBJ. 4

✔ 1. Total of Debit column: $285,000

PR 2-6B   Corrected trial balance

Elite Video has the following unadjusted trial balance as of October 31, 2012.

Elite Video
Unadjusted Trial Balance
October 31, 2012

	Debit Balances	Credit Balances
Cash	11,100	
Accounts Receivable...	17,560	
Supplies..	2,520	
Prepaid Insurance	1,840	
Equipment..	64,800	
Notes Payable..		31,600
Accounts Payable		6,160
Aimee Desanti, Capital...		39,140
Aimee Desanti, Drawing	11,600	
Fees Earned...		213,600
Wages Expense	122,400	
Rent Expense	25,020	
Advertising Expense..	13,140	
Gas, Electricity, and Water Expense	6,800	
	276,780	290,500

The debit and credit totals are not equal as a result of the following errors:

a. The balance of cash was overstated by $7,500.

b. A cash receipt of $7,200 was posted as a debit to Cash of $2,700.

c. A debit of $5,000 to Accounts Receivable was not posted.

d. A return of $350 of defective supplies was erroneously posted as a $530 credit to Supplies.

e. An insurance policy acquired at a cost of $1,000 was posted as a credit to Prepaid Insurance.

f. The balance of Notes Payable was overstated by $10,000.

g. A credit of $500 in Accounts Payable was overlooked when the balance of the account was determined.

h. A debit of $4,000 for a withdrawal by the owner was posted as a debit to Aimee Desanti, Capital.

i. The balance of $11,340 in Advertising Expense was entered as $13,140 in the trial balance.

j. Miscellaneous Expense, with a balance of $1,840, was omitted from the trial balance.

Instructions

1. Prepare a corrected unadjusted trial balance as of October 31 of the current year.

2. ➤ Does the fact that the unadjusted trial balance in (1) is balanced mean that there are no errors in the accounts? Explain.

Continuing Problem

✔ **4. Total of Debit column: $40,030**

The transactions completed by PS Music during June 2012 were described at the end of Chapter 1. The following transactions were completed during July, the second month of the business's operations:

July   1. Pat Sharpe made an additional investment in PS Music by depositing $4,000 in PS Music's checking account.

    1. Instead of continuing to share office space with a local real estate agency, Pat decided to rent office space near a local music store. Paid rent for July, $1,800.

    1. Paid a premium of $2,700 for a comprehensive insurance policy covering liability, theft, and fire. The policy covers a one-year period.

    2. Received $1,250 on account.

    3. On behalf of PS Music, Pat signed a contract with a local radio station, WHBD, to provide guest spots for the next three months. The contract requires PS Music to provide a guest disc jockey for 80 hours per month for a monthly fee of $3,600. Any additional hours beyond 80 will be billed to WHBD at $40 per hour. In accordance with the contract, Pat received $7,200 from WHBD as an advance payment for the first two months.

    3. Paid $250 on account.

    4. Paid an attorney $800 for reviewing the July 3rd contract with WHBD. (Record as Miscellaneous Expense.)

    5. Purchased office equipment on account from One-Stop Office Mart, $6,000.

    8. Paid for a newspaper advertisement, $200.

    11. Received $900 for serving as a disc jockey for a party.

    13. Paid $600 to a local audio electronics store for rental of digital recording equipment.

    14. Paid wages of $1,200 to receptionist and part-time assistant.

Enter the following transactions on Page 2 of the two-column journal.

16. Received $2,100 for serving as a disc jockey for a wedding reception.

18. Purchased supplies on account, $1,080.

21. Paid $620 to Upload Music for use of its current music demos in making various music sets.

22. Paid $800 to a local radio station to advertise the services of PS Music twice daily for the remainder of July.

23. Served as disc jockey for a party for $2,500. Received $750, with the remainder due August 4, 2012.

27. Paid electric bill, $760.

28. Paid wages of $1,200 to receptionist and part-time assistant.

29. Paid miscellaneous expenses, $370.

30. Served as a disc jockey for a charity ball for $1,800. Received $400, with the remainder due on August 9, 2012.

31. Received $2,800 for serving as a disc jockey for a party.

31. Paid $1,400 royalties (music expense) to National Music Clearing for use of various artists' music during July.

31. Withdrew $1,500 cash from PS Music for personal use.

PS Music's chart of accounts and the balance of accounts as of July 1, 2012 (all normal balances), are as follows:

11	Cash	$5,310	41	Fees Earned	$6,650
12	Accounts Receivable	1,250	50	Wages Expense	400
14	Supplies	170	51	Office Rent Expense	750
15	Prepaid Insurance	—	52	Equipment Rent Expense	700
17	Office Equipment	—	53	Utilities Expense	300
21	Accounts Payable	250	54	Music Expense	1,590
23	Unearned Revenue	—	55	Advertising Expense	450
31	Pat Sharpe, Capital	5,000	56	Supplies Expense	180
32	Pat Sharpe, Drawing	500	59	Miscellaneous Expense	300

Instructions

1. Enter the July 1, 2012, account balances in the appropriate balance column of a four-column account. Write *Balance* in the Item column, and place a check mark (✓) in the Posting Reference column. (*Hint:* Verify the equality of the debit and credit balances in the ledger before proceeding with the next instruction.)

2. Analyze and journalize each transaction in a two-column journal beginning on Page 1, omitting journal entry explanations.

3. Post the journal to the ledger, extending the account balance to the appropriate balance column after each posting.

4. Prepare an unadjusted trial balance as of July 31, 2012.

Cases & Projects

CP 2-1   Ethics and professional conduct in business

At the end of the current month, Jonni Rembert prepared a trial balance for Star Rescue Service. The credit side of the trial balance exceeds the debit side by a significant amount. Jonni has decided to add the difference to the balance of the miscellaneous expense account in order to complete the preparation of the current month's financial statements by a 5 o'clock deadline. Jonni will look for the difference next week when she has more time.

➤ Discuss whether Jonni is behaving in a professional manner.

CP 2-2 Account for revenue

Tucson College requires students to pay tuition each term before classes begin. Students who have not paid their tuition are not allowed to enroll or to attend classes.

What journal entry do you think Tucson College would use to record the receipt of the students' tuition payments? Describe the nature of each account in the entry.

CP 2-3 Record transactions

The following discussion took place between Erin Carr, the office manager of Panda Data Company, and a new accountant, Mark Goodell.

Mark: I've been thinking about our method of recording entries. It seems that it's inefficient.

Erin: In what way?

Mark: Well—correct me if I'm wrong—it seems like we have unnecessary steps in the process. We could easily develop a trial balance by posting our transactions directly into the ledger and bypassing the journal altogether. In this way, we could combine the recording and posting process into one step and save ourselves a lot of time. What do you think?

Erin: We need to have a talk.

➤ What should Erin say to Mark?

CP 2-4 Debits and credits

Group Project

The following excerpt is from a conversation between Boris Harris, the president and chief operating officer of Chesapeake Company, and his neighbor, Neil Liven.

Neil: Boris, I'm taking a course in night school, "Intro to Accounting." I was wondering—could you answer a couple of questions for me?

Boris: Well, I will if I can.

Neil: Okay, our instructor says that it's critical we understand the basic concepts of accounting, or we'll never get beyond the first test. My problem is with those rules of debit and credit . . . you know, assets increase with debits, decrease with credits, etc.

Boris: Yes, pretty basic stuff. You just have to memorize the rules. It shouldn't be too difficult.

Neil: Sure, I can memorize the rules, but my problem is I want to be sure I understand the basic concepts behind the rules. For example, why can't assets be increased with credits and decreased with debits like revenue? As long as everyone did it that way, why not? It would seem easier if we had the same rules for all increases and decreases in accounts. Also, why is the left side of an account called the debit side? Why couldn't it be called something simple . . . like the "LE" for Left Entry? The right side could be called just "RE" for Right Entry. Finally, why are there just two sides to an entry? Why can't there be three or four sides to an entry?

In a group of four or five, select one person to play the role of Boris and one person to play the role of Neil.

1. ➤ After listening to the conversation between Boris and Neil, help Boris answer Neil's questions.

2. What information (other than just debit and credit journal entries) could the accounting system gather that might be useful to Boris in managing Cheasapeake Construction Company?

CP 2-5 Transactions and income statement

Anwar Askari is planning to manage and operate AA Caddy Service at Mission Valley Golf and Country Club during June through August 2012. Anwar will rent a small maintenance building from the country club for $700 per month and will offer caddy services, including cart rentals, to golfers. Anwar has had no formal training in record keeping.

Anwar keeps notes of all receipts and expenses in a shoe box. An examination of Anwar's shoe box records for June revealed the following:

June 1. Transferred $3,500 from personal bank account to be used to operate the caddy service.

1. Paid rent expense to Mission Valley Golf and Country Club, $700.

2. Paid for golf supplies (practice balls, etc.), $800.

3. Arranged for the rental of 25 regular (pulling) golf carts and 10 gasoline-driven carts for $3,000 per month. Paid $500 in advance, with the remaining $2,500 due June 20.

7. Purchased supplies, including gasoline, for the golf carts on account, $600. Mission Valley Golf and Country Club has agreed to allow Anwar to store the gasoline in one of its fuel tanks at no cost.

15. Received cash for services from June 1–15, $4,150.

17. Paid cash to creditors on account, $600.

20. Paid remaining rental on golf carts, $2,500.

22. Purchased supplies, including gasoline, on account, $400.

25. Accepted IOUs from customers on account, $1,800.

28. Paid miscellaneous expenses, $350.

30. Received cash for services from June 16–30, $6,350.

30. Paid telephone and electricity (utilities) expenses, $340.

30. Paid wages of part-time employees, $850.

30. Received cash in payment of IOUs on account, $1,200.

30. Determined the amount of supplies on hand at the end of June, $500.

Anwar has asked you several questions concerning his financial affairs to date, and he has asked you to assist with his record keeping and reporting of financial data.

a. To assist Anwar with his record keeping, prepare a chart of accounts that would be appropriate for AA Caddy Service.

b. Prepare an income statement for June in order to help Anwar assess the profitability of AA Caddy Service. For this purpose, the use of T accounts may be helpful in analyzing the effects of each June transaction.

c. Based on Anwar's records of receipts and payments, compute the amount of cash on hand on June 30. For this purpose, a T account for cash may be useful.

d. ➤ A count of the cash on hand on June 30 totaled $8,390. Briefly discuss the possible causes of the difference between the amount of cash computed in (c) and the actual amount of cash on hand.

Internet Project

CP 2-6   Opportunities for accountants

The increasing complexity of the current business and regulatory environment has created an increased demand for accountants who can analyze business transactions and interpret their effects on the financial statements. In addition, a basic ability to analyze the effects of transactions is necessary to be successful in all fields of business as well as in other disciplines, such as law. To better understand the importance of accounting in today's environment, search the Internet or your local newspaper for job opportunities. One possible Internet site is **http://www.careerbuilder.com.** Then do one of the following:

1. Print a listing of one or two ads for accounting jobs. Alternatively, bring to class one or two newspaper ads for accounting jobs.

2. Print a listing of one or two ads for nonaccounting jobs for which some knowledge of accounting is preferred or necessary. Alternatively, bring to class one or two newspaper ads for such jobs.

Search for music

All the music you want.

Try it free

Learn More

JUST 10 BUCKS A MONTH.

Connect FROM ANYWHERE

Find THE MUSIC YOU LIKE

Play ANY SONG YOU WANT

Your opini
a chance

TAKE A SURVEY

safecount.net

Start »

10 Essential Disney Soundtracks

From the Lion King to Toy Story 3, we look back at the greatest Disney songs.

More

ew Releases

What Members Are Listening To

| Tracks | Albums | Artists |

The Adjusting Process

Rhapsody

Do you subscribe to an Internet-based music service such as Rhapsody®? Rhapsody began by providing digital music to its subscribers through Internet audio streaming. You can subscribe to "Rhapsody Premier" for $10.00 per month and listen to music by New Boyz, Coldplay, Flo Rida, or Carrie Underwood. Rhapsody, which is partially owned by RealNetworks®, has also expanded its services to include games and video content.

When should a company such as RealNetworks record revenue from its subscriptions? Subscription revenue is recorded when it is earned. Subscriptions revenue is earned when the service has been delivered to the customer. However, in many cases cash is received before the service is delivered. For example, the subscription to "Rhapsody Premier" is paid at the beginning of

the month. In this case, the cash received represents unearned revenue. As time passes and the services are delivered, the unearned revenue becomes earned and thus, becomes revenue. As a result, companies like RealNetworks must update their accounting records for items such as unearned subscriptions before preparing their financial statements. For example, RealNetworks reported in its financial statements that it had unearned (deferred) revenue of approximately $33 million as of December 31, 2009.

This chapter describes and illustrates the process by which companies update their accounting records before preparing financial statements. This discussion includes the adjustments for unearned revenues made at the end of the accounting period.

OBJ. 1 Describe the nature of the adjusting process.

Nature of the Adjusting Process

When preparing financial statements, the economic life of the business is divided into time periods. This **accounting period concept** requires that revenues and expenses be reported in the proper period. To determine the proper period, accountants use generally accepted accounting principles (GAAP), which requires the **accrual basis of accounting**.

Under the accrual basis of accounting, revenues are reported on the income statement in the period in which they are earned. For example, revenue is reported when the services are provided to customers. Cash may or may not be received from customers during this period. The accounting concept supporting this reporting of revenues is called the **revenue recognition concept**.

Under the accrual basis, expenses are reported in the same period as the revenues to which they relate. For example, utility expenses incurred in December are reported as an expense and matched against December's revenues even though the utility bill may not be paid until January. The accounting concept supporting reporting revenues and related expenses in the same period is called the **matching concept**, or **matching principle**. By matching revenues and expenses, net income or loss for the period is properly reported on the income statement.

Although GAAP requires the accrual basis of accounting, some businesses use the **cash basis of accounting**. Under the cash basis of accounting, revenues and expenses are reported on the income statement in the period in which cash is received or paid. For example, fees are recorded when cash is received from clients; likewise, wages are recorded when cash is paid to employees. The net income (or net loss) is the difference between the cash receipts (revenues) and the cash payments (expenses).

Small service businesses may use the cash basis, because they have few receivables and payables. For example, attorneys, physicians, and real estate agents often use the cash basis. For them, the cash basis provides financial statements similar to those of the accrual basis. For most large businesses, however, the cash basis will not provide accurate financial statements for user needs. For this reason, the accrual basis is used in this text.

American Airlines uses the accrual basis of accounting. Revenues are recognized when passengers take flights, not when the passenger makes the reservation or pays for the ticket.

The Adjusting Process

At the end of the accounting period, many of the account balances in the ledger are reported in the financial statements without change. For example, the balances of the cash and land accounts are normally the amount reported on the balance sheet.

Some accounts, however, require updating for the following reasons:[1]

1. Some expenses are not recorded daily. For example, the daily use of supplies would require many entries with small amounts. Also, the amount of supplies on hand on a day-to-day basis is normally not needed.

2. Some revenues and expenses are incurred as time passes rather than as separate transactions. For example, rent received in advance (unearned rent) expires and becomes revenue with the passage of time. Likewise, prepaid insurance expires and becomes an expense with the passage of time.

3. Some revenues and expenses may be unrecorded. For example, a company may have provided services to customers that it has not billed or recorded at the end of the accounting period. Likewise, a company may not pay its employees until the next accounting period even though the employees have earned their wages in the current period.

The analysis and updating of accounts at the end of the period before the financial statements are prepared is called the **adjusting process**. The journal entries that bring the accounts up to date at the end of the accounting period are called **adjusting entries**. All adjusting entries affect at least one income statement account and one balance sheet account. Thus, an adjusting entry will *always* involve a revenue or an expense account *and* an asset or a liability account.

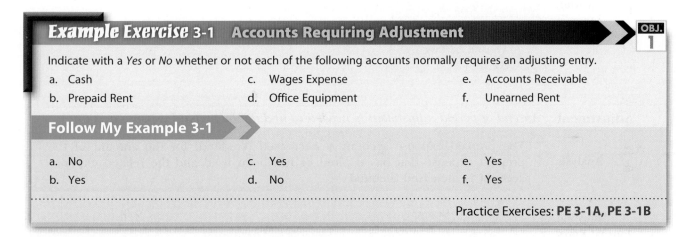

Example Exercise 3-1   Accounts Requiring Adjustment   OBJ. 1

Indicate with a *Yes* or *No* whether or not each of the following accounts normally requires an adjusting entry.

a. Cash   c. Wages Expense   e. Accounts Receivable
b. Prepaid Rent   d. Office Equipment   f. Unearned Rent

Follow My Example 3-1

a. No   c. Yes   e. Yes
b. Yes   d. No   f. Yes

Practice Exercises: **PE 3-1A, PE 3-1B**

Types of Accounts Requiring Adjustment

Four basic types of accounts require adjusting entries as shown below.

1. Prepaid expenses   3. Accrued revenues
2. Unearned revenues   4. Accrued expenses

Prepaid expenses are the advance payment of *future* expenses and are recorded as assets when cash is paid. Prepaid expenses become expenses over time or during normal operations. To illustrate, the following transaction of NetSolutions from Chapter 2 is used.

> Dec. 1   NetSolutions paid $2,400 as a premium on a one-year insurance policy.

On December 1, the cash payment of $2,400 was recorded as a debit to Prepaid Insurance and credit to Cash for $2,400. At the end of December, only $200 ($2,400 divided by 12 months) of the insurance premium is expired and has become an expense. The remaining $2,200 of prepaid insurance will become an expense in future months. Thus, the $200 is insurance expense of December and should be recorded with an adjusting entry.

---

1 Under the cash basis of accounting, accounts do not require adjusting. This is because transactions are recorded only when cash is received or paid. Thus, the matching concept is not used under the cash basis.

Other examples of prepaid expenses include supplies, prepaid advertising, and prepaid interest.

Exhibit 1 summarizes the nature of prepaid expenses.

EXHIBIT 1   Prepaid Expenses

Transaction   *Cash is paid in advance for an expense.*

Analysis   Advance payments of future expenses are recorded as assets when the cash is paid. The transaction is recorded as a debit to a prepaid expense account and a credit to the cash account.

Journal Entry

		Prepaid Expense		XXX	
		Cash			XXX
		Paid an expense in advance.			

Accounting Equation Impact

Assets	=	Liabilities	+	Owner's Equity

Cash

	XXX

Prepaid Expense

XXX	

Adjustment   *An end-of-period adjustment is needed to update the prepaid expense account.*

Analysis   The prepaid expense account is decreased (credited) for the amount of the prepaid expense that has expired or has been used and the related expense account is increased (debited).

Adjusting Journal Entry

		Expense		XXX	
		Prepaid Expense			XXX
		Adjustment for prepaid expense.			

Accounting Equation Impact

Assets	=	Liabilities	+	Owner's Equity (Expense)

Prepaid Expense

	XXX

Expense

XXX	

Unearned revenues are the advance receipt of *future* revenues and are recorded as liabilities when cash is received. Unearned revenues become earned revenues over time or during normal operations. To illustrate, the following December 1 transaction of NetSolutions is used.

> Dec. 1   NetSolutions received $360 from a local retailer to rent land for three months.

On December 1, the cash receipt of $360 was recorded as a debit to Cash and a credit to Unearned Rent for $360. At the end of December, $120 ($360 divided by 3 months) of the unearned rent has been earned. The remaining $240 will become rent revenue in future months. Thus, the $120 is rent revenue of December and should be recorded with an adjusting entry.

Other examples of unearned revenues include tuition received in advance by a school, an annual retainer fee received by an attorney, premiums received in advance by an insurance company, and magazine subscriptions received in advance by a publisher.

Exhibit 2 summarizes the nature of unearned revenues.

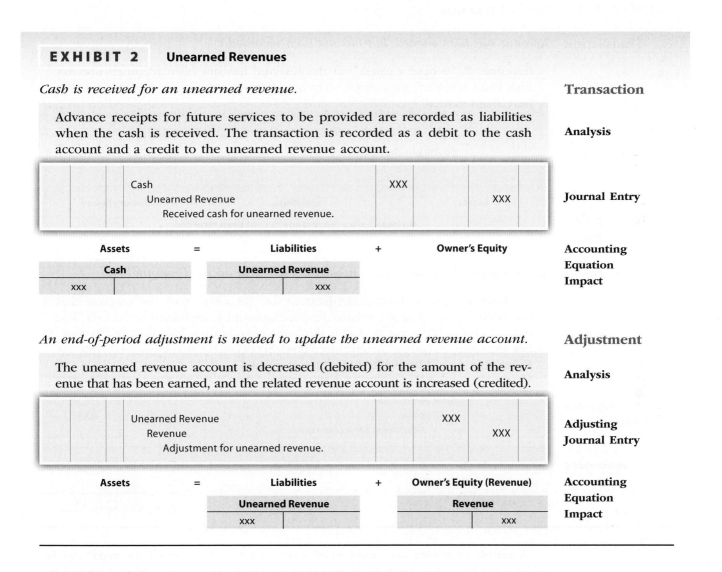

EXHIBIT 2   **Unearned Revenues**

Cash is received for an unearned revenue.   Transaction

Advance receipts for future services to be provided are recorded as liabilities when the cash is received. The transaction is recorded as a debit to the cash account and a credit to the unearned revenue account.   Analysis

Cash			XXX		
Unearned Revenue				XXX	
Received cash for unearned revenue.					

Journal Entry

Assets	=	Liabilities	+	Owner's Equity
Cash		**Unearned Revenue**		
XXX			XXX	

Accounting Equation Impact

An end-of-period adjustment is needed to update the unearned revenue account.   Adjustment

The unearned revenue account is decreased (debited) for the amount of the revenue that has been earned, and the related revenue account is increased (credited).   Analysis

Unearned Revenue			XXX		
Revenue				XXX	
Adjustment for unearned revenue.					

Adjusting Journal Entry

Assets	=	Liabilities	+	Owner's Equity (Revenue)
		Unearned Revenue		**Revenue**
		XXX		XXX

Accounting Equation Impact

Accrued revenues are unrecorded revenues that have been earned and for which cash has yet to be received. Fees for services that an attorney or a doctor has provided but not yet billed are accrued revenues. To illustrate, the following example involving NetSolutions and one of its customers is used.

Dec. 15   NetSolutions signed an agreement with Dankner Co. under which NetSolutions will bill Dankner Co. on the fifteenth of each month for services rendered at the rate of $20 per hour.

From December 16–31, NetSolutions provided 25 hours of service to Dankner Co. Although the revenue of $500 (25 hours × $20) has been earned, it will not be billed until January 15. Likewise, cash of $500 will not be received until Dankner pays its bill. Thus, the $500 of accrued revenue and the $500 of fees earned should be recorded with an adjusting entry on December 31.

Other examples of accrued revenues include accrued interest on notes receivable and accrued rent on property rented to others.

Exhibit 3 summarizes the nature of accrued revenues.

EXHIBIT 3	**Accrued Revenues**

Transaction	*Revenue has been earned, but has not been recorded.*
Analysis	Revenues have been earned, but the revenue has not been recorded nor has cash been received. No journal entry has been recorded even though revenues have been earned.
Journal Entry	No entry has been recorded.

Accounting Equation Impact	Assets	=	Liabilities	+	Owner's Equity
			No impact since the revenue has not been recorded.		

Adjustment	*An end-of-period adjustment is needed to recognize accrued revenue.*
Analysis	An asset account is increased (debited) for the amount of the revenue that has been earned, and the related revenue account is increased (credited). The type of receivable account that is debited depends upon the type of revenue. For example, Accounts Receivable would be debited for fees earned. Interest Receivable would be debited for interest earned.

Adjusting Journal Entry	Asset (Receivable) XXX
	    Revenue XXX
	      Adjustment for accrued revenue.

Accounting Equation Impact	Assets	=	Liabilities	+	Owner's Equity (Revenue)
	Receivable XXX				**Revenue** XXX

Accrued expenses are unrecorded expenses that have been incurred and for which cash has yet to be paid. Wages owed to employees at the end of a period but not yet paid are an accrued expense. To illustrate, the following example involving NetSolutions and its employees is used.

> Dec. 31   NetSolutions owes its employees wages of $250 for Monday and Tuesday, December 30 and 31.

NetSolutions paid wages of $950 on December 13 and $1,200 on December 27, 2011. These payments covered the biweekly pay periods that ended on those days. As of December 31, 2011, NetSolutions owes its employees wages of $250 for Monday and Tuesday, December 30 and 31. The wages of $250 will be paid on January 10, 2012; however, they are an expense of December. Thus, $250 of accrued wages should be recorded with an adjusting entry on December 31.

Other examples of accrued expenses include accrued interest on notes payable and accrued taxes.

Exhibit 4 summarizes the nature of accrued expenses.

EXHIBIT 4   Accrued Expenses

	Transaction
An expense has been incurred, but has not been recorded.	

An expense has been incurred, but the expense has not been recorded nor has cash been paid. No journal entry has been recorded even though an expense has been incurred.   **Analysis**

				Journal Entry
	No entry has been recorded.			

Assets	=	Liabilities	+	Owner's Equity	Accounting
					Equation
	No impact since the expense has not been recorded.				Impact

An end-of-period adjustment is needed to recognize the accrued expense.   **Adjustment**

An expense account is increased (debited) for the amount of the expense that has been incurred and the related liability account is increased (credited). The liability account that is credited depends upon the type of expense. For example, Wages Payable would be credited for wages expense. Interest Payable would be credited for interest expense.   **Analysis**

				Adjusting
Expense		XXX		Journal Entry
Liability (Payable)			XXX	
Adjustment for accrued expense.				

Assets	=	Liabilities	+	Owner's Equity (Expense)	Accounting
		Payable		**Expense**	Equation
		XXX		XXX	Impact

As illustrated in Exhibit 4, accrued revenues are earned revenues that are unrecorded. The cash receipts for accrued revenues are normally received in the next accounting period. Accrued expenses are expenses that have been incurred, but are unrecorded. The cash payments for accrued expenses are normally paid in the next accounting period.

Prepaid expenses and unearned revenues are sometimes referred to as *deferrals*. This is because the recording of the related expense or revenue is deferred to a future period. Accrued revenues and accrued expenses are sometimes referred to as *accruals*. This is because the related revenue or expense should be recorded or accrued in the current period.

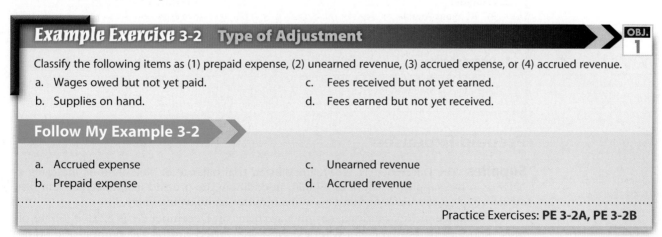

Example Exercise 3-2   Type of Adjustment   OBJ. 1

Classify the following items as (1) prepaid expense, (2) unearned revenue, (3) accrued expense, or (4) accrued revenue.

a. Wages owed but not yet paid.   c. Fees received but not yet earned.

b. Supplies on hand.   d. Fees earned but not yet received.

Follow My Example 3-2

a. Accrued expense   c. Unearned revenue

b. Prepaid expense   d. Accrued revenue

Practice Exercises: **PE 3-2A, PE 3-2B**

OBJ. 2 Journalize entries for accounts requiring adjustment.

Adjusting Entries

To illustrate adjusting entries, the December 31, 2011, unadjusted trial balance of NetSolutions shown in Exhibit 5 is used. An expanded chart of accounts for NetSolutions is shown in Exhibit 6. The additional accounts used in this chapter are shown in color. The rules of debit and credit shown in Exhibit 3 of Chapter 2 are used to record the adjusting entries.

EXHIBIT 5

Unadusted Trial Balance for NetSolutions

NetSolutions Unadusted Trial Balance December 31, 2011		
	Debit Balances	Credit Balances
Cash	2,065	
Accounts Receivable	2,220	
Supplies	2,000	
Prepaid Insurance	2,400	
Land	20,000	
Office Equipment	1,800	
Accounts Payable		900
Unearned Rent		360
Chris Clark, Capital		25,000
Chris Clark, Drawing	4,000	
Fees Earned		16,340
Wages Expense	4,275	
Rent Expense	1,600	
Utilities Expense	985	
Supplies Expense	800	
Miscellaneous Expense	455	
	42,600	42,600

EXHIBIT 6

Expanded Chart of Accounts for NetSolutions

Balance Sheet Accounts

1. Assets
- 11 Cash
- 12 Accounts Receivable
- 14 Supplies
- 15 Prepaid Insurance
- 17 Land
- 18 Office Equipment
- 19 Accumulated Depreciation—Office Equipment

2. Liabilities
- 21 Accounts Payable
- 22 Wages Payable
- 23 Unearned Rent

3. Owner's Equity
- 31 Chris Clark, Capital
- 32 Chris Clark, Drawing

Income Statement Accounts

4. Revenue
- 41 Fees Earned
- 42 Rent Revenue

5. Expenses
- 51 Wages Expense
- 52 Rent Expense
- 53 Depreciation Expense
- 54 Utilities Expense
- 55 Supplies Expense
- 56 Insurance Expense
- 59 Miscellaneous Expense

Prepaid Expenses

Supplies The December 31, 2011, unadjusted trial balance of NetSolutions indicates a balance in the supplies account of $2,000. In addition, the prepaid insurance account has a balance of $2,400. Each of these accounts requires an adjusting entry.

The balance in NetSolutions' supplies account on December 31 is $2,000. Some of these supplies (CDs, paper, envelopes, etc.) were used during December, and some are still on hand (not used). If either amount is known, the other can be determined. It is normally easier to determine the cost of the supplies on hand at the end of the month than to record daily supplies used.

Assuming that on December 31 the amount of supplies on hand is $760, the amount to be transferred from the asset account to the expense account is $1,240, computed as follows:

Supplies available during December (balance of account)	$2,000
Supplies on hand, December 31	760
Supplies used (amount of adjustment)	$1,240

At the end of December, the supplies expense account is increased (debited) for $1,240, and the supplies account is decreased (credited) for $1,240 to record the supplies used during December. The adjusting journal entry and T accounts for Supplies and Supplies Expense are as follows:

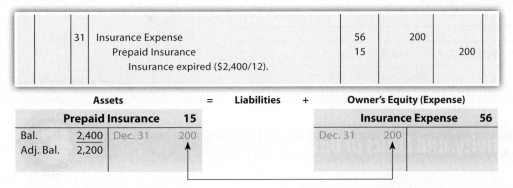

Journal   Page 5

Date	Description	Post. Ref.	Debit	Credit
2011 Dec. 31	Supplies Expense	55	1,240	
	Supplies	14		1,240
	Supplies used ($2,000 – $760).			

Adjusting Journal Entry

Assets = Liabilities + Owner's Equity (Expense)

Supplies			14
Bal.	2,000	Dec. 31	1,240
Adj. Bal.	760		

Supplies Expense		55
Bal.	800	
Dec. 31	1,240	
Adj. Bal.	2,040	

Accounting Equation Impact

The adjusting entry is shown in color in the T accounts to separate it from other transactions. After the adjusting entry is recorded and posted, the supplies account has a debit balance of $760. This balance is an asset that will become an expense in a future period.

Prepaid Insurance   The debit balance of $2,400 in NetSolutions' prepaid insurance account represents a December 1 prepayment of insurance for 12 months. At the end of December, the insurance expense account is increased (debited), and the prepaid insurance account is decreased (credited) by $200, the insurance for one month. The adjusting journal entry and T accounts for Prepaid Insurance and Insurance Expense are as follows:

	31	Insurance Expense	56	200	
		Prepaid Insurance	15		200
		Insurance expired ($2,400/12).			

Adjusting Journal Entry

Assets = Liabilities + Owner's Equity (Expense)

Prepaid Insurance			15
Bal.	2,400	Dec. 31	200
Adj. Bal.	2,200		

Insurance Expense		56
Dec. 31	200	

Accounting Equation Impact

After the adjusting entry is recorded and posted, the prepaid insurance account has a debit balance of $2,200. This balance is an asset that will become an expense in future periods. The insurance expense account has a debit balance of $200, which is an expense of the current period.

If the preceding adjustments for supplies ($1,240) and insurance ($200) are not recorded, the financial statements prepared as of December 31 will be misstated. On the income statement, Supplies Expense and Insurance Expense will be understated by a total of $1,440 ($1,240 + $200), and net income will be overstated by $1,440. On the balance sheet, Supplies and Prepaid Insurance will be overstated by a total of $1,440. Since net income increases owner's equity, Chris Clark, Capital will also be overstated by $1,440 on the balance sheet. The effects of omitting these adjusting entries on the income statement and balance sheet are as follows:

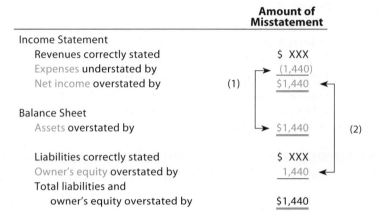

		Amount of Misstatement
Income Statement		
Revenues correctly stated		$ XXX
Expenses understated by		(1,440)
Net income overstated by	(1)	$1,440
Balance Sheet		
Assets overstated by		$1,440 (2)
Liabilities correctly stated		$ XXX
Owner's equity overstated by		1,440
Total liabilities and		
owner's equity overstated by		$1,440

Arrow (1) indicates the effect of the understated expenses on assets. Arrow (2) indicates the effect of the overstated net income on owner's equity.

Payments for prepaid expenses are sometimes made at the beginning of the period in which they will be *entirely used or consumed*. To illustrate, the following December 1 transaction of NetSolutions is used.

> Dec. 1   NetSolutions paid rent of $800 for the month.

On December 1, the rent payment of $800 represents Prepaid Rent. However, the Prepaid Rent expires daily, and at the end of December there will be no asset left. In such cases, the payment of $800 is recorded as Rent Expense rather than as Prepaid Rent. In this way, no adjusting entry is needed at the end of the period.[2]

Example Exercise 3-3   Adjustment for Prepaid Expense   OBJ. 2

The prepaid insurance account had a beginning balance of $6,400 and was debited for $3,600 of premiums paid during the year. Journalize the adjusting entry required at the end of the year assuming the amount of unexpired insurance related to future periods is $3,250.

Follow My Example 3-3

Insurance Expense.. 6,750
  Prepaid Insurance 6,750
    Insurance expired ($6,400 + $3,600 − $3,250).

Practice Exercises: PE 3-3A, PE 3-3B

Integrity, Objectivity, and Ethics in Business

FREE ISSUE

Office supplies are often available to employees on a "free issue" basis. This means that employees do not have to "sign" for the release of office supplies but merely obtain the necessary supplies from a local storage area as needed. Just because supplies are easily available, however, doesn't mean they can be taken for personal use. There are many instances where employees have been terminated for taking supplies home for personal use.

2 An alternative treatment of recording the cost of supplies, rent, and other prepayments of expenses is discussed in an appendix that can be downloaded from the book's companion Web site (**academic.cengage.com/accounting/warren**).

Unearned Revenues

The December 31 unadjusted trial balance of NetSolutions indicates a balance in the unearned rent account of $360. This balance represents the receipt of three months' rent on December 1 for December, January, and February. At the end of December, one months' rent has been earned. Thus, the unearned rent account is decreased (debited) by $120, and the rent revenue account is increased (credited) by $120. The $120 represents the rental revenue for one month ($360/3). The adjusting journal entry and T accounts are shown below.

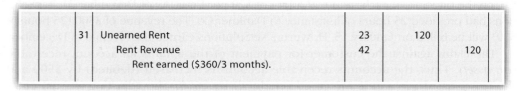

Adjusting Journal Entry

	31	Unearned Rent	23	120	
		Rent Revenue	42		120
		Rent earned ($360/3 months).			

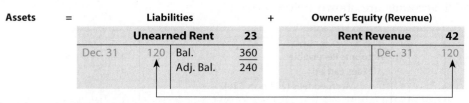

Accounting Equation Impact

Assets	=	Liabilities	+	Owner's Equity (Revenue)

Unearned Rent   23

| Dec. 31 | 120 | Bal. | 360 |
| | | Adj. Bal. | 240 |

Rent Revenue   42

| | | Dec. 31 | 120 |

After the adjusting entry is recorded and posted, the unearned rent account has a credit balance of $240. This balance is a liability that will become revenue in a future period. Rent Revenue has a balance of $120, which is revenue of the current period.[3]

If the preceding adjustment of unearned rent and rent revenue is not recorded, the financial statements prepared on December 31 will be misstated. On the income statement, Rent Revenue and the net income will be understated by $120. On the balance sheet, Unearned Rent will be overstated by $120, and Chris Clark, Capital will be understated by $120. The effects of omitting this adjusting entry are shown below.

Best Buy sells extended warranty contracts with terms between 12 and 36 months. The receipts from sales of these contracts are reported as unearned revenue on Best Buy's balance sheet. Revenue is recorded as the contracts expire.

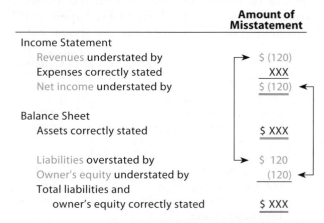

	Amount of Misstatement
Income Statement	
Revenues understated by	$ (120)
Expenses correctly stated	XXX
Net income understated by	$ (120)
Balance Sheet	
Assets correctly stated	$ XXX
Liabilities overstated by	$ 120
Owner's equity understated by	(120)
Total liabilities and	
owner's equity correctly stated	$ XXX

Example Exercise 3-4   Adjustment for Unearned Revenue   OBJ. 2

The balance in the unearned fees account, before adjustment at the end of the year, is $44,900. Journalize the adjusting entry required if the amount of unearned fees at the end of the year is $22,300.

Follow My Example 3-4

Unearned Fees	22,600	
Fees Earned		22,600
Fees earned ($44,900 − $22,300).		

Practice Exercises: **PE 3-4A, PE 3-4B**

---

3 An alternative treatment of recording revenues received in advance of their being earned is discussed in an appendix that can be downloaded from the book's companion Web site (**academic.cengage.com/accounting/warren**).

Accrued Revenues

RadioShack Corporation is engaged in consumer electronics retailing. RadioShack accrues revenue for finance charges and late payment charges related to its credit operations.

During an accounting period, some revenues are recorded only when cash is received. Thus, at the end of an accounting period, there may be revenue that has been earned *but has not been recorded*. In such cases, the revenue is recorded by increasing (debiting) an asset account and increasing (crediting) a revenue account.

To illustrate, assume that NetSolutions signed an agreement with Dankner Co. on December 15. The agreement provides that NetSolutions will answer computer questions and render assistance to Dankner Co.'s employees. The services will be billed to Dankner Co. on the fifteenth of each month at a rate of $20 per hour. As of December 31, NetSolutions had provided 25 hours of assistance to Dankner Co. The revenue of $500 (25 hours × $20) will be billed on January 15. However, NetSolutions earned the revenue in December.

The claim against the customer for payment of the $500 is an account receivable (*an asset*). Thus, the accounts receivable account is increased (debited) by $500 and the fees earned account is increased (credited) by $500. The adjusting journal entry and T accounts are shown below.

Adjusting Journal Entry

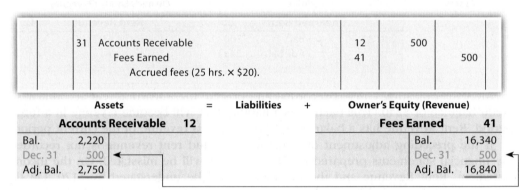

	31	Accounts Receivable	12	500	
		Fees Earned	41		500
		Accrued fees (25 hrs. × $20).			

Accounting Equation Impact

| Assets | = | Liabilities | + | Owner's Equity (Revenue) |

Accounts Receivable 12			Fees Earned 41
Bal. 2,220			Bal. 16,340
Dec. 31 500			Dec. 31 500
Adj. Bal. 2,750			Adj. Bal. 16,840

If the adjustment for the accrued revenue ($500) is not recorded, Fees Earned and the net income will be understated by $500 on the income statement. On the balance sheet, Accounts Receivable and Chris Clark, Capital will be understated by $500. The effects of omitting this adjusting entry are shown below.

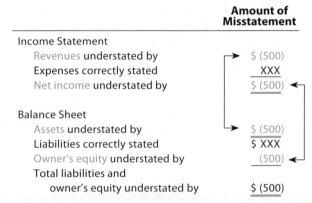

	Amount of Misstatement
Income Statement	
Revenues understated by	$ (500)
Expenses correctly stated	XXX
Net income understated by	$ (500)
Balance Sheet	
Assets understated by	$ (500)
Liabilities correctly stated	$ XXX
Owner's equity understated by	(500)
Total liabilities and owner's equity understated by	$ (500)

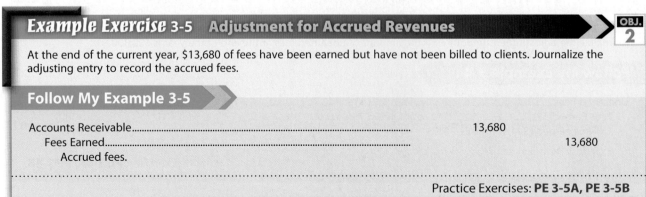

Example Exercise 3-5 Adjustment for Accrued Revenues **OBJ. 2**

At the end of the current year, $13,680 of fees have been earned but have not been billed to clients. Journalize the adjusting entry to record the accrued fees.

Follow My Example 3-5

Accounts Receivable	13,680	
Fees Earned		13,680
Accrued fees.		

Practice Exercises: **PE 3-5A, PE 3-5B**

Accrued Expenses

Some types of services used in earning revenues are paid for *after* the service has been performed. For example, wages expense is used hour by hour, but is paid only daily, weekly, biweekly, or monthly. At the end of the accounting period, the amount of such *accrued* but unpaid items is an expense and a liability.

For example, if the last day of the employees' pay period is not the last day of the accounting period, an accrued expense (wages expense) and the related liability (wages payable) must be recorded by an adjusting entry. This adjusting entry is necessary so that expenses are properly matched to the period in which they were incurred in earning revenue.

To illustrate, NetSolutions pays its employees biweekly. During December, NetSolutions paid wages of $950 on December 13 and $1,200 on December 27. These payments covered pay periods ending on those days as shown in Exhibit 7.

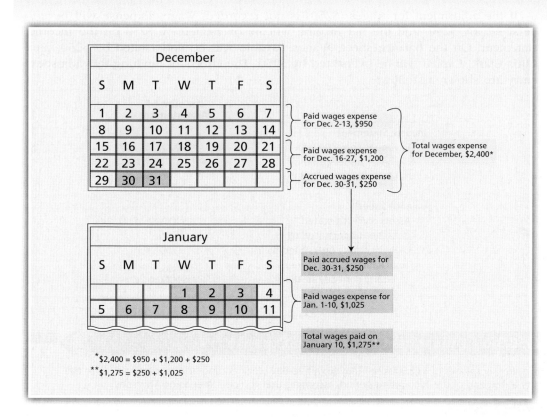

EXHIBIT 7

Accrued Wages

As of December 31, NetSolutions owes $250 of wages to employees for Monday and Tuesday, December 30 and 31. Thus, the wages expense account is increased (debited) by $250 and the wages payable account is increased (credited) by $250. The adjusting journal entry and T accounts are shown below.

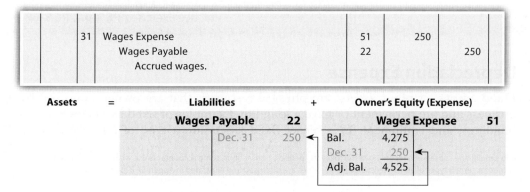

Adjusting
Journal Entry

Accounting
Equation
Impact

After the adjusting entry is recorded and posted, the debit balance of the wages expense account is $4,525. This balance of $4,525 is the wages expense for two months, November and December. The credit balance of $250 in Wages Payable is the liability for wages owed on December 31.

As shown in Exhibit 7, NetSolutions paid wages of $1,275 on January 10. This payment includes the $250 of accrued wages recorded on December 31. Thus, on January 10, the wages payable account is decreased (debited) by $250. Also, the wages expense account is increased (debited) by $1,025 ($1,275 – $250), which is the wages expense for January 1–10. Finally, the cash account is decreased (credited) by $1,275. The journal entry for the payment of wages on January 10 is shown below.[4]

Jan	10	Wages Expense	51	1,025	
		Wages Payable	22	250	
		Cash	11		1,275

If the adjustment for wages ($250) is not recorded, Wages Expense will be understated by $250, and the net income will be overstated by $250 on the income statement. On the balance sheet, Wages Payable will be understated by $250, and Chris Clark, Capital will be overstated by $250. The effects of omitting this adjusting entry are shown as follows:

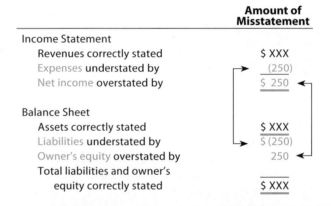

	Amount of Misstatement
Income Statement	
Revenues correctly stated	$ XXX
Expenses understated by	(250)
Net income overstated by	$ 250
Balance Sheet	
Assets correctly stated	$ XXX
Liabilities understated by	$ (250)
Owner's equity overstated by	250
Total liabilities and owner's equity correctly stated	$ XXX

Example Exercise 3-6 Adjustment for Accrued Expense — OBJ. 2

Sanregret Realty Co. pays weekly salaries of $12,500 on Friday for a five-day week ending on that day. Journalize the necessary adjusting entry at the end of the accounting period, assuming that the period ends on Thursday.

Follow My Example 3-6

Salaries Expense	10,000	
Salaries Payable		10,000
Accrued salaries [($12,500/5 days) × 4 days].		

Practice Exercises: **PE 3-6A, PE 3-6B**

Depreciation Expense

Fixed assets, or **plant assets**, are physical resources that are owned and used by a business and are permanent or have a long life. Examples of fixed assets include land, buildings, and equipment. In a sense, fixed assets are a type of *long-term* prepaid

4 To simplify the subsequent recording of the following period's transactions, some accountants use what is known as reversing entries for certain types of adjustments. Reversing entries are discussed and illustrated in Appendix B at the end of the textbook.

BusinessConnection

FORD MOTOR COMPANY WARRANTIES

Ford Motor Company provides warranties on the vehicles that it sells. For example, Ford offers "bumper-to-bumper" coverage in the United States for five years or 60,000 miles on its Ford brand. A bumper-to-bumper warranty normally implies that every part of a new car will be repaired or replaced if it is defective during the term of the warranty.

When Ford sells a new car, it estimates the future warranty costs that it will incur on the vehicle and accrues a warranty expense. Accruals for estimated warranty costs are based on historical warranty claim experience, which is adjusted for changes such as offering new types of vehicles. For example, Ford adjusted its warranty costs when it began selling its new fuel efficient Ford Escape Hybrid. The Ford Escape Hybrid has a gas-electric engine that automatically shuts off when the vehicle is stopped. The Escape also uses an electric motor to assist in accelerating or when the vehicle is coasting or slowing down.

Ford's warranty cost accruals (in millions) for the years ended December 31, 2009 and 2008 are as follows:

	2009	2008
Beginning balance	$ 3,346	$ 4,209
Payments during the year	(2,481)	(2,747)
Warranties issued during year	2,233	2,122
Other	121	(238)
Ending balance of accrued warranties	$ 3,219	$ 3,346

expense. However, because of their unique nature and long life, they are discussed separately from other prepaid expenses.

Fixed assets, such as office equipment, are used to generate revenue much like supplies are used to generate revenue. Unlike supplies, however, there is no visible reduction in the quantity of the equipment. Instead, as time passes, the equipment loses its ability to provide useful services. This decrease in usefulness is called **depreciation**.

All fixed assets, except land, lose their usefulness and, thus, are said to **depreciate**. As a fixed asset depreciates, a portion of its cost should be recorded as an expense. This periodic expense is called **depreciation expense**.

The adjusting entry to record depreciation expense is similar to the adjusting entry for supplies used. The depreciation expense account is increased (debited) for the amount of depreciation. However, the fixed asset account is not decreased (credited). This is because both the original cost of a fixed asset and the depreciation recorded since its purchase are reported on the balance sheet. Instead, an account entitled **Accumulated Depreciation** is increased (credited).

Accumulated depreciation accounts are called **contra accounts**, or **contra asset accounts**. This is because accumulated depreciation accounts are deducted from their related fixed asset accounts on the balance sheet. The normal balance of a contra account is opposite to the account from which it is deducted. Since the normal balance of a fixed asset account is a debit, the normal balance of an accumulated depreciation account is a credit.

The normal titles for fixed asset accounts and their related contra asset accounts are as follows:

Lowe's Companies, Inc., reported land, buildings, and store equipment at a cost of over $18 billion and accumulated depreciation of over $4.1 billion.

Fixed Asset Account	Contra Asset Account
Land	None—Land is not depreciated.
Buildings	Accumulated Depreciation—Buildings
Store Equipment	Accumulated Depreciation—Store Equipment
Office Equipment	Accumulated Depreciation—Office Equipment

The December 31, 2011, unadjusted trial balance of NetSolutions (Exhibit 5) indicates that NetSolutions owns two fixed assets: land and office equipment. Land does not depreciate; however, an adjusting entry is recorded for the depreciation of the office equipment for December. Assume that the office equipment depreciates $50 during December. The depreciation expense account is increased (debited) by $50, and the accumulated depreciation—office equipment account is increased (credited) by $50.[5] The adjusting journal entry and T accounts are shown below.

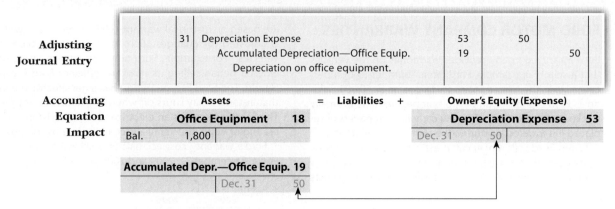

Adjusting Journal Entry

	31	Depreciation Expense	53	50	
		Accumulated Depreciation—Office Equip.	19		50
		Depreciation on office equipment.			

Accounting Equation Impact

Assets	= Liabilities +	Owner's Equity (Expense)

Office Equipment   18

Bal.   1,800

Depreciation Expense   53

Dec. 31   50

Accumulated Depr.—Office Equip. 19

Dec. 31   50

After the adjusting journal entry is recorded and posted, the office equipment account still has a debit balance of $1,800. This is the original cost of the office equipment that was purchased on December 4. The accumulated depreciation—office equipment account has a credit balance of $50. The difference between these two balances is the cost of the office equipment that has not yet been depreciated. This amount, called the **book value of the asset** (or **net book value**), is computed as shown below.

Book Value of Asset = Cost of the Asset – Accumulated Depreciation of Asset
Book Value of Office Equipment = Cost of Office Equipment – Accumulated Depre. of Office Equipment
Book Value of Office Equipment = $1,800 – $50
Book Value of Office Equipment = $1,750

The office equipment and its related accumulated depreciation are reported on the December 31, 2011, balance sheet as follows:

Office equipment	$1,800	
Less accumulated depreciation	50	$1,750

The market value of a fixed asset usually differs from its book value. This is because depreciation is an *allocation* method, not a *valuation* method. That is, depreciation allocates the cost of a fixed asset to expense over its estimated life. Depreciation does not measure changes in market values, which vary from year to year. Thus, on December 31, 2011, the market value of NetSolutions' office equipment could be more or less than $1,750.

If the adjustment for depreciation ($50) is not recorded, Depreciation Expense on the income statement will be understated by $50, and the net income will be overstated by $50. On the balance sheet, the book value of Office Equipment and Chris Clark, Capital will be overstated by $50. The effects of omitting the adjustment for depreciation are shown below.

	Amount of Misstatement
Income Statement	
Revenues correctly stated	$ XX
Expenses understated by	(50)
Net income overstated by	$ 50
Balance Sheet	
Assets overstated by	$ 50
Liabilities correctly stated	$ XX
Owner's equity overstated by	50
Total liabilities and owner's	
equity overstated by	$ 50

---

5 Methods of computing depreciation expense are described and illustrated in Chapter 10.

Example Exercise 3-7 Adjustment for Depreciation

The estimated amount of depreciation on equipment for the current year is $4,250. Journalize the adjusting entry to record the depreciation.

Follow My Example 3-7

Depreciation Expense	4,250	
Accumulated Depreciation—Equipment		4,250
Depreciation on equipment.		

Practice Exercises: **PE 3-7A, PE 3-7B**

Summary of Adjustment Process

Summarize the adjustment process.

A summary of the basic types of adjusting entries is shown in Exhibit 8 on page 120.

The adjusting entries for NetSolutions are shown in Exhibit 9 on page 121. The adjusting entries are dated as of the last day of the period. However, because collecting the adjustment data requires time, the entries are usually recorded at a later date. An explanation is normally included with each adjusting entry.

NetSolutions' adjusting entries are posted to the ledger shown in Exhibit 10 on pages 122–123. The adjustments are shown in color in Exhibit 10 to distinguish them from other transactions.

Example Exercise 3-8 Effect of Omitting Adjustments

For the year ending December 31, 2012, Mann Medical Co. mistakenly omitted adjusting entries for (1) $8,600 of unearned revenue that was earned, (2) earned revenue that was not billed of $12,500, and (3) accrued wages of $2,900. Indicate the combined effect of the errors on (a) revenues, (b) expenses, and (c) net income for the year ended December 31, 2012.

Follow My Example 3-8

a. Revenues were understated by $21,100 ($8,600 + $12,500).
b. Expenses were understated by $2,900.
c. Net income was understated by $18,200 ($8,600 + $12,500 − $2,900).

Practice Exercises: **PE 3-8A, PE 3-8B**

EXHIBIT 8 Summary of Adjustments

			PREPAID EXPENSES			
Examples	**Reason for Adjustment**	**Adjusting Entry**		**Examples from NetSolutions**		**Financial Statement Impact if Adjusting Entry Is Omitted**

Supplies, prepaid insurance	Prepaid expenses (assets) have been used or consumed in the business operations.	Expense Dr.
		  Asset Cr.
				Supplies Expense 1,240
				  Supplies 1,240
				Insurance Expense 200
				  Prepaid Insurance 200
						Income Statement:
						  Revenues No effect
						  Expenses Understated
						  Net income Overstated
						Balance Sheet:
						  Assets Overstated
						  Liabilities No effect
						  Owner's equity Overstated
						  (capital)

			UNEARNED REVENUES			

Unearned rent, magazine subscriptions received in advance, fees received in advance of services	Cash received before the services have been provided is recorded as a liability. Some services have been provided to customer before the end of the accounting period.	Liability Dr.
		  Revenue Cr.
				Unearned Rent 120
				  Rent Revenue 120
						Income Statement:
						  Revenues Understated
						  Expenses No effect
						  Net income Understated
						Balance Sheet:
						  Assets No effect
						  Liabilities Overstated
						  Owner's equity Understated
						  (capital)

			ACCRUED REVENUES			

Services performed but not billed, interest to be received	Services have been provided to the customer, but have not been billed or recorded. Interest has been earned, but has not been received or recorded.	Asset Dr.
		  Revenue Cr.
				Accounts Receivable 500
				  Fees Earned 500
						Income Statement:
						  Revenues Understated
						  Expenses No effect
						  Net income Understated
						Balance Sheet:
						  Assets Understated
						  Liabilities No effect
						  Owner's equity Understated
						  (capital)

			ACCRUED EXPENSES			

Wages or salaries incurred but not paid, interest incurred but not paid	Expenses have been incurred, but have not been paid or recorded.	Expense Dr.
		  Liability Cr.
				Wages Expense 250
				  Wages Payable 250
						Income Statement:
						  Revenues No effect
						  Expenses Understated
						  Net income Overstated
						Balance Sheet:
						  Assets No effect
						  Liabilities Understated
						  Owner's equity Overstated
						  (capital)

			DEPRECIATION			

Depreciation of equipment and buildings	Fixed assets depreciate as they are used or consumed in the business operations.	Expense Dr.
		  Contra Asset Cr.
				Depreciation Expense 50
				  Accum. Depreciation—
				   Office Equipment 50
						Income Statement:
						  Revenues No effect
						  Expenses Understated
						  Net income Overstated
						Balance Sheet:
						  Assets Overstated
						  Liabilities No effect
						  Owner's equity Overstated
						  (capital)

EXHIBIT 9

Adjusting Entries— NetSolutions

Date			Description	Post. Ref.	Debit	Credit
			Adjusting Entries			
2011 Dec	31		Supplies Expense	55	1,240	
			Supplies	14		1,240
			Supplies used ($2,000 – $760).			
	31		Insurance Expense	56	200	
			Prepaid Insurance	15		200
			Insurance expired ($2,400/12 months).			
	31		Unearned Rent	23	120	
			Rent Revenue	42		120
			Rent earned ($360/3 months).			
	31		Accounts Receivable	12	500	
			Fees Earned	41		500
			Accrued fees (25 hrs. × $20).			
	31		Wages Expense	51	250	
			Wages Payable	22		250
			Accrued wages.			
	31		Depreciation Expense	53	50	
			Accum. Depreciation—Office Equipment	19		50
			Depreciation on office equipment.			

An accountant may check whether all adjustments have been made by comparing current period adjustments with those of the prior period.

BusinessConnection

MICROSOFT CORPORATION

Microsoft Corporation develops, manufactures, licenses, and supports a wide range of computer software products, including Windows Vista, Windows 7, Windows XP, Word, Excel, and the Xbox® gaming system. When Microsoft sells its products, it incurs an obligation to support its software with technical support and periodic updates. As a result, not all the revenue is earned on the date of sale; some of the revenue on the date of sale is unearned. The portion of revenue related to support services, such as updates and technical support, is earned as time passes and support is provided to customers. Thus, each year Microsoft makes adjusting entries transferring some of its unearned revenue to revenue. The following excerpts were taken from Microsoft's financial statements:

The percentage of revenue recorded as unearned . . . ranges from approximately 15% to 25% of the sales price for Windows XP Home, approximately 5% to 15% of the sales price for Windows XP Professional, . . .

Unearned Revenue:

	June 30, 2009	June 30, 2008
Unearned revenue (in millions)	$14,284	$15,297

During the year ending June 30, 2010, Microsoft expects to record over $13,003 million of unearned revenue as revenue.

At the same time, Microsoft will record additional unearned revenue from current period sales.

Source: Taken from Microsoft's June 30, 2009, annual report.

EXHIBIT 10   Ledger with Adjusting Entries—NetSolutions

Account Cash   Account No. 11

Date	Item	Post. Ref.	Debit	Credit	Balance Debit	Balance Credit
2011						
Nov. 1		1	25,000		25,000	
5		1		20,000	5,000	
18		1	7,500		12,500	
30		1		3,650	8,850	
30		1		950	7,900	
30		2		2,000	5,900	
Dec. 1		2		2,400	3,500	
1		2		800	2,700	
1		2	360		3,060	
6		2		180	2,880	
11		2		400	2,480	
13		3		950	1,530	
16		3	3,100		4,630	
20		3		900	3,730	
21		3	650		4,380	
23		3		1,450	2,930	
27		3		1,200	1,730	
31		3		310	1,420	
31		4		225	1,195	
31		4	2,870		4,065	
31		4		2,000	2,065	

Account Accounts Receivable   Account No. 12

Date	Item	Post. Ref.	Debit	Credit	Balance Debit	Balance Credit
2011						
Dec. 16		3	1,750		1,750	
21		3		650	1,100	
31		4	1,120		2,220	
31	Adjusting	5	500		2,720	

Account Supplies   Account No. 14

Date	Item	Post. Ref.	Debit	Credit	Balance Debit	Balance Credit
2011						
Nov. 10		1	1,350		1,350	
30		1		800	550	
Dec. 23		3	1,450		2,000	
31	Adjusting	5		1,240	760	

Account Prepaid Insurance   Account No. 15

Date	Item	Post. Ref.	Debit	Credit	Balance Debit	Balance Credit
2011						
Dec. 1		2	2,400		2,400	
31	Adjusting	5		200	2,200	

Account Land   Account No. 17

Date	Item	Post. Ref.	Debit	Credit	Balance Debit	Balance Credit
2011						
Nov. 5		1	20,000		20,000	

Account Office Equipment   Account No. 18

Date	Item	Post. Ref.	Debit	Credit	Balance Debit	Balance Credit
2011						
Dec. 4		2	1,800		1,800	

Account Accum. Depr.—Office Equip.   Account No. 19

Date	Item	Post. Ref.	Debit	Credit	Balance Debit	Balance Credit
2011						
Dec. 1	Adjusting	5		50		50

Account Accounts Payable   Account No. 21

Date	Item	Post. Ref.	Debit	Credit	Balance Debit	Balance Credit
2011						
Nov. 10		1		1,350		1,350
30		1	950			400
Dec. 4		2		1,800		2,200
11		2	400			1,800
20		3	900			900

Account Wages Payable   Account No. 22

Date	Item	Post. Ref.	Debit	Credit	Balance Debit	Balance Credit
2011						
Dec. 31	Adjusting	5		250		250

Account Unearned Rent   Account No. 23

Date	Item	Post. Ref.	Debit	Credit	Balance Debit	Balance Credit
2011						
Dec. 1		2		360		360
31	Adjusting	5	120			240

Account Chris Clark, Capital   Account No. 31

Date	Item	Post. Ref.	Debit	Credit	Balance Debit	Balance Credit
2011						
Nov. 1		1		25,000		25,000

EXHIBIT 10 Ledger with Adjusting Entries—NetSolutions (*Concluded*)

Account *Chris Clark, Drawing* — Account No. 32

Date	Item	Post. Ref.	Debit	Credit	Balance Debit	Balance Credit
2011						
Nov. 30		2	2,000		2,000	
Dec. 31		4	2,000		4,000	

Account *Fees Earned* — Account No. 41

Date	Item	Post. Ref.	Debit	Credit	Balance Debit	Balance Credit
2011						
Nov. 18		1		7,500		7,500
Dec. 16		3		3,100		10,600
16		3		1,750		12,350
31		4		2,870		15,220
31		4		1,120		16,340
31	Adjusting	5		500		16,840

Account *Rent Revenue* — Account No. 42

Date	Item	Post. Ref.	Debit	Credit	Balance Debit	Balance Credit
2011						
Dec. 31	Adjusting	5		120		120

Account *Wages Expense* — Account No. 51

Date	Item	Post. Ref.	Debit	Credit	Balance Debit	Balance Credit
2011						
Nov. 30		1	2,125		2,125	
Dec. 13		3	950		3,075	
27		3	1,200		4,275	
31	Adjusting	5	250		4,525	

Account *Rent Expense* — Account No. 52

Date	Item	Post. Ref.	Debit	Credit	Balance Debit	Balance Credit
2011						
Nov. 30		1	800		800	
Dec. 1		2	800		1,600	

Account *Depreciation Expense* — Account No. 53

Date	Item	Post. Ref.	Debit	Credit	Balance Debit	Balance Credit
2011						
Dec. 31	Adjusting	5	50		50	

Account *Utilities Expense* — Account No. 54

Date	Item	Post. Ref.	Debit	Credit	Balance Debit	Balance Credit
2011						
Nov. 30		1	450		450	
Dec. 31		3	310		760	
31		4	225		985	

Account *Supplies Expense* — Account No. 55

Date	Item	Post. Ref.	Debit	Credit	Balance Debit	Balance Credit
2011						
Nov. 30		1	800		800	
Dec. 31	Adjusting	5	1,240		2,040	

Account *Insurance Expense* — Account No. 56

Date	Item	Post. Ref.	Debit	Credit	Balance Debit	Balance Credit
2011						
Dec. 31	Adjusting	5	200		200	

Account *Miscellaneous Expense* — Account No. 59

Date	Item	Post. Ref.	Debit	Credit	Balance Debit	Balance Credit
2011						
Nov. 30		1	275		275	
Dec. 6		2	180		455	

Adjusted Trial Balance

OBJ. 4 Prepare an adjusted trial balance.

After the adjusting entries are posted, an **adjusted trial balance** is prepared. The adjusted trial balance verifies the equality of the total debit and credit balances before the financial statements are prepared. If the adjusted trial balance does not balance, an error has occurred. However, as discussed in Chapter 2, errors may occur even though the adjusted trial balance totals agree. For example, if an adjusting entry were omitted, the adjusted trial balance totals would still agree.

Exhibit 11 shows the adjusted trial balance for NetSolutions as of December 31, 2011. Chapter 4 discusses how financial statements, including a classified balance sheet, are prepared from an adjusted trial balance.

EXHIBIT 11

Adjusted Trial Balance

NetSolutions Adjusted Trial Balance December 31, 2011	Debit Balances	Credit Balances
Cash	2,065	
Accounts Receivable..	2,720	
Supplies	760	
Prepaid Insurance	2,200	
Land	20,000	
Office Equipment	1,800	
Accumulated Depreciation—Office Equipment.............................		50
Accounts Payable		900
Wages Payable...		250
Unearned Rent...		240
Chris Clark, Capital		25,000
Chris Clark, Drawing..	4,000	
Fees Earned..		16,840
Rent Revenue		120
Wages Expense	4,525	
Rent Expense	1,600	
Depreciation Expense	50	
Utilities Expense	985	
Supplies Expense..	2,040	
Insurance Expense	200	
Miscellaneous Expense	455	
	43,400	43,400

Example Exercise 3-9   Effect of Errors on Adjusted Trial Balance

OBJ. 4

For each of the following errors, considered individually, indicate whether the error would cause the adjusted trial balance totals to be unequal. If the error would cause the adjusted trial balance totals to be unequal, indicate whether the debit or credit total is higher and by how much.

a. The adjustment for accrued fees of $5,340 was journalized as a debit to Accounts Payable for $5,340 and a credit to Fees Earned of $5,340.

b. The adjustment for depreciation of $3,260 was journalized as a debit to Depreciation Expense for $3,620 and a credit to Accumulated Depreciation for $3,260.

Follow My Example 3-9

a. The totals are equal even though the debit should have been to Accounts Receivable instead of Accounts Payable.

b. The totals are unequal. The debit total is higher by $360 ($3,620 − $3,260).

Practice Exercises: **PE 3-9A, PE 3-9B**

Financial Analysis and Interpretation: Vertical Analysis

F·A·I

Comparing each item in a financial statement with a total amount from the same statement is useful in analyzing relationships within the financial statement. **Vertical analysis** is the term used to describe such comparisons.

OBJ. 5 Describe and illustrate the use of vertical analysis in evaluating a company's performance and financial condition.

In vertical analysis of a balance sheet, each asset item is stated as a percent of the total assets. Each liability and owner's equity item is stated as a percent of total liabilities and owner's equity. In vertical analysis of an income statement, each item is stated as a percent of revenues or fees earned.

Vertical analysis is also useful for analyzing changes in financial statements over time. To illustrate, a vertical analysis of two years of income statements for J. Holmes, Attorney-at-Law, is shown below.

J. Holmes, Attorney-at-Law
Income Statements
For the Years Ended December 31, 2012 and 2011

	2012		2011	
	Amount	Percent	Amount	Percent
Fees earned	$187,500	100.0%	$150,000	100.0%
Operating expenses:				
Wages expense	$ 60,000	32.0%*	$ 45,000	30.0%**
Rent expense	15,000	8.0	12,000	8.0
Utilities expense	12,500	6.7	9,000	6.0
Supplies expense	2,700	1.4	3,000	2.0
Miscellaneous expense	2,300	1.2	1,800	1.2
Total operating expenses	$ 92,500	49.3%	$ 70,800	47.2%
Net income	$ 95,000	50.7%	$ 79,200	52.8%

*Rounded to one decimal place.
**$45,000 ÷ $150,000

The preceding vertical analysis indicates both favorable and unfavorable trends affecting the income statement of J. Holmes, Attorney-at-Law. The increase in wages expense of 2% (32.0% – 30.0%) is an unfavorable trend, as is the increase in utilities expense of 0.7% (6.7% – 6.0%). A favorable trend is the decrease in supplies expense of 0.6% (2.0% – 1.4%). Rent expense and miscellaneous expense as a percent of fees earned were constant. The net result of these trends is that net income decreased as a percent of fees earned from 52.8% to 50.7%.

The analysis of the various percentages shown for J. Holmes, Attorney-at-Law, can be enhanced by comparisons with industry averages. Such averages are published by trade associations and financial information services. Any major differences between industry averages should be investigated.

Vertical analysis of operating income taken from two years of income statements for RealNetworks is shown below.

RealNetworks
Income Statements
For the Years Ended December 31, 2009 and 2008

	2009		2008	
	Amount	Percent	Amount	Percent
Revenues	$562,264*	100.0%	$604,810	100.0%
Expenses:				
Cost of revenues	$ 222,142	39.5%	$233,244	38.6%
Selling expenses	199,148	35.4	256,135	42.3
Administrative expenses	79,164	14.1	69,981	11.6
Other expenses (net)	299,048	53.2	332,855	55.0
Total operating expenses	$799,502	142.2%	$892,215	147.5%
Operating income (loss)	$(237,238)	(42.2)%	$(287,405)	(47.5)%

*In millions

The preceding analysis indicates that RealNetworks experienced an operating loss of 42.2% of revenues in 2009. The analysis indicates that the cost of revenues was comparable across both years. Selling expenses decreased from 42.3% to 35.4%, while administrative expenses increased from 11.6% to 14.1%. The major cause of the losses in 2009 and 2008 was due to the other expenses, which were 53.2% and 55.0% of revenues for 2009 and 2008, respectively. The cause of these other expenses should be investigated. An examination of RealNetworks' annual report indicates that a large portion of these expenses was caused by the loss in value of some of its long-term assets due to the depressed economic conditions of the last several years.

Example Exercise 3-10 Vertical Analysis OBJ. 5

Two income statements for Fortson Company are shown below.

Fortson Company
Income Statements
For the Years Ended December 31, 2012 and 2011

	2012	2011
Fees earned	$425,000	$375,000
Operating expenses	263,500	210,000
Operating income	$161,500	$165,000

a. Prepare a vertical analysis of Fortson Company's income statements.

b. Does the vertical analysis indicate a favorable or unfavorable trend?

Follow My Example 3-10

a.
Fortson Company
Income Statements
For the Years Ended December 31, 2012 and 2011

	2012 Amount	2012 Percent	2011 Amount	2011 Percent
Fees earned	$425,000	100%	$375,000	100%
Operating expenses	263,500	62	210,000	56
Operating income	$161,500	38%	$165,000	44%

b. An unfavorable trend of increasing operating expenses and decreasing operating income is indicated.

Practice Exercises: **PE 3-10A, PE 3-10B**

At a Glance 3

OBJ. 1 Describe the nature of the adjusting process.

Key Points   The accrual basis of accounting requires that revenues are reported in the period in which they are earned and expenses are matched with the revenues they generate. The updating of accounts at the end of the accounting period is called the adjusting process. Each adjusting entry affects an income statement and balance sheet account. The four types of accounts requiring adjusting entries are prepaid expenses, unearned revenues, accrued revenues, and accrued expenses.

Learning Outcomes	Example Exercises	Practice Exercises
• Explain why accrual accounting requires adjusting entries.		
• List accounts that do and do NOT require adjusting entries at the end of the accounting period.	EE3-1	PE3-1A, 3-1B
• Give an example of a prepaid expense, unearned revenue, accrued revenue, and accrued expense.	EE3-2	PE3-2A, 3-2B

OBJ. 2 Journalize entries for accounts requiring adjustment.

Key Points At the end of the period, adjusting entries are needed for prepaid expenses, unearned revenues, accrued revenues, and accrued expenses. In addition, an adjusting entry is necessary to record depreciation on fixed assets.

Learning Outcomes	Example Exercises	Practice Exercises
• Prepare an adjusting entry for a prepaid expense.	EE3-3	PE3-3A, 3-3B
• Prepare an adjusting entry for an unearned revenue.	EE3-4	PE3-4A, 3-4B
• Prepare an adjusting entry for an accrued revenue.	EE3-5	PE3-5A, 3-5B
• Prepare an adjusting entry for an accrued expense.	EE3-6	PE3-6A, 3-6B
• Prepare an adjusting entry for depreciation expense.	EE3-7	PE3-7A, 3-7B

OBJ. 3 Summarize the adjustment process.

Key Points A summary of adjustments, including the type of adjustment, reason for the adjustment, the adjusting entry, and the effect of omitting an adjustment on the financial statements, is shown in Exhibit 8.

Learning Outcomes	Example Exercises	Practice Exercises
• Determine the effect on the income statement and balance sheet of omitting an adjusting entry for prepaid expense, unearned revenue, accrued revenue, accrued expense, and depreciation.	EE3-8	PE3-8A, 3-8B

OBJ. 4 Prepare an adjusted trial balance.

Key Points After all the adjusting entries have been posted, the equality of the total debit balances and total credit balances is verified by an adjusted trial balance.

Learning Outcomes	Example Exercises	Practice Exercises
• Prepare an adjusted trial balance.		
• Determine the effect of errors on the equality of the adjusted trial balance.	EE3-9	PE3-9A, 3-9B

OBJ. 5 Describe and illustrate the use of vertical analysis in evaluating a company's performance and financial condition.

Key Points Comparing each item on a financial statement with a total amount from the same statement is called vertical analysis. On the balance sheet, each asset is expressed as a percent of total assets and each liability and owner's equity is expressed as a percent of total liabilities and owner's equity. On the income statement, each revenue and expense is expressed as a percent of total revenues or fees earned.

Learning Outcomes	Example Exercises	Practice Exercises
• Describe vertical analysis.		
• Prepare a vertical analysis report of a financial statement.	EE3-10	PE3-10A, 3-10B

Key Terms

accounting period concept (104)
accrual basis of accounting (104)
accrued expenses (108)
accrued revenues (107)
Accumulated Depreciation (117)
adjusted trial balance (123)
adjusting entries (105)
adjusting process (105)

book value of the asset (or
  net book value) (118)
cash basis of accounting (104)
contra accounts (or contra
  asset accounts) (117)
depreciate (117)
depreciation (117)
depreciation expense (117)

fixed assets (or plant assets) (116)
matching concept (or matching
  principle) (104)
prepaid expenses (105)
revenue recognition concept (104)
unearned revenues (106)
vertical analysis (125)

Illustrative Problem

Three years ago, T. Roderick organized Harbor Realty. At July 31, 2012, the end of the current year, the unadjusted trial balance of Harbor Realty appears as shown below.

Harbor Realty
Unadjusted Trial Balance
July 31, 2012

	Debit Balances	Credit Balances
Cash	3,425	
Accounts Receivable	7,000	
Supplies	1,270	
Prepaid Insurance	620	
Office Equipment	51,650	
Accumulated Depreciation—Office Equipment		9,700
Accounts Payable		925
Wages Payable		0
Unearned Fees		1,250
T. Roderick, Capital		29,000
T. Roderick, Drawing	5,200	
Fees Earned		59,125
Wages Expense	22,415	
Depreciation Expense	0	
Rent Expense	4,200	
Utilities Expense	2,715	
Supplies Expense	0	
Insurance Expense	0	
Miscellaneous Expense	1,505	
	100,000	100,000

The data needed to determine year-end adjustments are as follows:

a. Supplies on hand at July 31, 2012, $380.

b. Insurance premiums expired during the year, $315.

c. Depreciation of equipment during the year, $4,950.

d. Wages accrued but not paid at July 31, 2012, $440.

e. Accrued fees earned but not recorded at July 31, 2012, $1,000.

f. Unearned fees on July 31, 2012, $750.

Instructions

1. Prepare the necessary adjusting journal entries. Include journal entry explanations.

2. Determine the balance of the accounts affected by the adjusting entries, and prepare an adjusted trial balance.

Solution

1.

	Journal				
Date	**Description**	**Post. Ref.**	**Debit**	**Credit**	
2012					
July 31	Supplies Expense		890		
	Supplies			890	
	Supplies used ($1,270 – $380).				
31	Insurance Expense		315		
	Prepaid Insurance			315	
	Insurance expired.				
31	Depreciation Expense		4,950		
	Accumulated Depreciation—Office Equipment			4,950	
	Depreciation expense.				
31	Wages Expense		440		
	Wages Payable			440	
	Accrued wages.				
31	Accounts Receivable		1,000		
	Fees Earned			1,000	
	Accrued fees.				
31	Unearned Fees		500		
	Fees Earned			500	
	Fees earned ($1,250 – $750).				

2.

Harbor Realty
Adjusted Trial Balance
July 31, 2012

	Debit Balances	Credit Balances
Cash	3,425	
Accounts Receivable.....	8,000	
Supplies	380	
Prepaid Insurance	305	
Office Equipment	51,650	
Accumulated Depreciation—Office Equipment.....		14,650
Accounts Payable		925
Wages Payable.....		440
Unearned Fees.....		750
T. Roderick, Capital		29,000
T. Roderick, Drawing.....	5,200	
Fees Earned.....		60,625
Wages Expense	22,855	
Depreciation Expense	4,950	
Rent Expense	4,200	
Utilities Expense	2,715	
Supplies Expense.....	890	
Insurance Expense	315	
Miscellaneous Expense	1,505	
	106,390	106,390

Discussion Questions

1. How are revenues and expenses reported on the income statement under (a) the cash basis of accounting and (b) the accrual basis of accounting?

2. Is the matching concept related to (a) the cash basis of accounting or (b) the accrual basis of accounting?

3. Why are adjusting entries needed at the end of an accounting period?

4. What is the difference between *adjusting entries* and *correcting entries*?

5. Identify the four different categories of adjusting entries frequently required at the end of an accounting period.

6. If the effect of the debit portion of an adjusting entry is to increase the balance of an asset account, which of the following statements describes the effect of the credit portion of the entry?

   a. Increases the balance of a revenue account.

   b. Increases the balance of an expense account.

   c. Increases the balance of a liability account.

7. If the effect of the credit portion of an adjusting entry is to increase the balance of a liability account, which of the following statements describes the effect of the debit portion of the entry?

   a. Increases the balance of a revenue account.

   b. Increases the balance of an expense account.

   c. Increases the balance of an asset account.

8. Does every adjusting entry have an effect on determining the amount of net income for a period? Explain.

9. On November 1 of the current year, a business paid the November rent on the building that it occupies. (a) Do the rights acquired at November 1 represent an asset or an expense? (b) What is the justification for debiting Rent Expense at the time of payment?

10. (a) Explain the purpose of the two accounts: Depreciation Expense and Accumulated Depreciation. (b) What is the normal balance of each account? (c) Is it customary for the balances of the two accounts to be equal in amount? (d) In what financial statements, if any, will each account appear?

Practice Exercises

Learning Objectives	Example Exercises	
OBJ. 1	EE 3-1 p. 105	**PE 3-1A Accounts requiring adjustment**

Indicate with a Yes or No whether or not each of the following accounts normally requires an adjusting entry.

a. Accumulated Depreciation   c. Office Equipment   e. Supplies

b. Albert Stucky, Drawing   d. Salaries Payable   f. Unearned Rent

| OBJ. 1 | EE 3-1 p. 105 | **PE 3-1B   Accounts requiring adjustment** |

Indicate with a Yes or No whether or not each of the following accounts normally requires an adjusting entry.

a. Building   c. Interest Expense   e. Pam Ingersoll, Capital

b. Cash   d. Miscellaneous Expense   f. Prepaid Insurance

| OBJ. 1 | EE 3-2 p. 109 | **PE 3-2A   Type of adjustment** |

Classify the following items as (1) prepaid expense, (2) unearned revenue, (3) accrued revenue, or (4) accrued expense.

a. Cash received for services not yet rendered   c. Rent revenue earned but not received

b. Insurance paid   d. Salaries owed but not yet paid

| OBJ. 1 | EE 3-2 p. 109 | **PE 3-2B   Type of adjustment** |

Classify the following items as (1) prepaid expense, (2) unearned revenue, (3) accrued revenue, or (4) accrued expense.

a. Cash received for use of land next month   c. Rent expense owed but not yet paid

b. Fees earned but not received   d. Supplies on hand

| OBJ. 2 | EE 3-3 p. 112 | **PE 3-3A   Adjustment for prepaid expense** |

The supplies account had a beginning balance of $2,400 and was debited for $3,975 for supplies purchased during the year. Journalize the adjusting entry required at the end of the year assuming the amount of supplies on hand is $1,375.

| OBJ. 2 | EE 3-3 p. 112 | **PE 3-3B   Adjustment for prepaid expense** |

The prepaid insurance account had a beginning balance of $7,200 and was debited for $4,800 of premiums paid during the year. Journalize the adjusting entry required at the end of the year assuming the amount of unexpired insurance related to future periods is $8,000.

| OBJ. 2 | EE 3-4 p. 113 | **PE 3-4A   Adjustment for unearned revenue** |

The balance in the unearned fees account, before adjustment at the end of the year, is $178,900. Journalize the adjusting entry required assuming the amount of unearned fees at the end of the year is $18,650.

| OBJ. 2 | EE 3-4 p. 113 | **PE 3-4B   Adjustment for unearned revenue** |

On August 1, 2012, Treadwell Co. received $10,500 for the rent of land for 12 months. Journalize the adjusting entry required for unearned rent on December 31, 2012.

| OBJ. 2 | EE 3-5 p. 114 | **PE 3-5A   Adjustment for accrued revenues** |

At the end of the current year, $11,600 of fees have been earned but have not been billed to clients. Journalize the adjusting entry to record the accrued fees.

Learning Objectives	Example Exercises	
OBJ. 2	EE 3-5 *p. 114*	

PE 3-5B   Adjustment for accrued revenues

At the end of the current year, $21,750 of fees have been earned but have not been billed to clients. Journalize the adjusting entry to record the accrued fees.

OBJ. 2	EE 3-6 *p. 116*	

PE 3-6A   Adjustment for accrued expense

Stress Free Realty Co. pays weekly salaries of $18,000 on Friday for a five-day workweek ending on that day. Journalize the necessary adjusting entry at the end of the accounting period assuming that the period ends on Thursday.

OBJ. 2	EE 3-6 *p. 116*	

PE 3-6B   Adjustment for accrued expense

ABC Realty Co. pays weekly salaries of $34,500 on Monday for a six-day workweek ending the preceding Saturday. Journalize the necessary adjusting entry at the end of the accounting period assuming that the period ends on Wednesday.

OBJ. 2	EE 3-7 *p. 119*	

PE 3-7A   Adjustment for depreciation

The estimated amount of depreciation on equipment for the current year is $11,500. Journalize the adjusting entry to record the depreciation.

OBJ. 2	EE 3-7 *p. 119*	

PE 3-7B   Adjustment for depreciation

The estimated amount of depreciation on equipment for the current year is $3,800. Journalize the adjusting entry to record the depreciation.

OBJ. 3	EE 3-8 *p. 119*	

PE 3-8A   Effect of omitting adjustments

For the year ending January 31, 2012, Balboa Medical Co. mistakenly omitted adjusting entries for (1) depreciation of $7,200, (2) fees earned that were not billed of $33,300, and (3) accrued wages of $6,000. Indicate the combined effect of the errors on (a) revenues, (b) expenses, and (c) net income for the year ended January 31, 2012.

OBJ. 3	EE 3-8 *p. 119*	

PE 3-8B   Effect of omitting adjustments

For the year ending June 30, 2012, Aspen Medical Services Co. mistakenly omitted adjusting entries for (1) $2,100 of supplies that were used, (2) unearned revenue of $13,900 that was earned, and (3) insurance of $12,000 that expired. Indicate the combined effect of the errors on (a) revenues, (b) expenses, and (c) net income for the year ended June 30, 2012.

OBJ. 4	EE 3-9 *p. 124*	

PE 3-9A   Effect of errors on adjusted trial balance

For each of the following errors, considered individually, indicate whether the error would cause the adjusted trial balance totals to be unequal. If the error would cause the adjusted trial balance totals to be unequal, indicate whether the debit or credit total is higher and by how much.

a. The adjustment of $17,520 for accrued fees earned was journalized as a debit to Accounts Receivable for $17,520 and a credit to Fees Earned for $17,250.

b. The adjustment of depreciation of $4,000 was omitted from the end-of-period adjusting entries.

OBJ. 4	EE 3-9 *p. 124*	

PE 3-9B   Effect of errors on adjusted trial balance

For each of the following errors, considered individually, indicate whether the error would cause the adjusted trial balance totals to be unequal. If the error would cause the adjusted trial balance totals to be unequal, indicate whether the debit or credit total is higher and by how much.

a. The adjustment for accrued wages of $3,600 was journalized as a debit to Wages Expense for $3,600 and a credit to Accounts Payable for $3,600.

b. The entry for $1,480 of supplies used during the period was journalized as a debit to Supplies Expense of $1,480 and a credit to Supplies of $1,840.

PE 3-10A   Vertical analysis

Two income statements for Fortson Company are shown below.

Fortson Company
Income Statements
For Years Ended December 31

	2012	2011
Fees earned	$425,000	$375,000
Operating expenses	263,500	225,000
Operating income	$161,500	$150,000

a. Prepare a vertical analysis of Fortson Company's income statements.

b. Does the vertical analysis indicate a favorable or unfavorable trend?

PE 3-10B   Vertical analysis

Two income statements for Bradford Company are shown below.

Bradford Company
Income Statements
For Years Ended December 31

	2012	2011
Fees earned	$825,000	$700,000
Operating expenses	684,750	602,000
Operating income	$140,250	$ 98,000

a. Prepare a vertical analysis of Bradford Company's income statements.

b. Does the vertical analysis indicate a favorable or unfavorable trend?

Exercises

OBJ. 1

EX 3-1   Classifying types of adjustments

Classify the following items as (a) prepaid expense, (b) unearned revenue, (c) accrued revenue, or (d) accrued expense.

1. A three-year premium paid on a fire insurance policy.

2. Fees earned but not yet received.

3. Fees received but not yet earned.

4. Salary owed but not yet paid.

5. Subscriptions received in advance by a magazine publisher.

6. Supplies on hand.

7. Taxes owed but payable in the following period.

8. Utilities owed but not yet paid.

OBJ. 1

EX 3-2   Classifying adjusting entries

The following accounts were taken from the unadjusted trial balance of Orion Co., a congressional lobbying firm. Indicate whether or not each account would normally require an adjusting entry. If the account normally requires an adjusting entry, use the following notation to indicate the type of adjustment:

AE—Accrued Expense

AR—Accrued Revenue

PE—Prepaid Expense

UR—Unearned Revenue

To illustrate, the answer for the first account is shown below.

Account	Answer
Accounts Receivable	Normally requires adjustment (AR).
Cash	
Interest Expense	
Interest Receivable	
Johann Atkins, Capital	
Land	
Office Equipment	
Prepaid Rent	
Supplies	
Unearned Fees	
Wages Expense	

OBJ. 2

EX 3-3 Adjusting entry for supplies

The balance in the supplies account, before adjustment at the end of the year, is $3,915. Journalize the adjusting entry required if the amount of supplies on hand at the end of the year is $1,750.

OBJ. 2

EX 3-4 Determining supplies purchased

The supplies and supplies expense accounts at December 31, after adjusting entries have been posted at the end of the first year of operations, are shown in the following T accounts:

Supplies			Supplies Expense	
Bal.	900		Bal.	2,750

Determine the amount of supplies purchased during the year.

OBJ. 2, 3

EX 3-5 Effect of omitting adjusting entry

At August 31, the end of the first month of operations, the usual adjusting entry transferring prepaid insurance expired to an expense account is omitted. Which items will be incorrectly stated, because of the error, on (a) the income statement for August and (b) the balance sheet as of August 31? Also indicate whether the items in error will be overstated or understated.

OBJ. 2

EX 3-6 Adjusting entries for prepaid insurance

The balance in the prepaid insurance account, before adjustment at the end of the year, is $14,800. Journalize the adjusting entry required under each of the following *alternatives* for determining the amount of the adjustment: (a) the amount of insurance expired during the year is $11,200; (b) the amount of unexpired insurance applicable to future periods is $3,600.

OBJ. 2

EX 3-7 Adjusting entries for prepaid insurance

The prepaid insurance account had a balance of $4,800 at the beginning of the year. The account was debited for $15,000 for premiums on policies purchased during the year. Journalize the adjusting entry required at the end of the year for each of the following situations: (a) the amount of unexpired insurance applicable to future periods is $5,000; (b) the amount of insurance expired during the year is $14,800.

OBJ. 2

✔ Amount of entry: $36,000

EX 3-8 Adjusting entries for unearned fees

The balance in the unearned fees account, before adjustment at the end of the year, is $45,000. Journalize the adjusting entry required if the amount of unearned fees at the end of the year is $9,000.

OBJ. 2, 3

EX 3-9 Effect of omitting adjusting entry

At the end of October, the first month of the business year, the usual adjusting entry transferring rent earned to a revenue account from the unearned rent account was omitted. Indicate which items will be incorrectly stated, because of the error, on (a) the income statement for October and (b) the balance sheet as of October 31. Also indicate whether the items in error will be overstated or understated.

OBJ. 2

EX 3-10 Adjusting entry for accrued fees

At the end of the current year, $12,300 of fees have been earned but have not been billed to clients.

a. Journalize the adjusting entry to record the accrued fees.

b. If the cash basis rather than the accrual basis had been used, would an adjusting entry have been necessary? Explain.

OBJ. 2

EX 3-11 Adjusting entries for unearned and accrued fees

The balance in the unearned fees account, before adjustment at the end of the year, is $96,000. Of these fees, $78,500 have been earned. In addition, $23,600 of fees have been earned but have not been billed. Journalize the adjusting entries (a) to adjust the unearned fees account and (b) to record the accrued fees.

OBJ. 2, 3

EX 3-12 Effect of omitting adjusting entry

The adjusting entry for accrued fees was omitted at July 31, the end of the current year. Indicate which items will be in error, because of the omission, on (a) the income statement for the current year and (b) the balance sheet as of July 31. Also indicate whether the items in error will be overstated or understated.

OBJ. 2

✔ a. Amount of entry: $3,750

EX 3-13 Adjusting entries for accrued salaries

Torrey Realty Co. pays weekly salaries of $9,375 on Friday for a five-day workweek ending on that day. Journalize the necessary adjusting entry at the end of the accounting period assuming that the period ends (a) on Tuesday and (b) on Thursday.

OBJ. 2

EX 3-14 Determining wages paid

The wages payable and wages expense accounts at January 31, after adjusting entries have been posted at the end of the first month of operations, are shown in the following T accounts:

Wages Payable		Wages Expense	
	Bal. 3,750	Bal. 41,250	

Determine the amount of wages paid during the month.

OBJ. 2, 3

EX 3-15 Effect of omitting adjusting entry

Accrued salaries owed to employees for December 30 and 31 are not considered in preparing the financial statements for the year ended December 31. Indicate which items will be erroneously stated, because of the error, on (a) the income statement for the year and (b) the balance sheet as of December 31. Also indicate whether the items in error will be overstated or understated.

OBJ. 2, 3

EX 3-16 Effect of omitting adjusting entry

Assume that the error in Exercise 3-15 was not corrected and that the accrued salaries were included in the first salary payment in January. Indicate which items will be erroneously stated, because of failure to correct the initial error, on (a) the income statement for the month of January and (b) the balance sheet as of January 31.

OBJ. 2

✔ b. $41,250

EX 3-17 Adjusting entries for prepaid and accrued taxes

Andular Financial Services was organized on April 1 of the current year. On April 2, Andular prepaid $9,000 to the city for taxes (license fees) for the *next* 12 months and debited the prepaid taxes account. Andular is also required to pay in January an annual tax (on property) for the *previous* calendar year. The estimated amount of the property tax for the current year (April 1 to December 31) is $34,500.

a. Journalize the two adjusting entries required to bring the accounts affected by the two taxes up to date as of December 31, the end of the current year.

b. What is the amount of tax expense for the current year?

OBJ. 2

EX 3-18 Adjustment for depreciation

The estimated amount of depreciation on equipment for the current year is $2,900. Journalize the adjusting entry to record the depreciation.

OBJ. 2

EX 3-19 Determining fixed asset's book value

The balance in the equipment account is $750,000, and the balance in the accumulated depreciation—equipment account is $425,000.

a. What is the book value of the equipment?

b. Does the balance in the accumulated depreciation account mean that the equipment's loss of value is $425,000? Explain.

OBJ. 2

EX 3-20 Book value of fixed assets

In a recent balance sheet, Microsoft Corporation reported *Property, Plant, and Equipment* of $15,082 million and *Accumulated Depreciation* of $7,547 million.

a. What was the book value of the fixed assets?

b. Would the book value of Microsoft Corporation's fixed assets normally approximate their fair market values?

OBJ. 2, 3

EX 3-21 Effects of errors on financial statements

For a recent period, the balance sheet for Costco Wholesale Corporation reported accrued expenses of $1,720 million. For the same period, Costco reported income before income taxes of $1,714 million. Assume that the adjusting entry for $1,720 million of accrued expenses was not recorded at the end of the current period. What would have been the income (loss) before income taxes?

OBJ. 2, 3

EX 3-22 Effects of errors on financial statements

For a recent year, the balance sheet for The Campbell Soup Company includes accrued expenses of $579 million. The income before taxes for The Campbell Soup Company for the year was $1,079 million.

a. Assume the adjusting entry for $579 million of accrued expenses was not recorded at the end of the year. By how much would income before taxes have been misstated?

b. What is the percentage of the misstatement in (a) to the reported income of $1,079 million? Round to one decimal place.

OBJ. 2, 3

✔ 1. a. Revenue understated, $18,000

EX 3-23 Effects of errors on financial statements

The accountant for Hallmark Medical Co., a medical services consulting firm, mistakenly omitted adjusting entries for (a) unearned revenue earned during the year ($18,000) and (b) accrued wages ($3,000). Indicate the effect of each error, considered individually, on the income statement for the current year ended May 31. Also indicate the effect of each error on the May 31 balance sheet. Set up a table similar to the following, and record your answers by inserting the dollar amount in the appropriate spaces. Insert a zero if the error does not affect the item.

	Error (a)		Error (b)	
	Over-stated	Under-stated	Over-stated	Under-stated
1. Revenue for the year would be	$ _____	$ _____	$ _____	$ _____
2. Expenses for the year would be	$ _____	$ _____	$ _____	$ _____
3. Net income for the year would be	$ _____	$ _____	$ _____	$ _____
4. Assets at May 31 would be	$ _____	$ _____	$ _____	$ _____
5. Liabilities at May 31 would be	$ _____	$ _____	$ _____	$ _____
6. Owner's equity at May 31 would be	$ _____	$ _____	$ _____	$ _____

OBJ. 2, 3

EX 3-24 Effects of errors on financial statements

If the net income for the current year had been $240,000 in Exercise 3-23, what would have been the correct net income if the proper adjusting entries had been made?

OBJ. 2, 3

EX 3-25 Adjusting entries for depreciation; effect of error

On December 31, a business estimates depreciation on equipment used during the first year of operations to be $14,500.

a. Journalize the adjusting entry required as of December 31.

b. If the adjusting entry in (a) were omitted, which items would be erroneously stated on (1) the income statement for the year and (2) the balance sheet as of December 31?

OBJ. 4

EX 3-26 Adjusting entries from trial balances

The unadjusted and adjusted trial balances for McWay Services Co. on August 31, 2012, are shown below.

McWay Services Co.
Trial Balance
August 31, 2012

	Unadjusted		Adjusted	
	Debit Balances	Credit Balances	Debit Balances	Credit Balances
Cash	8		8	
Accounts Receivable.................................	19		21	
Supplies...	6		5	
Prepaid Insurance	10		6	
Land	13		13	
Equipment..	20		20	
Accumulated Depreciation—Equipment		4		5
Accounts Payable		13		13
Wages Payable......................................		0		1
Chad McWay, Capital		46		46
Chad McWay, Drawing...............................	4		4	
Fees Earned...		37		39
Wages Expense	12		13	
Rent Expense	4		4	
Insurance Expense	0		4	
Utilities Expense	2		2	
Depreciation Expense	0		1	
Supplies Expense....................................	0		1	
Miscellaneous Expense	2		2	
	100	100	104	104

Journalize the five entries that adjusted the accounts at August 31, 2012. None of the accounts were affected by more than one adjusting entry.

OBJ. 4

✔ Corrected trial balance totals, $360,950

EX 3-27 Adjusting entries from trial balances

The accountant for E-Z Laundry prepared the following unadjusted and adjusted trial balances. Assume that all balances in the unadjusted trial balance and the amounts of the adjustments are correct. Identify the errors in the accountant's adjusting entries assuming that none of the accounts were affected by more than one adjusting entry.

E-Z Laundry
Trial Balance
July 31, 2012

	Unadjusted		Adjusted	
	Debit Balances	Credit Balances	Debit Balances	Credit Balances
Cash	7,500		7,500	
Accounts Receivable.................................	18,250		22,000	
Laundry Supplies....................................	3,750		5,500	
Prepaid Insurance*	5,200		1,400	
Laundry Equipment	190,000		184,000	
Accumulated Depreciation—Laundry Equipment.......		48,000		48,000
Accounts Payable		9,600		9,600
Wages Payable......................................				1,200
Myrna Lundy, Capital		110,300		110,300
Myrna Lundy, Drawing...............................	28,775		28,775	
Laundry Revenue....................................		182,100		182,100
Wages Expense	49,200		49,200	
Rent Expense	25,575		25,575	
Utilities Expense	18,500		18,500	
Depreciation Expense			6,000	
Laundry Supplies Expense			1,750	
Insurance Expense			800	
Miscellaneous Expense	3,250		3,250	
	350,000	350,000	354,250	351,200

* 3,800 of insurance expired during the year.

OBJ. 5

EX 3-28 Vertical analysis of income statement

The following data (in millions) are taken from the financial statements of Nike Inc. for the years ending May 31, 2009 and 2008:

	2009	2008
Net sales (revenues)	$19,176	$18,627
Net income	1,487	1,883

a. Determine the amount of change (in millions) and percent of change in net income for 2009. Round to one decimal place.

b. Determine the percentage relationship between net income and net sales (net income divided by net sales) for 2009 and 2008. Round to one decimal place.

c. What conclusions can you draw from your analysis?

OBJ. 5

EX 3-29 Vertical analysis of income statement

The following income statement data (in millions) for Dell Inc. and Hewlett-Packard Company (HP) were taken from their recent annual reports:

	Dell	Hewlett-Packard
Net sales	$ 61,101	$118,364
Cost of goods sold (expense)	(50,144)	(89,592)
Operating expenses	(7,767)	(17,970)
Operating income (loss)	$ 3,190	$ 10,802

a. Prepare a vertical analysis of the income statement for Dell. Round to one decimal place.

b. Prepare a vertical analysis of the income statement for HP. Round to one decimal place.

c. Based on (a) and (b), how does Dell compare to HP?

Problems Series A

OBJ. 2

PR 3-1A Adjusting entries

On October 31, 2012, the following data were accumulated to assist the accountant in preparing the adjusting entries for Dependable Realty:

a. The supplies account balance on October 31 is $3,975. The supplies on hand on October 31 are $1,050.

b. The unearned rent account balance on October 31 is $11,000, representing the receipt of an advance payment on October 1 of four months' rent from tenants.

c. Wages accrued but not paid at October 31 are $2,500.

d. Fees accrued but unbilled at October 31 are $4,900.

e. Depreciation of office equipment is $1,100.

Instructions

1. Journalize the adjusting entries required at October 31, 2012.

2. Briefly explain the difference between adjusting entries and entries that would be made to correct errors.

OBJ. 2, 3

PR 3-2A Adjusting entries

Selected account balances before adjustment for Newhouse Realty at March 31, 2012, the end of the current year, are as follows:

	Debits	Credits
Accounts Receivable	$ 80,000	
Equipment	150,000	
Accumulated Depreciation		$ 28,000
Prepaid Rent	6,000	

(Continued)

	Debits	Credits
Supplies	$ 3,000	
Wages Payable		—
Unearned Fees		$ 10,500
Fees Earned		410,000
Wages Expense	190,000	
Rent Expense	—	
Depreciation Expense	—	
Supplies Expense	—	

Data needed for year-end adjustments are as follows:

a. Unbilled fees at March 31, $13,500.

b. Supplies on hand at March 31, $950.

c. Rent expired, $4,000.

d. Depreciation of equipment during year, $1,500.

e. Unearned fees at March 31, $2,500.

f. Wages accrued but not paid at March 31, $2,200.

Instructions

1. Journalize the six adjusting entries required at March 31, based on the data presented.

2. What would be the effect on the income statement if adjustments (a) and (f) were omitted at the end of the year?

3. What would be the effect on the balance sheet if adjustments (a) and (f) were omitted at the end of the year?

4. What would be the effect on the "Net increase or decrease in cash" on the statement of cash flows if adjustments (a) and (f) were omitted at the end of the year?

OBJ. 2

PR 3-3A   Adjusting entries

Econo Company, an electronics repair store, prepared the unadjusted trial balance shown below at the end of its first year of operations.

Econo Company
Unadjusted Trial Balance
April 30, 2012

	Debit Balances	Credit Balances
Cash	13,800	
Accounts Receivable..	90,000	
Supplies..	21,600	
Equipment...	454,800	
Accounts Payable		21,000
Unearned Fees...		24,000
Randy Huntsinger, Capital		312,000
Randy Huntsinger, Drawing	18,000	
Fees Earned...		543,000
Wages Expense	126,000	
Rent Expense	96,000	
Utilities Expense	69,000	
Miscellaneous Expense	10,800	
	900,000	900,000

For preparing the adjusting entries, the following data were assembled:

a. Fees earned but unbilled on April 30 were $10,000.

b. Supplies on hand on April 30 were $8,150.

c. Depreciation of equipment was estimated to be $13,800 for the year.

d. The balance in unearned fees represented the April 1 receipt in advance for services to be provided. Only $19,000 of the services was provided between April 1 and April 30.

e. Unpaid wages accrued on April 30 were $1,770.

Instructions

1. Journalize the adjusting entries necessary on April 30, 2012.

2. Determine the revenues, expenses, and net income of Econo Company before the adjusting entries.

3. Determine the revenues, expense, and net income of Econo Company after the adjusting entries.

4. Determine the effect on Randy Huntsinger, Capital of the adjusting entries.

OBJ. 2, 3, 4

PR 3-4A Adjusting entries

Timken Company specializes in the repair of music equipment and is owned and operated by Secilia Timken. On April 30, 2012, the end of the current year, the accountant for Timken Company prepared the following trial balances:

Timken Company
Trial Balance
April 30, 2012

	Unadjusted		Adjusted	
	Debit Balances	Credit Balances	Debit Balances	Credit Balances
Cash	38,250		38,250	
Accounts Receivable...............................	109,500		109,500	
Supplies..	11,250		3,500	
Prepaid Insurance	14,250		2,700	
Equipment..	360,450		360,450	
Accumulated Depreciation—Equipment		94,500		107,000
Automobiles......................................	109,500		109,500	
Accumulated Depreciation—Automobiles		54,750		57,500
Accounts Payable		24,930		26,000
Salaries Payable...................................		—		7,500
Unearned Service Fees.............................		18,000		6,000
Secilia Timken, Capital		394,020		394,020
Secilia Timken, Drawing............................	75,000		75,000	
Service Fees Earned		733,800		745,800
Salary Expense....................................	516,900		524,400	
Rent Expense	54,000		54,000	
Supplies Expense..................................	—		7,750	
Depreciation Expense—Equipment..................	—		12,500	
Depreciation Expense—Automobiles	—		2,750	
Utilities Expense	12,900		13,970	
Taxes Expense.....................................	8,175		8,175	
Insurance Expense	—		11,550	
Miscellaneous Expense	9,825		9,825	
	1,320,000	1,320,000	1,343,820	1,343,820

Instructions

Journalize the seven entries that adjusted the accounts at June 30. None of the accounts were affected by more than one adjusting entry.

OBJ. 2, 3, 4

✔ 2. Total of Debit column: $819,550

PR 3-5A Adjusting entries and adjusted trial balances

Galloway Company is a small editorial services company owned and operated by Fran Briggs. On July 31, 2012, the end of the current year, Galloway Company's accounting clerk prepared the unadjusted trial balance shown on the next page.

The data needed to determine year-end adjustments are as follows:

a. Unexpired insurance at July 31, $4,800.

b. Supplies on hand at July 31, $600.

c. Depreciation of building for the year, $3,100.

d. Depreciation of equipment for the year, $2,700.

e. Rent unearned at July 31, $1,750.

f. Accrued salaries and wages at July 31, $3,000.

g. Fees earned but unbilled on July 31, $10,750.

Galloway Company
Unadjusted Trial Balance
July 31, 2012

	Debit Balances	Credit Balances
Cash	7,500	
Accounts Receivable	38,400	
Prepaid Insurance	7,200	
Supplies	1,980	
Land	112,500	
Building	200,250	
Accumulated Depreciation—Building		137,550
Equipment	135,300	
Accumulated Depreciation—Equipment		97,950
Accounts Payable		12,150
Unearned Rent		6,750
Fran Briggs, Capital		221,000
Fran Briggs, Drawing	15,000	
Fees Earned		324,600
Salaries and Wages Expense	193,370	
Utilities Expense	42,375	
Advertising Expense	22,800	
Repairs Expense	17,250	
Miscellaneous Expense	6,075	
	800,000	800,000

Instructions

1. Journalize the adjusting entries using the following additional accounts: Salaries and Wages Payable; Rent Revenue; Insurance Expense; Depreciation Expense—Building; Depreciation Expense—Equipment; and Supplies Expense.

2. Determine the balances of the accounts affected by the adjusting entries, and prepare an adjusted trial balance.

OBJ. 2, 3

✔ 2. Corrected net income: $92,300

PR 3-6A Adjusting entries and errors

At the end of June, the first month of operations, the following selected data were taken from the financial statements of Beth Cato, an attorney:

Net income for June	$ 80,000
Total assets at June 30	500,000
Total liabilities at June 30	200,000
Total owner's equity at June 30	300,000

In preparing the financial statements, adjustments for the following data were overlooked:

a. Supplies used during June, $1,500.

b. Unbilled fees earned at June 30, $18,000.

c. Depreciation of equipment for June, $3,000.

d. Accrued wages at June 30, $1,200.

Instructions

1. Journalize the entries to record the omitted adjustments.

2. Determine the correct amount of net income for June and the total assets, liabilities, and owner's equity at June 30. In addition to indicating the corrected amounts, indicate the effect of each omitted adjustment by setting up and completing a columnar table similar to the following. Adjustment (a) is presented as an example.

(Continued)

	Net Income	Total Assets	=	Total Liabilities	+	Total Owner's Equity
Reported amounts	$80,000	$500,000		$200,000		$300,000
Corrections:						
Adjustment (a)	−1,500	−1,500		0		−1,500
Adjustment (b)						
Adjustment (c)						
Adjustment (d)						
Corrected amounts						

Problems Series B

PR 3-1B   Adjusting entries

On January 31, 2012, the following data were accumulated to assist the accountant in preparing the adjusting entries for Oceanside Realty:

a. Fees accrued but unbilled at January 31 are $10,280.

b. The supplies account balance on January 31 is $6,100. The supplies on hand at January 31 are $1,300.

c. Wages accrued but not paid at January 31 are $3,000.

d. The unearned rent account balance at January 31 is $4,500, representing the receipt of an advance payment on January 1 of three months' rent from tenants.

e. Depreciation of office equipment is $1,400.

Instructions

1. Journalize the adjusting entries required at January 31, 2012.

2. Briefly explain the difference between adjusting entries and entries that would be made to correct errors.

PR 3-2B   Adjusting entries

Selected account balances before adjustment for Skylight Realty at June 30, 2012, the end of the current year, are shown below.

	Debits	Credits
Accounts Receivable	$ 75,000	
Accumulated Depreciation		$ 12,000
Depreciation Expense	—	
Equipment	250,000	
Fees Earned		400,000
Prepaid Rent	12,000	
Rent Expense	—	
Supplies	3,170	
Supplies Expense	—	
Unearned Fees		10,000
Wages Expense	140,000	
Wages Payable		—

Data needed for year-end adjustments are as follows:

a. Supplies on hand at June 30, $800.

b. Depreciation of equipment during year, $750.

c. Rent expired during year, $9,000.

d. Wages accrued but not paid at June 30, $1,700.

e. Unearned fees at June 30, $6,500.

f. Unbilled fees at June 30, $15,000.

Instructions

1. Journalize the six adjusting entries required at June 30, based on the data presented.

2. What would be the effect on the income statement if adjustments (b) and (e) were omitted at the end of the year?

3. What would be the effect on the balance sheet if adjustments (b) and (e) were omitted at the end of the year?

4. What would be the effect on the "Net increase or decrease in cash" on the statement of cash flows if adjustments (b) and (e) were omitted at the end of the year?

OBJ. 2

PR 3-3B Adjusting entries

Brown Trout Outfitters Co., an outfitter store for fishing treks, prepared the following unadjusted trial balance at the end of its first year of operations:

Brown Trout Outfitters Co.
Unadjusted Trial Balance
September 30, 2012

	Debit Balances	Credit Balances
Cash	26,400	
Accounts Receivable	87,600	
Supplies	7,200	
Equipment	162,000	
Accounts Payable		12,200
Unearned Fees		19,200
Jon Wolfe, Capital		222,800
Jon Wolfe, Drawing	10,000	
Fees Earned		295,800
Wages Expense	152,800	
Rent Expense	55,000	
Utilities Expense	42,000	
Miscellaneous Expense	7,000	
	550,000	550,000

For preparing the adjusting entries, the following data were assembled:

a. Supplies on hand on September 30 were $1,850.

b. Fees earned but unbilled on September 30 were $6,500.

c. Depreciation of equipment was estimated to be $2,800 for the year.

d. Unpaid wages accrued on September 30 were $1,275.

e. The balance in unearned fees represented the September 1 receipt in advance for services to be provided. Only $3,000 of the services was provided between September 1 and September 30.

Instructions

1. Journalize the adjusting entries necessary on September 30, 2012.

2. Determine the revenues, expenses, and net income of Brown Trout Outfitters Co. before the adjusting entries.

3. Determine the revenues, expense, and net income of Brown Trout Outfitters Co. after the adjusting entries.

4. Determine the effect on Jon Wolfe, Capital of the adjusting entries.

OBJ. 2, 3, 4

PR 3-4B Adjusting entries

Goldfinch Company specializes in the maintenance and repair of signs, such as billboards. On January 31, 2012, the accountant for Goldfinch Company prepared the following trial balances:

(*Continued*)

Goldfinch Company
Trial Balance
January 31, 2012

	Unadjusted		Adjusted	
	Debit Balances	Credit Balances	Debit Balances	Credit Balances
Cash	4,750		4,750	
Accounts Receivable................................	17,400		17,400	
Supplies	6,200		1,475	
Prepaid Insurance	9,000		2,700	
Land	50,000		50,000	
Buildings	120,000		120,000	
Accumulated Depreciation—Buildings...............		51,500		60,000
Trucks..	75,000		75,000	
Accumulated Depreciation—Trucks..................		12,000		13,550
Accounts Payable		6,920		8,000
Salaries Payable		—		750
Unearned Service Fees.............................		10,500		6,000
Marsha Parlik, Capital..............................		156,400		156,400
Marsha Parlik, Drawing	7,500		7,500	
Service Fees Earned		162,680		167,180
Salary Expense....................................	80,000		80,750	
Depreciation Expense—Trucks	—		1,550	
Rent Expense	11,900		11,900	
Supplies Expense..................................	—		4,725	
Utilities Expense	6,200		7,280	
Depreciation Expense—Buildings	—		8,500	
Taxes Expense	2,900		2,900	
Insurance Expense	—		6,300	
Miscellaneous Expense	9,150		9,150	
	400,000	400,000	411,880	411,880

Instructions

Journalize the seven entries that adjusted the accounts at January 31. None of the accounts were affected by more than one adjusting entry.

OBJ. 2, 3, 4

✔ 2. Total of Debit column: $340,075

PR 3-5B Adjusting entries and adjusted trial balances

Pacific Financial Services Co., which specializes in appliance repair services, is owned and operated by Eileen Hastings. Pacific Financial Services Co.'s accounting clerk prepared the unadjusted trial balance at October 31, 2012, shown below.

Pacific Financial Services Co.
Unadjusted Trial Balance
October 31, 2012

	Debit Balances	Credit Balances
Cash	10,200	
Accounts Receivable...	34,750	
Prepaid Insurance	6,000	
Supplies	1,725	
Land	50,000	
Building	80,750	
Accumulated Depreciation—Building............................		37,850
Equipment..	45,000	
Accumulated Depreciation—Equipment		17,650
Accounts Payable		3,750
Unearned Rent		3,600
Eileen Hastings, Capital		103,550
Eileen Hastings, Drawing	8,000	
Fees Earned...		158,600
Salaries and Wages Expense.....................................	56,850	
Utilities Expense	14,100	
Advertising Expense	7,500	
Repairs Expense..	6,100	
Miscellaneous Expense	4,025	
	325,000	325,000

The data needed to determine year-end adjustments are as follows:

a. Depreciation of building for the year, $1,900.

b. Depreciation of equipment for the year, $2,400.

c. Accrued salaries and wages at October 31, $1,375.

d. Unexpired insurance at October 31, $2,700.

e. Fees earned but unbilled on October 31, $9,400.

f. Supplies on hand at October 31, $325.

g. Rent unearned at October 31, $1,800.

Instructions

1. Journalize the adjusting entries using the following additional accounts: Salaries and Wages Payable; Rent Revenue; Insurance Expense; Depreciation Expense—Building; Depreciation Expense—Equipment; and Supplies Expense.

2. Determine the balances of the accounts affected by the adjusting entries and prepare an adjusted trial balance.

OBJ. 2, 3

✔ 2. Corrected net income: $150,500

PR 3-6B   Adjusting entries and errors

At the end of March, the first month of operations, the following selected data were taken from the financial statements of Kurt Reibel, an attorney:

Net income for March	$ 150,000
Total assets at March 31	1,000,000
Total liabilities at March 31	350,000
Total owner's equity at March 31	650,000

In preparing the financial statements, adjustments for the following data were overlooked:

a. Unbilled fees earned at March 31, $15,000.

b. Depreciation of equipment for March, $9,000.

c. Accrued wages at March 31, $3,500.

d. Supplies used during March, $2,000.

Instructions

1. Journalize the entries to record the omitted adjustments.

2. Determine the correct amount of net income for March and the total assets, liabilities, and owner's equity at March 31. In addition to indicating the corrected amounts, indicate the effect of each omitted adjustment by setting up and completing a columnar table similar to the following. Adjustment (a) is presented as an example.

	Net Income	Total Assets	+ Total Liabilities	= Total Owner's Equity
Reported amounts	$150,000	$1,000,000	$350,000	$650,000
Corrections:				
Adjustment (a)	+15,000	+15,000	0	+15,000
Adjustment (b)				
Adjustment (c)				
Adjustment (d)				
Corrected amounts				

Continuing Problem

✔ 3. Total of Debit column: $41,875

The unadjusted trial balance that you prepared for PS Music at the end of Chapter 2 should appear as shown on page 146.

PS Music
Unadjusted Trial Balance
July 31, 2012

	Debit Balances	Credit Balances
Cash	10,510	
Accounts Receivable	3,150	
Supplies	1,250	
Prepaid Insurance	2,700	
Office Equipment	6,000	
Accounts Payable		7,080
Unearned Revenue		7,200
Pat Sharpe, Capital		9,000
Pat Sharpe, Drawing	2,000	
Fees Earned		16,750
Music Expense	3,610	
Wages Expense	2,800	
Office Rent Expense	2,550	
Advertising Expense	1,450	
Equipment Rent Expense	1,300	
Utilities Expense	1,060	
Supplies Expense	180	
Miscellaneous Expense	1,470	
	40,030	40,030

The data needed to determine adjustments for the two-month period ending July 31, 2012, are as follows:

a. During July, PS Music provided guest disc jockeys for WHBD for a total of 120 hours. For information on the amount of the accrued revenue to be billed to WHBD, see the contract described in the July 3, 2012, transaction at the end of Chapter 2.

b. Supplies on hand at July 31, $400.

c. The balance of the prepaid insurance account relates to the July 1, 2012, transaction at the end of Chapter 2.

d. Depreciation of the office equipment is $75.

e. The balance of the unearned revenue account relates to the contract between PS Music and WHBD, described in the July 3, 2012, transaction at the end of Chapter 2.

f. Accrued wages as of July 31, 2012, were $170.

Instructions

1. Prepare adjusting journal entries. You will need the following additional accounts:

   18 Accumulated Depreciation—Office Equipment

   22 Wages Payable

   57 Insurance Expense

   58 Depreciation Expense

2. Post the adjusting entries, inserting balances in the accounts affected.

3. Prepare an adjusted trial balance.

Cases & Projects

CP 3-1   Ethics and professional conduct in business

Joshua Thorp opened Laser Co. on January 1, 2011. At the end of the first year, the business needed additional capital. On behalf of Laser, Joshua applied to Vermont National Bank for a loan of $500,000. Based on Laser financial statements, which had been prepared on a cash basis, the Vermont National Bank loan officer rejected the loan as too risky.

After receiving the rejection notice, Joshua instructed his accountant to prepare the financial statements on an accrual basis. These statements included $90,000 in accounts receivable and $35,000 in accounts payable. Joshua then instructed his accountant to record an additional $25,000 of accounts receivable for commissions on property for which a contract had been signed on December 28, 2011. The title to the property is to transfer on January 5, 2012, when an attorney formally records the transfer of the property to the buyer.

Joshua then applied for a $500,000 loan from NYC Bank, using the revised financial statements. On this application, Joshua indicated that he had not previously been rejected for credit. ━━━━▶ Discuss the ethical and professional conduct of Joshua Thorp in applying for the loan from NYC Bank.

CP 3-2   Accrued expense

On December 30, 2012, you buy a Ford 350F truck. It comes with a three-year, 48,000-mile warranty. On March 5, 2013, you return the truck to the dealership for some basic repairs covered under the warranty. The cost of the repairs to the dealership is $2,400. Assume that based upon past history, Ford Motor Company can reasonably estimate the cost of repairs for each model year for its Ford 350F. In what year, 2012 or 2013, should Ford recognize the cost of the warranty repairs as an expense?

CP 3-3   Accrued revenue

The following is an excerpt from a conversation between Kay Scott and Jeff Lee just before they boarded a flight to London on Delta Air Lines. They are going to London to attend their company's annual sales conference.

Kay: Jeff, aren't you taking an introductory accounting course at college?

Jeff: Yes, I decided it's about time I learned something about accounting. You know, our annual bonuses are based on the sales figures that come from the accounting department.

Kay: I guess I never really thought about it.

Jeff: You should think about it! Last year, I placed a $1,000,000 order on December 28. But when I got my bonus, the $1,000,000 sale wasn't included. They said it hadn't been shipped until January 5, so it would have to count in next year's bonus.

Kay: A real bummer!

Jeff: Right! I was counting on that bonus including the $1,000,000 sale.

Kay: Did you complain?

Jeff: Yes, but it didn't do any good. Lori, the head accountant, said something about matching revenues and expenses. Also, something about not recording revenues until the sale is final. I figure I'd take the accounting course and find out whether she's just messing with me.

Kay: I never really thought about it. When do you think Delta Air Lines will record its revenues from this flight?

Jeff: Hmmm . . . I guess it could record the revenue when it sells the ticket . . . or . . . when the boarding passes are scanned at the door . . . or . . . when we get off the plane . . . or when our company pays for the tickets . . . or . . . I don't know. I'll ask my accounting instructor.

━━━━▶ Discuss when Delta Air Lines should recognize the revenue from ticket sales to properly match revenues and expenses.

CP 3-4   Adjustments and financial statements

Several years ago, your brother opened Granite Appliance Repairs. He made a small initial investment and added money from his personal bank account as needed. He withdrew money for living expenses at irregular intervals. As the business grew, he hired an assistant. He is now considering adding more employees, purchasing additional service trucks, and purchasing the building he now rents. To secure funds for the expansion, your brother submitted a loan application to the bank and included the most recent financial statements (shown below) prepared from accounts maintained by a part-time bookkeeper.

Granite Appliance Repairs
Income Statement
For the Year Ended July 31, 2012

Service revenue		$225,000
Less: Rent paid	$62,400	
Wages paid	49,500	
Supplies paid	14,000	
Utilities paid	13,000	
Insurance paid	7,200	
Miscellaneous payments	18,200	164,300
Net income		$ 60,700

Granite Appliance Repairs
Balance Sheet
July 31, 2012

Assets

Cash	$ 31,800
Amounts due from customers	37,500
Truck	110,700
Total assets	$180,000

Equities

Owner's capital	$180,000

After reviewing the financial statements, the loan officer at the bank asked your brother if he used the accrual basis of accounting for revenues and expenses. Your brother responded that he did and that is why he included an account for "Amounts Due from Customers." The loan officer then asked whether or not the accounts were adjusted prior to the preparation of the statements. Your brother answered that they had not been adjusted.

a. Why do you think the loan officer suspected that the accounts had not been adjusted prior to the preparation of the statements?

b. Indicate possible accounts that might need to be adjusted before an accurate set of financial statements could be prepared.

CP 3-5 Codes of ethics

Obtain a copy of your college or university's student code of conduct. In groups of three or four, answer the following questions:

1. Compare this code of conduct with the accountant's Codes of Professional Conduct, which is linked to the text Web site at **www.cengage.com/accounting/warren**.

2. One of your classmates asks you for permission to copy your homework, which your instructor will be collecting and grading for part of your overall term grade. Although your instructor has not stated whether one student may or may not copy another student's homework, is it ethical for you to allow your classmate to copy your homework? Is it ethical for your classmate to copy your homework?

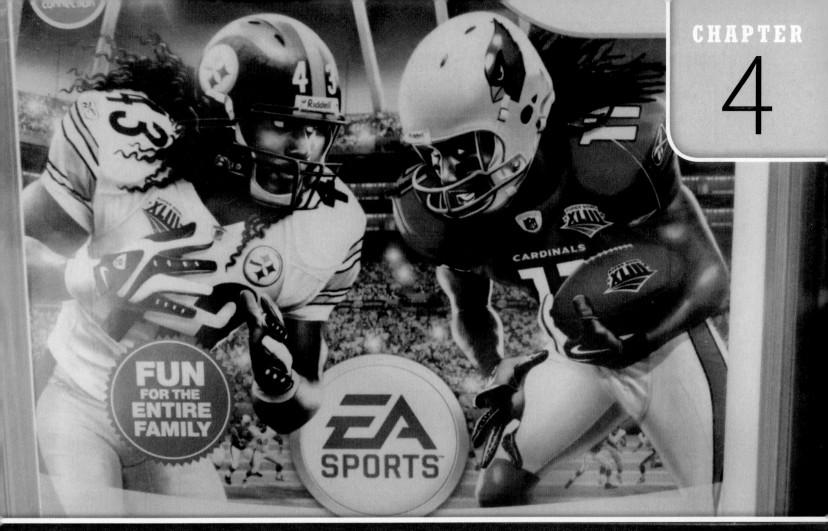

© AP Photo/Paul Sakuma

Completing the Accounting Cycle

Electronic Arts Inc.

Most of us have had to file a personal tax return. At the beginning of the year, you estimate your upcoming income and decide whether you need to increase your payroll tax withholdings or perhaps pay estimated taxes. During the year, you earn income and enter into tax-related transactions, such as making charitable contributions. At the end of the year, your employer sends you a tax withholding information (W-2) form, and you collect the tax records needed for completing your yearly tax forms. As the next year begins, you start the cycle all over again.

Businesses also go through a cycle of activities. For example, Electronic Arts Inc., the world's largest developer and marketer of electronic game software, begins its cycle by developing new or revised game titles, such as Madden NFL Football®, Need for Speed®, The Sims®, and The Lord of the Rings®. These games are marketed and sold throughout the year. During the year, operating transactions of the business are recorded.

For Electronic Arts, such transactions include the salaries of game developers, advertising expenditures, costs for producing and packaging games, and game revenues. At the end of the year, financial statements are prepared that summarize the operating activities for the year. Electronic Arts publishes these statements on its Web site at **http:// investor.ea.com**. Finally, before the start of the next year, the accounts are readied for recording the operations of the next year.

In Chapter 1, the initial cycle for NetSolutions began with Chris Clark's investment in the business on November 1, 2011. The cycle continued with recording NetSolutions' transactions for November and December, as we discussed and illustrated in Chapters 1 and 2. In Chapter 3, the cycle continued when the adjusting entries for the two months ending December 31, 2011, were recorded. In this chapter, the cycle is completed for NetSolutions by preparing financial statements and getting the accounts ready for recording transactions of the next period.

Learning Objectives

After studying this chapter, you should be able to:

		Example Exercises	Page
OBJ. 1	**Describe the flow of accounting information from the unadjusted trial balance into the adjusted trial balance and financial statements.**		
	Flow of Accounting Information	EE 4-1	152
OBJ. 2	**Prepare financial statements from adjusted account balances.**		
	Financial Statements		
	Income Statement		
	Statement of Owner's Equity	EE 4-2	154
	Balance Sheet	EE 4-3	155–156
OBJ. 3	**Prepare closing entries.**		
	Closing Entries		
	Journalizing and Posting Closing Entries	EE 4-4	159
	Post-Closing Trial Balance		
OBJ. 4	**Describe the accounting cycle.**		
	Accounting Cycle	EE 4-5	162
OBJ. 5	**Illustrate the accounting cycle for one period.**		
	Illustration of the Accounting Cycle		
OBJ. 6	**Explain what is meant by the fiscal year and the natural business year.**		
	Fiscal Year		
OBJ. 7	**Describe and illustrate the use of working capital and the current ratio in evaluating a company's financial condition.**		
	Financial Analysis and Interpretation: Working Capital and Current Ratio	EE 4-6	175–176

At a Glance 4 Page 176D

OBJ. 1 Describe the flow of accounting information from the unadjusted trial balance into the adjusted trial balance and financial statements.

Many companies use Microsoft's Excel® software to prepare end-of-period spreadsheets.

Flow of Accounting Information

The process of adjusting the accounts and preparing financial statements is one of the most important in accounting. Using the **NetSolutions** illustration from Chapters 1–3, the end-of-period spreadsheet and flow of accounting data in adjusting accounts and preparing financial statements are summarized in Exhibit 1.

The end-of-period spreadsheet in Exhibit 1 begins with the unadjusted trial balance. The unadjusted trial balance verifies that the total of the debit balances equals the total of the credit balances. If the trial balance totals are unequal, an error has occurred. Any errors must be found and corrected before the end-of-period process can continue.

The adjustments for NetSolutions from Chapter 3 are shown in the Adjustments columns of the spreadsheet. Cross-referencing (by letters) the debit and credit of each adjustment is useful in reviewing the effect of the adjustments on the unadjusted account balances. The adjustments are normally entered in the order in which the data are assembled. If the titles of the accounts to be adjusted do not appear in the unadjusted trial balance, the accounts are inserted in their proper order in the Account Title column. The total of the Adjustments columns verifies that the total debits equal the total credits for the adjusting entries. The total of the Debit column must equal the total of the Credit column.

The adjustments in the spreadsheet are added to or subtracted from the amounts in the Unadjusted Trial Balance columns to arrive at the amounts inserted in the Adjusted Trial Balance columns. In this way, the Adjusted Trial Balance columns of the spreadsheet illustrate the effect of the adjusting entries on the unadjusted accounts. The totals of the Adjusted Trial Balance columns verify that the totals of the debit and credit balances are equal after adjustment.

EXHIBIT 1

**End-of-Period
Spreadsheet
and Flow of
Accounting Data,
NetSolutions**

**NetSolutions
Balance Sheet
December 31, 2011**

Assets			Liabilities		
Current assets:			Current liabilities:		
Cash	$ 2,065		Accounts payable	$900	
Accounts receivable	2,720		Wages payable	250	
Supplies	760		Unearned rent	240	
Prepaid insurance	2,200		Total liabilities		$ 1,390
Total current assets		$ 7,745			
Property, plant, and equipment:					
Land	$20,000				
Office equipment	$1,800		**Owner's Equity**		
Less accum. depreciation	50	1,750			
Total property, plant,			Chris Clark, capital		28,105
and equipment		21,750	Total liabilities and		
Total assets		$29,495	owner's equity		$29,495

**NetSolutions
Statement of Owner's Equity
For the Two Months Ended December 31, 2011**

Chris Clark, capital, November 1, 2011		$ 0
Investment on November 1, 2011	$25,000	
Net income for November and December	7,105	
	$32,105	
Less withdrawals	4,000	
Increase in owner's equity		28,105
Chris Clark, capital, December 31, 2011		$28,105

**NetSolutions
Income Statement
For the Two Months Ended December 31, 2011**

Fees earned		$16,840
Rent revenue		120
Total revenues		$16,960
Expenses:		
Wages expense	$ 4,525	
Supplies expense	2,040	
Rent expense	1,600	
Utilities expense	985	
Insurance expense	200	
Depreciation expense	50	
Miscellaneous expense	455	
Total expenses		9,855
Net income		$ 7,105

NetSolutions
End-of-Period Spreadsheet
For the Two Months Ended December 31, 2011

	A	B	C	D	E	F	G
		Unadjusted		Adjustments		Adjusted	
		Trial Balance				Trial Balance	
6	Account Title	Dr.	Cr.	Dr.	Cr.	Dr.	Cr.
7							
8	Cash	2,065				2,065	
9	Accounts Receivable	2,220		(d) 500		2,720	
10	Supplies	2,000			(a) 1,240	760	
11	Prepaid Insurance	2,400			(b) 200	2,200	
12	Land	20,000				20,000	
13	Office Equipment	1,800				1,800	
14	Accumulated Depreciation				(f) 50		50
15	Accounts Payable		900				900
16	Wages Payable				(e) 250		250
17	Unearned Rent		360	(c) 120			240
18	Chris Clark, Capital		25,000				25,000
19	Chris Clark, Drawing	4,000				4,000	
20	Fees Earned		16,340		(d) 500		16,840
21	Rent Revenue				(c) 120		120
22	Wages Expense	4,275		(e) 250		4,525	
23	Supplies Expense	800		(a) 1,240		2,040	
24	Rent Expense	1,600				1,600	
25	Utilities Expense	985				985	
26	Insurance Expense			(b) 200		200	
27	Depreciation Expense			(f) 50		50	
28	Miscellaneous Expense	455				455	
29		42,600	42,600	2,360	2,360	43,400	43,400
30							

Exhibit 1 also illustrates the flow of accounts from the adjusted trial balance into the financial statements as follows:

1. The revenue and expense accounts (spreadsheet lines 20–28) flow into the income statement.
2. The owner's capital account, Chris Clark, Capital, (spreadsheet line 18) and owner's drawing account, Chris Clark, Drawing, (spreadsheet line 19) flow into the statement of owner's equity. The net income of $7,105 also flows into the statement of owner's equity from the income statement.
3. The asset and liability accounts (spreadsheet lines 8–17) flow into the balance sheet. The end-of-the-period owner's equity (Chris Clark, Capital of $28,105) also flows into the balance sheet from the statement of owner's equity.

To summarize, Exhibit 1 illustrates the process by which accounts are adjusted. In addition, Exhibit 1 illustrates how the adjusted accounts flow into the financial statements. The financial statements for NetSolutions can be prepared directly from Exhibit 1.

The spreadsheet in Exhibit 1 is not required. However, many accountants prepare such a spreadsheet, sometimes called a work sheet, as part of the normal end-of-period process. The primary advantage in doing so is that it allows managers and accountants to see the effect of adjustments on the financial statements. This is especially useful for adjustments that depend upon estimates. Such estimates and their effect on the financial statements are discussed in later chapters.[1]

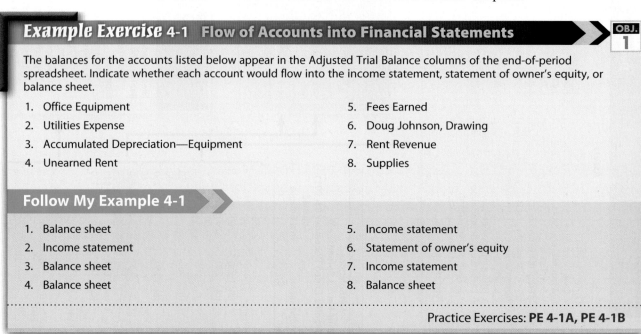

Example Exercise 4-1   Flow of Accounts into Financial Statements   OBJ. 1

The balances for the accounts listed below appear in the Adjusted Trial Balance columns of the end-of-period spreadsheet. Indicate whether each account would flow into the income statement, statement of owner's equity, or balance sheet.

1. Office Equipment
2. Utilities Expense
3. Accumulated Depreciation—Equipment
4. Unearned Rent

5. Fees Earned
6. Doug Johnson, Drawing
7. Rent Revenue
8. Supplies

Follow My Example 4-1

1. Balance sheet
2. Income statement
3. Balance sheet
4. Balance sheet

5. Income statement
6. Statement of owner's equity
7. Income statement
8. Balance sheet

Practice Exercises: **PE 4-1A, PE 4-1B**

OBJ. 2   Prepare financial statements from adjusted account balances.

Financial Statements

Using the adjusted trial balance shown in Exhibit 1, the financial statements for **NetSolutions** can be prepared. The income statement, the statement of owner's equity, and the balance sheet are shown in Exhibit 2.

Income Statement

The income statement is prepared directly from the Adjusted Trial Balance columns of the Exhibit 1 spreadsheet, beginning with fees earned of $16,840. The expenses in the income statement in Exhibit 2 are listed in order of size, beginning with the larger items. Miscellaneous expense is the last item, regardless of its amount.

1 The appendix to this chapter describes and illustrates how to prepare an end-of-period spreadsheet (work sheet) that includes financial statement columns.

EXHIBIT 2 Financial Statements, NetSolutions

NetSolutions
Income Statement
For the Two Months Ended December 31, 2011

Fees earned...	$16,840	
Rent revenue	120	
Total revenues		$16,960
Expenses:		
Wages expense...	$ 4,525	
Supplies expense...	2,040	
Rent expense	1,600	
Utilities expense...	985	
Insurance expense...	200	
Depreciation expense..	50	
Miscellaneous expense	455	
Total expenses		9,855
Net income		$ 7,105

NetSolutions
Statement of Owner's Equity
For the Two Months Ended December 31, 2011

Chris Clark, capital, November 1, 2011		$ 0
Investment on November 1, 2011...	$25,000	
Net income for November and December	7,105	
	$32,105	
Less withdrawals	4,000	
Increase in owner's equity		28,105
Chris Clark, capital, December 31, 2011		$28,105

NetSolutions
Balance Sheet
December 31, 2011

Assets			**Liabilities**		
Current assets:			Current liabilities:		
Cash....................................	$ 2,065		Accounts payable.....................	$900	
Accounts receivable	2,720		Wages payable	250	
Supplies	760		Unearned rent........................	240	
Prepaid insurance	2,200		Total liabilities.........................		$ 1,390
Total current assets..................		$ 7,745			
Property, plant, and equipment:					
Land..................................	$20,000				
Office equipment............	$1,800				
Less accum. depreciation.....	50	1,750	**Owner's Equity**		
Total property, plant,			Chris Clark, capital		28,105
and equipment		21,750	Total liabilities and		
Total assets.............................		$29,495	owner's equity		$29,495

Integrity, Objectivity, and Ethics in Business

CEO'S HEALTH?

How much and what information to disclose in financial statements and to investors presents a common ethical dilemma for managers and accountants. For example, Steve Jobs, co-founder and CEO of Apple Inc., has been diagnosed and treated for pancreatic cancer. Apple Inc., has insisted that the status of Steve Jobs's health is a "private" matter and does not have to be disclosed to investors. Apple maintains this position even though Jobs is a driving force behind Apple's innovation and financial success.

In January 2009, however, in response to increasing investor concerns and speculation, Jobs released a letter to investors on his health. The letter indicated that his recent weight loss was due to a hormone imbalance and not due to the recurrence of cancer.

Statement of Owner's Equity

The first item presented on the statement of owner's equity is the balance of the owner's capital account at the beginning of the period. The amount listed as owner's capital in the spreadsheet, however, is not always the account balance at the beginning of the period. The owner may have invested additional assets in the business during the period. For the beginning balance and any additional investments, it is necessary to refer to the owner's capital account in the ledger. These amounts, along with the net income (or net loss) and the drawing account balance, are used to determine the ending owner's capital account balance.

The basic form of the statement of owner's equity is shown in Exhibit 2. For Net-Solutions, the amount of drawings by the owner was less than the net income. If the owner's withdrawals had exceeded the net income, the order of the net income and the withdrawals would have been reversed. The difference between the two items would then be deducted from the beginning capital account balance. Other factors, such as additional investments or a net loss, also require some change in the form, as shown below.

Allan Johnson, capital, January 1, 2011	$39,000	
Additional investment during the year	6,000	
Total		$45,000
Net loss for the year	$ 5,600	
Withdrawals	9,500	
Decrease in owner's equity		15,100
Allan Johnson, capital, December 31, 2011		$29,900

Example Exercise 4-2 Statement of Owner's Equity

OBJ. 2

Zack Gaddis owns and operates Gaddis Employment Services. On January 1, 2011, Zack Gaddis, Capital had a balance of $186,000. During the year, Zack invested an additional $40,000 and withdrew $25,000. For the year ended December 31, 2011, Gaddis Employment Services reported a net income of $18,750. Prepare a statement of owner's equity for the year ended December 31, 2011.

Follow My Example 4-2

Gaddis Employment Services
Statement of Owner's Equity
For the Year Ended December 31, 2011

Zack Gaddis, capital, January 1, 2011	$186,000	
Additional investment during 2011	40,000	
Total		$226,000
Withdrawals	$ 25,000	
Less net income	18,750	
Decrease in owner's equity		6,250
Zack Gaddis, capital, December 31, 2011		$219,750

Practice Exercises: **PE 4-2A, PE 4-2B**

Balance Sheet

The balance sheet is prepared directly from the Adjusted Trial Balance columns of the Exhibit 1 spreadsheet, beginning with Cash of $2,065. The asset and liability amounts are taken from the spreadsheet. The owner's equity amount, however, is taken from the statement of owner's equity, as illustrated in Exhibit 2.

The balance sheet in Exhibit 2 shows subsections for assets and liabilities. Such a balance sheet is a *classified balance sheet*. These subsections are described next.

Assets Assets are commonly divided into two sections on the balance sheet: (1) current assets and (2) property, plant, and equipment.

Current Assets Cash and other assets that are expected to be converted to cash or sold or used up usually within one year or less, through the normal operations of the business, are called **current assets**. In addition to cash, the current assets may include notes receivable, accounts receivable, supplies, and other prepaid expenses.

Notes receivable are amounts that customers owe. They are written promises to pay the amount of the note and interest. Accounts receivable are also amounts customers owe, but they are less formal than notes. Accounts receivable normally result from providing services or selling merchandise on account. Notes receivable and accounts receivable are current assets because they are usually converted to cash within one year or less.

Property, Plant, and Equipment The property, plant, and equipment section may also be described as **fixed assets** or **plant assets**. These assets include equipment, machinery, buildings, and land. With the exception of land, as discussed in Chapter 3, fixed assets depreciate over a period of time. The original cost, accumulated depreciation, and book value of each major type of fixed asset are normally reported on the balance sheet or in the notes to the financial statements.

Liabilities Liabilities are the amounts the business owes to creditors. Liabilities are commonly divided into two sections on the balance sheet: (1) current liabilities and (2) long-term liabilities.

Current Liabilities Liabilities that will be due within a short time (usually one year or less) and that are to be paid out of current assets are called **current liabilities**. The most common liabilities in this group are notes payable and accounts payable. Other current liabilities may include Wages Payable, Interest Payable, Taxes Payable, and Unearned Fees.

Long-Term Liabilities Liabilities that will not be due for a long time (usually more than one year) are called **long-term liabilities**. If NetSolutions had long-term liabilities, they would be reported below the current liabilities. As long-term liabilities come due and are to be paid within one year, they are reported as current liabilities. If they are to be renewed rather than paid, they would continue to be reported as long term. When an asset is pledged as security for a liability, the obligation may be called a *mortgage note payable* or a *mortgage payable*.

Owner's Equity The owner's right to the assets of the business is presented on the balance sheet below the liabilities section. The owner's equity is added to the total liabilities, and this total must be equal to the total assets.

Note:
Two common classes of assets are current assets and property, plant, and equipment.

Note:
Two common classes of liabilities are current liabilities and long-term liabilities.

Example Exercise 4-3 Classified Balance Sheet
OBJ. 2

The following accounts appear in an adjusted trial balance of Hindsight Consulting. Indicate whether each account would be reported in the (a) current asset; (b) property, plant, and equipment; (c) current liability; (d) long-term liability; or (e) owner's equity section of the December 31, 2011, balance sheet of Hindsight Consulting.

1. Jason Corbin, Capital
2. Notes Receivable (due in 6 months)
3. Notes Payable (due in 2013)
4. Land

5. Cash
6. Unearned Rent (3 months)
7. Accumulated Depreciation—Equipment
8. Accounts Payable

(continued)

IFRS ▌ International Connection

INTERNATIONAL DIFFERENCES

Financial statements prepared under accounting practices in other countries often differ from those prepared under generally accepted accounting principles in the United States. This is to be expected, since cultures and market structures differ from country to country.

To illustrate, BMW Group prepares its financial statements under International Financial Reporting Standards as adopted by the European Union. In doing so, BMW's balance sheet reports fixed assets first, followed by current assets. It also reports owner's equity before the liabilities. In contrast, balance sheets prepared under U.S. accounting principles report current assets followed by fixed assets

and current liabilities followed by long-term liabilities and owner's equity. The U.S. form of balance sheet is organized to emphasize creditor interpretation and analysis. For example, current assets and current liabilities are presented first to facilitate their interpretation and analysis by creditors. Likewise, to emphasize their importance, liabilities are reported before owner's equity.*

Regardless of these differences, the basic principles underlying the accounting equation and the double-entry accounting system are the same in Germany and the United States. Even though differences in recording and reporting exist, the accounting equation holds true: the total assets still equal the total liabilities and owner's equity.

*Examples of U.S. and IFRS financial statement reporting differences are further discussed and illustrated in Appendix D.

OBJ. 3 Prepare closing entries.

Closing Entries

As discussed in Chapter 3, the adjusting entries are recorded in the journal at the end of the accounting period. For NetSolutions, the adjusting entries are shown in Exhibit 9 of Chapter 3.

After the adjusting entries are posted to NetSolutions' ledger, shown in Exhibit 6 (on pages 160–161), the ledger agrees with the data reported on the financial statements.

The balances of the accounts reported on the balance sheet are carried forward from year to year. Because they are relatively permanent, these accounts are called **permanent accounts** or **real accounts**. For example, Cash, Accounts Receivable, Equipment, Accumulated Depreciation, Accounts Payable, and Owner's Capital are permanent accounts.

The balances of the accounts reported on the income statement are not carried forward from year to year. Also, the balance of the owner's drawing account, which is reported on the statement of owner's equity, is not carried forward. Because these accounts report amounts for only one period, they are called **temporary accounts** or **nominal accounts**. Temporary accounts are not carried forward because they relate only to one period. For example, the Fees Earned of $16,840 and Wages Expense of $4,525 for NetSolutions shown in Exhibit 2 are for the two months ending December 31, 2011, and should not be carried forward to 2012.

Note:
Closing entries transfer the balances of temporary accounts to the owner's capital account.

At the beginning of the next period, temporary accounts should have zero balances. To achieve this, temporary account balances are transferred to permanent accounts at the end of the accounting period. The entries that transfer these balances are called **closing entries**. The transfer process is called the **closing process** and is sometimes referred to as **closing the books**.

The closing process involves the following four steps:

1. Revenue account balances are transferred to an account called Income Summary.

2. Expense account balances are transferred to an account called Income Summary.

3. The balance of Income Summary (net income or net loss) is transferred to the owner's capital account.
4. The balance of the owner's drawing account is transferred to the owner's capital account.

Exhibit 3 diagrams the closing process.

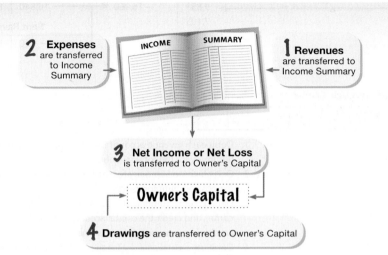

EXHIBIT 3

The Closing Process

Income Summary is a temporary account that is only used during the closing process. At the beginning of the closing process, Income Summary has no balance. During the closing process, Income Summary will be debited and credited for various amounts. At the end of the closing process, Income Summary will again have no balance. Because Income Summary has the effect of clearing the revenue and expense accounts of their balances, it is sometimes called a **clearing account**. Other titles used for this account include Revenue and Expense Summary, Profit and Loss Summary, and Income and Expense Summary.

> **Note:**
> The income summary account does not appear on the financial statements.

The four closing entries required in the closing process are as follows:

1. Debit each revenue account for its balance and credit Income Summary for the total revenue.
2. Credit each expense account for its balance and debit Income Summary for the total expenses.
3. Debit Income Summary for its balance and credit the owner's capital account.
4. Debit the owner's capital account for the balance of the drawing account and credit the drawing account.

In the case of a net loss, Income Summary will have a debit balance after the first two closing entries. In this case, credit Income Summary for the amount of its balance and debit the owner's capital account for the amount of the net loss.

Closing entries are recorded in the journal and are dated as of the last day of the accounting period. In the journal, closing entries are recorded immediately following the adjusting entries. The caption, *Closing Entries*, is often inserted above the closing entries to separate them from the adjusting entries.

It is possible to close the temporary revenue and expense accounts without using a clearing account such as Income Summary. In this case, the balances of the revenue and expense accounts are closed directly to the owner's capital account. This process may be used in a computerized accounting system.

Journalizing and Posting Closing Entries

A flowchart of the four closing entries for NetSolutions is shown in Exhibit 4. The balances in the accounts are those shown in the Adjusted Trial Balance columns of the end-of-period spreadsheet shown in Exhibit 1.

EXHIBIT 4 **Flowchart of Closing Entries for NetSolutions**

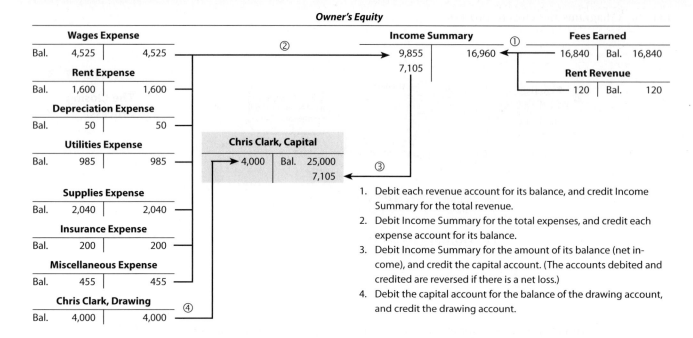

The closing entries for NetSolutions are shown in Exhibit 5. The account titles and balances for these entries may be obtained from the end-of-period spreadsheet, the adjusted trial balance, the income statement, the statement of owner's equity, or the ledger.

EXHIBIT 5

Closing Entries, NetSolutions

	Journal				Page 6
Date	**Description**	**Post. Ref.**	**Debit**	**Credit**	
	Closing Entries				
2011					
Dec. 31	Fees Earned	41	16,840		
	Rent Revenue	42	120		
	Income Summary	33		16,960	
31	Income Summary	33	9,855		
	Wages Expense	51		4,525	
	Rent Expense	52		1,600	
	Depreciation Expense	53		50	
	Utilities Expense	54		985	
	Supplies Expense	55		2,040	
	Insurance Expense	56		200	
	Miscellaneous Expense	59		455	
31	Income Summary	33	7,105		
	Chris Clark, Capital	31		7,105	
31	Chris Clark, Capital	31	4,000		
	Chris Clark, Drawing	32		4,000	

The closing entries are posted to NetSolutions' ledger as shown in Exhibit 6 (pages 160–161). Income Summary has been added to NetSolutions' ledger in Exhibit 6 as account number 33. After the closing entries are posted, NetSolutions' ledger has the following characteristics:

1. The balance of Chris Clark, Capital of $28,105 agrees with the amount reported on the statement of owner's equity and the balance sheet.
2. The revenue, expense, and drawing accounts will have zero balances.

As shown in Exhibit 6, the closing entries are normally identified in the ledger as "Closing." In addition, a line is often inserted in both balance columns after a closing entry is posted. This separates next period's revenue, expense, and withdrawal transactions from those of the current period. Next period's transactions will be posted directly below the closing entry.

Example Exercise 4-4   Closing Entries
OBJ. 3

After the accounts have been adjusted at July 31, the end of the fiscal year, the following balances are taken from the ledger of Cabriolet Services Co.:

Terry Lambert, Capital	$615,850
Terry Lambert, Drawing	25,000
Fees Earned	380,450
Wages Expense	250,000
Rent Expense	65,000
Supplies Expense	18,250
Miscellaneous Expense	6,200

Journalize the four entries required to close the accounts.

Follow My Example 4-4

July	31	Fees Earned	380,450	
		Income Summary		380,450
	31	Income Summary	339,450	
		Wages Expense		250,000
		Rent Expense		65,000
		Supplies Expense		18,250
		Miscellaneous Expense		6,200
	31	Income Summary	41,000	
		Terry Lambert, Capital		41,000
	31	Terry Lambert, Capital	25,000	
		Terry Lambert, Drawing		25,000

Practice Exercises: **PE 4-4A, PE 4-4B**

Post-Closing Trial Balance

A post-closing trial balance is prepared after the closing entries have been posted. The purpose of the post-closing (after closing) trial balance is to verify that the ledger is in balance at the beginning of the next period. The accounts and amounts should agree exactly with the accounts and amounts listed on the balance sheet at the end of the period. The post-closing trial balance for NetSolutions is shown in Exhibit 7.

EXHIBIT 6 Ledger, NetSolutions

Account Cash — Account No. 11

Date	Item	Post. Ref.	Debit	Credit	Balance Debit	Balance Credit
2011						
Nov. 1		1	25,000		25,000	
5		1		20,000	5,000	
18		1	7,500		12,500	
30		1		3,650	8,850	
30		1		950	7,900	
30		2		2,000	5,900	
Dec. 1		2		2,400	3,500	
1		2		800	2,700	
1		2	360		3,060	
6		2		180	2,880	
11		2		400	2,480	
13		3		950	1,530	
16		3	3,100		4,630	
20		3		900	3,730	
21		3	650		4,380	
23		3		1,450	2,930	
27		3		1,200	1,730	
31		3		310	1,420	
31		4		225	1,195	
31		4	2,870		4,065	
31		4		2,000	2,065	

Account Accounts Receivable — Account No. 12

Date	Item	Post. Ref.	Debit	Credit	Balance Debit	Balance Credit
2011						
Dec. 16		3	1,750		1,750	
21		3		650	1,100	
31		4	1,120		2,220	
31	Adjusting	5	500		2,720	

Account Supplies — Account No. 14

Date	Item	Post. Ref.	Debit	Credit	Balance Debit	Balance Credit
2011						
Nov. 10		1	1,350		1,350	
30		1		800	550	
Dec. 23		3	1,450		2,000	
31	Adjusting	5		1,240	760	

Account Prepaid Insurance — Account No. 15

Date	Item	Post. Ref.	Debit	Credit	Balance Debit	Balance Credit
2011						
Dec. 1		2	2,400		2,400	
31	Adjusting	5		200	2,200	

Account Land — Account No. 17

Date	Item	Post. Ref.	Debit	Credit	Balance Debit	Balance Credit
2011						
Nov. 5		1	20,000		20,000	

Account Office Equipment — Account No. 18

Date	Item	Post. Ref.	Debit	Credit	Balance Debit	Balance Credit
2011						
Dec. 4		2	1,800		1,800	

Account Accumulated Depreciation — Account No. 19

Date	Item	Post. Ref.	Debit	Credit	Balance Debit	Balance Credit
2011						
Dec. 31	Adjusting	5		50		50

Account Accounts Payable — Account No. 21

Date	Item	Post. Ref.	Debit	Credit	Balance Debit	Balance Credit
2011						
Nov. 10		1		1,350		1,350
30		1	950			400
Dec. 4		2		1,800		2,200
11		2	400			1,800
20		3	900			900

Account Wages Payable — Account No. 22

Date	Item	Post. Ref.	Debit	Credit	Balance Debit	Balance Credit
2011						
Dec. 31	Adjusting	5		250		250

Account Unearned Rent — Account No. 23

Date	Item	Post. Ref.	Debit	Credit	Balance Debit	Balance Credit
2011						
Dec. 1		2		360		360
31	Adjusting	5	120			240

Account Chris Clark, Capital — Account No. 31

Date	Item	Post. Ref.	Debit	Credit	Balance Debit	Balance Credit
2011						
Nov. 1		1		25,000		25,000
Dec. 31	Closing	6		7,105		32,105
31	Closing	6	4,000			28,105

EXHIBIT 6   Ledger, NetSolutions (*concluded*)

Account *Chris Clark, Drawing*   Account No. 32

Date	Item	Post. Ref.	Debit	Credit	Balance Debit	Balance Credit
2011						
Nov. 30		2	2,000		2,000	
Dec. 31		4	2,000		4,000	
31	Closing	6		4,000	—	—

Account *Income Summary*   Account No. 33

Date	Item	Post. Ref.	Debit	Credit	Balance Debit	Balance Credit
2011						
Dec. 31	Closing	6		16,960		16,960
31	Closing	6	9,855			7,105
31	Closing	6	7,105		—	—

Account *Fees Earned*   Account No. 41

Date	Item	Post. Ref.	Debit	Credit	Balance Debit	Balance Credit
2011						
Nov. 18		1		7,500		7,500
Dec. 16		3		3,100		10,600
16		3		1,750		12,350
31		4		2,870		15,220
31		4		1,120		16,340
31	Adjusting	5		500		16,840
31	Closing	6	16,840		—	—

Account *Rent Revenue*   Account No. 42

Date	Item	Post. Ref.	Debit	Credit	Balance Debit	Balance Credit
2011						
Dec. 31	Adjusting	5		120		120
31	Closing	6	120		—	—

Account *Wages Expense*   Account No. 51

Date	Item	Post. Ref.	Debit	Credit	Balance Debit	Balance Credit
2011						
Nov. 30		1	2,125		2,125	
Dec. 13		3	950		3,075	
27		3	1,200		4,275	
31	Adjusting	5	250		4,525	
31	Closing	6		4,525	—	—

Account *Rent Expense*   Account No. 52

Date	Item	Post. Ref.	Debit	Credit	Balance Debit	Balance Credit
2011						
Nov. 30		1	800		800	
Dec. 1		2	800		1,600	
31	Closing	6		1,600	—	—

Account *Depreciation Expense*   Account No. 53

Date	Item	Post. Ref.	Debit	Credit	Balance Debit	Balance Credit
2011						
Dec. 31	Adjusting	5	50		50	
31	Closing	6		50	—	—

Account *Utilities Expense*   Account No. 54

Date	Item	Post. Ref.	Debit	Credit	Balance Debit	Balance Credit
2011						
Nov. 30		1	450		450	
Dec. 31		3	310		760	
31		4	225		985	
31	Closing	6		985	—	—

Account *Supplies Expense*   Account No. 55

Date	Item	Post. Ref.	Debit	Credit	Balance Debit	Balance Credit
2011						
Nov. 30		1	800		800	
Dec. 31	Adjusting	5	1,240		2,040	
31	Closing	6		2,040	—	—

Account *Insurance Expense*   Account No. 56

Date	Item	Post. Ref.	Debit	Credit	Balance Debit	Balance Credit
2011						
Dec. 31	Adjusting	5	200		200	
31	Closing	6		200	—	—

Account *Miscellaneous Expense*   Account No. 59

Date	Item	Post. Ref.	Debit	Credit	Balance Debit	Balance Credit
2011						
Nov. 30		1	275		275	
Dec. 6		2	180		455	
31	Closing	6		455	—	—

EXHIBIT 7

Post-Closing Trial Balance, NetSolutions

	NetSolutions Post-Closing Trial Balance December 31, 2011		
		Debit Balances	**Credit Balances**
Cash...		2,065	
Accounts Receivable		2,720	
Supplies		760	
Prepaid Insurance.......................................		2,200	
Land...		20,000	
Office Equipment		1,800	
Accumulated Depreciation...........................			50
Accounts Payable			900
Wages Payable..			250
Unearned Rent			240
Chris Clark, Capital			28,105
		29,545	29,545

Describe the accounting cycle.

Accounting Cycle

The accounting process that begins with analyzing and journalizing transactions and ends with the post-closing trial balance is called the **accounting cycle**. The steps in the accounting cycle are as follows:

1. Transactions are analyzed and recorded in the journal.
2. Transactions are posted to the ledger.
3. An unadjusted trial balance is prepared.
4. Adjustment data are assembled and analyzed.
5. An optional end-of-period spreadsheet is prepared.
6. Adjusting entries are journalized and posted to the ledger.
7. An adjusted trial balance is prepared.
8. Financial statements are prepared.
9. Closing entries are journalized and posted to the ledger.
10. A post-closing trial balance is prepared.[2]

Example Exercise 4-5 Accounting Cycle

OBJ. 4

From the following list of steps in the accounting cycle, identify what two steps are missing.
a. Transactions are analyzed and recorded in the journal.
b. Transactions are posted to the ledger.
c. Adjustment data are assembled and analyzed.
d. An optional end-of-period spreadsheet is prepared.
e. Adjusting entries are journalized and posted to the ledger.
f. Financial statements are prepared.
g. Closing entries are journalized and posted to the ledger.
h. A post-closing trial balance is prepared.

Follow My Example 4-5

The following two steps are missing: (1) the preparation of an unadjusted trial balance and (2) the preparation of the adjusted trial balance. The unadjusted trial balance should be prepared after step (b). The adjusted trial balance should be prepared after step (e).

Practice Exercises: **PE 4-5A, PE 4-5B**

2 Some accountants include the journalizing and posting of "reversing entries" as the last step in the accounting cycle. Because reversing entries are not required, they are described and illustrated in Appendix B at the end of the book.

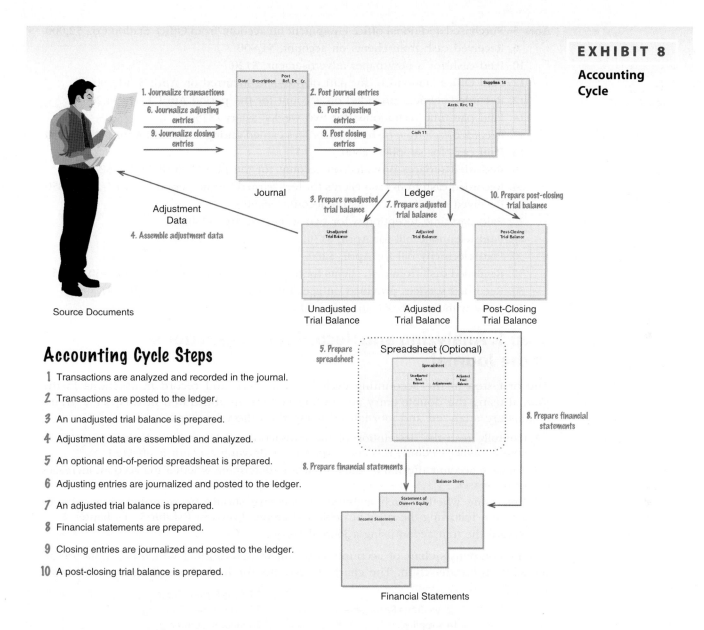

EXHIBIT 8

Accounting Cycle

Accounting Cycle Steps

1 Transactions are analyzed and recorded in the journal.

2 Transactions are posted to the ledger.

3 An unadjusted trial balance is prepared.

4 Adjustment data are assembled and analyzed.

5 An optional end-of-period spreadsheet is prepared.

6 Adjusting entries are journalized and posted to the ledger.

7 An adjusted trial balance is prepared.

8 Financial statements are prepared.

9 Closing entries are journalized and posted to the ledger.

10 A post-closing trial balance is prepared.

Exhibit 8 illustrates the accounting cycle in graphic form. It also illustrates how the accounting cycle begins with the source documents for a transaction and flows through the accounting system and into the financial statements.

Illustration of the Accounting Cycle

OBJ. 5 Illustrate the accounting cycle for one period.

In this section, the complete accounting cycle for one period is illustrated. Assume that for several years Kelly Pitney has operated a part-time consulting business from her home. As of April 1, 2012, Kelly decided to move to rented quarters and to operate the business on a full-time basis. The business will be known as Kelly Consulting. During April, Kelly Consulting entered into the following transactions:

Apr. 1. The following assets were received from Kelly Pitney: cash, $13,100; accounts receivable, $3,000; supplies, $1,400; and office equipment, $12,500. There were no liabilities received.

　　 1. Paid three months' rent on a lease rental contract, $4,800.

　　 2. Paid the premiums on property and casualty insurance policies, $1,800.

　　 4. Received cash from clients as an advance payment for services to be provided and recorded it as unearned fees, $5,000.

Apr. 5. Purchased additional office equipment on account from Office Station Co., $2,000.
6. Received cash from clients on account, $1,800.
10. Paid cash for a newspaper advertisement, $120.
12. Paid Office Station Co. for part of the debt incurred on April 5, $1,200.
12. Recorded services provided on account for the period April 1–12, $4,200.
14. Paid part-time receptionist for two weeks' salary, $750.
17. Recorded cash from cash clients for fees earned during the period April 1–16, $6,250.
18. Paid cash for supplies, $800.
20. Recorded services provided on account for the period April 13–20, $2,100.
24. Recorded cash from cash clients for fees earned for the period April 17–24, $3,850.
26. Received cash from clients on account, $5,600.
27. Paid part-time receptionist for two weeks' salary, $750.
29. Paid telephone bill for April, $130.
30. Paid electricity bill for April, $200.
30. Recorded cash from cash clients for fees earned for the period April 25–30, $3,050.
30. Recorded services provided on account for the remainder of April, $1,500.
30. Kelly withdrew $6,000 for personal use.

Step 1. Analyzing and Recording Transactions in the Journal

The first step in the accounting cycle is to analyze and record transactions in the journal using the double-entry accounting system. As illustrated in Chapter 2, transactions are analyzed and journalized using the following steps:

1. Carefully read the description of the transaction to determine whether an asset, liability, owner's equity, revenue, expense, or drawing account is affected.
2. For each account affected by the transaction, determine whether the account increases or decreases.
3. Determine whether each increase or decrease should be recorded as a debit or a credit, following the rules of debit and credit shown in Exhibit 3 of Chapter 2.
4. Record the transaction using a journal entry.

The company's chart of accounts is useful in determining which accounts are affected by the transaction. The chart of accounts for Kelly Consulting is as follows:

11 Cash	31 Kelly Pitney, Capital
12 Accounts Receivable	32 Kelly Pitney, Drawing
14 Supplies	33 Income Summary
15 Prepaid Rent	41 Fees Earned
16 Prepaid Insurance	51 Salary Expense
18 Office Equipment	52 Rent Expense
19 Accumulated Depreciation	53 Supplies Expense
21 Accounts Payable	54 Depreciation Expense
22 Salaries Payable	55 Insurance Expense
23 Unearned Fees	59 Miscellaneous Expense

After analyzing each of Kelly Consulting's transactions for April, the journal entries are recorded as shown in Exhibit 9.

Step 2. Posting Transactions to the Ledger

Periodically, the transactions recorded in the journal are posted to the accounts in the ledger. The debits and credits for each journal entry are posted to the accounts in the order in which they occur in the journal. As illustrated in Chapters 2 and 3, journal entries are posted to the accounts using the following four steps:

1. The date is entered in the Date column of the account.
2. The amount is entered into the Debit or Credit column of the account.
3. The journal page number is entered in the Posting Reference column.
4. The account number is entered in the Posting Reference (Post. Ref.) column in the journal.

EXHIBIT 9

Journal Entries for April, Kelly Consulting

		Journal			Page 1
Date		Description	Post. Ref.	Debit	Credit
2012 Apr.	1	Cash	11	13,100	
		Accounts Receivable	12	3,000	
		Supplies	14	1,400	
		Office Equipment	18	12,500	
		Kelly Pitney, Capital	31		30,000
	1	Prepaid Rent	15	4,800	
		Cash	11		4,800
	2	Prepaid Insurance	16	1,800	
		Cash	11		1,800
	4	Cash	11	5,000	
		Unearned Fees	23		5,000
	5	Office Equipment	18	2,000	
		Accounts Payable	21		2,000
	6	Cash	11	1,800	
		Accounts Receivable	12		1,800
	10	Miscellaneous Expense	59	120	
		Cash	11		120
	12	Accounts Payable	21	1,200	
		Cash	11		1,200
	12	Accounts Receivable	12	4,200	
		Fees Earned	41		4,200
	14	Salary Expense	51	750	
		Cash	11		750

		Journal			Page 2
Date		Description	Post. Ref.	Debit	Credit
2012 Apr.	17	Cash	11	6,250	
		Fees Earned	41		6,250
	18	Supplies	14	800	
		Cash	11		800
	20	Accounts Receivable	12	2,100	
		Fees Earned	41		2,100
	24	Cash	11	3,850	
		Fees Earned	41		3,850
	26	Cash	11	5,600	
		Accounts Receivable	12		5,600
	27	Salary Expense	51	750	
		Cash	11		750
	29	Miscellaneous Expense	59	130	
		Cash	11		130

(continued)

EXHIBIT 9

Journal Entries
for April, Kelly
Consulting
(*concluded*)

Journal					Page 2
Date		Description	Post. Ref.	Debit	Credit
2012 Apr. 30		Miscellaneous Expense	59	200	
		Cash	11		200
30		Cash	11	3,050	
		Fees Earned	41		3,050
30		Accounts Receivable	12	1,500	
		Fees Earned	41		1,500
30		Kelly Pitney, Drawing	32	6,000	
		Cash	11		6,000

The journal entries for Kelly Consulting have been posted to the ledger shown in Exhibit 17 on pages 172–173.

Step 3. Preparing an Unadjusted Trial Balance

An unadjusted trial balance is prepared to determine whether any errors have been made in posting the debits and credits to the ledger. The unadjusted trial balance shown in Exhibit 10 does not provide complete proof of the accuracy of the ledger. It indicates only that the debits and the credits are equal. This proof is of value, however, because errors often affect the equality of debits and credits. If the two totals of a trial balance are not equal, an error has occurred that must be discovered and corrected.

EXHIBIT 10

Unadjusted Trial
Balance, Kelly
Consulting

Kelly Consulting Unadjusted Trial Balance April 30, 2012	Debit Balances	Credit Balances
Cash	22,100	
Accounts Receivable	3,400	
Supplies	2,200	
Prepaid Rent	4,800	
Prepaid Insurance	1,800	
Office Equipment	14,500	
Accumulated Depreciation		0
Accounts Payable		800
Salaries Payable		0
Unearned Fees		5,000
Kelly Pitney, Capital		30,000
Kelly Pitney, Drawing	6,000	
Fees Earned		20,950
Salary Expense	1,500	
Rent Expense	0	
Supplies Expense	0	
Depreciation Expense	0	
Insurance Expense	0	
Miscellaneous Expense	450	
	56,750	56,750

The unadjusted account balances shown in Exhibit 10 were taken from Kelly Consulting's ledger shown in Exhibit 17, on pages 172–173, before any adjusting entries were recorded.

Step 4. Assembling and Analyzing Adjustment Data

Before the financial statements can be prepared, the accounts must be updated. The four types of accounts that normally require adjustment include prepaid expenses, unearned revenue, accrued revenue, and accrued expenses. In addition, depreciation expense must be recorded for fixed assets other than land. The following data have been assembled on April 30, 2012, for analysis of possible adjustments for Kelly Consulting:

a. Insurance expired during April is $300.

b. Supplies on hand on April 30 are $1,350.

c. Depreciation of office equipment for April is $330.

d. Accrued receptionist salary on April 30 is $120.

e. Rent expired during April is $1,600.

f. Unearned fees on April 30 are $2,500.

Step 5. Preparing an Optional End-of-Period Spreadsheet

Although an end-of-period spreadsheet is not required, it is useful in showing the flow of accounting information from the unadjusted trial balance to the adjusted trial balance. In addition, an end-of-period spreadsheet is useful in analyzing the impact of proposed adjustments on the financial statements. The end-of-period spreadsheet for Kelly Consulting is shown in Exhibit 11.

Step 6. Journalizing and Posting Adjusting Entries

Based on the adjustment data shown in Step 4, adjusting entries for Kelly Consulting are prepared as shown in Exhibit 12. Each adjusting entry affects at least one income statement account and one balance sheet account. Explanations for each adjustment including any computations are normally included with each adjusting entry.

EXHIBIT 11

End-of-Period Spreadsheet, Kelly Consulting

	A	B	C	D	E	F	G
1				Kelly Consulting			
2				End-of-Period Spreadsheet			
3				For the Month Ended April 30, 2012			
4		Unadjusted				Adjusted	
5		Trial Balance		Adjustments		Trial Balance	
6	Account Title	Dr.	Cr.	Dr.	Cr.	Dr.	Cr.
7							
8	Cash	22,100				22,100	
9	Accounts Receivable	3,400				3,400	
10	Supplies	2,200			(b) 850	1,350	
11	Prepaid Rent	4,800			(e) 1,600	3,200	
12	Prepaid Insurance	1,800			(a) 300	1,500	
13	Office Equipment	14,500				14,500	
14	Accum. Depreciation				(c) 330		330
15	Accounts Payable		800				800
16	Salaries Payable				(d) 120		120
17	Unearned Fees		5,000	(f) 2,500			2,500
18	Kelly Pitney, Capital		30,000				30,000
19	Kelly Pitney, Drawing	6,000				6,000	
20	Fees Earned		20,950		(f) 2,500		23,450
21	Salary Expense	1,500		(d) 120		1,620	
22	Rent Expense			(e) 1,600		1,600	
23	Supplies Expense			(b) 850		850	
24	Depreciation Expense			(c) 330		330	
25	Insurance Expense			(a) 300		300	
26	Miscellaneous Expense	450				450	
27		56,750	56,750	5,700	5,700	57,200	57,200
28							

EXHIBIT 12

Adjusting Entries, Kelly Consulting

			Journal			Page 3
Date			**Description**	**Post. Ref.**	**Debit**	**Credit**
2012 Apr.	30	Adjusting Entries				
		Insurance Expense		55	300	
			Prepaid Insurance	16		300
			Expired Insurance.			
	30	Supplies Expense		53	850	
			Supplies	14		850
			Supplies used ($2,200 – $1,350).			
	30	Depreciation Expense		54	330	
			Accumulated Depreciation	19		330
			Depreciation of office equipment.			
	30	Salary Expense		51	120	
			Salaries Payable	22		120
			Accrued salary.			
	30	Rent Expense		52	1,600	
			Prepaid Rent	15		1,600
			Rent expired during April.			
	30	Unearned Fees		23	2,500	
			Fees Earned	41		2,500
			Fees earned ($5,000 – $2,500).			

Each of the adjusting entries shown in Exhibit 12 is posted to Kelly Consulting's ledger shown in Exhibit 17 on pages 172–173. The adjusting entries are identified in the ledger as "Adjusting."

Step 7. Preparing an Adjusted Trial Balance

After the adjustments have been journalized and posted, an adjusted trial balance is prepared to verify the equality of the total of the debit and credit balances. This is the last step before preparing the financial statements. If the adjusted trial balance does not balance, an error has occurred and must be found and corrected. The adjusted trial balance for Kelly Consulting as of April 30, 2012, is shown in Exhibit 13.

Step 8. Preparing the Financial Statements

The most important outcome of the accounting cycle is the financial statements. The income statement is prepared first, followed by the statement of owner's equity and then the balance sheet. The statements can be prepared directly from the adjusted trial balance, the end-of-period spreadsheet, or the ledger. The net income or net loss shown on the income statement is reported on the statement of owner's equity along with any additional investments by the owner and any withdrawals. The ending owner's capital is reported on the balance sheet and is added with total liabilities to equal total assets.

The financial statements for Kelly Consulting are shown in Exhibit 14. Kelly Consulting earned net income of $18,300 for April. As of April 30, 2012, Kelly Consulting has total assets of $45,720, total liabilities of $3,420, and total owner's equity of $42,300.

EXHIBIT 13

Adjusted Trial Balance, Kelly Consulting

Kelly Consulting
Adjusted Trial Balance
April 30, 2012

	Debit Balances	Credit Balances
Cash	22,100	
Accounts Receivable	3,400	
Supplies	1,350	
Prepaid Rent	3,200	
Prepaid Insurance	1,500	
Office Equipment	14,500	
Accumulated Depreciation		330
Accounts Payable		800
Salaries Payable		120
Unearned Fees		2,500
Kelly Pitney, Capital		30,000
Kelly Pitney, Drawing	6,000	
Fees Earned		23,450
Salary Expense	1,620	
Rent Expense	1,600	
Supplies Expense	850	
Depreciation Expense	330	
Insurance Expense	300	
Miscellaneous Expense	450	
	57,200	57,200

EXHIBIT 14

Financial Statements, Kelly Consulting

Kelly Consulting
Income Statement
For the Month Ended April 30, 2012

Fees earned		$23,450
Expenses:		
Salary expense	$1,620	
Rent expense	1,600	
Supplies expense	850	
Depreciation expense	330	
Insurance expense	300	
Miscellaneous expense	450	
Total expenses		5,150
Net income		$18,300

Kelly Consulting
Statement of Owner's Equity
For the Month Ended April 30, 2012

Kelly Pitney, capital, April 1, 2012		$ 0
Investment during the month	$30,000	
Net income for the month	18,300	
	$48,300	
Less withdrawals	6,000	
Increase in owner's equity		42,300
Kelly Pitney, capital, April 30, 2012		$42,300

(continued)

EXHIBIT 14 **Financial Statements, Kelly Consulting (concluded)**

Kelly Consulting
Balance Sheet
April 30, 2012

Assets			Liabilities		
Current assets:			Current liabilities:		
Cash	$22,100		Accounts payable	$ 800	
Accounts receivable	3,400		Salaries payable	120	
Supplies	1,350		Unearned fees	2,500	
Prepaid rent	3,200		Total liabilities		$ 3,420
Prepaid insurance	1,500	$31,550			
Total current assets					
Property, plant, and equipment:					
Office equipment	$14,500				
Less accumulated depreciation	330		**Owner's Equity**		
Total property, plant,			Kelly Pitney, capital		42,300
and equipment		14,170	Total liabilities and		
Total assets		$45,720	owner's equity		$45,720

Step 9. Journalizing and Posting Closing Entries

As described earlier in this chapter, four closing entries are required at the end of an accounting period. These four closing entries are as follows:

1. Debit each revenue account for its balance and credit Income Summary for the total revenue.
2. Credit each expense account for its balance and debit Income Summary for the total expenses.
3. Debit Income Summary for its balance and credit the owner's capital account.
4. Debit the owner's capital account for the balance of the drawing account and credit the drawing account.

The four closing entries for Kelly Consulting are shown in Exhibit 15. The closing entries are posted to Kelly Consulting's ledger as shown in Exhibit 17 (pages 172–173). After the closing entries are posted, Kelly Consulting's ledger has the following characteristics:

1. The balance of Kelly Pitney, Capital of $42,300 agrees with the amount reported on the statement of owner's equity and the balance sheet.
2. The revenue, expense, and drawing accounts will have zero balances.

The closing entries are normally identified in the ledger as "Closing." In addition, a line is often inserted in both balance columns after a closing entry is posted. This separates next period's revenue, expense, and withdrawal transactions from those of the current period.

Step 10. Preparing a Post-Closing Trial Balance

A post-closing trial balance is prepared after the closing entries have been posted. The purpose of the post-closing trial balance is to verify that the ledger is in balance at the beginning of the next period. The accounts and amounts in the post-closing trial balance should agree exactly with the accounts and amounts listed on the balance sheet at the end of the period.

EXHIBIT 15

Closing Entries, Kelly Consulting

Journal				Page 4
Date	**Description**	**Post. Ref.**	**Debit**	**Credit**
	Closing Entries			
2012 Apr. 30	Fees Earned	41	23,450	
	Income Summary	33		23,450
30	Income Summary	33	5,150	
	Salary Expense	51		1,620
	Rent Expense	52		1,600
	Supplies Expense	53		850
	Depreciation Expense	54		330
	Insurance Expense	55		300
	Miscellaneous Expense	59		450
30	Income Summary	33	18,300	
	Kelly Pitney, Capital	31		18,300
30	Kelly Pitney, Capital	31	6,000	
	Kelly Pitney, Drawing	32		6,000

The post-closing trial balance for Kelly Consulting is shown in Exhibit 16. The balances shown in the post-closing trial balance are taken from the ending balances in the ledger shown in Exhibit 17. These balances agree with the amounts shown on Kelly Consulting's balance sheet in Exhibit 14.

EXHIBIT 16

Post-Closing Trial Balance, Kelly Consulting

Kelly Consulting Post-Closing Trial Balance April 30, 2012		
	Debit Balances	**Credit Balances**
Cash	22,100	
Accounts Receivable	3,400	
Supplies	1,350	
Prepaid Rent	3,200	
Prepaid Insurance	1,500	
Office Equipment	14,500	
Accumulated Depreciation		330
Accounts Payable		800
Salaries Payable		120
Unearned Fees		2,500
Kelly Pitney, Capital		42,300
	46,050	46,050

EXHIBIT 17   Ledger, Kelly Consulting

Ledger

Account Cash — Account No. 11

Date	Item	Post. Ref.	Debit	Credit	Balance Debit	Balance Credit
2012						
Apr. 1		1	13,100		13,100	
1		1		4,800	8,300	
2		1		1,800	6,500	
4		1	5,000		11,500	
6		1	1,800		13,300	
10		1		120	13,180	
12		1		1,200	11,980	
14		1		750	11,230	
17		2	6,250		17,480	
18		2		800	16,680	
24		2	3,850		20,530	
26		2	5,600		26,130	
27		2		750	25,380	
29		2		130	25,250	
30		2		200	25,050	
30		2	3,050		28,100	
30		2		6,000	22,100	

Account Accounts Receivable — Account No. 12

Date	Item	Post. Ref.	Debit	Credit	Balance Debit	Balance Credit
2012						
Apr. 1		1	3,000		3,000	
6		1		1,800	1,200	
12		1	4,200		5,400	
20		2	2,100		7,500	
26		2		5,600	1,900	
30		2	1,500		3,400	

Account Supplies — Account No. 14

Date	Item	Post. Ref.	Debit	Credit	Balance Debit	Balance Credit
2012						
Apr. 1		1	1,400		1,400	
18		2	800		2,200	
30	Adjusting	3		850	1,350	

Account Prepaid Rent — Account No. 15

Date	Item	Post. Ref.	Debit	Credit	Balance Debit	Balance Credit
2012						
Apr. 1		1	4,800		4,800	
30	Adjusting	3		1,600	3,200	

Account Prepaid Insurance — Account No. 16

Date	Item	Post. Ref.	Debit	Credit	Balance Debit	Balance Credit
2012						
Apr. 2		1	1,800		1,800	
30	Adjusting	3		300	1,500	

Account Office Equipment — Account No. 18

Date	Item	Post. Ref.	Debit	Credit	Balance Debit	Balance Credit
2012						
Apr. 1		1	12,500		12,500	
5		1	2,000		14,500	

Account Accumulated Depreciation — Account No. 19

Date	Item	Post. Ref.	Debit	Credit	Balance Debit	Balance Credit
2012						
Apr. 30	Adjusting	3		330		330

Account Accounts Payable — Account No. 21

Date	Item	Post. Ref.	Debit	Credit	Balance Debit	Balance Credit
2012						
Apr. 5		1		2,000		2,000
12		1	1,200			800

Account Salaries Payable — Account No. 22

Date	Item	Post. Ref.	Debit	Credit	Balance Debit	Balance Credit
2012						
Apr. 30	Adjusting	3		120		120

Account Unearned Fees — Account No. 23

Date	Item	Post. Ref.	Debit	Credit	Balance Debit	Balance Credit
2012						
Apr. 4		1		5,000		5,000
30	Adjusting	3	2,500			2,500

Account Kelly Pitney, Capital — Account No. 31

Date	Item	Post. Ref.	Debit	Credit	Balance Debit	Balance Credit
2012						
Apr. 1		1		30,000		30,000
30	Closing	4		18,300		48,300
30	Closing	4	6,000			42,300

EXHIBIT 17 Ledger, Kelly Consulting (*concluded*)

Account Kelly Pitney, Drawing — Account No. 32

Date	Item	Post. Ref.	Debit	Credit	Balance Debit	Balance Credit
2012 Apr. 30		2	6,000		6,000	
30	Closing	4		6,000	—	—

Account Income Summary — Account No. 33

Date	Item	Post. Ref.	Debit	Credit	Balance Debit	Balance Credit
2012 Apr. 30	Closing	4		23,450		23,450
30	Closing	4	5,150			18,300
30	Closing	4	18,300		—	—

Account Fees Earned — Account No. 41

Date	Item	Post. Ref.	Debit	Credit	Balance Debit	Balance Credit
2012 Apr. 12		1		4,200		4,200
17		2		6,250		10,450
20		2		2,100		12,550
24		2		3,850		16,400
30		2		3,050		19,450
30		2		1,500		20,950
30	Adjusting	3		2,500		23,450
30	Closing	4	23,450		—	—

Account Salary Expense — Account No. 51

Date	Item	Post. Ref.	Debit	Credit	Balance Debit	Balance Credit
2012 Apr. 14		1	750		750	
27		2	750		1,500	
30	Adjusting	3	120		1,620	
30	Closing	4		1,620	—	—

Account Rent Expense — Account No. 52

Date	Item	Post. Ref.	Debit	Credit	Balance Debit	Balance Credit
2012 Apr. 30	Adjusting	3	1,600		1,600	
30	Closing	4		1,600	—	—

Account Supplies Expense — Account No. 53

Date	Item	Post. Ref.	Debit	Credit	Balance Debit	Balance Credit
2012 Apr. 30	Adjusting	3	850		850	
30	Closing	4		850	—	—

Account Depreciation Expense — Account No. 54

Date	Item	Post. Ref.	Debit	Credit	Balance Debit	Balance Credit
2012 Apr. 30	Adjusting	3	330		330	
30	Closing	4		330	—	—

Account Insurance Expense — Account No. 55

Date	Item	Post. Ref.	Debit	Credit	Balance Debit	Balance Credit
2012 Apr. 30	Adjusting	3	300		300	
30	Closing	4		300	—	—

Account Miscellaneous Expense — Account No. 59

Date	Item	Post. Ref.	Debit	Credit	Balance Debit	Balance Credit
2012 Apr. 10		1	120		120	
29		2	130		250	
30		2	200		450	
30	Closing	4		450	—	—

Fiscal Year

OBJ. 6 Explain what is meant by the fiscal year and the natural business year.

The annual accounting period adopted by a business is known as its **fiscal year**. Fiscal years begin with the first day of the month selected and end on the last day of the following twelfth month. The period most commonly used is the calendar year. Other periods are not unusual, especially for businesses organized as corporations. For example, a corporation may adopt a fiscal year that ends when business activities have reached the lowest point in its annual operating cycle. Such a fiscal

Percentage of Companies with Fiscal Years Ending in:			
January	5%	July	2%
February	2	August	3
March	3	September	6
April	2	October	3
May	3	November	2
June	6	December	63

Source: *Accounting Trends & Techniques*, 63rd edition, 2009 (New York: American Institute of Certified Public Accountants).

year is called the **natural business year**. At the low point in its operating cycle, a business has more time to analyze the results of operations and to prepare financial statements.

Because companies with fiscal years often have highly seasonal operations, investors and others should be careful in interpreting partial-year reports for such companies. That is, you should expect the results of operations for these companies to vary significantly throughout the fiscal year.

The financial history of a business may be shown by a series of balance sheets and income statements for several fiscal years. If the life of a business is expressed by a line moving from left to right, the series of balance sheets and income statements may be graphed as follows:

Financial History of a Business

Income Statement for the year ended Dec. 31, 2010

Dec. 31 2010

Balance Sheet Dec. 31, 2010

Income Statement for the year ended Dec. 31, 2011

Dec. 31 2011

Balance Sheet Dec. 31, 2011

Income Statement for the year ended Dec. 31, 2012

Dec. 31 2012

Balance Sheet Dec. 31, 2012

BusinessConnection

CHOOSING A FISCAL YEAR

CVS Caremark Corporation (CVS) operates over 7,000 pharmacies throughout the United States and fills more than one billion prescriptions annually. CVS recently chose December 31 as its fiscal year-end described as follows:

.... *our Board of Directors approved a change in our fiscal year-end ... to December 31 of each year to better reflect our position in the health care ... industry.*

In contrast, most large retailers such as Walmart and Target use fiscal years ending January 31, when their operations are the slowest following the December holidays.

Financial Analysis and Interpretation: Working Capital and Current Ratio

OBJ. 7
Describe and illustrate the use of working capital and the current ratio in evaluating a company's financial condition.

The ability to convert assets into cash is called **liquidity**, while the ability of a business to pay its debts is called **solvency**. Two financial measures for evaluating a business's short-term liquidity and solvency are working capital and the current ratio.

Working capital is the excess of the current assets of a business over its current liabilities, as shown below.

Working Capital = Current Assets – Current Liabilities

Current assets are more liquid than long-term assets. Thus, an increase in a company's current assets increases or improves its liquidity. An increase in working capital increases or improves liquidity in the sense that current assets are available for uses other than paying current liabilities.

A positive working capital implies that the business is able to pay its current liabilities and is solvent. Thus, an increase in working capital increases or improves a company's solvency.

To illustrate, NetSolutions' working capital at the end of 2011 is $675 as computed below. This amount of working capital implies that NetSolutions is able to pay its current liabilities.

$$\text{Working Capital} = \text{Current Assets} - \text{Current Liabilities}$$
$$= \$7,745 - \$1,390$$
$$= \$6,355$$

The **current ratio** is another means of expressing the relationship between current assets and current liabilities. The current ratio is computed by dividing current assets by current liabilities, as shown below.

$$\text{Current Ratio} = \frac{\text{Current Assets}}{\text{Current Liabilities}}$$

To illustrate, the current ratio for NetSolutions at the end of 2011 is 1.5, computed as follows:

$$\text{Current Ratio} = \frac{\text{Current Assets}}{\text{Current Liabilities}}$$

$$= \frac{\$7,745}{\$1,390}$$

$$= 5.6 \text{ (Rounded)}$$

The current ratio is more useful than working capital in making comparisons across companies or with industry averages. To illustrate, the following data (in millions) were taken from the financial statements of Electronic Arts Inc. and Take-Two Interactive Software, Inc.

	Electronic Arts		Take-Two	
	Mar. 31, 2009	Mar. 31, 2008	Oct. 31, 2009	Oct. 31, 2008
Current assets	$3,120	$3,925	$628	$724
Current liabilities	1,136	1,299	354	365
Working capital	$1,984	$2,626	$274	$359
Current ratio	2.75	3.02	1.77	1.98
Operating income (loss)	($3,120 ÷ $1,136)	($3,925 ÷ $1,299)	($628 ÷ $354)	($724 ÷ $365)

Electronic Arts is larger than Take-Two and has 2009 working capital of $1,984 as compared to Take-Two's 2009 working capital of $274. Such size differences make comparisons across companies difficult. In contrast, the current ratio allows comparability across companies.

To illustrate, Electronic Arts has over seven times more working capital ($1,984) than does Take Two ($274). However, by using the current ratio the changes in liquidity of both companies can be directly compared. Specifically, Electronic Arts' current ratio declined from 3.02 to 2.75, or 0.27. Take Two's current ratio also declined from 1.98 to 1.77, or 0.21. Thus, both companies experienced a small decline in their liquidity in 2009.

Example Exercise 4-6 Working Capital and Current Ratio

OBJ. 7

Two income statements for Fortson Company are shown below.

	2012	2011
Current assets	$310,500	$262,500
Current liabilities	172,500	150,000

a. Determine the working capital and current ratio for 2012 and 2011.

b. Does the change in the current ratio from 2011 to 2012 indicate a favorable or an unfavorable trend?

(continued)

a.

	2012	**2011**
Current assets	$310,500	$262,500
Current liabilities	172,500	150,000
Working capital	$138,000	$112,500
Current ratio	1.80	1.75
	($310,500 ÷ $172,500)	($262,500 ÷ $150,000)

b. The change from 1.75 to 1.80 indicates a favorable trend.

Practice Exercises: **PE 4-6A, PE 4-6B**

APPENDIX 1

End-of-Period Spreadsheet (Work Sheet)

Accountants often use working papers for analyzing and summarizing data. Such working papers are not a formal part of the accounting records. This is in contrast to the chart of accounts, the journal, and the ledger, which are essential parts of an accounting system. Working papers are usually prepared by using a computer spreadsheet program such as Microsoft's Excel.™

The end-of-period spreadsheet shown in Exhibit 1 is a working paper used to summarize adjusting entries and their effects on the accounts. As illustrated in the chapter, the financial statements for **NetSolutions** can be prepared directly from the spreadsheet's Adjusted Trial Balance columns.

Some accountants prefer to expand the end-of-period spreadsheet shown in Exhibit 1 to include financial statement columns. Exhibits 18 through 22 illustrate the step-by-step process of how to prepare this expanded spreadsheet. As a basis for illustration, NetSolutions is used.

Step 1. Enter the Title

The spreadsheet is started by entering the following data:

1. Name of the business: *NetSolutions*
2. Type of working paper: *End-of-Period Spreadsheet*
3. The period of time: *For the Two Months Ended December 31, 2011*

Exhibit 18 shows the preceding data entered for NetSolutions.

Step 2. Enter the Unadjusted Trial Balance

Enter the unadjusted trial balance on the spreadsheet. The spreadsheet in Exhibit 18 shows the unadjusted trial balance for NetSolutions at December 31, 2011.

Step 3. Enter the Adjustments

The adjustments for NetSolutions from Chapter 3 are entered in the Adjustments columns, as shown in Exhibit 19. Cross-referencing (by letters) the debit and credit of each adjustment is useful in reviewing the spreadsheet. It is also helpful for identifying the adjusting entries that need to be recorded in the journal. This cross-referencing process is sometimes referred to as *keying* the adjustments.

The adjustments are normally entered in the order in which the data are assembled. If the titles of the accounts to be adjusted do not appear in the unadjusted trial balance, the accounts are inserted in their proper order in the Account Title column.

The adjusting entries for NetSolutions that are entered in the Adjustments columns are as follows:

(a) **Supplies**. The supplies account has a debit balance of $2,000. The cost of the supplies on hand at the end of the period is $760. The supplies expense for December is the difference between the two amounts, or $1,240 ($2,000 – $760). The adjustment is entered as (1) $1,240 in the Adjustments Debit column on the same line as Supplies Expense and (2) $1,240 in the Adjustments Credit column on the same line as Supplies.

(b) **Prepaid Insurance**. The prepaid insurance account has a debit balance of $2,400. This balance represents the prepayment of insurance for 12 months beginning December 1. Thus, the insurance expense for December is $200 ($2,400 ÷ 12). The adjustment is entered as (1) $200 in the Adjustments Debit column on the same line as Insurance Expense and (2) $200 in the Adjustments Credit column on the same line as Prepaid Insurance.

(c) **Unearned Rent**. The unearned rent account had a credit balance of $360. This balance represents the receipt of three months' rent, beginning with December. Thus, the rent revenue for December is $120 ($360 ÷ 3). The adjustment is entered as (1) $120 in the Adjustments Debit column on the same line as Unearned Rent and (2) $120 in the Adjustments Credit column on the same line as Rent Revenue.

Turn Exhibit 19

(d) **Accrued Fees**. Fees accrued at the end of December but not recorded total $500. This amount is an increase in an asset and an increase in revenue. The adjustment is entered as (1) $500 in the Adjustments Debit column on the same line as Accounts Receivable and (2) $500 in the Adjustments Credit column on the same line as Fees Earned.

(e) **Wages**. Wages accrued but not paid at the end of December total $250. This amount is an increase in expenses and an increase in liabilities. The adjustment is entered as (1) $250 in the Adjustments Debit column on the same line as Wages Expense and (2) $250 in the Adjustments Credit column on the same line as Wages Payable.

(f) **Depreciation**. Depreciation of the office equipment is $50 for December. The adjustment is entered as (1) $50 in the Adjustments Debit column on the same line as Depreciation Expense and (2) $50 in the Adjustments Credit column on the same line as Accumulated Depreciation.

After the adjustments have been entered, the Adjustments columns are totaled to verify the equality of the debits and credits. The total of the Debit column must equal the total of the Credit column.

Step 4. Enter the Adjusted Trial Balance

The adjusted trial balance is entered by combining the adjustments with the unadjusted balances for each account. The adjusted amounts are then extended to the Adjusted Trial Balance columns, as shown in Exhibit 20.

To illustrate, the cash amount of $2,065 is extended to the Adjusted Trial Balance Debit column since no adjustments affected Cash. Accounts Receivable has an initial balance of $2,220 and a debit adjustment of $500. Thus, $2,720 ($2,220 + $500) is entered in the Adjusted Trial Balance Debit column for Accounts Receivable. The same process continues until all account balances are extended to the Adjusted Trial Balance columns.

Turn Exhibit 20

After the accounts and adjustments have been extended, the Adjusted Trial Balance columns are totaled to verify the equality of debits and credits. The total of the Debit column must equal the total of the Credit column.

Step 5. Extend the Accounts to the Income Statement and Balance Sheet Columns

The adjusted trial balance amounts are extended to the Income Statement and Balance Sheet columns. The amounts for revenues and expenses are extended to the Income Statement column. The amounts for assets, liabilities, owner's capital, and drawing are extended to the Balance Sheet columns.[3]

Turn Exhibit 21

3 The balances of the owner's capital and drawing accounts are extended to the Balance Sheet columns because the spreadsheet does not have separate Statement of Owner's Equity columns.

EXHIBIT 18   Spreadsheet (Work Sheet) with Unadjusted Trial Balance Entered

	A	B	C	D	E	F	G	H	I	J	K
1			NetSolutions								
2			End-of-Period Spreadsheet (Work Sheet)								
3			For the Two Months Ended December 31, 2011								
4		Unadjusted				Adjusted					
5		Trial Balance		Adjustments		Trial Balance		Income Statement		Balance Sheet	
6	Account Title	Dr.	Cr.	Dr.	Cr.	Dr.	Cr.	Dr.	Cr.	Dr.	Cr.
7											
8	Cash	2,065									
9	Accounts Receivable	2,220									
10	Supplies	2,000									
11	Prepaid Insurance	2,400									
12	Land	20,000									
13	Office Equipment	1,800									
14	Accumulated Depreciation										
15	Accounts Payable		900								
16	Wages Payable										
17	Unearned Rent		360								
18	Chris Clark, Capital		25,000								
19	Chris Clark, Drawing	4,000									
20	Fees Earned		16,340								
21	Rent Revenue										
22	Wages Expense	4,275									
23	Supplies Expense	800									
24	Rent Expense	1,600									
25	Utilities Expense	985									
26	Insurance Expense										
27	Depreciation Expense										
28	Miscellaneous Expense	455									
29		42,600	42,600								
30											
31											
32											

The spreadsheet (work sheet) is used for summarizing the effects of adjusting entries. It also aids in preparing financial statements.

The first account listed in the Adjusted Trial Balance columns is Cash with a debit balance of $2,065. Cash is an asset, is listed on the balance sheet, and has a debit balance. Therefore, $2,065 is extended to the Balance Sheet Debit column. The Fees Earned balance of $16,840 is extended to the Income Statement Credit column. The same process continues until all account balances have been extended to the proper columns, as shown in Exhibit 21.

Turn Exhibit 21

Step 6. Total the Income Statement and Balance Sheet Columns, Compute the Net Income or Net Loss, and Complete the Spreadsheet

After the account balances are extended to the Income Statement and Balance Sheet columns, each of the columns is totaled. The difference between the two Income Statement column totals is the amount of the net income or the net loss for the period. This difference (net income or net loss) will also be the difference between the two Balance Sheet column totals.

If the Income Statement Credit column total (total revenue) is greater than the Income Statement Debit column total (total expenses), the difference is the net income. If the Income Statement Debit column total is greater than the Income Statement Credit column total, the difference is a net loss.

As shown in Exhibit 22, the total of the Income Statement Credit column is $16,960, and the total of the Income Statement Debit column is $9,855. Thus, the net income for NetSolutions is $7,105 as shown below.

Turn Exhibit 22

Total of Income Statement Credit column (revenues)	$16,960
Total of Income Statement Debit column (expenses)	9,855
Net income (excess of revenues over expenses)	$ 7,105

The amount of the net income, $7,105, is entered in the Income Statement Debit column and the Balance Sheet Credit column. *Net income* is also entered in the Account Title column. Entering the net income of $7,105 in the Balance Sheet Credit column has the effect of transferring the net balance of the revenue and expense accounts to the owner's capital account.

If there was a net loss instead of net income, the amount of the net loss would be entered in the Income Statement Credit column and the Balance Sheet Debit column. *Net loss* would also be entered in the Account Title column.

After the net income or net loss is entered on the spreadsheet, the Income Statement and Balance Sheet columns are totaled. The totals of the two Income Statement columns must now be equal. The totals of the two Balance Sheet columns must also be equal.

Preparing the Financial Statements from the Spreadsheet

The spreadsheet can be used to prepare the income statement, the statement of owner's equity, and the balance sheet shown in Exhibit 2. The income statement is normally prepared directly from the spreadsheet. The expenses are listed in the income statement in Exhibit 2 in order of size, beginning with the larger items. Miscellaneous expense is the last item, regardless of its amount.

The first item normally presented on the statement of owner's equity is the balance of the owner's capital account at the beginning of the period. The amount listed as owner's capital in the spreadsheet, however, is not always the account balance at the beginning of the period. The owner may have invested additional assets in the business during the period. Thus, for the beginning balance and any additional investments, it is necessary to refer to the capital account in the ledger. These amounts, along with the net income (or net loss) and the drawing amount shown in the spreadsheet, are used to determine the ending capital account balance.

The balance sheet can be prepared directly from the spreadsheet columns except for the ending balance of owner's capital. The ending balance of owner's capital is taken from the statement of owner's equity.

When a spreadsheet is used, the adjusting and closing entries are normally not journalized or posted until after the spreadsheet and financial statements have been prepared. The data for the adjusting entries are taken from the Adjustments columns of the spreadsheet. The data for the first two closing entries are taken from the Income Statement columns of the spreadsheet. The amount for the third closing entry is the net income or net loss appearing at the bottom of the spreadsheet. The amount for the fourth closing entry is the drawing account balance that appears in the Balance Sheet Debit column of the spreadsheet.

At a Glance 4

OBJ. 1

Describe the flow of accounting information from the unadjusted trial balance into the adjusted trial balance and financial statements.

Key Points   Exhibit 1 illustrates the end-of-period process by which accounts are adjusted and how the adjusted accounts flow into the financial statements.

Learning Outcomes	Example Exercises	Practice Exercises
• Using an end-of-period spreadsheet, describe how the unadjusted trial balance accounts are affected by adjustments and how the adjusted trial balance accounts flow into the income statement and balance sheet.	**EE4-1**	**PE4-1A, 4-1B**

OBJ. 2

Prepare financial statements from adjusted account balances.

Key Points   Using the end-of-period spreadsheet shown in Exhibit 1, the income statement and balance sheet for NetSolutions can be prepared. The statement of owner's equity is prepared by referring to transactions that have been posted to owner's capital accounts in the ledger. A classified balance sheet has sections for current assets; property, plant, and equipment; current liabilities; long-term liabilities; and owner's equity.

Learning Outcomes	Example Exercises	Practice Exercises
• Describe how the net income or net loss from the period can be determined from an end-of-period spreadsheet.		
• Prepare an income statement, statement of owner's equity, and a balance sheet.	**EE4-2**	**PE4-2A, 4-2B**
• Indicate how accounts would be reported on a classified balance sheet.	**EE4-3**	**PE4-3A, 4-3B**

3 Prepare closing entries.

Key Points Four entries are required in closing the temporary accounts. The first entry closes the revenue accounts to Income Summary. The second entry closes the expense accounts to Income Summary. The third entry closes the balance of Income Summary (net income or net loss) to the owner's capital account. The fourth entry closes the drawing account to the owner's capital account.

After the closing entries have been posted to the ledger, the balance in the capital account agrees with the amount reported on the statement of owner's equity and balance sheet. In addition, the revenue, expense, and drawing accounts will have zero balances.

Learning Outcomes	Example Exercises	Practice Exercises
• Prepare the closing entry for revenues.	EE4-4	PE4-4A, 4-4B
• Prepare the closing entry for expenses.	EE4-4	PE4-4A, 4-4B
• Prepare the closing entry for transferring the balance of Income Summary to the owner's capital account.	EE4-4	PE4-4A, 4-4B
• Prepare the closing entry for the owner's drawing account.	EE4-4	PE4-4A, 4-4B

4 Describe the accounting cycle.

Key Points The 10 basic steps of the accounting cycle are as follows:

1. Transactions are analyzed and recorded in the journal.
2. Transactions are posted to the ledger.
3. An unadjusted trial balance is prepared.
4. Adjustment data are assembled and analyzed.
5. An optional end-of-period spreadsheet is prepared.
6. Adjusting entries are journalized and posted to the ledger.
7. An adjusted trial balance is prepared.
8. Financial statements are prepared.
9. Closing entries are journalized and posted to the ledger.
10. A post-closing trial balance is prepared.

Learning Outcomes	Example Exercises	Practice Exercises
• List the 10 steps of the accounting cycle.		
• Determine whether any steps are out of order in a listing of accounting cycle steps.		
• Determine whether there are any missing steps in a listing of accounting cycle steps.	EE4-5	PE4-5A, 4-5B

5 Illustrate the accounting cycle for one period.

Key Points The complete accounting cycle for Kelly Consulting for the month of April is described and illustrated on pages 163–173.

Learning Outcomes

• Complete the accounting cycle for a period from beginning to end.

OBJ. 6 Explain what is meant by the fiscal year and the natural business year.

Key Points The annual accounting period adopted by a business is its fiscal year. A company's fiscal year that ends when business activities have reached the lowest point in its annual operating cycle is called the natural business year.

Learning Outcomes

• Explain why companies use a fiscal year that is different from the calendar year.

OBJ. 7 Describe and illustrate the use of working capital and the current ratio in evaluating a company's financial condition.

Key Points The ability to convert assets into cash is called liquidity, while the ability of a business to pay its debts is called solvency. Two financial measures for evaluating a business's short-term liquidity and solvency are working capital and the current ratio. Working capital is computed by subtracting current liabilities from current assets. An excess of current assets over current liabilities implies that the business is able to pay its current liabilities. The current ratio is computed by dividing current assets by current liabilities. The current ratio is more useful than working capital in making comparisons across companies or with industry averages.

Learning Outcomes	Example Exercises	Practice Exercises
• Define liquidity and solvency.		
• Compute working capital.	EE4-6	PE4-6A, 4-6B
• Compute the current ratio.	EE4-6	PE4-6A, 4-6B

Key Terms

accounting cycle (162)
clearing account (157)
closing entries (156)
closing process (156)
closing the books (156)
current assets (155)
current liabilities (155)

current ratio (175)
fiscal year (173)
fixed (plant) assets (155)
Income Summary (157)
liquidity (174)
long-term liabilities (155)
natural business year (174)

notes receivable (155)
real (permanent) accounts (156)
solvency (174)
temporary (nominal) accounts (156)
working capital (174)

Illustrative Problem

Three years ago, T. Roderick organized Harbor Realty. At July 31, 2012, the end of the current fiscal year, the following end-of-period spreadsheet was prepared:

	A	B	C	D	E	F	G
1		Harbor Realty					
2		End-of-Period Spreadsheet					
3		For the Year Ended July 31, 2012					
4		Unadjusted				Adjusted	
5		Trial Balance		Adjustments		Trial Balance	
6	**Account Title**	Dr.	Cr.	Dr.	Cr.	Dr.	Cr.
7							
8	Cash	3,425				3,425	
9	Accounts Receivable	7,000		(e) 1,000		8,000	
10	Supplies	1,270			(a) 890	380	
11	Prepaid Insurance	620			(b) 315	305	
12	Office Equipment	51,650				51,650	
13	Accum. Depreciation		9,700		(c) 4,950		14,650
14	Accounts Payable		925				925
15	Unearned Fees		1,250	(f) 500			750
16	Wages Payable				(d) 440		440
17	T. Roderick, Capital		29,000				29,000
18	T. Roderick, Drawing	5,200				5,200	
19	Fees Earned		59,125		(e) 1,000		60,625
20					(f) 500		
21	Wages Expense	22,415		(d) 440		22,855	
22	Depreciation Expense			(c) 4,950		4,950	
23	Rent Expense	4,200				4,200	
24	Utilities Expense	2,715				2,715	
25	Supplies Expense			(a) 890		890	
26	Insurance Expense			(b) 315		315	
27	Miscellaneous Expense	1,505				1,505	
28		100,000	100,000	8,095	8,095	106,390	106,390
29							

Instructions

1. Prepare an income statement, a statement of owner's equity (no additional investments were made during the year), and a balance sheet.

2. On the basis of the data in the end-of-period spreadsheet, journalize the closing entries.

Solution

1.

Harbor Realty Income Statement For the Year Ended July 31, 2012		
Fees earned...		$60,625
Expenses:		
Wages expense	$22,855	
Depreciation expense	4,950	
Rent expense	4,200	
Utilities expense	2,715	
Supplies expense	890	
Insurance expense	315	
Miscellaneous expense	1,505	
Total expenses....................................		37,430
Net income		$23,195

Harbor Realty Statement of Owner's Equity For the Year Ended July 31, 2012		
T. Roderick, capital, August 1, 2011..		$29,000
Net income for the year....................................	$23,195	
Less withdrawals	5,200	
Increase in owner's equity		17,995
T. Roderick, capital, July 31, 2012..		$46,995

Harbor Realty
Balance Sheet
July 31, 2012

Assets			Liabilities		
Current assets:			Current liabilities:		
Cash....................................	$ 3,425		Accounts payable.....................	$925	
Accounts receivable	8,000		Unearned fees	750	
Supplies	380		Wages payable	440	
Prepaid insurance	305		Total liabilities.........................		$ 2,115
Total current assets..................		$12,110			
Property, plant, and equipment:					
Office equipment......................	$51,650				
Less accum. depreciation...............	14,650		**Owner's Equity**		
Total property, plant,			T. Roderick, capital.....................		46,995
and equipment		37,000	Total liabilities and		
Total assets..............................		$49,110	owner's equity		$49,110

2.

		Journal			Page
Date		Description	Post. Ref.	Debit	Credit
2012 July 31		**Closing Entries** Fees Earned		60,625	
		Income Summary			60,625
	31	Income Summary		37,430	
		Wages Expense			22,855
		Depreciation Expense			4,950
		Rent Expense			4,200
		Utilities Expense			2,715
		Supplies Expense			890
		Insurance Expense			315
		Miscellaneous Expense			1,505
	31	Income Summary		23,195	
		T. Roderick, Capital			23,195
	31	T. Roderick, Capital		5,200	
		T. Roderick, Drawing			5,200

Discussion Questions

1. Why do some accountants prepare an end-of-period spreadsheet?

2. Describe the nature of the assets that compose the following sections of a balance sheet: (a) current assets, (b) property, plant, and equipment.

3. What is the difference between a current liability and a long-term liability?

4. What types of accounts are referred to as temporary accounts?

5. Why are closing entries required at the end of an accounting period?

6. What is the difference between adjusting entries and closing entries?

7. What is the purpose of the post-closing trial balance?

8. (a) What is the most important output of the accounting cycle? (b) Do all companies have an accounting cycle? Explain.

9. What is the natural business year?

10. The fiscal years for several well-known companies are as follows:

Company	Fiscal Year Ending	Company	Fiscal Year Ending
Sears	January 30	Home Depot	January 31
JCPenney	January 30	Tiffany & Co.	January 31
Target Corp.	January 30	Limited Brands, Inc.	January 31

What general characteristic shared by these companies explains why they do not have fiscal years ending December 31?

Practice Exercises

Learning Objectives	Example Exercises	
OBJ. 1	EE 4-1 *p. 152*	

PE 4-1A   Flow of accounts into financial statements

The balances for the accounts listed below appear in the Adjusted Trial Balance columns of the end-of-period spreadsheet. Indicate whether each account would flow into the income statement, statement of owner's equity, or balance sheet.

1. Accounts Receivable
2. Depreciation Expense—Equipment
3. Jean Kehler, Capital
4. Office Equipment

5. Rent Revenue
6. Supplies Expense
7. Unearned Revenue
8. Wages Payable

OBJ. 1   EE 4-1 *p. 152*

PE 4-1B   Flow of accounts into financial statements

The balances for the accounts listed below appear in the Adjusted Trial Balance columns of the end-of-period spreadsheet. Indicate whether each account would flow into the income statement, statement of owner's equity, or balance sheet.

1. Accumulated Depreciation—Building
2. Cash
3. Fees Earned
4. Insurance Expense

5. Prepaid Rent
6. Supplies
7. Vincent Schafer, Drawing
8. Wages Expense

OBJ. 2   EE 4-2 *p. 154*

PE 4-2A   Statement of owner's equity

Judy Flint owns and operates Derby Advertising Services. On January 1, 2011, Judy Flint, Capital had a balance of $290,000. During the year, Judy invested an additional $100,000 and withdrew $40,000. For the year ended December 31, 2011, Derby Advertising Services reported a net income of $93,750. Prepare a statement of owner's equity for the year ended December 31, 2011.

OBJ. 2   EE 4-2 *p. 154*

PE 4-2B   Statement of owner's equity

Mavis Curry owns and operates A2Z Delivery Services. On January 1, 2011, Mavis Curry, Capital had a balance of $600,000. During the year, Mavis made no additional investments and withdrew $45,000. For the year ended December 31, 2011, A2Z Delivery Services reported a net loss of $13,500. Prepare a statement of owner's equity for the year ended December 31, 2011.

OBJ. 2   EE 4-3 *p. 155*

PE 4-3A   Classified balance sheet

The following accounts appear in an adjusted trial balance of Pilot Consulting. Indicate whether each account would be reported in the (a) current asset; (b) property, plant, and equipment; (c) current liability; (d) long-term liability; or (e) owner's equity section of the December 31, 2011, balance sheet of Pilot Consulting.

1. Building
2. Marty Ramsey, Capital
3. Notes Payable (due in 2017)
4. Prepaid Rent

5. Salaries Payable
6. Supplies
7. Taxes Payable
8. Unearned Service Fees

Learning Objectives	Example Exercises	
OBJ. 2	EE 4-3 *p. 155*	**PE 4-3B Classified balance sheet**

The following accounts appear in an adjusted trial balance of F-18 Consulting. Indicate whether each account would be reported in the (a) current asset; (b) property, plant, and equipment; (c) current liability; (d) long-term liability; or (e) owner's equity section of the December 31, 2011, balance sheet of F-18 Consulting.

1. Accounts Payable
2. Accounts Receivable
3. Accumulated Depreciation—Building
4. Cash
5. Jess Garza, Capital
6. Note Payable (due in 2018)
7. Supplies
8. Wages Payable

OBJ. 3	EE 4-4 *p. 159*	**PE 4-4A Closing entries**

After the accounts have been adjusted at October 31, the end of the fiscal year, the following balances were taken from the ledger of Silver Gate Delivery Services Co.:

Mira Craig, Capital	$800,000
Mira Craig, Drawing	125,000
Fees Earned	700,000
Wages Expense	400,000
Rent Expense	75,000
Supplies Expense	16,000
Miscellaneous Expense	5,000

Journalize the four entries required to close the accounts.

OBJ. 3	EE 4-4 *p. 159*	**PE 4-4B Closing entries**

After the accounts have been adjusted at June 30, the end of the fiscal year, the following balances were taken from the ledger of Hillcrest Landscaping Co.:

Bryan Orr, Capital	$275,000
Bryan Orr, Drawing	25,000
Fees Earned	400,000
Wages Expense	280,000
Rent Expense	40,000
Supplies Expense	3,000
Miscellaneous Expense	12,000

Journalize the four entries required to close the accounts.

OBJ. 4	EE 4-5 *p. 162*	**PE 4-5A Accounting cycle**

From the following list of steps in the accounting cycle, identify what two steps are missing.

a. Transactions are analyzed and recorded in the journal.
b. An unadjusted trial balance is prepared.
c. Adjustment data are assembled and analyzed.
d. An optional end-of-period spreadsheet is prepared.
e. Adjusting entries are journalized and posted to the ledger.
f. An adjusted trial balance is prepared.
g. Closing entries are journalized and posted to the ledger.
h. A post-closing trial balance is prepared.

OBJ. 4	EE 4-5 *p. 162*	**PE 4-5B Accounting cycle**

From the following list of steps in the accounting cycle, identify what two steps are missing.

a. Transactions are analyzed and recorded in the journal.
b. Transactions are posted to the ledger.

c. An unadjusted trial balance is prepared.

d. An optional end-of-period spreadsheet is prepared.

e. Adjusting entries are journalized and posted to the ledger.

f. An adjusted trial balance is prepared.

g. Financial statements are prepared.

h. A post-closing trial balance is prepared.

OBJ. 7   EE 4-6 p. 175

PE 4-6A   Working capital and current ratio

The following balance sheet data for Mayer Company are shown below.

	2012	2011
Current assets	$840,000	$1,430,000
Current liabilities	600,000	550,000

a. Determine the working capital and current ratio for 2012 and 2011.

b. Does the change in the current ratio from 2011 to 2012 indicate a favorable or an unfavorable trend?

OBJ. 7   EE 4-6 p. 175

PE 4-6B   Working capital and current ratio

The following balance sheet data for Finn Company are shown below.

	2012	2011
Current assets	$288,000	$171,000
Current liabilities	120,000	90,000

a. Determine the working capital and current ratio for 2012 and 2011.

b. Does the change in the current ratio from 2011 to 2012 indicate a favorable or an unfavorable trend?

Exercises

OBJ. 1, 2

EX 4-1   Flow of accounts into financial statements

The balances for the accounts listed below appear in the Adjusted Trial Balance columns of the end-of-period spreadsheet. Indicate whether each account would flow into the income statement, statement of owner's equity, or balance sheet.

1. Accounts Payable
2. Accounts Receivable
3. Cash
4. Dora Kovar, Drawing
5. Fees Earned

6. Supplies
7. Unearned Rent
8. Utilities Expense
9. Wages Expense
10. Wages Payable

OBJ. 1, 2

EX 4-2   Classifying accounts

Balances for each of the following accounts appear in an adjusted trial balance. Identify each as (a) asset, (b) liability, (c) revenue, or (d) expense.

1. Accounts Receivable
2. Equipment
3. Fees Earned
4. Insurance Expense
5. Prepaid Advertising
6. Prepaid Rent

7. Rent Revenue
8. Salary Expense
9. Salary Payable
10. Supplies
11. Supplies Expense
12. Unearned Rent

OBJ. 1, 2

EX 4-3 Financial statements from the end-of-period spreadsheet

Pacifica Consulting is a consulting firm owned and operated by Tara Milsap. The end-of-period spreadsheet shown below was prepared for the year ended August 31, 2012.

	A	B	C	D	E	F	G
1		Pacifica Consulting					
2		End-of-Period Spreadsheet					
3		For the Year Ended August 31, 2012					
4		Unadjusted				Adjusted	
5		Trial Balance		Adjustments		Trial Balance	
6	Account Title	Dr.	Cr.	Dr.	Cr.	Dr.	Cr.
7							
8	Cash	9,500				9,500	
9	Accounts Receivable	22,500				22,500	
10	Supplies	2,400			(a) 2,000	400	
11	Office Equipment	18,500				18,500	
12	Accumulated Depreciation		2,500		(b) 1,200		3,700
13	Accounts Payable		6,100				6,100
14	Salaries Payable				(c) 300		300
15	Tara Milsap, Capital		22,600				22,600
16	Tara Milsap, Drawing	3,000				3,000	
17	Fees Earned		43,800				43,800
18	Salary Expense	17,250		(c) 300		17,550	
19	Supplies Expense			(a) 2,000		2,000	
20	Depreciation Expense			(b) 1,200		1,200	
21	Miscellaneous Expense	1,850				1,850	
22		75,000	75,000	3,500	3,500	76,500	76,500
23							

Based on the preceding spreadsheet, prepare an income statement, statement of owner's equity, and balance sheet for Pacifica Consulting.

OBJ. 1, 2

EX 4-4 Financial statements from the end-of-period spreadsheet

Three Winds Consulting is a consulting firm owned and operated by Gabriel Brull. The following end-of-period spreadsheet was prepared for the year ended June 30, 2012.

	A	B	C	D	E	F	G
1		Three Winds Consulting					
2		End-of-Period Spreadsheet					
3		For the Year Ended June 30, 2012					
4		Unadjusted				Adjusted	
5		Trial Balance		Adjustments		Trial Balance	
6	Account Title	Dr.	Cr.	Dr.	Cr.	Dr.	Cr.
7							
8	Cash	7,500				7,500	
9	Accounts Receivable	23,500				23,500	
10	Supplies	3,000			(a) 2,400	600	
11	Office Equipment	30,500				30,500	
12	Accumulated Depreciation		4,500		(b) 800		5,300
13	Accounts Payable		3,300				3,300
14	Salaries Payable				(c) 500		500
15	Gabriel Brull, Capital		32,200				32,200
16	Gabriel Brull, Drawing	2,000				2,000	
17	Fees Earned		60,000				60,000
18	Salary Expense	32,000		(c) 500		32,500	
19	Supplies Expense			(a) 2,400		2,400	
20	Depreciation Expense			(b) 800		800	
21	Miscellaneous Expense	1,500				1,500	
22		100,000	100,000	3,700	3,700	101,300	101,300
23							

Based on the preceding spreadsheet, prepare an income statement, statement of owner's equity, and balance sheet for Three Winds Consulting.

OBJ. 2

✔ Net income, $89,600

EX 4-5 **Income statement**

The following account balances were taken from the adjusted trial balance for On-Time Messenger Service, a delivery service firm, for the current fiscal year ended April 30, 2012:

Depreciation Expense	$ 6,400	Rent Expense	$ 48,400
Fees Earned	340,000	Salaries Expense	171,040
Insurance Expense	1,200	Supplies Expense	2,200
Miscellaneous Expense	2,600	Utilities Expense	18,560

Prepare an income statement.

OBJ. 2

✔ Net loss, $36,600

EX 4-6 **Income statement; net loss**

The following revenue and expense account balances were taken from the ledger of Graphics Services Co. after the accounts had been adjusted on February 29, 2012, the end of the current fiscal year:

Depreciation Expense	$ 9,000	Service Revenue	$250,000
Insurance Expense	4,000	Supplies Expense	3,000
Miscellaneous Expense	5,000	Utilities Expense	14,600
Rent Expense	36,000	Wages Expense	215,000

Prepare an income statement.

OBJ. 2

Internet Project

✔ a. Net income: $98

EX 4-7 **Income statement**

FedEx Corporation had the following revenue and expense account balances (in millions) at its fiscal year-end of May 31, 2009:

Depreciation	$1,975	Purchased Transportation	$ 4,534
Fuel	3,811	Rentals and Landing Fees	2,429
Maintenance and Repairs	1,898	Revenues	35,497
Other Expense (Income) Net	6,406	Salaries and Employee Benefits	13,767
Provision for Income Taxes	579		

a. Prepare an income statement.

b. ━━━▶ Compare your income statement with the related income statement that is available at the FedEx Corporation Web site, which is linked to the text's Web site at **academic.cengage .com/accounting/warren.** What similarities and differences do you see?

OBJ. 2

✔ Lisa DuBois, capital, Oct. 31, 2012: $635,000

EX 4-8 **Statement of owner's equity**

Fouts Systems Co. offers its services to residents in the Chicago area. Selected accounts from the ledger of Fouts Systems Co. for the current fiscal year ended October 31, 2012, are as follows:

Lisa DuBois, Capital				Lisa DuBois, Drawing			
Oct. 31	20,000	Nov. 1 (2011)	550,000	Jan. 31	5,000	Oct. 31	20,000
		Oct. 31	105,000	Apr. 30	5,000		
				July 31	5,000		
				Oct. 31	5,000		

Income Summary			
Oct. 31	375,000	Oct. 31	480,000
31	105,000		

Prepare a statement of owner's equity for the year.

OBJ. 2

✔ Erica Kilty, capital, June 30, 2012: $346,500

EX 4-9 **Statement of owner's equity; net loss**

Selected accounts from the ledger of Balboa Sports for the current fiscal year ended June 30, 2012, are as follows:

Erica Kilty, Capital				Erica Kilty, Drawing			
June 30	42,000	July 1 (2011)	398,500	Sept. 30	2,500	June 30	10,000
30	10,000			Dec. 31	2,500		
				May 31	2,500		
				June 30	2,500		

Income Summary				
June 30	402,000	June 30	360,000	
		30	42,000	

Prepare a statement of owner's equity for the year.

OBJ. 2

EX 4-10   Classifying assets

Identify each of the following as (a) a current asset or (b) property, plant, and equipment:

1. Accounts receivable
2. Building
3. Cash
4. Equipment
5. Prepaid Insurance
6. Supplies

OBJ. 2

EX 4-11   Balance sheet classification

At the balance sheet date, a business owes a mortgage note payable of $480,000, the terms of which provide for monthly payments of $2,500.

➤ Explain how the liability should be classified on the balance sheet.

OBJ. 2

✔ Total assets:
$750,000

EX 4-12   Balance sheet

My-Best Weight Co. offers personal weight reduction consulting services to individuals. After all the accounts have been closed on November 30, 2012, the end of the current fiscal year, the balances of selected accounts from the ledger of My-Best Weight Co. are as follows:

Accounts Payable	$ 34,500	Land	$400,000
Accounts Receivable	83,120	Prepaid Insurance	19,200
Accumulated Depreciation—Equipment	103,900	Prepaid Rent	12,000
Blanca Tierney, Capital	692,000	Salaries Payable	13,500
Cash	?	Supplies	2,080
Equipment	300,000	Unearned Fees	10,000

Prepare a classified balance sheet that includes the correct balance for Cash.

OBJ. 2

✔ Corrected balance sheet, total assets:
$525,000

EX 4-13   Balance sheet

List the errors you find in the following balance sheet. Prepare a corrected balance sheet.

Poshe Services Co.
Balance Sheet
For the Year Ended May 31, 2012

Assets			Liabilities		
Current assets:			Current liabilities:		
Cash	$ 14,000		Accounts receivable	$ 32,500	
Accounts payable	24,000		Accum. depr.—building . . .	155,000	
Supplies	6,500		Accum. depr.—equipment	25,000	
Prepaid insurance	12,000		Net income	135,000	
Land	180,000		Total liabilities		$347,500
Total current assets		$236,500			
Property, plant,			**Owner's Equity**		
and equipment:					
Building.	$375,000		Wages payable	$ 2,500	
Equipment.	85,000		Hector Delgado, capital	498,500	
Total property, plant,			Total owner's equity.		501,000
and equipment		612,000	Total liabilities and		
Total assets		$848,500	owner's equity		$848,500

OBJ. 3

EX 4-14   Identifying accounts to be closed

From the list at the top of the next page, identify the accounts that should be closed to Income Summary at the end of the fiscal year:

a. Accounts Payable
b. Accumulated Depreciation—Equipment
c. Depreciation Expense—Equipment
d. Equipment
e. Fauzi Hanna, Capital
f. Fauzi Hanna, Drawing

g. Fees Earned
h. Land
i. Supplies
j. Supplies Expense
k. Wages Expense
l. Wages Payable

OBJ. 3

EX 4-15 Closing entries

Prior to its closing, Income Summary had total debits of $815,000 and total credits of $1,280,000.

➤ Briefly explain the purpose served by the income summary account and the nature of the entries that resulted in the $815,000 and the $1,280,000.

OBJ. 3

EX 4-16 Closing entries with net income

After all revenue and expense accounts have been closed at the end of the fiscal year, Income Summary has a debit of $315,000 and a credit of $449,500. At the same date, Faye Barnes, Capital has a credit balance of $750,000, and Faye Barnes, Drawing has a balance of $40,000. (a) Journalize the entries required to complete the closing of the accounts. (b) Determine the amount of Faye Barnes, Capital at the end of the period.

OBJ. 3

EX 4-17 Closing entries with net loss

Imex Services Co. offers its services to individuals desiring to improve their personal images. After the accounts have been adjusted at March 31, the end of the fiscal year, the following balances were taken from the ledger of Imex Services Co.

Margo Hoskins, Capital	$300,000	Rent Expense	$40,000
Margo Hoskins, Drawing	15,000	Supplies Expense	20,000
Fees Earned	180,000	Miscellaneous Expense	7,500
Wages Expense	90,000		

Journalize the four entries required to close the accounts.

OBJ. 3

EX 4-18 Identifying permanent accounts

Which of the following accounts will usually appear in the post-closing trial balance?

a. Accounts Payable
b. Accumulated Depreciation
c. Anthony Adams, Capital
d. Anthony Adams, Drawing
e. Cash
f. Depreciation Expense

g. Fees Earned
h. Office Equipment
i. Salaries Expense
j. Salaries Payable
k. Supplies

OBJ. 3

✔ Correct column totals, $129,500

EX 4-19 Post-closing trial balance

An accountant prepared the following post-closing trial balance:

Gypsy Treasures Co.
Post-Closing Trial Balance
March 31, 2012

	Debit Balances	Credit Balances
Cash	18,000	
Accounts Receivable.	31,000	
Supplies		5,500
Equipment.		75,000
Accumulated Depreciation—Equipment	19,000	
Accounts Payable	11,000	
Salaries Payable.		1,000
Unearned Rent.	6,000	
Leticia Aloni, Capital.	92,500	
	177,500	81,500

Prepare a corrected post-closing trial balance. Assume that all accounts have normal balances and that the amounts shown are correct.

OBJ. 4

EX 4-20 Steps in the accounting cycle

Rearrange the following steps in the accounting cycle in proper sequence:

a. Financial statements are prepared.

b. An adjusted trial balance is prepared.

c. Adjustment data are asssembled and analyzed.

d. Adjusting entries are journalized and posted to the ledger.

e. Closing entries are journalized and posted to the ledger.

f. An unadjusted trial balance is prepared.

g. Transactions are posted to the ledger.

h. Transactions are analyzed and recorded in the journal.

i. An optional end-of-period spreadsheet (work sheet) is prepared.

j. A post-closing trial balance is prepared.

OBJ. 7

EX 4-21 Working capital and current ratio

The following data (in thousands) were taken from recent financial statements of Under Armour, Inc.:

	December 31	
	2008	**2007**
Current assets	$396,423	$322,245
Current liabilities	113,110	95,699

a. Compute the working capital and the current ratio as of December 31, 2008 and 2007. Round to two decimal places.

b. What conclusions concerning the company's ability to meet its financial obligations can you draw from part (a)?

OBJ. 7

EX 4-22 Working capital and current ratio

The following data (in thousands) were taken from recent financial statements of Starbucks Corporation:

	Sept. 27, 2009	Sept. 28, 2008
Current assets	$2,035,800	$1,748,000
Current liabilities	1,581,000	2,189,700

a. Compute the working capital and the current ratio as of September 27, 2009, and September 28, 2008. Round to two decimal places.

b. What conclusions concerning the company's ability to meet its financial obligations can you draw from part (a)?

Appendix
EX 4-23 Completing an end-of-period spreadsheet (work sheet)

List (a) through (j) in the order they would be performed in preparing and completing an end-of-period spreadsheet (work sheet).

a. Add the Debit and Credit columns of the Unadjusted Trial Balance columns of the spreadsheet (work sheet) to verify that the totals are equal.

b. Add the Debit and Credit columns of the Balance Sheet and Income Statement columns of the spreadsheet (work sheet) to verify that the totals are equal.

c. Add or deduct adjusting entry data to trial balance amounts, and extend amounts to the Adjusted Trial Balance columns.

(Continued)

d. Add the Debit and Credit columns of the Adjustments columns of the spreadsheet (work sheet) to verify that the totals are equal.

e. Add the Debit and Credit columns of the Balance Sheet and Income Statement columns of the spreadsheet (work sheet) to determine the amount of net income or net loss for the period.

f. Add the Debit and Credit columns of the Adjusted Trial Balance columns of the spreadsheet (work sheet) to verify that the totals are equal.

g. Enter the adjusting entries into the spreadsheet (work sheet), based on the adjustment data.

h. Enter the amount of net income or net loss for the period in the proper Income Statement column and Balance Sheet column.

i. Enter the unadjusted account balances from the general ledger into the Unadjusted Trial Balance columns of the spreadsheet (work sheet).

j. Extend the adjusted trial balance amounts to the Income Statement columns and the Balance Sheet columns.

✔ Total debits of Adjustments column: $27

Appendix
EX 4-24 Adjustment data on an end-of-period spreadsheet (work sheet)

Zeidman Security Services Co. offers security services to business clients. The trial balance for Zeidman Security Services Co. has been prepared on the end-of-period spreadsheet (work sheet) for the year ended July 31, 2012, shown below.

Zeidman Security Services Co.
End-of-Period Spreadsheet (Work Sheet)
For the Year Ended July 31, 2012

Account Title	Unadjusted Trial Balance		Adjustments		Adjusted Trial Balance	
	Dr.	Cr.	Dr.	Cr.	Dr.	Cr.
Cash	12					
Accounts Receivable	80					
Supplies	8					
Prepaid Insurance	12					
Land	100					
Equipment	40					
Accum. Depr.—Equipment		4				
Accounts Payable		36				
Wages Payable		0				
Alex Zeidman, Capital		170				
Alex Zeidman, Drawing	8					
Fees Earned		90				
Wages Expense	20					
Rent Expense	12					
Insurance Expense	0					
Utilities Expense	6					
Supplies Expense	0					
Depreciation Expense	0					
Miscellaneous Expense	2					
	300	300				

The data for year-end adjustments are as follows:

a. Fees earned, but not yet billed, $9.

b. Supplies on hand, $3.

c. Insurance premiums expired, $8.

d. Depreciation expense, $4.

e. Wages accrued, but not paid, $1.

Enter the adjustment data, and place the balances in the Adjusted Trial Balance columns.

✔ Net income: $41

Appendix
EX 4-25 Completing an end-of-period spreadsheet (work sheet)

Zeidman Security Services Co. offers security services to business clients. Complete the following end-of-period spreadsheet (work sheet) for Zeidman Security Services Co.

Zeidman Security Services Co.
End-of-Period Spreadsheet (Work Sheet)
For the Year Ended July 31, 2012

Account Title	Adjusted Trial Balance		Income Statement		Balance Sheet	
	Dr.	Cr.	Dr.	Cr.	Dr.	Cr.
Cash	12					
Accounts Receivable	89					
Supplies	3					
Prepaid Insurance	4					
Land	100					
Equipment	40					
Accum. Depr.—Equipment		8				
Accounts Payable		36				
Wages Payable		1				
Alex Zeidman, Capital		170				
Alex Zeidman, Drawing	8					
Fees Earned		99				
Wages Expense	21					
Rent Expense	12					
Insurance Expense	8					
Utilities Expense	6					
Supplies Expense	5					
Depreciation Expense	4					
Miscellaneous Expense	2					
	314	314				
Net income (loss)						

✔ Alex Zeidman,
capital, July 31,
2012: $203

Appendix
EX 4-26   Financial statements from an end-of-period spreadsheet (work sheet)

Based on the data in Exercise 4-25, prepare an income statement, statement of owner's equity, and balance sheet for Zeidman Security Services Co.

Appendix
EX 4-27   Adjusting entries from an end-of-period spreadsheet (work sheet)

Based on the data in Exercise 4-24, prepare the adjusting entries for Zeidman Security Services Co.

Appendix
EX 4-28   Appendix: Closing entries from an end-of-period spreadsheet (work sheet)

Based on the data in Exercise 4-25, prepare the closing entries for Zeidman Security Services Co.

Problems Series A

OBJ. 1, 2, 3

✔ 3. Total assets:
$239,500

PR 4-1A   Financial statements and closing entries

Beacon Company maintains and repairs warning lights, such as those found on radio towers and lighthouses. Beacon Company prepared the end-of-period spreadsheet shown on the next page at October 31, 2012, the end of the current fiscal year:

Instructions

1. Prepare an income statement for the year ended October 31.

2. Prepare a statement of owner's equity for the year ended October 31. No additional investments were made during the year.

3. Prepare a balance sheet as of October 31.

4. Based upon the end-of-period spreadsheet, journalize the closing entries.

(Continued)

5. Prepare a post-closing trial balance.

	A	B	C	D	E	F	G
1				Beacon Company			
2				End-of-Period Spreadsheet			
3				For the Year Ended October 31, 2012			
4		Unadjusted				Adjusted	
5		Trial Balance		Adjustments		Trial Balance	
6	Account Title	Dr.	Cr.	Dr.	Cr.	Dr.	Cr.
7	Cash	5,800				5,800	
8	Accounts Receivable	18,900		(a) 3,300		22,200	
9	Prepaid Insurance	4,200			(b) 2,500	1,700	
10	Supplies	2,730			(c) 1,730	1,000	
11	Land	98,000				98,000	
12	Building	200,000				200,000	
13	Accum. Depr.—Building		100,300		(d) 1,600		101,900
14	Equipment	101,000				101,000	
15	Accum. Depr.—Equipment		85,100		(e) 3,200		88,300
16	Accounts Payable		5,700				5,700
17	Salaries & Wages Payable				(f) 1,800		1,800
18	Unearned Rent		2,100	(g) 1,000			1,100
19	Neil Shepard, Capital		103,100				103,100
20	Neil Shepard, Drawing	10,000				10,000	
21	Fees Revenue		303,700		(a) 3,300		307,000
22	Rent Revenue				(g) 1,000		1,000
23	Salaries & Wages Expense	113,100		(f) 1,800		114,900	
24	Advertising Expense	21,700				21,700	
25	Utilities Expense	11,400				11,400	
26	Repairs Expense	8,850				8,850	
27	Depr. Exp.—Equipment			(e) 3,200		3,200	
28	Insurance Expense			(b) 2,500		2,500	
29	Supplies Expense			(c) 1,730		1,730	
30	Depr. Exp.—Building			(d) 1,600		1,600	
31	Misc. Expense	4,320				4,320	
32		600,000	600,000	15,130	15,130	609,900	609,900
33							

OBJ. 2, 3

✔ 1. Tom Wagner, capital, June 30: $284,300

PR 4-2A   Financial statements and closing entries

Info-Mart Company is an investigative services firm that is owned and operated by Tom Wagner. On June 30, 2012, the end of the current fiscal year, the accountant for Info-Mart Company prepared an end-of-period spreadsheet, a part of which is shown below.

	A	F	G
1		Info-Mart Company	
2		End-of-Period Spreadsheet	
3		For the Year Ended June 30, 2012	
4		Adjusted	
5		Trial Balance	
6	Account Title	Dr.	Cr.
7	Cash	20,000	
8	Accounts Receivable	47,200	
9	Supplies	7,500	
10	Prepaid Insurance	4,800	
11	Building	270,500	
12	Accumulated Depreciation—Building		55,200
13	Accounts Payable		6,000
14	Salaries Payable		1,500
15	Unearned Rent		3,000
16	Tom Wagner, Capital		255,300
17	Tom Wagner, Drawing	50,000	
18	Service Fees		500,000
19	Rent Revenue		25,000
20	Salaries Expense	350,000	
21	Rent Expense	62,500	
22	Supplies Expense	12,000	
23	Depreciation Expense—Equipment	6,000	
24	Utilities Expense	4,400	
25	Repairs Expense	3,200	
26	Insurance Expense	2,800	
27	Miscellaneous Expense	5,100	
28		846,000	846,000

Instructions

1. Prepare an income statement, statement of owner's equity (no additional investments were made during the year), and a balance sheet.

2. Journalize the entries that were required to close the accounts at June 30.

3. If Tom Wagner, Capital decreased $75,000 after the closing entries were posted, and the withdrawals remained the same, what was the amount of net income or net loss?

OBJ. 2 , 3

✔ **2. Net income: $39,300**

PR 4-3A   T accounts, adjusting entries, financial statements, and closing entries; optional end-of-period spreadsheet (work sheet)

The unadjusted trial balance of Launderland at November 30, 2012, the end of the current fiscal year, is shown below.

<table>
<thead>
<tr><th colspan="3">Launderland
Unadjusted Trial Balance
November 30, 2012</th></tr>
<tr><th></th><th>Debit
Balances</th><th>Credit
Balances</th></tr>
</thead>
<tbody>
<tr><td>Cash ....</td><td>9,000</td><td></td></tr>
<tr><td>Laundry Supplies...</td><td>20,900</td><td></td></tr>
<tr><td>Prepaid Insurance ....</td><td>9,600</td><td></td></tr>
<tr><td>Laundry Equipment ....</td><td>290,000</td><td></td></tr>
<tr><td>Accumulated Depreciation.................................</td><td></td><td>150,400</td></tr>
<tr><td>Accounts Payable ....</td><td></td><td>11,800</td></tr>
<tr><td>Gene Halsey, Capital.......................................</td><td></td><td>105,600</td></tr>
<tr><td>Gene Halsey, Drawing ....</td><td>8,400</td><td></td></tr>
<tr><td>Laundry Revenue...</td><td></td><td>232,200</td></tr>
<tr><td>Wages Expense ....</td><td>97,000</td><td></td></tr>
<tr><td>Rent Expense ....</td><td>40,000</td><td></td></tr>
<tr><td>Utilities Expense ....</td><td>19,700</td><td></td></tr>
<tr><td>Miscellaneous Expense ....</td><td>5,400</td><td></td></tr>
<tr><td></td><td>500,000</td><td>500,000</td></tr>
</tbody>
</table>

The data needed to determine year-end adjustments are as follows:

a. Laundry supplies on hand at November 30 are $5,000.

b. Insurance premiums expired during the year are $6,400.

c. Depreciation of equipment during the year is $7,000.

d. Wages accrued but not paid at November 30 are $1,500.

Instructions

1. For each account listed in the unadjusted trial balance, enter the balance in a T account. Identify the balance as "November 30 Bal." In addition, add T accounts for Wages Payable, Depreciation Expense, Laundry Supplies Expense, Insurance Expense, and Income Summary.

2. **Optional:** Enter the unadjusted trial balance on an end-of-period spreadsheet (work sheet) and complete the spreadsheet. Add the accounts listed in part (1) as needed.

3. Journalize and post the adjusting entries. Identify the adjustments by "Adj." and the new balances as "Adj. Bal."

4. Prepare an adjusted trial balance.

5. Prepare an income statement, a statement of owner's equity (no additional investments were made during the year), and a balance sheet.

6. Journalize and post the closing entries. Identify the closing entries by "Clos."

7. Prepare a post-closing trial balance.

OBJ. 2 , 3

✔ **4. Net income: $22,350**

PR 4-4A   Ledger accounts, adjusting entries, financial statements, and closing entries; optional end-of-period spreadsheet (work sheet)

If the working papers correlating with this textbook are not used, omit Problem 4-4A.

The ledger and trial balance of Wizard Services Co. as of July 31, 2012, the end of the first month of its current fiscal year, are presented in the working papers.

Data needed to determine the necessary adjusting entries are as follows:

a. Service revenue accrued at July 31 is $1,000.

b. Supplies on hand at July 31 are $3,900.

c. Insurance premiums expired during July are $1,100.

d. Depreciation of the building during July is $1,400.

e. Depreciation of equipment during July is $900.

f. Unearned rent at July 31 is $700.

g. Wages accrued at July 31 are $100.

Instructions

1. **Optional:** Complete the end-of-period spreadsheet (work sheet) using the adjustment data shown above.

2. Journalize and post the adjusting entries, inserting balances in the accounts affected.

3. Prepare an adjusted trial balance.

4. Prepare an income statement, a statement of owner's equity, and a balance sheet.

5. Journalize and post the closing entries. Indicate closed accounts by inserting a line in both Balance columns opposite the closing entry. Insert the new balance of the capital account.

6. Prepare a post-closing trial balance.

OBJ. 2, 3

✔ 5. Net income: $63,700

PR 4-5A Ledger accounts, adjusting entries, financial statements, and closing entries; optional spreadsheet (work sheet)

The unadjusted trial balance of Bruno's Hauling at February 29, 2012, the end of the current year, is shown below.

Bruno's Hauling
Unadjusted Trial Balance
February 29, 2012

		Debit Balances	Credit Balances
11	Cash	5,000	
13	Supplies	12,000	
14	Prepaid Insurance	3,600	
16	Equipment	110,000	
17	Accumulated Depreciation—Equipment		25,000
18	Trucks	60,000	
19	Accumulated Depreciation—Trucks		15,000
21	Accounts Payable		4,000
31	Bruno Shelton, Capital		71,000
32	Bruno Shelton, Drawing	15,000	
41	Service Revenue		160,000
51	Wages Expense	45,000	
53	Rent Expense	10,600	
54	Truck Expense	9,000	
59	Miscellaneous Expense	4,800	
		275,000	275,000

The data needed to determine year-end adjustments are as follows:

a. Supplies on hand at February 29 are $1,000.

b. Insurance premiums expired during year are $2,400.

c. Depreciation of equipment during year is $8,000.

d. Depreciation of trucks during year is $5,000.

e. Wages accrued but not paid at February 29 are $500.

Instructions

1. For each account listed in the trial balance, enter the balance in the appropriate Balance column of a four-column account and place a check mark (✓) in the Posting Reference column.

2. **Optional:** Enter the unadjusted trial balance on an end-of-period spreadsheet (work sheet) and complete the spreadsheet. Add the accounts listed in part (3) as needed.

3. Journalize and post the adjusting entries, inserting balances in the accounts affected. Record the adjusting entries on Page 26 of the journal. The following additional accounts from Bruno's Hauling's chart of accounts should be used: Wages Payable, 22; Supplies Expense, 52; Depreciation Expense—Equipment, 55; Depreciation Expense—Trucks, 56; Insurance Expense, 57.

4. Prepare an adjusted trial balance.

5. Prepare an income statement, a statement of owner's equity (no additional investments were made during the year), and a balance sheet.

6. Journalize and post the closing entries. Record the closing entries on Page 27 of the journal. (Income Summary is account #33 in the chart of accounts.) Indicate closed accounts by inserting a line in both Balance columns opposite the closing entry.

7. Prepare a post-closing trial balance.

OBJ. 4, 5

 8. Net income: $23,500

PR 4-6A Complete accounting cycle

For the past several years, Shane Banovich has operated a part-time consulting business from his home. As of October 1, 2012, Shane decided to move to rented quarters and to operate the business, which was to be known as Epic Consulting, on a full-time basis. Epic Consulting entered into the following transactions during October:

Oct. 1. The following assets were received from Shane Banovich: cash, $12,000; accounts receivable, $6,000; supplies, $1,500; and office equipment, $9,000. There were no liabilities received.

  1. Paid three months' rent on a lease rental contract, $4,800.

  2. Paid the premiums on property and casualty insurance policies, $3,000.

  4. Received cash from clients as an advance payment for services to be provided and recorded it as unearned fees, $4,000.

  5. Purchased additional office equipment on account from Office Station Co., $2,000.

  6. Received cash from clients on account, $3,500.

  10. Paid cash for a newspaper advertisement, $400.

  12. Paid Office Station Co. for part of the debt incurred on October 5, $1,000.

  12. Recorded services provided on account for the period October 1–12, $6,000.

  14. Paid part-time receptionist for two weeks' salary, $1,000.

Record the following transactions on Page 2 of the journal.

  17. Recorded cash from cash clients for fees earned during the period October 1–17, $7,500.

  18. Paid cash for supplies, $750.

  20. Recorded services provided on account for the period October 13–20, $5,200.

  24. Recorded cash from cash clients for fees earned for the period October 17–24, $3,700.

  26. Received cash from clients on account, $5,500.

  27. Paid part-time receptionist for two weeks' salary, $1,000.

  29. Paid telephone bill for October, $250.

  31. Paid electricity bill for October, $300.

  31. Recorded cash from cash clients for fees earned for the period October 25–31, $2,800.

  31. Recorded services provided on account for the remainder of October, $3,000.

  31. Shane withdrew $8,000 for personal use.

Instructions

1. Journalize each transaction in a two-column journal starting on Page 1, referring to the following chart of accounts in selecting the accounts to be debited and credited. (Do not insert the account numbers in the journal at this time.)

11 Cash	31 Shane Banovich, Capital
12 Accounts Receivable	32 Shane Banovich, Drawing
14 Supplies	41 Fees Earned
15 Prepaid Rent	51 Salary Expense
16 Prepaid Insurance	52 Rent Expense
18 Office Equipment	53 Supplies Expense
19 Accumulated Depreciation	54 Depreciation Expense
21 Accounts Payable	55 Insurance Expense
22 Salaries Payable	59 Miscellaneous Expense
23 Unearned Fees	

2. Post the journal to a ledger of four-column accounts.

3. Prepare an unadjusted trial balance.

4. At the end of October, the following adjustment data were assembled. Analyze and use these data to complete parts (5) and (6).

   a. Insurance expired during October is $250.

   b. Supplies on hand on October 31 are $700.

   c. Depreciation of office equipment for October is $300.

   d. Accrued receptionist salary on October 31 is $250.

   e. Rent expired during October is $1,600.

   f. Unearned fees on October 31 are $1,800.

5. **Optional:** Enter the unadjusted trial balance on an end-of-period spreadsheet (work sheet) and complete the spreadsheet.

6. Journalize and post the adjusting entries. Record the adjusting entries on Page 3 of the journal.

7. Prepare an adjusted trial balance.

8. Prepare an income statement, a statement of owner's equity, and a balance sheet.

9. Prepare and post the closing entries. (Income Summary is account #33 in the chart of accounts.) Record the closing entries on Page 4 of the journal. Indicate closed accounts by inserting a line in both the Balance columns opposite the closing entry.

10. Prepare a post-closing trial balance.

Problems Series B

PR 4-1B Financial statements and closing entries

DNA 4 U Company offers legal consulting advice to prison inmates. DNA 4 U Company prepared the end-of-period spreadsheet at the top of the following page at April 30, 2012, the end of the current fiscal year.

Instructions

1. Prepare an income statement for the year ended April 30.

2. Prepare a statement of owner's equity for the year ended April 30. No additional investments were made during the year.

3. Prepare a balance sheet as of April 30.

4. On the basis of the end-of-period spreadsheet, journalize the closing entries.

5. Prepare a post-closing trial balance.

	A	B	C	D	E	F	G
1				DNA 4U Company			
2				End-of-Period Spreadsheet			
3				For the Year Ended April 30, 2012			
4		Unadjusted				Adjusted	
5		Trial Balance		Adjustments		Trial Balance	
6	Account Title	Dr.	Cr.	Dr.	Cr.	Dr.	Cr.
7	Cash	5,100				5,100	
8	Accounts Receivable	12,750		(a) 1,250		14,000	
9	Prepaid Insurance	3,600			(b) 1,200	2,400	
10	Supplies	2,025			(c) 1,400	625	
11	Land	80,000				80,000	
12	Building	200,000				200,000	
13	Accum. Depr.—Building		90,000		(d) 2,500		92,500
14	Equipment	140,000				140,000	
15	Accum. Depr.—Equipment		54,450		(e) 5,000		59,450
16	Accounts Payable		9,750				9,750
17	Sal. & Wages Payable				(f) 1,900		1,900
18	Unearned Rent		4,500	(g) 3,000			1,500
19	Luis Cortes, Capital		311,300				311,300
20	Luis Cortes, Drawing	20,000				20,000	
21	Fees Revenue		280,000		(a) 1,250		281,250
22	Rent Revenue				(g) 3,000		3,000
23	Salaries & Wages Expense	145,100		(f) 1,900		147,000	
24	Advertising Expense	86,800				86,800	
25	Utilities Expense	30,000				30,000	
26	Travel Expense	18,750				18,750	
27	Depr. Exp.—Equipment			(e) 5,000		5,000	
28	Depr. Exp.—Building			(d) 2,500		2,500	
29	Supplies Expense			(c) 1,400		1,400	
30	Insurance Expense			(b) 1,200		1,200	
31	Misc. Expense	5,875				5,875	
32		750,000	750,000	16,250	16,250	760,650	760,650
33							

OBJ. 2, 3

PR 4-2B   Financial statements and closing entries

✔ 1. Lee Mather, capital, July 31: $468,000

Mather Services Company is a financial planning services firm owned and operated by Lee Mather. As of July 31, 2012, the end of the current fiscal year, the accountant for Mather Services Company prepared an end-of-period spreadsheet (work sheet), part of which is shown below.

	A	F	G
1	Mather Services Company		
2	End-of-Period Spreadsheet		
3	For the Year Ended July 31, 2012		
4		Adjusted	
5		Trial Balance	
6	Account Title	Dr.	Cr.
7	Cash	11,000	
8	Accounts Receivable	28,150	
9	Supplies	6,350	
10	Prepaid Insurance	9,500	
11	Land	100,000	
12	Buildings	360,000	
13	Accumulated Depreciation—Buildings		117,200
14	Equipment	260,000	
15	Accumulated Depreciation—Equipment		151,700
16	Accounts Payable		33,300
17	Salaries Payable		3,300
18	Unearned Rent		1,500
19	Lee Mather, Capital		407,000
20	Lee Mather, Drawing	25,000	
21	Service Fees		475,000
22	Rent Revenue		5,000
23	Salaries Expense	325,000	
24	Depreciation Expense—Equipment	17,500	
25	Rent Expense	15,500	
26	Supplies Expense	9,000	
27	Utilities Expense	8,500	
28	Depreciation Expense—Buildings	6,600	
29	Repairs Expense	3,450	
30	Insurance Expense	3,000	
31	Miscellaneous Expense	5,450	
32		1,194,000	1,194,000

Instructions

1. Prepare an income statement, a statement of owner's equity (no additional investments were made during the year), and a balance sheet.

2. Journalize the entries that were required to close the accounts at July 31.

3. If the balance of Lee Mather, Capital increased $40,000 after the closing entries were posted, and the withdrawals remained the same, what was the amount of net income or net loss?

OBJ. 2, 3

✔ 2. Net income:
$30,640

PR 4-3B   T accounts, adjusting entries, financial statements, and closing entries; optional end-of-period spreadsheet (work sheet)

The unadjusted trial balance of Laundry Basket at January 31, 2012, the end of the current fiscal year, is shown below.

Laundry Basket
Unadjusted Trial Balance
January 31, 2012

	Debit Balances	Credit Balances
Cash	3,480	
Laundry Supplies..	9,000	
Prepaid Insurance	5,760	
Laundry Equipment	130,800	
Accumulated Depreciation............................		49,200
Accounts Payable		7,440
Stacy Martinell, Capital		45,360
Stacy Martinell, Drawing..............................	2,400	
Laundry Revenue...		198,000
Wages Expense	85,800	
Rent Expense	43,200	
Utilities Expense	16,320	
Miscellaneous Expense	3,240	
	300,000	300,000

The data needed to determine year-end adjustments are as follows:

a. Wages accrued but not paid at January 31 arc $900.

b. Depreciation of equipment during the year is $7,000.

c. Laundry supplies on hand at January 31 are $2,100.

d. Insurance premiums expired during the year are $4,000.

Instructions

1. For each account listed in the unadjusted trial balance, enter the balance in a T account. Identify the balance as "Jan. 31 Bal." In addition, add T accounts for Wages Payable, Depreciation Expense, Laundry Supplies Expense, Insurance Expense, and Income Summary.

2. **Optional:** Enter the unadjusted trial balance on an end-of-period spreadsheet (work sheet) and complete the spreadsheet. Add the accounts listed in part (1) as needed.

3. Journalize and post the adjusting entries. Identify the adjustments by "Adj." and the new balances as "Adj. Bal."

4. Prepare an adjusted trial balance.

5. Prepare an income statement, a statement of owner's equity (no additional investments were made during the year), and a balance sheet.

6. Journalize and post the closing entries. Identify the closing entries by "Clos."

7. Prepare a post-closing trial balance.

OBJ. 2

✔ 4. Net income:
$22,150

PR 4-4B   Ledger accounts, adjusting entries, financial statements, and closing entries; optional end-of-period spreadsheet (work sheet)

If the working papers correlating with this textbook are not used, omit Problem 4-4B.

The ledger and trial balance of Sweetwater Services Co. as of July 31, 2012, the end of the first month of its current fiscal year, are presented in the working papers.

Data needed to determine the necessary adjusting entries are as follows:

a. Service revenue accrued at July 31 is $1,500.

b. Supplies on hand at July 31 are $3,800.

c. Insurance premiums expired during July are $1,200.

d. Depreciation of the building during July is $1,400.

e. Depreciation of equipment during July is $1,100.

f. Unearned rent at July 31 is $900.

g. Wages accrued but not paid at July 31 are $200.

Instructions

1. **Optional:** Complete the end-of-period spreadsheet (work sheet) using the adjustment data shown on the previous page.

2. Journalize and post the adjusting entries, inserting balances in the accounts affected.

3. Prepare an adjusted trial balance.

4. Prepare an income statement, a statement of owner's equity, and a balance sheet.

5. Journalize and post the closing entries. Indicate closed accounts by inserting a line in both Balance columns opposite the closing entry. Insert the new balance of the capital account.

6. Prepare a post-closing trial balance.

OBJ. 2, 3

✔ **5. Net income: $35,150**

PR 4-5B Ledger accounts, adjusting entries, financial statements, and closing entries; optional end-of-period spreadsheet (work sheet)

The unadjusted trial balance of Oak and Brass Interiors at December 31, 2012, the end of the current year, is shown below.

Oak and Brass Interiors
Unadjusted Trial Balance
December 31, 2012

		Debit Balances	Credit Balances
11	Cash	3,100	
13	Supplies	6,000	
14	Prepaid Insurance	7,500	
16	Equipment	90,000	
17	Accumulated Depreciation—Equipment		12,000
18	Trucks	50,000	
19	Accumulated Depreciation—Trucks		27,100
21	Accounts Payable		4,500
31	Sally Kriebel, Capital		66,400
32	Sally Kriebel, Drawing	3,000	
41	Service Revenue		140,000
51	Wages Expense	72,000	
52	Rent Expense	7,600	
53	Truck Expense	5,350	
59	Miscellaneous Expense	5,450	
		250,000	250,000

The data needed to determine year-end adjustments are as follows:

a. Supplies on hand at December 31 are $1,750.

b. Insurance premiums expired during the year are $2,000.

c. Depreciation of equipment during the year is $5,000.

d. Depreciation of trucks during the year is $2,200.

e. Wages accrued but not paid at December 31 are $1,000.

Instructions

1. For each account listed in the unadjusted trial balance, enter the balance in the appropriate Balance column of a four-column account and place a check mark (✓) in the Posting Reference column.

2. **Optional:** Enter the unadjusted trial balance on an end-of-period spreadsheet (work sheet) and complete the spreadsheet. Add the accounts listed in part (3) as needed.

3. Journalize and post the adjusting entries, inserting balances in the accounts affected. Record the adjusting entries on Page 26 of the journal. The following additional accounts from Oak and Brass Interiors' chart of accounts should be used: Wages Payable, 22; Depreciation Expense—Equipment, 54; Supplies Expense, 55; Depreciation Expense—Trucks, 56; Insurance Expense, 57.

4. Prepare an adjusted trial balance.

5. Prepare an income statement, a statement of owner's equity (no additional investments were made during the year), and a balance sheet.

(*Continued*)

6. Journalize and post the closing entries. Record the closing entries on Page 27 of the journal. (Income Summary is account #33 in the chart of accounts.) Indicate closed accounts by inserting a line in both Balance columns opposite the closing entry.

7. Prepare a post-closing trial balance.

OBJ. 4, 5

✔ 8. Net income:
$35,150

PR 4-6B Complete accounting cycle

For the past several years, Abby Brown has operated a part-time consulting business from her home. As of June 1, 2012, Abby decided to move to rented quarters and to operate the business, which was to be known as Square One Consulting, on a full-time basis. Square One Consulting entered into the following transactions during June:

June 1. The following assets were received from Abby Brown: cash, $30,000; accounts receivable, $7,500; supplies, $2,000; and office equipment, $15,000. There were no liabilities received.

  1. Paid three months' rent on a lease rental contract, $6,000.

  2. Paid the premiums on property and casualty insurance policies, $3,600.

  4. Received cash from clients as an advance payment for services to be provided and recorded it as unearned fees, $5,000.

  5. Purchased additional office equipment on account from Office Depot Co., $6,000.

  6. Received cash from clients on account, $4,000.

  10. Paid cash for a newspaper advertisement, $200.

  12. Paid Office Depot Co. for part of the debt incurred on June 5, $1,200.

  12. Recorded services provided on account for the period June 1–12, $13,000.

  14. Paid part-time receptionist for two weeks' salary, $1,500.

  Record the following transactions on Page 2 of the journal.

  17. Recorded cash from cash clients for fees earned during the period June 1–16, $9,000.

  18. Paid cash for supplies, $1,400.

  20. Recorded services provided on account for the period June 13–20, $8,500.

  24. Recorded cash from cash clients for fees earned for the period June 17–24, $6,300.

  26. Received cash from clients on account, $12,100.

  27. Paid part-time receptionist for two weeks' salary, $1,500.

  29. Paid telephone bill for June, $150.

  30. Paid electricity bill for June, $400.

  30. Recorded cash from cash clients for fees earned for the period June 25–30, $3,900.

  30. Recorded services provided on account for the remainder of June, $2,500.

  30. Abby withdrew $10,000 for personal use.

Instructions

1. Journalize each transaction in a two-column journal starting on Page 1, referring to the following chart of accounts in selecting the accounts to be debited and credited. (Do not insert the account numbers in the journal at this time.)

11 Cash	31 Abby Brown, Capital
12 Accounts Receivable	32 Abby Brown, Drawing
14 Supplies	41 Fees Earned
15 Prepaid Rent	51 Salary Expense
16 Prepaid Insurance	52 Supplies Expense
18 Office Equipment	53 Rent Expense
19 Accumulated Depreciation	54 Depreciation Expense
21 Accounts Payable	55 Insurance Expense
22 Salaries Payable	59 Miscellaneous Expense
23 Unearned Fees	

2. Post the journal to a ledger of four-column accounts.

3. Prepare an unadjusted trial balance.

4. At the end of June, the following adjustment data were assembled. Analyze and use these data to complete parts (5) and (6).

   a. Insurance expired during June is $200.

   b. Supplies on hand on June 30 are $600.

   c. Depreciation of office equipment for June is $250.

   d. Accrued receptionist salary on June 30 is $350.

   e. Rent expired during June is $2,500.

   f. Unearned fees on June 30 are $3,200.

5. **Optional:** Enter the unadjusted trial balance on an end-of-period spreadsheet (work sheet) and complete the spreadsheet.

6. Journalize and post the adjusting entries. Record the adjusting entries on Page 3 of the journal.

7. Prepare an adjusted trial balance.

8. Prepare an income statement, a statement of owner's equity, and a balance sheet.

9. Prepare and post the closing entries. Record the closing entries on Page 4 of the journal. (Income Summary is account #33 in the chart of accounts.) Indicate closed accounts by inserting a line in both the Balance columns opposite the closing entry.

10. Prepare a post-closing trial balance.

Continuing Problem

✔ 2. Net income:
$6,210

The unadjusted trial balance of PS Music as of July 31, 2012, along with the adjustment data for the two months ended July 31, 2012, are shown in Chapter 3.

Based upon the adjustment data, the adjusted trial balance shown below was prepared.

PS Music
Adjusted Trial Balance
July 31, 2012

	Debit Balances	Credit Balances
Cash	10,510	
Accounts Receivable	4,750	
Supplies	400	
Prepaid Insurance	2,475	
Office Equipment	6,000	
Accumulated Depreciation—Office Equipment		75
Accounts Payable		7,080
Wages Payable		170
Unearned Revenue		3,600
Pat Sharpe, Capital		9,000
Pat Sharpe, Drawing	2,000	
Fees Earned		21,950
Wages Expense	2,970	
Office Rent Expense	2,550	
Equipment Rent Expense	1,300	
Utilities Expense	1,060	
Music Expense	3,610	
Advertising Expense	1,450	
Supplies Expense	1,030	
Insurance Expense	225	
Depreciation Expense	75	
Miscellaneous Expense	1,470	
	41,875	41,875

Instructions

1. **Optional.** Using the data from Chapter 3, prepare an end-of-period spreadsheet (work sheet).

2. Prepare an income statement, a statement of owner's equity, and a balance sheet. (*Note:* Pat Sharpe made investments in PS Music on June 1 and July 1, 2012.)

3. Journalize and post the closing entries. The income summary account is #33 in the ledger of PS Music. Indicate closed accounts by inserting a line in both Balance columns opposite the closing entry.

4. Prepare a post-closing trial balance.

Comprehensive Problem 1

✔ 8. Net income, $25,680

GL
GENERAL
LEDGER

Kelly Pitney began her consulting business, Kelly Consulting, on April 1, 2012. The accounting cycle for Kelly Consulting for April, including financial statements, was illustrated on pages 163–173. During May, Kelly Consulting entered into the following transactions:

May   3. Received cash from clients as an advance payment for services to be provided and recorded it as unearned fees, $3,000.

   5. Received cash from clients on account, $2,100.

   9. Paid cash for a newspaper advertisement, $300.

  13. Paid Office Station Co. for part of the debt incurred on April 5, $400.

  15. Recorded services provided on account for the period May 1–15, $7,350.

  16. Paid part-time receptionist for two weeks' salary including the amount owed on April 30, $750.

  Record the following transactions on Page 6 of the journal.

  17. Recorded cash from cash clients for fees earned during the period May 1–16, $6,150.

  20. Purchased supplies on account, $600.

  21. Recorded services provided on account for the period May 16–20, $6,175.

  25. Recorded cash from cash clients for fees earned for the period May 17–23, $3,125.

  27. Received cash from clients on account, $11,250.

  28. Paid part-time receptionist for two weeks' salary, $750.

  30. Paid telephone bill for May, $120.

  31. Paid electricity bill for May, $290.

  31. Recorded cash from cash clients for fees earned for the period May 26–31, $2,800.

  31. Recorded services provided on account for the remainder of May, $1,900.

  31. Kelly withdrew $15,000 for personal use.

Instructions

1. The chart of accounts for Kelly Consulting is shown on page 164, and the post-closing trial balance as of April 30, 2012, is shown on page 171. For each account in the post-closing trial balance, enter the balance in the appropriate Balance column of a four-column account. Date the balances May 1, 2012, and place a check mark (✓) in the Posting Reference column. Journalize each of the May transactions in a two-column journal starting on Page 5 of the journal and using Kelly Consulting's chart of accounts. (Do not insert the account numbers in the journal at this time.)

2. Post the journal to a ledger of four-column accounts.

3. Prepare an unadjusted trial balance.

4. At the end of May, the following adjustment data were assembled. Analyze and use these data to complete parts (5) and (6).

   a. Insurance expired during May is $300.

   b. Supplies on hand on May 31 are $750.

   c. Depreciation of office equipment for May is $330.

    d. Accrued receptionist salary on May 31 is $300.

    e. Rent expired during May is $1,600.

    f. Unearned fees on May 31 are $1,500.

5. **Optional:** Enter the unadjusted trial balance on an end-of-period spreadsheet (work sheet) and complete the spreadsheet.

6. Journalize and post the adjusting entries. Record the adjusting entries on Page 7 of the journal.

7. Prepare an adjusted trial balance.

8. Prepare an income statement, a statement of owner's equity, and a balance sheet.

9. Prepare and post the closing entries. Record the closing entries on Page 8 of the journal. (Income Summary is account #33 in the chart of accounts.) Indicate closed accounts by inserting a line in both the Balance columns opposite the closing entry.

10. Prepare a post-closing trial balance.

Cases & Projects

CP 4-1   Ethics and professional conduct in business

Laser Graphics is a graphics arts design consulting firm. Spencer Lowry, its treasurer and vice president of finance, has prepared a classified balance sheet as of March 31, 2012, the end of its fiscal year. This balance sheet will be submitted with Laser Graphics' loan application to American Trust & Savings Bank.

    In the Current Assets section of the balance sheet, Spencer reported a $90,000 receivable from Jackie Doyle, the president of Laser Graphics, as a trade account receivable. Jackie borrowed the money from Laser Graphics in April 2010 for a down payment on a new home. She has orally assured Spencer that she will pay off the account receivable within the next year. Spencer reported the $90,000 in the same manner on the preceding year's balance sheet.

    ➤ Evaluate whether it is acceptable for Spencer to prepare the March 31, 2012, balance sheet in the manner indicated above.

CP 4-2   Financial statements

The following is an excerpt from a telephone conversation between Jared Bodine, president of Hometown Supplies Co., and Julie Sims, owner of Express Employment Co.

Jared: Julie, you're going to have to do a better job of finding me a new computer programmer. That last guy was great at programming, but he didn't have any common sense.

Julie: What do you mean? The guy had a master's degree with straight A's.

Jared: Yes, well, last month he developed a new financial reporting system. He said we could do away with manually preparing an end-of-period spreadsheet (work sheet) and financial statements. The computer would automatically generate our financial statements with "a push of a button."

Julie: So what's the big deal? Sounds to me like it would save you time and effort.

Jared: Right! The balance sheet showed a minus for supplies!

Julie: Minus supplies? How can that be?

Jared: That's what I asked.

Julie: So, what did he say?

Jared: Well, after he checked the program, he said that it must be right. The minuses were greater than the pluses. . . .

Julie: Didn't he know that Supplies can't have a credit balance—it must have a debit balance?

Jared: He asked me what a debit and credit were.

Julie: I see your point.

1.   ➤ Comment on (a) the desirability of computerizing Hometown Supplies Co.'s financial reporting system, (b) the elimination of the end-of-period spreadsheet (work sheet) in a computerized accounting system, and (c) the computer programmer's lack of accounting knowledge.

2.   ➤ Explain to the programmer why Supplies could not have a credit balance.

CP 4-3 Financial statements

Assume that you recently accepted a position with Frontier National Bank as an assistant loan officer. As one of your first duties, you have been assigned the responsibility of evaluating a loan request for $150,000 from Icancreateart.com, a small proprietorship. In support of the loan application, Tess Ramey, owner, submitted a "Statement of Accounts" (trial balance) for the first year of operations ended July 31, 2012.

Icancreateart.com
Statement of Accounts
July 31, 2012

Cash	5,000	
Billings Due from Others	40,000	
Supplies (chemicals, etc.)	7,500	
Building	122,300	
Equipment	25,000	
Amounts Owed to Others		11,000
Investment in Business		74,000
Service Revenue		215,000
Wages Expense	75,000	
Utilities Expense	10,000	
Rent Expense	8,000	
Insurance Expense	6,000	
Other Expenses	1,200	
	300,000	300,000

1. ▬▬▶ Explain to Tess Ramey why a set of financial statements (income statement, statement of owner's equity, and balance sheet) would be useful to you in evaluating the loan request.

2. In discussing the "Statement of Accounts" with Tess Ramey, you discovered that the accounts had not been adjusted at July 31. Analyze the "Statement of Accounts" and indicate possible adjusting entries that might be necessary before an accurate set of financial statements could be prepared.

3. ▬▬▶ Assuming that an accurate set of financial statements will be submitted by Tess Ramey in a few days, what other considerations or information would you require before making a decision on the loan request?

Internet Project

CP 4-4 Compare balance sheets

Group Project

In groups of three or four, compare the balance sheets of two different companies, and present to the class a summary of the similarities and differences of the two companies. You may obtain the balance sheets you need from one of the following sources:

1. Your school or local library.

2. The investor relations department of each company.

3. The company's Web site on the Internet.

4. EDGAR (Electronic Data Gathering, Analysis, and Retrieval), the electronic archives of financial statements filed with the Securities and Exchange Commission.

SEC documents can be retrieved using the EdgarScan™ service at **http://sec.gov.** To obtain annual report information, click on "Search for Company Filing," click on "Companies & Other Filers," type in the company name, and then click on "Find Companies." Click on the CIK related to the company name, search for Form 10-K, and click on "Retrieve Selected Findings." Finally, click on the "html" for the latest period and the related document.

© Pixland/Jupiter Images

Accounting Systems

Intuit Inc.

Whether you realize it or not, you likely interact with accounting systems. For example, your bank statement is a type of accounting system. When you make a deposit, the bank records an addition to your cash; when you withdraw cash, the bank records a reduction in your cash. Such a simple accounting system works well for a person with just a few transactions per month. However, over time, you may find that your financial affairs will become more complex and involve many different types of transactions, including investments and loan payments. At this point, relying on your bank statement may not be sufficient for managing your financial affairs. Personal financial planning software, such as Intuit's Quicken, can be useful when your financial affairs become more complex.

What happens if you decide to begin a small business? Transactions expand

to include customers, vendors, and employees. As a result, the accounting system will need to adjust to this complexity. Thus, many small businesses will use small-business accounting software, such as Intuit's QuickBooks, as their first accounting system. As a business grows, more sophisticated accounting systems will be needed. Companies such as SAP, Oracle, Microsoft, and Sage Software, Inc., offer accounting system solutions for businesses that become larger with more complex accounting needs.

Accounting systems used by large and small businesses employ the basic principles of the accounting cycle discussed in the previous chapters. However, these accounting systems include features that simplify the recording and summary process. In this chapter, we will discuss these simplifying procedures as they apply to both manual and computerized systems.

OBJ. 1 Define and describe an accounting system.

Basic Accounting Systems

In Chapters 1–4, an accounting system for NetSolutions was described and illustrated. An **accounting system** is the methods and procedures for collecting, classifying, summarizing, and reporting a business's financial and operating information. Most accounting systems, however, are more complex than NetSolutions'. For example, Southwest Airlines's accounting system not only records basic transaction data, but also records data on such items as ticket reservations, credit card collections, frequent-flier mileage, and aircraft maintenance.

As a business grows and changes, its accounting system also changes in a three-step process. This three-step process is as follows:

Step 1. *Analyze* user information needs.
Step 2. *Design* the system to meet the user needs.
Step 3. *Implement* the system.

For NetSolutions, our analysis determined that Chris Clark needed financial statements for the new business. We designed the system, using a basic manual system that included a chart of accounts, a two-column journal, and a general ledger. Finally, we implemented the system to record transactions and prepare financial statements.

Once a system has been implemented, input from users is used to analyze and improve the system. For example, in later chapters, NetSolutions expands its chart of accounts to record more complex transactions.

The accounting system design consists of:

1. internal controls and
2. information processing methods.

Internal controls are the policies and procedures that protect assets from misuse, ensure that business information is accurate, and ensure that laws and regulations are being followed. Internal controls are discussed in Chapter 8.

Processing methods are the means by which the accounting system collects, summarizes, and reports accounting information. These methods may be either *manual* or *computerized*. In the following sections, manual accounting systems that use special journals and subsidiary ledgers are described and illustrated. This is followed by a discussion of computerized accounting systems.

Manual Accounting Systems

 OBJ. 2 Journalize and post transactions in a manual accounting system that uses subsidiary ledgers and special journals.

Accounting systems are manual or computerized. Understanding a manual accounting system is useful in identifying relationships between accounting data and reports. Also, most computerized systems use principles from manual systems.

In prior chapters, the transactions for NetSolutions were manually recorded in an all-purpose (two-column) journal. The journal entries were then posted individually to the accounts in the ledger. Such a system is simple to use and easy to understand when there are a small number of transactions. However, when a business has a large number of *similar* transactions, using an all-purpose journal is inefficient and impractical. In such cases, subsidiary ledgers and special journals are useful.

Subsidiary Ledgers

A large number of individual accounts with a common characteristic can be grouped together in a separate ledger called a **subsidiary ledger**. The primary ledger, which contains all of the balance sheet and income statement accounts, is then called the **general ledger**. Each subsidiary ledger is represented in the general ledger by a summarizing account, called a **controlling account**. The sum of the balances of the accounts in a subsidiary ledger must equal the balance of the related controlling account. Thus, a subsidiary ledger is a secondary ledger that supports a controlling account in the general ledger.

Two of the most common subsidiary ledgers are as follows:

1. Accounts receivable subsidiary ledger
2. Accounts payable subsidiary ledger

The **accounts receivable subsidiary ledger**, or *customers ledger*, lists the individual customer accounts in alphabetical order. The controlling account in the general ledger that summarizes the debits and credits to the individual customer accounts is Accounts Receivable.

The **accounts payable subsidiary ledger**, or *creditors ledger*, lists individual creditor accounts in alphabetical order. The related controlling account in the general ledger is Accounts Payable.

The relationship between the general ledger and the accounts receivable and accounts payable subsidiary ledgers is illustrated in Exhibit 1.

Many businesses use subsidiary ledgers for other accounts in addition to Accounts Receivable and Accounts Payable. For example, businesses often use an equipment subsidiary ledger to keep track of each item of equipment purchased, its cost, location, and other data.

Special Journals

One method of processing transactions more efficiently in a manual system is to use special journals. **Special journals** are designed to record a single kind of

EXHIBIT 1 **General Ledger and Subsidiary Ledgers**

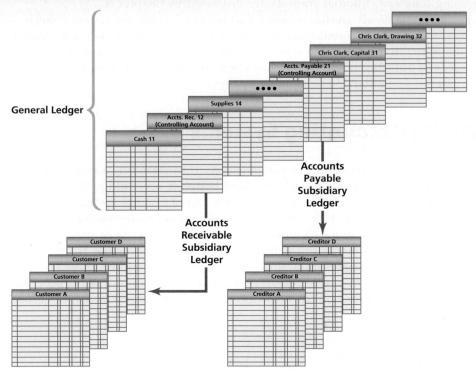

transaction that occurs frequently. For example, since most businesses have many transactions in which cash is paid out, they will likely use a special journal for recording cash payments. Likewise, they will use another special journal for recording cash receipts.

The format and number of special journals that a business uses depends on the nature of the business. The common transactions and their related special journals used by small service businesses are as follows:

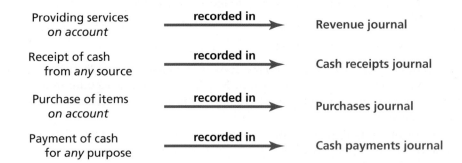

	recorded in	
Providing services *on account*	→	Revenue journal
Receipt of cash from *any* source	→	Cash receipts journal
Purchase of items *on account*	→	Purchases journal
Payment of cash for *any* purpose	→	Cash payments journal

The all-purpose two-column journal, called the **general journal** or simply the *journal,* can be used for entries that do not fit into any of the special journals. For example, adjusting and closing entries are recorded in the general journal.

The following types of transactions, special journals, and subsidiary ledgers are described and illustrated for **NetSolutions**:

Transaction	Special Journal	Subsidiary Ledger
Fees earned on account	Revenue journal	Accounts receivable subsidiary ledger
Cash receipts	Cash receipts journal	Accounts receivable subsidiary ledger
Purchases on account	Purchases journal	Accounts payable subsidiary ledger
Cash payments	Cash payments journal	Accounts payable subsidiary ledger

As shown above, transactions that are recorded in the revenue and cash receipts journals will affect the accounts receivable subsidiary ledger. Likewise, transactions that are recorded in the purchases and cash payments journals will affect the accounts payable subsidiary ledger.

We will assume that NetSolutions had the following selected general ledger balances on March 1, 2012:

Account Number	Account	Balance
11	Cash	$6,200
12	Accounts Receivable	3,400
14	Supplies	2,500
18	Office Equipment	2,500
21	Accounts Payable	1,230

Revenue Journal

Fees earned on account would be recorded in the **revenue journal**. *Cash fees earned* would be recorded in the cash receipts journal.

To illustrate the efficiency of using a revenue journal, an example for NetSolutions is used. Specifically, assume that NetSolutions recorded the following four revenue transactions for March in its general journal:

2012					
Mar.	2	Accounts Receivable—Accessories By Claire	12/✓	2,200	
		Fees Earned	41		2,200
	6	Accounts Receivable—RapZone	12/✓	1,750	
		Fees Earned	41		1,750
	18	Accounts Receivable—Web Cantina	12/✓	2,650	
		Fees Earned	41		2,650
	27	Accounts Receivable—Accessories By Claire	12/✓	3,000	
		Fees Earned	41		3,000

For the above entries, NetSolutions recorded eight account titles and eight amounts. In addition, NetSolutions made 12 postings to the ledgers—four to Accounts Receivable in the general ledger, four to the accounts receivable subsidiary ledger (indicated by each check mark), and four to Fees Earned in the general ledger.

The preceding revenue transactions could be recorded more efficiently in a revenue journal, as shown in Exhibit 2. In each revenue transaction, the amount of the debit to Accounts Receivable is the same as the amount of the credit to Fees Earned. Thus, only a single amount column is necessary. The date, invoice number, customer name, and amount are entered separately for each transaction.

Revenues are normally recorded in the revenue journal when the company sends an invoice to the customer. An **invoice** is the bill that is sent to the customer by the company. Each invoice is normally numbered in sequence for future reference.

To illustrate, assume that on March 2 NetSolutions issued Invoice No. 615 to Accessories By Claire for fees earned of $2,200. This transaction is entered in the revenue journal, shown in Exhibit 2, by entering the following items:

1. Date column: *Mar. 2*
2. Invoice No. column: *615*

EXHIBIT 2 **Revenue Journal**

			Revenue Journal		Page 35
Date	Invoice No.		Account Debited	Post. Ref.	Accts. Rec. Dr. Fees Earned Cr.
2012					
Mar. 2	615		Accessories By Claire		2,200
6	616		RapZone		1,750
18	617		Web Cantina		2,650
27	618		Accessories By Claire		3,000
31					9,600

3. Account Debited column: *Accessories By Claire*
4. Accts. Rec. Dr./Fees Earned Cr. column: *2,200*

The process of posting from a revenue journal, shown in Exhibit 3, is as follows:

1. Each transaction is posted individually to a customer account in the accounts receivable subsidiary ledger. Postings to customer accounts should be made on a regular basis. In this way, the customer's account will show a current balance. Since the balances in the customer accounts are usually debit balances, the three-column account form is shown in Exhibit 3.

   To illustrate, Exhibit 3 shows the posting of the $2,200 debit to Accessories By Claire in the accounts receivable subsidiary ledger. After the posting, Accessories By Claire has a debit balance of $2,200.

2. To provide a trail of the entries posted to the subsidiary and general ledger, the source of these entries is indicated in the Posting Reference column of each account by inserting the letter R (for revenue journal) and the page number of the revenue journal.

   To illustrate, Exhibit 3 shows that after $2,200 is posted to Accessories By Claire's account, R35 is inserted into the Post. Ref. column of the account.

3. To indicate that the transaction has been posted to the accounts receivable subsidiary ledger, a check mark (✓) is inserted in the Post. Ref. column of the revenue journal, as shown in Exhibit 3.

   To illustrate, Exhibit 3 shows that a check mark (✓) has been inserted in the Post. Ref. column next to Accessories By Claire in the revenue journal to indicate that the $2,200 has been posted.

4. A single monthly total is posted to Accounts Receivable and Fees Earned in the general ledger. This total is equal to the sum of the month's debits to the individual accounts in the subsidiary ledger. It is posted in the general ledger as a debit to Accounts Receivable and a credit to Fees Earned, as shown in Exhibit 3. The accounts receivable account number (12) and the fees earned account number (41) are then inserted below the total in the revenue journal to indicate that the posting is completed.

   To illustrate, Exhibit 3 shows the monthly total of $9,600 was posted as a debit to Accounts Receivable (12) and as a credit to Fees Earned (41).

Exhibit 3 illustrates the efficiency gained by using the revenue journal rather than the general journal. Specifically, all of the transactions for fees earned during the month are posted to the general ledger only once—at the end of the month.

EXHIBIT 3 **Revenue Journal and Postings**

Revenue Journal
Page 35

Date	Invoice No.	Account Debited	Post. Ref.	Accts. Rec. Dr. Fees Earned Cr.
2012				
Mar. 2	615	Accessories By Claire	✓	2,200
6	616	RapZone	✓	1,750
18	617	Web Cantina	✓	2,650
27	618	Accessories By Claire	✓	3,000
31				9,600
				(12) (41)

General Ledger

Account Accounts Receivable — Account No. 12

Date	Item	Post. Ref.	Debit	Credit	Balance Debit	Balance Credit
2012						
Mar. 1	Balance	✓			3,400	
31		R35	9,600		13,000	

Account Fees Earned — Account No. 41

Date	Item	Post. Ref.	Debit	Credit	Balance Debit	Balance Credit
2012						
Mar. 31		R35		9,600		9,600

Accounts Receivable Subsidiary Ledger

Name: Accessories By Claire

Date	Item	Post. Ref.	Debit	Credit	Balance
2012					
Mar. 2		R35	2,200		2,200
27		R35	3,000		5,200

Name: RapZone

Date	Item	Post. Ref.	Debit	Credit	Balance
2012					
Mar. 6		R35	1,750		1,750

Name: Web Cantina

Date	Item	Post. Ref.	Debit	Credit	Balance
2012					
Mar. 1	Balance	✓			3,400
18		R35	2,650		6,050

Example Exercise 5-1 Revenue Journal
OBJ. 2

The following revenue transactions occurred during December:

Dec. 5. Issued Invoice No. 302 to Butler Company for services provided on account, $5,000.
9. Issued Invoice No. 303 to JoJo Enterprises for services provided on account, $2,100.
15. Issued Invoice No. 304 to Double D Inc. for services provided on account, $3,250.

Record these transactions in a revenue journal as illustrated in Exhibit 2.

Follow My Example 5-1

REVENUE JOURNAL

Date	Invoice No.	Account Debited	Post. Ref.	Accts. Rec. Dr. Fees Earned Cr.
Dec. 5	302	Butler Company		5,000
9	303	JoJo Enterprises		2,100
15	304	Double D Inc.		3,250

Practice Exercises: **PE 5-1A, PE 5-1B**

Cash Receipts Journal

All transactions that involve the receipt of cash are recorded in a **cash receipts journal**. The cash receipts journal for NetSolutions is shown in Exhibit 4.

The cash receipts journal shown in Exhibit 4 has a Cash Dr. column. The kinds of transactions in which cash is received and how often they occur determine the titles of the other columns. For example, NetSolutions often receives cash from customers on account. Thus, the cash receipts journal in Exhibit 4 has an Accounts Receivable Cr. column.

To illustrate, on March 28 Accessories By Claire made a payment of $2,200 on its account. This transaction is recorded in the cash receipts journal, shown in Exhibit 4, by entering the following items:

1. Date column: *Mar. 28*
2. Account Credited column: *Accessories By Claire*

EXHIBIT 4   **Cash Receipts Journal and Postings**

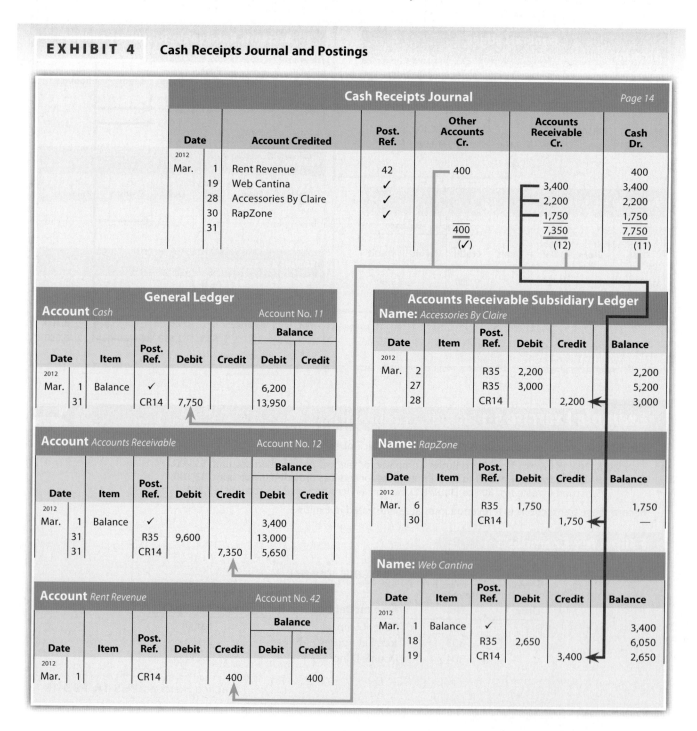

3. Accounts Receivable Cr. column: *2,200*

4. Cash Dr. column: *2,200*

The Other Accounts Cr. column in Exhibit 4 is used for recording credits to any account for which there is no special credit column. For example, NetSolutions received cash on March 1 for rent. Since no special column exists for Rent Revenue, Rent Revenue is entered in the Account Credited column. Thus, this transaction is recorded in the cash receipts journal, shown in Exhibit 4, by entering the following items:

1. Date column: *Mar. 1*

2. Account Credited column: *Rent Revenue*

3. Other Accounts Cr. column: *400*

4. Cash Dr. column: *400*

At the end of the month, all of the amount columns are totaled. The debits must equal the credits. If the debits do not equal the credits, an error has occurred. Before proceeding further, the error must be found and corrected.

The process of posting from the cash receipts journal, shown in Exhibit 4, is:

1. Each transaction involving the receipt of cash on account is posted individually to a customer account in the accounts receivable subsidiary ledger. Postings to customer accounts should be made on a regular basis. In this way, the customer's account will show a current balance.

   To illustrate, Exhibit 4 shows on March 19 the receipt of $3,400 on account from Web Cantina. The posting of the $3,400 credit to Web Cantina in the accounts receivable subsidiary ledger is also shown in Exhibit 4. After the posting, Web Cantina has a debit balance of $2,650. If a posting results in a customer's account with a credit balance, the credit balance is indicated by an asterisk or parentheses in the Balance column. If an account's balance is zero, a line may be drawn in the Balance column.

2. To provide a trail of the entries posted to the subsidiary ledger, the source of these entries is indicated in the Posting Reference column of each account by inserting the letter CR (for cash receipts journal) and the page number of the cash receipts journal.

   To illustrate, Exhibit 4 shows that after $3,400 is posted to Web Cantina's account in the accounts receivable subsidiary ledger, CR14 is inserted into the Post. Ref. column of the account.

3. To indicate that the transaction has been posted to the accounts receivable subsidiary ledger, a check mark (✓) is inserted in the Posting Reference column of the cash receipts journal.

   To illustrate, Exhibit 4 shows that a check mark (✓) has been inserted in the Post. Ref. column next to Web Cantina to indicate that the $3,400 has been posted.

4. A single monthly total of the Accounts Receivable Cr. column is posted to the accounts receivable general ledger account. This is the total cash received on account and is posted as a credit to Accounts Receivable. The accounts receivable account number (12) is then inserted below the Accounts Receivable Cr. column to indicate that the posting is complete.

   To illustrate, Exhibit 4 shows the monthly total of $7,350 was posted as a credit to Accounts Receivable (12).

5. A single monthly total of the Cash Dr. column is posted to the cash general ledger account. This is the total cash received during the month and is posted as a debit to Cash. The cash account number (11) is then inserted below the Cash Dr. column to indicate that the posting is complete.

   To illustrate, Exhibit 4 shows the monthly total of $7,750 was posted as a debit to Cash (11).

6. The accounts listed in the Other Accounts Cr. column are posted on a regular basis as a separate credit to each account. The account number is then inserted in the Post. Ref. column to indicate that the posting is complete. Because accounts in the Other Accounts Cr. column are posted individually, a check mark is placed below the column total at the end of the month to show that no further action is needed.

   To illustrate, Exhibit 4 shows that $400 was posted as a credit to Rent Revenue in the general ledger, and the rent revenue account number (42) was entered in the Post. Ref. column of the cash receipts journal. Also, at the end of the month a check mark (✓) is entered below the Other Accounts Cr. column to indicate that no further action is needed.

Accounts Receivable Control Account and Subsidiary Ledger

After all posting has been completed for the month, the balances in the accounts receivable subsidiary ledger should be totaled. This total should then be compared with the balance of the accounts receivable controlling account in the general ledger. If the controlling account and the subsidiary ledger do not agree, an error has occurred. Before proceeding further, the error must be located and corrected.

The total of NetSolutions' accounts receivable subsidiary ledger is $5,650. This total agrees with the balance of its accounts receivable control account on March 31, 2012, as shown below.

Accounts Receivable (Control)		NetSolutions Accounts Receivable Customer Balances March 31, 2012	
Balance, March 1, 2012	$ 3,400	Accessories By Claire	$3,000
Total debits (from revenue journal)	9,600	RapZone	0
Total credits (from cash receipts journal)	(7,350)	Web Cantina	2,650
Balance, March 31, 2012	$ 5,650	Total accounts receivable	$5,650

Equal debit balances

Example Exercise 5-2 Accounts Receivable Subsidiary Ledger

OBJ. 2

The debits and credits from two transactions are presented in the following customer account:

NAME   Sweet Tooth Confections
ADDRESS   1212 Lombard St.

Date	Item	Post. Ref.	Debit	Credit	Balance
July 1	Balance				625
7	Invoice 35	R12	86		711
31	Invoice 31	CR4		122	589

Describe each transaction and the source of each posting.

Follow My Example 5-2

July 7. Provided $86 of services on account to Sweet Tooth Confections, itemized on Invoice No. 35. Amount posted from page 12 of the revenue journal.

31. Collected cash of $122 from Sweet Tooth Confections (Invoice No. 31). Amount posted from page 4 of the cash receipts journal.

Practice Exercises: **PE 5-2A, PE 5-2B**

Purchases Journal

All *purchases on account* are recorded in the **purchases journal**. *Cash purchases would be recorded in the cash payments journal.* The purchases journal for NetSolutions is shown in Exhibit 5.

The amounts purchased on account are recorded in the purchases journal in an Accounts Payable Cr. column. The items most often purchased on account determine the titles of the other columns. For example, NetSolutions often purchases supplies on account. Thus, the purchases journal in Exhibit 5 has a Supplies Dr. column.

To illustrate, on March 3 NetSolutions purchased $600 of supplies on account from Howard Supplies. This transaction is recorded in the purchases journal, shown in Exhibit 5, by entering the following items:

1. Date column: *Mar. 3*

2. Account Credited column: *Howard Supplies*

3. Accounts Payable Cr. column: *600*

4. Supplies Dr. column: *600*

The Other Accounts Dr. column in Exhibit 5 is used to record purchases on account of any item for which there is no special debit column. The title of the account to be debited is entered in the Other Accounts Dr. column, and the amount is entered in the Amount column.

EXHIBIT 5 **Purchases Journal and Postings**

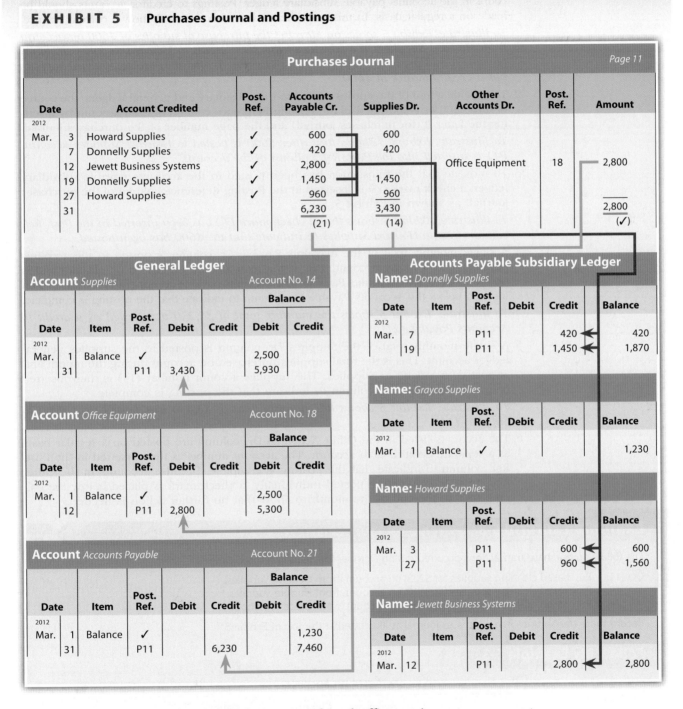

To illustrate, on March 12 NetSolutions purchased office equipment on account from Jewett Business Systems for $2,800. This transaction is recorded in the purchases journal shown in Exhibit 5 by entering the following items:

1. Date column: *Mar. 12*
2. Account Credited column: *Jewett Business Systems*
3. Accounts Payable Cr. column: *2,800*
4. Other Accounts Dr. column: *Office Equipment*
5. Amount column: *2,800*

At the end of the month, all of the amount columns are totaled. The debits must equal the credits. If the debits do not equal the credits, an error has occurred. Before proceeding further, the error must be found and corrected.

The process of posting from the purchases journal shown in Exhibit 5 is as follows:

1. Each transaction involving a purchase on account is posted individually to a creditor's account in the accounts payable subsidiary ledger. Postings to creditor accounts should be made on a regular basis. In this way, the creditor's account will show a current balance.

   To illustrate, Exhibit 5 shows on March 3 the purchase of supplies of $600 on account from Howard Supplies. The posting of the $600 credit to Howard Supplies accounts payable subsidiary ledger is also shown in Exhibit 5. After the posting, Howard Supplies has a credit balance of $600.

2. To provide a trail of the entries posted to the subsidiary and general ledgers, the source of these entries is indicated in the Posting Reference column of each account by inserting the letter P (for purchases journal) and the page number of the purchases journal.

   To illustrate, Exhibit 5 shows that after $600 is posted to Howard Supplies account, P11 is inserted into the Post. Ref. column of the account.

3. To indicate that the transaction has been posted to the accounts payable subsidiary ledger, a check mark (✓) is inserted in the Posting Reference column of the purchases journal, as shown in Exhibit 5.

   To illustrate, Exhibit 5 shows that a check mark (✓) has been inserted in the Post. Ref. column next to Howard Supplies to indicate that the $600 has been posted.

4. A single monthly total of the Accounts Payable Cr. column is posted to the accounts payable general ledger account. This is the total amount purchased on account and is posted as a credit to Accounts Payable. The accounts payable account number (21) is then inserted below the Accounts Payable Cr. column to indicate that the posting is complete.

   To illustrate, Exhibit 5 shows the monthly total of $6,230 was posted as a credit to Accounts Payable (21).

5. A single monthly total of the Supplies Dr. column is posted to the supplies general ledger account. This is the total supplies purchased on account during the month and is posted as a debit to Supplies. The supplies account number (14) is then inserted below the Supplies Dr. column to indicate that the posting is complete.

   To illustrate, Exhibit 5 shows the monthly total of $3,430 was posted as a debit to Supplies (14).

6. The accounts listed in the Other Accounts Dr. column are posted on a regular basis as a separate debit to each account. The account number is then inserted in the Post. Ref. column to indicate that the posting is complete. Because accounts in the Other Accounts Dr. column are posted individually, a check mark is placed below the column total at the end of the month to show that no further action is needed.

Example Exercise 5-3 Purchases Journal

OBJ. 2

The following purchase transactions occurred during October for Helping Hand Cleaners:

Oct. 11. Purchased cleaning supplies for $235, on account, from General Supplies.
   19. Purchased cleaning supplies for $110, on account, from Hubble Supplies.
   24. Purchased office equipment for $850, on account, from Office Warehouse.

Record these transactions in a purchases journal as illustrated at the top of Exhibit 5.

Follow My Example 5-3

PURCHASES JOURNAL

Date	Account Credited	Post. Ref.	Accounts Payable Cr.	Cleaning Supplies Dr.	Other Accounts Dr.	Post. Ref.	Amount
Oct. 11	General Supplies		235	235			
19	Hubble Supplies		110	110			
24	Office Warehouse		850		Office Equipment		850

Practice Exercises: **PE 5-3A, PE 5-3B**

To illustrate, Exhibit 5 shows that $2,800 was posted as a debit to Office Equipment in the general ledger, and the office equipment account number (18) was entered in the Post. Ref. column of the purchases journal. Also, at end of month, a check mark (✓) is entered below the Amount column to indicate no further action is needed.

Cash Payments Journal

All transactions that involve the payment of cash are recorded in a **cash payments journal**. The cash payments journal for NetSolutions is shown in Exhibit 6.

The cash payments journal shown in Exhibit 6 has a Cash Cr. column. The kinds of transactions in which cash is paid and how often they occur determine the titles of the other columns. For example, NetSolutions often pays cash to creditors on account. Thus, the cash payments journal in Exhibit 6 has an Accounts Payable Dr. column. In addition, NetSolutions makes all payments by check. Thus, a check number is entered for each payment in the Ck. No. (Check Number) column to the right of the Date column. The check numbers are helpful in controlling cash payments and provide a useful cross-reference.

To illustrate, on March 15 NetSolutions issued Check No. 151 for $1,230 to Grayco Supplies for payment on its account. This transaction is recorded in the cash payments journal shown in Exhibit 6 by entering the following items:

1. Date column: *Mar. 15*
2. Ck. No. column: *151*
3. Account Debited column: *Grayco Supplies*
4. Accounts Payable Dr. column: *1,230*
5. Cash Cr. column: *1,230*

The Other Accounts Dr. column in Exhibit 6 is used for recording debits to any account for which there is no special debit column. For example, NetSolutions issued Check No. 150 on March 2 for $1,600 in payment of March rent. This transaction is recorded in the cash payments journal, shown in Exhibit 6, by entering these items:

1. Date column: *Mar. 2*
2. Ck. No. column: *150*
3. Account Debited column: *Rent Expense*
4. Other Accounts Dr. column: *1,600*
5. Cash Cr. column: *1,600*

At the end of the month, all of the amount columns are totaled. The debits must equal the credits. If the debits do not equal the credits, an error has occurred. Before proceeding further, the error must be found and corrected.

The process of posting from the cash payments journal, Exhibit 6, is as follows:

1. Each transaction involving the payment of cash on account is posted individually to a creditor account in the accounts payable subsidiary ledger. Postings to creditor accounts should be made on a regular basis. In this way, the creditor's account will show a current balance.
   To illustrate, Exhibit 6 shows on March 22 the payment of $420 on account to Donnelly Supplies. The posting of the $420 debit to Donnelly Supplies in the accounts payable subsidiary ledger is also shown in Exhibit 6. After the posting, Donnelly Supplies has a credit balance of $1,450.
2. To provide a trail of the entries posted to the subsidiary and general ledgers, the source of these entries is indicated in the Posting Reference column of each account by inserting the letter CP (for cash payments journal) and the page number of the cash payments journal.
   To illustrate, Exhibit 6 shows that after $420 is posted to Donnelly Supplies account, CP7 is inserted into the Post. Ref. column of the account.
3. To indicate that the transaction has been posted to the accounts payable subsidiary ledger, a check mark (✓) is inserted in the Posting Reference column of the cash payments journal.
   To illustrate, Exhibit 6 shows that a check mark (✓) has been inserted in the Post. Ref. column next to Donnelly Supplies to indicate that the $420 has been posted.

EXHIBIT 6   Cash Payments Journal and Postings

Cash Payments Journal — Page 7

Date		Ck. No.	Account Debited	Post. Ref.	Other Accounts Dr.	Accounts Payable Dr.	Cash Cr.
2012							
Mar.	2	150	Rent Expense	52	1,600		1,600
	15	151	Grayco Supplies	✓		1,230	1,230
	21	152	Jewett Business Systems	✓		2,800	2,800
	22	153	Donnelly Supplies	✓		420	420
	30	154	Utilities Expense	54	1,050		1,050
	31	155	Howard Supplies	✓		600	600
	31				2,650	5,050	7,700
					(✓)	(21)	(11)

General Ledger

Account Cash   **Account No. 11**

Date		Item	Post. Ref.	Debit	Credit	Balance Debit	Balance Credit
2012							
Mar.	1	Balance	✓			6,200	
	31		CR14	7,750		13,950	
	31		CP7		7,700	6,250	

Account Accounts Payable   **Account No. 21**

Date		Item	Post. Ref.	Debit	Credit	Balance Debit	Balance Credit
2012							
Mar.	1	Balance	✓				1,230
	31		P11		6,230		7,460
	31		CP7	5,050			2,410

Account Rent Expense   **Account No. 52**

Date		Item	Post. Ref.	Debit	Credit	Balance Debit	Balance Credit
2012							
Mar.	2		CP7	1,600		1,600	

Account Utilities Expense   **Account No. 54**

Date		Item	Post. Ref.	Debit	Credit	Balance Debit	Balance Credit
2012							
Mar.	30		CP7	1,050		1,050	

Accounts Payable Subsidiary Ledger

Name: Donnelly Supplies

Date		Item	Post. Ref.	Debit	Credit	Balance
2012						
Mar.	7		P11		420	420
	19		P11		1,450	1,870
	22		CP7	420		1,450

Name: Grayco Supplies

Date		Item	Post. Ref.	Debit	Credit	Balance
2012						
Mar.	1	Balance	✓			1,230
	15		CP7	1,230		—

Name: Howard Supplies

Date		Item	Post. Ref.	Debit	Credit	Balance
2012						
Mar.	3		P11		600	600
	27		P11		960	1,560
	31		CP7	600		960

Name: Jewett Business Systems

Date		Item	Post. Ref.	Debit	Credit	Balance
2012						
Mar.	12		P11		2,800	2,800
	21		CP7	2,800		—

4. A single monthly total of the Accounts Payable Dr. column is posted to the accounts payable general ledger account. This is the total cash paid on account and is posted as a debit to Accounts Payable. The accounts payable account number (21) is then inserted below the Accounts Payable Dr. column to indicate that the posting is complete. *To illustrate, Exhibit 6 shows the monthly total of $5,050 was posted as a debit to Accounts Payable (21).*

5. A single monthly total of the Cash Cr. column is posted to the cash general ledger account. This is the total cash payments during the month and is posted as a credit to Cash. The cash account number (11) is then inserted below the Cash Cr. column to indicate that the posting is complete.

   To illustrate, Exhibit 6 shows the monthly total of $7,700 was posted as a credit to Cash (11).

6. The accounts listed in the Other Accounts Dr. column are posted on a regular basis as a separate debit to each account. The account number is then inserted in the Post. Ref. column to indicate that the posting is complete. Because accounts in the Other Accounts Dr. column are posted individually, a check mark is placed below the column total at the end of the month to show that no further action is needed.

   To illustrate, Exhibit 6 shows that $1,600 was posted as a debit to Rent Expense (52) and $1,050 was posted as a debit to Utilities Expense (54) in the general ledger. The account numbers (52 and 54, respectively) were entered in the Post. Ref. column of the cash payments journal. Also, at the end of the month, a check mark (✓) is entered below the Other Accounts Dr. column to indicate that no further action is needed.

Accounts Payable Control Account and Subsidiary Ledger

After all posting has been completed for the month, the balances in the accounts payable subsidiary ledger should be totaled. This total should then be compared with the balance of the accounts payable controlling account in the general ledger. If the controlling account and the subsidiary ledger do not agree, an error has occurred. Before proceeding, the error must be located and corrected.

The total of NetSolutions' accounts payable subsidiary ledger is $2,410. This total agrees with the balance of its accounts payable control account on March 31, 2012, as shown below.

Accounts Payable (Control)		NetSolutions Accounts Payable Creditor Balances March 31, 2012	
Balance, March 1, 2012	$1,230	Donnelly Supplies	$1,450
Total credits (from purchases journal)	6,230	Grayco Supplies	0
Total debits		Howard Supplies	960
(from cash payments journal)	(5,050)	Jewett Business Systems	0
Balance, March 31, 2012	$2,410	Total	$2,410

Equal credit balances

Example Exercise 5-4   Accounts Payable Subsidiary Ledger

OBJ. 2

The debits and credits from two transactions are presented in the following creditor's (supplier's) account:

NAME   Lassiter Services Inc.
ADDRESS   301 St. Bonaventure Ave.

Date	Item	Post. Ref.	Debit	Credit	Balance
Aug. 1	Balance				320
12	Invoice No. 101	CP36	200		120
22	Invoice No. 106	P16		140	260

Describe each transaction and the source of each posting.

Follow My Example 5-4

Aug. 12   Paid $200 to Lassiter Services Inc. on account (Invoice No. 101). Amount posted from page 36 of the cash payments journal.

   22   Purchased $140 of services on account from Lassiter Services Inc. itemized on Invoice No. 106. Amount posted from page 16 of the purchases journal.

Practice Exercises: **PE 5-4A, PE 5-4B**

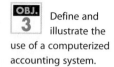

Define and illustrate the use of a computerized accounting system.

Computerized Accounting Systems

Computerized accounting systems are widely used by even the smallest of companies. Computerized accounting systems have the following three main advantages over manual systems:

1. Computerized systems simplify the record-keeping process by recording transactions in electronic forms and, at the same time, posting them electronically to general and subsidiary ledger accounts.
2. Computerized systems are generally more accurate than manual systems.
3. Computerized systems provide management with current account balance information to support decision making, since account balances are posted as the transactions occur.

The popular QuickBooks accounting software for small- to medium-sized businesses is used to illustrate a computerized accounting system for **NetSolutions**. To simplify, the illustration is limited to transactions involving revenue earned on

BusinessConnection

ACCOUNTING SYSTEMS AND PROFIT MEASUREMENT

A Greek restaurant owner in Canada had his own system of accounting. He kept his accounts payable in a cigar box on the left-hand side of his cash register, his daily cash returns in the cash register, and his receipts for paid bills in another cigar box on the right. A truly "manual" system.

When his youngest son graduated as an accountant, he was appalled by his father's primitive methods. "I don't

know how you can run a business that way," he said. "How do you know what your profits are?"

"Well, son," the father replied, "when I got off the boat from Greece, I had nothing but the pants I was wearing. Today, your brother is a doctor. You are an accountant. Your sister is a speech therapist. Your mother and I have a nice car, a city house, and a country home. We have a good business, and everything is paid for...."

"So, you add all that together, subtract the pants, and there's your profit!"

account and the subsequent recording of cash collections. Exhibit 7 illustrates the use of QuickBooks for NetSolutions to record transactions as follows:

Large companies have their accounting systems integrated within the automated business systems of the firm. Such integrated software is termed ERP, or enterprise resource planning.

Step 1. Record fees by completing an electronic invoice form.

Sales transactions are entered onto the computer screen using an electronic invoice form. The electronic form appears like a paper form with spaces, or fields, to input transaction data. The data spaces may have pull-down lists to ease data entry. After the form is completed, it is printed out and mailed, or e-mailed, to the customer.

To illustrate, on March 2, NetSolutions earned $2,200 on account from Accessories By Claire. As shown in Exhibit 7, Invoice No. 615 was created using an electronic form. Upon submitting the invoice form, QuickBooks automatically posts a $2,200 debit to the Accessories By Claire customer account and a credit to Fees Earned. An invoice is either e-mailed or printed for mailing to Accessories By Claire.

Step 2. Record collection of payment by completing a "receive payment" form.

Upon collection from the customer, a "receive payment" electronic form is opened and completed. As with the "invoice form," data are input into the various spaces directly or by using pull-down lists.

To illustrate, a $2,200 payment was collected from Accessories By Claire on March 28. As shown in Exhibit 7, the $2,200 was applied to Invoice No. 615, as shown by the check mark (✓) next to the March 2 date at the bottom of the form. As shown at the bottom of the form, the March 27 invoice of $3,000 remains uncollected. When the screen is completed, a debit of $2,200 is automatically posted to the cash account, and a credit for $2,200 is posted to the Accessories By Claire account. This causes the balance of the Accessories By Claire account to be reduced from $5,200 to $3,000.

EXHIBIT 7 **Revenue and Cash Receipts in QuickBooks**

1. **Record fees by completing an electronic invoice form.**

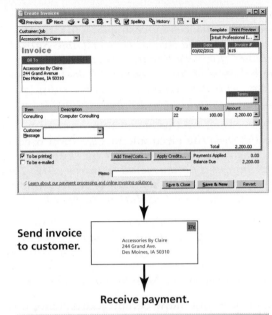

Journal Entry Equivalent

	Dr.	Cr.
Accounts Receivable—		
Accessories By Claire	2,200	
Fees Earned		2,200

Send invoice to customer.

Accessories By Claire
244 Grand Ave.
Des Moines, IA 50310

Receive payment.

2. **Record collection of payment by completing a "receive payment" form.**

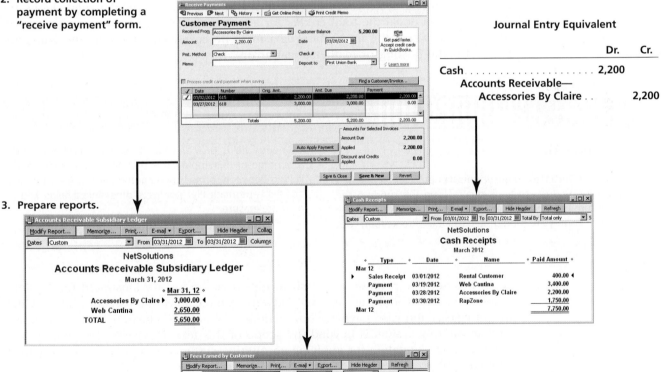

Journal Entry Equivalent

	Dr.	Cr.
Cash	2,200	
Accounts Receivable—		
Accessories By Claire		2,200

3. **Prepare reports.**

NetSolutions
Accounts Receivable Subsidiary Ledger
March 31, 2012

	Mar 31, 12
Accessories By Claire	3,000.00
Web Cantina	2,650.00
TOTAL	5,650.00

NetSolutions
Cash Receipts
March 2012

Type	Date	Name	Paid Amount
Mar 12			
Sales Receipt	03/01/2012	Rental Customer	400.00
Payment	03/19/2012	Web Cantina	3,400.00
Payment	03/28/2012	Accessories By Claire	2,200.00
Payment	03/30/2012	RapZone	1,750.00
Mar 12			7,750.00

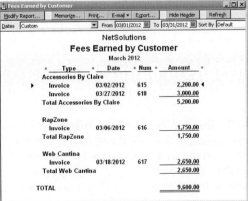

NetSolutions
Fees Earned by Customer
March 2012

Type	Date	Num	Amount
Accessories By Claire			
Invoice	03/02/2012	615	2,200.00
Invoice	03/27/2012	618	3,000.00
Total Accessories By Claire			5,200.00
RapZone			
Invoice	03/06/2012	616	1,750.00
Total RapZone			1,750.00
Web Cantina			
Invoice	03/18/2012	617	2,650.00
Total Web Cantina			2,650.00
TOTAL			9,600.00

Step 3. Prepare reports.

At any time, managers may request reports from the software. Three such reports include the following:

1. "Accounts Receivable Subsidiary Ledger" lists as of a specific date the accounts receivable balances by customer.

   To illustrate, the Accounts Receivable Subsidiary Ledger report shown in Exhibit 7 for NetSolutions was generated as of March 31, 2012. The total of the balances of the Accounts Receivable Subsidiary Ledger report of $5,650 agrees with the accounts receivable subsidiary balance total we illustrated using a manual system for NetSolutions on page 214.

2. "Fees Earned by Customer" lists revenue by customer for the month. It is created from the electronic invoice form used in step 1.

   To illustrate, the Fees Earned by Customer report shown in Exhibit 7 for NetSolutions is for the month of March 2012. The total fees earned by customer of $9,600 agree with the total of the revenue journal we illustrated using a manual system for NetSolutions in Exhibits 2 and 3.

3. *"Cash Receipts"* lists the cash receipts during the month.

   To illustrate, the Cash Receipts report shown in Exhibit 7 for NetSolutions is for the month of March 2012. The total cash receipts of $7,750 agree with the total of the Cash Dr. column of the cash receipts journal we illustrated using a manual system for NetSolutions in Exhibit 4.

The computer does not allow certain journalizing errors. For example, a computerized accounting system will not process a transaction unless the total debits for the transaction equal the total credits for a transaction. Instead, an error screen will notify the user that the transaction data must be corrected. Likewise, the computer will not make posting or mathematical errors.

BusinessConnection

TURBOTAX

Intuit sells TurboTax®, one of the most popular tax preparation software products for individuals. Using this product, the tax return is prepared using electronic tax forms. Thus, the familiar Form 1040 is presented as an electronic form with data-entry fields provided for the various line items. The advantage of this approach is that all the arithmetic and linking between forms is done automatically. A change in one field automatically updates all other linked fields. Thus, no more erasure.

In this section, revenue and cash receipt transactions are illustrated for NetSolutions using QuickBooks accounting software. Similar illustrations could be provided for purchases and cash payment transactions. A complete illustration of a computerized accounting system is beyond the scope of this text. However, this chapter provides a solid foundation for applying accounting system concepts in either a manual or a computerized system.

Integrity, Objectivity, and Ethics in Business

ONLINE FRAUD

Fraud accounted for over $3.3 billion in e-commerce losses in 2009, or approximately 1.2% of all online revenue. As a result, online retailers are using address verification and credit card security codes as additional security measures. Address verification matches the customer's address to the address on file with the credit card company, while the security code is the additional four-digit code designed to reduce fictitious credit card transactions.

Source: 11th Annual CyberSource fraud survey, *CyberSource*, November 19, 2009.

E-Commerce

The U.S. Census Bureau indicates that e-commerce sales are over $130 billion in retail sales. This represents over 3% of all retail sales.[1] Using the Internet to perform business transactions is termed **e-commerce.** When transactions are between a company and a consumer, it is termed B2C (business-to-consumer) e-commerce. Examples of companies engaged in B2C e-commerce include Amazon.com, priceline.com Incorporated, and Dell Inc.

The B2C business allows consumers to shop and receive goods at home, rather than going to the store. For example, Whirlpool Corporation allows consumers to use its Web site to order appliances, selecting color and other features. After paying with a credit card, customers can receive delivery of the appliance from the Whirlpool factory.

When transactions are conducted between two companies, it is termed B2B (business-to-business) e-commerce. Examples of companies engaged in B2B e-commerce include Cisco Systems, Inc., an Internet equipment manufacturer, and Bristol-Myers Squibb Company (BMS), a pharmaceutical company. BMS, for example, uses e-commerce to purchase supplies and equipment from its suppliers. E-commerce streamlines purchases and payments by automating transactions and eliminating paperwork. BMS claims over $90 million in savings by placing its purchase/payment cycle on the Internet.

A new trend is toward application service provider (ASP) software solutions whereby the accounting system is managed and distributed over the Internet by a third party. Under this model, the software is "rented," while analysis, design, and implementation are largely provided by the ASP vendor.

The Internet creates opportunities for improving the speed and efficiency of transactions. Many companies are realizing these benefits of using e-commerce as illustrated above. Three additional areas where the Internet is being used for business purposes are as follows:

1. **Supply chain management (SCM):** Internet applications to plan and coordinate suppliers.
2. **Customer relationship management (CRM):** Internet applications to plan and coordinate marketing and sales effort.
3. **Product life-cycle management (PLM):** Internet applications to plan and coordinate the product development and design process.

E-commerce also provides opportunities for faster business processes that operate at lower costs. New Internet applications are continually being introduced as the Internet develops into a preferred method of conducting business.

Financial Analysis and Interpretation: Segment Analysis

Accounting systems often use computers to collect, classify, summarize, and report financial and operating information in a variety of ways. One way is to report revenue earned by different segments of business. Businesses may be segmented by region, by product or service, or by type of customer. Segment revenues are determined from the invoice data that are entered into the accounting system.

For example, Intuit Inc. uses invoice data from the accounting system to determine the amount of revenue earned by different products and services. Segment analysis uses horizontal and vertical comparisons to analyze the contributions of various segments to the total operating performance of a company. To illustrate, selected product and service segment revenue information from the notes to Intuit's financial statements for the fiscal years ending July 31, 2009 and 2008, is presented on the following page.

Segment	2009 (in thousands)	2008 (in thousands)
Financial Management Solutions	$ 578,801	$ 592,106
Employee Management Solutions	364,831	336,880
Payments Solutions	290,974	253,560
Consumer Tax	996,413	929,429
Accounting Professionals	351,747	326,723
Financial Institutions	311,105	298,540
Other Businesses	288,666	333,736
Total revenues	$3,182,537	$3,070,974

This segment information can be used to perform horizontal analysis using 2008 as the base year as follows:

Segment	2009 (in thousands)	2008 (in thousands)	Increase (Decrease) Amount	Percent
Financial Management Solutions	$ 578,801	$ 592,106	$ (13,305)	(2.2)%
Employee Management Solutions	364,831	336,880	27,951	8.3
Payments Solutions	290,974	253,560	37,414	14.8
Consumer Tax	996,413	929,429	66,984	7.2
Accounting Professionals	351,747	326,723	25,024	7.7
Financial Institutions	311,105	298,540	12,565	4.2
Other Businesses	288,666	333,736	(45,070)	(13.5)
Total revenues	$3,182,537	$3,070,974	$111,563	3.6

Intuit Inc. increased total revenue by 3.6% from 2008 to 2009. This increase came from strong revenue gains in the Employee Management Solutions, Payments Solutions, Consumer Tax, and Accounting Professionals segments combined with revenue losses in the Financial Management Solutions and Other Businesses segments. The Payments Solutions segment had the largest revenue increase from 2008 to 2009, at 14.8%.

In addition, vertical analysis could be performed on the segment disclosures as follows:

Segment	2009 Amount (in thousands)	Percent	2008 Amount (in thousands)	Percent
Financial Management Solutions	$ 578,801	18.2%	$ 592,106	19.3%
Employee Management Solutions	364,831	11.5	336,880	11.0
Payments Solutions	290,974	9.1	253,560	8.3
Consumer Tax	996,413	31.3	929,429	30.3
Accounting Professionals	351,747	11.1	326,723	10.6
Financial Institutions	311,105	9.8	298,540	9.7
Other Businesses	288,666	9.1	333,736	10.9
Total revenues	$3,182,537	100.0%*	$3,070,974	100.0%*

*Percentages do not add exactly to 100% due to rounding.

The preceding analysis shows that revenue in the Financial Management Solutions and Other Businesses segments declined as a percent of total revenues from 2008 to 2009. The remaining segments all increased as a percent of total revenues from 2008 to 2009.

Both analyses indicate that Intuit's second largest business segment, the Financial Management Solutions segment, is declining. This segment consists of Quicken and Quickbooks products. However, the remaining segments are more than compensating for the revenue decline. For example, Intuit's largest segment, Consumer Tax, is still growing with such products as TurboTax.

Example Exercise 5-5 · Segment Analysis

OBJ. 5

Morse Company does business in two regional segments: East and West. The following annual revenue information was determined from the accounting system's invoice information:

Segment	2012	2011
East	$25,000	$20,000
West	50,000	60,000
Total revenues	$75,000	$80,000

Prepare horizontal and vertical analyses of the segments.

Follow My Example 5-5

Horizontal analysis:

			Increase (Decrease)	
Segment	2012	2011	Amount	Percent
East	$25,000	$20,000	$ 5,000	25.0%
West	50,000	60,000	(10,000)	(16.7)
Total revenues	$75,000	$80,000	$ (5,000)	(6.3)

Vertical analysis:

	2012		2011	
Segment	Amount	Percent	Amount	Percent
East	$25,000	33.3%	$20,000	25.0%
West	50,000	66.7	60,000	75.0
Total revenues	$75,000	100.0%	$80,000	100.0%

Practice Exercises: **PE 5-5A, PE 5-5B**

At a Glance 5

OBJ. 1

Define and describe an accounting system.

Key Points An accounting system is the methods and procedures for collecting, classifying, summarizing, and reporting a business's financial information. The three steps through which an accounting system evolves are: (1) analysis of information needs, (2) design of the system, and (3) implementation of the system design.

Learning Outcomes	Example Exercises	Practice Exercises
• Define an accounting system.		
• Describe the three steps for designing an accounting system: (1) analysis, (2) design, and (3) implementation.		

OBJ.
2
Journalize and post transactions in a manual accounting system that uses subsidiary ledgers and special journals.

Key Points   Subsidiary ledgers may be used to maintain separate records for customers and creditors (vendors). A controlling account in the general ledger summarizes the subsidiary ledger accounts. The sum of the subsidiary ledger account balances must agree with the balance in the related controlling account.

Learning Outcomes	Example Exercises	Practice Exercises
• Prepare a revenue journal and post services provided on account to individual customer accounts and the column total to the corresponding general ledger accounts.	EE5-1	PE5-1A, 5-1B
• Prepare a cash receipts journal and post collections on account to individual customer accounts. Post Other Accounts column entries individually and special column totals to the corresponding general ledger accounts.	EE5-2	PE5-2A, 5-2B
• Prepare a purchases journal and post amounts owed to individual creditor accounts. Post Other Accounts column entries individually and special column totals to the corresponding general ledger accounts.	EE5-3	PE5-3A, 5-3B
• Prepare a cash payments journal and post the amounts paid to individual creditor accounts. Post Other Accounts column entries individually and special column totals to the corresponding general ledger accounts.	EE5-4	PE5-4A, 5-4B

OBJ.
3
Describe and illustrate the use of a computerized accounting system.

Key Points   Computerized accounting systems are similar to manual systems. The main advantages of a computerized accounting system are the simultaneous recording and posting of transactions, high degree of accuracy, and timeliness of reporting.

Learning Outcomes	Example Exercises	Practice Exercises
• Differentiate between a manual and a computerized accounting system.		
• Illustrate revenue and cash receipts transactions using QuickBooks.		

OBJ.
4
Describe the basic features of e-commerce.

Key Points   Using the Internet to perform business transactions is termed e-commerce. B2C e-commerce involves Internet transactions between a business and consumer, while B2B e-commerce involves Internet transactions between businesses. More elaborate e-commerce involves planning and coordinating suppliers, customers, and product design.

Learning Outcomes	Example Exercises	Practice Exercises
• Define e-commerce and describe the major trends in e-commerce.		

OBJ. 5

Use segment analysis in evaluating the operating performance of a company.

Key Points   Businesses may be segmented by region, by product or service, or by type of customer. Segment revenues can be analyzed using horizontal and vertical analyses. Such analyses are useful to management for evaluating the causes of business performance.

Learning Outcomes	Example Exercises	Practice Exercises
• Prepare horizontal and vertical analyses for business segments.	EE5-5	PE5-5A, 5-5B

Key Terms

accounting system (206)

accounts payable subsidiary ledger (207)

accounts receivable subsidiary ledger (207)

cash payments journal (217)

cash receipts journal (212)

controlling account (207)

e-commerce (223)

general journal (208)

general ledger (207)

internal controls (207)

invoice (209)

purchases journal (214)

revenue journal (209)

special journals (207)

subsidiary ledger (207)

Illustrative Problem

Selected transactions of O'Malley Co. for the month of May are as follows:

a. May   1. Issued Check No. 1001 in payment of rent for May, $1,200.

b.   2. Purchased office supplies on account from McMillan Co., $3,600.

c.   4. Issued Check No. 1003 in payment of freight charges on the supplies purchased on May 2, $320.

d.   8. Provided services on account to Waller Co., Invoice No. 51, $4,500.

e.   9. Issued Check No. 1005 for office supplies purchased, $450.

f.   10. Received cash for office supplies sold to employees at cost, $120.

g.   11. Purchased office equipment on account from Fender Office Products, $15,000.

h.   12. Issued Check No. 1010 in payment of the supplies purchased from McMillan Co. on May 2, $3,600.

i.   16. Provided services on account to Riese Co., Invoice No. 58, $8,000.

j.   18. Received $4,500 from Waller Co. in payment of May 8 invoice.

k.   20. Invested additional cash in the business, $10,000.

l.   25. Provided services for cash, $15,900.

m.   30. Issued Check No. 1040 for withdrawal of cash for personal use, $1,000.

n.   30. Issued Check No. 1041 in payment of electricity and water invoices, $690.

o. May 30. Issued Check No. 1042 in payment of office and sales salaries for May, $15,800.

p. 31. Journalized adjusting entries from the work sheet prepared for the fiscal year ended May 31.

O'Malley Co. maintains a revenue journal, a cash receipts journal, a purchases journal, a cash payments journal, and a general journal. In addition, accounts receivable and accounts payable subsidiary ledgers are used.

Instructions

1. Indicate the journal in which each of the preceding transactions, (a) through (p), would be recorded.

2. Indicate whether an account in the accounts receivable or accounts payable subsidiary ledgers would be affected for each of the preceding transactions.

3. Journalize transactions (b), (c), (d), (h), and (j) in the appropriate journals.

Solution

1. Journal	2. Subsidiary Ledger
a. Cash payments journal	
b. Purchases journal	Accounts payable ledger
c. Cash payments journal	
d. Revenue journal	Accounts receivable ledger
e. Cash payments journal	
f. Cash receipts journal	
g. Purchases journal	Accounts payable ledger
h. Cash payments journal	Accounts payable ledger
i. Revenue journal	Accounts receivable ledger
j. Cash receipts journal	Accounts receivable ledger
k. Cash receipts journal	
l. Cash receipts journal	
m. Cash payments journal	
n. Cash payments journal	
o. Cash payments journal	
p. General journal	

3.

Transaction (b):

Purchases Journal

Date	Account Credited	Post. Ref.	Accounts Payable Cr.	Office Supplies Dr.	Other Accounts Dr.	Post. Ref.	Amount
May 2	McMillan Co.		3,600	3,600			

Transactions (c) and (h):

Cash Payments Journal

Date	Ck. No.	Account Debited	Post. Ref.	Other Accounts Dr.	Accounts Payable Dr.	Cash Cr.
May 4	1003	Freight Expense		320		320
12	1010	McMillan Co.			3,600	3,600

Transaction (d):

Revenue Journal					
Date	Invoice No.	Account Debited	Post. Ref.	Accts. Rec. Dr. Fees Earned Cr.	
May 8	51	Waller Co.		4,500	

Transaction (j):

Cash Receipts Journal					
Date	Account Credited	Post. Ref.	Other Accounts Cr.	Accounts Receivable Cr.	Cash Dr.
May 18	Waller Co.			4,500	4,500

Discussion Questions

1. Why would a company maintain separate accounts receivable ledgers for each customer, as opposed to maintaining a single accounts receivable ledger for all customers?

2. What are the major advantages of the use of special journals?

3. In recording 400 fees earned on account during a single month, how many times will it be necessary to write Fees Earned (a) if each transaction, including fees earned, is recorded individually in a two-column general journal; (b) if each transaction for fees earned is recorded in a revenue journal?

4. How many postings to Fees Earned for the month would be needed in Discussion Question 3 if the procedure described in (a) had been used; if the procedure described in (b) had been used?

5. During the current month, the following errors occurred in recording transactions in the purchases journal or in posting from it.

   a. An invoice for $1,875 of supplies from Kelly Co. was recorded as having been received from Kelley Co., another supplier.
   b. A credit of $420 to Blackstone Company was posted as $240 in the subsidiary ledger.

   c. An invoice for equipment of $4,800 was recorded as $4,000.
   d. The Accounts Payable column of the purchases journal was overstated by $3,600.

   How will each error come to the bookkeeper's attention, other than by chance discovery?

6. Assuming the use of a two-column general journal, a purchases journal, and a cash payments journal as illustrated in this chapter, indicate the journal in which each of the following transactions should be recorded:

   a. Purchase of office supplies on account.
   b. Purchase of supplies for cash.
   c. Purchase of store equipment on account.
   d. Payment of cash on account to creditor.
   e. Payment of cash for office supplies.

7. What is an electronic form, and how is it used in a computerized accounting system?

8. Do computerized systems use controlling accounts to verify the accuracy of the subsidiary accounts?

9. What happens to the special journal in a computerized accounting system that uses electronic forms?

10. How would e-commerce improve the revenue/collection cycle?

Practice Exercises

Learning Objectives   *Example Exercises*

OBJ. 2   EE 5-1 *p. 211*

PE 5-1A   Revenue journal

The following revenue transactions occurred during October:

Oct.   7.   Issued Invoice No. 121 to Darcy Co. for services provided on account, $320.

17.   Issued Invoice No. 122 to Triple A Inc. for services provided on account, $470.

21.   Issued Invoice No. 123 to Whaley Co. for services provided on account, $530.

Record these three transactions into the following revenue journal format:

		REVENUE JOURNAL		
Date	Invoice No.	Account Debited	Post. Ref.	Accts. Rec. Dr. Fees Earned Cr.

OBJ. 2   EE 5-1 *p. 211*

PE 5-1B   Revenue journal

The following revenue transactions occurred during May:

May   6.   Issued Invoice No. 78 to Lemon Co. for services provided on account, $1,240.

9.   Issued Invoice No. 79 to Hitchcock Inc. for services provided on account, $3,420.

19.   Issued Invoice No. 80 to Conrad Inc. for services provided on account, $1,470.

Record these three transactions into the following revenue journal format:

		REVENUE JOURNAL		
Date	Invoice No.	Account Debited	Post. Ref.	Accts. Rec. Dr. Fees Earned Cr.

OBJ. 2   EE 5-2 *p. 214*

PE 5-2A   Accounts receivable subsidiary ledger

The debits and credits from two transactions are presented in the following customer account:

NAME   Signal Communications Inc.
ADDRESS   76 Oak Ridge Rd.

Date	Item	Post. Ref.	Debit	Credit	Balance
June 1	Balance	✓			280
20	Invoice 579	CR106		95	185
28	Invoice 527	R92	75		260

Describe each transaction and the source of each posting.

OBJ. 2   EE 5-2 *p. 214*

PE 5-2B   Accounts receivable subsidiary ledger

The debits and credits from two transactions are presented in the following customer account:

NAME   Mobility Products Inc.
ADDRESS   46 W. Main St.

Date	Item	Post. Ref.	Debit	Credit	Balance
Sept. 1	Balance	✓			1,200
8	Invoice 119	R24	840		2,040
17	Invoice 106	CR46		590	1,450

Describe each transaction and the source of each posting.

PE 5-3A   Purchases journal

The following purchase transactions occurred during August for Elegance Catering Service:

Aug. 11. Purchased party supplies for $390, on account from Party Zone Supplies Inc.

     14. Purchased party supplies for $290, on account from Fun 4 All Supplies Inc.

     29. Purchased office furniture for $3,560, on account from Office Space Inc.

Record these transactions in the following purchases journal format:

PURCHASES JOURNAL

Date	Accounts Credited	Post. Ref.	Accounts Payable Cr.	Office Supplies Dr.	Other Account Dr.	Post. Ref.	Amount

PE 5-3B   Purchases journal

The following purchase transactions occurred during December for Rehoboth Inc.:

Dec. 6. Purchased office supplies for $415, on account from Supply Hut Inc.

     14. Purchased office equipment for $1,950, on account from Zell Computer Inc.

     19. Purchased office supplies for $450, on account from Supply Hut Inc.

Record these transactions in the following purchases journal format:

PURCHASES JOURNAL

Date	Accounts Credited	Post. Ref.	Accounts Payable Cr.	Office Supplies Dr.	Other Account Dr.	Post. Ref.	Amount

PE 5-4A   Accounts payable subsidiary ledger

The debits and credits from two transactions are presented in the following supplier's (creditor's) account:

NAME   *Newton Computer Services Inc.*
ADDRESS   *2199 Technology Place*

Date	Item	Post. Ref.	Debit	Credit	Balance
Nov. 1	Balance				9,400
11	Invoice 75	P8		2,790	12,190
21	Invoice 43	CP46	6,550		5,640

Describe each transaction and the source of each posting.

PE 5-4B   Accounts payable subsidiary ledger

The debits and credits from two transactions are presented in the following supplier's (creditor's) account:

NAME   *Daisy Inc.*
ADDRESS   *5000 Grand Ave.*

Date	Item	Post. Ref.	Debit	Credit	Balance
Feb. 1	Balance				92
11	Invoice 122	CP71	79		13
20	Invoice 139	P55		57	70

Describe each transaction and the source of each posting.

PE 5-5A   Segment analysis

Harrow Company does business in two customer segments, Retail and Wholesale. The following annual revenue information was determined from the accounting system's invoice information:

	2012	2011
Retail	$ 80,000	$ 75,000
Wholesale	120,000	140,000
Total revenue	$200,000	$215,000

Prepare a horizontal and vertical analysis of the segments. Round to one decimal place.

OBJ. 5   EE 5-5 *p. 225*   **PE 5-5B   Segment analysis**

Outdoor Country, Inc. does business in two product segments, Camping and Fishing. The following annual revenue information was determined from the accounting system's invoice information:

	2012	2011
Camping	$250,000	$280,000
Fishing	100,000	60,000
Total revenue	$350,000	$340,000

Prepare a horizontal and vertical analysis of the segments. Round to one decimal place.

Exercises

OBJ. 2

EX 5-1   Identify postings from revenue journal

Using the following revenue journal for Gamma Services Inc., identify each of the posting references, indicated by a letter, as representing (1) posting to general ledger accounts or (2) posting to subsidiary ledger accounts.

REVENUE JOURNAL

Date	Invoice No.	Account Debited	Post. Ref.	Accounts Rec. Dr. Fees Earned Cr.
2012				
June 1	112	Hazmat Safety Co.	(a)	$2,625
10	113	Masco Co.	(b)	980
18	114	Eco-Systems	(c)	1,600
27	115	Nero Enterprises	(d)	1,240
30				$6,445
				(e)

OBJ. 2

✔ d. Total accounts
receivable, $6,975

EX 5-2   Accounts receivable ledger

Based on the data presented in Exercise 5-1, assume that the beginning balances for the customer accounts were zero, except for Nero Enterprises, which had a $530 beginning balance. In addition, there were no collections during the period.

a. Set up a T account for Accounts Receivable and T accounts for the four accounts needed in the customer ledger.

b. Post to the T accounts.

c. Determine the balance in the accounts.

d. Prepare a listing of the accounts receivable subsidiary ledger account balances as of June 30, 2012.

OBJ. 2

EX 5-3   Identify journals

Assuming the use of a two-column (all-purpose) general journal, a revenue journal, and a cash receipts journal as illustrated in this chapter, indicate the journal in which each of the following transactions should be recorded:

a. Sale of office supplies on account, at cost, to a neighboring business.

b. Receipt of cash from sale of office equipment.

c. Closing of drawing account at the end of the year.

d. Providing services for cash.

e. Receipt of cash refund from overpayment of taxes.

f. Adjustment to record accrued salaries at the end of the year.

g. Receipt of cash for rent.

h. Receipt of cash on account from a customer.

i. Providing services on account.

j. Investment of additional cash in the business by the owner.

OBJ. 2

EX 5-4   Identify journals

Assuming the use of a two-column (all-purpose) general journal, a purchases journal, and a cash payments journal as illustrated in this chapter, indicate the journal in which each of the following transactions should be recorded:

a. Purchase of an office computer on account.

b. Purchase of services on account.

c. Purchase of office supplies on account.

d. Adjustment to prepaid rent at the end of the month.

e. Adjustment to record accrued salaries at the end of the period.

f. Purchase of office supplies for cash.

g. Advance payment of a one-year fire insurance policy on the office.

h. Purchase of office equipment for cash.

i. Adjustment to prepaid insurance at the end of the month.

j. Adjustment to record depreciation at the end of the month.

k. Payment of six months' rent in advance.

OBJ. 2

EX 5-5   Identify transactions in accounts receivable ledger

The debits and credits from three related transactions are presented in the following customer's account taken from the accounts receivable subsidiary ledger.

| NAME | Casey By Design | | | | |
| ADDRESS | 1319 Elm Street | | | | |

Date	Item	Post. Ref.	Debit	Credit	Balance
2012					
Feb. 3		R44	740		740
6		J11		80	660
16		CR81		660	—

Describe each transaction, and identify the source of each posting.

OBJ. 2

EX 5-6   Prepare journal entries in a revenue journal

Madison Services Company had the following transactions during the month of April:

Apr.   2. Issued Invoice No. 201 to Triple Play Corp. for services rendered on account, $345.

3. Issued Invoice No. 202 to Mid States Inc. for services rendered on account, $410.

14. Issued Invoice No. 203 to Triple Play Corp. for services rendered on account, $110.

25. Issued Invoice No. 204 to Parker Co. for services rendered on account, $830.

28. Collected Invoice No. 201 from Triple Play Corp.

a. Prepare a revenue journal with the following headings to record the April revenue transactions for Madison Services Company.

(Continued)

REVENUE JOURNAL

Date	Invoice No.	Account Debited	Post. Ref.	Accts. Rec. Dr. Fees Earned Cr.

b. What is the total amount posted to the accounts receivable and fees earned accounts from the revenue journal for April?

c. What is the April 30 balance of the Triple Play Corp. customer account assuming a zero balance on April 1?

OBJ. 2, 3

EX 5-7 Posting a revenue journal

The revenue journal for Tech-Aid Consulting Inc. is shown below. The accounts receivable control account has a July 1, 2012, balance of $805 consisting of an amount due from Astro Star Co. There were no collections during July.

REVENUE JOURNAL   Page *12*

Date	Invoice No.	Account Debited	Post. Ref.	Accts. Rec. Dr. Fees Earned Cr.
2012				
July 4	355	Borman Co.		1,960
9	356	Life Star Inc.		3,220
14	357	Astro Star Co.		1,490
22	359	Borman Co.		2,650
				9,320

a. Prepare a T account for the accounts receivable customer accounts.

b. Post the transactions from the revenue journal to the customer accounts, and determine their ending balances.

c. Prepare T accounts for the accounts receivable and fees earned accounts. Post control totals to the two accounts, and determine the ending balances.

d. Prepare a schedule of the customer account balances to verify the equality of the sum of the customer account balances and the accounts receivable account balance.

e. How might a computerized system differ from a revenue journal in recording revenue transactions?

OBJ. 2

✔ Accounts Receivable balance, May 31, $5,490

EX 5-8 Accounts receivable subsidiary ledger

The revenue and cash receipts journals for Amazon Productions Inc. are shown below. The accounts receivable control account has a May 1, 2012, balance of $3,910, consisting of an amount due from Bishop Studios Inc.

REVENUE JOURNAL   Page *16*

Date	Invoice No.	Account Debited	Post. Ref.	Accts. Rec. Dr. Fees Earned Cr.
2012				
May 6	1	Chandler Broadcasting Co.	✓	1,250
14	2	Gold Coast Media Inc.	✓	5,700
22	3	Chandler Broadcasting Co.	✓	2,200
27	4	Bishop Studios Inc.	✓	1,250
28	5	Amber Communications Inc.	✓	2,040
30				12,440
				(12) (41)

CASH RECEIPTS JOURNAL   Page *36*

Date	Account Credited	Post. Ref.	Fees Earned Cr.	Accts. Rec. Cr.	Cash Dr.
2012					
May 6	Bishop Studios Inc.	✓	—	3,910	3,910
11	Fees Earned		3,200		3,200
18	Chandler Broadcasting Co	✓	—	1,250	1,250
28	Gold Coast Media Inc.	✓	—	5,700	5,700
30			3,200	10,860	14,060
			(41)	(12)	(11)

Prepare a listing of the accounts receivable subsidiary ledger account balances and verify that the total agrees with the ending balance of the accounts receivable account.

OBJ. 2

EX 5-9 Revenue and cash receipts journals

Transactions related to revenue and cash receipts completed by Main Line Inc. during the month of August 2012 are as follows:

Aug. 2. Issued Invoice No. 512 to Boston Co., $780.

4. Received cash from CMI Inc., on account, for $195.

8. Issued Invoice No. 513 to Gabriel Co., $275.

12. Issued Invoice No. 514 to Dockers Inc., $690.

19. Received cash from Dockers Inc., on account, $525.

22. Issued Invoice No. 515 to Electronic Central Inc., $150.

27. Received cash from Marshall Inc. for services provided, $115.

29. Received cash from Boston Co. for invoice of August 2.

31. Received cash from McCleary Co. for services provided, $65.

Prepare a single-column revenue journal and a cash receipts journal to record these transactions. Use the following column headings for the cash receipts journal: Fees Earned Cr., Accounts Receivable Cr., and Cash Dr. Place a check mark (✓) in the Post. Ref. column to indicate when the accounts receivable subsidiary ledger should be posted.

OBJ. 2

✔ Revenue journal total, $10,160

EX 5-10 Revenue and cash receipts journals

Essential Paris, Inc. has $2,290 in the December 1 balance of the accounts receivable account consisting of $940 from Chrystal Co. and $1,350 from Venus Co. Transactions related to revenue and cash receipts completed by Essential Paris, Inc. during the month of December 2012 are as follows:

Dec. 3. Issued Invoice No. 622 for services provided to Palace Corp., $1,920.

5. Received cash from Chrystal Co., on account, for $940.

8. Issued Invoice No. 623 for services provided to Sunstream Aviation Inc., $3,450.

12. Received cash from Venus Co., on account, for $1,350.

18. Issued Invoice No. 624 for services provided to Amex Services Inc., $2,600.

23. Received cash from Palace Corp. for Invoice No. 622.

28. Issued Invoice No. 625 to Venus Co., on account, for $2,190.

30. Received cash from Rogers Co. for services provided, $80.

a. Prepare a single-column revenue journal and a cash receipts journal to record these transactions. Use the following column headings for the cash receipts journal: Fees Earned Cr., Accounts Receivable Cr., and Cash Dr. Place a check mark (✓) in the Post. Ref. column to indicate when the accounts receivable subsidiary ledger should be posted.

b. Prepare a listing of the accounts receivable subsidiary ledger account balances and verify that the total of the accounts receivable subsidiary ledger equals the balance of the accounts receivable account on December 31, 2012.

c. Why does Essential Paris use a subsidiary ledger for accounts receivable?

OBJ. 2

EX 5-11 Identify postings from purchases journal

Using the following purchases journal, identify each of the posting references, indicated by a letter, as representing (1) a posting to a general ledger account, (2) a posting to a subsidiary ledger account, or (3) that no posting is required.

PURCHASES JOURNAL   Page *49*

Date	Account Credited	Post. Ref.	Accounts Payable Cr.	Store Supplies Dr.	Office Supplies Dr.	Other Accounts Dr.	Post. Ref.	Amount
2012								
Mar. 4	Arrow Supply Co.	(a)	4,000		4,000			
6	Coastal Equipment Co.	(b)	5,325			Warehouse Equipment	(c)	5,325
9	Thorton Products	(d)	1,875	1,600	275			
14	Office Warehouse	(e)	2,200			Office Equipment	(f)	2,200
20	Office Warehouse	(g)	6,000			Store Equipment	(h)	6,000
25	Monroe Supply Co.	(i)	2,740	2,740				
30			22,140	4,340	4,275			13,525
			(j)	(k)	(l)			(m)

OBJ. 2

EX 5-12   Identify postings from cash payments journal

Using the following cash payments journal, identify each of the posting references, indicated by a letter, as representing (1) a posting to a general ledger account, (2) a posting to a subsidiary ledger account, or (3) that no posting is required.

CASH PAYMENTS JOURNAL   Page *46*

Date	Ck. No.	Account Debited	Post. Ref.	Other Accounts Dr.	Accounts Payable Dr.	Cash Cr.
2012						
Aug. 3	611	Energy Systems Co.	(a)		4,000	4,000
5	612	Utilities Expense	(b)	310		310
10	613	Prepaid Rent	(c)	3,200		3,200
16	614	Flowers to Go, Inc.	(d)		1,250	1,250
19	615	Advertising Expense	(e)	640		640
22	616	Office Equipment	(f)	3,600		3,600
25	617	Office Supplies	(g)	250		250
26	618	Echo Co.	(h)		5,500	5,500
31	619	Salaries Expense	(i)	1,750		1,750
31				9,750	10,750	20,500
				(j)	(k)	(l)

OBJ. 2

EX 5-13   Identify transactions in accounts payable ledger account

The debits and credits from three related transactions are presented in the following creditor's account taken from the accounts payable ledger.

NAME   *Apex Performance Co.*
ADDRESS   *101 W. Stratford Ave.*

Date	Item	Post. Ref.	Debit	Credit	Balance
2012					
Mar. 6		P44		12,000	12,000
11		J12	400		11,600
16		CP23	11,600		—

Describe each transaction, and identify the source of each posting.

OBJ. 2

EX 5-14   Prepare journal entries in a purchases journal

Sentry Security Company had the following transactions during the month of January:

Jan.   4.   Purchased office supplies from Office Universe Inc. on account, $550.

     9.   Purchased office equipment on account from Tek Village, Inc., $2,300.

   16.   Purchased office supplies from Office Universe Inc. on account, $90.

   21.   Purchased office supplies from Paper-to-Go Inc. on account, $170.

   27.   Paid invoice on January 4 purchase from Office Universe Inc.

a.   Prepare a purchases journal with the following headings to record the January purchase transactions for Sentry Security Company.

PURCHASES JOURNAL

Date	Account Credited	Post. Ref.	Accts. Payable Cr.	Office Supplies Dr.	Other Accounts Dr.	Post. Ref.	Amount

b. What is the total amount posted to the accounts payable and office supplies accounts from the purchases journal for January?

c. What is the January 31 balance of the Office Universe Inc. creditor account assuming a zero balance on January 1?

OBJ. 2, 3
✔ d. Total, $4,215

EX 5-15   Posting a purchases journal

The purchases journal for Crystal View Window Cleaners Inc. is shown below. The accounts payable account has a January 1, 2012, balance of $365 of an amount due from Little Co. There were no payments made on creditor invoices during January.

PURCHASES JOURNAL   Page 16

Date	Account Credited	Post. Ref.	Accts. Payable Cr.	Cleaning Supplies Dr.	Other Accounts Dr.	Post. Ref.	Amount
2012							
Jan. 4	Kleen-Mate Supplies Inc.		570	570			
15	Little Co.		250	250			
19	Office Mate Inc.		2,700		Office Equipment		2,700
26	Kleen-Mate Supplies Inc.		330	330			
31			3,850	1,150			2,700

a. Prepare a T account for the accounts payable creditor accounts.

b. Post the transactions from the purchases journal to the creditor accounts, and determine their ending balances.

c. Prepare T accounts for the accounts payable control and cleaning supplies accounts. Post control totals to the two accounts, and determine their ending balances.

d. Prepare a schedule of the creditor account balances to verify the equality of the sum of the creditor account balances and the accounts payable account balance.

e. How might a computerized accounting system differ from the use of a purchases journal in recording purchase transactions?

OBJ. 2
✔ Accts. Pay., June 30, $15,860

EX 5-16   Accounts payable subsidiary ledger

The cash payments and purchases journals for Out of Eden Landscaping Co. are shown below. The accounts payable control account has a June 1, 2012, balance of $2,450, consisting of an amount owed to Augusta Sod Co.

CASH PAYMENTS JOURNAL   Page 31

Date	Ck. No.	Account Debited	Post. Ref.	Other Accounts Dr.	Accounts Payable Dr.	Cash Cr.
2012						
June 4	203	Augusta Sod Co	✓		2,450	2,450
5	204	Utilities Expense	54	410		410
15	205	Kopp Lumber Co.	✓		5,135	5,135
24	206	Schott's Fertilizer	✓		820	820
30				410	8,405	8,815
				(✓)	(21)	(11)

PURCHASES JOURNAL   Page 22

Date	Account Credited	Post. Ref.	Accounts Payable Cr.	Landscaping Supplies Dr.	Other Accounts Dr	Post. Ref.	Amount
2012							
June 3	Kopp Lumber Co.	✓	5,135	5,135			
7	Concrete Equipment Co.	✓	2,650		Equipment	18	2,650
14	Schott's Fertilizer	✓	820	820			
24	Augusta Sod Co.	✓	6,010	6,010			
29	Kopp Lumber Co.	✓	7,200	7,200			
30			21,815	19,165			2,650
			(21)	(14)			(✓)

(Continued)

Prepare a schedule of the accounts payable subsidiary ledger balances, and determine that the total agrees with the ending balance of the accounts payable account.

OBJ. 2

✔ Purchases journal, Accts. Pay., Total, $815

EX 5-17 Purchases and cash payments journals

Transactions related to purchases and cash payments completed by Marion Cleaning Services Inc. during the month of August 2012 are as follows:

Aug. 1. Issued Check No. 57 to Liquid Klean Supplies Inc. in payment of account, $275.

     3. Purchased cleaning supplies on account from Sani-Fresh Products Inc., $160.

     8. Issued Check No. 58 to purchase equipment from Carson Equipment Sales, $2,400.

    12. Purchased cleaning supplies on account from Porter Products Inc., $250.

    15. Issued Check No. 59 to Abbott Laundry Service in payment of account, $120.

    18. Purchased supplies on account from Liquid Klean Supplies Inc., $265.

    20. Purchased laundry services from Abbott Laundry Service on account, $140.

    26. Issued Check No. 60 to Sani-Fresh Products Inc. in payment of August 3 invoice.

    31. Issued Check No. 61 in payment of salaries, $5,200.

Prepare a purchases journal and a cash payments journal to record these transactions. The forms of the journals are similar to those illustrated in the text. Place a check mark (✓) in the Post. Ref. column to indicate when the accounts payable subsidiary ledger should be posted. Marion Cleaning Services Inc. uses the following accounts:

Cash	11
Cleaning Supplies	14
Equipment	18
Accounts Payable	21
Salary Expense	51
Laundry Service Expense	53

OBJ. 2

EX 5-18 Purchases and cash payments journals

Happy Tails Inc. has a September 1 accounts payable balance of $525, which consists of $340 due Labradore Inc. and $185 due Meow Mart Inc. Transactions related to purchases and cash payments completed by Happy Tails Inc. during the month of September 2012 are as follows:

Sept. 4. Purchased pet supplies from Best Friend Supplies Inc. on account, $230.

     6. Issued Check No. 345 to Labradore Inc. in payment of account, $340.

    13. Purchased pet supplies from Poodle Pals Inc., $660.

    18. Issued Check No. 346 to Meow Mart Inc. in payment of account, $185.

    19. Purchased office equipment from Office Helper Inc. on account, $2,250.

    23. Issued Check No. 347 to Best Friend Supplies Inc. in payment of account from purchase made on September 4.

    27. Purchased pet supplies from Meow Mart Inc. on account, $350.

    30. Issued Check No. 348 to Sanders Inc. for cleaning expenses, $50.

a. Prepare a purchases journal and a cash payments journal to record these transactions. The forms of the journals are similar to those used in the text. Place a check mark (✓) in the Post. Ref. column to indicate when the accounts payable subsidiary ledger should be posted. Happy Tails Inc. uses the following accounts:

Cash	11
Office Equipment	13
Pet Supplies	14
Accounts Payable	21
Cleaning Expense	54

b. Prepare a listing of accounts payable subsidiary ledger balances on September 30, 2012. Verify that the total of the accounts payable subsidiary ledger balances equals the balance of the accounts payable control account on September 30, 2012.

c. Why does Happy Tails use a subsidiary ledger for accounts payable?

EX 5-19 Error in accounts payable ledger and accounts payable subsidiary ledger

After Gold Rush Assay Services Inc. had completed all postings for March in the current year (2012), the sum of the balances in the following accounts payable ledger did not agree with the $37,900 balance of the controlling account in the general ledger.

NAME *C. D. Greer and Son*
ADDRESS *972 S. Tenth Street*

Date	Item	Post. Ref.	Debit	Credit	Balance
2012					
Mar. 17		P30		3,750	3,750
27		P31		12,000	15,750

NAME *Chester Chemical Supplies Inc.*
ADDRESS *1170 Mattis Avenue*

Date	Item	Post. Ref.	Debit	Credit	Balance
2012					
Mar. 1	Balance	✓			8,300
9		P30		6,200	14,000
12		J7	300		13,700
20		CP23	5,800		7,900

NAME *Cutler and Powell*
ADDRESS *717 Elm Street*

Date	Item	Post. Ref.	Debit	Credit	Balance
2012					
Mar. 1	Balance	✓			6,100
18		CP23	6,100		—
29		P31		7,800	7,800

NAME *Montana Minerals Co.*
ADDRESS *1240 W. Main Street*

Date	Item	Post. Ref.	Debit	Credit	Balance
2012					
Mar. 1	Balance	✓			4,750
10		CP22	4,750		—
17		P30		3,700	3,700
25		J7	900		1,800

NAME *Valley Power*
ADDRESS *915 E. Walnut Street*

Date	Item	Post. Ref.	Debit	Credit	Balance
2012					
Mar. 5		P30		3,150	3,150

Assuming that the controlling account balance of $37,900 has been verified as correct, (a) determine the error(s) in the preceding accounts and (b) prepare a listing of accounts payable subsidiary ledger balances (from the corrected accounts payable subsidiary ledger).

EX 5-20 Identify postings from special journals

ViewPoint Consulting Company makes most of its sales and purchases on credit. It uses the five journals described in this chapter (revenue, cash receipts, purchases, cash payments, and general journals). Identify the journal most likely used in recording the postings for selected transactions indicated by letter in the T accounts on the following page:

Cash				Prepaid Rent	
a.	10,940	b.	6,500	e.	1,200

Accounts Receivable				Accounts Payable			
c.	11,790	a.	10,940	b.	6,500	d.	7,400

Office Supplies		Fees Earned	
d.	7,400	c.	11,790

Rent Expense	
e.	1,200

OBJ. 2

EX 5-21 Cash receipts journal

The following cash receipts journal headings have been suggested for a small service firm. List the errors you find in the headings.

			CASH RECEIPTS JOURNAL			Page *12*
Date	Account Credited	Post. Ref.	Fees Earned Cr.	Accts. Rec. Cr.	Cash Cr.	Other Accounts Dr.

OBJ. 3

EX 5-22 Computerized accounting systems

Most computerized accounting systems use electronic forms to record transaction information, such as the invoice form illustrated at the top of Exhibit 7.

a. Identify the key input fields (spaces) in an electronic invoice form.

b. What accounts are posted from an electronic invoice form?

c. Why aren't special journal totals posted to control accounts at the end of the month in an electronic accounting system?

OBJ. 3, 4

EX 5-23 Computerized accounting systems and e-commerce

Apple Corporation's iTunes® provides digital products, such as music, video, and software, which can be downloaded to portable devices such as iPhone® and iPod®. Purchases made on iTunes are made with a credit card that is on file with the credit card processing company. Such transactions are considered cash transactions. Once the purchase is made, the consumer can download the requested digital product to their portable device for their enjoyment and the charge will show up on their credit card bill.

a. What kind of e-commerce application is described by Apple iTunes?

b. Assume you purchased 12 songs for $1 each on iTunes. Provide the journal entry generated by Apple's e-commerce application.

c. If a special journal were used, what type of special journal would be used to record this sales transaction?

d. If an electronic form were used, what type of electronic form would be used to record this sales transaction?

e. How might you expect revenues to be recorded for a B2C e-commerce transaction?

OBJ. 4

EX 5-24 E-commerce

For each of the following companies, determine if their e-commerce strategy is primarily business-to-consumer (B2C), business-to-business (B2B), or both. Use the Internet to investigate each company's site in conducting your research.

a. Amazon.com

b. Dell Inc.

c. Dupont

d. Intuit Inc.

e. L.L. Bean, Inc.

f. W.W. Grainger, Inc.

OBJ. 5

EX 5-25 Segment revenue horizontal analysis

Starbucks Corporation reported the following geographical segment revenues for fiscal years 2009 and 2008:

	2009 (in millions)	2008 (in millions)
United States	$7,104	$ 7,532
International	1,920	2,103
Global consumer products	750	748
Total revenues	$9,774	$10,383

a. Prepare a horizontal analysis of the segment data using 2008 as the base year.

b. Prepare a vertical analysis of the segment data.

c. What conclusions can be drawn from your analyses?

OBJ. 5

EX 5-26 Segment revenue vertical analysis

News Corporation is one of the world's largest entertainment companies that includes Twentieth Century Fox films, Fox Broadcasting, Fox News, the FX, and various satellite, cable, and publishing properties. The company provided revenue disclosures by its major product segments in the notes to its financial statements as follows:

Major Product Segments	For the Year Ended June 30, 2009 (in millions)
Filmed Entertainment	$ 5,936
Television	4,602
Cable Network Programming	5,580
Direct Broadcast Satellite Television	3,760
Magazines and Inserts	1,168
Newspapers and Information Services	5,858
Book Publishing	1,141
Other	2,378
Total revenues	$30,423

a. Provide a vertical analysis of the product segment revenues.

b. Are the revenues of News Corporation diversified or concentrated within a product segment? Explain.

OBJ. 5

EX 5-27 Segment revenue horizontal and vertical analyses

The comparative regional segment revenues for McDonald's Corporation is as follows:

	2009 (in millions)	2008 (in millions)
United States	$ 7,943.8	$ 8,078.3
Europe	9,273.8	9,922.9
APMEA*	4,337.0	4,230.8
Other Countries & Corporate	1,190.1	1,290.4
Total revenues	$22,744.7	$23,522.4

*APMEA = Asia/Pacific, Middle East, Africa

a. Provide a horizontal analysis of the regional segment revenues using 2008 as the base year. Round whole percents to one digit.

b. Provide a vertical analysis of the regional segment revenues for both years. Round whole percents to one digit.

c. What conclusions can be drawn from your analyses?

Problems Series A

OBJ. 2, 3

✔ 1. Revenue
journal, total fees
earned, $830

PR 5-1A **Revenue journal; accounts receivable and general ledgers**

Newton Learning Centers was established on October 20, 2012, to provide educational services. The services provided during the remainder of the month are as follows:

Oct. 21. Issued Invoice No. 1 to J. Dunlop for $60 on account.

22. Issued Invoice No. 2 to K. Todd for $255 on account.

24. Issued Invoice No. 3 to T. Patrick for $55 on account.

25. Provided educational services, $100, to K. Todd in exchange for educational supplies.

27. Issued Invoice No. 4 to F. Mintz for $150 on account.

30. Issued Invoice No. 5 to D. Chase for $135 on account.

30. Issued Invoice No. 6 to K. Todd for $105 on account.

31. Issued Invoice No. 7 to T. Patrick for $70 on account.

Instructions

1. Journalize the transactions for October, using a single-column revenue journal and a two-column general journal. Post to the following customer accounts in the accounts receivable ledger, and insert the balance immediately after recording each entry: D. Chase; J. Dunlop; F. Mintz; T. Patrick; K. Todd.

2. Post the revenue journal and the general journal to the following accounts in the general ledger, inserting the account balances only after the last postings:

12	Accounts Receivable
13	Supplies
41	Fees Earned

3. a. What is the sum of the balances of the accounts in the subsidiary ledger at October 31?

   b. What is the balance of the controlling account at October 31?

4. Assume Newton Learning Centers began using a computerized accounting system to record the sales transactions on November 1. What are some of the benefits of the computerized system over the manual system?

OBJ. 2, 3

✔ 3. Total cash
receipts, $32,870

PR 5-2A **Revenue and cash receipts journals; accounts receivable and general ledgers**

Transactions related to revenue and cash receipts completed by Aspen Architects Co. during the period June 2–30, 2012, are as follows:

June 2. Issued Invoice No. 793 to Nickle Co., $4,900.

5. Received cash from Mendez Co. for the balance owed on its account.

6. Issued Invoice No. 794 to Preston Co., $1,760.

13. Issued Invoice No. 795 to Shilo Co., $2,630.

   Post revenue and collections to the accounts receivable subsidiary ledger.

15. Received cash from Preston Co. for the balance owed on June 1.

16. Issued Invoice No. 796 to Preston Co., $5,500.

   Post revenue and collections to the accounts receivable subsidiary ledger.

19. Received cash from Nickle Co. for the balance due on invoice of June 2.

20. Received cash from Preston Co. for invoice of June 6.

22. Issued Invoice No. 797 to Mendez Co., $7,240.

25. Received $2,000 note receivable in partial settlement of the balance due on the Shilo Co. account.

30. Recorded cash fees earned, $12,350.

   Post revenue and collections to the accounts receivable subsidiary ledger.

Instructions

1. Insert the following balances in the general ledger as of June 1:

11	Cash	$11,350
12	Accounts Receivable	13,860
14	Notes Receivable	6,000
41	Fees Earned	—

2. Insert the following balances in the accounts receivable subsidiary ledger as of June 1:

Mendez Co.	$7,970
Nickle Co.	—
Preston Co.	5,890
Shilo Co.	—

3. Prepare a single-column revenue journal (p. 40) and a cash receipts journal (p. 36). Use the following column headings for the cash receipts journal: Fees Earned Cr., Accounts Receivable Cr., and Cash Dr. The Fees Earned column is used to record cash fees. Insert a check mark (✓) in the Post. Ref. column when recording cash fees.

4. Using the two special journals and the two-column general journal (p. 1), journalize the transactions for June. Post to the accounts receivable subsidiary ledger, and insert the balances at the points indicated in the narrative of transactions. Determine the balance in the customer's account before recording a cash receipt.

5. Total each of the columns of the special journals, and post the individual entries and totals to the general ledger. Insert account balances after the last posting.

6. Determine that the subsidiary ledger agrees with the controlling account in the general ledger.

7. Why would an automated system omit postings to a control account as performed in step 5 for Accounts Receivable?

OBJ. 2, 4

✔ **5b. Total accounts payable credit, $14,195**

PR 5-3A   Purchases, accounts payable account, and accounts payable ledger

English Garden Landscaping designs and installs landscaping. The landscape designers and office staff use office supplies, while field supplies (rock, bark, etc.) are used in the actual landscaping. Purchases on account completed by English Garden Landscaping during January 2012 are as follows:

Jan. 2. Purchased office supplies on account from Meade Co., $350.

5. Purchased office equipment on account from Peach Computers Co., $3,150.

9. Purchased office supplies on account from Executive Office Supply Co., $290.

13. Purchased field supplies on account from Yamura Co., $1,140.

14. Purchased field supplies on account from Naples Co., $2,680.

17. Purchased field supplies on account from Yamura Co., $1,050.

24. Purchased field supplies on account from Naples Co., $3,240.

29. Purchased office supplies on account from Executive Office Supply Co., $260.

31. Purchased field supplies on account from Naples Co., $1,000.

Instructions

1. Insert the following balances in the general ledger as of January 1:

14	Field Supplies	$ 5,920
15	Office Supplies	750
18	Office Equipment	12,300
21	Accounts Payable	1,035

2. Insert the following balances in the accounts payable subsidiary ledger as of January 1:

Executive Office Supply Co.	$340
Meade Co.	695
Naples Co.	—
Peach Computers Co.	—
Yamura Co.	—

3. Journalize the transactions for January, using a purchases journal (p. 30) similar to the one illustrated in this chapter. Prepare the purchases journal with columns for Accounts

(Continued)

Payable, Field Supplies, Office Supplies, and Other Accounts. Post to the creditor accounts in the accounts payable subsidiary ledger immediately after each entry.

4. Post the purchases journal to the accounts in the general ledger.

5. a. What is the sum of the balances in the subsidiary ledger at January 31?

   b. What is the balance of the controlling account at January 31?

6. What type of e-commerce application would be used to plan and coordinate suppliers?

OBJ. 2

✔ 1. Total cash
payments, $93,615

PR 5-4A   Purchases and cash payments journals; accounts payable and general ledgers

Green Mountain Water Testing Service was established on November 16, 2012. Green Mountain uses field equipment and field supplies (chemicals and other supplies) to analyze water for unsafe contaminants in streams, lakes, and ponds. Transactions related to purchases and cash payments during the remainder of November are as follows:

Nov. 16. Issued Check No. 1 in payment of rent for the remainder of November, $1,700.

16. Purchased field supplies on account from Hydro Supply Co., $4,380.

16. Purchased field equipment on account from Test-Rite Equipment Co., $16,900.

17. Purchased office supplies on account from Best Office Supply Co., $375.

19. Issued Check No. 2 in payment of field supplies, $2,560, and office supplies, $300.

   Post the journals to the accounts payable subsidiary ledger.

23. Purchased office supplies on account from Best Office Supply Co., $580.

23. Issued Check No. 3 to purchase land, $45,000.

24. Issued Check No. 4 to Hydro Supply Co. in payment of invoice, $4,380.

26. Issued Check No. 5 to Test-Rite Equipment Co. in payment of invoice, $16,900.

   Post the journals to the accounts payable subsidiary ledger.

30. Acquired land in exchange for field equipment having a cost of $8,000.

30. Purchased field supplies on account from Hydro Supply Co., $5,900.

30. Issued Check No. 6 to Best Office Supply Co. in payment of invoice, $375.

30. Purchased the following from Test-Rite Equipment Co. on account: field supplies, $900, and field equipment, $3,700.

30. Issued Check No. 7 in payment of salaries, $22,400.

   Post the journals to the accounts payable subsidiary ledger.

Instructions

1. Journalize the transactions for November. Use a purchases journal and a cash payments journal, similar to those illustrated in this chapter, and a two-column general journal. Use debit columns for Field Supplies, Office Supplies, and Other Accounts in the purchases journal. Refer to the following partial chart of accounts:

11	Cash	19	Land
14	Field Supplies	21	Accounts Payable
15	Office Supplies	61	Salary Expense
17	Field Equipment	71	Rent Expense

At the points indicated in the narrative of transactions, post to the following accounts in the accounts payable subsidiary ledger:

Best Office Supply Co.

Hydro Supply Co.

Test-Rite Equipment Co.

2. Post the individual entries (Other Accounts columns of the purchases journal and the cash payments journal and both columns of the general journal) to the appropriate general ledger accounts.

3. Total each of the columns of the purchases journal and the cash payments journal, and post the appropriate totals to the general ledger. (Because the problem does not include transactions related to cash receipts, the cash account in the ledger will have a credit balance.)

4. Sum the balances of the accounts payable subsidiary ledger.

5. Why might Green Mountain consider using a subsidiary ledger for the field equipment?

OBJ. 2

✔ 2. Total cash
receipts, $58,160

PR 5-5A   All journals and general ledger; trial balance

The transactions completed by Sure N' Safe Courier Company during July 2012, the first month of the fiscal year, were as follows:

July 1. Issued Check No. 610 for July rent, $7,500.

2. Issued Invoice No. 940 to Capps Co., $2,680.

3. Received check for $6,700 from Trimble Co. in payment of account.

5. Purchased a vehicle on account from Browning Transportation, $34,600.

6. Purchased office equipment on account from Austin Computer Co., $5,200.

6. Issued Invoice No. 941 to Dawar Co., $5,970.

9. Issued Check No. 611 for fuel expense, $900.

10. Received check from Sing Co. in payment of $3,980 invoice.

10. Issued Check No. 612 for $1,040 to Office To Go Inc. in payment of invoice.

10. Issued Invoice No. 942 to Joy Co., $2,640.

11. Issued Check No. 613 for $3,670 to Essential Supply Co. in payment of account.

11. Issued Check No. 614 for $725 to Porter Co. in payment of account.

12. Received check from Capps Co. in payment of $2,680 invoice.

13. Issued Check No. 615 to Browning Transportation in payment of $34,600 balance.

16. Issued Check No. 616 for $42,100 for cash purchase of a vehicle.

16. Cash fees earned for July 1–16, $18,900.

17. Issued Check No. 617 for miscellaneous administrative expense, $750.

18. Purchased maintenance supplies on account from Essential Supply Co., $1,950.

19. Purchased the following on account from McClain Co.: maintenance supplies, $1,900; office supplies, $470.

20. Issued Check No. 618 in payment of advertising expense, $2,350.

20. Used $4,000 maintenance supplies to repair delivery vehicles.

23. Purchased office supplies on account from Office To Go Inc., $600.

24. Issued Invoice No. 943 to Sing Co., $7,000.

24. Issued Check No. 619 to J. Bourne as a personal withdrawal, $3,000.

25. Issued Invoice No. 944 to Dawar Co., $6,450.

25. Received check for $4,500 from Trimble Co. in payment of balance.

26. Issued Check No. 620 to Austin Computer Co. in payment of $5,200 invoice of July 6.

30. Issued Check No. 621 for monthly salaries as follows: driver salaries, $18,900; office salaries, $8,300.

31. Cash fees earned for July 17–31, $21,400.

31. Issued Check No. 622 in payment for office supplies, $800.

Instructions

1. Enter the following account balances in the general ledger as of July 1:

11	Cash	$167,900	32	J. Bourne, Drawing	—
12	Accounts Receivable	15,180	41	Fees Earned	—
14	Maintenance Supplies	10,850	51	Driver Salaries Expense	—
15	Office Supplies	4,900	52	Maintenance Supplies Exp.	—
16	Office Equipment	28,500	53	Fuel Expense	—
17	Accum. Depr.—Office Equip.	6,900	61	Office Salaries Expense	—
18	Vehicles	95,900	62	Rent Expense	—
19	Accum. Depr.—Vehicles	14,700	63	Advertising Expense	—
21	Accounts Payable	5,435	64	Miscellaneous Administrative Expense	—
31	J. Bourne, Capital	296,195			

(*Continued*)

2. Journalize the transactions for July 2012, using the following journals similar to those illustrated in this chapter: cash receipts journal (p. 31), purchases journal (p. 37, with columns for Accounts Payable, Maintenance Supplies, Office Supplies, and Other Accounts), single-column revenue journal (p. 35), cash payments journal (p. 34), and two-column general journal (p. 1). Assume that the daily postings to the individual accounts in the accounts payable ledger and the accounts receivable ledger have been made.

3. Post the appropriate individual entries to the general ledger.

4. Total each of the columns of the special journals, and post the appropriate totals to the general ledger; insert the account balances.

5. Prepare a trial balance.

Problems Series B

OBJ. 2, 3

✔ 1. Revenue journal, total fees earned, $2,320

PR 5-1B   Revenue journal; accounts receivable and general ledgers

Sentinel Security Services was established on March 15, 2012, to provide security services. The services provided during the remainder of the month are listed below.

Mar. 18. Issued Invoice No. 1 to Murphy Co. for $410 on account.

20. Issued Invoice No. 2 to Qwik-Mart Co. for $290 on account.

24. Issued Invoice No. 3 to Goforth Co. for $625 on account.

27. Issued Invoice No. 4 to Carson Co. for $510 on account.

28. Issued Invoice No. 5 to Amber Waves Co. for $100 on account.

28. Provided security services, $90, to Qwik-Mart Co. in exchange for supplies.

30. Issued Invoice No. 6 to Qwik-Mart Co. for $140 on account.

31. Issued Invoice No. 7 to Goforth Co. for $245 on account.

Instructions

1. Journalize the transactions for March, using a single-column revenue journal and a two-column general journal. Post to the following customer accounts in the accounts receivable ledger, and insert the balance immediately after recording each entry: Amber Waves Co.; Carson Co.; Goforth Co.; Murphy Co.; Qwik-Mart Co.

2. Post the revenue journal to the following accounts in the general ledger, inserting the account balances only after the last postings:

12	Accounts Receivable
14	Supplies
41	Fees Earned

3. a. What is the sum of the balances of the accounts in the subsidiary ledger at March 31?

   b. What is the balance of the controlling account at March 31?

4. Assume Sentinel Security Services began using a computerized accounting system to record the sales transactions on April 1. What are some of the benefits of the computerized system over the manual system?

OBJ. 2, 3

✔ 3. Total cash receipts, $7,690

PR 5-2B   Revenue and cash receipts journals; accounts receivable and general ledgers

Transactions related to revenue and cash receipts completed by Pinnacle Engineering Services during the period April 2–30, 2012, are as follows:

Apr. 2. Issued Invoice No. 717 to Yee Co., $950.

3. Received cash from Auto-Flex Co. for the balance owed on its account.

7. Issued Invoice No. 718 to Park Development Co., $530.

10. Issued Invoice No. 719 to Ridge Communities, $2,350.

Post revenue and collections to the accounts receivable subsidiary ledger.

Apr. 14. Received cash from Park Development Co. for the balance owed on April 1.

16. Issued Invoice No. 720 to Park Development Co., $325.

Post revenue and collections to the accounts receivable subsidiary ledger.

18. Received cash from Yee Co. for the balance due on invoice of April 2.

20. Received cash from Park Development Co. for invoice of April 7.

23. Issued Invoice No. 721 to Auto-Flex Co., $790.

30. Recorded cash fees earned, $3,950.

30. Received office equipment of $1,500 in partial settlement of balance due on the Ridge Communities account.

Post revenue and collections to the accounts receivable subsidiary ledger.

Instructions

1. Insert the following balances in the general ledger as of April 1:

11	Cash	$18,340
12	Accounts Receivable	2,260
18	Office Equipment	34,700
41	Fees Earned	—

2. Insert the following balances in the accounts receivable subsidiary ledger as of April 1:

Auto-Flex Co.	$1,460
Park Development Co.	800
Ridge Communities	—
Yee Co.	—

3. Prepare a single-column revenue journal (p. 40) and a cash receipts journal (p. 36). Use the following column headings for the cash receipts journal: Fees Earned Cr., Accounts Receivable Cr., and Cash Dr. The Fees Earned column is used to record cash fees. Insert a check mark (✓) in the Post. Ref. column when recording cash fees.

4. Using the two special journals and the two-column general journal (p. 1), journalize the transactions for April. Post to the accounts receivable subsidiary ledger, and insert the balances at the points indicated in the narrative of transactions. Determine the balance in the customer's account before recording a cash receipt.

5. Total each of the columns of the special journals, and post the individual entries and totals to the general ledger. Insert account balances after the last posting.

6. Determine that the subsidiary ledger agrees with the controlling account in the general ledger.

7. Why would an automated system omit postings to a control account as performed in step 5 for Accounts Receivable?

OBJ. 2, 4

✔ 5a. Total accounts payable credit, $27,370

PR 5-3B   Purchases, accounts payable account, and accounts payable ledger

True Plumb Surveyors provides survey work for construction projects. The office staff use office supplies, while surveying crews use field supplies. Purchases on account completed by True Plumb Surveyors during August 2012 are as follows:

Aug. 1. Purchased field supplies on account from Wendell Co., $2,670.

3. Purchased office supplies on account from Lassiter Co., $290.

8. Purchased field supplies on account from Ready Supplies, $3,900.

12. Purchased field supplies on account from Wendell Co., $2,950.

15. Purchased office supplies on account from J-Mart Co., $400.

19. Purchased office equipment on account from Accu-Vision Supply Co., $7,350.

23. Purchased field supplies on account from Ready Supplies, $2,140.

26. Purchased office supplies on account from J-Mart Co., $205.

30. Purchased field supplies on account from Ready Supplies, $2,750.

Instructions

1. Insert the following balances in the general ledger as of August 1:

14	Field Supplies	$ 6,200
15	Office Supplies	1,490
18	Office Equipment	19,400
21	Accounts Payable	4,715

2. Insert the following balances in the accounts payable subsidiary ledger as of August 1:

Accu-Vision Supply Co.	$3,600
J-Mart Co.	690
Lassiter Co.	425
Ready Supplies	—
Wendell Co.	—

3. Journalize the transactions for August, using a purchases journal (p. 30) similar to the one illustrated in this chapter. Prepare the purchases journal with columns for Accounts Payable, Field Supplies, Office Supplies, and Other Accounts. Post to the creditor accounts in the accounts payable ledger immediately after each entry.

4. Post the purchases journal to the accounts in the general ledger.

5. a. What is the sum of the balances in the subsidiary ledger at August 31?

   b. What is the balance of the controlling account at August 31?

6. What type of e-commerce application would be used to plan and coordinate suppliers?

OBJ. 2

✔ 1. Total cash payments, $265,000

PR 5-4B   Purchases and cash payments journals; accounts payable and general ledgers

Texas Tea Exploration Co. was established on July 15, 2012, to provide oil-drilling services. Texas Tea uses field equipment (rigs and pipe) and field supplies (drill bits and lubricants) in its operations. Transactions related to purchases and cash payments during the remainder of July are as follows:

July 16. Issued Check No. 1 in payment of rent for the remainder of July, $6,000.

16. Purchased field equipment on account from Petro Services Inc., $26,400.

17. Purchased field supplies on account from Culver Supply Co., $8,750.

18. Issued Check No. 2 in payment of field supplies, $3,150, and office supplies, $500.

20. Purchased office supplies on account from A-One Office Supply Co., $1,200.

   Post the journals to the accounts payable subsidiary ledger.

24. Issued Check No. 3 to Petro Services Inc., in payment of July 16 invoice.

26. Issued Check No. 4 to Culver Supply Co. in payment of July 17 invoice.

28. Issued Check No. 5 to purchase land, $190,000.

28. Purchased office supplies on account from A-One Office Supply Co., $2,970.

   Post the journals to the accounts payable subsidiary ledger.

30. Purchased the following from Petro Services Inc. on account: field supplies, $22,980 and office equipment, $4,200.

30. Issued Check No. 6 to A-One Office Supply Co. in payment of July 20 invoice.

30. Purchased field supplies on account from Culver Supply Co., $10,200.

31. Issued Check No. 7 in payment of salaries, $29,000.

31. Rented building for one year in exchange for field equipment having a cost of $14,000.

   Post the journals to the accounts payable subsidiary ledger.

Instructions

1. Journalize the transactions for July. Use a purchases journal and a cash payments journal, similar to those illustrated in this chapter, and a two-column general journal. Set debit columns for Field Supplies, Office Supplies, and Other Accounts in the purchases journal. Refer to the following partial chart of accounts:

11 Cash	18 Office Equipment
14 Field Supplies	19 Land
15 Office Supplies	21 Accounts Payable
16 Prepaid Rent	61 Salary Expense
17 Field Equipment	71 Rent Expense

At the points indicated in the narrative of transactions, post to the following subsidiary accounts in the accounts payable ledger:

A-One Office Supply Co.

Culver Supply Co.

Petro Services Inc.

2. Post the individual entries (Other Accounts columns of the purchases journal and the cash payments journal; both columns of the general journal) to the appropriate general ledger accounts.

3. Total each of the columns of the purchases journal and the cash payments journal, and post the appropriate totals to the general ledger. (Because the problem does not include transactions related to cash receipts, the cash account in the ledger will have a credit balance.)

4. Sum the balances of the accounts payable subsidiary ledger.

5. Why might Texas Tea consider using a subsidiary ledger for the field equipment?

OBJ. 2

✔ 2. Total cash receipts, $84,390

PR 5-5B All journals and general ledger; trial balance

The transactions completed by By Tomorrow Express Company during May 2012, the first month of the fiscal year, were as follows:

May 1. Issued Check No. 205 for May rent, $1,500.

2. Purchased a vehicle on account from McIntyre Sales Co., $23,700.

3. Purchased office equipment on account from Office Mate Inc., $640.

5. Issued Invoice No. 91 to Martin Co., $6,000.

6. Received check for $6,890 from Chavez Co. in payment of invoice.

7. Issued Invoice No. 92 to Trent Co., $8,650.

9. Issued Check No. 206 for fuel expense, $710.

10. Received check for $9,500 from Sajeev Co. in payment of invoice.

10. Issued Check No. 207 to Office City in payment of $500 invoice.

10. Issued Check No. 208 to Bastille Co. in payment of $1,450 invoice.

11. Issued Invoice No. 93 to Jarvis Co., $6,900.

11. Issued Check No. 209 to Porter Co. in payment of $375 invoice.

12. Received check for $6,000 from Martin Co. in payment of invoice.

13. Issued Check No. 210 to McIntyre Sales Co. in payment of $23,700 invoice.

16. Cash fees earned for May 1–16, $24,600.

16. Issued Check No. 211 for purchase of a vehicle, $24,000.

17. Issued Check No. 212 for miscellaneous administrative expense, $4,360.

18. Purchased maintenance supplies on account from Bastille Co., $1,790.

18. Received check for rent revenue on office space, $2,500.

19. Purchased the following on account from Master Supply Co.: maintenance supplies, $2,500, and office supplies, $2,000.

20. Issued Check No. 213 in payment of advertising expense, $7,810.

20. Used maintenance supplies with a cost of $4,200 to repair vehicles.

21. Purchased office supplies on account from Office City, $790.

24. Issued Invoice No. 94 to Sajeev Co., $8,000.

25. Received check for $12,500 from Chavez Co. in payment of invoice.

May 25. Issued Invoice No. 95 to Trent Co., $5,900.

26. Issued Check No. 214 to Office Mate Inc. in payment of $640 invoice.

27. Issued Check No. 215 to J. Wu as a personal withdrawal, $3,500.

30. Issued Check No. 216 in payment of driver salaries, $29,300.

31. Issued Check No. 217 in payment of office salaries, $19,400.

31. Issued Check No. 218 for office supplies, $560.

31. Cash fees earned for May 17–31, $22,400.

Instructions

1. Enter the following account balances in the general ledger as of May 1:

11	Cash	$ 65,200	32	J. Wu, Drawing	—
12	Accounts Receivable	28,890	41	Fees Earned	—
14	Maintenance Supplies	7,240	42	Rent Revenue	—
15	Office Supplies	3,690	51	Driver Salaries Expense	—
16	Office Equipment	17,300	52	Maintenance Supplies Expense	—
17	Accum. Depr.—Office Equip.	4,250	53	Fuel Expense	—
18	Vehicles	62,400	61	Office Salaries Expense	—
19	Accum. Depr.—Vehicles	17,800	62	Rent Expense	—
21	Accounts Payable	2,325	63	Advertising Expense	—
31	J. Wu, Capital	160,345	64	Miscellaneous Administrative Exp.	—

2. Journalize the transactions for May 2012, using the following journals similar to those illustrated in this chapter: single-column revenue journal (p. 35), cash receipts journal (p. 31), purchases journal (p. 37, with columns for Accounts Payable, Maintenance Supplies, Office Supplies, and Other Accounts), cash payments journal (p. 34), and two-column general journal (p. 1). Assume that the daily postings to the individual accounts in the accounts payable ledger and the accounts receivable ledger have been made.

3. Post the appropriate individual entries to the general ledger.

4. Total each of the columns of the special journals, and post the appropriate totals to the general ledger; insert the account balances.

5. Prepare a trial balance.

Cases & Projects

CP 5-1 Ethics and professional conduct in business

E-Biz Financial, Inc., provides accounting applications for business customers on the Internet for a monthly subscription. E-Biz Financial customers run their accounting system on the Internet; thus, the business data and accounting software reside on the servers of E-Biz Financial, Inc. The senior management of E-Biz believes that once a customer begins to use E-Biz Financial it would be very difficult to cancel the service. That is, customers are "locked in" because it would be difficult to move the business data from E-Biz Financial to another accounting application, even though the customers own their own data. Therefore, E-Biz Financial has decided to entice customers with an initial low monthly price that is half of the normal monthly rate for the first year of services. After a year, the price will be increased to the regular monthly rate. E-Biz Financial management believes that customers will have to accept the full price because customers will be "locked in" after one year of use.

a. Discuss whether the half-price offer is an ethical business practice.

b. Discuss whether customer "lock in" is an ethical business practice.

CP 5-2 Manual vs. computerized accounting systems

The following conversation took place between Merit Construction Co.'s bookkeeper, Dan Essex, and the accounting supervisor, Sarah Nelson:

Sarah: Dan, I'm thinking about bringing in a new computerized accounting system to replace our manual system. I guess this will mean that you will need to learn how to do computerized accounting.

Dan: What does computerized accounting mean?

Sarah: I'm not sure, but you'll need to prepare for this new way of doing business.

Dan: I'm not so sure we need a computerized system. I've been looking at some of the sample reports from the software vendor. It looks to me as if the computer will not add much to what we are already doing.

Sarah: What do you mean?

Dan: Well, look at these reports. This Sales by Customer Report looks like our revenue journal, and the Deposit Detail Report looks like our cash receipts journal. Granted, the computer types them, so they look much neater than my special journals, but I don't see that we're gaining much from this change.

Sarah: Well, surely there's more to it than nice-looking reports. I've got to believe that a computerized system will save us time and effort someplace.

Dan: I don't see how. We still need to key in transactions into the computer. If anything, there may be more work when it's all said and done.

➤ Do you agree with Dan? Why might a computerized environment be preferred over the manual system?

CP 5-3 Accounts receivable and accounts payable

A subsidiary ledger is used for accounts receivable and accounts payable. Thus, transactions that are made "on account" are posted to the individual customer or vendor accounts.

a. Why do companies use subsidiary ledgers for accounts payable and accounts receivable?

b. Identify another account that may benefit from using a subsidiary ledger.

CP 5-4 Design of accounting systems

For the past few years, your client, Professional Health Services (PHS), has operated a small medical practice. PHS's current annual revenues are $945,000. Because the accountant has been spending more and more time each month recording all transactions in a two-column journal and preparing the financial statements, PHS is considering improving the accounting system by adding special journals and subsidiary ledgers. PHS has asked you to help with this project and has compiled the following information:

Type of Transaction	Estimated Frequency per Month
Fees earned on account	240
Purchase of medical supplies on account	190
Cash receipts from patients on account	175
Cash payments on account	160
Cash receipts from patients at time services provided	120
Purchase of office supplies on account	35
Purchase of magazine subscriptions on account	5
Purchase of medical equipment on account	4
Cash payments for office salaries	3
Cash payments for utilities expense	3

1. ➤ Briefly discuss the circumstances under which special journals would be used in place of a two-column (all-purpose) journal. Include in your answer your recommendations for PHS's medical practice.

2. Assume that PHS has decided to use a revenue journal and a purchases journal. Design the format for each journal, giving special consideration to the needs of the medical practice.

3. Which subsidiary ledgers would you recommend for the medical practice?

Internet Project

CP 5-5 Internet-based accounting systems

Internet-based accounting software is a recent trend in business computing. Major software firms such as Oracle, SAP, and NetSuites are running their core products on the Internet. NetSuite Inc. is one of the most popular small business Internet-based accounting systems.

➡ Go to the text's Web site at **academic.cengage.com/accounting/warren** and click on the link to the NetSuite Inc. site. Read about the product from the site, and prepare a memo to management, defining Internet-based accounting. Also, outline the advantages and disadvantages of Internet-based accounting compared to running software on a company's internal computer network.

Internet Project

CP 5-6 SCM and CRM

Group Project

The two leading software application providers for supply chain management (SCM) and customer relationship management (CRM) software are I2 Technologies and Salesforce .com, respectively. In groups of two or three, go to the Web site for each company (linked to the text's Web site at **academic.cengage.com/accounting/warren**) and list the functions provided by each company's application.

© Susan Van Etten

Accounting for Merchandising Businesses

Dollar Tree Stores, Inc.

When you are low on cash but need to pick up party supplies, housewares, or other consumer items, where do you go? Many shoppers are turning to **Dollar Tree Stores, Inc.,** the nation's largest single price point dollar retailer with over 3,400 stores in 48 states. For the fixed price of $1 on merchandise in its stores, Dollar Tree has worked hard providing "new treasures" every week for the entire family.

Despite the fact that items cost only $1, the accounting for a merchandiser, like Dollar Tree, is more complex than for a service company. This is because a service company sells only services and has no inventory. With Dollar Tree's locations and merchandise, the company must design its accounting system to not only record the receipt

of goods for resale, but also to keep track of what merchandise is available for sale as well as where the merchandise is located. In addition, Dollar Tree must record the sales and costs of the goods sold for each of its stores. Finally, Dollar Tree must record such data as delivery costs, merchandise discounts, and merchandise returns.

This chapter focuses on the accounting principles and concepts for a merchandising business. In doing so, the basic differences between merchandiser and service company activities are highlighted. The financial statements of a merchandising business and accounting for merchandise transactions are also described and illustrated.

OBJ. 1 Distinguish between the activities and financial statements of service and merchandising businesses.

Nature of Merchandising Businesses

The activities of a service business differ from those of a merchandising business. These differences are illustrated in the following condensed income statements:

Service Business		Merchandising Business	
Fees earned	$XXX	Sales	$XXX
Operating expenses	–XXX	Cost of merchandise sold	–XXX
Net income	$XXX	Gross profit	$XXX
		Operating expenses	–XXX
		Net income	$XXX

The revenue activities of a service business involve providing services to customers. On the income statement for a service business, the revenues from services are reported as *fees earned*. The operating expenses incurred in providing the services are subtracted from the fees earned to arrive at *net income*.

In contrast, the revenue activities of a merchandising business involve the buying and selling of merchandise. A merchandising business first purchases merchandise to sell to its customers. When this merchandise is sold, the revenue is reported as sales, and its cost is recognized as an expense. This expense is called the **cost of merchandise sold**. The cost of merchandise sold is subtracted from sales to arrive at gross profit. This amount is called **gross profit** because it is the profit *before* deducting operating expenses.

Merchandise on hand (not sold) at the end of an accounting period is called **merchandise inventory**. Merchandise inventory is reported as a current asset on the balance sheet.

Example Exercise 6-1 Gross Profit

OBJ. 1

During the current year, merchandise is sold for $250,000 cash and for $975,000 on account. The cost of the merchandise sold is $735,000. What is the amount of the gross profit?

Follow My Example 6-1

The gross profit is $490,000 ($250,000 + $975,000 − $735,000).

Practice Exercises: **PE 6-1A, PE 6-1B**

The Operating Cycle

The operations of a merchandising business involve the purchase of merchandise for sale (purchasing), the sale of the products to customers (sales), and the receipt of cash from customers (collection). This overall process is referred to as the *operating cycle*. Thus, the operating cycle begins with spending cash, and it ends with receiving cash from customers. The operating cycle for a merchandising business is shown to the right.

Operating cycles for retailers are usually shorter than for manufacturers because retailers purchase goods in a form ready for sale to the customer. Of course, some retailers will have shorter operating cycles than others because of the nature of their products. For example, a jewelry store or an automobile dealer normally has a longer operating cycle than a consumer electronics store or a grocery store.

Businesses with longer operating cycles normally have higher profit margins on their products than businesses with shorter operating cycles. For example, it is not unusual for jewelry stores to price their jewelry at 30%–50% above cost. In contrast, grocery stores operate on very small profit margins, often below 5%. Grocery stores make up the difference by selling their products more quickly.

Financial Statements for a Merchandising Business

OBJ. 2 Describe and illustrate the financial statements of a merchandising business.

This section illustrates the financial statements for **NetSolutions** after it becomes a retailer of computer hardware and software. During 2011, Chris Clark implemented the second phase of NetSolutions' business plan. In doing so, Chris notified clients that beginning July 1, 2012, NetSolutions would no longer offer consulting services. Instead, it would become a retailer.

NetSolutions' business strategy is to offer personalized service to individuals and small businesses who are upgrading or purchasing new computer systems. NetSolutions' personal service includes a no-obligation, on-site assessment of the customer's computer needs. By providing personalized service and follow-up, Chris feels that NetSolutions can compete effectively against such retailers as Best Buy and Office Depot, Inc.

Multiple-Step Income Statement

The 2013 income statement for NetSolutions is shown in Exhibit 1.[1] This form of income statement, called a **multiple-step income statement**, contains several sections, subsections, and subtotals.

---

1 The NetSolutions income statement for 2013 is used because it allows a better illustration of the computation of the cost of merchandise sold in the appendix to this chapter.

Revenue from Sales This section of the multiple-step income statement consists of sales, sales returns and allowances, sales discounts, and net sales. This section, as shown in Exhibit 1, is as follows:

Revenue from sales:			
Sales			$720,185
Less: Sales returns and allowances	$6,140		
Sales discounts	5,790	11,930	
Net sales			$708,255

Sales is the total amount charged customers for merchandise sold, including cash sales and sales on account. During 2013, NetSolutions sold merchandise of $720,185 for cash or on account.

Sales returns and allowances are granted by the seller to customers for damaged or defective merchandise. In such cases, the customer may either return the merchandise or accept an allowance from the seller. NetSolutions reported $6,140 of sales returns and allowances during 2013.

Sales discounts are granted by the seller to customers for early payment of amounts owed. For example, a seller may offer a customer a 2% discount on a sale of $10,000 if the customer pays within 10 days. If the customer pays within the 10-day period, the seller receives cash of $9,800, and the buyer receives a discount of $200 ($10,000 × 2%). NetSolutions reported $5,790 of sales discounts during 2013.

EXHIBIT 1

Multiple-Step Income Statement

NetSolutions
Income Statement
For the Year Ended December 31, 2013

Revenue from sales:			
Sales		$720,185	
Less: Sales returns and allowances	$ 6,140		
Sales discounts	5,790	11,930	
Net sales			$708,255
Cost of merchandise sold			525,305
Gross profit			$182,950
Operating expenses:			
Selling expenses:			
Sales salaries expense	$53,430		
Advertising expense	10,860		
Depreciation expense—store equipment	3,100		
Delivery expense	2,800		
Miscellaneous selling expense	630		
Total selling expenses		$ 70,820	
Administrative expenses:			
Office salaries expense	$21,020		
Rent expense	8,100		
Depreciation expense—office equipment	2,490		
Insurance expense	1,910		
Office supplies expense	610		
Miscellaneous administrative expense	760		
Total administrative expenses		34,890	
Total operating expenses			105,710
Income from operations			$ 77,240
Other income and expense:			
Rent revenue		$ 600	
Interest expense		(2,440)	(1,840)
Net income			$ 75,400

Net sales is determined by subtracting sales returns and allowances and sales discounts from sales. As shown in Exhibit 1, NetSolutions reported $708,255 of net sales during 2013. Some companies report only net sales and report sales, sales returns and allowances, and sales discounts in notes to the financial statements.

Cost of Merchandise Sold   As shown in Exhibit 1, NetSolutions reported cost of merchandise sold of $525,305 during 2013. The cost of merchandise sold is the cost of merchandise sold to customers. Merchandise costs consist of all the costs of acquiring the merchandise and readying it for sale, such as purchase and freight costs. Recording these costs is described and illustrated later in this chapter.

Two systems of accounting for recording and reporting the cost of merchandise sold are:

For many merchandising businesses, the cost of merchandise sold is usually the largest expense. For example, the approximate percentage of cost of merchandise sold to sales is 63% for JCPenney and 66% for The Home Depot.

1. Periodic inventory system
2. Perpetual inventory system

Under the **periodic inventory system**, the inventory records do not show the amount available for sale or the amount sold during the period. Instead, the cost of merchandise sold and the merchandise on hand are determined at the end of the period by physically counting the inventory. The periodic inventory system is described and illustrated in the appendix to this chapter.

Under the **perpetual inventory system**, each purchase and sale of merchandise is recorded in the inventory and the cost of merchandise sold accounts. As a result, the amounts of merchandise available for sale and sold are continuously (perpetually) updated in the inventory records. Because many retailers use computerized systems, the perpetual inventory system is widely used.

Under a perpetual inventory system, the cost of merchandise sold is reported as a single line on the income statement. An example of such reporting is illustrated in Exhibit 1 for NetSolutions. Because of its wide use, the perpetual inventory system is used in the remainder of this chapter.

Gross Profit   Gross profit is computed by subtracting the cost of merchandise sold from net sales, as shown below.

Retailers, such as Best Buy, Sears Holding Corporation, and Walmart, and grocery store chains, such as Winn-Dixie Stores, Inc. and Kroger, use bar codes and optical scanners as part of their computerized inventory systems.

Net sales	$708,255
Cost of merchandise sold	525,305
Gross profit	$182,950

As shown above and in Exhibit 1, NetSolutions has gross profit of $182,950 in 2013.

Income from Operations   **Income from operations**, sometimes called operating income, is determined by subtracting operating expenses from gross profit. Operating expenses are normally classified as either selling expenses or administrative expenses.

Selling expenses are incurred directly in the selling of merchandise. Examples of selling expenses include sales salaries, store supplies used, depreciation of store equipment, delivery expense, and advertising.

Administrative expenses, sometimes called **general expenses**, are incurred in the administration or general operations of the business. Examples of administrative expenses include office salaries, depreciation of office equipment, and office supplies used.

Each selling and administrative expense may be reported separately as shown in Exhibit 1. However, many companies report selling, administrative, and operating expenses as single line items as shown below for NetSolutions.

See Appendix D for more information

Gross profit		$182,950
Operating expenses:		
Selling expenses	$70,820	
Administrative expenses	34,890	
Total operating expenses		105,710
Income from operations		$ 77,240

Other Income and Expense Other income and expense items are not related to the primary operations of the business. **Other income** is revenue from sources other than the primary operating activity of a business. Examples of other income include income from interest, rent, and gains resulting from the sale of fixed assets. **Other expense** is an expense that cannot be traced directly to the normal operations of the business. Examples of other expenses include interest expense and losses from disposing of fixed assets.

Other income and other expense are offset against each other on the income statement. If the total of other income exceeds the total of other expense, the difference is added to income from operations to determine net income. If the reverse is true, the difference is subtracted from income from operations. The other income and expense items of NetSolutions are reported as shown below and in Exhibit 1.

Income from operations		$77,240
Other income and expense:		
Rent revenue	$ 600	
Interest expense	(2,440)	(1,840)
Net income		$75,400

Single-Step Income Statement

An alternate form of income statement is the **single-step income statement.** As shown in Exhibit 2, the income statement for NetSolutions deducts the total of all expenses *in one step* from the total of all revenues.

The single-step form emphasizes total revenues and total expenses in determining net income. A criticism of the single-step form is that gross profit and income from operations are not reported.

Statement of Owner's Equity

The statement of owner's equity for NetSolutions is shown in Exhibit 3. This statement is prepared in the same manner as for a service business.

Balance Sheet

The balance sheet may be presented with assets on the left-hand side and the liabilities and owner's equity on the right-hand side. This form of the balance sheet is called the **account form.** The balance sheet may also be presented in a downward sequence in

EXHIBIT 2

Single-Step Income Statement

NetSolutions Income Statement For the Year Ended December 31, 2013		
Revenues:		
Net sales..		$708,255
Rent revenue		600
Total revenues		$708,855
Expenses:		
Cost of merchandise sold	$525,305	
Selling expenses	70,820	
Administrative expenses......................................	34,890	
Interest expense...	2,440	
Total expenses		633,455
Net income		$ 75,400

EXHIBIT 3

Statement of Owner's Equity for Merchandising Business

NetSolutions Statement of Owner's Equity For the Year Ended December 31, 2013		
Chris Clark, capital, January 1, 2013		$153,800
Net income for the year	$75,400	
Less withdrawals	18,000	
Increase in owner's equity		57,400
Chris Clark, capital, December 31, 2013		$211,200

three sections. This form of balance sheet is called the **report form.** The report form of balance sheet for NetSolutions is shown in Exhibit 4. In Exhibit 4, merchandise inventory is reported as a current asset and the current portion of the note payable of $5,000 is reported as a current liability.

EXHIBIT 4

Report Form of Balance Sheet

NetSolutions Balance Sheet December 31, 2013			
Assets			
Current assets:			
Cash		$52,950	
Accounts receivable		91,080	
Merchandise inventory		62,150	
Office supplies		480	
Prepaid insurance		2,650	
Total current assets			$209,310
Property, plant, and equipment:			
Land		$20,000	
Store equipment	$27,100		
Less accumulated depreciation	5,700	21,400	
Office equipment	$15,570		
Less accumulated depreciation	4,720	10,850	
Total property, plant, and equipment			52,250
Total assets			$261,560
Liabilities			
Current liabilities:			
Accounts payable		$22,420	
Note payable (current portion)		5,000	
Salaries payable		1,140	
Unearned rent		1,800	
Total current liabilities			$ 30,360
Long-term liabilities:			
Note payable (final payment due 2023)			20,000
Total liabilities			$ 50,360
Owner's Equity			
Chris Clark, capital			211,200
Total liabilities and owner's equity			$261,560

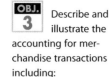

BusinessConnection

H&R BLOCK VERSUS THE HOME DEPOT

H&R Block is a service business that primarily offers tax planning and preparation to its customers. The Home Depot is a large home improvement retailer. The differences in the operations of a service and merchandise business are illustrated in their income statements, as shown below.

H&R Block
Condensed Income Statement
For the Year Ending April 30, 2009
(in millions)

Revenue	$4,084
Operating expenses	3,245
Operating income	$ 839
Other expense (net)	28
Income before taxes	$ 811
Income taxes	326
Net income	$ 485

As discussed in a later chapter, corporations are subject to income taxes. Thus, the income statements of H&R Block and The Home Depot report "income taxes" as a deduction from "income before income taxes" in arriving at net income. This is in contrast to a proprietorship such as NetSolutions, which is not subject to income taxes.

The Home Depot
Condensed Income Statement
For the Year Ending February 1, 2009
(in millions)

Net sales	$71,288
Cost of merchandise sold	47,298
Gross profit	$23,990
Operating expenses	19,631
Operating income	$ 4,359
Other expense (net)	821
Income before taxes	$ 3,538
Income taxes	1,278
Net income	$ 2,260

OBJ. 3 Describe and illustrate the accounting for merchandise transactions including:
- sale of merchandise
- purchase of merchandise
- freight
- sales taxes and trade discounts
- dual nature of merchandising transactions

Merchandising Transactions

The prior section described and illustrated the financial statements of a merchandising business, **NetSolutions**. This section describes and illustrates the recording of merchandise transactions, including the use of a chart of accounts for a merchandising business.

Chart of Accounts for a Merchandising Business

The chart of accounts for a merchandising business should reflect the elements of the financial statements. The chart of accounts for NetSolutions is shown in Exhibit 5. The accounts related to merchandising transactions are shown in color.

As shown in Exhibit 5, NetSolutions' chart of accounts consists of three-digit account numbers. The first digit indicates the major financial statement classification (1 for assets, 2 for liabilities, and so on). The second digit indicates the subclassification (e.g., 11 for current assets, 12 for noncurrent assets). The third digit identifies the specific account (e.g., 110 for Cash, 123 for Store Equipment). Using a three-digit numbering system makes it easier to add new accounts as they are needed.

Sales Transactions

Merchandise transactions are recorded using the rules of debit and credit that we described and illustrated in Chapter 2. Exhibit 3, shown on page 57 of Chapter 2, summarizes these rules.

Special journals may be used, or transactions may be entered, recorded, and posted using a computerized accounting system. To simplify, a two-column general journal is used in this chapter.

EXHIBIT 5

Chart of Accounts for NetSolutions, a Merchandising Business

Balance Sheet Accounts	Income Statement Accounts
100 Assets	**400 Revenues**
110 Cash	410 Sales
112 Accounts Receivable	411 Sales Returns and Allowances
115 Merchandise Inventory	412 Sales Discounts
116 Office Supplies	**500 Costs and Expenses**
117 Prepaid Insurance	510 Cost of Merchandise Sold
120 Land	520 Sales Salaries Expense
123 Store Equipment	521 Advertising Expense
124 Accumulated Depreciation—	522 Depreciation Expense—
Store Equipment	Store Equipment
125 Office Equipment	523 Delivery Expense
126 Accumulated Depreciation—	529 Miscellaneous Selling Expense
Office Equipment	530 Office Salaries Expense
	531 Rent Expense
200 Liabilities	532 Depreciation Expense—
210 Accounts Payable	Office Equipment
211 Salaries Payable	533 Insurance Expense
212 Unearned Rent	534 Office Supplies Expense
215 Notes Payable	539 Misc. Administrative Expense
300 Owner's Equity	**600 Other Income**
310 Chris Clark, Capital	610 Rent Revenue
311 Chris Clark, Drawing	**700 Other Expense**
312 Income Summary	710 Interest Expense

Cash Sales A business may sell merchandise for cash. Cash sales are normally entered (rung up) on a cash register and recorded in the accounts. To illustrate, assume that on January 3, NetSolutions sells merchandise for $1,800. These cash sales are recorded as follows:

		Journal			Page 25
Date		**Description**	**Post. Ref.**	**Debit**	**Credit**
2013 Jan.	3	Cash		1,800	
		Sales			1,800
		To record cash sales.			

Using the perpetual inventory system, the cost of merchandise sold and the decrease in merchandise inventory are also recorded. In this way, the merchandise inventory account indicates the amount of merchandise on hand (not sold).

To illustrate, assume that the cost of merchandise sold on January 3 is $1,200. The entry to record the cost of merchandise sold and the decrease in the merchandise inventory is as follows:

Jan.	3	Cost of Merchandise Sold		1,200	
		Merchandise Inventory			1,200
		To record the cost of merchandise sold.			

Sales may be made to customers using credit cards such as MasterCard or VISA. Such sales are recorded as cash sales. This is because these sales are normally processed by a clearing-house that contacts the bank that issued the card. The issuing bank then electronically transfers cash directly to the retailer's bank account.[2] Thus, the retailer normally receives cash within a few days of making the credit card sale.

If the customers in the preceding sales had used MasterCards to pay for their purchases, the sales would be recorded exactly as shown in the preceding entry. Any processing fees charged by the clearing-house or issuing bank are periodically recorded as an expense. This expense is normally reported on the income statement as an administrative expense. To illustrate, assume that NetSolutions paid credit card processing fees of $48 on January 31. These fees would be recorded as follows:

Jan.	31	Credit Card Expense	48	
		Cash		48
		To record service charges on credit card sales for the month.		

A retailer may accept MasterCard or VISA but not American Express. Why? American Express Co.'s service fees are normally higher than MasterCard's or VISA's. As a result, some retailers choose not to accept American Express cards. The disadvantage of this practice is that the retailer may lose customers to competitors who do accept American Express cards.

Instead of using MasterCard or VISA, a customer may use a credit card that is not issued by a bank. For example, a customer might use an American Express card. If the seller uses a clearing-house, the clearing-house will collect the receivable and transfer the cash to the retailer's bank account similar to the way it would have if the customer had used MasterCard or VISA. Large businesses, however, may not use a clearing-house. In such cases, nonbank credit card sales must first be reported to the card company before cash is received. Thus, a receivable is created with the nonbank credit card company. However, since most retailers use clearing-houses to process both bank and nonbank credit cards, all credit card sales will be recorded as cash sales.

Sales on Account A business may sell merchandise on account. The seller records such sales as a debit to Accounts Receivable and a credit to Sales. An example of an entry for a NetSolutions sale on account of $510 follows. The cost of merchandise sold was $280.

Jan.	12	Accounts Receivable—Sims Co.	510	
		Sales		510
		Invoice No. 7172.		
	12	Cost of Merchandise Sold	280	
		Merchandise Inventory		280
		Cost of merch. sold on Invoice No. 7172.		

Sales Discounts The terms of a sale are normally indicated on the **invoice** or bill that the seller sends to the buyer. An example of a sales invoice for NetSolutions is shown in Exhibit 6.

The terms for when payments for merchandise are to be made are called the **credit terms.** If payment is required on delivery, the terms are *cash* or *net cash.* Otherwise, the buyer is allowed an amount of time, known as the **credit period,** in which to pay.

The credit period usually begins with the date of the sale as shown on the invoice. If payment is due within a stated number of days after the invoice date, such as 30 days, the terms are *net 30 days.* These terms may be written as *n/30.*[3] If payment

2 CyberSource is one of the major credit card clearing-houses. For a more detailed description of how credit card sales are processed, see the following CyberSource Web page: **http://www.cybersource.com/products_and_services/global_payment_services/credit_card_processing/howitworks.xml**.

3 The word *net* as used here does not have the usual meaning of a number after deductions have been subtracted, as in *net income.*

NetSolutions			106-8

NetSolutions
5101 Washington Ave.
Cincinnati, OH 45227-5101

Invoice   Made in U.S.A.

SOLD TO   **CUSTOMER'S ORDER NO. & DATE**
Omega Technologies   412 Jan. 4, 2013
1000 Matrix Blvd.
San Jose, CA. 95116-1000

DATE SHIPPED	**HOW SHIPPED AND ROUTE**	**TERMS**	**INVOICE DATE**
Jan. 7, 2013	US Express Trucking Co.	2/10, n/30	Jan. 7, 2013

FROM	**F.O.B.**		
Cincinnati	Cincinnati		

QUANTITY	**DESCRIPTION**	**UNIT PRICE**	**AMOUNT**
10	3COM Wireless PC Card	150.00	1,500.00

EXHIBIT 6

Invoice

is due by the end of the month in which the sale was made, the terms are written as *n/eom*.

To encourage the buyer to pay before the end of the credit period, the seller may offer a discount. For example, a seller may offer a 2% discount if the buyer pays within 10 days of the invoice date. If the buyer does not take the discount, the total amount is due within 30 days. These terms are expressed as *2/10, n/30* and are read as *2% discount if paid within 10 days, net amount due within 30 days*. The credit terms of 2/10, n/30 are summarized in Exhibit 7, using the invoice in Exhibit 6.

Discounts taken by the buyer for early payment are recorded as sales discounts by the seller. Managers usually want to know the amount of the sales discounts for a period. For this reason, sales discounts are recorded in a separate sales discounts account, which is a *contra* (or *offsetting*) account to Sales.

To illustrate, assume that NetSolutions receives $1,470 on January 17 for the invoice shown in Exhibit 6. Since the invoice was paid within the discount period (10 days), the buyer deducted $30 ($1,500 × 2%) from the invoice amount. Net-Solutions would record the receipt of the cash as follows:

Jan.	17	Cash	1,470	
		Sales Discounts	30	
		Accounts Receivable—Omega Technologies		1,500
		Collection on Invoice No. 106-8, less 2%		
		discount.		

Sales Returns and Allowances
Merchandise sold may be returned to the seller (sales return). In other cases, the seller may reduce the initial selling price (sales allowance). This might occur if the merchandise is defective, damaged during shipment, or does not meet the buyer's expectations.

If the return or allowance is for a sale on account, the seller usually issues the buyer a **credit memorandum**, often called a **credit memo**. A credit memo authorizes

EXHIBIT 7

Credit Terms

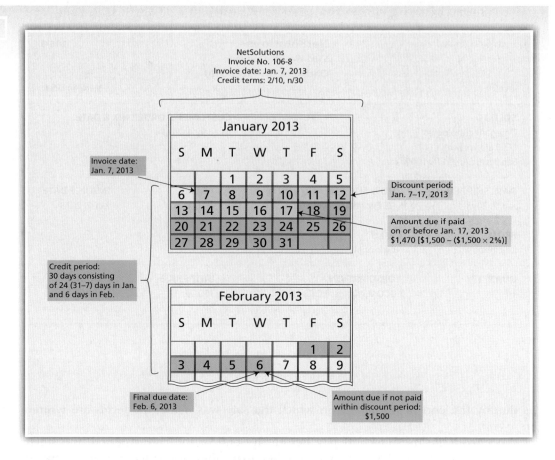

a credit to (decreases) the buyer's account receivable. A credit memo indicates the amount and reason for the credit. An example of a credit memo issued by NetSolutions is shown in Exhibit 8.

Like sales discounts, sales returns and allowances reduce sales revenue. Also, returns often result in additional shipping and handling expenses. Thus, managers usually want to know the amount of returns and allowances for a period. For this reason, sales returns and allowances are recorded in a separate sales returns and allowances account, which is a *contra* (or *offsetting*) account to Sales.

The seller debits Sales Returns and Allowances for the amount of the return or allowance. If the sale was on account, the seller credits Accounts Receivable. Using a perpetual inventory system, the seller must also debit (increase) Merchandise Inventory and decrease (credit) Cost of Merchandise Sold for the cost of the returned merchandise.

EXHIBIT 8

Credit Memo

NetSolutions		**No. 32**
5101 Washington Ave.		
Cincinnati, OH 45227-5101		

CREDIT MEMO

TO	**DATE**
Krier Company	January 13, 2013
7608 Melton Avenue	
Los Angeles, CA 90025-3942	

WE CREDIT YOUR ACCOUNT AS FOLLOWS

1	Graphic Video Card	225.00

To illustrate, the credit memo shown in Exhibit 8 is used. The selling price of the merchandise returned in Exhibit 8 is $225. Assuming that the cost of the merchandise returned is $140, the sales return and allowance would be recorded as follows:

Jan.	13	Sales Returns and Allowances	225	
		Accounts Receivable—Krier Company		225
		Credit Memo No. 32.		
	13	Merchandise Inventory	140	
		Cost of Merchandise Sold		140
		Cost of merchandise returned, Credit		
		Memo No. 32.		

A buyer may pay for merchandise and then later return it. In this case, the seller may do one of the following:

1. Issue a credit that is applied against the buyer's other receivables.
2. Issue a cash refund.

If the credit is applied against the buyer's other receivables, the seller records the credit with entries similar to those shown above. If cash is refunded, the seller debits Sales Returns and Allowances and credits Cash.

Example Exercise 6-2   Sales Transactions

OBJ. 3

Journalize the following merchandise transactions:
a. Sold merchandise on account, $7,500 with terms 2/10, n/30. The cost of the merchandise sold was $5,625.
b. Received payment less the discount.

Follow My Example 6-2

a. Accounts Receivable..	7,500	
Sales...		7,500
Cost of Merchandise Sold...	5,625	
Merchandise Inventory.....................................		5,625
b. Cash..	7,350	
Sales Discounts..	150	
Accounts Receivable		7,500

Practice Exercises: **PE 6-2A, PE 6-2B**

Integrity, Objectivity, and Ethics in Business

THE CASE OF THE FRAUDULENT PRICE TAGS

One of the challenges for a retailer is policing its sales return policy. There are many ways in which customers can unethically or illegally abuse such policies. In one case, a couple was accused of attaching Marshalls' store price tags to cheaper merchandise bought or obtained elsewhere. The couple then returned the cheaper goods and received the substantially higher refund amount. Company security officials discovered the fraud and had the couple arrested after they had allegedly bilked the company for over $1 million.

Purchase Transactions

Under the perpetual inventory system, cash purchases of merchandise are recorded as follows:

Journal					Page 24
Date	**Description**		**Post. Ref.**	**Debit**	**Credit**
2013 Jan. 3	Merchandise Inventory			2,510	
	Cash				2,510
	Purchased inventory from Bowen Co.				

Purchases of merchandise on account are recorded as follows:

Jan. 4	Merchandise Inventory			9,250	
	Accounts Payable—Thomas Corporation				9,250
	Purchased inventory on account.				

Purchases Discounts   A buyer may receive a discount from the seller (sales discount) for early payment of the amount owed. From the buyer's perspective, such discounts are called **purchases discounts**.

Purchases discounts taken by a buyer reduce the cost of the merchandise purchased. Even if the buyer has to borrow to pay within a discount period, it is normally to the buyer's advantage to do so. For this reason, accounting systems are normally designed so that all available discounts are taken.

To illustrate, assume that NetSolutions purchased merchandise from Alpha Technologies as follows:

Invoice Date	Invoice Amount	Terms
March 12	$3,000	2/10, n/30

The last day of the discount period is March 22 (March 12 + 10 days). Assume that in order to pay the invoice on March 22, NetSolutions borrows $2,940, which is $3,000 less the discount of $60 ($3,000 × 2%). If we also assume an annual interest rate of 6% and a 360-day year, the interest on the loan of $2,940 for the remaining 20 days of the credit period is $9.80 ($2,940 × 6% × 20/360).

The net savings to NetSolutions of taking the discount is $50.20, computed as follows:

Discount of 2% on $3,000	$60.00
Interest for 20 days at a rate of 6% on $2,940	9.80
Savings from taking the discount	$50.20

The savings can also be seen by comparing the interest rate on the money *saved* by taking the discount and the interest rate on the money *borrowed* to take the discount. The interest rate on the money saved in the prior example is estimated by converting 2% for 20 days to a yearly rate, as follows:

$$2\% \times \frac{360 \text{ days}}{20 \text{ days}} = 2\% \times 18 = 36\%$$

NetSolutions borrowed $2,940 at 6% to take the discount. If NetSolutions does not take the discount, it *pays* an estimated interest rate of 36% for using the $2,940 for the remaining 20 days of the credit period. Thus, buyers should normally take all available purchase discounts.

Under the perpetual inventory system, the buyer initially debits Merchandise Inventory for the amount of the invoice. When paying the invoice within the discount period, the buyer credits Merchandise Inventory for the amount of the discount. In this way, Merchandise Inventory shows the *net* cost to the buyer.

To illustrate, NetSolutions would record the Alpha Technologies invoice and its payment at the end of the discount period as follows:

Mar.	12	Merchandise Inventory	3,000	
		Accounts Payable—Alpha Technologies		3,000
	22	Accounts Payable—Alpha Technologies	3,000	
		Cash		2,940
		Merchandise Inventory		60

Assume that NetSolutions does not take the discount, but instead pays the invoice on April 11. In this case, NetSolutions would record the payment on April 11 as follows:

Apr.	11	Accounts Payable—Alpha Technologies	3,000	
		Cash		3,000

Purchases Returns and Allowances   A buyer may receive an allowance for merchandise that is returned (purchases return) or a price allowance (purchases allowance) for damaged or defective merchandise. From a buyer's perspective, such sales returns and allowances are called **purchases returns and allowances**. In both cases, the buyer normally sends the seller a debit memorandum.

A **debit memorandum**, often called a **debit memo**, is shown in Exhibit 9. A debit memo informs the seller of the amount the buyer proposes to *debit* to the account payable due the seller. It also states the reasons for the return or the request for the price allowance.

The buyer may use the debit memo as the basis for recording the return or allowance or wait for approval from the seller (creditor). In either case, the buyer debits Accounts Payable and credits Merchandise Inventory.

EXHIBIT 9

Debit Memo

NetSolutions			**No. 18**
5101 Washington Ave.			
Cincinnati, OH 45227-5101			

DEBIT MEMO

TO	**DATE**
Maxim Systems	March 7, 2013
7519 East Wilson Ave.	
Seattle, WA 98101-7519	

WE DEBITED YOUR ACCOUNT AS FOLLOWS

10	Server Network Interface Cards, your invoice No. 7291,	@90.00	900.00
	are being returned via parcel post. Our order specified No. 825X.		

To illustrate, NetSolutions records the return of the merchandise indicated in the debit memo in Exhibit 9 as follows:

Mar.	7	Accounts Payable—Maxim Systems	900	
		Merchandise Inventory		900
		Debit Memo No. 18.		

A buyer may return merchandise or be granted a price allowance before paying an invoice. In this case, the amount of the debit memo is deducted from the invoice. The amount is deducted before the purchase discount is computed.

To illustrate, assume the following data concerning a purchase of merchandise by NetSolutions on May 2:

May   2. Purchased $5,000 of merchandise on account from Delta Data Link, terms 2/10, n/30.

     4. Returned $3,000 of the merchandise purchased on March 2.

   12. Paid for the purchase of May 2 less the return and discount.

NetSolutions would record these transactions as follows:

May	2	Merchandise Inventory	5,000	
		Accounts Payable—Delta Data Link		5,000
		Purchased merchandise.		
	4	Accounts Payable—Delta Data Link	3,000	
		Merchandise Inventory		3,000
		Returned portion of merch. purchased.		
	12	Accounts Payable—Delta Data Link	2,000	
		Cash		1,960
		Merchandise Inventory		40
		Paid invoice [($5,000 – $3,000) × 2%		
		= $40; $2,000 – $40 = $1,960].		

Example Exercise 6-3   Purchase Transactions

OBJ. 3

Rofles Company purchased merchandise on account from a supplier for $11,500, terms 2/10, n/30. Rofles Company returned $3,000 of the merchandise and received full credit.

a. If Rofles Company pays the invoice within the discount period, what is the amount of cash required for the payment?

b. Under a perpetual inventory system, what account is credited by Rofles Company to record the return?

Follow My Example 6-3

a. $8,330. Purchase of $11,500 less the return of $3,000 less the discount of $170 [($11,500 – $3,000) × 2%].

b. Merchandise Inventory

Practice Exercises: **PE 6-3A, PE 6-3B**

Freight

Purchases and sales of merchandise often involve freight. The terms of a sale indicate when ownership (title) of the merchandise passes from the seller to the buyer. This point determines whether the buyer or the seller pays the freight costs.[4]

The ownership of the merchandise may pass to the buyer when the seller delivers the merchandise to the freight carrier. In this case, the terms are said to be **FOB (free on board) shipping point**. This term means that the buyer pays the freight costs from the shipping point to the final destination. Such costs are part of the buyer's total cost of purchasing inventory and are added to the cost of the inventory by debiting Merchandise Inventory.

To illustrate, assume that on June 10, NetSolutions purchased merchandise as follows:

June 10. Purchased merchandise from Magna Data, $900, terms FOB shipping point.
   10. Paid freight of $50 on June 10 purchase from Magna Data.

NetSolutions would record these two transactions as follows:

June	10	Merchandise Inventory	900	
		Accounts Payable—Magna Data		900
		Purchased merchandise, terms FOB		
		shipping point.		
	10	Merchandise Inventory	50	
		Cash		50
		Paid shipping cost on merchandise		
		purchased.		

The ownership of the merchandise may pass to the buyer when the buyer receives the merchandise. In this case, the terms are said to be **FOB (free on board) destination**. This term means that the seller pays the freight costs from the shipping point to the buyer's final destination. When the seller pays the delivery charges, the seller debits Delivery Expense or Freight Out. Delivery Expense is reported on the seller's income statement as a selling expense.

To illustrate, assume that NetSolutions sells merchandise as follows:

June 15. Sold merchandise to Kranz Company on account, $700, terms FOB destination. The cost of the merchandise sold is $480.
   15. NetSolutions pays freight of $40 on the sale of June 15.

NetSolutions records the sale, the cost of the sale, and the freight cost as follows:

June	15	Accounts Receivable—Kranz Company	700	
		Sales		700
		Sold merchandise, terms FOB destination.		
	15	Cost of Merchandise Sold	480	
		Merchandise Inventory		480
		Recorded cost of merchandise sold to		
		Kranz Company.		
	15	Delivery Expense	40	
		Cash		40
		Paid shipping cost on merch. sold.		

Note:
The buyer bears the freight costs if the shipping terms are FOB shipping point.

Sometimes FOB shipping point and FOB destination are expressed in terms of a specific location at which the title to the merchandise passes to the buyer. For example, if Toyota Motor Corporation's assembly plant in Osaka, Japan, sells automobiles to a dealer in Chicago, FOB shipping point is expressed as FOB Osaka. Likewise, FOB destination is expressed as FOB Chicago.

Note:
The seller bears the freight costs if the shipping terms are FOB destination.

4 The passage of title also determines whether the buyer or seller must pay other costs, such as the cost of insurance, while the merchandise is in transit.

The seller may prepay the freight, even though the terms are FOB shipping point. The seller will then add the freight to the invoice. The buyer debits Merchandise Inventory for the total amount of the invoice, including the freight. Any discount terms would not apply to the prepaid freight.

To illustrate, assume that NetSolutions sells merchandise as follows:

June 20. Sold merchandise to Planter Company on account, $800, terms FOB shipping point. NetSolutions paid freight of $45, which was added to the invoice. The cost of the merchandise sold is $360.

NetSolutions records the sale, the cost of the sale, and the freight as follows:

June	20	Accounts Receivable—Planter Company		800	
		Sales			800
		Sold merch., terms FOB shipping point.			
	20	Cost of Merchandise Sold		360	
		Merchandise Inventory			360
		Recorded cost of merchandise sold to Planter Company.			
	20	Accounts Receivable—Planter Company		45	
		Cash			45
		Prepaid shipping cost on merch. sold.			

Shipping terms, the passage of title, and whether the buyer or seller is to pay the freight costs are summarized in Exhibit 10.

EXHIBIT 10 Freight Terms

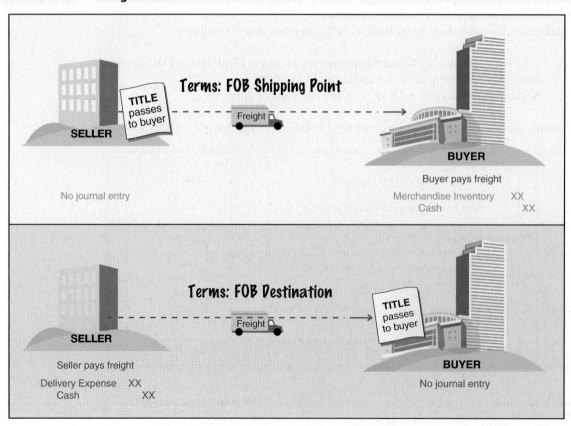

Example Exercise 6-4   Freight Terms

OBJ.
3

Determine the amount to be paid in full settlement of each of invoices (a) and (b), assuming that credit for returns and allowances was received prior to payment and that all invoices were paid within the discount period.

	Merchandise	Freight Paid by Seller	Freight Terms	Returns and Allowances
a.	$4,500	$200	FOB shipping point, 1/10, n/30	$ 800
b.	5,000	60	FOB destination, 2/10, n/30	2,500

Follow My Example 6-4

a. $3,863. Purchase of $4,500 less return of $800 less the discount of $37 [($4,500 − $800) × 1%] plus $200 of shipping.

b. $2,450. Purchase of $5,000 less return of $2,500 less the discount of $50 [($5,000 − $2,500) × 2%].

Practice Exercises: **PE 6-4A, PE 6-4B**

Summary: Recording Merchandise Inventory

Recording merchandise inventory transactions under the perpetual inventory system has been described and illustrated in the preceding sections. These transactions involved purchases, purchases discounts, purchases returns and allowances, freight, sales, and sales returns from customers. Exhibit 11 summarizes how these transactions are recorded in T account form.

EXHIBIT 11

Recording Merchandise Inventory

Merchandise Inventory

Purchases of merchandise for sale	XXX	Purchases discounts	XXX
Freight for merchandise purchased FOB shipping point	XXX	Purchases returns and allowances	XXX
Merchandise returned from customer	XXX	Cost of merchandise sold	XXX

Cost of Merchandise Sold

Cost of merchandise sold	XXX	Merchandise returned from customer	XXX

Sales Taxes and Trade Discounts

Sales of merchandise often involve sales taxes. Also, the seller may offer buyers trade discounts.

Sales Taxes Almost all states levy a tax on sales of merchandise.[5] The liability for the sales tax is incurred when the sale is made.

---

5 Businesses that purchase merchandise for resale to others are normally exempt from paying sales taxes on their purchases. Only final buyers of merchandise normally pay sales taxes.

At the time of a cash sale, the seller collects the sales tax. When a sale is made on account, the seller charges the tax to the buyer by debiting Accounts Receivable. The seller credits the sales account for the amount of the sale and credits the tax to Sales Tax Payable. For example, the seller would record a sale of $100 on account, subject to a tax of 6%, as follows:

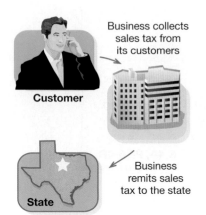

Business collects sales tax from its customers

Customer

Business remits sales tax to the state

State

Aug.	12	Accounts Receivable—Lemon Co.	106	
		Sales		100
		Sales Tax Payable		6
		Invoice No. 339.		

On a regular basis, the seller pays to the taxing authority (state) the amount of the sales tax collected. The seller records such a payment as follows:

Sept.	15	Sales Tax Payable	2,900	
		Cash		2,900
		Payment for sales taxes collected during August.		

BusinessConnection

SALES TAXES

While there is no federal sales tax, most states have enacted state-wide sales taxes. In addition, many states allow counties and cities to collect a "local option" sales taxes. Delaware, Montana, New Hampshire, and Oregon have no state or local sales taxes. Tennessee (9.4%), California (9.15%), Washington (8.75%), and Louisiana (8.75%) have the highest average combined rates (including state and local option taxes). Several towns in Tuscaloosa County, Alabama, have the highest

combined rates in the United States of 11%, while Chicago, Illinois, has the highest combined city rate of 10.25%.

What about companies that sell merchandise through the Internet? The general rule is that if the company ships merchandise to a customer in a state where the company does not have a physical location, no sales tax is due. For example, a customer in Montana who purchases merchandise online from a New York retailer (and no physical location in Montana) does not have to pay sales tax to either Montana or New York.

Source: The Sales Tax Clearinghouse at **www.thestc.com/FAQ.stm** (accessed May 6, 2010).

Trade Discounts Wholesalers are companies that sell merchandise to other businesses rather than to the public. Many wholesalers publish sales catalogs. Rather than updating their catalogs, wholesalers may publish price updates. These updates may include large discounts from the catalog list prices. In addition, wholesalers often offer special discounts to government agencies or businesses that order large quantities. Such discounts are called **trade discounts**.

Sellers and buyers do not normally record the list prices of merchandise and trade discounts in their accounts. For example, assume that an item has a list price of $1,000 and a 40% trade discount. The seller records the sale of the item at $600 [$1,000 less the trade discount of $400 ($1,000 × 40%)]. Likewise, the buyer records the purchase at $600.

Dual Nature of Merchandise Transactions

Each merchandising transaction affects a buyer and a seller. In the following illustration, the same transactions for a seller and buyer are recorded. In this example, the seller is Scully Company and the buyer is Burton Co.

Transaction	Scully Company (Seller)		Burton Co. (Buyer)	
July 1. Scully Company sold merchandise on account to Burton Co., $7,500, terms FOB shipping point, n/45. The cost of the merchandise sold was $4,500.	Accounts Receivable—Burton Co. .	7,500	Merchandise Inventory	7,500
	Sales.		7,500	Accounts Payable—Scully Co. . .		7,500
	Cost of Merchandise Sold	4,500		
	Merchandise Inventory.		4,500		
July 2. Burton Co. paid freight of $150 on July 1 purchase from Scully Company.	No journal entry.		Merchandise Inventory	150
			Cash.		150
July 5. Scully Company sold merchandise on account to Burton Co., $5,000, terms FOB destination, n/30. The cost of the merchandise sold was $3,500.	Accounts Receivable—Burton Co. . ..	5,000	Merchandise Inventory	5,000
	Sales.		5,000	Accounts Payable—Scully Co. . .		5,000
	Cost of Merchandise Sold	3,500		
	Merchandise Inventory.		3,500		
July 7. Scully Company paid freight of $250 for delivery of merchandise sold to Burton Co. on July 5.	Delivery Expense	250	No journal entry.	
	Cash.		250		
July 13. Scully Company issued Burton Co. a credit memo for merchandise returned, $1,000. The merchandise had been purchased by Burton Co. on account on July 5. The cost of the merchandise returned was $700.	Sales Returns and Allowances.	1,000	Accounts Payable—Scully Co.	1,000
	Accounts Receivable—Burton Co.		1,000	Merchandise Inventory.		1,000
	Merchandise Inventory	700		
	Cost of Merchandise Sold.		700		
July 15. Scully Company received payment from Burton Co. for purchase of July 5.	Cash	4,000	Accounts Payable—Scully Co.	4,000
	Accounts Receivable—Burton Co.		4,000	Cash.		4,000
July 18. Scully Company sold merchandise on account to Burton Co.,$12,000, terms FOB shipping point, 2/10, n/eom. Scully Company prepaid freight of $500, which was added to the invoice. The cost of the merchandise sold was $7,200.	Accounts Receivable—Burton Co. . ..	12,000	Merchandise Inventory	12,500
	Sales.		12,000	Accounts Payable—Scully Co. . .		12,500
	Accounts Receivable—Burton Co. .	500		
	Cash.		500		
	Cost of Merchandise Sold	7,200		
	Merchandise Inventory.		7,200		
July 28. Scully Company received payment from Burton Co. for purchase of July 18, less discount (2% × $12,000).	Cash	12,260	Accounts Payable—Scully Co.	12,500
	Sales Discounts.	240	Merchandise Inventory.		240
	Accounts Receivable—Burton Co.		12,500	Cash.		12,260

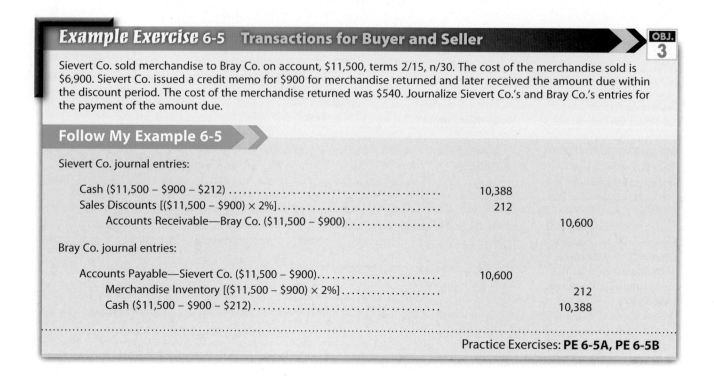

Example Exercise 6-5 Transactions for Buyer and Seller

OBJ. 3

Sievert Co. sold merchandise to Bray Co. on account, $11,500, terms 2/15, n/30. The cost of the merchandise sold is $6,900. Sievert Co. issued a credit memo for $900 for merchandise returned and later received the amount due within the discount period. The cost of the merchandise returned was $540. Journalize Sievert Co.'s and Bray Co.'s entries for the payment of the amount due.

Follow My Example 6-5

Sievert Co. journal entries:

Cash ($11,500 − $900 − $212)	10,388	
Sales Discounts [($11,500 − $900) × 2%]	212	
Accounts Receivable—Bray Co. ($11,500 − $900)		10,600

Bray Co. journal entries:

Accounts Payable—Sievert Co. ($11,500 − $900)	10,600	
Merchandise Inventory [($11,500 − $900) × 2%]		212
Cash ($11,500 − $900 − $212)		10,388

Practice Exercises: **PE 6-5A, PE 6-5B**

OBJ. 4 Describe the adjusting and closing process for a merchandising business.

The Adjusting and Closing Process

Thus far, the chart of accounts and the recording of transactions for a merchandising business have been described and illustrated. The preparation of financial statements for **NetSolutions** has also been illustrated. In the remainder of this chapter, the adjusting and closing process for a merchandising business will be described. In this discussion, the focus will be on the elements of the accounting cycle that differ from those of a service business.

Adjusting Entry for Inventory Shrinkage

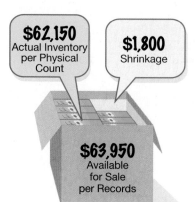

Under the perpetual inventory system, the merchandise inventory account is continually updated for purchase and sales transactions. As a result, the balance of the merchandise inventory account is the amount of merchandise available for sale at that point in time. However, retailers normally experience some loss of inventory due to shoplifting, employee theft, or errors. Thus, the physical inventory on hand at the end of the accounting period is usually less than the balance of Merchandise Inventory. This difference is called **inventory shrinkage** or **inventory shortage**.

To illustrate, NetSolutions' inventory records indicate the following on December 31, 2013:

	Dec. 31, 2013
Account balance of Merchandise Inventory	$63,950
Physical merchandise inventory on hand	62,150
Inventory shrinkage	$ 1,800

At the end of the accounting period, inventory shrinkage is recorded by the following adjusting entry:

			Adjusting Entry		
Dec.	31	Cost of Merchandise Sold		1,800	
		Merchandise Inventory			1,800
		Inventory shrinkage ($63,950 − $62,150).			

After the preceding entry is recorded, the balance of Merchandise Inventory agrees with the physical inventory on hand at the end of the period. Since inventory shrinkage cannot be totally eliminated, it is considered a normal cost of operations. If, however, the amount of the shrinkage is unusually large, it may be disclosed separately on the income statement. In such cases, the shrinkage may be recorded in a separate account, such as Loss from Merchandise Inventory Shrinkage.[6]

Example Exercise 6-6   Inventory Shrinkage

OBJ. 4

Pulmonary Company's perpetual inventory records indicate that $382,800 of merchandise should be on hand on March 31, 2012. The physical inventory indicates that $371,250 of merchandise is actually on hand. Journalize the adjusting entry for the inventory shrinkage for Pulmonary Company for the year ended March 31, 2012. Assume that the inventory shrinkage is a normal amount.

Follow My Example 6-6

Mar. 31	Cost of Merchandise Sold	11,550	
	Merchandise Inventory....................................		11,550
	Inventory shrinkage ($382,800 – $371,250).		

Practice Exercises: **PE 6-6A, PE 6-6B**

Closing Entries

The closing entries for a merchandising business are similar to those for a service business. The four closing entries for a merchandising business are as follows:

1. Debit each temporary account with a credit balance, such as Sales, for its balance and credit Income Summary.
2. Credit each temporary account with a debit balance, such as the various expenses, and credit Income Summary. Since Sales Returns and Allowances, Sales Discounts, and Cost of Merchandise Sold are temporary accounts with debit balances, they are credited for their balances.
3. Debit Income Summary for the amount of its balance (net income) and credit the owner's capital account. The accounts debited and credited are reversed if there is a net loss.
4. Debit the owner's capital account for the balance of the drawing account and credit the drawing account.

The four closing entries for NetSolutions are shown at the top of the following page.

NetSolutions' income summary account after the closing entries have been posted is as follows:

Account *Income Summary*						Account No. *312*	
			Post.			**Balance**	
Date		Item	Ref.	**Debit**	**Credit**	**Debit**	**Credit**
2013 Dec.	31	Revenues	29		720,785		720,785
	31	Expenses	29	645,385			75,400
	31	Net income	29	75,400		—	—

After the closing entries are posted to the accounts, a post-closing trial balance is prepared. The only accounts that should appear on the post-closing trial balance are the asset, contra asset, liability, and owner's capital accounts with balances. These are the same accounts that appear on the end-of-period balance sheet. If the two totals of the trial balance columns are not equal, an error has occurred that must be found and corrected.

6 The adjusting process for a merchandising business may be aided by preparing an end-of-period spreadsheet (work sheet). An end-of-period spreadsheet (work sheet) for a merchandising business is described and illustrated in an online appendix at **cengage.com/accounting/warren**.

		Journal			Page 29
Date		**Item**	**Post. Ref.**	**Debit**	**Credit**
		Closing Entries			
2013 Dec.	31	Sales	410	720,185	
		Rent Revenue	610	600	
		Income Summary	312		720,785
	31	Income Summary	312	645,385	
		Sales Returns and Allowances	411		6,140
		Sales Discounts	412		5,790
		Cost of Merchandise Sold	510		525,305
		Sales Salaries Expense	520		53,430
		Advertising Expense	521		10,860
		Depr. Expense—Store Equipment	522		3,100
		Delivery Expense	523		2,800
		Miscellaneous Selling Expense	529		630
		Office Salaries Expense	530		21,020
		Rent Expense	531		8,100
		Depr. Expense—Office Equipment	532		2,490
		Insurance Expense	533		1,910
		Office Supplies Expense	534		610
		Misc. Administrative Expense	539		760
		Interest Expense	710		2,440
	31	Income Summary	312	75,400	
		Chris Clark, Capital	310		75,400
	31	Chris Clark, Capital	310	18,000	
		Chris Clark, Drawing	311		18,000

FAI

OBJ. 5 Describe and illustrate the use of the ratio of net sales to assets in evaluating a company's operating performance.

Financial Analysis and Interpretation: Ratio of Net Sales to Assets

The **ratio of net sales to assets** measures how effectively a business is using its assets to generate sales. A high ratio indicates an effective use of assets. The assets used in computing the ratio may be the total assets at the end of the year, the average of the total assets at the beginning and end of the year, or the average of the monthly assets. For our purposes, the average of the total assets at the beginning and end of the year is used.

The ratio of net sales to assets is computed as follows:

$$\text{Ratio of Net Sales to Assets} = \frac{\text{Net Sales}}{\text{Average Total Assets}}$$

To illustrate the use of this ratio, the following data (in millions) were taken from the annual reports of Dollar Tree, Inc.:

	For Years Ended	
	January 31, 2009	**February 2, 2008**
Total revenues (net sales)	$4,645	$4,243
Total assets:		
Beginning of year	1,788	1,873
End of year	2,036	1,788

The ratios of net sales to assets for each year are as follows:

	For Years Ended	
	January 31, 2009	**February 2, 2008**
Ratio of net sales to assets	2.43	2.32
	$4,645/[($1,788 + $2,036)/2]	$4,243/[($1,873 + $1,788)/2]

Based on the preceding ratios, Dollar Tree improved its ratio of net sales to assets from 2.32 in 2008 to 2.43 in 2009. Thus, Dollar Tree improved the utilization of its assets to generate sales in 2009.

Using the ratio of net sales to assets for comparisons to competitors and with industry averages could also be beneficial in interpreting Dollar Tree's use of its assets. For example, the following data (in millions) were taken from the annual reports of Dollar General Corporation for the year ended January 30, 2009:

	For Year Ended January 30, 2009
Total revenues (net sales)	$10,458
Total assets:	
Beginning of year	8,656
End of year	8,889

Dollar General's ratio of net sales to assets for 2009 is as follows:

	For Year Ended January 30, 2009
Ratio of net sales to assets	1.19
	$10,458/[($8,656 + $8,889)/2]

Comparing Dollar General's 2009 ratio of 1.19 to Dollar Tree's 2009 ratio of 2.43 implies Dollar Tree is using its assets more efficiently than Dollar General.

Example Exercise 6-7   Ratio of Net Sales to Assets   OBJ. 5

The following financial statement data for the years ending December 31, 2012 and 2011, for Gilbert Company are shown below.

	2012	2011
Net sales	$1,305,000	$962,500
Total assets:		
Beginning of year	840,000	700,000
End of year	900,000	840,000

a. Determine the ratio of net sales to assets for 2012 and 2011.

b. Does the change in the current ratio from 2011 to 2012 indicate a favorable or an unfavorable trend?

Follow My Example 6-7

a.

	2012	2011
Ratio of net sales to assets	1.50	1.25
	$1,305,000/[($840,000 + $900,000)/2]	$962,500/[($840,000 + $700,000)/2]

b. The change from 1.25 to 1.50 indicates a favorable trend in using assets to generate sales.

Practice Exercises: **PE 6-7A, PE 6-7B**

A P P E N D I X

The Periodic Inventory System

Throughout this chapter, the perpetual inventory system was used to record purchases and sales of merchandise. Not all merchandise businesses, however, use the perpetual inventory system. For example, small merchandise businesses, such as a local hardware store, may use a manual accounting system. A manual perpetual inventory system is time consuming and costly to maintain. In this case, the periodic inventory system may be used.

Cost of Merchandise Sold Using the Periodic Inventory System

In the periodic inventory system, sales are recorded in the same manner as in the perpetual inventory system. However, cost of merchandise sold is not recorded on the date of sale. Instead, cost of merchandise sold is determined at the end of the period as shown in Exhibit 12 for **NetSolutions**.

EXHIBIT 12

Determining Cost of Merchandise Sold Using the Periodic System

Merchandise inventory, January 1, 2013			$ 59,700
Purchases		$521,980	
Less: Purchases returns and allowances	$9,100		
Purchases discounts	2,525	11,625	
Net purchases		$510,355	
Add freight in		17,400	
Cost of merchandise purchased			527,755
Merchandise available for sale			$587,455
Less merchandise inventory, December 31, 2013			62,150
Cost of merchandise sold			$525,305

Chart of Accounts Under the Periodic Inventory System

The chart of accounts under a periodic inventory system is shown in Exhibit 13. The accounts used to record transactions under the periodic inventory system are highlighted in Exhibit 13.

Balance Sheet Accounts	Income Statement Accounts

100 Assets
   110 Cash
   111 Notes Receivable
   112 Accounts Receivable
   115 Merchandise Inventory
   116 Office Supplies
   117 Prepaid Insurance
   120 Land
   123 Store Equipment
   124 Accumulated Depreciation—
         Store Equipment
   125 Office Equipment
   126 Accumulated Depreciation—
         Office Equipment

200 Liabilities
   210 Accounts Payable
   211 Salaries Payable
   212 Unearned Rent
   215 Notes Payable

300 Owner's Equity
   310 Chris Clark, Capital
   311 Chris Clark, Drawing
   312 Income Summary

400 Revenues
   410 Sales
   411 Sales Returns and Allowances
   412 Sales Discounts

500 Costs and Expenses
   510 Purchases
   511 Purchases Returns and
         Allowances
   512 Purchases Discounts
   513 Freight In
   520 Sales Salaries Expense
   521 Advertising Expense
   522 Depreciation Expense—
         Store Equipment
   523 Delivery Expense
   529 Miscellaneous Selling Expense
   530 Office Salaries Expense
   531 Rent Expense
   532 Depreciation Expense—
         Office Equipment
   533 Insurance Expense
   534 Office Supplies Expense
   539 Misc. Administrative Expense

600 Other Income
   610 Rent Revenue

700 Other Expense
   710 Interest Expense

EXHIBIT 13

Chart of Accounts Under the Periodic Inventory System

Recording Merchandise Transactions Under the Periodic Inventory System

Using the periodic inventory system, purchases of inventory are not recorded in the merchandise inventory account. Instead, purchases, purchases discounts, and purchases returns and allowances accounts are used. In addition, the sales of merchandise are not recorded in the inventory account. Thus, there is no detailed record of the amount of inventory on hand at any given time. At the end of the period, a physical count of merchandise inventory on hand is taken. This physical count is used to determine the cost of merchandise sold as shown in Exhibit 12.

The use of purchases, purchases discounts, purchases returns and allowances, and freight in accounts are described below.

Purchases Purchases of inventory are recorded in a purchases account rather than in the merchandise inventory account. Purchases is debited for the invoice amount of a purchase.

Purchases Discounts Purchases discounts are normally recorded in a separate purchases discounts account. The balance of the purchases discounts account is reported as a deduction from Purchases for the period. Thus, Purchases Discounts is a contra (or offsetting) account to Purchases.

Purchases Returns and Allowances Purchases returns and allowances are recorded in a similar manner as purchases discounts. A separate purchases returns and allowances account is used to record returns and allowances. Purchases returns and allowances are reported as a deduction from Purchases for the period. Thus, Purchases Returns and Allowances is a contra (or offsetting) account to Purchases.

Freight In When merchandise is purchased FOB shipping point, the buyer pays for the freight. Under the periodic inventory system, freight paid when purchasing merchandise FOB shipping point is debited to Freight In, Transportation In, or a similar account.

The preceding periodic inventory accounts and their effect on the cost of merchandise purchased are summarized below.

Account	Entry to Increase	Normal Balance	Effect on Cost of Merchandise Purchased
Purchases	Debit	Debit	Increases
Purchases Discounts	Credit	Credit	Decreases
Purchases Returns and Allowances	Credit	Credit	Decreases
Freight In	Debit	Debit	Increases

Exhibit 14 illustrates the recording of merchandise transactions using the periodic system. As a review, Exhibit 14 also illustrates how each transaction would have been recorded using the perpetual system.

EXHIBIT 14 **Transactions Using the Periodic and Perpetual Inventory Systems**

Transaction	Periodic Inventory System	Perpetual Inventory System

June 5. Purchased $30,000 of merchandise on account, terms 2/10, n/30.	Purchases 30,000
	  Accounts Payable 30,000
		Merchandise Inventory 30,000
		  Accounts Payable 30,000

June 8. Returned merchandise purchased on account on June 5, $500.	Accounts Payable 500
	  Purchases Returns and
	    Allowances 500
		Accounts Payable 500
		  Merchandise Inventory 500

June 15. Paid for purchase of June 5, less return of $500 and discount of $590 [($30,000 − $500) × 2%].	Accounts Payable 29,500
	  Cash 28,910
	  Purchases Discounts 590
		Accounts Payable 29,500
		  Cash 28,910
		  Merchandise Inventory 590

June 18. Sold merchandise on account, $12,500, 1/10, n/30. The cost of the merchandise sold was $9,000.	Accounts Receivable 12,500
	  Sales 12,500
		Accounts Receivable 12,500
		  Sales 12,500
		Cost of Merchandise Sold 9,000
		  Merchandise Inventory 9,000

June 21. Received merchandise returned on account, $4,000. The cost of the merchandise returned was $2,800.	Sales Returns and Allowances.. 4,000
	  Accounts Receivable 4,000
		Sales Returns and Allowances.... 4,000
		  Accounts Receivable 4,000
		Merchandise Inventory 2,800
		  Cost of Merchandise Sold ... 2,800

June 22. Purchased merchandise, $15,000, terms FOB shipping point, 2/15, n/30, with prepaid freight of $750 added to the invoice.	Purchases 15,000
	Freight In 750
	  Accounts Payable 15,750
		Merchandise Inventory 15,750
		  Accounts Payable 15,750

June 28. Received $8,415 as payment on account from June 18 sale less return of June 21 and less discount of $85 [($12,500 − $4,000) × 1%].	Cash 8,415
	Sales Discounts 85
	  Accounts Receivable 8,500
		Cash 8,415
		Sales Discounts 85
		  Accounts Receivable 8,500

June 29. Received $19,600 from cash sales. The cost of the merchandise sold was $13,800.	Cash 19,600
	  Sales 19,600
		Cash 19,600
		  Sales 19,600
		Cost of Merchandise Sold 13,800
		  Merchandise Inventory 13,800

Adjusting Process Under the Periodic Inventory System

The adjusting process is the same under the periodic and perpetual inventory systems except for the inventory shrinkage adjustment. The ending merchandise inventory is determined by a physical count under both systems.

Under the perpetual inventory system, the ending inventory physical count is compared to the balance of Merchandise Inventory. The difference is the amount of inventory shrinkage. The inventory shrinkage is then recorded as a debit to Cost of Merchandise Sold and a credit to Merchandise Inventory.

Under the periodic inventory system, the merchandise inventory account is not kept up to date for purchases and sales. As a result, the inventory shrinkage cannot be directly determined. Instead, any inventory shrinkage is included indirectly in the computation of cost of merchandise sold as shown in Exhibit 12. This is a major disadvantage of the periodic inventory system. That is, under the periodic inventory system, inventory shrinkage is not separately determined.

Financial Statements Under the Periodic Inventory System

The financial statements are similar under the perpetual and periodic inventory systems. When the multiple-step format of income statement is used, cost of merchandise sold may be reported as shown in Exhibit 12.

Closing Entries Under the Periodic Inventory System

The closing entries differ in the periodic inventory system in that there is no cost of merchandise sold account to close to Income Summary. Instead, the purchases, purchases discounts, purchases returns and allowances, and freight in accounts are closed to Income Summary. In addition, the merchandise inventory account is adjusted to the end-of-period physical inventory count during the closing process.

The four closing entries under the periodic inventory system are as follows:

1. Debit each temporary account with a credit balance, such as Sales, for its balance and credit Income Summary. Since Purchases Discounts and Purchases Returns and Allowances are temporary accounts with credit balances, they are debited for their balances. In addition, Merchandise Inventory is debited for its end-of-period balance based on the end-of-period physical inventory.

2. Credit each temporary account with a debit balance, such as the various expenses, and debit Income Summary. Since Sales Returns and Allowances, Sales Discounts, Purchases, and Freight In are temporary accounts with debit balances, they are credited for their balances. In addition, Merchandise Inventory is credited for its balance as of the beginning of the period.

3. Debit Income Summary for the amount of its balance (net income) and credit the owner's capital account. The accounts debited and credited are reversed if there is a net loss.

4. Debit the owner's capital account for the balance of the drawing account and credit the drawing account.

The four closing entries for NetSolutions under the periodic inventory system are shown on the next page.

				Journal				
Date				**Item**	**Post. Ref.**	**Debit**	**Credit**	
2013				Closing Entries				
Dec.	31		Merchandise Inventory		115	62,150		
			Sales		410	720,185		
			Purchases Returns and Allowances		511	9,100		
			Purchases Discounts		512	2,525		
			Rent Revenue		610	600		
			Income Summary		312		794,560	
	31		Income Summary		312	719,160		
			Merchandise Inventory		115		59,700	
			Sales Returns and Allowances		411		6,140	
			Sales Discounts		412		5,790	
			Purchases		510		521,980	
			Freight In		513		17,400	
			Sales Salaries Expense		520		53,430	
			Advertising Expense		521		10,860	
			Depreciation Expense—Store Equipment		522		3,100	
			Delivery Expense		523		2,800	
			Miscellaneous Selling Expense		529		630	
			Office Salaries Expense		530		21,020	
			Rent Expense		531		8,100	
			Depreciation Expense—Office Equipment		532		2,490	
			Insurance Expense		533		1,910	
			Office Supplies Expense		534		610	
			Miscellaneous Administrative Expense		539		760	
			Interest Expense		710		2,440	
	31		Income Summary		312	75,400		
			Chris Clark, Capital		310		75,400	
	31		Chris Clark, Capital		310	18,000		
			Chris Clark, Drawing		311		18,000	

In the first closing entry, Merchandise Inventory is debited for $62,150. This is the ending physical inventory count on December 31, 2013. In the second closing entry, Merchandise Inventory is credited for its January 1, 2013, balance of $59,700. In this way, the closing entries highlight the importance of the beginning and ending balances of Merchandise Inventory in determining cost of merchandise sold, as shown in Exhibit 12. After the closing entries are posted, Merchandise Inventory will have a balance of $62,150. This is the amount reported on the December 31, 2013, balance sheet.

In the preceding closing entries, the periodic accounts are highlighted in color. Under the perpetual inventory system, the highlighted periodic inventory accounts are replaced by the cost of merchandise sold account.

At a Glance 6

OBJ. 1

Distinguish between the activities and financial statements of service and merchandising businesses.

Key Points Merchandising businesses purchase merchandise for selling to customers.

On a merchandising business's income statement, revenue from selling merchandise is reported as sales. The cost of the merchandise sold is subtracted from sales to arrive at gross profit. The operating expenses are subtracted from gross profit to arrive at net income. Merchandise inventory, which is merchandise not sold, is reported as a current asset on the balance sheet.

Learning Outcomes	Example Exercises	Practice Exercises
• Describe how the activities of a service and a merchandising business differ.		
• Describe the differences between the income statements of a service and a merchandising business.		
• Compute gross profit.	EE6-1	PE6-1A, 6-1B
• Describe how merchandise inventory is reported on the balance sheet.		

OBJ. 2

Describe and illustrate the financial statements of a merchandising business.

Key Points The multiple-step income statement of a merchandiser reports sales, sales returns and allowances, sales discounts, and net sales. The cost of the merchandise sold is subtracted from net sales to determine the gross profit. Operating income is determined by subtracting selling and administrative expenses from gross profit. Net income is determined by adding or subtracting the net of other income and expense. The income statement may also be reported in a single-step form.

The statement of owner's equity is similar to that for a service business.

The balance sheet reports merchandise inventory at the end of the period as a current asset.

Learning Outcomes	Example Exercises	Practice Exercises
• Prepare a multiple-step income statement for a merchandising business.		
• Prepare a single-step income statement.		
• Prepare a statement of owner's equity for a merchandising business.		
• Prepare a balance sheet for a merchandising business.		

OBJ. 3

Describe and illustrate the accounting for merchandise transactions including:
- **sale of merchandise**
- **purchase of merchandise**
- **freight**
- **sales taxes and trade discounts**
- **dual nature of merchandising transactions**

Key Points The chart of accounts for a merchandising business (NetSolutions) is shown in Exhibit 5. Sales of merchandise for cash or on account are recorded as sales. The cost of merchandise sold and the reduction in merchandise inventory are also recorded at the time of sale. Discounts for early payment of sales on account are recorded as sales discounts. Price adjustments and returned merchandise are recorded as sales returns and allowances.

Purchases of merchandise for cash or on account are recorded as merchandise inventory. Discounts for early payment of purchases on account are recorded as purchases discounts. Price adjustments or returned merchandise are recorded as purchases returns and allowances.

When merchandise is shipped FOB shipping point, the buyer pays the freight and debits Merchandise Inventory. When merchandise is shipped FOB destination, the seller pays the freight and debits Delivery Expense or Freight Out.

The liability for sales tax is incurred when the sale is made and is recorded by the seller as a credit to the sales tax payable account. Trade discounts are discounts off the list price of merchandise.

Each merchandising transaction affects a buyer and a seller.

Learning Outcomes	Example Exercises	Practice Exercises
• Prepare journal entries to record sales of merchandise for cash or using a credit card.		
• Prepare journal entries to record sales of merchandise on account.	EE6-2	PE6-2A, 6-2B
• Prepare journal entries to record sales discounts and sales returns and allowances.	EE6-2	PE6-2A, 6-2B
• Prepare journal entries to record the purchase of merchandise for cash.		
• Prepare journal entries to record the purchase of merchandise on account.	EE6-3	PE6-3A, 6-3B
• Prepare journal entries to record purchases discounts and purchases returns and allowances.	EE6-3	PE6-3A, 6-3B
• Prepare journal entries for freight from the point of view of the buyer and seller.		
• Determine the total cost of the purchase of merchandise under differing freight terms.	EE6-4	PE6-4A, 6-4B
• Prepare journal entries for the collection and payment of sales taxes by the seller.		
• Determine the cost of merchandise purchased when a trade discount is offered by the seller.		
• Record the same merchandise transactions for the buyer and seller.	EE6-5	PE6-5A, 6-5B

OBJ. 4

Describe the adjusting and closing process for a merchandising business.

Key Points The normal adjusting entry for inventory shrinkage is to debit Cost of Merchandise Sold and credit Merchandise Inventory.

The closing entries for a merchandising business are similar to those for a service business except that the cost of merchandise sold, sales discounts, and sales returns and allowances accounts are also closed to Income Summary.

Learning Outcomes	Example Exercises	Practice Exercises
• Prepare the adjusting journal entry for inventory shrinkage.	EE6-6	PE6-6A, 6-6B
• Prepare the closing entries for a merchandising business.		

OBJ. 5 Describe and illustrate the use of the ratio of net sales to assets in evaluating a company's operating performance.

Key Points The ratio of net sales to assets measures how effectively a business is using its assets to generate sales. A high ratio indicates an effective use of assets. Using the average of the total assets at the beginning and end of the year, the ratio is computed as follows:

$$\text{Ratio of Net Sales to Assets} = \frac{\text{Net Sales}}{\text{Average Total Assets}}$$

Learning Outcomes	Example Exercises	Practice Exercises
• Interpret a high ratio of net sales to assets.		
• Compute the ratio of net sales to assets.	EE6-7	PE6-7A, 6-7B

Key Terms

account form (258)

administrative expenses (general expenses) (257)

cost of merchandise sold (254)

credit memorandum (credit memo) (263)

credit period (262)

credit terms (262)

debit memorandum (debit memo) (267)

FOB (free on board) destination (269)

FOB (free on board) shipping point (269)

gross profit (254)

income from operations (operating income) (257)

inventory shrinkage (inventory shortage) (274)

invoice (262)

merchandise inventory (254)

multiple-step income statement (255)

net sales (257)

other expense (258)

other income (258)

periodic inventory system (257)

perpetual inventory system (257)

purchases discounts (266)

purchases returns and allowances (267)

ratio of net sales to assets (276)

report form (259)

sales (256)

sales discounts (256)

sales returns and allowances (256)

selling expenses (257)

single-step income statement (258)

trade discounts (272)

Illustrative Problem

The following transactions were completed by Montrose Company during May of the current year. Montrose Company uses a perpetual inventory system.

May 3. Purchased merchandise on account from Floyd Co., $4,000, terms FOB shipping point, 2/10, n/30, with prepaid freight of $120 added to the invoice.

5. Purchased merchandise on account from Kramer Co., $8,500, terms FOB destination, 1/10, n/30.

6. Sold merchandise on account to C. F. Howell Co., list price $4,000, trade discount 30%, terms 2/10, n/30. The cost of the merchandise sold was $1,125.

8. Purchased office supplies for cash, $150.

10. Returned merchandise purchased on May 5 from Kramer Co., $1,300.

13. Paid Floyd Co. on account for purchase of May 3, less discount.

May 14. Purchased merchandise for cash, $10,500.

15. Paid Kramer Co. on account for purchase of May 5, less return of May 10 and discount.

16. Received cash on account from sale of May 6 to C. F. Howell Co., less discount.

19. Sold merchandise on MasterCard credit cards, $2,450. The cost of the merchandise sold was $980.

22. Sold merchandise on account to Comer Co., $3,480, terms 2/10, n/30. The cost of the merchandise sold was $1,400.

24. Sold merchandise for cash, $4,350. The cost of the merchandise sold was $1,750.

25. Received merchandise returned by Comer Co. from sale on May 22, $1,480. The cost of the returned merchandise was $600.

31. Paid a service processing fee of $140 for MasterCard sales.

Instructions

1. Journalize the preceding transactions.

2. Journalize the adjusting entry for merchandise inventory shrinkage, $3,750.

Solution

1.	May	3	Merchandise Inventory	4,120	
			Accounts Payable—Floyd Co.		4,120
		5	Merchandise Inventory	8,500	
			Accounts Payable—Kramer Co.		8,500
		6	Accounts Receivable—C. F. Howell Co.	2,800	
			Sales		2,800
			[$4,000 – (30% × $4,000)]		
		6	Cost of Merchandise Sold	1,125	
			Merchandise Inventory		1,125
		8	Office Supplies	150	
			Cash		150
		10	Accounts Payable—Kramer Co.	1,300	
			Merchandise Inventory		1,300
		13	Accounts Payable—Floyd Co.	4,120	
			Merchandise Inventory		80
			Cash		4,040
			[$4,000 – (2% × $4,000) + $120]		
		14	Merchandise Inventory	10,500	
			Cash		10,500
		15	Accounts Payable—Kramer Co.	7,200	
			Merchandise Inventory		72
			Cash		7,128
			[($8,500 – $1,300) × 1% = $72;		
			$8,500 – $1,300 – $72 = $7,128]		
		16	Cash	2,744	
			Sales Discounts	56	
			Accounts Receivable—C. F. Howell Co.		2,800
		19	Cash	2,450	
			Sales		2,450
		19	Cost of Merchandise Sold	980	
			Merchandise Inventory		980
		22	Accounts Receivable—Comer Co.	3,480	
			Sales		3,480
		22	Cost of Merchandise Sold	1,400	
			Merchandise Inventory		1,400
		24	Cash	4,350	
			Sales		4,350

May	24	Cost of Merchandise Sold		1,750	
		Merchandise Inventory			1,750
	25	Sales Returns and Allowances		1,480	
		Accounts Receivable—Comer Co.			1,480
	25	Merchandise Inventory		600	
		Cost of Merchandise Sold			600
	31	Credit Card Expense		140	
		Cash			140
2.	May 31	Cost of Merchandise Sold		3,750	
		Merchandise Inventory			3,750
		Inventory shrinkage.			

Discussion Questions

1. What distinguishes a merchandising business from a service business?

2. Can a business earn a gross profit but incur a net loss? Explain.

3. Name at least three accounts that would normally appear in the chart of accounts of a merchandising business but would not appear in the chart of accounts of a service business.

4. How are sales to customers using MasterCard and VISA recorded?

5. The credit period during which the buyer of merchandise is allowed to pay usually begins with what date?

6. What is the meaning of (a) 1/15, n/60; (b) n/30; (c) n/eom?

7. What is the nature of (a) a credit memo issued by the seller of merchandise, (b) a debit memo issued by the buyer of merchandise?

8. Who bears the freight when the terms of sale are (a) FOB shipping point, (b) FOB destination?

9. Mountain Gear Inc., which uses a perpetual inventory system, experienced a normal inventory shrinkage of $21,950. What accounts would be debited and credited to record the adjustment for the inventory shrinkage at the end of the accounting period?

10. Assume that Mountain Gear Inc. in Discussion Question 9 experienced an abnormal inventory shrinkage of $263,750. Mountain Gear Inc. has decided to record the abnormal inventory shrinkage so that it would be separately disclosed on the income statement. What account would be debited for the abnormal inventory shrinkage?

Practice Exercises

Learning Objectives	Example Exercises	
OBJ. 1	EE 6-1 *p. 255*	**PE 6-1A Gross profit**

During the current year, merchandise is sold for $275,000 cash and $990,000 on account. The cost of the merchandise sold is $950,000. What is the amount of the gross profit?

OBJ. 1	EE 6-1 *p. 255*	**PE 6-1B Gross profit**

During the current year, merchandise is sold for $40,000 cash and $415,000 on account. The cost of the merchandise sold is $360,000. What is the amount of the gross profit?

OBJ. 3	EE 6-2 *p. 265*	**PE 6-2A Sales transactions**

Journalize the following merchandise transactions:

a. Sold merchandise on account, $29,000 with terms 2/10, n/30. The cost of the merchandise sold was $21,750.

b. Received payment less the discount.

OBJ. 3	EE 6-2 *p. 265*	**PE 6-2B Sales transactions**

Journalize the following merchandise transactions:

a. Sold merchandise on account, $60,000 with terms 1/10, n/30. The cost of the merchandise sold was $40,000.

b. Received payment less the discount.

OBJ. 3	EE 6-3 *p. 268*	**PE 6-3A Purchase transactions**

MR Tile Company purchased merchandise on account from a supplier for $9,000, terms 2/10, n/30. MR Tile Company returned $1,500 of the merchandise and received full credit.

a. If MR Tile Company pays the invoice within the discount period, what is the amount of cash required for the payment?

b. Under a perpetual inventory system, what account is credited by MR Tile Company to record the return?

OBJ. 3	EE 6-3 *p. 268*	**PE 6-3B Purchase transactions**

Piedmont Company purchased merchandise on account from a supplier for $30,000, terms 1/10, n/30. Piedmont Company returned $4,000 of the merchandise and received full credit.

a. If Piedmont Company pays the invoice within the discount period, what is the amount of cash required for the payment?

b. Under a perpetual inventory system, what account is debited by Piedmont Company to record the return?

OBJ. 3	EE 6-4 *p. 271*	**PE 6-4A Freight terms**

Determine the amount to be paid in full settlement of each of invoices (a) and (b), assuming that credit for returns and allowances was received prior to payment and that all invoices were paid within the discount period.

Learning Objectives	Example Exercises			Merchandise	Freight Paid by Seller	Freight Terms	Returns and Allowances
			a.	$120,000	$5,000	FOB shipping point, 1/10, n/30	$15,000
			b.	90,000	1,000	FOB destination, 2/10, n/30	2,000

OBJ. 3 EE 6-4 *p. 271*

PE 6-4B Freight terms

Determine the amount to be paid in full settlement of each of invoices (a) and (b), assuming that credit for returns and allowances was received prior to payment and that all invoices were paid within the discount period.

	Merchandise	Freight Paid by Seller	Freight Terms	Returns and Allowances
a.	$20,000	$500	FOB destination, 1/10, n/30	$2,000
b.	18,000	250	FOB shipping point, 2/10, n/30	1,000

OBJ. 3 EE 6-5 *p. 274*

PE 6-5A Transactions for buyer and seller

Storall Co. sold merchandise to Bunting Co. on account, $8,000, terms 2/15, n/30. The cost of the merchandise sold is $3,000. Storall Co. issued a credit memo for $1,000 for merchandise returned and later received the amount due within the discount period. The cost of the merchandise returned was $400. Journalize Storall Co.'s and Bunting Co.'s entries for the payment of the amount due.

OBJ. 3 EE 6-5 *p. 274*

PE 6-5B Transactions for buyer and seller

SPA Co. sold merchandise to Boyd Co. on account, $25,000, terms FOB shipping point, 2/10, n/30. The cost of the merchandise sold is $16,000. SPA Co. paid freight of $675 and later received the amount due within the discount period. Journalize SPA Co.'s and Boyd Co.'s entries for the payment of the amount due.

OBJ. 4 EE 6-6 *p. 275*

PE 6-6A Inventory shrinkage

House of Clean Company's perpetual inventory records indicate that $375,000 of merchandise should be on hand on June 30, 2012. The physical inventory indicates that $366,500 of merchandise is actually on hand. Journalize the adjusting entry for the inventory shrinkage for House of Clean Company for the year ended June 30, 2012. Assume that the inventory shrinkage is a normal amount.

OBJ. 4 EE 6-6 *p. 275*

PE 6-6B Inventory shrinkage

Zurich Company's perpetual inventory records indicate that $1,380,000 of merchandise should be on hand on August 31, 2012. The physical inventory indicates that $1,315,900 of merchandise is actually on hand. Journalize the adjusting entry for the inventory shrinkage for Zurich Company for the year ended August 31, 2012. Assume that the inventory shrinkage is a normal amount.

OBJ. 5 EE 6-7 *p. 277*

PE 6-7A Ratio of net sales to assets

The following financial statement data for years ending December 31 for Foodworks Company are shown below.

	2012	2011
Net sales	$880,000	$787,500
Total assets:		
Beginning of year	500,000	375,000
End of year	600,000	500,000

a. Determine the ratio of net sales to assets for 2012 and 2011.

b. Does the change in the ratio of net sales to assets from 2011 to 2012 indicate a favorable or an unfavorable trend?

Learning *Example*
Objectives *Exercises*

OBJ. 5 EE 6-7 *p. 277*

PE 6-7B Ratio of net sales to assets

The following financial Statement data for years ending December 31 for Beading Company are shown below.

	2012	2011
Net sales	$675,000	$475,000
Total assets:		
Beginning of year	200,000	180,000
End of year	250,000	200,000

a. Determine the ratio of net sales to assets for 2012 and 2011.

b. Does the change in the ratio of net sales to assets from 2011 to 2012 indicate a favorable or an unfavorable trend?

Exercises

OBJ. 1

EX 6-1 Determining gross profit

During the current year, merchandise is sold for $775,000. The cost of the merchandise sold is $426,250.

a. What is the amount of the gross profit?

b. Compute the gross profit percentage (gross profit divided by sales).

c. ➤ Will the income statement necessarily report a net income? Explain.

OBJ. 1

EX 6-2 Determining cost of merchandise sold

For the year ended February 28, 2009, Best Buy reported revenue of $45,015 million. Its gross profit was $10,998 million. What was the amount of Best Buy's cost of merchandise sold?

OBJ. 2

EX 6-3 Income statement for merchandiser

For the fiscal year, sales were $6,750,000, sales discounts were $120,000, sales returns and allowances were $90,000, and the cost of merchandise sold was $4,000,000.

a. What was the amount of net sales?

b. What was the amount of gross profit?

c. If total operating expenses were $1,200,000, could you determine net income?

OBJ. 2

EX 6-4 Income statement for merchandiser

The following expenses were incurred by a merchandising business during the year. In which expense section of the income statement should each be reported: (a) selling, (b) administrative, or (c) other?

1. Advertising expense
2. Depreciation expense on store equipment
3. Insurance expense on office equipment
4. Interest expense on notes payable
5. Rent expense on office building
6. Salaries of office personnel
7. Salary of sales manager
8. Sales supplies used

OBJ. 2

✔ Net income:
$1,075,000

EX 6-5 Single-step income statement

Summary operating data for Heartland Company during the current year ended November 30, 2012, are as follows: cost of merchandise sold, $2,500,000; administrative expenses, $300,000; interest expense, $20,000; rent revenue, $95,000; net sales, $4,200,000; and selling expenses, $400,000. Prepare a single-step income statement.

OBJ. 2

EX 6-6 Multiple-step income statement

Identify the errors in the following income statement:

Keepsakes Company
Income Statement
For the Year Ended February 29, 2012

Revenue from sales:			
Sales..		$7,200,000	
Add: Sales returns and allowances	$275,000		
Sales discounts	130,000	405,000	
Gross sales			$7,605,000
Cost of merchandise sold............................			4,075,000
Income from operations			$3,530,000
Expenses:			
Selling expenses..		$ 950,000	
Administrative expenses		475,000	
Delivery expense		125,000	
Total expenses			1,550,000
			$1,980,000
Other expense:			
Interest revenue			30,000
Gross profit			$1,950,000

OBJ. 2

✔ a. $30,000
✔ h. $515,000

EX 6-7 Determining amounts for items omitted from income statement

Two items are omitted in each of the following four lists of income statement data. Determine the amounts of the missing items, identifying them by letter.

Sales	$300,000	$600,000	$850,000	$ (g)
Sales returns and allowances	(a)	30,000	(e)	10,000
Sales discounts	20,000	18,000	70,000	25,000
Net sales	250,000	(c)	775,000	(h)
Cost of merchandise sold	(b)	330,000	(f)	400,000
Gross profit	100,000	(d)	300,000	115,000

OBJ. 2

✔ a. Net income:
$370,000

EX 6-8 Multiple-step income statement

On December 31, 2012, the balances of the accounts appearing in the ledger of Warm Place Furnishings Company, a furniture wholesaler, are as follows:

Administrative Expenses	$ 250,000	Rhonda Sipes, Capital	$ 741,000
Building	1,025,000	Rhonda Sipes, Drawing	50,000
Cash	97,000	Salaries Payable	6,000
Cost of Merchandise Sold	1,700,000	Sales	3,000,000
Interest Expense	30,000	Sales Discounts	40,000
Merchandise Inventory	260,000	Sales Returns and Allowances	160,000
Notes Payable	400,000	Selling Expenses	450,000
Office Supplies	20,000	Store Supplies	65,000

a. Prepare a multiple-step income statement for the year ended December 31, 2012.

b. Compare the major advantages and disadvantages of the multiple-step and single-step forms of income statements.

OBJ. 3

EX 6-9   Chart of accounts

Do-Right Paints Co. is a newly organized business with a list of accounts arranged in alphabetical order below.

Accounts Payable	Miscellaneous Administrative Expense
Accounts Receivable	Miscellaneous Selling Expense
Accumulated Depreciation—Office Equipment	Notes Payable
Accumulated Depreciation—Store Equipment	Office Equipment
Advertising Expense	Office Salaries Expense
Cash	Office Supplies
Cost of Merchandise Sold	Office Supplies Expense
Delivery Expense	Prepaid Insurance
Depreciation Expense—Office Equipment	Rent Expense
Depreciation Expense—Store Equipment	Salaries Payable
Income Summary	Sales
Insurance Expense	Sales Discounts
Interest Expense	Sales Returns and Allowances
Jamie Ricardi, Capital	Sales Salaries Expense
Jamie Ricardi, Drawing	Store Equipment
Land	Store Supplies
Merchandise Inventory	Store Supplies Expense

Construct a chart of accounts, assigning account numbers and arranging the accounts in balance sheet and income statement order, as illustrated in Exhibit 5. Each account number is three digits: the first digit is to indicate the major classification ("1" for assets, and so on); the second digit is to indicate the subclassification ("11" for current assets, and so on); and the third digit is to identify the specific account ("110" for Cash, "112" for Accounts Receivable, "114" for Merchandise Inventory, "115" for Store Supplies, and so on).

OBJ. 3

EX 6-10   Sales-related transactions, including the use of credit cards

Journalize the entries for the following transactions:

a. Sold merchandise for cash, $30,000. The cost of the merchandise sold was $18,000.

b. Sold merchandise on account, $120,000. The cost of the merchandise sold was $72,000.

c. Sold merchandise to customers who used MasterCard and VISA, $100,000. The cost of the merchandise sold was $70,000.

d. Sold merchandise to customers who used American Express, $45,000. The cost of the merchandise sold was $27,000.

e. Received an invoice from National Credit Co. for $9,000, representing a service fee paid for processing MasterCard, VISA, and American Express sales.

OBJ. 3

EX 6-11   Sales returns and allowances

During the year, sales returns and allowances totaled $80,000. The cost of the merchandise returned was $48,000. The accountant recorded all the returns and allowances by debiting the sales account and crediting Cost of Merchandise Sold for $80,000.

➤ Was the accountant's method of recording returns acceptable? Explain. In your explanation, include the advantages of using a sales returns and allowances account.

OBJ. 3

EX 6-12   Sales-related transactions

After the amount due on a sale of $40,000, terms 2/10, n/eom, is received from a customer within the discount period, the seller consents to the return of the entire shipment. The cost of the merchandise returned was $24,000. (a) What is the amount of the refund owed to the customer? (b) Journalize the entries made by the seller to record the return and the refund.

OBJ. 3

EX 6-13   Sales-related transactions

The debits and credits for three related transactions are presented in the following T accounts. Describe each transaction.

Cash		
(5)	32,340	

Accounts Receivable		
(1)	35,000	(3)	2,000
		(5)	33,000

Merchandise Inventory		
(4)	1,200	(2)	21,000

Sales		
		(1)	35,000

Sales Discounts		
(5)	660	

Sales Returns and Allowances		
(3)	2,000	

Cost of Merchandise Sold		
(2)	21,000	(4)	1,200

OBJ. 3

✔ d. $18,240

EX 6-14   Sales-related transactions

Merchandise is sold on account to a customer for $18,000, terms FOB shipping point, 2/10, n/30. The seller paid the freight of $600. Determine the following: (a) amount of the sale, (b) amount debited to Accounts Receivable, (c) amount of the discount for early payment, and (d) amount due within the discount period.

OBJ. 3

EX 6-15   Purchase-related transaction

Bergquist Company purchased merchandise on account from a supplier for $12,000, terms 1/10, n/30. Bergquist Company returned $3,000 of the merchandise and received full credit.

a. If Bergquist Company pays the invoice within the discount period, what is the amount of cash required for the payment?

b. Under a perpetual inventory system, what account is credited by Bergquist Company to record the return?

OBJ. 3

EX 6-16   Purchase-related transactions

A retailer is considering the purchase of 100 units of a specific item from either of two suppliers. Their offers are as follows:

E: $300 a unit, total of $30,000, 1/10, n/30, no charge for freight.

F: $295 a unit, total of $29,500, 2/10, n/30, plus freight of $375.

Which of the two offers, E or F, yields the lower price?

OBJ. 3

EX 6-17   Purchase-related transactions

The debits and credits from four related transactions are presented in the following T accounts. Describe each transaction.

Cash		
		(2)	400
		(4)	11,760

Merchandise Inventory		
(1)	15,000	(3)	3,000
(2)	400	(4)	240

Accounts Payable		
(3)	3,000	(1)	15,000
(4)	12,000		

OBJ. 3

✔ (c) Cash, cr. $31,360

EX 6-18   Purchase-related transactions

Mayn Co., a women's clothing store, purchased $36,000 of merchandise from a supplier on account, terms FOB destination, 2/10, n/30. Mayn Co. returned $4,000 of the merchandise, receiving a credit memo, and then paid the amount due within the discount period. Journalize Mayn Co.'s entries to record (a) the purchase, (b) the merchandise return, and (c) the payment.

OBJ. 3

✔ (e) Cash, dr. $2,400

EX 6-19 Purchase-related transactions

Journalize entries for the following related transactions of Blue Moon Company:

a. Purchased $60,000 of merchandise from Sierra Co. on account, terms 1/10, n/30.

b. Paid the amount owed on the invoice within the discount period.

c. Discovered that $10,000 of the merchandise was defective and returned items, receiving credit.

d. Purchased $7,500 of merchandise from Sierra Co. on account, terms n/30.

e. Received a check for the balance owed from the return in (c), after deducting for the purchase in (d).

OBJ. 3

✔ a. $35,000

EX 6-20 Determining amounts to be paid on invoices

Determine the amount to be paid in full settlement of each of the following invoices, assuming that credit for returns and allowances was received prior to payment and that all invoices were paid within the discount period.

	Merchandise	Freight Paid by Seller		Returns and Allowances
a.	$36,000	—	FOB destination, n/30	$1,000
b.	10,000	$375	FOB shipping point, 2/10, n/30	1,200
c.	8,250	—	FOB shipping point, 1/10, n/30	750
d.	4,000	200	FOB shipping point, 2/10, n/30	500
e.	8,500	—	FOB destination, 1/10, n/30	—

OBJ. 3

✔ c. $29,960

EX 6-21 Sales tax

A sale of merchandise on account for $28,000 is subject to a 7% sales tax. (a) Should the sales tax be recorded at the time of sale or when payment is received? (b) What is the amount of the sale? (c) What is the amount debited to Accounts Receivable? (d) What is the title of the account to which the $1,960 ($28,000 × 7%) is credited?

OBJ. 3

EX 6-22 Sales tax transactions

Journalize the entries to record the following selected transactions:

a. Sold $12,900 of merchandise on account, subject to a sales tax of 4%. The cost of the merchandise sold was $7,800.

b. Paid $32,750 to the state sales tax department for taxes collected.

OBJ. 3

EX 6-23 Sales-related transactions

Skycrest Co., a furniture wholesaler, sells merchandise to Boyle Co. on account, $45,000, terms 2/10, n/30. The cost of the merchandise sold is $27,000. Skycrest Co. issues a credit memo for $9,000 for merchandise returned and subsequently receives the amount due within the discount period. The cost of the merchandise returned is $5,400. Journalize Skycrest Co.'s entries for (a) the sale, including the cost of the merchandise sold, (b) the credit memo, including the cost of the returned merchandise, and (c) the receipt of the check for the amount due from Boyle Co.

OBJ. 3

EX 6-24 Purchase-related transactions

Based on the data presented in Exercise 6-23, journalize Boyle Co.'s entries for (a) the purchase, (b) the return of the merchandise for credit, and (c) the payment of the invoice within the discount period.

OBJ. 3

EX 6-25 Normal balances of merchandise accounts

What is the normal balance of the following accounts: (a) Cost of Merchandise Sold, (b) Delivery Expense, (c) Merchandise Inventory, (d) Sales, (e) Sales Discounts, (f) Sales Returns and Allowances, (g) Sales Tax Payable?

OBJ. 4

EX 6-26   Adjusting entry for merchandise inventory shrinkage

Old Faithful Tile Co.'s perpetual inventory records indicate that $715,950 of merchandise should be on hand on December 31, 2012. The physical inventory indicates that $693,675 of merchandise is actually on hand. Journalize the adjusting entry for the inventory shrinkage for Old Faithful Tile Co. for the year ended December 31, 2012.

OBJ. 4

EX 6-27   Closing the accounts of a merchandiser

From the following list, identify the accounts that should be closed to Income Summary at the end of the fiscal year under a perpetual inventory system: (a) Accounts Payable, (b) Advertising Expense, (c) Cost of Merchandise Sold, (d) Merchandise Inventory, (e) Sales, (f) Sales Discounts, (g) Sales Returns and Allowances, (h) Supplies, (i) Supplies Expense, (j) Tyler Royce, Drawing, (k) Wages Payable.

OBJ. 4

EX 6-28   Closing entries; net income

Based on the data presented in Exercise 6-8, journalize the closing entries.

OBJ. 4

EX 6-29   Closing entries

On August 31, 2012, the balances of the accounts appearing in the ledger of Wood Interiors Company, a furniture wholesaler, are as follows:

Accumulated Depr.—Building	$142,000	Notes Payable	$ 25,000
Administrative Expenses	90,000	Sales	800,000
Building	400,000	Sales Discounts	18,000
Cash	55,000	Sales Returns and Allow.	12,000
Cost of Merchandise Sold	350,000	Sales Tax Payable	3,000
Interest Expense	1,000	Selling Expenses	150,000
Kate Archer, Capital	172,000	Store Supplies	15,000
Kate Archer, Drawing	5,000	Store Supplies Expenses	20,000
Merchandise Inventory	26,000		

Prepare the August 31, 2012, closing entries for Wood Interiors Company.

OBJ. 5

EX 6-30   Ratio of net sales to assets

The Home Depot reported the following data (in millions) in its financial statements:

	2009	2008
Net sales	$71,288	$77,349
Total assets at the end of the year	41,164	44,324
Total assets at the beginning of the year	44,324	52,263

a. Determine the ratio of net sales to assets for The Home Depot for 2009 and 2008. Round to two decimal places.

b. What conclusions can be drawn from these ratios concerning the trend in the ability of The Home Depot to effectively use its assets to generate sales?

OBJ. 5

EX 6-31   Ratio of net sales to assets

Kroger, a national supermarket chain, reported the following data (in millions) in its financial statements for the year ended January 31, 2009:

Total revenue	$76,000
Total assets at end of year	23,211
Total assets at beginning of year	22,299

a. Compute the ratio of net sales to assets for 2009. Round to two decimal places.

b. ━━━▶ Tiffany & Co. is a large North American retailer of jewelry, with a ratio of net sales to assets of 0.95. Why would Tiffany's ratio of net sales to assets be lower than that of Kroger?

Appendix
EX 6-32 Identify items missing in determining cost of merchandise sold

For (a) through (d), identify the items designated by "X" and "Y."

a. Purchases − (X + Y) = Net purchases.

b. Net purchases + X = Cost of merchandise purchased.

c. Merchandise inventory (beginning) + Cost of merchandise purchased = X.

d. Merchandise available for sale − X = Cost of merchandise sold.

✔ a. Cost of merchandise sold, $1,948,500

Appendix
EX 6-33 Cost of merchandise sold and related items

The following data were extracted from the accounting records of Danhof Company for the year ended June 30, 2012:

Merchandise inventory, July 1, 2011	$ 250,000
Merchandise inventory, June 30, 2012	325,000
Purchases	2,100,000
Purchases returns and allowances	50,000
Purchases discounts	39,000
Sales	3,250,000
Freight in	12,500

a. Prepare the cost of merchandise sold section of the income statement for the year ended June 30, 2012, using the periodic inventory system.

b. Determine the gross profit to be reported on the income statement for the year ended June 30, 2012.

c. Would gross profit be different if the perpetual inventory system was used instead of the periodic inventory system?

Appendix
EX 6-34 Cost of merchandise sold

Based on the following data, determine the cost of merchandise sold for April:

Merchandise inventory, April 1	$ 15,000
Merchandise inventory, April 30	28,000
Purchases	290,000
Purchases returns and allowances	10,000
Purchases discounts	5,800
Freight in	4,200

Appendix
EX 6-35 Cost of merchandise sold

Based on the following data, determine the cost of merchandise sold for March:

Merchandise inventory, March 1	$100,000
Merchandise inventory, March 31	90,000
Purchases	800,000
Purchases returns and allowances	15,000
Purchases discounts	12,000
Freight in	8,000

✔ Correct cost of merchandise sold, $885,000

Appendix
EX 6-36 Cost of merchandise sold

Identify the errors in the following schedule of cost of merchandise sold for the current year ended March 31, 2012:

Cost of merchandise sold:			
Merchandise inventory, March 31, 2012			$ 75,000
Purchases		$900,000	
Plus: Purchases returns and allowances........................	$18,000		
Purchases discounts	12,000	30,000	
Gross purchases		$930,000	
Less freight in		10,000	
Cost of merchandise purchased...............................			920,000
Merchandise available for sale			$995,000
Less merchandise inventory, April 1, 2011			80,000
Cost of merchandise sold......................................			$915,000

Appendix
EX 6-37 Rules of debit and credit for periodic inventory accounts

Complete the following table by indicating for (a) through (g) whether the proper answer is debit or credit.

Account	Increase	Decrease	Normal Balance
Purchases	(a)	credit	(b)
Purchases Discounts	(c)	debit	credit
Purchases Returns and Allowances	(d)	debit	(e)
Freight in	(f)	(g)	debit

Appendix
EX 6-38 Journal entries using the periodic inventory system

The following selected transactions were completed by Burton Company during July of the current year. Burton Company uses the periodic inventory system.

July   2. Purchased $24,000 of merchandise on account, FOB shipping point, terms 2/15, n/30.

5. Paid freight of $500 on the July 2 purchase.

6. Returned $4,000 of the merchandise purchased on July 2.

13. Sold merchandise on account, $15,000, FOB destination, 1/10, n/30. The cost of merchandise sold was $9,000.

15. Paid freight of $100 for the merchandise sold on July 13.

17. Paid for the purchase of July 2 less the return and discount.

23. Received payment on account for the sale of July 13 less the discount.

Journalize the entries to record the transactions of Burton Company.

Appendix
Ex 6-39 Journal entries using perpetual inventory system

Using the data shown in Exercise 6-38, journalize the entries for the transactions assuming that Burton Company uses the perpetual inventory system.

Appendix
Ex 6-40 Closing entries using periodic inventory system

Pyramid Company is a small rug retailer owned and operated by Rosemary Endecott. After the accounts have been adjusted on January 31, the following selected account balances were taken from the ledger:

Advertising Expense	$ 40,000
Depreciation Expense	15,000
Freight In	8,000
Merchandise Inventory, January 1	250,000
Merchandise Inventory, January 31	300,000
Miscellaneous Expense	29,000
Purchases	750,000
Purchases Discounts	12,000
Purchases Returns and Allowances	8,000
Rosemary Endecott, Drawing	60,000
Salaries Expense	175,000
Sales	1,200,000
Sales Discounts	20,000
Sales Returns and Allowances	30,000

Journalize the closing entries on January 31.

Problems Series A

OBJ. 1, 2

✔ 1. Net income: $775,000

PR 6-1A Multiple-step income statement and report form of balance sheet

The following selected accounts and their current balances appear in the ledger of Carpet Land Co. for the fiscal year ended October 31, 2012:

Cash	$ 274,000	Sales Returns and Allowances	$ 70,000
Accounts Receivable	425,000	Sales Discounts	55,000
Merchandise Inventory	525,000	Cost of Merchandise Sold	3,600,000
Office Supplies	12,000	Sales Salaries Expense	925,000
Prepaid Insurance	9,000	Advertising Expense	150,000
Office Equipment	315,000	Depreciation Expense—	
Accumulated Depreciation—		Store Equipment	35,000
Office Equipment	187,000	Miscellaneous Selling Expense	40,000
Store Equipment	900,000	Office Salaries Expense	315,000
Accumulated Depreciation—		Rent Expense	115,000
Store Equipment	293,000	Depreciation Expense—	
Accounts Payable	193,000	Office Equipment	22,000
Salaries Payable	12,000	Insurance Expense	18,000
Note Payable		Office Supplies Expense	9,000
(final payment due 2037)	400,000	Miscellaneous Administrative Exp.	11,000
Maggie Young, Capital	750,000	Interest Expense	15,000
Maggie Young, Drawing	150,000		
Sales	6,155,000		

Instructions

1. Prepare a multiple-step income statement.

2. Prepare a statement of owner's equity.

3. Prepare a report form of balance sheet, assuming that the current portion of the note payable is $16,000.

4. Briefly explain (a) how multiple-step and single-step income statements differ and (b) how report-form and account-form balance sheets differ.

OBJ. 2, 4

✔ 3. Total assets: $1,980,000

PR 6-2A   Single-step income statement and account form of balance sheet

Selected accounts and related amounts for Carpet Land Co. for the fiscal year ended October 31, 2012, are presented in Problem 6-1A.

Instructions

1. Prepare a single-step income statement in the format shown in Exhibit 2.

2. Prepare a statement of owner's equity.

3. Prepare an account form of balance sheet, assuming that the current portion of the note payable is $16,000.

4. Prepare closing entries as of October 31, 2012.

OBJ. 3

PR 6-3A   Sales-related transactions

The following selected transactions were completed by Artic Supply Co., which sells office supplies primarily to wholesalers and occasionally to retail customers:

Jan. 2. Sold merchandise on account to Mammoth Co., $15,000, terms FOB destination, 1/10, n/30. The cost of the merchandise sold was $9,000.

3. Sold merchandise for $8,000 plus 8% sales tax to retail cash customers. The cost of merchandise sold was $6,000.

4. Sold merchandise on account to Sando Co., $12,500, terms FOB shipping point, n/eom. The cost of merchandise sold was $7,500.

5. Sold merchandise for $10,000 plus 8% sales tax to retail customers who used MasterCard. The cost of merchandise sold was $6,000.

12. Received check for amount due from Mammoth Co. for sale on January 2.

14. Sold merchandise to customers who used American Express cards, $9,000. The cost of merchandise sold was $5,500.

16. Sold merchandise on account to Malloy Co., $18,700, terms FOB shipping point, 1/10, n/30. The cost of merchandise sold was $11,250.

Jan. 18. Issued credit memo for $2,700 to Malloy Co. for merchandise returned from sale on January 16. The cost of the merchandise returned was $1,600.

19. Sold merchandise on account to Savin Co., $21,500, terms FOB shipping point, 2/10, n/30. Added $500 to the invoice for prepaid freight. The cost of merchandise sold was $12,900.

26. Received check for amount due from Malloy Co. for sale on January 16 less credit memo of January 18 and discount.

28. Received check for amount due from Savin Co. for sale of January 19.

31. Received check for amount due from Sando Co. for sale of January 4.

31. Paid Eagle Delivery Service $6,190 for merchandise delivered during January to customers under shipping terms of FOB destination.

Feb. 3. Paid City Bank $1,350 for service fees for handling MasterCard and American Express sales during January.

15. Paid $2,100 to state sales tax division for taxes owed on sales.

Instructions

Journalize the entries to record the transactions of Artic Supply Co.

OBJ. 3

PR 6-4A   Purchase-related transactions

The following selected transactions were completed by Gourmet Company during January of the current year:

Jan. 1. Purchased merchandise from Bearcat Co., $19,000, terms FOB destination, n/30.

3. Purchased merchandise from Alvarado Co., $28,500, terms FOB shipping point, 2/10, n/eom. Prepaid freight of $650 was added to the invoice.

4. Purchased merchandise from Fogel Co., $11,000, terms FOB destination, 2/10, n/30.

6. Issued debit memo to Fogel Co. for $1,000 of merchandise returned from purchase on January 4.

13. Paid Alvarado Co. for invoice of January 3, less discount.

14. Paid Fogel Co. for invoice of January 4, less debit memo of January 6 and discount.

19. Purchased merchandise from Unitrust Co., $32,900, terms FOB shipping point, n/eom.

19. Paid freight of $750 on January 19 purchase from Unitrust Co.

20. Purchased merchandise from Lenn Co., $10,000, terms FOB destination, 1/10, n/30.

30. Paid Lenn Co. for invoice of January 20, less discount.

31. Paid Bearcat Co. for invoice of January 1.

31. Paid Unitrust Co. for invoice of January 19.

Instructions

Journalize the entries to record the transactions of Gourmet Company for January.

OBJ. 3

PR 6-5A   Sales-related and purchase-related transactions

The following were selected from among the transactions completed by The Grill Company during April of the current year:

Apr. 3. Purchased merchandise on account from Grizzly Co., list price $60,000, trade discount 30%, terms FOB destination, 2/10, n/30.

4. Sold merchandise for cash, $23,750. The cost of the merchandise sold was $14,000.

Apr. 5. Purchased merchandise on account from Ferraro Co., $26,000, terms FOB shipping point, 2/10, n/30, with prepaid freight of $600 added to the invoice.

6. Returned $7,000 ($10,000 list price less trade discount of 30%) of merchandise purchased on April 3 from Grizzly Co.

11. Sold merchandise on account to Logan Co., list price $12,000, trade discount 25%, terms 1/10, n/30. The cost of the merchandise sold was $5,000.

13. Paid Grizzly Co. on account for purchase of April 3, less return of April 6 and discount.

14. Sold merchandise on VISA, $90,000. The cost of the merchandise sold was $55,000.

15. Paid Ferraro Co. on account for purchase of April 5, less discount.

21. Received cash on account from sale of April 11 to Logan Co., less discount.

24. Sold merchandise on account to Half Moon Co., $17,500, terms 1/10, n/30. The cost of the merchandise sold was $10,000.

28. Paid VISA service fee of $4,000.

30. Received merchandise returned by Half Moon Co. from sale on April 24, $2,500. The cost of the returned merchandise was $1,400.

Instructions
Journalize the transactions.

OBJ. 3

PR 6-6A Sales-related and purchase-related transactions for seller and buyer
The following selected transactions were completed during May between Sky Company and Big Co.:

May 1. Sky Company sold merchandise on account to Big Co., $72,000, terms FOB destination, 2/15, n/eom. The cost of the merchandise sold was $43,200.

2. Sky Company paid freight of $3,000 for delivery of merchandise sold to Big Co. on May 1.

5. Sky Company sold merchandise on account to Big Co., $48,500, terms FOB shipping point, n/eom. The cost of the merchandise sold was $30,000.

6. Big Co. returned $12,000 of merchandise purchased on account on May 1 from Sky Company. The cost of the merchandise returned was $7,200.

9. Big Co. paid freight of $1,800 on May 5 purchase from Sky Company.

15. Sky Company sold merchandise on account to Big Co., $64,000, terms FOB shipping point, 1/10, n/30. Sky Company paid freight of $2,500, which was added to the invoice. The cost of the merchandise sold was $38,400.

16. Big Co. paid Sky Company for purchase of May 1, less discount and less return of May 6.

25. Big Co. paid Sky Company on account for purchase of May 15, less discount.

31. Big Co. paid Sky Company on account for purchase of May 5.

Instructions
Journalize the May transactions for (1) Sky Company and (2) Big Co.

Appendix
PR 6-7A Purchase-related transactions using periodic inventory system
Selected transactions for Gourmet Company during January of the current year are listed in Problem 6-4A.

Instructions
Journalize the entries to record the transactions of Gourmet Company for January using the periodic inventory system.

Appendix
PR 6-8A   Sales-related and purchase-related transactions using periodic inventory system

Selected transactions for The Grill Company during April of the current year are listed in Problem 6-5A.

Instructions
Journalize the entries to record the transactions of The Grill Company for April using the periodic inventory system.

Appendix
PR 6-9A   Sales-related and purchase-related transactions for buyer and seller using periodic inventory system

Selected transactions during May between Sky Company and Big Co. are listed in Problem 6-6A.

Instructions
Journalize the entries to record the transactions for (1) Sky Company and (2) Big Co. assuming that both companies use the periodic inventory system.

✔ 2. Net income,
$345,000

Appendix
PR 6-10A   Periodic inventory accounts, multiple-step income statement, closing entries

On July 31, 2012, the balances of the accounts appearing in the ledger of Sagebrush Company are as follows:

Cash	$ 18,300	Sales Discounts	$ 8,000
Accounts Receivable	72,000	Purchases	700,000
Merchandise Inventory,		Purchases Returns and Allowances	6,000
August 1, 2011	90,000	Purchases Discounts	4,000
Office Supplies	3,000	Freight In	30,000
Prepaid Insurance	4,500	Sales Salaries Expense	300,000
Land	300,000	Advertising Expense	55,000
Store Equipment	270,000	Delivery Expense	9,000
Accumulated Depreciation—		Depreciation Expense—	
Store Equipment	55,900	Store Equipment	6,000
Office Equipment	78,500	Miscellaneous Selling Expense	10,000
Accumulated Depreciation—		Office Salaries Expense	150,000
Office Equipment	16,000	Rent Expense	30,000
Accounts Payable	27,800	Insurance Expense	3,000
Salaries Payable	3,000	Office Supplies Expense	2,000
Unearned Rent	8,300	Depreciation Expense—	
Notes Payable	50,000	Office Equipment	1,500
Peter Richards, Capital	355,300	Miscellaneous Administrative Expense	3,500
Peter Richards, Drawing	35,000	Rent Revenue	7,000
Sales	1,660,000	Interest Expense	2,000
Sales Returns and Allowances	12,000		

Instructions
1. Does Sagebrush Company use a periodic or perpetual inventory system? Explain.

2. Prepare a multiple-step income statement for Sagebrush Company for the year ended July 31, 2012. The merchandise inventory as of July 31, 2012, was $80,000.

3. Prepare the closing entries for Sagebrush Company as of July 31, 2012.

4. What would be the net income if the perpetual inventory system had been used?

Problems Series B

OBJ. 1, 2

✔ 1. Net income:
$360,000

PR 6-1B   Multiple-step income statement and report form of balance sheet

The following selected accounts and their current balances appear in the ledger of Black Lab Co. for the fiscal year ended April 30, 2012:

Cash	$ 42,000	Sales Returns and Allowances	$ 40,000
Accounts Receivable	150,000	Sales Discounts	15,000
Merchandise Inventory	180,000	Cost of Merchandise Sold	1,855,000
Office Supplies	5,000	Sales Salaries Expense	400,000
Prepaid Insurance	12,000	Advertising Expense	120,000
Office Equipment	120,000	Depreciation Expense—	
Accumulated Depreciation—		Store Equipment	15,000
Office Equipment	28,000	Miscellaneous Selling Expense	18,000
Store Equipment	500,000	Office Salaries Expense	240,000
Accumulated Depreciation—		Rent Expense	38,000
Store Equipment	87,500	Insurance Expense	24,000
Accounts Payable	48,500	Depreciation Expense—	
Salaries Payable	4,000	Office Equipment	7,000
Note Payable		Office Supplies Expense	4,000
(final payment due 2032)	140,000	Miscellaneous Administrative Exp.	6,000
Cindy Worley, Capital	386,000	Interest Expense	8,000
Cindy Worley, Drawing	45,000		
Sales	3,150,000		

Instructions

1. Prepare a multiple-step income statement.

2. Prepare a statement of owner's equity.

3. Prepare a report form of balance sheet, assuming that the current portion of the note payable is $7,000.

4. Briefly explain (a) how multiple-step and single-step income statements differ and (b) how report-form and account-form balance sheets differ.

OBJ. 2, 4

✔ 3. Total assets:
$893,500

PR 6-2B   Single-step income statement and account form of balance sheet

Selected accounts and related amounts for Black Lab Co. for the fiscal year ended April 30, 2012, are presented in Problem 6-1B.

Instructions

1. Prepare a single-step income statement in the format shown in Exhibit 2.

2. Prepare a statement of owner's equity.

3. Prepare an account form of balance sheet, assuming that the current portion of the note payable is $7,000.

4. Prepare closing entries as of April 30, 2012.

OBJ. 3

PR 6-3B   Sales-related transactions

The following selected transactions were completed by Lawn Supplies Co., which sells irrigation supplies primarily to wholesalers and occasionally to retail customers:

Mar. 1.   Sold merchandise on account to Green Grass Co., $18,000, terms FOB shipping point, n/eom. The cost of merchandise sold was $11,000.

2.   Sold merchandise for $42,000 plus 7% sales tax to retail cash customers. The cost of merchandise sold was $25,200.

5.   Sold merchandise on account to Jones Company, $30,000, terms FOB destination, 1/10, n/30. The cost of merchandise sold was $19,500.

Mar.   8.   Sold merchandise for $20,000 plus 7% sales tax to retail customers who used VISA cards. The cost of merchandise sold was $14,000.

13.   Sold merchandise to customers who used MasterCard cards, $15,800. The cost of merchandise sold was $9,500.

14.   Sold merchandise on account to Haynes Co., $8,000, terms FOB shipping point, 1/10, n/30. The cost of merchandise sold was $5,000.

15.   Received check for amount due from Jones Company for sale on March 5.

16.   Issued credit memo for $1,800 to Haynes Co. for merchandise returned from sale on March 14. The cost of the merchandise returned was $1,000.

18.   Sold merchandise on account to Horton Company, $6,850, terms FOB shipping point, 2/10, n/30. Paid $210 for freight and added it to the invoice. The cost of merchandise sold was $4,100.

24.   Received check for amount due from Haynes Co. for sale on March 14 less credit memo of March 16 and discount.

28.   Received check for amount due from Horton Company for sale of March 18.

31.   Paid First Delivery Service $5,750 for merchandise delivered during March to customers under shipping terms of FOB destination.

31.   Received check for amount due from Green Grass Co. for sale of March 1.

Apr.   3.   Paid First Federal Bank $1,650 for service fees for handling MasterCard and VISA sales during March.

10.   Paid $6,175 to state sales tax division for taxes owed on sales.

Instructions
Journalize the entries to record the transactions of Lawn Supplies Co.

OBJ. 3

PR 6-4B   Purchase-related transactions

The following selected transactions were completed by Britt Co. during October of the current year:

Oct.   1.   Purchased merchandise from Mable Co., $17,500, terms FOB shipping point, 2/10, n/eom. Prepaid freight of $300 was added to the invoice.

5.   Purchased merchandise from Conway Co., $22,600, terms FOB destination, n/30.

10.   Paid Mable Co. for invoice of October 1, less discount.

13.   Purchased merchandise from Larson Co., $12,750, terms FOB destination, 2/10, n/30.

14.   Issued debit memo to Larson Co. for $1,500 of merchandise returned from purchase on October 13.

18.   Purchased merchandise from Lakey Company, $12,250, terms FOB shipping point, n/eom.

18.   Paid freight of $275 on October 18 purchase from Lakey Company.

19.   Purchased merchandise from Adler Co., $14,200, terms FOB destination, 2/10, n/30.

23.   Paid Larson Co. for invoice of October 13, less debit memo of October 14 and discount.

29.   Paid Adler Co. for invoice of October 19, less discount.

31.   Paid Lakey Company for invoice of October 18.

31.   Paid Conway Co. for invoice of October 5.

Instructions
Journalize the entries to record the transactions of Britt Co. for October.

OBJ. 3

PR 6-5B Sales-related and purchase-related transactions

The following were selected from among the transactions completed by Wild Adventures Company during December of the current year:

Dec. 3. Purchased merchandise on account from Miramar Co., list price $45,000, trade discount 20%, terms FOB shipping point, 2/10, n/30, with prepaid freight of $1,200 added to the invoice.

5. Purchased merchandise on account from Grand Canyon Co., $19,000, terms FOB destination, 2/10, n/30.

6. Sold merchandise on account to Arches Co., list price $30,000, trade discount 25%, terms 2/10, n/30. The cost of the merchandise sold was $14,000.

7. Returned $3,000 of merchandise purchased on December 5 from Grand Canyon Co.

13. Paid Miramar Co. on account for purchase of December 3, less discount.

15. Paid Grand Canyon Co. on account for purchase of December 5, less return of December 7 and discount.

16. Received cash on account from sale of December 6 to Arches Co., less discount.

19. Sold merchandise on MasterCard, $41,950. The cost of the merchandise sold was $25,000.

22. Sold merchandise on account to Yellowstone River Co., $20,000, terms 2/10, n/30. The cost of the merchandise sold was $9,000.

23. Sold merchandise for cash, $57,500. The cost of the merchandise sold was $34,500.

28. Received merchandise returned by Yellowstone River Co. from sale on December 22, $4,000. The cost of the returned merchandise was $1,800.

31. Paid MasterCard service fee of $1,700.

Instructions
Journalize the transactions.

OBJ. 3

PR 6-6B Sales-related and purchase-related transactions for seller and buyer

The following selected transactions were completed during June between Salinas Company and Brokaw Company:

June 2. Salinas Company sold merchandise on account to Brokaw Company, $20,000, terms FOB shipping point, 2/10, n/30. Salinas Company paid freight of $675, which was added to the invoice. The cost of the merchandise sold was $12,000.

8. Salinas Company sold merchandise on account to Brokaw Company, $34,750, terms FOB destination, 1/15, n/eom. The cost of the merchandise sold was $19,850.

8. Salinas Company paid freight of $800 for delivery of merchandise sold to Brokaw Company on June 8.

12. Brokaw Company returned $5,750 of merchandise purchased on account on June 8 from Salinas Company. The cost of the merchandise returned was $3,000.

12. Brokaw Company paid Salinas Company for purchase of June 2, less discount.

23. Brokaw Company paid Salinas Company for purchase of June 8, less discount and less return of June 12.

24. Salinas Company sold merchandise on account to Brokaw Company, $31,800, terms FOB shipping point, n/eom. The cost of the merchandise sold was $20,500.

26. Brokaw Company paid freight of $475 on June 24 purchase from Salinas Company.

30. Brokaw Company paid Salinas Company on account for purchase of June 24.

Instructions
Journalize the June transactions for (1) Salinas Company and (2) Brokaw Company.

Appendix
PR 6-7B Purchase-related transactions using periodic inventory system

Selected transactions for Britt Co. during October of the current year are listed in Problem 6-4B.

Instructions

Journalize the entries to record the transactions of Britt Co. for October using the periodic inventory system.

Appendix
PR 6-8B Sales-related and purchase-related transactions using periodic inventory system

Selected transactions for Wild Adventures Company during December of the current year are listed in Problem 6-5B.

Instructions

Journalize the entries to record the transactions of Wild Adventures Company for December using the periodic inventory system.

Appendix
PR 6-9B Sales-related and purchase-related transactions for buyer and seller using periodic inventory system

Selected transactions during June between Salinas Company and Brokaw Company are listed in Problem 6-6B.

Instructions

Journalize the entries to record the transactions for (1) Salinas Company and (2) Brokaw Company assuming that both companies use the periodic inventory system.

✔ 2. Net income, $395,000

Appendix
PR 6-10B Periodic inventory accounts, multiple-step income statement, closing entries

On April 30, 2012, the balances of the accounts appearing in the ledger of Heritage Company are as follows:

Cash	$ 60,000	Sales Discounts	$ 35,000
Accounts Receivable	150,000	Purchases	1,770,000
Merchandise Inventory, May 1, 2011	290,000	Purchases Returns and Allowances	12,000
Office Supplies	7,000	Purchases Discounts	8,000
Prepaid Insurance	18,000	Freight In	25,000
Land	70,000	Sales Salaries Expense	450,000
Store Equipment	400,000	Advertising Expense	200,000
Accumulated Depreciation—		Delivery Expense	18,000
Store Equipment	190,000	Depreciation Expense—	
Office Equipment	250,000	Store Equipment	12,000
Accumulated Depreciation—		Miscellaneous Selling Expense	28,000
Office Equipment	110,000	Office Salaries Expense	200,000
Accounts Payable	85,000	Rent Expense	45,000
Salaries Payable	9,000	Insurance Expense	6,000
Unearned Rent	6,000	Office Supplies Expense	5,000
Notes Payable	50,000	Depreciation Expense—	
Mary Diaz, Capital	525,000	Office Equipment	3,000
Mary Diaz, Drawing	100,000	Miscellaneous Administrative Expense	13,000
Sales	3,175,000	Rent Revenue	27,000
Sales Returns and Allowances	40,000	Interest Expense	2,000

Instructions

1. Does Heritage Company use a periodic or perpetual inventory system? Explain.

2. Prepare a multiple-step income statement for Heritage Company for the year ended April 30, 2012. The merchandise inventory as of April 30, 2012, was $315,000.

3. Prepare the closing entries for Heritage Company as of April 30, 2012.

4. What would be the net income if the perpetual inventory system had been used?

Comprehensive Problem 2

✔ 8. Net income:
$710,760

Ocean Atlantic Co. is a merchandising business. The account balances for Ocean Atlantic Co. as of July 1, 2012 (unless otherwise indicated), are as follows:

110	Cash	$ 63,600
112	Accounts Receivable	153,900
115	Merchandise Inventory	602,400
116	Prepaid Insurance	16,800
117	Store Supplies	11,400
123	Store Equipment	469,500
124	Accumulated Depreciation—Store Equipment	56,700
210	Accounts Payable	96,600
211	Salaries Payable	—
310	Kevin Gilmour, Capital, August 1, 2011	555,300
311	Kevin Gilmour, Drawing	135,000
312	Income Summary	—
410	Sales	3,221,100
411	Sales Returns and Allowances	92,700
412	Sales Discounts	59,400
510	Cost of Merchandise Sold	1,623,000
520	Sales Salaries Expense	334,800
521	Advertising Expense	81,000
522	Depreciation Expense	—
523	Store Supplies Expense	—
529	Miscellaneous Selling Expense	12,600
530	Office Salaries Expense	182,100
531	Rent Expense	83,700
532	Insurance Expense	—
539	Miscellaneous Administrative Expense	7,800

During July, the last month of the fiscal year, the following transactions were completed:

July 1. Paid rent for July, $4,000.

3. Purchased merchandise on account from Lingard Co., terms 2/10, n/30, FOB shipping point, $25,000.

4. Paid freight on purchase of July 3, $1,000.

6. Sold merchandise on account to Holt Co., terms 2/10, n/30, FOB shipping point, $40,000. The cost of the merchandise sold was $24,000.

7. Received $18,000 cash from Flatt Co. on account, no discount.

10. Sold merchandise for cash, $90,000. The cost of the merchandise sold was $50,000.

13. Paid for merchandise purchased on July 3, less discount.

14. Received merchandise returned on sale of July 6, $7,000. The cost of the merchandise returned was $4,500.

15. Paid advertising expense for last half of July, $9,000.

16. Received cash from sale of July 6, less return of July 14 and discount.

19. Purchased merchandise for cash, $22,000.

19. Paid $23,100 to Carino Co. on account, no discount.

Record the following transactions on Page 21 of the journal.

20. Sold merchandise on account to Reedley Co., terms 1/10, n/30, FOB shipping point, $40,000. The cost of the merchandise sold was $25,000.

21. For the convenience of the customer, paid freight on sale of July 20, $1,100.

21. Received $17,600 cash from Owen Co. on account, no discount.

21. Purchased merchandise on account from Munson Co., terms 1/10, n/30, FOB destination, $32,000.

July 24. Returned $5,000 of damaged merchandise purchased on July 21, receiving credit from the seller.

26. Refunded cash on sales made for cash, $12,000. The cost of the merchandise returned was $7,200.

28. Paid sales salaries of $22,800 and office salaries of $15,200.

29. Purchased store supplies for cash, $2,400.

30. Sold merchandise on account to Dix Co., terms 2/10, n/30, FOB shipping point, $18,750. The cost of the merchandise sold was $11,250.

30. Received cash from sale of July 20, less discount, plus freight paid on July 21.

31. Paid for purchase of July 21, less return of July 24 and discount.

Instructions

1. Enter the balances of each of the accounts in the appropriate balance column of a four-column account. Write *Balance* in the item section, and place a check mark (✓) in the Posting Reference column. Journalize the transactions for July starting on Page 20 of the journal.

2. Post the journal to the general ledger, extending the month-end balances to the appropriate balance columns after all posting is completed. In this problem, you are not required to update or post to the accounts receivable and accounts payable subsidiary ledgers.

3. Prepare an unadjusted trial balance.

4. At the end of July, the following adjustment data were assembled. Analyze and use these data to complete (5) and (6).

a.	Merchandise inventory on July 31		$565,000
b.	Insurance expired during the year		13,400
c.	Store supplies on hand on July 31		3,900
d.	Depreciation for the current year		11,500
e.	Accrued salaries on July 31:		
	Sales salaries	$3,200	
	Office salaries	1,300	4,500

5. **Optional:** Enter the unadjusted trial balance on a 10-column end-of-period spreadsheet (work sheet), and complete the spreadsheet.

6. Journalize and post the adjusting entries. Record the adjusting entries on Page 22 of the journal.

7. Prepare an adjusted trial balance.

8. Prepare an income statement, a statement of owner's equity, and a balance sheet.

9. Prepare and post the closing entries. Record the closing entries on Page 23 of the journal. Indicate closed accounts by inserting a line in both the Balance columns opposite the closing entry. Insert the new balance in the owner's capital account.

10. Prepare a post-closing trial balance.

Cases & Projects

CP 6-1 Ethics and professional conduct in business

On March 13, 2012, Plant-Wise Company, a garden retailer, purchased $18,000 of seed, terms 2/10, n/30, from Premium Seed Co. Even though the discount period had expired, Brendan Morton subtracted the discount of $360 when he processed the documents for payment on March 26, 2012.

━━━━━━ Discuss whether Brendan Morton behaved in a professional manner by subtracting the discount, even though the discount period had expired.

CP 6-2 Purchases discounts and accounts payable

Bud's Video Store Co. is owned and operated by Jim Budeski. The following is an excerpt from a conversation between Jim Budeski and Ann Pavik, the chief accountant for Bud's Video Store.

Jim: Ann, I've got a question about this recent balance sheet.

Ann: Sure, what's your question?

Jim: Well, as you know, I'm applying for a bank loan to finance our new store in Coronado, and I noticed that the accounts payable are listed as $235,000.

Ann: That's right. Approximately $190,000 of that represents amounts due our suppliers, and the remainder is miscellaneous payables to creditors for utilities, office equipment, supplies, etc.

Jim: That's what I thought. But as you know, we normally receive a 2% discount from our suppliers for earlier payment, and we always try to take the discount.

Ann: That's right. I can't remember the last time we missed a discount.

Jim: Well, in that case, it seems to me the accounts payable should be listed minus the 2% discount. Let's list the accounts payable due suppliers as $186,200, rather than $190,000. Every little bit helps. You never know. It might make the difference between getting the loan and not.

➤ How would you respond to Jim Budeski's request?

CP 6-3 Determining cost of purchase

The following is an excerpt from a conversation between Jon Akers and Deb Flack. Jon is debating whether to buy a stereo system from Old Town Audio, a locally owned electronics store, or Sound Pro, an online electronics company.

Jon: Deb, I don't know what to do about buying my new stereo.

Deb: What's the problem?

Jon: Well, I can buy it locally at Old Town Audio for $1,400.00. However, Sound Pro has the same system listed for $1,150.00.

Deb: So what's the big deal? Buy it from Sound Pro.

Jon: It's not quite that simple. Sound Pro charges $39.99 for shipping and handling. If I have them send it next-day air, it'll cost $69.99 for shipping and handling.

Deb: I guess it is a little confusing.

Jon: That's not all. Old Town Audio will give an additional 2% discount if I pay cash. Otherwise, they will let me use my VISA, or I can pay it off in three monthly installments. In addition, if I buy it from Old Town Audio I have to pay 8% sales tax. I won't have to pay sales tax if I buy it from Sound Pro since they are out of state.

Deb: Anything else???

Jon: Well ... Sound Pro says I have to charge it on my VISA. They don't accept checks.

Deb: I am not surprised. Many online stores don't accept checks.

Jon: I give up. What would you do?

1. Assuming that Sound Pro doesn't charge sales tax on the sale to Jon, which company is offering the best buy?
2. ➤ What might be some considerations other than price that might influence Jon's decision on where to buy the stereo system?

CP 6-4 Sales discounts

Your sister operates Budget Parts Company, an online boat parts distributorship that is in its third year of operation. The income statement is shown below and was recently prepared for the year ended July 31, 2012.

Budget Parts Company
Income Statement
For the Year Ended July 31, 2012

Revenues:		
Net sales		$600,000
Interest revenue		7,500
Total revenues		$607,500
Expenses:		
Cost of merchandise sold	$360,000	
Selling expenses	67,500	
Administrative expenses	36,000	
Interest expense	11,250	
Total expenses		474,750
Net income		$132,750

Your sister is considering a proposal to increase net income by offering sales discounts of 2/15, n/30, and by shipping all merchandise FOB shipping point. Currently, no sales discounts are allowed and merchandise is shipped FOB destination. It is estimated that these credit terms will increase net sales by 15%. The ratio of the cost of merchandise sold to net sales is expected to be 60%. All selling and administrative expenses are expected to remain unchanged, except for store supplies, miscellaneous selling, office supplies, and miscellaneous administrative expenses, which are expected to increase proportionately with increased net sales. The amounts of these preceding items for the year ended July 31, 2012, were as follows:

Store supplies expense	$9,000
Miscellaneous selling expense	2,400
Office supplies expense	2,000
Miscellaneous administrative expense	1,000

The other income and other expense items will remain unchanged. The shipment of all merchandise FOB shipping point will eliminate all delivery expense, which for the year ended July 31, 2012, were $12,000.

1. Prepare a projected single-step income statement for the year ending July 31, 2013, based on the proposal. Assume all sales are collected within the discount period.

2. a. ▬▬▶ Based on the projected income statement in (1), would you recommend the implementation of the proposed changes?

   b. Describe any possible concerns you may have related to the proposed changes described in (1).

CP 6-5 Shopping for a television

Group Project
Assume that you are planning to purchase a 52-inch LCD, flat screen television. In groups of three or four, determine the lowest cost for the television, considering the available alternatives and the advantages and disadvantages of each alternative. For example, you could purchase locally, through mail order, or through an Internet shopping service. Consider such factors as delivery charges, interest-free financing, discounts, coupons, and availability of warranty services. Prepare a report for presentation to the class.

© Ryan McVay/Digital Vision/Getty Images

Inventories

Best Buy

Assume that in September you purchased a Sony HDTV plasma television from **Best Buy**. At the same time, you purchased a Denon surround sound system for $399.99. You liked your surround sound so well that in November you purchased an identical Denon system on sale for $349.99 for your bedroom TV. Over the holidays, you moved to a new apartment and in the process of unpacking discovered that one of the Denon surround sound systems was missing. Luckily, your renters/homeowners insurance policy will cover the theft, but the insurance company needs to know the cost of the system that was stolen.

The Denon systems were identical. However, to respond to the insurance company, you will need to identify which system was stolen. Was it the first system, which cost $399.99, or was it the second system, which cost $349.99? Whichever assumption you make may determine the amount that you receive from the insurance company.

Merchandising businesses such as Best Buy make similar assumptions when identical merchandise is purchased at different costs. For example, Best Buy may have purchased thousands of Denon surround sound systems over the past year at different costs. At the end of a period, some of the Denon systems will still be in inventory, and some will have been sold. But which costs relate to the sold systems, and which costs relate to the Denon systems still in inventory? Best Buy's assumption about inventory costs can involve large dollar amounts and, thus, can have a significant impact on the financial statements. For example, Best Buy reported $4,753 million of inventory on February 28, 2009, and net income of $1,003 million for the year.

This chapter discusses such issues as how to determine the cost of merchandise in inventory and the cost of merchandise sold. However, this chapter begins by discussing the importance of control over inventory.

Control of Inventory

OBJ. 1 Describe the importance of control over inventory.

Two primary objectives of control over inventory are as follows:[1]

1. Safeguarding the inventory from damage or theft.
2. Reporting inventory in the financial statements.

Safeguarding Inventory

Controls for safeguarding inventory begin as soon as the inventory is ordered. The following documents are often used for inventory control:

Purchase order
Receiving report
Vendor's invoice

The **purchase order** authorizes the purchase of the inventory from an approved vendor. As soon as the inventory is received, a receiving report is completed. The **receiving report** establishes an initial record of the receipt of the inventory. To make

---

1 Additional controls used by businesses are described and illustrated in Chapter 8, "Sarbanes-Oxley, Internal Control, and Cash."

sure the inventory received is what was ordered, the receiving report is compared with the company's purchase order. The price, quantity, and description of the item on the purchase order and receiving report are then compared to the vendor's invoice. If the receiving report, purchase order, and vendor's invoice agree, the inventory is recorded in the accounting records. If any differences exist, they should be investigated and reconciled.

Recording inventory using a perpetual inventory system is also an effective means of control. The amount of inventory is always available in the **subsidiary inventory ledger**. This helps keep inventory quantities at proper levels. For example, comparing inventory quantities with maximum and minimum levels allows for the timely reordering of inventory and prevents ordering excess inventory.

Finally, controls for safeguarding inventory should include security measures to prevent damage and customer or employee theft. Some examples of security measures include the following:

1. Storing inventory in areas that are restricted to only authorized employees.
2. Locking high-priced inventory in cabinets.
3. Using two-way mirrors, cameras, security tags, and guards.

Best Buy uses scanners to screen customers as they leave the store for merchandise that has not been purchased. In addition, Best Buy stations greeters at the store's entrance to keep customers from bringing in bags that can be used to shoplift merchandise.

Reporting Inventory

A **physical inventory** or count of inventory should be taken near year-end to make sure that the quantity of inventory reported in the financial statements is accurate. After the quantity of inventory on hand is determined, the cost of the inventory is assigned for reporting in the financial statements. Most companies assign costs to inventory using one of three inventory cost flow assumptions. If a physical count is not possible or inventory records are not available, the inventory cost may be estimated as described in the appendix at the end of this chapter.

Inventory Cost Flow Assumptions

OBJ. 2 Describe three inventory cost flow assumptions and how they impact the income statement and balance sheet.

An accounting issue arises when identical units of merchandise are acquired at different unit costs during a period. In such cases, when an item is sold, it is necessary to determine its cost using a cost flow assumption and related inventory cost flow method. Three common cost flow assumptions and related inventory cost flow methods are shown below.

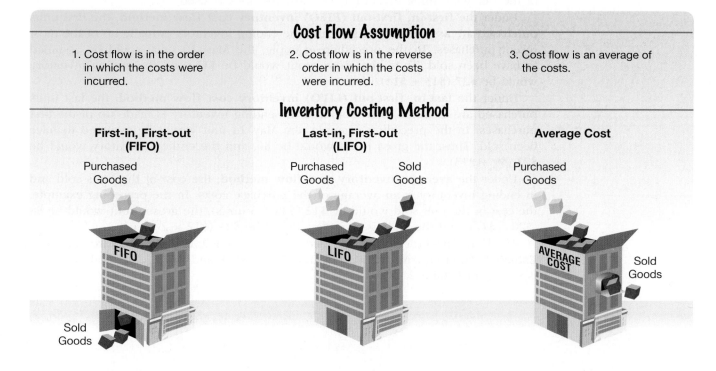

Cost Flow Assumption

1. Cost flow is in the order in which the costs were incurred.

2. Cost flow is in the reverse order in which the costs were incurred.

3. Cost flow is an average of the costs.

Inventory Costing Method

First-in, First-out (FIFO)

Last-in, First-out (LIFO)

Average Cost

To illustrate, assume that three identical units of merchandise are purchased during May, as follows:

			Units	Cost
May	10	Purchase	1	$ 9
	18	Purchase	1	13
	24	Purchase	1	14
Total			3	$36

Average cost per unit: $12 ($36 ÷ 3 units)

Assume that one unit is sold on May 30 for $20. Depending upon which unit was sold, the gross profit varies from $11 to $6 as shown below.

	May 10 Unit Sold	May 18 Unit Sold	May 24 Unit Sold
Sales	$20	$20	$20
Cost of merchandise sold	9	13	14
Gross profit	$11	$ 7	$ 6
Ending inventory	$27	$23	$22
	($13 + $14)	($9 + $14)	($9 + $13)

The specific identification method is normally used by automobile dealerships, jewelry stores, and art galleries.

Under the **specific identification inventory cost flow method**, the unit sold is identified with a specific purchase. The ending inventory is made up of the remaining units on hand. Thus, the gross profit, cost of merchandise sold, and ending inventory can vary as shown above. For example, if the May 18 unit was sold, the cost of merchandise sold is $13, the gross profit is $7, and the ending inventory is $23.

The specific identification method is not practical unless each inventory unit can be separately identified. For example, an automobile dealer may use the specific identification method since each automobile has a unique serial number. However, most businesses cannot identify each inventory unit separately. In such cases, one of the following three inventory cost flow methods is used.

Under the **first-in, first-out (FIFO) inventory cost flow method**, the first units purchased are assumed to be sold and the ending inventory is made up of the most recent purchases. In the preceding example, the May 10 unit would be assumed to have been sold. Thus, the gross profit would be $11, and the ending inventory would be $27 ($13 + $14).

Under the **last-in, first-out (LIFO) inventory cost flow method**, the last units purchased are assumed to be sold and the ending inventory is made up of the first purchases. In the preceding example, the May 24 unit would be assumed to have been sold. Thus, the gross profit would be $6, and the ending inventory would be $22 ($9 + $13).

Under the **average inventory cost flow method**, the cost of the units sold and in ending inventory is an average of the purchase costs. In the preceding example, the cost of the unit sold would be $12 ($36 ÷ 3 units), the gross profit would be $8 ($20 – $12), and the ending inventory would be $24 ($12 × 2 units).

The three inventory cost flow methods, FIFO, LIFO, and average, are shown in Exhibit 1. The frequency with which the FIFO, LIFO, and average methods are used is shown in Exhibit 2.

EXHIBIT 1 **Inventory Costing Methods**

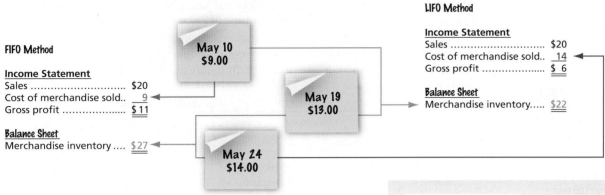

Purchases

FIFO Method

Income Statement
Sales $20
Cost of merchandise sold.. __9__
Gross profit .... $ 11

Balance Sheet
Merchandise inventory $27

LIFO Method

Income Statement
Sales $20
Cost of merchandise sold.. __14__
Gross profit .... $ 6

Balance Sheet
Merchandise inventory..... $22

Average Cost
[($9 + $13 + $14)/3 = $12]

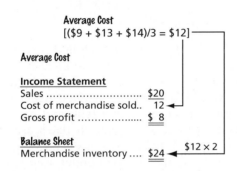

Average Cost

Income Statement
Sales $20
Cost of merchandise sold.. __12__
Gross profit .... $ 8

Balance Sheet
Merchandise inventory .... $24 $12 × 2

EXHIBIT 2 **Use of Inventory Costing Methods***

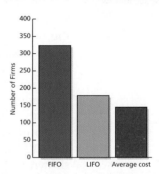

Source: *Accounting Trends and Techniques*, 63rd edition, 2009
(New York: American Institute of Certified Public Accountants).
*Firms may be counted more than once for using multiple methods.

Example Exercise 7-1   Cost Flow Methods   OBJ. 2

Three identical units of Item QBM are purchased during February, as shown below.

Item QBM		Units	Cost
Feb. 8	Purchase	1	$ 45
15	Purchase	1	48
26	Purchase	1	51
Total		3	$144
Average cost per unit			$ 48 ($144 ÷ 3 units)

Assume that one unit is sold on February 27 for $70.

Determine the gross profit for February and ending inventory on February 28 using the (a) first-in, first-out (FIFO); (b) last-in, first-out (LIFO); and (c) average cost methods.

Follow My Example 7-1

	Gross Profit	Ending Inventory
a. First-in, first-out (FIFO)................	$25 ($70 − $45)	$99 ($48 + $51)
b. Last-in, first-out (LIFO)................	$19 ($70 − $51)	$93 ($45 + $48)
c. Average cost	$22 ($70 − $48)	$96 ($48 × 2)

Practice Exercises: **PE 7-1A, PE 7-1B**

OBJ. 3 Determine the cost of inventory under the perpetual inventory system, using the FIFO, LIFO, and average cost methods.

Inventory Costing Methods Under a Perpetual Inventory System

As illustrated in the prior section, when identical units of an item are purchased at different unit costs, an inventory cost flow method must be used. This is true regardless of whether the perpetual or periodic inventory system is used.

In this section, the FIFO, LIFO, and average cost methods are illustrated under a perpetual inventory system. For purposes of illustration, the data for Item 127B are used, as shown below.

Item 127B		Units	Cost
Jan. 1	Inventory	100	$20
4	Sale at $30 per unit	70	
10	Purchase	80	21
22	Sale at $30 per unit	40	
28	Sale at $30 per unit	20	
30	Purchase	100	22

First-In, First-Out Method

When the FIFO method is used, costs are included in cost of merchandise sold in the order in which they were purchased. This is often the same as the physical flow of the merchandise. Thus, the FIFO method often provides results that are about the same as those that would have been obtained using the specific identification method. For example, grocery stores shelve milk and other perishable products by expiration dates. Products with early expiration dates are stocked in front. In this way, the oldest products (earliest purchases) are sold first.

To illustrate, Exhibit 3 shows use of FIFO under a perpetual inventory system for Item 127B. The journal entries and the subsidiary inventory ledger for Item 127B are shown in Exhibit 3 as follows:

1. The beginning balance on January 1 is $2,000 (100 units at a unit cost of $20).
2. On January 4, 70 units were sold at a price of $30 each for sales of $2,100 (70 units × $30). The cost of merchandise sold is $1,400 (70 units at a unit cost of $20). After the sale, there remains $600 of inventory (30 units at a unit cost of $20).

EXHIBIT 3 **Entries and Perpetual Inventory Account (FIFO)**

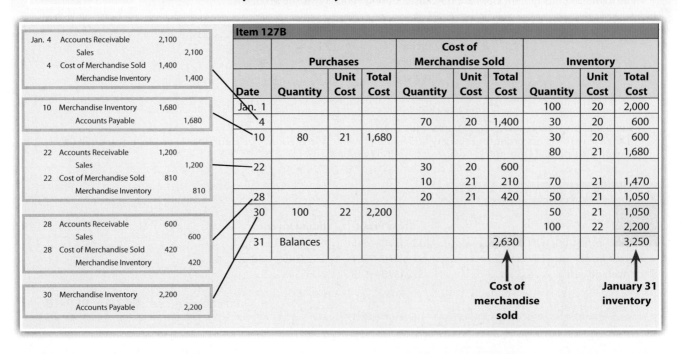

Jan. 4	Accounts Receivable	2,100	
	Sales		2,100
4	Cost of Merchandise Sold	1,400	
	Merchandise Inventory		1,400
10	Merchandise Inventory	1,680	
	Accounts Payable		1,680
22	Accounts Receivable	1,200	
	Sales		1,200
22	Cost of Merchandise Sold	810	
	Merchandise Inventory		810
28	Accounts Receivable	600	
	Sales		600
28	Cost of Merchandise Sold	420	
	Merchandise Inventory		420
30	Merchandise Inventory	2,200	
	Accounts Payable		2,200

Item 127B

		Purchases			Cost of Merchandise Sold			Inventory		
Date	Quantity	Unit Cost	Total Cost	Quantity	Unit Cost	Total Cost	Quantity	Unit Cost	Total Cost
Jan. 1							100	20	2,000
4				70	20	1,400	30	20	600
10	80	21	1,680				30	20	600
							80	21	1,680
22				30	20	600			
				10	21	210	70	21	1,470
28				20	21	420	50	21	1,050
30	100	22	2,200				50	21	1,050
							100	22	2,200
31	Balances					2,630			3,250

Cost of merchandise sold

January 31 inventory

3. On January 10, $1,680 is purchased (80 units at a unit cost of $21). After the purchase, the inventory is reported on two lines, $600 (30 units at a unit cost of $20) from the beginning inventory and $1,680 (80 units at a unit cost of $21) from the January 10 purchase.

4. On January 22, 40 units are sold at a price of $30 each for sales of $1,200 (40 units × $30). Using FIFO, the cost of merchandise sold of $810 consists of $600 (30 units at a unit cost of $20) from the beginning inventory plus $210 (10 units at a unit cost of $21) from the January 10 purchase. After the sale, there remains $1,470 of inventory (70 units at a unit cost of $21) from the January 10 purchase.

5. The January 28 sale and January 30 purchase are recorded in a similar manner.

6. The ending balance on January 31 is $3,250. This balance is made up of two layers of inventory as follows:

	Date of Purchase	Quantity	Unit Cost	Total Cost
Layer 1:	Jan. 10	50	$21	$1,050
Layer 2:	Jan. 30	100	22	2,200
Total		150		$3,250

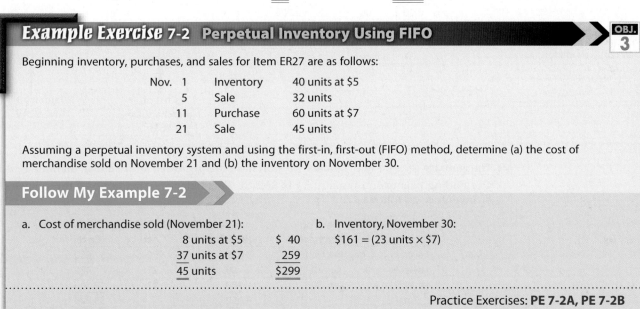

Example Exercise 7-2   Perpetual Inventory Using FIFO

OBJ. 3

Beginning inventory, purchases, and sales for Item ER27 are as follows:

Nov.	1	Inventory	40 units at $5
	5	Sale	32 units
	11	Purchase	60 units at $7
	21	Sale	45 units

Assuming a perpetual inventory system and using the first-in, first-out (FIFO) method, determine (a) the cost of merchandise sold on November 21 and (b) the inventory on November 30.

Follow My Example 7-2

a. Cost of merchandise sold (November 21):

8 units at $5	$ 40
37 units at $7	259
45 units	$299

b. Inventory, November 30:

$161 = (23 units × $7)

Practice Exercises: **PE 7-2A, PE 7-2B**

Last-In, First-Out Method

When the LIFO method is used, the cost of the units sold is the cost of the most recent purchases. The LIFO method was originally used in those rare cases where the units sold were taken from the most recently purchased units. However, for tax purposes, LIFO is now widely used even when it does not represent the physical flow of units. The tax impact of LIFO is discussed later in this chapter.

See Appendix D for more information

To illustrate, Exhibit 4 shows the use of LIFO under a perpetual inventory system for Item 127B. The journal entries and the subsidiary inventory ledger for Item 127B are shown in Exhibit 4 as follows:

1. The beginning balance on January 1 is $2,000 (100 units at a unit of cost of $20).

2. On January 4, 70 units were sold at a price of $30 each for sales of $2,100 (70 units × $30). The cost of merchandise sold is $1,400 (70 units at a unit cost of $20). After the sale, there remains $600 of inventory (30 units at a unit cost of $20).

3. On January 10, $1,680 is purchased (80 units at a unit cost of $21). After the purchase, the inventory is reported on two lines, $600 (30 units at a unit cost of $20) from the beginning inventory and $1,680 (80 units at $21 per unit) from the January 10 purchase.

4. On January 22, 40 units are sold at a price of $30 each for sales of $1,200 (40 units × $30). Using LIFO, the cost of merchandise sold is $840 (40 units at unit cost of $21) from the January 10 purchase. After the sale, there remains $1,440 of inventory consisting of $600 (30 units at a unit cost of $20) from the beginning inventory and $840 (40 units at a unit cost of $21) from the January 10 purchase.

EXHIBIT 4 Entries and Perpetual Inventory Account (LIFO)

Jan. 4	Accounts Receivable	2,100	
	Sales		2,100
4	Cost of Merchandise Sold	1,400	
	Merchandise Inventory		1,400

| 10 | Merchandise Inventory | 1,680 | |
| | Accounts Payable | | 1,680 |

22	Accounts Receivable	1,200	
	Sales		1,200
22	Cost of Merchandise Sold	840	
	Merchandise Inventory		840

28	Accounts Receivable	600	
	Sales		600
28	Cost of Merchandise Sold	420	
	Merchandise Inventory		420

| 30 | Merchandise Inventory | 2,200 | |
| | Accounts Payable | | 2,200 |

Item 127B

| | | Purchases | | | Cost of Merchandise Sold | | | Inventory | | |
| | | | Unit | Total | | Unit | Total | | Unit | Total |
Date	Quantity	Cost	Cost	Quantity	Cost	Cost	Quantity	Cost	Cost
Jan. 1							100	20	2,000
4				70	20	1,400	30	20	600
10	80	21	1,680				30	20	600
							80	21	1,680
22				40	21	840	30	20	600
							40	21	840
28				20	21	420	30	20	600
							20	21	420
30	100	22	2,200				30	20	600
							20	21	420
							100	22	2,200
31	Balances					2,660			3,220

↑ Cost of merchandise sold

↑ January 31 inventory

5. The January 28 sale and January 30 purchase are recorded in a similar manner.

6. The ending balance on January 31 is $3,220. This balance is made up of three layers of inventory as follows:

	Date of Purchase	Quantity	Unit Cost	Total Cost
Layer 1:	Beg. inv. (Jan. 1)	30	$20	$ 600
Layer 2:	Jan. 10	20	21	420
Layer 3:	Jan. 30	100	22	2,200
Total		150		$3,220

When the LIFO method is used, the subsidiary inventory ledger is sometimes maintained in units only. The units are converted to dollars when the financial statements are prepared at the end of the period.

Example Exercise 7-3 Perpetual Inventory Using LIFO

OBJ. 3

Beginning inventory, purchases, and sales for Item ER27 are as follows:

Nov.	1	Inventory	40 units at $5
	5	Sale	32 units
	11	Purchase	60 units at $7
	21	Sale	45 units

Assuming a perpetual inventory system and using the last-in, first-out (LIFO) method, determine (a) the cost of the merchandise sold on November 21 and (b) the inventory on November 30.

Follow My Example 7-3

a. Cost of merchandise sold (November 21):
$315 = (45 units × $7)

b. Inventory, November 30:

8 units at $5	$ 40
15 units at $7	105
23 units	$145

Practice Exercises: PE 7-3A, PE 7-3B

Average Cost Method

When the average cost method is used in a perpetual inventory system, an average unit cost for each item is computed each time a purchase is made. This unit cost is used to determine the cost of each sale until another purchase is made and a new average is computed. This technique is called a *moving average.* Since the average cost method is rarely used in a perpetual inventory system, it is not illustrated.

Computerized Perpetual Inventory Systems

A perpetual inventory system may be used in a manual accounting system. However, if there are many inventory transactions, such a system is costly and time consuming. In most cases, perpetual inventory systems are computerized.

Computerized perpetual inventory systems are useful to managers in controlling and managing inventory. For example, fast-selling items can be reordered before the stock runs out. Sales patterns can also be analyzed to determine when to mark down merchandise or when to restock seasonal merchandise. Finally, inventory data can be used in evaluating advertising campaigns and sales promotions.

Inventory Costing Methods Under a Periodic Inventory System

OBJ. 4 Determine the cost of inventory under the periodic inventory system, using the FIFO, LIFO, and average cost methods.

When the periodic inventory system is used, only revenue is recorded each time a sale is made. No entry is made at the time of the sale to record the cost of the merchandise sold. At the end of the accounting period, a physical inventory is taken to determine the cost of the inventory and the cost of the merchandise sold.[2]

Like the perpetual inventory system, a cost flow assumption must be made when identical units are acquired at different unit costs during a period. In such cases, the FIFO, LIFO, or average cost method is used.

First-In, First-Out Method

To illustrate the use of the FIFO method in a periodic inventory system, we use the same data for Item 127B as in the perpetual inventory example. The beginning inventory entry and purchases of Item 127B in January are as follows:

Jan. 1	Inventory	100 units at	$20	$2,000
10	Purchase	80 units at	21	1,680
30	Purchase	100 units at	22	2,200
Available for sale during month	280			$5,880

2 Determining the cost of merchandise sold using the periodic system was illustrated in the appendix to Chapter 6.

The physical count on January 31 shows that 150 units are on hand. Using the FIFO method, the cost of the merchandise on hand at the end of the period is made up of the most recent costs. The cost of the 150 units in ending inventory on January 31 is determined as follows:

Most recent costs, January 30 purchase	100 units at	$22	$2,200
Next most recent costs, January 10 purchase	50 units at	$21	1,050
Inventory, January 31	150 units		$3,250

Deducting the cost of the January 31 inventory of $3,250 from the cost of merchandise available for sale of $5,880 yields the cost of merchandise sold of $2,630, as shown below.

Beginning inventory, January 1	$2,000
Purchases ($1,680 + $2,200)	3,880
Cost of merchandise available for sale in January	$5,880
Less ending inventory, January 31	3,250
Cost of merchandise sold	$2,630

The $3,250 cost of the ending merchandise inventory on January 31 is made up of the most recent costs. The $2,630 cost of merchandise sold is made up of the beginning inventory and the earliest costs. Exhibit 5 shows the relationship of the cost of merchandise sold for January and the ending inventory on January 31.

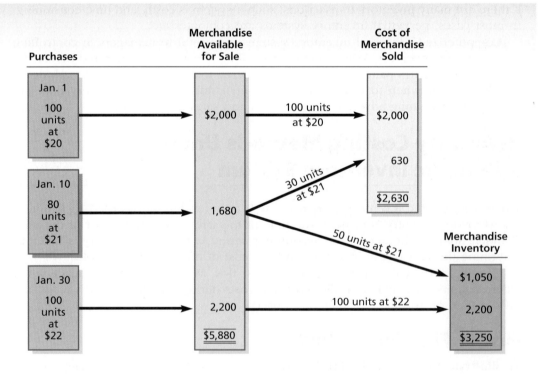

EXHIBIT 5

First-In, First-Out Flow of Costs

Last-In, First-Out Method

See Appendix D for more information

When the LIFO method is used, the cost of merchandise on hand at the end of the period is made up of the earliest costs. Based on the same data as in the FIFO example, the cost of the 150 units in ending inventory on January 31 is determined as follows:

Beginning inventory, January 1	100 units at	$20	$2,000
Next earliest costs, January 10	50 units at	$21	1,050
Inventory, January 31	150 units		$3,050

Deducting the cost of the January 31 inventory of $3,050 from the cost of merchandise available for sale of $5,880 yields the cost of merchandise sold of $2,830, as shown below.

Beginning inventory, January 1	$2,000
Purchases ($1,680 + $2,200)	3,880
Cost of merchandise available for sale in January	$5,880
Less ending inventory, January 31	3,050
Cost of merchandise sold	$2,830

The $3,050 cost of the ending merchandise inventory on January 31 is made up of the earliest costs. The $2,830 cost of merchandise sold is made up of the most recent costs. Exhibit 6 shows the relationship of the cost of merchandise sold for January and the ending inventory on January 31.

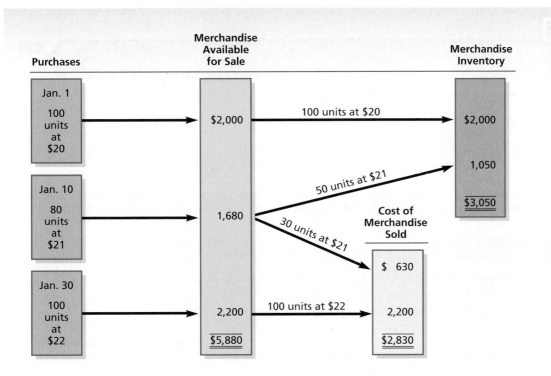

EXHIBIT 6

Last-In, First-Out Flow of Costs

Average Cost Method

The average cost method is sometimes called the *weighted average method*. The average cost method uses the average unit cost for determining cost of merchandise sold and the ending merchandise inventory. If purchases are relatively uniform during a period, the average cost method provides results that are similar to the physical flow of goods.

The weighted average unit cost is determined as follows:

$$\text{Average Unit Cost} = \frac{\text{Total Cost of Units Available for Sale}}{\text{Units Available for Sale}}$$

To illustrate, we use the data for Item 127B as follows:

$$\text{Average Unit Cost} = \frac{\text{Total Cost of Units Available for Sale}}{\text{Units Available for Sale}} = \frac{\$5,880}{280 \text{ units}}$$

$$= \$21 \text{ per unit}$$

The cost of the January 31 ending inventory is as follows:

Inventory, January 31: $3,150 (150 units × $21)

Deducting the cost of the January 31 inventory of $3,150 from the cost of merchandise available for sale of $5,880 yields the cost of merchandise sold of $2,730, as shown below.

Beginning inventory, January 1	$2,000
Purchases ($1,680 + $2,200)	3,880
Cost of merchandise available for sale in January	$5,880
Less ending inventory, January 31	3,150
Cost of merchandise sold	$2,730

The cost of merchandise sold could also be computed by multiplying the number of units sold by the average cost as follows:

Cost of merchandise sold: $2,730 (130 units × $21)

Example Exercise 7-4   Periodic Inventory Using FIFO, LIFO, Average Cost Methods   **OBJ. 4**

The units of an item available for sale during the year were as follows:

Jan.	1	Inventory	6 units at $50	$ 300
Mar.	20	Purchase	14 units at $55	770
Oct.	30	Purchase	20 units at $62	1,240
		Available for sale	40 units	$2,310

There are 16 units of the item in the physical inventory at December 31. The periodic inventory system is used. Determine the inventory cost using (a) the first-in, first-out (FIFO) method, (b) the last-in, first-out (LIFO) method, and (c) the average cost method.

Follow My Example 7-4

a. First-in, first-out (FIFO) method: $992 = (16 units × $62)
b. Last-in, first-out (LIFO) method: $850 = (6 units × $50) + (10 units × $55)
c. Average cost method: $924 (16 units × $57.75), where average cost = $57.75 = $2,310/40 units

Practice Exercises: **PE 7-4A, PE 7-4B**

OBJ. 5 Compare and contrast the use of the three inventory costing methods.

Comparing Inventory Costing Methods

A different cost flow is assumed for the FIFO, LIFO, and average inventory cost flow methods. As a result, the three methods normally yield different amounts for the following:

1. Cost of merchandise sold
2. Gross profit
3. Net income
4. Ending merchandise inventory

Using the periodic inventory system illustration with sales of $3,900 (130 units × $30), these differences are illustrated below.[3]

See Appendix D for
more information

Partial Income Statements

	First-In, First-Out		Average Cost		Last-In, First-Out	
Net sales		$3,900		$3,900		$3,900
Cost of merchandise sold:						
Beginning inventory	$2,000		$2,000		$2,000	
Purchases	3,880		3,880		3,880	
Merchandise available for sale	$5,880		$5,880		$5,880	
Less ending inventory	3,250		3,150		3,050	
Cost of merchandise sold		2,630		2,730		2,830
Gross profit		$1,270		$1,170		$1,070

The preceding differences show the effect of increasing costs (prices). If costs (prices) remain the same, all three methods would yield the same results. However, costs (prices) normally do change. The effects of changing costs (prices) on the FIFO and LIFO methods are summarized in Exhibit 7. The average cost method will always yield results between those of FIFO and LIFO.

FIFO reports higher gross profit and net income than the LIFO method when costs (prices) are increasing, as shown in Exhibit 7. However, in periods of rapidly rising costs, the inventory that is sold must be replaced at increasingly higher costs. In such cases, the larger FIFO gross profit and net income are sometimes called *inventory profits* or *illusory profits*.

During a period of increasing costs, LIFO matches more recent costs against sales on the income statement. Thus, it can be argued that the LIFO method more nearly matches current costs with current revenues. LIFO also offers an income tax savings during periods of increasing costs. This is because LIFO reports the lowest amount of gross profit and, thus, taxable net income.[4] However, under LIFO, the ending inventory on the balance sheet may be quite different from its current replacement cost. In such cases, the financial statements normally include a note that estimates what the inventory would have been if FIFO had been used.

The average cost method is, in a sense, a compromise between FIFO and LIFO. The effect of cost (price) trends is averaged in determining the cost of merchandise sold and the ending inventory. For a series of purchases, the average cost will be the same, regardless of whether costs are increasing or decreasing. For example, reversing the sequence of unit costs presented in the prior illustration does not affect the average unit cost nor the amounts reported for cost of merchandise sold, gross profit, or ending inventory.

EXHIBIT 7

Effects of Changing Costs (Prices): FIFO and LIFO Cost Methods

	Increasing Costs (Prices)		Decreasing Costs (Prices)	
	Highest Amount	Lowest Amount	Highest Amount	Lowest Amount
Cost of merchandise sold	LIFO	FIFO	FIFO	LIFO
Gross profit	FIFO	LIFO	LIFO	FIFO
Net income	FIFO	LIFO	LIFO	FIFO
Ending merchandise inventory	FIFO	LIFO	LIFO	FIFO

3 Similar results would also occur when comparing inventory costing methods under a perpetual inventory system.

4 A proposal currently exists before the U.S. Congress to not allow the use of LIFO for tax purposes.

Integrity, Objectivity, and Ethics in Business

WHERE'S THE BONUS?

Managers are often given bonuses based on reported earnings numbers. This can create a conflict. LIFO can improve the value of the company through lower taxes. However, in periods of rising costs (prices), LIFO also produces a lower earnings number and, therefore, lower management

bonuses. Ethically, managers should select accounting procedures that will maximize the value of the firm, rather than their own compensation. Compensation specialists can help avoid this ethical dilemma by adjusting the bonus plan for the accounting procedure differences.

 Describe and illustrate the reporting of merchandise inventory in the financial statements.

Reporting Merchandise Inventory in the Financial Statements

Cost is the primary basis for valuing and reporting inventories in the financial statements. However, inventory may be valued at other than cost in the following cases:

1. The cost of replacing items in inventory is below the recorded cost.
2. The inventory cannot be sold at normal prices due to imperfections, style changes, or other causes.

Valuation at Lower of Cost or Market

See Appendix D for more information

If the cost of replacing inventory is lower than its recorded purchase cost, the **lower-of-cost-or-market (LCM) method** is used to value the inventory. *Market,* as used in *lower of cost or market*, is the cost to replace the inventory. The market value is based on normal quantities that would be purchased from suppliers.

The lower-of-cost-or-market method can be applied in one of three ways. The cost, market price, and any declines could be determined for the following:

1. Each item in the inventory.
2. Each major class or category of inventory.
3. Total inventory as a whole.

The amount of any price decline is included in the cost of merchandise sold. This, in turn, reduces gross profit and net income in the period in which the price declines occur. This matching of price declines to the period in which they occur is the primary advantage of using the lower-of-cost-or-market method.

To illustrate, assume the following data for 400 identical units of Item A in inventory on December 31, 2012:

Unit purchased cost	$10.25
Replacement cost on December 31, 2012	9.50

Since Item A could be replaced at $9.50 a unit, $9.50 is used under the lower-of-cost-or-market method.

Exhibit 8 illustrates applying the lower-of-cost-or-market method to each inventory item (A, B, C, and D). As applied on an item-by-item basis, the total lower-of-cost-or-market is $15,070, which is a market decline of $450 ($15,520 − $15,070). This market decline of $450 is included in the cost of merchandise sold.

In Exhibit 8, Items A, B, C, and D could be viewed as a class of inventory items. If the lower-of-cost-or-market method is applied to the class, the inventory would be valued at $15,472, which is a market decline of $48 ($15,520 − $15,472). Likewise, if Items A, B, C, and D make up the total inventory, the lower-of-cost-or-market method as applied to the total inventory would be the same amount, $15,472.

EXHIBIT 8

Determining
Inventory at
Lower of Cost
or Market

	A	B	C	D	E	F	G
1			Unit	Unit		Total	
2		Inventory	Cost	Market			Lower
3	Item	Quantity	Price	Price	Cost	Market	of C or M
4	A	400	$10.25	$ 9.50	$ 4,100	$ 3,800	$ 3,800
5	B	120	22.50	24.10	2,700	2,892	2,700
6	C	600	8.00	7.75	4,800	4,650	4,650
7	D	280	14.00	14.75	3,920	4,130	3,920
8	Total				$15,520	$15,472	$15,070
9							

Example Exercise 7-5 Lower-of-Cost-or-Market Method

OBJ. 6

On the basis of the following data, determine the value of the inventory at the lower of cost or market. Apply lower of cost or market to each inventory item as shown in Exhibit 8.

Item	Inventory Quantity	Unit Cost Price	Unit Market Price
C17Y	10	$ 39	$40
B563	7	110	98

Follow My Example 7-5

	A	B	C	D	E	F	G
1			Unit	Unit		Total	
2		Inventory	Cost	Market			Lower
3	Item	Quantity	Price	Price	Cost	Market	of C or M
4	C17Y	10	$ 39	$ 40	$ 390	$ 400	$ 390
5	B563	7	110	98	770	686	686
6	Total				$1,160	$1,086	$1,076
7							

Practice Exercises: **PE 7-5A, PE 7-5B**

Valuation at Net Realizable Value

Merchandise that is out of date, spoiled, or damaged can often be sold only at a price below its original cost. Such merchandise should be valued at its **net realizable value**. Net realizable value is determined as follows:

Net Realizable Value = Estimated Selling Price – Direct Costs of Disposal

Direct costs of disposal include selling expenses such as special advertising or sales commissions. To illustrate, assume the following data about an item of damaged merchandise:

Original cost	$1,000
Estimated selling price	800
Selling expenses	150

The merchandise should be valued at its net realizable value of $650 as shown below.

Net Realizable Value = $800 – $150 = $650

BusinessConnection

INVENTORY WRITE-DOWNS

Worthington Industries, Inc., is a diversified metal processing company that manufactures metal products, such as metal framing and pressure cylinders. During the year ended May 31, 2009, the company experienced rapidly changing business conditions. Due to the global financial crisis and recession, steel prices underwent a severe and rapid decline. As a result, the company recorded an inventory write-down of $105 million and an overall net loss of $108 million for the year.

Merchandise Inventory on the Balance Sheet

See Appendix D for more information

Merchandise inventory is usually reported in the Current Assets section of the balance sheet. In addition to this amount, the following are reported:

1. The method of determining the cost of the inventory (FIFO, LIFO, or average)
2. The method of valuing the inventory (cost or the lower of cost or market)

The financial statement reporting for the topics covered in Chapters 7–15 are illustrated using excerpts from the financial statements of Mornin' Joe. Mornin' Joe is a fictitious company that offers drip and espresso coffee in a coffeehouse setting. The complete financial statements of Mornin' Joe are illustrated at the end of Chapter 15 (pages 713–716).

The balance sheet presentation for merchandise inventory for Mornin' Joe is as follows:

Mornin' Joe Balance Sheet December 31, 2012		
Current assets:		
Cash and cash equivalents		$235,000
Trading investments (at cost)....................................	$420,000	
Plus valuation allowance on trading investments	45,000	465,000
Accounts receivable	$305,000	
Less allowance for doubtful accounts	12,300	292,700
Merchandise inventory—at lower of cost (first-in, first-out method) or market		120,000

It is not unusual for a large business to use different costing methods for segments of its inventories. Also, a business may change its inventory costing method. In such cases, the effect of the change and the reason for the change are disclosed in the financial statements.

Effect of Inventory Errors on the Financial Statements

Any errors in merchandise inventory will affect the balance sheet and income statement. Some reasons that inventory errors may occur include the following:

1. Physical inventory on hand was miscounted.
2. Costs were incorrectly assigned to inventory. For example, the FIFO, LIFO, or average cost method was incorrectly applied.
3. Inventory in transit was incorrectly included or excluded from inventory.
4. Consigned inventory was incorrectly included or excluded from inventory.

Inventory errors often arise from merchandise that is in transit at year-end. As discussed in Chapter 6, shipping terms determine when the title to merchandise passes. When goods are purchased or sold *FOB shipping point*, title passes to the buyer when the goods are shipped. When the terms are *FOB destination*, title passes to the buyer when the goods are received.

To illustrate, assume that SysExpress ordered the following merchandise from American Products:

Date ordered:	December 27, 2011
Amount:	$10,000
Terms:	FOB shipping point, 2/10, n/30
Date shipped by seller:	December 30
Date delivered:	January 3, 2012

When SysExpress counts its physical inventory on December 31, 2011, the merchandise is still in transit. In such cases, it would be easy for SysExpress to not include the $10,000 of merchandise in its December 31 physical inventory. However, since the merchandise was purchased *FOB shipping point*, SysExpress owns the merchandise. Thus, it should be included in the ending December 31 inventory even though it is not on hand. Likewise, any merchandise *sold* by SysExpress *FOB destination* is still SysExpress's inventory even if it is in transit to the buyer on December 31.

Inventory errors often arise from **consigned inventory**. Manufacturers sometimes ship merchandise to retailers who act as the manufacturer's selling agent. The manufacturer, called the **consignor**, retains title until the goods are sold. Such merchandise is said to be shipped *on consignment* to the retailer, called the **consignee**. Any unsold merchandise at year-end is a part of the manufacturer's (consignor's) inventory, even though the merchandise is in the hands of the retailer (consignee). At year-end, it would be easy for the retailer (consignee) to incorrectly include the consigned merchandise in its physical inventory. Likewise, the manufacturer (consignor) should include consigned inventory in its physical inventory even though the inventory is not on hand.

Income Statement Effects   Inventory errors will misstate the income statement amounts for cost of merchandise sold, gross profit, and net income. The effects of inventory errors on the current period's income statement are summarized in Exhibit 9.

EXHIBIT 9

Effect of Inventory Errors on Current Period's Income Statement

	Income Statement Effect		
Inventory Error	**Cost of Merchandise Sold**	**Gross Profit**	**Net Income**
Beginning inventory is:			
Understated	*Understated*	*Overstated*	*Overstated*
Overstated	*Overstated*	*Understated*	*Understated*
Ending inventory is:			
Understated	*Overstated*	*Understated*	*Understated*
Overstated	*Understated*	*Overstated*	*Overstated*

To illustrate, the income statements of SysExpress shown in Exhibit 10 are used.[5] On December 31, 2011, assume that SysExpress incorrectly records its physical inventory as $50,000 instead of the correct amount of $60,000. Thus, the December 31, 2011, inventory is understated by $10,000 ($60,000 − $50,000). As a result, the cost of merchandise sold is overstated by $10,000. The gross profit and the net income for the year will also be understated by $10,000.

The December 31, 2011, merchandise inventory becomes the January 1, 2012, inventory. Thus, the beginning inventory for 2012 is understated by $10,000. As a result, the cost of merchandise sold is understated by $10,000 for 2012. The gross profit and net income for 2012 will be overstated by $10,000.

As shown in Exhibit 10, since the ending inventory of one period is the beginning inventory of the next period, the effects of inventory errors carry forward to the next period. Specifically, if uncorrected, the effects of inventory errors reverse themselves

5 The effect of inventory errors will be illustrated using the periodic system. This is because it is easier to see the impact of inventory errors on the income statement using the periodic system. The effect of inventory errors would be the same under the perpetual inventory system.

EXHIBIT 10 **Effects of Inventory Errors on Two Years' Income Statements**

	2011		2012	
SysExpress Income Statement For the Years Ended December 31, 2011 and 2012				
	Correct	Incorrect	Incorrect	Correct
Net sales	$980,000	$980,000	$1,100,000	$1,100,000
Merchandise inventory, January 1	$ 55,000	$ 55,000	$ 50,000	$ 60,000
Purchases	650,000	650,000	700,000	700,000
Merchandise available for sale	$705,000	$705,000	$750,000	$760,000
Less merchandise inventory, December 31	60,000	50,000	70,000	70,000
Cost of merchandise sold	645,000	655,000	680,000	690,000
Gross profit	$335,000	$325,000	$ 420,000	$ 410,000
Operating expenses	100,000	100,000	120,000	120,000
Net income	$235,000	$225,000	$ 300,000	$ 290,000

$10,000
Understatement
of Net Income

$10,000
Overstatement
of Net Income

Net Effect Is Zero for Two Years
The inventory errors reverse (or cancel) so that the combined net
income for the two years of $525,000 ($225,000 + $300,000) is correct.

in the next period. In Exhibit 10, the combined net income for the two years of $525,000 is correct even though the 2011 and 2012 income statements were incorrect.

Balance Sheet Effects Inventory errors misstate the merchandise inventory, current assets, total assets, and owner's equity on the balance sheet. The effects of inventory errors on the current period's balance sheet are summarized in Exhibit 11.

EXHIBIT 11

Effect of Inventory Errors on Current Period's Balance Sheet

	Balance Sheet Effect			
Ending Inventory Error	Merchandise Inventory	Current Assets	Total Assets	Owner's Equity (Capital)
Understated	Understated	Understated	Understated	Understated
Overstated	Overstated	Overstated	Overstated	Overstated

For the SysExpress illustration shown in Exhibit 10, the December 31, 2011, ending inventory was understated by $10,000. As a result, the merchandise inventory, current assets, and total assets would be understated by $10,000 on the December 31, 2011, balance sheet. Because the ending physical inventory is understated, the cost of merchandise sold for 2011 will be overstated by $10,000. Thus, the gross profit and the net income for 2011 are understated by $10,000. Since the net income is closed to owner's equity (capital) at the end of the period, the owner's equity on the December 31, 2011, balance sheet is also understated by $10,000.

As discussed above, inventory errors reverse themselves within two years. As a result, the balance sheet will be correct as of December 31, 2012. Using the SysExpress illustration from Exhibit 10, these effects are summarized on the next page.

	Amount of Misstatement	
Balance Sheet:	December 31, 2011	December 31, 2012
Merchandise inventory overstated (understated)	$(10,000)	Correct
Current assets overstated (understated)	(10,000)	Correct
Total assets overstated (understated)	(10,000)	Correct
Owner's equity overstated (understated)	(10,000)	Correct
Income Statement:	2011	2012
Cost of merchandise sold overstated (understated)	$ 10,000	$(10,000)
Gross profit overstated (understated)	(10,000)	10,000
Net income overstated (understated)	(10,000)	10,000

Example Exercise 7-6 Effect of Inventory Errors

OBJ. 6

Zula Repair Shop incorrectly counted its December 31, 2012, inventory as $250,000 instead of the correct amount of $220,000. Indicate the effect of the misstatement on Zula's December 31, 2012, balance sheet and income statement for the year ended December 31, 2012.

Follow My Example 7-6

	Amount of Misstatement Overstatement (Understatement)
Balance Sheet:	
Merchandise inventory overstated	$ 30,000
Current assets overstated	30,000
Total assets overstated	30,000
Owner's equity overstated	30,000
Income Statement:	
Cost of merchandise sold understated	$(30,000)
Gross profit overstated	30,000
Net income overstated	30,000

Practice Exercises: **PE 7-6A, PE 7-6B**

BusinessConnection

RAPID INVENTORY AT COSTCO

Costco Wholesale Corporation operates over 500 membership warehouses that offer members low prices on a limited selection of nationally branded and selected private label products. Costco emphasizes high sales volumes and rapid inventory turnover. This enables Costco to operate profitably at lower gross margins than traditional wholesalers, discount retailers, and supermarkets. In addition, Costco's rapid inventory turnover allows it to conserve its working capital, as described below.

Because of our high sales volume and rapid inventory turnover, we generally have the opportunity to sell and be paid for inventory before we are required to pay ... our merchandise vendors....As sales increase and inventory turnover becomes more rapid, a greater percentage of inventory is financed through *payment terms provided by suppliers rather than by our working capital.*

Source: Costco Wholesale Corporation, Annual Report on Form 10-K for the fiscal year ended August 31, 2009.

Financial Analysis and Interpretation: Inventory Turnover and Number of Days' Sales in Inventory

A merchandising business should keep enough inventory on hand to meet its customers' needs. A failure to do so may result in lost sales. However, too much inventory ties up funds that could be used to improve operations. Also, excess inventory increases expenses such as storage and property taxes. Finally, excess inventory increases the risk of losses due to price declines, damage, or changes in customer tastes.

Two measures to analyze the efficiency and effectiveness of inventory management are:

1. inventory turnover and
2. number of days' sales in inventory.

Inventory turnover measures the relationship between cost of merchandise sold and the amount of inventory carried during the period. It is computed as follows:

$$\text{Inventory Turnover} = \frac{\text{Cost of Merchandise Sold}}{\text{Average Inventory}}$$

To illustrate, inventory turnover for Best Buy is computed from the following data (in millions) taken from two recent annual reports.

	For the Year Ended	
	February 28, 2009	**March 1, 2008**
Cost of merchandise sold	$34,017	$30,477
Inventories:		
Beginning of year	4,708	4,028
End of year	4,753	4,708
Average inventory:		
($4,708 + $4,753) ÷ 2	4,731	
($4,028 + $4,708) ÷ 2		4,368
Inventory turnover:		
$34,017 ÷ $4,731	7.2	
$30,477 ÷ $4,368		7.0

Generally, the larger the inventory turnover the more efficient and effective the company is managing inventory. As shown above, inventory turnover increased from 7.0 to 7.2 during 2009, and thus Best Buy improved its inventory efficiency.

The **number of days' sales in inventory** measures the length of time it takes to acquire, sell, and replace the inventory. It is computed as follows:

$$\text{Number of Days' Sales in Inventory} = \frac{\text{Average Inventory}}{\text{Average Daily Cost of Merchandise Sold}}$$

The average daily cost of merchandise sold is determined by dividing the cost of merchandise sold by 365. Based upon the preceding data, the number of days' sales in inventory for Best Buy is computed below.

	For the Year Ended	
	February 28, 2009	**March 1, 2008**
Cost of merchandise sold	$34,017	$30,477
Average daily cost of merchandise sold:		
$34,017 ÷ 365 days	93	
$30,477 ÷ 365 days		84
Average inventory:		
($4,708 + $4,753) ÷ 2	4,731	
($4,028 + $4,708) ÷ 2		4,368
Number of days' sales in inventory:		
$4,731 ÷ $93	51 days	
$4,368 ÷ $84		52 days

Generally, the lower the number of days' sales in inventory, the more efficient and effective the company is in managing inventory. As shown above, the number of days' sales in inventory decreased from 52 to 51 during 2009, and thus Best Buy improved its inventory management. This is consistent with the increase in inventory during the year.

As with most financial ratios, differences exist among industries. To illustrate, Zale Corporation is a large retailer of fine jewelry in the United States. Since jewelry doesn't sell as rapidly as Best Buy's consumer electronics, Zale's inventory turnover and number of days' sales in inventory should be significantly different than Best Buy's. For 2009, this is confirmed as shown below.

	Best Buy	Zale
Inventory turnover	7.2	1.3
Number of days' sales in inventory	51 days	292 days

Example Exercise 7-7   Inventory Turnover and Number of Days' Sales in Inventory

OBJ. 7

Financial statement data for years ending December 31 for Beadle Company are shown below.

	2012	2011
Cost of merchandise sold	$877,500	$615,000
Inventories:		
Beginning of year	225,000	225,000
End of year	315,000	185,000

a. Determine inventory turnover for 2012 and 2011.
b. Determine the number of days' sales in inventory for 2012 and 2011.
c. Does the change in inventory turnover and the number of days' sales in inventory from 2011 to 2012 indicate a favorable or an unfavorable trend?

Follow My Example 7-7

a. Inventory turnover:

	2012	2011
Average inventory:		
($225,000 + $315,000) ÷ 2	$270,000	
($185,000 + $225,000) ÷ 2		$205,000
Inventory turnover:		
$877,500 ÷ $270,000	3.25	
$615,000 ÷ $205,000		3.00

b. Number of days' sales in inventory:

	2012	2011
Average daily cost of merchandise sold:		
$877,500 ÷ 365 days	$2,404	
$615,000 ÷ 365 days		$1,685
Average inventory:		
($225,000 + $315,000) ÷ 2	$270,000	
($185,000 + $225,000) ÷ 2		$205,000
Number of days' sales in inventory:		
$270,000 ÷ $2,404	112.3 days	
$205,000 ÷ $1,685		121.7 days

c. The increase in the inventory turnover from 3.00 to 3.25 and the decrease in the number of days' sales in inventory from 121.7 days to 112.3 days indicate favorable trends in managing inventory.

Practice Exercises: **PE 7-7A, PE 7-7B**

A P P E N D I X

Estimating Inventory Cost

A business may need to estimate the amount of inventory for the following reasons:

1. Perpetual inventory records are not maintained.
2. A disaster such as a fire or flood has destroyed the inventory records and the inventory.
3. Monthly or quarterly financial statements are needed, but a physical inventory is taken only once a year.

This appendix describes and illustrates two widely used methods of estimating inventory cost.

Retail Method of Inventory Costing

The **retail inventory method** of estimating inventory cost requires costs and retail prices to be maintained for the merchandise available for sale. A ratio of cost to retail price is then used to convert ending inventory at retail to estimate the ending inventory cost.

The retail inventory method is applied as follows:

Step 1. Determine the total merchandise available for sale at cost and retail.
Step 2. Determine the ratio of the cost to retail of the merchandise available for sale.
Step 3. Determine the ending inventory at retail by deducting the net sales from the merchandise available for sale at retail.
Step 4. Estimate the ending inventory cost by multiplying the ending inventory at retail by the cost to retail ratio.

Exhibit 12 illustrates the retail inventory method.

EXHIBIT 12

Determining Inventory by the Retail Method

	A	B	C
1		Cost	Retail
2	Merchandise inventory, January 1	$19,400	$ 36,000
3	Purchases in January (net)	42,600	64,000
Step 1 → 4	Merchandise available for sale	$62,000	$100,000
Step 2 → 5	Ratio of cost to retail price: $\dfrac{\$62,000}{\$100,000} = 62\%$		
6	Sales for January (net)		70,000
Step 3 → 7	Merchandise inventory, January 31, at retail		$ 30,000
Step 4 → 8	Merchandise inventory, January 31, at estimated cost		
9	($30,000 × 62%)		$ 18,600
10			

When estimating the cost to retail ratio, the mix of items in the ending inventory is assumed to be the same as the merchandise available for sale. If the ending inventory is made up of different classes of merchandise, cost to retail ratios may be developed for each class of inventory.

An advantage of the retail method is that it provides inventory figures for preparing monthly statements. Department stores and similar retailers often determine gross profit and operating income each month, but may take a physical inventory only once or twice a year. Thus, the retail method allows management to monitor operations more closely.

The retail method may also be used as an aid in taking a physical inventory. In this case, the items are counted and recorded at their retail (selling) prices instead of their costs. The physical inventory at retail is then converted to cost by using the cost to retail ratio.

Gross Profit Method of Inventory Costing

The **gross profit method** uses the estimated gross profit for the period to estimate the inventory at the end of the period. The gross profit is estimated from the preceding year, adjusted for any current-period changes in the cost and sales prices.

The gross profit method is applied as follows:

Step 1. Determine the merchandise available for sale at cost.

Step 2. Determine the estimated gross profit by multiplying the net sales by the gross profit percentage.

Step 3. Determine the estimated cost of merchandise sold by deducting the estimated gross profit from the net sales.

Step 4. Estimate the ending inventory cost by deducting the estimated cost of merchandise sold from the merchandise available for sale.

Exhibit 13 illustrates the gross profit method.

EXHIBIT 13

Estimating Inventory by Gross Profit Method

	A	B	C
1			Cost
2	Merchandise inventory, January 1		$ 57,000
3	Purchases in January (net)		180,000
Step 1 → 4	Merchandise available for sale		$237,000
5	Sales for January (net)	$250,000	
Step 2 → 6	Less estimated gross profit ($250,000 × 30%)	75,000	
Step 3 → 7	Estimated cost of merchandise sold		175,000
Step 4 → 8	Estimated merchandise inventory, January 31		$ 62,000
9			

The gross profit method is useful for estimating inventories for monthly or quarterly financial statements. It is also useful in estimating the cost of merchandise destroyed by fire or other disasters.

At a Glance 7

OBJ. 1

Describe the importance of control over inventory.

Key Points   Two objectives of inventory control are safeguarding the inventory and properly reporting it in the financial statements. The perpetual inventory system and physical count enhance control over inventory.

Learning Outcomes	Example Exercises	Practice Exercises
• Describe controls for safeguarding inventory.		
• Describe how a perpetual inventory system enhances control over inventory.		
• Describe why taking a physical inventory enhances control over inventory.		

Describe three inventory cost flow assumptions and how they impact the income statement and balance sheet.

Key Points   The three common inventory cost flow assumptions used in business are the (1) first-in, first-out method (FIFO); (2) last-in, first-out method (LIFO); and (3) average cost method. The cost flow assumption affects the income statement and balance sheet.

Learning Outcomes	Example Exercises	Practice Exercises
• Describe the FIFO, LIFO, and average cost flow methods.		
• Describe how choice of a cost flow method affects the income statement and balance sheet.	EE7-1	PE7-1A, 7-1B

Determine the cost of inventory under the perpetual inventory system, using the FIFO, LIFO, and average cost methods.

Key Points   In a perpetual inventory system, the number of units and the cost of each type of merchandise are recorded in a subsidiary inventory ledger, with a separate account for each type of merchandise.

Learning Outcomes	Example Exercises	Practice Exercises
• Determine the cost of inventory and cost of merchandise sold using a perpetual inventory system under the FIFO method.	EE7-2	PE7-2A, 7-2B
• Determine the cost of inventory and cost of merchandise sold using a perpetual inventory system under the LIFO method.	EE7-3	PE7-3A, 7-3B

Determine the cost of inventory under the periodic inventory system, using the FIFO, LIFO, and average cost methods.

Key Points   In a periodic inventory system, a physical inventory is taken to determine the cost of the inventory and the cost of merchandise sold.

Learning Outcomes	Example Exercises	Practice Exercises
• Determine the cost of inventory and cost of merchandise sold using a periodic inventory system under the FIFO method.	EE7-4	PE7-4A, 7-4B
• Determine the cost of inventory and cost of merchandise sold using a periodic inventory system under the LIFO method.	EE7-4	PE7-4A, 7-4B
• Determine the cost of inventory and cost of merchandise sold using a periodic inventory system under the average cost method.	EE7-4	PE7-4A, 7-4B

OBJ. 5

Compare and contrast the use of the three inventory costing methods.

Key Points   The three inventory costing methods will normally yield different amounts for (1) the ending inventory, (2) the cost of merchandise sold for the period, and (3) the gross profit (and net income) for the period.

Learning Outcomes	Example Exercises	Practice Exercises
• Indicate which inventory cost flow method will yield the highest and lowest ending inventory and net income during periods of increasing prices.		
• Indicate which inventory cost flow method will yield the highest and lowest ending inventory and net income during periods of decreasing prices.		

OBJ.
6   **Describe and illustrate the reporting of merchandise inventory in the financial statements.**

Key Points   The lower of cost or market is used to value inventory. Inventory that is out of date, spoiled, or damaged is valued at its net realizable value.

Merchandise inventory is usually presented in the Current Assets section of the balance sheet, following receivables. The method of determining the cost and valuing the inventory is reported.

Errors in reporting inventory based on the physical inventory will affect the balance sheet and income statement.

Learning Outcomes	Example Exercises	Practice Exercises
• Determine inventory using lower of cost or market.	EE7-5	PE7-5A, 7-5B
• Illustrate the use of net realizable value for spoiled or damaged inventory.		
• Prepare the Current Assets section of the balance sheet that includes inventory.		
• Determine the effect of inventory errors on the balance sheet and income statement.	EE7-6	PE7-6A, 7-6B

OBJ.
7   **Describe and illustrate the inventory turnover and the number of days' sales in inventory in analyzing the efficiency and effectiveness of inventory management.**

Key Points   Two measures to analyze the efficiency and effectiveness of inventory management are (1) inventory turnover and (2) number of days' sales in inventory

Learning Outcomes	Example Exercises	Practice Exercises
• Describe the use of inventory turnover and number of days' sales in inventory in analyzing how well a company manages inventory.		
• Compute the inventory turnover.	EE7-7	PE7-7A, 7-7B
• Compute the number of days' sales in inventory.	EE7-7	PE7-7A, 7-7B

Key Terms

average inventory cost
  flow method (314)
consigned inventory (327)
consignee (327)
consignor (327)
first-in, first-out (FIFO) inventory
  cost flow method (314)
gross profit method (333)

inventory turnover (330)
last-in, first-out (LIFO) inventory
  cost flow method (314)
lower-of-cost-or-market
  (LCM) method (324)
net realizable value (325)
number of days' sales in
  inventory (330)

physical inventory (313)
purchase order (312)
receiving report (312)
retail inventory method (332)
specific identification inventory
  cost flow method (314)
subsidiary inventory ledger (313)

Illustrative Problem

Stewart Co.'s beginning inventory and purchases during the year ended December 31, 2012, were as follows:

		Unit	Units Cost	Total Cost
January 1	Inventory	1,000	$50.00	$ 50,000
March 10	Purchase	1,200	52.50	63,000
June 25	Sold 800 units			
August 30	Purchase	800	55.00	44,000
October 5	Sold 1,500 units			
November 26	Purchase	2,000	56.00	112,000
December 31	Sold 1,000 units			
	Total	5,000		$269,000

Instructions

1. Determine the cost of inventory on December 31, 2012, using the perpetual inventory system and each of the following inventory costing methods:
   a. first-in, first-out
   b. last-in, first-out

2. Determine the cost of inventory on December 31, 2012, using the periodic inventory system and each of the following inventory costing methods:
   a. first-in, first-out
   b. last-in, first-out
   c. average cost

3. Appendix: Assume that during the fiscal year ended December 31, 2012, sales were $290,000 and the estimated gross profit rate was 40%. Estimate the ending inventory at December 31, 2012, using the gross profit method.

Solution

1. a. First-in, first-out method: $95,200
   b. Last-in, first-out method: $91,000 ($35,000 + $56,000)

2. a. First-in, first-out method:
   1,700 units at $56 = $95,200

   b. Last-in, first-out method:

1,000 units at $50.00	$50,000
700 units at $52.50	36,750
1,700 units	$86,750

1. a. First-in, first-out method: $95,200

Date	Purchases			Cost of Merchandise Sold			Inventory		
	Quantity	Unit Cost	Total Cost	Quantity	Unit Cost	Total Cost	Quantity	Unit Cost	Total Cost
2012 Jan. 1							1,000	50.00	50,000
Mar. 10	1,200	52.50	63,000				1,000	50.00	50,000
							1,200	52.50	63,000
June 25				800	50.00	40,000	200	50.00	10,000
							1,200	52.50	63,000
Aug. 30	800	55.00	44,000				200	50.00	10,000
							1,200	52.50	63,000
							800	55.00	44,000
Oct. 5				200	50.00	10,000	700	55.00	38,500
				1,200	52.50	63,000			
				100	55.00	5,500			
Nov. 26	2,000	56.00	112,000				700	55.00	38,500
							2,000	56.00	112,000
Dec. 31				700	55.00	38,500	1,700	56.00	95,200
				300	56.00	16,800			
31	Balances					173,800			95,200

b. Last-in, first-out method: $91,000 ($35,000 + $56,000)

Date	Purchases			Cost of Merchandise Sold			Inventory		
	Quantity	Unit Cost	Total Cost	Quantity	Unit Cost	Total Cost	Quantity	Unit Cost	Total Cost
2012 Jan. 1							1,000	50.00	50,000
Mar. 10	1,200	52.50	63,000				1,000	50.00	50,000
							1,200	52.50	63,000
June 25				800	52.50	42,000	1,000	50.00	50,000
							400	52.50	21,000
Aug. 30	800	55.00	44,000				1,000	50.00	50,000
							400	52.50	21,000
							800	55.00	44,000
Oct. 5				800	55.00	44,000	700	50.00	35,000
				400	52.50	21,000			
				300	50.00	15,000			
Nov. 26	2,000	56.00	112,000				700	50.00	35,000
							2,000	56.00	112,000
Dec. 31				1,000	56.00	56,000	700	50.00	35,000
							1,000	56.00	56,000
31	Balances					178,000			91,000

c. Average cost method:

Average cost per unit: $269,000/5,000 units = $53.80

Inventory, December 31, 2012: 1,700 units at $53.80 = $91,460

3. Appendix:

Merchandise inventory, January 1, 2012		$ 50,000
Purchases (net)		219,000
Merchandise available for sale		$269,000
Sales (net)	$290,000	
Less estimated gross profit ($290,000 × 40%)	116,000	
Estimated cost of merchandise sold		174,000
Estimated merchandise inventory, December 31, 2012		$ 95,000

Discussion Questions

1. Before inventory purchases are recorded, the receiving report should be reconciled to what documents?

2. Why is it important to periodically take a physical inventory when using a perpetual inventory system?

3. Do the terms *FIFO* and *LIFO* refer to techniques used in determining quantities of the various classes of merchandise on hand? Explain.

4. If merchandise inventory is being valued at cost and the price level is decreasing, which of the three methods of costing—FIFO, LIFO, or average cost—will yield (a) the highest inventory cost, (b) the lowest inventory cost, (c) the highest gross profit, and (d) the lowest gross profit?

5. Which of the three methods of inventory costing—FIFO, LIFO, or average cost—will in general yield an inventory cost most nearly approximating current replacement cost?

6. If inventory is being valued at cost and the price level is steadily rising, which of the three methods of costing—FIFO, LIFO, or average cost—will yield the lowest annual income tax expense? Explain.

7. Because of imperfections, an item of merchandise cannot be sold at its normal selling price. How should this item be valued for financial statement purposes?

8. The inventory at the end of the year was understated by $23,950. (a) Did the error cause an overstatement or an understatement of the gross profit for the year? (b) Which items on the balance sheet at the end of the year were overstated or understated as a result of the error?

9. X-mas Co. sold merchandise to Mistletoe Company on October 31, FOB shipping point. If the merchandise is in transit on October 31, the end of the fiscal year, which company would report it in its financial statements? Explain.

10. A manufacturer shipped merchandise to a retailer on a consignment basis. If the merchandise is unsold at the end of the period, in whose inventory should the merchandise be included?

Practice Exercises

Learning Objectives	Example Exercises	
OBJ. 2	EE 7-1 *p. 315*	**PE 7-1A Cost flow methods**

Three identical units of Item K113 are purchased during July, as shown below.

		Item JC07	Units	Cost
July	9	Purchase	1	$160
	17	Purchase	1	168
	26	Purchase	1	176
	Total		3	$504
	Average cost per unit			$168 ($504 ÷ 3 units)

Assume that one unit is sold on July 31 for $225.

Determine the gross profit for July and ending inventory on July 31 using the (a) first-in, first-out (FIFO); (b) last-in, first-out (LIFO); and (c) average cost methods.

Learning Objectives	Example Exercises	
OBJ. 2	EE 7-1 *p. 315*	**PE 7-1B Cost flow methods**

Three identical units of Item ZE9 are purchased during April, as shown below.

		Item WH4	Units	Cost
Apr.	2	Purchase	1	$10
	12	Purchase	1	12
	23	Purchase	1	14
	Total		3	$36
	Average cost per unit			$12 ($36 ÷ 3 units)

Assume that one unit is sold on April 27 for $29.

Determine the gross profit for April and ending inventory on April 30 using the (a) first-in, first-out (FIFO); (b) last-in, first-out (LIFO); and (c) average cost methods.

Learning Objectives	Example Exercises	
OBJ. 3	EE 7-2 *p. 317*	**PE 7-2A Perpetual inventory using FIFO**

Beginning inventory, purchases, and sales for Item B901 are as follows:

Aug.	1	Inventory	50 units at $80
	9	Sale	30 units
	13	Purchase	40 units at $85
	28	Sale	25 units

Assuming a perpetual inventory system and using the first-in, first-out (FIFO) method, determine (a) the cost of merchandise sold on August 28 and (b) the inventory on August 31.

Learning Objectives	Example Exercises	
OBJ. 3	EE 7-2 *p. 317*	**PE 7-2B Perpetual inventory using FIFO**

Beginning inventory, purchases, and sales for Item CSW15 are as follows:

Mar.	1	Inventory	100 units at $15
	7	Sale	88 units
	15	Purchase	125 units at $18
	24	Sale	75 units

Assuming a perpetual inventory system and using the first-in, first-out (FIFO) method, determine (a) the cost of merchandise sold on March 24 and (b) the inventory on March 31.

Learning Objectives *Example Exercises*

OBJ. 3   EE 7-3 p. 318

PE 7-3A   Perpetual inventory using LIFO

Beginning inventory, purchases, and sales for Item QED9 are as follows:

Nov.	1	Inventory	90 units at $50
	4	Sale	72 units
	23	Purchase	100 units at $60
	26	Sale	84 units

Assuming a perpetual inventory system and using the last-in, first-out (LIFO) method, determine (a) the cost of merchandise sold on November 26 and (b) the inventory on November 30.

OBJ. 3   EE 7-3 p. 318

PE 7-3B   Perpetual inventory using LIFO

Beginning inventory, purchases, and sales for Item MMM8 are as follows:

Jan.	1	Inventory	90 units at $17
	8	Sale	75 units
	15	Purchase	125 units at $18
	27	Sale	80 units

Assuming a perpetual inventory system and using the last-in, first-out (LIFO) method, determine (a) the cost of merchandise sold on January 27 and (b) the inventory on January 31.

OBJ. 4   EE 7-4 p. 322

PE 7-4A   Periodic inventory using FIFO, LIFO, average cost methods

The units of an item available for sale during the year were as follows:

Jan.	1	Inventory	12 units at $45	$ 540
July	7	Purchase	18 units at $50	900
Nov.	23	Purchase	15 units at $54	810
		Available for sale	45 units	$2,250

There are 11 units of the item in the physical inventory at December 31. The periodic inventory system is used. Determine the inventory cost using (a) the first-in, first-out (FIFO) method; (b) the last-in, first-out (LIFO) method; and (c) the average cost method.

OBJ. 4   EE 7-4 p. 322

PE 7-4B   Periodic inventory using FIFO, LIFO, average cost methods

The units of an item available for sale during the year were as follows:

Jan.	1	Inventory	10 units at $120	$ 1,200
Apr.	13	Purchase	130 units at $114	14,820
Sept.	30	Purchase	20 units at $119	2,380
		Available for sale	160 units	$18,400

There are 23 units of the item in the physical inventory at December 31. The periodic inventory system is used. Determine the inventory cost using (a) the first-in, first-out (FIFO) method; (b) the last-in, first-out (LIFO) method; and (c) the average cost method.

OBJ. 6   EE 7-5 p. 325

PE 7-5A   Lower-of-cost-or-market method

On the basis of the following data, determine the value of the inventory at the lower of cost or market. Apply lower of cost or market to each inventory item as shown in Exhibit 8.

Item	Inventory Quantity	Unit Cost Price	Unit Market Price
IA17	200	$40	$38
TX24	150	55	60

OBJ. 6   EE 7-5 p. 325

PE 7-5B   Lower-of-cost-or-market method

On the basis of the following data, determine the value of the inventory at the lower of cost or market. Apply lower of cost or market to each inventory item as shown in Exhibit 8.

Item	Inventory Quantity	Unit Cost Price	Unit Market Price
MT22	1,500	$ 7	$ 4
WY09	900	22	25

Learning Objectives	Example Exercises	

OBJ. 6   EE 7-6 *p. 329*   **PE 7-6A   Effect of inventory errors**

During the taking of its physical inventory on December 31, 2012, Kate's Interiors Company incorrectly counted its inventory as $83,175 instead of the correct amount of $90,700. Indicate the effect of the misstatement on Kate's Interiors' December 31, 2012, balance sheet and income statement for the year ended December 31, 2012.

OBJ. 6   EE 7-6 *p. 329*   **PE 7-6B   Effect of inventory errors**

During the taking of its physical inventory on December 31, 2012, Russian Bath Company incorrectly counted its inventory as $580,000 instead of the correct amount of $545,000. Indicate the effect of the misstatement on Russian Bath's December 31, 2012, balance sheet and income statement for the year ended December 31, 2012.

OBJ. 7   EE 7-7 *p. 331*   **PE 7-7A   Inventory turnover and number of days' sales in inventory**

The following financial statement data for years ending December 31 for Gillispie Company are shown below.

	2012	2011
Cost of merchandise sold	$882,000	$680,000
Inventories:		
Beginning of year	$200,000	$140,000
End of year	290,000	200,000

a. Determine inventory turnover for 2012 and 2011.

b. Determine the number of days' sales in inventory for 2012 and 2011. Round to one decimal place.

c. Does the change in inventory turnover and the number of days' sales in inventory from 2011 to 2012 indicate a favorable or unfavorable trend?

OBJ. 7   EE 7-7 *p. 331*   **PE 7-7B   Inventory turnover and number of days' sales in inventory**

The following financial statement data for years ending December 31 for Pinnell Company are shown below.

	2012	2011
Cost of merchandise sold	$1,800,000	$1,428,000
Inventories:		
Beginning of year	$570,000	$450,000
End of year	630,000	570,000

a. Determine inventory turnover for 2012 and 2011.

b. Determine the number of days' sales in inventory for 2012 and 2011. Round to one decimal place.

c. Does the change in inventory turnover and the number of days' sales in inventory from 2011 to 2012 indicate a favorable or unfavorable trend?

Exercises

OBJ. 1   **EX 7-1   Control of inventories**

A4A Hardware Store currently uses a periodic inventory system. Ray Ballard, the owner, is considering the purchase of a computer system that would make it feasible to switch to a perpetual inventory system.

Ray is unhappy with the periodic inventory system because it does not provide timely information on inventory levels. Ray has noticed on several occasions that the store runs out of good-selling items, while too many poor-selling items are on hand.

Ray is also concerned about lost sales while a physical inventory is being taken. A4A Hardware currently takes a physical inventory twice a year. To minimize distractions, the store is closed on the day inventory is taken. Ray believes that closing the store is the only way to get an accurate inventory count.

━━━━━━▶ Will switching to a perpetual inventory system strengthen A4A Hardware's control over inventory items? Will switching to a perpetual inventory system eliminate the need for a physical inventory count? Explain.

OBJ. 1

EX 7-2 Control of inventories

Lincoln Luggage Shop is a small retail establishment located in a large shopping mall. This shop has implemented the following procedures regarding inventory items:

a. Since the shop carries mostly high-quality, designer luggage, all inventory items are tagged with a control device that activates an alarm if a tagged item is removed from the store.

b. Since the display area of the store is limited, only a sample of each piece of luggage is kept on the selling floor. Whenever a customer selects a piece of luggage, the salesclerk gets the appropriate piece from the store's stockroom. Since all salesclerks need access to the stockroom, it is not locked. The stockroom is adjacent to the break room used by all mall employees.

c. Whenever Lincoln receives a shipment of new inventory, the items are taken directly to the stockroom. Lincoln's accountant uses the vendor's invoice to record the amount of inventory received.

━━━━━━▶ State whether each of these procedures is appropriate or inappropriate. If it is inappropriate, state why.

OBJ. 2, 3

✔ Inventory balance, June 30, $5,070

EX 7-3 Perpetual inventory using FIFO

Beginning inventory, purchases, and sales data for portable DVD players are as follows:

June	1	Inventory	75 units at $40
	6	Sale	60 units
	14	Purchase	90 units at $42
	19	Sale	50 units
	25	Sale	20 units
	30	Purchase	80 units at $45

The business maintains a perpetual inventory system, costing by the first-in, first-out method.

a. Determine the cost of the merchandise sold for each sale and the inventory balance after each sale, presenting the data in the form illustrated in Exhibit 3.

b. Based upon the preceding data, would you expect the inventory to be higher or lower using the last-in, first-out method?

OBJ. 2, 3

✔ Inventory balance, June 30, $5,040

EX 7-4 Perpetual inventory using LIFO

Assume that the business in Exercise 7-3 maintains a perpetual inventory system, costing by the last-in, first-out method. Determine the cost of merchandise sold for each sale and the inventory balance after each sale, presenting the data in the form illustrated in Exhibit 4.

OBJ. 2, 3

✔ Inventory balance, July 31, $23,900

EX 7-5 Perpetual inventory using LIFO

Beginning inventory, purchases, and sales data for prepaid cell phones for July are as follows:

Inventory		Purchases		Sales	
July 1	800 units at $45	July 10	500 units at $50	July 12	700 units
		20	450 units at $52	14	300 units
				31	250 units

a. Assuming that the perpetual inventory system is used, costing by the LIFO method, determine the cost of merchandise sold for each sale and the inventory balance after each sale, presenting the data in the form illustrated in Exhibit 4.

b. Based upon the preceding data, would you expect the inventory to be higher or lower using the first-in, first-out method?

EX 7-6 Perpetual inventory using FIFO

Assume that the business in Exercise 7-5 maintains a perpetual inventory system, costing by the first-in, first-out method. Determine the cost of merchandise sold for each sale and the inventory balance after each sale, presenting the data in the form illustrated in Exhibit 3.

EX 7-7 FIFO, LIFO costs under perpetual inventory system

The following units of a particular item were available for sale during the year:

Beginning inventory	180 units at $80
Sale	120 units at $125
First purchase	400 units at $82
Sale	300 units at $125
Second purchase	300 units at $84
Sale	275 units at $125

The firm uses the perpetual inventory system, and there are 185 units of the item on hand at the end of the year. What is the total cost of the ending inventory according to (a) FIFO, (b) LIFO?

EX 7-8 Periodic inventory by three methods

The units of an item available for sale during the year were as follows:

Jan.	1	Inventory	9 units at $360
Feb.	17	Purchase	18 units at $414
July	21	Purchase	21 units at $468
Nov.	23	Purchase	12 units at $495

There are 16 units of the item in the physical inventory at December 31. The periodic inventory system is used. Determine the inventory cost by (a) the first-in, first-out method, (b) the last-in, first-out method, and (c) the average cost method.

EX 7-9 Periodic inventory by three methods; cost of merchandise sold

The units of an item available for sale during the year were as follows:

Jan.	1	Inventory	21 units at $180
Mar.	10	Purchase	29 units at $195
Aug.	30	Purchase	10 units at $204
Dec.	12	Purchase	15 units at $210

There are 24 units of the item in the physical inventory at December 31. The periodic inventory system is used. Determine the inventory cost and the cost of merchandise sold by three methods, presenting your answers in the following form:

	Cost	
Inventory Method	**Merchandise Inventory**	**Merchandise Sold**
a. First-in, first-out	$	$
b. Last-in, first-out		
c. Average cost		

EX 7-10 Comparing inventory methods

Assume that a firm separately determined inventory under FIFO and LIFO and then compared the results.

a. In each space below, place the correct sign [less than (<), greater than (>), or equal (=)] for each comparison, assuming periods of rising prices.

1. FIFO inventory	_____	LIFO inventory
2. FIFO cost of goods sold	_____	LIFO cost of goods sold
3. FIFO net income	_____	LIFO net income
4. FIFO income tax	_____	LIFO income tax

b. Why would management prefer to use LIFO over FIFO in periods of rising prices?

OBJ. 6

✔ LCM: $10,320

EX 7-11 Lower-of-cost-or-market inventory

On the basis of the following data, determine the value of the inventory at the lower of cost or market. Assemble the data in the form illustrated in Exhibit 8.

Commodity	Inventory Quantity	Unit Cost Price	Unit Market Price
AL65	40	$28	$30
CA22	50	70	65
LA98	110	6	5
SC16	30	40	30
UT28	75	60	62

OBJ. 6

EX 7-12 Merchandise inventory on the balance sheet

Based on the data in Exercise 7-11 and assuming that cost was determined by the FIFO method, show how the merchandise inventory would appear on the balance sheet.

OBJ. 6

EX 7-13 Effect of errors in physical inventory

Hydro White Water Co. sells canoes, kayaks, whitewater rafts, and other boating supplies. During the taking of its physical inventory on December 31, 2012, Hydro White Water incorrectly counted its inventory as $439,650 instead of the correct amount of $451,000.

a. State the effect of the error on the December 31, 2012, balance sheet of Hydro White Water.

b. State the effect of the error on the income statement of Hydro White Water for the year ended December 31, 2012.

c. If uncorrected, what would be the effect of the error on the 2013 income statement?

d. If uncorrected, what would be the effect of the error on the December 31, 2013, balance sheet?

OBJ. 6

EX 7-14 Effect of errors in physical inventory

Eclipse Motorcycle Shop sells motorcycles, ATVs, and other related supplies and accessories. During the taking of its physical inventory on December 31, 2012, Eclipse Motorcycle Shop incorrectly counted its inventory as $350,000 instead of the correct amount of $338,000.

a. State the effect of the error on the December 31, 2012, balance sheet of Eclipse Motorcycle Shop.

b. State the effect of the error on the income statement of Eclipse Motorcycle Shop for the year ended December 31, 2012.

c. If uncorrected, what would be the effect of the error on the 2013 income statement?

d. If uncorrected, what would be the effect of the error on the December 31, 2013, balance sheet?

OBJ. 6

EX 7-15 Error in inventory

During 2012, the accountant discovered that the physical inventory at the end of 2011 had been understated by $18,000. Instead of correcting the error, however, the accountant assumed that an $18,000 overstatement of the physical inventory in 2012 would balance out the error.

➤ Are there any flaws in the accountant's assumption? Explain.

OBJ. 7

EX 7-16 Inventory turnover

The following data were taken from recent annual reports of Apple Computer, Inc., a manufacturer of personal computers and related products, and American Greetings Corporation, a manufacturer and distributor of greeting cards and related products:

	Apple	American Greetings
Cost of goods sold	$23,397,000,000	$809,956,000
Inventory, end of year	455,000,000	203,873,000
Inventory, beginning of the year	509,000,000	216,671,000

a. Determine the inventory turnover for Apple and American Greetings. Round to one decimal place.

b. Would you expect American Greetings' inventory turnover to be higher or lower than Apple's? Why?

OBJ. 7

✔ a. Kroger, 30 days' sales in inventory

EX 7-17   Inventory turnover and number of days' sales in inventory

Kroger, Safeway Inc., and Winn-Dixie Stores Inc. are three grocery chains in the United States. Inventory management is an important aspect of the grocery retail business. Recent balance sheets for these three companies indicated the following merchandise inventory information:

	Merchandise Inventory	
	End of Year (in millions)	Beginning of Year (in millions)
Kroger	$4,859	$4,855
Safeway	2,591	2,798
Winn-Dixie	665	649

The cost of goods sold for each company were:

	Cost of Goods Sold (in millions)
Kroger	$58,564
Safeway	31,589
Winn-Dixie	5,269

a. Determine the number of days' sales in inventory and inventory turnover for the three companies. Round to the nearest day and one decimal place.

b. Interpret your results in part (a).

c. If Winn-Dixie had Kroger's number of days' sales in inventory, how much additional cash flow (round to nearest million) would have been generated from the smaller inventory relative to its actual average inventory position?

Appendix
EX 7-18   Retail inventory method

A business using the retail method of inventory costing determines that merchandise inventory at retail is $780,000. If the ratio of cost to retail price is 65%, what is the amount of inventory to be reported on the financial statements?

Appendix
EX 7-19   Retail inventory method

A business using the retail method of inventory costing determines that merchandise inventory at retail is $475,000. If the ratio of cost to retail price is 80%, what is the amount of inventory to be reported on the financial statements?

Appendix
EX 7-20   Retail inventory method

A business using the retail method of inventory costing determines that merchandise inventory at retail is $900,000. If the ratio of cost to retail price is 72%, what is the amount of inventory to be reported on the financial statements?

✔ Inventory, November 30: $337,500

Appendix
EX 7-21   Retail inventory method

On the basis of the following data, estimate the cost of the merchandise inventory at November 30 by the retail method:

		Cost	Retail
November 1	Merchandise inventory	$ 300,000	$ 400,000
November 1–30	Purchases (net)	2,100,000	2,800,000
November 1–30	Sales (net)		2,750,000

✔ a. Merchandise destroyed: $620,000

Appendix
EX 7-22   Gross profit inventory method

The merchandise inventory was destroyed by fire on December 13. The following data were obtained from the accounting records:

Jan. 1	Merchandise inventory	$ 500,000
Jan. 1–Dec. 13	Purchases (net)	4,280,000
	Sales (net)	6,500,000
	Estimated gross profit rate	36%

a. Estimate the cost of the merchandise destroyed.

b. Briefly describe the situations in which the gross profit method is useful.

Appendix
EX 7-23   Gross profit method

Based on the following data, estimate the cost of ending merchandise inventory:

Sales (net)	$5,260,000
Estimated gross profit rate	40%
Beginning merchandise inventory	$ 180,000
Purchases (net)	3,200,000
Merchandise available for sale	$3,380,000

Appendix
EX 7-24   Gross profit method

Based on the following data, estimate the cost of ending merchandise inventory:

Sales (net)	$2,080,000
Estimated gross profit rate	37%
Beginning merchandise inventory	$ 75,000
Purchases (net)	1,325,000
Merchandise available for sale	$1,400,000

Problems Series A

OBJ. 2, 3

✔ 3. $28,725

PR 7-1A   FIFO perpetual inventory

The beginning inventory at Keats Office Supplies and data on purchases and sales for a three-month period are as follows:

Date		Transaction	Number of Units	Per Unit	Total
Mar.	1	Inventory	300	$20	$ 6,000
	10	Purchase	500	21	10,500
	28	Sale	400	35	14,000
	30	Sale	250	40	10,000
Apr.	5	Sale	80	40	3,200
	10	Purchase	450	22	9,900
	16	Sale	250	42	10,500
	28	Sale	150	45	6,750
May	5	Purchase	175	24	4,200
	14	Sale	160	50	8,000
	25	Purchase	150	25	3,750
	30	Sale	140	50	7,000

Instructions

1. Record the inventory, purchases, and cost of merchandise sold data in a perpetual inventory record similar to the one illustrated in Exhibit 3, using the first-in, first-out method.

2. Determine the total sales and the total cost of merchandise sold for the period. Journalize the entries in the sales and cost of merchandise sold accounts. Assume that all sales were on account.

3. Determine the gross profit from sales for the period.

4. Determine the ending inventory cost.

5. Based upon the preceding data, would you expect the inventory using the last-in, first-out method to be higher or lower?

OBJ. 2, 3

✔ 2. Gross profit, $28,210

PR 7-2A LIFO perpetual inventory

The beginning inventory at Keats Office Supplies and data on purchases and sales for a three-month period are shown in Problem 7-1A.

Instructions

1. Record the inventory, purchases, and cost of merchandise sold data in a perpetual inventory record similar to the one illustrated in Exhibit 4, using the last-in, first-out method.

2. Determine the total sales, the total cost of merchandise sold, and the gross profit from sales for the period.

3. Determine the ending inventory cost.

OBJ. 2, 4

✔ 1. $6,756

PR 7-3A Periodic inventory by three methods

Bulldog Appliances uses the periodic inventory system. Details regarding the inventory of appliances at September 1, 2011, purchases invoices during the next 12 months, and the inventory count at August 31, 2012, are summarized as follows:

| Model | Inventory, September 1 | Purchases Invoices | | | Inventory Count, August 31 |
		1st	2nd	3rd	
AZ09	—	4 at $ 32	4 at $ 35	4 at $ 38	5
GA85	8 at $ 88	4 at $ 79	3 at $ 85	6 at $ 92	7
HI71	3 at 75	3 at 65	15 at 68	9 at 70	5
KS32	7 at 242	6 at 250	5 at 260	10 at 259	9
MS17	12 at 80	10 at 82	16 at 89	16 at 90	13
ND52	2 at 108	2 at 110	3 at 128	3 at 130	5
WV63	5 at 160	4 at 170	4 at 175	7 at 180	8

Instructions

1. Determine the cost of the inventory on August 31, 2012, by the first-in, first-out method. Present data in columnar form, using the following headings:

Model	Quantity	Unit Cost	Total Cost

If the inventory of a particular model comprises one entire purchase plus a portion of another purchase acquired at a different unit cost, use a separate line for each purchase.

2. Determine the cost of the inventory on August 31, 2012, by the last-in, first-out method, following the procedures indicated in (1).

3. Determine the cost of the inventory on August 31, 2012, by the average cost method, using the columnar headings indicated in (1).

4. ➡ Discuss which method (FIFO or LIFO) would be preferred for income tax purposes in periods of (a) rising prices and (b) declining prices.

OBJ. 6

✔ Total LCM, $44,621

PR 7-4A Lower-of-cost-or-market inventory

If the working papers correlating with this textbook are not used, omit Problem 7-4A.

Data on the physical inventory of Rhino Company as of December 31, 2012, are presented in the working papers. The quantity of each commodity on hand has been determined and recorded on the inventory sheet. Unit market prices have also been determined as of December 31 and recorded on the sheet. The inventory is to be determined at cost and also at the lower of cost or market, using the first-in, first-out method. Quantity and cost data from the last purchases invoice of the year and the next-to-the-last purchases invoice are summarized as follows:

Description	Last Purchases Invoice Quantity Purchased	Last Purchases Invoice Unit Cost	Next-to-the-Last Purchases Invoice Quantity Purchased	Next-to-the-Last Purchases Invoice Unit Cost
Alpha	30	$ 60	30	$ 59
Beta	35	175	20	180
Charlie	20	130	25	129
Echo	130	24	100	25
Frank	10	565	10	560
George	100	15	100	14
Killo	10	385	5	384
Quebec	500	8	500	7
Romeo	80	22	50	21
Sierra	5	250	4	260
Whiskey	100	21	100	19
X-Ray	10	750	9	745

Instructions

Record the appropriate unit costs on the inventory sheet, and complete the pricing of the inventory. When there are two different unit costs applicable to an item, proceed as follows:

1. Draw a line through the quantity, and insert the quantity and unit cost of the last purchase.

2. On the following line, insert the quantity and unit cost of the next-to-the-last purchase.

3. Total the cost and market columns and insert the lower of the two totals in the Lower of C or M column. The first item on the inventory sheet has been completed as an example.

✔ 1. $175,000

Appendix
PR 7-5A Retail method; gross profit method

Selected data on merchandise inventory, purchases, and sales for Myrina Co. and Lemnos Co. are as follows:

	Cost	Retail
Myrina Co.		
Merchandise inventory, May 1	$ 130,000	$ 185,000
Transactions during May:		
Purchases (net)	1,382,000	1,975,000
Sales		1,950,000
Sales returns and allowances		40,000
Lemnos Co.		
Merchandise inventory, July 1	$ 280,000	
Transactions during July through September:		
Purchases (net)	3,400,000	
Sales	5,300,000	
Sales returns and allowances	100,000	
Estimated gross profit rate	35%	

Instructions

1. Determine the estimated cost of the merchandise inventory of Myrina Co. on May 31 by the retail method, presenting details of the computations.

2. a. Estimate the cost of the merchandise inventory of Lemnos Co. on September 30 by the gross profit method, presenting details of the computations.

   b. Assume that Lemnos Co. took a physical inventory on September 30 and discovered that $269,750 of merchandise was on hand. What was the estimated loss of inventory due to theft or damage during July through September?

Problems Series B

OBJ. 2, 3

✔ 3. $642,500

PR 7-1B   FIFO perpetual inventory

The beginning inventory of merchandise at Francesca Co. and data on purchases and sales for a three-month period are as follows:

Date		Transaction	Number of Units	Per Unit	Total
July	3	Inventory	75	$1,500	$112,500
	8	Purchase	150	1,800	270,000
	11	Sale	90	3,000	270,000
	30	Sale	45	3,000	135,000
Aug.	8	Purchase	125	2,000	250,000
	10	Sale	110	3,000	330,000
	19	Sale	80	3,000	240,000
	28	Purchase	100	2,200	220,000
Sept.	5	Sale	60	3,500	210,000
	16	Sale	50	3,500	175,000
	21	Purchase	180	2,400	432,000
	28	Sale	90	3,500	315,000

Instructions

1. Record the inventory, purchases, and cost of merchandise sold data in a perpetual inventory record similar to the one illustrated in Exhibit 3, using the first-in, first-out method.

2. Determine the total sales and the total cost of merchandise sold for the period. Journalize the entries in the sales and cost of merchandise sold accounts. Assume that all sales were on account.

3. Determine the gross profit from sales for the period.

4. Determine the ending inventory cost.

5. Based upon the preceding data, would you expect the inventory using the last-in, first-out method to be higher or lower?

OBJ. 2, 3

✔ 2. Gross profit, $629,000

PR 7-2B   LIFO perpetual inventory

The beginning inventory for Francesca Co and data on purchases and sales for a three-month period are shown in Problem 7-1B.

Instructions

1. Record the inventory, purchases, and cost of merchandise sold data in a perpetual inventory record similar to the one illustrated in Exhibit 4, using the last-in, first-out method.

2. Determine the total sales, the total cost of merchandise sold, and the gross profit from sales for the period.

3. Determine the ending inventory cost.

PR 7-3B Periodic inventory by three methods

Artic Appliances uses the periodic inventory system. Details regarding the inventory of appliances at January 1, 2012, purchases invoices during the year, and the inventory count at December 31, 2012, are summarized as follows:

Model	Inventory, January 1	Purchases Invoices 1st	2nd	3rd	Inventory Count, December 31
AK82	3 at $520	3 at $527	3 at $530	3 at $535	5
CO62	9 at 213	7 at 215	6 at 222	6 at 225	12
DE03	5 at 60	3 at 65	1 at 65	1 at 70	2
FL12	6 at 305	3 at 310	3 at 316	4 at 317	4
ME09	6 at 520	8 at 531	4 at 549	6 at 542	7
NM57	—	4 at 222	4 at 232	—	2
TN33	4 at 35	6 at 36	8 at 37	7 at 39	5

Instructions

1. Determine the cost of the inventory on December 31, 2012, by the first-in, first-out method. Present data in columnar form, using the following headings:

Model	Quantity	Unit Cost	Total Cost

  If the inventory of a particular model comprises one entire purchase plus a portion of another purchase acquired at a different unit cost, use a separate line for each purchase.

2. Determine the cost of the inventory on December 31, 2012, by the last-in, first-out method, following the procedures indicated in (1).

3. Determine the cost of the inventory on December 31, 2012, by the average cost method, using the columnar headings indicated in (1).

4. ━━━▶ Discuss which method (FIFO or LIFO) would be preferred for income tax purposes in periods of (a) rising prices and (b) declining prices.

PR 7-4B Lower-of-cost-or-market inventory

If the working papers correlating with this textbook are not used, omit Problem 7-4B.

Data on the physical inventory of Chiron Co. as of December 31, 2012, are presented in the working papers. The quantity of each commodity on hand has been determined and recorded on the inventory sheet. Unit market prices have also been determined as of December 31 and recorded on the sheet. The inventory is to be determined at cost and also at the lower of cost or market, using the first-in, first-out method. Quantity and cost data from the last purchases invoice of the year and the next-to-the-last purchases invoice are summarized as follows:

Description	Last Purchases Invoice Quantity Purchased	Unit Cost	Next-to-the-Last Purchases Invoice Quantity Purchased	Unit Cost
Alpha	30	$ 60	40	$ 59
Beta	25	170	15	180
Charlie	20	130	15	128
Echo	150	25	100	27
Frank	6	550	15	540
George	90	16	100	15
Killo	8	395	4	394
Quebec	500	6	500	7
Romeo	75	25	80	26
Sierra	5	250	4	260
Whiskey	100	17	115	16
X-Ray	10	750	8	740

Instructions

Record the appropriate unit costs on the inventory sheet, and complete the pricing of the inventory. When there are two different unit costs applicable to an item:

1. Draw a line through the quantity, and insert the quantity and unit cost of the last purchase.

2. On the following line, insert the quantity and unit cost of the next-to-the-last purchase.

3. Total the cost and market columns and insert the lower of the two totals in the Lower of C or M column. The first item on the inventory sheet has been completed as an example.

✔ 1. $409,500

Appendix
PR 7-5B   Retail method; gross profit method

Selected data on merchandise inventory, purchases, and sales for Segal Co. and Iroquois Co. are as follows:

	Cost	Retail
Segal Co.		
Merchandise inventory, March 1	$ 298,000	$ 375,000
Transactions during March:		
Purchases (net)	4,850,000	6,225,000
Sales		6,320,000
Sales returns and allowances		245,000
Iroquois Co.		
Merchandise inventory, January 1	$ 300,000	
Transactions during January thru March:		
Purchases (net)	4,150,000	
Sales	6,900,000	
Sales returns and allowances	175,000	
Estimated gross profit rate	40%	

Instructions

1. Determine the estimated cost of the merchandise inventory of Segal Co. on March 31 by the retail method, presenting details of the computations.

2. a. Estimate the cost of the merchandise inventory of Iroquois Co. on March 31 by the gross profit method, presenting details of the computations.

   b. Assume that Iroquois Co. took a physical inventory on March 31 and discovered that $396,500 of merchandise was on hand. What was the estimated loss of inventory due to theft or damage during January thru March?

Cases & Projects

CP 7-1   Ethics and professional conduct in business

Contours Co. is experiencing a decrease in sales and operating income for the fiscal year ending July 31, 2012. Mark Irwin, controller of Contours Co., has suggested that all orders received before the end of the fiscal year be shipped by midnight, July 31, 2012, even if the shipping department must work overtime. Since Contours Co. ships all merchandise FOB shipping point, it would record all such shipments as sales for the year ending July 31, 2012, thereby offsetting some of the decreases in sales and operating income.

➤ Discuss whether Mark Irwin is behaving in a professional manner.

CP 7-2   LIFO and inventory flow

The following is an excerpt from a conversation between Gary Ortiz, the warehouse manager for Ivey Foods Wholesale Co., and its accountant, Lori Cray. Ivey Foods operates a large regional warehouse that supplies produce and other grocery products to grocery stores in smaller communities.

Gary: Lori, can you explain what's going on here with these monthly statements?

Lori: Sure, Gary. How can I help you?

Gary: I don't understand this last-in, first-out inventory procedure. It just doesn't make sense.

Lori: Well, what it means is that we assume that the last goods we receive are the first ones sold. So the inventory consists of the items we purchased first.

Gary: Yes, but that's my problem. It doesn't work that way! We always distribute the oldest produce first. Some of that produce is perishable! We can't keep any of it very long or it'll spoil.

Lori: Gary, you don't understand. We only *assume* that the products we distribute are the last ones received. We don't actually have to distribute the goods in this way.

Gary: I always thought that accounting was supposed to show what really happened. It all sounds like "make believe" to me! Why not report what really happens?

 Respond to Gary's concerns.

CP 7-3   Costing inventory

White Dove Company began operations in 2012 by selling a single product. Data on purchases and sales for the year were as follows:

Purchases:

Date	Units Purchased	Unit Cost	Total Cost
April 6	62,000	$12.20	$ 756,400
May 18	66,000	13.00	858,000
June 6	80,000	13.20	1,056,000
July 10	80,000	14.00	1,120,000
August 10	54,400	14.25	775,200
October 25	25,600	14.50	371,200
November 4	16,000	14.95	239,200
December 10	16,000	16.00	256,000
	400,000		$5,432,000

Sales:

April	32,000 units
May	32,000
June	40,000
July	48,000
August	56,000
September	56,000
October	36,000
November	20,000
December	16,000
Total units	336,000
Total sales	$5,200,000

On January 4, 2013, the president of the company, Joel McLees, asked for your advice on costing the 64,000-unit physical inventory that was taken on December 31, 2012. Moreover, since the firm plans to expand its product line, he asked for your advice on the use of a perpetual inventory system in the future.

1. Determine the cost of the December 31, 2012, inventory under the periodic system, using the (a) first-in, first-out method, (b) last-in, first-out method, and (c) average cost method.

2. Determine the gross profit for the year under each of the three methods in (1).

3. a. Explain varying viewpoints why each of the three inventory costing methods may best reflect the results of operations for 2012.

    b. Which of the three inventory costing methods may best reflect the replacement cost of the inventory on the balance sheet as of December 31, 2012?

    c. Which inventory costing method would you choose to use for income tax purposes? Why?

    d. Discuss the advantages and disadvantages of using a perpetual inventory system. From the data presented in this case, is there any indication of the adequacy of inventory levels during the year?

CP 7-4 Inventory ratios for Dell and HP

Dell Inc. and Hewlett-Packard Development Company, L.P. (HP) are both manufacturers of computer equipment and peripherals. However, the two companies follow two different strategies. Dell follows primarily a build-to-order strategy, where the consumer orders the computer from a Web page. The order is then manufactured and shipped to the customer within days of the order. In contrast, HP follows a build-to-stock strategy, where the computer is first built for inventory, then sold from inventory to retailers, such as Best Buy. The two strategies can be seen in the difference between the inventory turnover and number of days' sales in inventory ratios for the two companies. The following financial statement information is provided for Dell and HP for a recent fiscal year (in millions):

	Dell	HP
Inventory, beginning of period	$ 1,180	$ 7,879
Inventory, end of period	867	6,128
Cost of goods sold	50,144	87,524

a. Determine the inventory turnover ratio and number of days' sales in inventory ratio for each company. Round to one decimal place.

b. Interpret the difference between the ratios for the two companies.

CP 7-5 Comparing inventory ratios for two companies

Tiffany Co. is a high-end jewelry retailer, while Amazon.com uses its e-commerce services, features, and technologies to sell its products through the Internet. Recent balance sheet inventory disclosures for Tiffany and Amazon.com (in millons) are as follows:

	End-of-Period Inventory	Beginning-of-Period Inventory
Tiffany Co.	$1,601	$1,242
Amazon.com	1,399	1,200

The cost of merchandise sold reported by each company was as follows:

	Tiffany Co.	Amazon.com
Cost of merchandise sold	$1,215	$14,896

a. Determine the inventory turnover and number of days' sales in inventory for Tiffany and Amazon.com. Round to two decimal places and nearest day.

b. Interpret your results.

CP 7-6 Comparing inventory ratios for three companies

The general merchandise retail industry has a number of segments represented by the following companies:

Company Name	Merchandise Concept
Costco Wholesale Corporation	Membership warehouse
Wal-Mart	Discount general merchandise
JCPenney	Department store

For a recent year, the following cost of merchandise sold and beginning and ending inventories have been provided from corporate annual reports (in millions) for these three companies:

	Costco	Wal-Mart	JCPenney
Cost of merchandise sold	$62,335	$306,158	$11,571
Merchandise inventory, beginning	5,039	35,180	3,641
Merchandise inventory, ending	5,405	34,511	3,259

a. Determine the inventory turnover ratio for all three companies. Round to one decimal place.

b. Determine the number of days' sales in inventory for all three companies. Round to one decimal place.

c. Interpret these results based on each company's merchandise concept.

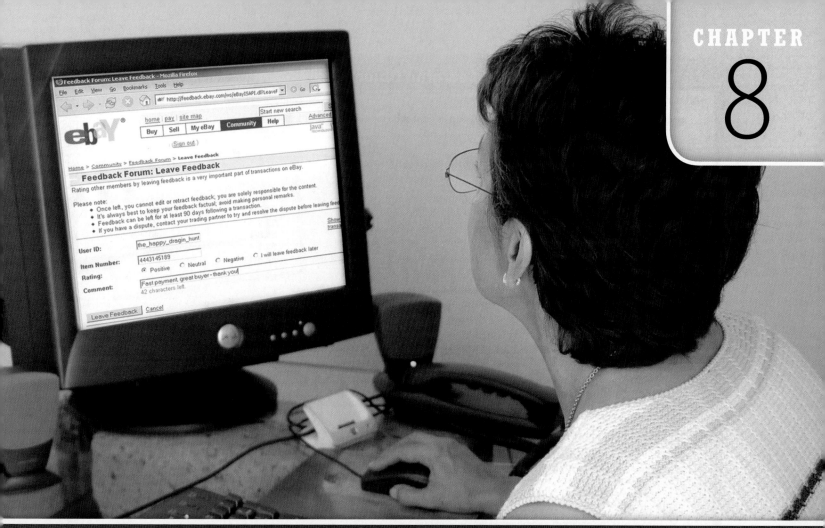
© Kemie Guaida/iStockphoto Inc.

CHAPTER

8

Sarbanes-Oxley, Internal Control, and Cash

eBay Inc.

Controls are a part of your everyday life. At one extreme, laws are used to limit your behavior. For example, speed limits are designed to control your driving for traffic safety. In addition, you are also affected by many nonlegal controls. For example, you can keep credit card receipts in order to compare your transactions to the monthly credit card statement. Comparing receipts to the monthly statement is a control designed to catch mistakes made by the credit card company. In addition, banks give you a personal identification number (PIN) as a control against unauthorized access to your cash if you lose your automated teller machine (ATM) card. Dairies use freshness dating on their milk containers as a control to prevent the purchase or sale of soured milk. As you can see, you use and encounter controls every day.

Just as there are many examples of controls throughout society, businesses must also implement controls to help guide the behavior of their managers, employees, and customers. For example, **eBay Inc.** maintains an Internet-based marketplace for the sale of

goods and services. Using eBay's online platform, buyers and sellers can browse, buy, and sell a wide variety of items including antiques and used cars. However, in order to maintain the integrity and trust of its buyers and sellers, eBay must have controls to ensure that buyers pay for their items and sellers don't misrepresent their items or fail to deliver sales. One such control eBay uses is a feedback forum that establishes buyer and seller reputations. A prospective buyer or seller can view the member's reputation and feedback comments before completing a transaction. Dishonest or unfair trading can lead to a negative reputation and even suspension or cancellation of the member's ability to trade on eBay.

This chapter discusses controls that can be included in accounting systems to provide reasonable assurance that the financial statements are reliable. Controls to discover and prevent errors to a bank account are also discussed. This chapter begins by discussing the Sarbanes-Oxley Act of 2002 and its impact on controls and financial reporting.

Learning Objectives

OBJ. 1 Describe the Sarbanes-Oxley Act of 2002 and its impact on internal controls and financial reporting.

Sarbanes-Oxley Act of 2002

During the financial scandals of the early 2000s, stockholders, creditors, and other investors lost billions of dollars.[1] As a result, the U.S. Congress passed the **Sarbanes-Oxley Act of 2002**. This act, often referred to as *Sarbanes-Oxley*, is one of the most important laws affecting U.S. companies in recent history. The purpose of Sarbanes-Oxley is to restore public confidence and trust in the financial reporting of companies.

Sarbanes-Oxley applies only to companies whose stock is traded on public exchanges, referred to as *publicly held companies*. However, Sarbanes-Oxley highlighted the importance of assessing the financial controls and reporting of all companies. As a result, companies of all sizes have been influenced by Sarbanes-Oxley.

Sarbanes-Oxley emphasizes the importance of effective internal control.[2] **Internal control** is defined as the procedures and processes used by a company to:

1. Safeguard its assets.
2. Process information accurately.
3. Ensure compliance with laws and regulations.

Sarbanes-Oxley requires companies to maintain effective internal controls over the recording of transactions and the preparing of financial statements. Such controls are important because they deter fraud and prevent misleading financial statements as shown on the next page.

---

1 Exhibit 2 in Chapter 1 briefly summarizes these scandals.

2 Sarbanes-Oxley also has important implications for corporate governance and the regulation of the public accounting profession. This chapter, however, focuses on the internal control implications of Sarbanes-Oxley.

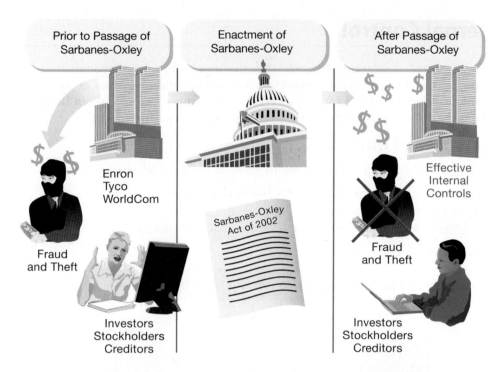

Sarbanes-Oxley also requires companies and their independent accountants to report on the effectiveness of the company's internal controls.[3] These reports are required to be filed with the company's annual 10-K report with the Securities and Exchange Commission. Companies are also encouraged to include these reports in their annual reports to stockholders. An example of such a report by the management of Nike is shown in Exhibit 1.

Management's Annual Report on Internal Control Over Financial Reporting

Management is responsible for establishing and maintaining adequate internal control over financial reporting . . . , Under the supervision and with the participation of our Chief Executive Officer and Chief Financial Officer, our management conducted an evaluation of the effectiveness of our internal control over financial reporting based upon the framework in *Internal Control—Integrated Framework* issued by the Committee of Sponsoring Organizations of the Treadway Commission. Based on that evaluation, our management concluded that our internal control over financial reporting is effective as of May 31, 2009. . . .

PricewaterhouseCoopers LLP, an independent registered public accounting firm, has audited . . . management's assessment of the effectiveness of our internal control over financial reporting . . . and . . . the effectiveness of our internal control over financial reporting . . . as stated in their report. . . .

MARK G. PARKER
Chief Executive Officer and President

DONALD W. BLAIR
Chief Financial Officer

EXHIBIT 1

Sarbanes-Oxley Report of Nike

Exhibit 1 indicates that Nike based its evaluation of internal controls on *Internal Control—Integrated Framework*, which was issued by the Committee of Sponsoring Organizations (COSO) of the Treadway Commission. This framework is the standard by which companies design, analyze, and evaluate internal controls. For this reason, this framework is used as the basis for discussing internal controls.

Information on *Internal Control—Integrated Framework* can be found on COSO's Web site at **http://www.coso.org/.**

3 These reporting requirements are required under Section 404 of the act. As a result, these requirements and reports are often referred to as 404 requirements and 404 reports.

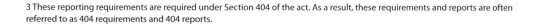

Describe and illustrate the objectives and elements of internal control.

Internal Control

Internal Control—Integrated Framework is the standard by which companies design, analyze, and evaluate internal control.[4] In this section, the objectives of internal control are described followed by a discussion of how these objectives can be achieved through the *Integrated Framework's* five elements of internal control.

Objectives of Internal Control

The objectives of internal control are to provide reasonable assurance that:

1. Assets are safeguarded and used for business purposes.
2. Business information is accurate.
3. Employees and managers comply with laws and regulations.

These objectives are illustrated below.

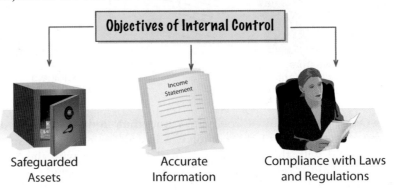

Safeguarded
Assets

Accurate
Information

Compliance with Laws
and Regulations

Internal control can safeguard assets by preventing theft, fraud, misuse, or misplacement. A serious concern of internal control is preventing employee fraud. **Employee fraud** is the intentional act of deceiving an employer for personal gain. Such fraud may range from minor overstating of a travel expense report to stealing millions of dollars. Employees stealing from a business often adjust the accounting records in order to hide their fraud. Thus, employee fraud usually affects the accuracy of business information.

Accurate information is necessary to successfully operate a business. Businesses must also comply with laws, regulations, and financial reporting standards. Examples of such standards include environmental regulations, safety regulations, and generally accepted accounting principles (GAAP).

Elements of Internal Control

The three internal control objectives can be achieved by applying the five **elements of internal control** set forth by the *Integrated Framework*.[5] These elements are as follows:

1. Control environment
2. Risk assessment

4 *Internal Control—Integrated Framework* by the Committee of Sponsoring Organizations of the Treadway Commission, 1992.
5 Ibid., pp. 12–14.

3. Control procedures
4. Monitoring
5. Information and communication

The elements of internal control are illustrated in Exhibit 2.

EXHIBIT 2

Elements of Internal Control

In Exhibit 2, the elements of internal control form an umbrella over the business to protect it from control threats. The control environment is the size of the umbrella. Risk assessment, control procedures, and monitoring are the fabric of the umbrella, which keep it from leaking. Information and communication connect the umbrella to management.

Control Environment

The **control environment** is the overall attitude of management and employees about the importance of controls. Three factors influencing a company's control environment are as follows:

1. Management's philosophy and operating style
2. The company's organizational structure
3. The company's personnel policies

Control Environment

Management's philosophy and operating style relates to whether management emphasizes the importance of internal controls. An emphasis on controls and adherence to control policies creates an effective control environment. In contrast, overemphasizing operating goals and tolerating deviations from control policies creates an ineffective control environment.

The business's organizational structure is the framework for planning and controlling operations. For example, a retail store chain might organize each of its stores as separate business units. Each store manager has full authority over pricing and other operating activities. In such a structure, each store manager has the responsibility for establishing an effective control environment.

The business's personnel policies involve the hiring, training, evaluation, compensation, and promotion of employees. In addition, job descriptions, employee codes of ethics, and conflict-of-interest policies are part of the personnel policies. Such policies can enhance the internal control environment if they provide reasonable assurance that only competent, honest employees are hired and retained.

Risk Assessment

All businesses face risks such as changes in customer requirements, competitive threats, regulatory changes, and changes in economic factors. Management should identify such risks, analyze their significance, assess their likelihood of occurring, and take any necessary actions to minimize them.

Control Procedures

Control procedures provide reasonable assurance that business goals will be achieved, including the prevention of fraud. Control procedures, which constitute one of the most important elements of internal control, include the following as shown in Exhibit 3.

1. Competent personnel, rotating duties, and mandatory vacations
2. Separating responsibilities for related operations
3. Separating operations, custody of assets, and accounting
4. Proofs and security measures

EXHIBIT 3

Internal Control Procedures

Competent Personnel, Rotating Duties, and Mandatory Vacations A successful company needs competent employees who are able to perform the duties that they are assigned. Procedures should be established for properly training and supervising employees. It is also advisable to rotate duties of accounting personnel and mandate vacations for all employees. In this way, employees are encouraged to adhere to procedures. Cases of employee fraud are often discovered when a long-term employee, who never took vacations, missed work because of an illness or another unavoidable reason.

Separating Responsibilities for Related Operations The responsibility for related operations should be divided among two or more persons. This decreases the possibility of errors and fraud. For example, if the same person orders supplies, verifies the receipt of the supplies, and pays the supplier, the following abuses may occur:

1. Orders may be placed on the basis of friendship with a supplier, rather than on price, quality, and other objective factors.
2. The quantity and quality of supplies received may not be verified; thus, the company may pay for supplies not received or that are of poor quality.
3. Supplies may be stolen by the employee.
4. The validity and accuracy of invoices may not be verified; hence, the company may pay false or inaccurate invoices.

For the preceding reasons, the responsibilities for purchasing, receiving, and paying for supplies should be divided among three persons or departments.

Separating Operations, Custody of Assets, and Accounting The responsibilities for operations, custody of assets, and accounting should be separated. In this way, the accounting records serve as an independent check on the operating managers and the employees who have custody of assets.

To illustrate, employees who handle cash receipts should not record cash receipts in the accounting records. To do so would allow employees to borrow or steal cash and hide the theft in the accounting records. Likewise, operating managers should not also record the results of operations. To do so would allow the managers to distort the accounting reports to show favorable results, which might allow them to receive larger bonuses.

Proofs and Security Measures Proofs and security measures are used to safeguard assets and ensure reliable accounting data. Proofs involve procedures such as authorization, approval, and reconciliation. For example, an employee planning to travel on company business may be required to complete a "travel request" form for a manager's authorization and approval.

Documents used for authorization and approval should be prenumbered, accounted for, and safeguarded. Prenumbering of documents helps prevent transactions from being recorded more than once or not at all. In addition, accounting for and

Integrity, Objectivity, and Ethics in Business

TIPS ON PREVENTING EMPLOYEE FRAUD IN SMALL COMPANIES

- Do not have the same employee write company checks and keep the books. Look for payments to vendors you don't know or payments to vendors whose names appear to be misspelled.
- If your business has a computer system, restrict access to accounting files as much as possible. Also, keep a backup copy of your accounting files and store it at an off-site location.
- Be wary of anybody working in finance that declines to take vacations. They may be afraid that a replacement will uncover fraud.
- Require and monitor supporting documentation (such as vendor invoices) before signing checks.

- Track the number of credit card bills you sign monthly.
- Limit and monitor access to important documents and supplies, such as blank checks and signature stamps.
- Check W-2 forms against your payroll annually to make sure you're not carrying any fictitious employees.
- Rely on yourself, not on your accountant, to spot fraud.

Source: Steve Kaufman, "Embezzlement Common at Small Companies," Knight-Ridder Newspapers, reported in *Athens Daily News/Athens Banner-Herald*, March 10, 1996, p. 4D.

safeguarding prenumbered documents helps prevent fraudulent transactions from being recorded. For example, blank checks are prenumbered and safeguarded. Once a payment has been properly authorized and approved, the checks are filled out and issued.

Reconciliations are also an important control. Later in this chapter, the use of bank reconciliations as an aid in controlling cash is described and illustrated.

Security measures involve measures to safeguard assets. For example, cash on hand should be kept in a cash register or safe. Inventory not on display should be stored in a locked storeroom or warehouse. Accounting records such as the accounts receivable subsidiary ledger should also be safeguarded to prevent their loss. For example, electronically maintained accounting records should be safeguarded with access codes and backed up so that any lost or damaged files could be recovered if necessary.

Monitoring

Monitoring the internal control system is used to locate weaknesses and improve controls. Monitoring often includes observing employee behavior and the accounting system for indicators of control problems. Some such indicators are shown in Exhibit 4.[6]

Evaluations of controls are often performed when there are major changes in strategy, senior management, business structure, or operations. Internal auditors, who are independent of operations, usually perform such evaluations. Internal auditors are also responsible for day-to-day monitoring of controls. External auditors also evaluate and report on internal control as part of their annual financial statement audit.

EXHIBIT 4

Warning Signs of Internal Control Problems

Warning signs with regard to people

1. Abrupt change in lifestyle (without winning the lottery).
2. Close social relationships with suppliers.
3. Refusing to take a vacation.
4. Frequent borrowing from other employees.
5. Excessive use of alcohol or drugs.

Warning signs from the accounting system

1. Missing documents or gaps in transaction numbers (could mean documents are being used for fraudulent transactions).
2. An unusual increase in customer refunds (refunds may be phony).
3. Differences between daily cash receipts and bank deposits (could mean receipts are being pocketed before being deposited).
4. Sudden increase in slow payments (employee may be pocketing the payments).
5. Backlog in recording transactions (possibly an attempt to delay detection of fraud).

Information and Communication

Information and communication is an essential element of internal control. Information about the control environment, risk assessment, control procedures, and monitoring is used by management for guiding operations and ensuring compliance with reporting, legal, and regulatory requirements. Management also uses external information to assess events and conditions that impact decision making and external

6 Edwin C. Bliss, "Employee Theft," *Boardroom Reports*, July 15, 1994, pp. 5–6.

reporting. For example, management uses pronouncements of the Financial Accounting Standards Board (FASB) to assess the impact of changes in reporting standards on the financial statements.

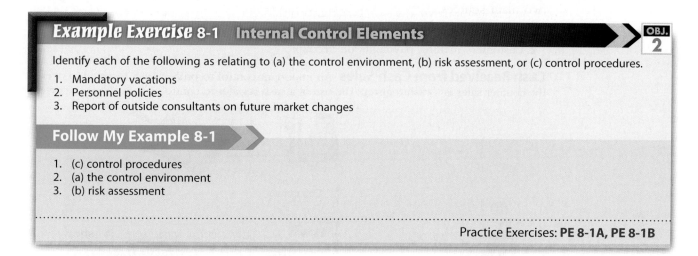

Example Exercise 8-1 Internal Control Elements

OBJ. 2

Identify each of the following as relating to (a) the control environment, (b) risk assessment, or (c) control procedures.

1. Mandatory vacations
2. Personnel policies
3. Report of outside consultants on future market changes

Follow My Example 8-1

1. (c) control procedures
2. (a) the control environment
3. (b) risk assessment

Practice Exercises: **PE 8-1A, PE 8-1B**

Limitations of Internal Control

Internal control systems can provide only reasonable assurance for safeguarding assets, processing accurate information, and compliance with laws and regulations. In other words, internal controls are not a guarantee. This is due to the following factors:

1. The human element of controls
2. Cost-benefit considerations

The *human element* recognizes that controls are applied and used by humans. As a result, human errors can occur because of fatigue, carelessness, confusion, or misjudgment. For example, an employee may unintentionally shortchange a customer or miscount the amount of inventory received from a supplier. In addition, two or more employees may collude together to defeat or circumvent internal controls. This latter case often involves fraud and the theft of assets. For example, the cashier and the accounts receivable clerk might collude to steal customer payments on account.

Cost-benefit considerations recognize that cost of internal controls should not exceed their benefits. For example, retail stores could eliminate shoplifting by searching all customers before they leave the store. However, such a control procedure would upset customers and result in lost sales. Instead, retailers use cameras or signs saying *We prosecute all shoplifters.*

Cash Controls Over Receipts and Payments

OBJ. 3 Describe and illustrate the application of internal controls to cash.

Cash includes coins, currency (paper money), checks, and money orders. Money on deposit with a bank or other financial institution that is available for withdrawal is also considered cash. Normally, you can think of cash as anything that a bank would accept for deposit in your account. For example, a check made payable to you could normally be deposited in a bank and, thus, is considered cash.

Businesses usually have several bank accounts. For example, a business might have one bank account for general cash payments and another for payroll. A separate ledger account is normally used for each bank account. For example, a bank account at City Bank could be identified in the ledger as *Cash in Bank—City Bank.* To simplify, this chapter assumes that a company has only *one* bank account, which is identified in the ledger as *Cash.*

Cash is the asset most likely to be stolen or used improperly in a business. For this reason, businesses must carefully control cash and cash transactions.

Control of Cash Receipts

To protect cash from theft and misuse, a business must control cash from the time it is received until it is deposited in a bank. Businesses normally receive cash from two main sources.

1. Customers purchasing products or services
2. Customers making payments on account

Cash Received from Cash Sales   An important control to protect cash received in over-the-counter sales is a cash register. The use of a cash register to control cash is shown below.

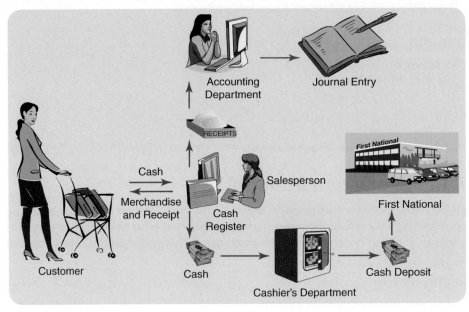

A cash register controls cash as follows:

1. At the beginning of every work shift, each cash register clerk is given a cash drawer containing a predetermined amount of cash. This amount is used for making change for customers and is sometimes called a *change fund*.
2. When a salesperson enters the amount of a sale, the cash register displays the amount to the customer. This allows the customer to verify that the clerk has charged the correct amount. The customer also receives a cash receipt.
3. At the end of the shift, the clerk and the supervisor count the cash in the clerk's cash drawer. The amount of cash in each drawer should equal the beginning amount of cash plus the cash sales for the day.
4. The supervisor takes the cash to the Cashier's Department where it is placed in a safe.
5. The supervisor forwards the clerk's cash register receipts to the Accounting Department.
6. The cashier prepares a bank deposit ticket.
7. The cashier deposits the cash in the bank, or the cash is picked up by an armored car service, such as Wells Fargo.
8. The Accounting Department summarizes the cash receipts and records the day's cash sales.
9. When cash is deposited in the bank, the bank normally stamps a duplicate copy of the deposit ticket with the amount received. This bank receipt is returned to the Accounting Department, where it is compared to the total amount that should have been deposited. This control helps ensure that all the cash is deposited and that no cash is lost or stolen on the way to the bank. Any shortages are thus promptly detected.

Salespersons may make errors in making change for customers or in ringing up cash sales. As a result, the amount of cash on hand may differ from the amount of cash sales. Such differences are recorded in a **cash short and over account**.

To illustrate, assume the following cash register data for May 3:

Cash register total for cash sales	$35,690
Cash receipts from cash sales	35,668

The cash sales, receipts, and shortage of $22 ($35,690 − $35,668) would be recorded as follows:

May	3	Cash		35,668	
		Cash Short and Over		22	
		Sales			35,690

If there had been cash over, Cash Short and Over would have been credited for the overage. At the end of the accounting period, a debit balance in Cash Short and Over is included in miscellaneous expense on the income statement. A credit balance is included in the Other Income section. If a salesperson consistently has large cash short and over amounts, the supervisor may require the clerk to take additional training.

Cash Received in the Mail Cash is received in the mail when customers pay their bills. This cash is usually in the form of checks and money orders. Most companies design their invoices so that customers return a portion of the invoice, called a *remittance advice*, with their payment. Remittance advices may be used to control cash received in the mail as follows:

1. An employee opens the incoming mail and compares the amount of cash received with the amount shown on the remittance advice. If a customer does not return a remittance advice, the employee prepares one. The remittance advice serves as a record of the cash initially received. It also helps ensure that the posting to the customer's account is for the amount of cash received.
2. The employee opening the mail stamps checks and money orders "For Deposit Only" in the bank account of the business.
3. The remittance advices and their summary totals are delivered to the Accounting Department.
4. All cash and money orders are delivered to the Cashier's Department.
5. The cashier prepares a bank deposit ticket.
6. The cashier deposits the cash in the bank, or the cash is picked up by an armored car service, such as Wells Fargo.
7. An accounting clerk records the cash received and posts the amounts to the customer accounts.
8. When cash is deposited in the bank, the bank normally stamps a duplicate copy of the deposit ticket with the amount received. This bank receipt is returned to the Accounting Department, where it is compared to the total amount that should have been deposited. This control helps ensure that all cash is deposited and that no cash is lost or stolen on the way to the bank. Any shortages are thus promptly detected.

Separating the duties of the Cashier's Department, which handles cash, and the Accounting Department, which records cash, is a control. If Accounting Department employees both handle and record cash, an employee could steal cash and change the accounting records to hide the theft.

Cash Received by EFT Cash may also be received from customers through **electronic funds transfer (EFT)**. For example, customers may authorize automatic electronic transfers from their checking accounts to pay monthly bills for such items as cell phone, Internet, and electric services. In such cases, the company sends the customer's bank a signed form from the customer authorizing the monthly electronic transfers. Each month, the company notifies the customer's bank of the amount of the transfer and the date the transfer should take place. On the due date, the company records the electronic transfer as a receipt of cash to its bank account and posts the amount paid to the customer's account.

Companies encourage customers to use EFT for the following reasons:

1. EFTs cost less than receiving cash payments through the mail.
2. EFTs enhance internal controls over cash since the cash is received directly by the bank without any employees handling cash.
3. EFTs reduce late payments from customers and speed up the processing of cash receipts.

Control of Cash Payments

Howard Schultz & Associates (HS&A) specializes in reviewing cash payments for its clients. HS&A searches for errors, such as duplicate payments, failures to take discounts, and inaccurate computations. Amounts recovered for clients range from thousands to millions of dollars.

The control of cash payments should provide reasonable assurance that:

1. Payments are made for only authorized transactions.
2. Cash is used effectively and efficiently. For example, controls should ensure that all available purchase discounts are taken.

In a small business, an owner/manager may authorize payments based on personal knowledge. In a large business, however, purchasing goods, inspecting the goods received, and verifying the invoices are usually performed by different employees. These duties must be coordinated to ensure that proper payments are made to creditors. One system used for this purpose is the voucher system.

Voucher System

A **voucher system** is a set of procedures for authorizing and recording liabilities and cash payments. A **voucher** is any document that serves as proof of authority to pay cash or issue an electronic funds transfer. An invoice that has been approved for payment could be considered a voucher. In many businesses, however, a voucher is a special form used to record data about a liability and the details of its payment.

In a manual system, a voucher is normally prepared after all necessary supporting documents have been received. For the purchase of goods, a voucher is supported by the supplier's invoice, a purchase order, and a receiving report. After a voucher is prepared, it is submitted for approval. Once approved, the voucher is recorded in the accounts and filed by due date. Upon payment, the voucher is recorded in the same manner as the payment of an account payable.

In a computerized system, data from the supporting documents (such as purchase orders, receiving reports, and suppliers' invoices) are entered directly into computer files. At the due date, the checks are automatically generated and mailed to creditors. At that time, the voucher is electronically transferred to a paid voucher file.

Cash Paid by EFT

Cash can also be paid by electronic funds transfer (EFT) systems. For example, you can withdraw cash from your bank account using an ATM machine. Your withdrawal is a type of EFT transfer.

Companies also use EFT transfers. For example, many companies pay their employees via EFT. Under such a system, employees authorize the deposit of their payroll checks directly into their checking accounts. Each pay period, the company transfers the employees' net pay to their checking accounts through the use of EFT. Many companies also use EFT systems to pay their suppliers and other vendors.

 Describe the nature of a bank account and its use in controlling cash.

Bank Accounts

A major reason that companies use bank accounts is for internal control. Some of the control advantages of using bank accounts are as follows:

1. Bank accounts reduce the amount of cash on hand.
2. Bank accounts provide an independent recording of cash transactions. Reconciling the balance of the cash account in the company's records with the cash balance according to the bank is an important control.
3. Use of bank accounts facilitates the transfer of funds using EFT systems.

Bank Statement

Banks usually maintain a record of all checking account transactions. A summary of all transactions, called a **bank statement**, is mailed to the company (depositor) or made available online, usually each month. The bank statement shows the beginning balance, additions, deductions, and the ending balance. A typical bank statement is shown in Exhibit 5.

Checks or copies of the checks listed in the order that they were paid by the bank may accompany the bank statement. If paid checks are returned, they are stamped "Paid," together with the date of payment. Many banks no longer return checks or check copies. Instead, the check payment information is available online.

EXHIBIT 5

Bank Statement

```
                    MEMBER FDIC                                 PAGE    1

VALLEY NATIONAL BANK                      ACCOUNT NUMBER    1627042
OF LOS ANGELES
                                          FROM  6/30/11    TO  7/31/11
LOS ANGELES, CA 90020-4253    (310)555-5151
                                          BALANCE              4,218.60

                                       22 DEPOSITS            13,749.75

    POWER NETWORKING                   52 WITHDRAWALS         14,698.57
    1000 Belkin Street
    Los Angeles, CA 90014 -1000         3 OTHER DEBITS
                                          AND CREDITS            90.00CR

                                          NEW BALANCE          3,359.78
```

* — CHECKS AND OTHER DEBITS — — — — — —	* — — — — — — DEPOSITS — * —DATE * BALANCE *

No. 850	819.40	No. 852	122.54	585.75	07/01	3,862.41
No. 854	369.50	No. 853	20.15	421.53	07/02	3,894.29
No. 851	600.00	No. 856	190.70	781.30	07/03	3,884.89
No. 855	25.93	No. 857	52.50		07/04	3,806.46
No. 860	921.20	No. 858	160.00	662.50	07/05	3,387.76
No. 862	91.07	NSF	300.00	503.18	07/07	3,499.87

No. 880	32.26	No. 877	535.09	ACH 932.00	07/29	4,136.66
No. 881	21.10	No. 879	732.26	705.21	07/30	4,088.51
No. 882	126.20	SC	18.00	MS 408.00	07/30	4,352.31
No. 874	26.12	ACH	1,615.13	648.72	07/31	3,359.78

```
    EC — ERROR CORRECTION          ACH — AUTOMATED CLEARING HOUSE
    MS — MISCELLANEOUS
    NSF — NOT SUFFICIENT FUNDS      SC — SERVICE CHARGE

* * *                  * * *                      * * *

        THE RECONCILEMENT OF THIS STATEMENT WITH YOUR RECORDS IS ESSENTIAL.
           ANY ERROR OR EXCEPTION SHOULD BE REPORTED IMMEDIATELY.
```

The company's checking account balance *in the bank records* is a liability. Thus, in the bank's records, the company's account has a credit balance. Since the bank statement is prepared from the bank's point of view, a credit memo entry on the bank statement indicates an increase (a credit) to the company's account. Likewise, a debit memo entry on the bank statement indicates a decrease (a debit) in the company's account. This relationship is shown below.

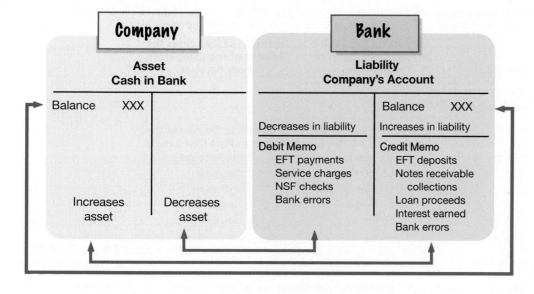

A bank makes credit entries (issues credit memos) for the following:

1. Deposits made by electronic funds transfer (EFT)
2. Collections of note receivable for the company
3. Proceeds for a loan made to the company by the bank
4. Interest earned on the company's account
5. Correction (if any) of bank errors

A bank makes debit entries (issues debit memos) for the following:

1. Payments made by electronic funds transfer (EFT)
2. Service charges
3. Customer checks returned for not sufficient funds
4. Correction (if any) of bank errors

Customers' checks returned for not sufficient funds, called *NSF checks*, are customer checks that were initially deposited, but were not paid by the customer's bank. Since the company's bank credited the customer's check to the company's account when it was deposited, the bank debits the company's account (issues a debit memo) when the check is returned without payment.

The reason for a credit or debit memo entry is indicated on the bank statement. Exhibit 5 identifies the following types of credit and debit memo entries:

EC: Error correction to correct bank error
NSF: Not sufficient funds check
SC: Service charge
ACH: Automated clearing house entry for electronic funds transfer
MS: Miscellaneous item such as collection of a note receivable on behalf of the company or receipt of a loan by the company from the bank

The above list includes the notation "ACH" for electronic funds transfers. ACH is a network for clearing electronic funds transfers among individuals, companies, and banks.[7] Because electronic funds transfers may be either deposits or payments, ACH entries may indicate either a debit or credit entry to the company's account. Likewise, entries to correct bank errors and miscellaneous items may indicate a debit or credit entry to the company's account.

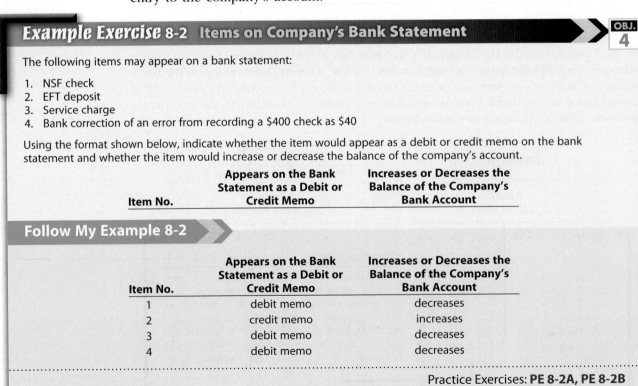

Example Exercise 8-2 Items on Company's Bank Statement

OBJ. 4

The following items may appear on a bank statement:

1. NSF check
2. EFT deposit
3. Service charge
4. Bank correction of an error from recording a $400 check as $40

Using the format shown below, indicate whether the item would appear as a debit or credit memo on the bank statement and whether the item would increase or decrease the balance of the company's account.

Item No.	Appears on the Bank Statement as a Debit or Credit Memo	Increases or Decreases the Balance of the Company's Bank Account

Follow My Example 8-2

Item No.	Appears on the Bank Statement as a Debit or Credit Memo	Increases or Decreases the Balance of the Company's Bank Account
1	debit memo	decreases
2	credit memo	increases
3	debit memo	decreases
4	debit memo	decreases

Practice Exercises: **PE 8-2A, PE 8-2B**

7 For further information on ACH, go to **http://www.nacha.org/**. Click on "About Us," and then click on "Intro to NACHA".

Using the Bank Statement as a Control Over Cash

The bank statement is a primary control that a company uses over cash. A company uses the bank's statement as a control by comparing the company's recording of cash transactions to those recorded by the bank.

The cash balance shown by a bank statement is usually different from the company's cash balance, as shown in Exhibit 6.

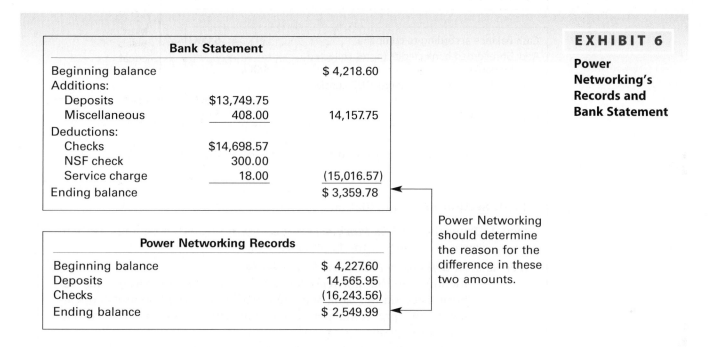

EXHIBIT 6

Power Networking's Records and Bank Statement

Bank Statement		
Beginning balance		$ 4,218.60
Additions:		
Deposits	$13,749.75	
Miscellaneous	408.00	14,157.75
Deductions:		
Checks	$14,698.57	
NSF check	300.00	
Service charge	18.00	(15,016.57)
Ending balance		$ 3,359.78

Power Networking should determine the reason for the difference in these two amounts.

Power Networking Records	
Beginning balance	$ 4,227.60
Deposits	14,565.95
Checks	(16,243.56)
Ending balance	$ 2,549.99

Differences between the company and bank balance may arise because of a delay by either the company or bank in recording transactions. For example, there is normally a time lag of one or more days between the date a check is written and the date that it is paid by the bank. Likewise, there is normally a time lag between when the company mails a deposit to the bank (or uses the night depository) and when the bank receives and records the deposit.

Differences may also arise because the bank has debited or credited the company's account for transactions that the company will not know about until the bank statement is received. Finally, differences may arise from errors made by either the company or the bank. For example, the company may incorrectly post to Cash a check written for $4,500 as $450. Likewise, a bank may incorrectly record the amount of a check.

Bank Reconciliation

OBJ. 5 Describe and illustrate the use of a bank reconciliation in controlling cash.

A **bank reconciliation** is an analysis of the items and amounts that result in the cash balance reported in the bank statement to differ from the balance of the cash account in the ledger. The adjusted cash balance determined in the bank reconciliation is reported on the balance sheet.

A bank reconciliation is usually divided into two sections as follows:

1. The *bank section* begins with the cash balance according to the bank statement and ends with the *adjusted balance*.
2. The *company section* begins with the cash balance according to the company's records and ends with the *adjusted balance*.

The *adjusted balance* from bank and company sections must be equal. The format of the bank reconciliation is shown below.

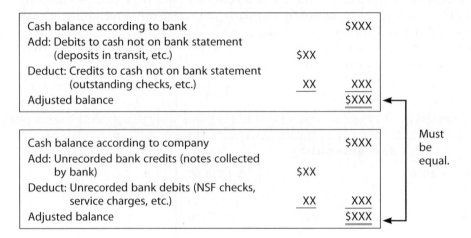

Cash balance according to bank		$XXX
Add: Debits to cash not on bank statement (deposits in transit, etc.)	$XX	
Deduct: Credits to cash not on bank statement (outstanding checks, etc.)	XX	XXX
Adjusted balance		$XXX

Cash balance according to company		$XXX
Add: Unrecorded bank credits (notes collected by bank)	$XX	
Deduct: Unrecorded bank debits (NSF checks, service charges, etc.)	XX	XXX
Adjusted balance		$XXX

Must be equal.

A bank reconciliation is prepared using the following steps:

Bank Section of Reconciliation

Step 1. Enter the *Cash balance according to bank* from the ending cash balance according to the bank statement.

Step 2. *Add deposits not recorded by the bank.*
Identify deposits not recorded by the bank by comparing each deposit listed on the bank statement with unrecorded deposits appearing in the preceding period's reconciliation and with the current period's deposits.
Examples: Deposits in transit at the end of the period.

Step 3. *Deduct outstanding checks that have not been paid by the bank.*
Identify outstanding checks by comparing paid checks with outstanding checks appearing on the preceding period's reconciliation and with recorded checks.
Examples: Outstanding checks at the end of the period.

Step 4. Determine the *Adjusted balance* by adding Step 2 and deducting Step 3.

Company Section of Reconciliation

Step 5. Enter the *Cash balance according to company* from the ending cash balance in the ledger.

Step 6. *Add credit memos that have not been recorded.*
Identify the bank credit memos that have not been recorded by comparing the bank statement credit memos to entries in the journal.
Examples: A note receivable and interest that the bank has collected for the company.

Step 7. *Deduct debit memos that have not been recorded.*
Identify the bank debit memos that have not been recorded by comparing the bank statement debit memos to entries in the journal.
Examples: Customers' not sufficient funds (NSF) checks; bank service charges.

Step 8. Determine the *Adjusted balance* by adding Step 6 and deducting Step 7.

Step 9. Verify that the adjusted balances determined in Steps 4 and 8 are equal.

The adjusted balances in the bank and company sections of the reconciliation must be equal. If the balances are not equal, an item has been overlooked and must be found.

Sometimes, the adjusted balances are not equal because either the company or the bank has made an error. In such cases, the error is often discovered by comparing the amount of each item (deposit and check) on the bank statement with that in the company's records.

Any bank or company errors discovered should be added or deducted from the bank or company section of the reconciliation depending on the nature of the error. For example, assume that the bank incorrectly recorded a company check for $50 as $500. This bank error of $450 ($500 – $50) would be added to the bank balance in the bank section of the reconciliation. In addition, the bank would be notified of the error so that it could be corrected. On the other hand, assume that the company recorded a deposit of $1,200 as $2,100. This company error of $900 ($2,100 – $1,200) would be deducted from the cash balance in the company section of the bank reconciliation. The company would later correct the error using a journal entry.

To illustrate, the bank statement for Power Networking in Exhibit 5 on page 367 is used. This bank statement shows a balance of $3,359.78 as of July 31. The cash balance in Power Networking's ledger on the same date is $2,549.99. Using the preceding steps, the following reconciling items were identified:

Step 2. Deposit of July 31, not recorded on bank statement: $816.20
Step 3. Outstanding checks:

Check No. 812	$1,061.00
Check No. 878	435.39
Check No. 883	48.60
Total	$1,544.99

Step 6. Note receivable of $400 plus interest of $8 collected by bank not recorded in the journal as indicated by a credit memo of $408.
Step 7. Check from customer (Thomas Ivey) for $300 returned by bank because of insufficient funds (NSF) as indicated by a debit memo of $300.00.
Bank service charges of $18, not recorded in the journal as indicated by a debit memo of $18.00.

In addition, an error of $9 was discovered. This error occurred when Check No. 879 for $732.26 to Taylor Co., on account, was recorded in the company's journal as $723.26.

The bank reconciliation, based on the Exhibit 5 bank statement and the preceding reconciling items, is shown in Exhibit 7.

The company's records do not need to be updated for any items in the *bank section* of the reconciliation. This section begins with the cash balance according to the bank statement. However, the bank should be notified of any errors that need to be corrected.

The company's records do need to be updated for any items in the *company section* of the bank reconciliation. The company's records are updated using journal entries. For example, journal entries should be made for any unrecorded bank memos and any company errors.

The journal entries for Power Networking, based on the bank reconciliation shown in Exhibit 7, are as follows:

July	31	Cash		408	
		Notes Receivable			400
		Interest Revenue			8
	31	Accounts Receivable—Thomas Ivey		300	
		Miscellaneous Expense		18	
		Accounts Payable—Taylor Co.		9	
		Cash			327

EXHIBIT 7   **Bank Reconciliation for Power Networking**

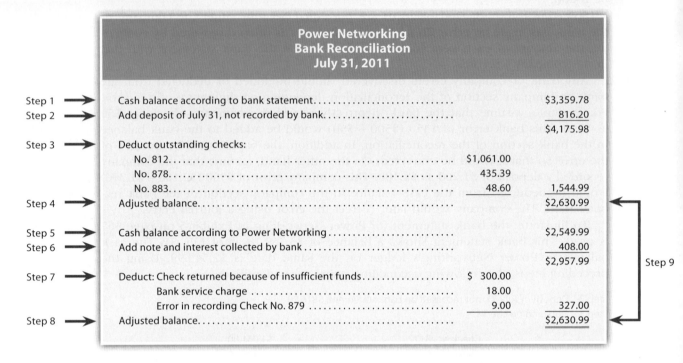

Step 1 →	Cash balance according to bank statement..............................		$3,359.78
Step 2 →	Add deposit of July 31, not recorded by bank..........................		816.20
			$4,175.98
Step 3 →	Deduct outstanding checks:		
	No. 812..	$1,061.00	
	No. 878..	435.39	
	No. 883..	48.60	1,544.99
Step 4 →	Adjusted balance..		$2,630.99
Step 5 →	Cash balance according to Power Networking.........................		$2,549.99
Step 6 →	Add note and interest collected by bank.............................		408.00
			$2,957.99
Step 7 →	Deduct: Check returned because of insufficient funds...................	$ 300.00	
	Bank service charge	18.00	
	Error in recording Check No. 879	9.00	327.00
Step 8 →	Adjusted balance..		$2,630.99

Step 9

After the preceding journal entries are recorded and posted, the cash account will have a debit balance of $2,630.99. This cash balance agrees with the adjusted balance shown on the bank reconciliation. This is the amount of cash on July 31 and is the amount that is reported on Power Networking's July 31 balance sheet.

Businesses may reconcile their bank accounts in a slightly different format from that shown in Exhibit 7. Regardless, the objective is to control cash by reconciling the company's records with the bank statement. In doing so, any errors or misuse of cash may be detected.

To enhance internal control, the bank reconciliation should be prepared by an employee who does not take part in or record cash transactions. Otherwise, mistakes may occur, and it is more likely that cash will be stolen or misapplied. For example, an employee who handles cash and also reconciles the bank statement could steal a cash deposit, omit the deposit from the accounts, and omit it from the reconciliation.

Bank reconciliations are also an important part of computerized systems where deposits and checks are stored in electronic files and records. Some systems use computer software to determine the difference between the bank statement and company cash balances. The software then adjusts for deposits in transit and outstanding checks. Any remaining differences are reported for further analysis.

Example Exercise 8-3   Bank Reconciliation   OBJ. 5

The following data were gathered to use in reconciling the bank account of Photo Op:

Balance per bank...	$14,500
Balance per company records...	13,875
Bank service charges	75
Deposit in transit	3,750
NSF check..	800
Outstanding checks	5,250

a. What is the adjusted balance on the bank reconciliation?

b. Journalize any necessary entries for Photo Op based on the bank reconciliation.

(continued)

Integrity, Objectivity, and Ethics in Business

BANK ERROR IN YOUR FAVOR

You may sometime have a bank error in your favor, such as a misposted deposit. Such errors are not a case of "found money," as in the Monopoly® game. Bank control systems quickly discover most errors and make automatic adjustments. Even so, you have a legal responsibility to report the error and return the money to the bank.

Special-Purpose Cash Funds

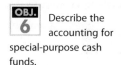

OBJ. 6 Describe the accounting for special-purpose cash funds.

A company often has to pay small amounts for such items as postage, office supplies, or minor repairs. Although small, such payments may occur often enough to total a significant amount. Thus, it is desirable to control such payments. However, writing a check for each small payment is not practical. Instead, a special cash fund, called a **petty cash fund**, is used.

A petty cash fund is established by estimating the amount of payments needed from the fund during a period, such as a week or a month. A check is then written and cashed for this amount. The money obtained from cashing the check is then given to an employee, called the *petty cash custodian*. The petty cash custodian disburses monies from the fund as needed. For control purposes, the company may place restrictions on the maximum amount and the types of payments that can be made from the fund. Each time money is paid from petty cash, the custodian records the details on a petty cash receipts form.

The petty cash fund is normally replenished at periodic intervals, when it is depleted, or reaches a minimum amount. When a petty cash fund is replenished, the accounts debited are determined by summarizing the petty cash receipts. A check is then written for this amount, payable to Petty Cash.

To illustrate, assume that a petty cash fund of $500 is established on August 1. The entry to record this transaction is as follows:

Aug.	1	Petty Cash		500	
		Cash			500

The only time Petty Cash is debited is when the fund is initially established, as shown in the preceding entry, or when the fund is being increased. The only time Petty Cash is credited is when the fund is being decreased.

At the end of August, the petty cash receipts indicate expenditures for the following items:

Office supplies	$380
Postage (debit Office Supplies)	22
Store supplies	35
Miscellaneous administrative expense	30
Total	$467

The entry to replenish the petty cash fund on August 31 is as follows:

Aug.	31	Office Supplies	402	
		Store Supplies	35	
		Miscellaneous Administrative Expense	30	
		Cash		467

Petty Cash is not debited when the fund is replenished. Instead, the accounts affected by the petty cash disbursements are debited, as shown in the preceding entry. Replenishing the petty cash fund restores the fund to its original amount of $500.

Companies often use other cash funds for special needs, such as payroll or travel expenses. Such funds are called **special-purpose funds**. For example, each salesperson might be given $1,000 for travel-related expenses. Periodically, each salesperson submits an expense report, and the fund is replenished. Special-purpose funds are established and controlled in a manner similar to that of the petty cash fund.

Example Exercise 8-4 Petty Cash Fund

OBJ. 6

Prepare journal entries for each of the following:

a. Issued a check to establish a petty cash fund of $500.

b. The amount of cash in the petty cash fund is $120. Issued a check to replenish the fund, based on the following summary of petty cash receipts: office supplies, $300 and miscellaneous administrative expense, $75. Record any missing funds in the cash short and over account.

Follow My Example 8-4

a.	Petty Cash	500	
	Cash		500
b.	Office Supplies	300	
	Miscellaneous Administrative Expense	75	
	Cash Short and Over	5	
	Cash		380

Practice Exercises: **PE 8-4A, PE 8-4B**

OBJ. 7 Describe and illustrate the reporting of cash and cash equivalents in the financial statements.

Financial Statement Reporting of Cash

Cash is normally listed as the first asset in the Current Assets section of the balance sheet. Most companies present only a single cash amount on the balance sheet by combining all their bank and cash fund accounts.

A company may temporarily have excess cash. In such cases, the company normally invests in highly liquid investments in order to earn interest. These investments are called **cash equivalents**.[8] Examples of cash equivalents include U.S. Treasury bills,

---

8 To be classified a cash equivalent, according to FASB Statement No. 95, the investment is expected to be converted to cash within 90 days.

notes issued by major corporations (referred to as commercial paper), and money market funds. In such cases, companies usually report *Cash and cash equivalents* as one amount on the balance sheet.

The balance sheet presentation for cash for Mornin' Joe is shown below.

Mornin' Joe Balance Sheet December 31, 2012	
Assets	
Current assets:	
Cash and cash equivalents	$235,000

Banks may require that companies maintain minimum cash balances in their bank accounts. Such a balance is called a **compensating balance**. This is often required by the bank as part of a loan agreement or line of credit. A *line of credit* is a preapproved amount the bank is willing to lend to a customer upon request. Compensating balance requirements are normally disclosed in notes to the financial statements.

Financial Analysis and Interpretation: Ratio of Cash to Monthly Cash Expenses

OBJ. 8 Describe and illustrate the use of the ratio of cash to monthly cash expenses to assess the ability of a company to continue in business.

For startup companies or companies in financial distress, cash is critical for survival. In their first few years, startup companies often report losses and negative net cash flows from operations. Moreover, companies in financial distress can also report losses and negative cash flows from operations. In such cases, the **ratio of cash to monthly cash expenses** is useful for assessing how long a company can continue to operate without:

1. Additional financing, or
2. Generating positive cash flows from operations

The ratio of cash to monthly cash expenses is computed as follows:

$$\text{Ratio of Cash to Monthly Cash Expenses} = \frac{\text{Cash as of Year-End}}{\text{Monthly Cash Expenses}}$$

The cash, including any cash equivalents, is taken from the balance sheet as of year-end. The monthly cash expenses, sometimes called *cash burn*, are estimated from the operating activities section of the statement of cash flows as follows:

$$\text{Monthly Cash Expenses} = \frac{\text{Negative Cash Flow from Operations}}{12}$$

To illustrate, Evergreen Solar, Inc. manufactures solar products including solar panels that convert sunlight into electricity. The following data (in thousands) were taken from the financial statements of Evergreen Solar:

	For Years Ending December 31			
	2009	**2008**	**2007**	**2006**
Cash and cash equivalents at year-end	$112,368	$100,888	$ 70,428	$ 6,828
Cash flow from operations	(37,094)	(65,881)	(11,996)	(10,328)

Based on the preceding data, the monthly cash expenses and ratio of cash to monthly expenses are computed below.

	For Years Ending December 31			
	2009	**2008**	**2007**	**2006**
Monthly cash expenses:				
$37,094 ÷ 12.............................	$3,091			
$65,881 ÷ 12.............................		$5,490		
$11,996 ÷ 12.............................			$1,000	
$10,328 ÷ 12.............................				$861
Ratio of cash to monthly cash expenses:				
$112,368 ÷ $3,091.........................	36.4 months			
$100,888 ÷ $5,490.........................		18.4 months		
$70,428 ÷ $1,000..........................			70.4 months	
$6,828 ÷ $861.............................				7.9 months

The preceding computations indicate that Evergreen Solar had only 7.9 months of cash available as of December 31, 2006. During 2007, Evergreen raised additional cash of approximately $175 million by issuing stock. This enabled Evergreen to continue to operate in 2007 and resulted in Evergreen having 70.4 months of cash available as of December 31, 2007.

During 2008, Evergreen's monthly cash expenses (cash burn) increased to $5,490 from $1,000 in 2007. Evergreen also raised additional cash of approximately $490 million while investing approximately $350 million in plant and equipment. The result is that as of December 31, 2008, Evergreen had 18.4 months of cash with which to continue to operate.

During 2009, Evergreen decreased its monthly cash expenses from $5,490 in 2008 to $3,091. In addition, Evergreen raised additional cash of $105 million by issuing stock and obtaining a loan. As a result, at the end of 2009 Evergreen had 36.4 months of cash with which to continue to operate. In the long-term, however, Evergreen will need to generate positive cash flows from operations to survive.

Example Exercise 8-5 Ratio of Cash to Monthly Cash Expenses   OBJ. 8

Financial data for Chapman Company are as follows:

	For Year Ending December 31, 2012
Cash on December 31, 2012	$ 102,000
Cash flow from operations	(144,000)

a. Compute the ratio of cash to monthly cash expenses.

b. Interpret the results computed in (a).

Follow My Example 8-5

a. $\text{Monthly Cash Expenses} = \dfrac{\text{Negative Cash Flow from Operations}}{12} = \dfrac{\$144,000}{12} = \$12,000 \text{ per month}$

$\dfrac{\text{Ratio of Cash to}}{\text{Monthly Cash Expenses}} = \dfrac{\text{Cash as of Year-End}}{\text{Monthly Cash Expenses}} = \dfrac{\$102,000}{\$12,000 \text{ per month}} = 8.5 \text{ months}$

b. The preceding computations indicate that Chapman Company has 8.5 months of cash remaining as of December 31, 2012. To continue operations beyond 8.5 months, Chapman Company will need to generate positive cash flows from operations or raise additional financing from its owners or by issuing debt.

Practice Exercises: **PE 8-5A, PE 8-5B**

BusinessConnection

MICROSOFT CORPORATION

Microsoft Corporation develops, manufactures, licenses, and supports software products for computing devices. Microsoft software products include computer operating systems, such as Windows®, and application software, such

as Microsoft Word® and Excel®. Microsoft is actively involved in the video game market through its Xbox® and is also involved in online products and services.

Microsoft is known for its strong cash position. Microsoft's June 30, 2009, balance sheet reported over $31 billion of cash and short-term investments, as shown below.

Balance Sheet
June 30, 2009
(In millions)

Assets

Current assets:

Cash and equivalents...	$ 6,076
Short-term investments	25,371
Total cash and short-term investments.....................	$31,447

The cash and cash equivalents of $6,076 million are further described in the notes to the financial statements, as shown below.

Cash and equivalents:

Cash	$2,064
Mutual funds...	900
Commercial paper	400
U.S. government and agency securities........................	2,369
Certificates of deposit	275
Municipal securities	68
Total cash and equivalents.................................	$6,076

At a Glance 8

OBJ. 1

Describe the Sarbanes-Oxley Act of 2002 and its impact on internal controls and financial reporting.

Key Points Sarbanes-Oxley requires companies to maintain strong and effective internal controls and to report on the effectiveness of the internal controls.

Learning Outcomes	Example Exercises	Practice Exercises
• Describe why Congress passed Sarbanes-Oxley.		
• Describe the purpose of Sarbanes-Oxley.		
• Define internal control.		

OBJ. 2

Describe and illustrate the objectives and elements of internal control.

Key Points The objectives of internal control are to provide reasonable assurance that (1) assets are safeguarded and used for business purposes, (2) business information is accurate, and (3) laws and regulations are complied with. The elements of internal control are the control environment, risk assessment, control procedures, monitoring, and information and communication.

Learning Outcomes	Example Exercises	Practice Exercises
• List the objectives of internal control.		
• List the elements of internal control.		
• Describe each element of internal control and factors influencing each element.	EE8-1	PE8-1A, 8-1B

OBJ. 3

Describe and illustrate the application of internal controls to cash.

Key Points A cash register is a control for protecting cash received in over-the-counter sales. A remittance advice is a control for cash received through the mail. Separating the duties of handling cash and recording cash is also a control. A voucher system is a control system for cash payments. Many companies use electronic funds transfers for cash receipts and cash payments.

Learning Outcomes	Example Exercises	Practice Exercises
• Describe and give examples of controls for cash received from cash sales, cash received in the mail, and cash received by EFT.		
• Describe and give examples of controls for cash payments made using a voucher system and cash payments made by EFT.		

OBJ. 4

Describe the nature of a bank account and its use in controlling cash.

Key Points Bank accounts control cash by reducing the amount of cash on hand and facilitating the transfer of cash between businesses and locations. In addition, the bank statement allows a business to reconcile the cash transactions recorded in the accounting records to those recorded by the bank.

Learning Outcomes	Example Exercises	Practice Exercises
• Describe how the use of bank accounts helps control cash.		
• Describe a bank statement and provide examples of items that appear on a bank statement as debit and credit memos.	EE8-2	PE8-2A, 8-2B

OBJ. 5

Describe and illustrate the use of a bank reconciliation in controlling cash.

Key Points A bank reconciliation is prepared using nine steps as summarized on page 370. The items in the company section of a bank reconciliation must be journalized on the company's records.

Learning Outcomes	Example Exercises	Practice Exercises
• Describe a bank reconciliation.		
• Prepare a bank reconciliation.	EE8-3	PE8-3A, 8-3B
• Journalize any necessary entries on the company's records based on the bank reconciliation.	EE8-3	PE8-3A, 8-3B

OBJ. 6   Describe the accounting for special-purpose cash funds.

Key Points   Special-purpose cash funds, such as a petty cash fund or travel funds, are used by businesses to meet specific needs. Each fund is established by cashing a check for the amount of cash needed. At periodic intervals, the fund is replenished and the disbursements recorded.

Learning Outcomes	Example Exercises	Practice Exercises
• Describe the use of special-purpose cash funds.		
• Journalize the entry to establish a petty cash fund.	EE8-4	PE8-4A, 8-4B
• Journalize the entry to replenish a petty cash fund.	EE8-4	PE8-4A, 8-4B

OBJ. 7   Describe and illustrate the reporting of cash and cash equivalents in the financial statements.

Key Points   Cash is listed as the first asset in the Current assets section of the balance sheet. Companies that have invested excess cash in highly liquid investments usually report *Cash and cash equivalents* on the balance sheet.

Learning Outcomes	Example Exercises	Practice Exercises
• Describe the reporting of cash and cash equivalents in the financial statements.		
• Illustrate the reporting of cash and cash equivalents in the financial statements.		

OBJ. 8   Describe and illustrate the use of the ratio of cash to monthly cash expenses to assess the ability of a company to continue in business.

Key Points   The ratio of cash to monthly cash expenses is useful for assessing how long a company can continue to operate without (1) additional financing or (2) generating positive cash flows from operations.

Learning Outcomes	Example Exercises	Practice Exercises
• Describe the use of the ratio of cash to monthly cash expenses.		
• Compute the ratio of cash to monthly cash expenses.	EE8-5	PE 8-5A, 8-5B

Key Terms

bank reconciliation (369)
bank statement (366)
cash (363)
cash equivalents (374)
cash short and over account (364)
compensating balance (375)

control environment (359)
electronic funds transfer (EFT) (365)
elements of internal control (358)
employee fraud (358)
internal control (356)
petty cash fund (373)

ratio of cash to monthly
  cash expenses (375)
Sarbanes-Oxley Act of 2002 (356)
special-purpose funds (374)
voucher (366)
voucher system (366)

Illustrative Problem

The bank statement for Urethane Company for June 30, 2011, indicates a balance of $9,143.11. All cash receipts are deposited each evening in a night depository, after banking hours. The accounting records indicate the following summary data for cash receipts and payments for June:

Cash balance as of June 1	$ 3,943.50
Total cash receipts for June	28,971.60
Total amount of checks issued in June	28,388.85

Comparing the bank statement and the accompanying canceled checks and memos with the records reveals the following reconciling items:

a. The bank had collected for Urethane Company $1,030 on a note left for collection. The face amount of the note was $1,000.

b. A deposit of $1,852.21, representing receipts of June 30, had been made too late to appear on the bank statement.

c. Checks outstanding totaled $5,265.27.

d. A check drawn for $139 had been incorrectly charged by the bank as $157.

e. A check for $30 returned with the statement had been recorded in the company's records as $240. The check was for the payment of an obligation to Avery Equipment Company for the purchase of office supplies on account.

f. Bank service charges for June amounted to $18.20.

Instructions

1. Prepare a bank reconciliation for June.

2. Journalize the entries that should be made by Urethane Company.

Solution

1.

Urethane Company Bank Reconciliation June 30, 2011			
Cash balance according to bank statement			$ 9,143.11
Add: Deposit of June 30 not recorded by bank		$1,852.21	
Bank error in charging check as $157			
instead of $139		18.00	1,870.21
			$11,013.32
Deduct: Outstanding checks			5,265.27
Adjusted balance			$ 5,748.05
Cash balance according to company's records			$ 4,526.25*
Add: Proceeds of note collected by bank,			
including $30 interest		$1,030.00	
Error in recording check		210.00	1,240.00
			$ 5,766.25
Deduct: Bank service charges			18.20
Adjusted balance			$ 5,748.05

*$3,943.50 + $28,971.60 − $28,388.85

2.

June	30	Cash		1,240.00	
		Notes Receivable			1,000.00
		Interest Revenue			30.00
		Accounts Payable—Avery Equipment Company			210.00
	30	Miscellaneous Administrative Expense		18.20	
		Cash			18.20

Discussion Questions

1. (a) Name and describe the five elements of internal control. (b) Is any one element of internal control more important than another?

2. Why should the employee who handles cash receipts not have the responsibility for maintaining the accounts receivable records? Explain.

3. The ticket seller at a movie theater doubles as a ticket taker for a few minutes each day while the ticket taker is on a break. Which control procedure of a business's system of internal control is violated in this situation?

4. Why should the responsibility for maintaining the accounting records be separated from the responsibility for operations? Explain.

5. Assume that Peggy Gyger, accounts payable clerk for Patmen Inc., stole $193,750 by paying fictitious invoices for goods that were never received. The clerk set up accounts in the names of the fictitious companies and cashed the checks at a local bank. Describe a control procedure that would have prevented or detected the fraud.

6. Before a voucher for the purchase of merchandise is approved for payment, supporting documents should be compared to verify the accuracy of the liability. Give an example of supporting documents for the purchase of merchandise.

7. The balance of Cash is likely to differ from the bank statement balance. What two factors are likely to be responsible for the difference?

8. What is the purpose of preparing a bank reconciliation?

9. Smyrna Inc. has a petty cash fund of $900. (a) Since the petty cash fund is only $900, should Smyrna Inc. implement controls over petty cash? (b) What controls, if any, could be used for the petty cash fund?

10. (a) How are cash equivalents reported in the financial statements? (b) What are some examples of cash equivalents?

Practice Exercises

Learning Objectives

OBJ. 2

Example Exercises

EE 8-1 *p. 363*

PE 8-1A Internal control elements

Identify each of the following as relating to (a) the control environment, (b) control procedures, or (c) information and communication.

1. Separating related operations
2. Report of internal auditors
3. Management's philosophy and operating style

OBJ. 2   EE 8-1 *p. 363*

PE 8-1B Internal control elements

Identify each of the following as relating to (a) the control environment, (b) control procedures, or (c) monitoring.

1. Personnel policies
2. Safeguarding inventory in a locked warehouse
3. Hiring of external auditors to review the adequacy of controls

OBJ. 4   EE 8-2 *p. 368*

PE 8-2A Items on company's bank statement

The following items may appear on a bank statement:

1. EFT payment
2. Note collected for company
3. Bank correction of an error from recording a $7,200 deposit as $2,700
4. Service charge

Using the format shown below, indicate whether each item would appear as a debit or credit memo on the bank statement and whether the item would increase or decrease the balance of the company's account.

Item No.	Appears on the Bank Statement as a Debit or Credit Memo	Increases or Decreases the Balance of the Company's Bank Account

OBJ. 4   EE 8-2 *p. 368*

PE 8-2B Items on company's bank statement

The following items may appear on a bank statement:

1. NSF check
2. Bank correction of an error from posting another customer's check to the company's account
3. Loan proceeds
4. EFT deposit

Using the format shown below, indicate whether each item would appear as a debit or credit memo on the bank statement and whether the item would increase or decrease the balance of the company's account.

Item No.	Appears on the Bank Statement as a Debit or Credit Memo	Increases or Decreases the Balance of the Company's Bank Account

Learning Objectives	Example Exercises	
OBJ. 5	EE 8-3 p. 372	

PE 8-3A   Bank reconciliation

The following data were gathered to use in reconciling the bank account of Azalea Company:

Balance per bank	$25,500
Balance per company records	27,475
Bank service charges	75
Deposit in transit	7,500
NSF check	3,400
Outstanding checks	9,000

a. What is the adjusted balance on the bank reconciliation?

b. Journalize any necessary entries for Azalea Company based on the bank reconciliation.

OBJ. 5   EE 8-3 p. 372

PE 8-3B   Bank reconciliation

The following data were gathered to use in reconciling the bank account of Bradford Company:

Balance per bank	$17,400
Balance per company records	5,765
Bank service charges	125
Deposit in transit	3,000
Note collected by bank with $360 interest	9,360
Outstanding checks	5,400

a. What is the adjusted balance on the bank reconciliation?

b. Journalize any necessary entries for Bradford Company based on the bank reconciliation.

OBJ. 6   EE 8-4 p. 374

PE 8-4A   Petty cash fund

Prepare journal entries for each of the following:

a. Issued a check to establish a petty cash fund of $800.

b. The amount of cash in the petty cash fund is $225. Issued a check to replenish the fund, based on the following summary of petty cash receipts: repair expense, $450 and miscellaneous selling expense, $75. Record any missing funds in the cash short and over account.

OBJ. 6   EE 8-4 p. 374

PE 8-4B   Petty cash fund

Prepare journal entries for each of the following:

a. Issued a check to establish a petty cash fund of $750.

b. The amount of cash in the petty cash fund is $325. Issued a check to replenish the fund, based on the following summary of petty cash receipts: store supplies, $300 and miscellaneous selling expense, $100. Record any missing funds in the cash short and over account.

OBJ. 8   EE 8-5 p. 376

FAI

PE 8-5A   Ratio of cash to monthly cash expenses

Financial data for Hauser Company are shown below.

	For Year Ending December 31, 2012
Cash on December 31, 2012	$ 58,800
Cash flow from operations	(72,000)

a. Compute the ratio of cash to monthly cash expenses.

b. Interpret the results computed in (a).

OBJ. 8   EE 8-5 p. 376

FAI

PE 8-5B   Ratio of cash to monthly cash expenses

Financial data for Preston Company are shown below.

	For Year Ending December 31, 2012
Cash on December 31, 2012	$ 184,800
Cash flow from operations	(158,400)

a. Compute the ratio of cash to monthly cash expenses.

b. Interpret the results computed in (a).

Exercises

OBJ. 1

EX 8-1 Sarbanes-Oxley internal control report

Using Wikpedia (**www.wikpedia.com**), look up the entry for Sarbanes-Oxley Act. Look over the table of contents and find the section that describes Section 404.

➤ What does Section 404 require of management's internal control report?

OBJ. 2, 3

EX 8-2 Internal controls

Joan Whalen has recently been hired as the manager of Jittery Coffee Shop. Jittery Coffee Shop is a national chain of franchised coffee shops. During her first month as store manager, Joan encountered the following internal control situations:

a. Since only one employee uses the cash register, that employee is responsible for counting the cash at the end of the shift and verifying that the cash in the drawer matches the amount of cash sales recorded by the cash register. Joan expects each cashier to balance the drawer to the penny *every* time—no exceptions.

b. Joan caught an employee putting a case of 400 single-serving tea bags in her car. Not wanting to create a scene, Joan smiled and said, "I don't think you're putting those tea bags on the right shelf. Don't they belong inside the coffee shop?" The employee returned the tea bags to the stockroom.

c. Jittery Coffee Shop has one cash register. Prior to Joan's joining the coffee shop, each employee working on a shift would take a customer order, accept payment, and then prepare the order. Joan made one employee on each shift responsible for taking orders and accepting the customer's payment. Other employees prepare the orders.

➤ State whether you agree or disagree with Joan's method of handling each situation and explain your answer.

OBJ. 2, 3

EX 8-3 Internal controls

Meridian Clothing is a retail store specializing in women's clothing. The store has established a liberal return policy for the holiday season in order to encourage gift purchases. Any item purchased during November and December may be returned through January 31, with a receipt, for cash or exchange. If the customer does not have a receipt, cash will still be refunded for any item under $50. If the item is more than $50, a check is mailed to the customer.

Whenever an item is returned, a store clerk completes a return slip, which the customer signs. The return slip is placed in a special box. The store manager visits the return counter approximately once every two hours to authorize the return slips. Clerks are instructed to place the returned merchandise on the proper rack on the selling floor as soon as possible.

This year, returns at Meridian Clothing have reached an all-time high. There are a large number of returns under $50 without receipts.

a. ➤ How can sales clerks employed at Meridian Clothing use the store's return policy to steal money from the cash register?

b. ➤ What internal control weaknesses do you see in the return policy that make cash thefts easier?

c. ➤ Would issuing a store credit in place of a cash refund for all merchandise returned without a receipt reduce the possibility of theft? List some advantages and disadvantages of issuing a store credit in place of a cash refund.

d. ➤ Assume that Meridian Clothing is committed to the current policy of issuing cash refunds without a receipt. What changes could be made in the store's procedures regarding customer refunds in order to improve internal control?

OBJ. 2, 3

EX 8-4 Internal controls for bank lending

Evergreen Bank provides loans to businesses in the community through its Commercial Lending Department. Small loans (less than $250,000) may be approved by an individual loan officer, while larger loans (greater than $250,000) must be approved by a board of loan officers. Once a loan is approved, the funds are made available to the loan applicant under agreed-upon terms. The president of Evergreen Bank has instituted a policy whereby he has the individual authority to approve loans up to $10,000,000. The president believes that this policy will allow flexibility to approve loans to valued clients much quicker than under the previous policy.

━━━━► As an internal auditor of Evergreen Bank, how would you respond to this change in policy?

OBJ. 2, 3

EX 8-5 Internal controls

One of the largest losses in history from unauthorized securities trading involved a securities trader for the French bank, Societe Generale. The trader was able to circumvent internal controls and create over $7 billion in trading losses in six months. The trader apparently escaped detection by using knowledge of the bank's internal control systems learned from a previous back-office monitoring job. Much of this monitoring involved the use of software to monitor trades. In addition, traders were usually kept to tight trading limits. Apparently, these controls failed in this case.

━━━━► What general weaknesses in Societe Generale's internal controls contributed to the occurrence and size of the losses?

OBJ. 2, 3

EX 8-6 Internal controls

An employee of JHT Holdings, Inc., a trucking company, was responsible for resolving roadway accident claims under $25,000. The employee created fake accident claims and wrote settlement checks of between $5,000 and $25,000 to friends or acquaintances acting as phony "victims." One friend recruited subordinates at his place of work to cash some of the checks. Beyond this, the JHT employee also recruited lawyers, who he paid to represent both the trucking company and the fake victims in the bogus accident settlements. When the lawyers cashed the checks, they allegedly split the money with the corrupt JHT employee. This fraud went undetected for two years.

━━━━► Why would it take so long to discover such a fraud?

OBJ. 2, 3

EX 8-7 Internal controls

Frog Sound Co. discovered a fraud whereby one of its front office administrative employees used company funds to purchase goods, such as computers, digital cameras, compact disk players, and other electronic items for her own use. The fraud was discovered when employees noticed an increase in delivery frequency from vendors and the use of unusual vendors. After some investigation, it was discovered that the employee would alter the description or change the quantity on an invoice in order to explain the cost on the bill.

━━━━► What general internal control weaknesses contributed to this fraud?

OBJ. 2, 3

EX 8-8 Financial statement fraud

A former chairman, CFO, and controller of Donnkenny, Inc., an apparel company that makes sportswear for Pierre Cardin and Victoria Jones, pleaded guilty to financial statement fraud. These managers used false journal entries to record fictitious sales, hid inventory in public warehouses so that it could be recorded as "sold," and required sales orders to be backdated so that the sale could be moved back to an earlier period. The combined effect of these actions caused $25 million out of $40 million in quarterly sales to be phony.

a. ━━━━► Why might control procedures listed in this chapter be insufficient in stopping this type of fraud?

b. ━━━━► How could this type of fraud be stopped?

OBJ. 2, 3

EX 8-9 Internal control of cash receipts

The procedures used for over-the-counter receipts are as follows. At the close of each day's business, the sales clerks count the cash in their respective cash drawers, after which they determine the amount recorded by the cash register and prepare the memo cash form, noting any discrepancies. An employee from the cashier's office counts the cash, compares the total with the memo, and takes the cash to the cashier's office.

a. ━━━━► Indicate the weak link in internal control.

b. ━━━━► How can the weakness be corrected?

OBJ. 2, 3

EX 8-10 Internal control of cash receipts

Mel Lane works at the drive-through window of Bison Burgers. Occasionally, when a drive-through customer orders, Mel fills the order and pockets the customer's money. He does not ring up the order on the cash register.

➤ Identify the internal control weaknesses that exist at Bison Burgers, and discuss what can be done to prevent this theft.

OBJ. 2, 3

EX 8-11 Internal control of cash receipts

The mailroom employees send all remittances and remittance advices to the cashier. The cashier deposits the cash in the bank and forwards the remittance advices and duplicate deposit slips to the Accounting Department.

a. ➤ Indicate the weak link in internal control in the handling of cash receipts.

b. ➤ How can the weakness be corrected?

OBJ. 2, 3

EX 8-12 Entry for cash sales; cash short

The actual cash received from cash sales was $27,943, and the amount indicated by the cash register total was $28,000. Journalize the entry to record the cash receipts and cash sales.

OBJ. 2, 3

EX 8-13 Entry for cash sales; cash over

The actual cash received from cash sales was $13,590, and the amount indicated by the cash register total was $13,540. Journalize the entry to record the cash receipts and cash sales.

OBJ. 2, 3

EX 8-14 Internal control of cash payments

Signs-A-Rama Co. is a small merchandising company with a manual accounting system. An investigation revealed that in spite of a sufficient bank balance, a significant amount of available cash discounts had been lost because of failure to make timely payments. In addition, it was discovered that the invoices for several purchases had been paid twice.

➤ Outline procedures for the payment of vendors' invoices, so that the possibilities of losing available cash discounts and of paying an invoice a second time will be minimized.

OBJ. 2, 3

EX 8-15 Internal control of cash payments

Digit Tech Company, a communications equipment manufacturer, recently fell victim to a fraud scheme developed by one of its employees. To understand the scheme, it is necessary to review Digit Tech's procedures for the purchase of services.

The purchasing agent is responsible for ordering services (such as repairs to a photocopy machine or office cleaning) after receiving a service requisition from an authorized manager. However, since no tangible goods are delivered, a receiving report is not prepared. When the Accounting Department receives an invoice billing Digit Tech for a service call, the accounts payable clerk calls the manager who requested the service in order to verify that it was performed.

The fraud scheme involves Loretta Trent, the manager of plant and facilities. Loretta arranged for her uncle's company, Laser Systems, to be placed on Digit Tech's approved vendor list. Loretta did not disclose the family relationship.

On several occasions, Loretta would submit a requisition for services to be provided by Laser Systems. However, the service requested was really not needed, and it was never performed. Laser Systems would bill Digit Tech for the service and then split the cash payment with Loretta.

➤ Explain what changes should be made to Digit Tech's procedures for ordering and paying for services in order to prevent such occurrences in the future.

OBJ. 5

EX 8-16   Bank reconciliation

Identify each of the following reconciling items as: (a) an addition to the cash balance according to the bank statement, (b) a deduction from the cash balance according to the bank statement, (c) an addition to the cash balance according to the company's records, or (d) a deduction from the cash balance according to the company's records. (None of the transactions reported by bank debit and credit memos have been recorded by the company.)

1. Bank service charges, $120.
2. Check of a customer returned by bank to company because of insufficient funds, $4,200.
3. Check for $240 incorrectly recorded by the company as $420.
4. Check for $1,000 incorrectly charged by bank as $10,000.
5. Deposit in transit, $24,950.
6. Outstanding checks, $18,100.
7. Note collected by bank, $15,600.

OBJ. 5

EX 8-17   Entries based on bank reconciliation

Which of the reconciling items listed in Exercise 8-16 require an entry in the company's accounts?

OBJ. 5

✔ Adjusted balance:
$16,000

EX 8-18   Bank reconciliation

The following data were accumulated for use in reconciling the bank account of Maplewood Co. for July:

1. Cash balance according to the company's records at July 31, $15,600.
2. Cash balance according to the bank statement at July 31, $16,230.
3. Checks outstanding, $3,180.
4. Deposit in transit, not recorded by bank, $2,950.
5. A check for $270 in payment of an account was erroneously recorded in the check register as $720.
6. Bank debit memo for service charges, $50.

a. Prepare a bank reconciliation, using the format shown in Exhibit 7.

b. If the balance sheet were prepared for Maplewood Co. on July 31, what amount should be reported for cash?

c. Must a bank reconciliation always balance (reconcile)?

OBJ. 5

EX 8-19   Entries for bank reconciliation

Using the data presented in Exercise 8-18, journalize the entry or entries that should be made by the company.

OBJ. 5

EX 8-20   Entries for note collected by bank

Accompanying a bank statement for O'Fallon Company is a credit memo for $21,200, representing the principal ($20,000) and interest ($1,200) on a note that had been collected by the bank. The company had been notified by the bank at the time of the collection, but had made no entries. Journalize the entry that should be made by the company to bring the accounting records up to date.

OBJ. 5

✔ Adjusted balance:
$14,000

EX 8-21   Bank reconciliation

An accounting clerk for Muskegon Co. prepared the following bank reconciliation:

Muskegon Co.
Bank Reconciliation
May 31, 2012

Cash balance according to company's records		$ 5,110
Add: Outstanding checks	$2,500	
Error by Muskegon Co. in recording Check		
No. 2219 as $810 instead of $180	630	
Note for $8,000 collected by bank, including interest.	8,320	11,450
		$16,560
Deduct: Deposit in transit on May 31	$5,200	
Bank service charges	60	5,260
Cash balance according to bank statement.		$11,300

a. From the data in the above bank reconciliation, prepare a new bank reconciliation for Muskegon Co., using the format shown in the illustrative problem.

b. If a balance sheet were prepared for Muskegon Co. on May 31, 2012, what amount should be reported for cash?

EX 8-22   Bank reconciliation

Identify the errors in the following bank reconciliation:

Alma Co.
Bank Reconciliation
For the Month Ended November 30, 2012

Cash balance according to bank statement.		$12,090
Add outstanding checks:		
No. 915.	$ 850	
960.	615	
964.	850	
965.	775	3,090
		$15,180
Deduct deposit of November 30, not recorded by bank		4,000
Adjusted balance.		$11,180
Cash balance according to company's records		$ 4,430
Add: Proceeds of note collected by bank:		
Principal.	$5,000	
Interest.	200	$5,200
Service charges		30	5,230
		$ 9,660
Deduct: Check returned because of insufficient funds.	$1,100	
Error in recording November 23 deposit of $6,100 as $1,600 . .	4,500	5,600
Adjusted balance.		$ 4,060

EX 8-23   Using bank reconciliation to determine cash receipts stolen

Lasting Impressions Co. records all cash receipts on the basis of its cash register tapes. Lasting Impressions Co. discovered during April 2012 that one of its sales clerks had stolen an undetermined amount of cash receipts when she took the daily deposits to the bank. The following data have been gathered for April:

Cash in bank according to the general ledger	$ 8,900
Cash according to the April 30, 2012, bank statement	20,500
Outstanding checks as of April 30, 2012	6,800
Bank service charge for April	100
Note receivable, including interest collected by bank in April	10,400

No deposits were in transit on April 30.

a. Determine the amount of cash receipts stolen by the sales clerk.

b. ▬▬▬▶ What accounting controls would have prevented or detected this theft?

OBJ. 6

EX 8-24 Petty cash fund entries

Journalize the entries to record the following:

a. Check No. 6300 is issued to establish a petty cash fund of $1,200.

b. The amount of cash in the petty cash fund is now $200. Check No. 6527 is issued to replenish the fund, based on the following summary of petty cash receipts: office supplies, $650; miscellaneous selling expense, $230; miscellaneous administrative expense, $90. (Since the amount of the check to replenish the fund plus the balance in the fund do not equal $1,200, record the discrepancy in the cash short and over account.)

OBJ. 7

EX 8-25 Variation in cash flows

Mattel, Inc., designs, manufactures, and markets toy products worldwide. Mattel's toys include Barbie™ fashion dolls and accessories, Hot Wheels™, and Fisher-Price brands. For a recent year, Mattel reported the following net cash flows from operating activities (in thousands):

First quarter ending March 31	$ (214,807)
Second quarter ending June 30	(135,003)
Third quarter ending September 30	31,003
Fourth quarter December 31	1,102,915

Explain why Mattel reported negative net cash flows from operating activities during the first two quarters, a small positive net cash flow in the third quarter, and a large positive cash flow for the fourth quarter with overall net positive cash flow for the year.

OBJ. 8

EX 8-26 Cash to monthly cash expenses ratio

During 2012, Pierport Inc. has monthly cash expenses of $400,000. On December 31, 2012, the cash balance is $3,600,000.

a. Compute the ratio of cash to monthly cash expenses.

b. Based on (a), what are the implications for Pierport Inc.?

OBJ. 8

EX 8-27 Cash to monthly cash expenses ratio

Delta Air Lines, one of the world's largest airlines, provides passenger and cargo services throughout the United States and the world. Delta reported the following financial data (in millions) for the year ended December 31, 2008:

Net cash flows from operating activities	$(1,7 07)
Cash and cash equivalents, December 31, 2008	4,255

a. Determine the monthly cash expenses. Round to one decimal place.

b. Determine the ratio of cash to monthly cash expenses. Round to one decimal place.

c. Based on your analysis, do you believe that Delta will remain in business?

OBJ. 8

EX 8-28 Cash to monthly cash expenses ratio

Allos Therapeutics, Inc., is a biopharmaceutical company that develops drugs for the treatment of cancer. Allos Therapeutics reported the following financial data (in thousands) for the years ending December 31, 2008, 2007, and 2006.

	For Years Ending December 31		
	2008	**2007**	**2006**
Cash and cash equivalents	$ 30,696	$ 16,103	$ 10,437
Net cash flows from operations	(42,850)	(30,823)	(25,147)

a. Determine the monthly cash expenses for 2008, 2007, and 2006. Round to one decimal place.

b. Determine the ratio of cash to monthly cash expenses as of December 31, 2008, 2007, and 2006. Round to one decimal place.

c. ━━━━▶ Based on (a) and (b), comment on Allos Therapeutics' ratio of cash to monthly operating expenses for 2008, 2007, and 2006.

Problems Series A

OBJ. 2, 3

PR 8-1A   Evaluating internal control of cash

The following procedures were recently installed by Pine Creek Company:

a. Along with petty cash expense receipts for postage, office supplies, etc., several post-dated employee checks are in the petty cash fund.

b. After necessary approvals have been obtained for the payment of a voucher, the treasurer signs and mails the check. The treasurer then stamps the voucher and supporting documentation as paid and returns the voucher and supporting documentation to the accounts payable clerk for filing.

c. At the end of each day, all cash receipts are placed in the bank's night depository.

d. The accounts payable clerk prepares a voucher for each disbursement. The voucher along with the supporting documentation is forwarded to the treasurer's office for approval.

e. At the end of each day, an accounting clerk compares the duplicate copy of the daily cash deposit slip with the deposit receipt obtained from the bank.

f. The bank reconciliation is prepared by the cashier, who works under the supervision of the treasurer.

g. All mail is opened by the mail clerk, who forwards all cash remittances to the cashier. The cashier prepares a listing of the cash receipts and forwards a copy of the list to the accounts receivable clerk for recording in the accounts.

h. At the end of the day, cash register clerks are required to use their own funds to make up any cash shortages in their registers.

Instructions

━━━━▶ Indicate whether each of the procedures of internal control over cash represents (1) a strength or (2) a weakness. For each weakness, indicate why it exists.

OBJ. 3, 6

PR 8-2A   Transactions for petty cash, cash short and over

Picasso Restoration Company completed the following selected transactions during August 2012:

Aug. 1. Established a petty cash fund of $750.

   10. The cash sales for the day, according to the cash register records, totaled $9,780. The actual cash received from cash sales was $9,800.

   31. Petty cash on hand was $240. Replenished the petty cash fund for the following disbursements, each evidenced by a petty cash receipt:

   Aug. 3. Store supplies, $251.

       7. Express charges on merchandise sold, $60 (Delivery Expense).

       9. Office supplies, $20.

      13. Office supplies, $30.

      19. Postage stamps, $11 (Office Supplies).

      21. Repair to office file cabinet lock, $40 (Miscellaneous Administrative Expense).

Aug. 22. Postage due on special delivery letter, $18 (Miscellaneous Administrative Expense).

24. Express charges on merchandise sold, $50 (Delivery Expense).

30. Office supplies, $15.

31. The cash sales for the day, according to the cash register records, totaled $11,200. The actual cash received from cash sales was $11,130.

31. Decreased the petty cash fund by $100.

Instructions
Journalize the transactions.

OBJ. 5

✔ 1. Adjusted balance: $11,400

PR 8-3A   Bank reconciliation and entries

The cash account for Online Medical Co. at June 30, 2012, indicated a balance of $9,375. The bank statement indicated a balance of $10,760 on June 30, 2012. Comparing the bank statement and the accompanying canceled checks and memos with the records revealed the following reconciling items:

a. Checks outstanding totaled $3,900.

b. A deposit of $4,000, representing receipts of June 30, had been made too late to appear on the bank statement.

c. The bank had collected $2,100 on a note left for collection. The face of the note was $2,000.

d. A check for $550 returned with the statement had been incorrectly recorded by Online Medical Co. as $500. The check was for the payment of an obligation to Hirsch Co. for the purchase on account.

e. A check drawn for $60 had been erroneously charged by the bank as $600.

f. Bank service charges for June amounted to $25.

Instructions

1. Prepare a bank reconciliation.

2. Journalize the necessary entries. The accounts have not been closed.

3. If a balance sheet were prepared for Online Medical Co. on June 30, 2012, what amount should be reported as cash?

OBJ. 5

✔ 1. Adjusted balance: $23,750

PR 8-4A   Bank reconciliation and entries

The cash account for Bravo Bike Co. at May 1, 2012, indicated a balance of $15,085. During May, the total cash deposited was $75,100 and checks written totaled $69,750. The bank statement indicated a balance of $25,460 on May 31. Comparing the bank statement, the canceled checks, and the accompanying memos with the records revealed the following reconciling items:

a. Checks outstanding totaled $11,360.

b. A deposit of $9,200, representing receipts of May 31, had been made too late to appear on the bank statement.

c. The bank had collected for Bravo Bike Co. $4,725 on a note left for collection. The face of the note was $4,500.

d. A check for $490 returned with the statement had been incorrectly charged by the bank as $940.

e. A check for $410 returned with the statement had been recorded by Bravo Bike Co. as $140. The check was for the payment of an obligation to Portage Co. on account.

f. Bank service charges for July amounted to $40.

g. A check for $1,100 from Elkhart Co. was returned by the bank because of insufficient funds.

Instructions

1. Prepare a bank reconciliation as of May 31.
2. Journalize the necessary entries. The accounts have not been closed.
3. If a balance sheet were prepared for Bravo Bike Co. on May 31, 2012, what amount should be reported as cash?

OBJ. 5

✔ 1. Adjusted
balance: $13,900.50

PR 8-5A   Bank reconciliation and entries

Oneida Furniture Company deposits all cash receipts each Wednesday and Friday in a night depository, after banking hours. The data required to reconcile the bank statement as of June 30 have been taken from various documents and records and are reproduced as follows. The sources of the data are printed in capital letters. All checks were written for payments on account.

CASH ACCOUNT:

Balance as of June 1	$9,317.40
CASH RECEIPTS FOR MONTH OF JUNE	$9,524.16

DUPLICATE DEPOSIT TICKETS:

Date and amount of each deposit in June:

Date	Amount	Date	Amount	Date	Amount
June 1	$1,080.50	June 10	$ 896.61	June 22	$ 897.34
3	854.17	15	882.95	24	942.71
8	845.00	17	1,607.64	30	1,517.24

CHECKS WRITTEN:

Number and amount of each check issued in June:

Check No.	Amount	Check No.	Amount	Check No.	Amount
740	$237.50	747	Void	754	$ 449.75
741	495.15	748	$450.90	755	272.75
742	501.90	749	640.13	756	113.95
743	671.30	750	276.77	757	407.95
744	560.88	751	299.37	758	259.60
745	117.25	752	537.01	759	901.50
746	298.66	753	380.95	760	486.39
Total amount of checks issued in June					$8,359.66

BANK RECONCILIATION FOR PRECEDING MONTH:

Oneida Furniture Company
Bank Reconciliation
May 31, 20—

Cash balance according to bank statement..........................		$ 9,447.20
Add deposit for May 31, not recorded by bank......................		690.25
		$10,137.45
Deduct outstanding checks:		
No. 731	$162.15	
736	345.95	
738	251.40	
739	60.55	820.05
Adjusted balance..		$ 9,317.40
Cash balance according to company's records		$ 9,352.50
Deduct service charges		35.10
Adjusted balance..		$ 9,317.40

JUNE BANK STATEMENT:

				MEMBER FDIC		PAGE 1	
		AMERICAN NATIONAL BANK			ACCOUNT NUMBER		
		OF CHICAGO			FROM 6/01/20– TO 6/30/20–		
	CHICAGO, IL 60603 (312)441-1239				BALANCE	9,447.20	
					9 DEPOSITS	8,691.77	
					20 WITHDRAWALS	8,014.37	
	ONEIDA FURNITURE COMPANY				4 OTHER DEBITS AND CREDITS	3,370.00CR	
					NEW BALANCE	13,494.60	

* – – – CHECKS AND OTHER DEBITS – – – *				– DEPOSITS – – *	– DATE – *	– – BALANCE – – *
No.731	162.15	No.736	345.95	690.25	6/01	9,629.35
No.739	60.55	No.740	237.50	1,080.50	6/02	10,411.80
No.741	495.15	No.742	501.90	854.17	6/04	10,268.92
No.743	671.30	No.744	506.88	840.50	6/09	9,931.24
No.745	117.25	No.746	298.66	MS 3,500.00	6/09	13,015.33
No.748	450.90	No.749	640.13	MS 210.00	6/09	12,134.30
No.750	276.77	No.751	299.37	896.61	6/11	12,454.77
No.752	537.01	No.753	380.95	882.95	6/16	12,419.76
No.754	449.75	No.755	272.75	1,606.74	6/18	13,304.00
No.757	407.95	No.759	901.50	897.34	6/23	12,891.89
				942.71	6/25	13,834.60
		NSF	300.00		6/28	13,534.60
		SC	40.00		6/30	13,494.60

EC — ERROR CORRECTION   OD — OVERDRAFT
MS — MISCELLANEOUS   PS — PAYMENT STOPPED
NSF — NOT SUFFICIENT FUNDS   SC — SERVICE CHARGE

* * *   * * *   * * *

THE RECONCILEMENT OF THIS STATEMENT WITH YOUR RECORDS IS ESSENTIAL.
ANY ERROR OR EXCEPTION SHOULD BE REPORTED IMMEDIATELY.

Instructions

1. Prepare a bank reconciliation as of June 30. If errors in recording deposits or checks are discovered, assume that the errors were made by the company. Assume that all deposits are from cash sales. All checks are written to satisfy accounts payable.

2. Journalize the necessary entries. The accounts have not been closed.

3. What is the amount of Cash that should appear on the balance sheet as of June 30?

4. ➤ Assume that a canceled check for $270 has been incorrectly recorded by the bank as $720. Briefly explain how the error would be included in a bank reconciliation and how it should be corrected.

Problems Series B

OBJ. 2, 3

PR 8-1B   **Evaluate internal control of cash**

The following procedures were recently installed by The Blind Shop:

a. At the end of a shift, each cashier counts the cash in his or her cash register, unlocks the cash register record, and compares the amount of cash with the amount on the record to determine cash shortages and overages.

b. Checks received through the mail are given daily to the accounts receivable clerk for recording collections on account and for depositing in the bank.

c. Each cashier is assigned a separate cash register drawer to which no other cashier has access.

d. Vouchers and all supporting documents are perforated with a PAID designation after being paid by the treasurer.

e. All sales are rung up on the cash register, and a receipt is given to the customer. All sales are recorded on a record locked inside the cash register.

f. Disbursements are made from the petty cash fund only after a petty cash receipt has been completed and signed by the payee.

g. The bank reconciliation is prepared by the cashier.

Instructions

Indicate whether each of the procedures of internal control over cash represents (1) a strength or (2) a weakness. For each weakness, indicate why it exists.

OBJ. 3, 6

PR 8-2B Transactions for petty cash, cash short and over

Cedar Springs Company completed the following selected transactions during November 2012:

Nov. 1. Established a petty cash fund of $850.

12. The cash sales for the day, according to the cash register records, totaled $16,100. The actual cash received from cash sales was $16,175.

30. Petty cash on hand was $70. Replenished the petty cash fund for the following disbursements, each evidenced by a petty cash receipt:

Nov. 2. Store supplies, $100.

10. Express charges on merchandise purchased, $260 (Merchandise Inventory).

14. Office supplies, $125.

15. Office supplies, $80.

18. Postage stamps, $70 (Office Supplies).

20. Repair to fax, $35 (Miscellaneous Administrative Expense).

21. Repair to office door lock, $15 (Miscellaneous Administrative Expense).

22. Postage due on special delivery letter, $40 (Miscellaneous Administrative Expense).

28. Express charges on merchandise purchased, $40 (Merchandise Inventory).

30. The cash sales for the day, according to the cash register records, totaled $19,415. The actual cash received from cash sales was $19,350.

30. Increased the petty cash fund by $150.

Instructions

Journalize the transactions.

OBJ. 5

✔ 1. Adjusted balance: $27,000

PR 8-3B Bank reconciliation and entries

The cash account for Ambulance Systems at February 29, 2012, indicated a balance of $20,580. The bank statement indicated a balance of $24,750 on February 29, 2012. Comparing the bank statement and the accompanying canceled checks and memos with the records reveals the following reconciling items:

a. Checks outstanding totaled $9,300.

b. A deposit of $12,000, representing receipts of February 29, had been made too late to appear on the bank statement.

c. The bank had collected $6,240 on a note left for collection. The face of the note was $6,000.

d. A check for $140 returned with the statement had been incorrectly recorded by Ambulance Systems as $410. The check was for the payment of an obligation to Holland Co. for the purchase of office supplies on account.

e. A check drawn for $725 had been incorrectly charged by the bank as $275.

f. Bank service charges for February amounted to $90.

Instructions

1. Prepare a bank reconciliation.

2. Journalize the necessary entries. The accounts have not been closed.

3. If a balance sheet were prepared for Ambulance Systems on February 29, 2012, what amount should be reported as cash?

PR 8-4B Bank reconciliation and entries

The cash account for South Bay Sports Co. on April 1, 2012, indicated a balance of $35,025. During April, the total cash deposited was $83,150, and checks written totaled $90,000. The bank statement indicated a balance of $34,345 on April 30, 2012. Comparing the bank statement, the canceled checks, and the accompanying memos with the records revealed the following reconciling items:

a. Checks outstanding totaled $7,700.

b. A deposit of $3,800, representing receipts of April 30, had been made too late to appear on the bank statement.

c. A check for $960 had been incorrectly charged by the bank as $690.

d. A check for $150 returned with the statement had been recorded by South Bay Sports Co. as $1,500. The check was for the payment of an obligation to Jones Co. on account.

e. The bank had collected for South Bay Sports Co. $2,600 on a note left for collection. The face of the note was $2,500.

f. Bank service charges for June amounted to $50.

g. A check for $1,900 from Valley Schools Academy was returned by the bank because of insufficient funds.

Instructions

1. Prepare a bank reconciliation as of April 30.

2. Journalize the necessary entries. The accounts have not been closed.

3. If a balance sheet were prepared for South Bay Sports Co. on April 30, 2012, what amount should be reported as cash?

PR 8-5B Bank reconciliation and entries

La Casa Interiors deposits all cash receipts each Wednesday and Friday in a night depository, after banking hours. The data required to reconcile the bank statement as of July 31 have been taken from various documents and records and are reproduced as follows. The sources of the data are printed in capital letters. All checks were written for payments on account.

BANK RECONCILIATION FOR PRECEDING MONTH (DATED JUNE 30):

Cash balance according to bank statement........................		$ 9,422.80
Add deposit of June 30, not recorded by bank......................		780.80
		$10,203.60
Deduct outstanding checks:		
No. 580	$310.10	
No. 602	85.50	
No. 612	92.50	
No. 613	137.50	625.60
Adjusted balance...		$ 9,578.00
Cash balance according to company's records		$ 9,605.70
Deduct service charges		27.70
Adjusted balance...		$ 9,578.00
CASH ACCOUNT:		
Balance as of July 1		$ 9,578.00

CHECKS WRITTEN:

Number and amount of each check issued in July:

Check No.	Amount	Check No.	Amount	Check No.	Amount
614	$243.50	621	$309.50	628	$ 837.70
615	350.10	622	Void	629	329.90
616	279.90	623	Void	630	882.80
617	395.50	624	707.01	631	1,081.56
618	435.40	625	185.63	632	325.40
619	320.10	626	550.03	633	310.08
620	238.87	627	318.73	634	241.71
Total amount of checks issued in July					$8,343.42

CASH RECEIPTS FOR MONTH OF JULY   6,247.12
DUPLICATE DEPOSIT TICKETS:
    Date and amount of each deposit in July:

Date	Amount	Date	Amount	Date	Amount
July 2	$569.50	July 12	$580.70	July 23	$731.45
5	701.80	16	600.10	26	601.50
9	812.94	19	701.26	31	947.87

JULY BANK STATEMENT:

```
                                    MEMBER FDIC                          PAGE   1
    A
    N B   AMERICAN NATIONAL BANK           ACCOUNT NUMBER
          OF DETROIT
                                           FROM   7/01/20–   TO   7/31/20–
    DETROIT, MI 48201-2500   (313)933-8547
                                           BALANCE               9,422.80

                                      9  DEPOSITS                 6,086.35

                                     20  WITHDRAWALS              8,237.41

          LA CASA INTERIORS           4  OTHER DEBITS
                                         AND CREDITS              3,685.00CR

                                         NEW BALANCE            10,956.74

    *------ CHECKS AND OTHER DEBITS ------*-- DEPOSITS -*- DATE -*- BALANCE- *

    No.580  310.10   No.612    92.50           780.80    07/01      9,801.00
    No.602   85.50   No.614   243.50           569.50    07/03     10,041.50
    No.615  350.10   No.616   279.90           701.80    07/06     10,113.30
    No.617  395.50   No.618   435.40           819.24    07/11     10,101.64
    No.619  320.10   No.620   238.87           580.70    07/13     10,123.37
    No.621  309.50   No.624   707.01      MS 4,000.00    07/14     13,106.86
    No.625  158.63   No.626   550.03      MS   160.00    07/14     12,558.20
    No.627  318.73   No.629   329.90           600.10    07/17     12,509.67
    No.630  882.80   No.631 1,081.56  NSF 450.00         07/20     10,095.31
    No.628  837.70   No.633   310.08           701.26    07/21      9,648.79
                                             731.45    07/24     10,380.24
                                             601.50    07/28     10,981.74
                              SC    25.00              07/31     10,956.74

        EC — ERROR CORRECTION                OD — OVERDRAFT
        MS — MISCELLANEOUS                   PS — PAYMENT STOPPED
        NSF — NOT SUFFICIENT FUNDS           SC — SERVICE CHARGE
    * * *                        * * *                              * * *
           THE RECONCILEMENT OF THIS STATEMENT WITH YOUR RECORDS IS ESSENTIAL.
             ANY ERROR OR EXCEPTION SHOULD BE REPORTED IMMEDIATELY.
```

Instructions

1. Prepare a bank reconciliation as of July 31. If errors in recording deposits or checks are discovered, assume that the errors were made by the company. Assume that all deposits are from cash sales. All checks are written to satisfy accounts payable.

2. Journalize the necessary entries. The accounts have not been closed.

3. What is the amount of Cash that should appear on the balance sheet as of July 31?

4. ➤ Assume that a canceled check for $325 has been incorrectly recorded by the bank as $3,250. Briefly explain how the error would be included in a bank reconciliation and how it should be corrected.

Cases & Projects

CP 8-1   Ethics and professional conduct in business

During the preparation of the bank reconciliation for Regal Concepts Co., Misty Watts, the assistant controller, discovered that Windsor National Bank incorrectly recorded a $15,750 check written by Regal Concepts Co. as $1,575. Misty has decided not to notify the bank but wait for the bank to detect the error. Misty plans to record the $14,175 error as Other Income if the bank fails to detect the error within the next three months.

➤ Discuss whether Misty is behaving in a professional manner.

CP 8-2   Internal controls

The following is an excerpt from a conversation between two sales clerks, Craig Rice and Jill Allen. Craig and Jill are employed by Ogden Electronics, a locally owned and operated electronics retail store.

Craig: Did you hear the news?

Jill: What news?

Craig: Kate and Steve were both arrested this morning.

Jill: What? Arrested? You're putting me on!

Craig: No, really! The police arrested them first thing this morning. Put them in handcuffs, read them their rights—the whole works. It was unreal!

Jill: What did they do?

Craig: Well, apparently they were filling out merchandise refund forms for fictitious customers and then taking the cash.

Jill: I guess I never thought of that. How did they catch them?

Craig: The store manager noticed that returns were twice that of last year and seemed to be increasing. When he confronted Kate, she became flustered and admitted to taking the cash, apparently over $10,000 in just three months. They're going over the last six months' transactions to try to determine how much Steve stole. He apparently started stealing first.

➤ Suggest appropriate control procedures that would have prevented or detected the theft of cash.

CP 8-3   Internal controls

The following is an excerpt from a conversation between the store manager of Dozier Brothers Grocery Stores, Amy Blankenship, and Mike Ulrich, president of Dozier Brothers Grocery Stores.

Mike: Amy, I'm concerned about this new scanning system.

Amy: What's the problem?

Mike: Well, how do we know the clerks are ringing up all the merchandise?

Amy: That's one of the strong points about the system. The scanner automatically rings up each item, based on its bar code. We update the prices daily, so we're sure that the sale is rung up for the right price.

Mike: That's not my concern. What keeps a clerk from pretending to scan items and then simply not charging his friends? If his friends were buying 10-15 items, it would be easy for the clerk to pass through several items with his finger over the bar code or just pass the merchandise through the scanner with the wrong side showing. It would look normal for anyone observing. In the old days, we at least could hear the cash register ringing up each sale.

Amy: I see your point.

➤ Suggest ways that Dozier Brothers Grocery Stores could prevent or detect the theft of merchandise as described.

CP 8-4   Ethics and professional conduct in business

Eric Inman and Darcy Getz are both cash register clerks for Farmer John's Markets. Nancy McNeil is the store manager for Farmer John's Markets. The following is an excerpt of a conversation between Eric and Darcy:

Eric: Darcy, how long have you been working for Farmer John's Markets?

Darcy: Almost five years this June. You just started two weeks ago . . . right?

Eric: Yes. Do you mind if I ask you a question?

Darcy: No, go ahead.

Eric: What I want to know is, have they always had this rule that if your cash register is short at the end of the day, you have to make up the shortage out of your own pocket?

Darcy: Yes, as long as I've been working here.

Eric: Well, it's the pits. Last week I had to pay in almost $25.

Darcy: It's not that big a deal. I just make sure that I'm not short at the end of the day.

Eric: How do you do that?

Darcy: I just shortchange a few customers early in the day. There are a few jerks that deserve it anyway. Most of the time, their attention is elsewhere and they don't think to check their change.

Eric: What happens if you're over at the end of the day?

Darcy: Nancy lets me keep it as long as it doesn't get to be too large. I've not been short in over a year. I usually clear about $10 to $15 extra per day.

 Discuss this case from the viewpoint of proper controls and professional behavior.

CP 8-5   Bank reconciliation and internal control

The records of Diamondale Company indicate a May 31 cash balance of $10,550, which includes undeposited receipts for May 30 and 31. The cash balance on the bank statement as of May 31 is $8,575. This balance includes a note of $5,000 plus $200 interest collected by the bank but not recorded in the journal. Checks outstanding on May 31 were as follows: No. 670, $900; No. 679, $750; No. 690, $1,650; No. 1148, $225; No. 1149, $300; and No. 1151, $600.

On May 3, the cashier resigned, effective at the end of the month. Before leaving on May 31, the cashier prepared the following bank reconciliation:

Cash balance per books, May 31		$10,550
Add outstanding checks:		
No. 1148	$225	
1149	300	
1151	600	1,025
		$11,575
Less undeposited receipts		3,000
Cash balance per bank, May 31		$ 8,575
Deduct unrecorded note with interest		5,200
True cash, May 31		$ 3,375

```
Calculator Tape of Outstanding Checks:
              0*
            225+
            300+
            600+
          1,025*
```

Subsequently, the owner of Diamondale Company discovered that the cashier had stolen an unknown amount of undeposited receipts, leaving only $1,000 to be deposited on May 31. The owner, a close family friend, has asked your help in determining the amount that the former cashier has stolen.

1. Determine the amount the cashier stole from Diamondale Company. Show your computations in good form.

2. How did the cashier attempt to conceal the theft?

3. a. Identify two major weaknesses in internal controls, which allowed the cashier to steal the undeposited cash receipts.

   b. ➤ Recommend improvements in internal controls, so that similar types of thefts of undeposited cash receipts can be prevented.

CP 8-6   Observe internal controls over cash

Group Project

Select a business in your community and observe its internal controls over cash receipts and cash payments. The business could be a bank or a bookstore, restaurant, department store, or other retailer. In groups of three or four, identify and discuss the similarities and differences in each business's cash internal controls.

CP 8-7   Cash to monthly cash expenses ratio

OccuLogix, Inc., is a health care company that specializes in developing diagnostic devices for eye disease. OccuLogix reported the following data (in thousands) for the years ending December 31, 2008, 2007, and 2006:

	For Years Ending December 31		
	2008	**2007**	**2006**
Cash and cash equivalents	$ 2,565	$ 2,236	$ 5,741
Net cash flows from operations	(9,434)	(17,217)	(14,548)

1. Determine the monthly cash expenses for 2008, 2007, and 2006. Round to one decimal place.

2. Determine the ratio of cash to monthly cash expenses as of December 31, 2008, 2007, and 2006. Round to one decimal place.

3. ➤ Based on (1) and (2), comment on OccuLogix's ratio of cash to monthly operating expenses for 2008, 2007, and 2006.

© Erik Isakson/Tetra Images/Jupiter Images

Receivables

CHAPTER 9

Oakley, Inc.

The sale and purchase of merchandise involves the exchange of goods for cash. However, the point at which cash actually changes hands varies with the transaction. Consider transactions by **Oakley, Inc.,** a worldwide leader in the design, development, manufacture, and distribution of premium sunglasses, goggles, prescription eyewear, apparel, footwear, and accessories. Not only does the company sell its products through three different company-owned retail chains, but it also has approximately 10,000 independent distributors.

If you were to buy a pair of sunglasses at an Oakley Vault, which is one of the company's retail outlet stores, you would have to pay cash or use a credit card to pay for the glasses before you left the store. However, Oakley allows

its distributors to purchase sunglasses "on account." These sales on account are recorded as receivables due from the distributors.

As an individual, you also might build up a trusted financial history with a local company or department store that would allow you to purchase merchandise on account. Like Oakley's distributors, your purchase on account would be recorded as an account receivable. Such credit transactions facilitate sales and are a significant current asset for many businesses.

This chapter describes common classifications of receivables, illustrates how to account for uncollectible receivables, and demonstrates the reporting of receivables on the balance sheet.

OBJ. 1 Describe the common classes of receivables.

Classification of Receivables

The receivables that result from sales on account are normally accounts receivable or notes receivable. The term **receivables** includes all money claims against other entities, including people, companies, and other organizations. Receivables are usually a significant portion of the total current assets.

Accounts Receivable

The most common transaction creating a receivable is selling merchandise or services on account (on credit). The receivable is recorded as a debit to Accounts Receivable. Such **accounts receivable** are normally collected within a short period, such as 30 or 60 days. They are classified on the balance sheet as a current asset.

An annual report of La-Z-Boy Incorporated reported that receivables made up over 46% of La-Z-Boy's current assets.

Notes Receivable

Notes receivable are amounts that customers owe for which a formal, written instrument of credit has been issued. If notes receivable are expected to be collected within a year, they are classified on the balance sheet as a current asset.

Notes are often used for credit periods of more than 60 days. For example, an automobile dealer may require a down payment at the time of sale and accept a note or a series of notes for the remainder. Such notes usually provide for monthly payments.

Notes may also be used to settle a customer's account receivable. Notes and accounts receivable that result from sales transactions are sometimes called *trade receivables*. In this chapter, all notes and accounts receivable are from sales transactions.

Other Receivables

Other receivables include interest receivable, taxes receivable, and receivables from officers or employees. Other receivables are normally reported separately on the balance sheet. If they are expected to be collected within one year, they are classified as current assets. If collection is expected beyond one year, they are classified as noncurrent assets and reported under the caption *Investments.*

Uncollectible Receivables

OBJ. 2 Describe the accounting for uncollectible receivables.

In prior chapters, the accounting for sales of merchandise or services on account (on credit) was described and illustrated. A major issue that has not yet been discussed is that some customers will not pay their accounts. That is, some accounts receivable will be uncollectible.

Companies may shift the risk of uncollectible receivables to other companies. For example, some retailers do not accept sales on account, but will only accept cash or credit cards. Such policies shift the risk to the credit card companies.

Companies may also sell their receivables. This is often the case when a company issues its own credit card. For example, Macy's and JCPenney issue their own credit cards. Selling receivables is called *factoring* the receivables. The buyer of the receivables is called a *factor.* An advantage of factoring is that the company selling its receivables immediately receives cash for operating and other needs. Also, depending on the factoring agreement, some of the risk of uncollectible accounts is shifted to the factor.

Regardless of how careful a company is in granting credit, some credit sales will be uncollectible. The operating expense recorded from uncollectible receivables is called **bad debt expense**, *uncollectible accounts expense,* or *doubtful accounts expense.*

There is no general rule for when an account becomes uncollectible. Some indications that an account may be uncollectible include the following:

1. The receivable is past due.
2. The customer does not respond to the company's attempts to collect.
3. The customer files for bankruptcy.
4. The customer closes its business.
5. The company cannot locate the customer.

Adams, Stevens & Bradley, Ltd. is a collection agency that operates on a contingency basis. That is, its fees are based on what it collects.

If a customer doesn't pay, a company may turn the account over to a collection agency. After the collection agency attempts to collect payment, any remaining balance in the account is considered worthless.

The two methods of accounting for uncollectible receivables are as follows:

1. The **direct write-off method** records bad debt expense only when an account is determined to be worthless.
2. The **allowance method** records bad debt expense by estimating uncollectible accounts at the end of the accounting period.

The direct write-off method is often used by small companies and companies with few receivables.[1] Generally accepted accounting principles (GAAP), however, require companies with a large amount of receivables to use the allowance method. As a result, most well-known companies such as General Electric, Pepsi, Intel, and FedEx use the allowance method.

Direct Write-Off Method for Uncollectible Accounts

OBJ. 3 Describe the direct write-off method of accounting for uncollectible receivables.

Under the direct write-off method, Bad Debt Expense is not recorded until the customer's account is determined to be worthless. At that time, the customer's account receivable is written off.

---

1 The direct write-off method is also required for federal income tax purposes.

To illustrate, assume that a $4,200 account receivable from D. L. Ross has been determined to be uncollectible. The entry to write off the account is as follows:

May	10	Bad Debt Expense	4,200	
		Accounts Receivable—D. L. Ross		4,200

An account receivable that has been written off may be collected later. In such cases, the account is reinstated by an entry that reverses the write-off entry. The cash received in payment is then recorded as a receipt on account.

To illustrate, assume that the D. L. Ross account of $4,200 written off on May 10 is later collected on November 21. The reinstatement and receipt of cash is recorded as follows:

Nov.	21	Accounts Receivable—D. L. Ross	4,200	
		Bad Debt Expense		4,200
	21	Cash	4,200	
		Accounts Receivable—D. L. Ross		4,200

The direct write-off method is used by businesses that sell most of their goods or services for cash or through the acceptance of MasterCard or VISA, which are recorded as cash sales. In such cases, receivables are a small part of the current assets and any bad debt expense is small. Examples of such businesses are a restaurant, a convenience store, and a small retail store.

Example Exercise 9-1   Direct Write-off Method

OBJ. 3

Journalize the following transactions using the direct write-off method of accounting for uncollectible receivables:

July 9.   Received $1,200 from Jay Burke and wrote off the remainder owed of $3,900 as uncollectible.
Oct. 11.   Reinstated the account of Jay Burke and received $3,900 cash in full payment.

Follow My Example 9-1

July 9	Cash	1,200	
	Bad Debt Expense...	3,900	
	Accounts Receivable—Jay Burke		5,100
Oct. 11	Accounts Receivable—Jay Burke..............................	3,900	
	Bad Debt Expense..		3,900
11	Cash	3,900	
	Accounts Receivable—Jay Burke		3,900

Practice Exercises: **PE 9-1A, PE 9-1B**

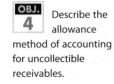
Describe the allowance method of accounting for uncollectible receivables.

Allowance Method for Uncollectible Accounts

The allowance method estimates the uncollectible accounts receivable at the end of the accounting period. Based on this estimate, Bad Debt Expense is recorded by an adjusting entry.

To illustrate, assume that ExTone Company began operations August 1. As of the end of its accounting period on December 31, 2011, ExTone has an accounts receivable balance of $200,000. This balance includes some past due accounts. Based on industry averages, ExTone estimates that $30,000 of the December 31 accounts receivable will be uncollectible. However, on December 31, ExTone doesn't know which customer accounts will be uncollectible. Thus, specific customer accounts cannot be decreased or credited. Instead, a contra asset account, **Allowance for Doubtful Accounts**, is credited for the estimated bad debts.

Using the $30,000 estimate, the following adjusting entry is made on December 31:

2011					
Dec.	31	Bad Debt Expense		30,000	
		Allowance for Doubtful Accounts			30,000
		Uncollectible accounts estimate.			

The preceding adjusting entry affects the income statement and balance sheet. On the income statement, the $30,000 of Bad Debt Expense will be matched against the related revenues of the period. On the balance sheet, the value of the receivables is reduced to the amount that is expected to be collected or realized. This amount, $170,000 ($200,000 − $30,000), is called the **net realizable value** of the receivables.

Note:
The adjusting entry reduces receivables to their net realizable value and matches the uncollectible expense with revenues.

After the preceding adjusting entry is recorded, Accounts Receivable still has a debit balance of $200,000. This balance is the total amount owed by customers on account on December 31 as supported by the accounts receivable subsidiary ledger. The accounts receivable contra account, Allowance for Doubtful Accounts, has a credit balance of $30,000.

Integrity, Objectivity, and Ethics in Business

SELLER BEWARE

A company in financial distress will still try to purchase goods and services on account. In these cases, rather than "buyer beware," it is more like "seller beware." Sellers must be careful in advancing credit to such companies, because trade creditors have low priority for cash payments in the event of bankruptcy. To help suppliers, third-party services specialize in evaluating court actions and payment decisions of financially distressed companies.

Write-Offs to the Allowance Account

When a customer's account is identified as uncollectible, it is written off against the allowance account. This requires the company to remove the specific accounts receivable and an equal amount from the allowance account.

To illustrate, on January 21, 2012, John Parker's account of $6,000 with ExTone Company is written off as follows:

2012					
Jan.	21	Allowance for Doubtful Accounts		6,000	
		Accounts Receivable—John Parker			6,000

At the end of a period, Allowance for Doubtful Accounts will normally have a balance. This is because Allowance for Doubtful Accounts is based on an estimate. As a result, the total write-offs to the allowance account during the period will rarely equal the balance of the account at the beginning of the period. The allowance account will have a credit balance at the end of the period if the write-offs during the period are less than the beginning balance. It will have a debit balance if the write-offs exceed the beginning balance.

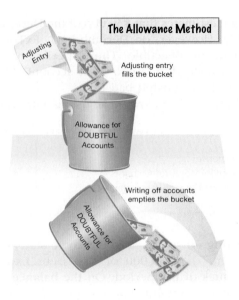

To illustrate, assume that during 2012 ExTone Company writes off $26,750 of uncollectible accounts, including the $6,000 account of John Parker recorded on January 21. Allowance for Doubtful Accounts will have a credit balance of $3,250 ($30,000 – $26,750), as shown below.

ALLOWANCE FOR DOUBTFUL ACCOUNTS

				Jan. 1	Balance	30,000
Total accounts	Jan.	21	6,000			
written off $26,750	Feb.	2	3,900			
	⋮		⋮			
				Dec. 31	Unadjusted balance	3,250

If ExTone Company had written off $32,100 in accounts receivable during 2012, Allowance for Doubtful Accounts would have a debit balance of $2,100, as shown below.

ALLOWANCE FOR DOUBTFUL ACCOUNTS

				Jan. 1	Balance	30,000
Total accounts	Jan.	21	6,000			
written off $32,100	Feb.	2	3,900			
	⋮		⋮			
Dec. 31	Unadjusted balance	2,100			

The allowance account balances (credit balance of $3,250 and debit balance of $2,100) in the preceding illustrations are *before* the end-of-period adjusting entry. After the end-of-period adjusting entry is recorded, Allowance for Doubtful Accounts should always have a credit balance.

An account receivable that has been written off against the allowance account may be collected later. Like the direct write-off method, the account is reinstated by an entry that reverses the write-off entry. The cash received in payment is then recorded as a receipt on account.

To illustrate, assume that Nancy Smith's account of $5,000 which was written off on April 2 is collected later on June 10. ExTone Company records the reinstatement and the collection as follows:

June	10	Accounts Receivable—Nancy Smith	5,000	
		Allowance for Doubtful Accounts		5,000
	10	Cash	5,000	
		Accounts Receivable—Nancy Smith		5,000

Example Exercise 9-2   Allowance Method

OBJ. 4

Journalize the following transactions using the allowance method of accounting for uncollectible receivables.

July   9.   Received $1,200 from Jay Burke and wrote off the remainder owed of $3,900 as uncollectible.
Oct. 11.   Reinstated the account of Jay Burke and received $3,900 cash in full payment.

Follow My Example 9-2

July 9	Cash	1,200	
	Allowance for Doubtful Accounts.............................	3,900	
	Accounts Receivable—Jay Burke		5,100
Oct. 11	Accounts Receivable—Jay Burke.............................	3,900	
	Allowance for Doubtful Accounts...........................		3,900
11	Cash	3,900	
	Accounts Receivable—Jay Burke		3,900

Practice Exercises: **PE 9-2A, PE 9-2B**

Estimating Uncollectibles

The allowance method requires an estimate of uncollectible accounts at the end of the period. This estimate is normally based on past experience, industry averages, and forecasts of the future.

The two methods used to estimate uncollectible accounts are as follows:

1. Percent of sales method.
2. Analysis of receivables method.

Percent of Sales Method   Since accounts receivable are created by credit sales, uncollectible accounts can be estimated as a percent of credit sales. If the portion of credit sales to sales is relatively constant, the percent may be applied to total sales or net sales.

BusinessConnection

ALLOWANCE PERCENTAGES ACROSS COMPANIES

The percent of the allowance for doubtful accounts to total accounts receivable will vary across companies and industries. For example, the following percentages were computed from recent annual reports:

HCA's higher percent of allowance for doubtful accounts to total accounts receivable is due in part because Medicare reimbursements are often less than the amounts billed patients.

Company	Industry	Percent of Allowance for Doubtful Accounts to Total Accounts Receivable
Apple Inc.	Computer/technology products	1.5%
Deere & Company	Farm machinery & equipment	17.1
Delta Air Lines	Transportation services	2.8
HCA Inc.	Health services	59.0
Sears	Retail	4.8

To illustrate, assume the following data for ExTone Company on December 31, 2012, before any adjustments:

Balance of Accounts Receivable	$ 240,000
Balance of Allowance for Doubtful Accounts	3,250 (Cr.)
Total credit sales	3,000,000
Bad debt as a percent of credit sales	¾%

Bad Debt Expense of $22,500 is estimated as follows:

Bad Debt Expense = Credit Sales × Bad Debt as a Percent of Credit Sales
Bad Debt Expense = $3,000,000 × ¾% = $22,500

The adjusting entry for uncollectible accounts on December 31, 2012, is as follows:

Dec.	31	Bad Debt Expense	22,500	
		Allowance for Doubtful Accounts		22,500
		Uncollectible accounts estimate		
		($3,000,000 × ¾% = $22,500).		

After the adjusting entry is posted to the ledger, Bad Debt Expense will have an adjusted balance of $22,500. Allowance for Doubtful Accounts will have an adjusted balance of $25,750 ($3,250 + $22,500). Both T accounts are shown below.

BAD DEBT EXPENSE

Dec. 31	Adjusting entry	22,500	◄
Dec. 31	Adjusted balance	22,500	

ALLOWANCE FOR DOUBTFUL ACCOUNTS

				Jan. 1	Balance	30,000
Total accounts	Jan. 21	6,000				
written off $26,750	Feb. 2	3,900				
	⋮	⋮				
				Dec. 31	Unadjusted balance	3,250
				Dec. 31	Adjusting entry	22,500 ◄
				Dec. 31	Adjusted balance	25,750

Under the percent of sales method, the amount of the adjusting entry is the amount estimated for Bad Debt Expense. This estimate is credited to whatever the unadjusted balance is for Allowance for Doubtful Accounts.

To illustrate, assume that in the preceding example the unadjusted balance of Allowance for Doubtful Accounts on December 31, 2012, had been a $2,100 debit balance instead of a $3,250 credit balance. The adjustment would still have been $22,500. However, the December 31, 2012, ending adjusted balance of Allowance for Doubtful Accounts would have been $20,400 ($22,500 − $2,100).

Note:
The estimate based on sales is added to any balance in Allowance for Doubtful Accounts.

Example Exercise 9-3 Percent of Sales Method

OBJ.
4

At the end of the current year, Accounts Receivable has a balance of $800,000; Allowance for Doubtful Accounts has a credit balance of $7,500; and net sales for the year total $3,500,000. Bad debt expense is estimated at ½ of 1% of net sales.
 Determine (a) the amount of the adjusting entry for uncollectible accounts; (b) the adjusted balances of Accounts Receivable, Allowance for Doubtful Accounts, and Bad Debt Expense; and (c) the net realizable value of accounts receivable.

Follow My Example 9-3

a. $17,500 ($3,500,000 × 0.005)

	Adjusted Balance
b. Accounts Receivable	$800,000
Allowance for Doubtful Accounts ($7,500 + $17,500)	25,000
Bad Debt Expense...	17,500

c. $775,000 ($800,000 − $25,000)

Practice Exercises: **PE 9-3A, PE 9-3B**

Analysis of Receivables Method The analysis of receivables method is based on the assumption that the longer an account receivable is outstanding, the less likely that it will be collected. The analysis of receivables method is applied as follows:

Step 1. The due date of each account receivable is determined.

Step 2. The number of days each account is past due is determined. This is the number of days between the due date of the account and the date of the analysis.

Step 3. Each account is placed in an aged class according to its days past due. Typical aged classes include the following:

> Not past due
> 1–30 days past due
> 31–60 days past due
> 61–90 days past due
> 91–180 days past due
> 181–365 days past due
> Over 365 days past due

Step 4. The totals for each aged class are determined.

Step 5. The total for each aged class is multiplied by an estimated percentage of uncollectible accounts for that class.

Step 6. The estimated total of uncollectible accounts is determined as the sum of the uncollectible accounts for each aged class.

The preceding steps are summarized in an aging schedule, and this overall process is called **aging the receivables**.

To illustrate, assume that ExTone Company uses the analysis of receivables method instead of the percent of sales method. ExTone prepared an aging schedule for its accounts receivable of $240,000 as of December 31, 2012, as shown in Exhibit 1.

EXHIBIT 1   **Aging of Receivables Schedule, December 31, 2012**

		A	B	C	D	E	F	G	H	I
	1			Not			Days Past Due			
	2			Past						Over
	3	Customer	Balance	Due	1–30	31–60	61–90	91–180	181–365	365
	4	Ashby & Co.	1,500			1,500				
	5	B. T. Barr	6,100					3,500	2,600	
	6	Brock Co.	4,700	4,700						
Steps 1–3	21									
	22	Saxon Woods Co.	600					600		
Step 4 →	23	Total	240,000	125,000	64,000	13,100	8,900	5,000	10,000	14,000
Step 5 →	24	Percent uncollectible			2%	5%	10%	20%	30%	50%	80%
Step 6 →	25	Estimate of uncollectible accounts	26,490	2,500	3,200	1,310	1,780	1,500	5,000	11,200

Assume that ExTone Company sold merchandise to Saxon Woods Co. on August 29 with terms 2/10, n/30. Thus, the due date (Step 1) of Saxon Woods' account is September 28, as shown below.

Credit terms, net	30 days
Less: Aug. 29 to Aug. 31	2 days
Days in September	28 days

As of December 31, Saxon Woods' account is 94 days past due (Step 2), as shown below.

Number of days past due in September	2 days (30 – 28)
Number of days past due in October	31 days
Number of days past due in November	30 days
Number of days past due in December	31 days
Total number of days past due	94 days

Exhibit 1 shows that the $600 account receivable for Saxon Woods Co. was placed in the 91–180 days past due class (Step 3).

The total for each of the aged classes is determined (Step 4). Exhibit 1 shows that $125,000 of the accounts receivable are not past due, while $64,000 are 1–30 days past due. ExTone Company applies a different estimated percentage of uncollectible accounts to the totals of each of the aged classes (Step 5). As shown in Exhibit 1, the percent is 2% for accounts not past due, while the percent is 80% for accounts over 365 days past due.

The sum of the estimated uncollectible accounts for each aged class (Step 6) is the estimated uncollectible accounts on December 31, 2012. This is the desired adjusted balance for Allowance for Doubtful Accounts. For ExTone Company, this amount is $26,490, as shown in Exhibit 1.

Comparing the estimate of $26,490 with the unadjusted balance of the allowance account determines the amount of the adjustment for Bad Debt Expense. For ExTone, the unadjusted balance of the allowance account is a credit balance of $3,250. The amount to be added to this balance is therefore $23,240 ($26,490 – $3,250). The adjusting entry is as follows:

Note:
The estimate based on receivables is compared to the balance in the allowance account to determine the amount of the adjusting entry.

Dec.	31	Bad Debt Expense	23,240	
		Allowance for Doubtful Accounts		23,240
		Uncollectible accounts estimate		
		($26,490 – $3,250).		

After the preceding adjusting entry is posted to the ledger, Bad Debt Expense will have an adjusted balance of $23,240. Allowance for Doubtful Accounts will have an adjusted balance of $26,490, and the net realizable value of the receivables is $213,510 ($240,000 – $26,490). Both T accounts are shown below.

BAD DEBT EXPENSE

Dec. 31	Adjusting entry	23,240
Dec. 31	Adjusted balance	23,240

ALLOWANCE FOR DOUBTFUL ACCOUNTS

Dec. 31	Unadjusted balance	3,250
Dec. 31	Adjusting entry	23,240
Dec. 31	Adjusted balance	26,490

Under the analysis of receivable method, the amount of the adjusting entry is the amount that will yield an adjusted balance for Allowance for Doubtful Accounts equal to that estimated by the aging schedule.

To illustrate, if the unadjusted balance of the allowance account had been a debit balance of $2,100, the amount of the adjustment would have been $28,590 ($26,490 + $2,100). In this case, Bad Debt Expense would have an adjusted balance of $28,590. However, the adjusted balance of Allowance for Doubtful Accounts would still have been $26,490. After the adjusting entry is posted, both T accounts are shown below.

BAD DEBT EXPENSE

Dec. 31	Adjusting entry	28,590
Dec. 31	Adjusted balance	28,590

ALLOWANCE FOR DOUBTFUL ACCOUNTS

Dec. 31	Unadjusted balance	2,100

Dec. 31	Adjusting entry	28,590
Dec. 31	Adjusted balance	26,490

Example Exercise 9-4   Analysis of Receivables Method

OBJ. 4

At the end of the current year, Accounts Receivable has a balance of $800,000; Allowance for Doubtful Accounts has a credit balance of $7,500; and net sales for the year total $3,500,000. Using the aging method, the balance of Allowance for Doubtful Accounts is estimated as $30,000.

   Determine (a) the amount of the adjusting entry for uncollectible accounts; (b) the adjusted balances of Accounts Receivable, Allowance for Doubtful Accounts, and Bad Debt Expense; and (c) the net realizable value of accounts receivable.

Follow My Example 9-4

a. $22,500 ($30,000 – $7,500)

	Adjusted Balance
b. Accounts Receivable	$800,000
Allowance for Doubtful Accounts...	30,000
Bad Debt Expense...	22,500

c. $770,000 ($800,000 – $30,000)

Practice Exercises: **PE 9-4A, PE 9-4B**

Comparing Estimation Methods Both the percent of sales and analysis of receivables methods estimate uncollectible accounts. However, each method has a slightly different focus and financial statement emphasis.

Under the percent of sales method, Bad Debt Expense is the focus of the estimation process. The percent of sales method places more emphasis on matching revenues and expenses and, thus, emphasizes the income statement. That is, the amount of the adjusting entry is based on the estimate of Bad Debt Expense for the period. Allowance for Doubtful Accounts is then credited for this amount.

Under the analysis of receivables method, Allowance for Doubtful Accounts is the focus of the estimation process. The analysis of receivables method places more emphasis on the net realizable value of the receivables and, thus, emphasizes the balance sheet. That is, the amount of the adjusting entry is the amount that will yield an adjusted balance for Allowance for Doubtful Accounts equal to that estimated by the aging schedule. Bad Debt Expense is then debited for this amount.

Exhibit 2 summarizes these differences between the percent of sales and the analysis of receivables methods. Exhibit 2 also shows the results of the ExTone Company illustration for the percent of sales and analysis of receivables methods. The amounts shown in Exhibit 2 assume an unadjusted credit balance of $3,250 for Allowance for

EXHIBIT 2

Difference Between Estimation Methods

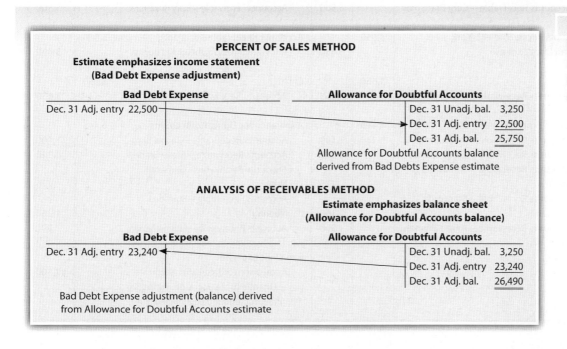

Doubtful Accounts. While the methods normally yield different amounts for any one period, over several periods the amounts should be similar.

OBJ. 5 Compare the direct write-off and allowance methods of accounting for uncollectible accounts.

Comparing Direct Write-Off and Allowance Methods

Journal entries for the direct write-off and allowance methods are illustrated and compared in this section. As a basis for illustration, the following transactions, taken from the records of Hobbs Co. for the year ending December 31, 2011, are used:

Mar. 1. Wrote off account of C. York, $3,650.

Apr. 12. Received $2,250 as partial payment on the $5,500 account of Cary Bradshaw. Wrote off the remaining balance as uncollectible.

June 22. Received the $3,650 from C. York, which had been written off on March 1. Reinstated the account and recorded the cash receipt.

Sept. 7. Wrote off the following accounts as uncollectible (record as one journal entry):

Jason Bigg	$1,100	Stanford Noonan	$1,360
Steve Bradey	2,220	Aiden Wyman	990
Samantha Neeley	775		

Dec. 31. Hobbs Company uses the percent of credit sales method of estimating uncollectible expenses. Based on past history and industry averages, 1.25% of credit sales are expected to be uncollectible. Hobbs recorded $3,400,000 of credit sales during 2011.

Exhibit 3 illustrates the journal entries for Hobbs Company using the direct write-off and allowance methods. Using the direct write-off method, there is no adjusting entry on December 31 for uncollectible accounts. In contrast, the allowance method records an adjusting entry for estimated uncollectible accounts of $42,500.

EXHIBIT 3 **Comparing Direct Write-Off and Allowance Methods**

		Direct Write-Off Method			Allowance Method		
2011							
Mar.	1	Bad Debt Expense	3,650		Allowance for Doubtful Accounts	3,650	
		Accounts Receivable—C. York		3,650	Accounts Receivable—C. York		3,650
Apr.	12	Cash	2,250		Cash	2,250	
		Bad Debt Expense	3,250		Allowance for Doubtful Accounts	3,250	
		Accounts Receivable—Cary Bradshaw		5,500	Accounts Receivable—Cary Bradshaw		5,500
June	22	Accounts Receivable—C. York	3,650		Accounts Receivable—C. York	3,650	
		Bad Debt Expense		3,650	Allowance for Doubtful Accounts		3,650
	22	Cash	3,650		Cash	3,650	
		Accounts Receivable—C. York		3,650	Accounts Receivable—C. York		3,650
Sept.	7	Bad Debt Expense	6,445		Allowance for Doubtful Accounts	6,445	
		Accounts Receivable—Jason Bigg		1,100	Accounts Receivable—Jason Bigg		1,100
		Accounts Receivable—Steve Bradey		2,220	Accounts Receivable—Steve Bradey		2,220
		Accounts Receivable—Samantha Neeley		775	Accounts Receivable—Samantha Neeley		775
		Accounts Receivable—Stanford Noonan		1,360	Accounts Receivable—Stanford Noonan		1,360
		Accounts Receivable—Aiden Wyman		990	Accounts Receivable—Aiden Wyman		990
Dec.	31	No Entry			Bad Debt Expense	42,500	
					Allowance for Doubtful Accounts		42,500
					Uncollectible accounts estimate ($3,400,000 × 0.0125 = $42,500).		

The primary differences between the direct write-off and allowance methods are summarized below.

	Direct Write-Off Method	**Allowance Method**
Bad debt expense is recorded	When the specific customer accounts are determined to be uncollectible.	Using estimate based on (1) a percent of sales or (2) an analysis of receivables.
Allowance account	No allowance account is used.	The allowance account is used.
Primary users	Small companies and companies with few receivables.	Large companies and those with a large amount of receivables.

Notes Receivable

Describe the accounting for notes receivable.

A note has some advantages over an account receivable. By signing a note, the debtor recognizes the debt and agrees to pay it according to its terms. Thus, a note is a stronger legal claim.

Characteristics of Notes Receivable

A promissory note is a written promise to pay the face amount, usually with interest, on demand or at a date in the future.[2] Characteristics of a promissory note are as follows:

1. The *maker* is the party making the promise to pay.
2. The *payee* is the party to whom the note is payable.
3. The *face amount* is the amount for which the note is written on its face.
4. The *issuance date* is the date a note is issued.
5. The *due date* or *maturity date* is the date the note is to be paid.
6. The *term* of a note is the amount of time between the issuance and due dates.
7. The *interest rate* is that rate of interest that must be paid on the face amount for the term of the note.

Exhibit 4 illustrates a promissory note. The maker of the note is Selig Company, and the payee is Pearland Company. The face value of the note is $2,000, and the issuance date is March 16, 2011. The term of the note is 90 days, which results in a due date of June 14, 2011, as shown below.

Days in March	31 days
Minus issuance date of note	16
Days remaining in March	15 days
Add days in April	30
Add days in May	31
Add days in June (due date of June 14)	14
Term of note	90 days

Due Date of 90-Day Note

In Exhibit 4, the term of the note is 90 days and has an interest rate of 10%.

---

2 You may see references to noninterest-bearing notes. Such notes are not widely used and carry an assumed or implicit interest rate.

EXHIBIT 4 **Promissory Note**

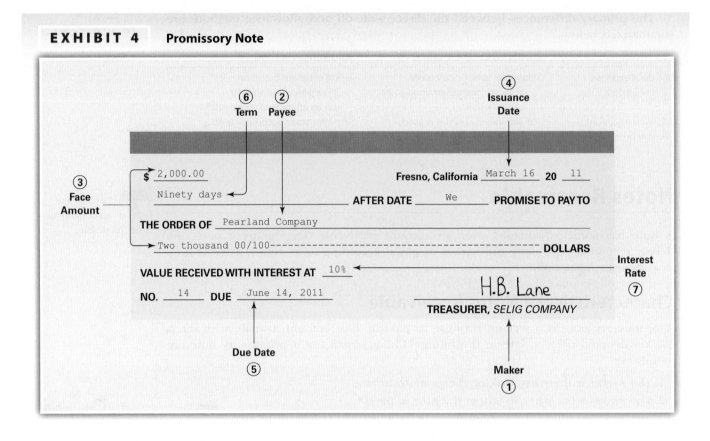

The interest on a note is computed as follows:

$$\text{Interest} = \text{Face Amount} \times \text{Interest Rate} \times (\text{Term}/360 \text{ days})$$

The interest rate is stated on an annual (yearly) basis, while the term is expressed as days. Thus, the interest on the note in Exhibit 4 is computed as follows:

$$\text{Interest} = \$2,000 \times 10\% \times (90/360) = \$50$$

To simplify, 360 days per year will be used. In practice, companies such as banks and mortgage companies use the exact number of days in a year, 365.

The **maturity value** is the amount that must be paid at the due date of the note, which is the sum of the face amount and the interest. The maturity value of the note in Exhibit 4 is $2,050 ($2,000 + $50).

Accounting for Notes Receivable

A promissory note may be received by a company from a customer to replace an account receivable. In such cases, the promissory note is recorded as a note receivable.[3]

To illustrate, assume that a company accepts a 30-day, 12% note dated November 21, 2012, in settlement of the account of W. A. Bunn Co., which is past due and has a balance of $6,000. The company records the receipt of the note as follows:

Nov.	21	Notes Receivable—W. A. Bunn Co.	6,000	
		Accounts Receivable—W. A. Bunn Co.		6,000

3 The accounting for notes payable is described and illustrated in Chapter 14.

At the due date, the company records the receipt of $6,060 ($6,000 face amount plus $60 interest) as follows:

Dec.	21	Cash	6,060	
		Notes Receivable—W. A. Bunn Co.		6,000
		Interest Revenue		60
		[$6,060 = $6,000 + ($6,000 × 12% × 30/360)].		

If the maker of a note fails to pay the note on the due date, the note is a **dishonored note receivable**. A company that holds a dishonored note transfers the face amount of the note plus any interest due back to an accounts receivable account. For example, assume that the $6,000, 30-day, 12% note received from W. A. Bunn Co. and recorded on November 21 is dishonored. The company holding the note transfers the note and interest back to the customer's account as follows:

Dec.	21	Accounts Receivable—W. A. Bunn Co.	6,060	
		Notes Receivable—W. A. Bunn Co.		6,000
		Interest Revenue		60

The company has earned the interest of $60, even though the note is dishonored. If the account receivable is uncollectible, the company will write off $6,060 against Allowance for Doubtful Accounts.

A company receiving a note should record an adjusting entry for any accrued interest at the end of the period. For example, assume that Crawford Company issues a $4,000, 90-day, 12% note dated December 1, 2012, to settle its account receivable. If the accounting period ends on December 31, the company receiving the note would record the following entries:

2012				
Dec.	1	Notes Receivable—Crawford Company	4,000	
		Accounts Receivable—Crawford Company		4,000
	31	Interest Receivable	40	
		Interest Revenue		40
		Accrued interest		
		($4,000 × 12% × 30/360).		
2013				
Mar.	1	Cash	4,120	
		Notes Receivable—Crawford Company		4,000
		Interest Receivable		40
		Interest Revenue		80
		Total interest of $120		
		($4,000 × 12% × 90/360).		

The interest revenue account is closed at the end of each accounting period. The amount of interest revenue is normally reported in the Other Income section of the income statement.

Example Exercise 9-5   Note Receivable

OBJ. 6

Same Day Surgery Center received a 120-day, 6% note for $40,000, dated March 14 from a patient on account.

a. Determine the due date of the note.

b. Determine the maturity value of the note.

c. Journalize the entry to record the receipt of the payment of the note at maturity.

(continued)

a. The due date of the note is July 12, determined as follows:

March	17 days (31 − 14)
April	30 days
May	31 days
June	30 days
July	12 days
Total	120 days

b. $40,800 [$40,000 + ($40,000 × 6% × 120/360)]

c.
July 12	Cash	40,800	
	Notes Receivable...		40,000
	Interest Revue..		800

Practice Exercises: **PE 9-5A, PE 9-5B**

OBJ.
7
Describe the reporting of receivables on the balance sheet.

Reporting Receivables on the Balance Sheet

All receivables that are expected to be realized in cash within a year are reported in the Current assets section of the balance sheet. Current assets are normally reported in the order of their liquidity, beginning with cash and cash equivalents.

The balance sheet presentation for receivables for Mornin' Joe is shown below.

Mornin' Joe Balance Sheet December 31, 2012		
Assets		
Current assets:		
Cash and cash equivalents		$235,000
Trading investments (at cost)...............................	$420,000	
Plus valuation allowance for trading investments	45,000	465,000
Accounts receivable	$305,000	
Less allowance for doubtful accounts	12,300	292,700

In Mornin' Joe's financial statements, the allowance for doubtful accounts is subtracted from accounts receivable. Some companies report receivables at their net realizable value with a note showing the amount of the allowance.

Other disclosures related to receivables are reported either on the face of the financial statements or in the financial statement notes. Such disclosures include the market (fair) value of the receivables. In addition, if unusual credit risks exist within the receivables, the nature of the risks are disclosed. For example, if the majority of the receivables are due from one customer or are due from customers located in one area of the country or one industry, these facts are disclosed.[4]

OBJ.
8
Describe and illustrate the use of accounts receivable turnover and number of days' sales in receivables to evaluate a company's efficiency in collecting its receivables.

Financial Analysis and Interpretation: Accounts Receivable Turnover and Number of Days' Sales in Receivables

Two financial measures that are especially useful in evaluating efficiency in collecting receivables are (1) the accounts receivable turnover and (2) the number of days' sales in receivables.

4 *FASB Accounting Standards Codification*, Section 210-10-50.

The **accounts receivable turnover** measures how frequently during the year the accounts receivable are being converted to cash. For example, with credit terms of n/30, the accounts receivable should turn over about 12 times per year.

The accounts receivable turnover is computed as follows:[5]

$$\text{Accounts Receivable Turnover} = \frac{\text{Net Sales}}{\text{Average Accounts Receivable}}$$

The average accounts receivable can be determined by using monthly data or by simply adding the beginning and ending accounts receivable balances and dividing by two. For example, using the following financial data (in millions) for FedEx, the 2009 and 2008 accounts receivable turnover is computed as 8.1 as shown below.

	2009	2008
Net sales	$35,497	$37,953
Accounts receivable:		
Beginning of year	4,903	4,478
End of year	3,902	4,903
Average accounts receivable:		
($3,902 + $4,903)/2	4,403	
($4,903 + $4,478)/2		4,691
Accounts receivable turnover:		
$35,497/$4,403	8.1	
$37,953/$4,691		8.1

The **number of days' sales in receivables** is an estimate of the length of time the accounts receivable have been outstanding. With credit terms of n/30, the number of days' sales in receivables should be about 30 days. It is computed as follows:

$$\text{Number of Days' Sales in Receivables} = \frac{\text{Average Accounts Receivable}}{\text{Average Daily Sales}}$$

Average daily sales are determined by dividing net sales by 365 days. For example, using the preceding data for FedEx, the number of days' sales in receivables is 45.3 and 45.1 for 2009 and 2008, as shown below.

	2009	2008
Average daily sales:		
$35,497/365	97.3	
$37,953/365		104.0
Number of days' sales in receivables:		
$4,403/97.3	45.3	
$4,691/104.0		45.1

Example Exercise 9-6 Accounts Receivable Turnover and Number of Days' Sales in Receivables

OBJ. 8

Financial statement data for years ending December 31 for Osterman Company are as follows:

	2012	2011
Net sales	$4,284,000	$3,040,000
Accounts receivable:		
Beginning of year	550,000	400,000
End of year	640,000	550,000

a. Determine accounts receivable turnover for 2012 and 2011.

b. Determine the number of days' sales in receivables for 2012 and 2011.

c. Does the change in accounts receivable turnover and the number of days' sales in receivable from 2011 to 2012 indicate a favorable or an unfavorable trend?

(continued)

5 If known, credit sales can be used in the numerator. However, because credit sales are not normally disclosed to external users, most analysts use net sales in the numerator.

Follow My Example 9-6

a. Accounts receivable turnover:

	2012	2011
Average accounts receivable:		
($550,000 + $640,000)/2	$595,000	
($400,000 + $550,000)/2		$475,000
Accounts receivable turnover:		
$4,284,000/$595,000	7.2	
$3,040,000/$475,000		6.4

b. Number of days' sales in receivables:

	2012	2011
Average daily sales:		
$4,284,000/365 days	$11,737	
$3,040,000/365 days		$8,329
Number of days' sales in receivables:		
$595,000/$11,737	50.7 days	
$475,000/$8,329		57.0 days

c. The increase in the accounts receivable turnover from 6.4 to 7.2 and the decrease in the number of days' sales in receivables from 57.0 days to 50.7 days indicate favorable trends in the efficiency of collecting accounts receivable.

Practice Exercises: **PE 9-6A, PE 9-6B**

The number of days' sales in receivables confirms that FedEx's efficiency in collecting accounts receivable has remained the same during 2009 and 2008. Generally, the efficiency in collecting accounts receivable has improved when the accounts receivable turnover increases or the number of days' sales in receivables decreases.

BusinessConnection

DELTA AIR LINES

Delta Air Lines is a major air carrier that services cities throughout the United States and the world. In its operations, Delta generates accounts receivable as reported in the following note to its financial statements:

Our accounts receivable are generated largely from the sale of passenger airline tickets and cargo transportation services. The majority of these sales are processed through major credit card companies, resulting in accounts receivable... We also have receivables from the sale of mileage credits under our Sky-Miles and WorldPerks

Programs to participating airlines and nonairline businesses such as credit card companies, hotels, and car rental agencies. We believe the credit risk associated with these receivables is minimal and that the allowance for uncollectible accounts that we have provided is appropriate.

In its December 31, 2008, balance sheet, Delta reported the following accounts receivable (in millions):

	Dec. 31, 2009	Dec. 31, 2008
Current Assets:		
...		
Accounts receivable, net of an allowance for uncollectible accounts of $47 at December 31, 2009 and $42 at December 31, 2008	$1,353	$1,513

At a Glance 9

OBJ. 1   Describe the common classes of receivables.

Key Points   *Receivables* includes all money claims against other entities. Receivables are normally classified as accounts receivable, notes receivable, or other receivables.

Learning Outcomes	Example Exercises	Practice Exercises
• Define the term *receivables*.		
• List some common classifications of receivables.		

OBJ. 2   Describe the accounting for uncollectible receivables.

Key Points   The operating expense recorded from uncollectible receivables is called *bad debt expense*. The two methods of accounting for uncollectible receivables are the direct write-off method and the allowance method.

Learning Outcomes	Example Exercises	Practice Exercises
• Describe how a company may shift the risk of uncollectible receivables to other companies.		
• List factors that indicate an account receivable is uncollectible		
• Describe two methods of accounting for uncollectible accounts receivable.		

OBJ. 3   Describe the direct write-off method of accounting for uncollectible receivables.

Key Points   Under the direct write-off method, the entry to write off an account debits Bad Debt Expense and credits Accounts Receivable. Neither an allowance account nor an adjusting entry is needed at the end of the period.

Learning Outcomes	Example Exercises	Practice Exercises
• Prepare journal entries to write off an account using the direct write-off method.	EE9-1	PE9-1A, 9-1B
• Prepare journal entries for the reinstatement and collection of an account previously written off.	EE9-1	PE9-1A, 9-1B

OBJ. 4

Describe the allowance method of accounting for uncollectible receivables.

Key Points   Under the allowance method, an adjusting entry is made for uncollectible accounts. When an account is determined to be uncollectible, it is written off against the allowance account. The allowance account normally has a credit balance after the adjusting entry has been posted and is a contra asset account.

The estimate of uncollectibles may be based on a percent of sales or an analysis of receivables. Exhibit 2 compares and contrasts these two methods..

Learning Outcomes	Example Exercises	Practice Exercises
• Prepare journal entries to write off an account using the allowance method.	EE9-2	PE9-2A, 9-2B
• Prepare journal entries for the reinstatement and collection of an account previously written off.	EE9-2	PE9-2A, 9-2B
• Determine the adjustment, bad debt expense, and net realizable value of accounts receivable using the percent of sales method.	EE9-3	PE9-3A, 9-3B
• Determine the adjustment, bad debt expense, and net realizable value of accounts receivable using the analysis of receivables method.	EE9-4	PE9-4A, 9-4B

OBJ. 5

Compare the direct write-off and allowance methods of accounting for uncollectible accounts.

Key Points   Exhibit 3 illustrates the differences between the direct write-off and allowance methods of accounting for uncollectible accounts.

Learning Outcomes	Example Exercises	Practice Exercises
• Describe the differences in accounting for uncollectible accounts under the direct write-off and allowance methods.		
• Record journal entries using the direct write-off and allowance methods.		

OBJ. 6

Describe the accounting for notes receivable.

Key Points   A note received to settle an account receivable is recorded as a debit to Notes Receivable and a credit to Accounts Receivable. When a note is paid at maturity, Cash is debited, Notes Receivable is credited, and Interest Revenue is credited. If the maker of a note fails to pay, the dishonored note is recorded by debiting an accounts receivable account for the amount due from the maker of the note.

Learning Outcomes	Example Exercises	Practice Exercises
• Describe the characteristics of a note receivable.		
• Determine the due date and maturity value of a note receivable.	EE9-5	PE9-5A, 9-5B
• Prepare journal entries for the receipt of the payment of a note receivable.	EE9-5	PE9-5A, 9-5B
• Prepare a journal entry for the dishonored note receivable.		

OBJ. 7   **Describe the reporting of receivables on the balance sheet.**

Key Points   All receivables that are expected to be realized in cash within a year are reported in the Current Assets section of the balance sheet. In addition to the allowance for doubtful accounts, additional receivable disclosures include the market (fair) value and unusual credit risks.

Learning Outcomes	Example Exercises	Practice Exercises
• Describe how receivables are reported in the Current Assets section of the balance sheet.		
• Describe disclosures related to receivables that should be reported in the financial statements.		

OBJ. 8   **Describe and illustrate the use of accounts receivable turnover and number of days' sales in receivables to evaluate a company's efficiency in collecting its receivables.**

Key Points   Two financial measures that are especially useful in evaluating efficiency in collecting receivables are (1) the accounts receivable turnover and (2) the number of days' sales in receivables. Generally, the efficiency in collecting accounts receivable has improved when the accounts receivable turnover increases or there is a decrease in the number of days' sales in receivables.

Learning Outcomes	Example Exercises	Practice Exercises
• Describe two measures of the efficiency of managing receivables.		
• Compute and interpret the accounts receivable turnover and number of days' sales in receivables.	EE9-6	PE9-6A, 9-6B

Key Terms

accounts receivable (402)

accounts receivable turnover (417)

aging the receivables (409)

Allowance for Doubtful Accounts (405)

allowance method (403)

bad debt expense (403)

direct write-off method (403)

dishonored note receivable (415)

maturity value (414)

net realizable value (405)

notes receivable (402)

number of days' sales in receivables (417)

receivables (402)

Illustrative Problem

Ditzler Company, a construction supply company, uses the allowance method of accounting for uncollectible accounts receivable. Selected transactions completed by Ditzler Company are as follows:

Feb. 1. Sold merchandise on account to Ames Co., $8,000. The cost of the merchandise sold was $4,500.

Mar. 15. Accepted a 60-day, 12% note for $8,000 from Ames Co. on account.

Apr. 9. Wrote off a $2,500 account from Dorset Co. as uncollectible.

21. Loaned $7,500 cash to Jill Klein, receiving a 90-day, 14% note.

May 14. Received the interest due from Ames Co. and a new 90-day, 14% note as a renewal of the loan. (Record both the debit and the credit to the notes receivable account.)

June 13. Reinstated the account of Dorset Co., written off on April 9, and received $2,500 in full payment.

July 20. Jill Klein dishonored her note.

Aug. 12. Received from Ames Co. the amount due on its note of May 14.

19. Received from Jill Klein the amount owed on the dishonored note, plus interest for 30 days at 15%, computed on the maturity value of the note.

Dec. 16. Accepted a 60-day, 12% note for $12,000 from Global Company on account.

31. It is estimated that 3% of the credit sales of $1,375,000 for the year ended December 31 will be uncollectible.

Instructions

1. Journalize the transactions.

2. Journalize the adjusting entry to record the accrued interest on December 31 on the Global Company note.

Solution

1.

Feb.	1	Accounts Receivable—Ames Co.	8,000.00	
		Sales		8,000.00
	1	Cost of Merchandise Sold	4,500.00	
		Merchandise Inventory		4,500.00
Mar.	15	Notes Receivable—Ames Co.	8,000.00	
		Accounts Receivable—Ames Co.		8,000.00
Apr.	9	Allowance for Doubtful Accounts	2,500.00	
		Accounts Receivable—Dorset Co.		2,500.00
	21	Notes Receivable—Jill Klein	7,500.00	
		Cash		7,500.00
May	14	Notes Receivable—Ames Co.	8,000.00	
		Cash	160.00	
		Notes Receivable—Ames Co.		8,000.00
		Interest Revenue		160.00
June	13	Accounts Receivable—Dorset Co.	2,500.00	
		Allowance for Doubtful Accounts		2,500.00
	13	Cash	2,500.00	
		Accounts Receivable—Dorset Co.		2,500.00
July	20	Accounts Receivable—Jill Klein	7,762.50	
		Notes Receivable—Jill Klein		7,500.00
		Interest Revenue		262.50
Aug.	12	Cash	8,280.00	
		Notes Receivable—Ames Co.		8,000.00
		Interest Revenue		280.00
	19	Cash	7,859.53	
		Accounts Receivable—Jill Klein		7,762.50
		Interest Revenue		97.03
		($7,762.50 × 15% × 30/360).		
Dec.	16	Notes Receivable—Global Company	12,000.00	
		Accounts Receivable—Global Company		12,000.00
	31	Bad Debt Expense	41,250.00	
		Allowance for Doubtful Accounts		41,250.00
		Uncollectible accounts estimate		
		($1,375,000 × 3%).		

2.

Dec.	31	Interest Receivable	60.00	
		Interest Revenue		60.00
		Accrued interest		
		($12,000 × 12% × 15/360).		

Discussion Questions

1. What are the three classifications of receivables?

2. Elite Hardware is a small hardware store in the rural township of Rexburg that rarely extends credit to its customers in the form of an account receivable. The few customers that are allowed to carry accounts receivable are long-time residents of Rexburg and have a history of doing business at Elite Hardware. What method of accounting for uncollectible receivables should Elite Hardware use? Why?

3. What kind of an account (asset, liability, etc.) is Allowance for Doubtful Accounts, and is its normal balance a debit or a credit?

4. After the accounts are adjusted and closed at the end of the fiscal year, Accounts Receivable has a balance of $471,200 and Allowance for Doubtful Accounts has a balance of $27,500. Describe how the accounts receivable and the allowance for doubtful accounts are reported on the balance sheet.

5. A firm has consistently adjusted its allowance account at the end of the fiscal year by adding a fixed percent of the period's net sales on account. After seven years, the balance in Allowance for Doubtful Accounts has become very large in relationship to the balance in Accounts Receivable. Give two possible explanations.

6. Which of the two methods of estimating uncollectibles provides for the most accurate estimate of the current net realizable value of the receivables?

7. Calypso Company issued a note receivable to Kearny Company. (a) Who is the payee? (b) What is the title of the account used by Kearny Company in recording the note?

8. If a note provides for payment of principal of $150,000 and interest at the rate of 4%, will the interest amount to $6,000? Explain.

9. The maker of a $60,000, 5%, 90-day note receivable failed to pay the note on the due date of April 30. What accounts should be debited and credited by the payee to record the dishonored note receivable?

10. The note receivable dishonored in Discussion Question 9 is paid on May 30 by the maker, plus interest for 30 days, 8%. What entry should be made to record the receipt of the payment?

Practice Exercises

Learning Objectives	Example Exercises	
OBJ. 3	EE 9-1 *p. 404*	

PE 9-1A   Direct write-off method

Journalize the following transactions using the direct write-off method of accounting for uncollectible receivables:

Jan. 17. Received $250 from Ian Kearns and wrote off the remainder owed of $750 as uncollectible.

Apr.   6. Reinstated the account of Ian Kearns and received $750 cash in full payment.

OBJ. 3   EE 9-1 *p. 404*

PE 9-1B   Direct write-off method

Journalize the following transactions using the direct write-off method of accounting for uncollectible receivables:

July   7. Received $500 from Betty Williams and wrote off the remainder owed of $2,000 as uncollectible.

Nov. 13. Reinstated the account of Betty Williams and received $2,000 cash in full payment.

OBJ. 4   EE 9-2 *p. 407*

PE 9-2A   Allowance method

Journalize the following transactions using the allowance method of accounting for uncollectible receivables:

Jan. 17. Received $250 from Ian Kearns and wrote off the remainder owed of $750 as uncollectible.

Apr.   6. Reinstated the account of Ian Kearns and received $750 cash in full payment.

OBJ. 4   EE 9-2 *p. 407*

PE 9-2B   Allowance method

Journalize the following transactions using the allowance method of accounting for uncollectible receivables:

July   7. Received $500 from Betty Williams and wrote off the remainder owed of $2,000 as uncollectible.

Nov. 13. Reinstated the account of Betty Williams and received $2,000 cash in full payment.

OBJ. 4   EE 9-3 *p. 408*

PE 9-3A   Percent of sales method

At the end of the current year, Accounts Receivable has a balance of $325,000; Allowance for Doubtful Accounts has a credit balance of $3,900; and net sales for the year total $4,500,000. Bad debt expense is estimated at ½ of 1% of net sales.

Determine (a) the amount of the adjusting entry for uncollectible accounts; (b) the adjusted balances of Accounts Receivable, Allowance for Doubtful Accounts, and Bad Debt Expense; and (c) the net realizable value of accounts receivable.

OBJ. 4   EE 9-3 *p. 408*

PE 9-3B   Percent of sales method

At the end of the current year, Accounts Receivable has a balance of $2,500,000; Allowance for Doubtful Accounts has a debit balance of $9,000; and net sales for the year total $32,000,000. Bad debt expense is estimated at ¼ of 1% of net sales.

Determine (a) the amount of the adjusting entry for uncollectible accounts; (b) the adjusted balances of Accounts Receivable, Allowance for Doubtful Accounts, and Bad Debt Expense; and (c) the net realizable value of accounts receivable.

PE 9-4A   Analysis of receivables method

At the end of the current year, Accounts Receivable has a balance of $325,000; Allowance for Doubtful Accounts has a credit balance of $3,900; and net sales for the year total $4,500,000. Using the aging method, the balance of Allowance for Doubtful Accounts is estimated as $25,000.

Determine (a) the amount of the adjusting entry for uncollectible accounts; (b) the adjusted balances of Accounts Receivable, Allowance for Doubtful Accounts, and Bad Debt Expense; and (c) the net realizable value of accounts receivable.

PE 9-4B   Analysis of receivables method

At the end of the current year, Accounts Receivable has a balance of $2,500,000; Allowance for Doubtful Accounts has a debit balance of $9,000; and net sales for the year total $32,000,000. Using the aging method, the balance of Allowance for Doubtful Accounts is estimated as $76,000.

Determine (a) the amount of the adjusting entry for uncollectible accounts; (b) the adjusted balances of Accounts Receivable, Allowance for Doubtful Accounts, and Bad Debt Expense; and (c) the net realizable value of accounts receivable.

PE 9-5A   Note receivable

Vista Supply Company received a 30-day, 4% note for $90,000, dated September 8 from a customer on account.

a. Determine the due date of the note.

b. Determine the maturity value of the note.

c. Journalize the entry to record the receipt of the payment of the note at maturity.

PE 9-5B   Note receivable

Gorilla Supply Company received a 120-day, 5% note for $150,000, dated March 27 from a customer on account.

a. Determine the due date of the note.

b. Determine the maturity value of the note.

c. Journalize the entry to record the receipt of the payment of the note at maturity.

PE 9-6A   Accounts receivable turnover and number of days' sales in receivables

Financial statement data for years ending December 31 for Blum Company are shown below.

	2012	2011
Net sales	$2,430,000	$1,920,000
Accounts receivable:		
Beginning of year	180,000	120,000
End of year	225,000	180,000

a. Determine the accounts receivable turnover for 2012 and 2011.

b. Determine the number of days' sales in receivables for 2012 and 2011. Round to one decimal place.

c. Does the change in accounts receivable turnover and the number of days' sales in receivables from 2011 to 2012 indicate a favorable or an unfavorable trend?

PE 9-6B   Accounts receivable turnover and number of days' sales in receivables

Financial statement data for years ending December 31 for Sherick Company are shown below.

	2012	2011
Net sales	$4,514,000	$4,200,000
Accounts receivable:		
Beginning of year	280,000	320,000
End of year	330,000	280,000

a. Determine the accounts receivable turnover for 2012 and 2011.

b. Determine the number of days' sales in receivables for 2012 and 2011. Round to one decimal place.

c. Does the change in accounts receivable turnover and the number of days' sales in receivables from 2011 to 2012 indicate a favorable or an unfavorable trend?

Exercises

OBJ. 1

EX 9-1 Classifications of receivables

Boeing is one of the world's major aerospace firms, with operations involving commercial aircraft, military aircraft, missiles, satellite systems, and information and battle management systems. As of December 31, 2009, Boeing had $3,090 million of receivables involving U.S. government contracts and $1,206 million of receivables involving commercial aircraft customers, such as Delta Air Lines and United Airlines.

Should Boeing report these receivables separately in the financial statements, or combine them into one overall accounts receivable amount? Explain.

OBJ. 2

✔ a. 20.9%

EX 9-2 Nature of uncollectible accounts

The MGM Mirage owns and operates casinos including the MGM Grand and the Bellagio in Las Vegas, Nevada. As of December 31, 2009, The MGM Mirage reported accounts and notes receivable of $465,580,000 and allowance for doubtful accounts of $97,106,000. Johnson & Johnson manufactures and sells a wide range of health care products including Band-Aids and Tylenol. As of December 31, 2009, Johnson & Johnson reported accounts receivable of $9,979,000,000 and allowance for doubtful accounts of $333,000,000.

a. Compute the percentage of the allowance for doubtful accounts to the accounts and notes receivable as of December 31, 2009, for The MGM Mirage. Round to one decimal place.

b. Compute the percentage of the allowance for doubtful accounts to the accounts receivable as of December 31, 2009, for Johnson & Johnson. Round to one decimal place.

c. Discuss possible reasons for the difference in the two ratios computed in (a) and (b).

OBJ. 3

EX 9-3 Entries for uncollectible accounts, using direct write-off method

Journalize the following transactions in the accounts of Cecena Medical Co., a medical equipment company that uses the direct write-off method of accounting for uncollectible receivables:

Feb. 13. Sold merchandise on account to Dr. Ben Katz, $120,000. The cost of the merchandise sold was $72,000.

May 4. Received $90,000 from Dr. Ben Katz and wrote off the remainder owed on the sale of February 13 as uncollectible.

Nov. 19. Reinstated the account of Dr. Ben Katz that had been written off on May 4 and received $30,000 cash in full payment.

OBJ. 4

EX 9-4 Entries for uncollectible receivables, using allowance method

Journalize the following transactions in the accounts of Metromark Company, a restaurant supply company that uses the allowance method of accounting for uncollectible receivables:

Feb. 11. Sold merchandise on account to Dakota Co., $29,000. The cost of the merchandise sold was $17,400.

Apr. 15. Received $7,500 from Dakota Co. and wrote off the remainder owed on the sale of February 11 as uncollectible.

Sept. 3. Reinstated the account of Dakota Co. that had been written off on April 15 and received $21,500 cash in full payment.

OBJ. 3, 4

EX 9-5 Entries to write off accounts receivable

Acropolis Company, a computer consulting firm, has decided to write off the $12,950 balance of an account owed by a customer, Aaron Guzman. Journalize the entry to record the write-off, assuming that (a) the direct write-off method is used and (b) the allowance method is used.

OBJ. 4

✔ a. $80,000

✔ b. $82,000

EX 9-6 Providing for doubtful accounts

At the end of the current year, the accounts receivable account has a debit balance of $1,275,000 and net sales for the year total $16,000,000. Determine the amount of the adjusting entry to provide for doubtful accounts under each of the following assumptions:

a. The allowance account before adjustment has a debit balance of $5,000. Bad debt expense is estimated at ½ of 1% of net sales.

b. The allowance account before adjustment has a debit balance of $5,000. An aging of the accounts in the customer ledger indicates estimated doubtful accounts of $77,000.

c. The allowance account before adjustment has a credit balance of $7,500. Bad debt expense is estimated at ¼ of 1% of net sales.

d. The allowance account before adjustment has a credit balance of $7,500. An aging of the accounts in the customer ledger indicates estimated doubtful accounts of $43,500.

OBJ. 4

✔ Alpha Auto, 77 days

EX 9-7   Number of days past due

Honest Abe's Auto Supply distributes new and used automobile parts to local dealers throughout the Northeast. Honest Abe's credit terms are n/30. As of the end of business on July 31, the following accounts receivable were past due:

Account	Due Date	Amount
Alpha Auto	May 15	$ 9,000
Best Auto	July 8	3,000
Downtown Repair	March 18	7,500
Lucky's Auto Repair	June 1	5,000
Pit Stop Auto	June 3	750
Sally's	April 12	13,000
Trident Auto	May 31	1,500
Washburn Repair & Tow	March 2	1,500

Determine the number of days each account is past due.

OBJ. 4

EX 9-8   Aging of receivables schedule

The accounts receivable clerk for Quigley Industries prepared the following partially completed aging of receivables schedule as of the end of business on November 30:

	A	B	C	D	E	F	G
1			Not		Days Past Due		
2			Past				Over
3	Customer	Balance	Due	1–30	31–60	61–90	90
4	Able Brothers Inc.	3,000	3,000				
5	Accent Company	4,500		4,500			
21	Zumpano Company	5,000			5,000		
22	Subtotals	830,000	500,000	180,000	80,000	45,000	25,000

The following accounts were unintentionally omitted from the aging schedule and not included in the subtotals above:

Customer	Balance	Due Date
Beltran Industries	$12,000	July 10
Doodle Company	8,000	September 20
La Corp Inc.	17,000	October 17
VIP Sales Company	10,000	November 4
We-Go Company	23,000	December 21

a. Determine the number of days past due for each of the preceding accounts.

b. Complete the aging-of-receivables schedule by adding the omitted accounts to the bottom of the schedule and updating the totals.

OBJ. 4

✔ $68,130

EX 9-9   Estimating allowance for doubtful accounts

Quigley Industries has a past history of uncollectible accounts, as shown below. Estimate the allowance for doubtful accounts, based on the aging of receivables schedule you completed in Exercise 9-8.

Age Class	Percent Uncollectible
Not past due	1%
1–30 days past due	4
31–60 days past due	15
61–90 days past due	35
Over 90 days past due	60

OBJ. 4

EX 9-10   Adjustment for uncollectible accounts

Using data in Exercise 9-9, assume that the allowance for doubtful accounts for Quigley Industries has a credit balance of $14,280 before adjustment on November 30. Journalize the adjusting entry for uncollectible accounts as of November 30.

OBJ. 4

EX 9-11   Estimating doubtful accounts

Imperial Bikes Co. is a wholesaler of motorcycle supplies. An aging of the company's accounts receivable on December 31, 2012, and a historical analysis of the percentage of uncollectible accounts in each age category are as follows:

Age Interval	Balance	Percent Uncollectible
Not past due	$600,000	¼%
1–30 days past due	120,000	2
31–60 days past due	60,000	3
61–90 days past due	45,000	10
91–180 days past due	26,000	40
Over 180 days past due	24,000	75
	$875,000	

Estimate what the proper balance of the allowance for doubtful accounts should be as of December 31, 2012.

OBJ. 4

EX 9-12   Entry for uncollectible accounts

Using the data in Exercise 9-11, assume that the allowance for doubtful accounts for Imperial Bikes Co. had a debit balance of $1,400 as of December 31, 2012.

Journalize the adjusting entry for uncollectible accounts as of December 31, 2012.

OBJ. 5

✔ c. $14,900 higher

EX 9-13   Entries for bad debt expense under the direct write-off and allowance methods

The following selected transactions were taken from the records of Aprilla Company for the first year of its operations ending December 31, 2012:

Jan. 27. Wrote off account of C. Knoll, $6,000.

Feb. 17. Received $1,000 as partial payment on the $3,000 account of Joni Lester. Wrote off the remaining balance as uncollectible.

Mar.   3. Received $6,000 from C. Knoll, which had been written off on January 27. Reinstated the account and recorded the cash receipt.

Dec. 31. Wrote off the following accounts as uncollectible (record as one journal entry):

Jason Short	$4,500
Kim Snider	1,500
Sue Pascall	1,100
Tracy Lane	3,500
Randy Pape	500

31. If necessary, record the year-end adjusting entry for uncollectible accounts.

a. Journalize the transactions for 2012 under the direct write-off method.

b. Journalize the transactions for 2012 under the allowance method. Aprilla Company uses the percent of credit sales method of estimating uncollectible accounts expense. Based on past history and industry averages, 1¾% of credit sales are expected to be uncollectible. Aprilla Company recorded $1,600,000 of credit sales during 2012.

c. ▬▬▶ How much higher (lower) would Aprilla Company's net income have been under the direct write-off method than under the allowance method?

OBJ. 5

✔ c. $200 higher

EX 9-14 Entries for bad debt expense under the direct write-off and allowance methods

The following selected transactions were taken from the records of Silhouette Company for the year ending December 31, 2012:

Mar. 4. Wrote off account of Myron Rimando, $7,500.

May 19. Received $2,000 as partial payment on the $10,000 account of Shirley Mason. Wrote off the remaining balance as uncollectible.

Aug. 7. Received the $7,500 from Myron Rimando, which had been written off on March 4. Reinstated the account and recorded the cash receipt.

Dec. 31. Wrote off the following accounts as uncollectible (record as one journal entry):

Brandon Peele	$ 5,000
Clyde Stringer	9,000
Ned Berry	13,000
Mary Adams	2,000
Gina Bowers	4,500

Dec. 31. If necessary, record the year-end adjusting entry for uncollectible accounts.

a. Journalize the transactions for 2012 under the direct write-off method.

b. Journalize the transactions for 2012 under the allowance method, assuming that the allowance account had a beginning balance of $45,000 on January 1, 2012, and the company uses the analysis of receivables method. Silhouette Company prepared the following aging schedule for its accounts receivable:

Aging Class (Number of Days Past Due)	Receivables Balance on December 31	Estimated Percent of Uncollectible Accounts
0–30 days	$300,000	1%
31–60 days	80,000	4
61–90 days	20,000	15
91–120 days	10,000	40
More than 120 days	40,000	80
Total receivables	$450,000	

c. ━━━▶ How much higher (lower) would Silhouette's 2012 net income have been under the direct write-off method than under the allowance method?

OBJ. 5

EX 9-15 Effect of doubtful accounts on net income

During its first year of operations, Filippi's Plumbing Supply Co. had net sales of $4,800,000, wrote off $65,000 of accounts as uncollectible using the direct write-off method, and reported net income of $375,000. Determine what the net income would have been if the allowance method had been used, and the company estimated that 1½% of net sales would be uncollectible.

OBJ. 5

✔ b. $19,500 credit balance

EX 9-16 Effect of doubtful accounts on net income

Using the data in Exercise 9-15, assume that during the second year of operations Filippi's Plumbing Supply Co. had net sales of $5,500,000, wrote off $70,000 of accounts as uncollectible using the direct write-off method, and reported net income of $450,000.

a. Determine what net income would have been in the second year if the allowance method (using 1½% of net sales) had been used in both the first and second years.

b. Determine what the balance of the allowance for doubtful accounts would have been at the end of the second year if the allowance method had been used in both the first and second years.

OBJ. 5

✔ c. $16,000 higher

EX 9-17 Entries for bad debt expense under the direct write-off and allowance methods

Spangler Company wrote off the following accounts receivable as uncollectible for the first year of its operations ending December 31, 2012:

Customer	Amount
Will Boyette	$10,000
Stan Frey	8,000
Tammy Imes	5,000
Shana Wagner	6,000
Total	$29,000

a. Journalize the write-offs for 2012 under the direct write-off method.

b. Journalize the write-offs for 2012 under the allowance method. Also, journalize the adjusting entry for uncollectible accounts. The company recorded $3,000,000 of credit sales during 2012. Based on past history and industry averages, 1½% of credit sales are expected to be uncollectible.

c. How much higher (lower) would Spangler Company's 2012 net income have been under the direct write-off method than under the allowance method?

OBJ. 5

EX 9-18   Entries for bad debt expense under the direct write-off and allowance methods

Magnetics International wrote off the following accounts receivable as uncollectible for the year ending December 31, 2012:

Customer	Amount
Trey Betts	$15,500
Cheryl Carson	9,000
Irene Harris	29,700
Renee Putman	3,100
Total	$57,300

The company prepared the following aging schedule for its accounts receivable on December 31, 2012:

Aging Class (Number of Days Past Due)	Receivables Balance on December 31	Estimated Percent of Uncollectible Accounts
0–30 days	$600,000	1%
31–60 days	150,000	2
61–90 days	75,000	18
91–120 days	50,000	30
More than 120 days	60,000	50
Total receivables	$935,000	

a. Journalize the write-offs for 2012 under the direct write-off method.

b. Journalize the write-offs and the year-end adjusting entry for 2012 under the allowance method, assuming that the allowance account had a beginning balance of $55,000 on January 1, 2012, and the company uses the analysis of receivables method.

c. How much higher (lower) would Magnetics International's 2012 net income have been under the allowance method than under the direct write-off method?

OBJ. 6

✔ a. Aug. 13, $600

EX 9-19   Determine due date and interest on notes

Determine the due date and the amount of interest due at maturity on the following notes:

	Date of Note	Face Amount	Interest Rate	Term of Note
a.	May 15	$40,000	6%	90 days
b.	March 20	15,000	4	60 days
c.	May 19	24,000	3	60 days
d.	October 1	10,500	8	60 days
e.	August 30	18,000	5	120 days

OBJ. 6

✔ b. $91,350

EX 9-20 Entries for notes receivable

Oregon Interior Decorators issued a 90-day, 6% note for $90,000, dated April 9, to Corvallis Furniture Company on account.

a. Determine the due date of the note.

b. Determine the maturity value of the note.

c. Journalize the entries to record the following: (1) receipt of the note by Corvallis Furniture and (2) receipt of payment of the note at maturity.

OBJ. 6

EX 9-21 Entries for notes receivable

The series of seven transactions recorded in the following T accounts were related to a sale to a customer on account and the receipt of the amount owed. Briefly describe each transaction.

	CASH				NOTES RECEIVABLE		
(7)	40,602			(5)	40,000	(6)	40,000

	ACCOUNTS RECEIVABLE				SALES RETURNS AND ALLOWANCES		
(1)	50,000	(3)	10,000	(3)	10,000		
(6)	40,400	(5)	40,000				
		(7)	40,400				

	MERCHANDISE INVENTORY				COST OF MERCHANDISE SOLD		
(4)	6,000	(2)	30,000	(2)	30,000	(4)	6,000

	SALES				INTEREST REVENUE		
		(1)	50,000			(6)	400
						(7)	202

OBJ. 6

EX 9-22 Entries for notes receivable, including year-end entries

The following selected transactions were completed by Zip-Up Co., a supplier of zippers for clothing:

2011

Dec. 10. Received from Point Loma Clothing & Bags Co., on account, a $36,000, 90-day, 4% note dated December 10.

    31. Recorded an adjusting entry for accrued interest on the note of December 10.

    31. Recorded the closing entry for interest revenue.

2012

Mar. 9. Received payment of note and interest from Point Loma Clothing & Bags Co.

Journalize the transactions.

OBJ. 6

EX 9-23 Entries for receipt and dishonor of note receivable

Journalize the following transactions of Frankenstein Productions:

May 3. Received a $150,000, 120-day, 6% note dated May 3 from Sunrider Co. on account.

Aug. 31. The note is dishonored by Sunrider Co.

Oct. 30. Received the amount due on the dishonored note plus interest for 60 days at 9% on the total amount charged to Sunrider Co. on August 31.

OBJ. 4, 6

EX 9-24 Entries for receipt and dishonor of notes receivable

Journalize the following transactions in the accounts of Jamba Co., which operates a riverboat casino:

Mar. 1. Received an $80,000, 60-day, 6% note dated March 1 from Tomekia Co. on account.

18. Received a $75,000, 60-day, 8% note dated March 18 from Mystic Co. on account.

Apr. 30. The note dated March 1 from Tomekia Co. is dishonored, and the customer's account is charged for the note, including interest.

May 17. The note dated March 18 from Mystic Co. is dishonored, and the customer's account is charged for the note, including interest.

July 29. Cash is received for the amount due on the dishonored note dated March 1 plus interest for 90 days at 8% on the total amount debited to Tomekia Co. on April 30.

Aug. 23. Wrote off against the allowance account the amount charged to Mystic Co. on May 17 for the dishonored note dated March 18.

OBJ. 7

EX 9-25 Receivables on the balance sheet

List any errors you can find in the following partial balance sheet:

Tulips Company
Balance Sheet
December 31, 2012

Assets		
Current assets:		
Cash		$138,000
Notes receivable	$400,000	
Less interest receivable	20,000	380,000
Accounts receivable	$795,000	
Plus allowance for doubtful accounts	14,500	809,500

OBJ. 8

✔ a. 2009: 8.6

EX 9-26 Accounts receivable turnover and days' sales in receivables

Polo Ralph Lauren Corporation designs, markets, and distributes a variety of apparel, home decor, accessory, and fragrance products. The company's products include such brands as Polo by Ralph Lauren, Ralph Lauren Purple Label, Ralph Lauren, Polo Jeans Co., and Chaps. Polo Ralph Lauren reported the following (in thousands):

	For the Period Ending	
	March 29, 2009	**March 29, 2008**
Net sales	$5,018,900	$4,880,100
Accounts receivable	576,700	585,000

Assume that accounts receivable (in millions) were $511,900 at the beginning of the 2008 fiscal year.

a. Compute the accounts receivable turnover for 2009 and 2008. Round to one decimal place.

b. Compute the days' sales in receivables for 2009 and 2008. Round to one decimal place.

c. ➤ What conclusions can be drawn from these analyses regarding Ralph Lauren's efficiency in collecting receivables?

OBJ. 8

✔ a. 2009: 8.7

EX 9-27 Accounts receivable turnover and days' sales in receivables

H.J. Heinz Company was founded in 1869 at Sharpsburg, Pennsylvania, by Henry J. Heinz. The company manufactures and markets food products throughout the world, including ketchup, condiments and sauces, frozen food, pet food, soups, and tuna. For the fiscal years 2009 and 2008, H.J. Heinz reported the following (in thousands):

	Year Ending	
	April 29, 2009	April 30, 2008
Net sales	$10,148,082	$10,070,778
Accounts receivable	1,171,797	1,161,481

Assume that the accounts receivable (in thousands) were $996,852 at the beginning of fiscal year 2008.

a. Compute the accounts receivable turnover for 2009 and 2008. Round to one decimal place.

b. Compute the days' sales in receivables at the end of 2009 and 2008. Round to one decimal place.

c. ➤ What conclusions can be drawn from these analyses regarding Heinz's efficiency in collecting receivables?

OBJ. 8

EX 9-28   Accounts receivable turnover and days' sales in receivables

The Limited Brands Inc. sells women's clothing and personal health care products through specialty retail stores including Victoria's Secret and Bath & Body Works stores. The Limited Brands reported the following (in millions):

	For the Period Ending	
	Jan. 31, 2010	Jan. 31, 2009
Net sales	$8,632	$9,043
Accounts receivable	249	313

Assume that accounts receivable (in millions) were $355 at the beginning of fiscal year 2009.

a. Compute the accounts receivable turnover for 2010 and 2009. Round to one decimal place.

b. Compute the day's sales in receivables for 2010 and 2009. Round to one decimal place.

c. What conclusions can be drawn from these analyses regarding The Limited Brands' efficiency in collecting receivables?

OBJ. 8

EX 9-29   Accounts receivable turnover

Use the data in Exercises 9-27 and 9-28 to analyze the accounts receivable turnover ratios of H.J. Heinz Company and The Limited Brands Inc.

a. Compute the average accounts receivable turnover ratio for The Limited Brands Inc. and H.J. Heinz Company for the years shown in Exercises 9-27 and 9-28.

b. ➤ Does The Limited Brands or H.J. Heinz Company have the higher average accounts receivable turnover ratio?

c. ➤ Explain the logic underlying your answer in (b).

Problems Series A

OBJ. 4

✔ 3. $1,140,000

PR 9-1A   Entries related to uncollectible accounts

The following transactions were completed by Axiom Management Company during the current fiscal year ended December 31:

Feb. 17. Received 25% of the $30,000 balance owed by Gillespie Co., a bankrupt business, and wrote off the remainder as uncollectible.

Apr. 11. Reinstated the account of Colleen Bertram, which had been written off in the preceding year as uncollectible. Journalized the receipt of $4,250 cash in full payment of Colleen's account.

July 6. Wrote off the $9,000 balance owed by Covered Wagon Co., which has no assets.

Nov. 20. Reinstated the account of Dugan Co., which had been written off in the preceding year as uncollectible. Journalized the receipt of $5,900 cash in full payment of the account.

Dec. 31. Wrote off the following accounts as uncollectible (compound entry): Kipp Co., $3,000; Moore Co., $4,000; Butte Distributors, $8,000; Parker Towers, $6,700.

31. Based on an analysis of the $1,200,000 of accounts receivable, it was estimated that $60,000 will be uncollectible. Journalized the adjusting entry.

Instructions

1. Record the January 1 credit balance of $40,000 in a T account for Allowance for Doubtful Accounts.

2. Journalize the transactions. Post each entry that affects the following selected T accounts and determine the new balances:

Allowance for Doubtful Accounts

Bad Debt Expense

3. Determine the expected net realizable value of the accounts receivable as of December 31.

4. Assuming that instead of basing the provision for uncollectible accounts on an analysis of receivables, the adjusting entry on December 31 had been based on an estimated expense of ¾ of 1% of the net sales of $7,500,000 for the year, determine the following:

a. Bad debt expense for the year.

b. Balance in the allowance account after the adjustment of December 31.

c. Expected net realizable value of the accounts receivable as of December 31.

OBJ. 4

✔ 3. $111,095

PR 9-2A   Aging of receivables; estimating allowance for doubtful accounts

Angler's Dream Company supplies flies and fishing gear to sporting goods stores and outfitters throughout the western United States. The accounts receivable clerk for Angler's Dream prepared the following partially completed aging of receivables schedule as of the end of business on December 31, 2011:

	A	B	C	D	E	F	G	H
1			Not			Days Past Due		
2			Past					
3	Customer	Balance	Due	1–30	31–60	61–90	91–120	Over 120
4	AAA Fishery	20,000	20,000					
5	Blue Ribbon Flies	7,500			7,500			
30	Z Fish Co.	4,000		4,000				
31	Subtotals	1,060,000	500,000	315,000	120,000	40,000	25,000	60,000

The following accounts were unintentionally omitted from the aging schedule:

Customer	Due Date	Balance
Antelope Sports & Flies	June 21, 2011	$ 3,000
Big Hole Flies	Aug. 30, 2011	6,500
Charlie's Fish Co.	Sept. 8, 2011	12,000
Deschutes Sports	Oct. 20, 2011	4,000
Green River Sports	Nov. 7, 2011	3,500
Smith River Co.	Nov. 28, 2011	1,500
Wild Trout Company	Dec. 5, 2011	5,000
Wolfe Sports	Jan. 7, 2012	4,500

Angler's Dream has a past history of uncollectible accounts by age category, as follows:

Age Class	Percent Uncollectible
Not past due	1%
1–30 days past due	4
31–60 days past due	8
61–90 days past due	25
91–120 days past due	45
Over 120 days past due	80

Instructions

1. Determine the number of days past due for each of the preceding accounts.

2. Complete the aging of receivables schedule by adding the omitted accounts to the bottom of the schedule and updating the totals.

3. Estimate the allowance for doubtful accounts, based on the aging of receivables schedule.

4. Assume that the allowance for doubtful accounts for Angler's Dream Company has a debit balance of $1,405 before adjustment on December 31, 2011. Journalize the adjusting entry for uncollectible accounts.

5. Assume that the adjusting entry in (4) was inadvertently omitted, how would the omission affect the balance sheet and income statement?

OBJ. 3, 4, 5

✔ 1. Year 4: Balance of allowance account, end of year, $14,950

PR 9-3A Compare two methods of accounting for uncollectible receivables

Tel-Com Company, a telephone service and supply company, has just completed its fourth year of operations. The direct write-off method of recording bad debt expense has been used during the entire period. Because of substantial increases in sales volume and the amount of uncollectible accounts, the company is considering changing to the allowance method. Information is requested as to the effect that an annual provision of ¾% of sales would have had on the amount of bad debt expense reported for each of the past four years. It is also considered desirable to know what the balance of Allowance for Doubtful Accounts would have been at the end of each year. The following data have been obtained from the accounts:

			Year of Origin of Accounts Receivable Written Off as Uncollectible			
Year	Sales	Uncollectible Accounts Written off	1st	2nd	3rd	4th
1st	$ 700,000	$2,000	$2,000			
2nd	900,000	3,400	1,800	$1,600		
3rd	1,200,000	6,450	1,000	3,700	$1,750	
4th	2,000,000	9,200		1,260	3,700	$4,240

Instructions

1. Assemble the desired data, using the following column headings:

	Bad Debt Expense			
Year	Expense Actually Reported	Expense Based on Estimate	Increase (Decrease) in Amount of Expense	Balance of Allowance Account, End of Year

2. ━━━▶ Experience during the first four years of operations indicated that the receivables were either collected within two years or had to be written off as uncollectible. Does the estimate of ¾% of sales appear to be reasonably close to the actual experience with uncollectible accounts originating during the first two years? Explain.

OBJ. 6

✔ 1. Note 2: Due
date, July 24; Interest
due at maturity, $90

PR 9-4A   Details of notes receivable and related entries

Old Town Co. wholesales bathroom fixtures. During the current fiscal year, Old Town Co. received the following notes:

	Date	Face Amount	Term	Interest Rate
1.	Apr. 10	$45,000	60 days	4%
2.	June 24	18,000	30 days	6
3.	July 1	36,000	120 days	6
4.	Oct. 31	36,000	60 days	9
5.	Nov. 15	54,000	60 days	6
6.	Dec. 27	40,500	30 days	4

Instructions

1. Determine for each note (a) the due date and (b) the amount of interest due at maturity, identifying each note by number.

2. Journalize the entry to record the dishonor of Note (3) on its due date.

3. Journalize the adjusting entry to record the accrued interest on Notes (5) and (6) on December 31.

4. Journalize the entries to record the receipt of the amounts due on Notes (5) and (6) in January.

OBJ. 6

PR 9-5A   Notes receivable entries

The following data relate to notes receivable and interest for Viking Co., a cable manufacturer and supplier. (All notes are dated as of the day they are received.)

June   3. Received a $24,000, 4%, 60-day note on account.

July   26. Received a $27,000, 5%, 120-day note on account.

Aug.   2. Received $24,160 on note of June 3.

Sept.   4. Received a $60,000, 3%, 60-day note on account.

Nov.   3. Received $60,300 on note of September 4.

5. Received a $36,000, 7%, 30-day note on account.

23. Received $27,450 on note of July 26.

30. Received an $18,000, 5%, 30-day note on account.

Dec.   5. Received $36,210 on note of November 5.

30. Received $18,075 on note of November 30.

Instructions

Journalize entries to record the transactions.

OBJ. 6

PR 9-6A   Sales and notes receivable transactions

The following were selected from among the transactions completed by Sorento Co. during the current year. Sorento Co. sells and installs home and business security systems.

Jan.   5. Loaned $17,500 cash to Marc Jager, receiving a 90-day, 8% note.

Feb.   4. Sold merchandise on account to Tedra & Co., $19,000. The cost of the merchandise sold was $11,000.

13. Sold merchandise on account to Centennial Co., $30,000. The cost of merchandise sold was $17,600.

Mar.   6. Accepted a 60-day, 6% note for $19,000 from Tedra & Co. on account.

14. Accepted a 60-day, 9% note for $30,000 from Centennial Co. on account.

Apr. 5. Received the interest due from Marc Jager and a new 120-day, 9% note as a renewal of the loan of January 5. (Record both the debit and the credit to the notes receivable account.)

May 5. Received from Tedra & Co. the amount due on the note of March 6.

13. Centennial Co. dishonored its note dated March 14.

July 12. Received from Centennial Co. the amount owed on the dishonored note, plus interest for 60 days at 12% computed on the maturity value of the note.

Aug. 3. Received from Marc Jager the amount due on his note of April 5.

Sept. 7. Sold merchandise on account to Lock-It Co., $9,000. The cost of the merchandise sold was $5,000.

17. Received from Lock-It Co. the amount of the invoice of September 7, less 1% discount.

Instructions
Journalize the transactions.

Problems Series B

OBJ. 4

✔ 3. $1,830,000

PR 9-1B   Entries related to uncollectible accounts

The following transactions were completed by The Spencer Gallery during the current fiscal year ended December 31:

Mar. 15. Reinstated the account of Brad Atwell, which had been written off in the preceding year as uncollectible. Journalized the receipt of $3,750 cash in full payment of Brad's account.

May 20. Wrote off the $15,000 balance owed by Glory Rigging Co., which is bankrupt.

Aug. 13. Received 40% of the $18,000 balance owed by Coastal Co., a bankrupt business, and wrote off the remainder as uncollectible.

Sept. 2. Reinstated the account of Lorie Kidd, which had been written off two years earlier as uncollectible. Recorded the receipt of $6,500 cash in full payment.

Dec. 31. Wrote off the following accounts as uncollectible (compound entry): Kimbro Co., $9,000; McHale Co., $2,500; Summit Furniture, $7,500; Wes Riggs, $2,000.

31. Based on an analysis of the $1,880,000 of accounts receivable, it was estimated that $50,000 will be uncollectible. Journalized the adjusting entry.

Instructions

1. Record the January 1 credit balance of $38,500 in a T account for Allowance for Doubtful Accounts.

2. Journalize the transactions. Post each entry that affects the following T accounts and determine the new balances:

    Allowance for Doubtful Accounts
    Bad Debt Expense

3. Determine the expected net realizable value of the accounts receivable as of December 31.

4. Assuming that instead of basing the provision for uncollectible accounts on an analysis of receivables, the adjusting entry on December 31 had been based on an estimated expense of ½ of 1% of the net sales of $9,600,000 for the year, determine the following:

    a. Bad debt expense for the year.

    b. Balance in the allowance account after the adjustment of December 31.

    c. Expected net realizable value of the accounts receivable as of December 31.

OBJ. 4

✔ 3. $72,290

PR 9-2B   Aging of receivables; estimating allowance for doubtful accounts

Capri Wigs Company supplies wigs and hair care products to beauty salons throughout California and the Pacific Northwest. The accounts receivable clerk for Capri Wigs prepared the following partially completed aging of receivables schedule as of the end of business on December 31, 2011:

	A	B	C	D	E	F	G	H
1			Not			Days Past Due		
2			Past					
3	Customer	Balance	Due	1–30	31–60	61–90	91–120	Over 120
4	Absolute Beauty	15,000	15,000					
5	Blonde Wigs	8,000			8,000			
30	Zensational Beauty	3,000			3,000			
31	Subtotals	700,000	287,000	180,000	150,000	40,000	18,000	25,000

The following accounts were unintentionally omitted from the aging schedule:

Customer	Due Date	Balance
Shining Beauty	May 28, 2011	$4,000
Paradise Beauty Store	Sept. 7, 2011	7,000
Amazing Hair Products	Oct. 17, 2011	1,000
Hairy's Hair Care	Oct. 24, 2011	1,500
Golden Images	Nov. 23, 2011	1,600
Oh The Hair	Nov. 29, 2011	3,500
All About Hair	Dec. 2, 2011	4,000
Lasting Images	Jan. 5, 2012	9,400

Capri Wigs has a past history of uncollectible accounts by age category, as follows:

Age Class	Percent Uncollectible
Not past due	2%
1–30 days past due	5
31–60 days past due	12
61–90 days past due	16
91–120 days past due	40
Over 120 days past due	75

Instructions

1. Determine the number of days past due for each of the preceding accounts.
2. Complete the aging of receivables schedule by adding the omitted accounts to the bottom of the schedule and updating the totals.
3. Estimate the allowance for doubtful accounts, based on the aging of receivables schedule.
4. Assume that the allowance for doubtful accounts for Capri Wigs has a credit balance of $3,040 before adjustment on December 31, 2011. Journalize the adjustment for uncollectible accounts.
5. Assume that the adjusting entry in (4) was inadvertently omitted, how would the omission affect the balance sheet and income statement?

OBJ. 3, 4, 5

✔ 1. Year 4: Balance of allowance account, end of year, $13,900

PR 9-3B   Compare two methods of accounting for uncollectible receivables

Cyber Tech Company, which operates a chain of 25 electronics supply stores, has just completed its fourth year of operations. The direct write-off method of recording bad debt expense has been used during the entire period. Because of substantial increases in sales volume and the amount of uncollectible accounts, the firm is considering changing to the allowance method. Information is requested as to the effect that an annual provision of ½% of sales would have had on the amount of bad debt expense reported for each of the past four years. It is also considered desirable to know what the balance of Allowance for Doubtful Accounts would have been at the end of each year. The following data have been obtained from the accounts:

			Year of Origin of Accounts Receivable Written Off as Uncollectible			
Year	Sales	Uncollectible Accounts Written Off	1st	2nd	3rd	4th
1st	$1,400,000	$ 1,300	$1,300			
2nd	2,000,000	3,600	1,500	$2,100		
3rd	3,000,000	13,500	4,000	3,300	$6,200	
4th	3,600,000	17,700		4,000	6,100	$7,600

Instructions

1. Assemble the desired data, using the following column headings:

	Bad Debt Expense			
Year	Expense Actually Reported	Expense Based on Estimate	Increase (Decrease) in Amount of Expense	Balance of Allowance Account, End of Year

2. ━━━━▶ Experience during the first four years of operations indicated that the receivables were either collected within two years or had to be written off as uncollectible. Does the estimate of ½% of sales appear to be reasonably close to the actual experience with uncollectible accounts originating during the first two years? Explain.

OBJ. 6

✔ 1. Note 1: Due date, June 2; Interest due at maturity, $100

PR 9-4B Details of notes receivable and related entries

Media Ads Co. produces advertising videos. During the last six months of the current fiscal year, Media Ads Co. received the following notes:

	Date	Face Amount	Term	Interest Rate
1.	Apr. 3	$15,000	60 days	4%
2.	May 19	57,600	45 days	6
3.	Aug. 7	50,000	90 days	5
4.	Sept. 4	20,000	90 days	6
5.	Nov. 21	27,000	60 days	8
6.	Dec. 16	21,600	60 days	6

Instructions

1. Determine for each note (a) the due date and (b) the amount of interest due at maturity, identifying each note by number.

2. Journalize the entry to record the dishonor of Note (3) on its due date.

3. Journalize the adjusting entry to record the accrued interest on Notes (5) and (6) on December 31.

4. Journalize the entries to record the receipt of the amounts due on Notes (5) and (6) in January and February.

OBJ. 6

PR 9-5B Notes receivable entries

The following data relate to notes receivable and interest for El Rayo Co., a financial services company. (All notes are dated as of the day they are received.)

Mar. 1. Received a $90,000, 6%, 60-day note on account.

  25. Received a $10,000, 4%, 90-day note on account.

Apr. 30. Received $90,900 on note of March 1.

May 16. Received a $36,000, 7%, 90-day note on account.

  31. Received a $25,000, 6%, 30-day note on account.

June 23. Received $10,100 on note of March 25.

     30. Received $25,125 on note of May 31.

July   1. Received a $28,000, 9%, 30-day note on account.

    31. Received $28,210 on note of July 1.

Aug. 14. Received $36,630 on note of May 16.

Instructions
Journalize the entries to record the transactions.

OBJ. 6

PR 9-6B Sales and notes receivable transactions

The following were selected from among the transactions completed during the current year by Indigo Co., an appliance wholesale company:

Jan. 13. Sold merchandise on account to Boylan Co., $32,000. The cost of merchandise sold was $19,200.

Mar. 10. Accepted a 60-day, 6% note for $32,000 from Boylan Co. on account.

May   9. Received from Boylan Co. the amount due on the note of March 10.

June 10. Sold merchandise on account to Holen for $18,000. The cost of merchandise sold was $10,000.

    15. Loaned $24,000 cash to Angie Jones, receiving a 30-day, 7% note.

    20. Received from Holen the amount due on the invoice of June 10, less 2% discount.

July 15. Received the interest due from Angie Jones and a new 60-day, 9% note as a renewal of the loan of June 15. (Record both the debit and the credit to the notes receivable account.)

Sept. 13. Received from Angie Jones the amount due on her note of July 15.

    13. Sold merchandise on account to Aztec Co., $40,000. The cost of merchandise sold was $25,000.

Oct. 12. Accepted a 60-day, 6% note for $40,000 from Aztec Co. on account.

Dec. 11. Aztec Co. dishonored the note dated October 12.

    26. Received from Aztec Co. the amount owed on the dishonored note, plus interest for 15 days at 12% computed on the maturity value of the note.

Instructions
Journalize the transactions.

Cases & Projects

CP 9-1 Ethics and professional conduct in business

Stacey Ball, vice president of operations for Clinton County Bank, has instructed the bank's computer programmer to use a 365-day year to compute interest on depository accounts (liabilities). Stacey also instructed the programmer to use a 360-day year to compute interest on loans (assets).

➡ Discuss whether Stacey is behaving in a professional manner.

CP 9-2 Estimate uncollectible accounts

For several years, Dolphin Co.'s sales have been on a "cash only" basis. On January 1, 2009, however, Dolphin Co. began offering credit on terms of n/30. The amount of the adjusting entry to record the estimated uncollectible receivables at the end of each year has been ¼ of 1% of credit sales, which is the rate reported as the average for the industry. Credit sales and the year-end credit balances in Allowance for Doubtful Accounts for the past four years are as follows:

Year	Credit Sales	Allowance for Doubtful Accounts
2009	$3,000,000	$ 3,200
2010	3,150,000	5,500
2011	3,400,000	8,000
2012	3,800,000	10,300

Hugh Lopez, president of Dolphin Co., is concerned that the method used to account for and write off uncollectible receivables is unsatisfactory. He has asked for your advice in the analysis of past operations in this area and for recommendations for change.

1. Determine the amount of (a) the addition to Allowance for Doubtful Accounts and (b) the accounts written off for each of the four years.

2. a. ➤ Advise Hugh Lopez as to whether the estimate of ¼ of 1% of credit sales appears reasonable.

   b. ➤ Assume that after discussing (a) with Hugh Lopez, he asked you what action might be taken to determine what the balance of Allowance for Doubtful Accounts should be at December 31, 2012, and what possible changes, if any, you might recommend in accounting for uncollectible receivables. How would you respond?

CP 9-3 Accounts receivable turnover and days' sales in receivables

Best Buy is a specialty retailer of consumer electronics, including personal computers, entertainment software, and appliances. Best Buy operates retail stores in addition to the Best Buy, Media Play, On Cue, and Magnolia Hi-Fi Web sites. For two recent years, Best Buy reported the following (in millions):

	Year Ending	
	Feb. 28, 2009	Mar. 1, 2008
Net sales	$45,015	$40,023
Accounts receivable at end of year	1,868	549

Assume that the accounts receivable (in millions) were $548 at the beginning of fiscal year 2008.

1. Compute the accounts receivable turnover for 2009 and 2008. Round to one decimal place.

2. Compute the days' sales in receivables at the end of 2009 and 2008. Round to one decimal place.

3. ➤ What conclusions can be drawn from (1) and (2) regarding Best Buy's efficiency in collecting receivables?

4. ➤ What assumption did we make about sales for the Best Buy ratio computations that might distort the ratios and therefore cause the ratios not to be comparable for 2009 and 2008?

CP 9-4 Accounts receivable turnover and days' sales in receivables

Apple Computer, Inc., designs, manufactures, and markets personal computers and related personal computing and communicating solutions for sale primarily to education, creative, consumer, and business customers. Substantially all of the company's net sales over the last five years are from sales of its Macs, iPods, iPads, and related software and peripherals. For two recent fiscal years, Apple reported the following (in millions):

	Year Ending	
	Sept. 26, 2009	Sept. 27, 2008
Net sales	$36,537	$32,479
Accounts receivable at end of year	3,361	2,422

Assume that the accounts receivable (in millions) were $1,637 at the beginning of fiscal year 2008.

1. Compute the accounts receivable turnover for 2009 and 2008. Round to one decimal place.

2. Compute the days' sales in receivables at the end of 2009 and 2008. Round to one decimal place.

3. ➤ What conclusions can be drawn from (1) and (2) regarding Apple's efficiency in collecting receivables?

CP 9-5   Accounts receivable turnover and days' sales in receivables

EarthLink, Inc., is a nationwide Internet Service Provider (ISP). EarthLink provides a variety of services to its customers, including narrowband access, broadband or high-speed access, and Web hosting services. For two recent years, EarthLink reported the following (in thousands):

	Year Ending	
	Dec. 31, 2009	Dec. 31, 2008
Net sales	$723,729	$955,577
Accounts receivable at end of year	66,623	50,823

Assume that the accounts receivable (in thousands) were $41,483 at January 1, 2008.

1. Compute the accounts receivable turnover for 2009 and 2008. Round to one decimal place.

2. Compute the days' sales in receivables at the end of 2009 and 2008. Round to one decimal place.

3. ➤ What conclusions can be drawn from (1) and (2) regarding EarthLink's efficiency in collecting receivables?

4. ➤ Given the nature of EarthLink's operations, do you believe EarthLink's accounts receivable turnover ratio would be higher or lower than a typical manufacturing company, such as Boeing or Kellogg Company? Explain.

CP 9-6   Accounts receivable turnover

The accounts receivable turnover ratio will vary across companies, depending on the nature of the company's operations. For example, an accounts receivable turnover of 6 for an Internet Service Provider is unacceptable but might be excellent for a manufacturer of specialty milling equipment. A list of well-known companies follows.

Alcoa Inc.	The Coca-Cola Company	Kroger
AutoZone, Inc.	Delta Air Lines	Procter & Gamble
Barnes & Noble, Inc.	The Home Depot	Wal-Mart
Caterpillar	IBM	Whirlpool Corporation

1. Categorize each of the preceding companies as to whether its turnover ratio is likely to be above or below 15.

2. ➤ Based on (1), identify a characteristic of companies with accounts receivable turnover ratios above 15.

© AP Photo/W. A. Harewood

Fixed Assets and Intangible Assets

Fatburger Inc.

Do you remember purchasing your first car? You probably didn't buy your first car like you would buy a CD. Purchasing a new or used car is expensive. In addition, you would drive (use) the car for the next 3–5 years or longer. As a result, you might spend hours or weeks considering different makes and models, safety ratings, warranties, and operating costs before deciding on the final purchase.

Like buying her first car, Lovie Yancey spent a lot of time before deciding to open her first restaurant. In 1952, she created the biggest, juiciest hamburger that anyone had ever seen. She called it a Fatburger. The restaurant initially started as a 24-hour operation to cater to the schedules of professional musicians. As a fan of popular music and its performers, Yancey played rhythm and blues, jazz, and blues recordings for her customers. Fatburger's popularity with entertainers was illustrated when its name was used in a 1992 rap by Ice Cube. "Two in the mornin' got the Fatburger," Cube said, in "It Was a Good Day," a track on his *Predator* album.

The demand for this incredible burger was such that, in 1980, Ms. Yancey decided to offer Fatburger franchise

opportunities. In 1990, with the goal of expanding Fatburger throughout the world, **Fatburger Inc.** purchased the business from Ms. Yancey. Today, Fatburger has grown to a multi-restaurant chain with owners and investors such as talk show host Montel Williams, former Cincinnati Bengals' tackle Willie Anderson, comedian David Spade, and musicians Cher, Janet Jackson, and Pharrell.

So, how much would it cost you to open a Fatburger restaurant? On average, the total investment begins at over $700,000 per restaurant. Thus, in starting a Fatburger restaurant, you would be making a significant investment that would affect your life for years to come.

This chapter discusses the accounting for investments in fixed assets such as those used to open a Fatburger restaurant. How to determine the portion of the fixed asset that becomes an expense over time is also discussed. Finally, the accounting for the disposal of fixed assets and accounting for intangible assets such as patents and copyrights are discussed.

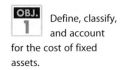

OBJ. 1 Define, classify, and account for the cost of fixed assets.

Nature of Fixed Assets

Fixed assets are long-term or relatively permanent assets such as equipment, machinery, buildings, and land. Other descriptive titles for fixed assets are *plant assets* or *property, plant, and equipment*. Fixed assets have the following characteristics:

1. They exist physically and, thus, are *tangible* assets.
2. They are owned and used by the company in its normal operations.
3. They are not offered for sale as part of normal operations.

Exhibit 1 shows the percent of fixed assets to total assets for some select companies. As shown in Exhibit 1, fixed assets are often a significant portion of the total assets of a company.

EXHIBIT 1   **Fixed Assets as a Percent of Total Assets—Selected Companies**

	Fixed Assets as a Percent of Total Assets
Alcoa Inc.	47%
ExxonMobil Corporation	53
Ford Motor Company	25
Kroger	57
Office Depot Inc.	30
United Parcel Service, Inc.	57
Verizon Communications	43
Walgreen Co.	43
Wal-Mart	59

Classifying Costs

A cost that has been incurred may be classified as a fixed asset, an investment, or an expense. Exhibit 2 shows how to determine the proper classification of a cost and how it should be recorded. As shown in Exhibit 2, classifying a cost involves the following steps:

See Appendix D for more information

Step 1.   Is the purchased item long-lived?

If *yes*, the item is recorded as an asset on the balance sheet, either as a fixed asset or an investment. Proceed to Step 2.

If *no*, the item is classified and recorded as an *expense*.

Step 2.   Is the asset used in normal operations?

If *yes*, the asset is classified and recorded as a *fixed asset*.

If *no*, the asset is classified and recorded as an *investment*.

Items that are classified and recorded as fixed assets include land, buildings, or equipment. Such assets normally last more than a year and are used in the normal operations. However, standby equipment for use during peak periods or when other equipment breaks down is still classified as a fixed asset even though it is not used very often. In contrast, fixed assets that have been abandoned or are no longer used in operations are not classified as fixed assets.

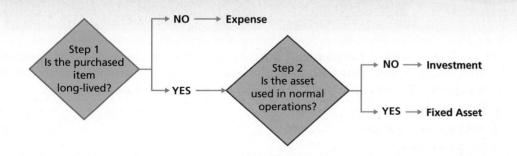

EXHIBIT 2

Classifying Costs

Although fixed assets may be sold, they should not be offered for sale as part of normal operations. For example, cars and trucks offered for sale by an automotive dealership are not fixed assets of the dealership. On the other hand, a tow truck used in the normal operations of the dealership is a fixed asset of the dealership.

Investments are long-lived assets that are not used in the normal operations and are held for future resale. Such assets are reported on the balance sheet in a section entitled *Investments*. For example, undeveloped land acquired for future resale would be classified and reported as an investment, not land.

The Cost of Fixed Assets

In addition to purchase price, costs of acquiring fixed assets include all amounts spent getting the asset in place and ready for use. For example, freight costs and the costs of installing equipment are part of the asset's total cost.

Exhibit 3 summarizes some of the common costs of acquiring fixed assets. These costs are recorded by debiting the related fixed asset account, such as Land,[1] Building, Land Improvements, or Machinery and Equipment.

EXHIBIT 3   Costs of Acquiring Fixed Assets

Building

- Architects' fees
- Engineers' fees
- Insurance costs incurred during construction
- Interest on money borrowed to finance construction
- Walkways to and around the building
- Sales taxes
- Repairs (purchase of existing building)
- Reconditioning (purchase of existing building)
- Modifying for use
- Permits from government agencies

Machinery & Equipment

- Sales taxes
- Freight
- Installation
- Repairs (purchase of used equipment)
- Reconditioning (purchase of used equipment)
- Insurance while in transit
- Assembly
- Modifying for use
- Testing for use
- Permits from government agencies

Land

- Purchase price
- Sales taxes
- Permits from government agencies
- Broker's commissions
- Title fees
- Surveying fees
- Delinquent real estate taxes
- Removing unwanted building less any salvage
- Grading and leveling
- Paving a public street bordering the land

Land Improvements

- Trees and shrubs
- Fences
- Outdoor lighting
- Paved parking areas

Only costs necessary for preparing the fixed asset for use are included as a cost of the asset. Unnecessary costs that do not increase the asset's usefulness are recorded as an expense. For example, the following costs are included as an expense:

1. Vandalism
2. Mistakes in installation
3. Uninsured theft
4. Damage during unpacking and installing
5. Fines for not obtaining proper permits from governmental agencies

A company may incur costs associated with constructing a fixed asset such as a new building. The direct costs incurred in the construction, such as labor and

---

1 As discussed here, land is assumed to be used only as a location or site and not for its mineral deposits or other natural resources.

lease liability account. The asset is then written off as an expense (amortized) over the life of the capital lease. The accounting for capital leases is discussed in more advanced accounting texts.

An **operating lease** is accounted for as if the lessee is renting the asset for the lease term. The lessee records operating lease payments by debiting *Rent Expense* and crediting *Cash*. The lessee's future lease obligations are not recorded in the accounts. However, such obligations are disclosed in notes to the financial statements.

The asset rentals described in earlier chapters of this text were accounted for as operating leases. To simplify, all leases are assumed to be operating leases throughout this text.

Accounting for Depreciation

OBJ. 2 Compute depreciation, using the following methods: straight-line method, units-of-production method, and double-declining-balance method.

Over time, fixed assets, with the exception of land, lose their ability to provide services. Thus, the costs of fixed assets such as equipment and buildings should be recorded as an expense over their useful lives. This periodic recording of the cost of fixed assets as an expense is called **depreciation**. Because land has an unlimited life, it is not depreciated.

The adjusting entry to record depreciation debits *Depreciation Expense* and credits a *contra asset* account entitled *Accumulated Depreciation* or *Allowance for Depreciation*. The use of a contra asset account allows the original cost to remain unchanged in the fixed asset account.

Note:
The adjusting entry to record depreciation debits Depreciation Expense and credits Accumulated Depreciation.

Depreciation can be caused by physical or functional factors.

1. *Physical depreciation* factors include wear and tear during use or from exposure to weather.
2. *Functional depreciation* factors include obsolescence and changes in customer needs that cause the asset to no longer provide services for which it was intended. For example, equipment may become obsolete due to changing technology.

Two common misunderstandings that exist about *depreciation* as used in accounting include:

1. Depreciation does not measure a decline in the market value of a fixed asset. Instead, depreciation is an allocation of a fixed asset's cost to expense over the asset's useful life. Thus, the book value of a fixed asset (cost less accumulated depreciation) usually does not agree with the asset's market value. This is justified in accounting because a fixed asset is for use in a company's operations rather than for resale.
2. Depreciation does not provide cash to replace fixed assets as they wear out. This misunderstanding may occur because depreciation, unlike most expenses, does not require an outlay of cash when it is recorded.

Factors in Computing Depreciation Expense

Three factors determine the depreciation expense for a fixed asset. These three factors are as follows:

1. The asset's initial cost
2. The asset's expected useful life
3. The asset's estimated residual value

The initial *cost* of a fixed asset is determined using the concepts discussed and illustrated earlier in this chapter.

The *expected useful life* of a fixed asset is estimated at the time the asset is placed into service. Estimates of expected useful lives are available from industry trade associations. The Internal Revenue Service also publishes guidelines for useful lives, which may be helpful for financial reporting purposes. However, it is not uncommon for different companies to use a different useful life for similar assets.

The **residual value** of a fixed asset at the end of its useful life is estimated at the time the asset is placed into service. Residual value is sometimes referred to as *scrap* *value, salvage value,* or *trade-in value.* The difference between a fixed asset's initial cost and its residual value is called the asset's *depreciable cost.* The depreciable cost is the amount of the asset's cost that is allocated over its useful life as depreciation expense. If a fixed asset has no residual value, then its entire cost should be allocated to depreciation.

Exhibit 4 shows the relationship between depreciation expense and a fixed asset's initial cost, expected useful life, and estimated residual value.

EXHIBIT 4

Depreciation Expense Factors

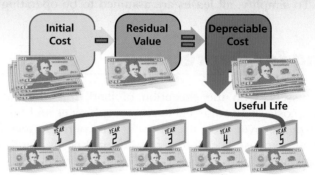

For an asset placed into or taken out of service during the first half of a month, many companies compute depreciation on the asset for the entire month. That is, the asset is treated as having been purchased or sold on the first day of *that* month. Likewise, purchases and sales during the second half of a month are treated as having occurred on the first day of the *next* month. To simplify, this practice is used in this chapter.

The three depreciation methods used most often are as follows:[2]

1. Straight-line depreciation
2. Units-of-production depreciation
3. Double-declining-balance depreciation

Exhibit 5 shows how often these methods are used in financial statements.

EXHIBIT 5

Use of Depreciation Methods

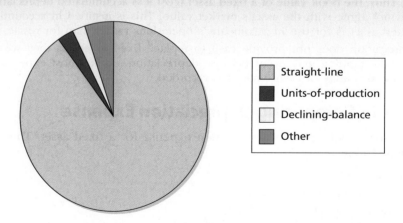

Source: *Accounting Trends & Techniques,* 63rd ed., American Institute of Certified Public Accountants, New York, 2009.

It is not necessary for a company to use only one method of computing depreciation for all of its fixed assets. For example, a company may use one method for depreciating equipment and another method for depreciating buildings.

2 Another method not often used today, called the *sum-of-the-years-digits method,* is described and illustrated in an online appendix located at **www.cengage.com/accounting/warren**.

A company may also use different methods for determining income and property taxes.

Straight-Line Method

The **straight-line method** provides for the same amount of depreciation expense for each year of the asset's useful life. As shown in Exhibit 5, the straight-line method is by far the most widely used depreciation method.

To illustrate, assume that equipment was purchased on January 1 as follows:

Initial cost	$24,000
Expected useful life	5 years
Estimated residual value	$2,000

The annual straight-line depreciation of $4,400 is computed below.

$$\text{Annual Depreciation} = \frac{\text{Cost} - \text{Residual Value}}{\text{Useful Life}} = \frac{\$24,000 - \$2,000}{5 \text{ Years}} = \$4,400$$

If an asset is used for only part of a year, the annual depreciation is prorated. For example, assume that the preceding equipment was purchased and placed into service on October 1. The depreciation for the year ending December 31 would be **$1,100**, computed as follows:

$$\textit{First-Year Partial Depreciation} = \$4,400 \times 3/12 = \$1,100$$

The computation of straight-line depreciation may be simplified by converting the annual depreciation to a percentage of depreciable cost.[3] The straight-line percentage is determined by dividing 100% by the number of years of expected useful life, as shown below.

Expected Years of Useful Life	Straight-Line Percentage
5 years	20% (100%/5)
8 years	12.5% (100%/8)
10 years	10% (100%/10)
20 years	5% (100%/20)
25 years	4% (100%/25)

For the preceding equipment, the annual depreciation of $4,400 can be computed by multiplying the depreciable cost of $22,000 by 20% (100%/5).

Example Exercise 10-2 Straight-Line Depreciation   OBJ. 2

Equipment acquired at the beginning of the year at a cost of $125,000 has an estimated residual value of $5,000 and an estimated useful life of 10 years. Determine (a) the depreciable cost, (b) the straight-line rate, and (c) the annual straight-line depreciation.

Follow My Example 10-2

a. $120,000 ($125,000 − $5,000)

b. 10% = 1/10

c. $12,000 ($120,000 × 10%), or ($120,000/10 years)

Practice Exercises: **PE 10-2A, PE 10-2B**

---

[3] The depreciation rate may also be expressed as a fraction. For example, the annual straight-line rate for an asset with a three-year useful life is 1/3.

As shown on the previous page, the straight-line method is simple to use. When an asset's revenues are about the same from period to period, straight-line depreciation provides a good matching of depreciation expense with the asset's revenues.

Norfolk Southern Corporation depreciates its train engines based on hours of operation.

Units-of-Production Method

The **units-of-production method** provides the same amount of depreciation expense for each unit of production. Depending on the asset, the units of production can be expressed in terms of hours, miles driven, or quantity produced.

The units-of-production method is applied in two steps.

Step 1.   Determine the depreciation per unit as:

$$\text{Depreciation per Unit} = \frac{\text{Cost} - \text{Residual Value}}{\text{Total Units of Production}}$$

Step 2.   Compute the depreciation expense as:

$$\text{Depreciation Expense} = \text{Depreciation per Unit} \times \text{Total Units of Production Used}$$

To illustrate, assume that the equipment in the preceding example is expected to have a useful life of 10,000 operating hours. During the year, the equipment was operated 2,100 hours. The units-of-production depreciation for the year is $4,620, as shown below.

Step 1.   Determine the depreciation per hour as:

$$\text{Depreciation per Hour} = \frac{\text{Cost} - \text{Residual Value}}{\text{Total Units of Production}} = \frac{\$24,000 - \$2,000}{10,000 \text{ Hours}} = \$2.20 \text{ per Hour}$$

Step 2.   Compute the depreciation expense as:

$$\text{Depreciation Expense} = \text{Depreciation per Unit} \times \text{Total Units of Production Used}$$

$$\text{Depreciation Expense} = \$2.20 \text{ per Hour} \times 2,100 \text{ Hours} = \$4,620$$

The units-of-production method is often used when a fixed asset's in-service time (or use) varies from year to year. In such cases, the units-of-production method matches depreciation expense with the asset's revenues.

Example Exercise 10-3   Units-of-Production Depreciation

OBJ. 2

Equipment acquired at a cost of $180,000 has an estimated residual value of $10,000, has an estimated useful life of 40,000 hours, and was operated 3,600 hours during the year. Determine (a) the depreciable cost, (b) the depreciation rate, and (c) the units-of-production depreciation for the year.

Follow My Example 10-3

a. $170,000 ($180,000 − $10,000)
b. $4.25 per hour ($170,000/40,000 hours)
c. $15,300 (3,600 hours × $4.25)

Practice Exercises: **PE 10-3A, PE 10-3B**

Double-Declining-Balance Method

The **double-declining-balance method** provides for a declining periodic expense over the expected useful life of the asset. The double-declining-balance method is applied in three steps.

Step 1.   Determine the straight-line percentage using the expected useful life.
Step 2.   Determine the double-declining-balance rate by multiplying the straight-line rate from Step 1 by 2.
Step 3.   Compute the depreciation expense by multiplying the double-declining-balance rate from Step 2 times the book value of the asset.

To illustrate, the equipment purchased in the preceding example is used to compute double-declining-balance depreciation. For the first year, the depreciation is **$9,600**, as shown below.

Step 1.   Straight-line percentage = 20% (100%/5)
Step 2.   Double-declining-balance rate = 40% (20% × 2)
Step 3.   Depreciation expense = $9,600 ($24,000 × 40%)

For the first year, the book value of the equipment is its initial cost of $24,000. After the first year, the **book value** (cost minus accumulated depreciation) declines and, thus, the depreciation also declines. The double-declining-balance depreciation for the full five-year life of the equipment is shown below.

Year	Cost	Acc. Dep. at Beginning of Year	Book Value at Beginning of Year	Double-Declining-Balance Rate	Depreciation for Year	Book Value at End of Year
1	$24,000		$24,000.00	× 40%	$9,600.00	$14,400.00
2	24,000	$ 9,600.00	14,400.00	× 40%	5,760.00	8,640.00
3	24,000	15,360.00	8,640.00	× 40%	3,456.00	5,184.00
4	24,000	18,816.00	5,184.00	× 40%	2,073.60	3,110.40
5	24,000	20,889.60	3,110.40	—	1,110.40	2,000.00

When the double-declining-balance method is used, the estimated residual value is *not* considered. However, the asset should not be depreciated below its estimated residual value. In the above example, the estimated residual value was $2,000. Therefore, the depreciation for the fifth year is $1,110.40 ($3,110.40 − $2,000.00) instead of $1,244.16 (40% × $3,110.40).

Like straight-line depreciation, if an asset is used for only part of a year, the annual depreciation is prorated. For example, assume that the preceding equipment was purchased and placed into service on October 1. The depreciation for the year ending December 31 would be $2,400, computed as follows:

First-Year Partial Depreciation = $9,600 × 3/12 = $2,400

The depreciation for the second year would then be $8,640, computed as follows:

Second-Year Depreciation = $8,640 = [40% × ($24,000 − $2,400)]

The double-declining-balance method provides a higher depreciation in the first year of the asset's use, followed by declining depreciation amounts. For this reason, the double-declining-balance method is called an **accelerated depreciation method**.

An asset's revenues are often greater in the early years of its use than in later years. In such cases, the double-declining-balance method provides a good matching of depreciation expense with the asset's revenues.

Example Exercise 10-4 Double-Declining-Balance Depreciation OBJ. 2

Equipment acquired at the beginning of the year at a cost of $125,000 has an estimated residual value of $5,000 and an estimated useful life of 10 years. Determine (a) the double-declining-balance rate and (b) the double-declining-balance depreciation for the first year.

Follow My Example 10-4

a. 20% [(1/10) × 2]
b. $25,000 ($125,000 × 20%)

Practice Exercises: **PE 10-4A, PE 10-4B**

Comparing Depreciation Methods

The three depreciation methods are summarized in Exhibit 6. All three methods allocate a portion of the total cost of an asset to an accounting period, while never depreciating an asset below its residual value.

EXHIBIT 6

Summary of Depreciation Methods

Method	Useful Life	Depreciable Cost	Depreciation Rate	Depreciation Expense
Straight-line	Years	Cost less residual value	Straight-line rate*	Constant
Units-of-production	Total units of production	Cost less residual value	$\dfrac{\text{Cost} - \text{Residual value}}{\text{Total units of production}}$	Variable
Double-declining-balance	Years	Declining book value, but not below residual value	Straight-line rate* × 2	Declining

*Straight-line rate = (1/Useful life)

The straight-line method provides for the same periodic amounts of depreciation expense over the life of the asset. The units-of-production method provides for periodic amounts of depreciation expense that vary, depending on the amount the asset is used. The double-declining-balance method provides for a higher depreciation amount in the first year of the asset's use, followed by declining amounts.

The depreciation for the straight-line, units-of-production, and double-declining-balance methods is shown in Exhibit 7. The depreciation in Exhibit 7 is based on the

EXHIBIT 7

Comparing Depreciation Methods

	Depreciation Expense		
Year	Straight-Line Method	Units-of-Production Method	Double-Declining-Balance Method
1	$ 4,400*	$ 4,620 ($2.20 × 2,100 hrs.)	$ 9,600.00 ($24,000 × 40%)
2	4,400	3,300 ($2.20 × 1,500 hrs.)	5,760.00 ($14,400 × 40%)
3	4,400	5,720 ($2.20 × 2,600 hrs.)	3,456.00 ($8,640 × 40%)
4	4,400	3,960 ($2.20 × 1,800 hrs.)	2,073.60 ($5,184 × 40%)
5	4,400	4,400 ($2.20 × 2,000 hrs.)	1,110.40**
Total	$22,000	$22,000	$22,000.00

*$4,400 = ($24,000 − $2,000)/5 years
**$3,110.40 − $2,000.00 because the equipment cannot be depreciated below its residual value of $2,000.

equipment purchased in our prior illustrations. For the units-of-production method, we assume that the equipment was used as follows:

Year 1	2,100 hours
Year 2	1,500
Year 3	2,600
Year 4	1,800
Year 5	2,000
Total	10,000 hours

Depreciation for Federal Income Tax

The Internal Revenue Code uses the *Modified Accelerated Cost Recovery System (MACRS)* to compute depreciation for tax purposes. MACRS has eight classes of useful life and depreciation rates for each class. Two of the most common classes are the five-year class and the seven-year class.[4] The five-year class includes automobiles and light-duty trucks. The seven-year class includes most machinery and equipment. Depreciation for these two classes is similar to that computed using the double-declining-balance method.

In using the MACRS rates, residual value is ignored. Also, all fixed assets are assumed to be put in and taken out of service in the middle of the year. For the five-year-class assets, depreciation is spread over six years, as shown below.

Year	MACRS 5-Year-Class Depreciation Rates
1	20.0%
2	32.0
3	19.2
4	11.5
5	11.5
6	5.8
	100.0%

To simplify, a company will sometimes use MACRS for both financial statement and tax purposes. This is acceptable if MACRS does not result in significantly different amounts than would have been reported using one of the three depreciation methods discussed in this chapter.

BusinessConnection

DEPRECIATING ANIMALS?

Under MACRS, various farm animals may be depreciated. The period (years) over which some common classes of farm animals may be depreciated are shown in the table to the right.

Depreciation for farm animals begins when the animal reaches the age of maturity, which is normally when it can be worked, milked, or bred. For race horses, depreciation begins when a horse is put into training.

Class of Animal	Years
Dairy or breeding cattle	7–10
Goats and sheep	5
Hogs	3
Horses	3–12

---

4 Real estate is in either a 27½-year or a 31½-year class and is depreciated by the straight-line method.

Revising Depreciation Estimates

Estimates of residual values and useful lives of fixed assets may change due to abnormal wear and tear or obsolescence. When new estimates are determined, they are used to determine the depreciation expense in future periods. The depreciation expense recorded in earlier years is not affected.[5]

To illustrate, assume the following data for a machine that was purchased on January 1, 2011.

Initial machine cost	$140,000
Expected useful life	5 years
Estimated residual value	$10,000
Annual depreciation using the straight-line method	
[($140,000 − $10,000)/5 years]	$26,000

At the end of 2012, the machine's book value (undepreciated cost) is $88,000, as shown below.

Initial machine cost	$140,000
Less accumulated depreciation ($26,000 per year × 2 years)	52,000
Book value (undepreciated cost), end of second year	$ 88,000

During 2013, the company estimates that the machine's remaining useful life is eight years (instead of three) and that its residual value is $8,000 (instead of $10,000). The depreciation expense for each of the remaining eight years is $10,000, computed as follows:

Book value (undepreciated cost), end of second year	$88,000
Less revised estimated residual value	8,000
Revised remaining depreciable cost	$80,000
Revised annual depreciation expense	
[($88,000 − $8,000)/8 years]	$10,000

Exhibit 8 shows the book value of the asset over its original and revised lives. After the depreciation is revised at the end of 2012, book value declines at a slower rate. At the end of year 2020, the book value reaches the revised residual value of $8,000.

EXHIBIT 8

Book Value of Asset with Change in Estimate

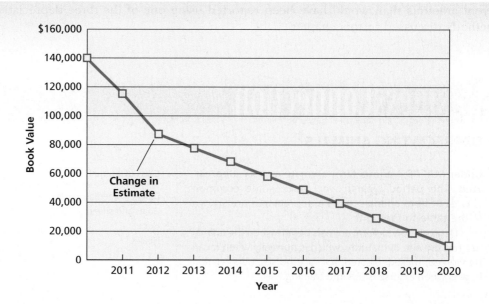

Example Exercise 10-5 **Revision of Depreciation**

A warehouse with a cost of $500,000 has an estimated residual value of $120,000, has an estimated useful life of 40 years, and is depreciated by the straight-line method. (a) Determine the amount of the annual depreciation. (b) Determine the book value at the end of the twentieth year of use. (c) Assuming that at the start of the twenty-first year the remaining life is estimated to be 25 years and the residual value is estimated to be $150,000, determine the depreciation expense for each of the remaining 25 years.

Follow My Example 10-5

a. $9,500 [($500,000 – $120,000)/40]
b. $310,000 [$500,000 – ($9,500 × 20)]
c. $6,400 [($310,000 – $150,000)/25]

Practice Exercises: **PE 10-5A, PE 10-5B**

Disposal of Fixed Assets

Journalize entries for the disposal of fixed assets.

Fixed assets that are no longer useful may be discarded or sold.[6] In such cases, the fixed asset is removed from the accounts. Just because a fixed asset is fully depreciated, however, does not mean that it should be removed from the accounts.

If a fixed asset is still being used, its cost and accumulated depreciation should remain in the ledger even if the asset is fully depreciated. This maintains accountability for the asset in the ledger. If the asset was removed from the ledger, the accounts would contain no evidence of the continued existence of the asset. In addition, cost and accumulated depreciation data on such assets are often needed for property tax and income tax reports.

Discarding Fixed Assets

If a fixed asset is no longer used and has no residual value, it is discarded. For example, assume that a fixed asset that is fully depreciated and has no residual value is discarded. The entry to record the discarding removes the asset and its related accumulated depreciation from the ledger.

To illustrate, assume that equipment acquired at a cost of $25,000 is fully depreciated at December 31, 2011. On February 14, 2012, the equipment is discarded. The entry to record the discard is as follows:

Feb.	14	Accumulated Depreciation—Equipment	25,000	
		Equipment		25,000
		To write off equipment discarded.		

Note:
The entry to record the disposal of a fixed asset removes the cost of the asset and its accumulated depreciation from the accounts.

If an asset has not been fully depreciated, depreciation should be recorded before removing the asset from the accounting records.

To illustrate, assume that equipment costing $6,000 with no estimated residual value is depreciated at a straight-line rate of 10%. On December 31, 2011, the accumulated depreciation balance, after adjusting entries, is $4,750. On March 24, 2012, the asset is removed from service and discarded. The entry to record the depreciation for the three months of 2012 before the asset is discarded is as follows:

Mar.	24	Depreciation Expense—Equipment	150	
		Accumulated Depreciation—Equipment		150
		To record current depreciation on		
		equipment discarded ($600 × 3/12).		

6 The accounting for the exchange of fixed assets is described and illustrated in the appendix at the end of this chapter.

The discarding of the equipment is then recorded as follows:

Mar.	24	Accumulated Depreciation—Equipment	4,900	
		Loss on Disposal of Equipment	1,100	
		Equipment		6,000
		To write off equipment discarded.		

The loss of $1,100 is recorded because the balance of the accumulated depreciation account ($4,900) is less than the balance in the equipment account ($6,000). Losses on the discarding of fixed assets are nonoperating items and are normally reported in the Other expense section of the income statement.

Selling Fixed Assets

The entry to record the sale of a fixed asset is similar to the entries for discarding an asset. The only difference is that the receipt of cash is also recorded. If the selling price is more than the book value of the asset, a gain is recorded. If the selling price is less than the book value, a loss is recorded.

To illustrate, assume that equipment is purchased at a cost of $10,000 with no estimated residual value and is depreciated at a straight-line rate of 10%. The equipment is sold for cash on October 12 of the eighth year of its use. The balance of the accumulated depreciation account as of the preceding December 31 is $7,000. The entry to update the depreciation for the nine months of the current year is as follows:

Oct.	12	Depreciation Expense—Equipment	750	
		Accumulated Depreciation—Equipment		750
		To record current depreciation on		
		equipment sold ($10,000 × $\frac{9}{12}$ × 10%).		

After the current depreciation is recorded, the book value of the asset is $2,250 ($10,000 − $7,750). The entries to record the sale, assuming three different selling prices, are as follows:

Sold at book value, for $2,250. No gain or loss.

Oct.	12	Cash	2,250	
		Accumulated Depreciation—Equipment	7,750	
		Equipment		10,000

Sold below book value, for $1,000. Loss of $1,250.

Oct.	12	Cash	1,000	
		Accumulated Depreciation—Equipment	7,750	
		Loss on Sale of Equipment	1,250	
		Equipment		10,000

Sold above book value, for $2,800. Gain of $550.

Oct.	12	Cash	2,800	
		Accumulated Depreciation—Equipment	7,750	
		Equipment		10,000
		Gain on Sale of Equipment		550

Example Exercise 10-6 Sale of Equipment

Equipment was acquired at the beginning of the year at a cost of $91,000. The equipment was depreciated using the straight-line method based on an estimated useful life of nine years and an estimated residual value of $10,000.

a. What was the depreciation for the first year?

b. Assuming the equipment was sold at the end of the second year for $78,000, determine the gain or loss on sale of the equipment.

c. Journalize the entry to record the sale.

Follow My Example 10-6

a. $9,000 [($91,000 − $10,000)/9]

b. $5,000 gain {$78,000 − [$91,000 − ($9,000 × 2)]}

c.
Cash	78,000	
Accumulated Depreciation—Equipment..............................	18,000	
Equipment...		91,000
Gain on Sale of Equipment		5,000

Practice Exercises: **PE 10-6A, PE 10-6B**

Natural Resources

OBJ. 4 Compute depletion and journalize the entry for depletion.

The fixed assets of some companies include timber, metal ores, minerals, or other natural resources. As these resources are harvested or mined and then sold, a portion of their cost is debited to an expense account. This process of transferring the cost of natural resources to an expense account is called **depletion**.

Depletion is determined as follows:[7]

Step 1.   Determine the depletion rate as:

$$\text{Depletion Rate} = \frac{\text{Cost of Resource}}{\text{Estimated Total Units of Resource}}$$

Step 2.   Multiply the depletion rate by the quantity extracted from the resource during the period.

$$\text{Depletion Expense} = \text{Depletion Rate} \times \text{Quantity Extracted}$$

To illustrate, assume that Karst Company purchased mining rights as follows:

Cost of mineral deposit	$400,000
Estimated total units of resource	1,000,000 tons
Tons mined during year	90,000 tons

The depletion expense of $36,000 for the year is computed, as shown below.

Step 1.

$$\text{Depletion Rate} = \frac{\text{Cost of Resource}}{\text{Estimated Total Units of Resource}} = \frac{\$400,000}{1,000,000 \text{ Tons}} = \$0.40 \text{ per Ton}$$

Step 2.

$$\text{Depletion Expense} = \$0.40 \text{ per Ton} \times 90,000 \text{ Tons} = \$36,000$$

The adjusting entry to record the depletion is shown below.

Dec.	31	Depletion Expense		36,000	
		Accumulated Depletion			36,000
		Depletion of mineral deposit.			

[7] We assume that there is no significant residual value left after all the natural resource is extracted.

Like the accumulated depreciation account, Accumulated Depletion is a *contra asset* account. It is reported on the balance sheet as a deduction from the cost of the mineral deposit.

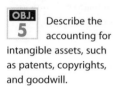

Example Exercise 10-7 **Depletion**

OBJ. 4

Earth's Treasures Mining Co. acquired mineral rights for $45,000,000. The mineral deposit is estimated at 50,000,000 tons. During the current year, 12,600,000 tons were mined and sold.

a. Determine the depletion rate.

b. Determine the amount of depletion expense for the current year.

c. Journalize the adjusting entry on December 31 to recognize the depletion expense.

Follow My Example 10-7

a. $0.90 per ton ($45,000,000/50,000,000 tons)

b. $11,340,000 (12,600,000 tons × $0.90 per ton)

c. Dec. 31 Depletion Expense 11,340,000
                Accumulated Depreciation   11,340,000
            Depletion of mineral deposit.

Practice Exercises: **PE 10-7A, PE 10-7B**

OBJ. 5 Describe the accounting for intangible assets, such as patents, copyrights, and goodwill.

Intangible Assets

Patents, copyrights, trademarks, and goodwill are long-lived assets that are used in the operations of a business and are not held for sale. These assets are called **intangible assets** because they do not exist physically.

The accounting for intangible assets is similar to that for fixed assets. The major issues are:

IFRS ◄ IFRS

See Appendix D for more information

1. Determining the initial cost.
2. Determining the **amortization**, which is the amount of cost to transfer to expense.

Amortization results from the passage of time or a decline in the usefulness of the intangible asset.

Patents

Manufacturers may acquire exclusive rights to produce and sell goods with one or more unique features. Such rights are granted by **patents,** which the federal government issues to inventors. These rights continue in effect for 20 years. A business may purchase patent rights from others, or it may obtain patents developed by its own research and development.

The initial cost of a purchased patent, including any legal fees, is debited to an asset account. This cost is written off, or amortized, over the years of the patent's expected useful life. The expected useful life of a patent may be less than its legal life. For example, a patent may become worthless due to changing technology or consumer tastes.

Patent amortization is normally computed using the straight-line method. The amortization is recorded by debiting an amortization expense account and crediting the patents account. A separate contra asset account is usually *not* used for intangible assets.

To illustrate, assume that at the beginning of its fiscal year, a company acquires patent rights for $100,000. Although the patent will not expire for 14 years, its remaining useful life is estimated as five years. The adjusting entry to amortize the patent at the end of the year is as follows:

Dec.	31	Amortization Expense—Patents		20,000	
		Patents			20,000
		Patent amortization ($100,000/5).			

Some companies develop their own patents through research and development. In such cases, any *research and development costs* are usually recorded as current operating expenses in the period in which they are incurred. This accounting for research and development costs is justified on the basis that any future benefits from research and development are highly uncertain.

InternationalConnection

INTERNATIONAL FINANCIAL REPORTING STANDARDS (IFRS)

IFRS allow certain research and development (R&D) costs to be recorded as assets when incurred. Typically, R&D costs are classified as either research costs or development costs. If certain criteria are met, research costs can be recorded as an expense, while development costs can be recorded as an asset. This criterion includes such considerations as the company's intent to use or to sell the intangible asset. For example, Nokia Corporation (Finland) reported capitalized development costs of €143 million on its December 31, 2009, statement of financial position (balance sheet), where € represents the euro, the common currency of the European Economic Union.*

*Differences between U.S. GAAP and IFRS are further discussed and illustrated in Appendix D.

Copyrights and Trademarks

The exclusive right to publish and sell a literary, artistic, or musical composition is granted by a **copyright**. Copyrights are issued by the federal government and extend for 70 years beyond the author's death. The costs of a copyright include all costs of creating the work plus any other costs of obtaining the copyright. A copyright that is purchased is recorded at the price paid for it. Copyrights are amortized over their estimated useful lives.

A **trademark** is a name, term, or symbol used to identify a business and its products. Most businesses identify their trademarks with ® in their advertisements and on their products.

Under federal law, businesses can protect their trademarks by registering them for 10 years and renewing the registration for 10-year periods. Like a copyright, the legal costs of registering a trademark are recorded as an asset.

If a trademark is purchased from another business, its cost is recorded as an asset. In such cases, the cost of the trademark is considered to have an indefinite useful life. Thus, trademarks are not amortized. Instead, trademarks are reviewed periodically for impaired value. When a trademark is impaired, the trademark should be written down and a loss recognized.

Goodwill

Goodwill refers to an intangible asset of a business that is created from such favorable factors as location, product quality, reputation, and managerial skill. Goodwill allows a business to earn a greater rate of return than normal.

Generally accepted accounting principles (GAAP) allow goodwill to be recorded only if it is objectively determined by a transaction. An example of such a transaction is the purchase of a business at a price in excess of the fair value of its net assets (assets – liabilities). The excess is recorded as goodwill and reported as an intangible asset.

Unlike patents and copyrights, goodwill is not amortized. However, a loss should be recorded if the future prospects of the purchased firm become impaired. This loss would normally be disclosed in the Other expense section of the income statement.

To illustrate, assume that on December 31 FaceCard Company has determined that $250,000 of the goodwill created from the purchase of Electronic Systems is impaired. The entry to record the impairment is as follows:

Dec.	31	Loss from Impaired Goodwill	250,000	
		Goodwill		250,000
		Impaired goodwill.		

Exhibit 9 shows intangible asset disclosures for 500 large firms. Goodwill is the most often reported intangible asset. This is because goodwill arises from merger transactions, which are common.

EXHIBIT 9

Frequency of Intangible Asset Disclosures for 500 Firms

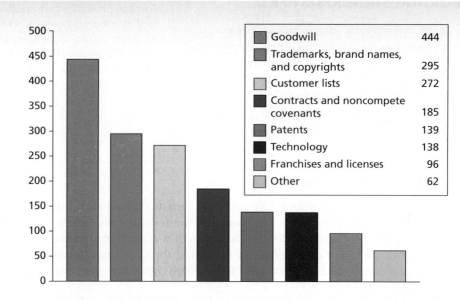

Goodwill	444
Trademarks, brand names, and copyrights	295
Customer lists	272
Contracts and noncompete covenants	185
Patents	139
Technology	138
Franchises and licenses	96
Other	62

Source: *Accounting Trends & Techniques,* 63rd ed., American Institute of Certified Public Accountants, New York, 2009.
Note: Some firms have multiple disclosures.

Exhibit 10 summarizes the characteristics of intangible assets.

EXHIBIT 10

Comparison of Intangible Assets

Intangible Asset	Description	Amortization Period	Periodic Expense
Patent	Exclusive right to benefit from an innovation.	Estimated useful life not to exceed legal life.	Amortization expense.
Copyright	Exclusive right to benefit from a literary, artistic, or musical composition.	Estimated useful life not to exceed legal life.	Amortization expense.
Trademark	Exclusive use of a name, term, or symbol.	None	Impairment loss if fair value less than carrying value (impaired).
Goodwill	Excess of purchase price of a business over the fair value of its net assets (assets − liabilities).	None	Impairment loss if fair value less than carrying value (impaired).

Example Exercise 10-8 Impaired Goodwill and Amortization of Patent

OBJ. 5

On December 31, it was estimated that goodwill of $40,000 was impaired. In addition, a patent with an estimated useful economic life of 12 years was acquired for $84,000 on July 1.

a. Journalize the adjusting entry on December 31 for the impaired goodwill.

b. Journalize the adjusting entry on December 31 for the amortization of the patent rights.

Follow My Example 10-8

a.	Dec. 31	Loss from Impaired Goodwill	40,000	
		Goodwill		40,000
		Impaired goodwill.		
b.	Dec. 31	Amortization Expense—Patents	3,500	
		Patents		3,500
		Amortized patent rights [($84,000/12) × (6/12)].		

Practice Exercises: **PE 10-8A, PE 10-8B**

Financial Reporting for Fixed Assets and Intangible Assets

OBJ. 6 Describe how depreciation expense is reported in an income statement and prepare a balance sheet that includes fixed assets and intangible assets.

In the income statement, depreciation and amortization expense should be reported separately or disclosed in a note. A description of the methods used in computing depreciation should also be reported.

In the balance sheet, each class of fixed assets should be disclosed on the face of the statement or in the notes. The related accumulated depreciation should also be disclosed, either by class or in total. The fixed assets may be shown at their *book value* (cost less accumulated depreciation), which can also be described as their *net* amount.

If there are many classes of fixed assets, a single amount may be presented in the balance sheet, supported by a note with a separate listing. Fixed assets may be reported under the more descriptive caption of property, plant, and equipment.

Intangible assets are usually reported in the balance sheet in a separate section following fixed assets. The balance of each class of intangible assets should be disclosed net of any amortization.

The balance sheet presentation for Mornin' Joe's fixed and intangible assets is shown below.

Mornia' Joe
Balance Sheet
December 31, 2012

Property, plant, and equipment:			
Land		$1,850,000	
Buildings	$2,650,000		
Less accumulated depreciation	420,000	2,230,000	
Office equipment	$ 350,000		
Less accumulated depreciation	102,000	248,000	
Total property, plant, and equipment			$4,328,000
Intangible assets:			
Patents			140,000

The cost and related accumulated depletion of mineral rights are normally shown as part of the Fixed Assets section of the balance sheet. The mineral rights may be shown net of depletion on the face of the balance sheet. In such cases, a supporting note discloses the accumulated depletion.

Financial Analysis and Interpretation: Fixed Asset Turnover Ratio

OBJ. 7 Describe and illustrate the fixed asset turnover ratio to assess the efficiency of a company's use of its fixed assets.

A measure of a company's efficiency in using its fixed assets to generate revenue is the fixed asset turnover ratio. The **fixed asset turnover ratio** measures the number of dollars of sales earned per dollar of fixed assets. It is computed as follows:

$$\text{Fixed Asset Turnover Ratio} = \frac{\text{Net Sales}}{\text{Average Book Value of Fixed Assets}}$$

To illustrate, the following data (in millions) are used for Starbucks Corp.

	Sept. 27, 2009	Sept. 28, 2008
Net sales	$9,775	$10,383
Fixed assets (net):		
Beginning of year	2,956	2,890
End of year	2,536	2,956

Starbucks' fixed asset turnover ratios for 2009 and 2008 are computed as follows:

	2009	2008
Net sales	$9,775	$10,383
Average fixed assets	$2,746	$ 2,923
	[($2,536 + $2,956) ÷ 2]	[($2,956 + $2,890) ÷ 2]
Fixed asset turnover ratio	3.56	3.55
	($9,775 ÷ $2,746)	($10,383 ÷ $2,923)

BusinessConnection

HUB-AND-SPOKE OR POINT-TO-POINT?

Southwest Airlines Co. uses a simple fare structure, featuring low, unrestricted, unlimited, everyday coach fares. These fares are made possible by Southwest's use of a point-to-point, rather than a hub-and-spoke, business approach.

United Airlines, Inc., Delta Air Lines, and American Airlines employ a hub-and-spoke approach in which an airline establishes major hubs that serve as connecting links to other cities. For example, Delta has major connecting hubs in Atlanta and Salt Lake City.

In contrast, Southwest focuses on nonstop, point-to-point service between selected cities. As a result, Southwest minimizes connections, delays, and total trip time. This operating approach permits Southwest to achieve high utilization of its fixed assets, such as its 737 aircraft.

© AP Photo/Matt Slocum

The higher the fixed asset turnover, the more efficiently a company is using its fixed assets in generating sales. For example, in 2009 Starbucks earned $3.56 of sales for every dollar of fixed assets, which is slightly more than $3.55 of sales for every dollar of fixed assets it earned in 2008. Thus, Starbucks used its fixed assets slightly more efficiently in 2009.

As illustrated above, the fixed asset turnover ratio can be compared across time for a single company. In addition, the ratio can be compared across companies. For example, the fixed asset turnover ratio for a number of different companies and industries is shown below.

Company (industry)	Fixed Asset Turnover Ratio
Comcast Corporation (cable)	1.43
Google (Internet)	4.70
Manpower Inc. (temporary employment)	99.32
Norfolk Southern Corporation (railroad)	0.49
Ruby Tuesday, Inc. (restaurant)	1.20
Southwest Airlines Co. (airline)	1.01

The smaller ratios are associated with companies that require large fixed asset investments. The larger fixed asset turnover ratios are associated with firms that are more labor-intensive and require smaller fixed asset investments.

Example Exercise 10-9 Fixed Asset Turnover Ratio

OBJ. 7

Financial statement data for years ending December 31 for Broadwater Company are shown below.

	2012	2011
Net sales	$2,862,000	$2,025,000
Fixed assets:		
Beginning of year	750,000	600,000
End of year	840,000	750,000

a. Determine the fixed asset turnover ratio for 2012 and 2011.
b. Does the change in the fixed asset turnover ratio from 2011 to 2012 indicate a favorable or an unfavorable trend?

Follow My Example 10-9

a. Fixed asset turnover:

	2012	2011
Net sales	$2,862,000	$2,025,000
Fixed assets:		
Beginning of year	$750,000	$600,000
End of year	$840,000	$750,000
Average fixed assets	$795,000	$675,000
	[($750,000 + $840,000) ÷ 2]	[($600,000 + $750,000) ÷ 2]
Fixed asset turnover	3.6	3.0
	($2,862,000 ÷ $795,000)	($2,025,000 ÷ $675,000)

b. The increase in the fixed asset turnover ratio from 3.0 to 3.6 indicates a favorable trend in the efficiency of using fixed assets to generate sales.

Practice Exercises: **PE 10-9A, PE 10-9B**

A P P E N D I X

Exchanging Similar Fixed Assets

Old equipment is often traded in for new equipment having a similar use. In such cases, the seller allows the buyer an amount for the old equipment traded in. This amount, called the **trade-in allowance**, may be either greater or less than the book value of the old equipment. The remaining balance—the amount owed—is either paid in cash or recorded as a liability. It is normally called **boot**, which is its tax name.

Accounting for the exchange of similar assets depends on whether the transaction has *commercial substance*.[8] An exchange has commercial substance if future cash flows change as a result of the exchange. If an exchange of similar assets has commercial substance, a gain or loss is recognized based on the difference between the book value of the asset given up (exchanged) and the fair market value of the asset received. In such cases, the exchange is accounted for similar to that of a sale of a fixed asset.

Gain on Exchange

To illustrate a gain on an exchange of similar assets, assume the following:

Similar equipment acquired (new):

Price (fair market value) of new equipment	$5,000
Trade-in allowance on old equipment	1,100
Cash paid at June 19, date of exchange	$3,900

Equipment traded in (old):

Cost of old equipment	$4,000
Accumulated depreciation at date of exchange	3,200
Book value at June 19, date of exchange	$ 800

The entry to record this exchange and payment of cash is as follows:

Date	Account	Debit	Credit
June 19	Accumulated Depreciation—Equipment	3,200	
	Equipment (new equipment)	5,000	
	Equipment (old equipment)		4,000
	Cash		3,900
	Gain on Exchange of Equipment		300

The gain on the exchange, $300, is the difference between the fair market value of the new asset of $5,000 and the book value of the old asset traded in of $800 plus the cash paid of $3,900 as shown below.

Price (fair market value) of new equipment		$5,000
Less assets given up in exchange:		
Book value of old equipment ($4,000 – $3,200)	$ 800	
Cash paid on the exchange	3,900	4,700
Gain on exchange of assets		$ 300

Loss on Exchange

To illustrate a loss on an exchange of similar assets, assume that instead of a trade-in allowance of $1,100, a trade-in allowance of only $675 was allowed in the preceding example. In this case, the cash paid on the exchange is $4,325 as shown on the next page.

8 *FASB Accounting Standards Codification,* Section 360-10-30.

Price (fair market value) of new equipment	$5,000
Trade-in allowance of old equipment	675
Cash paid at June 19, date of exchange	$4,325

The entry to record this exchange and payment of cash is as follows:

June 19	Accumulated Depreciation—Equipment	3,200	
	Equipment (new equipment)	5,000	
	Loss on Exchange of Equipment	125	
	Equipment (old equipment)		4,000
	Cash		4,325

The loss on the exchange, $125, is the difference between the fair market value of the new asset ($5,000) and the book value of the old asset traded in ($800) plus the cash paid ($4,325), as shown below.

Price (fair market value) of new equipment		$5,000
Less assets given up in exchange:		
Book value of old equipment ($4,000 – $3,200)	$ 800	
Cash paid on the exchange	4,325	5,125
Loss on exchange of assets		$ (125)

In those cases where an asset exchange *lacks commercial substance*, no gain is recognized on the exchange. Instead, the cost of the new asset is adjusted for any gain. For example, in the first illustration, the gain of $300 would be subtracted from the purchase price of $5,000 and the new asset would be recorded at $4,700. Accounting for the exchange of assets that lack commercial substance is discussed in more advanced accounting texts.[9]

9 The exchange of similar assets also involves complex tax issues which are discussed in advanced accounting courses.

At a Glance 10

OBJ. 1

Define, classify, and account for the cost of fixed assets.

Key Points Fixed assets are long-term tangible assets used in the normal operations of the business such as equipment, buildings, and land. The initial cost of a fixed asset includes all amounts spent to get the asset in place and ready for use. Revenue expenditures include ordinary repairs and maintenance. Capital expenditures include asset improvements and extraordinary repairs.

Learning Outcomes	Example Exercises	Practice Exercises
• Define *fixed assets*.		
• List types of costs that should be included in the cost of a fixed asset.		
• Provide examples of ordinary repairs, asset improvements, and extraordinary repairs.		
• Prepare journal entries for ordinary repairs, asset improvements, and extraordinary repairs.	EE10-1	PE10-1A, 10-1B

OBJ. 2

Compute depreciation, using the following methods: straight-line method, units-of-production method, and double-declining-balance method.

Key Points All fixed assets except land should be depreciated over time. Three factors are considered in determining depreciation: (1) the fixed asset's initial cost, (2) the useful life of the asset, and (3) the residual value of the asset.

Depreciation may be determined using the straight-line, units-of-production, and double-declining-balance methods.

Depreciation may be revised into the future for changes in an asset's useful life or residual value.

Learning Outcomes	Example Exercises	Practice Exercises
• Define and describe *depreciation*.		
• List the factors used in determining depreciation.		
• Compute straight-line depreciation.	EE10-2	PE10-2A, 10-2B
• Compute units-of-production depreciation.	EE10-3	PE10-3A, 10-3B
• Compute double-declining-balance depreciation.	EE10-4	PE10-4A, 10-4B
• Compute revised depreciation for a change in an asset's useful life and residual value.	EE10-5	PE10-5A, 10-5B

OBJ. 3

Journalize entries for the disposal of fixed assets.

Key Points When discarding a fixed asset, any depreciation for the current period should be recorded, and the book value of the asset is then removed from the accounts.

When a fixed asset is sold, the book value is removed, and the cash or other asset received is recorded. If the selling price is more than the book value of the asset, the transaction results in a gain. If the selling price is less than the book value, there is a loss.

Learning Outcomes	Example Exercises	Practice Exercises
• Prepare the journal entry for discarding a fixed asset.		
• Prepare journal entries for the sale of a fixed asset.	EE10-6	PE10-6A, 10-6B

OBJ. 4

Compute depletion and journalize the entry for depletion.

Key Points The amount of periodic depletion is computed by multiplying the quantity of minerals extracted during the period by a depletion rate. The depletion rate is computed by dividing the cost of the mineral deposit by its estimated total units of resource. The entry to record depletion debits a depletion expense account and credits an accumulated depletion account.

Learning Outcomes	Example Exercises	Practice Exercises
• Define and describe *depletion*.		
• Compute a depletion rate.	EE10-7	PE10-7A, 10-7B
• Prepare the journal entry to record depletion.	EE10-7	PE10-7A, 10-7B

OBJ.
5 Describe the accounting for intangible assets, such as patents, copyrights, and goodwill.

Key Points Long-term assets such as patents, copyrights, trademarks, and goodwill are intangible assets. The cost of patents and copyrights should be amortized over the years of the asset's expected usefulness by debiting an expense account and crediting the intangible asset account. Trademarks and goodwill are not amortized, but are written down only upon impairment.

Learning Outcomes	Example Exercises	Practice Exercises
• Define, describe, and provide examples of intangible assets.		
• Prepare a journal entry for the purchase of an intangible asset.		
• Prepare a journal entry to amortize the costs of patents and copyrights.	EE10-8	PE10-8A, 10-8B
• Prepare the journal entry to record the impairment of goodwill.	EE10-8	PE10-8A, 10-8B

OBJ.
6 Describe how depreciation expense is reported in an income statement and prepare a balance sheet that includes fixed assets and intangible assets.

Key Points The amount of depreciation expense and depreciation methods should be disclosed in the financial statements. Each major class of fixed assets should be disclosed, along with the related accumulated depreciation. Intangible assets are usually presented in a separate section following fixed assets. Each major class of intangible assets should be disclosed net of the amortization recorded to date.

Learning Outcomes	Example Exercises	Practice Exercises
• Describe and illustrate how fixed assets are reported on the income statement and balance sheet.		
• Describe and illustrate how intangible assets are reported on the income statement and balance sheet.		

OBJ.
7 Describe and illustrate the fixed asset turnover ratio to assess the efficiency of a company's use of its fixed assets.

Key Points A measure of a company's efficiency in using its fixed assets to generate sales is the fixed asset turnover ratio. The fixed asset turnover ratio measures the number of dollars of sales earned per dollar of fixed assets and is computed by dividing net sales by the average book value of fixed assets.

Learning Outcomes	Example Exercises	Practice Exercises
• Describe a measure of the efficiency of a company's use of fixed assets to generate revenue.		
• Compute and interpret the fixed asset turnover ratio.	EE10-9	PE10-9A, 10-9B

Key Terms

accelerated depreciation
method (455)

amortization (462)

book value (455)

boot (468)

capital expenditures (449)

capital lease (450)

copyright (463)

depletion (461)

depreciation (451)

double-declining-balance
method (455)

fixed asset turnover ratio (466)

fixed assets (446)

goodwill (463)

intangible assets (462)

operating lease (451)

patents (462)

residual value (451)

revenue expenditures (449)

straight-line method (453)

trade-in allowance (468)

trademark (463)

units-of-production method (454)

Illustrative Problem

McCollum Company, a furniture wholesaler, acquired new equipment at a cost of $150,000 at the beginning of the fiscal year. The equipment has an estimated life of five years and an estimated residual value of $12,000. Ellen McCollum, the president, has requested information regarding alternative depreciation methods.

Instructions

1. Determine the annual depreciation for each of the five years of estimated useful life of the equipment, the accumulated depreciation at the end of each year, and the book value of the equipment at the end of each year by (a) the straight-line method and (b) the double-declining-balance method.

2. Assume that the equipment was depreciated under the double-declining-balance method. In the first week of the fifth year, the equipment was sold for $10,000. Journalize the entry to record the sale.

Solution

1.

	Year	Depreciation Expense	Accumulated Depreciation, End of Year	Book Value, End of Year
a.	1	$27,600*	$ 27,600	$122,400
	2	27,600	55,200	94,800
	3	27,600	82,800	67,200
	4	27,600	110,400	39,600
	5	27,600	138,000	12,000

*$27,600 = ($150,000 − $12,000) ÷ 5

	Year	Depreciation Expense	Accumulated Depreciation, End of Year	Book Value, End of Year
b.	1	$60,000**	$ 60,000	$ 90,000
	2	36,000	96,000	54,000
	3	21,600	117,600	32,400
	4	12,960	130,560	19,440
	5	7,440***	138,000	12,000

**$60,000 = $150,000 × 40%

***The asset is not depreciated below the estimated residual value of $12,000.
$7,440 = $150,000 − $130,560 − $12,000

2.

Cash			10,000	
Accumulated Depreciation—Equipment			130,560	
Loss on Sale of Equipment			9,440	
Equipment				150,000

Discussion Questions

1. Arentz Office Supplies has a fleet of automobiles and trucks for use by salespersons and for delivery of office supplies and equipment. Universal Auto Sales Co. has automobiles and trucks for sale. Under what caption would the automobiles and trucks be reported in the balance sheet of (a) Arentz Office Supplies and (b) Universal Auto Sales Co.?

2. Cleanway Co. acquired an adjacent vacant lot with the hope of selling it in the future at a gain. The lot is not intended to be used in Cleanway's business operations. Where should such real estate be listed in the balance sheet?

3. Airy Company solicited bids from several contractors to construct an addition to its office building. The lowest bid received was for $575,000. Airy Company decided to construct the addition itself at a cost of $435,000. What amount should be recorded in the building account?

4. Distinguish between the accounting for capital expenditures and revenue expenditures.

5. Immediately after a used truck is acquired, a new motor is installed at a total cost of $4,150. Is this a capital expenditure or a revenue expenditure?

6. Biggest Company purchased a machine that has a manufacturer's suggested life of 18 years. The company plans to use the machine on a special project that will last 10 years. At the completion of the project, the machine will be sold. Over how many years should the machine be depreciated?

7. Is it necessary for a business to use the same method of computing depreciation (a) for all classes of its depreciable assets and (b) for financial statement purposes and in determining income taxes?

8. a. Under what conditions is the use of an accelerated depreciation method most appropriate?
   b. Why is an accelerated depreciation method often used for income tax purposes?
   c. What is the Modified Accelerated Cost Recovery System (MACRS), and under what conditions is it used?

9. For some of the fixed assets of a business, the balance in Accumulated Depreciation is exactly equal to the cost of the asset. (a) Is it permissible to record additional depreciation on the assets if they are still useful to the business? Explain. (b) When should an entry be made to remove the cost and the accumulated depreciation from the accounts?

10. a. Over what period of time should the cost of a patent acquired by purchase be amortized?
    b. In general, what is the required accounting treatment for research and development costs?
    c. How should goodwill be amortized?

Practice Exercises

Learning Objectives	Example Exercises	
OBJ. 1	EE 10-1 p. 450	**PE 10-1A Capital and revenue expenditures**

On September 30, Madison River Inflatables Co. paid $1,425 to install a hydraulic lift and $35 for an air filter for one of its delivery trucks. Journalize the entries for the new lift and air filter expenditures.

OBJ. 1   EE 10-1 p. 450   **PE 10-1B   Capital and revenue expenditures**

On June 9, Martin Associates Co. paid $1,300 to repair the transmission on one of its delivery vans. In addition, Martin Associates paid $600 to install a GPS system in its van. Journalize the entries for the transmission and GPS system expenditures.

OBJ. 2   EE 10-2 p. 453   **PE 10-2A   Straight-line depreciation**

Equipment acquired at the beginning of the year at a cost of $275,000 has an estimated residual value of $30,000 and an estimated useful life of 10 years. Determine (a) the depreciable cost, (b) the straight-line rate, and (c) the annual straight-line depreciation.

OBJ. 2   EE 10-2 p. 453   **PE 10-2B   Straight-line depreciation**

A building acquired at the beginning of the year at a cost of $980,000 has an estimated residual value of $60,000 and an estimated useful life of 20 years. Determine (a) the depreciable cost, (b) the straight-line rate, and (c) the annual straight-line depreciation.

OBJ. 2   EE 10-3 p. 454   **PE 10-3A   Units-of-production depreciation**

A tractor acquired at a cost of $315,000 has an estimated residual value of $27,000, has an estimated useful life of 90,000 hours, and was operated 3,700 hours during the year. Determine (a) the depreciable cost, (b) the depreciation rate, and (c) the units-of-production depreciation for the year.

OBJ. 2   EE 10-3 p. 454   **PE 10-3B   Units-of-production depreciation**

A truck acquired at a cost of $150,000 has an estimated residual value of $40,000, has an estimated useful life of 400,000 miles, and was driven 80,000 miles during the year. Determine (a) the depreciable cost, (b) the depreciation rate, and (c) the units-of-production depreciation for the year.

OBJ. 2   EE 10-4 p. 456   **PE 10-4A   Double-declining-balance depreciation**

Equipment acquired at the beginning of the year at a cost of $190,000 has an estimated residual value of $30,000 and an estimated useful life of eight years. Determine (a) the double-declining-balance rate and (b) the double-declining-balance depreciation for the first year.

OBJ. 2   EE 10-4 p. 456   **PE 10-4B   Double-declining-balance depreciation**

A building acquired at the beginning of the year at a cost of $820,000 has an estimated residual value of $100,000 and an estimated useful life of 50 years. Determine (a) the double-declining-balance rate and (b) the double-declining-balance depreciation for the first year.

Learning Objectives	Example Exercises	
OBJ. 2	EE 10-5 *p. 459*	

PE 10-5A   Revision of depreciation

A truck with a cost of $94,000 has an estimated residual value of $20,500, has an estimated useful life of 15 years, and is depreciated by the straight-line method. (a) Determine the amount of the annual depreciation. (b) Determine the book value at the end of the seventh year of use. (c) Assuming that at the start of the eighth year the remaining life is estimated to be six years and the residual value is estimated to be $15,000, determine the depreciation expense for each of the remaining six years.

OBJ. 2   EE 10-5 *p. 459*   **PE 10-5B   Revision of depreciation**

Equipment with a cost of $300,000 has an estimated residual value of $42,000, has an estimated useful life of 24 years, and is depreciated by the straight-line method. (a) Determine the amount of the annual depreciation. (b) Determine the book value at the end of the fourteenth year of use. (c) Assuming that at the start of the fifteenth year the remaining life is estimated to be five years and the residual value is estimated to be $20,000, determine the depreciation expense for each of the remaining five years.

OBJ. 3   EE 10-6 *p. 461*   **PE 10-6A   Sale of equipment**

Equipment was acquired at the beginning of the year at a cost of $215,000. The equipment was depreciated using the straight-line method based on an estimated useful life of 18 years and an estimated residual value of $39,500.

a.   What was the depreciation for the first year?

b.   Assuming the equipment was sold at the end of the eighth year for $128,000, determine the gain or loss on the sale of the equipment.

c.   Journalize the entry to record the sale.

OBJ. 3   EE 10-6 *p. 461*   **PE 10-6B   Sale of equipment**

Equipment was acquired at the beginning of the year at a cost of $450,000. The equipment was depreciated using the double-declining-balance method based on an estimated useful life of 10 years and an estimated residual value of $60,000.

a.   What was the depreciation for the first year?

b.   Assuming the equipment was sold at the end of the second year for $319,500, determine the gain or loss on the sale of the equipment.

c.   Journalize the entry to record the sale.

OBJ. 4   EE 10-7 *p. 462*   **PE 10-7A   Depletion**

Big Horn Mining Co. acquired mineral rights for $90,000,000. The mineral deposit is estimated at 250,000,000 tons. During the current year, 30,000,000 tons were mined and sold.

a.   Determine the depletion rate.

b.   Determine the amount of depletion expense for the current year.

c.   Journalize the adjusting entry on December 31 to recognize the depletion expense.

OBJ. 4   EE 10-7 *p. 462*   **PE 10-7B   Depletion**

Silver Tip Mining Co. acquired mineral rights for $300,000,000. The mineral deposit is estimated at 400,000,000 tons. During the current year, 84,000,000 tons were mined and sold.

a.   Determine the depletion rate.

b.   Determine the amount of depletion expense for the current year.

c.   Journalize the adjusting entry on December 31 to recognize the depletion expense.

Learning Objectives	*Example Exercises*

OBJ. 5   EE 10-8 p. 465

PE 10-8A   Impaired goodwill and amortization of patent

On December 31, it was estimated that goodwill of $750,000 was impaired. In addition, a patent with an estimated useful economic life of 18 years was acquired for $864,000 on August 1.

a. Journalize the adjusting entry on December 31 for the impaired goodwill.

b. Journalize the adjusting entry on December 31 for the amortization of the patent rights.

OBJ. 5   EE 10-8 p. 465

PE 10-8B   Impaired goodwill and amortization of patent

On December 31, it was estimated that goodwill of $1,200,000 was impaired. In addition, a patent with an estimated useful economic life of 12 years was acquired for $288,000 on April 1.

a. Journalize the adjusting entry on December 31 for the impaired goodwill.

b. Journalize the adjusting entry on December 31 for the amortization of the patent rights.

OBJ. 7   EE 10-9 p. 467

PE 10-9A   Fixed asset turnover ratio

Financial statement data for years ending December 31 for Winnett Company are shown below.

	2012	2011
Net sales	$3,572,000	$3,526,000
Fixed assets:		
Beginning of year	900,000	820,000
End of year	980,000	900,000

a. Determine the fixed asset turnover ratio for 2012 and 2011.

b. Does the change in the fixed asset turnover ratio from 2011 to 2012 indicate a favorable or an unfavorable trend?

OBJ. 7   EE 10-9 p. 467

PE 10-9B   Fixed asset turnover ratio

Financial statement data for years ending December 31 for Fallon Company are shown below.

	2012	2011
Net sales	$740,000	$520,000
Fixed assets:		
Beginning of year	425,000	375,000
End of year	500,000	425,000

a. Determine the fixed asset turnover ratio for 2012 and 2011.

b. Does the change in the fixed asset turnover ratio from 2011 to 2012 indicate a favorable or an unfavorable trend?

Exercises

OBJ. 1

EX 10-1   Costs of acquiring fixed assets

Les Bancroft owns and operates Crown Print Co. During January, Crown Print Co. incurred the following costs in acquiring two printing presses. One printing press was new, and the other was used by a business that recently filed for bankruptcy.

Costs related to new printing press:

1. Sales tax on purchase price

2. Insurance while in transit

3. Freight

4. Special foundation

5. Fee paid to factory representative for installation

6. New parts to replace those damaged in unloading

Costs related to used printing press:

7. Fees paid to attorney to review purchase agreement

8. Freight

9. Installation

10. Replacement of worn-out parts

11. Repair of damage incurred in reconditioning the press

12. Repair of vandalism during installation

a. Indicate which costs incurred in acquiring the new printing press should be debited to the asset account.

b. Indicate which costs incurred in acquiring the used printing press should be debited to the asset account.

OBJ. 1

EX 10-2   Determine cost of land

Alpine Ski Co. has developed a tract of land into a ski resort. The company has cut the trees, cleared and graded the land and hills, and constructed ski lifts. (a) Should the tree cutting, land clearing, and grading costs of constructing the ski slopes be debited to the land account? (b) If such costs are debited to Land, should they be depreciated?

OBJ. 1

✔ $346,600

EX 10-3   Determine cost of land

Discount Delivery Company acquired an adjacent lot to construct a new warehouse, paying $25,000 and giving a short-term note for $300,000. Legal fees paid were $2,100, delinquent taxes assumed were $14,000, and fees paid to remove an old building from the land were $9,000. Materials salvaged from the demolition of the building were sold for $3,500. A contractor was paid $800,000 to construct a new warehouse. Determine the cost of the land to be reported on the balance sheet.

OBJ. 1

EX 10-4   Capital and revenue expenditures

Emerald Lines Co. incurred the following costs related to trucks and vans used in operating its delivery service:

1. Installed security systems on four of the newer trucks.

2. Rebuilt the transmission on one of the vans that had been driven 40,000 miles. The van was no longer under warranty.

3. Installed a hydraulic lift to a van.

4. Replaced a truck's suspension system with a new suspension system that allows for the delivery of heavier loads.

5. Removed a two-way radio from one of the trucks and installed a new radio with a greater range of communication.

6. Repaired a flat tire on one of the vans.

7. Changed the radiator fluid on a truck that had been in service for the past four years.

8. Tinted the back and side windows of one of the vans to discourage theft of contents.

9. Changed the oil and greased the joints of all the trucks and vans.

10. Overhauled the engine on one of the trucks purchased three years ago.

Classify each of the costs as a capital expenditure or a revenue expenditure.

OBJ. 1

EX 10-5 Capital and revenue expenditures

Aubrey Seagars owns and operates Diamond Transport Co. During the past year, Aubrey incurred the following costs related to an 18-wheel truck:

1. Installed a television in the sleeping compartment of the truck.
2. Replaced the old radar detector with a newer model that is fastened to the truck with a locking device that prevents its removal.
3. Installed a wind deflector on top of the cab to increase fuel mileage.
4. Modified the factory-installed turbo charger with a special-order kit designed to add 50 more horsepower to the engine performance.
5. Replaced a headlight that had burned out.
6. Replaced the hydraulic brake system that had begun to fail during his latest trip through the Rocky Mountains.
7. Changed engine oil.
8. Replaced a shock absorber that had worn out.
9. Replaced fog and cab light bulbs.
10. Removed the old CB radio and replaced it with a newer model with a greater range.

Classify each of the costs as a capital expenditure or a revenue expenditure.

OBJ. 1

EX 10-6 Capital and revenue expenditures

Reliable Move Company made the following expenditures on one of its delivery trucks:

Feb. 4. Replaced transmission at a cost of $4,300.

May 6. Paid $1,900 for installation of a hydraulic lift.

Sept. 10. Paid $60 to change the oil and air filter.

Prepare journal entries for each expenditure.

OBJ. 2

EX 10-7 Nature of depreciation

Butte Ironworks Co. reported $7,500,000 for equipment and $6,175,000 for accumulated depreciation—equipment on its balance sheet.

Does this mean (a) that the replacement cost of the equipment is $7,500,000 and (b) that $6,175,000 is set aside in a special fund for the replacement of the equipment? Explain.

OBJ. 2
✔ c. 10%

EX 10-8 Straight-line depreciation rates

Convert each of the following estimates of useful life to a straight-line depreciation rate, stated as a percentage: (a) 4 years, (b) 8 years, (c) 10 years, (d) 16 years, (e) 25 years, (f) 40 years, (g) 50 years.

OBJ. 2
✔ $6,625

EX 10-9 Straight-line depreciation

A refrigerator used by a meat processor has a cost of $120,000, an estimated residual value of $14,000, and an estimated useful life of 16 years. What is the amount of the annual depreciation computed by the straight-line method?

OBJ. 2
✔ $518

EX 10-10 Depreciation by units-of-production method

A diesel-powered tractor with a cost of $185,000 and estimated residual value of $37,000 is expected to have a useful operating life of 40,000 hours. During February, the generator was operated 140 hours. Determine the depreciation for the month.

OBJ. 2

✔ a. Truck #1,
credit Accumulated
Depreciation, $5,850

EX 10-11   Depreciation by units-of-production method

Prior to adjustment at the end of the year, the balance in Trucks is $275,900 and the balance in Accumulated Depreciation—Trucks is $91,350. Details of the subsidiary ledger are as follows:

Truck No.	Cost	Estimated Residual Value	Estimated Useful Life	Accumulated Depreciation at Beginning of Year	Miles Operated During Year
1	$75,000	$15,000	200,000 miles	—	19,500 miles
2	38,000	3,000	200,000	$ 8,050	36,000
3	72,900	9,900	300,000	60,900	25,000
4	90,000	20,000	250,000	22,400	26,000

a. Determine the depreciation rates per mile and the amount to be credited to the accumulated depreciation section of each of the subsidiary accounts for the miles operated during the current year.

b. Journalize the entry to record depreciation for the year.

OBJ. 2

✔ a. $3,200

EX 10-12   Depreciation by two methods

A Kubota tractor acquired on January 9 at a cost of $80,000 has an estimated useful life of 25 years. Assuming that it will have no residual value, determine the depreciation for each of the first two years (a) by the straight-line method and (b) by the double-declining-balance method.

OBJ. 2

✔ a. $18,375

EX 10-13   Depreciation by two methods

A storage tank acquired at the beginning of the fiscal year at a cost of $344,000 has an estimated residual value of $50,000 and an estimated useful life of 16 years. Determine the following: (a) the amount of annual depreciation by the straight-line method and (b) the amount of depreciation for the first and second years computed by the double-declining-balance method.

OBJ. 2

✔ a. First year,
$5,625

EX 10-14   Partial-year depreciation

Sandblasting equipment acquired at a cost of $64,000 has an estimated residual value of $4,000 and an estimated useful life of eight years. It was placed in service on April 1 of the current fiscal year, which ends on December 31. Determine the depreciation for the current fiscal year and for the following fiscal year by (a) the straight-line method and (b) the double-declining-balance method.

OBJ. 2

✔ a. $16,250

EX 10-15   Revision of depreciation

A building with a cost of $900,000 has an estimated residual value of $250,000, has an estimated useful life of 40 years, and is depreciated by the straight-line method. (a) What is the amount of the annual depreciation? (b) What is the book value at the end of the twenty-fourth year of use? (c) If at the start of the twenty-fifth year it is estimated that the remaining life is nine years and that the residual value is $240,000, what is the depreciation expense for each of the remaining nine years?

OBJ. 1, 2

✔ b. Depreciation
Expense, $625

EX 10-16   Capital expenditure and depreciation

Viking Company purchased and installed carpet in its new general offices on June 30 for a total cost of $15,000. The carpet is estimated to have a 12-year useful life and no residual value.

a. Prepare the journal entries necessary for recording the purchase of the new carpet.

b. Record the December 31 adjusting entry for the partial-year depreciation expense for the carpet, assuming that Viking Company uses the straight-line method.

OBJ. 3

EX 10-17 Entries for sale of fixed asset

Equipment acquired on January 5, 2009, at a cost of $380,000, has an estimated useful life of 16 years, has an estimated residual value of $40,000, and is depreciated by the straight-line method.

a. What was the book value of the equipment at December 31, 2012, the end of the year?

b. Assuming that the equipment was sold on July 1, 2013, for $270,000, journalize the entries to record (1) depreciation for the six months until the sale date, and (2) the sale of the equipment.

OBJ. 3

✔ b. $305,000

EX 10-18 Disposal of fixed asset

Equipment acquired on January 4, 2009, at a cost of $425,000, has an estimated useful life of nine years and an estimated residual value of $65,000.

a. What was the annual amount of depreciation for the years 2009, 2010, and 2011, using the straight-line method of depreciation?

b. What was the book value of the equipment on January 1, 2012?

c. Assuming that the equipment was sold on January 9, 2012, for $290,000, journalize the entry to record the sale.

d. Assuming that the equipment had been sold on January 9, 2012, for $310,000 instead of $290,000, journalize the entry to record the sale.

OBJ. 4

✔ a. $3,000,000

EX 10-19 Depletion entries

Ashwood Mining Co. acquired mineral rights for $15,000,000. The mineral deposit is estimated at 120,000,000 tons. During the current year, 24,000,000 tons were mined and sold.

a. Determine the amount of depletion expense for the current year.

b. Journalize the adjusting entry to recognize the depletion expense.

OBJ. 5

✔ a. $33,000

EX 10-20 Amortization entries

Greenleaf Company acquired patent rights on January 6, 2009, for $300,000. The patent has a useful life equal to its legal life of 12 years. On January 3, 2012, Greenleaf successfully defended the patent in a lawsuit at a cost of $72,000.

a. Determine the patent amortization expense for the current year ended December 31, 2012.

b. Journalize the adjusting entry to recognize the amortization.

OBJ. 6

EX 10-21 Book value of fixed assets

Apple Computer, Inc., designs, manufactures, and markets personal computers and related software. Apple also manufactures and distributes music players (iPod) and mobile phones (iPhone) along with related accessories and services including online distribution of third-party music, videos, and applications. The following information was taken from a recent annual report of Apple:

Property, Plant, and Equipment (in millions):

	Current Year	Preceding Year
Land and buildings	$ 955	$ 810
Machinery, equipment, and internal-use software	1,932	1,491
Office furniture and equipment	115	122
Other fixed assets related to leases	1,665	1,324
Accumulated depreciation and amortization	1,713	1,292

a. Compute the book value of the fixed assets for the current year and the preceding year and explain the differences, if any.

b. ━━━▶ Would you normally expect the book value of fixed assets to increase or decrease during the year?

OBJ. 6

EX 10-22 Balance sheet presentation

List the errors you find in the following partial balance sheet:

Contours Company
Balance Sheet
December 31, 2012

Assets

Total current assets.. $350,000

Property, plant, and equipment:	Replacement Cost	Accumulated Depreciation	Book Value	
Land..	$100,000	$ 25,000	$ 75,000	
Buildings..................................	256,000	90,000	166,000	
Factory equipment	297,000	110,000	187,000	
Office equipment........................	72,000	48,000	24,000	
Patents	48,000	—	48,000	
Goodwill..................................	27,000	7,000	20,000	
Total property, plant, and equipment........	$800,000	$280,000		$520,000

OBJ. 7

EX 10-23 Fixed asset turnover ratio

Verizon Communications is a major telecommunications company in the United States. Verizon's balance sheet disclosed the following information regarding fixed assets:

	Dec. 31, 2009 (in millions)	Dec. 31, 2008 (in millions)
Plant, property, and equipment	$228,518	$215,605
Less accumulated depreciation	137,052	129,059
	$ 91,466	$ 86,546

Verizon's revenue for 2009 was $107,808 million. The fixed asset turnover for the telecommunications industry averages 1.10.

a. Determine Verizon's fixed asset turnover ratio. Round to two decimal places.

b. ━━━▶ Interpret Verizon's fixed asset turnover ratio.

OBJ. 7

EX 10-24 Fixed asset turnover ratio

The following table shows the revenue and average net fixed assets (in millions) for a recent fiscal year for Best Buy and RadioShack:

	Revenue	Average Net Fixed Assets
Best Buy	$45,015	$3,740
RadioShack	4,225	312

a. Compute the fixed asset turnover for each company. Round to two decimal places.

b. Which company uses its fixed assets more efficiently? Explain.

✔ a. $225,000

Appendix
EX 10-25 Asset traded for similar asset

A printing press priced at a fair market value of $400,000 is acquired in a transaction that has commercial substance by trading in a similar press and paying cash for the difference between the trade-in allowance and the price of the new press.

a. Assuming that the trade-in allowance is $175,000, what is the amount of cash given?

b. Assuming that the book value of the press traded in is $160,000, what is the gain or loss on the exchange?

✔ b. $10,000 loss

Appendix
EX 10-26   Asset traded for similar asset

Assume the same facts as in Exercise 10-25, except that the book value of the press traded in is $185,000. (a) What is the amount of cash given? (b) What is the gain or loss on the exchange?

Appendix
EX 10-27   Entries for trade of fixed asset

On April 1, Clear Water Co., a water distiller, acquired new bottling equipment with a list price (fair market value) of $350,000. Clear Water received a trade-in allowance of $50,000 on the old equipment of a similar type and paid cash of $300,000. The following information about the old equipment is obtained from the account in the equipment ledger: cost, $280,000; accumulated depreciation on December 31, the end of the preceding fiscal year, $216,000; annual depreciation, $18,000. Assuming the exchange has commercial substance, journalize the entries to record (a) the current depreciation of the old equipment to the date of trade-in and (b) the exchange transaction on April 1.

Appendix
EX 10-28   Entries for trade of fixed asset

On July 1, Potts Delivery Services acquired a new truck with a list price (fair market value) of $80,000. Potts received a trade-in allowance of $15,000 on an old truck of similar type and paid cash of $65,000. The following information about the old truck is obtained from the account in the equipment ledger: cost, $60,000; accumulated depreciation on December 31, the end of the preceding fiscal year, $42,000; annual depreciation, $7,500. Assuming the exchange has commercial substance, journalize the entries to record (a) the current depreciation of the old truck to the date of trade-in and (b) the transaction on July 1.

Problems Series A

OBJ. 1

✔ Land, $402,500

PR 10-1A   Allocate payments and receipts to fixed asset accounts

The following payments and receipts are related to land, land improvements, and buildings acquired for use in a wholesale ceramic business. The receipts are identified by an asterisk.

a.	Fee paid to attorney for title search	$ 3,000
b.	Cost of real estate acquired as a plant site: Land	320,000
	Building	30,000
c.	Special assessment paid to city for extension of water main to the property	18,000
d.	Cost of razing and removing building	5,000
e.	Proceeds from sale of salvage materials from old building	3,000*
f.	Delinquent real estate taxes on property, assumed by purchaser	12,000
g.	Premium on one-year insurance policy during construction	4,200
h.	Cost of filling and grading land	17,500
i.	Architect's and engineer's fees for plans and supervision	44,000
j.	Money borrowed to pay building contractor	750,000*
k.	Cost of repairing windstorm damage during construction	5,500
l.	Cost of paving parking lot to be used by customers	15,000
m.	Cost of trees and shrubbery planted	9,000
n.	Cost of floodlights installed on parking lot	1,000
o.	Cost of repairing vandalism damage during construction	2,500
p.	Proceeds from insurance company for windstorm and vandalism damage	6,000*
q.	Payment to building contractor for new building	800,000
r.	Interest incurred on building loan during construction	37,500
s.	Refund of premium on insurance policy (g) canceled after 11 months	350*

Instructions

1. Assign each payment and receipt to Land (unlimited life), Land Improvements (limited life), Building, or Other Accounts. Indicate receipts by an asterisk. Identify each item by letter and list the amounts in columnar form, as follows:

Item	Land	Land Improvements	Building	Other Accounts

2. Determine the amount debited to Land, Land Improvements, and Building.

3. ➡ The costs assigned to the land, which is used as a plant site, will not be depreciated, while the costs assigned to land improvements will be depreciated. Explain this seemingly contradictory application of the concept of depreciation.

4. What would be the effect on the income statement and balance sheet if the cost of filling and grading land of $17,500 [payment (h)] was incorrectly classified as Land Improvements rather than Land? Assume Land Improvements are depreciated over a 20-year life using the double-declining-balance method.

OBJ. 2

✔ a. 2010: straight-line depreciation, $31,250

PR 10-2A   Compare three depreciation methods

Breyer Company purchased packaging equipment on January 3, 2010, for $101,250. The equipment was expected to have a useful life of three years, or 25,000 operating hours, and a residual value of $7,500. The equipment was used for 9,500 hours during 2010, 8,400 hours in 2011, and 7,100 hours in 2012.

Instructions

1. Determine the amount of depreciation expense for the years ended December 31, 2010, 2011, and 2012, by (a) the straight-line method, (b) the units-of-production method, and (c) the double-declining-balance method. Also determine the total depreciation expense for the three years by each method. The following columnar headings are suggested for recording the depreciation expense amounts:

	Depreciation Expense		
Year	Straight-Line Method	Units-of-Production Method	Double-Declining-Balance Method

2. What method yields the highest depreciation expense for 2010?

3. What method yields the most depreciation over the three–year life of the equipment?

OBJ. 2

✔ a. 2010: $21,500

PR 10-3A   Depreciation by three methods; partial years

Security IDs Company purchased equipment on July 1, 2010, for $135,000. The equipment was expected to have a useful life of three years, or 12,000 operating hours, and a residual value of $6,000. The equipment was used for 1,500 hours during 2010, 3,500 hours in 2011, 5,000 hours in 2012, and 2,000 hours in 2013.

Instructions

Determine the amount of depreciation expense for the years ended December 31, 2010, 2011, 2012, and 2013, by (a) the straight-line method, (b) the units-of-production method, and (c) the double-declining-balance method. Round to the nearest dollar.

OBJ. 2, 3

✔ b. Year 1: $315,000 depreciation expense

PR 10-4A   Depreciation by two methods; sale of fixed asset

New lithographic equipment, acquired at a cost of $787,500 at the beginning of a fiscal year, has an estimated useful life of five years and an estimated residual value of $67,500. The manager requested information regarding the effect of alternative methods on the amount of depreciation expense each year. On the basis of the data presented to the manager, the double-declining-balance method was selected.

In the first week of the fifth year, the equipment was sold for $115,000.

Instructions

1. Determine the annual depreciation expense for each of the estimated five years of use, the accumulated depreciation at the end of each year, and the book value of the equipment at the end of each year by (a) the straight-line method and (b) the

(*Continued*)

double-declining-balance method. The following columnar headings are suggested for each schedule:

Year	Depreciation Expense	Accumulated Depreciation, End of Year	Book Value, End of Year

2. Journalize the entry to record the sale.

3. Journalize the entry to record the sale, assuming that the equipment was sold for $98,900 instead of $115,000.

OBJ. 1, 2, 3

PR 10-5A   Transactions for fixed assets, including sale

The following transactions, adjusting entries, and closing entries were completed by D. Hurd Furniture Co. during a three-year period. All are related to the use of delivery equipment. The double-declining-balance method of depreciation is used.

2010

Jan. 9. Purchased a used delivery truck for $30,000, paying cash.

Mar. 17. Paid garage $400 for miscellaneous repairs to the truck.

Dec. 31. Recorded depreciation on the truck for the year. The estimated useful life of the truck is four years, with a residual value of $6,000 for the truck.

2011

Jan. 2. Purchased a new truck for $48,000, paying cash.

Aug 1. Sold the used truck for $12,500. (Record depreciation to date in 2011 for the truck.)

Sept. 23. Paid garage $325 for miscellaneous repairs to the truck.

Dec. 31. Record depreciation for the new truck. It has an estimated residual value of $11,000 and an estimated life of five years.

2012

July 1. Purchased a new truck for $52,000, paying cash.

Oct. 2. Sold the truck purchased January 2, 2011, for $17,000. (Record depreciation for the year.)

Dec. 31. Recorded depreciation on the remaining truck. It has an estimated residual value of $14,000 and an estimated useful life of eight years.

Instructions

Journalize the transactions and the adjusting entries.

OBJ. 4, 5

✔ 1. a. $360,000

PR 10-6A   Amortization and depletion entries

Data related to the acquisition of timber rights and intangible assets during the current year ended December 31 are as follows:

a. Timber rights on a tract of land were purchased for $864,000 on July 10. The stand of timber is estimated at 3,600,000 board feet. During the current year, 1,500,000 board feet of timber were cut and sold.

b. On December 31, the company determined that $4,000,000 of goodwill was impaired.

c. Governmental and legal costs of $1,170,000 were incurred on April 10 in obtaining a patent with an estimated economic life of 12 years. Amortization is to be for three-fourths of a year.

Instructions

1. Determine the amount of the amortization, depletion, or impairment for the current year for each of the foregoing items.

2. Journalize the adjusting entries required to record the amortization, depletion, or impairment for each item.

Problems Series B

OBJ. 1

✔ Land, $597,500

PR 10-1B Allocate payments and receipts to fixed asset accounts

The following payments and receipts are related to land, land improvements, and buildings acquired for use in a wholesale apparel business. The receipts are identified by an asterisk.

a.	Finder's fee paid to real estate agency	$ 5,000
b.	Cost of real estate acquired as a plant site: Land	500,000
	Building	40,000
c.	Fee paid to attorney for title search	2,500
d.	Delinquent real estate taxes on property, assumed by purchaser	15,000
e.	Architect's and engineer's fees for plans and supervision	36,000
f.	Cost of removing building purchased with land in (b)	10,000
g.	Proceeds from sale of salvage materials from old building	4,000*
h.	Cost of filling and grading land	20,000
i.	Premium on one-year insurance policy during construction	6,000
j.	Money borrowed to pay building contractor	750,000*
k.	Special assessment paid to city for extension of water main to the property	9,000
l.	Cost of repairing windstorm damage during construction	3,000
m.	Cost of repairing vandalism damage during construction	2,000
n.	Cost of trees and shrubbery planted	12,000
o.	Cost of paving parking lot to be used by customers	14,500
p.	Interest incurred on building loan during construction	45,000
q.	Proceeds from insurance company for windstorm and vandalism damage	3,000*
r.	Payment to building contractor for new building	800,000
s.	Refund of premium on insurance policy (i) canceled after 10 months	1,000*

Instructions

1. Assign each payment and receipt to Land (unlimited life), Land Improvements (limited life), Building, or Other Accounts. Indicate receipts by an asterisk. Identify each item by letter and list the amounts in columnar form, as follows:

Item	Land	Land Improvements	Building	Other Accounts

2. Determine the amount debited to Land, Land Improvements, and Building.

3. ━━━━ The costs assigned to the land, which is used as a plant site, will not be depreciated, while the costs assigned to land improvements will be depreciated. Explain this seemingly contradictory application of the concept of depreciation.

4. What would be the effect on the income statement and balance sheet if the cost of paving the parking lot of $14,500 [payment (o)] was incorrectly classified as Land rather than Land Improvements? Assume Land Improvements are depreciated over a 10-year life using the double-declining-balance method.

OBJ. 2

✔ a. 2011: straight-line depreciation, $100,000

PR 10-2B Compare three depreciation methods

Plum Coatings Company purchased waterproofing equipment on January 2, 2011, for $450,000. The equipment was expected to have a useful life of four years, or 10,000 operating hours, and a residual value of $50,000. The equipment was used for 3,000 hours during 2011, 4,000 hours in 2012, 2,500 hours in 2013, and 500 hours in 2014.

Instructions

1. Determine the amount of depreciation expense for the years ended December 31, 2011, 2012, 2013, and 2014, by (a) the straight-line method, (b) the units-of-production method, and (c) the double-declining-balance method. Also determine the total depreciation expense for the four years by each method. The following columnar headings are suggested for recording the depreciation expense amounts:

	Depreciation Expense		
Year	Straight-Line Method	Units-of-Production Method	Double-Declining-Balance Method

(Continued)

2. What method yields the highest depreciation expense for 2011?

3. What method yields the most depreciation over the four-year life of the equipment?

PR 10-3B **Depreciation by three methods; partial years**

Helix Company purchased tool sharpening equipment on April 1, 2010, for $72,000. The equipment was expected to have a useful life of three years, or 9,000 operating hours, and a residual value of $2,700. The equipment was used for 2,400 hours during 2010, 4,000 hours in 2011, 2,000 hours in 2012, and 600 hours in 2013.

Instructions

Determine the amount of depreciation expense for the years ended December 31, 2010, 2011, 2012, and 2013, by (a) the straight-line method, (b) the units-of-production method, and (c) the double-declining-balance method.

PR 10-4B **Depreciation by two methods; sale of fixed asset**

New tire retreading equipment, acquired at a cost of $72,000 at the beginning of a fiscal year, has an estimated useful life of four years and an estimated residual value of $5,400. The manager requested information regarding the effect of alternative methods on the amount of depreciation expense each year. On the basis of the data presented to the manager, the double-declining-balance method was selected.

In the first week of the fourth year, the equipment was sold for $13,750.

Instructions

1. Determine the annual depreciation expense for each of the estimated four years of use, the accumulated depreciation at the end of each year, and the book value of the equipment at the end of each year by (a) the straight-line method and (b) the double-declining-balance method. The following columnar headings are suggested for each schedule:

Year	Depreciation Expense	Accumulated Depreciation, End of Year	Book Value, End of Year

2. Journalize the entry to record the sale.

3. Journalize the entry to record the sale, assuming that the equipment sold for $3,700 instead of $13,750.

PR 10-5B **Transactions for fixed assets, including sale**

The following transactions, adjusting entries, and closing entries were completed by McHenry Furniture Co. during a three-year period. All are related to the use of delivery equipment. The double-declining-balance method of depreciation is used.

2010

Jan. 4. Purchased a used delivery truck for $54,000, paying cash.

Feb. 24. Paid garage $275 for changing the oil, replacing the oil filter, and tuning the engine on the delivery truck.

Dec. 31. Recorded depreciation on the truck for the fiscal year. The estimated useful life of the truck is eight years, with a residual value of $12,000 for the truck.

2011

Jan. 3. Purchased a new truck for $60,000, paying cash.

Mar. 7. Paid garage $300 to tune the engine and make other minor repairs on the used truck.

Apr. 30 Sold the used truck for $35,000. (Record depreciation to date in 2011 for the truck.)

Dec. 31. Record depreciation for the new truck. It has an estimated residual value of $16,000 and an estimated life of 10 years.

2012

July   1.   Purchased a new truck for $64,000, paying cash.

Oct.   7.   Sold the truck purchased January 3, 2011, for $45,000. (Record depreciation for the year.)

Dec. 31.   Recorded depreciation on the remaining truck. It has an estimated residual value of $17,500 and an estimated useful life of 10 years.

Instructions
Journalize the transactions and the adjusting entries.

OBJ. 4, 5

✔ b. $45,000

PR 10-6B   Amortization and depletion entries

Data related to the acquisition of timber rights and intangible assets during the current year ended December 31 are as follows:

a.   On December 31, the company determined that $1,800,000 of goodwill was impaired.

b.   Governmental and legal costs of $900,000 were incurred on June 30 in obtaining a patent with an estimated economic life of 10 years. Amortization is to be for one-half year.

c.   Timber rights on a tract of land were purchased for $1,560,000 on February 4. The stand of timber is estimated at 12,000,000 board feet. During the current year, 3,200,000 board feet of timber were cut and sold.

Instructions

1.   Determine the amount of the amortization, depletion, or impairment for the current year for each of the foregoing items.

2.   Journalize the adjusting entries to record the amortization, depletion, or impairment for each item.

Cases & Projects

CP 10-1   Ethics and professional conduct in business

Rosa Salinas, CPA, is an assistant to the controller of Zebra Consulting Co. In her spare time, Rosa also prepares tax returns and performs general accounting services for clients. Frequently, Rosa performs these services after her normal working hours, using Zebra Consulting Co.'s computers and laser printers. Occasionally, Rosa's clients will call her at the office during regular working hours.

⟶ Discuss whether Rosa is performing in a professional manner.

CP 10-2   Financial vs. tax depreciation

The following is an excerpt from a conversation between two employees of Omni Technologies, Jay Bach and Cora Hardaway. Jay is the accounts payable clerk, and Cora is the cashier.

Jay: Cora, could I get your opinion on something?

Cora: Sure, Jay.

Jay: Do you know Jo, the fixed assets clerk?

Cora: I know who she is, but I don't know her real well. Why?

Jay: Well, I was talking to her at lunch last Monday about how she liked her job, etc. You know, the usual . . . and she mentioned something about having to keep two sets of books . . . one for taxes and one for the financial statements. That can't be good accounting, can it? What do you think?

Cora: Two sets of books? It doesn't sound right.

Jay: It doesn't seem right to me either. I was always taught that you had to use generally accepted accounting principles. How can there be two sets of books? What can be the difference between the two?

⟶ How would you respond to Jay and Cora if you were Jo?

CP 10-3   Effect of depreciation on net income

Atlas Construction Co. specializes in building replicas of historic houses. Paul Raines, president of Atlas Construction, is considering the purchase of various items of equipment on July 1, 2010, for $500,000. The equipment would have a useful life of five years and no residual value. In the past, all equipment has been leased. For tax purposes, Paul is considering depreciating the equipment by the straight-line method. He discussed the matter with his CPA and learned that, although the straight-line method could be elected, it was to his advantage to use the Modified Accelerated Cost Recovery System (MACRS) for tax purposes. He asked for your advice as to which method to use for tax purposes.

1. Compute depreciation for each of the years (2010, 2011, 2012, 2013, 2014, and 2015) of useful life by (a) the straight-line method and (b) MACRS. In using the straight-line method, one-half year's depreciation should be computed for 2010 and 2015. Use the MACRS rates presented on page 457.

2. Assuming that income before depreciation and income tax is estimated to be $900,000 uniformly per year and that the income tax rate is 40%, compute the net income for each of the years 2010, 2011, 2012, 2013, 2014, and 2015 if (a) the straight-line method is used and (b) MACRS is used.

3. ➡ What factors would you present for Paul's consideration in the selection of a depreciation method?

CP 10-4   Applying for patents, copyrights, and trademarks

Group Project

Go to the Internet and review the procedures for applying for a patent, a copyright, and a trademark. You may find information available on Wikipedia (Wikipedia.org) useful for this purpose. Prepare a brief written summary of these procedures.

CP 10-5   Fixed asset turnover: three industries

The following table shows the revenues and average net fixed assets for a recent fiscal year for three different companies from three different industries: retailing, manufacturing, and communications.

	Revenues (in millions)	Average Net Fixed Assets (in millions)
Wal-Mart	$405,607	$96,335
Occidental Petroleum Corporation	15,403	32,856
Comcast Corporation	34,256	24,034

a. For each company, determine the fixed asset turnover ratio. Round to two decimal places.

b. Explain Wal-Mart's ratio relative to the other two companies.

Current Liabilities and Payroll

Panera Bread

B uying goods on credit is probably as old as business itself. In fact, the ancient Babylonians were lending money to support trade as early as 1300 B.C. The use of credit makes transactions more convenient and improves buying power. For *individuals*, the most common form of short-term credit is a credit card. Credit cards allow individuals to purchase items before they are paid for, while removing the need for individuals to carry large amounts of cash. They also provide documentation of purchases through a monthly credit card statement.

Short-term credit is also used by *businesses* to make purchasing items for manufacture or resale more convenient. Short-term credit also gives a business control over the payment for goods and services. For example, **Panera Bread**, a chain of bakery-cafés located throughout the United States, uses short-term trade credit, or accounts payable, to purchase ingredients for making bread products in its bakeries. Short-term trade credit gives Panera control over cash payments by separating the purchase function from the payment function. Thus, the employee responsible for purchasing the bakery ingredients is separated from the employee responsible for paying for the purchase. This separation of duties can help prevent unauthorized purchases or payments.

In addition to accounts payable, a business like Panera Bread can also have current liabilities related to payroll, payroll taxes, employee benefits, short-term notes, unearned revenue, and contingencies. This chapter discusses each of these types of current liabilities.

OBJ. 1 Describe and illustrate current liabilities related to accounts payable, current portion of long-term debt, and notes payable.

Current Liabilities

When a company or a bank advances *credit*, it is making a loan. The company or bank is called a *creditor* (or *lender*). The individuals or companies receiving the loan are called *debtors* (or *borrowers*).

Debt is recorded as a liability by the debtor. *Long-term liabilities* are debts due beyond one year. Thus, a 30-year mortgage used to purchase property is a long-term liability. *Current liabilities* are debts that will be paid out of current assets and are due within one year.

Three types of current liabilities are discussed in this section—accounts payable, the current portion of long-term debt, and short-term notes payable.

Accounts Payable

Accounts payable transactions have been described and illustrated in earlier chapters. These transactions involved a variety of purchases on account, including the purchase of merchandise and supplies. For most companies, accounts payable is the largest current liability. Exhibit 1 shows the accounts payable balance as a percent of total current liabilities for a number of companies.

EXHIBIT 1

Accounts Payable as a Percent of Total Current Liabilities

Company	Accounts Payable as a Percent of Total Current Liabilities
Alcoa Inc.	36%
AT&T	57
Gap Inc.	47
IBM	17
Rite Aid Corp.	55
Chevron Corp.	52

Current Portion of Long-Term Debt

Long-term liabilities are often paid back in periodic payments, called *installments*. Such installments that are due *within* the coming year are classified as a current liability. The installments due *after* the coming year are classified as a long-term liability.

To illustrate, The Coca-Cola Company reported the following debt payments schedule in its December 31, 2009, annual report to shareholders:

Fiscal year ending	
2010	$ 51,000,000
2011	573,000,000
2012	153,000,000
2013	178,000,000
2014	912,000,000
Thereafter	3,243,000,000
Total principal payments	$5,110,000,000

The debt of $51,000,000 due in 2010 would be reported as a current liability on the December 31, 2009, balance sheet. The remaining debt of $5,059,000,000 ($5,110,000,000 − $51,000,000) would be reported as a long-term liability on the balance sheet.

Short-Term Notes Payable

Notes may be issued to purchase merchandise or other assets. Notes may also be issued to creditors to satisfy an account payable created earlier.[1]

To illustrate, assume that Nature's Sunshine Company issued a 90-day, 12% note for $1,000, dated August 1, 2011, to Murray Co. for a $1,000 overdue account. The entry to record the issuance of the note is as follows:

Aug.	1	Accounts Payable—Murray Co.	1,000	
		Notes Payable		1,000
		Issued a 90-day, 12% note on account.		

When the note matures, the entry to record the payment of $1,000 plus $30 interest ($1,000 × 12% × 90/360) is as follows:

Oct.	30	Notes Payable	1,000	
		Interest Expense	30	
		Cash		1,030
		Paid principal and interest due on note.		

---

1 The accounting for notes received to satisfy an account receivable was described and illustrated in Chapter 9, Receivables.

The interest expense is reported in the Other Expense section of the income statement for the year ended December 31, 2011. The interest expense account is closed at December 31.

Each note transaction affects a debtor (borrower) and creditor (lender). The following illustration shows how the same transactions are recorded by the debtor and creditor. In this illustration, the debtor (borrower) is Bowden Co., and the creditor (lender) is Coker Co.

	Bowden Co. (Borrower)			Coker Co. (Creditor)		

May 1. Bowden Co. purchased merchandise on account from Coker Co., $10,000, 2/10, n/30. The merchandise cost Coker Co. $7,500.	Merchandise Inventory
	    Accounts Payable
		10,000	10,000	Accounts Receivable
				    Sales
				
				Cost of Merchandise Sold
				    Merchandise Inventory
					10,000
					
					7,500
						10,000
						
						7,500

May 31. Bowden Co. issued a 60-day, 12% note for $10,000 to Coker Co. on account.	Accounts Payable
	    Notes Payable
		10,000	10,000	Notes Receivable
				    Accounts Receivable
					10,000	10,000

July 30. Bowden Co. paid Coker Co. the amount due on the note of May 31. Interest: $10,000 × 12% × 60/360.	Notes Payable
	Interest Expense
	    Cash
		10,000
		200
			10,200	Cash
				    Interest Revenue
				    Notes Receivable
					10,200	200
						10,000

A company may also borrow from a bank by issuing a note. To illustrate, assume that on September 19 Iceburg Company borrowed cash from First National Bank by issuing a $4,000, 90-day, 15% note to the bank. The entry to record the issuance of the note and the cash proceeds is as follows:

Sept.	19	Cash		4,000	
		Notes Payable			4,000
		Issued a 90-day, 15% note to First National Bank.			

On the due date of the note (December 18), Iceburg Company owes First National Bank $4,000 plus interest of $150 ($4,000 × 15% × 90/360). The entry to record the payment of the note is as follows:

Dec.	18	Notes Payable		4,000	
		Interest Expense		150	
		Cash			4,150
		Paid principal and interest due on note.			

In some cases, a *discounted note* may be issued rather than an interest-bearing note. A discounted note has the following characteristics:

1. The interest rate on the note is called the *discount rate*.
2. The amount of interest on the note, called the *discount*, is computed by multiplying the discount rate times the face amount of the note.
3. The debtor (borrower) receives the face amount of the note less the discount, called the *proceeds*.
4. The debtor must repay the face amount of the note on the due date.

To illustrate, assume that on August 10, Cary Company issues a $20,000, 90-day discounted note to Western National Bank. The discount rate is 15%, and the amount of the discount is $750 ($20,000 × 15% × 90/360). Thus, the proceeds received by Cary Company are $19,250. The entry by Cary Company is as follows:

Aug.	10	Cash	19,250	
		Interest Expense	750	
		Notes Payable		20,000
		Issued a 90-day discounted note to Western		
		National Bank at a 15% discount rate.		

The entry when Cary Company pays the discounted note on November 8 is as follows:[2]

Nov.	8	Notes Payable	20,000	
		Cash		20,000
		Paid note due.		

Other current liabilities that have been discussed in earlier chapters include accrued expenses, unearned revenue, and interest payable. The accounting for wages and salaries, termed *payroll accounting*, is discussed next.

Example Exercise 11-1 Proceeds from Notes Payable   **OBJ. 1**

On July 1, Bella Salon Company issued a 60-day note with a face amount of $60,000 to Delilah Hair Products Company for merchandise inventory.

a. Determine the proceeds of the note, assuming the note carries an interest rate of 6%.

b. Determine the proceeds of the note, assuming the note is discounted at 6%.

Follow My Example 11-1

a. $60,000

b. $59,400 [$60,000 − ($60,000 × 6% × 60/360)]

Practice Exercises: **PE 11-1A, PE 11-1B**

Payroll and Payroll Taxes

OBJ. 2 Determine employer liabilities for payroll, including liabilities arising from employee earnings and deductions from earnings.

In accounting, **payroll** refers to the amount paid to employees for services they provided during the period. A company's payroll is important for the following reasons:

1. Payroll and related payroll taxes significantly affect the net income of most companies.
2. Payroll is subject to federal and state regulations.
3. Good employee morale requires payroll to be paid timely and accurately.

Liability for Employee Earnings

Salary usually refers to payment for managerial and administrative services. Salary is normally expressed in terms of a month or a year. *Wages* usually refers to payment for employee manual labor. The rate of wages is normally stated on an hourly or a weekly basis. The salary or wage of an employee may be increased by bonuses, commissions, profit sharing, or cost-of-living adjustments.

Note:
Employee salaries and wages are expenses to an employer.

---

2 If the accounting period ends before a discounted note is paid, an adjusting entry should record the prepaid (deferred) interest that is not yet an expense. This deferred interest would be deducted from Notes Payable in the Current Liabilities section of the balance sheet.

Companies engaged in interstate commerce must follow the Fair Labor Standards Act. This act, sometimes called the Federal Wage and Hour Law, requires employers to pay a minimum rate of 1½ times the regular rate for all hours worked in excess of 40 hours per week. Exemptions are provided for executive, administrative, and some supervisory positions. Increased rates for working overtime, nights, or holidays are common, even when not required by law. These rates may be as much as twice the regular rate.

To illustrate computing an employee's earnings, assume that John T. McGrath is a salesperson employed by McDermott Supply Co. McGrath's regular rate is $34 per hour, and any hours worked in excess of 40 hours per week are paid at 1½ times the regular rate. McGrath worked 42 hours for the week ended December 27. His earnings of **$1,462** for the week are computed as follows:

Earnings at regular rate (40 hrs. × $34)	$1,360
Earnings at overtime rate [2 hrs. × ($34 × 1½)]	102
Total earnings	$1,462

Deductions from Employee Earnings

The total earnings of an employee for a payroll period, including any overtime pay, are called **gross pay**. From this amount is subtracted one or more *deductions* to arrive at the **net pay**. Net pay is the amount paid the employee. The deductions normally include federal, state, and local income taxes, medical insurance, and pension contributions.

Income Taxes Employers normally withhold a portion of employee earnings for payment of the employees' federal income tax. Each employee authorizes the amount to be withheld by completing an "Employee's Withholding Allowance Certificate," called a W-4. Exhibit 2 is the W-4 form submitted by John T. McGrath.

On the W-4, an employee indicates marital status and the number of withholding allowances. A single employee may claim one withholding allowance. A married employee may claim an additional allowance for a spouse. An employee may also claim an allowance for each dependent other than a spouse. Each allowance reduces the federal income tax withheld from the employee's pay. Exhibit 2 indicates that John T. McGrath is single and, thus, claimed one withholding allowance.

The federal income tax withheld depends on each employee's gross pay and W-4 allowance. Withholding tables issued by the Internal Revenue Service (IRS) are used to determine amounts to withhold. Exhibit 3 is an example of an IRS wage withholding table for a single person who is paid weekly.[3]

EXHIBIT 2

Employee's Withholding Allowance Certificate (W-4 Form)

3 IRS withholding tables are also available for married employees and for pay periods other than weekly.

In Exhibit 3, each row is the employee's wages after deducting the employee's withholding allowances. Each year, the amount of the standard withholding allowance is determined by the IRS. For ease of computation and because this amount changes each year, we assume that the standard withholding allowance to be deducted in Exhibit 3 for a single person paid weekly is $70.[4] Thus, if two withholding allowances are claimed, $140 ($70 × 2) is deducted.

To illustrate, John T. McGrath made $1,462 for the week ended December 27. McGrath's W-4 claims one withholding allowance of $70. Thus, the wages used in determining McGrath's withholding bracket in Exhibit 3 are $1,392 ($1,462 − $70).

After the person's withholding wage bracket has been computed, the federal income tax to be withheld is determined as follows:

Step 1. Locate the proper withholding wage bracket in Exhibit 3.

McGrath's wages after deducting one standard IRS withholding allowance are $1,392 ($1,462 − $70). Therefore, the wage bracket for McGrath is $1,302–$1,624.

Step 2. Compute the withholding for the proper wage bracket using the directions in the two right-hand columns in Exhibit 3.

For McGrath's wage bracket, the withholding is computed as "$234.60. plus 27% of the excess over $1,302." Hence, McGrath's withholding is $258.90, as shown below.

Initial withholding from wage bracket	$234.60
Plus [27% × ($1,392 − $1,302)]	24.30
Total withholding	$258.90

EXHIBIT 3 Wage Bracket Withholding Table

Table for Percentage Method of Withholding WEEKLY Payroll Period

(a) SINGLE person (including head of household)—

If the amount of wages (after subtracting withholding allowances) is: The amount of income tax to withhold is:

Not over $116 . . . . $0

Over—	But not over—		of excess over —
$116	— $200	. . . 10%	— $116
$200	— $693	. . . $8.40 plus 15%	— $200
$693	— $1,302	. . . $82.35 plus 25%	— $693
$1,302	— $1,624	. . . $234.60 plus 27%	— $1,302	← McGrath wage bracket
$1,624	— $1,687	. . . $321.54 plus 30%	— $1,624
$1,687	— $3,344	. . . $340.44 plus 28%	— $1,687
$3,344	— $7,225	. . . $804.40 plus 33%	— $3,344
$7,225	. . . .	$2,085.13 plus 35%	— $7,225

Source: Publication 15, *Employer's Tax Guide*, Internal Revenue Service, 2010.

Residents of New York City must pay federal, state, and city income taxes.

Employers may also be required to withhold state or city income taxes. The amounts to be withheld are determined on state-by-state and city-by-city bases.

Example Exercise 11-2 Federal Income Tax Withholding **OBJ. 2**

Karen Dunn's weekly gross earnings for the present week were $2,250. Dunn has two exemptions. Using the wage bracket withholding table in Exhibit 3 with a $70 standard withholding allowance for each exemption, what is Dunn's federal income tax withholding?

(continued)

4 The actual IRS standard withholding allowance changes every year and was $70.19 for 2010.

Follow My Example 11-2

Total wage payment...		$ 2,250
One allowance (provided by IRS)..	$70	
Multiplied by allowances claimed on Form W-4	× 2	140
Amount subject to withholding..		$ 2,110
Initial withholding from wage bracket in Exhibit 3.........................		$340.44
Plus additional withholding: 28% of excess over $1,687		118.44*
Federal income tax withholding..		$458.88

*28% × ($2,110 – $1,687)

Practice Exercises: **PE 11-2A, PE 11-2B**

FICA Tax Employers are required by the Federal Insurance Contributions Act (FICA) to withhold a portion of the earnings of each employee. The **FICA tax** withheld contributes to the following two federal programs:

1. *Social security*, which provides payments for retirees, survivors, and disability insurance.
2. *Medicare*, which provides health insurance for senior citizens.

The amount withheld from each employee is based on the employee's earnings *paid* in the *calendar* year. The withholding tax rates and maximum earnings subject to tax are often revised by Congress.[5] To simplify, this chapter assumes the following rates and earnings subject to tax:

1. Social security: 6% on all earnings
2. Medicare: 1.5% on all earnings

To illustrate, assume that John T. McGrath's earnings for the week ending December 27 are $1,462 and the total FICA tax to be withheld is **$109.65**, as shown below.

Earnings subject to 6% social security tax........................	$1,462	
Social security tax rate	× 6%	
Social security tax		$ 87.72
Earnings subject to 1.5% Medicare tax...........................	$1,462	
Medicare tax rate	× 1.5%	
Medicare tax		21.93
Total FICA tax...		$109.65

Other Deductions Employees may choose to have additional amounts deducted from their gross pay. For example, an employee may authorize deductions for retirement savings, for charitable contributions, or life insurance. A union contract may also require the deduction of union dues.

Computing Employee Net Pay

Gross earnings less payroll deductions equals *net pay*, sometimes called *take-home pay*. Assuming that John T. McGrath authorized deductions for retirement savings and

5 As of January 1, 2010, the social security tax rate was 6.2% and the Medicare tax rate was 1.45%. Earnings subject to the social security tax are limited to an annual threshold amount, but for text examples and problems, assume all accumulated annual earnings are below this threshold and subject to the tax.

for a United Fund contribution, McGrath's net pay for the week ended December 27 is $1,068.45, as shown below.

Gross earnings for the week		$1,462.00
Deductions:		
Social security tax	$ 87.72	
Medicare tax	21.93	
Federal income tax	258.90	
Retirement savings	20.00	
United Fund	5.00	
Total deductions		393.55
Net pay		$1,068.45

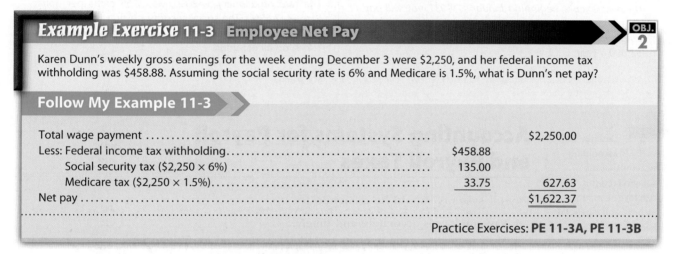

Example Exercise 11-3 Employee Net Pay

> OBJ.
> 2

Karen Dunn's weekly gross earnings for the week ending December 3 were $2,250, and her federal income tax withholding was $458.88. Assuming the social security rate is 6% and Medicare is 1.5%, what is Dunn's net pay?

Follow My Example 11-3

Total wage payment		$2,250.00
Less: Federal income tax withholding...	$458.88	
Social security tax ($2,250 × 6%)	135.00	
Medicare tax ($2,250 × 1.5%)..	33.75	627.63
Net pay		$1,622.37

Practice Exercises: **PE 11-3A, PE 11-3B**

Liability for Employer's Payroll Taxes

Employers are subject to the following payroll taxes for amounts paid their employees:

1. *FICA Tax*: Employers must match the employee's FICA tax contribution.
2. *Federal Unemployment Compensation Tax (FUTA)*: This employer tax provides for temporary payments to those who become unemployed. The tax collected by the federal government is allocated among the states for use in state programs rather than paid directly to employees. Congress often revises the FUTA tax rate and maximum earnings subject to tax.
3. *State Unemployment Compensation Tax (SUTA)*: This employer tax also provides temporary payments to those who become unemployed. The FUTA and SUTA programs are closely coordinated, with the states distributing the unemployment checks.[6] SUTA tax rates and earnings subject to tax vary by state.[7]

The preceding employer taxes are an operating expense of the company. Exhibit 4 summarizes the responsibility for employee and employer payroll taxes.

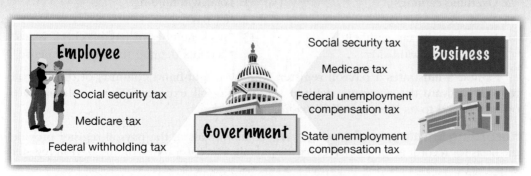

EXHIBIT 4

Responsibility for Tax Payments

6 This rate may be reduced to 0.8% for credits for state unemployment compensation tax.

7 As of January 1, 2010, the maximum state rate credited against the federal unemployment rate was 5.4% of the first $7,000 of each employee's earnings during a calendar year.

BusinessConnection

THE MOST YOU WILL EVER PAY

In 1936, the Social Security Board described how the tax was expected to affect a worker's pay, as follows:

The taxes called for in this law will be paid both by your employer and by you. For the next 3 years you will pay maybe 15 cents a week, maybe 25 cents a week, maybe 30 cents or more, according to what you earn. That is to say, during the next 3 years, beginning January 1, 1937, you will pay 1 cent for every dollar you earn, and at the same time your employer will pay 1 cent for every dollar you earn, up to $3,000 a year. . . .

. . . Beginning in 1940 you will pay, and your employer will pay, 1½ cents for each dollar you earn, up to $3,000 a year . . . and then beginning in 1943, you will pay 2 cents, and so will your employer, for every dollar you earn for the next three years. After that, you and your employer will each pay half a cent more for 3 years, and finally, beginning in 1949, . . . you and your employer will each pay 3 cents on each dollar you earn, up to $3,000 a year. That is the most you will ever pay.

The rate on January 1, 2010, was 7.65 cents per dollar earned (7.65%). The social security portion was 6.20% on the first $106,800 of earnings. The Medicare portion was 1.45% on all earnings.

Source: Arthur Lodge, "That Is the Most You Will Ever Pay," *Journal of Accountancy*, October 1985, p. 44.

OBJ. 3 Describe payroll accounting systems that use a payroll register, employee earnings records, and a general journal.

Accounting Systems for Payroll and Payroll Taxes

Payroll systems should be designed to:

1. Pay employees accurately and timely.
2. Meet regulatory requirements of federal, state, and local agencies.
3. Provide useful data for management decision-making needs.

Although payroll systems differ among companies, the major elements of most payroll systems are:

1. Payroll register
2. Employee's earnings record
3. Payroll checks

Payroll Register

The **payroll register** is a multicolumn report used for summarizing the data for each payroll period. Although payroll registers vary by company, a payroll register normally includes the following columns:

1. Employee name
2. Total hours worked
3. Regular earnings
4. Overtime earnings
5. Total gross earnings
6. Social security tax withheld
7. Medicare tax withheld
8. Federal income tax withheld
9. Retirement savings withheld
10. Miscellaneous items withheld
11. Total withholdings
12. Net pay
13. Check number of payroll check issued
14. Accounts debited for payroll expense

Exhibit 5 illustrates a payroll register. The two right-hand columns of the payroll register indicate the accounts debited for the payroll expense. These columns are often referred to as the *payroll distribution*.

Recording Employees' Earnings The column totals of the payroll register provide the basis for recording the journal entry for payroll. The entry based on the payroll register in Exhibit 5 is shown on the next page.

Recording and Paying Payroll Taxes Payroll taxes are recorded as liabilities when the payroll is *paid* to employees. In addition, employers compute and report payroll taxes on a *calendar-year* basis, which may differ from the company's fiscal year.

Note:
Payroll taxes become a liability to the employer when the payroll is paid.

Dec.	27	Sales Salaries Expense	11,122.00	
		Office Salaries Expense	2,780.00	
		Social Security Tax Payable		834.12
		Medicare Tax Payable		208.53
		Employees Federal Income Tax Payable		3,332.00
		Retirement Savings Deductions Payable		680.00
		United Fund Deductions Payable		520.00
		Salaries Payable		8,327.35
		Payroll for week ended December 27.		

Example Exercise 11-4 Journalize Period Payroll

OBJ. 3

The payroll register of Chen Engineering Services indicates $900 of social security withheld and $225 of Medicare tax withheld on total salaries of $15,000 for the period. Federal withholding for the period totaled $2,925.
   Provide the journal entry for the period's payroll.

Follow My Example 11-4

Salaries Expense...	15,000	
Social Security Tax Payable....................................		900
Medicare Tax Payable		225
Employees Federal Withholding Tax Payable		2,925
Salaries Payable...		10,950

Practice Exercises: **PE 11-4A, PE 11-4B**

On December 27, McDermott Supply has the following payroll data:

Sales salaries	$11,122
Office salaries owed	2,780
Wages owed employees on December 27...............	$13,902
Wages subject to payroll taxes:	
Social security tax (6%)................................	$13,902
Medicare tax (1.5%)	13,902
State (5.4%) and federal (0.8%)	
unemployment compensation tax	2,710

Employers must match the employees' social security and Medicare tax contributions. In addition, the employer must pay state unemployment compensation tax (SUTA) of 5.4% and federal unemployment compensation tax (FUTA) of 0.8%. When payroll is paid on December 27, these payroll taxes are computed as follows:

Social security tax	$ 834.12 ($13,902 × 6%, and from Social Security Tax column of Exhibit 5)
Medicare tax	208.53 ($13,902 × 1.5%, and from Medicare Tax column of Exhibit 5)
SUTA	146.34 ($2,710 × 5.4%)
FUTA	21.68 ($2,710 × 0.8%)
Total payroll taxes	$1,210.67

The entry to journalize the payroll tax expense for Exhibit 5 is shown below.

Dec.	27	Payroll Tax Expense	1,210.67	
		Social Security Tax Payable		834.12
		Medicare Tax Payable		208.53
		State Unemployment Tax Payable		146.34
		Federal Unemployment Tax Payable		21.68
		Payroll taxes for week ended December 27.		

EXHIBIT 5   Payroll Register

	Employee Name	Total Hours	Earnings			
			Regular	Overtime	Total	
1	Abrams, Julie S.	40	500.00		500.00	1
2	Elrod, Fred G.	44	392.00	58.80	450.80	2
3	Gomez, Jose C.	40	840.00		840.00	3
4	McGrath, John T.	42	1,360.00	102.00	1,462.00	4
25	Wilkes, Glenn K.	40	480.00		480.00	25
26	Zumpano, Michael W.	40	600.00		600.00	26
27	Total		13,328.00	574.00	13,902.00	27
28						28

The preceding entry records a liability for each payroll tax. When the payroll taxes are paid, an entry is recorded debiting the payroll tax liability accounts and crediting Cash.

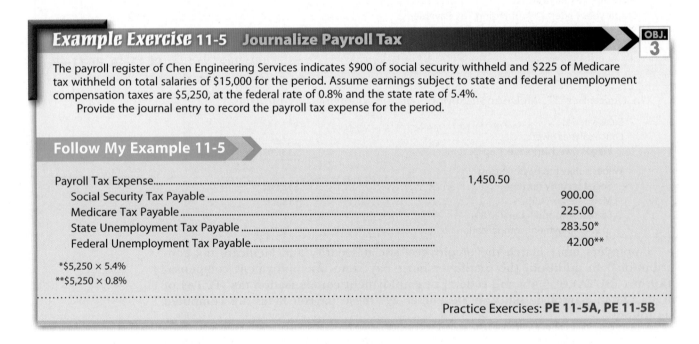

Example Exercise 11-5   **Journalize Payroll Tax**   OBJ. 3

The payroll register of Chen Engineering Services indicates $900 of social security withheld and $225 of Medicare tax withheld on total salaries of $15,000 for the period. Assume earnings subject to state and federal unemployment compensation taxes are $5,250, at the federal rate of 0.8% and the state rate of 5.4%.

    Provide the journal entry to record the payroll tax expense for the period.

Follow My Example 11-5

Payroll Tax Expense	1,450.50	
Social Security Tax Payable		900.00
Medicare Tax Payable		225.00
State Unemployment Tax Payable		283.50*
Federal Unemployment Tax Payable		42.00**

*$5,250 × 5.4%
**$5,250 × 0.8%

Practice Exercises: **PE 11-5A, PE 11-5B**

Employee's Earnings Record

Each employee's earnings to date must be determined at the end of each payroll period. This total is necessary for computing the employee's social security tax withholding and the employer's payroll taxes. Thus, detailed payroll records must be kept for each employee. This record is called an **employee's earnings record**.

Exhibit 6, on pages 502–503, shows a portion of John T. McGrath's employee's earnings record. An employee's earnings record and the payroll register are interrelated. For example, McGrath's earnings record for December 27 can be traced to the fourth line of the payroll register in Exhibit 5.

As shown in Exhibit 6, an employee's earnings record has quarterly and yearly totals. These totals are used for tax, insurance, and other reports. For example, one such report is the Wage and Tax Statement, commonly called a *W-2*. This form is

EXHIBIT 5 (Concluded)

	Social Security Tax	Medicare Tax	Federal Income Tax	Retirement Savings	Misc.		Total	Net Pay	Check No.	Sales Salaries Expense	Office Salaries Expense	
	Deductions Withheld							**Paid**		**Accounts Debited**		
1	30.00	7.50	74.00	20.00	UF	10.00	141.50	358.50	6857	500.00		1
2	27.05	6.76	62.00		UF	50.00	145.81	304.99	6858		450.80	2
3	50.40	12.60	131.00	25.00	UF	10.00	229.00	611.00	6859	840.00		3
4	87.72	21.93	258.90	20.00	UF	5.00	393.55	1,068.45	6860	1,462.00		4
25	28.80	7.20	69.00	10.00			115.00	365.00	6880	480.00		25
26	36.00	9.00	79.00	5.00	UF	2.00	131.00	469.00	6881		600.00	26
27	834.12	208.53	3,332.00	680.00	UF	520.00	5,574.65	8,327.35		11,122.00	2,780.00	27
28												28

Miscellaneous Deductions: UF—United Fund

provided annually to each employee as well as to the Social Security Administration. The W-2 shown below is based on John T. McGrath's employee's earnings record shown in Exhibit 6.

22222	Void ☐	a Employee's social security number 381-48-9120	For Official Use Only ▶ OMB No. 1545-0008	

b Employer identification number (EIN) 61-8436524	1 Wages, tips, other compensation 100,500.00	2 Federal income tax withheld 21,387.65
c Employer's name, address, and ZIP code McDermott Supply Co. 415 8th Ave. So. Dubuque, IA 52736-0142	3 Social security wages 100,500.00	4 Social security tax withheld 6,030.00
	5 Medicare wages and tips 100,500.00	6 Medicare tax withheld 1,507.50
	7 Social security tips	8 Allocated tips
d Control number	9 Advance EIC payment	10 Dependent care benefits
e Employee's first name and initial: John T. Last name: McGrath Suff.	11 Nonqualified plans	12a See instructions for box 12
1830 4th St. Clinton, IA 52732-6142	13 Statutory employee ☐ Retirement plan ☐ Third-party sick pay ☐	12b
	14 Other	12c
		12d
f Employee's address and ZIP code		

15 State IA	Employer's state ID number	16 State wages, tips, etc.	17 State income tax	18 Local wages, tips, etc.	19 Local income tax	20 Locality name Dubuque

Form **W-2** Wage and Tax Statement **2011**

Department of the Treasury—Internal Revenue Service
For Privacy Act and Paperwork Reduction Act Notice, see back of Copy D.
Cat. No. 10134D

Copy A For Social Security Administration — Send this entire page with Form W-3 to the Social Security Administration; photocopies are **not** acceptable.

Do Not Cut, Fold, or Staple Forms on This Page — Do Not Cut, Fold, or Staple Forms on This Page

Payroll Checks

Companies may pay employees, especially part-time employees, by issuing *payroll checks*. Each check includes a detachable statement showing how the net pay was computed. Exhibit 7, on page 504, illustrates a payroll check for John T. McGrath.

Most companies issuing payroll checks use a special payroll bank account. In such cases, payroll is processed as follows:

1. The total net pay for the period is determined from the payroll register.
2. The company authorizes an electronic funds transfer (EFT) from its regular bank account to the special payroll bank account for the total net pay.
3. Individual payroll checks are written from the payroll account.
4. The numbers of the payroll checks are inserted in the payroll register.

EXHIBIT 6

Employee's
Earnings Record

John T. McGrath
1830 4th St.
Clinton, IA 52732-6142   PHONE: 555-3148

SINGLE	NUMBER OF WITHHOLDING ALLOWANCES: 1	PAY RATE: $1,360.00 Per Week
OCCUPATION: Salesperson		EQUIVALENT HOURLY RATE: $34

	Period Ending	Total Hours	Regular Earnings	Overtime Earnings	Total Earnings	Total	
42	SEPT. 27	53	1,360.00	663.00	2,023.00	75,565.00	42
43	THIRD QUARTER		17,680.00	7,605.00	25,285.00		43
44	OCT. 4	51	1,360.00	561.00	1,921.00	77,486.00	44
50	NOV. 15	50	1,360.00	510.00	1,870.00	89,382.00	50
51	NOV. 22	53	1,360.00	663.00	2,023.00	91,405.00	51
52	NOV. 29	47	1,360.00	357.00	1,717.00	93,122.00	52
53	DEC. 6	53	1,360.00	663.00	2,023.00	95,145.00	53
54	DEC.13	52	1,360.00	612.00	1,972.00	97,117.00	54
55	DEC. 20	51	1,360.00	561.00	1,921.00	99,038.00	55
56	DEC. 27	42	1,360.00	102.00	1,462.00	100,500.00	56
57	FOURTH QUARTER		17,680.00	7,255.00	24,935.00		57
58	YEARLY TOTAL		70,720.00	29,780.00	100,500.00		58

An advantage of using a separate payroll bank account is that reconciling the bank statements is simplified. In addition, a payroll bank account establishes control over payroll checks and, thus, prevents their theft or misuse.

Many companies use electronic funds transfer to pay their employees. In such cases, each pay period an employee's net pay is deposited directly into the employee checking account. Later, employees receive a payroll statement summarizing how the net pay was computed.

Payroll System Diagram

The inputs into a payroll system may be classified as:

1. Constants, which are data that remain unchanged from payroll to payroll.

   Examples: Employee names, social security numbers, marital status, number of income tax withholding allowances, rates of pay, tax rates, and withholding tables.

2. Variables, which are data that change from payroll to payroll.

   Examples: Number of hours or days worked for each employee, accrued days of sick leave, vacation credits, total earnings to date, and total taxes withheld.

In a computerized accounting system, constants are stored within a payroll file. The variables are input each pay period by a payroll clerk. In some systems, employees swipe their identification (ID) cards when they report for and leave work. In such cases, the hours worked by each employee are automatically updated.

A computerized payroll system also maintains electronic versions of the payroll register and employee earnings records. Payroll system outputs, such as payroll checks, EFTs, and tax records, are automatically produced each pay period.

EXHIBIT 6   (Concluded)

SOC. SEC. NO.: 381-48-9120   EMPLOYEE NO.: 814

DATE OF BIRTH: February 15, 1982

DATE EMPLOYMENT TERMINATED:

| | Deductions | | | | | | Paid | | |
	Social Security Tax	Medicare Tax	Federal Income Tax	Retirement Savings	Other		Total	Net Amount	Check No.	
42	121.38	30.35	429.83	20.00			601.56	1,421.44	6175	42
43	1,517.10	379.28	5,391.71	260.00	UF	40.00	7,588.09	17,696.91		43
44	115.26	28.82	401.27	20.00			565.35	1,355.65	6225	44
50	112.20	28.05	386.99	20.00			547.24	1,322.76	6530	50
51	121.38	30.35	429.83	20.00			601.56	1,421.44	6582	51
52	103.02	25.76	344.15	20.00			492.93	1,224.07	6640	52
53	121.38	30.35	429.83	20.00	UF	5.00	606.56	1,416.44	6688	53
54	118.32	29.58	415.55	20.00			583.45	1,388.55	6743	54
55	115.26	28.82	401.27	20.00			565.35	1,355.65	6801	55
56	87.72	21.93	258.90	20.00	UF	5.00	393.55	1,068.45	6860	56
57	1,496.10	374.03	5,293.71	260.00	UF	15.00	7,438.84	17,496.16		57
58	6,030.00	1,507.50	21,387.65	1,040.00	UF	100.00	30,065.15	70,434.85		58

Internal Controls for Payroll Systems

The cash payment controls described in Chapter 8, *Sarbanes-Oxley, Internal Control, and Cash*, also apply to payrolls. Some examples of payroll controls include the following:

1. If a check-signing machine is used, blank payroll checks and access to the machine should be restricted to prevent their theft or misuse.
2. The hiring and firing of employees should be properly authorized and approved in writing.
3. All changes in pay rates should be properly authorized and approved in writing.
4. Employees should be observed when arriving for work to verify that employees are "checking in" for work only once and only for themselves. Employees may "check in" for work by using a time card or by swiping their employee ID card.
5. Payroll checks should be distributed by someone other than employee supervisors.
6. A special payroll bank account should be used.

Integrity, Objectivity, and Ethics in Business

$8 MILLION FOR 18 MINUTES OF WORK

Computer system controls can be very important in issuing payroll checks. In one case, a Detroit schoolteacher was paid $4,015,625 after deducting $3,884,375 in payroll deductions for 18 minutes of overtime work. The error was caused by a computer glitch when the teacher's employee identification number was substituted incorrectly in the "hourly wage" field and wasn't caught by the payroll software. After six days, the error was discovered and the money was returned. "One of the things that came with (the software) is a fail-safe that prevents that. It doesn't work," a financial officer said. The district has since installed a program to flag any paycheck exceeding $10,000.

Source: Associated Press, September 27, 2002.

EXHIBIT 7

Payroll Check

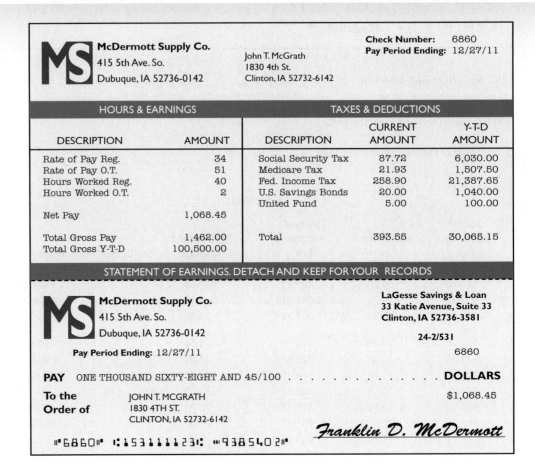

Employees' Fringe Benefits

Many companies provide their employees benefits in addition to salary and wages earned. Such **fringe benefits** may include vacation, medical, and retirement benefits.

The cost of employee fringe benefits is recorded as an expense by the employer. To match revenues and expenses, the estimated cost of fringe benefits is recorded as an expense during the period in which the employees earn the benefits.

Vacation Pay

Note:

Vacation pay becomes the employer's liability as the employee earns vacation rights.

Most employers provide employees vacations, sometimes called *compensated absences*. The liability to pay for employee vacations could be accrued as a liability at the end of each pay period. However, many companies wait and record an adjusting entry for accrued vacation at the end of the year.

To illustrate, assume that employees earn one day of vacation for each month worked. The estimated vacation pay for the year ending December 31 is $325,000. The adjusting entry for the accrued vacation is shown below.

Dec.	31	Vacation Pay Expense	325,000	
		Vacation Pay Payable		325,000
		Accrued vacation pay for the year.		

Employees may be required to take all their vacation time within one year. In such cases, any accrued vacation pay will be paid within one year. Thus, the vacation pay payable is reported as a current liability on the balance sheet. If employees are allowed to accumulate their vacation pay, the estimated vacation pay payable that will *not* be taken within a year is reported as a long-term liability.

When employees take vacations, the liability for vacation pay is decreased by debiting Vacation Pay Payable. Salaries or Wages Payable and the other related payroll accounts for taxes and withholdings are credited.

Pensions

A **pension** is a cash payment to retired employees. Pension rights are accrued by employees as they work, based on the employer's pension plan. Two basic types of pension plans are:

1. Defined contribution plan
2. Defined benefit plan

In a **defined contribution plan**, the company invests contributions on behalf of the employee during the employee's working years. Normally, the employee and employer contribute to the plan. The employee's pension depends on the total contributions and the investment returns earned on those contributions.

One of the more popular defined contribution plans is the 401k plan. Under this plan, employees contribute a portion of their gross pay to investments, such as mutual funds. A 401k plan offers employees two advantages.

1. The employee contribution is deducted before taxes.
2. The contributions and related earnings are not taxed until withdrawn at retirement.

In most cases, the employer matches some portion of the employee's contribution. The employer's cost is debited to *Pension Expense*. To illustrate, assume that Heaven Scent Perfumes Company contributes 10% of employee monthly salaries to an employee 401k plan. Assuming $500,000 of monthly salaries, the journal entry to record the monthly contribution is shown below.

Dec.	31	Pension Expense	50,000	
		Cash		50,000
		Contributed 10% of monthly salaries to pension plan.		

In a **defined benefit plan**, the company pays the employee a fixed annual pension based on a formula. The formula is normally based on such factors as the employee's years of service, age, and past salary.

Annual Pension = 1.5% × Years of Service × Highest 3-Year Average Salary

In a defined benefit plan, the employer is obligated to pay for (fund) the employee's future pension benefits. As a result, many companies are replacing their defined benefit plans with defined contribution plans.

The pension cost of a defined benefit plan is debited to *Pension Expense*. Cash is credited for the amount contributed (funded) by the employer. Any unfunded amount is credited to *Unfunded Pension Liability*.

To illustrate, assume that the defined benefit plan of Hinkle Co. requires an annual pension cost of $80,000. This annual contribution is based on estimates of Hinkle's future pension liabilities. On December 31, Hinkle Co. pays $60,000 to the pension fund. The entry to record the payment and unfunded liability is shown below.

Dec.	31	Pension Expense	80,000	
		Cash		60,000
		Unfunded Pension Liability		20,000
		Annual pension cost and contribution.		

If the unfunded pension liability is to be paid within one year, it is reported as a current liability on the balance sheet. Any portion of the unfunded pension liability that will be paid beyond one year is a long-term liability.

The accounting for pensions is complex due to the uncertainties of estimating future pension liabilities. These estimates depend on such factors as employee life expectancies, employee turnover, expected employee compensation levels, and investment income on pension contributions. Additional accounting and disclosures related to pensions are covered in advanced accounting courses.

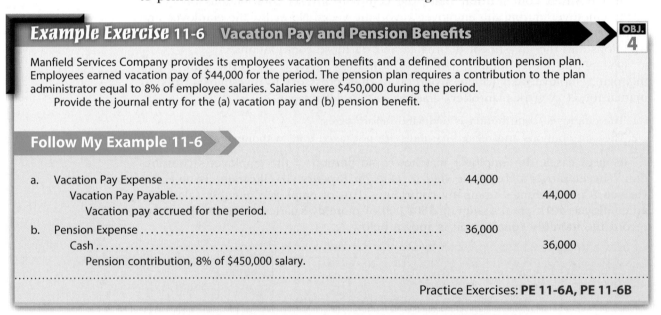

Example Exercise 11-6   **Vacation Pay and Pension Benefits**   OBJ. 4

Manfield Services Company provides its employees vacation benefits and a defined contribution pension plan. Employees earned vacation pay of $44,000 for the period. The pension plan requires a contribution to the plan administrator equal to 8% of employee salaries. Salaries were $450,000 during the period.
    Provide the journal entry for the (a) vacation pay and (b) pension benefit.

Follow My Example 11-6

a.	Vacation Pay Expense..	44,000	
	Vacation Pay Payable...		44,000
	Vacation pay accrued for the period.		
b.	Pension Expense..	36,000	
	Cash..		36,000
	Pension contribution, 8% of $450,000 salary.		

Practice Exercises: **PE 11-6A, PE 11-6B**

Postretirement Benefits Other than Pensions

Employees may earn rights to other postretirement benefits from their employer. Such benefits may include dental care, eye care, medical care, life insurance, tuition assistance, tax services, and legal services.

The accounting for other postretirement benefits is similar to that of defined benefit pension plans. The estimate of the annual benefits expense is recorded by debiting *Postretirement Benefits Expense*. If the benefits are fully funded, Cash is credited for the same amount. If the benefits are not fully funded, a postretirement benefits plan liability account is also credited.

The financial statements should disclose the nature of the postretirement benefit liabilities. These disclosures are usually included as notes to the financial statements. Additional accounting and disclosures for postretirement benefits are covered in advanced accounting courses.

Current Liabilities on the Balance Sheet

Accounts payable, the current portion of long-term debt, notes payable, and any other debts that are due within one year are reported as current liabilities on the balance sheet. The balance sheet presentation of current liabilities for Mornin' Joe is as shown on the next page.

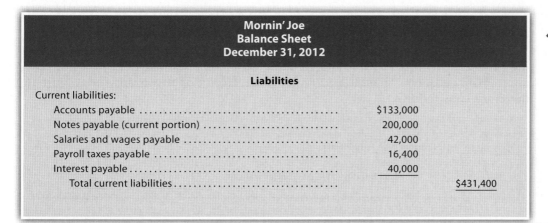

Mornin' Joe
Balance Sheet
December 31, 2012

Liabilities

Current liabilities:

Accounts payable	$133,000
Notes payable (current portion)	200,000
Salaries and wages payable	42,000
Payroll taxes payable	16,400
Interest payable	40,000
Total current liabilities.................................	$431,400

BusinessConnection

GENERAL MOTORS PENSION PROBLEMS

In June 2009, General Motors Company, the world's second-largest automaker, filed for bankruptcy. The company's troubles began decades earlier when the company agreed to provide employees with large pension benefits instead of giving them wage increases. While this strategy was initially successful, by the mid-1990s large numbers of employees began to retire, and the increasing pension costs began to put a financial strain on the company. In 2003, the company issued $18.5 billion in debt to fund its growing unfunded pension liability, but this only provided a temporary fix. From 1993 to 2007, General Motors spent $103 billion on pension and health care benefits for retirees, and the company had 4.61 retired union employees for every one active union employee. By June 2009, the combination of growing pension obligations and deteriorating sales forced the company into bankruptcy.

Source: R. Lowenstein, "Siphoning GM's Future," *The New York Times*, July 10, 2008.

Contingent Liabilities

OBJ.
5
Describe the accounting treatment for contingent liabilities and journalize entries for product warranties.

Some liabilities may arise from past transactions if certain events occur in the future. These *potential* liabilities are called **contingent liabilities**.

The accounting for contingent liabilities depends on the following two factors:

1. Likelihood of occurring: Probable, reasonably possible, or remote
2. Measurement: Estimable or not estimable

The likelihood that the event creating the liability occurring is classified as *probable*, *reasonably possible*, or *remote*. The ability to estimate the potential liability is classified as *estimable* or *not estimable*.

Probable and Estimable

If a contingent liability is *probable* and the amount of the liability can be *reasonably estimated*, it is recorded and disclosed. The liability is recorded by debiting an expense and crediting a liability.

To illustrate, assume that during June a company sold a product for $60,000 that includes a 36-month warranty for repairs. The average cost of repairs over the warranty period is 5% of the sales price. The entry to record the estimated product warranty expense for June is as shown below.

June	30	Product Warranty Expense	3,000	
		Product Warranty Payable		3,000
		Warranty expense for June, 5% × $60,000.		

The estimated costs of warranty work on new car sales are a contingent liability for Ford Motor Company.

The preceding entry records warranty expense in the same period in which the sale is recorded. In this way, warranty expense is matched with the related revenue (sales).

If the product is repaired under warranty, the repair costs are recorded by debiting *Product Warranty Payable* and crediting *Cash, Supplies, Wages Payable*, or other appropriate accounts. Thus, if a $200 part is replaced under warranty on August 16, the entry is as follows:

Aug.	16	Product Warranty Payable	200	
		Supplies		200
		Replaced defective part under warranty.		

Example Exercise 11-7 Estimated Warranty Liability

OBJ. 5

Cook-Rite Co. sold $140,000 of kitchen appliances during August under a six-month warranty. The cost to repair defects under the warranty is estimated at 6% of the sales price. On September 11, a customer required a $200 part replacement plus $90 of labor under the warranty.

Provide the journal entry for (a) the estimated warranty expense on August 31 and (b) the September 11 warranty work.

Follow My Example 11-7

a. Product Warranty Expense 8,400

    Product Warranty Payable... 8,400

        To record warranty expense for August, 6% × $140,000.

b. Product Warranty Payable... 290

    Supplies 200

    Wages Payable... 90

        Replaced defective part under warranty.

Practice Exercises: **PE 11-7A, PE 11-7B**

Probable and Not Estimable

A contingent liability may be probable, but cannot be estimated. In this case, the contingent liability is disclosed in the notes to the financial statements. For example, a company may have accidentally polluted a local river by dumping waste products. At the end of the period, the cost of the cleanup and any fines may not be able to be estimated.

Reasonably Possible

A contingent liability may be only possible. For example, a company may have lost a lawsuit for infringing on another company's patent rights. However, the verdict is under appeal and the company's lawyers feel that the verdict will be reversed or significantly reduced. In this case, the contingent liability is disclosed in the notes to the financial statements.

Remote

A contingent liability may be remote. For example, a ski resort may be sued for injuries incurred by skiers. In most cases, the courts have found that a skier accepts the risk of injury when participating in the activity. Thus, unless the ski resort is grossly negligent, the resort will not incur a liability for ski injuries. In such cases, no disclosure needs to be made in the notes to the financial statements.

The accounting treatment of contingent liabilities is summarized in Exhibit 8.

Common examples of contingent liabilities disclosed in notes to the financial statements are litigation, environmental matters, guarantees, and contingencies from the sale of receivables.

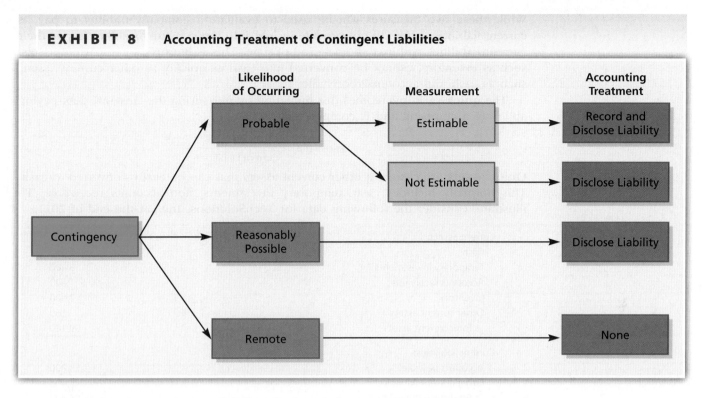

EXHIBIT 8 Accounting Treatment of Contingent Liabilities

An example of a contingent liability disclosure from a recent annual report of Google Inc. is shown below.

> *We have also had copyright claims filed against us alleging that features of certain of our products and services, including Google Web Search, Google News, Google Video, Google Image Search, Google Book Search and YouTube, infringe their rights. Adverse results in these lawsuits may include awards of substantial monetary damages, costly royalty or licensing agreements or orders preventing us from offering certain functionalities, and may also result in a change in our business practices, which could result in a loss of revenue for us or otherwise harm our business. . . .*
>
> *Although the results of litigation and claims cannot be predicted with certainty, we believe that the final outcome of the matters discussed above will not have a material adverse effect on our business . . .*

Professional judgment is necessary in distinguishing between classes of contingent liabilities. This is especially the case when distinguishing between probable and reasonably possible contingent liabilities.

Financial Analysis and Interpretation: Quick Ratio

Current position analysis helps creditors evaluate a company's ability to pay its current liabilities. This analysis is based on the following three measures:

OBJ. 6 Describe and illustrate the use of the quick ratio in analyzing a company's ability to pay its current liabilities.

1. Working capital
2. Current ratio
3. Quick ratio

Working capital and the current ratio were discussed in Chapter 4, and are computed as follows:

$$\text{Working Capital} = \text{Current Assets} - \text{Current Liabilities}$$

$$\text{Current Ratio} = \frac{\text{Current Assets}}{\text{Current Liabilities}}$$

While these two measures can be used to evaluate a company's ability to pay its current liabilities, they do not provide insight into the company's ability to pay their current liabilities within a short period of time. This is because some current assets, such as inventory, cannot be converted into cash as quickly as other current assets, such as cash and accounts receivable.

The **quick ratio** overcomes this limitation by measuring the "instant" debt-paying ability of a company and is computed as follows:

$$\text{Quick Ratio} = \frac{\text{Quick Assets}}{\text{Current Liabilities}}$$

Quick assets are cash and other current assets that can be easily converted to cash. This normally includes cash, temporary investments, and accounts receivable. To illustrate, consider the following data for TechSolutions, Inc., at the end of 2011:

Current assets:	
Cash	$2,020
Temporary investments	3,400
Accounts receivable	1,600
Inventory	2,000
Other current assets	160
Total current assets	$9,180
Current liabilities:	
Accounts payable	$3,000
Other current liabilities	2,400
Total current liabilities	$5,400
Working capital (current assets – current liabilities)	$3,780
Current ratio (current assets/current liabilities)	1.7

The quick ratio for TechSolutions, Inc., is computed as follows:

$$\text{Quick Ratio} = \frac{\$2,020 + \$3,400 + \$1,600}{\$5,400} = 1.3$$

The quick ratio of 1.3 indicates that the company has more than enough quick assets to pay its current liabilities in a short period of time. A quick ratio below 1.0 would indicate that the company does not have enough quick assets to cover its current liabilities.

Like the current ratio, the quick ratio is particularly useful in making comparisons across companies. To illustrate, the following selected balance sheet data (excluding ratios) were taken from the 2008 financial statements of Panera Bread Company and Starbucks Corporation (in thousands):

	Panera Bread	Starbucks
Current assets:		
Cash and cash equivalents	$ 74,710	$ 599,800
Temporary investments	2,400	66,300
Accounts receivable	35,079	557,600
Inventory	11,959	664,900
Other current assets	14,265	147,200
Total current assets	$138,413	$2,035,800
Current liabilities:		
Accounts payable	$114,014	$1,192,100
Other current liabilities	—	388,900
Total current liabilities	$114,014	$1,581,000
Working capital (current assets – current liabilities)	$ 24,399	$ 454,800
Current ratio (current assets/current liabilities)	1.2	1.3
Quick ratio (quick assets/current liabilities)*	1.0	0.8

*The quick ratio for each company is computed as follows:
Panera Bread: ($74,710 + $2,400 + $35,079)/$114,014 = 1.0
Starbucks: ($599,800 + $66,300 + $557,600)/$1,581,000 = 0.8

Starbucks is larger than Panera Bread and has over 18 times the amount of working capital. Such size differences make working capital comparisons between companies difficult. In contrast, the current and quick ratios provide better comparisons across companies. In this example, Panera Bread has a slightly lower current ratio than Starbucks. However, Starbucks' 0.8 quick ratio reveals that it does not have enough quick assets to cover its current liabilities, while Panera Bread's quick ratio of 1.0 indicates that the company has just enough quick assets to meet its current liabilities.

Example Exercise 11-8 Quick Ratio

OBJ. 6

Sayer Company reported the following current assets and current liabilities for the years ended December 31, 2012 and 2011:

	2012	2011
Cash	$1,250	$1,000
Temporary investments	1,925	1,650
Accounts receivable	1,775	1,350
Inventory	1,900	1,700
Accounts payable	2,750	2,500

a. Compute the quick ratio for 2012 and 2011.

b. Interpret the company's quick ratio across the two time periods.

Follow My Example 11-8

a. December 31, 2012:
  Quick Ratio = Quick Assets/Current Liabilities
  Quick Ratio = ($1,250 + $1,925 + $1,775)/$2,750
  Quick Ratio = 1.8

  December 31, 2011:
  Quick Ratio = Quick Assets/Current Liabilities
  Quick Ratio = ($1,000 + $1,650 + $1,350)/$2,500
  Quick Ratio = 1.6

b. The quick ratio of Sayer Company has improved from 1.6 in 2011 to 1.8 in 2012. This increase is the result of a large increase in the three types of quick assets (cash, temporary investments, and accounts receivable) compared to a relatively smaller increase in the current liability, accounts payable.

Practice Exercises: **PE 11-8A, PE 11-8B**

At a Glance 11

1

Describe and illustrate current liabilities related to accounts payable, current portion of long-term debt, and notes payable.

Key Points   Current liabilities are obligations that are to be paid out of current assets and are due within a short time, usually within one year. The three primary types of current liabilities are accounts payable, notes payable, and current portion of long-term debt.

Learning Outcomes	Example Exercises	Practice Exercises
• Identify and define the most frequently reported current liabilities on the balance sheet.		
• Determine the interest from interest-bearing and discounted notes payable.	**EE11-1**	**PE11-1A, 11-1B**

2

Determine employer liabilities for payroll, including liabilities arising from employee earnings and deductions from earnings.

Key Points   An employer's liability for payroll is determined from employee total earnings, including overtime pay. From this amount, employee deductions are subtracted to arrive at the net pay to be paid to each employee. Most employers also incur liabilities for payroll taxes, such as social security tax, Medicare tax, federal unemployment compensation tax, and state unemployment compensation tax.

Learning Outcomes	Example Exercises	Practice Exercises
• Compute the federal withholding tax from a wage bracket withholding table.	**EE11-2**	**PE11-2A, 11-2B**
• Compute employee net pay, including deductions for social security and Medicare tax.	**EE11-3**	**PE11-3A, 11-3B**

3

Describe payroll accounting systems that use a payroll register, employee earnings records, and a general journal.

Key Points   The payroll register is used in assembling and summarizing the data needed for each payroll period. The payroll register is supported by a detailed payroll record for each employee, called an *employee's earnings record*.

Learning Outcomes	Example Exercises	Practice Exercises
• Journalize the employee's earnings, net pay, and payroll liabilities from the payroll register.	**EE11-4**	**PE11-4A, 11-4B**
• Journalize the payroll tax expense.	**EE11-5**	**PE11-5A, 11-5B**
• Describe elements of a payroll system, including the employee's earnings record, payroll checks, and internal controls.		

OBJ. 4

Journalize entries for employee fringe benefits, including vacation pay and pensions.

Key Points   Fringe benefits are expenses of the period in which the employees earn the benefits. Fringe benefits are recorded by debiting an expense account and crediting a liability account.

Learning Outcomes	Example Exercises	Practice Exercises
• Journalize vacation pay.	EE11-6	PE11-6A, 11-6B
• Distinguish and journalize defined contribution and defined benefit pension plans.	EE11-6	PE11-6A, 11-6B

OBJ. 5

Describe the accounting treatment for contingent liabilities and journalize entries for product warranties.

Key Points   A contingent liability is a potential obligation that results from a past transaction but depends on a future event. The accounting for contingent liabilities is summarized in Exhibit 8.

Learning Outcomes	Example Exercises	Practice Exercises
• Describe the accounting for contingent liabilities.		
• Journalize estimated warranty obligations and services granted under warranty.	EE11-7	PE11-7A, 11-7B

OBJ. 6

Describe and illustrate the use of the quick ratio in analyzing a company's ability to pay its current liabilities.

Key Points   The quick ratio is a measure of a company's ability to pay current liabilities within a short period of time. The quick ratio is computed by dividing quick assets by current liabilities. Quick assets include cash, temporary investments, accounts receivable, and other current assets that can be easily converted into cash. A quick ratio exceeding 1.0 is usually desirable.

Learning Outcomes	Example Exercises	Practice Exercises
• Describe the quick ratio.		
• Compute and evaluate the quick ratio.	EE11-8	PE11-8A, 11-8B

Key Terms

contingent liabilities (507)	FICA tax (496)	payroll register (498)
current position analysis (509)	fringe benefits (504)	pension (505)
defined benefit plan (505)	gross pay (494)	quick assets (510)
defined contribution plan (505)	net pay (494)	quick ratio (510)
employee's earnings record (500)	payroll (493)	

Illustrative Problem

Selected transactions of Taylor Company, completed during the fiscal year ended December 31, are as follows:

Mar. 1. Purchased merchandise on account from Kelvin Co., $20,000.

Apr. 10. Issued a 60-day, 12% note for $20,000 to Kelvin Co. on account.

June 9. Paid Kelvin Co. the amount owed on the note of April 10.

Aug. 1. Issued a $50,000, 90-day note to Harold Co. in exchange for a building. Harold Co. discounted the note at 15%.

Oct. 30. Paid Harold Co. the amount due on the note of August 1.

Dec. 27. Journalized the entry to record the biweekly payroll. A summary of the payroll record follows:

Salary distribution:		
Sales	$63,400	
Officers	36,600	
Office	10,000	$110,000
Deductions:		
Social security tax	$ 6,600	
Medicare tax	1,650	
Federal income tax withheld	17,600	
State income tax withheld	4,950	
Savings bond deductions	850	
Medical insurance deductions	1,120	32,770
Net amount		$ 77,230

27. Journalized the entry to record payroll taxes for social security and Medicare from the biweekly payroll.

30. Issued a check in payment of liabilities for employees' federal income tax of $17,600, social security tax of $13,200, and Medicare tax of $3,300.

31. Issued a check for $9,500 to the pension fund trustee to fully fund the pension cost for December.

31. Journalized an entry to record the employees' accrued vacation pay, $36,100.

31. Journalized an entry to record the estimated accrued product warranty liability, $37,240.

Instructions

Journalize the preceding transactions.

Solution

Mar.	1	Merchandise Inventory	20,000	
		Accounts Payable—Kelvin Co.		20,000
Apr.	10	Accounts Payable—Kelvin Co.	20,000	
		Notes Payable		20,000
June	9	Notes Payable	20,000	
		Interest Expense	400	
		Cash		20,400
Aug.	1	Building	48,125	
		Interest Expense	1,875	
		Notes Payable		50,000
Oct.	30	Notes Payable	50,000	
		Cash		50,000
Dec.	27	Sales Salaries Expense	63,400	
		Officers Salaries Expense	36,600	
		Office Salaries Expense	10,000	
		Social Security Tax Payable		6,600
		Medicare Tax Payable		1,650
		Employees Federal Income Tax Payable		17,600
		Employees State Income Tax Payable		4,950
		Bond Deductions Payable		850
		Medical Insurance Payable		1,120
		Salaries Payable		77,230
	27	Payroll Tax Expense	8,250	
		Social Security Tax Payable		6,600
		Medicare Tax Payable		1,650
	30	Employees Federal Income Tax Payable	17,600	
		Social Security Tax Payable	13,200	
		Medicare Tax Payable	3,300	
		Cash		34,100
	31	Pension Expense	9,500	
		Cash		9,500
		Fund pension cost.		
	31	Vacation Pay Expense	36,100	
		Vacation Pay Payable		36,100
		Accrue vacation pay.		
	31	Product Warranty Expense	37,240	
		Product Warranty Payable		37,240
		Accrue warranty expense.		

Discussion Questions

1. Does a discounted note payable provide credit without interest? Discuss.

2. Employees are subject to taxes withheld from their paychecks.

   a. List the federal taxes withheld from most employee paychecks.
   b. Give the title of the accounts credited by amounts withheld.

3. Why are deductions from employees' earnings classified as liabilities for the employer?

4. For each of the following payroll-related taxes, indicate whether they generally apply to (a) employees only, (b) employers only, or (c) both employees and employers:

   1. Federal income tax
   2. Medicare tax
   3. Social security tax
   4. Federal unemployment compensation tax
   5. State unemployment compensation tax

5. What are the principal reasons for using a special payroll checking account?

6. Explain how a payroll system that is properly designed and operated tends to ensure that wages paid are based on hours actually worked.

7. To match revenues and expenses properly, should the expense for employee vacation pay be recorded in the period during which the vacation privilege is earned or during the period in which the vacation is taken? Discuss.

8. Identify several factors that influence the future pension obligation of an employer under a defined benefit pension plan.

9. When should the liability associated with a product warranty be recorded? Discuss.

10. General Motors Corporation reported $7.0 billion of product warranties in the Current Liabilities section of a recent balance sheet. How would costs of repairing a defective product be recorded?

Practice Exercises

Learning Objectives	Example Exercises	
OBJ. 1	EE 11-1 *p. 493*	**PE 11-1A Proceeds from notes payable**

On September 1, Rongo Co. issued a 45-day note with a face amount of $80,000 to Simone Co. for merchandise inventory.

a. Determine the proceeds of the note, assuming the note carries an interest rate of 8%.

b. Determine the proceeds of the note, assuming the note is discounted at 8%.

OBJ. 1	EE 11-1 *p. 493*	**PE 11-1B Proceeds from notes payable**

On February 1, Tectronic Co. issued a 60-day note with a face amount of $120,000 to Tokai Warehouse Co. for cash.

a. Determine the proceeds of the note, assuming the note carries an interest rate of 9%.

b. Determine the proceeds of the note, assuming the note is discounted at 9%.

OBJ. 2	EE 11-2 *p. 495*	**PE 11-2A Federal income tax withholding**

Bob Tappert's weekly gross earnings for the present week were $1,600. Tappert has one exemption. Using the wage bracket withholding table in Exhibit 3 with a $70 standard withholding allowance for each exemption, what is Tappert's federal income tax withholding?

OBJ. 2	EE 11-2 *p. 495*	**PE 11-2B Federal income tax withholding**

John Wolfe's weekly gross earnings for the present week were $2,200. Wolfe has two exemptions. Using the wage bracket withholding table in Exhibit 3 with a $70 standard withholding allowance for each exemption, what is Wolfe's federal income tax withholding?

OBJ. 2	EE 11-3 *p. 497*	**PE 11-3A Employee net pay**

Bob Tappert's weekly gross earnings for the week ending December 18 were $1,600, and his federal income tax withholding was $296.16. Assuming the social security rate is 6% and Medicare is 1.5% of all earnings, what is Tappert's net pay?

OBJ. 2	EE 11-3 *p. 497*	**PE 11-3B Employee net pay**

John Wolfe's weekly gross earnings for the week ending September 5 were $2,200, and his federal income tax withholding was $444.88. Assuming the social security rate is 6% and Medicare is 1.5% of all earnings, what is Wolfe's net pay?

OBJ. 3	EE 11-4 *p. 499*	**PE 11-4A Journalize period payroll**

The payroll register of Gregory Communications Co. indicates $4,080 of social security withheld and $1,020 of Medicare tax withheld on total salaries of $68,000 for the period. Federal withholding for the period totaled $13,464.

Provide the journal entry for the period's payroll.

OBJ. 3	EE 11-4 *p. 499*	**PE 11-4B Journalize period payroll**

The payroll register of Russert Construction Co. indicates $18,000 of social security withheld and $4,500 of Medicare tax withheld on total salaries of $300,000 for the period.

Retirement savings withheld from employee paychecks were $18,000 for the period. Federal withholding for the period totaled $59,400.

Provide the journal entry for the period's payroll.

OBJ. 3 **EE 11-5** *p. 500*

PE 11-5A **Journalize payroll tax**

The payroll register of Gregory Communications Co. indicates $4,080 of social security withheld and $1,020 of Medicare tax withheld on total salaries of $68,000 for the period. Assume earnings subject to state and federal unemployment compensation taxes are $12,500, at the federal rate of 0.8% and the state rate of 5.4%.

Provide the journal entry to record the payroll tax expense for the period.

OBJ. 3 **EE 11-5** *p. 500*

PE 11-5B **Journalize payroll tax**

The payroll register of Russert Construction Co. indicates $18,000 of social security withheld and $4,500 of Medicare tax withheld on total salaries of $300,000 for the period. Assume earnings subject to state and federal unemployment compensation taxes are $13,000, at the federal rate of 0.8% and the state rate of 5.4%.

Provide the journal entry to record the payroll tax expense for the period.

OBJ. 4 **EE 11-6** *p. 506*

PE 11-6A **Vacation pay and pension benefits**

Lutes Company provides its employees with vacation benefits and a defined contribution pension plan. Employees earned vacation pay of $25,500 for the period. The pension plan requires a contribution to the plan administrator equal to 8% of employee salaries. Salaries were $340,000 during the period.

Provide the journal entry for the (a) vacation pay and (b) pension benefit.

OBJ. 4 **EE 11-6** *p. 506*

PE 11-6B **Vacation pay and pension benefits**

Wang Equipment Company provides its employees vacation benefits and a defined benefit pension plan. Employees earned vacation pay of $42,000 for the period. The pension formula calculated a pension cost of $273,000. Only $210,000 was contributed to the pension plan administrator.

Provide the journal entry for the (a) vacation pay and (b) pension benefit.

OBJ. 5 **EE 11-7** *p. 508*

PE 11-7A **Estimated warranty liability**

Zinn Co. sold $500,000 of equipment during May under a one-year warranty. The cost to repair defects under the warranty is estimated at 5% of the sales price. On October 10, a customer required a $100 part replacement, plus $65 of labor under the warranty.

Provide the journal entry for (a) the estimated warranty expense on May 31 and (b) the October 10 warranty work.

OBJ. 5 **EE 11-7** *p. 508*

PE 11-7B **Estimated warranty liability**

Caldwell Industries sold $410,000 of consumer electronics during August under a nine-month warranty. The cost to repair defects under the warranty is estimated at 4% of the sales price. On October 15, a customer was given $110 cash under terms of the warranty.

Provide the journal entry for (a) the estimated warranty expense on August 31 and (b) the October 15 cash payment.

OBJ. 6 **EE 11-8** *p. 511*

F·A·I

PE 11-8A **Quick ratio**

Grangel Company reported the following current assets and liabilities for December 31, 2012 and 2011:

	Dec. 31, 2012	Dec. 31, 2011
Cash	$ 620	$ 560
Temporary investments	1,330	1,250
Accounts receivable	850	830
Inventory	1,000	1,000
Accounts payable	2,800	2,200

a. Compute the quick ratio for December 31, 2012 and 2011.

b. Interpret the company's quick ratio. Is the quick ratio improving or declining?

OBJ. 6   EE 11-8 *p. 511*

PE 11-8B   Quick ratio

Tappert Company reported the following current assets and liabilities for December 31, 2012 and 2011:

	Dec. 31, 2012	Dec. 31, 2011
Cash	$ 990	$ 860
Temporary investments	1,910	1,500
Accounts receivable	1,600	1,280
Inventory	2,000	1,400
Accounts payable	3,000	2,800

a. Compute the quick ratio for December 31, 2012 and 2011.

b. Interpret the company's quick ratio. Is the quick ratio improving or declining?

Exercises

OBJ. 1

✔ Total current
liabilities, $782,500

EX 11-1   Current liabilities

New Wave Co. sold 10,000 annual subscriptions of *Game Life* for $75 during December 2012. These new subscribers will receive monthly issues, beginning in January 2013. In addition, the business had taxable income of $550,000 during the first calendar quarter of 2013. The federal tax rate is 40%. A quarterly tax payment will be made on April 7, 2013.

Prepare the Current Liabilities section of the balance sheet for New Wave Co. on March 31, 2013.

OBJ. 1

EX 11-2   Entries for discounting notes payable

TKR Enterprises issues a 30-day note for $570,000 to Sweeney Industries for merchandise inventory. Sweeney Industries discounts the note at 8%.

a. Journalize TKR Enterprises' entries to record:

   1. the issuance of the note.

   2. the payment of the note at maturity.

b. Journalize Sweeney Industries' entries to record:

   1. the receipt of the note.

   2. the receipt of the payment of the note at maturity.

OBJ. 1

EX 11-3   Evaluate alternative notes

A borrower has two alternatives for a loan: (1) issue a $180,000, 45-day, 10% note or (2) issue a $180,000, 45-day note that the creditor discounts at 10%.

a. Calculate the amount of the interest expense for each option.

b. Determine the proceeds received by the borrower in each situation.

c. ➤ Which alternative is more favorable to the borrower? Explain.

OBJ. 1

EX 11-4   Entries for notes payable

A business issued a 45-day, 6% note for $80,000 to a creditor on account. Journalize the entries to record (a) the issuance of the note and (b) the payment of the note at maturity, including interest.

OBJ. 1

EX 11-5   Entries for discounted note payable

A business issued a 30-day note for $72,000 to a creditor on account. The note was discounted at 7%. Journalize the entries to record (a) the issuance of the note and (b) the payment of the note at maturity.

OBJ. 1

EX 11-6   Fixed asset purchases with note

On June 30, Beahm Management Company purchased land for $250,000 and a building for $350,000, paying $300,000 cash and issuing an 8% note for the balance, secured by a mortgage on the property. The terms of the note provide for 20 semiannual payments of $15,000 on the principal plus the interest accrued from the date of the preceding payment. Journalize the entry to record (a) the transaction on June 30, (b) the payment of the first installment on December 31, and (c) the payment of the second installment the following June 30.

OBJ. 1

EX 11-7   Current portion of long-term debt

Burger King Holdings, Inc., the operator and franchisor of Burger King restaurants, reported the following information about its long-term debt in the notes to a recent financial statement:

Long-term debt is comprised of the following:

	June 30	
	2009	**2008**
Notes payable	$823,100,000	$876,200,000
Less current portion	(67,500,000)	(7,400,000)
Long-term debt	$755,600,000	$868,800,000

a. How much of the notes payable was disclosed as a current liability on the June 30, 2009, balance sheet?

b. How much did the total current liabilities change between 2008 and 2009 as a result of the current portion of long-term debt?

c. If Burger King did not issue additional notes payable during 2010, what would be the total notes payable on June 30, 2010?

OBJ. 2

✔ b. Net pay, 2,725.75

EX 11-8   Calculate payroll

An employee earns $60 per hour and 1.5 times that rate for all hours in excess of 40 hours per week. Assume that the employee worked 55 hours during the week, Assume further that the social security tax rate was 6.0%, the Medicare tax rate was 1.5%, and federal income tax to be withheld was $743.

a. Determine the gross pay for the week.

b. Determine the net pay for the week.

OBJ. 2

✔ Administrator net pay, $1,776.92

EX 11-9   Calculate payroll

Donohue Professional Services has three employees—a consultant, a computer programmer, and an administrator. The following payroll information is available for each employee:

	Consultant	Computer Programmer	Administrator
Regular earnings rate	$2,800 per week	$30 per hour	$42 per hour
Overtime earnings rate	Not applicable	1.5 times hourly rate	2 times hourly rate
Number of withholding allowances	3	2	1

For the current pay period, the computer programmer worked 60 hours and the administrator worked 50 hours. The federal income tax withheld for all three employees, who are single, can be determined from the wage bracket withholding table in Exhibit 3 in the chapter. Assume further that the social security tax rate was 6.0%, the Medicare tax rate was 1.5%, and one withholding allowance is $70.

Determine the gross pay and the net pay for each of the three employees for the current pay period.

OBJ. 2, 3

✔ a. (3) Total earnings, $900,000

EX 11-10 Summary payroll data

In the following summary of data for a payroll period, some amounts have been intentionally omitted:

Earnings:	
1. At regular rate	?
2. At overtime rate	$135,000
3. Total earnings	?
Deductions:	
4. Social security tax	54,000
5. Medicare tax	13,500
6. Income tax withheld	225,000
7. Medical insurance	31,500
8. Union dues	?
9. Total deductions	335,250
10. Net amount paid	564,750
Accounts debited:	
11. Factory Wages	475,000
12. Sales Salaries	?
13. Office Salaries	200,000

a. Calculate the amounts omitted in lines (1), (3), (8), and (12).

b. Journalize the entry to record the payroll accrual.

c. Journalize the entry to record the payment of the payroll.

OBJ. 3

✔ a. $85,000

EX 11-11 Payroll tax entries

According to a summary of the payroll of Brooks Industries Co., $1,100,000 was subject to the 6.0% social security tax and the 1.5% Medicare tax. Also, $50,000 was subject to state and federal unemployment taxes.

a. Calculate the employer's payroll taxes, using the following rates: state unemployment, 4.2%; federal unemployment, 0.8%.

b. Journalize the entry to record the accrual of payroll taxes.

OBJ. 3

EX 11-12 Payroll entries

The payroll register for Robinson Company for the week ended November 18 indicated the following:

Salaries	$1,300,000
Social security tax withheld	61,100
Medicare tax withheld	19,500
Federal income tax withheld	260,000

In addition, state and federal unemployment taxes were calculated at the rate of 5.2% and 0.8%, respectively, on $240,000 of salaries.

a. Journalize the entry to record the payroll for the week of November 18.

b. Journalize the entry to record the payroll tax expense incurred for the week of November 18.

OBJ. 3

EX 11-13 Payroll entries

Faber Company had gross wages of $110,000 during the week ended June 17. The amount of wages subject to social security tax was $110,000, while the amount of wages subject to federal and state unemployment taxes was $15,000. Tax rates are as follows:

Social security	6.0%
Medicare	1.5%
State unemployment	5.4%
Federal unemployment	0.8%

The total amount withheld from employee wages for federal taxes was $22,000.

a. Journalize the entry to record the payroll for the week of June 17.

b. Journalize the entry to record the payroll tax expense incurred for the week of June 17.

OBJ. 3

EX 11-14 Payroll internal control procedures

Big Dave's Pizza is a pizza restaurant specializing in the sale of pizza by the slice. The store employs 10 full-time and 15 part-time workers. The store's weekly payroll averages $5,600 for all 25 workers.

Big Dave's Pizza uses a personal computer to assist in preparing paychecks. Each week, the store's accountant collects employee time cards and enters the hours worked into the payroll program. The payroll program calculates each employee's pay and prints a paycheck. The accountant uses a check-signing machine to sign the paychecks. Next, the restaurant's owner authorizes the transfer of funds from the restaurant's regular bank account to the payroll account.

For the week of June 11, the accountant accidentally recorded 200 hours worked instead of 40 hours for one of the full-time employees.

Does Big Dave's Pizza have internal controls in place to catch this error? If so, how will this error be detected?

OBJ. 3

EX 11-15 Internal control procedures

Matt's Bikes is a small manufacturer of specialty bicycles. The company employs 18 production workers and four administrative persons. The following procedures are used to process the company's weekly payroll:

a. Whenever an employee receives a pay raise, the supervisor must fill out a wage adjustment form, which is signed by the company president. This form is used to change the employee's wage rate in the payroll system.

b. All employees are required to record their hours worked by clocking in and out on a time clock. Employees must clock out for lunch break. Due to congestion around the time clock area at lunch time, management has not objected to having one employee clock in and out for an entire department.

c. Whenever a salaried employee is terminated, Personnel authorizes Payroll to remove the employee from the payroll system. However, this procedure is not required when an hourly worker is terminated. Hourly employees only receive a paycheck if their time cards show hours worked. The computer automatically drops an employee from the payroll system when that employee has six consecutive weeks with no hours worked.

d. Paychecks are signed by using a check-signing machine. This machine is located in the main office so that it can be easily accessed by anyone needing a check signed.

e. Matt's Bikes maintains a separate checking account for payroll checks. Each week, the total net pay for all employees is transferred from the company's regular bank account to the payroll account.

State whether each of the procedures is appropriate or inappropriate after considering the principles of internal control. If a procedure is inappropriate, describe the appropriate procedure.

OBJ. 4

EX 11-16 Accrued vacation pay

A business provides its employees with varying amounts of vacation per year, depending on the length of employment. The estimated amount of the current year's vacation pay is $61,200.

a. Journalize the adjusting entry required on January 31, the end of the first month of the current year, to record the accrued vacation pay.

b. How is the vacation pay reported on the company's balance sheet? When is this amount removed from the company's balance sheet?

OBJ. 4

EX 11-17 Pension plan entries

Wren Co. operates a chain of gift shops. The company maintains a defined contribution pension plan for its employees. The plan requires quarterly installments to be paid to the funding agent, Whims Funds, by the fifteenth of the month following the end of each quarter. Assume that the pension cost is $141,500 for the quarter ended March 31.

a. Journalize the entries to record the accrued pension liability on March 31 and the payment to the funding agent on April 15.

b. How does a defined contribution plan differ from a defined benefit plan?

OBJ. 4

EX 11-18 Defined benefit pension plan terms

In a recent year's financial statements, Procter & Gamble showed an unfunded pension liability of $3,706 million and a periodic pension cost of $341 million.

Explain the meaning of the $3,706 million unfunded pension liability and the $341 million periodic pension cost.

OBJ. 5

EX 11-19 Accrued product warranty

Parker Products Co. warrants its products for one year. The estimated product warranty is 3% of sales. Assume that sales were $442,000 for September. In October, a customer received warranty repairs requiring $110 of parts and $86 of labor.

a. Journalize the adjusting entry required at September 30, the end of the first month of the current fiscal year, to record the accrued product warranty.

b. Journalize the entry to record the warranty work provided in October.

OBJ. 5

EX 11-20 Accrued product warranty

General Motors Corporation disclosed estimated product warranty payable for comparative years as follows:

	(in millions)	
	12/31/08	12/31/07
Current estimated product warranty payable	$3,792	$4,655
Noncurrent estimated product warranty payable	4,699	4,960
Total	$8,491	$9,615

GM's sales were $177,594 million in 2007 and decreased to $147,732 million in 2008. Assume that the total paid on warranty claims during 2008 was $5,000 million.

a. Why are short- and long-term estimated warranty liabilities separately disclosed?

b. Provide the journal entry for the 2008 product warranty expense.

c. What two conditions must be met in order for a product warranty liability to be reported in the financial statements?

OBJ. 5

EX 11-21 Contingent liabilities

Several months ago, Reiltz Industries, Inc. experienced a hazardous materials spill at one of its plants. As a result, the Environmental Protection Agency (EPA) fined the company $570,000. The company is contesting the fine. In addition, an employee is seeking $560,000 in damages related to the spill. Lastly, a homeowner has sued the company for $364,000. The homeowner lives 35 miles from the plant, but believes that the incident has reduced the home's resale value by $364,000.

Reiltz's legal counsel believes that it is probable that the EPA fine will stand. In addition, counsel indicates that an out-of-court settlement of $238,000 has recently been reached with the employee. The final papers will be signed next week. Counsel believes that the homeowner's case is much weaker and will be decided in favor of Reiltz. Other litigation related to the spill is possible, but the damage amounts are uncertain.

a. Journalize the contingent liabilities associated with the hazardous materials spill. Use the account "Damage Awards and Fines" to recognize the expense for the period.

b. ━━━▶ Prepare a note disclosure relating to this incident.

OBJ. 6

✔ a. 2012: 1.0

FAI

EX 11-22 Quick ratio

CCB Co. had the following current assets and liabilities for two comparative years:

	Dec. 31, 2012	Dec. 31, 2011
Current assets:		
Cash	$ 506,000	$ 524,000
Accounts receivable	354,000	364,000
Inventory	240,000	200,000
Total current assets	$1,100,000	$1,088,000
Current liabilities:		
Current portion of long-term debt	$ 160,000	$ 120,000
Accounts payable	265,000	220,000
Accrued and other current liabilities	435,000	400,000
Total current liabilities	$ 860,000	$ 740,000

a. Determine the quick ratio for December 31, 2012 and 2011.

b. ━━━▶ Interpret the change in the quick ratio between the two balance sheet dates.

OBJ. 6

✔ a. Apple, 2.4

 FAI

EX 11-23 Quick ratio

The current assets and current liabilities for Apple Computer, Inc., and Dell Inc. are shown as follows at the end of a recent fiscal period:

	Apple Computer, Inc. (in millions) Sept. 26, 2009	Dell Inc. (in millions) Jan. 29, 2010
Current assets:		
Cash and cash equivalents	$ 5,263	$10,635
Short-term investments	18,201	373
Accounts receivable	4,496	8,543
Inventories	455	1,051
Other current assets*	3,140	3,643
Total current assets	$31,555	$24,245
Current liabilities:		
Accounts payable	$ 9,453	$15,257
Accrued and other current liabilities	2,053	3,703
Total current liabilities	$11,506	$18,960

*These represent prepaid expense and other nonquick current assets.

a. Determine the quick ratio for both companies.

b. Interpret the quick ratio difference between the two companies.

Problems Series A

OBJ. 1, 5

PR 11-1A   Liability transactions

The following items were selected from among the transactions completed by Isis Co. during the current year:

Feb   15.   Purchased merchandise on account from Viper Co., $260,000, terms n/30.

Mar.   17.   Issued a 45-day, 5% note for $260,000 to Viper Co., on account.

May   1.   Paid Viper Co. the amount owed on the note of March 17.

June   15.   Borrowed $300,000 from Ima Bank, issuing a 60-day, 9% note.

July   21.   Purchased tools by issuing a $240,000, 60-day note to Charger Co., which discounted the note at the rate of 7%.

Aug.   14.   Paid Ima Bank the interest due on the note of June 15 and renewed the loan by issuing a new 30-day, 10% note for $300,000. (Journalize both the debit and credit to the notes payable account.)

Sept.   13.   Paid Ima Bank the amount due on the note of August 14.

19.   Paid Charger Co. the amount due on the note of July 21.

Dec.   1.   Purchased office equipment from Challenger Co. for $235,000, paying $35,000 and issuing a series of ten 7.5% notes for $20,000 each, coming due at 30-day intervals.

12.   Settled a product liability lawsuit with a customer for $121,600, payable in January. Isis accrued the loss in a litigation claims payable account.

31.   Paid the amount due Challenger Co. on the first note in the series issued on December 1.

Instructions

1. Journalize the transactions.

2. Journalize the adjusting entry for each of the following accrued expenses at the end of the current year: (a) product warranty cost, $26,240; (b) interest on the nine remaining notes owed to Challenger Co.

OBJ. 2, 3

✔ 1. (b) Dr. Payroll Tax Expense, $42,465

PR 11-2A   Entries for payroll and payroll taxes

The following information about the payroll for the week ended December 30 was obtained from the records of Arnsparger Equipment Co.:

Salaries:		Deductions:	
Sales salaries	$270,000	Income tax withheld	$ 95,920
Warehouse salaries	142,000	Social security tax withheld	32,700
Office salaries	133,000	Medicare tax withheld	8,175
	$545,000	U.S. savings bonds	11,990
		Group insurance	9,810
			$158,595

Tax rates assumed:
Social security, 6%
Medicare, 1.5%
State unemployment (employer only), 4.5%
Federal unemployment (employer only), 0.8%

Instructions

1. Assuming that the payroll for the last week of the year is to be paid on December 31, journalize the following entries:

a. December 30, to record the payroll.

b. December 30, to record the employer's payroll taxes on the payroll to be paid on December 31. Of the total payroll for the last week of the year, $30,000 is subject to unemployment compensation taxes.

(continued)

2. Assuming that the payroll for the last week of the year is to be paid on January 5 of the following fiscal year, journalize the following entries:

    a. December 30, to record the payroll.

    b. January 5, to record the employer's payroll taxes on the payroll to be paid on January 5. Since it is a new fiscal year, all $545,000 in salaries is subject to unemployment compensation taxes.

PR 11-3A   Wage and tax statement data on employer FICA tax

Courtside Concepts Co. began business on January 2, 2011. Salaries were paid to employees on the last day of each month, and social security tax, Medicare tax, and federal income tax were withheld in the required amounts. An employee who is hired in the middle of the month receives half the monthly salary for that month. All required payroll tax reports were filed, and the correct amount of payroll taxes was remitted by the company for the calendar year. Early in 2012, before the Wage and Tax Statements (Form W-2) could be prepared for distribution to employees and for filing with the Social Security Administration, the employees' earnings records were inadvertently destroyed.

None of the employees resigned or were discharged during the year, and there were no changes in salary rates. The social security tax was withheld at the rate of 6.0% and Medicare tax at the rate of 1.5% on salary. Data on dates of employment, salary rates, and employees' income taxes withheld, which are summarized as follows, were obtained from personnel records and payroll records:

Employee	Date First Employed	Monthly Salary	Monthly Income Tax Withheld
Garnett	Jan. 2	$ 4,400	$ 706
Kidd	Oct. 1	7,200	1,442
J. O'Neal	Apr. 16	3,600	506
Bryant	Nov. 1	3,000	356
S. O'Neal	Jan. 16	12,800	3,012
Marbury	Dec. 1	5,000	856
Duncan	Feb. 1	11,200	2,564

Instructions

1. Calculate the amounts to be reported on each employee's Wage and Tax Statement (Form W-2) for 2011, arranging the data in the following form:

Employee	Gross Earnings	Federal Income Tax Withheld	Social Security Tax Withheld	Medicare Tax Withheld

2. Calculate the following employer payroll taxes for the year: (a) social security; (b) Medicare; (c) state unemployment compensation at 4.6% on the first $10,000 of each employee's earnings; (d) federal unemployment compensation at 0.8% on the first $10,000 of each employee's earnings; (e) total.

PR 11-4A   Payroll register

If the working papers correlating with this textbook are not used, omit Problem 11-4A. The payroll register for Knapp Co. for the week ended September 14, 2012, is presented in the working papers.

Instructions

1. Journalize the entry to record the payroll for the week.

2. Journalize the entry to record the issuance of the checks to employees.

3. Journalize the entry to record the employer's payroll taxes for the week. Assume the following tax rates: state unemployment, 3.6%; federal unemployment, 0.8%. Of the earnings, $2,000 is subject to unemployment taxes.

4. Journalize the entry to record a check issued on September 17 to Fourth National Bank in payment of employees' income taxes, $2,062.17, social security taxes, $1,463.88, and Medicare taxes, $365.98.

OBJ. 2, 3

✔ 1. Total net amount
payable, $11,180.93

OBJ. 2, 3

PR 11-5A   Payroll register

The following data for Throwback Industries, Inc. relate to the payroll for the week ended December 7, 2012:

Employee	Hours Worked	Hourly Rate	Weekly Salary	Federal Income Tax	U.S. Savings Bonds
Blanda	48	$44.00		$526.24	$ 45
Dawson	42	38.00		351.31	50
Fouts	44	46.00		402.04	55
Griese	36	32.00		241.92	65
Namath	45	40.00		399.00	0
Marino			$2,200	528.00	44
Staubach	35	29.00		152.25	110
Starr			2,450	539.00	102
Unitas	41	38.00		315.40	0

Employees Marino and Starr are office staff, and all of the other employees are sales personnel. All sales personnel are paid 1½ times the regular rate for all hours in excess of 40 hours per week. The social security tax rate is 6.0%, and Medicare tax is 1.5% of each employee's annual earnings. The next payroll check to be used is No. 625.

Instructions

1. Prepare a payroll register for Throwback Industries, Inc. for the week ended December 7, 2012. Use the following columns for the payroll register: Name, Total Hours, Regular Earnings, Overtime Earnings, Total Earnings, Social Security Tax, Medicare Tax, Federal Income Tax, U.S. Savings Bonds, Total Deductions, Net Pay, Ck. No., Sales Salaries Expense, and Office Salaries Expense.

2. Journalize the entry to record the payroll sales for the week.

OBJ. 2, 3, 4

GL
GENERAL
LEDGER

PR 11-6A   Payroll accounts and year-end entries

The following accounts, with the balances indicated, appear in the ledger of Quinn Co. on December 1 of the current year:

311	Salaries Payable	—		318	Bond Deductions Payable	$ 4,200
312	Social Security Tax Payable	$10,830		319	Medical Insurance Payable	33,000
313	Medicare Tax Payable	2,850		511	Operations Salaries Expense	1,150,000
314	Employees Federal Income Tax Payable	17,575		611	Officers Salaries Expense	750,000
315	Employees State Income Tax Payable	17,100		612	Office Salaries Expense	190,000
316	State Unemployment Tax Payable	1,800		619	Payroll Tax Expense	163,680
317	Federal Unemployment Tax Payable	600				

The following transactions relating to payroll, payroll deductions, and payroll taxes occurred during December:

Dec. 2. Issued Check No. 210 for $4,200 to Ace Bank to purchase U.S. savings bonds for employees.

  5. Issued Check No. 211 to Ace Bank for $31,255 in payment of $10,830 of social security tax, $2,850 of Medicare tax, and $17,575 of employees' federal income tax due.

  16. Journalized the entry to record the biweekly payroll. A summary of the payroll record follows:

Salary distribution:			
Operations		$52,200	
Officers		34,100	
Office		8,650	$94,950
Deductions:			
Social security tax		$ 5,697	
Medicare tax		1,424	
Federal income tax withheld		17,566	
State income tax withheld		4,273	
Savings bond deductions		2,100	
Medical insurance deductions		5,500	36,560
Net amount			$58,390

Dec. 16. Issued Check No. 220 in payment of the net amount of the biweekly payroll.

16. Journalized the entry to record payroll taxes on employees' earnings of December 16: social security tax, $5,697; Medicare tax, $1,424; state unemployment tax, $450; federal unemployment tax, $150.

19. Issued Check No. 224 to Ace Bank for $31,048, in payment of $11,394 of social security tax, $2,848 of Medicare tax, and $17,566 of employees' federal income tax due.

19. Issued Check No. 229 to Blackwood Insurance Company for $33,000, in payment of the semiannual premium on the group medical insurance policy.

30. Journalized the entry to record the biweekly payroll. A summary of the payroll record follows:

Salary distribution:		
Operations	$51,400	
Officers	34,100	
Office	8,400	$93,900
Deductions:		
Social security tax	$ 5,634	
Medicare tax	1,409	
Federal income tax withheld	17,184	
State income tax withheld	4,226	
Savings bond deductions	2,100	30,553
Net amount		$63,347

30. Issued Check No. 341 in payment of the net amount of the biweekly payroll.

30. Journalized the entry to record payroll taxes on employees' earnings of December 30: social security tax, $5,634; Medicare tax, $1,409; state unemployment tax, $225; federal unemployment tax, $75.

30. Issued Check No. 243 for $25,599 to State Department of Revenue in payment of employees' state income tax due on December 31.

30. Issued Check No. 245 to Ace Bank for $4,200 to purchase U.S. savings bonds for employees.

31. Paid $50,000 to the employee pension plan. The annual pension cost is $65,000. (Record both the payment and unfunded pension liability.)

Instructions

1. Journalize the transactions.

2. Journalize the following adjusting entries on December 31:

   a. Salaries accrued: operations salaries, $5,140; officers salaries, $3,410; office salaries, $840. The payroll taxes are immaterial and are not accrued.

   b. Vacation pay, $17,500.

Problems Series B

OBJ. 1, 5

PR 11-1B Liability transactions

The following items were selected from among the transactions completed by Javelin, Inc. during the current year:

Mar. 1. Borrowed $80,000 from Nova Company, issuing a 30-day, 9% note for that amount.

15. Purchased equipment by issuing a $180,000, 180-day note to Shelby Manufacturing Co., which discounted the note at the rate of 7.5%.

31. Paid Nova Company the interest due on the note of March 1 and renewed the loan by issuing a new 60-day, 9% note for $80,000. (Record both the debit and credit to the notes payable account.)

May 30. Paid Nova Company the amount due on the note of March 31.

July 6. Purchased merchandise on account from Pacer Co., $56,000, terms, n/30.

Aug. 5. Issued a 45-day, 8% note for $56,000 to Pacer Co., on account.

Sept. 11. Paid Shelby Manufacturing Co. the amount due on the note of March 15.

19. Paid Pacer Co. the amount owed on the note of August 5.

Nov. 16. Purchased store equipment from Gremlin Co. for $190,000, paying $40,000 and issuing a series of fifteen 6% notes for $10,000 each, coming due at 30-day intervals.

Dec. 16. Paid the amount due Gremlin Co. on the first note in the series issued on November 16.

21. Settled a personal injury lawsuit with a customer for $55,250, to be paid in January. Javelin, Inc. accrued the loss in a litigation claims payable account.

Instructions

1. Journalize the transactions.

2. Journalize the adjusting entry for each of the following accrued expenses at the end of the current year:

   a. Product warranty cost, $13,520.

   b. Interest on the 14 remaining notes owed to Gremlin Co.

OBJ. 2, 3

✔ 1. (b) Dr. Payroll Tax Expense, $67,248

PR 11-2B Entries for payroll and payroll taxes

The following information about the payroll for the week ended December 30 was obtained from the records of Dart Co.:

Salaries:		Deductions:	
Sales salaries	$546,000	Income tax withheld	$172,480
Warehouse salaries	116,000	Social security tax withheld	52,800
Office salaries	218,000	Medicare tax withheld	13,200
	$880,000	U.S. savings bonds	26,400
		Group insurance	39,600
			$304,480

Tax rates assumed:

Social security, 6%

Medicare, 1.5%

State unemployment (employer only), 4.0%

Federal unemployment (employer only), 0.8%

Instructions

1. Assuming that the payroll for the last week of the year is to be paid on December 31, journalize the following entries:

   a. December 30, to record the payroll.

   b. December 30, to record the employer's payroll taxes on the payroll to be paid on December 31. Of the total payroll for the last week of the year, $26,000 is subject to unemployment compensation taxes.

2. Assuming that the payroll for the last week of the year is to be paid on January 4 of the following fiscal year, journalize the following entries:

   a. December 30, to record the payroll.

   b. January 4, to record the employer's payroll taxes on the payroll to be paid on January 4. Since it is a new fiscal year, all $880,000 in salaries is subject to unemployment compensation taxes.

OBJ. 2, 3

✔ 2. (e) $23,977.00

PR 11-3B Wage and tax statement data and employer FICA tax

Diamond Industries, Inc., began business on January 2, 2011. Salaries were paid to employees on the last day of each month, and social security tax, Medicare tax, and federal income tax were withheld in the required amounts. An employee who is hired in the middle of the month receives half the monthly salary for that month. All required payroll tax reports were filed, and the correct amount of payroll taxes was remitted by the company for the calendar year. Early in 2012, before the Wage and Tax Statements

(Form W-2) could be prepared for distribution to employees and for filing with the Social Security Administration, the employees' earnings records were inadvertently destroyed.

None of the employees resigned or were discharged during the year, and there were no changes in salary rates. The social security tax was withheld at the rate of 6.0% and Medicare tax at the rate of 1.5% on salary. Data on dates of employment, salary rates, and employees' income taxes withheld, which are summarized as follows, were obtained from personnel records and payroll records:

Employee	Date First Employed	Monthly Salary	Monthly Income Tax Withheld
Beltran	Jan. 1	$ 4,300	$ 681
Jeter	Apr. 16	11,000	2,508
Lee	Aug. 1	7,800	1,612
Rodriguez	Nov. 16	3,000	356
Santana	Mar. 1	6,120	1,145
Ramirez	May 16	3,840	566
Ordonez	Dec. 1	4,000	606

Instructions

1. Calculate the amounts to be reported on each employee's Wage and Tax Statement (Form W-2) for 2011, arranging the data in the following form:

Employee	Gross Earnings	Federal Income Tax Withheld	Social Security Tax Withheld	Medicare Tax Withheld

2. Calculate the following employer payroll taxes for the year: (a) social security; (b) Medicare; (c) state unemployment compensation at 4.4% on the first $9,000 of each employee's earnings; (d) federal unemployment compensation at 0.8% on the first $9,000 of each employee's earnings; (e) total.

OBJ. 2, 3

✔ 3. Dr. Payroll Tax Expense, $1,188.61

PR 11-4B Payroll register

If the working papers correlating with this textbook are not used, omit Problem 11-4B.

The payroll register for Ritchie Manufacturing Co. for the week ended September 14, 2012, is presented in the working papers.

Instructions

1. Journalize the entry to record the payroll for the week.

2. Journalize the entry to record the issuance of the checks to employees.

3. Journalize the entry to record the employer's payroll taxes for the week. Assume the following tax rates: state unemployment, 3.4%; federal unemployment, 0.8%. Of the earnings, $2,200 is subject to unemployment taxes.

4. Journalize the entry to record a check issued on September 17 to Second National Bank in payment of employees' income taxes, $2,464.97, social security taxes, $1,753.92, and Medicare taxes, $438.50.

OBJ. 2, 3

✔ 1. Total net amount payable, $9,583.80

PR 11-5B Payroll register

The following data for Gridiron Industries, Inc., relate to the payroll for the week ended December 7, 2012:

Employee	Hours Worked	Hourly Rate	Weekly Salary	Federal Income Tax	U.S. Savings Bonds
Aikman	50	$26.00		$328.90	$45
Csonka			$3,400	731.00	0
Dickerson	35	28.00		186.20	38
Elway	44	34.00		328.44	30
Harris	38	22.00		175.56	45
Motley			2,000	480.00	68
Nagurski	45	26.00		185.25	0
Sanders	45	27.00		282.15	45
Swann	42	25.00		215.00	0

Employees Csonka and Motley are office staff, and all of the other employees are sales personnel. All sales personnel are paid 1½ times the regular rate for all hours in excess of 40 hours per week. The social security tax rate is 6.0% of each employee's annual earnings, and Medicare tax is 1.5% of each employee's annual earnings. The next payroll check to be used is No. 328.

Instructions

1. Prepare a payroll register for Gridiron Industries, Inc., for the week ended December 7, 2012. Use the following columns for the payroll register: Name, Total Hours, Regular Earnings, Overtime Earnings, Total Earnings, Social Security Tax, Medicare Tax, Federal Income Tax, U.S. Savings Bonds, Total Deductions, Net Pay, Ck. No., Sales Salaries Expense, and Office Salaries Expense.

2. Journalize the entry to record the payroll sales for the week.

OBJ. 2, 3, 4

PR 11-6B Payroll accounts and year-end entries

The following accounts, with the balances indicated, appear in the ledger of Codigo Co. on December 1 of the current year:

111	Salaries Payable	—	118	Bond Deductions Payable	$ 2,520
112	Social Security Tax Payable	$ 6,847	119	Medical Insurance Payable	2,800
113	Medicare Tax Payable	1,763	411	Sales Salaries Expense	778,000
114	Employees Federal Income Tax Payable	10,873	511	Officers Salaries Expense	375,000
115	Employees State Income Tax Payable	9,874	611	Office Salaries Expense	140,000
116	State Unemployment Tax Payable	1,400	618	Payroll Tax Expense	104,610
117	Federal Unemployment Tax Payable	400			

The following transactions relating to payroll, payroll deductions, and payroll taxes occurred during December:

Dec. 1. Issued Check No. 615 to Canal Insurance Company for $2,800, in payment of the semiannual premium on the group medical insurance policy.

1. Issued Check No. 616 to Green Bank for $19,483, in payment for $6,847 of social security tax, $1,763 of Medicare tax, and $10,873 of employees' federal income tax due.

2. Issued Check No. 617 for $2,520 to Green Bank to purchase U.S. savings bonds for employees.

12. Journalized the entry to record the biweekly payroll. A summary of the payroll record follows:

Salary distribution:		
Sales	$35,300	
Officers	17,000	
Office	6,300	$58,600
Deductions:		
Social security tax	$ 3,516	
Medicare tax	879	
Federal income tax withheld	10,431	
State income tax withheld	2,637	
Savings bond deductions	1,260	
Medical insurance deductions	467	19,190
Net amount		$39,410

12. Issued Check No. 622 in payment of the net amount of the biweekly payroll.

12. Journalized the entry to record payroll taxes on employees' earnings of December 12: social security tax, $3,516; Medicare tax, $879; state unemployment tax, $350; federal unemployment tax, $100.

15. Issued Check No. 630 to Green Bank for $18,635, in payment for $7,032 of social security tax, $1,758 of Medicare tax, and $10,431 of employees' federal income tax due.

Dec. 26. Journalized the entry to record the biweekly payroll. A summary of the payroll record follows:

Salary distribution:		
Sales	$35,400	
Officers	17,250	
Office	6,400	$59,050
Deductions:		
Social security tax	$ 3,543	
Medicare tax	886	
Federal income tax withheld	10,511	
State income tax withheld	2,657	
Savings bond deductions	1,260	18,857
Net amount		$40,193

26. Issued Check No. 640 for the net amount of the biweekly payroll.

26. Journalized the entry to record payroll taxes on employees' earnings of December 26: social security tax, $3,543; Medicare tax, $886; state unemployment tax, $170; federal unemployment tax, $45.

30. Issued Check No. 651 for $15,168 to State Department of Revenue, in payment of employees' state income tax due on December 31.

30. Issued Check No. 652 to Green Bank for $2,520 to purchase U.S. savings bonds for employees.

31. Paid $61,600 to the employee pension plan. The annual pension cost is $72,800. (Record both the payment and the unfunded pension liability.)

Instructions

1. Journalize the transactions.

2. Journalize the following adjusting entries on December 31:

   a. Salaries accrued: sales salaries, $10,620; officers salaries, $5,175; office salaries, $1,920. The payroll taxes are immaterial and are not accrued.

   b. Vacation pay, $14,840.

Comprehensive Problem 3

✔ 5. Total assets, $2,563,840

Selected transactions completed by Gampfer Company during its first fiscal year ending December 31 were as follows:

Jan. 2. Issued a check to establish a petty cash fund of $3,200.

Mar. 14. Replenished the petty cash fund, based on the following summary of petty cash receipts: office supplies, $1,200; miscellaneous selling expense, $410; miscellaneous administrative expense, $620.

Apr. 21. Purchased $22,400 of merchandise on account, terms 1/10, n/30. The perpetual inventory system is used to account for inventory.

May 20. Paid the invoice of April 21 after the discount period had passed.

23. Received cash from daily cash sales for $15,120. The amount indicated by the cash register was $15,152.

June 15. Received a 60-day, 10% note for $127,500 on the Cady account.

Aug. 14. Received amount owed on June 15 note, plus interest at the maturity date.

18. Received $5,440 on the Yoder account and wrote off the remainder owed on a $6,400 accounts receivable balance. (The allowance method is used in accounting for uncollectible receivables.)

Sept. 9. Reinstated the Yoder account written off on August 18 and received $960 cash in full payment.

15. Purchased land by issuing a $480,000, 90-day note to Ace Development Co., which discounted it at 8%.

Oct. 17. Sold office equipment in exchange for $96,000 cash plus receipt of a $64,000, 90-day, 6% note. The equipment had a cost of $224,000 and accumulated depreciation of $44,800 as of October 17.

Nov. 30. Journalized the monthly payroll for November, based on the following data:

Salaries		Deductions	
Sales salaries	$ 96,640	Income tax withheld	$28,090
Office salaries	55,200	Social security tax withheld	9,110
	$151,840	Medicare tax withheld	2,278

Unemployment tax rates:	
State unemployment	4.0%
Federal unemployment	0.8%
Amount subject to unemployment taxes:	
State unemployment	$5,000
Federal unemployment	5,000

30. Journalized the employer's payroll taxes on the payroll.

Dec. 14. Journalized the payment of the September 15 note at maturity.

31. The pension cost for the year was $136,000, of which $99,840 was paid to the pension plan trustee.

Instructions

1. Journalize the selected transactions.

2. Based on the following data, prepare a bank reconciliation for December of the current year:

   a. Balance according to the bank statement at December 31, $202,240.

   b. Balance according to the ledger at December 31, $175,440.

   c. Checks outstanding at December 31, $48,960.

   d. Deposit in transit, not recorded by bank, $21,120.

   e. Bank debit memo for service charges, $540.

   f. A check for $11,520 in payment of an invoice was incorrectly recorded in the accounts as $11,020.

3. Based on the bank reconciliation prepared in (2), journalize the entry or entries to be made by Gampfer Company.

4. Based on the following selected data, journalize the adjusting entries as of December 31 of the current year:

   a. Estimated uncollectible accounts at December 31, $11,520, based on an aging of accounts receivable. The balance of Allowance for Doubtful Accounts at December 31 was $1,200 (debit).

   b. The physical inventory on December 31 indicated an inventory shrinkage of $2,360.

   c. Prepaid insurance expired during the year, $16,300.

   d. Office supplies used during the year, $2,800.

   e. Depreciation is computed as follows:

Asset	Cost	Residual Value	Acquisition Date	Useful Life in Years	Depreciation Method Used
Buildings	$650,000	$ 0	January 2	50	Double-declining-balance
Office Equip.	176,000	16,000	January 3	5	Straight-line
Store Equip.	80,000	8,000	July 1	10	Straight-line

   f. A patent costing $36,000 when acquired on January 2 has a remaining legal life of eight years and is expected to have value for six years.

   g. The cost of mineral rights was $390,000. Of the estimated deposit of 650,000 tons of ore, 38,400 tons were mined and sold during the year.

(Continued)

h. Vacation pay expense for December, $7,500.

i. A product warranty was granted beginning December 1 and covering a one-year period. The estimated cost is 3% of sales, which totaled $1,350,000 in December.

j. Interest was accrued on the note receivable received on October 17.

5. Based on the following information and the post-closing trial balance shown below, prepare a balance sheet in report form at December 31 of the current year.

The merchandise inventory is stated at cost by the LIFO method.
The product warranty payable is a current liability.

Vacation pay payable:
Current liability	$5,100
Long-term liability	2,400

The unfunded pension liability is a long-term liability.

Notes payable:
Current liability	$ 50,000
Long-term liability	450,000

Gampfer Company
Post-Closing Trial Balance
December 31, 2012

	Debit Balances	Credit Balances
Petty Cash	3,200	
Cash	174,400	
Notes Receivable	64,000	
Accounts Receivable	336,000	
Allowance for Doubtful Accounts		11,520
Merchandise Inventory	230,000	
Interest Receivable	800	
Prepaid Insurance	32,600	
Office Supplies	9,600	
Land	470,400	
Buildings	650,000	
Accumulated Depreciation—Buildings		26,000
Office Equipment	176,000	
Accumulated Depreciation—Office Equipment		32,000
Store Equipment	80,000	
Accumulated Depreciation—Store Equipment		3,600
Mineral Rights	390,000	
Accumulated Depletion		23,040
Patents	30,000	
Social Security Tax Payable		13,513
Medicare Tax Payable		3,378
Employees Federal Income Tax Payable		28,090
State Unemployment Tax Payable		40
Federal Unemployment Tax Payable		200
Salaries Payable		112,612
Accounts Payable		224,000
Interest Payable		20,207
Product Warranty Payable		40,500
Vacation Pay Payable		7,500
Unfunded Pension Liability		36,160
Notes Payable		500,000
J. Gampfer, Capital		1,564,640
	2,647,000	2,647,000

Cases & Projects

CP 11-1 Ethics and professional conduct in business

Lisa Deuel is a certified public accountant (CPA) and staff accountant for Bratz and Bratz, a local CPA firm. It had been the policy of the firm to provide a holiday bonus equal to two weeks' salary to all employees. The firm's new management team announced on November 15 that a bonus equal to only one week's salary would be made available to employees this year. Lisa thought that this policy was unfair because she and her co-workers planned on the full two-week bonus. The two-week bonus had been given for 10 straight years, so it seemed as though the firm had breached an implied commitment. Thus, Lisa decided that she would make up the lost bonus week by working an extra six hours of overtime per week over the next five weeks until the end of the year. Bratz and Bratz's policy is to pay overtime at 150% of straight time.

Lisa's supervisor was surprised to see overtime being reported, since there is generally very little additional or unusual client service demands at the end of the calendar year. However, the overtime was not questioned, since firm employees are on the "honor system" in reporting their overtime.

➤ Discuss whether the firm is acting in an ethical manner by changing the bonus. Is Lisa behaving in an ethical manner?

CP 11-2 Recognizing pension expense

The annual examination of Wave Company's financial statements by its external public accounting firm (auditors) is nearing completion. The following conversation took place between the controller of Wave Company (Tommy) and the audit manager from the public accounting firm (Jaclyn).

Jaclyn: You know, Tommy, we are about to wrap up our audit for this fiscal year. Yet, there is one item still to be resolved.

Tommy: What's that?

Jaclyn: Well, as you know, at the beginning of the year, Wave began a defined benefit pension plan. This plan promises your employees an annual payment when they retire, using a formula based on their salaries at retirement and their years of service. I believe that a pension expense should be recognized this year, equal to the amount of pension earned by your employees.

Tommy: Wait a minute. I think you have it all wrong. The company doesn't have a pension expense until it actually pays the pension in cash when the employee retires. After all, some of these employees may not reach retirement, and if they don't, the company doesn't owe them anything.

Jaclyn: You're not really seeing this the right way. The pension is earned by your employees during their working years. You actually make the payment much later—when they retire. It's like one long accrual—much like incurring wages in one period and paying them in the next. Thus, I think that you should recognize the expense in the period the pension is earned by the employees.

Tommy: Let me see if I've got this straight. I should recognize an expense this period for something that may or may not be paid to the employees in 20 or 30 years, when they finally retire. How am I supposed to determine what the expense is for the current year? The amount of the final retirement depends on many uncertainties: salary levels, employee longevity, mortality rates, and interest earned on investments to fund the pension. I don't think that an amount can be determined, even if I accepted your arguments.

➤ Evaluate Jaclyn's position. Is she right or is Tommy correct?

CP 11-3   Ethics and professional conduct in business

Gloria Seuss was discussing summer employment with Ella Kitt, president of Hotel California Construction Service:

Ella: I'm glad that you're thinking about joining us for the summer. We could certainly use the help.

Gloria: Sounds good. I enjoy outdoor work, and I could use the money to help with next year's school expenses.

Ella: I've got a plan that can help you out on that. As you know, I'll pay you $14 per hour, but in addition, I'd like to pay you with cash. Since you're only working for the summer, it really doesn't make sense for me to go to the trouble of formally putting you on our payroll system. In fact, I do some jobs for my clients on a strictly cash basis, so it would be easy to just pay you that way.

Gloria: Well, that's a bit unusual, but I guess money is money.

Ella: Yeah, not only that, it's tax-free!

Gloria: What do you mean?

Ella: Didn't you know? Any money that you receive in cash is not reported to the IRS on a W-2 form; therefore, the IRS doesn't know about the income—hence, it's the same as tax-free earnings.

a. ➤ Why does Ella Kitt want to conduct business transactions using cash (not check or credit card)?

b. ➤ How should Gloria respond to Ella's suggestion?

Internet Project

CP 11-4   Payroll forms

Group Project

Payroll accounting involves the use of government-supplied forms to account for payroll taxes. Three common forms are the W-2, Form 940, and Form 941. Form a team with three of your classmates and retrieve copies of each of these forms. They may be obtained from a local IRS office, a library, or downloaded from the Internet at **http://www.irs.gov** (go to forms and publications).

➤ Briefly describe the purpose of each of the three forms.

Internet Project

CP 11-5   Contingent liabilities

Altria Group, Inc., has over 12 pages dedicated to describing contingent liabilities in the notes to recent financial statements. These pages include extensive descriptions of multiple contingent liabilities. Use the Internet to research Altria Group, Inc., at **http://www.altria.com**.

a. What are the major business units of Altria Group?

b. Based on your understanding of this company, why would Altria Group require 11 pages of contingency disclosure?

© Chris Hondros/Newsmakers/Getty Images

Accounting for Partnerships and Limited Liability Companies

Razor USA, LLC

Most good ideas begin as the solution to a problem, such as with Gino Tsai. Gino's legs got tired as he walked around his Taiwanese bicycle factory. As a result, Gino spent five years designing what is now known as the Razor scooter. Little did he know that his new, lightweight foldable scooter would be used by people of all ages, as well as being an Xtreme sport for youth. Today the Razor scooter, along with other Razor products, are sold worldwide by Razor USA, LLC. The letters "LLC" stand for limited liability company. Unlike sole proprietorships illustrated in prior chapters, a LLC is a business form that normally has multiple owners.

The entity form chosen by a business has an important impact on the owners' legal liability, taxation, and ability to raise money. The four major forms of business entities discussed in this text are the proprietorship, partnership, limited liability company, and corporation. Proprietorships have been discussed in prior chapters. Partnerships and limited liability companies will be discussed in this chapter, and corporations will be introduced in the next chapter.

OBJ. 1 Describe the characteristics of proprietorships, partnerships, and limited liability companies.

Proprietorships, Partnerships, and Limited Liability Companies

The four most common legal forms for organizing and operating a business are as follows:

1. Proprietorship
2. Corporation
3. Partnership
4. Limited liability company

In this section, the characteristics of proprietorships, partnerships, and limited liability companies are described. The characteristics of corporations are described in Chapter 13.

Proprietorships

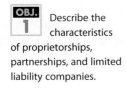

The Internal Revenue Service (IRS) estimates that proprietorships file 70% of business tax returns, but earn only 5% of all business revenues.

A proprietorship is a company owned by a single individual. The most common type of proprietorships are professional service providers, such as lawyers, architects, realtors, and physicians.

Characteristics of proprietorships include the following:

1. *Simple to form.* There are no legal restrictions or forms to file.
2. *No limitation on legal liability.* The owner is personally liable for any debts or legal claims against the business. Thus, creditors can take the personal assets of the owner if the business debts exceed the owner's investment in the company.

3. *Not taxable.* For federal income tax purposes, a proprietorship is not taxed. Instead, the proprietorship's income or loss is "passed through" to the owner's individual income tax return.[1]

4. *Limited life.* When the owner dies or retires, the proprietorship ceases to exist.

5. *Limited ability to raise capital (funds).* The ability to raise capital (funds) is limited to what the owner can provide from personal resources or through borrowing.

Partnerships

A **partnership** is an association of two or more persons who own and manage a business for profit.[2] Partnerships are less widely used than proprietorships.

Characteristics of a partnership include the following:

1. *Moderately complex to form.* A partnership requires only an agreement between two or more persons to organize. However, the **partnership agreement**, sometimes called the *articles of partnership*, includes matters such as amounts to be invested, limits on withdrawals, distributions of income and losses, and admission and withdrawal of partners. Thus, an attorney is often used in forming a partnership.

2. *No limitation on legal liability.* The partners are personally liable for any debts or legal claims against the partnership. Therefore, creditors can take the personal assets of the partners if the business debts exceed the partners' investment in the business.

3. *Not taxable.* For federal income tax purposes, a partnership is not taxed. Instead, the partnership's income or loss is "passed through" to the partners' individual income tax returns. However, partnerships must still report revenues, expenses, and income or loss annually to the Internal Revenue Service.

4. *Limited life.* When a partner dies or retires, the partnership ceases to exist. Likewise, the admission of a new partner dissolves the old partnership, and a new partnership must be formed if operations are to continue.

> **Note:**
> A partnership is a nontaxable entity that has a limited life and unlimited liability.

5. *Limited ability to raise capital (funds).* The ability to raise capital (funds) for the partnership is limited to what the partners can provide from personal resources or through borrowing.

In addition to those characteristics, some unique aspects of partnerships are:

1. *Co-ownership of partnership property.* The property invested in a partnership by a partner becomes the joint property of all the partners. When a partnership is dissolved, each partner's share of the partnership assets is the balance in their capital account.

2. *Mutual agency.* Each partner is an agent of the partnership and may act on behalf of the entire partnership. Thus, any liabilities created by one partner become liabilities of all the partners.

3. *Participation in income.* Net income and net loss are distributed among the partners according to their partnership agreement. If the partnership agreement does not provide for distribution of income and losses, then income and losses are divided equally among the partners.

BusinessConnection

BREAKING UP IS HARD TO DO

In August 7, 2008, Kristen Hall, founding member of the country music group Sugarland, filed a lawsuit against her other two band members. Kristen felt entitled to one-third of the profits the band earned on its double platinum album, *Enjoy the Ride*, after she left the band to pursue a song-writing career. However, the band did not have a formal partnership agreement and, thus, there was no way to easily determine what she should receive. Without a partnership agreement, the case will be decided using Georgia partnership law. This dispute and related lawsuit might have been avoided by a formal partnership agreement.

---

1 The proprietor's statement of income is included on Schedule C of the individual 1040 tax return.

2 The definition of a partnership is included in the Uniform Partnership Act, which has been adopted by most states.

A partnership may be organized as a limited partnership. A *limited partnership* is a unique legal form that provides partners who are not involved in the operations of the partnership with limited liability. In such a form, at least one *general partner* operates the partnership and has unlimited liability. The remaining partners are considered *limited partners*.

Limited Liability Companies

A **limited liability company (LLC)** is a form of legal entity that provides limited liability to its owners, but is treated as a partnership for tax purposes. The LLC is a relatively new form of business entity that has become widely used for small companies. LLCs, which may be owned by one or more persons or entities, are designed to overcome some of the disadvantages of a partnership.

Many companies have joint ventures organized as LLCs. For example, Walt Disney Company has a 42% interest in A&E Television Networks, LLC.

Characteristics of an LLC include the following:

1. *Moderately complex to form.* An LLC requires an agreement among the owners who are called members. The *operating agreement*, sometimes called *articles of organization*, includes matters such as amounts to be invested, limits on withdrawals, distributions of income and losses, and admission and withdrawal of members. An attorney is normally used in forming an LCC.
2. *Limited legal liability.* The members have *limited liability* even if they are active in the company. Thus, the members' personal assets are legally protected against creditor claims made against the LLC. That is, only the members' investments in the company are subject to claims of creditors.
3. *Not taxable.* An LLC may elect to be treated as a partnership for tax purposes. In this way, income passes through the LLC and is taxed on the individual members' tax returns.[3]
4. *Unlimited life.* Most LLC operating agreements specify continuity of life for the LLC, even when a member withdraws or new members join the LLC.
5. *Moderate ability to raise capital (funds).* Because of their limited liability, LLCs are attractive to many investors, thus allowing for greater access to capital (funds) than is normally the case in a partnership.

An LLC may elect to operate as a *member-managed* or a *manager-managed* company. In a member-managed LLC, individual members may legally bind the LLC, like partners bind a partnership. In a manager-managed LLC, only authorized members may legally bind the LLC. Thus, in a manager-managed LLC, members may share in the income of the LLC without concern for managing the company. As a result, manager-managed LLCs are attractive to many investors.

Comparing Proprietorships, Partnerships, and Limited Liability Companies

Exhibit 1 summarizes the characteristics of proprietorships, partnerships, and limited liability companies.

EXHIBIT 1   Characteristics of Proprietorships, Partnerships, and Limited Liability Companies

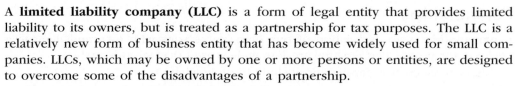

Organizational Form	Complexity of Formation	Legal Liability	Taxation	Limitation on Life of Entity	Access to Capital
Proprietorship	Simple	No limitation	Nontaxable (pass-through) entity	Limited	Limited
Partnership	Moderate	No limitation	Nontaxable (pass-through) entity	Limited	Limited
Limited Liability Company	Moderate	Limited liability	Nontaxable (pass-through) entity by election	Unlimited	Moderate

3 An LLC may also be taxed as a separate entity. However, doing so would remove these tax benefits, making this a less common election.

BusinessConnection

ORGANIZATIONAL FORMS IN THE ACCOUNTING INDUSTRY

The four major accounting firms, KPMG LLP, Ernst & Young, PricewaterhouseCoopers, and Deloitte & Touche, all began as partnerships. This form was legally required due to the theory of mutual agency. That is, the partnership form was thought to create public trust by requiring all partners to be jointly liable and responsible for each other's judgments.

In addition, investment in the partnerships was limited to practicing accountants. This prevented any pressures from outside investors affecting professional decisions.

As these firms grew and the risk increased, all of these firms were allowed to change, by law, to limited liability partnerships (LLPs). Thus, while remaining a partnership, the liability of the partners was limited to their investment in the firm. The LLP form is very similar to an LLC, except that investment is restricted to professionals.

Forming and Dividing Income of a Partnership

OBJ. 2 Describe and illustrate the accounting for forming a partnership and for dividing the net income and net loss of a partnership.

Most of the day-to-day accounting for a partnership or an LLC is similar to that illustrated in earlier chapters. However, the formation, division of net income or net loss, dissolution, and liquidation of partnerships and LLCs give rise to unique transactions.

In the remainder of this chapter, the unique transactions for partnerships and LLCs are described and illustrated. The accounting for an LLC is the same as a partnership, except that the terms "member" and "members' equity" are used rather than "partner" or "owners' capital." For this reason, the journal entries for an LLC are shown alongside the partnership entries.

Forming a Partnership

In forming a partnership, the investments of each partner are recorded in separate entries. The assets contributed by a partner are debited to the partnership asset accounts. If any liabilities are assumed by the partnership, the partnership liability accounts are credited. The partner's capital account is credited for the net amount.

To illustrate, assume that Joseph Stevens and Earl Foster, owners of competing hardware stores, agree to combine their businesses in a partnership. Stevens agrees to contribute the following:

Cash	$ 7,200	Office equipment	$2,500
Accounts receivable	16,300	Allowance for doubtful accounts	1,500
Merchandise inventory	28,700	Accounts payable	2,600
Store equipment	5,400		

The entry to record the assets and liabilities contributed by Stevens is as follows:

LLC

Cash	7,200	
Accounts Receivable	16,300	
Merchandise Inventory	28,700	
Store Equipment	5,400	
Office Equipment	2,500	
Allowance for Doubtful Accounts		1,500
Accounts Payable		2,600
Joseph Stevens, Member Equity		56,000

Apr.	1	Cash	7,200	
		Accounts Receivable	16,300	
		Merchandise Inventory	28,700	
		Store Equipment	5,400	
		Office Equipment	2,500	
		Allowance for Doubtful Accounts		1,500
		Accounts Payable		2,600
		Joseph Stevens, Capital		56,000

In the preceding entry, the noncash assets are recorded at values agreed upon by the partners. These values are normally based on current market values. As a result, the book value of the assets contributed by the partners normally differs from that recorded by the new partnership.

To illustrate, the store equipment contributed by Stevens may have had a book value of $3,500 in Stevens' ledger (cost of $10,000 less accumulated depreciation of $6,500). However, the store equipment is recorded at its current market value of $5,400 in the preceding entry. The contributions of Foster would be recorded in an entry similar to the entry for Stevens.

Example Exercise 12-1 **Journalize Partner's Original Investment**   OBJ. 2

Reese Howell contributed equipment, inventory, and $34,000 cash to a partnership. The equipment had a book value of $23,000 and a market value of $29,000. The inventory had a book value of $60,000, but only had a market value of $15,000, due to obsolescence. The partnership also assumed a $12,000 note payable owed by Howell that was used originally to purchase the equipment.
   Provide the journal entry for Howell's contribution to the partnership.

Follow My Example 12-1

Cash...	34,000	
Inventory..	15,000	
Equipment	29,000	
Notes Payable		12,000
Reese Howell, Capital		66,000

Practice Exercises: **PE 12-1A, PE 12-1B**

Dividing Income

Income or losses of the partnership are divided *equally* if no partnership agreement exists or the partnership agreement does not specify how the division is to occur. Most partnership agreements, however, do specify how income or losses are to be divided.
   Common methods of dividing partnership income are based on:

1. Services of the partners
2. Services and investments of the partners

Dividing Income—Services of Partners One method of dividing partnership income is based on the services provided by each partner to the partnership. These services are often recognized by partner salary allowances. Such allowances reflect differences in partners' abilities and time devoted to the partnership. Since partners are not employees, such allowances are recorded as divisions of net income and are credited to the partners' capital accounts.
   To illustrate, assume that the partnership agreement of Jennifer Stone and Crystal Mills provides for the following:

	Monthly Salary Allowance
Jennifer Stone	$5,000
Crystal Mills	4,000
Remaining net income:	Divided Equally

The division of income may be reported at the bottom of the partnership income statement. Using this format, the division of $150,000 of net income would be reported on the bottom of the partnership income statement as follows:

Net income.. $150,000

Division of net income:

	J. Stone	C. Mills	Total
Annual salary allowance	$ 60,000	$ 48,000	$ 108,000
Remaining income	21,000	21,000	42,000
Net income	$81,000	$69,000	$150,000

The division of net income may also be reported as a separate statement accompanying the balance sheet and the income statement or in a statement of partnership capital.

The net income division is recorded as a closing entry, even if the partners do not withdraw the amounts of their salary allowances. The entry for closing Income Summary and dividing net income is as follows:

LLC

Income Summary	150,000	
Jennifer Stone, Member Equity		81,000
Crystal Mills, Member Equity		69,000

Dec.	31	Income Summary		150,000	
		Jennifer Stone, Capital			81,000
		Crystal Mills, Capital			69,000

If Stone and Mills withdraw their salary allowances monthly, the withdrawals are debited to their drawing accounts. At the end of the year, the drawing account debit balances of $60,000 and $48,000 are then closed to the partners' capital accounts.

Dividing Income—Services of Partners and Investments

A partnership agreement may divide income not only based upon services, but also based upon the amount invested by each partner. In doing so, the partnership may pay interest on the capital balance of each partner. In this way, partners with more invested in the partnership are rewarded by receiving more of the partnership income. One such method of dividing partnership income would be as follows:

1. Partner salary allowances
2. Interest on capital investments
3. Any remaining income equally

To illustrate, assume that the partnership agreement for Stone and Mills provides for the following:

1.

	Monthly Salary Allowance
Jennifer Stone	$5,000
Crystal Mills	4,000

2. Interest of 12% on each partner's capital balance as of January 1.

Capital, Jennifer Stone, January 1	$160,000
Capital, Crystal Mills, January 1	120,000

3. Remaining income: Divided Equally

The $150,000 net income for the year is divided as follows:

Net income.. **$150,000**

Division of net income:

	J. Stone	C. Mills	Total
Annual salary allowance	$ 60,000	$ 48,000	$ 108,000
Interest allowance	19,200[1]	14,400[2]	33,600
Remaining income	4,200	4,200	8,400
Net income	$83,400	$66,600	$150,000

[1] 12% × $160,000
[2] 12% × $120,000

The entry for closing Income Summary and dividing net income is as follows:

LLC

Income Summary	150,000	
Jennifer Stone, Member Equity		83,400
Crystal Mills, Member Equity		66,600

Dec.	31	Income Summary		150,000	
		Jennifer Stone, Capital			83,400
		Crystal Mills, Capital			66,600

Integrity, Objectivity, and Ethics in Business

TYRANNY OF THE MAJORITY

Some partnerships involve the contribution of money by one partner and the contribution of effort and expertise by another. This can create a conflict between the two partners, since one works and the other doesn't. Without a properly developed partnership agreement, the working partner could take income in the form of a salary allowance, leaving little for the investor partner. Thus, partnership agreements often require all partners to agree on salary allowances provided to working partners.

Dividing Income—Allowances Exceed Net Income

In the preceding example, the net income is $150,000. The total of the salary ($108,000) and interest ($33,600) allowances is $141,600. Thus, the net income exceeds the salary and interest allowances. In some cases, however, the net income may be less than the total of the allowances. In this case, the remaining net income to divide is a *negative* amount. This negative amount is divided among the partners as though it were a net loss.

To illustrate, assume the same salary and interest allowances as in the preceding example, but that the net income is $100,000. In this case, the total of the allowances of $141,600 exceeds the net income by $41,600 ($100,000 − $141,600). This amount is divided equally between Stone and Mills. Thus, $20,800 ($41,600/2) is deducted from each partner's share of the allowances. The final division of net income between Stone and Mills is shown below.

Net income **$100,000**

Division of net income:

	J. Stone	C. Mills	Total
Annual salary allowance	$ 60,000	$ 48,000	$ 108,000
Interest allowance	19,200	14,400	33,600
Total	$ 79,200	$ 62,400	$ 141,600
Deduct excess of allowances over income	20,800	20,800	41,600
Net income	**$58,400**	**$41,600**	**$100,000**

The entry for closing Income Summary and dividing net income is as follows:[4]

LLC

Income Summary	100,000	
Jennifer Stone, Member Equity		58,400
Crystal Mills, Member Equity		41,600

Dec.	31	Income Summary		100,000	
		Jennifer Stone, Capital			58,400
		Crystal Mills, Capital			41,600

Example Exercise 12-2 Dividing Partnership Net Income

OBJ. 2

Steve Prince and Chelsy Bernard formed a partnership, dividing income as follows:

1. Annual salary allowance to Prince of $42,000.
2. Interest of 9% on each partner's capital balance on January 1.
3. Any remaining net income divided equally.

Prince and Bernard had $20,000 and $150,000 in their January 1 capital balances, respectively. Net income for the year was $240,000.

How much net income should be distributed to Prince?

(Continued)

4 In the event of a net loss, the amount deducted from the total allowances would be the "excess of allowances over loss" or the sum of the net loss and the allowances, divided according to the sharing ratio.

Follow My Example 12-2

	Steve Prince	Chelsy Bernard	Total
Annual salary...	$ 42,000	$ 0	$ 42,000
Interest..	1,800[1]	13,500[2]	15,300
Remaining income..................................	91,350[3]	91,350	182,700
Total distributed to Prince...........................	$135,150	$104,850	$240,000

[1] $20,000 × 9%
[2] $150,000 × 9%
[3] ($240,000 − $42,000 − $15,300) × 50%

Practice Exercises: **PE 12-2A, PE 12-2B**

Partner Admission and Withdrawal

OBJ. 3 Describe and illustrate the accounting for partner admission and withdrawal.

Many partnerships provide for admitting new partners and for partner withdrawals by amending the existing partnership agreement. In this way, the company may continue operating without having to form a new partnership and prepare a new partnership agreement.

Admitting a Partner

As shown in Exhibit 2, a person may be admitted to a partnership by either of the following:

1. Purchasing an interest from one or more of the existing partners
2. Contributing assets to the partnership

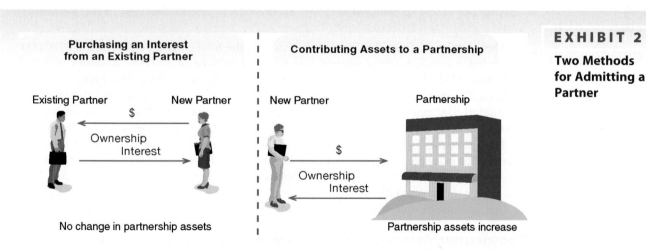

EXHIBIT 2

Two Methods for Admitting a Partner

When a new partner is admitted by *purchasing an interest* from one or more of the existing partners, the total assets and the total owners' equity of the partnership are not affected. The capital (equity) of the new partner is recorded by transferring capital (equity) from the existing partners.

When a new partner is admitted by *contributing assets* to the partnership, the total assets and the total owners' equity of the partnership are increased. The capital (equity) of the new partner is recorded as the amount of assets contributed to the partnership by the new partner.

Purchasing an Interest from Existing Partners When a new partner is admitted by purchasing an interest from one or more of the existing partners, the transaction is between the new and existing partners acting as individuals. The admission of the new partner is recorded by transferring owners' equity amounts from the capital accounts of the selling partners to the capital account of the new partner.

To illustrate, assume that on June 1 Tom Andrews and Nathan Bell each sell one-fifth of their partnership equity of Bring It Consulting to Joe Canter for $10,000 in cash. On June 1, the partnership has net assets of $100,000 and both existing partners have capital balances of $50,000 each. This transaction is between Andrews, Bell, and Canter. The only entry required by Bring It Consulting is to record the transfer of capital (equity) from Andrews and Bell to Canter, as shown below.

LLC			June	1	Tom Andrews, Capital	10,000	
Tom Andrews, Member Equity	10,000				Nathan Bell, Capital	10,000	
Nathan Bell, Member Equity	10,000				Joe Canter, Capital		20,000
Joe Canter, Member Equity		20,000				

The effect of the transaction on the partnership accounts is shown in the following diagram:

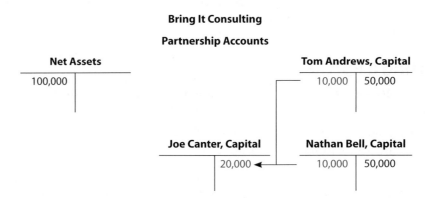

Bring It Consulting

Partnership Accounts

After Canter is admitted to Bring It Consulting, the total owners' equity is still $100,000. Canter has a one-fifth (20%) interest and a capital balance of $20,000. Andrews and Bell each own two-fifths (40%) interest and have capital balances of $40,000 each.

Even though Canter has a one-fifth (20%) interest in the partnership, he may not be entitled to a one-fifth share of the partnership net income. The division of the net income or net loss is made according to the new or amended partnership agreement.

The preceding entry is not affected by the amount paid by Canter for the one-fifth interest. For example, if Canter had paid $15,000 to Andrews and Bell instead of $10,000, the entry would still be the same. This is because the transaction is between Andrews, Bell, and Canter, rather than the partnership. Any gain or loss by Andrews and Bell on the sale of their partnership interest is theirs as individuals and does not affect the partnership.

Contributing Assets to a Partnership When a new partner is admitted by contributing assets to the partnership, the total assets and the total owners' equity of the partnership are increased. This is because the transaction is between the new partner and the partnership.

To illustrate, assume that instead of purchasing a one-fifth ownership in Bring It Consulting directly from Tom Andrews and Nathan Bell, Joe Canter contributes $20,000 cash to Bring It Consulting for ownership equity of $20,000. The entry to record this transaction is as follows:

LLC			June	1	Cash	20,000	
Cash	20,000				Joe Canter, Capital		20,000
Joe Canter, Member Equity		20,000				

The effect of the transaction on the partnership accounts is shown in the following diagram:

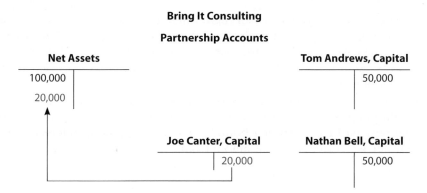

Bring It Consulting

Partnership Accounts

After the admission of Canter, the net assets and total owners' equity of Bring It Consulting increase to $120,000, of which Joe Canter has a $20,000 interest. In contrast, in the prior example, the net assets and total owners' equity of Bring It Consulting did not change from $100,000.

Revaluation of Assets   Before a new partner is admitted, the balances of a partnership's asset accounts should be stated at current values. If necessary, the accounts should be adjusted. Any net adjustment (increase or decrease) in asset values is divided among the capital accounts of the existing partners similar to the division of income.

To illustrate, assume that in the preceding example the balance of the merchandise inventory account is $14,000 and the current replacement value is $17,000. If Andrews and Bell share net income equally, the revaluation is recorded as follows:

LLC

Merchandise Inventory	3,000	
Tom Andrews, Member Equity		1,500
Nathan Bell, Member Equity		1,500

June	1	Merchandise Inventory		3,000	
		Tom Andrews, Capital			1,500
		Nathan Bell, Capital			1,500

Failure to adjust the partnership accounts for current values before admission of a new partner may result in the new partner sharing in asset gains or losses that arose in prior periods.

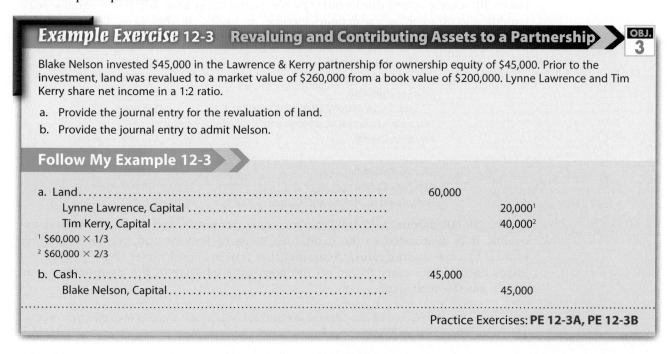

Example Exercise 12-3   Revaluing and Contributing Assets to a Partnership   OBJ. 3

Blake Nelson invested $45,000 in the Lawrence & Kerry partnership for ownership equity of $45,000. Prior to the investment, land was revalued to a market value of $260,000 from a book value of $200,000. Lynne Lawrence and Tim Kerry share net income in a 1:2 ratio.

a.   Provide the journal entry for the revaluation of land.
b.   Provide the journal entry to admit Nelson.

Follow My Example 12-3

a. Land.. 60,000
     Lynne Lawrence, Capital .... 20,000[1]
     Tim Kerry, Capital .... 40,000[2]
[1] $60,000 × 1/3
[2] $60,000 × 2/3

b. Cash... 45,000
     Blake Nelson, Capital... 45,000

Practice Exercises: **PE 12-3A, PE 12-3B**

Partner Bonuses A new partner may pay existing partners a bonus to join a partnership. In other cases, existing partners may pay a new partner a bonus to join the partnership.

Bonuses are usually paid because of higher than normal profits the new or existing partners are expected to contribute in the future. For example, a new partner may bring special qualities or skills to the partnership. Celebrities such as actors, musicians, or sports figures often provide name recognition that is expected to increase a partnership's profits.

Partner bonuses are illustrated in Exhibit 3. Existing partners receive a bonus when the ownership interest received by the new partner is less than the amount paid. In contrast, the new partner receives a bonus when the ownership interest received by the new partner is greater than the amount paid.

EXHIBIT 3
Partner Bonuses

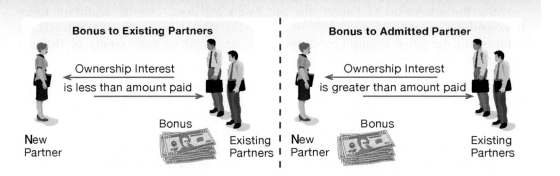

To illustrate, assume that on March 1 the partnership of Marsha Jenkins and Helen Kramer is considering a new partner, Alex Diaz. After the assets of the partnership have been adjusted to current market values, the capital balances of Jenkins and Kramer are as follows:

Marsha Jenkins, Capital	$20,000
Helen Kramer, Capital	24,000
Total owners' equity *before* admitting Diaz	$44,000

Jenkins and Kramer agree to admit Diaz to the partnership for $31,000. In return, Diaz will receive a one-third equity in the partnership and will share equally with Jenkins and Kramer in partnership income or losses. In this case, Diaz is paying Jenkins and Kramer a $6,000 bonus to join the partnership, computed as follows:

Marsha Jenkins, Capital	$20,000
Helen Kramer, Capital	24,000
Diaz's contribution	31,000
Total owners' equity *after* admitting Diaz	$75,000
Diaz's equity interest after admission	× 1/3
Alex Diaz, Capital	$25,000
Diaz's contribution	$31,000
Alex Diaz, Capital	25,000
Bonus paid to Jenkins and Kramer	$ 6,000

The $6,000 bonus paid by Diaz increases Jenkins's and Kramer's capital accounts. It is distributed to the capital accounts of Jenkins and Kramer according to their income-sharing ratio.[5] Assuming that Jenkins and Kramer share profits and losses equally, the entry to record the admission of Diaz to the partnership is as shown on the next page:

5 Another method used to record the admission of partners attributes goodwill rather than a bonus to the partners. This method is discussed in advanced accounting textbooks.

LLC		
Cash	31,000	
Alex Diaz, Member Equity		25,000
Marsha Jenkins, Member Equity		3,000
Helen Kramer, Member Equity		3,000

	Mar.	1	Cash	31,000	
			Alex Diaz, Capital		25,000
			Marsha Jenkins, Capital		3,000
			Helen Kramer, Capital		3,000

Existing partners may agree to pay the new partner a bonus to join a partnership. To illustrate, assume that after adjusting assets to market values, the capital balances of Janice Cowen and Steve Dodd are as follows:

Janice Cowen, Capital	$ 80,000
Steve Dodd, Capital	40,000
Total owners' equity *before* admitting Chou	$120,000

Cowen and Dodd agree to admit Ellen Chou to the partnership on June 1 for an investment of $30,000. In return, Chou will receive a one-fourth equity interest in the partnership and will share in one-fourth of the profits and losses. In this case, Cowen and Dodd are paying Chou a $7,500 bonus to join the partnership, computed as follows:

Janice Cowen, Capital	$ 80,000
Steve Dodd, Capital	40,000
Chou's contribution	30,000
Total owners' equity *after* admitting Chou	$150,000
Chou's equity interest after admission	× ¼
Ellen Chou, Capital	$ 37,500
Ellen Chou, Capital	$ 37,500
Chou's contribution	30,000
Bonus paid to Chou	$ 7,500

The $7,500 bonus paid to Chou decreases Cowen's and Dodd's capital accounts. It is distributed to the capital accounts of Cowen and Dodd according to their income-sharing ratio. Assuming that the income-sharing ratio of Cowen and Dodd was 2:1 before the admission of Chou, the entry to record the admission of Chou to the partnership is as follows:

LLC		
Cash	30,000	
Janice Cowen, Member Equity	5,000¹	
Steve Dodd, Member Equity	2,500²	
Ellen Chou, Member Equity		37,500

	June	1	Cash	30,000	
			Janice Cowen, Capital	5,000¹	
			Steve Dodd, Capital	2,500²	
			Ellen Chou, Capital		37,500

¹ $7,500 × 2/3
² $7,500 × 1/3

Example Exercise 12-4   Partner Bonus

OBJ. 3

Lowman has a capital balance of $45,000 after adjusting assets to fair market value. Conrad contributes $26,000 to receive a 30% interest in a new partnership with Lowman.
    Determine the amount and recipient of the partner bonus.

Follow My Example 12-4

Equity of Lowman	$45,000
Conrad's contribution	26,000
Total equity after admitting Conrad	$71,000
Conrad's equity interest	× 30%
Conrad's equity after admission	$21,300
Conrad's contribution	$26,000
Conrad's equity after admission	21,300
Bonus paid to Lowman	$ 4,700

Practice Exercises: **PE 12-4A, PE 12-4B**

Withdrawal of a Partner

A partner may retire or withdraw from a partnership. In such cases, the withdrawing partner's interest is normally sold to the:

1. Existing partners or
2. Partnership

A partner generally cannot withdraw without permission of the remaining partners, nor can a partner be forced to withdraw by the other partners. In this sense, a partnership is like a marriage, "for better or for worse."

If the *existing partners* purchase the withdrawing partner's interest, the purchase and sale of the partnership interest is between the partners as individuals. The only entry on the partnership's records is to debit the capital account of the partner withdrawing and to credit the capital account of the partner or partners buying the additional interest.

If the *partnership purchases* the withdrawing partner's interest, the assets and the owners' equity of the partnership are reduced by the purchase price. Before the purchase, the asset accounts should be adjusted to current values. The net amount of any adjustment should be divided among the capital accounts of the partners according to their income-sharing ratio.

The entry to record the purchase debits the capital account of the withdrawing partner and credits Cash for the amount of the purchase. If not enough partnership cash is available to pay the withdrawing partner, a liability may be created (credited) for the amount owed the withdrawing partner.

Death of a Partner

When a partner dies, the partnership accounts should be closed as of the date of death. The net income for the current period should then be determined and divided among the partners' capital accounts. The asset accounts should also be adjusted to current values and the amount of any adjustment divided among the capital accounts of the partners.

After the income is divided and any assets revalued, an entry is recorded to close the deceased partner's capital account. The entry debits the deceased partner's capital account for its balance and credits a liability account, which is payable to the deceased's estate. The remaining partner or partners may then decide to continue the business or liquidate it.

 Describe and illustrate the accounting for liquidating a partnership.

Liquidating Partnerships

When a partnership goes out of business, it sells the assets, pays the creditors, and distributes the remaining cash or other assets to the partners. This winding-up process is called the **liquidation** of the partnership. Although *liquidating* refers to the payment of liabilities, it includes the entire winding-up process.

When the partnership goes out of business and the normal operations are discontinued, the accounts should be adjusted and closed. The only accounts remaining open will be the asset, contra asset, liability, and owners' equity accounts.

The liquidation process is illustrated in Exhibit 4. The steps in the liquidation process are as follows:

Note:
In liquidation, cash is distributed to partners according to their capital balances.

Step 1. Sell the partnership assets. This step is called **realization.**
Step 2. Distribute any gains or losses from realization to the partners based on their income-sharing ratio.
Step 3. Pay the claims of creditors using the cash from step 1 realization.
Step 4. Distribute the remaining cash to the partners based on the balances in their capital accounts.

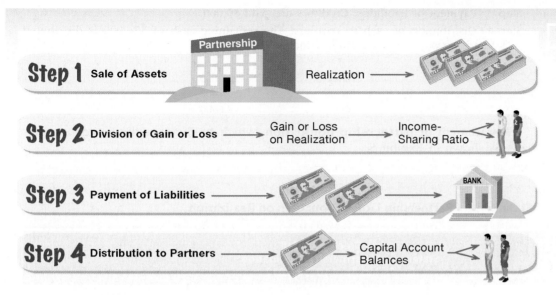

EXHIBIT 4

Steps in Liquidating a Partnership

To illustrate, assume that Farley, Green, and Hall decide to liquidate their partnership. On April 9, after discontinuing business operations of the partnership and closing the accounts, the following trial balance is prepared:

Farley, Green, and Hall Post-Closing Trial Balance April 9, 2012		
	Debit Balances	**Credit Balances**
Cash...	11,000	
Noncash Assets...	64,000	
Liabilities..		9,000
Jean Farley, Capital		22,000
Brad Green, Capital		22,000
Alice Hall, Capital		22,000
	75,000	75,000

Farley, Green, and Hall share income and losses in a ratio of 5:3:2 (50%, 30%, 20%). To simplify, assume that all noncash assets are sold in a single transaction and that all liabilities are paid at one time. In addition, Noncash Assets and Liabilities will be used as account titles in place of the various asset, contra asset, and liability accounts.

Gain on Realization

Assume that Farley, Green, and Hall sell all noncash assets for $72,000. Thus, a gain of $8,000 ($72,000 − $64,000) is realized. The partnership is liquidated during April as follows:

Step 1. Sale of assets: $72,000 is realized from sale of all the noncash assets.

Step 2. Division of gain: The gain of $8,000 is distributed to Farley, Green, and Hall in the income-sharing ratio of 5:3:2. Thus, the partner capital accounts are credited as follows:

Farley	$4,000 ($8,000 × 50%)
Green	2,400 ($8,000 × 30%)
Hall	1,600 ($8,000 × 20%)

Step 3. Payment of liabilities: Creditors are paid $9,000.

Step 4. Distribution of cash to partners: The remaining cash of $74,000 is distributed to the partners according to their capital balances as follows:

Farley	$26,000
Green	24,400
Hall	23,600

A **statement of partnership liquidation**, which summarizes the liquidation process, is shown in Exhibit 5.

EXHIBIT 5   **Statement of Partnership Liquidation: Gain on Realization**

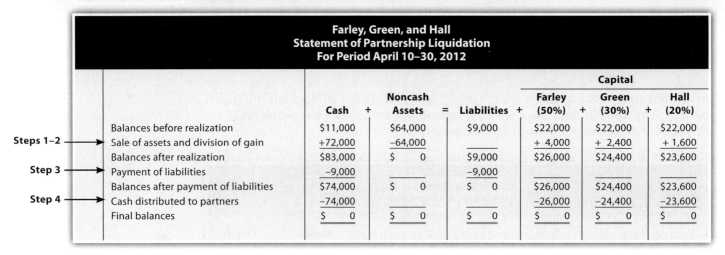

	Cash	+	Noncash Assets	=	Liabilities	+	Farley (50%)	+	Green (30%)	+	Hall (20%)
Farley, Green, and Hall											
Statement of Partnership Liquidation											
For Period April 10–30, 2012											
									Capital		
Balances before realization	$11,000		$64,000		$9,000		$22,000		$22,000		$22,000
Sale of assets and division of gain	+72,000		−64,000				+ 4,000		+ 2,400		+ 1,600
Balances after realization	$83,000		$ 0		$9,000		$26,000		$24,400		$23,600
Payment of liabilities	−9,000				−9,000						
Balances after payment of liabilities	$74,000		$ 0		$ 0		$26,000		$24,400		$23,600
Cash distributed to partners	−74,000						−26,000		−24,400		−23,600
Final balances	$ 0		$ 0		$ 0		$ 0		$ 0		$ 0

Steps 1–2 → Sale of assets and division of gain
Step 3 → Payment of liabilities
Step 4 → Cash distributed to partners

The entries to record the steps in the liquidating process are as follows:

Sale of assets (Step 1):

LLC

Cash	72,000	
Noncash Assets		64,000
Gain on Realization		8,000

Cash	72,000	
Noncash Assets		64,000
Gain on Realization		8,000

Division of gain (Step 2):

LLC

Gain on Realization	8,000	
Jean Farley, Member Equity		4,000
Brad Green, Member Equity		2,400
Alice Hall, Member Equity		1,600

Gain on Realization	8,000	
Jean Farley, Capital		4,000
Brad Green, Capital		2,400
Alice Hall, Capital		1,600

Payment of liabilities (Step 3):

LLC

Liabilities	9,000	
Cash		9,000

Liabilities	9,000	
Cash		9,000

Distribution of cash to partners (Step 4):

LLC		
Jean Farley, Member Equity	26,000	
Brad Green, Member Equity	24,400	
Alice Hall, Member Equity	23,600	
Cash		74,000

Jean Farley, Capital	26,000	
Brad Green, Capital	24,400	
Alice Hall, Capital	23,600	
Cash		74,000

As shown in Exhibit 5, *the cash is distributed to the partners based on the balances of their capital accounts.* These balances are determined after the gain on realization has been divided among the partners and the liabilities paid. The *income-sharing ratio should not be used as a basis for distributing the cash to partners.*

Loss on Realization

Assume that Farley, Green, and Hall sell all noncash assets for $44,000. Thus, a loss of $20,000 ($64,000 – $44,000) is realized. The liquidation of the partnership is as follows:

Step 1. Sale of assets: $44,000 is realized from the sale of all the noncash assets.

Step 2. Division of loss: The loss of $20,000 is distributed to Farley, Green, and Hall in the income-sharing ratio of 5:3:2. Thus, the partner capital accounts are debited as follows:

Farley	$10,000 ($20,000 × 50%)
Green	6,000 ($20,000 × 30%)
Hall	4,000 ($20,000 × 20%)

Step 3. Payment of liabilities: Creditors are paid $9,000.

Step 4. Distribution of cash to partners: The remaining cash of $46,000 is distributed to the partners according to their capital balances as follows:

Farley	$12,000
Green	16,000
Hall	18,000

The steps in liquidating the partnership are summarized in the statement of partnership liquidation shown in Exhibit 6.

EXHIBIT 6   **Statement of Partnership Liquidation: Loss on Realization**

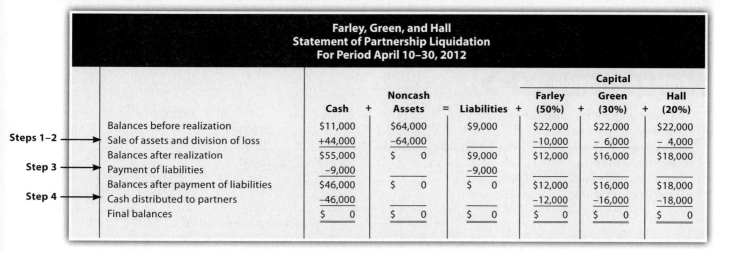

		Cash	+	Noncash Assets	=	Liabilities	+	Farley (50%)	+	Green (30%)	+	Hall (20%)
	Balances before realization	$11,000		$64,000		$9,000		$22,000		$22,000		$22,000
Steps 1–2	Sale of assets and division of loss	+44,000		−64,000				−10,000		− 6,000		− 4,000
	Balances after realization	$55,000		$ 0		$9,000		$12,000		$16,000		$18,000
Step 3	Payment of liabilities	−9,000				−9,000						
	Balances after payment of liabilities	$46,000		$ 0		$ 0		$12,000		$16,000		$18,000
Step 4	Cash distributed to partners	−46,000						−12,000		−16,000		−18,000
	Final balances	$ 0		$ 0		$ 0		$ 0		$ 0		$ 0

Farley, Green, and Hall
Statement of Partnership Liquidation
For Period April 10–30, 2012

The entries to liquidate the partnership are as follows:

Sale of assets (Step 1):

LLC

Cash	44,000	
Loss on Realization	20,000	
Noncash Assets		64,000

Cash	44,000	
Loss on Realization	20,000	
Noncash Assets		64,000

Division of loss (Step 2):

LLC

Jean Farley, Member Equity	10,000	
Brad Green, Member Equity	6,000	
Alice Hall, Member Equity	4,000	
Loss on Realization		20,000

Jean Farley, Capital	10,000	
Brad Green, Capital	6,000	
Alice Hall, Capital	4,000	
Loss on Realization		20,000

Payment of liabilities (Step 3):

LLC

Liabilities	9,000	
Cash		9,000

Liabilities	9,000	
Cash		9,000

Distribution of cash to partners (Step 4):

LLC

Jean Farley, Member Equity	12,000	
Brad Green, Member Equity	16,000	
Alice Hall, Member Equity	18,000	
Cash		46,000

Jean Farley, Capital	12,000	
Brad Green, Capital	16,000	
Alice Hall, Capital	18,000	
Cash		46,000

Example Exercise 12-5 Liquidating Partnerships

Prior to liquidating their partnership, Todd and Gentry had capital accounts of $50,000 and $100,000, respectively. Prior to liquidation, the partnership had no other cash assets than what was realized from the sale of assets. These assets were sold for $220,000. The partnership had $20,000 of liabilities. Todd and Gentry share income and losses equally. Determine the amount received by Gentry as a final distribution from the liquidation of the partnership.

Follow My Example 12-5

Gentry's equity prior to liquidation		$100,000
Realization of asset sale	$220,000	
Book value of assets ($50,000 + $100,000 + $20,000)	170,000	
Gain on liquidation	$ 50,000	
Gentry's share of gain (50% × $50,000)		25,000
Gentry's cash distribution		$125,000

Practice Exercises: **PE 12-5A, PE 12-5B**

Loss on Realization—Capital Deficiency

The share of a loss on realization may be greater than the balance in a partner's capital account. The resulting debit balance in the capital account is called a **deficiency**. It represents a claim of the partnership against the partner.

To illustrate, assume that Farley, Green, and Hall sell all noncash assets for $10,000. Thus, a loss of $54,000 ($64,000 – $10,000) is realized. The liquidation of the partnership is as follows:

Step 1. Sale of assets: $10,000 is realized from the sale of all the noncash assets.

Step 2. Division of loss: The loss of $54,000 is distributed to Farley, Green, and Hall in the income-sharing ratio of 5:3:2. The partner capital accounts are debited as follows:

Farley	$27,000 ($54,000 × 50%)
Green	16,200 ($54,000 × 30%)
Hall	10,800 ($54,000 × 20%)

Step 3. Payment of liabilities: Creditors are paid $9,000.

Step 4. Distribution of cash to partners: The share of the loss allocated to Farley, $27,000 (50% × $54,000), exceeds the $22,000 balance in her capital account. This $5,000 deficiency represents an amount that Farley owes the partnership. Assuming that Farley pays the deficiency, the cash of $17,000 is distributed to the partners according to their capital balances as follows:

Farley	$ 0
Green	5,800
Hall	11,200

The steps in liquidating the partnership are summarized in the statement of partnership liquidation shown in Exhibit 7.

The entries to liquidate the partnership are as follows:

Sale of assets (Step 1):

LLC

Cash	10,000	
Loss on Realization	54,000	
Noncash Assets		64,000

Cash	10,000	
Loss on Realization	54,000	
Noncash Assets		64,000

EXHIBIT 7   Statement of Partnership Liquidation: Loss on Realization—Capital Deficiency

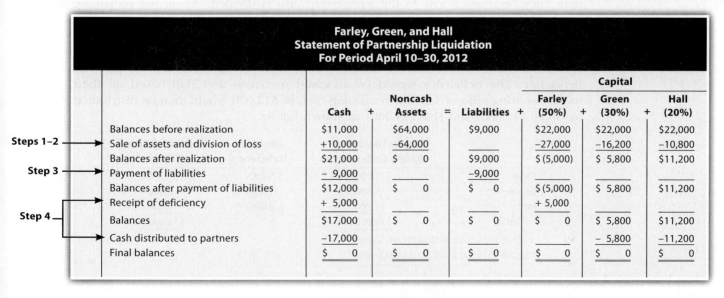

Farley, Green, and Hall
Statement of Partnership Liquidation
For Period April 10–30, 2012

	Cash +	Noncash Assets =	Liabilities +	Farley (50%) +	Green (30%) +	Hall (20%)
Steps 1–2 → Balances before realization	$11,000	$64,000	$9,000	$22,000	$22,000	$22,000
Sale of assets and division of loss	+10,000	−64,000		−27,000	−16,200	−10,800
Balances after realization	$21,000	$ 0	$9,000	$ (5,000)	$ 5,800	$11,200
Step 3 → Payment of liabilities	− 9,000		−9,000			
Balances after payment of liabilities	$12,000	$ 0	$ 0	$ (5,000)	$ 5,800	$11,200
Receipt of deficiency	+ 5,000			+ 5,000		
Step 4 → Balances	$17,000	$ 0	$ 0	$ 0	$ 5,800	$11,200
Cash distributed to partners	−17,000				− 5,800	−11,200
Final balances	$ 0	$ 0	$ 0	$ 0	$ 0	$ 0

Division of loss (Step 2):

LLC		
Jean Farley, Member Equity	27,000	
Brad Green, Member Equity	16,200	
Alice Hall, Member Equity	10,800	
Loss on Realization		54,000

Jean Farley, Capital		27,000	
Brad Green, Capital		16,200	
Alice Hall, Capital		10,800	
Loss on Realization			54,000

Payment of liabilities (Step 3):

LLC		
Liabilities	9,000	
Cash		9,000

Liabilities		9,000	
Cash			9,000

Receipt of deficiency (Step 4):

LLC		
Cash	5,000	
Jean Farley, Member Equity		5,000

Cash		5,000	
Jean Farley, Capital			5,000

Distribution of cash to partners (Step 4):

LLC		
Brad Green, Member Equity	5,800	
Alice Hall, Member Equity	11,200	
Cash		17,000

Brad Green, Capital		5,800	
Alice Hall, Capital		11,200	
Cash			17,000

If the deficient partner does not pay the partnership their deficiency, there will not be sufficient partnership cash to pay the remaining partners in full. Any uncollected deficiency becomes a loss to the partnership and is divided among the remaining partners' capital balances based on their income-sharing ratio. The cash balance will then equal the sum of the capital account balances. The cash can then be distributed to the remaining partners, based on the balances of their capital accounts.

To illustrate, assume that in the preceding example Farley could not pay her deficiency. The deficiency would be allocated to Green and Hall based on their income-sharing ratio of 3:2. The remaining cash of $12,000 would then be distributed to Green ($2,800) and Hall ($9,200) as shown below.

	Capital Balances *Before* Deficiency	Allocated (Deficiency)	Capital Balances *After* Deficiency
Farley	$ (5,000)	$ 5,000	$ 0
Green	5,800	(3,000)*	2,800
Hall	11,200	(2,000)**	9,200
Total	$12,000		$12,000

*$3,000 = [$5,000 × (3/5)] or ($5,000 × 60%)
**$2,000 = [$5,000 × (2/5)] or ($5,000 × 40%)

The entries to allocate Farley's deficiency and distribute the cash are as follows:

Allocation of deficiency (Step 4):

LLC		
Brad Green, Member Equity	3,000	
Alice Hall, Member Equity	2,000	
Jean Farley, Member Equity		5,000

Brad Green, Capital		3,000	
Alice Hall, Capital		2,000	
Jean Farley, Capital			5,000

Distribution of cash to partners (Step 4):

LLC		
Brad Green, Member Equity	2,800	
Alice Hall, Member Equity	9,200	
Cash		12,000

Brad Green, Capital		2,800	
Alice Hall, Capital		9,200	
Cash			12,000

Example Exercise 12-6   Liquidating Partnerships—Deficiency

OBJ. 4

Prior to liquidating their partnership, Short and Bain had capital accounts of $20,000 and $80,000, respectively. The partnership assets were sold for $40,000. The partnership had no liabilities. Short and Bain share income and losses equally.

a. Determine the amount of Short's deficiency.

b. Determine the amount distributed to Bain, assuming Short is unable to satisfy the deficiency.

Follow My Example 12-6

a.		
Short's equity prior to liquidation...		$ 20,000
Realization of asset sale	$ 40,000	
Book value of assets ($20,000 + $80,000).................................	100,000	
Loss on liquidation	$ 60,000	
Short's share of loss (50% × $60,000)..		30,000
Short's deficiency		$(10,000)

b. $40,000. $80,000 – $30,000 share of loss – $10,000 Short deficiency.

Practice Exercises: **PE 12-6A, PE 12-6B**

Statement of Partnership Equity

OBJ. 5 Prepare the statement of partnership equity.

Reporting changes in partnership capital accounts is similar to that for a proprietorship. The primary difference is that there is a capital account for each partner. The changes in partner capital accounts for a period of time are reported in a **statement of partnership equity**.

Exhibit 8 illustrates a statement of partnership equity for Investors Associates, a partnership of Dan Cross and Kelly Baker. Each partner's capital account is shown as a separate column. The partner capital accounts may change due to capital additions, net income, or withdrawals.

The equity reporting for an LLC is similar to that of a partnership. Instead of a statement of partnership capital, a statement of members' equity is prepared. The **statement of members' equity** reports the changes in member equity for a period.

EXHIBIT 8

Statement of Partnership Equity

Investors Associates Statement of Partnership Equity For the Year Ended December 31, 2012			
	Dan Cross, Capital	Kelly Baker, Capital	Total Partnership Capital
Balance, January 1, 2012	$245,000	$365,000	$610,000
Capital additions	50,000		50,000
Net income for the year	40,000	80,000	120,000
Less partner withdrawals	(5,000)	(45,000)	(50,000)
Balance, December 31, 2012	$330,000	$400,000	$730,000

The statement is similar to Exhibit 8, except that the columns represent member equity rather than partner equity.

Financial Analysis and Interpretation: Revenue per Employee

OBJ. 6 Analyze and interpret employee efficiency.

Many partnerships and LLCs operate as service-oriented enterprises. This is the case for many professions, such as medical, advertising, and accounting. The performance of such firms can be measured by the amount of net income per partner, as illustrated in this chapter. Another measure used to assess the performance of a service-oriented business is revenue per employee.

Revenue per employee is a measure of the efficiency of the business in generating revenues. It is computed as follows:

$$\text{Revenue per Employee} = \frac{\text{Revenue}}{\text{Number of Employees}}$$

In a partnership, the number of partners may be included with employees or partners may be evaluated separately. Generally, the higher the revenue per employee the more efficient the company is in generating revenue from its employees. In evaluating revenue per employee, changes over time as well as comparisons with industry averages are often used.

To illustrate comparisons over time, assume Washburn & Lovett, CPAs, has the following information for two years:

	2013	2012
Revenues	$220,000,000	$180,000,000
Number of employees	1,600	1,500

For Washburn & Lovett, the revenue per employee ratio is computed for 2013 and 2012 as follows:

$$\text{Revenue per employee, 2013:} \frac{\$220,000,000}{1,600 \text{ employees}} = \$137,500 \text{ per employee}$$

$$\text{Revenue per employee, 2012:} \frac{\$180,000,000}{1,500 \text{ employees}} = \$120,000 \text{ per employee}$$

Washburn & Lovett increased revenues by $40,000,000 ($220,000,000 − $180,000,000), or 22.2% ($40,000,000/$180,000,000) from 2012 to 2013. The number of employees increased by 100, or 6.7% (100 employees/1,500 employees) between the two years. Thus, the firm increased revenues at a rate faster than the increase in employees. As a result, the revenue per employee improved from $120,000 to $137,500 between the two years, suggesting improved efficiency in generating revenues.

To illustrate comparison within an industry, the revenue per employee for Starbucks and McDonald's for a recent year are as computed below.

$$\text{Starbucks: } \frac{\$10,383,000,000}{172,000 \text{ employees}} = \$60,366 \text{ per employee}$$

$$\text{McDonald's: } \frac{\$23,500,000,000}{400,000 \text{ employees}} = \$58,750 \text{ per employee}$$

The difference in the preceding ratios is small enough to conclude that Starbucks and McDonald's are equally efficient in their ability to generate revenue per employee.

The importance of comparing revenue per employee within an industry is further illustrated by comparing Apple, Inc., and Dell Inc. The revenue per employee for Apple, Inc., is $1,014,969. In contrast, Dell has revenue per employee of $756,700. Thus, Apple has higher revenue per employee efficiency than does Dell.

Finally, you should note that comparisons across industries are often misleading. For example, Apple's revenue per employee of $1,014,969 is much higher than Starbucks' $60,366. However, Apple is a much different company than Starbucks; thus, this comparison is misleading. McDonald's is a better comparison for Starbucks, as is Dell for Apple.

Example Exercise 12-7   Revenue per Employee

OBJ. 6

AccuTax, CPAs earned $4,200,000 during 2012 using 20 employees. During 2013, the firm grew revenues to $4,560,000 and expanded the staff to 24 employees.

a. Determine the revenue per employee for each year.
b. Interpret the results.

Follow My Example 12-7

a. 2012: $\dfrac{\$4,200,000}{20 \text{ employees}} = \$210,000$ per employee

  2013: $\dfrac{\$4,560,000}{24 \text{ employees}} = \$190,000$ per employee

b. While AccuTax grew revenues by $360,000 ($4,560,000 – $4,200,000), or 8.6% ($360,000/$4,200,000), the number of employees expanded by 4, or 20% (4/20). The growth in revenue was less than the growth in the number of employees; thus, the revenue per employee declined between the two years. The firm was less efficient in generating revenues from its employees in 2013.

Practice Exercises: **PE 12-7A, PE 12-7B**

At a Glance 12

OBJ. 1

Describe the characteristics of proprietorships, partnerships, and limited liability companies.

Key Points   The advantages and disadvantages of proprietorships, partnerships, and limited liability companies are summarized in Exhibit 1.

Learning Outcomes	Example Exercises	Practice Exercises
• Identify the advantages and disadvantages of proprietorships, partnerships, and limited liability companies.		

OBJ. 2

Describe and illustrate the accounting for forming a partnership and for dividing the net income and net loss of a partnership.

Key Points When a partnership is formed, accounts are debited for contributed assets and credited for assumed liabilities, and the partner's capital account is credited for the net amount. The net income of a partnership may be divided among the partners on the basis of services rendered, interest earned on the capital account balance, and the income-sharing ratio.

Learning Outcomes	Example Exercises	Practice Exercises
• Journalize the initial formation of a partnership and establish partner capital.	EE12-1	PE12-1A, 12-1B
• Determine and journalize the income distributed to each partner.	EE12-2	PE12-2A, 12-2B

OBJ. 3

Describe and illustrate the accounting for partner admission and withdrawal.

Key Points Partnership assets should be restated to current values prior to admission or withdrawal of a partner. A new partner may be admitted into a partnership by either purchasing an interest from an existing partner or by purchasing an interest directly from the partnership.

Learning Outcomes	Example Exercises	Practice Exercises
• Prepare for partner admission by revaluing assets to approximate current values.	EE12-3	PE12-3A, 12-3B
• Distinguish between partner admission through purchase from an existing partner or purchase from the partnership.	EE12-3	PE12-3A, 12-3B
• Determine partner bonuses.	EE12-4	PE12-4A, 12-4B

OBJ. 4

Describe and illustrate the accounting for liquidating a partnership.

Key Points A partnership is liquidated by the (1) sale of partnership assets (realization), (2) distribution of gain or loss on realization to the partners, (3) payments to creditors, and (4) distribution of the remaining cash to partners according to their capital account balances. A partner may be deficient when the amount of loss distribution exceeds the capital balance.

Learning Outcomes	Example Exercises	Practice Exercises
• Apply the four steps of liquidating a partnership for either gain or loss on realization.	EE12-5	PE12-5A, 12-5B
• Apply the four steps of partnership liquidation when there is a partner deficiency.	EE12-6	PE12-6A, 12-6B

OBJ. 5

Prepare the statement of partnership equity.

Key Points A statement of partnership equity reports the changes in partnership equity from capital additions, net income, and withdrawals.

Learning Outcomes	Example Exercises	Practice Exercises
• Prepare a statement of partnership equity.		

Analyze and interpret employee efficiency.

Key Points The revenue per employee ratio is calculated as the total annual revenues divided by the total employees. This ratio measures the total revenue earned by each employee, and thus, is a measure of the efficiency of each employee in revenue terms. The ratio is often used to measure efficiency trends over time and across similar firms.

Learning Outcomes	Example Exercises	Practice Exercises
• Analyze and interpret the revenue per employee ratio.	EE12-7	PE12-7A, 12-7B

Key Terms

deficiency (555)

limited liability company (LLC) (540)

liquidation (550)

partnership (539)

partnership agreement (539)

realization (550)

revenue per employee (558)

statement of members' equity (557)

statement of partnership equity (557)

statement of partnership liquidation (552)

Illustrative Problem

Radcliffe, Sonders, and Towers, who share in income and losses in the ratio of 2:3:5, decided to discontinue operations as of April 30, 2012, and liquidate their partnership. After the accounts were closed on April 30, 2012, the following trial balance was prepared:

Radcliffe, Sonders, and Towers Post-Closing Trial Balance April 30, 2012		
	Debit Balances	**Credit Balances**
Cash	5,900	
Noncash Assets	109,900	
Liabilities		26,800
Radcliffe, Capital		14,600
Sonders, Capital		27,900
Towers, Capital		46,500
	115,800	115,800

Between May 1 and May 18, the noncash assets were sold for $27,400, and the liabilities were paid.

Instructions

1. Assuming that the partner with the capital deficiency pays the entire amount owed to the partnership, prepare a statement of partnership liquidation.

2. Journalize the entries to record (a) the sale of the assets, (b) the division of loss on the sale of the assets, (c) the payment of the liabilities, (d) the receipt of the deficiency, and (e) the distribution of cash to the partners.

Solution

1.

Radcliffe, Sonders, and Towers Statement of Partnership Liquidation For Period May 1–18, 2012							
					Capital		
	Cash +	Noncash Assets =	Liabilities +	Radcliffe (20%) +	Sonders (30%) +	Towers (50%)
Balances before realization	$ 5,900	$109,000	$26,800	$14,600	$27,900	$46,500
Sale of assets and division of loss	+27,400	−109,000		−16,500	−24,750	−41,250
Balances after realization	$33,300	$ 0	$26,800	$ (1,900)	$ 3,150	$ 5,250
Payment of liabilities	−26,800		−26,800			
Balances after payment of liabilities	$ 6,500	$ 0	$ 0	$ (1,900)	$ 3,150	$ 5,250
Receipt of deficiency	+ 1,900			+ 1,900		
Balances	$ 8,400	$ 0	$ 0	$ 0	$ 3,150	$ 5,250
Cash distributed to partners	−8,400				− 3,150	− 5,250
Final balances	$ 0	$ 0	$ 0	$ 0	$ 0	$ 0

2.a.

Cash	27,400	
Loss on Realization	82,500	
Noncash Assets		109,900

b.

Radcliffe, Capital	16,500	
Sonders, Capital	24,750	
Towers, Capital	41,250	
Loss on Realization		82,500

c.

Liabilities	26,800	
Cash		26,800

d.

Cash	1,900	
Radcliffe, Capital		1,900

e.

Sonders, Capital		3,150	
Towers, Capital		5,250	
Cash			8,400

Discussion Questions

1. What are the main advantages of (a) proprietorships, (b) partnerships, and (c) limited liability companies?

2. What are the disadvantages of a partnership over a limited liability company form of organization for a profit-making business?

3. Emilio Alvarez and Graciela Zavala joined together to form a partnership. Is it possible for them to lose a greater amount than the amount of their investment in the partnership? Explain.

4. What are the major features of a partnership agreement for a partnership, or an operating agreement for a limited liability company?

5. Josiah Barlow, Patty DuMont, and Owen Maholic are contemplating the formation of a partnership. According to the partnership agreement, Barlow is to invest $60,000 and devote one-half time, DuMont is to invest $40,000 and devote three-fourths time, and Maholic is to make no investment and devote full time. Would Maholic be correct in assuming that, since he is not contributing any assets to the firm, he is risking nothing? Explain.

6. During the current year, Marsha Engles withdrew $4,000 monthly from the partnership of Engles and Cox Water Management Consultants. Is it possible that her share of partnership net income for the current year might be more or less than $48,000? Explain.

7. a. What accounts are debited and credited to record a partner's cash withdrawal in lieu of salary?

   b. The articles of partnership provide for a salary allowance of $6,000 per month to partner C. If C withdrew only $4,000 per month, would this affect the division of the partnership net income?

   c. At the end of the fiscal year, what accounts are debited and credited to record the division of net income among partners?

8. Explain the difference between the admission of a new partner to a partnership (a) by purchase of an interest from another partner and (b) by contribution of assets to the partnership.

9. Why is it important to state all partnership assets in terms of current prices at the time of the admission of a new partner?

10. Why might a partnership pay a bonus to a newly admitted partner?

Practice Exercises

Learning Objectives	Example Exercises	
OBJ. 2	EE 12-1 *p. 542*	**PE 12-1A Journalize partner's original investment**

Brittany Adams contributed a patent, accounts receivable, and $61,000 cash to a partnership. The patent had a book value of $56,000. However, the technology covered by the patent appeared to have significant market potential. Thus, the patent was appraised at $240,000. The accounts receivable control account was $78,000, with an allowance for doubtful accounts of $4,000. The partnership also assumed a $15,000 account payable from Adams.

Provide the journal entry for Adams' contribution to the partnership.

OBJ. 2	EE 12-1 *p. 542*	**PE 12-1B Journalize partner's original investment**

Kevin LaRoche contributed land, inventory, and $28,000 cash to a partnership. The land had a book value of $65,000 and a market value of $135,000. The inventory had a book value of $60,000 and a market value of $51,000. The partnership also assumed a $50,000 note payable owed by LaRoche that was used originally to purchase the land.

Provide the journal entry for LaRoche's contribution to the partnership.

OBJ. 2	EE 12-2 *p. 544*	**PE 12-2A Dividing partnership net income**

Cody Paulson and Hannah O'Brien formed a partnership, dividing income as follows:

1. Annual salary allowance to Paulson of $26,000.

2. Interest of 5% on each partner's capital balance on January 1.

3. Any remaining net income divided to Paulson and O'Brien, 2:1.

Paulson and O'Brien had $50,000 and $120,000, respectively, in their January 1 capital balances. Net income for the year was $33,000.

How much net income should be distributed to Paulson?

OBJ. 2	EE 12-2 *p. 544*	**PE 12-2B Dividing partnership net income**

Alex Conyers and Shaunika Stevens formed a partnership, dividing income as follows:

1. Annual salary allowance to Stevens of $45,000.

2. Interest of 8% on each partner's capital balance on January 1.

3. Any remaining net income divided equally.

Conyers and Stevens had $50,000 and $160,000, respectively, in their January 1 capital balances. Net income for the year was $200,000.

How much net income should be distributed to Stevens?

OBJ. 3	EE 12-3 *p. 547*	**PE 12-3A Revaluing and contributing assets to a partnership**

Antoine Dodd purchased one-half of Kyle Bryan's interest in the Rich and Bryan partnership for $24,000. Prior to the investment, land was revalued to a market value of $110,000 from a book value of $84,000. Zach Rich and Kyle Bryan share net income equally. Bryan had a capital balance of $25,000 prior to these transactions.

a. Provide the journal entry for the revaluation of land.

b. Provide the journal entry to admit Dodd.

OBJ. 3   EE 12-3 *p. 547*   **PE 12-3B   Revaluing and contributing assets to a partnership**

Naseef Asad invested $75,000 in the Lionel and Morehouse partnership for ownership equity of $75,000. Prior to the investment, equipment was revalued to a market value of $57,000 from a book value of $33,000. Justin Lionel and Courtney Morehouse share net income in a 2:1 ratio.

a. Provide the journal entry for the revaluation of equipment.

b. Provide the journal entry to admit Asad.

OBJ. 3   EE 12-4 *p. 549*   **PE 12-4A   Partner bonus**

Sharpe has a capital balance of $300,000 after adjusting assets to fair market value. Rojas contributes $250,000 to receive a 60% interest in a new partnership with Sharpe.
    Determine the amount and recipient of the partner bonus.

OBJ. 3   EE 12-4 *p. 549*   **PE 12-4B   Partner bonus**

Joshi has a capital balance of $80,000 after adjusting assets to fair market value. Costas contributes $40,000 to receive a 40% interest in a new partnership with Joshi.
    Determine the amount and recipient of the partner bonus.

OBJ. 4   EE 12-5 *p. 554*   **PE 12-5A   Liquidating partnerships**

Prior to liquidating their partnership, Fowler and Ericson had capital accounts of $26,000 and $40,000, respectively. Prior to liquidation, the partnership had no cash assets other than what was realized from the sale of assets. These partnership assets were sold for $86,000. The partnership had $12,000 of liabilities. Fowler and Ericson share income and losses equally. Determine the amount received by Fowler as a final distribution from liquidation of the partnership.

OBJ. 4   EE 12-5 *p. 554*   **PE 12-5B   Liquidating partnerships**

Prior to liquidating their partnership, Quinn and Kestor had capital accounts of $200,000 and $120,000, respectively. Prior to liquidation, the partnership had no cash assets other than what was realized from the sale of assets. These partnership assets were sold for $240,000. The partnership had $30,000 of liabilities. Quinn and Kestor share income and losses equally. Determine the amount received by Quinn as a final distribution from liquidation of the partnership.

OBJ. 4   EE 12-6 *p. 557*   **PE 12-6A   Liquidating partnerships—deficiency**

Prior to liquidating their partnership, Jolly and Haines had capital accounts of $80,000 and $45,000, respectively. The partnership assets were sold for $30,000. The partnership had no liabilities. Jolly and Haines share income and losses equally.

a. Determine the amount of Haines' deficiency.

b. Determine the amount distributed to Jolly, assuming Haines is unable to satisfy the deficiency.

OBJ. 4   EE 12-6 *p. 557*   **PE 12-6B   Liquidating partnerships—deficiency**

Prior to liquidating their partnership, Chow and Fuentes had capital accounts of $85,000 and $165,000, respectively. The partnership assets were sold for $45,000. The partnership had no liabilities. Chow and Fuentes share income and losses equally.

a. Determine the amount of Chow's deficiency.

b. Determine the amount distributed to Fuentes, assuming Chow is unable to satisfy the deficiency.

OBJ. 6   EE 12-7 *p. 559*

PE 12-7A   Revenue per employee

Aaron and Rogers, CPAs earned $12,600,000 during 2012 using 90 employees. During 2013, the firm grew revenues to $14,400,000 and expanded the staff to 96 employees.

a. Determine the revenue per employee for each year.

b. Interpret the results.

OBJ. 6   EE 12-7 *p. 559*

PE 12-7B   Revenue per employee

TechSystems, Architects earned $3,600,000 during 2012 using 20 employees. During 2013, the firm reduced revenues to $3,200,000 and reduced the staff to 16 employees.

a. Determine the revenue per employee for each year.

b. Interpret the results.

Exercises

OBJ. 2

EX 12-1   Record partner's original investment

Amber Moss and Latoya Pell decide to form a partnership by combining the assets of their separate businesses. Moss contributes the following assets to the partnership: cash, $15,000; accounts receivable with a face amount of $159,000 and an allowance for doubtful accounts of $9,700; merchandise inventory with a cost of $100,000; and equipment with a cost of $155,000 and accumulated depreciation of $100,000.

The partners agree that $6,000 of the accounts receivable are completely worthless and are not to be accepted by the partnership, that $11,400 is a reasonable allowance for the uncollectibility of the remaining accounts, that the merchandise inventory is to be recorded at the current market price of $91,450, and that the equipment is to be valued at $62,500.

Journalize the partnership's entry to record Moss's investment.

OBJ. 2

EX 12-2   Record partner's original investment

Jessica Kimble and Carlos Segura form a partnership by combining assets of their former businesses. The following balance sheet information is provided by Kimble, sole proprietorship:

Cash		$ 50,000
Accounts receivable	$100,000	
Less: Allowance for doubtful accounts	5,900	94,100
Land		180,000
Equipment	$ 70,000	
Less: Accumulated depreciation—equipment	43,000	27,000
Total assets		$351,100
Accounts payable		$ 22,500
Notes payable		80,000
Jessica Kimble, capital		248,600
Total liabilities and owner's equity		$351,100

Kimble obtained appraised values for the land and equipment as follows:

Land	$284,000
Equipment	19,000

An analysis of the accounts receivable indicated that the allowance for doubtful accounts should be increased to $7,000.

Journalize the partnership's entry for Kimble's investment.

OBJ. 2

✔ b. Wyatt, $315,000

EX 12-3 Dividing partnership income

Jennifer Wyatt and Megan Truett formed a partnership, investing $330,000 and $110,000, respectively. Determine their participation in the year's net income of $420,000 under each of the following independent assumptions: (a) no agreement concerning division of net income; (b) divided in the ratio of original capital investment; (c) interest at the rate of 8% allowed on original investments and the remainder divided in the ratio of 2:3; (d) salary allowances of $50,000 and $70,000, respectively, and the balance divided equally; (e) allowance of interest at the rate of 8% on original investments, salary allowances of $50,000 and $70,000, respectively, and the remainder divided equally.

OBJ. 2

✔ c. Wyatt, $76,320

EX 12-4 Dividing partnership income

Determine the income participation of Wyatt and Truett, according to each of the five assumptions as to income division listed in Exercise 12-3 if the year's net income is $160,000.

OBJ. 2

EX 12-5 Dividing partnership net loss

Ashley Adams and Michael Rovell formed a partnership in which the partnership agreement provided for salary allowances of $45,000 and $35,000, respectively. Determine the division of a $30,000 net loss for the current year.

OBJ. 2

EX 12-6 Negotiating income-sharing ratio

Sixty-year-old Mary Filmore retired from her computer consulting business in Boston and moved to Florida. There she met 27-year-old Emily Wright, who had just graduated from Eldon Community College with an associate degree in computer science. Mary and Emily formed a partnership called F&W Computer Consultants. Mary contributed $35,000 for startup costs and devoted one-half time to the business. Emily devoted full time to the business. The monthly drawings were $2,000 for Mary and $4,000 for Emily.

At the end of the first year of operations, the two partners disagreed on the division of net income. Mary reasoned that the division should be equal. Although she devoted only one-half time to the business, she contributed all of the startup funds. Emily reasoned that the income-sharing ratio should be 2:1 in her favor because she devoted full time to the business and her monthly drawings were twice those of Mary.

a. Can you identify any flaws in the partners' reasoning regarding the income-sharing ratio?

b. How could an income-sharing agreement resolve this dispute?

OBJ. 2

✔ a. Richards, $85,200

EX 12-7 Dividing LLC income

Joshua Richards and Taylor Clark formed a limited liability company with an operating agreement that provided a salary allowance of $60,000 and $50,000 to each member, respectively. In addition, the operating agreement specified an income-sharing ratio of 3:2. The two members withdrew amounts equal to their salary allowances.

a. Determine the division of $152,000 net income for the year.

b. Provide journal entries to close the (1) income summary and (2) drawing accounts for the two members.

c. If the net income were less than the sum of the salary allowances, how would income be divided between the two members of the LLC?

OBJ. 2, 5

✔ a. Nelson, $269,890

EX 12-8 Dividing LLC net income and statement of members' equity

Macro Media, LLC, has three members: WLKT Partners, Amanda Nelson, and Daily Sentinel Newspaper, LLC. On January 1, 2012, the three members had equity of $250,000, $50,000, and $140,000, respectively. WLKT Partners contributed an additional $50,000 to Macro Media, LLC, on June 1, 2012. Amanda Nelson received an annual salary allowance of $88,700 during 2012. The members' equity accounts are also credited with 10% interest on each member's January 1 capital balance. Any remaining income is to be shared in the ratio of 4:3:3 among the three members. The net income for Macro Media, LLC, for 2012 was $720,000. Amounts equal to the salary and interest allowances were withdrawn by the members.

a. Determine the division of income among the three members.

b. Prepare the journal entry to close the net income and withdrawals to the individual member equity accounts.

c. Prepare a statement of members' equity for 2012.

d. What are the advantages of an income-sharing agreement for the members of this LLC?

OBJ. 2

EX 12-9   Partner income and withdrawal journal entries

The notes to the annual report for KPMG LLP (U.K.) indicated the following policies regarding the partners' capital:

> *The allocation of profits to those who were partners during the financial year occurs following the finalization of the annual financial statements. During the year, partners receive monthly drawings and, from time to time, additional profit distributions. Both the monthly drawings and profit distributions represent payments on account of current-year profits and are reclaimable from partners until profits have been allocated.*

Assume that the partners draw £40 million per month for 2012 and the net income for the year is £600 million. Journalize the partner capital and partner drawing control accounts in the following requirements:

a. Provide the journal entry for the monthly partner drawing for January.

b. Provide the journal entry to close the income summary account at the end of the year.

c. Provide the journal entry to close the drawing account at the end of the year.

d. Why would partner drawings be considered "reclaimable" until profits have been allocated?

OBJ. 3

EX 12-10   Admitting new partners

Lily Yuan and Kayla Dunn are partners who share in the income equally and have capital balances of $180,000 and $62,500, respectively. Yuan, with the consent of Dunn, sells one-third of her interest to Rachel Burnett. What entry is required by the partnership if the sales price is (a) $40,000? (b) $80,000?

OBJ. 3

✔ b. Faber, $120,000

EX 12-11   Admitting new partners who buy an interest and contribute assets

The capital accounts of Jonathan Faber and Faheem Ahmad have balances of $150,000 and $110,000, respectively. Lauren Wells and Rachel Lee are to be admitted to the partnership. Wells buys one-fifth of Faber's interest for $35,000 and one-fourth of Ahmad's interest for $25,000. Lee contributes $70,000 cash to the partnership, for which she is to receive an ownership equity of $70,000.

a. Journalize the entries to record the admission of (1) Wells and (2) Lee.

b. What are the capital balances of each partner after the admission of the new partners?

OBJ. 3

✔ b. Rivas, $65,000

EX 12-12   Admitting new partner who contributes assets

After the tangible assets have been adjusted to current market prices, the capital accounts of Brandon Newman and Latrell Osbourne have balances of $75,000 and $125,000, respectively. Juan Rivas is to be admitted to the partnership, contributing $50,000 cash to the partnership, for which he is to receive an ownership equity of $65,000. All partners share equally in income.

a. Journalize the entry to record the admission of Rivas, who is to receive a bonus of $15,000.

b. What are the capital balances of each partner after the admission of the new partner?

c. Why are tangible assets adjusted to current market prices, prior to admitting a new partner?

OBJ. 3

EX 12-13   Admitting new partner with bonus

Andrew Hall and Brian Li formed a partnership to provide landscaping services. Hall and Li shared profits and losses equally. After all the tangible assets have been adjusted to current market prices, the capital accounts of Andrew Hall and Brian Li have balances of $54,000 and $71,000, respectively. Kristin Lane has expertise with using the computer to prepare landscape designs, cost estimates, and renderings. Hall and Li deem these skills useful; thus, Lane is admitted to the partnership at a 30% interest for a purchase price of $35,000.

a. Determine the recipient and amount of the partner bonus.

b. Provide the journal entry to admit Lane into the partnership.

c. Why would a bonus be paid in this situation?

OBJ. 3

✔ b. (2) Bonus paid to Mann, $15,000

EX 12-14   Admitting a new LLC member with bonus

HealthSource, LLC, consists of two doctors, Drew and Moore, who share in all income and losses according to a 2:3 income-sharing ratio. Dr. Mann has been asked to join the LLC. Prior to admitting Mann, the assets of HealthSource were revalued to reflect their current market values. The revaluation resulted in medical equipment being increased by $35,000. Prior to the revaluation, the equity balances for Drew and Moore were $201,000 and $289,000, respectively.

a. Provide the journal entry for the asset revaluation.

b. Provide the journal entry for the bonus under the following independent situations:

　　1. Mann purchased a 30% interest in HealthSource, LLC, for $285,000.

　　2. Mann purchased a 25% interest in HealthSource, LLC, for $155,000.

OBJ. 3

✔ b. (1) Bonus paid to Jenkins, $11,000

EX 12-15   Admitting new partner with bonus

J. Witt and K. Torres are partners in Whole Earth Consultants. Witt and Torres share income equally. L. Jenkins will be admitted to the partnership. Prior to the admission, equipment was revalued downward by $12,000. The capital balances of each partner are $106,000 and $141,000, respectively, prior to the revaluation.

a. Provide the journal entry for the asset revaluation.

b. Provide the journal entry for Jenkins' admission under the following independent situations:

　　1. Jenkins purchased a 20% interest for $45,000.

　　2. Jenkins purchased a 30% interest for $135,000.

OBJ. 2, 3, 5

✔ Wilson capital, Dec. 31, 2012, $191,700

EX 12-16   Partner bonuses, statement of partners' equity

The partnership of Angel Investor Associates began operations on January 1, 2012, with contributions from two partners as follows:

Scott Wilson	$120,000
Michael Goforth	80,000

The following additional partner transactions took place during the year:

1. In early January, Lance McGinnis is admitted to the partnership by contributing $50,000 cash for a 20% interest.

2. Net income of $250,000 was earned in 2012. In addition, Scott Wilson received a salary allowance of $45,000 for the year. The three partners agree to an income-sharing ratio equal to their capital balances after admitting McGinnis.

3. The partners' withdrawals are equal to half of the increase in their capital balances from salary allowance and income.

Prepare a statement of partnership equity for the year ended December 31, 2012.

OBJ. 3

EX 12-17   Withdrawal of partner

David Winner is to retire from the partnership of Winner and Associates as of March 31, the end of the current fiscal year. After closing the accounts, the capital balances of the partners are as follows: David Winner, $210,000; Alexis Richards, $125,000; and Marcus Williams, $140,000. They have shared net income and net losses in the ratio of 3:2:2. The partners agree that the merchandise inventory should be increased by $32,000, and the allowance for doubtful accounts should be increased by $4,000. Winner agrees to accept a note for $150,000 in partial settlement of his ownership equity. The remainder of his claim is to be paid in cash. Richards and Williams are to share equally in the net income or net loss of the new partnership.

Journalize the entries to record (a) the adjustment of the assets to bring them into agreement with current market prices and (b) the withdrawal of Winner from the partnership.

OBJ. 2, 3, 5

✔ a. 2:3

EX 12-18   Statement of members' equity, admitting new member

The statement of members' equity for Bonanza, LLC, is shown below.

Bonanza, LLC
Statement of Members' Equity
For the Years Ended December 31, 2012 and 2013

	Idaho Properties, LLC, Member Equity	Silver Holdings, LLC, Member Equity	Justin Thomas Member Equity	Total Members' Equity
Members' equity, December 31, 2011	$552,000	$420,500		$ 972,500
Net income	128,000	192,000		320,000
Members' equity, December 31, 2012	$680,000	$612,500		$1,292,500
Thomas contribution, January 1, 2013	8,000	12,000	$250,000	270,000
Net income	90,000	225,000	135,000	450,000
Less member withdrawals	(32,000)	(48,000)	(50,000)	(130,000)
Members' equity, December 31, 2013	$746,000	$801,500	$335,000	$1,882,500

a. What was the income-sharing ratio in 2012?

b. What was the income-sharing ratio in 2013?

c. How much cash did Justin Thomas contribute to Bonanza, LLC, for his interest?

d. Why do the member equity accounts of Idaho Properties, LLC, and Silver Holdings, LLC, have positive entries for Justin Thomas' contribution?

e. What percentage interest of Bonanza did Justin Thomas acquire?

f. Why are withdrawals less than net income?

OBJ. 4

✔ a. $6,000 loss

EX 12-19   Distribution of cash upon liquidation

Lyle and Fisher are partners, sharing gains and losses equally. They decide to terminate their partnership. Prior to realization, their capital balances are $15,000 and $7,000, respectively. After all noncash assets are sold and all liabilities are paid, there is a cash balance of $16,000.

a. What is the amount of a gain or loss on realization?

b. How should the gain or loss be divided between Lyle and Fisher?

c. How should the cash be divided between Lyle and Fisher?

OBJ. 4

✔ Mason, $40,000

EX 12-20   Distribution of cash upon liquidation

Daniel Mason and Srini Kumar, with capital balances of $34,000 and $36,000, respectively, decide to liquidate their partnership. After selling the noncash assets and paying the liabilities, there is $82,000 of cash remaining. If the partners share income and losses equally, how should the cash be distributed?

OBJ. 4

✔ b. $79,500

EX 12-21   Liquidating partnerships—capital deficiency

Gifford, Lawrence, and Ma share equally in net income and net losses. After the partnership sells all assets for cash, divides the losses on realization, and pays the liabilities, the balances in the capital accounts are as follows: Gifford, $32,000 Cr.; Lawrence, $62,500 Cr.; Ma, $15,000 Dr.

a. What term is applied to the debit balance in Ma's capital account?

b. What is the amount of cash on hand?

c. Journalize the transaction that must take place for Gifford and Lawrence to receive cash in the liquidation process equal to their capital account balances.

OBJ. 4

✔ a. Deacon, $650

EX 12-22   Distribution of cash upon liquidation

Deacon, Raines, and Francis arranged to import and sell orchid corsages for a university dance. They agreed to share equally the net income or net loss of the venture. Deacon and Raines advanced $300 and $450 of their own respective funds to pay for advertising and other expenses. After collecting for all sales and paying creditors, the partnership has $1,800 in cash.

a. How should the money be distributed?

b. Assuming that the partnership has only $600 instead of $1,800, do any of the three partners have a capital deficiency? If so, how much?

OBJ. 4

EX 12-23   Liquidating partnerships—capital deficiency

Arnold, Peters, and Suzuki are partners sharing income 3:2:1. After the firm's loss from liquidation is distributed, the capital account balances were: Arnold, $18,000 Dr.; Peters, $75,000 Cr.; and Suzuki, $55,000 Cr. If Arnold is personally bankrupt and unable to pay any of the $18,000, what will be the amount of cash received by Peters and Suzuki upon liquidation?

OBJ. 4

EX 12-24   Statement of partnership liquidation

After closing the accounts on July 1, prior to liquidating the partnership, the capital account balances of Jessup, King, and Oliver are $70,000, $43,000, and $22,000, respectively. Cash, noncash assets, and liabilities total $62,000, $108,000, and $35,000, respectively. Between July 1 and July 29, the noncash assets are sold for $90,000, the liabilities are paid, and the remaining cash is distributed to the partners. The partners share net income and loss in the ratio of 3:2:1. Prepare a statement of partnership liquidation for the period July 1–29, 2012.

OBJ. 4

EX 12-25   Statement of LLC liquidation

Hall, Lang, and Das are members of Evergreen Sales, LLC, sharing income and losses in the ratio of 2:2:1, respectively. The members decide to liquidate the limited liability company. The members' equity prior to liquidation and asset realization on May 1, 2012, are as follows:

Hall	$37,000
Lang	40,000
Das	18,000
Total	$95,000

In winding up operations during the month of May, noncash assets with a book value of $107,000 are sold for $123,000, and liabilities of $25,000 are satisfied. Prior to realization, Evergreen Sales has a cash balance of $13,000.

a. Prepare a statement of LLC liquidation.

b. Provide the journal entry for the final cash distribution to members.

c. What is the role of the income- and loss-sharing ratio in liquidating a LLC?

EX 12-26 Partnership entries and statement of partners' equity

The capital accounts of Gary Menendez and Melissa Breeden have balances of $75,000 and $55,000, respectively, on January 1, 2012, the beginning of the current fiscal year. On April 10, Menendez invested an additional $12,000. During the year, Menendez and Breeden withdrew $44,000 and $35,000, respectively, and net income for the year was $92,000. The articles of partnership make no reference to the division of net income.

a. Journalize the entries to close (1) the income summary account and (2) the drawing accounts.

b. Prepare a statement of partners' equity for the current year for the partnership of Menendez and Breeden.

EX 12-27 Revenue per professional staff

The accounting firm of Deloitte & Touche is the largest international accounting firm in the world as ranked by total revenues. For the last two years, Deloitte & Touche reported the following for its U.S. operations:

	2009	2008
Revenue (in billions)	$26.1	$27.4
Number of professional staff (including partners)	139,760	133,100

a. For 2009 and 2008, determine the revenue per professional staff. Round to the nearest thousand dollars.

b. Interpret the trend between the two years.

EX 12-28 Revenue per employee

Commerical Cleaning Services, LLC, provides cleaning services for office buildings. The firm has 10 members in the LLC, which did not change between 2012 and 2013. During 2013, the business terminated two commercial contracts. The following revenue and employee information is provided:

	2013	2012
Revenues (in thousands)	$20,000	$22,400
Number of employees (excluding members)	160	200

a. For 2013 and 2012, determine the revenue per employee (excluding members).

b. Interpret the trend between the two years.

Problems Series A

PR 12-1A Entries and balance sheet for partnership

On August 1, 2012, Wardell Cole and Marva Landers form a partnership. Cole agrees to invest $15,600 in cash and merchandise inventory valued at $62,400. Landers invests certain business assets at valuations agreed upon, transfers business liabilities, and contributes sufficient cash to bring her total capital to $60,000. Details regarding the book values of the business assets and liabilities, and the agreed valuations, follow:

	Landers' Ledger Balance	Agreed-Upon Valuation
Accounts Receivable	$25,300	$23,700
Allowance for Doubtful Accounts	1,500	1,900
Equipment	92,300 }	57,900
Accumulated Depreciation—Equipment	35,600 }	
Accounts Payable	20,000	20,000
Notes Payable	30,000	30,000

The partnership agreement includes the following provisions regarding the division of net income: interest on original investments at 10%, salary allowances of $22,500 (Cole) and $30,400 (Landers), and the remainder equally.

Instructions

1. Journalize the entries to record the investments of Cole and Landers in the partnership accounts.

2. Prepare a balance sheet as of August 1, 2012, the date of formation of the partnership of Cole and Landers.

3. After adjustments and the closing of revenue and expense accounts at July 31, 2013, the end of the first full year of operations, the income summary account has a credit balance of $100,500, and the drawing accounts have debit balances of $25,000 (Cole) and $30,400 (Landers). Journalize the entries to close the income summary account and the drawing accounts at July 31, 2013.

OBJ. 2

✔ 1. f. Dyer net income, $41,600

PR 12-2A   Dividing partnership income

Dyer and Salinas have decided to form a partnership. They have agreed that Dyer is to invest $120,000 and that Salinas is to invest $40,000. Dyer is to devote one-half time to the business and Salinas is to devote full time. The following plans for the division of income are being considered:

a. Equal division.

b. In the ratio of original investments.

c. In the ratio of time devoted to the business.

d. Interest of 12% on original investments and the remainder equally.

e. Interest of 12% on original investments, salary allowances of $32,000 to Dyer and $64,000 to Salinas, and the remainder equally.

f. Plan (e), except that Salinas is also to be allowed a bonus equal to 20% of the amount by which net income exceeds the total salary allowances.

Instructions

For each plan, determine the division of the net income under each of the following assumptions: (1) net income of $108,000 and (2) net income of $150,000. Present the data in tabular form, using the following columnar headings:

Plan	$108,000		$150,000	
	Dyer	**Salinas**	**Dyer**	**Salinas**

OBJ. 2, 5

✔ 2. Dec. 31 capital—Adkins, $85,000

PR 12-3A   Financial statements for partnership

The ledger of Aiden Durant and Jasmine Adkins, attorneys-at-law, contains the following accounts and balances after adjustments have been recorded on December 31, 2012:

Aiden, Durant, Adkins
Trial Balance
December 31, 2012

	Debit Balances	Credit Balances
Cash	42,000	
Accounts Receivable	42,300	
Supplies	1,500	
Land	100,000	
Building	108,100	
Accumulated Depreciation—Building		62,500
Office Equipment	46,000	
Accumulated Depreciation—Office Equipment		19,400
Accounts Payable		29,800
Salaries Payable		3,200
Aiden Durant, Capital		100,000
Aiden Durant, Drawing	45,000	

Jasmine Adkins, Capital		60,000
Jasmine Adkins, Drawing	65,000	
Professional Fees		364,500
Salary Expense	146,000	
Depreciation Expense—Building	14,500	
Property Tax Expense	9,000	
Heating and Lighting Expense	7,200	
Supplies Expense	5,200	
Depreciation Expense—Office Equipment	4,500	
Miscellaneous Expense	3,100	
	639,400	639,400

The balance in Adkins' capital account includes an additional investment of $10,000 made on August 10, 2012.

Instructions

1. Prepare an income statement for 2012, indicating the division of net income. The articles of partnership provide for salary allowances of $40,000 to Durant and $50,000 to Adkins, allowances of 10% on each partner's capital balance at the beginning of the fiscal year, and equal division of the remaining net income or net loss.

2. Prepare a statement of partners' equity for 2012.

3. Prepare a balance sheet as of the end of 2012.

OBJ. 3

✔ 3. Total assets, $282,500

PR 12-4A   Admitting new partner

Tosio Kato and Angela Gordon have operated a successful firm for many years, sharing net income and net losses equally. Tricia McCay is to be admitted to the partnership on May 1 of the current year, in accordance with the following agreement:

a. Assets and liabilities of the old partnership are to be valued at their book values as of April 30, except for the following:

   • Accounts receivable amounting to $2,400 are to be written off, and the allowance for doubtful accounts is to be increased to 5% of the remaining accounts.

   • Merchandise inventory is to be valued at $63,200.

   • Equipment is to be valued at $141,900.

b. McCay is to purchase $60,000 of the ownership interest of Gordon for $65,000 cash and to contribute another $35,000 cash to the partnership for a total ownership equity of $95,000.

The post-closing trial balance of Kato and Gordon as of April 30 is as follows:

Kato and Gordon
Post-Closing Trial Balance
April 30, 2012

	Debit Balances	Credit Balances
Cash	6,000	
Accounts Receivable	38,400	
Allowance for Doubtful Accounts		1,400
Merchandise Inventory	59,000	
Prepaid Insurance	2,200	
Equipment	165,000	
Accumulated Depreciation—Equipment		51,700
Accounts Payable		9,500
Notes Payable		40,000
Tosio Kato, Capital		90,000
Angela Gordon, Capital		78,000
	270,600	270,600

Instructions

1. Journalize the entries as of April 30 to record the revaluations, using a temporary account entitled Asset Revaluations. The balance in the accumulated depreciation account is to be eliminated. After journalizing the revaluations, close the balance of the asset revaluations account to the capital accounts of Tosio Kato and Angela Gordon.

2. Journalize the additional entries to record McCay's entrance to the partnership on May 1, 2012.

3. Present a balance sheet for the new partnership as of May 1, 2012.

OBJ. 4

PR 12-5A   Statement of partnership liquidation

After the accounts are closed on July 3, 2012, prior to liquidating the partnership, the capital accounts of Rebecca Adams, Austin Cooper, and Ricardo Ruiz are $22,400, $5,300, and $31,900, respectively. Cash and noncash assets total $8,800 and $68,800, respectively. Amounts owed to creditors total $18,000. The partners share income and losses in the ratio of 2:1:1. Between July 3 and July 29, the noncash assets are sold for $33,200, the partner with the capital deficiency pays his deficiency to the partnership, and the liabilities are paid.

Instructions

1. Prepare a statement of partnership liquidation, indicating (a) the sale of assets and division of loss, (b) the payment of liabilities, (c) the receipt of the deficiency (from the appropriate partner), and (d) the distribution of cash.

2. Assume the partner with the capital deficiency declares bankruptcy and is unable to pay the deficiency. Journalize the entries to (a) allocate the partner's deficiency and (b) distribute the remaining cash.

OBJ. 4

PR 12-6A   Statement of partnership liquidation

On October 1, 2012, the firm of Sams, Price, and Ladd decided to liquidate their partnership. The partners have capital balances of $54,000, $77,000, and $12,000, respectively. The cash balance is $26,000, the book values of noncash assets total $155,000, and liabilities total $38,000. The partners share income and losses in the ratio of 2:2:1.

Instructions

1. Prepare a statement of partnership liquidation, covering the period October 1–30 2012, for each of the following independent assumptions:

   a. All of the noncash assets are sold for $212,000 in cash, the creditors are paid, and the remaining cash is distributed to the partners.

   b. All of the noncash assets are sold for $70,000 in cash, the creditors are paid, the partner with the debit capital balance pays the amount owed to the firm, and the remaining cash is distributed to the partners.

2. Assume the partner with the capital deficiency in part (b) above declares bankruptcy and is unable to pay the deficiency. Journalize the entries to (a) allocate the partner's deficiency and (b) distribute the remaining cash.

Problems Series B

OBJ. 2

✔ 3. Harber net income, $56,900

PR 12-1B   Entries and balance sheet for partnership

On June 1, 2011, Anne Harber and Heather Lamb form a partnership. Harber agrees to invest $16,000 cash and merchandise inventory valued at $42,000. Lamb invests certain business assets at valuations agreed upon, transfers business liabilities, and contributes sufficient cash to bring her total capital to $80,000. Details regarding the book values of the business assets and liabilities, and the agreed valuations, follow:

	Lamb's Ledger Balance	Agreed-Upon Balance
Accounts Receivable	$21,400	$19,400
Allowance for Doubtful Accounts	1,000	1,300
Merchandise Inventory	24,300	25,900
Equipment	44,000	34,000
Accumulated Depreciation—Equipment	14,000	
Accounts Payable	7,000	7,000
Notes Payable	5,000	5,000

The partnership agreement includes the following provisions regarding the division of net income: interest of 10% on original investments, salary allowances of $36,000 (Harber) and $22,000 (Lamb), and the remainder equally.

Instructions

1. Journalize the entries to record the investments of Harber and Lamb in the partnership accounts.

2. Prepare a balance sheet as of June 1, 2011, the date of formation of the partnership of Harber and Lamb.

3. After adjustments and the closing of revenue and expense accounts at May 31, 2012, the end of the first full year of operations, the income summary account has a credit balance of $102,000, and the drawing accounts have debit balances of $40,000 (Harber) and $25,000 (Lamb). Journalize the entries to close the income summary account and the drawing accounts at May 31, 2012.

OBJ. 2

✔ 1. f. Snyder net income, $128,900

PR 12-2B   Dividing partnership income

Tim Snyder and Jay Wise have decided to form a partnership. They have agreed that Snyder is to invest $30,000 and that Wise is to invest $40,000. Snyder is to devote full time to the business, and Wise is to devote one-half time. The following plans for the division of income are being considered:

a. Equal division.

b. In the ratio of original investments.

c. In the ratio of time devoted to the business.

d. Interest of 10% on original investments and the remainder in the ratio of 3:2.

e. Interest of 10% on original investments, salary allowances of $34,000 to Snyder and $17,000 to Wise, and the remainder equally.

f. Plan (e), except that Snyder is also to be allowed a bonus equal to 20% of the amount by which net income exceeds the total salary allowances.

Instructions

For each plan, determine the division of the net income under each of the following assumptions: (1) net income of $210,000 and (2) net income of $84,000. Present the data in tabular form, using the following columnar headings:

	$210,000		$84,000	
Plan	Snyder	Wise	Snyder	Wise

OBJ. 2, 5

✔ 2. Dec. 31 capital— Hoffman, $201,200

PR 12-3B   Financial statements for partnerships

The ledger of Jin Ding and Paul Hoffman, attorneys-at-law, contains the following accounts and balances after adjustments have been recorded on December 31, 2012:

Ding and Hoffman
Trial Balance
December 31, 2012

	Debit Balances	Credit Balances
Cash	26,900	
Accounts Receivable	41,300	
Supplies	6,700	
Land	140,000	
Building	160,000	
Accumulated Depreciation—Building		52,000
Office Equipment	62,000	
Accumulated Depreciation—Office Equipment		21,300
Accounts Payable		3,400
Salaries Payable		5,200
Jin Ding, Capital		130,000
Jin Ding, Drawing	50,000	
Paul Hoffman, Capital		170,000
Paul Hoffman, Drawing	60,000	
Professional Fees		583,200
Salary Expense	315,700	
Depreciation Expense—Building	75,000	
Heating and Lighting Expense	11,900	
Depreciation Expense—Office Equipment	6,700	
Property Tax Expense	3,500	
Supplies Expense	3,400	
Miscellaneous Expense	2,000	
	965,100	965,100

The balance in Hoffman's capital account includes an additional investment of $20,000 made on April 5, 2012.

Instructions

1. Prepare an income statement for the current fiscal year, indicating the division of net income. The articles of partnership provide for salary allowances of $60,000 to Ding and $75,000 to Hoffman, allowances of 12% on each partner's capital balance at the beginning of the fiscal year, and equal division of the remaining net income or net loss.

2. Prepare a statement of partners' equity for 2012.

3. Prepare a balance sheet as of the end of 2012.

OBJ. 3

✔ 3. Total assets,
$227,300

PR 12-4B   Admitting new partner

Anthony Simpson and Shawna Ryder have operated a successful firm for many years, sharing net income and net losses equally. Blaine Evans is to be admitted to the partnership on June 1 of the current year, in accordance with the following agreement:

a. Assets and liabilities of the old partnership are to be valued at their book values as of May 31, except for the following:

  • Accounts receivable amounting to $3,400 are to be written off, and the allowance for doubtful accounts is to be increased to 5% of the remaining accounts.

  • Merchandise inventory is to be valued at $64,300.

  • Equipment is to be valued at $88,000.

b. Evans is to purchase $32,000 of the ownership interest of Ryder for $37,500 cash and to contribute $40,000 cash to the partnership for a total ownership equity of $72,000.

The post-closing trial balance of Simpson and Ryder as of May 31 follows.

Simpson and Ryder
Post-Closing Trial Balance
May 31, 2012

	Debit Balances	Credit Balances
Cash	14,400	
Accounts Receivable	21,400	
Allowance for Doubtful Accounts		500
Merchandise Inventory	58,600	
Prepaid Insurance	3,500	
Equipment	97,000	
Accumulated Depreciation—Equipment		25,700
Accounts Payable		14,700
Notes Payable		12,000
Anthony Simpson, Capital		80,000
Shawna Ryder, Capital		62,000
	194,900	194,900

Instructions

1. Journalize the entries as of May 31 to record the revaluations, using a temporary account entitled Asset Revaluations. The balance in the accumulated depreciation account is to be eliminated. After journalizing the revaluations, close the balance of the asset revaluations account to the capital accounts of Anthony Simpson and Shawna Ryder.

2. Journalize the additional entries to record Evans' entrance to the partnership on May 31, 2012.

3. Present a balance sheet for the new partnership as of June 1, 2012.

OBJ. 4

PR 12-5B   Statement of partnership liquidation

After the accounts are closed on September 10, 2012, prior to liquidating the partnership, the capital accounts of Randy Campbell, Ken Thayer, and Linda Tipton are $38,000, $6,400, and $28,500, respectively. Cash and noncash assets total $17,700 and $64,200, respectively. Amounts owed to creditors total $9,000. The partners share income and losses in the ratio of 1:1:2. Between September 10 and September 30, the noncash assets are sold for $35,000, the partner with the capital deficiency pays his or her deficiency to the partnership, and the liabilities are paid.

Instructions

1. Prepare a statement of partnership liquidation, indicating (a) the sale of assets and division of loss, (b) the payment of liabilities, (c) the receipt of the deficiency (from the appropriate partner), and (d) the distribution of cash.

2. Assume the partner with the capital deficiency declares bankruptcy and is unable to pay the deficiency. Journalize the entries to (a) allocate the partner's deficiency and (b) distribute the remaining cash.

OBJ. 4

PR 12-6B   Statement of partnership liquidation

On June 3, 2012, the firm of Lyon, Malone, and Chen decided to liquidate their partnership. The partners have capital balances of $12,000, $76,000, and $104,000, respectively. The cash balance is $19,000, the book values of noncash assets total $218,000, and liabilities total $45,000. The partners share income and losses in the ratio of 1:2:2.

Instructions

1. Prepare a statement of partnership liquidation, covering the period June 3–29, 2012, for each of the following independent assumptions:

   a. All of the noncash assets are sold for $272,000 in cash, the creditors are paid, and the remaining cash is distributed to the partners.

   b. All of the noncash assets are sold for $105,000 in cash, the creditors are paid, the partner with the debit capital balance pays the amount owed to the firm, and the remaining cash is distributed to the partners.

2. Assume the partner with the capital deficiency in part (b) above declares bankruptcy and is unable to pay the deficiency. Journalize the entries to (a) allocate the partner's deficiency and (b) distribute the remaining cash.

Cases & Projects

CP 12-1   Partnership agreement

Colin Maples, M.D., and Daniel Graham, M.D., are sole owners of two medical practices that operate in the same medical building. The two doctors agree to combine assets and liabilities of the two businesses to form a partnership. The partnership agreement calls for dividing income equally between the two doctors. After several months, the following conversation takes place between the two doctors:

Maples: I've noticed that your patient load has dropped over the last couple of months. When we formed our partnership, we were seeing about the same number of patients per week. However, now our patient records show that you have been seeing about half as many patients as I have. Are there any issues that I should be aware of?

Graham: There's nothing going on. When I was working on my own, I was really putting in the hours. One of the reasons I formed this partnership was to enjoy life a little more and scale back a little bit.

Maples: I see. Well, I find that I'm working as hard as I did when I was on my own, yet making less than I did previously. Essentially, you're sharing in half of my billings and I'm sharing in half of yours. Since you are working much less than I am, I end up on the short end of the bargain.

Graham: Well, I don't know what to say. An agreement is an agreement. The partnership is based on a 50/50 split. That's what a partnership is all about.

Maples: If that's so, then it applies equally well on the effort end of the equation as on the income end.

➤ Discuss whether Graham is acting in an ethical manner. How could Maples renegotiate the partnership agreement to avoid this dispute?

CP 12-2   Dividing partnership income

Jerry Graves and Bonnie Moss decide to form a partnership. Graves will contribute $300,000 to the partnership, while Moss will contribute only $30,000. However, Moss will be responsible for running the day-to-day operations of the partnership, which are anticipated to require about 45 hours per week. In contrast, Graves will only work five hours per week for the partnership. The two partners are attempting to determine a formula for dividing partnership net income. Graves believes the partners should divide income in the ratio of 7:3, favoring Graves, since Graves provides the majority of the capital. Moss believes the income should be divided 7:3, favoring Moss, since Moss provides the majority of effort in running the partnership business.

➤ How would you advise the partners in developing a method for dividing income?

CP 12-3   Revenue per employee

The following table shows key operating statistics for the four largest public accounting firms:

	U.S. Net Revenues (in millions)	No. of Partners	No. of Professional Staff
Deloitte & Touche	$10,980	2,949	32,857
Ernst & Young	8,232	2,350	20,250
PricewaterhouseCoopers	7,578	2,198	22,100
KPMG LLP	5,679	1,818	16,564

Source: The 2009 *Accounting Today* Top 100 Firms.

a. Determine the revenue per partner and revenue per professional staff for each firm. Round to the nearest dollar.

b. Interpret the differences between the firms in terms of your answer in (a) and the table information.

CP 12-4   Partnership agreement

Karen Pratt has agreed to invest $200,000 into an LLC with Jennifer Stahl and Don Keene. Stahl and Keene will not invest any money, but will provide effort and expertise to the LLC. Stahl and Keene have agreed that the net income of the LLC should be divided so that Pratt is to receive a 10% preferred return on her capital investment prior to any remaining income being divided equally among the partners. In addition, Stahl and Keene have suggested that the operating agreement be written so that all matters are settled by majority vote, with each partner having a one-third voting interest in the LLC.

━━━━▶ If you were providing Karen Pratt counsel, what might you suggest in forming the final agreement?

CP 12-5   Information on LLC

Group Project

In an assigned group or individually (if so assigned), go to the Web site for Chrysler Group LLC at **http://www.chryslergroupllc.com.** Using this Web site and other Internet information about Chrysler Group LLC, answer the following questions:

a. Briefly describe the business of Chrysler Group LLC.

b. When was Chrysler Group LLC formed?

c. Describe the membership structure of Chrysler Group LLC.

d. Is Chrysler Group LLC a public company?

COMMON STOCK

THIS CERTIFICATE IS TRANSFERABLE
IN CANTON, MA, JERSEY CITY, NJ
AND NEW YORK CITY, NY

HASBRO, INC.

(A RHODE ISLAND CORPORATION)

COMMON STO

SEE REVERSE FOR CERTAIN DEFINITIONS

One

COUNTERSIGNED AND REGISTERED:
EquiServe Trust Company, N.A.

TRANSFER AGENT
AND REGISTRAR

BY

AUTHORIZED SIGNATURE

FULLY PAID AND NON-ASSESSABLE SHARES OF THE COMMON STOCK OF THE PAR VALUE OF 50¢ EACH OF

CERTIFICATE OF STOCK

Hasbro, Inc. Transfers of these shares will be registered on the books of the Corporation maintained for that purpose ... This Certificate is not valid unless countersigned and registered by the Transfer Agent and Registrar.

Witness the seal of the Corporation and the signatures of its duly authorized officers.

Dated: March 1, 2005

SECRETARY

CHAIRMAN OF THE BOARD

HASBRO INC.
INCORPORATED
1926
RHODE ISLAND

Used by permission of Hasbro

Corporations: Organization, Stock Transactions, and Dividends

Hasbro

If you purchase a share of stock from **Hasbro**, you own a small interest in the company. You may request a Hasbro stock certificate as an indication of your ownership.

As you may know, Hasbro is one of the world's largest toy manufacturers and produces popular children's toys such as G.I. Joe, Play-Doh, Tonka toys, Mr. Potato Head, and NERF. In addition, Hasbro manufactures family entertainment products such as Monopoly, Scrabble, and Trivial Pursuit under the Milton Bradley and Parker Brothers labels. In fact, the stock certificate of Hasbro has a picture of Mr. Monopoly, the Monopoly game icon, printed on it.

Purchasing a share of stock from Hasbro may be a great gift idea for the "hard-to-shop-for person." However, a stock certificate represents more than just a picture that you can frame. In fact, the stock certificate is a document that reflects legal ownership of the future financial prospects of Hasbro. In addition, as a shareholder, it represents your claim against the assets and earnings of the corporation.

If you are purchasing Hasbro stock as an investment, you should analyze Hasbro's financial statements and management's plans for the future. For example, Hasbro has a unique relationship with Disney that allows it to produce and sell licensed Disney products. Should this Disney relationship affect how much you are willing to pay for the stock? Also, you might want to know if Hasbro plans to pay cash dividends or whether management is considering issuing additional shares of stock.

This chapter describes and illustrates the nature of corporations including the accounting for stock and dividends. This discussion will aid you in making decisions such as whether or not to buy Hasbro stock.

OBJ. 1 Describe the nature of the corporate form of organization.

Nature of a Corporation

Most large businesses are organized as corporations. As a result, corporations generate more than 90% of the total business dollars in the United States. In contrast, most small businesses are organized as proprietorships, partnerships, or limited liability companies.

Characteristics of a Corporation

A corporation was defined in the Dartmouth College case of 1819, in which Chief Justice Marshall of the U.S. Supreme Court stated: "A corporation is an artificial being, invisible, intangible, and existing only in contemplation of the law."

A *corporation* is a legal entity, distinct and separate from the individuals who create and operate it. As a legal entity, a corporation may acquire, own, and dispose of property in its own name. It may also incur liabilities and enter into contracts. Most importantly, it can sell shares of ownership, called **stock**. This characteristic gives corporations the ability to raise large amounts of capital.

The **stockholders** or *shareholders* who own the stock own the corporation. They can buy and sell stock without affecting the corporation's operations or continued existence. Corporations whose shares of stock are traded in public markets are called *public corporations*. Corporations whose shares are not traded publicly are usually owned by a small group of investors and are called *nonpublic* or *private corporations*.

The stockholders of a corporation have *limited liability*. This means that creditors usually may not go beyond the assets of the corporation to satisfy their claims. Thus, the financial loss that a stockholder may suffer is limited to the amount invested.

The stockholders control a corporation by electing a *board of directors*. This board meets periodically to establish corporate policies. It also selects the chief executive officer (CEO) and other major officers to manage the corporation's day-to-day affairs. Exhibit 1 shows the organizational structure of a corporation.

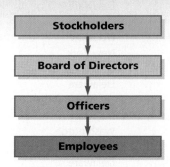

EXHIBIT 1

Organizational Structure of a Corporation

As a separate entity, a corporation is subject to taxes. For example, corporations must pay federal income taxes on their income.[1] Thus, corporate income that is distributed to stockholders in the form of *dividends* has already been taxed. In turn, stockholders must pay income taxes on the dividends they receive. This *double taxation* of corporate earnings is a major disadvantage of the corporate form. The advantages and disadvantages of the corporate form are listed in Exhibit 2.

Note:
Corporations have a separate legal existence, transferable units of ownership, and limited stockholder liability.

EXHIBIT 2   Advantages and Disadvantages of the Corporate Form

Advantages	Explanation
Separate legal existence	A corporation exists separately from its owners.
Continuous life	A corporation's life is separate from its owners; therefore, it exists indefinitely.
Raising large amounts of capital	The corporate form is suited for raising large amounts of money from shareholders.
Ownership rights are easily transferable	A corporation sells shares of ownership, called *stock*. The stockholders of a public company can transfer their shares of stock to other stockholders through stock markets, such as the New York Stock Exchange.
Limited liability	A corporation's creditors usually may not go beyond the assets of the corporation to satisfy their claims. Thus, the financial loss that a stockholder may suffer is limited to the amount invested.

Disadvantages	Explanation
Owner is separate from management	Stockholders control management through a board of directors. The board of directors should represent shareholder interests; however, the board is often more closely tied to management than to shareholders. As a result, the board of directors and management may not always behave in the best interests of stockholders.
Double taxation of dividends	As a separate legal entity, a corporation is subject to taxation. Thus, net income distributed as dividends will be taxed once at the corporation level, and then again at the individual level.
Regulatory costs	Corporations must satisfy many requirements such as those required by the Sarbanes-Oxley Act of 2002.

Forming a Corporation

The first step in forming a corporation is to file an *application of incorporation* with the state. State incorporation laws differ, and corporations often organize in those states with the more favorable laws. For this reason, more than half of the largest companies are incorporated in Delaware. Exhibit 3 lists some corporations, their states of incorporation, and the location of their headquarters.

After the application of incorporation has been approved, the state grants a *charter* or *articles of incorporation*. The articles of incorporation formally create the corporation.[2]

---

1 A majority of states also require corporations to pay income taxes.

2 The articles of incorporation may also restrict a corporation's activities in certain areas, such as owning certain types of real estate, conducting certain types of business activities, or purchasing its own stock.

Corporation	State of Incorporation	Headquarters
Caterpillar	Delaware	Peoria, Ill.
Delta Air Lines	Delaware	Atlanta, Ga.
The Dow Chemical Company	Delaware	Midland, Mich.
General Electric Company	New York	Fairfield, Conn.
The Home Depot	Delaware	Atlanta, Ga.
Kellogg Company	Delaware	Battle Creek, Mich.
3M	Delaware	St. Paul, Minn.
R.J. Reynolds Tobacco Company	Delaware	Winston-Salem, N.C.
Starbucks Corporation	Washington	Seattle, Wash.
Sun Microsystems, Inc.	Delaware	Palo Alto, Calif.
The Washington Post Company	Delaware	Washington, D.C.
Whirlpool Corporation	Delaware	Benton Harbor, Mich.

The corporate management and board of directors then prepare a set of *bylaws*, which are the rules and procedures for conducting the corporation's affairs.

Costs may be incurred in organizing a corporation. These costs include legal fees, taxes, state incorporation fees, license fees, and promotional costs. Such costs are debited to an expense account entitled *Organizational Expenses.*

To illustrate, a corporation's organizing costs of $8,500 on January 5 are recorded as shown below.

Jan.	5	Organizational Expenses	8,500	
		Cash		8,500
		Paid costs of organizing the corporation.		

OBJ. 2 Describe the two main sources of stockholders' equity.

Stockholders' Equity

The owners' equity in a corporation is called **stockholders' equity**, *shareholders' equity, shareholders' investment,* or *capital.* On the balance sheet, stockholders' equity is reported by its two main sources.

1. Capital contributed to the corporation by the stockholders, called **paid-in capital** or *contributed capital.*
2. Net income retained in the business, called **retained earnings**.

A Stockholders' Equity section of a balance sheet is shown below.[3]

Stockholders' Equity

Paid-in capital:		
Common stock	$330,000	
Retained earnings	80,000	
Total stockholders' equity		$410,000

The paid-in capital contributed by the stockholders is recorded in separate accounts for each class of stock. If there is only one class of stock, the account is entitled *Common Stock* or *Capital Stock.*

Retained earnings is a corporation's cumulative net income that has not been distributed as dividends. **Dividends** are distributions of a corporation's earnings to stockholders. Sometimes retained earnings that are not distributed as dividends are referred to in the financial statements as *earnings retained for use in the business* and *earnings reinvested in the business.*

3 The reporting of stockholders' equity is further discussed and illustrated later in this chapter.

Net income increases retained earnings, while a net loss and dividends decrease retained earnings. The net increase or decrease in retained earnings for a period is recorded by the following closing entries:

1. The balance of Income Summary (the net income or net loss) is transferred to Retained Earnings. For *net income,* Income Summary is debited and Retained Earnings is credited. For a *net loss,* Retained Earnings is debited and Income Summary is credited.
2. The balance of the dividends account, which is similar to the drawing account for a proprietorship, is transferred to Retained Earnings. Retained Earnings is debited and Dividends is credited for the balance of the dividends account.

Most companies generate net income. In addition, most companies do not pay out all of their net income in dividends. As a result, Retained Earnings normally has a credit balance. However, in some cases, a debit balance in Retained Earnings may occur. A debit balance in Retained Earnings is called a **deficit**. Such a balance often results from accumulated net losses. In the Stockholders' Equity section, a deficit is deducted from paid-in capital in determining total stockholders' equity.

The balance of Retained Earnings does not represent surplus cash or cash left over for dividends. This is because cash generated from operations is normally used to improve or expand operations. As cash is used, its balance decreases; however, the balance of the retained earnings account is unaffected. As a result, over time the balance in Retained Earnings becomes less and less related to the balance of Cash.

Paid-In Capital from Issuing Stock

OBJ. 3

Describe and illustrate the characteristics of stock, classes of stock, and entries for issuing stock.

The two main sources of stockholders' equity are paid-in capital (or contributed capital) and retained earnings. The main source of paid-in capital is from issuing stock.

Characteristics of Stock

The number of shares of stock that a corporation is *authorized* to issue is stated in its charter. The term *issued* refers to the shares issued to the stockholders. A corporation may reacquire some of the stock that it has issued. The stock remaining in the hands of stockholders is then called **outstanding stock**. The relationship between authorized, issued, and outstanding stock is shown in the graphic at the right.

Upon request, corporations may issue stock certificates to stockholders to document their ownership. Printed on a stock certificate is the name of the company, the name of the stockholder, and the number of shares owned. The stock certificate may also indicate a dollar amount assigned to each share of stock, called **par** value. Stock may be issued without par, in which case it is called *no-par stock.* In some states, the board of directors of a corporation is required to assign a *stated value* to no-par stock.

Number of shares authorized, issued, and outstanding

Corporations have limited liability and, thus, creditors have no claim against stockholders' personal assets. To protect creditors, however, some states require corporations to maintain a minimum amount of paid-in capital. This minimum amount, called *legal capital,* usually includes the par or stated value of the shares issued.

The major rights that accompany ownership of a share of stock are as follows:

1. The right to vote in matters concerning the corporation.
2. The right to share in distributions of earnings.
3. The right to share in assets upon liquidation.

These stock rights normally vary with the class of stock.

Classes of Stock

When only one class of stock is issued, it is called **common stock**. Each share of common stock has equal rights.

Note:
The two primary classes of paid-in capital are common stock and preferred stock.

A corporation may also issue one or more classes of stock with various preference rights such as a preference to dividends. Such a stock is called a **preferred stock**. The dividend rights of preferred stock are stated either as dollars per share or as a percent of par. For example, a $50 par value preferred stock with a $4 per share dividend may be described as either:[4]

$4 preferred stock, $50 par

or

8% preferred stock, $50 par

Because they have first rights (preference) to any dividends, preferred stockholders have a greater chance of receiving dividends than common stockholders. However, since dividends are normally based on earnings, a corporation cannot guarantee dividends even to preferred stockholders.

The payment of dividends is authorized by the corporation's board of directors. When authorized, the directors are said to have *declared* a dividend.

Cumulative preferred stock has a right to receive regular dividends that were not declared (paid) in prior years. Noncumulative preferred stock does not have this right.

Cumulative preferred stock dividends that have not been paid in prior years are said to be **in arrears**. Any preferred dividends in arrears must be paid before any common stock dividends are paid. In addition, any dividends in arrears are normally disclosed in notes to the financial statements.

To illustrate, assume that a corporation has issued the following preferred and common stock:

1,000 shares of $4 cumulative preferred stock, $50 par
4,000 shares of common stock, $15 par

The corporation was organized on January 1, 2010, and paid no dividends in 2010 and 2011. In 2012, the corporation paid $22,000 in dividends, of which $12,000 was paid to preferred stockholders and $10,000 was paid to common stockholders as shown below.

Total dividends paid		$ 22,000
Preferred stockholders:		
2010 dividends in arrears (1,000 shares × $4)	$4,000	
2011 dividends in arrears (1,000 shares × $4)	4,000	
2012 dividend (1,000 shares × $4)	4,000	
Total preferred dividends paid		(12,000)
Dividends available to common stockholders		$10,000

As a result, preferred stockholders received $12.00 per share ($12,000 ÷ 1,000 shares) in dividends, while common stockholders received $2.50 per share ($10,000 ÷ 4,000 shares).

In addition to dividend preference, preferred stock may be given preferences to assets if the corporation goes out of business and is liquidated. However, claims of creditors must be satisfied first. Preferred stockholders are next in line to receive any remaining assets, followed by the common stockholders.

Issuing Stock

A separate account is used for recording the amount of each class of stock issued to investors in a corporation. For example, assume that a corporation is authorized to issue 10,000 shares of $100 par preferred stock and 100,000 shares of $20 par common stock. The corporation issued 5,000 shares of preferred stock and 50,000

---

4 In some cases, preferred stock may receive additional dividends if certain conditions are met. Such stock, called *participating preferred stock*, is not often issued.

Example Exercise 13-1 Dividends per Share

OBJ. 3

Sandpiper Company has 20,000 shares of 1% cumulative preferred stock of $100 par and 100,000 shares of $50 par common stock. The following amounts were distributed as dividends:

Year 1 $10,000
Year 2   45,000
Year 3   80,000

Determine the dividends per share for preferred and common stock for each year.

Follow My Example 13-1

	Year 1	Year 2	Year 3
Amount distributed	$10,000	$45,000	$80,000
Preferred dividend (20,000 shares)	10,000	30,000*	20,000
Common dividend (100,000 shares)	$ 0	$15,000	$60,000
*($10,000 + $20,000)			
Dividends per share:			
Preferred stock	$0.50	$1.50	$1.00
Common stock	None	$0.15	$0.60

Practice Exercises: **PE 13-1A, PE 13-1B**

shares of common stock at par for cash. The corporation's entry to record the stock issue is as follows:[5]

	Cash			1,500,000		
	Preferred Stock					500,000
	Common Stock					1,000,000
	Issued preferred stock and common					
	stock at par for cash.					

Stock is often issued by a corporation at a price other than its par. The price at which stock is sold depends on a variety of factors, such as the following:

1. The financial condition, earnings record, and dividend record of the corporation.
2. Investor expectations of the corporation's potential earning power.
3. General business and economic conditions and expectations.

If stock is issued (sold) for a price that is more than its par, the stock has been sold at a **premium**. For example, if common stock with a par of $50 is sold for $60 per share, the stock has sold at a premium of $10.

If stock is issued (sold) for a price that is less than its par, the stock has been sold at a **discount**. For example, if common stock with a par of $50 is sold for $45 per share, the stock has sold at a discount of $5. Many states do not permit stock to be sold at a discount. In other states, stock may be sold at a discount in only unusual cases. Since stock is rarely sold at a discount, it is not illustrated.

In order to distribute dividends, financial statements, and other reports, a corporation must keep track of its stockholders. Large public corporations normally use a financial institution, such as a bank, for this purpose.[6] In such cases, the financial institution is referred to as a *transfer agent* or *registrar*.

---

[5] The accounting for investments in stocks from the point of view of the investor is discussed in Chapter 15.

[6] Small corporations may use a subsidiary ledger, called a *stockholders ledger*. in this case, the stock accounts (Preferred Stock and Common Stock) are controlling accounts for the subsidiary ledger.

Premium on Stock

When stock is issued at a premium, Cash is debited for the amount received. Common Stock or Preferred Stock is credited for the par amount. The excess of the amount paid over par is part of the paid-in capital. An account entitled *Paid-In Capital in Excess of Par* is credited for this amount.

To illustrate, assume that Caldwell Company issues 2,000 shares of $50 par preferred stock for cash at $55. The entry to record this transaction is as follows:

	Cash		110,000	
	Preferred Stock			100,000
	Paid-In Capital in Excess of Par—Preferred Stock			10,000
	Issued $50 par preferred stock at $55.			

When stock is issued in exchange for assets other than cash, such as land, buildings, and equipment, the assets acquired are recorded at their fair market value. If this value cannot be determined, the fair market price of the stock issued is used.

To illustrate, assume that a corporation acquired land with a fair market value that cannot be determined. In exchange, the corporation issued 10,000 shares of its $10 par common. If the stock has a market price of $12 per share, the transaction is recorded as follows:

	Land		120,000	
	Common Stock			100,000
	Paid-In Capital in Excess of Par			20,000
	Issued $10 par common stock, valued at $12 per share, for land.			

No-Par Stock

In most states, no-par preferred and common stock may be issued. When no-par stock is issued, Cash is debited and Common Stock is credited for the proceeds. As no-par stock is issued over time, this entry is the same even if the issuing price varies.

To illustrate, assume that on January 9 a corporation issues 10,000 shares of no-par common stock at $40 a share. On June 27, the corporation issues an additional 1,000 shares at $36. The entries to record these issuances of the no-par stock are as follows:

Jan.	9	Cash		400,000	
		Common Stock			400,000
		Issued 10,000 shares of no-par common at $40.			
June	27	Cash		36,000	
		Common Stock			36,000
		Issued 1,000 shares of no-par common at $36.			

In some states, no-par stock may be assigned a *stated value per share*. The stated value is recorded like a par value. Any excess of the proceeds over the stated value is credited to *Paid-In Capital in Excess of Stated Value*.

BusinessConnection

CISCO SYSTEMS, INC.

Cisco Systems, Inc., manufactures and sells networking and communications products worldwide. Some excerpts of its bylaws are shown below.

ARTICLE 2
SHAREHOLDERS' MEETINGS
Section 2.01 Annual Meetings. The annual meeting of the shareholders of the Corporation . . . shall be held each year on the second Thursday in November at 10:00 A.M. . . .

ARTICLE 3
BOARD OF DIRECTORS
Section 3.02 Number and Qualification of Directors. The number of authorized directors of this Corporation shall

be not less than eight (8) nor more than fifteen (15), . . . to be (determined) by . . . the Board of Directors or shareholders.

ARTICLE 4
OFFICERS
Section 4.01 Number and Term. The officers of the Corporation shall include a President, a Secretary and a Chief Financial Officer, all of which shall be chosen by the Board of Directors. . . .

Section 4.06 President. The President shall be the general manager and chief executive officer of the Corporation, . . . shall preside at all meetings of shareholders, shall have general supervision of the affairs of the Corporation. . . .

To illustrate, assume that in the preceding example the no-par common stock is assigned a stated value of $25. The issuance of the stock on January 9 and June 27 is recorded as follows:

Jan.	9	Cash	400,000	
		Common Stock		250,000
		Paid-In Capital in Excess of Stated Value		150,000
		Issued 10,000 shares of no-par common at $40; stated value, $25.		
June	27	Cash	36,000	
		Common Stock		25,000
		Paid-In Capital in Excess of Stated Value		11,000
		Issued 1,000 shares of no-par common at $36; stated value, $25.		

Example Exercise 13-2   Entries for Issuing Stock   OBJ. 3

On March 6, Limerick Corporation issued for cash 15,000 shares of no-par common stock at $30. On April 13, Limerick issued at par 1,000 shares of 4%, $40 par preferred stock for cash. On May 19, Limerick issued for cash 15,000 shares of 4%, $40 par preferred stock at $42.

Journalize the entries to record the March 6, April 13, and May 19 transactions.

Follow My Example 13-2

Mar. 6	Cash	450,000	
	Common Stock		450,000
	(15,000 shares × $30).		
Apr. 13	Cash	40,000	
	Preferred Stock		40,000
	(1,000 shares × $40).		
May 19	Cash	630,000	
	Preferred Stock		600,000
	Paid-In Capital in Excess of Par		30,000
	(15,000 shares × $42).		

Practice Exercises: **PE 13-2A, PE 13-2B**

InternationalConnection

IFRS FOR SMES

In 2010, the International Accounting Standards Board (IASB) issued a set of accounting standards specifically designed for small- and medium-sized enterprises (SMEs) called International Financial Reporting Standards (IFRS) for SMEs. SMEs in the United States are private companies and such small corporations that they do not report to the Securities and Exchange Commission (SEC). IFRS for SMEs consist of only 230 pages, compared to 2,700

pages for full IFRS. These standards are designed to be cost effective for SMEs. Thus, IFRS for SMEs require fewer disclosures and contain no industry-specific standards or exceptions.

The American Institute of CPAs (AICPA) has accepted IFRS for SMEs as part of U.S. Generally Accepted Accounting Principles (GAAP) for private companies not reporting to the SEC. If users, such as bankers and investors, accept these financial statements, IFRS for SMEs may become popular in the United States.*

*Differences between U.S. GAAP and IFRS are further discussed and illustrated in Appendix D.

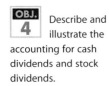

OBJ. 4 Describe and illustrate the accounting for cash dividends and stock dividends.

Accounting for Dividends

When a board of directors declares a cash dividend, it authorizes the distribution of cash to stockholders. When a board of directors declares a stock dividend, it authorizes the distribution of its stock. In both cases, declaring a dividend reduces the retained earnings of the corporation.[7]

Cash Dividends

A cash distribution of earnings by a corporation to its shareholders is a **cash dividend**. Although dividends may be paid in other assets, cash dividends are the most common.

Three conditions for a cash dividend are as follows:

1. Sufficient retained earnings
2. Sufficient cash
3. Formal action by the board of directors

There must be a sufficient (large enough) balance in Retained Earnings to declare a cash dividend. That is, the balance of Retained Earnings must be large enough so that the dividend does not create a debit balance in the retained earnings account. However, a large Retained Earnings balance does not mean that there is cash available to pay dividends. This is because the balances of Cash and Retained Earnings are often unrelated.

Even if there are sufficient retained earnings and cash, a corporation's board of directors is not required to pay dividends. Nevertheless, many corporations pay quarterly cash dividends to make their stock more attractive to investors. *Special* or *extra* dividends may also be paid when a corporation experiences higher than normal profits.

Three dates included in a dividend announcement are as follows:

1. Date of declaration
2. Date of record
3. Date of payment

The *date of declaration* is the date the board of directors formally authorizes the payment of the dividend. On this date, the corporation incurs the liability to pay the amount of the dividend.

---

7 In rare cases, when a corporation is reducing its operations or going out of business, a dividend may be a distribution of paid-in capital. Such a dividend is called a *liquidating dividend*.

The *date of record* is the date the corporation uses to determine which stockholders will receive the dividend. During the period of time between the date of declaration and the date of record, the stock price is quoted as selling *with-dividends*. This means that any investors purchasing the stock before the date of record will receive the dividend.

The *date of payment* is the date the corporation will pay the dividend to the stockholders who owned the stock on the date of record. During the period of time between the record date and the payment date, the stock price is quoted as selling *ex-dividends*. This means that since the date of record has passed, any new investors will not receive the dividend.

To illustrate, assume that on October 1 Hiber Corporation declares the cash dividends shown below with a date of record of November 10 and a date of payment of December 2.

Microsoft Corporation declared a dividend of $0.13 per share on December 9, 2009, to common stockholders of record as of February 18, 2010, payable on March 11, 2010.

	Dividend per Share	Total Dividends
Preferred stock, $100 par, 5,000 shares outstanding.....................	$2.50	$12,500
Common stock, $10 par, 100,000 shares outstanding	$0.30	30,000
Total		$42,500

On October 1, the declaration date, Hiber Corporation records the following entry:

Oct.	1	Cash Dividends		42,500	
		Cash Dividends Payable			42,500
		Declared cash dividends.			

Declaration Date

On November 10, the date of record, no entry is necessary. This date merely ***Date of Record*** determines which stockholders will receive the dividends.

On December 2, the date of payment, Hiber Corporation records the payment of the dividends as follows:

Dec.	2	Cash Dividends Payable		42,500	
		Cash			42,500
		Paid cash dividends.			

Date of Payment

At the end of the accounting period, the balance in Cash Dividends will be transferred to Retained Earnings as part of the closing process. This closing entry debits Retained Earnings and credits Cash Dividends for the balance of the cash dividends account. If the cash dividends have not been paid by the end of the period, Cash Dividends Payable will be reported on the balance sheet as a current liability.

Example Exercise 13-3 Entries for Cash Dividends

OBJ. 4

The important dates in connection with a cash dividend of $75,000 on a corporation's common stock are February 26, March 30, and April 2. Journalize the entries required on each date.

Follow My Example 13-3

Feb. 26	Cash Dividends...	75,000	
	Cash Dividends Payable...............................		75,000
Mar. 30	No entry required.		
Apr. 2	Cash Dividends Payable..................................	75,000	
	Cash...		75,000

Practice Exercises: **PE 13-3A, PE 13-3B**

Integrity, Objectivity, and Ethics in Business

THE PROFESSOR WHO KNEW TOO MUCH

A major Midwestern university released a quarterly "American Customer Satisfaction Index" based on its research of customers of popular U.S. products and services. Before the release of the index to the public, the professor in charge of the research bought and sold stocks of some of the companies in the report. The professor was quoted as saying that he thought it was important to test his theories of customer satisfaction with "real" [his own] money.

Is this proper or ethical? Apparently, the dean of the Business School didn't think so. In a statement to the press,

the dean stated: "I have instructed anyone affiliated with the (index) not to make personal use of information gathered in the course of producing the quarterly index, prior to the index's release to the general public, and they [the researchers] have agreed."

Sources: Jon E. Hilsenrath and Dan Morse, "Researcher Uses Index to Buy, Short Stocks," *The Wall Street Journal*, February 18, 2003; and Jon E. Hilsenrath, "Satisfaction Theory: Mixed Results," *The Wall Street Journal*, February 19, 2003.

Stock Dividends

A **stock dividend** is a distribution of shares of stock to stockholders. Stock dividends are normally declared only on common stock and issued to common stockholders.

A stock dividend affects only stockholders' equity. Specifically, the amount of the stock dividend is transferred from Retained Earnings to Paid-In Capital. The amount transferred is normally the fair value (market price) of the shares issued in the stock dividend.[8]

To illustrate, assume that the stockholders' equity accounts of Hendrix Corporation as of December 15 are as follows:

Common Stock, $20 par (2,000,000 shares issued)	$40,000,000
Paid-In Capital in Excess of Par—Common Stock	9,000,000
Retained Earnings	26,600,000

On December 15, Hendrix Corporation declares a stock dividend of 5% or 100,000 shares (2,000,000 shares × 5%) to be issued on January 10 to stockholders of record on December 31. The market price of the stock on December 15 (the date of declaration) is $31 per share.

The entry to record the stock dividend is as follows:

Dec.	15	Stock Dividends	3,100,000	
		Stock Dividends Distributable		2,000,000
		Paid-In Capital in Excess of Par—Common Stock		1,100,000
		Declared 5% (100,000 share) stock dividend on $20 par common stock with a market price of $31 per share.		

After the preceding entry is recorded, Stock Dividends will have a debit balance of $3,100,000. Like cash dividends, the stock dividends account is closed to Retained Earnings at the end of the accounting period. This closing entry debits Retained Earnings and credits Stock Dividends.

At the end of the period, the *stock dividends distributable* and *paid-in capital in excess of par—common stock* accounts are reported in the Paid-In Capital section of the balance sheet. Thus, the effect of the preceding stock dividend is to transfer $3,100,000 of retained earnings to paid-in capital.

8 The use of fair market value is justified as long as the number of shares issued for the stock dividend is small (less than 25% of the shares outstanding).

On January 10, the stock dividend is distributed to stockholders by issuing 100,000 shares of common stock. The issuance of the stock is recorded by the following entry:

Jan.	10	Stock Dividends Distributable	2,000,000	
		Common Stock		2,000,000
		Issued stock as stock dividend.		

A stock dividend does not change the assets, liabilities, or total stockholders' equity of a corporation. Likewise, a stock dividend does not change an individual stockholder's proportionate interest (equity) in the corporation.

To illustrate, assume a stockholder owns 1,000 of a corporation's 10,000 shares outstanding. If the corporation declares a 6% stock dividend, the stockholder's proportionate interest will not change as shown below.

	Before Stock Dividend	After Stock Dividend
Total shares issued	10,000	10,600 [10,000 + (10,000 × 6%)]
Number of shares owned	1,000	1,060 [1,000 + (1,000 × 6%)]
Proportionate ownership	10% (1,000/10,000)	10% (1,060/10,600)

Example Exercise 13-4   Entries for Stock Dividends   OBJ. 4

Vienna Highlights Corporation has 150,000 shares of $100 par common stock outstanding. On June 14, Vienna Highlights declared a 4% stock dividend to be issued August 15 to stockholders of record on July 1. The market price of the stock was $110 per share on June 14.

Journalize the entries required on June 14, July 1, and August 15.

Follow My Example 13-4

June 14	Stock Dividends (150,000 × 4% × $110).........................	660,000	
	Stock Dividends Distributable (6,000 × $100)		600,000
	Paid-In Capital in Excess of Par—Common Stock ($660,000 – $600,000)...		60,000
July 1	No entry required.		
Aug. 15	Stock Dividends Distributable	600,000	
	Common Stock		600,000

Practice Exercises: **PE 13-4A, PE 13-4B**

Treasury Stock Transactions

OBJ. 5   Describe and illustrate the accounting for treasury stock transactions.

Treasury stock is stock that a corporation has issued and then reacquired. A corporation may reacquire (purchase) its own stock for a variety of reasons, including the following:

1. To provide shares for resale to employees
2. To reissue as bonuses to employees, or
3. To support the market price of the stock

The *cost method* is normally used for recording the purchase and resale of treasury stock.[9] Using the cost method, *Treasury Stock* is debited for the cost (purchase price) of the stock. When the stock is resold, Treasury Stock is credited for its cost. Any difference between the cost and the selling price is debited or credited to *Paid-In Capital from Sale of Treasury Stock*.

The 2009 edition of *Accounting Trends & Techniques* indicated that over 70% of the companies surveyed reported treasury stock.

To illustrate, assume that a corporation has the following paid-in capital on January 1:

Common stock, $25 par (20,000 shares authorized and issued)	$500,000
Excess of issue price over par	150,000
	$650,000

9 Another method that is infrequently used, called the *par value method*, is discussed in advanced accounting texts.

On February 13, the corporation purchases 1,000 shares of its common stock at $45 per share. The entry to record the purchase of the treasury stock is as follows:

Feb.	13	Treasury Stock	45,000	
		Cash		45,000
		Purchased 1,000 shares of treasury stock at $45.		

On April 29, the corporation sells 600 shares of the treasury stock for $60. The entry to record the sale is as follows:

Apr.	29	Cash	36,000	
		Treasury Stock		27,000
		Paid-In Capital from Sale of Treasury Stock		9,000
		Sold 600 shares of treasury stock at $60.		

A sale of treasury stock may result in a decrease in paid-in capital. To the extent that Paid-In Capital from Sale of Treasury Stock has a credit balance, it is debited for any such decrease. Any remaining decrease is then debited to the retained earnings account.

To illustrate, assume that on October 4, the corporation sells the remaining 400 shares of treasury stock for $40 per share. The entry to record the sale is as follows:

Oct.	4	Cash	16,000	
		Paid-In Capital from Sale of Treasury Stock	2,000	
		Treasury Stock		18,000
		Sold 400 shares of treasury stock at $40.		

The October 4 entry shown above decreases paid-in capital by $2,000. Since Paid-In Capital from Sale of Treasury Stock has a credit balance of $9,000, the entire $2,000 was debited to Paid-In Capital from Sale of Treasury Stock.

No dividends (cash or stock) are paid on the shares of treasury stock. To do so would result in the corporation earning dividend revenue from itself.

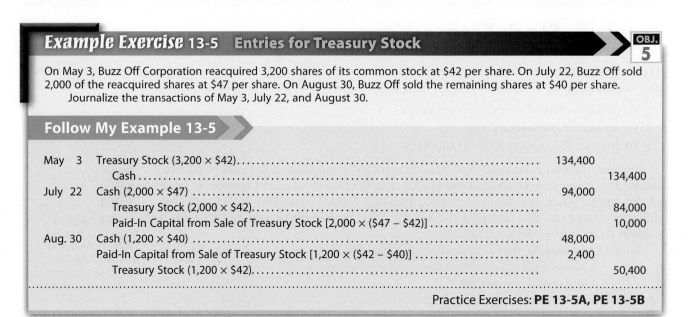

Example Exercise 13-5   Entries for Treasury Stock   OBJ. 5

On May 3, Buzz Off Corporation reacquired 3,200 shares of its common stock at $42 per share. On July 22, Buzz Off sold 2,000 of the reacquired shares at $47 per share. On August 30, Buzz Off sold the remaining shares at $40 per share. Journalize the transactions of May 3, July 22, and August 30.

Follow My Example 13-5

May	3	Treasury Stock (3,200 × $42)...	134,400	
		Cash...		134,400
July	22	Cash (2,000 × $47)	94,000	
		Treasury Stock (2,000 × $42)...............................		84,000
		Paid-In Capital from Sale of Treasury Stock [2,000 × ($47 − $42)]		10,000
Aug.	30	Cash (1,200 × $40)	48,000	
		Paid-In Capital from Sale of Treasury Stock [1,200 × ($42 − $40)]	2,400	
		Treasury Stock (1,200 × $42)...............................		50,400

Practice Exercises: **PE 13-5A, PE 13-5B**

Reporting Stockholders' Equity

OBJ. 6   Describe and illustrate the reporting of stockholders' equity.

As with other sections of the balance sheet, alternative terms and formats may be used in reporting stockholders' equity. Also, changes in retained earnings and paid-in capital may be reported in separate statements or notes to the financial statements.

Stockholders' Equity on the Balance Sheet

Exhibit 4 shows two methods for reporting stockholders' equity for the December 31, 2012, balance sheet for Telex Inc.

Method 1.   Each class of stock is reported, followed by its related paid-in capital accounts. Retained earnings is then reported followed by a deduction for treasury stock.

Method 2.   The stock accounts are reported, followed by the paid-in capital reported as a single item, Additional paid-in capital. Retained earnings is then reported followed by a deduction for treasury stock.

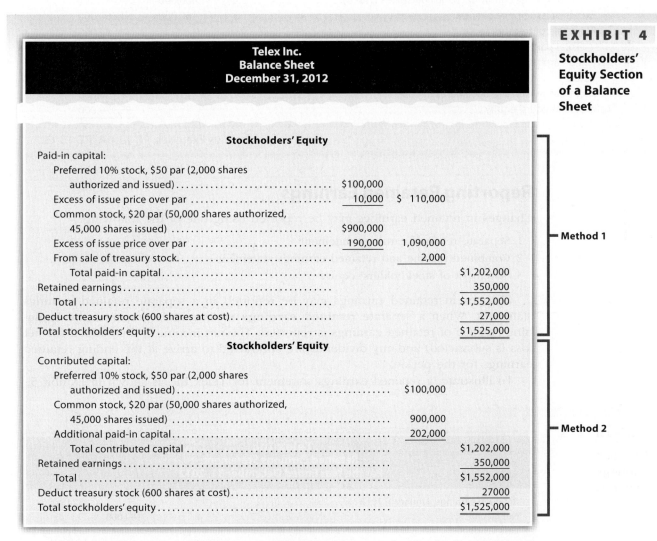

EXHIBIT 4

Stockholders' Equity Section of a Balance Sheet

Telex Inc.
Balance Sheet
December 31, 2012

Stockholders' Equity

Paid-in capital:

Preferred 10% stock, $50 par (2,000 shares authorized and issued) $100,000

Excess of issue price over par .... 10,000 $ 110,000

Common stock, $20 par (50,000 shares authorized, 45,000 shares issued) $900,000

Excess of issue price over par 190,000   1,090,000

From sale of treasury stock.................................. 2,000

Total paid-in capital.................................... $1,202,000

Retained earnings... 350,000

Total $1,552,000

Deduct treasury stock (600 shares at cost)................... 27,000

Total stockholders' equity $1,525,000

— Method 1

Stockholders' Equity

Contributed capital:

Preferred 10% stock, $50 par (2,000 shares authorized and issued)........................... $100,000

Common stock, $20 par (50,000 shares authorized, 45,000 shares issued) 900,000

Additional paid-in capital................................ 202,000

Total contributed capital $1,202,000

Retained earnings... 350,000

Total $1,552,000

Deduct treasury stock (600 shares at cost)................ 27000

Total stockholders' equity $1,525,000

— Method 2

Significant changes in stockholders' equity during a period may also be presented in a statement of stockholders' equity or in the notes to the financial statements. The statement of stockholders' equity is illustrated later in this section.

Relevant rights and privileges of the various classes of stock outstanding should also be reported.[10] Examples include dividend and liquidation preferences, conversion rights, and redemption rights. Such information may be disclosed on the face of the balance sheet or in the notes to the financial statements.

10 *FASB Accounting Standards Codification*, Section 505-10-50.

Example Exercise 13-6 Reporting Stockholders' Equity

OBJ. 6

Using the following accounts and balances, prepare the Stockholders' Equity section of the balance sheet. Forty thousand shares of common stock are authorized, and 5,000 shares have been reacquired.

Common Stock, $50 par	$1,500,000
Paid-In Capital in Excess of Par	160,000
Paid-In Capital from Sale of Treasury Stock	44,000
Retained Earnings	4,395,000
Treasury Stock	120,000

Follow My Example 13-6

Stockholders' Equity

Paid-in capital:		
Common stock, $50 par		
(40,000 shares authorized, 30,000 shares issued)	$1,500,000	
Excess of issue price over par	160,000	$1,660,000
From sale of treasury stock		44,000
Total paid-in capital		$1,704,000
Retained earnings		4,395,000
Total		$6,099,000
Deduct treasury stock (5,000 shares at cost)		120,000
Total stockholders' equity		$5,979,000

Practice Exercises: **PE 13-6A, PE 13-6B**

Reporting Retained Earnings

Changes in retained earnings may be reported using one of the following:

1. Separate retained earnings statement
2. Combined income and retained earnings statement
3. Statement of stockholders' equity

Changes in retained earnings may be reported in a separate retained earnings statement. When a separate **retained earnings statement** is prepared, the beginning balance of retained earnings is reported. The net income is then added (or net loss is subtracted) and any dividends are subtracted to arrive at the ending retained earnings for the period.

To illustrate, a retained earnings statement for Telex Inc. is shown in Exhibit 5.

EXHIBIT 5

Retained Earnings Statement

Telex Inc.
Retained Earnings Statement
For the Year Ended December 31, 2012

Retained earnings, January 1, 2012			$245,000
Net income		$180,000	
Less dividends:			
Preferred stock	$10,000		
Common stock	65,000	75,000	
Increase in retained earnings			105,000
Retained earnings, December 31, 2012			$350,000

Changes in retained earnings may also be reported in combination with the income statement. This format emphasizes net income as the connecting link between the income statement and ending retained earnings. Since this format is not often used, we do not illustrate it.

Changes in retained earnings may also be reported in a statement of stockholders' equity. An example of reporting changes in retained earnings in a statement of stockholders' equity for Telex Inc. is shown in Exhibit 6.

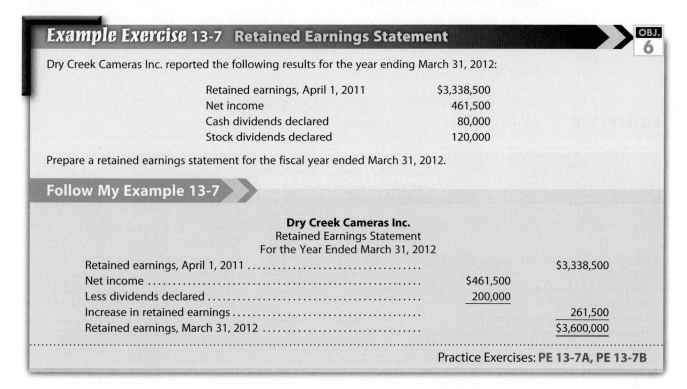

Example Exercise 13-7 Retained Earnings Statement

> OBJ.
> 6

Dry Creek Cameras Inc. reported the following results for the year ending March 31, 2012:

Retained earnings, April 1, 2011	$3,338,500
Net income	461,500
Cash dividends declared	80,000
Stock dividends declared	120,000

Prepare a retained earnings statement for the fiscal year ended March 31, 2012.

Follow My Example 13-7

Dry Creek Cameras Inc.
Retained Earnings Statement
For the Year Ended March 31, 2012

Retained earnings, April 1, 2011		$3,338,500
Net income	$461,500	
Less dividends declared	200,000	
Increase in retained earnings		261,500
Retained earnings, March 31, 2012		$3,600,000

Practice Exercises: **PE 13-7A, PE 13-7B**

Restrictions The use of retained earnings for payment of dividends may be restricted by action of a corporation's board of directors. Such **restrictions,** sometimes called *appropriations,* remain part of the retained earnings.

Restrictions of retained earnings are classified as:

1. *Legal.* State laws may require a restriction of retained earnings.

    Example: States may restrict retained earnings by the amount of treasury stock purchased. In this way, legal capital cannot be used for dividends.

2. *Contractual.* A corporation may enter into contracts that require restrictions of retained earnings.

    Example: A bank loan may restrict retained earnings so that money for repaying the loan cannot be used for dividends.

3. *Discretionary.* A corporation's board of directors may restrict retained earnings voluntarily.

    Example: The board may restrict retained earnings and, thus, limit dividend distributions so that more money is available for expanding the business.

Restrictions of retained earnings must be disclosed in the financial statements. Such disclosures are usually included in the notes to the financial statements.

Prior Period Adjustments An error may arise from a mathematical mistake or from a mistake in applying accounting principles. Such errors may not be discovered within the same period in which they occur. In such cases, the effect of the error should not affect the current period's net income. Instead, the correction of the error, called a **prior period adjustment**, is reported in the retained earnings statement. Such corrections are reported as an adjustment to the beginning balance of retained earnings.[11]

11 Prior period adjustments are illustrated in advanced texts.

Statement of Stockholders' Equity

When the only change in stockholders' equity is due to net income or net loss and dividends, a retained earnings statement is sufficient. However, when a corporation also has changes in stock and paid-in capital accounts, a **statement of stockholders' equity** is normally prepared.

A statement of stockholders' equity is normally prepared in a columnar format. Each column is a major stockholders' equity classification. Changes in each classification are then described in the left-hand column. Exhibit 6 illustrates a statement of stockholders' equity for Telex Inc.

EXHIBIT 6   **Statement of Stockholders' Equity**

Telex Inc. **Statement of Stockholders' Equity** **For the Year Ended December 31, 2012**						
	Preferred Stock	Common Stock	Additional Paid-In Capital	Retained Earnings	Treasury Stock	Total
Balance, January 1, 2012	$100,000	$850,000	$177,000	$245,000	$(17,000)	$1,355,000
Net income				180,000		180,000
Dividends on preferred stock				(10,000)		(10,000)
Dividends on common stock				(65,000)		(65,000)
Issuance of additional common stock		50,000	25,000			75,000
Purchase of treasury stock					(10,000)	(10,000)
Balance, December 31, 2012	$100,000	$900,000	$202,000	$350,000	$(27,000)	$1,525,000

Reporting Stockholders' Equity for Mornin' Joe

Mornin' Joe reports stockholders' equity in its balance sheet. Mornin' Joe also includes a retained earnings statement and statement of stockholders' equity in its financial statements.

The Stockholders' Equity section of Mornin' Joe's balance sheet as of December 31, 2012, is shown below.

Mornin' Joe **Balance Sheet** **December 31, 2012**			
Stockholders' Equity			
Paid-in capital:			
Preferred 10% stock, $50 par (6,000 shares			
authorized and issued)		$ 300,000	
Excess of issue price over par		50,000	$ 350,000
Common stock, $20 par (50,000 shares authorized,			
45,000 shares issued)		$ 900,000	
Excess of issue price over par		1,450,000	2,350,000
Total paid-in capital			$2,700,000
Retained earnings			1,200,300
Total			$3,900,300
Deduct treasury stock (1,000 shares at cost)			46,000
Total stockholders' equity			$3,854,300
Total liabilities and stockholders' equity			$6,169,700

Mornin' Joe's retained earnings statement for the year ended December 31, 2012, is as follows:

Mornin' Joe Retained Earnings Statment For the Year Ended December 31, 2012		
Retained earnings, January 1, 2012		$ 852,700
Net income	$421,600	
Less dividends:		
Preferred stock	$30,000	
Common stock	44,000	74,000
Increase in retained earnings......................		347,600
Retained earnings, December 31, 2012..............		$1,200,300

The statement of stockholders' equity for Mornin' Joe is shown below.

Mornin' Joe Statement of Stockholders' Equity For the Year Ended December 31, 2012						
	Preferred Stock	Common Stock	Additional Paid-In Capital	Retained Earnings	Treasury Stock	Total
Balance, January 1, 2012	$300,000	$800,000	$1,325,000	$ 852,700	$(36,000)	$3,241,700
Net income				421,600		421,600
Dividends on preferred stock.......				(30,000)		(30,000)
Dividends on common stock				(44,000)		(44,000)
Issuance of additional common stock		100,000	175,000			275,000
Purchase of treasury stock					(10,000)	(10,000)
Balance, December 31, 2012	$300,000	$900,000	$1,500,000	$1,200,300	$(46,000)	$3,854,300

Stock Splits

OBJ. 7 Describe the effect of stock splits on corporate financial statements.

A **stock split** is a process by which a corporation reduces the par or stated value of its common stock and issues a proportionate number of additional shares. A stock split applies to all common shares including the unissued, issued, and treasury shares.

A major objective of a stock split is to reduce the market price per share of the stock. This attracts more investors and broadens the types and numbers of stockholders.

To illustrate, assume that Rojek Corporation has 10,000 shares of $100 par common stock outstanding with a current market price of $150 per share. The board of directors declares the following stock split:

1. Each common shareholder will receive 5 shares for each share held. This is called a 5-for-1 stock split. As a result, 50,000 shares (10,000 shares × 5) will be outstanding.
2. The par of each share of common stock will be reduced to $20 ($100/5).

The par value of the common stock outstanding is $1,000,000 both before and after the stock split as shown below.

	Before Split	After Split
Number of shares	10,000	50,000
Par value per share	× $100	× $20
Total	$1,000,000	$1,000,000

4 shares, $100 par

20 shares, $20 par

$400 total par value   **$400 total par value**

Note:
A stock split does not
require a journal entry.

In addition, each Rojek Corporation shareholder owns the same total par amount of stock before and after the stock split. For example, a stockholder who owned 4 shares of $100 par stock before the split (total par of $400) would own 20 shares of $20 par stock after the split (total par of $400). Only the number of shares and the par value per share have changed.

Since there are more shares outstanding after the stock split, the market price of the stock should decrease. For example, in the preceding example, there would be 5 times as many shares outstanding after the split. Thus, the market price of the stock would be expected to fall from $150 to about $30 ($150/5).

Stock splits do not require a journal entry since only the par (or stated) value and number of shares outstanding have changed. However, the details of stock splits are normally disclosed in the notes to the financial statements.

BusinessConnection

BUFFETT ON STOCK SPLITS

Warren E. Buffett, chairman and chief executive officer of Berkshire Hathaway Inc., opposes stock splits on the basis that they add no value to the company. Since its inception, Berkshire Hathaway has never declared a stock split on its primary (Class A) common stock. As a result, Berkshire Hathaway's Class A common stock sells well above $100,000 per share, which is the most expensive stock on the

New York Stock Exchange. Such a high price doesn't bother Buffet since he believes that high stock prices attract more sophisticated and long-term investors and discourage stock speculators and short-term investors.

In contrast, Microsoft Corporation has split its stock nine times since it went public in 1986. As a result, one share of Microsoft purchased in 1986 is equivalent to 288 shares today, which would be worth approximately $7,500.

Financial Analysis and Interpretation: Earnings per Share

OBJ. 8 Describe and illustrate the use of earnings per share in evaluating a company's profitability.

Net income is often used by investors and creditors in evaluating a company's profitability. However, net income by itself is difficult to use in comparing companies of different sizes. Also, trends in net income may be difficult to evaluate if there have been significant changes in a company's stockholders' equity. Thus, the profitability of companies is often expressed as earnings per share.

Earnings per common share (EPS), sometimes called *basic earnings per share,* is the net income per share of common stock outstanding during a period.[12] Corporations whose stock is traded in a public market must report earnings per common share on their income statements.

Earnings per share is computed as follows:

$$\text{Earnings per Share} = \frac{\text{Net Income} - \text{Preferred Dividends}}{\text{Average Number of Common Shares Outstanding}}$$

If a company has preferred stock outstanding, any preferred dividends are subtracted from net income. This is because the numerator represents only those earnings available to the common shareholders.

To illustrate, the following data (in thousands) were taken from Hasbro's financial statements:

12 For complex capital structures, earnings per share assuming dilution may also be reported as described in Chapter 17.

	2009	**2008**
Net income............................	$374,930	$306,766
Average number of common shares outstanding	139,487 shares	140,877 shares
Earnings per share.......................	$2.69	$2.18
	($374,930 ÷ 139,487 shares)	($306,766 ÷ 140,877 shares)

Hasbro had no preferred stock outstanding during 2008; thus, no preferred dividends were subtracted in computing earnings per share. As shown above, Hasbro's earnings per share increased from $2.18 in 2008 to $2.69 in 2009. An increase in earnings per share is generally considered a favorable trend.

Earnings per share can be used to compare two companies with different net incomes. For example, the following data (in millions) were taken from a recent year's financial statements for Bank of America Corporation and JP Morgan Chase & Co.

	Bank of America	**JP Morgan Chase**
Net income...................................	$4,008	$5,605
Preferred dividends...........................	$1,452	$674
Average number of common shares outstanding........................	4,592 shares	3,501 shares

Bank of America:

$$\text{Earnings per Share} = \frac{\text{Net Income} - \text{Preferred Dividends}}{\text{Average Number of Common Shares Outstanding}} = \frac{\$4,008 - \$1,452}{4,592 \text{ shares}} = \frac{\$2,556}{4,592 \text{ shares}} = \$0.56$$

JP Morgan Chase:

$$\text{Earnings per Share} = \frac{\text{Net Income} - \text{Preferred Dividends}}{\text{Average Number of Common Shares Outstanding}} = \frac{\$5,605 - \$674}{3,501 \text{ shares}} = \frac{\$4,931}{3,501 \text{ shares}} = \$1.41$$

On the bases of net income and earnings per share, JP Morgan Chase is more profitable than Bank of America.

Example Exercise 13-8 Earnings per Share

OBJ. 8

Financial statement data for years ending December 31 for Finnegan Company are shown below.

	2012	**2011**
Net income	$350,000	$195,000
Preferred dividends	$20,000	$15,000
Average number of common shares outstanding	75,000 shares	50,000 shares

a. Determine earnings per share for 2012 and 2011.
b. Does the change in the earnings per share from 2011 to 2012 indicate a favorable or an unfavorable trend?

Follow My Example 13-8

a.

2012:

$$\text{Earnings per Share} = \frac{\text{Net Income} - \text{Preferred Dividends}}{\text{Average Number of Common Shares Outstanding}} = \frac{\$350,000 - \$20,000}{75,000 \text{ shares}} = \frac{\$330,000}{75,000 \text{ shares}} = \$4.40$$

2011:

$$\text{Earnings per Share} = \frac{\text{Net Income} - \text{Preferred Dividends}}{\text{Average Number of Common Shares Outstanding}} = \frac{\$195,000 - \$15,000}{50,000 \text{ shares}} = \frac{\$180,000}{50,000 \text{ shares}} = \$3.60$$

b. The increase in the earnings per share from $3.60 to $4.40 indicates a favorable trend in the company's profitability.

Practice Exercises: **PE 13-8A, PE 13-8B**

At a Glance 13

OBJ. 1 Describe the nature of the corporate form of organization.

Key Points Corporations have a separate legal existence, transferable units of stock, unlimited life, and limited stockholders' liability. The advantages and disadvantages of the corporate form are summarized in Exhibit 2. Costs incurred in organizing a corporation are debited to Organizational Expenses.

Learning Outcomes	Example Exercises	Practice Exercises
• Describe the characteristics of corporations.		
• List the advantages and disadvantages of the corporate form.		
• Prepare a journal entry for the costs of organizing a corporation.		

OBJ. 2 Describe the two main sources of stockholders' equity.

Key Points The two main sources of stockholders' equity are (1) capital contributed by the stockholders and others, called *paid-in capital*, and (2) net income retained in the business, called *retained earnings*. Stockholders' equity is reported in a corporation balance sheet according to these two sources.

Learning Outcomes	Example Exercises	Practice Exercises
• Describe what is meant by paid-in capital.		
• Describe what is meant by net income retained in the business.		
• Prepare a simple Stockholders' Equity section of the balance sheet.		

OBJ. 3 Describe and illustrate the characteristics of stock, classes of stock, and entries for issuing stock.

Key Points The main source of paid-in capital is from issuing common and preferred stock. Stock issued at par is recorded by debiting Cash and crediting the class of stock issued for its par amount. Stock issued for more than par is recorded by debiting Cash, crediting the class of stock for its par, and crediting Paid-In Capital in Excess of Par for the difference. When no-par stock is issued, the entire proceeds are credited to the stock account. No-par stock may be assigned a stated value per share, and the excess of the proceeds over the stated value may be credited to Paid-In Capital in Excess of Stated Value.

Learning Outcomes	Example Exercises	Practice Exercises
• Describe the characteristics of common and preferred stock including rights to dividends.	EE13-1	13-1A, 13-1B
• Journalize the entry for common and preferred stock issued at par.	EE13-2	13-2A, 13-2B
• Journalize the entry for common and preferred stock issued at more than par.	EE13-2	13-2A, 13-2B
• Journalize the entry for issuing no-par stock.	EE13-2	13-2A, 13-2B

Describe and illustrate the accounting for cash dividends and stock dividends.

Key Points   The entry to record a declaration of cash dividends debits Dividends and credits Dividends Payable. When a stock dividend is declared, Stock Dividends is debited for the fair value of the stock to be issued. Stock Dividends Distributable is credited for the par or stated value of the common stock to be issued. The difference between the fair value of the stock and its par or stated value is credited to Paid-In Capital in Excess of Par—Common Stock. When the stock is issued on the date of payment, Stock Dividends Distributable is debited and Common Stock is credited for the par or stated value of the stock issued.

Learning Outcomes	Example Exercises	Practice Exercises
• Journalize the entries for the declaration and payment of cash dividends.	EE13-3	PE13-3A, 13-3B
• Journalize the entries for the declaration and payment of stock dividends.	EE13-4	PE13-4A, 13-4B

Describe and illustrate the accounting for treasury stock transactions.

Key Points   When a corporation buys its own stock, the cost method of accounting is normally used. Treasury Stock is debited for its cost, and Cash is credited. If the stock is resold, Treasury Stock is credited for its cost and any difference between the cost and the selling price is normally debited or credited to Paid-In Capital from Sale of Treasury Stock.

Learning Outcomes	Example Exercises	Practice Exercises
• Define treasury stock.		
• Describe the accounting for treasury stock.		
• Journalize entries for the purchase and sale of treasury stock.	EE13-5	PE13-5A, 13-5B

Describe and illustrate the reporting of stockholders' equity.

Key Points   Two alternatives for reporting stockholders' equity are shown in Exhibit 4. Changes in retained earnings are reported in a retained earnings statement, as shown in Exhibit 5. Restrictions to retained earnings should be disclosed. Any prior period adjustments are reported in the retained earnings statement. Changes in stockholders' equity may be reported on a statement of stockholders' equity, as shown in Exhibit 6.

Learning Outcomes	Example Exercises	Practice Exercises
• Prepare the Stockholders' Equity section of the balance sheet.	EE13-6	PE13-6A, 13-6B
• Prepare a retained earnings statement.	EE13-7	PE13-7A, 13-7B
• Describe retained earnings restrictions and prior period adjustments.		
• Prepare a statement of stockholders' equity.		

OBJ. 7

Describe the effect of stock splits on corporate financial statements.

Key Points When a corporation reduces the par or stated value of its common stock and issues a proportionate number of additional shares, a stock split has occurred. There are no changes in the balances of any accounts, and no entry is required for a stock split.

Learning Outcomes	Example Exercises	Practice Exercises
• Define and give an example of a stock split.		
• Describe the accounting for and effects of a stock split on the financial statements.		

OBJ. 8

Describe and illustrate the use of earnings per share in evaluating a company's profitability.

Key Points The profitability of companies is often expressed as earnings per share. Earnings per share is computed by subtracting preferred dividends from net income and dividing by the average number of common shares outstanding.

Learning Outcomes	Example Exercises	Practice Exercises
• Describe the use of earnings per share in evaluating a company's profitability.		
• Compute and interpret earnings per share.	EE13-8	PE13-8A, 13-8B

Key Terms

cash dividend (590)
common stock (585)
cumulative preferred stock (586)
deficit (585)
discount (587)
dividends (584)
earnings per common share (EPS) (600)

in arrears (586)
outstanding stock (585)
paid-in capital (584)
par (585)
preferred stock (586)
premium (587)
prior period adjustments (597)
restrictions (597)
retained earnings (584)

retained earnings statement (596)
statement of stockholders' equity (598)
stock (582)
stock dividend (592)
stock split (599)
stockholders (582)
stockholders' equity (584)
treasury stock (593)

Illustrative Problem

Altenburg Inc. is a lighting fixture wholesaler located in Arizona. During its current fiscal year, ended December 31, 2012, Altenburg Inc. completed the following selected transactions:

Feb. 3. Purchased 2,500 shares of its own common stock at $26, recording the stock at cost. (Prior to the purchase, there were 40,000 shares of $20 par common stock outstanding.)

May 1. Declared a semiannual dividend of $1 on the 10,000 shares of preferred stock and a 30¢ dividend on the common stock to stockholders of record on May 31, payable on June 15.

June 15. Paid the cash dividends.

Sept. 23. Sold 1,000 shares of treasury stock at $28, receiving cash.

Nov. 1. Declared semiannual dividends of $1 on the preferred stock and 30¢ on the common stock. In addition, a 5% common stock dividend was declared on the common stock outstanding, to be capitalized at the fair market value of the common stock, which is estimated at $30.

Dec. 1. Paid the cash dividends and issued the certificates for the common stock dividend.

Instructions

Journalize the entries to record the transactions for Altenburg Inc.

Solution

2012					
Feb.	3	Treasury Stock		65,000	
		Cash			65,000
May	1	Cash Dividends		21,250	
		Cash Dividends Payable			21,250
		(10,000 × $1) + [(40,000 − 2,500) × $0.30].			
June	15	Cash Dividends Payable		21,250	
		Cash			21,250
Sept.	23	Cash		28,000	
		Treasury Stock			26,000
		Paid-In Capital from Sale of Treasury Stock			2,000
Nov.	1	Cash Dividends		21,550	
		Cash Dividends Payable			21,550
		(10,000 × $1) + [(40,000 − 1,500) × $0.30].			
	1	Stock Dividends		57,750*	
		Stock Dividends Distributable			38,500
		Paid-In Capital in Excess of			
		Par—Common Stock			19,250
		*(40,000 − 1,500) × 5% × $30.			
Dec.	1	Cash Dividends Payable		21,550	
		Stock Dividends Distributable		38,500	
		Cash			21,550
		Common Stock			38,500

Discussion Questions

1. Of two corporations organized at approximately the same time and engaged in competing businesses, one issued $150 par common stock, and the other issued $1.00 par common stock. Do the par designations provide any indication as to which stock is preferable as an investment? Explain.

2. A stockbroker advises a client to "buy preferred stock. . . . With that type of stock, . . . [you] will never have to worry about losing the dividends." Is the broker right?

3. A corporation with both preferred stock and common stock outstanding has a substantial credit balance in its retained earnings account at the beginning of the current fiscal year. Although net income for the current year is sufficient to pay the preferred dividend of $90,000 each quarter and a common dividend of $275,000 each quarter, the board of directors declares dividends only on the preferred stock. Suggest possible reasons for passing the dividends on the common stock.

4. An owner of 1,000 shares of Simmons Company common stock receives a stock dividend of 6 shares.

   a. What is the effect of the stock dividend on the stockholder's proportionate interest (equity) in the corporation?

   b. How does the total equity of 1,006 shares compare with the total equity of 1,000 shares before the stock dividend?

5. a. Where should a declared but unpaid cash dividend be reported on the balance sheet?

   b. Where should a declared but unissued stock dividend be reported on the balance sheet?

6. A corporation reacquires 25,000 shares of its own $10 par common stock for $1,000,000, recording it at cost.

   a. What effect does this transaction have on revenue or expense of the period?

   b. What effect does it have on stockholders' equity?

7. The treasury stock in Discussion Question 6 is resold for $1,200,000.

   a. What is the effect on the corporation's revenue of the period?

   b. What is the effect on stockholders' equity?

8. What are the three classifications of restrictions of retained earnings, and how are such restrictions normally reported on the financial statements?

9. Indicate how prior period adjustments would be reported on the financial statements presented only for the current period.

10. What is the primary purpose of a stock split?

Practice Exercises

Learning Objectives	Example Exercises

OBJ. 3   EE 13-1 p. 587   **PE 13-1A   Dividends per share**

Hays-Smith Company has 18,000 shares of 4% cumulative preferred stock of $125 par and 50,000 shares of $40 par common stock. The following amounts were distributed as dividends:

Year 1	$ 72,000
Year 2	125,000
Year 3	160,000

Determine the dividends per share for preferred and common stock for each year.

OBJ. 3   EE 13-1 p. 587   **PE 13-1B   Dividends per share**

Lasers4U Company has 10,000 shares of 2% cumulative preferred stock of $50 par and 25,000 shares of $100 par common stock. The following amounts were distributed as dividends:

Year 1	$18,000
Year 2	7,500
Year 3	35,000

Determine the dividends per share for preferred and common stock for each year.

OBJ. 3   EE 13-2 p. 589   **PE 13-2A   Entries for issuing stock**

On February 23, Muir Corporation issued for cash 75,000 shares of no-par common stock (with a stated value of $80) at $125. On October 6, Muir issued 20,000 shares of 1%, $50 preferred stock at par for cash. On November 4, Muir issued for cash 12,000 shares of 1%, $50 par preferred stock at $59.

Journalize the entries to record the February 23, October 6, and November 4 transactions.

OBJ. 3   EE 13-2 p. 589   **PE 13-2B   Entries for issuing stock**

On August 7, Asian Artifacts Corporation issued for cash 300,000 shares of no-par common stock at $1.75. On September 1, Asian Artifacts issued 25,000 shares of 2%, $40 preferred stock at par for cash. On November 2, Asian Artifacts issued for cash 10,000 shares of 2%, $40 par preferred stock at $52.

Journalize the entries to record the August 7, September 1, and November 2 transactions.

OBJ. 4   EE 13-3 p. 591   **PE 13-3A   Entries for cash dividends**

The declaration, record, and payment dates in connection with a cash dividend of $115,000 on a corporation's common stock are October 15, November 14, and December 14. Journalize the entries required on each date.

OBJ. 4   EE 13-3 p. 591   **PE 13-3B   Entries for cash dividends**

The declaration, record, and payment dates in connection with a cash dividend of $275,000 on a corporation's common stock are March 3, April 2, and May 2. Journalize the entries required on each date.

OBJ. 4   EE 13-4 p. 593   **PE 13-4A   Entries for stock dividends**

Arroyo Corporation has 100,000 shares of $60 par common stock outstanding. On February 8, Arroyo Corporation declared a 6% stock dividend to be issued April 11 to stockholders of record on March 10. The market price of the stock was $94 per share on February 8.

Journalize the entries required on February 8, March 10, and April 11.

OBJ. 4   EE 13-4 *p. 593*   **PE 13-4B   Entries for stock dividends**

U-Store Corporation has 250,000 shares of $15 par common stock outstanding. On July 20, U-Store Corporation declared a 3% stock dividend to be issued September 18 to stockholders of record on August 19. The market price of the stock was $54 per share on July 20.
Journalize the entries required on July 20, August 19, and September 18.

OBJ. 5   EE 13-5 *p. 594*   **PE 13-5A   Entries for treasury stock**

On March 8, Golf Resorts Inc. reacquired 13,000 shares of its common stock at $42 per share. On May 16, Golf Resorts sold 9,500 of the reacquired shares at $50 per share. On August 30, Golf Resorts sold the remaining shares at $40 per share.
Journalize the transactions of March 8, May 16, and August 30.

OBJ. 5   EE 13-5 *p. 594*   **PE 13-5B   Entries for treasury stock**

On September 9, Palin Clothing Inc. reacquired 9,000 shares of its common stock at $24 per share. On October 7, Palin Clothing sold 4,800 of the reacquired shares at $29 per share. On December 20, Palin Clothing sold the remaining shares at $22 per share.
Journalize the transactions of September 9, October 7, and December 20.

OBJ. 6   EE 13-6 *p. 596*   **PE 13-6A   Reporting stockholders' equity**

Using the following accounts and balances, prepare the Stockholders' Equity section of the balance sheet. Fifty thousand shares of common stock are authorized, and 2,500 shares have been reacquired.

Common Stock, $120 par	$4,800,000
Paid-In Capital in Excess of Par	600,000
Paid-In Capital from Sale of Treasury Stock	59,000
Retained Earnings	7,138,500
Treasury Stock	287,500

OBJ. 6   EE 13-6 *p. 596*   **PE 13-6B   Reporting stockholders' equity**

Using the following accounts and balances, prepare the Stockholders' Equity section of the balance sheet. Two-hundred thousand shares of common stock are authorized, and 24,000 shares have been reacquired.

Common Stock, $15 par	$2,400,000
Paid-In Capital in Excess of Par	480,000
Paid-In Capital from Sale of Treasury Stock	100,000
Retained Earnings	5,275,000
Treasury Stock	336,000

OBJ. 6   EE 13-7 *p. 597*   **PE 13-7A   Retained earnings statement**

Emmy Leaders Inc. reported the following results for the year ending August 31, 2012:

Retained earnings, September 1, 2011	$740,000
Net income	145,000
Cash dividends declared	5,000
Stock dividends declared	30,000

Prepare a retained earnings statement for the fiscal year ended August 31, 2012.

OBJ. 6   EE 13-7 *p. 597*   **PE 13-7B   Retained earnings statement**

Auckland Cruises Inc. reported the following results for the year ending April 30, 2012:

Retained earnings, May 1, 2011	$3,180,000
Net income	515,000
Cash dividends declared	100,000
Stock dividends declared	125,000

Prepare a retained earnings statement for the fiscal year ended April 30, 2012.

Learning Objectives	Example Exercises
OBJ. 8	EE 13-8 *p. 601*

PE 13-8A Earnings per share

Financial statement data for years ending December 31 for Jardine Company are shown below.

	2012	2011
Net income	$117,000	$104,000
Preferred dividends	$18,000	$18,000
Average number of common shares outstanding	50,000 shares	40,000 shares

a. Determine the earnings per share for 2012 and 2011.

b. Does the change in the earnings per share from 2011 to 2012 indicate a favorable or an unfavorable trend?

OBJ. 8	EE 13-8 *p. 601*

PE 13-8B Earnings per share

Financial statement data for years ending December 31 for Duffner Company are shown below.

	2012	2011
Net income	$971,000	$692,000
Preferred dividends	$35,000	$35,000
Average number of common shares outstanding	120,000 shares	90,000 shares

a. Determine the earnings per share for 2012 and 2011.

b. Does the change in the earnings per share from 2011 to 2012 indicate a favorable or an unfavorable trend?

Exercises

OBJ. 3

✔ Preferred stock, 1st year: $1.25

EX 13-1 Dividends per share

Baxter Inc., a developer of radiology equipment, has stock outstanding as follows: 18,000 shares of cumulative 2%, preferred stock of $75 par, and 40,000 shares of $10 par common. During its first four years of operations, the following amounts were distributed as dividends: first year, $22,500; second year, $28,800; third year, $40,100; fourth year, $77,000. Calculate the dividends per share on each class of stock for each of the four years.

OBJ. 3

✔ Preferred stock, 1st year: $0.30

EX 13-2 Dividends per share

Wings Inc., a software development firm, has stock outstanding as follows: 25,000 shares of cumulative 1%, preferred stock of $40 par, and 50,000 shares of $120 par common. During its first four years of operations, the following amounts were distributed as dividends: first year, $7,500; second year, $10,500; third year, $25,000; fourth year, $60,000. Calculate the dividends per share on each class of stock for each of the four years.

OBJ. 3

EX 13-3 Entries for issuing par stock

On January 14, Mountain Rocks Inc., a marble contractor, issued for cash 24,000 shares of $25 par common stock at $32, and on March 17, it issued for cash 60,000 shares of $10 par preferred stock at $11.

a. Journalize the entries for January 14 and March 17.

b. What is the total amount invested (total paid-in capital) by all stockholders as of March 17?

OBJ. 3

EX 13-4 Entries for issuing no-par stock

On July 12, Lasting Carpet Inc., a carpet wholesaler, issued for cash 300,000 shares of no-par common stock (with a stated value of $4) at $9, and on November 18, it issued for cash 40,000 shares of $90 par preferred stock at $100.

a. Journalize the entries for July 12 and November 18, assuming that the common stock is to be credited with the stated value.

b. What is the total amount invested (total paid-in capital) by all stockholders as of November 18?

OBJ. 3

EX 13-5 Issuing stock for assets other than cash

On April 15, Hass Corporation, a wholesaler of hydraulic lifts, acquired land in exchange for 17,500 shares of $20 par common stock with a current market price of $30. Journalize the entry to record the transaction.

OBJ. 3

EX 13-6 Selected stock transactions

Fantastic Sounds Corp., an electric guitar retailer, was organized by Pam Mikhail, Jane Lo, and Dale Nadal. The charter authorized 400,000 shares of common stock with a par of $50. The following transactions affecting stockholders' equity were completed during the first year of operations:

a. Issued 20,000 shares of stock at par to Pam Mikhail for cash.

b. Issued 1,000 shares of stock at par to Dale Nadal for promotional services provided in connection with the organization of the corporation, and issued 15,000 shares of stock at par to Dale Nadal for cash.

c. Purchased land and a building from Jane Lo. The building is mortgaged for $300,000 for 20 years at 5%, and there is accrued interest of $2,500 on the mortgage note at the time of the purchase. It is agreed that the land is to be priced at $200,000 and the building at $500,000, and that Jane Lo's equity will be exchanged for stock at par. The corporation agreed to assume responsibility for paying the mortgage note and the accrued interest.

Journalize the entries to record the transactions.

OBJ. 3

EX 13-7 Issuing stock

Wildwood Nursery, with an authorization of 50,000 shares of preferred stock and 400,000 shares of common stock, completed several transactions involving its stock on June 1, the first day of operations. The trial balance at the close of the day follows:

Cash	1,584,000	
Land	350,000	
Buildings	910,000	
Preferred 3% Stock, $120 par		1,200,000
Paid-In Capital in Excess of Par—Preferred Stock		60,000
Common Stock, $50 par		1,500,000
Paid-In Capital in Excess of Par—Common Stock		84,000
	2,844,000	2,844,000

All shares within each class of stock were sold at the same price. The preferred stock was issued in exchange for the land and buildings.

Journalize the two entries to record the transactions summarized in the trial balance.

OBJ. 3

EX 13-8 Issuing stock

Baird Products Inc., a wholesaler of office products, was organized on January 30 of the current year, with an authorization of 80,000 shares of 2% preferred stock, $75 par and 800,000 shares of $20 par common stock. The following selected transactions were completed during the first year of operations:

Jan. 30. Issued 300,000 shares of common stock at par for cash.

31. Issued 750 shares of common stock at par to an attorney in payment of legal fees for organizing the corporation.

Feb. 21. Issued 32,000 shares of common stock in exchange for land, buildings, and equipment with fair market prices of $150,000, $460,000, and $90,000, respectively.

Mar. 2. Issued 15,000 shares of preferred stock at $77.50 for cash.

Journalize the transactions.

OBJ. 4

EX 13-9   Entries for cash dividends

The declaration, record, and payment dates in connection with a cash dividend of $365,850 on a corporation's common stock are April 1, May 1, and June 3. Journalize the entries required on each date.

OBJ. 4

✔ b. (1) $18,060,000
    (3) $93,556,000

EX 13-10   Entries for stock dividends

Organic Life Co. is an HMO for businesses in the Portland area. The following account balances appear on the balance sheet of Organic Life Co.: Common stock (250,000 shares authorized), $125 par, $17,500,000; Paid-in capital in excess of par—common stock, $560,000; and Retained earnings, $75,496,000. The board of directors declared a 3% stock dividend when the market price of the stock was $132 a share. Organic Life Co. reported no income or loss for the current year.

a. Journalize the entries to record (1) the declaration of the dividend, capitalizing an amount equal to market value, and (2) the issuance of the stock certificates.

b. Determine the following amounts before the stock dividend was declared: (1) total paid-in capital, (2) total retained earnings, and (3) total stockholders' equity.

c. Determine the following amounts after the stock dividend was declared and closing entries were recorded at the end of the year: (1) total paid-in capital, (2) total retained earnings, and (3) total stockholders' equity.

OBJ. 5

✔ b. $102,000 credit

EX 13-11   Treasury stock transactions

Deer Creek Inc. bottles and distributes spring water. On April 27 of the current year, Deer Creek reacquired 15,000 shares of its common stock at $60 per share. On July 13, Deer Creek sold 9,000 of the reacquired shares at $72 per share. The remaining 6,000 shares were sold at $59 per share on October 8.

a. Journalize the transactions of April 27, July 13, and October 8.

b. What is the balance in Paid-In Capital from Sale of Treasury Stock on December 31 of the current year?

c. ▬▬▬▶ For what reasons might Deer Creek have purchased the treasury stock?

OBJ. 5, 6

✔ b. $94,000 credit

EX 13-12   Treasury stock transactions

Golden Gardens Inc. develops and produces spraying equipment for lawn maintenance and industrial uses. On June 19 of the current year, Golden Gardens Inc. reacquired 24,000 shares of its common stock at $64 per share. On August 30, 19,000 of the reacquired shares were sold at $68 per share, and on September 6, 3,000 of the reacquired shares were sold at $70.

a. Journalize the transactions of June 19, August 30, and September 6.

b. What is the balance in Paid-In Capital from Sale of Treasury Stock on December 31 of the current year?

c. What is the balance in Treasury Stock on December 31 of the current year?

d. How will the balance in Treasury Stock be reported on the balance sheet?

OBJ. 5, 6

✔ b. $24,000 credit

EX 13-13   Treasury stock transactions

Conyers Water Inc. bottles and distributes spring water. On July 5 of the current year, Conyers Water Inc. reacquired 12,500 shares of its common stock at $80 per share. On November 3, Conyers Water Inc. sold 7,000 of the reacquired shares at $85 per share. The remaining 5,500 shares were sold at $78 per share on December 10.

a. Journalize the transactions of July 5, November 3, and December 10.

b. What is the balance in Paid-In Capital from Sale of Treasury Stock on December 31 of the current year?

c. Where will the balance in Paid-In Capital from Sale of Treasury Stock be reported on the balance sheet?

d. ▬▬▬▶ For what reasons might Conyers Water Inc. have purchased the treasury stock?

OBJ. 6

✔ Total paid-in capital, $7,720,000

EX 13-14 Reporting paid-in capital

The following accounts and their balances were selected from the unadjusted trial balance of CW Group Inc., a freight forwarder, at March 31, the end of the current fiscal year:

Preferred 1% Stock, $75 par	$ 4,500,000
Paid-In Capital in Excess of Par—Preferred Stock	180,000
Common Stock, no par, $8 stated value	2,400,000
Paid-In Capital in Excess of Stated Value—Common Stock	450,000
Paid-In Capital from Sale of Treasury Stock	190,000
Retained Earnings	11,570,000

Prepare the Paid-In Capital portion of the Stockholders' Equity section of the balance sheet. There are 500,000 shares of common stock authorized and 100,000 shares of preferred stock authorized.

OBJ. 6

✔ Total stockholders' equity, $11,677,000

EX 13-15 Stockholders' equity section of balance sheet

The following accounts and their balances appear in the ledger of Cline Properties Inc. on April 30 of the current year:

Common Stock, $90 par	$2,700,000
Paid-In Capital in Excess of Par	120,000
Paid-In Capital from Sale of Treasury Stock	36,000
Retained Earnings	9,173,000
Treasury Stock	352,000

Prepare the Stockholders' Equity section of the balance sheet as of April 30. Fifty thousand shares of common stock are authorized, and 4,000 shares have been reacquired.

OBJ. 6

✔ Total stockholders' equity, $31,308,000

EX 13-16 Stockholders' equity section of balance sheet

Furious and Fast Car Inc. retails racing products for BMWs, Porsches, and Ferraris. The following accounts and their balances appear in the ledger of Furious and Fast Car Inc. on November 30, the end of the current year:

Common Stock, $8 par	$ 3,000,000
Paid-In Capital in Excess of Par—Common Stock	525,000
Paid-In Capital in Excess of Par—Preferred Stock	280,000
Paid-In Capital from Sale of Treasury Stock—Common	175,000
Preferred 2% Stock, $125 par	5,000,000
Retained Earnings	23,120,000
Treasury Stock—Common	792,000

Sixty thousand shares of preferred and 500,000 shares of common stock are authorized. There are 88,000 shares of common stock held as treasury stock.

Prepare the Stockholders' Equity section of the balance sheet as of November 30, the end of the current year.

OBJ. 6

✔ Retained earnings, October 31, $966,750

EX 13-17 Retained earnings statement

Sandusky Corporation, a manufacturer of industrial pumps, reports the following results for the year ending October 31, 2012:

Retained earnings, November 1, 2011	$796,750
Net income	215,000
Cash dividends declared	15,000
Stock dividends declared	30,000

Prepare a retained earnings statement for the fiscal year ended October 31, 2012.

OBJ. 6

✔ Corrected total stockholders' equity, $53,527,000

EX 13-18 Stockholders' equity section of balance sheet

List the errors in the following Stockholders' Equity section of the balance sheet prepared as of the end of the current year.

Stockholders' Equity

Paid-in capital:		
Preferred 1% stock, $200 par		
(25,000 shares authorized and issued)................	$5,000,000	
Excess of issue price over par	75,000	$ 5,075,000
Retained earnings		41,750,000
Treasury stock (45,000 shares at cost)		648,000
Dividends payable...		175,000
Total paid-in capital		$ 47,648,000
Common stock, $14 par (800,000 shares		
authorized, 500,000 shares issued).....................		7,600,000
Organizing costs		250,000
Total stockholders' equity		$55,498,000

OBJ. 6

✔ Total stockholders' equity, Dec. 31, $10,773,000

EX 13-19 Statement of stockholders' equity

The stockholders' equity T accounts of Life's Greeting Cards Inc. for the current fiscal year ended December 31, 2012, are as follows. Prepare a statement of stockholders' equity for the fiscal year ended December 31, 2012.

COMMON STOCK

	Jan. 1	Balance	3,000,000
	Mar. 7	Issued	
		27,000 shares	1,350,000
	Dec. 31	Balance	4,350,000

PAID-IN CAPITAL IN EXCESS OF PAR

	Jan. 1	Balance	480,000
	Mar. 7	Issued	
		27,000 shares	324,000
	Dec. 31	Balance	804,000

TREASURY STOCK

Aug. 7	Purchased		
	4,500 shares	216,000	

RETAINED EARNINGS

Mar. 31	Dividend	37,500	Jan. 1	Balance	5,220,000
June 30	Dividend	37,500	Dec. 31	Closing	
Sept. 30	Dividend	37,500		(net income)	765,000
Dec. 31	Dividend	37,500	Dec. 31	Balance	5,835,000

OBJ. 7

EX 13-20 Effect of stock split

Gino's Restaurant Corporation wholesales ovens and ranges to restaurants throughout the Midwest. Gino's Restaurant Corporation, which had 100,000 shares of common stock outstanding, declared a 5-for-1 stock split (4 additional shares for each share issued).

a. What will be the number of shares outstanding after the split?

b. If the common stock had a market price of $200 per share before the stock split, what would be an approximate market price per share after the split?

OBJ. 4, 7

EX 13-21 Effect of cash dividend and stock split

Indicate whether the following actions would (+) increase, (–) decrease, or (0) not affect Indigo Inc.'s total assets, liabilities, and stockholders' equity:

	Assets	Liabilities	Stockholders' Equity
(1) Authorizing and issuing stock certificates in a stock split	_____	_____	_____
(2) Declaring a stock dividend	_____	_____	_____
(3) Issuing stock certificates for the stock dividend declared in (2)	_____	_____	_____
(4) Declaring a cash dividend	_____	_____	_____
(5) Paying the cash dividend declared in (4)	_____	_____	_____

OBJ. 4, 7

EX 13-22 Selected dividend transactions, stock split

Selected transactions completed by Gene's Boating Corporation during the current fiscal year are as follows:

Feb. 10. Split the common stock 3 for 1 and reduced the par from $60 to $20 per share. After the split, there were 300,000 common shares outstanding.

May 1. Declared semiannual dividends of $2.00 on 40,000 shares of preferred stock and $0.12 on the common stock payable on June 15.

June 15. Paid the cash dividends.

Nov. 1. Declared semiannual dividends of $2.00 on the preferred stock and $0.08 on the common stock (before the stock dividend). In addition, a 2% common stock dividend was declared on the common stock outstanding. The fair market value of the common stock is estimated at $28.

Dec. 15. Paid the cash dividends and issued the certificates for the common stock dividend.

Journalize the transactions.

OBJ. 8

EX 13-23 EPS

Malen Arts, Inc., had earnings of $133,750 for 2012. The company had 25,000 shares of common stock outstanding during the year. In addition, the company issued 10,000 shares of $100 par value preferred stock on January 3, 2012. The preferred stock has a dividend of $4 per share. There were no transactions in either common or preferred stock during 2012.

Determine the basic earnings per share for Malen Arts.

OBJ. 8

EX 13-24 EPS

Procter & Gamble (P&G) is one of the largest consumer products companies in the world, famous for such brands as Crest® and Tide®. Financial information for the company for three recent years is as follows:

	Fiscal Years Ended (in millions)		
	2009	**2008**	**2007**
Net income	$11,293	$11,798	$10,063
Preferred dividends	$192	$176	$161
Average number of common shares outstanding	2,952	3,081	3,159

a. Determine the earnings per share for fiscal years 2009, 2008, and 2007. Round to the nearest cent.

b. Evaluate the growth in earnings per share for the three years in comparison to the growth in net income for the three years.

OBJ. 8

EX 13-25 EPS

OfficeMax and Staples are two companies competing in the retail office supply business. OfficeMax had a net income of $667,000 for a recent year, while Staples had a net income of $738,671,000. OfficeMax had preferred stock of $36,479,000 with preferred dividends of $2,818,000. Staples had no preferred stock. The outstanding common shares for each company were as follows:

	Average Number of Common Shares Outstanding
OfficeMax	77,483,000
Staples	721,838,000

a. Determine the earnings per share for each company. Round to the nearest cent.

b. Evaluate the relative profitability of the two companies.

Problems Series A

OBJ. 3

✔ 1. Common
dividends in 2009:
$9,000

PR 13-1A Dividends on preferred and common stock

Love Theatre Inc. owns and operates movie theaters throughout New Mexico and Utah. Love Theatre has declared the following annual dividends over a six-year period: 2007, $16,000; 2008, $48,000; 2009, $65,000; 2010, $90,000; 2011, $115,000; and 2012, $140,000. During the entire period ending December 31 of each year, the outstanding stock of the company was composed of 25,000 shares of cumulative, 2% preferred stock, $80 par, and 100,000 shares of common stock, $4 par.

Instructions

1. Calculate the total dividends and the per-share dividends declared on each class of stock for each of the six years. There were no dividends in arrears on January 1, 2007. Summarize the data in tabular form, using the following column headings:

Year	Total Dividends	Preferred Dividends		Common Dividends	
		Total	Per Share	Total	Per Share
2007	$ 16,000				
2008	48,000				
2009	65,000				
2010	90,000				
2011	115,000				
2012	140,000				

2. Calculate the average annual dividend per share for each class of stock for the six-year period.

3. Assuming a market price per share of $128 for the preferred stock and $7.80 for the common stock, calculate the average annual percentage return on initial shareholders' investment, based on the average annual dividend per share (a) for preferred stock and (b) for common stock.

OBJ. 3

PR 13-2A Stock transactions for corporate expansion

On March 1 of the current year, the following accounts and their balances appear in the ledger of Mocha Corp., a coffee processor:

Preferred 2% Stock, $25 par (300,000 shares authorized, 120,000 shares issued)..	$ 3,000,000
Paid-In Capital in Excess of Par—Preferred Stock	480,000
Common Stock, $100 par (800,000 shares authorized, 250,000 shares issued)..	25,000,000
Paid-In Capital in Excess of Par—Common Stock	2,000,000
Retained Earnings...	50,000,000

At the annual stockholders' meeting on April 18, the board of directors presented a plan for modernizing and expanding plant operations at a cost of approximately $14,000,000. The plan provided (a) that a building, valued at $3,500,000, and the land on which it is located, valued at $5,000,000, be acquired in accordance with preliminary negotiations by the issuance of 80,000 shares of common stock, (b) that 85,000 shares of the unissued preferred stock be issued through an underwriter, and (c) that the corporation borrow $3,000,000. The plan was approved by the stockholders and accomplished by the following transactions:

June 5. Issued 80,000 shares of common stock in exchange for land and a building, according to the plan.

    16. Issued 85,000 shares of preferred stock, receiving $30 per share in cash.

    29. Borrowed $3,000,000 from First City Bank, giving a 6% mortgage note.

No other transactions occurred during June.

Instructions

Journalize the entries to record the foregoing transactions.

PR 13-3A Selected stock transactions

The following selected accounts appear in the ledger of Patton Environmental Inc. on July 1, 2012, the beginning of the current fiscal year:

Preferred 2% Stock, $75 par (40,000 shares authorized, 20,000 shares issued)	$ 1,500,000
Paid-In Capital in Excess of Par—Preferred Stock	240,000
Common Stock, $15 par (500,000 shares authorized, 260,000 shares issued)	3,900,000
Paid-In Capital in Excess of Par—Common Stock	400,000
Retained Earnings	12,750,000

During the year, the corporation completed a number of transactions affecting the stockholders' equity. They are summarized as follows:

a. Issued 50,000 shares of common stock at $20, receiving cash.

b. Issued 10,000 shares of preferred 2% stock at $92.

c. Purchased 30,000 shares of treasury common for $480,000.

d. Sold 15,000 shares of treasury common for $322,500.

e. Sold 10,000 shares of treasury common for $155,000.

f. Declared cash dividends of $1.50 per share on preferred stock and $0.04 per share on common stock.

g. Paid the cash dividends.

Instructions

Journalize the entries to record the transactions. Identify each entry by letter.

PR 13-4A Entries for selected corporate transactions

Tolbert Enterprises Inc. manufactures bathroom fixtures. The stockholders' equity accounts of Tolbert Enterprises Inc., with balances on January 1, 2012, are as follows:

Common Stock, $10 stated value (600,000 shares authorized, 400,000 shares issued)	$4,000,000
Paid-In Capital in Excess of Stated Value	750,000
Retained Earnings	9,150,000
Treasury Stock (40,000 shares, at cost)	600,000

The following selected transactions occurred during the year:

Jan. 4. Paid cash dividends of $0.13 per share on the common stock. The dividend had been properly recorded when declared on December 1 of the preceding fiscal year for $46,800.

Apr. 3. Issued 75,000 shares of common stock for $1,200,000.

June 6. Sold all of the treasury stock for $725,000.

July 1. Declared a 4% stock dividend on common stock, to be capitalized at the market price of the stock, which is $18 per share.

Aug. 15. Issued the certificates for the dividend declared on July 1.

Nov. 10. Purchased 25,000 shares of treasury stock for $500,000.

Dec. 27. Declared a $0.16-per-share dividend on common stock.

31. Closed the credit balance of the income summary account, $950,000.

31. Closed the two dividends accounts to Retained Earnings.

Instructions

1. Enter the January 1 balances in T accounts for the stockholders' equity accounts listed. Also prepare T accounts for the following: Paid-In Capital from Sale of Treasury Stock; Stock Dividends Distributable; Stock Dividends; Cash Dividends.

2. Journalize the entries to record the transactions, and post to the eight selected accounts.

3. Prepare a retained earnings statement for the year ended December 31, 2012.

4. Prepare the Stockholders' Equity section of the December 31, 2012, balance sheet.

OBJ. 3, 4, 5, 7

✔ Nov. 15, cash
dividends, $159,400

PR 13-5A Entries for selected corporate transactions

Selected transactions completed by Big Water Boating Corporation during the current fiscal year are as follows:

Jan. 3. Split the common stock 3 for 1 and reduced the par from $90 to $30 per share. After the split, there were 750,000 common shares outstanding.

Apr. 7. Purchased 50,000 shares of the corporation's own common stock at $33, recording the stock at cost.

May 1. Declared semiannual dividends of $1.40 on 35,000 shares of preferred stock and $0.09 on the common stock to stockholders of record on May 15, payable on June 1.

June 1. Paid the cash dividends.

July 29. Sold 36,000 shares of treasury stock at $40, receiving cash.

Nov. 15. Declared semiannual dividends of $1.40 on the preferred stock and $0.15 on the common stock (before the stock dividend). In addition, a 2% common stock dividend was declared on the common stock outstanding. The fair market value of the common stock is estimated at $41.

Dec. 31. Paid the cash dividends and issued the certificates for the common stock dividend.

Instructions
Journalize the transactions.

Problems Series B

OBJ. 3

✔ 1. Common
dividends in 2009:
$2,000

PR 13-1B Dividends on preferred and common stock

Boise Bike Corp. manufactures mountain bikes and distributes them through retail outlets in Montana, Idaho, Oregon, and Washington. Boise Bike Corp. has declared the following annual dividends over a six-year period ending December 31 of each year: 2007, $8,000; 2008, $24,000; 2009, $60,000; 2010, $75,000; 2011, $80,000; and 2012, $98,000. During the entire period, the outstanding stock of the company was composed of 20,000 shares of 2% cumulative preferred stock, $75 par, and 50,000 shares of common stock, $5 par.

Instructions

1. Determine the total dividends and the per-share dividends declared on each class of stock for each of the six years. There were no dividends in arrears on January 1, 2007. Summarize the data in tabular form, using the following column headings:

Year	Total Dividends	Preferred Dividends		Common Dividends	
		Total	Per Share	Total	Per Share
2007	$ 8,000				
2008	24,000				
2009	60,000				
2010	75,000				
2011	80,000				
2012	98,000				

2. Determine the average annual dividend per share for each class of stock for the six-year period.

3. Assuming a market price of $125 for the preferred stock and $13.75 for the common stock, calculate the average annual percentage return on initial shareholders' investment, based on the average annual dividend per share (a) for preferred stock and (b) for common stock.

PR 13-2B **Stock transaction for corporate expansion**

Picasso Optics produces medical lasers for use in hospitals. The accounts and their balances appear in the ledger of Picasso Optics on November 30 of the current year as follows:

Preferred 2% Stock, $80 par (150,000 shares authorized, 75,000 shares issued)	$ 6,000,000
Paid-In Capital in Excess of Par—Preferred Stock	225,000
Common Stock, $100 par (500,000 shares authorized, 150,000 shares issued)	15,000,000
Paid-In Capital in Excess of Par—Common Stock	1,800,000
Retained Earnings	50,250,000

At the annual stockholders' meeting on December 10, the board of directors presented a plan for modernizing and expanding plant operations at a cost of approximately $15,500,000. The plan provided (a) that the corporation borrow $6,000,000, (b) that 45,000 shares of the unissued preferred stock be issued through an underwriter, and (c) that a building, valued at $5,000,000, and the land on which it is located, valued at $487,500, be acquired in accordance with preliminary negotiations by the issuance of 52,500 shares of common stock. The plan was approved by the stockholders and accomplished by the following transactions:

Jan. 12. Borrowed $6,000,000 from Livingston National Bank, giving a 5% mortgage note.

18. Issued 45,000 shares of preferred stock, receiving $85 per share in cash.

25. Issued 52,500 shares of common stock in exchange for land and a building, according to the plan.

No other transactions occurred during January.

Instructions

Journalize the entries to record the foregoing transactions.

PR 13-3B **Selected stock transactions**

Daley Welding Corporation sells and services pipe welding equipment in Illinois. The following selected accounts appear in the ledger of Daley Welding Corporation on May 1, 2012, the beginning of the current fiscal year:

Preferred 2% Stock, $40 par (50,000 shares authorized, 40,000 shares issued)	$ 1,600,000
Paid-In Capital in Excess of Par—Preferred Stock	240,000
Common Stock, $8 par (1,000,000 shares authorized, 750,000 shares issued)	6,000,000
Paid-In Capital in Excess of Par—Common Stock	2,500,000
Retained Earnings	43,175,000

During the year, the corporation completed a number of transactions affecting the stockholders' equity. They are summarized as follows:

a. Purchased 100,000 shares of treasury common for $1,500,000.

b. Sold 60,000 shares of treasury common for $1,080,000.

c. Issued 8,000 shares of preferred 2% stock at $50.

d. Issued 150,000 shares of common stock at $21, receiving cash.

e. Sold 25,000 shares of treasury common for $362,500.

f. Declared cash dividends of $0.80 per share on preferred stock and $0.11 per share on common stock.

g. Paid the cash dividends.

Instructions

Journalize the entries to record the transactions. Identify each entry by letter.

PR 13-4B   Entries for selected corporate transactions

Ruffalo Enterprises Inc. produces aeronautical navigation equipment. The stockholders' equity accounts of Ruffalo Enterprises Inc., with balances on January 1, 2012, are as follows:

Common Stock, $8 stated value (250,000 shares authorized, 175,000 shares issued)	$1,400,000
Paid-In Capital in Excess of Stated Value	700,000
Retained Earnings	1,840,000
Treasury Stock (40,000 shares, at cost)	400,000

The following selected transactions occurred during the year:

Jan.   9. Paid cash dividends of $0.10 per share on the common stock. The dividend had been properly recorded when declared on November 30 of the preceding fiscal year for $13,500.

Mar. 15. Sold all of the treasury stock for $540,000.

May 13. Issued 50,000 shares of common stock for $680,000.

June 14. Declared a 2% stock dividend on common stock, to be capitalized at the market price of the stock, which is $15 per share.

July 16. Issued the certificates for the dividend declared on June 14.

Oct. 30. Purchased 25,000 shares of treasury stock for $320,000.

Dec. 30. Declared a $0.12-per-share dividend on common stock.

31. Closed the credit balance of the income summary account, $775,000.

31. Closed the two dividends accounts to Retained Earnings.

Instructions

1. Enter the January 1 balances in T accounts for the stockholders' equity accounts listed. Also prepare T accounts for the following: Paid-In Capital from Sale of Treasury Stock; Stock Dividends Distributable; Stock Dividends; Cash Dividends.

2. Journalize the entries to record the transactions, and post to the eight selected accounts.

3. Prepare a retained earnings statement for the year ended December 31, 2012.

4. Prepare the Stockholders' Equity section of the December 31, 2012, balance sheet.

PR 13-5B   Entries for selected corporate transactions

Maui Outfitters Corporation manufactures and distributes leisure clothing. Selected transactions completed by Maui Outfitters during the current fiscal year are as follows:

Feb. 19. Split the common stock 4 for 1 and reduced the par from $80 to $20 per share. After the split, there were 600,000 common shares outstanding.

Mar.   1. Declared semiannual dividends of $1.20 on 75,000 shares of preferred stock and $0.08 on the 600,000 shares of $20 par common stock to stockholders of record on March 31, payable on April 30.

Apr. 30. Paid the cash dividends.

June 27. Purchased 90,000 shares of the corporation's own common stock at $24, recording the stock at cost.

Aug. 17. Sold 40,000 shares of treasury stock at $30, receiving cash.

Sept. 1. Declared semiannual dividends of $1.20 on the preferred stock and $0.12 on the common stock (before the stock dividend). In addition, a 1% common stock dividend was declared on the common stock outstanding, to be capitalized at the fair market value of the common stock, which is estimated at $28.

Oct. 31. Paid the cash dividends and issued the certificates for the common stock dividend.

Instructions

Journalize the transactions.

Cases & Projects

CP 13-1 Board of directors' actions

Bernie Ebbers, the CEO of WorldCom, a major telecommunications company, was having personal financial troubles. Ebbers pledged a large stake of his WorldCom stock as security for some personal loans. As the price of WorldCom stock sank, Ebbers' bankers threatened to sell his stock in order to protect their loans. To avoid having his stock sold, Ebbers asked the board of directors of WorldCom to loan him nearly $400 million of corporate assets at 2.5% interest to pay off his bankers. The board agreed to lend him the money.

➤ Comment on the decision of the board of directors in this situation.

CP 13-2 Ethics and professional conduct in business

Hazel Holden and Cedric Dalton are organizing Calgary Metals Unlimited Inc. to undertake a high-risk gold-mining venture in Canada. Hazel and Cedric tentatively plan to request authorization for 100,000,000 shares of common stock to be sold to the general public. Hazel and Cedric have decided to establish par of $0.02 per share in order to appeal to a wide variety of potential investors. Hazel and Cedric feel that investors would be more willing to invest in the company if they received a large quantity of shares for what might appear to be a "bargain" price.

➤ Discuss whether Hazel and Cedric are behaving in a professional manner.

CP 13-3 Issuing stock

Bio Engineering Inc. began operations on January 2, 2012, with the issuance of 250,000 shares of $80 par common stock. The sole stockholders of Bio Engineering Inc. are Jean Cushing and Dr. Louis Fong, who organized Bio Engineering Inc. with the objective of developing a new flu vaccine. Dr. Fong claims that the flu vaccine, which is nearing the final development stage, will protect individuals against 95% of the flu types that have been medically identified. To complete the project, Bio Engineering Inc. needs $40,000,000 of additional funds. The local banks have been unwilling to loan the funds because of the lack of sufficient collateral and the riskiness of the business.

The following is a conversation between Jean Cushing, the chief executive officer of Bio Engineering Inc., and Louis Fong, the leading researcher.

Jean: What are we going to do? The banks won't loan us any more money, and we've got to have $40 million to complete the project. We are so close! It would be a disaster to quit now. The only thing I can think of is to issue additional stock. Do you have any suggestions?

Louis: I guess you're right. But if the banks won't loan us any more money, how do you think we can find any investors to buy stock?

Jean: I've been thinking about that. What if we promise the investors that we will pay them 5% of net sales until they have received an amount equal to what they paid for the stock?

Louis: What happens when we pay back the $40 million? Do the investors get to keep the stock? If they do, it'll dilute our ownership.

Jean: How about, if after we pay back the $40 million, we make them turn in their stock for $120 per share? That's one and one-half times what they paid for it, plus they would have already gotten all their money back. That's a $120 profit per share for the investors.

Louis: It could work. We get our money, but don't have to pay any interest, dividends, or the $80 per share until we start generating net sales. At the same time, the investors could get their money back plus $120 per share profit.

Jean: We'll need current financial statements for the new investors. I'll get our accountant working on them and contact our attorney to draw up a legally binding contract for the new investors. Yes, this could work.

In late 2012, the attorney and the various regulatory authorities approved the new stock offering, and 500,000 shares of common stock were privately sold to new investors at the stock's par of $80.

In preparing financial statements for 2012, Jean Cushing and Todd Nash, the controller for Bio Engineering Inc., have the following conversation:

Todd: Jean, I've got a problem.

Jean: What's that, Todd?

Todd: Issuing common stock to raise that additional $40 million was a great idea. But . . .

Jean: But what?

Todd: I've got to prepare the 2012 annual financial statements, and I am not sure how to classify the common stock.

Jean: What do you mean? It's common stock.

Todd: I'm not so sure. I called the auditor and explained how we are contractually obligated to pay the new stockholders 5% of net sales until $80 per share is paid. Then, we may be obligated to pay them $120 per share.

Jean: So . . .

Todd: So the auditor thinks that we should classify the additional issuance of $40 million as debt, not stock! And, if we put the $40 million on the balance sheet as debt, we will violate our other loan agreements with the banks. And, if these agreements are violated, the banks may call in all our debt immediately. If they do that, we are in deep trouble. We'll probably have to file for bankruptcy. We just don't have the cash to pay off the banks.

1. ▬▬▬▶ Discuss the arguments for and against classifying the issuance of the $40 million of stock as debt.

2. ▬▬▬▶ What do you think might be a practical solution to this classification problem?

CP 13-4   Interpret stock exchange listing

The following stock exchange data for General Electric (GE) were taken from the Yahoo! Finance Web site on April 29, 2010:

Gen Electric Co (NYSE: GE)

Last Trade:	19.49	Prev. Clos:	18.95
Trade Time:	4:00 PM EST	1y Target Est:	22.09
Change:	0.54	Day's Range:	19.03–19.49
	(2.85%)	52wk Range:	10.50–19.69
		Volume:	70,066,312
		Div & Yield:	0.40 (2.40%)

a. If you owned 500 shares of GE, what amount would you receive as a quarterly dividend?

b. Compute the percentage increase in price from the Previous Close to the Last Trade. Round to two decimal places.

c. What is GE's percentage change in market price from the 52-week low to the Previous Close on April 28, 2010? Round to one decimal place.

d. If you bought 500 shares of GE at the Last Trade price on April 29, 2010, how much would it cost, and who gets the money?

CP 13-5   Dividends

Cikan Designs Inc. has paid quarterly cash dividends since 2001. These dividends have steadily increased from $0.02 per share to the latest dividend declaration of $0.40 per share. The board of directors would like to continue this trend and is hesitant to suspend or decrease the amount of quarterly dividends. Unfortunately, sales dropped sharply in the fourth quarter of 2012 because of worsening economic conditions and increased competition. As a result, the board is uncertain as to whether it should declare a dividend for the last quarter of 2012.

On November 1, 2012, Cikan Designs Inc. borrowed $3,600,000 from Metro National Bank to use in modernizing its retail stores and to expand its product line in reaction to its competition. The terms of the 10-year, 6% loan require Cikan Designs Inc. to:

a. Pay monthly interest on the last day of the month.

b. Pay $360,000 of the principal each November 1, beginning in 2013.

c. Maintain a current ratio (current assets/current liabilities) of 2.

d. Maintain a minimum balance (a compensating balance) of $100,000 in its Metro National Bank account.

On December 31, 2012, $900,000 of the $3,600,000 loan had been disbursed in modernization of the retail stores and in expansion of the product line. Cikan Designs Inc.'s balance sheet as of December 31, 2012, is shown below.

Cikan Designs Inc.
Balance Sheet
December 31, 2012

Assets

Current assets:			
Cash		$ 250,000	
Marketable securities		2,700,000	
Accounts receivable	$ 700,000		
Less allowance for doubtful accounts	50,000	650,000	
Merchandise inventory		2,680,000	
Prepaid expenses		20,000	
Total current assets			$ 6,300,000
Property, plant, and equipment:			
Land		$ 500,000	
Buildings	$4,750,000		
Less accumulated depreciation...........	1,140,000	3,610,000	
Equipment	$2,320,000		
Less accumulated depreciation	730,000	1,590,000	
Total property, plant, and equipment			5,700,000
Total assets......................................			$12,000,000

Liabilities

Current liabilities:		
Accounts payable	$1,430,000	
Notes payable (Metro National Bank)........	360,000	
Salaries payable...........................	10,000	
Total current liabilities...................		$1,800,000
Long-term liabilities:		
Notes payable (Metro National Bank)........		3,240,000
Total liabilities		$5,040,000

Stockholders' Equity

Paid-in capital:		
Common stock, $25 par (200,000 shares		
authorized, 180,000 shares issued)	$4,500,000	
Excess of issue price over par	270,000	
Total paid-in capital	$4,770,000	
Retained earnings............................	2,190,000	
Total stockholders' equity.....................		6,960,000
Total liabilities and stockholders' equity.......		$12,000,000

The board of directors is scheduled to meet January 8, 2013, to discuss the results of operations for 2012 and to consider the declaration of dividends for the fourth quarter of 2012. The chairman of the board has asked for your advice on the declaration of dividends.

1. ▬▬▬ What factors should the board consider in deciding whether to declare a cash dividend?

2. ▬▬▬ The board is considering the declaration of a stock dividend instead of a cash dividend. Discuss the issuance of a stock dividend from the point of view of (a) a stockholder and (b) the board of directors.

Internet Project

CP 13-6   Profiling a corporation

Group Project

Select a public corporation you are familiar with or which interests you. Using the Internet, your school library, and other sources, develop a short (1 to 2 pages) profile of the corporation. Include in your profile the following information:

1. Name of the corporation.
2. State of incorporation.
3. Nature of its operations.
4. Total assets for the most recent balance sheet.
5. Total revenues for the most recent income statement.
6. Net income for the most recent income statement.
7. Classes of stock outstanding.
8. Market price of the stock outstanding.
9. High and low price of the stock for the past year.
10. Dividends paid for each share of stock during the past year.

In groups of three or four, discuss each corporate profile. Select one of the corporations, assuming that your group has $100,000 to invest in its stock. Summarize why your group selected the corporation it did and how financial accounting information may have affected your decision. Keep track of the performance of your corporation's stock for the remainder of the term.

Note: Most major corporations maintain "home pages" on the Internet. This home page provides a variety of information on the corporation and often includes the corporation's financial statements. In addition, the New York Stock Exchange Web site **(http://www.nyse .com)** includes links to the home pages of many listed companies. Financial statements can also be accessed using EDGAR, the electronic archives of financial statements filed with the Securities and Exchange Commission (SEC).

SEC documents can also be retrieved using the EdgarScan™ service at **http://www.sec .gov/edgar/searchedgar/companysearch.html.** To obtain annual report information, key in a company name in the appropriate space. Edgar will list the reports available to you for the company you've selected. Select the most recent annual report filing, identified as a 10-K or 10-K405.

© Under Armour®/PRNewsFoto/AP Photos Publicity

Long-Term Liabilities: Bonds and Notes

Under Armour®

Most of us don't have enough money in our bank accounts to buy a house or a car by simply writing a check. Just imagine if you had to save the entire purchase price of a house before you could buy it! To help us make these types of purchases, banks will typically lend us the money, as long as we agree to repay the loan with interest in smaller future payments. Loans such as this, or long-term debt, allow us to purchase assets such as houses and cars today, which benefit us over the long term.

The use of debt can also help a business reach its objectives. Most businesses have to borrow money in order to acquire assets that they will use to generate income. For example, **Under Armour®**, a maker of performance athletic clothing, uses debt to acquire assets that

it needs to manufacture and sell its products. Since it began in 1995, the company has used long-term debt to transform itself from a small business to a leading athletic wear company. The company now sells products in over 8,000 retail stores across the world. In addition, Under Armour® products are used by a number of teams in the National Football League, Major League Baseball, the National Hockey League, and in Olympic sports.

While debt can help companies like Under Armour® grow to achieve financial success, too much debt can be a financial burden that may even lead to bankruptcy. Just like individuals, businesses must manage debt wisely. In this chapter, we will discuss the nature of, accounting for, analysis of, and investments in long-term debt.

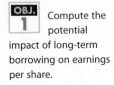

OBJ. 1 Compute the potential impact of long-term borrowing on earnings per share.

Financing Corporations

Corporations finance their operations using the following sources:

1. Short-term debt, such as purchasing goods or services on account.
2. Long-term debt, such as issuing bonds or notes payable.
3. Equity, such as issuing common or preferred stock.

Short-term debt including the purchase of goods and services on account and the issuance of short-term notes payable was discussed in Chapter 11, while issuing equity in the form of common or preferred stock was discussed in Chapter 13. This chapter focuses on the use of long-term debt such as bonds and notes payable to finance a company's operations.

A **bond** is a form of an interest-bearing note. Like a note, a bond requires periodic interest payments with the face amount to be repaid at the maturity date. As creditors of the corporation, bondholder claims on the corporation's assets rank ahead of stockholders.

To illustrate the effects of long-term financing, assume Huckadee Corporation is considering the following plans to issue debt and equity:

	Plan 1		Plan 2		Plan 3	
	Amount	**Percent**	**Amount**	**Percent**	**Amount**	**Percent**
Issue 12% bonds	—	0%	—	0%	$2,000,000	50%
Issue 9% preferred stock, $50 par value	—	0	$2,000,000	50	1,000,000	25
Issue common stock, $10 par value	$4,000,000	100	2,000,000	50	1,000,000	25
Total amount of financing	$4,000,000	100%	$4,000,000	100%	$4,000,000	100%

Each of the preceding plans finances some of the corporation's operations by issuing common stock. However, the percentage financed by common stock varies from 100% (Plan 1) to 25% (Plan 3). In deciding among financing plans, the effect on earnings per share is often considered.

Earnings per share (EPS) measures the income earned by each share of common stock. It is computed as follows:[1]

$$\text{Earnings per Share} = \frac{\text{Net Income} - \text{Preferred Dividends}}{\text{Number of Common Shares Outstanding}}$$

To illustrate, assume the following data for Huckadee Corporation:

1. Earnings before interest and income taxes are $800,000.
2. The tax rate is 40%.
3. All bonds or stocks are issued at their par or face amount.

The effect of the preceding financing plans on Huckadee's net income and earnings per share is shown in Exhibit 1.

	Plan 1	Plan 2	Plan 3
12% bonds	—	—	$2,000,000
Preferred 9% stock, $50 par	—	$2,000,000	1,000,000
Common stock, $10 par	$4,000,000	2,000,000	1,000,000
Total	$4,000,000	$4,000,000	$4,000,000
Earnings before interest and income tax	$ 800,000	$ 800,000	$ 800,000
Deduct interest on bonds	—	—	240,000
Income before income tax	$ 800,000	$ 800,000	$ 560,000
Deduct income tax	320,000	320,000	224,000
Net income	$ 480,000	$ 480,000	$ 336,000
Dividends on preferred stock	—	180,000	90,000
Available for dividends on common stock	$ 480,000	$ 300,000	$ 246,000
Shares of common stock outstanding	÷ 400,000	÷ 200,000	÷ 100,000
Earnings per share on common stock	$ 1.20	$ 1.50	$ 2.46

EXHIBIT 1

Effect of Alternative Financing Plans—$800,000 Earnings

Exhibit 1 indicates that Plan 3 yields the highest earnings per share on common stock and, thus, is the most attractive for common stockholders. If the estimated earnings are more than $800,000, the difference between the earnings per share to common stockholders under Plans 1 and 3 is even greater.[2]

If smaller earnings occur, however, Plans 1 and 2 become more attractive to common stockholders. To illustrate, Exhibit 2 shows the effect on earnings per share if estimated earnings are $440,000 rather than $800,000 as estimated in Exhibit 1.

	Plan 1	Plan 2	Plan 3
12% bonds	—	—	$2,000,000
Preferred 9% stock, $50 par	—	$2,000,000	1,000,000
Common stock, $10 par	$4,000,000	2,000,000	1,000,000
Total	$4,000,000	$4,000,000	$4,000,000
Earnings before interest and income tax	$ 440,000	$ 440,000	$ 440,000
Deduct interest on bonds	—	—	240,000
Income before income tax	$ 440,000	$ 440,000	$ 200,000
Deduct income tax	176,000	176,000	80,000
Net income	$ 264,000	$ 264,000	$ 120,000
Dividends on preferred stock	—	180,000	90,000
Available for dividends on common stock	$ 264,000	$ 84,000	$ 30,000
Shares of common stock outstanding	÷ 400,000	÷ 200,000	÷ 100,000
Earnings per share on common stock	$ 0.66	$ 0.42	$ 0.30

EXHIBIT 2

Effect of Alternative Financing Plans—$440,000 Earnings

1 Earnings per share is also discussed in the *Financial Analysis and Interpretation* section of Chapter 13 and in Chapter 17.

2 The higher earnings per share under Plan 3 is due to a finance concept known as *leverage*. This concept is discussed further in Chapter 17.

In addition to earnings per share, the corporation should consider other factors in deciding among the financing plans. For example, if bonds are issued, the interest and the face value of the bonds at maturity must be paid. If these payments are not made, the bondholders could seek court action and force the company into bankruptcy. In contrast, a corporation is not legally obligated to pay dividends on preferred or common stock.

Example Exercise 14-1 **Alternative Financing Plans** **OBJ. 1**

Gonzales Co. is considering the following alternative plans for financing its company:

	Plan 1	Plan 2
Issue 10% bonds (at face value)	—	$2,000,000
Issue common stock, $10 par	$3,000,000	1,000,000

Income tax is estimated at 40% of income.

Determine the earnings per share of common stock under the two alternative financing plans, assuming income before bond interest and income tax is $750,000.

Follow My Example 14-1

	Plan 1	Plan 2
Earnings before bond interest and income tax	$750,000	$750,000
Bond interest	0	200,000[2]
Balance	$750,000	$550,000
Income tax	300,000[1]	220,000[3]
Net income	$450,000	$330,000
Dividends on preferred stock	0	0
Earnings available for common stock	$450,000	$330,000
Number of common shares	÷300,000	÷100,000
Earnings per share on common stock	$ 1.50	$ 3.30

[1]$750,000 × 40%   [2]$2,000,000 × 10%   [3]$550,000 × 40%

Practice Exercises: **PE 14-1A, PE 14-1B**

OBJ. 2 Describe the characteristics and terminology of bonds payable.

Nature of Bonds Payable

Corporate bonds normally differ in face amount, interest rates, interest payment dates, and maturity dates. Bonds also differ in other ways such as whether corporate assets are pledged in support of the bonds.

Bond Characteristics and Terminology

Dow Chemical Company's 8.55% bonds, maturing in 2019, sold for 119.753 on January 19, 2010.

The underlying contract between the company issuing bonds and the bondholders is called a **bond indenture** or *trust indenture*. A bond issue is normally divided into a number of individual bonds. The face amount of each bond is call the principal. This is the amount that must be repaid on the dates the bonds mature. The principal is usually $1,000, or a multiple of $1,000. The interest on bonds may be payable annually, semiannually, or quarterly. Most bonds pay interest semiannually.

When all bonds of an issue mature at the same time, they are called *term bonds*. If the bonds mature over several dates, they are called *serial bonds*. For example, one-tenth of an issue of $1,000,000 bonds, or $100,000, may mature 16 years from the issue date, another $100,000 in the 17th year, and so on.

Bonds that may be exchanged for other securities, such as common stock, are called *convertible bonds*. Bonds that a corporation reserves the right to redeem before their maturity are called *callable bonds*. Bonds issued on the basis of the general credit of the corporation are called *debenture bonds*.

Proceeds from Issuing Bonds

When a corporation issues bonds, the proceeds received for the bonds depend on:

1. The face amount of the bonds, which is the amount due at the maturity date.
2. The interest rate on the bonds.
3. The market rate of interest for similar bonds.

The face amount and the interest rate on the bonds are identified in the bond indenture. The interest rate to be paid on the face amount of the bond is called the **contract rate** or *coupon rate*.

The **market rate of interest**, sometimes called the **effective rate of interest**, is the rate determined from sales and purchases of similar bonds. The market rate of interest is affected by a variety of factors, including investors' expectations of current and future economic conditions.

By comparing the market and contract rates of interest, it can be determined whether the bonds will sell for more than, less than, or at their face amount, as shown below.

If the market rate equals the contract rate, bonds will sell at the **face amount**.

If the market rate is greater than the contract rate, the bonds will sell for less than their face value. The face amount of the bonds less the selling price is called a **discount**. A bond sells at a discount because buyers are not willing to pay the full face amount for bonds whose contract rate is lower than the market rate.

If the market rate is less than the contract rate, the bonds will sell for more than their face value. The selling price of the bonds less the face amount is called a **premium**. A bond sells at a premium because buyers are willing to pay more than the face amount for bonds whose contract rate is higher than the market rate.

The price of a bond is quoted as a percentage of the bond's face value. For example, a $1,000 bond quoted at 98 could be purchased or sold for $980 ($1,000 × 0.98). Likewise, bonds quoted at 109 could be purchased or sold for $1,090 ($1,000 × 1.09).

U.S. GOVERNMENT DEBT

Like many corporations, the U.S. government issues debt to finance its operations. The debt is issued by the U.S. Treasury Department in the form of U.S. Treasury bills, notes, and bonds, which have the following characteristics:

	Issued at	Interest Paid	Maturity
U.S. Treasury bills	Discount	None	1 year or less
U.S. Treasury notes	Face value	Semiannual	1 to 10 years
U.S. Treasury bonds	Face value	Semiannual	10 years or more

At the end of 2008, total U.S. government debt issued by the federal government was $9,985 billion. The Congressional Budget Office estimated that this amount would grow to $18,350 billion by 2014.

Source: Historical Tables: Budget of the U.S. Government, Fiscal Year 2010, U.S. Office of Management and Budget.

Journalize entries for bonds payable.

Accounting for Bonds Payable

Bonds may be issued at their face amount, a discount, or a premium. When bonds are issued at less or more than their face amount, the discount or premium must be amortized over the life of the bonds. At the maturity date, the face amount must be repaid. In some situations, a corporation may redeem bonds before their maturity date by repurchasing them from investors.

Bonds Issued at Face Amount

If the market rate of interest is equal to the contract rate of interest, the bonds will sell for their face amount or a price of 100. To illustrate, assume that on January 1, 2011, Eastern Montana Communications Inc. issued the following bonds:

Face amount	$100,000
Contract rate of interest	12%
Interest paid semiannually on June 30 and December 31.	
Term of bonds	5 years
Market rate of interest	12%

Since the contract rate of interest and the market rate of interest are the same, the bonds will sell at their face amount. The entry to record the issuance of the bonds is as follows:

2011 Jan.	1	Cash		100,000	
		Bonds Payable			100,000
		Issued $100,000 bonds payable at face amount.			

Every six months (on June 30 and December 31) after the bonds are issued, interest of $6,000 ($100,000 × 12% × ½) is paid. The first interest payment on June 30, 2011, is recorded as follows:

2011 June	30	Interest Expense		6,000	
		Cash			6,000
		Paid six months' interest on bonds.			

At the maturity date, the payment of the principal of $100,000 is recorded as follows:

2015 Dec.	31	Bonds Payable		100,000	
		Cash			100,000
		Paid bond principal at maturity date.			

Bonds Issued at a Discount

If the market rate of interest is more than the contract rate of interest, the bonds will sell for less than their face amount. This is because investors are not willing to pay the full face amount for bonds that pay a lower contract rate of interest than the rate they could earn on similar bonds (market rate). The difference between the face amount and the selling price of the bonds is the bond discount.[3]

To illustrate, assume that on January 1, 2011, Western Wyoming Distribution Inc. issued the following bonds:

3 The price that investors are willing to pay for the bonds depends on present value concepts. Present value concepts, including the computation of bond prices, are described and illustrated in Appendix 1 at the end of this chapter.

Face amount	$100,000
Contract rate of interest	12%
Interest paid semiannually on June 30 and December 31.	
Term of bonds.	5 years
Market rate of interest	13%

Note:
Bonds will sell at a discount when the market rate of interest is higher than the contract rate.

Since the contract rate of interest is less than the market rate of interest, the bonds will sell at less than their face amount. Assuming the bonds sell for $96,406, the entry to record the issuance of the bonds is as follows:

2011					
Jan.	1	Cash		96,406	
		Discount on Bonds Payable		3,594	
		Bonds Payable			100,000
		Issued $100,000 bonds at discount.			

The $96,406 may be viewed as the amount investors are willing to pay for bonds that have a lower contract rate of interest (12%) than the market rate (13%). The discount is the market's way of adjusting the contract rate of interest to the higher market rate of interest.

The account, Discount on Bonds Payable, is a contra account to Bonds Payable and has a normal debit balance. It is subtracted from Bonds Payable to determine the carrying amount (or book value) of the bonds payable. Thus, after the preceding entry, the carrying amount of the bonds payable is $96,406 ($100,000 − $3,594).

Example Exercise 14-2   Issuing Bonds at a Discount   OBJ. 3

On the first day of the fiscal year, a company issues a $1,000,000, 6%, five-year bond that pays semiannual interest of $30,000 ($1,000,000 × 6% × ½), receiving cash of $936,420. Journalize the entry to record the issuance of the bonds.

Follow My Example 14-2

Cash	936,420	
Discount on Bonds Payable	63,580	
Bonds Payable		1,000,000

Practice Exercises: **PE 14-2A, PE 14-2B**

Amortizing a Bond Discount

A bond discount must be amortized to interest expense over the life of the bond. The entry to amortize a bond discount is shown below.

		Interest Expense		XXX	
		Discount on Bonds Payable			XXX

The preceding entry may be made annually as an adjusting entry, or it may be combined with the semiannual interest payment. In the latter case, the entry would be as follows:

		Interest Expense		XXX	
		Discount on Bonds Payable			XXX
		Cash (amount of semiannual interest)			XXX

The two methods of computing the amortization of a bond discount are:

1. *Straight-line method*
2. *Effective interest rate method,* sometimes called the *interest method*

The **effective interest rate method** is required by generally accepted accounting principles. However, the straight-line method may be used if the results do not differ significantly from the interest method. The straight-line method is used in this chapter. The effective interest rate method is described and illustrated in Appendix 2 at the end of this chapter.

The straight-line method provides equal amounts of amortization. To illustrate, amortization of the Western Wyoming Distribution bond discount of $3,594 is computed below.

Discount on bonds payable	$3,594
Term of bonds	5 years
Semiannual amortization	$359.40 ($3,594/10 periods)

The combined entry to record the first interest payment and the amortization of the discount is as follows:

2011					
June	30	Interest Expense		6,359.40	
		Discount on Bonds Payable			359.40
		Cash			6,000.00
		Paid semiannual interest and			
		amortized ¹⁄₁₀ of bond discount.			

The preceding entry is made on each interest payment date. Thus, the amount of the semiannual interest expense on the bonds ($6,359.40) remains the same over the life of the bonds.

The effect of the discount amortization is to increase the interest expense from $6,000.00 to $6,359.40 on every semiannual interest payment date. In effect, this increases the contract rate of interest from 12% to a rate of interest that approximates the market rate of 13%. In addition, as the discount is amortized, the carrying amount of the bonds increases until it equals the face amount of the bonds on the maturity date.

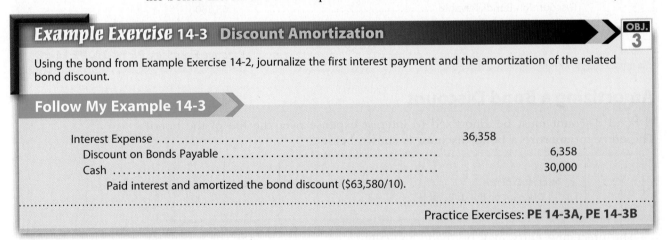

Example Exercise 14-3 **Discount Amortization** **OBJ. 3**

Using the bond from Example Exercise 14-2, journalize the first interest payment and the amortization of the related bond discount.

Follow My Example 14-3

Interest Expense	36,358	
Discount on Bonds Payable		6,358
Cash		30,000
Paid interest and amortized the bond discount ($63,580/10).		

Practice Exercises: **PE 14-3A, PE 14-3B**

Note:
Bonds will sell at a premium when the market rate of interest is less than the contract rate.

Bonds Issued at a Premium

If the market rate of interest is less than the contract rate of interest, the bonds will sell for more than their face amount. This is because investors are willing to pay more for bonds that pay a higher contract rate of interest than the rate they could earn on similar bonds (market rate).

To illustrate, assume that on January 1, 2011, Northern Idaho Transportation Inc. issued the following bonds:

Face amount	$100,000
Contract rate of interest	12%
Interest paid semiannually on	
June 30 and December 31.	
Term of bonds	5 years
Market rate of interest	11%

Since the contract rate of interest is more than the market rate of interest, the bonds will sell at more than their face amount. Assuming the bonds sell for $103,769, the entry to record the issuance of the bonds is as follows:

2011					
Jan.	1	Cash		103,769	
		Bonds Payable			100,000
		Premium on Bonds Payable			3,769
		Issued $100,000 bonds at a premium.			

The $3,769 premium may be viewed as the extra amount investors are willing to pay for bonds that have a higher contract rate of interest (12%) than the market rate (11%). The premium is the market's way of adjusting the contract rate of interest to the lower market rate of interest.

The account, Premium on Bonds Payable, has a normal credit balance. It is added to Bonds Payable to determine the carrying amount (or book value) of the bonds payable. Thus, after the preceding entry, the carrying amount of the bonds payable is $103,769 ($100,000 + $3,769).

Example Exercise 14-4 Issuing Bonds at a Premium

OBJ. 3

A company issues a $2,000,000, 12%, five-year bond that pays semiannual interest of $120,000 ($2,000,000 × 12% × ½), receiving cash of $2,154,440. Journalize the bond issuance.

Follow My Example 14-4

Cash	2,154,440	
Premium on Bonds Payable		154,440
Bonds Payable		2,000,000

Practice Exercises: **PE 14-4A, PE 14-4B**

Amortizing a Bond Premium

Like bond discounts, a bond premium must be amortized over the life of the bond. The amortization can be computed using either the straight-line or the effective interest rate method. The entry to amortize a bond premium is shown below.

		Premium on Bonds Payable		XXX	
		Interest Expense			XXX

The preceding entry may be made annually as an adjusting entry, or it may be combined with the semiannual interest payment. In the latter case, it would be:

		Interest Expense		XXX	
		Premium on Bonds Payable		XXX	
		Cash (amount of semiannual interest)			XXX

To illustrate, amortization of the preceding premium of $3,769 is computed using the straight-line method as shown below.

Premium on bonds payable...................	$3,769
Term of bonds...............................	5 years
Semiannual amortization	$376.90 ($3,769/10 periods)

The combined entry to record the first interest payment and the amortization of the discount is as follows:

2011					
June	30	Interest Expense		5,623.10	
		Premium on Bonds Payable		376.90	
		Cash			6,000.00
		Paid semiannual interest and			
		amortized $^{1}/_{10}$ of bond discount.			

The preceding entry is made on each interest payment date. Thus, the amount of the semiannual interest expense ($5,623.10) on the bonds remains the same over the life of the bonds.

The effect of the premium amortization is to decrease the interest expense from $6,000.00 to $5,623.10. In effect, this decreases the rate of interest from 12% to a rate of interest that approximates the market rate of 11%. In addition, as the premium is amortized, the carrying amount of the bonds decreases until it equals the face amount of bonds on the maturity date.

Example Exercise 14-5 Premium Amortization

OBJ. 3

Using the bond from Example Exercise 14-4, journalize the first interest payment and the amortization of the related bond premium.

Follow My Example 14-5

Interest Expense	104,556	
Premium on Bonds Payable	15,444	
Cash...		120,000
Paid interest and amortized the bond premium ($154,440/10).		

Practice Exercises: **PE 14-5A, PE 14-5B**

BusinessConnection

GENERAL MOTORS BONDS

In June 2009, after years of losses and weakening financial condition, General Motors Corporation, maker of Chevrolet, Saturn, Pontiac, and Saab cars and trucks, was forced to file for bankruptcy. As part of the bankruptcy and restructuring plan, the U.S. government made a multibillion-dollar cash investment in the company in exchange for 60% of the restructured company's common stock. In addition, General Motors' bondholders were forced to exchange their bonds for the remaining common shares in the restructured company, which were worth only a fraction of the bonds' face value. Bondholders also lost the security of interest payments and repayment of the bonds' face value at maturity.

Source: C. Isidore, "GM Bankruptcy: End of an Era," *CNNMoney.com*, June 2, 2009.

Bond Redemption

A corporation may redeem or call bonds before they mature. This is often done when the market rate of interest declines below the contract rate of interest. In such cases, the corporation may issue new bonds at a lower interest rate and use the proceeds to redeem the original bond issue.

Callable bonds can be redeemed by the issuing corporation within the period of time and at the price stated in the bond indenture. Normally, the call price is above the face value. A corporation may also redeem its bonds by purchasing them on the open market.[4]

A corporation usually redeems its bonds at a price different from the carrying amount (or book value) of the bonds. The **carrying amount** of bonds payable is the face amount of the bonds less any unamortized discount or plus any unamortized premium. A gain or loss may be realized on a bond redemption as follows:

1. A *gain* is recorded if the price paid for redemption is below the bond carrying amount.
2. A *loss* is recorded if the price paid for the redemption is above the carrying amount.

Gains and losses on the redemption of bonds are reported in the *Other income (loss)* section of the income statement.

To illustrate, assume that on June 30, 2011, a corporation has the following bond issue:

Face amount of bonds	$100,000
Premium on bonds payable	4,000

On June 30, 2011, the corporation redeemed one-fourth ($25,000) of these bonds in the market for $24,000. The entry to record the redemption is as follows:

2011					
June	30	Bonds Payable		25,000	
		Premium on Bonds Payable		1,000	
		Cash			24,000
		Gain on Redemption of Bonds			2,000
		Redeemed $25,000 bonds for $24,000.			

In the preceding entry, only the portion of the premium related to the redeemed bonds ($4,000 × 25% = $1,000) is written off. The difference between the carrying amount of the bonds redeemed, $26,000 ($25,000 + $1,000), and the redemption price, $24,000, is recorded as a gain.

Assume that the corporation calls the remaining $75,000 of outstanding bonds, which are held by a private investor, for $79,500 on July 1, 2011. The entry to record the redemption is as follows:

2011					
July	1	Bonds Payable		75,000	
		Premium on Bonds Payable		3,000	
		Loss on Redemption of Bonds		1,500	
		Cash			79,500
		Redeemed $75,000 bonds for $79,500.			

Example Exercise 14-6   Redemption of Bonds Payable

OBJ. 3

A $500,000 bond issue on which there is an unamortized discount of $40,000 is redeemed for $475,000. Journalize the redemption of the bonds.

(Continued)

[4] Some bond indentures require the corporation issuing the bonds to transfer cash to a special cash fund, called a *sinking fund,* over the life of the bond. Such funds help assure investors that there will be adequate cash to pay the bonds at their maturity date.

OBJ. 4 Describe and illustrate the accounting for installment notes.

Individuals typically use mortgage notes when buying a house or car.

Installment Notes

Corporations often finance their operations by issuing bonds payable. As an alternative, corporations may issue installment notes. An **installment note** is a debt that requires the borrower to make equal periodic payments to the lender for the term of the note. Unlike bonds, each note payment includes the following:

1. Payment of a portion of the amount initially borrowed, called the *principal*
2. Payment of interest on the outstanding balance

At the end of the note's term, the principal will have been repaid in full.

Installment notes are often used to purchase specific assets such as equipment, and are often secured by the purchased asset. When a note is secured by an asset, it is called a **mortgage note**. If the borrower fails to pay a mortgage note, the lender has the right to take possession of the pledged asset and sell it to pay off the debt. Mortgage notes are typically issued by an individual bank.

Issuing an Installment Note

When an installment note is issued, an entry is recorded debiting Cash and crediting Notes Payable. To illustrate, assume that Lewis Company issues the following installment note to City National Bank on January 1, 2010.

Principal amount of note	$24,000
Interest rate	6%
Term of note	5 years
Annual payments	$5,698[5]

The entry to record the issuance of the note is as follows:

2010					
Jan.	1	Cash		24,000	
		Notes Payable			24,000
		Issued installment note for cash.			

Annual Payments

The preceding note payable requires Lewis Company to repay the principal and interest in equal payments of $5,698 beginning December 3, 2010, for each of the next five years. Unlike bonds, however, each installment note payment includes an interest and principal component.

The interest portion of an installment note payment is computed by multiplying the interest rate by the carrying amount (book value) of the note at the beginning of the period. The principal portion of the payment is then computed as the difference between the total installment note payment (cash paid) and the interest component. These computations are illustrated in Exhibit 3 as follows:

[5] The amount of the annual payment is calculated by using the present value concepts discussed in Appendix 1. The annual payment of $5,698 is computed by dividing the $24,000 loan amount by the present value of an annuity of $1 for 5 periods at 6% (4.21236) from Exhibit 5 (rounded to the nearest dollar).

EXHIBIT 3   **Amortization of Installment Notes**

For the Year Ending	A January 1 Carrying Amount	B Note Payment (cash paid)	C Interest Expense (6% of January 1 Note Carrying Amount)	D Decrease in Notes Payable (B – C)	E December 31 Carrying Amount (A – D)
December 31, 2010	$24,000	$ 5,698	$ 1,440 (6% of $24,000)	$ 4,258	$19,742
December 31, 2011	19,742	5,698	1,185 (6% of $19,742)	4,513	15,229
December 31, 2012	15,229	5,698	914 (6% of $15,229)	4,784	10,445
December 31, 2013	10,445	5,698	627 (6% of $10,445)	5,071	5,374
December 31, 2014	5,374	5,698	324* (6% of $5,374)	5,374	0
		$28,490	$4,490	$24,000	

*Rounded ($5,374 – $5,698).

1. The January 1, 2010, carrying value (Column A) equals the amount borrowed from the bank. The January 1 balance in the following years equals the December 31 balance from the prior year.
2. The note payment (Column B) remains constant at $5,698, the annual cash payments required by the bank.
3. The interest expense (Column C) is computed at 6% of the installment note carrying amount at the beginning of each year. As a result, the interest expense decreases each year.
4. Notes payable decreases each year by the amount of the principal repayment (Column D). The principal repayment is computed by subtracting the interest expense (Column C) from the total payment (Column B). The principal repayment (Column D) increases each year as the interest expense decreases (Column C).
5. The carrying amount on December 31 (Column E) of the note decreases from $24,000, the initial amount borrowed, to $0 at the end of the five years.

The entry to record the first payment on December 31, 2010, is as follows:

2010 Dec.	31	Interest Expense		1,440	
		Notes Payable		4,258	
		Cash			5,698
		Paid principal and interest on installment note.			

The entry to record the second payment on December 31, 2011, is as follows:

2011 Dec.	31	Interest Expense		1,185	
		Notes Payable		4,513	
		Cash			5,698
		Paid principal and interest on installment note.			

As the prior entries show, the cash payment is the same in each year. The interest and principal repayment, however, change each year. This is because the carrying amount (book value) of the note decreases each year as principal is repaid, which decreases the interest component the next period.

The entry to record the final payment on December 31, 2014, is as follows:

2014 Dec.	31	Interest Expense		324	
		Notes Payable		5,374	
		Cash			5,698
		Paid principal and interest on installment note.			

After the final payment, the carrying amount on the note is zero, indicating that the note has been paid in full. Any assets that secure the note would then be released by the bank.

Example Exercise 14-7 Journalizing Installment Notes

OBJ. 4

On the first day of the fiscal year, a company issues a $30,000, 10%, five-year installment note that has annual payments of $7,914. The first note payment consists of $3,000 of interest and $4,914 of principal repayment.

a. Journalize the entry to record the issuance of the installment note.
b. Journalize the first annual note payment.

Follow My Example 14-7

a.

Cash			30,000	
Notes Payable				30,000
Issued $30,000 of installment note for cash.				

b.

Interest Expense			3,000	
Notes Payable			4,914	
Cash				7,914
Paid principal and interest on installment note.				

Practice Exercises: **PE 14-7A, PE 14-7B**

Integrity, Objectivity, and Ethics in Business

LIAR'S LOANS

One of the main causes of the 2008 financial crisis was a widespread inability of homeowners to repay their home mortgages. While the weak economy contributed to these problems, many mortgage defaults were the result of unethical lending practices in the form of "stated income" or "liar's" loans. In a conventional home mortgage, lenders base the amount of a loan on the borrower's income, expenses, and total assets. These amounts are verified by reviewing the borrower's tax returns, bank statements, and payroll records. Liar's loans, however, based the amount of the loan on the borrower's "stated income," without verifying it through sources such as tax returns, W-2 statements, or payroll records. Without independent verification, borrowers often falsified or lied about their "stated income" in order to obtain a larger loan than they were qualified for. Once in their homes, many of these borrowers were unable to make their loan payments, causing them to default on their home mortgages.

OBJ. 5

Describe and illustrate the reporting of long-term liabilities including bonds and notes payable.

Reporting Long-Term Liabilities

Bonds payable and notes payable are reported as liabilities on the balance sheet. Any portion of the bonds or notes that is due within one year is reported as a current liability. Any remaining bonds or notes are reported as a long-term liability.

Any unamortized premium is reported as an addition to the face amount of the bonds. Any unamortized discount is reported as a deduction from the face amount of the bonds. A description of the bonds and notes should also be reported either on the face of the financial statements or in the accompanying notes.

The reporting of bonds and notes payable for Mornin' Joe is shown below.

Mornin' Joe
Balance Sheet
December 31, 2012

Current liabilities:		
Accounts payable	$133,000	
Notes payable (current portion)	200,000	
Salaries and wages payable	42,000	
Payroll taxes payable	16,400	
Interest payable	40,000	
Total current liabilities		$ 431,400
Long-term liabilities:		
Bonds payable, 8%, due December 31, 2030	$500,000	
Less unamortized discount	16,000	$ 484,000
Notes payable		1,400,000
Total long-term liabilities		$1,884,000
Total liabilities		$2,315,400

Financial Analysis and Interpretation: Number of Times Interest Charges Are Earned

As we have discussed, the assets of a company are subject to the (1) claims of creditors and (2) the rights of owners. As creditors, bondholders are primarily concerned with the company's ability to make its periodic interest payments and repay the face amount of the bonds at maturity.

Analysts assess the risk that bondholders will not receive their interest payments by computing the **number of times interest charges are earned** during the year as follows:

$$\text{Number of Times Interest Charges Are Earned} = \frac{\text{Income Before Income Tax} + \text{Interest Expense}}{\text{Interest Expense}}$$

OBJ.
6 Describe and illustrate how the number of times interest charges are earned is used to evaluate a company's financial condition.

This ratio computes the number of times interest payments could be paid out of current period earnings, measuring the company's ability to make its interest payments. Because interest payments reduce income tax expense, the ratio is computed using income before tax.

To illustrate, the following data were taken from the 2008 annual report of Under Armour, Inc. (in thousands):

Interest expense	$ 850
Income before income tax	69,900

The number of times interest charges are earned for Under Armour, Inc., is computed as follows:

$$\text{Number of Times Interest Charges Are Earned} = \frac{\$69,900 + \$850}{\$850} = 83.24$$

Compare this to the number of times interest charges are earned for Southwest Airlines (an airline), and Verizon Communications (a telecommunications company) shown on the next page (in thousands):

	Under Armour	Southwest Airlines	Verizon Communications
Interest expense	$850	$105,000	$1,819,000
Income before income tax expense	$69,900	$278,000	$9,759,000
Number of times interest charges are earned	83.24	3.65	6.37

Under Armour's number of times interest charges are earned is 83.24, indicating that the company generates enough income before taxes to pay (cover) its interest payments 83.24 times. As a result, debtholders have extremely good protection in the event of an earnings decline. Compare this to Southwest Airlines, which only generates enough income before taxes to pay (cover) its interest payments 3.65 times. A small decrease in Southwest Airlines' earnings could jeopardize the payment of interest. Verizon Communications falls in between, with a ratio of 6.37.

Example Exercise 14-8 Number of Times Interest Charges Are Earned

OBJ. 6

Harris Industries reported the following on the company's income statement in 2012 and 2011:

	2012	2011
Interest expense	$ 200,000	$180,000
Income before income tax expense	1,000,000	720,000

a. Determine the number of times interest charges were earned for 2012 and 2011. Round to one decimal place.
b. Is the number of times interest charges are earned improving or declining?

Follow My Example 14-8

a. 2012:

$$\text{Number of times interest charges are earned: } 6.0 = \frac{\$1,000,000 + \$200,000}{\$200,000}$$

2011:

$$\text{Number of times interest charges are earned: } 5.0 = \frac{\$720,000 + \$180,000}{\$180,000}$$

b. The number of times interest charges are earned has increased from 5.0 in 2011 to 6.0 in 2012. Thus, the debtholders have improved confidence in the company's ability to make its interest payments.

Practice Exercises: **PE 14-8A, PE 14-8B**

A P P E N D I X 1

Present Value Concepts and Pricing Bonds Payable

When a corporation issues bonds, the price that investors are willing to pay for the bonds depends on the following:

1. The face amount of the bonds, which is the amount due at the maturity date.
2. The periodic interest to be paid on the bonds.
3. The market rate of interest.

An investor determines how much to pay for the bonds by computing the present value of the bond's future cash receipts, using the market rate of interest. A bond's future cash receipts include its face value at maturity and the periodic interest payments.

Present Value Concepts

The concept of present value is based on the time value of money. The *time value of money concept* recognizes that cash received today is worth more than the same amount of cash to be received in the future.

To illustrate, what would you rather have: $1,000 today or $1,000 one year from now? You would rather have the $1,000 today because it could be invested to earn interest. For example, if the $1,000 could be invested to earn 10% per year, the $1,000 will accumulate to $1,100 ($1,000 plus $100 interest) in one year. In this sense, you can think of the $1,000 in hand today as the **present value** of $1,100 to be received a year from today. This present value is illustrated below.

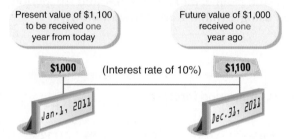

A related concept to present value is **future value**. To illustrate, using the preceding example, the $1,100 to be received on December 31, 2011, is the *future value* of $1,000 on January 1, 2011, assuming an interest rate of 10%.

Present Value of an Amount   To illustrate the present value of an amount, assume that $1,000 is to be received in one year. If the market rate of interest is 10%, the present value of the $1,000 is $909.09 ($1,000/1.10). This present value is illustrated below.

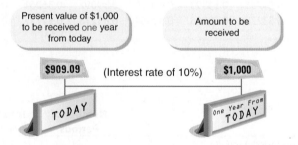

If the $1,000 is to be received in two years, with interest of 10% compounded at the end of the first year, the present value is $826.45 ($909.09/1.10).[6] This present value is illustrated below.

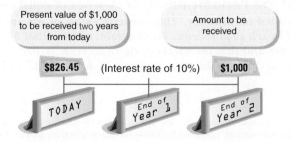

6 Note that the future value of $826.45 in two years, at an interest rate of 10% compounded annually, is $1,000.

Spreadsheet software with built-in present value functions can be used to calculate present values.

The present value of an amount to be received in the future can be determined by a series of divisions such as illustrated on the previous page. In practice, however, it is easier to use a table of present values.

The *present value of $1* table is used to find the present value factor for $1 to be received after a number of periods in the future. The amount to be received is then multiplied by this factor to determine its present value.

To illustrate, Exhibit 4 is a partial table of the present value of $1.[7] Exhibit 4 indicates that the present value of $1 to be received in two years with a market rate of interest of 10% a year is 0.82645. Multiplying $1,000 to be received in two years by 0.82645 yields $826.45 ($1,000 × 0.82645). This amount is the same amount computed earlier. In Exhibit 4, the Periods column represents the number of compounding periods, and the percentage columns represent the compound interest rate per period. Thus, the present value factor from Exhibit 4 for 12% for five years is 0.56743. If the interest is compounded semiannually, the interest rate is 6% (12% divided by 2), and the number of periods is 10 (5 years × 2 times per year). Thus, the present value factor from Exhibit 4 for 6% and 10 periods is 0.55840. Some additional examples using Exhibit 4 are shown below.

EXHIBIT 4 **Present Value of $1 at Compound Interest**

Periods	5%	5½%	6%	6½%	7%	10%	11%	12%	13%	14%
1	0.95238	0.94787	0.94340	0.93897	0.93458	0.90909	0.90090	0.89286	0.88496	0.87719
2	0.90703	0.89845	0.89000	0.88166	0.87344	0.82645	0.81162	0.79719	0.78315	0.76947
3	0.86384	0.85161	0.83962	0.82785	0.81630	0.75132	0.73119	0.71178	0.69305	0.67497
4	0.82270	0.80722	0.79209	0.77732	0.76290	0.68301	0.65873	0.63552	0.61332	0.59208
5	0.78353	0.76513	0.74726	0.72988	0.71299	0.62092	0.59345	0.56743	0.54276	0.51937
6	0.74622	0.72525	0.70496	0.68533	0.66634	0.56447	0.53464	0.50663	0.48032	0.45559
7	0.71068	0.68744	0.66506	0.64351	0.62275	0.51316	0.48166	0.45235	0.42506	0.39964
8	0.67684	0.65160	0.62741	0.60423	0.58201	0.46651	0.43393	0.40388	0.37616	0.35056
9	0.64461	0.61763	0.59190	0.56735	0.54393	0.42410	0.39092	0.36061	0.33288	0.30751
10	0.61391	0.58543	0.55840	0.53273	0.50835	0.38554	0.35218	0.32197	0.29459	0.26974

	Number of Periods	Interest Rate	Present Value of $1 Factor from Exhibit 4
10% for *two* years compounded *annually*	2	10%	0.82645
10% for *two* years compounded *semiannually*	4	5%	0.82270
10% for *three* years compounded *semiannually*	6	5%	0.74622
12% for *five* years compounded *semiannually*	10	6%	0.55840

Present Value of the Periodic Receipts A series of equal cash receipts spaced equally in time is called an **annuity**. The **present value of an annuity** is the sum of the present values of each cash receipt. To illustrate, assume that $100 is to be received annually for two years and that the market rate of interest is 10%. Using Exhibit 4, the present value of the receipt of the two amounts of $100 is $173.55, as shown on the next page.

---

7 To simplify the illustrations and homework assignments, the tables presented in this chapter are limited to 10 periods for a small number of interest rates, and the amounts are carried to only five decimal places. Computer programs are available for determining present value factors for any number of interest rates, decimal places, or periods. More complete interest tables are presented in Appendix A of the text.

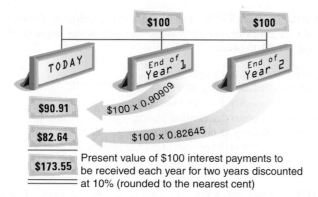

Present value of $100 interest payments to be received each year for two years discounted at 10% (rounded to the nearest cent)

Instead of using present value of $1 tables to determine the present value of each cash flow separately, such as Exhibit 4, the present value of an annuity can be computed in a single step. Using a value from the present value of an annuity of $1 table in Exhibit 5, the present value of the entire annuity can be calculated by multiplying the equal cash payment times the appropriate present value of an annuity of $1.

EXHIBIT 5   **Present Value of an Annuity of $1 at Compound Interest**

Periods	5%	5½%	6%	6½%	7%	10%	11%	12%	13%	14%
1	0.95238	0.94787	0.94340	0.93897	0.93458	0.90909	0.90090	0.89286	0.88496	0.87719
2	1.85941	1.84632	1.83339	1.82063	1.80802	1.73554	1.71252	1.69005	1.66810	1.64666
3	2.72325	2.69793	2.67301	2.64848	2.62432	2.48685	2.44371	2.40183	2.36115	2.32163
4	3.54595	3.50515	3.46511	3.42580	3.38721	3.16987	3.10245	3.03735	2.97447	2.91371
5	4.32948	4.27028	4.21236	4.15568	4.10020	3.79079	3.69590	3.60478	3.51723	3.43308
6	5.07569	4.99553	4.91732	4.84101	4.76654	4.35526	4.23054	4.11141	3.99755	3.88867
7	5.78637	5.68297	5.58238	5.48452	5.38929	4.86842	4.71220	4.56376	4.42261	4.28830
8	6.46321	6.33457	6.20979	6.08875	5.97130	5.33493	5.14612	4.96764	4.79677	4.63886
9	7.10782	6.95220	6.80169	6.65610	6.51523	5.75902	5.53705	5.32825	5.13166	4.94637
10	7.72174	7.53763	7.36009	7.18883	7.02358	6.14457	5.88923	5.65022	5.42624	5.21612

To illustrate, the present value of $100 to be received at the end of each of the next two years at 10% compound interest per period is $173.55 ($100 × 1.73554). This amount is the same amount computed above using the present value of $1.

Pricing Bonds

The selling price of a bond is the sum of the present values of:

1. The face amount of the bonds due at the maturity date
2. The periodic interest to be paid on the bonds

The market rate of interest is used to compute the present value of both the face amount and the periodic interest.

To illustrate the pricing of bonds, assume that Southern Utah Communications Inc. issued the following bond on January 1, 2011:

Face amount	$100,000
Contract rate of interest	12%
Interest paid semiannually on June 30 and December 31.	
Term of bonds.	5 years

Market Rate of Interest of 12%
Assuming a market rate of interest of 12%, the bonds would sell for their face amount. As shown by the following present value computations, the bonds would sell for $100,000.

Present value of face amount of $100,000 due in 5 years,
   at 12% compounded semiannually: $100,000 × 0.55840
   (present value of $1 for 10 periods at 6% from Exhibit 4)................................ $ 55,840
Present value of 10 semiannual interest payments of $6,000,
   at 12% compounded semiannually: $6,000 × 7.36009
   (present value of an annuity of $1 for 10 periods at 6% from Exhibit 5) 44,160
Total present value of bonds.. $100,000

Market Rate of Interest of 13%
Assuming a market rate of interest of 13%, the bonds would sell at a discount. As shown by the following present value computations, the bonds would sell for $96,406.[8]

Present value of face amount of $100,000 due in 5 years,
   at 13% compounded semiannually: $100,000 × 0.53273
   (present value of $1 for 10 periods at 6½% from Exhibit 4)............................... $53,273
Present value of 10 semiannual interest payments of $6,000,
   at 13% compounded semiannually: $6,000 × 7.18883
   (present value of an annuity of $1 for 10 periods at 6½% from Exhibit 5) 43,133
Total present value of bonds.. $96,406

Market Rate of Interest of 11%
Assuming a market rate of interest of 11%, the bonds would sell at a premium. As shown by the following present value computations, the bonds would sell for $103,769.

Present value of face amount of $100,000 due in 5 years,
   at 11% compounded semiannually: $100,000 × 0.58543
   (present value of $1 for 10 periods at 5½% from Exhibit 4)............................... $ 58,543
Present value of 10 semiannual interest payments of $6,000,
   at 11% compounded semiannually: $6,000 × 7.53763
   (present value of an annuity of $1 for 10 periods at 5½% from Exhibit 5) 45,226
Total present value of bonds.. $103,769

As shown above, the selling price of the bond varies with the present value of the bond's face amount at maturity, interest payments, and the market rate of interest.

APPENDIX 2

Effective Interest Rate Method of Amortization

The effective interest rate method of amortization provides for a constant *rate* of interest over the life of the bonds. As the discount or premium is amortized, the carrying amount of the bonds changes. As a result, interest expense also changes each period. This is in contrast to the straight-line method, which provides for a constant *amount* of interest expense each period.

The interest rate used in the effective interest rate method of amortization, sometimes called the *interest method*, is the market rate on the date the bonds are issued. The carrying amount of the bonds is multiplied by this interest rate to determine the interest expense for the period. The difference between the interest expense and the interest payment is the amount of discount or premium to be amortized for the period.

8 Some corporations issue bonds called **zero-coupon bonds** that provide for only the payment of the face amount at maturity. Such bonds sell for large discounts. In this example, such a bond would sell for $53,273, which is the present value of the face amount.

Amortization of Discount by the Interest Method

To illustrate, the following data taken from the chapter illustration of issuing bonds at a discount are used:

Face value of 12%, 5-year bonds, interest compounded semiannually	$100,000
Present value of bonds at effective (market) rate of interest of 13%	96,406
Discount on bonds payable.	$ 3,594

Exhibit 6 illustrates the interest method for the preceding bonds. Exhibit 6 begins with six columns. The first column is not lettered. The remaining columns are lettered A through E. The exhibit was then prepared as follows:

Step 1. List the interest payments dates in the first column, which for the preceding bond are 10 interest payment dates (semiannual interest over five years). Also, list on the first line the initial amount of discount in Column D and the initial carrying amount (selling price) of the bonds in Column E.

Step 2. List in Column A the semiannual interest payments, which for the preceding bond is $6,000 ($100,000 × 6%).

Step 3. Compute the interest expense in Column B by multiplying the bond carrying amount at the beginning of each period times 6½%, which is the effective interest (market) rate.

Step 4. Compute the discount to be amortized each period in Column C by subtracting the interest payment in Column A ($6,000) from the interest expense for the period shown in Column B.

Step 5. Compute the remaining unamortized discount by subtracting the amortized discount in Column C for the period from the unamortized discount at the beginning of the period in Column D.

Step 6. Compute the bond carrying amount at the end of the period by subtracting the unamortized discount at the end of the period in Column D from the face amount of the bonds ($100,000).

Steps 3–6 are repeated for each interest payment.

As shown in Exhibit 6, the interest expense increases each period as the carrying amount of the bond increases. Also, the unamortized discount decreases each period to zero at the maturity date. Finally, the carrying amount of the bonds increases from $96,406 to $100,000 (the face amount) at maturity.

EXHIBIT 6   **Amortization of Discount on Bonds Payable**

Interest Payment Date	A Interest Paid (6% of Face Amount)	B Interest Expense (6½% of Bond Carrying Amount)	C Discount Amortization (B – A)	D Unamortized Discount (D – C)	E Bond Carrying Amount ($100,000 – D)
				$3,594	$ 96,406
June 30, 2011	$6,000	$6,266 (6½% of $96,406)	$266	3,328	96,672
Dec. 31, 2011	6,000	6,284 (6½% of $96,672)	284	3,044	96,956
June 30, 2012	6,000	6,302 (6½% of $96,956)	302	2,742	97,258
Dec. 31, 2012	6,000	6,322 (6½% of $97,258)	322	2,420	97,580
June 30, 2013	6,000	6,343 (6½% of $97,580)	343	2,077	97,923
Dec. 31, 2013	6,000	6,365 (6½% of $97,923)	365	1,712	98,288
June 30, 2014	6,000	6,389 (6½% of $98,288)	389	1,323	98,677
Dec. 31, 2014	6,000	6,414 (6½% of $98,677)	414	909	99,091
June 30, 2015	6,000	6,441 (6½% of $99,091)	441	468	99,532
Dec. 31, 2015	6,000	6,470 (6½% of $99,532)	468*	—	100,000

*Cannot exceed unamortized discount.

The entry to record the first interest payment on June 30, 2011, and the related discount amortization is as follows:

2011				
June	30	Interest Expense	6,266	
		Discount on Bonds Payable		266
		Cash		6,000
		Paid semiannual interest and amortized bond discount for ½ year.		

If the amortization is recorded only at the end of the year, the amount of the discount amortized on December 31, 2011, would be $550. This is the sum of the first two semiannual amortization amounts ($266 and $284) from Exhibit 6.

Amortization of Premium by the Interest Method

To illustrate, the following data taken from the chapter illustration of issuing bonds at a premium are used:

Present value of bonds at effective (market) rate of interest of 11%. $103,769
Face value of 12%, 5-year bonds, interest compounded semiannually 100,000
Premium on bonds payable. . . . . $ 3,769

Exhibit 7 illustrates the interest method for the preceding bonds. Exhibit 7 begins with six columns. The first column is not lettered. The remaining columns are lettered A through E. The exhibit was then prepared as follows:

Step 1. List the number of interest payments in the first column, which for the preceding bond are 10 interest payments (semiannual interest over 5 years). Also, list on the first line the initial amount of premium in Column D and the initial carrying amount of the bonds in Column E.

Step 2. List in Column A the semiannual interest payments, which for the preceding bond is $6,000 ($100,000 × 6%).

Step 3. Compute the interest expense in Column B by multiplying the bond carrying amount at the beginning of each period times 5½%, which is the effective interest (market) rate.

Step 4. Compute the premium to be amortized each period in Column C by subtracting the interest expense for the period shown in Column B from the interest payment in Column A ($6,000).

EXHIBIT 7   **Amortization of Premium on Bonds Payable**

Interest Payment Date	A Interest Paid (6% of Face Amount)	B Interest Expense (5½% of Bond Carrying Amount)	C Premium Amortization (A – B)	D Unamortized Premium (D – C)	E Bond Carrying Amount ($100,000 + D)
				$3,769	$103,769
June 30, 2011	$6,000	$5,707 (5½% of $103,769)	$293	3,476	103,476
Dec. 31, 2011	6,000	5,691 (5½% of $103,476)	309	3,167	103,167
June 30, 2012	6,000	5,674 (5½% of $103,167)	326	2,841	102,841
Dec. 31, 2012	6,000	5,656 (5½% of $102,841)	344	2,497	102,497
June 30, 2013	6,000	5,637 (5½% of $102,497)	363	2,134	102,134
Dec. 31, 2013	6,000	5,617 (5½% of $102,134)	383	1,751	101,751
June 30, 2014	6,000	5,596 (5½% of $101,751)	404	1,347	101,347
Dec. 31, 2014	6,000	5,574 (5½% of $101,347)	426	921	100,921
June 30, 2015	6,000	5,551 (5½% of $100,921)	449	472	100,472
Dec. 31, 2015	6,000	5,526 (5½% of $100,472)	472*	—	100,000

*Cannot exceed unamortized premium.

Step 5. Compute the remaining unamortized premium by subtracting the amortized premium in Column C for the period from the unamortized premium at the beginning of the period in Column D.

Step 6. Compute the bond carrying amount at the end of the period in Column D by adding the unamortized premium at the end of the period to the face amount of the bonds ($100,000).

Steps 3–6 are repeated for each interest payment.

As shown in Exhibit 7, the interest expense decreases each period as the carrying amount of the bond decreases. Also, the unamortized premium decreases each period to zero at the maturity date. Finally, the carrying amount of the bonds decreases from $103,769 to $100,000 (the face amount) at maturity.

The entry to record the first interest payment on June 30, 2011, and the related premium amortization is as follows:

2011					
June	30	Interest Expense	5,707	
		Premium on Bonds Payable	293	
		Cash		6,000
		Paid semiannual interest and amortized bond premium for ½ year.		

If the amortization is recorded only at the end of the year, the amount of the premium amortized on December 31, 2011, would be $602. This is the sum of the first two semiannual amortization amounts ($293 and $309) from Exhibit 7.

At a Glance 14

Compute the potential impact of long-term borrowing on earnings per share.

Key Points   Corporations can finance their operations by issuing short-term debt, long-term debt, or equity. One of the many factors that influence a corporation's decision on whether it should issue long-term debt or equity is the effect each alternative has on earnings per share.

Learning Outcomes	Example Exercises	Practice Exercises
• Define the concept of a bond.		
• Calculate and compare the effect of alternative long-term financing plans on earnings per share.	EE14-1	PE14-1A, 14-1B

Describe the characteristics and terminology of bonds payable.

Key Points   A corporation that issues bonds enters into a contract, or bond indenture.

When a corporation issues bonds, the price that buyers are willing to pay for the bonds depends on (1) the face amount of the bonds, (2) the periodic interest to be paid on the bonds, and (3) the market rate of interest.

Learning Outcomes	Example Exercises	Practice Exercises
• Define the characteristics of a bond.		
• Describe the various types of bonds.		
• Describe the factors that determine the price of a bond.		

OBJ. 3 Journalize entries for bonds payable.

Key Points   The journal entry for issuing bonds payable debits Cash and credits Bonds Payable. Any difference between the face amount of the bonds and the selling price is debited to Discount on Bonds Payable or credited to Premium on Bonds Payable when the bonds are issued. The discount or premium on bonds payable is amortized to interest expense over the life of the bonds.

   At the maturity date, the entry to record the repayment of the face value of a bond is a debit to Bonds Payable and a credit to Cash.

   When a corporation redeems bonds before they mature, Bonds Payable is debited for the face amount of the bonds, the premium (discount) on bonds payable account is debited (credited) for its unamoritzed balance, Cash is credited, and any gain or loss on the redemption is recorded.

Learning Outcomes	Example Exercises	Practice Exercises
• Journalize the issuance of bonds at face value and the payment of periodic interest.		
• Journalize the issuance of bonds at a discount.	EE14-2	PE14-2A, 14-2B
• Journalize the amortization of a bond discount.	EE14-3	PE14-3A, 14-3B
• Journalize the issuance of bonds at a premium.	EE14-4	PE14-4A, 14-4B
• Journalize the amortization of a bond premium.	EE14-5	PE14-5A, 14-5B
• Describe bond redemptions.		
• Journalize the redemption of bonds payable.	EE14-6	PE14-6A, 14-6B

OBJ. 4 Describe and illustrate the accounting for installment notes.

Key Points   An installment note requires the borrower to make equal periodic payments to the lender for the term of the note. Unlike bonds, the annual payment in an installment note consists of both principal and interest. The journal entry for the annual payment debits Interest Expense and Notes Payable and credits Cash for the amount of the payment. After the final payment, the carrying amount on the note is zero.

Learning Outcomes	Example Exercises	Practice Exercises
• Define the characteristics of an installment note.		
• Journalize the issuance of installment notes.	EE14-7	PE14-7A, 14-7B
• Journalize the annual payment for an installment note.		

OBJ. 5 Describe and illustrate the reporting of long-term liabilities including bonds and notes payable.

Key Points   Bonds payable and notes payable are usually reported as long-term liabilities. If the balance sheet date is within one year, they are reported as a current liability. A discount on bonds should be reported as a deduction from the related bonds payable. A premium on bonds should be reported as an addition to related bonds payable.

Learning Outcome	Example Exercises	Practice Exercises
• Illustrate the balance sheet presentation of bonds payable and notes payable.		

Describe and illustrate how the number of times interest charges are earned is used to evaluate a company's financial condition.

Key Points The number of times interest charges are earned measures the risk to bondholders that a company will not be able to make its interest payments. It is computed by dividing income before income tax plus interest expense by interest expense. This ratio measures the number of times interest payments could be paid (covered) by current period earnings.

Learning Outcomes	Example Exercises	Practice Exercises
• Describe and compute the number of times interest charges are earned.	EE14-8	PE14-8A, 14-8B
• Interpret the number of times interest charges are earned.		

Key Terms

bond (626)
bond indenture (628)
carrying amount (635)
contract rate (629)
discount (629)

earnings per share (EPS) (627)
effective interest rate method (632)
effective rate of interest (629)
face amount (629)
installment note (636)

market rate of interest (629)
mortgage notes (636)
number of times interest
   charges are earned (639)
premium (629)

Illustrative Problem

The fiscal year of Russell Inc., a manufacturer of acoustical supplies, ends December 31. Selected transactions for the period 2011 through 2018, involving bonds payable issued by Russell Inc., are as follows:

2011

June 30. Issued $2,000,000 of 25-year, 7% callable bonds dated June 30, 2011, for cash of $1,920,000. Interest is payable semiannually on June 30 and December 31.

Dec. 31. Paid the semiannual interest on the bonds.

   31. Recorded straight-line amortization of $1,600 of discount on the bonds.

   31. Closed the interest expense account.

2012

June 30. Paid the semiannual interest on the bonds.

Dec. 31. Paid the semiannual interest on the bonds.

   31. Recorded straight-line amortization of $3,200 of discount on the bonds.

   31. Closed the interest expense account.

2018

June 30. Recorded the redemption of the bonds, which were called at 101.5. The balance in the bond discount account is $57,600 after the payment of interest and amortization of discount have been recorded. (Record the redemption only.)

Instructions

1. Journalize entries to record the preceding transactions.

2. Determine the amount of interest expense for 2011 and 2012.

3. Determine the carrying amount of the bonds as of December 31, 2012.

Solution

1.

2011					
June	30	Cash		1,920,000	
		Discount on Bonds Payable		80,000	
		Bonds Payable			2,000,000
Dec.	31	Interest Expense		70,000	
		Cash			70,000
	31	Interest Expense		1,600	
		Discount on Bonds Payable			1,600
		Amortization of discount from July 1 to December 31.			
	31	Income Summary		71,600	
		Interest Expense			71,600
2012					
June	30	Interest Expense		70,000	
		Cash			70,000
Dec.	31	Interest Expense		70,000	
		Cash			70,000
	31	Interest Expense		3,200	
		Discount on Bonds Payable			3,200
		Amortization of discount from January 1 to December 31.			
	31	Income Summary		143,200	
		Interest Expense			143,200
2018					
June	30	Bonds Payable		2,000,000	
		Loss on Redemption of Bonds Payable		87,600	
		Discount on Bonds Payable			57,600
		Cash			2,030,000

2. a. 2011: $71,600 = $70,000 + $1,600

b. 2012: $143,200 = $70,000 + $70,000 + $3,200

3.
Initial carrying amount of bonds	$1,920,000
Discount amortized on December 31, 2011	1,600
Discount amortized on December 31, 2012	3,200
Carrying amount of bonds, December 31, 2012	$1,924,800

Discussion Questions

1. Describe the two distinct obligations incurred by a corporation when issuing bonds.

2. Explain the meaning of each of the following terms as they relate to a bond issue: (a) convertible, (b) callable, and (c) debenture.

3. If you asked your broker to purchase for you a 12% bond when the market interest rate for such bonds was 11%, would you expect to pay more or less than the face amount for the bond? Explain.

4. A corporation issues $18,000,000 of 10% bonds to yield interest at the rate of 8%. (a) Was the amount of cash received from the sale of the bonds greater or less than $18,000,000? (b) Identify the following terms related to the bond issue: (1) face amount, (2) market or effective rate of interest, (3) contract rate of interest, and (4) maturity amount.

5. If bonds issued by a corporation are sold at a premium, is the market rate of interest greater or less than the contract rate?

6. The following data relate to a $200,000,000, 5% bond issued for a selected semiannual interest period:

Bond carrying amount at beginning of period	$216,221,792
Interest paid during period	5,000,000
Interest expense allocable to the period	4,864,990

(a) Were the bonds issued at a discount or at a premium? (b) What is the unamortized amount of the discount or premium account at the beginning of the period? (c) What account was debited to amortize the discount or premium?

7. Bonds Payable has a balance of $3,500,000 and Discount on Bonds Payable has a balance of $125,000. If the issuing corporation redeems the bonds at 97, is there a gain or loss on the bond redemption?

8. What is a mortgage note?

9. Fleeson Company needs additional funds to purchase equipment for a new production facility and is considering either issuing bonds payable or borrowing the money from a local bank in the form of an installment note. How does an installment note differ from a bond payable?

10. How would a bond payable be reported on the balance sheet if: (a) it is payable within one year and (b) it is payable beyond one year?

Practice Exercises

Learning Objectives	Example Exercises	
OBJ. 1	EE 14-1 *p. 628*	**PE 14-1A Alternative financing plans**

Baker Co. is considering the following alternative financing plans:

	Plan 1	Plan 2
Issue 5% bonds (at face value)	$3,000,000	$1,500,000
Issue preferred $4 stock, $25 par	—	2,500,000
Issue common stock, $40 par	3,000,000	2,000,000

Income tax is estimated at 40% of income.

Determine the earnings per share of common stock, assuming income before bond interest and income tax is $1,000,000.

OBJ. 1	EE 14-1 *p. 628*	**PE 14-1B Alternative financing plans**

Fly Co. is considering the following alternative financing plans:

	Plan 1	Plan 2
Issue 12% bonds (at face value)	$10,000,000	$5,000,000
Issue preferred $1.75 stock, $20 par	—	8,000,000
Issue common stock, $20 par	10,000,000	7,000,000

Income tax is estimated at 40% of income.

Determine the earnings per share of common stock, assuming income before bond interest and income tax is $2,000,000.

OBJ. 3	EE 14-2 *p. 631*	**PE 14-2A Issuing bonds at a discount**

On the first day of the fiscal year, a company issues a $4,000,000, 10%, 10-year bond that pays semiannual interest of $200,000 ($4,000,000 × 10% × ½), receiving cash of $3,760,992. Journalize the bond issuance.

OBJ. 3	EE 14-2 *p. 631*	**PE 14-2B Issuing bonds at a discount**

On the first day of the fiscal year, a company issues a $1,500,000, 9%, five-year bond that pays semiannual interest of $67,500 ($1,500,000 × 9% × ½), receiving cash of $1,334,398. Journalize the bond issuance.

OBJ. 3	EE 14-3 *p. 632*	**PE 14-3A Discount amortization**

Using the bond from Practice Exercise 14-2A, journalize the first interest payment and the amortization of the related bond discount. Round to the nearest dollar.

OBJ. 3	EE 14-3 *p. 632*	**PE 14-3B Discount amortization**

Using the bond from Practice Exercise 14-2B, journalize the first interest payment and the amortization of the related bond discount. Round to the nearest dollar.

OBJ. 3	EE 14-4 *p. 633*	**PE 14-4A Issuing bonds at a premium**

A company issues a $2,000,000, 9%, five-year bond that pays semiannual interest of $90,000 ($2,000,000 × 9% × ½), receiving cash of $2,166,332. Journalize the bond issuance.

OBJ. 3	EE 14-4 *p. 633*	**PE 14-4B Issuing bonds at a premium**

A company issues a $6,000,000, 12%, five-year bond that pays semiannual interest of $360,000 ($6,000,000 × 12% × ½), receiving cash of $6,463,304. Journalize the bond issuance.

Learning Objectives	Example Exercises	
OBJ. 3	EE 14-5 *p. 634*	**PE 14-5A Premium amortization**

Using the bond from Practice Exercise 14-4A, journalize the first interest payment and the amortization of the related bond premium. Round to the nearest dollar.

OBJ. 3	EE 14-5 *p. 634*	**PE 14-5B Premium amortization**

Using the bond from Practice Exercise 14-4B, journalize the first interest payment and the amortization of the related bond premium. Round to the nearest dollar.

OBJ. 3	EE 14-6 *p. 635*	**PE 14-6A Redemption of bonds payable**

An $800,000 bond issue on which there is an unamortized discount of $60,000 is redeemed for $760,000. Journalize the redemption of the bonds.

OBJ. 3	EE 14-6 *p. 635*	**PE 14-6B Redemption of bonds payable**

A $450,000 bond issue on which there is an unamortized premium of $25,000 is redeemed for $441,000. Journalize the redemption of the bonds.

OBJ. 4	EE 14-7 *p. 638*	**PE 14-7A Journalizing installment notes**

On the first day of the fiscal year, a company issues $100,000, 8%, six-year installment notes that have annual payments of $21,632. The first note payment consists of $8,000 of interest and $13,632 of principal repayment.

a. Journalize the entry to record the issuance of the installment notes.

b. Journalize the first annual note payment.

OBJ. 4	EE 14-7 *p. 638*	**PE 14-7B Journalizing installment notes**

On the first day of the fiscal year, a company issues $55,000, 9%, five-year installment notes that have annual payments of $14,140. The first note payment consists of $4,950 of interest and $9,190 of principal repayment.

a. Journalize the entry to record the issuance of the installment notes.

b. Journalize the first annual note payment.

OBJ. 6	EE 14-8 *p. 640*	**PE 14-8A Number of times interest charges are earned**

Katula Company reported the following on the company's income statement in 2012 and 2011:

	2012	2011
Interest expense	$ 250,000	$ 275,000
Income before income tax expense	3,100,000	4,400,000

a. Determine the number of times interest charges were earned for 2011 and 2012. Round to one decimal place.

b. Is the number of times interest charges are earned improving or declining?

OBJ. 6	EE 14-8 *p. 640*	**PE 14-8B Number of times interest charges are earned**

Marsh Products, Inc., reported the following on the company's income statement in 2012 and 2011:

	2012	2011
Interest expense	$ 420,000	$ 375,000
Income before income tax expense	4,200,000	3,000,000

a. Determine the number of times interest charges were earned for 2011 and 2012. Round to one decimal place.

b. Is the number of times interest charges are earned improving or declining?

Exercises

OBJ. 1

✔ a. $1.30

EX 14-1 Effect of financing on earnings per share

Kelton Co., which produces and sells skiing equipment, is financed as follows:

Bonds payable, 8% (issued at face amount)	$20,000,000
Preferred $2 stock, $10 par	20,000,000
Common stock, $25 par	20,000,000

Income tax is estimated at 40% of income.

Determine the earnings per share of common stock, assuming that the income before bond interest and income tax is (a) $10,000,000, (b) $12,000,000, and (c) $14,000,000.

OBJ. 1

EX 14-2 Evaluate alternative financing plans

Based on the data in Exercise 14-1, what factors other than earnings per share should be considered in evaluating these alternative financing plans?

OBJ. 1

EX 14-3 Corporate financing

The financial statements for Nike, Inc., are presented in Appendix C at the end of the text. What is the major source of financing for Nike?

OBJ. 3

EX 14-4 Bond price

Procter and Gamble's 4.7% bonds due in 2019 were reported as selling for 104.797.

Were the bonds selling at a premium or at a discount? Why is Proctor & Gamble able to sell its bonds at this price?

OBJ. 3

EX 14-5 Entries for issuing bonds

Austin Co. produces and distributes semiconductors for use by computer manufacturers. Austin Co. issued $15,000,000 of 12-year, 12% bonds on May 1 of the current year, with interest payable on May 1 and November 1. The fiscal year of the company is the calendar year. Journalize the entries to record the following selected transactions for the current year:

May 1. Issued the bonds for cash at their face amount.

Nov. 1. Paid the interest on the bonds.

Dec. 31. Recorded accrued interest for two months.

OBJ. 3

✔ b. $2,867,977

EX 14-6 Entries for issuing bonds and amortizing discount by straight-line method

On the first day of its fiscal year, Keller Company issued $25,000,000 of five–year, 10% bonds to finance its operations of producing and selling home improvement products. Interest is payable semiannually. The bonds were issued at a market (effective) interest rate of 12%, resulting in Keller Company receiving cash of $23,160,113.

a. Journalize the entries to record the following:

1. Sale of the bonds.

2. First semiannual interest payment. (Amortization of discount is to be recorded annually.)

3. Second semiannual interest payment.

4. Amortization of discount at the end of the first year, using the straight-line method. (Round to the nearest dollar.)

b. Determine the amount of the bond interest expense for the first year.

c. Explain why the company was able to issue the bonds for only $23,160,113 rather than for the face amount of $25,000,000.

OBJ. 2, 3

EX 14-7   Entries for issuing bonds and amortizing premium by straight-line method

McCool Corporation wholesales repair products to equipment manufacturers. On April 1, 2010, McCool Corporation issued $30,000,000 of five-year, 10% bonds at a market (effective) interest rate of 8%, receiving cash of $32,446,500. Interest is payable semiannually on April 1 and October 1. Journalize the entries to record the following:

a. Sale of bonds on April 1, 2012.

b. First interest payment on October 1, 2012, and amortization of bond premium for six months, using the straight-line method. (Round to the nearest dollar.)

c. Explain why the company was able to issue the bonds for $32,446,500 rather than for the face amount of $30,000,000.

OBJ. 3

EX 14-8   Entries for issuing and calling bonds; loss

Dillip Corp., a wholesaler of office equipment, issued $45,000,000 of 10-year, 10% callable bonds on March 1, 2012, with interest payable on March 1 and September 1. The fiscal year of the company is the calendar year. Journalize the entries to record the following selected transactions:

2012

Mar. 1.   Issued the bonds for cash at their face amount.

Sept. 1.   Paid the interest on the bonds.

2016

Sept. 1.   Called the bond issue at 103, the rate provided in the bond indenture. (Omit entry for payment of interest.)

OBJ. 3

EX 14-9   Entries for issuing and calling bonds; gain

Fogel Corp. produces and sells renewable energy equipment. To finance its operations, Fogel Corp. issued $32,000,000 of 20-year, 11% callable bonds on January 1, 2012, with interest payable on January 1 and July 1. The fiscal year of the company is the calendar year. Journalize the entries to record the following selected transactions:

2012

Jan. 1.   Issued the bonds for cash at their face amount.

July 1.   Paid the interest on the bonds.

2018

July 1.   Called the bond issue at 97, the rate provided in the bond indenture. (Omit entry for payment of interest.)

OBJ. 4

EX 14-10   Entries for issuing installment note transactions

On the first day of the fiscal year, Harris Company borrowed $65,000 by giving a 10-year, 6% installment note to Cuba Bank. The note requires annual payments of $8,832, with the first payment occurring on the last day of the fiscal year. The first payment consists of interest of $3,900 and principal repayment of $4,932.

a. Journalize the entries to record the following:

1. Issued the installment note for cash on the first day of the fiscal year.

2. Paid the first annual payment on the note.

b. Explain how the notes payable would be reported on the balance sheet at the end of the first year.

OBJ. 4

EX 14-11   Entries for issuing installment note transactions

On January 1, 2012, Averill Company issued a $120,000, 8-year, 10% installment note from Deacon Bank. The note requires annual payments of $22,493, beginning on December 31, 2012. Journalize the entries to record the following:

2012

Jan.   1. Issued the notes for cash at their face amount.

Dec. 31. Paid the annual payment on the note, which consisted of interest of $12,000 and principal of $10,493.

2017

Dec. 31. Paid the annual payment on the note, which consisted of interest of $5,594 and principal of $16,899.

OBJ. 4

EX 14-12   Entries for issuing installment note transactions

On January 1, 2012, Daan Company obtained a $28,000, four-year, 9% installment note from Poklers Bank. The note requires annual payments of $8,642, beginning on December 31, 2012.

a. Prepare an amortization table for this installment note, similar to the one presented in Exhibit 3.

b. Journalize the entries for the issuance of the note and the four annual note payments.

c. Describe how the annual note payment would be reported in the 2012 income statement.

OBJ. 5

EX 14-13   Reporting bonds

At the beginning of the current year, two bond issues (Putnam Industries 5% 10-year bonds and Rucker Corporation 6% five-year bonds) were outstanding. During the year, the Putnam Industries bonds were redeemed and a significant loss on the redemption of bonds was reported as an extraordinary item on the income statement. At the end of the year, the Rucker Corporation bonds were reported as a noncurrent liability. The maturity date on the Rucker Corporation bonds was early in the following year.

➤ Identify the flaws in the reporting practices related to the two bond issues.

OBJ. 6

EX 14-14   Number of times interest charges are earned

The following data were taken from recent annual reports of Southwest Airlines, which operates a low-fare airline service to over 50 cities in the United States.

	Current Year	Preceding Year
Interest expense	$105,000,000	$69,000,000
Income before income tax	278,000,000	1,058,000

a. Determine the number of times interest charges were earned for the current and preceding years. Round to one decimal place.

b. ➤ What conclusions can you draw?

OBJ. 6

FAI

EX 14-15   Number of times interest charges are earned

Quansi, Inc., reported the following on the company's income statement in 2012 and 2011:

	2012	2011
Interest expense	$ 10,000,000	$ 12,500,000
Income before income tax expense	240,000,000	375,000,000

a. Determine the number of times interest charges were earned for 2011 and 2012. Round to one decimal place.

b. ➤ Is the number of times interest charges are earned improving or declining?

OBJ. 6

FAI

EX 14-16   Number of times interest charges are earned

Vixeron Company reported the following on the company's income statement for 2012 and 2011:

	2012	2011
Interest expense	$3,000,000	$3,000,000
Income before income tax	1,200,000	3,600,000

a. Determine the number of times interest charges were earned for 2011 and 2012. Round to one decimal place.

b. ➤ What conclusions can you draw?

Appendix 1
EX 14-17   Present value of amounts due

Determine the present value of $750,000 to be received in three years, using an interest rate of 12%, compounded annually.

a. Use the present value table in Exhibit 4.

b. Why is the present value less than the $750,000 to be received in the future?

Appendix 1
EX 14-18   Present value of an annuity

Determine the present value of $150,000 to be received at the end of each of four years, using an interest rate of 7%, compounded annually, as follows:

a. By successive computations, using the present value table in Exhibit 4.

b. By using the present value table in Exhibit 5.

c. Why is the present value of the four $150,000 cash receipts less than the $600,000 to be received in the future?

✔ $79,077,130

Appendix 1
EX 14-19   Present value of an annuity

On January 1, 2012, you win $110,000,000 in the state lottery. The $110,000,000 prize will be paid in equal installments of $11,000,000 over 10 years. The payments will be made on December 31 of each year, beginning on December 31, 2012. If the current interest rate is 6.5%, determine the present value of your winnings. Use the present value tables in Appendix A.

Appendix 1
EX 14-20   Present value of an annuity

Assume the same data as in Appendix 1 Exercise 14–19, except that the current interest rate is 13%.

➤ Will the present value of your winnings using an interest rate of 13% be one-half the present value of your winnings using an interest rate of 6.5%? Why or why not?

Appendix 1
EX 14-21   Present value of bonds payable; discount

Baliga Co. produces and sells high-quality audio equipment. To finance its operations, Baliga Co. issued $18,000,000 of five-year, 8% bonds with interest payable semiannually at a market (effective) interest rate of 10%. Determine the present value of the bonds payable, using the present value tables in Exhibits 4 and 5. Round to the nearest dollar.

✔ $86,030,076

Appendix 1
EX 14-22   Present value of bonds payable; premium

Herbst Co. issued $80,000,000 of five-year, 13% bonds with interest payable semiannually, at a market (effective) interest rate of 11%. Determine the present value of the bonds payable, using the present value tables in Exhibits 4 and 5. Round to the nearest dollar.

✔ b. $3,396,512

Appendix 2
EX 14-23   Amortize discount by interest method

On the first day of its fiscal year, Ramsey Company issued $35,000,000 of 10-year, 9% bonds to finance its operations. Interest is payable semiannually. The bonds were issued at a market (effective) interest rate of 11%, resulting in Ramsey Company receiving cash of $30,817,399. The company uses the interest method.

a. Journalize the entries to record the following:

1. Sale of the bonds.

2. First semiannual interest payment, including amortization of discount. Round to the nearest dollar.

(continued)

3. Second semiannual interest payment, including amortization of discount. Round to the nearest dollar.

b. Compute the amount of the bond interest expense for the first year.

c. Explain why the company was able to issue the bonds for only $30,817,399 rather than for the face amount of $35,000,000.

✔ b. $1,879,754

Appendix 2

EX 14-24 Amortize premium by interest method

Knight Corporation wholesales auto parts to auto manufacturers. On March 1, 2012, Knight Corporation issued $17,500,000 of five-year, 12% bonds at a market (effective) interest rate of 10%, receiving cash of $18,851,252. Interest is payable semiannually. Knight Corporation's fiscal year begins on March 1. The company uses the interest method.

a. Journalize the entries to record the following:

1. Sale of the bonds.

2. First semiannual interest payment, including amortization of premium. Round to the nearest dollar.

3. Second semiannual interest payment, including amortization of premium. Round to the nearest dollar.

b. Determine the bond interest expense for the first year.

c. Explain why the company was able to issue the bonds for $18,851,252 rather than for the face amount of $17,500,000.

✔ a. $53,680,315
✔ c. $295,932

Appendix 1 and Appendix 2

EX 14-25 Compute bond proceeds, amortizing premium by interest method, and interest expense

Evans Co. produces and sells motorcycle parts. On the first day of its fiscal year, Evans Co. issued $50,000,000 of five-year, 14% bonds at a market (effective) interest rate of 12%, with interest payable semiannually. Compute the following, presenting figures used in your computations.

a. The amount of cash proceeds from the sale of the bonds. Use the tables of present values in Exhibits 4 and 5. Round to the nearest dollar.

b. The amount of premium to be amortized for the first semiannual interest payment period, using the interest method. Round to the nearest dollar.

c. The amount of premium to be amortized for the second semiannual interest payment period, using the interest method. Round to the nearest dollar.

d. The amount of the bond interest expense for the first year.

✔ a. $53,530,290
✔ b. $479,469

Appendix 1 and Appendix 2

EX 14-26 Compute bond proceeds, amortizing discount by interest method, and interest expense

Lewis Co. produces and sells aviation equipment. On the first day of its fiscal year, Lewis Co. issued $60,000,000 of five-year, 10% bonds at a market (effective) interest rate of 13%, with interest payable semiannually. Compute the following, presenting figures used in your computations.

a. The amount of cash proceeds from the sale of the bonds. Use the tables of present values in Exhibits 4 and 5. Round to the nearest dollar.

b. The amount of discount to be amortized for the first semiannual interest payment period, using the interest method. Round to the nearest dollar.

c. The amount of discount to be amortized for the second semiannual interest payment period, using the interest method. Round to the nearest dollar.

d. The amount of the bond interest expense for the first year.

Problems Series A

PR 14-1A   Effect of financing on earnings per share

Three different plans for financing a $200,000,000 corporation are under consideration by its organizers. Under each of the following plans, the securities will be issued at their par or face amount, and the income tax rate is estimated at 40% of income.

	Plan 1	Plan 2	Plan 3
11% bonds	—	—	$100,000,000
Preferred 5% stock, $40 par	—	$100,000,000	50,000,000
Common stock, $25 par	$200,000,000	100,000,000	50,000,000
Total	$200,000,000	$200,000,000	$200,000,000

Instructions

1. Determine for each plan the earnings per share of common stock, assuming that the income before bond interest and income tax is $30,000,000.

2. Determine for each plan the earnings per share of common stock, assuming that the income before bond interest and income tax is $16,000,000.

3. ━━━━▶ Discuss the advantages and disadvantages of each plan.

PR 14-2A   Bond discount, entries for bonds payable transactions

On July 1, 2012, Bliss Industries Inc. issued $24,000,000 of 20-year, 11% bonds at a market (effective) interest rate of 14%, receiving cash of $19,200,577. Interest on the bonds is payable semiannually on December 31 and June 30. The fiscal year of the company is the calendar year.

Instructions

1. Journalize the entry to record the amount of cash proceeds from the sale of the bonds.

2. Journalize the entries to record the following:

   a. The first semiannual interest payment on December 31, 2012, and the amortization of the bond discount, using the straight-line method. (Round to the nearest dollar.)

   b. The interest payment on June 30, 2013, and the amortization of the bond discount, using the straight-line method. (Round to the nearest dollar.)

3. Determine the total interest expense for 2012.

4. Will the bond proceeds always be less than the face amount of the bonds when the contract rate is less than the market rate of interest?

5. (Appendix 1) Compute the price of $19,200,577 received for the bonds by using the tables of present value in Appendix A at the end of the text. (Round to the nearest dollar.)

PR 14-3A   Bond premium, entries for bonds payable transactions

Fabulator, Inc. produces and sells fashion clothing. On July 1, 2012, Fabulator, Inc. issued $120,000,000 of 20-year, 14% bonds at a market (effective) interest rate of 11%, receiving cash of $148,882,608. Interest on the bonds is payable semiannually on December 31 and June 30. The fiscal year of the company is the calendar year.

Instructions

1. Journalize the entry to record the amount of cash proceeds from the sale of the bonds.

2. Journalize the entries to record the following:

   a. The first semiannual interest payment on December 31, 2012, and the amortization of the bond premium, using the straight-line method. (Round to the nearest dollar.)

   b. The interest payment on June 30, 2013, and the amortization of the bond premium, using the straight-line method. (Round to the nearest dollar.)

3. Determine the total interest expense for 2012.

4. Will the bond proceeds always be greater than the face amount of the bonds when the contract rate is greater than the market rate of interest?

(continued)

5. (Appendix 1) Compute the price of $148,882,608 received for the bonds by using the tables of present value in Appendix A at the end of the text. (Round to the nearest dollar.)

OBJ. 3, 4

✔ 3. $58,236,896

PR 14-4A Entries for bonds payable and installment note transactions

The following transactions were completed by Simmons Inc., whose fiscal year is the calendar year:

2012

July 1. Issued $64,000,000 of 10-year, 12% callable bonds dated July 1, 2012, at a market (effective) rate of 14%, receiving cash of $57,219,878. Interest is payable semiannually on December 31 and June 30.

Oct. 1. Borrowed $320,000 as a five-year, 6% installment note from Ibis Bank. The note requires annual payments of $75,967, with the first payment occurring on September 30, 2013.

Dec. 31. Accrued $4,800 of interest on the installment note. The interest is payable on the date of the next installment note payment.

31. Paid the semiannual interest on the bonds. The bond discount is amortized annually in a separate journal entry.

31. Recorded bond discount amortization of $339,006, which was determined using the straight-line method.

31. Closed the interest expense account.

2013

June 30. Paid the semiannual interest on the bonds.

Sept. 30. Paid the annual payment on the note, which consisted of interest of $19,200 and principal of $56,767.

Dec. 31. Accrued $3,948 of interest on the installment note. The interest is payable on the date of the next installment note payment.

31. Paid the semiannual interest on the bonds. The bond discount is amortized annually in a separate journal entry.

31. Recorded bond discount amortization of $678,012, which was determined using the straight-line method.

31. Closed the interest expense account.

2014

June 30. Recorded the redemption of the bonds, which were called at 98. The balance in the bond discount account is $5,424,098 after payment of interest and amortization of discount have been recorded. (Record the redemption only.)

Sept. 30. Paid the second annual payment on the note, which consisted of interest of $15,794 and principal of $60,173.

Instructions

1. Journalize the entries to record the foregoing transactions.

2. Indicate the amount of the interest expense in (a) 2012 and (b) 2013.

3. Determine the carrying amount of the bonds as of December 31, 2013.

✔ 3. $1,344,040

Appendix 1 and Appendix 2
PR 14-5A Bond discount, entries for bonds payable transactions, interest method of amortizing bond discount

On July 1, 2012, Bliss Industries, Inc. issued $24,000,000 of 20-year, 11% bonds at a market (effective) interest rate of 14%, receiving cash of $19,200,577. Interest on the bonds is payable semiannually on December 31 and June 30. The fiscal year of the company is the calendar year.

Instructions

1. Journalize the entry to record the amount of cash proceeds from the sale of the bonds.

2. Journalize the entries to record the following:

a. The first semiannual interest payment on December 31, 2012, and the amortization of the bond discount, using the interest method. (Round to the nearest dollar.)

b. The interest payment on June 30, 2013, and the amortization of the bond discount, using the interest method. (Round to the nearest dollar.)

3. Determine the total interest expense for 2012.

✔ 3. $8,188,543

Appendix 1 and Appendix 2
PR 14-6A   Bond premium, entries for bonds payable transactions, interest method of amortizing bond discount

Fabulator, Inc. produces and sells fashion clothing. On July 1, 2012, Fabulator, Inc. issued $120,000,000 of 20-year, 14% bonds at a market (effective) interest rate of 11%, receiving cash of $148,882,608. Interest on the bonds is payable semiannually on December 31 and June 30. The fiscal year of the company is the calendar year.

Instructions

1. Journalize the entry to record the amount of cash proceeds from the sale of the bonds.

2. Journalize the entries to record the following:

   a. The first semiannual interest payment on December 31, 2012, and the amortization of the bond discount, using the interest method. (Round to the nearest dollar.)

   b. The interest payment on June 30, 2013, and the amortization of the bond discount, using the interest method. (Round to the nearest dollar.)

3. Determine the total interest expense for 2012.

Problems Series B

OBJ. 1

✔ 1. Plan 3: $4.75

PR 14-1B   Effect of financing on earnings per share

Three different plans for financing a $40,000,000 corporation are under consideration by its organizers. Under each of the following plans, the securities will be issued at their par or face amount, and the income tax rate is estimated at 40% of income.

	Plan 1	Plan 2	Plan 3
10% bonds	—	—	$20,000,000
Preferred $2.50 stock, $50 par	—	$20,000,000	10,000,000
Common stock, $25 par	$40,000,000	20,000,000	10,000,000
Total	$40,000,000	$40,000,000	$40,000,000

Instructions

1. Determine for each plan the earnings per share of common stock, assuming that the income before bond interest and income tax is $6,000,000.

2. Determine for each plan the earnings per share of common stock, assuming that the income before bond interest and income tax is $3,200,000.

3. ━━━➤ Discuss the advantages and disadvantages of each plan.

OBJ. 2, 3

✔ 3. $2,100,119

PR 14-2B   Bond discount, entries for bonds payable transactions

On July 1, 2012, Hallo Corporation, a wholesaler of communication equipment, issued $34,000,000 of 20-year, 12% bonds at a market (effective) interest rate of 13%, receiving cash of $31,595,241. Interest on the bonds is payable semiannually on December 31 and June 30. The fiscal year of the company is the calendar year.

Instructions

1. Journalize the entry to record the amount of cash proceeds from the sale of the bonds.

2. Journalize the entries to record the following:

   a. The first semiannual interest payment on December 31, 2012, and the amortization of the bond discount, using the straight-line method. (Round to the nearest dollar.)

(continued)

b. The interest payment on June 30, 2013, and the amortization of the bond discount, using the straight-line method. (Round to the nearest dollar.)

3. Determine the total interest expense for 2012.

4. Will the bond proceeds always be less than the face amount of the bonds when the contract rate is less than the market rate of interest?

5. (Appendix 1) Compute the price of $31,595,241 received for the bonds by using the tables of present value in Appendix A at the end of the text. (Round to the nearest dollar.)

OBJ. 2, 3

✔ 3. $803,316

PR 14-3B   Bond premium, entries for bonds payable transactions

Buddie Corporation produces and sells baseball gloves. On July 1, 2012, Buddie Corporation issued $12,500,000 of 10-year, 14% bonds at a market (effective) interest rate of 12%, receiving cash of $13,933,680. Interest on the bonds is payable semiannually on December 31 and June 30. The fiscal year of the company is the calendar year.

Instructions

1. Journalize the entry to record the amount of cash proceeds from the sale of the bonds.

2. Journalize the entries to record the following:

    a. The first semiannual interest payment on December 31, 2012, and the amortization of the bond premium, using the straight-line method. (Round to the nearest dollar.)

    b. The interest payment on June 30, 2013, and the amortization of the bond premium, using the straight-line method. (Round to the nearest dollar.)

3. Determine the total interest expense for 2012.

4. Will the bond proceeds always be greater than the face amount of the bonds when the contract rate is greater than the market rate of interest?

5. (Appendix 1) Compute the price of $13,933,680 received for the bonds by using the tables of present value in Appendix A at the end of the text. (Round to the nearest dollar.)

OBJ. 3, 4

✔ 3. $48,673,530

PR 14-4B   Entries for bonds payable and installment note transactions

The following transactions were completed by Wilkerson Inc., whose fiscal year is the calendar year:

2012

July   1. Issued $42,000,000 of 10-year, 13% callable bonds dated July 1, 2012, at a market (effective) rate of 10%, receiving cash of $49,851,213. Interest is payable semiannually on December 31 and June 30.

Oct.   1. Borrowed $510,000 as a six-year, 9% installment note from Challenger Bank. The note requires annual payments of $113,689, with the first payment occurring on September 30, 2013.

Dec. 31. Accrued $11,475 of interest on the installment note. The interest is payable on the date of the next installment note payment.

      31. Paid the semiannual interest on the bonds. The bond discount is amortized annually in a separate journal entry.

      31. Recorded bond premium amortization of $392,561, which was determined using the straight-line method.

      31. Closed the interest expense account.

2013

June 30. Paid the semiannual interest on the bonds.

Sept. 30. Paid the annual payment on the note, which consisted of interest of $45,900 and principal of $67,789.

Dec. 31. Accrued $9,950 of interest on the installment note. The interest is payable on the date of the next installment note payment.

Dec. 31. Paid the semiannual interest on the bonds. The bond discount is amortized annually in a separate journal entry.

31. Recorded bond premium amortization of $785,122, which was determined using the straight-line method.

31. Closed the interest expense account.

2014

June 30. Recorded the redemption of the bonds, which were called at 102. The balance in the bond premium account is $6,280,969 after payment of interest and amortization of premium have been recorded. (Record the redemption only.)

Sept. 30. Paid the second annual payment on the note, which consisted of interest of $39,799 and principal of $73,890.

Instructions

1. Journalize the entries to record the foregoing transactions.

2. Indicate the amount of the interest expense in (a) 2012 and (b) 2013.

3. Determine the carrying amount of the bonds as of December 31, 2013.

✔ 3. $2,053,691

Appendix 1 and Appendix 2
PR 14-5B   Bond discount, entries for bonds payable transactions, interest method of amortizing bond discount

On July 1, 2012, Hallo Corporation, a wholesaler of communication equipment, issued $34,000,000 of 20-year, 12% bonds at a market (effective) interest rate of 13%, receiving cash of $31,595,241. Interest on the bonds is payable semiannually on December 31 and June 30. The fiscal year of the company is the calendar year.

Instructions

1. Journalize the entry to record the amount of cash proceeds from the sale of the bonds.

2. Journalize the entries to record the following:

   a. The first semiannual interest payment on December 31, 2012, and the amortization of the bond discount, using the interest method. (Round to the nearest dollar.)

   b. The interest payment on June 30, 2013, and the amortization of the bond discount, using the interest method. (Round to the nearest dollar.)

3. Determine the total interest expense for 2012.

✔ 3. $836,021

Appendix 1 and Appendix 2
PR 14-6B   Bond premium, entries for bonds payable transactions, interest method of amortizing bond premium

Buddie Corporation produces and sells baseball gloves. On July 1, 2012, Buddie Corporation issued $12,500,000 of 10-year, 14% bonds at a market (effective) interest rate of 12%, receiving cash of $13,933,680. Interest on the bonds is payable semiannually on December 31 and June 30. The fiscal year of the company is the calendar year.

Instructions

1. Journalize the entry to record the amount of cash proceeds from the sale of the bonds.

2. Journalize the entries to record the following:

   a. The first semiannual interest payment on December 31, 2012, and the amortization of the bond premium, using the interest method. (Round to the nearest dollar.)

   b. The interest payment on June 30, 2013, and the amortization of the bond premium, using the interest method. (Round to the nearest dollar.)

3. Determine the total interest expense for 2012.

Cases & Projects

CP 14-1 General Electric bond issuance

General Electric Capital, a division of General Electric, uses long-term debt extensively. In a recent year, GE Capital issued $11 billion in long-term debt to investors, then within days filed legal documents to prepare for another $50 billion long-term debt issue. As a result of the $50 billion filing, the price of the initial $11 billion offering declined (due to higher risk of more debt).

> Bill Gross, a manager of a bond investment fund, "denounced a 'lack in candor' related to GE's recent debt deal. 'It was the most recent and most egregious example of how bondholders are mistreated.' Gross argued that GE was not forthright when GE Capital recently issued $11 billion in bonds, one of the largest issues ever from a U.S. corporation. What bothered Gross is that three days after the issue the company announced its intention to sell as much as $50 billion in additional debt, warrants, preferred stock, guarantees, letters of credit and promissory notes at some future date."

In your opinion, did GE Capital act unethically by selling $11 billion of long-term debt without telling those investors that a few days later it would be filing documents to prepare for another $50 billion debt offering?

Source: Jennifer Ablan, "Gross Shakes the Bond Market; GE Calms It, a Bit," *Barron's,* March 25, 2002.

CP 14-2 Ethics and professional conduct in business

Juicy Energy Industries develops and produces bio mass, an alternative energy source. The company has an outstanding $10,000,000, 30-year, 10% bond issue dated July 1, 2007. The bond issue is due June 30, 2037. Some bond indentures require the corporation issuing the bonds to transfer cash to a special cash fund, called a sinking fund, over the life of the bond. Such funds help assure investors that there will be adequate cash to pay the bonds at their maturity date.

The bond indenture requires a bond sinking fund, which has a balance of $1,200,000 as of July 1, 2012. The company is currently experiencing a shortage of funds due to a recent acquisition. Dillip Fogel, the company's treasurer, is considering using the funds from the bond sinking fund to cover payroll and other bills that are coming due at the end of the month. Dillip's brother-in-law is a trustee in a sinking fund, who has indicated willingness to allow Dillip to use the funds from the sinking fund to temporarily meet the company's cash needs.

Discuss whether Dillip's proposal is appropriate.

CP 14-3 Present values

Bailey Mills recently won the jackpot in the New Jersey lottery while he was visiting his parents. When he arrived at the lottery office to collect his winnings, he was offered the following three payout options:

a. Receive $40,000,000 in cash today.

b. Receive $10,000,000 today and $3,600,000 per year for 10 years, with the first payment being received one year from today.

c. Receive $5,000,000 per year for 20 years, with the first payment being received one year from today.

Assuming that the effective rate of interest is 10%, which payout option should Bailey select? Explain your answer and provide any necessary supporting calculations.

CP 14-4 Preferred stock vs. bonds

Accusport Inc. has decided to expand its operations to owning and operating golf courses. The following is an excerpt from a conversation between the chief executive officer, Tucker Thorup, and the vice president of finance, Don Clark.

Tucker: Don, have you given any thought to how we're going to finance the acquisition of Knotty Pines Golf Course?

Don: Well, the two basic options, as I see it, are to issue either preferred stock or bonds. The equity market is a little depressed right now. The rumor is that the Federal Reserve Bank's going to increase the interest rates either this month or next.

Tucker: Yes, I've heard the rumor. The problem is that we can't wait around to see what's going to happen. We'll have to move on this next week if we want any chance to complete the acquisition of Knotty Pines Golf Course.

Don: Well, the bond market is strong right now. Maybe we should issue debt this time around.

Tucker: That's what I would have guessed as well. Knotty Pines Golf Course's financial statements look pretty good, except for the volatility of its income and cash flows. But that's characteristic of the industry.

➤ Discuss the advantages and disadvantages of issuing preferred stock versus bonds.

CP 14-5   Financing business expansion

You hold a 25% common stock interest in the family-owned business, a construction equipment company. Your sister, who is the manager, has proposed an expansion of plant facilities at an expected cost of $10,000,000. Two alternative plans have been suggested as methods of financing the expansion. Each plan is briefly described as follows:

Plan 1.   Issue $10,000,000 of 20-year, 10% notes at face amount.

Plan 2.   Issue an additional 200,000 shares of $10 par common stock at $20 per share, and $6,000,000 of 20-year, 10% notes at face amount.

The balance sheet as of the end of the previous fiscal year is as follows:

Thacker, Inc.
Balance Sheet
December 31, 2012

Assets	
Current assets	$ 6,000,000
Property, plant, and equipment	9,000,000
Total assets	$15,000,000

Liabilities and Stockholders' Equity	
Liabilities	$ 4,500,000
Common stock, $10	1,600,000
Paid-in capital in excess of par	200,000
Retained earnings	8,700,000
Total liabilities and stockholders' equity	$15,000,000

Net income has remained relatively constant over the past several years. The expansion program is expected to increase yearly income before bond interest and income tax from $800,000 in the previous year to $1,500,000 for this year. Your sister has asked you, as the company treasurer, to prepare an analysis of each financing plan.

1. Prepare a table indicating the expected earnings per share on the common stock under each plan. Assume an income tax rate of 40%. Round to the nearest cent.

2. a. ➤ Discuss the factors that should be considered in evaluating the two plans.

   b. ➤ Which plan offers the greater benefit to the present stockholders? Give reasons for your opinion.

CP 14-6   Number of times interest charges are earned

The following financial data were taken from the financial statements of Williams-Sonoma, Inc.

	Fiscal Year		
	2009	**2008**	**2007**
Interest expense	$ 1,480	$ 2,099	$ 2,125
Earnings before taxes	41,953	316,340	337,186

1. What is the number of times interest charges are earned for Williams-Sonoma in 2009, 2008, and 2007? (Round your answers to one decimal place.)

2. Evaluate this ratio for Williams-Sonoma.

© Fred Prouser/Reuters/Landov

Investments and Fair Value Accounting

News Corporation

You invest cash to earn more cash. For example, you could deposit cash in a bank account to earn interest. You could also invest cash in preferred or common stocks and in corporate or U.S. government notes and bonds.

Preferred and common stock can be purchased through a stock exchange, such as the **New York Stock Exchange (NYSE)**. Preferred stock is purchased primarily with the expectation of earning dividends. Common stock is purchased with the expectation of earning dividends or realizing gains from a price increase in the stock.

Corporate and U.S. government bonds can also be purchased through a bond exchange. Bonds are purchased with the primary expectation of earning interest revenue.

Companies make investments for many of the same reasons that you would as an

individual. For example, **News Corporation**, a diversified media company, which produces such popular television shows as *The Simpsons* and *American Idol*, has invested $150 million of available cash in stocks and bonds. These investments are held by News Corporation for interest, dividends, and expected price increases.

Unlike most individuals, however, companies also purchase significant amounts of the outstanding common stock of other companies for strategic reasons. For example, News Corporation invested in 32% of the Hulu, an online video joint venture with other major media companies.

Investments in debt and equity securities give rise to a number of accounting issues. These issues are described and illustrated in this chapter.

OBJ. 1 Describe why companies invest in debt and equity securities.

Why Companies Invest

Most companies generate cash from their operations. This cash can be used for the following purposes:

1. Investing in current operations
2. Investing in temporary investments to earn additional revenue
3. Investing in long-term investments in stock of other companies for strategic reasons

Investing Cash in Current Operations

Cash is often used to support the current operating activities of a company. For example, cash may be used to replace worn-out equipment or to purchase new, more efficient, and productive equipment. In addition, cash may be reinvested in the company to expand its current operations. For example, a retailer based in the northwest United States might decide to expand by opening stores in the midwest.

To support its current level of operations, a company also uses cash to pay:

1. expenses.
2. suppliers of merchandise and other assets.
3. interest to creditors.
4. dividends to stockholders.

The accounting for the use of cash in current operations has been described and illustrated in earlier chapters. For example, Chapter 10, "Fixed Assets and Intangible

Assets," illustrated the use of cash for purchasing property, plant, and equipment. In this chapter, we describe and illustrate the use of cash for investing in temporary investments and stock of other companies.

Investing Cash in Temporary Investments

A company may temporarily have excess cash that is not needed for use in its current operations. This is often the case when a company has a seasonal operating cycle. For example, a significant portion of the annual merchandise sales of a retailer occurs during the fall holiday season. As a result, retailers often experience a large increase in cash during this period, which is not needed until the spring buying season.

Instead of letting excess cash remain idle in a checking account, most companies invest their excess cash in temporary investments. In doing so, companies invest in securities such as:

1. **Debt securities**, which are notes and bonds that pay interest and have a fixed maturity date.
2. **Equity securities**, which are preferred and common stock that represent ownership in a company and do not have a fixed maturity date.

Investments in debt and equity securities, termed **Investments** or *Temporary Investments*, are reported in the Current Assets section of the balance sheet.

The primary objective of investing in temporary investments is to:

1. earn interest revenue
2. receive dividends
3. realize gains from increases in the market price of the securities.

Investments in certificates of deposit and other securities that do not normally change in value are disclosed on the balance sheet as *cash and cash equivalents*. Such investments are held primarily for their interest revenue.

Investing Cash in Long-Term Investments

A company may invest cash in the debt or equity of another company as a long-term investment. Long-term investments may be held for the same investment objectives as temporary investments. However, long-term investments often involve the purchase of a significant portion of the stock of another company. Such investments usually have a strategic purpose, such as:

1. *Reduction of costs*: When one company buys another company, the combined company may be able to reduce administrative expenses. For example, a combined company does not need two chief executive officers (CEOs) or chief financial officers (CFOs).
2. *Replacement of management*: If the purchased company has been mismanaged, the acquiring company may replace the company's management and, thus, improve operations and profits.
3. *Expansion*: The acquiring company may purchase a company because it has a complementary product line, territory, or customer base. The new combined company may be able to serve customers better than the two companies could separately.
4. *Integration*: A company may integrate operations by acquiring a supplier or customer. Acquiring a supplier may provide a more stable or uninterrupted supply of resources. Acquiring a customer may also provide a market for the company's products or services.

The Walt Disney Company purchased Marvel Entertainment in order to expand into action/adventure characters, movies, and products.

Accounting for Debt Investments

OBJ. 2   Describe and illustrate the accounting for debt investments.

Debt securities include notes and bonds, issued by corporations and governmental organizations. Most companies invest excess cash in bonds as investments to earn interest revenue.

The accounting for bond investments[1] includes recording the following:

1. Purchase of bonds
2. Interest revenue
3. Sale of bonds

Purchase of Bonds

The purchase of bonds is recorded by debiting an investments account for the purchase price of the bonds, including any brokerage commissions. If the bonds are purchased between interest dates, the purchase price includes accrued interest since the last interest payment. This is because the seller has earned the accrued interest, but the buyer will receive the accrued interest when it is paid.

To illustrate, assume that Homer Company purchases $18,000 of U.S. Treasury bonds at their par value on March 17, 2012, plus accrued interest for 45 days. The bonds have an interest rate of 6%, payable on July 31 and January 31.

The entry to record the purchase of Treasury bonds is as follows:

2012				
Mar.	17	Investments—U.S. Treasury Bonds	18,000	
		Interest Receivable	135	
		Cash		18,135
		Purchased $18,000, 6% Treasury bonds.		

Since Homer Company purchased the bonds on March 17, it is also purchasing the accrued interest for 45 days (January 31 to March 17) as shown in Exhibit 1. The accrued interest of $135 is computed as follows:[2]

$$\text{Accrued Interest} = \$18,000 \times 6\% \times (45/360) = \$135$$

The accrued interest is recorded by debiting Interest Receivable for $135. Bond Investments is debited for the purchase price of the bonds of $18,000.

Interest Revenue

On July 31, Homer Company receives a semiannual interest payment of $540 ($18,000 × 6% × 1 ½). The $540 interest includes the $135 accrued interest that Homer Company purchased with the bonds on March 17. Thus, Homer Company has earned $405 ($540 − $135) of interest revenue since purchasing the bonds as shown in Exhibit 1.

The receipt of the interest on July 31 is recorded as follows:

2012				
July	31	Cash	540	
		Interest Receivable		135
		Interest Revenue		405
		Received semiannual interest.		

Homer Company's accounting period ends on December 31. Thus, an adjusting entry must be made to accrue interest for five months (August 1 to December 31) of $450 ($18,000 × 6% × 5/12) as shown in Exhibit 1. The adjusting entry to record the accrued interest is as follows:

2012				
Dec.	31	Interest Receivable	450	
		Interest Revenue		450
		Accrue interest.		

---

1 Debt investments may also include installment notes and short-term notes. The basic accounting for notes is similar to bonds and, thus, is not illustrated.

2 To simplify, a 360-day year is used to compute interest.

> ### EXHIBIT 1   Interest Timeline
>
>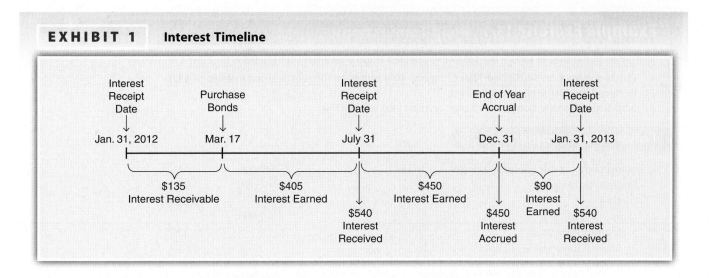

For the year ended December 31, 2012, Homer Company would report *Interest revenue* of $855 ($405 + $450) as part of *Other income* on its income statement.

The receipt of the semiannual interest of $540 on January 31, 2013, is recorded as follows:

2013				
Jan.	31	Cash	540	
		Interest Revenue		90
		Interest Receivable		450
		Received interest on Treasury bonds.		

Sale of Bonds

The sale of a bond investment normally results in a gain or loss. If the proceeds from the sale exceed the book value (cost) of the bonds, then a gain is recorded. If the proceeds are less than the book value (cost) of the bonds, a loss is recorded.

To illustrate, on January 31, 2013, Homer Company sells the Treasury bonds at 98, which is a price equal to 98% of par value. The sale results in a loss of $360, as shown below.

Proceeds from sale	$17,640*
Less book value (cost) of the bonds	18,000
Loss on sale of bonds	$ (360)

*($18,000 × 98%)

The entry to record the sale is as follows:

2013				
Jan.	31	Cash	17,640	
		Loss on Sale of Investment	360	
		Investments—U.S. Treasury Bonds		18,000
		Sale of U.S. Treasury bonds.		

There is no accrued interest upon the sale since the interest payment date is also January 31. If the sale were between interest dates, interest accrued since the last interest payment date would be added to the sale proceeds and credited to Interest Revenue. The loss on the sale of bond investments is reported as part of *Other income (loss)* on Homer Company's income statement.

Example Exercise 15-1 **Bond Transactions**

OBJ. 2

Journalize the entries to record the following selected bond investment transactions for Tyler Company:

1. Purchased for cash $40,000 of Tyler Company 10% bonds at 100 plus accrued interest of $320.
2. Received the first semiannual interest.
3. Sold $30,000 of the bonds at 102 plus accrued interest of $110.

Follow My Example 15-1

1.	Investments—Tyler Company Bonds	40,000	
	Interest Receivable	320	
	Cash		40,320
2.	Cash	2,000*	
	Interest Receivable		320
	Interest Revenue		1,680
	*$40,000 × 10% × ½		
3.	Cash	30,710*	
	Interest Revenue		110
	Gain on Sale of Investments		600
	Investments—Tyler Company Bonds		30,000

*Sale proceeds ($30,000 × 102%)	$30,600
Accrued interest	110
Total proceeds from sale	$30,710

Practice Exercises: **PE 15-1A, PE 15-1B**

OBJ. 3

Describe and illustrate the accounting for equity investments.

Accounting for Equity Investments

A company may invest in the preferred or common stock of another company. The company investing in another company's stock is the **investor**. The company whose stock is purchased is the **investee**.

The percent of the investee's outstanding stock purchased by the investor determines the degree of control that the investor has over the investee. This, in turn, determines the accounting method used to record the stock investment as shown in Exhibit 2.

EXHIBIT 2

Stock Investments

Percent of Outstanding Stock Owned by Investor	Degree of Control of Investor over Investee	Accounting Method
Less than 20%	No control	Cost method
Between 20% and 50%	Significant influence	Equity method
Greater than 50%	Control	Consolidation

Less Than 20% Ownership

If the investor purchases less than 20% of the outstanding stock of the investee, the investor is considered to have no control over the investee. In this case, it is assumed that the investor purchased the stock primarily to earn dividends or realize gains on price increases of the stock.

Investments of less than 20% of the investee's outstanding stock are accounted for using the **cost method**. Under the cost method, entries are recorded for the following transactions:

1. Purchase of stock
2. Receipt of dividends
3. Sale of stock

Purchase of Stock

The purchase of stock is recorded at its cost. Any brokerage commissions are included as part of the cost.

To illustrate, assume that on May 1, Bart Company purchases 2,000 shares of Lisa Company common stock at $49.90 per share plus a brokerage fee of $200. The entry to record the purchase of the stock is as follows:

May	1	Investments—Lisa Company Stock		100,000	
		Cash			100,000
		Purchased 2,000 shares of Lisa Company common stock [($49.90 × 2,000 shares) + $200].			

Receipt of Dividends

On July 31, Bart Company receives a dividend of $0.40 per share from Lisa Company. The entry to record the receipt of the dividend is as follows:

July	31	Cash		800	
		Dividend Revenue			800
		Received dividend on Lisa Company common stock (2,000 shares × $0.40).			

Dividend revenue is reported as part of *Other income* on Bart Company's income statement.

Sale of Stock

The sale of a stock investment normally results in a gain or loss. A gain is recorded if the proceeds from the sale exceed the book value (cost) of the stock. A loss is recorded if the proceeds from the sale are less than the book value (cost).

To illustrate, on September 1, Bart Company sells 1,500 shares of Lisa Company stock for $54.50 per share, less a $160 commission. The sale results in a gain of $6,590, as shown below.

Proceeds from sale	$81,590*
Book value (cost) of the stock	75,000**
Gain on sale	$ 6,590

*($54.50 × 1,500 shares) – $160
**($100,000/2,000 shares) × 1,500 shares

The entry to record the sale is as follows:

Sept.	1	Cash		81,590	
		Gain on Sale of Investments			6,590
		Investments—Lisa Company Stock			75,000
		Sale of 1,500 shares of Lisa Company common stock.			

The gain on the sale of investments is reported as part of *Other income* on Bart Company's income statement.

Example Exercise 15-2 Stock Transactions

OBJ. 3

On September 1, 1,500 shares of Monroe Company are acquired at a price of $24 per share plus a $40 brokerage fee. On October 14, a $0.60 per share dividend was received on the Monroe Company stock. On November 11, 750 shares (half) of Monroe Company stock were sold for $20 per share, less a $45 brokerage fee. Prepare the journal entries for the original purchase, dividend, and sale.

Follow My Example 15-2

Sept. 1	Investments—Monroe Company Stock	36,040*	
	Cash		36,040
	*(1,500 shares × $24 per share) + $40		
Oct. 14	Cash	900*	
	Dividend Revenue		900
	*$0.60 per share × 1,500 shares		
Nov. 11	Cash	14,955*	
	Loss on Sale of Investments	3,065	
	Investments—Monroe Company Stock		18,020**

*(750 shares × $20) − $45
**$36,040 × ½

Practice Exercises: **PE 15-2A, PE 15-2B**

Between 20%–50% Ownership

If the investor purchases between 20% and 50% of the outstanding stock of the investee, the investor is considered to have a significant influence over the investee. In this case, it is assumed that the investor purchased the stock primarily for strategic reasons such as developing a supplier relationship.

Investments of between 20% and 50% of the investee's outstanding stock are accounted for using the **equity method**. Under the equity method, the stock is recorded initially at its cost, including any brokerage commissions. This is the same as under the cost method.

Under the equity method, the investment account is adjusted for the investor's share of the *net income* and *dividends* of the investee. These adjustments are as follows:

1. *Net Income:* The investor records its share of the net income of the investee as an increase in the investment account. Its share of any net loss is recorded as a decrease in the investment account.

2. *Dividends:* The investor's share of cash dividends received from the investee decreases the investment account.

Purchase of Stock To illustrate, assume that Simpson Inc. purchased its 40% interest in Flanders Corporation's common stock on January 2, 2012, for $350,000. The entry to record the purchase is as follows:

2012 Jan.	2	Investment in Flanders Corporation Stock		350,000	
		Cash			350,000
		Purchased 40% of Flanders			
		Corporation stock.			

Recording Investee Net Income For the year ended December 31, 2012, Flanders Corporation reported net income of $105,000. Under the equity method, Simpson Inc. (the investor) records its share of Flanders net income as shown on the next page.

2012					
Dec.	31	Investment in Flanders Corporation Stock		42,000	
		Income of Flanders Corporation			42,000
		Record 40% share of Flanders			
		Corporation net income, $105,000 × 40%.			

Income of Flanders Corporation is reported on Simpson Inc.'s income statement. Depending on its significance, it may be reported separately or as part of *Other income.* If Flanders Corporation had a loss during the period, then the journal entry would be a debit to Loss of Flanders Corporation and a credit to the investment account.

Recording Investee Dividends During the year, Flanders declared and paid cash dividends of $45,000. Under the equity method, Simpson Inc. (the investor) records its share of Flanders dividends as follows:

2012					
Dec.	31	Cash		18,000	
		Investment in Flanders Corporation Stock			18,000
		Record 40% share of Flanders			
		Corporation dividends, $45,000 × 40%.			

The effect of recording 40% of Flanders Corporation's net income and dividends is to increase the investment account by $24,000 ($42,000 – $18,000). Thus, Investment in Flanders Corporation Stock increases from $350,000 to $374,000, as shown below.

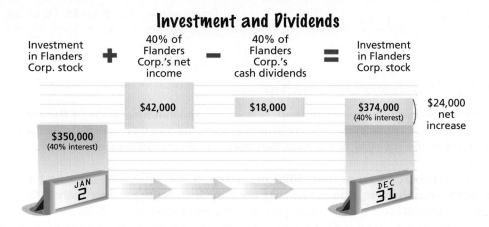

Investment and Dividends

Under the equity method, the investment account reflects the investor's proportional changes in the net book value of the investee. For example, Flanders Corporation's net book value increased by $60,000 (net income of $105,000 less dividends of $45,000) during the year. As a result, Simpson's share of Flanders' net book value increased by $24,000 ($60,000 × 40%). Investments accounted for under the equity method are classified on the balance sheet as noncurrent assets.

Sale of Stock Under the equity method, a gain or loss is normally recorded from the sale of an investment. A gain is recorded if the proceeds exceed the *book value* of the investment. A loss is recorded if the proceeds are less than the *book value* of the investment.

To illustrate, if Simpson Inc. sold Flanders Corporation's stock on January 1, 2013, for $400,000, a gain of $26,000 would be reported, as shown below.

Proceeds from sale	$400,000
Book value of stock investment	374,000
Gain on sale	$ 26,000

The entry to record the sale is as follows:

2013					
Jan.	1	Cash		400,000	
		Investment in Flanders Corporation Stock			374,000
		Gain on Sale of Flanders Corporation Stock			26,000
		Sale of Flanders Corporation stock.			

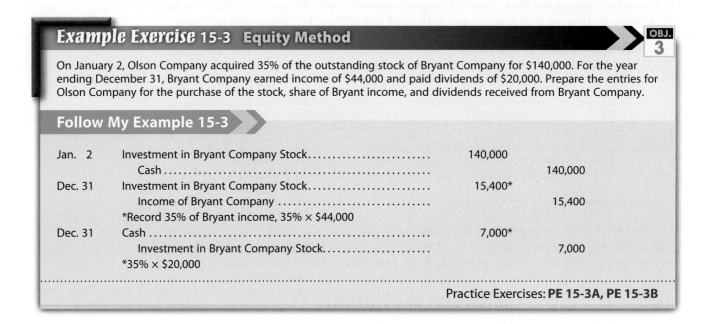

Example Exercise 15-3 Equity Method   OBJ. 3

On January 2, Olson Company acquired 35% of the outstanding stock of Bryant Company for $140,000. For the year ending December 31, Bryant Company earned income of $44,000 and paid dividends of $20,000. Prepare the entries for Olson Company for the purchase of the stock, share of Bryant income, and dividends received from Bryant Company.

Follow My Example 15-3

Jan. 2	Investment in Bryant Company Stock.........................	140,000	
	Cash		140,000
Dec. 31	Investment in Bryant Company Stock.........................	15,400*	
	Income of Bryant Company		15,400
	*Record 35% of Bryant income, 35% × $44,000		
Dec. 31	Cash	7,000*	
	Investment in Bryant Company Stock......................		7,000
	*35% × $20,000		

Practice Exercises: **PE 15-3A, PE 15-3B**

More Than 50% Ownership

If the investor purchases more than 50% of the outstanding stock of the investee, the investor is considered to have control over the investee. In this case, it is assumed that the investor purchased the stock of the investee primarily for strategic reasons.

The purchase of more than 50% ownership of the investee's stock is termed a **business combination**. Companies may combine in order to produce more efficiently, diversify product lines, expand geographically, or acquire know-how.

A corporation owning all or a majority of the voting stock of another corporation is called a **parent company**. The corporation that is controlled is called the **subsidiary company**.

Parent and subsidiary corporations often continue to maintain separate accounting records and prepare their own financial statements. In such cases, at the end of the year, the financial statements of the parent and subsidiary are combined and reported as a single company. These combined financial statements are called **consolidated financial statements**. Such statements are normally identified by adding *and Subsidiary(ies)* to the name of the parent corporation or by adding *Consolidated* to the statement title.

To the external stakeholders of the parent company, consolidated financial statements are more meaningful than separate statements for each corporation. This is because the parent company, in substance, controls the subsidiaries. The accounting for business combinations, including preparing consolidated financial statements, is decribed and illustrated in advanced accounting courses and textbooks.

Valuing and Reporting Investments

OBJ. 4 Describe and illustrate valuing and reporting investments in the financial statements.

Debt and equity securities are *financial assets* that are often traded on public exchanges such as the New York Stock Exchange. As a result, their market value can be observed and, thus, objectively determined.

For this reason, generally accepted accounting principles (GAAP) allow some debt and equity securities to be valued in the accounting records and financial statements at their fair market values. In contrast, GAAP requires tangible assets such as property, plant, and equipment to be valued and reported at their net book values (cost less accumulated depreciation).

For purposes of valuing and reporting, debt and equity securities are classified as follows:

1. Trading securities
2. Available-for-sale securities
3. Held-to-maturity securities

Trading Securities

Trading securities are debt and equity securities that are purchased and sold to earn short-term profits from changes in their market prices. Trading securities are often held by banks, mutual funds, insurance companies, and other financial institutions.

Since trading securities are held as a short-term investment, they are reported as a current asset on the balance sheet. Trading securities are valued as a portfolio (group) of securities using the securities' fair values. **Fair value** is the market price that the company would receive for a security if it were sold. Changes in fair value of the portfolio (group) of trading securities are recognized as an **unrealized gain or loss** for the period.

SunTrust Banks Inc. holds $10 billion in trading securities as current assets.

To illustrate, assume Maggie Company purchased a portfolio of trading securities during 2012. On December 31, 2012, the cost and fair values of the securities were as follows:

Name	Number of Shares	Total Cost	Total Fair Value
Armour Company	400	$ 5,000	$ 7,200
Maven, Inc.	500	11,000	7,500
Polaris Co.	200	8,000	10,600
Total		$24,000	$25,300

The portfolio of trading securities is reported at its fair value of $25,300. An adjusting entry is made to record the increase in fair value of $1,300 ($25,300 − $24,000). In order to maintain a record of the original cost of the securities, a valuation account, called *Valuation Allowance for Trading Investments*, is debited for $1,300 and *Unrealized Gain on Trading Investments* is credited for $1,300.[3] The adjusting entry on December 31, 2012, to record the fair value of the portfolio of trading securities is shown below.

2012				
Dec.	31	Valuation Allowance for Trading Investments	1,300	
		Unrealized Gain on Trading Investments		1,300
		To record increase in fair value of		
		trading securities.		

The *Unrealized Gain on Trading Investments* is reported on the income statement. Depending on its significance, it may be reported separately or as *Other income* on the income statement. The valuation allowance is reported on the December 31, 2012, balance sheet as follows:

Maggie Company
Balance Sheet (selected items)
December 31, 2012

Current assets:		
Cash..		$120,000
Trading investments (at cost)...........................	$24,000	
Plus valuation allowance for trading investments	1,300	
Trading investments (at fair value)		25,300

If the fair value was less than the cost, then the adjustment would debit *Unrealized Loss on Trading Investments* and credit *Valuation Allowance for Trading Investments* for the difference. Unrealized Loss on Trading Investments would be reported on the income statement as Other expenses. Valuation Allowance for Trading Investments would be shown on the balance sheet as a *deduction* from Trading Investments (at cost).

Over time, the valuation allowance account is adjusted to reflect the difference between the cost and fair value of the portfolio. Thus, increases in the valuation allowance account from the beginning of the period will result in an adjustment to record an unrealized gain, similar to the journal entry illustrated above. Likewise, decreases in the valuation allowance account from the beginning of the period will result in an adjustment to record an unrealized loss.

Example Exercise 15-4 Valuing Trading Securities at Fair Value

OBJ. 4

On January 1, 2012, Valuation Allowance for Trading Investments had a zero balance. On December 31, 2012, the cost of the trading securities portfolio was $79,200, and the fair value was $76,800. Prepare the December 31, 2012, adjusting journal entry to record the unrealized gain or loss on trading investments.

(Continued)

---

3 We assume that the valuation allowance account has a beginning balance of zero to simplify our illustrations.

Follow My Example 15-4

2012			
Dec. 31	Unrealized Loss on Trading Investments.......................	2,400	
	Valuation Allowance for Trading Investments...............		2,400*
	To record decrease in fair value of trading investments.		

*Trading investments at fair value, December 31, 2012	$ 76,800
Less: Trading investments at cost, December 31, 2012	79,200
Unrealized loss on trading investments	$ (2,400)

Practice Exercises: **PE 15-4A, PE 15-4B**

Integrity, Objectivity, and Ethics in Business

LOAN LOSS WOES

During the economic crisis of 2008, many of the largest U.S. banks were accused of having provided mortgages to marginally qualified borrowers. Such loans, called "sub-prime" and "Alt-A" loans, were made to earn mortgage fees. When the borrowers were unable to pay their mortgages, the banks incurred large losses on defaulted loans. These losses were so large that the U.S. government had to provide money (TARP funds) to many banks to bail them out of their financial distress.

During the middle of the crisis, the FASB voted to provide banks more flexibility in applying fair value accounting for bank assets, such as defaulted loans. These FASB rule changes allowed banks to minimize the impact of their defaulted loan write-downs and improve their earnings. Some criticized the FASB as succumbing to political pressure, and reducing overall financial statement fairness.

Source: Ian Katz, "FASB Eases Fair-Value Rules Amid Lawmaker Pressure," *Bloomberg*, April 2, 2009.

Available-for-Sale Securities

Available-for-sale securities are debt and equity securities that are neither held for trading, held to maturity, or held for strategic reasons.

The accounting for available-for-sale securities is similar to the accounting for trading securities except for the reporting of changes in fair values. Specifically, changes in the fair values of *trading securities* are reported as an unrealized gain or loss on the income statement. In contrast, changes in the fair values of *available-for-sale securities* are reported as part of stockholders' equity and, thus, excluded from the income statement.

To illustrate, assume that Maggie Company purchased the three securities during 2012 as available-for-sale securities instead of trading securities. On December 31, 2012, the cost and fair values of the securities were as follows:

Name	Number of Shares	Total Cost	Total Fair Value
Armour Company	400	$ 5,000	$ 7,200
Maven, Inc.	500	11,000	7,500
Polaris Co.	200	8,000	10,600
Total		$24,000	$25,300

Microsoft Corporation holds over $25 billion in available-for-sale securities as current assets.

The portfolio of available-for-sale securities is reported at its fair value of $25,300. An adjusting entry is made to record the increase in fair value of $1,300 ($25,300 – $24,000). In order to maintain a record of the original cost of the securities, a valuation account, called *Valuation Allowance for Available-for-Sale Investments*, is debited for $1,300. This account is similar to the valuation account used for trading securities.

Unlike trading securities, the December 31, 2012, adjusting entry credits a stockholders' equity account instead of an income statement account.[4] The $1,300 increase in fair value is credited to *Unrealized Gain (Loss) on Available-for-Sale Investments.*

The adjusting entry on December 31, 2012, to record the fair value of the portfolio of available-for-sale securities is as follows:

2012				
Dec.	31	Valuation Allowance for Available-for-Sale Investments	1,300	
		Unrealized Gain (Loss) on Available-for-Sale Investments		1,300
		To record increase in fair value of available-for-sale investments.		

A credit balance in Unrealized Gain (Loss) on Available-for-Sale Investments is added to stockholders' equity, while a debit balance is subtracted from stockholders' equity.

The valuation allowance and the unrealized gain are reported on the December 31, 2012, balance sheet as follows:

Maggie Company
Balance Sheet
December 31, 2012

Current assets:
Cash $120,000
Available-for-sale investments (at cost) $24,000
Plus valuation allowance for available-for-sale investments 1,300
Available-for-sale investments (at fair value) 25,300

Stockholders' equity:
Common stock . . . . $ 10,000
Paid-in capital in excess of par value 150,000
Retained earnings 250,000
Unrealized gain (loss) on available-for-sale investments 1,300
Total stockholders' equity $411,300

Equal

As shown above, Unrealized Gain (Loss) on Available-for-Sale Investments is reported as an addition to stockholders' equity. In future years, the cumulative effects of unrealized gains and losses are reported in this account. Since 2012 was the first year that Maggie Company purchased available-for-sale securities, the unrealized gain is reported as the balance of *Unrealized Gain (Loss) on Available-for-Sale Investments.* This treatment is supported under the theory that available-for-sale securities will be held longer than trading securities, so changes in fair value over time have a greater opportunity to cancel out. Thus, these changes are not reported on the income statement as is the case with trading securities.

If the fair value was less than the cost, then the adjustment would debit Unrealized Gain (Loss) on Available-for-Sale Investments and credit Valuation Allowance for Available-for-Sale Investments for the difference. Unrealized Gain (Loss) on Trading Investments would be reported in the Stockholders' Equity section as

4 This is a rare exception to the rule that every adjusting entry must affect an income statement and a balance sheet account.

a negative item. Valuation Allowance for Available-for-Sale Investments would be shown on the balance sheet as a deduction from Available-for-Sale Investments (at cost).

Over time, the valuation allowance account is adjusted to reflect the difference between the cost and fair value of the portfolio. Thus, increases in the valuation allowance from the beginning of the period will result in an adjustment to record an increase in the valuation and unrealized gain (loss) accounts, similar to the journal entry illustrated earlier. Likewise, decreases in valuation allowance from the beginning of the period will result in an adjustment to record decreases in the valuation and unrealized gain (loss) accounts.

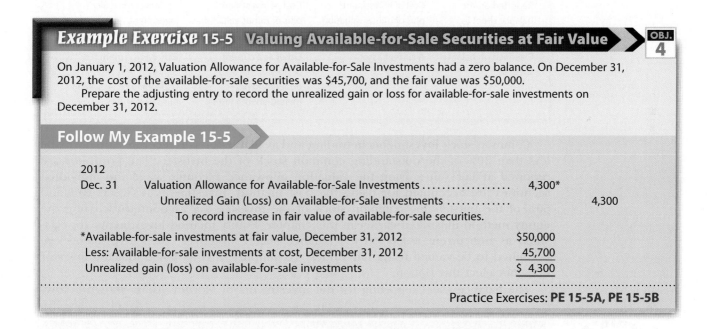

Example Exercise 15-5   **Valuing Available-for-Sale Securities at Fair Value**   OBJ. 4

On January 1, 2012, Valuation Allowance for Available-for-Sale Investments had a zero balance. On December 31, 2012, the cost of the available-for-sale securities was $45,700, and the fair value was $50,000.

Prepare the adjusting entry to record the unrealized gain or loss for available-for-sale investments on December 31, 2012.

Follow My Example 15-5

2012
Dec. 31   Valuation Allowance for Available-for-Sale Investments 4,300*
          Unrealized Gain (Loss) on Available-for-Sale Investments   4,300
          To record increase in fair value of available-for-sale securities.

*Available-for-sale investments at fair value, December 31, 2012	$50,000
Less: Available-for-sale investments at cost, December 31, 2012	45,700
Unrealized gain (loss) on available-for-sale investments	$ 4,300

Practice Exercises: **PE 15-5A, PE 15-5B**

Held-to-Maturity Securities

Held-to-maturity securities are debt investments, such as notes or bonds, that a company intends to hold until their maturity date. Held-to-maturity securities are primarily purchased to earn interest revenue.

If a held-to-maturity security will mature within a year, it is reported as a current asset on the balance sheet. Held-to-maturity securities maturing beyond a year are reported as noncurrent assets.

Only securities with maturity dates such as corporate notes and bonds are classified as held-to-maturity securities. Equity securities are not held-to-maturity securities because they have no maturity date.

Held-to-maturity bond investments are recorded at their cost, including any brokerage commissions, as illustrated earlier in this chapter. If the interest rate on the bonds differs from the market rate of interest, the bonds may be purchased at a premium or discount. In such cases, the premium or discount is amortized over the life of the bonds.

Held-to-maturity bond investments are reported on the balance sheet at their amortized cost. The accounting for held-to-maturity investments, including premium and discount amortization, is described in advanced accounting texts.

Summary

Exhibit 3 summarizes the valuation and balance sheet reporting of trading, available-for-sale, and held-to-maturity securities.

EXHIBIT 3

Summary of
Valuing and
Reporting of
Investments

	Trading Securities	Available-for-Sale Securities	Held-to-Maturity Securities
Valued at:	**Fair Value**	**Fair Value**	**Amortized Cost**
Changes in valuation are reported as:	Unrealized gain or loss is reported on income statement as Other income (loss).	Accumulated unrealized gain or loss is reported in stockholders' equity on the balance sheet.	Premium or discount amortization is reported as part of interest revenue on the income statement.
Reported on the balance sheet as:	Cost of investments plus or minus valuation allowance.	Cost of investments plus or minus valuation allowance.	Amortized cost of investment.
Classified on balance sheet as:	A current asset.	Either as a current or noncurrent asset, depending on management's intent.	Either as a current or noncurrent asset, depending on remaining term to maturity.

Common stock investments in trading and available-for-sale securities are normally less than 20% of the outstanding common stock of the investee. The portfolios are reported at fair value using the valuation allowance account, while the individual securities are accounted for using the cost method. Investments between 20% and 50% of the outstanding common stock of the investee are accounted for using the equity method illustrated earlier in this chapter. Equity method investments are classified as noncurrent assets on the balance sheet. Moreover, such investments are permitted to be valued using fair values. To simplify, it is assumed that the investor does not elect this option.

The balance sheet reporting for the investments of Mornin' Joe is shown below.

Mornin' Joe
Balance Sheet
December 31, 2012

Assets

Current assets:

Cash and cash equivalents		$235,000
Trading investments (at cost)	$420,000	
Plus valuation allowance for trading investments	45,000	465,000
Accounts receivable	$305,000	
Less allowance for doubtful accounts	12,300	292,700
Merchandise inventory—at lower of cost		
(first-in, first-out method) or market		120,000
Prepaid insurance		24,000
Total current assets...................................		$1,136,700

Investments:

Investment in AM Coffee (equity method)		565,000

Property, plant, and equipment:

Mornin' Joe invests in trading securities and does not have investments in held-to-maturity or available-for-sale securities. Mornin' Joe also owns 40% of AM Coffee Corporation, which is accounted for using the equity method. Mornin' Joe intends to keep its investment in AM Coffee indefinitely for strategic reasons; thus, its investment in AM Coffee is classified as a noncurrent asset. Such investments are normally reported before property, plant, and equipment.

Mornin' Joe reported an Unrealized Gain on Trading Investments of $5,000 and Equity Income in AM Coffee of $57,000 in the Other income and expense section of its income statement, as shown below.

Mornin' Joe		
Income Statement		
For the Year Ended December 31, 2012		
Revenue from sales:		
Sales		$5,450,000
Less: Sales returns and allowances	$26,500	
Sales discounts	21,400	47,900
Net sales.....................................		$5,402,100
Cost of merchandise sold		2,160,000
Gross profit		$3,242,100
Total operating expenses		2,608,700
Income from operations		$ 633,400
Other income and expense:		
Interest revenue..............................	$ 18,000	
Interest expense..............................	(136,000)	
Loss on disposal of fixed asset	(23,000)	
Unrealized gain on trading investments	5,000	
Equity income in AM Coffee	57,000	(79,000)
Income before income taxes		$ 554,400
Income tax expense		132,800
Net income		$ 421,600

BusinessConnection

WARREN BUFFETT: THE SAGE OF OMAHA

Beginning in 1962, Warren Buffett, one of the world's wealthiest and most successful investors, began buying shares of Berkshire Hathaway. He eventually took control of the company and transformed it from a textile manufacturing company into an investment holding company. Today, Berkshire Hathaway holds over $125 billion in cash and cash equivalents, equity securities, and debt securities. Berkshire's largest holdings include The Coca-Cola Company, American Express, Wells Fargo, and Procter & Gamble. Berkshire Class A common stock trades near $115,000 per share, the highest priced share on the New York Stock Exchange. These shares would have given an investor a nearly 1,400% return since 1990.

Buffett compares his investment style to hitting a baseball: "Ted Williams, one of the greatest hitters in the game, stated, 'my argument is, to be a good hitter, you've got to get a good ball to hit. It's the first rule of the book. If I have to bite at stuff that is out of my happy zone, I'm not a .344 hitter. I might only be a .250 hitter.'" Buffett states, "Charlie (Buffett's partner) and I agree and will try to wait for (investment) opportunities that are well within our 'happy zone.'"[5] One of Buffet's recent "happy zone" investments was the acquisition of Burlington Northern Santa Fe Railroad for $34 billion.

Warren Buffett as the CEO of Berkshire Hathaway earns a salary of only $100,000 per year, which is the lowest CEO salary for a company of its size in the United States. However, he personally owns approximately 38% of the company, making him worth over $40 billion. What will Buffett do with this wealth? He has decided to give nearly all of it to philanthropic causes through the Bill and Melinda Gates Foundation.

5 Warren E. Buffett, *The Essays of Warren Buffett: Lessons for Corporate America*, edited by Lawrence A. Cunningham, p. 234.

Describe fair value accounting and its implications for the future.

Fair Value Accounting

Fair value is the price that would be received for selling an asset or paying off a liability. Fair value assumes that the asset is sold or the liability paid off under *normal* rather than under distressed conditions.

As illustrated earlier, generally accepted accounting principles require the use of fair values for valuing and reporting debt and equity securities held as trading or available-for-sale investments. In addition, accounts receivable is recorded and reported at an amount that approximates its fair value. Likewise, accounts payable are recorded and reported at approximately their fair value.

In contrast, many assets and liabilities are recorded and reported at amounts that differ significantly from their fair values. For example, when equipment or other property, plant, and equipment assets are purchased, they are initially recorded at their fair values. That is, they are recorded at their purchase price, called *historical cost*, and depreciated over its useful life. As a result, the book value of property, plant, and equipment normally differs significantly from its fair value. Likewise, held-to-maturity securities are valued at their amortized cost rather than at their fair values.

Trend to Fair Value Accounting

A current trend is for the Financial Accounting Standards Board (FASB) and other accounting regulators to adopt accounting principles using fair values for valuing and reporting assets and liabilities. Factors contributing to this trend include the following:

1. Current generally accepted accounting principles are a hybrid of varying measurement methods that often conflict with one another. For example, property, plant, and equipment are normally reported at their depreciated book values. However, GAAP require that if a fixed asset value is *impaired*, that it be written down to its fair value. Such conflicting accounting principles could confuse users of financial statements.

2. A greater percentage of the total assets of many companies consists of financial assets such as receivables and securities. Fair values for such assets can often be readily obtained from stock market quotations or computed using current interest rates and present values. Likewise, many liabilities can be readily valued using market quotations or current interest rates and present values.

See Appendix D for more information

3. The world economy has compelled accounting regulators to adopt a worldwide set of accounting principles and standards. *International Financial Reporting Standards (IFRSs)* are issued by the International Accounting Standards Board *(IASB)* and are used by the European Economic Union (EU). As a result, the FASB is under increasing pressure to conform U.S. accounting standards to international standards. One area where differences exist is in the use of fair values, which are more often used by International Financial Reporting Standards.

While there is an increasing trend to fair value accounting, using fair values has several potential disadvantages. Some of these disadvantages include the following:

1. Fair values may not be readily obtainable for some assets or liabilities. As a result, accounting reports may become more subjective and less reliable. For example, fair values (market quotations) are normally available for trading and available-for-sale securities. However, fair values may not be as available for assets such as property, plant, and equipment or intangible assets such as goodwill.

2. Fair values make it more difficult to compare companies if companies use different methods of determining (measuring) fair values. This would be especially true for assets and liabilities for which fair values are not readily available.

3. Using fair values could result in more fluctuations in accounting reports because fair values normally change from year to year. Such volatility may confuse users of the financial statements. It may also make it more difficult for users to determine current operating trends and to predict future trends.

Effect of Fair Value Accounting on the Financial Statements

The use of fair values for valuing assets and liabilities affects the financial statements. Specifically, the balance sheet and income statement could be affected.

Balance Sheet When an asset or a liability is reported at its fair value, any difference between the asset's original cost or prior period's fair value must be recorded. As we illustrated for trading and available-for-sale securities, one method for doing this is to use a valuation allowance. The account, *Valuation Allowance for Trading Investments,* was used earlier in this chapter to adjust trading securities to their fair values.

Available-for-sale securities are recorded at fair value. Changes in their fair values are not recognized on the income statement, but are included as part of stockholders' equity.

Income Statement Instead of recording the unrealized gain or loss on changes in fair values as part of stockholders' equity, the unrealized gains or losses may be reported on the income statement. This method was illustrated earlier in this chapter for *trading* securities.

As shown above, differences exist as to how to best report changes in fair values— that is, whether to report gains or losses on fair values on the income statement or the balance sheet.

In an attempt to bridge these differences, the FASB introduced the concepts of *comprehensive income* and *accumulated other comprehensive income.* These concepts are described in the appendix to this chapter.

Financial Analysis and Interpretation: Dividend Yield

OBJ. 6   Describe and illustrate the computation of dividend yield.

The **dividend yield** measures the rate of return to stockholders based on cash dividends. Dividend is most often computed for common stock because preferred stock has a stated dividend rate. In contrast, the cash dividends paid on common stock normally varies with the profitability of the corporation.

The dividend yield is computed as follows:

$$\text{Dividend Yield} = \frac{\text{Dividends per Share of Common Stock}}{\text{Market Price per Share of Common Stock}}$$

To illustrate, the market price of News Corporation was $15.50 on February 12, 2010. During the preceding year, News Corporation had paid dividends of $0.12 per share. Thus, the dividend yield of News Corporation's common stock is computed as follows:

$$\text{Dividend Yield} = \frac{\text{Dividends per Share of Common Stock}}{\text{Market Price per Share of Common Stock}} = \frac{\$0.12}{\$15.50} = 0.77\%$$

News Corporation pays a dividend yield of less than 1%. The dividend yield is first a function of a company's profitability, or ability to pay a dividend. For example, many banks nearly eliminated their dividends during the banking crisis of the late 2000s because they had significant losses. News Corporation has sufficient profitability to pay a dividend. Secondly, a company's dividend yield is a function of management's alternative use of funds. If a company has sufficient growth opportunities, funds may be directed toward internal investment, rather than toward paying dividends. This would explain News Corporation's small dividend yield.

The dividend yield will vary from day to day, because the market price of a corporation's stock varies day to day. Current dividend yields are provided with newspaper listings of market prices and most Internet quotation services, such as from either Yahoo's or Google's Finance Web site.

Recent dividend yields for some selected companies are as follows:

Company	Dividend Yield (%)
Apple	None
Best Buy	1.57
Coca-Cola Company	3.04
Duke Energy	5.94
Hewlett-Packard	0.48
Microsoft	1.86
Starbucks	None
Verizon Communications	6.57

As can be seen, the dividend yield varies widely across firms. Growth firms tend to retain their earnings to fund future growth. Thus, Apple and Starbucks pay no dividends, and Hewlett-Packard has a very small dividend. Common stockholders of these companies expect to earn most of their return from stock price appreciation. In contrast, Duke Energy and Verizon Communications are regulated utilities that provide a return to common stockholders mostly through their dividend. Best Buy, Coca-Cola, and Microsoft provide a mix of dividend and expected stock price appreciation to their common stockholders.

Example Exercise 15-6 Dividend Yield   OBJ. 6

On March 11, 2012, Sheldon Corporation had a market price per share of common stock of $58. For the previous year, Sheldon paid an annual dividend of $2.90. Compute the dividend yield for Sheldon Corporation.

Follow My Example 15-6

$$\text{Dividend Yield} = \frac{\text{Dividends per Share of Common Stock}}{\text{Market Price per Share of Common Stock}}$$

$$\text{Dividend Yield} = \frac{\$2.90}{\$58} = 0.05, \text{ or } 5\%$$

Practice Exercises: **PE 15-6A, PE 15-6B**

A P P E N D I X

Comprehensive Income

Comprehensive income is defined as all changes in stockholders' equity during a period, except those resulting from dividends and stockholders' investments. Comprehensive income is computed by adding or subtracting *other comprehensive income* from net income as follows:

Net income	$XXX
Other comprehensive income	XXX
Comprehensive income	$XXX

Other comprehensive income items include unrealized gains and losses on available-for-sale securities as well as other items such as foreign currency and pension liability adjustments. The *cumulative* effect of other comprehensive income is reported on the balance sheet, as **accumulated other comprehensive income**.

Companies may report comprehensive income in the financial statements as follows:

1. On the income statement
2. In a separate statement of comprehensive income
3. In the statement of stockholders' equity

Companies may use terms other than comprehensive income, such as *total non-owner changes in equity*.

In the earlier illustration, Maggie Company had reported an unrealized gain on available-for-sale investments of $1,300. This unrealized gain would be reported in the Stockholders' Equity section of its 2012 balance sheet as follows:

Maggie Company
Balance Sheet
December 31, 2012

Stockholders' equity:	
Common stock..	$ 10,000
Paid-in capital in excess of par value..	150,000
Retained earnings...	250,000
Unrealized gain (loss) on available-for-sale investments..........................	1,300
Total stockholders' equity...	$411,300

Alternatively, Maggie Company could have reported the unrealized gain as part of accumulated other comprehensive income as follows:

Maggie Company
Balance Sheet
December 31, 2012

Stockholders' equity:	
Common stock..	$ 10,000
Paid-in capital in excess of par value..	150,000
Retained earnings...	250,000
Accumulated other comprehensive income:	
Unrealized gain on available-for-sale investments..............................	1,300
Total stockholders' equity...	$411,300

At a Glance 15

Describe why companies invest in debt and equity securities.

Key Points   Cash can be used to (1) invest in current operations, (2) invest to earn additional revenue in marketable securities, or (3) invest in marketable securities for strategic reasons.

Learning Outcomes	Example Exercises	Practice Exercises
• Describe the ways excess cash is used by a business.		
• Describe the purpose of temporary investments.		
• Describe the strategic purpose of long-term investments.		

Describe and illustrate the accounting for debt investments.

Key Points   The accounting for debt investments includes recording the purchase, interest revenue, and sale of the debt. Both the purchase and sale date may include accrued interest.

Learning Outcomes	Example Exercises	Practice Exercises
• Prepare journal entries to record the purchase of a debt investment, including accrued interest.	EE15-1	PE15-1A, 15-1B
• Prepare journal entries for interest revenue from debt investments.	EE15-1	PE15-1A, 15-1B
• Prepare journal entries to record the sale of a debt investment at a gain or loss.	EE15-1	PE15-1A, 15-1B

Describe and illustrate the accounting for equity investments.

Key Points   The accounting for equity investments differs depending on the degree of control. Accounting for investments of less than 20% of the outstanding stock (no control) of the investee includes recording the purchase of stock, receipt of dividends, and sale of stock at a gain or loss. Influential investments of 20%–50% of the outstanding stock of an investee are accounted for under the *equity method*. An investment for more than 50% of the outstanding stock of an investee is treated as a *business combination* and accounted for using *consolidated financial statements*.

Learning Outcomes	Example Exercises	Practice Exercises
• Describe the accounting for less than 20%, 20%–50%, and greater than 50% investments.		
• Prepare journal entries to record the purchase of a stock investment.	EE15-2	PE15-2A, 15-2B
• Prepare journal entries for receipt of dividends.	EE15-2	PE15-2A, 15-2B
• Prepare journal entries for the sale of a stock investment at a gain or loss.	EE15-2	PE15-2A, 15-2B
• Prepare journal entries for the equity earnings of an equity method investee.	EE15-3	PE15-3A, 15-3B
• Prepare journal entries for the dividends received from an equity method investee.	EE15-3	PE15-3A, 15-3B
• Describe a business combination, parent company, and subsidiary company.		
• Describe consolidated financial statements.		

OBJ. 4

Describe and illustrate valuing and reporting investments in the financial statements.

Key Points Debt and equity securities are classified as (1) trading securities, (2) available-for-sale securities, and (3) held-to-maturity securities for reporting and valuation purposes. *Trading securities* are valued at *fair value*, with unrealized gains and losses reported on the income statement. *Available-for-sale securities* are debt and equity securities that are not classified as trading or held-to-maturity. Available-for-sale securities are reported at fair value with unrealized gains or losses reported in the Stockholders' Equity section of the balance sheet. *Held-to-maturity* investments are debt securities that are intended to be held until their maturity date. Held-to-maturity debt investments are valued at amortized cost.

Learning Outcomes	Example Exercises	Practice Exercises
• Describe trading securities, held-to-maturity securities, and available-for-sale securities.		
• Prepare journal entries to record the change in the fair value of a trading security portfolio.	**EE15-4**	**PE15-4A, 15-4B**
• Describe and illustrate the reporting of trading securities on the balance sheet.		
• Prepare journal entries to record the change in fair value of an available-for-sale security portfolio.	**EE15-5**	**PE15-5A, 15-5B**
• Describe and illustrate the reporting of available-for-sale securities on the balance sheet.		
• Describe the accounting for held-to-maturity debt securities.		

OBJ. 5

Describe fair value accounting and its implications for the future.

Key Points There is a trend toward fair value accounting in generally accepted accounting principles (GAAP). Fair value provides relevance at the sacrifice of objectivity for assets without established market prices.

Learning Outcomes	Example Exercises	Practice Exercises
• Describe the reasons why there is a trend toward fair value accounting.		
• Describe the disadvantages of fair value accounting.		
• Describe how fair value accounting impacts the balance sheet and income statement.		
• Describe the future of fair value accounting.		

OBJ. 6

Describe and illustrate the computation of dividend yield.

Key Points The dividend yield measures the cash return from common dividends as a percent of the market price. The ratio is computed as dividends per share of common stock divided by the market price per share of common stock.

Learning Outcomes	Example Exercises	Practice Exercises
• Compute dividend yield.	**EE15-6**	**PE15-6A, 15-6B**
• Describe how dividend yield measures the return to stockholders from dividends.		

Key Terms

accumulated other comprehensive income (687)

available-for-sale securities (679)

business combination (676)

comprehensive income (686)

consolidated financial statements (676)

cost method (673)

debt securities (669)

dividend yield (685)

equity method (674)

equity securities (669)

fair value (677)

held-to-maturity securities (681)

investee (672)

investments (669)

investor (672)

other comprehensive income (686)

parent company (676)

subsidiary company (676)

trading securities (677)

unrealized gain or loss (677)

Illustrative Problem

The following selected investment transactions were completed by Rosewell Company during 2012, its first year of operations:

2012

Jan. 11. Purchased 800 shares of Bryan Company stock as an available-for-sale security at $23 per share plus an $80 brokerage commission.

Feb. 6. Purchased $40,000 of 8% U.S. Treasury bonds at par value plus accrued interest for 36 days. The bonds pay interest on January 1 and July 1. The bonds were classified as held-to-maturity securities.

Mar. 3. Purchased 1,900 shares of Cohen Company stock as a trading security at $48 per share plus a $152 brokerage commission.

Apr. 5. Purchased 2,400 shares of Lyons Inc. stock as an available-for-sale security at $68 per share plus a $120 brokerage commission.

May 12. Purchased 200,000 shares of Myers Company at $37 per share plus an $8,000 brokerage commission. Myers Company has 800,000 common shares issued and outstanding. The equity method was used for this investment.

July 1. Received semiannual interest on bonds purchased on February 6.

Aug. 29. Sold 1,200 shares of Cohen Company stock at $61 per share less a $90 brokerage commission.

Oct. 5. Received an $0.80-per-share dividend on Bryan Company stock.

Nov. 11. Received a $1.10-per-share dividend on Myers Company stock.

16. Purchased 3,000 shares of Morningside Company stock as a trading security for $52 per share plus a $150 brokerage commission.

Dec. 31. Accrued interest on February 6 bonds.

31. Myers Company earned $1,200,000 during the year. Rosewell recorded its share of Myers Company earnings using the equity method.

31. Prepared adjusting entries for the portfolios of trading and available-for-sale securities based upon the following fair values (stock prices):

Bryan Company	$21
Cohen Company	43
Lyons Inc.	88
Myers Company	40
Morningside Company	45

Instructions

1. Journalize the preceding transactions.

2. Prepare the balance sheet disclosure for Rosewell Company's investments on December 31, 2012. Assume held-to-maturity investments are classified as noncurrent assets.

Solution

1.

2012				
Jan.	11	Available-for-Sale Investments—Bryan Company	18,480*	
		Cash		18,480
		*(800 shares × $23 per share) + $80		

Feb.	6	Investments—U.S. Treasury Bonds	40,000	
		Interest Receivable	320*	
		Cash		40,320
		*$40,000 × 8% × (36 days/360 days)		

Mar.	3	Trading Investments—Cohen Company	91,352*	
		Cash		91,352
		*(1,900 shares × $48 per share) + $152		

Apr.	5	Available-for-Sale Investments—Lyons Inc.	163,320*	
		Cash		163,320
		*(2,400 shares × $68 per share) + $120		

May	12	Investment in Myers Company	7,408,000*	
		Cash		7,408,000
		*(200,000 shares × $37 per share) + $8,000		

July	1	Cash	1,600*	
		Interest Receivable		320
		Interest Revenue		1,280
		*$40,000 × 8% × ½		

Aug.	29	Cash	73,110*	
		Trading Investments—Cohen Company		57,696**
		Gain on Sale of Investments		15,414
		*(1,200 shares × $61 per share) – $90		
		**1,200 shares × ($91,352/1,900 shares)		

2012 Oct.	5	Cash	640	
		Dividend Revenue		640
		*800 shares × $0.80 per share		

Nov.	11	Cash	220,000	
		Investment in Myers Company Stock		220,000
		*200,000 shares × $1.10 per share		

Nov.	16	Trading Investments—Morningside Company	156,150*	
		Cash		156,150
		*(3,000 shares × $52 per share) + $150		

Dec.	31	Interest Receivable	1,600	
		Interest Revenue		1,600
		Accrue interest, $40,000 × 8% × ½.		

Dec.	31	Investment in Myers Company Stock	300,000	
		Income of Myers Company		300,000
		Record equity income,		
		$1,200,000 × (200,000 shares/800,000 shares).		

Dec.	31	Unrealized Loss on Trading Investments	24,706	
		Valuation Allowance for Trading Investments		24,706
		Record decease in fair value of trading		
		investments, $165,100 –$189,806.		

Name	Number of Shares	Total Cost	Total Fair Value
Cohen Company	700	$ 33,656	$ 30,100*
Morningside Company	3,000	156,150	135,000**
Total		$189,806	$165,100

*700 shares × $43 per share
**3,000 shares × $45 per share

Note: Myers Company is valued using the equity method; thus, the fair value is not used.

Dec.	31	Valuation Allowance for Available-for-Sale		
		Investments	46,200	
		Unrealized Gain (Loss) on Available-for-		
		Sale Investments		46,200
		Record increase in fair value of available-for-		
		sale investments, $228,000 – $181,800.		

Name	Number of Shares	Total Cost	Total Fair Value
Bryan Company	800	$ 18,480	$ 16,800*
Lyons Inc.	2,400	163,320	211,200**
Total		$181,800	$228,000

*800 shares × $21 per share
**2,400 shares × $88 per share

2.

Rosewell Company
Balance Sheet (Selected)
December 31, 2012

Current assets:		
Cash..		$ XXX,XXX
Trading investments (at cost).................................	$189,806	
Less valuation allowance for trading investments.............	24,706	
Trading investments at fair value.............................		165,100
Available-for-sale investments (at cost)......................	$181,800	
Plus valuation allowance for available-for-sale investments....	46,200	
Available-for-sale investments at fair value..................		228,000
Noncurrent investments:		
Held-to-maturity investments................................		$ 40,000
Investments in Myers Company (equity method)..............		7,488,000
Stockholders' equity:		
Common stock...		$ XX,XXX
Paid-in capital in excess of par value........................		XXX,XXX
Retained earnings...		XXX,XXX
Plus unrealized gain (loss) on available-for-sale investments...		46,200
Total stockholders' equity...................................		$ XXX,XXX

Discussion Questions

1. Why might a business invest in another company's stock?

2. Why would there be a gain or loss on the sale of a bond investment?

3. When is using the cost method the appropriate accounting for equity investments?

4. How does the accounting for a dividend received differ between the cost method and the equity method?

5. If an investor owns more than 50% of an investee, how is this treated on the investor's financial statements?

6. What is the major difference in the accounting for a portfolio of trading securities and a portfolio of available-for-sale securities?

7. If Valuation Allowance for Trading Investments has a credit balance, how is it treated on the balance sheet?

8. How would a debit balance in Unrealized Gain (Loss) on Available-for-Sale Investments be disclosed in the financial statements?

9. What is the evidence of the trend toward fair value accounting?

10. What are some potential disadvantages of fair value accounting?

Practice Exercises

Learning Objectives	Example Exercises	
OBJ. 2	EE 15-1 p.672	**PE 15-1A Bond transactions**

Journalize the entries to record the following selected bond investment transactions for Capital Trust:

a. Purchased for cash $250,000 of Belmont City 4% bonds at 100 plus accrued interest of $1,500.

b. Received first semiannual interest.

c. Sold $80,000 of the bonds at 97 plus accrued interest of $500.

OBJ. 2	EE 15-1 p.672	**PE 15-1B Bond transactions**

Journalize the entries to record the following selected bond investment transactions for Jennings Products:

a. Purchased for cash $40,000 of Tech Grove, Inc. 6% bonds at 100 plus accrued interest of $850.

b. Received first semiannual interest.

c. Sold $15,000 of the bonds at 102 plus accrued interest of $150.

OBJ. 3	EE 15-2 p.674	**PE 15-2A Stock transactions**

On February 12, 5,000 shares of Mid-Ex Company are acquired at a price of $24 per share plus a $200 brokerage fee. On April 22, a $0.36-per-share dividend was received on the Mid-Ex Company stock. On May 10, 4,000 shares of the Mid-Ex Company stock were sold for $31 per share less a $160 brokerage fee. Prepare the journal entries for the original purchase, dividend, and sale.

OBJ. 3	EE 15-2 p.674	**PE 15-2B Stock transactions**

On August 15, 1,600 shares of Birch Company are acquired at a price of $44 per share plus a $160 brokerage fee. On September 10, a $0.75-per-share dividend was received on the Birch Company stock. On October 5, 500 shares of the Birch Company stock were sold for $35 per share less a $50 brokerage fee. Prepare the journal entries for the original purchase, dividend, and sale.

OBJ. 3	EE 15-3 p.676	**PE 15-3A Equity method**

On January 2, THT Company acquired 40% of the outstanding stock of First Alert Company for $155,000. For the year ending December 31, First Alert Company earned income of $42,000 and paid dividends of $12,000. Prepare the entries for THT Company for the purchase of the stock, share of First Alert income, and dividends received from First Alert Company.

OBJ. 3	EE 15-3 p.676	**PE 15-3B Equity method**

On January 2, Bassett Company acquired 30% of the outstanding stock of Nassim Company for $400,000. For the year ending December 31, Nassim Company earned income of $110,000 and paid dividends of $46,000. Prepare the entries for Bassett Company for the purchase of the stock, share of Nassim income, and dividends received from Nassim Company.

PE 15-4A   Valuing trading securities at fair value

On January 1, 2012, Valuation Allowance for Trading Investments had a zero balance. On December 31, 2012, the cost of the trading securities portfolio was $105,800 and the fair value was $101,600. Prepare the December 31, 2012, adjusting journal entry to record the unrealized gain or loss on trading investments.

PE 15-4B   Valuing trading securities at fair value

On January 1, 2012, Valuation Allowance for Trading Investments had a zero balance. On December 31, 2012, the cost of the trading securities portfolio was $33,200, and the fair value was $39,500. Prepare the December 31, 2012, adjusting journal entry to record the unrealized gain or loss on trading investments.

PE 15-5A   Valuing available-for-sale securities at fair value

On January 1, 2012, Valuation Allowance for Available-for-Sale Securities had a zero balance. On December 31, 2012, the cost of the available-for-sale securities was $62,400, and the fair value was $56,900. Prepare the adjusting entry to record the unrealized gain or loss for available-for-sale securities on December 31, 2012.

PE 15-5B   Valuing available-for-sale securities at fair value

On January 1, 2012, Valuation Allowance for Available-for-Sale Securities had a zero balance. On December 31, 2012, the cost of the available-for-sale securities was $7,600, and the fair value was $9,500. Prepare the adjusting entry to record the unrealized gain or loss for available-for-sale securities on December 31, 2012.

PE 15-6A   Dividend yield

On September 25, 2012, Lucas Corporation had a market price per share of common stock of $8. For the previous year, Lucas paid an annual dividend of $0.16. Compute the dividend yield for Lucas Corporation.

PE 15-6B   Dividend yield

On June 12, 2012, Mid State Power and Electric Company had a market price per share of common stock of $48. For the previous year, Mid State paid an annual dividend of $2.88. Compute the dividend yield for Mid State Power and Electric Company.

Exercises

EX 15-1   Entries for investment in bonds, interest, and sale of bonds

Dristol Company acquired $56,000 Reynolds Company, 4.5% bonds on April 1, 2012, at par value. Interest is paid semiannually on April 1 and October 1. On October 1, 2012, Dristol sold $20,000 of the bonds for 99.

Journalize entries to record the following:

a. The initial acquisition of the bonds on April 1.

b. The semiannual interest received on October 1.

c. The sale of the bonds on October 1.

d. The accrual of $637 interest on December 31, 2012.

OBJ. 2

EX 15-2 Entries for investments in bonds, interest, and sale of bonds

Jupiter Investments acquired $40,000 Carlisle Corp., 9% bonds at par value on September 1, 2012. The bonds pay interest on September 1 and March 1. On March 1, 2013, Jupiter sold $40,000 par value Carlisle Corp. bonds at 103.

Journalize the entries to record the following:

a. The initial acquisition of the Carlisle Corp. bonds on September 1, 2012.

b. The adjusting entry for four months of accrued interest earned on the Carlisle Corp. bonds on December 31, 2012.

c. The receipt of semiannual interest on March 1, 2013.

d. The sale of $10,000 Carlisle Corp. bonds on March 1, 2013, at 103.

OBJ. 2

✔ Dec. 1, Loss on sale of investments, $220

EX 15-3 Entries for investment in bonds, interest, and sale of bonds

Afton Co. purchased $24,000 of 4%, 10-year Davis County bonds on July 12, 2012, directly from the county at par value. The bonds pay semiannual interest on May 1 and November 1. On December 1, 2012, Afton Co. sold $6,000 of the Davis County bonds at 98 plus $20 accrued interest, less a $100 brokerage commission.

Provide the journal entries for:

a. the purchase of the bonds on July 12, plus 72 days of accrued interest.

b. semiannual interest on November 1.

c. sale of the bonds on December 1.

d. adjusting entry for accrued interest of $120 on December 31, 2012.

OBJ. 2

✔ Sept. 5, Loss on sale of investments, $720

EX 15-4 Entries for investment in bonds, interest, and sale of bonds

The following bond investment transactions were completed during 2012 by Mission Company:

Jan. 21. Purchased 50, $1,000 par value government bonds at 100 plus 20 days' accrued interest. The bonds pay 4.5% annual interest on June 30 and January 1.

June 30. Received semiannual interest on bond investment.

Sept. 5. Sold 24, $1,000 par value bonds at 97 plus $201 accrued interest.

a. Journalize the entries for these transactions.

b. Provide the December 31, 2012, adjusting journal entry for semiannual interest earned from the bond coupon.

OBJ. 2

EX 15-5 Interest on bond investments

On May 1, 2012, Todd Company purchased $66,000 of 5%, 12-year Lincoln Company bonds at par plus two months' accrued interest. The bonds pay interest on March 1 and September 1. On October 1, 2012, Todd Company sold $24,000 of the Lincoln Company bonds acquired on May 1, plus one month accrued interest. On December 31, 2012, four months' interest was accrued for the remaining bonds.

Determine the interest earned by Todd Company on Lincoln Company bonds for 2012.

OBJ. 3

✔ c. Gain on sale of investments, $5,625

EX 15-6 Entries for investment in stock, receipt of dividends, and sale of shares

On February 17, Walters Corporation acquired 4,000 shares of the 100,000 outstanding shares of Lycore Co. common stock at $22.50 plus commission charges of $200. On July 11, a cash dividend of $0.80 per share was received. On December 4, 1,000 shares were sold at $28.30, less commission charges of $125.

Record the entries for (a) the purchase of stock, (b) the receipt of dividends, and (c) the sale of 1,000 shares.

OBJ. 3

✔ June 3, Loss on sale of investments, $4,097

EX 15-7 Entries for investment in stock, receipt of dividends, and sale of shares

The following equity investment-related transactions were completed by Kindle Company in 2012:

Jan. 12. Purchased 1,400 shares of Inskip Company for a price of $48.90 per share plus a brokerage commission of $112.

Apr. 10. Received a quarterly dividend of $0.22 per share on the Inskip Company investment.

June 3. Sold 900 shares for a price of $44.50 per share less a brokerage commission of $65.

Journalize the entries for these transactions.

OBJ. 3

✔ Nov. 14, Dividend revenue, $60

EX 15-8 Entries for stock investments, dividends, and sale of stock

Archway Tech Corp. manufactures surveying equipment. Journalize the entries to record the following selected equity investment transactions completed by Archway during 2012:

Feb.   2. Purchased for cash 800 shares of Parr Inc. stock for $28 per share plus a $120 brokerage commission.

Apr. 16. Received dividends of $0.12 per share on Parr Inc. stock.

June 17. Purchased 600 shares of Parr Inc. stock for $33 per share plus a $150 brokerage commission.

Aug. 19. Sold 1,000 shares of Parr Inc. stock for $41 per share less a $200 brokerage commission. Archway assumes that the first investments purchased are the first investments sold.

Nov. 14. Received dividends of $0.15 per share on Parr Inc. stock.

OBJ. 3

EX 15-9 Entries for stock investments, dividends, and sale of stock

Hombolt Industries, Inc. buys and sells investments as part of its ongoing cash management. The following investment transactions were completed during the year:

Feb.   6. Acquired 500 shares of Randolph Co. stock for $112 per share plus a $125 brokerage commission.

Apr. 21. Acquired 1,400 shares of Sterling Co. stock for $28 per share plus a $98 commission.

Aug. 15. Sold 200 shares of Randolph Co. stock for $124 per share less an $80 brokerage commission.

Sept. 8. Sold 500 shares of Sterling Co. stock for $22.50 per share less a $70 brokerage commission.

Oct. 31. Received dividends of $0.26 per share on Randolph Co. stock.

Journalize the entries for these transactions.

OBJ. 3

EX 15-10 Equity method for stock investment

At a total cost of $660,000, Penn Corporation acquired 60,000 shares of Teller Corp. common stock as a long-term investment. Penn Corporation uses the equity method of accounting for this investment. Teller Corp. has 200,000 shares of common stock outstanding, including the shares acquired by Penn Corporation.

Journalize the entries by Penn Corporation to record the following information:

a. Teller Corp. reports net income of $940,000 for the current period.

b. A cash dividend of $2.50 per common share is paid by Teller Corp. during the current period.

c. Why is the equity method appropriate for the Teller Corp. investment?

EX 15-11 Equity method for stock investment

On January 15, 2012, Outdoor Life Inc. purchased 94,500 shares of Escape Tours Inc. directly from one of the founders for a price of $38 per share. Escape Tours has 225,000 shares outstanding, including the Outdoor Life shares. On July 2, 2012, Escape Tours paid $230,000 in total dividends to its shareholders. On December 31, 2012, Escape Tours reported a net income of $695,000 for the year. Outdoor Life uses the equity method in accounting for its investment in Escape Tours.

a. Provide the Outdoor Life Inc. journal entries for the transactions involving its investment in Escape Tours Inc. during 2012.

b. Determine the December 31, 2012, balance of Investment in Escape Tours Inc. Stock.

EX 15-12 Equity method for stock investment with loss

On January 10, 2012, Badger Co. purchased 30% of the outstanding stock of Crest Co. for $123,000. Crest paid total dividend to all shareholders of $15,000 on July 15. Crest had a net loss of $25,000 for 2012.

a. Journalize Badger's purchase of the stock, receipt of dividend, and adjusting entry for the equity loss in Crest Co. stock.

b. Compute the balance of Investment in Crest Co. Stock for December 31, 2012.

c. How does valuing an investment under the equity method differ from valuing an investment at fair value?

EX 15-13 Equity method for stock investment

Jarvis Company's balance sheet disclosed its long-term investment in Moss Company under the equity method for comparative years as follows:

	Dec. 31, 2013	Dec. 31, 2012
Investment in Moss Company stock (in millions)	$105	$116

In addition, the 2013 Jarvis Company income statement disclosed equity earnings in the Moss Company investment as $15 million. Jarvis Company neither purchased nor sold Moss Company stock during 2013. The fair value of Moss Company stock investment on December 31, 2013, was $125 million.

Explain the change in the Investment in Moss Company Stock balance sheet account from December 31, 2012, to December 31, 2013.

EX 15-14 Missing statement items, trading investments

KVS Capital, Inc., makes investments in trading securities. Selected income statement items for the years ended December 31, 2012 and 2013, plus selected items from comparative balance sheets, are as follows:

KVS Capital, Inc.
Selected Income Statement Items
For the Years Ended December 31, 2012 and 2013

	2012	2013
Operating income	a.	e.
Unrealized gain (loss)	b.	$(3,000)
Net income	c.	19,000

KVS Capital, Inc.
Selected Balance Sheet Items
December 31, 2011, 2012, and 2013

	Dec. 31, 2011	Dec. 31, 2012	Dec. 31, 2013
Trading investments, at cost	$123,000	$146,000	$172,000
Valuation allowance for trading investments	(4,000)	9,000	g.
Trading investments, at fair value	d.	f.	h.
Retained earnings	$156,000	$192,000	i.

There were no dividends.

Determine the missing lettered items.

OBJ. 3, 4

EX 15-15 **Fair value journal entries, trading investments**

The investments of Giving Tree, Inc. include a single investment: 9,000 shares of Cardio Solutions, Inc. common stock purchased on March 3, 2012, for $22 per share including brokerage commission. These shares were classified as trading securities. As of the December 31, 2012, balance sheet date, the share price increased to $29 per share.

a. Journalize the entries to acquire the investment on March 3, and record the adjustment to fair value on December 31, 2012.

b. How is the unrealized gain or loss for trading investments disclosed on the financial statements?

OBJ. 3, 4

EX 15-16 **Fair value journal entries, trading investments**

Acorn Bancorp Inc. purchased a portfolio of trading securities during 2012. The cost and fair value of this portfolio on December 31, 2012, was as follows:

Name	Number of Shares	Total Cost	Total Fair Value
Apex, Inc.	1,200	$16,000	$17,500
Evans Company	700	23,000	19,000
Quaker Company	300	9,000	8,600
Total		$48,000	$45,100

On April 3, 2013, Acorn Bancorp Inc. purchased 500 shares of Luke, Inc., at $36 per share plus a $100 brokerage fee.

Provide the journal entries to record the following:

a. The adjustment of the trading security portfolio to fair value on December 31, 2012.

b. The April 3, 2013, purchase of Luke, Inc., stock.

OBJ. 3, 4

✔ a. Dec. 31, 2012,
Unrealized gain on
trading investments,
$12,600

EX 15-17 **Fair value journal entries, trading investments**

First Guarantee Financial, Inc., purchased the following trading securities during 2012, its first year of operations:

Name	Number of Shares	Cost
B&T Transportation, Inc.	3,400	$ 74,200
Citrus Foods, Inc.	1,500	26,500
Stuart Housewares, Inc.	800	45,200
Total		$145,900

The market price per share for the trading security portfolio on December 31, 2012, was as follows:

	Market Price per Share
	Dec. 31, 2012
B&T Transportation, Inc.	$26
Citrus Foods, Inc.	19
Stuart Housewares, Inc.	52

a. Provide the journal entry to adjust the trading security portfolio to fair value on December 31, 2012.

b. Assume the market prices of the portfolio were the same on December 31, 2013, as they were on December 31, 2012. What would be the journal entry to adjust the portfolio to fair value?

OBJ. 4

EX 15-18 Financial statement disclosure, trading investments

The income statement for Tri-Con, Inc., for the year ended December 31, 2012, was as follows:

Tri-Con, Inc.
Income Statement (selected items)
For the Year Ended December 31, 2012

Income from operations	$148,000
Gain on sale of investments	12,000
Less unrealized loss on trading investments	34,000
Net income	$126,000

The balance sheet dated December 31, 2011, showed a Retained Earnings balance of $614,000. During 2012, the company purchased trading investments for the first time at a cost of $166,000. In addition, trading investments with a cost of $45,000 were sold at a gain during 2012. The company paid $35,000 in dividends during 2012.

a. Determine the December 31, 2012, Retained Earnings balance.

b. Provide the December 31, 2012, balance sheet disclosure for Trading Investments.

OBJ. 4

✔ f. ($9,000)

EX 15-19 Missing statement items, available-for-sale securities

Oceanic Airways makes investments in available-for-sale securities. Selected income statement items for the years ended December 31, 2012 and 2013, plus selected items from comparative balance sheets, are as follows:

Oceanic Airways
Selected Income Statement Items
For the Years Ended December 31, 2012 and 2013

	2012	2013
Operating income	a.	g.
Gain (loss) from sale of investments	$4,000	$ (8,000)
Net income (loss)	b.	(15,000)

Oceanic Airways
Selected Balance Sheet Items
December 31, 2011, 2012, and 2013

	Dec. 31, 2011	Dec. 31, 2012	Dec. 31, 2013
Assets			
Available-for-sale investments, at cost	$ 78,000	$ 68,000	$95,000
Valuation allowance for available-for-sale investments	6,000	(9,000)	h.
Available-for-sale investments, at fair value	c.	e.	i.
Stockholders' Equity			
Unrealized gain (loss) on available-for- sale investments	d.	f.	(11,000)
Retained earnings	$151,000	$201,000	j.

There were no dividends.
Determine the missing lettered items.

OBJ. 3, 4

EX 15-20 Fair value journal entries, available-for-sale investments

The investments of Macon, Inc. include a single investment: 8,000 shares of Pacific Wave, Inc. common stock purchased on August 10, 2012, for $8 per share including brokerage commission. These shares were classified as available-for-sale securities. As of the December 31, 2012, balance sheet date, the share price declined to $6 per share.

a. Journalize the entries to acquire the investment on August 10, and record the adjustment to fair value on December 31, 2012.

b. How is the unrealized gain or loss for available-for-sale investments disclosed on the financial statements?

OBJ. 3, 4

EX 15-21 Fair value journal entries, available-for-sale investments

Arnott Inc. purchased a portfolio of available-for-sale securities in 2012, its first year of operations. The cost and fair value of this portfolio on December 31, 2012, was as follows:

Name	Number of Shares	Total Cost	Total Fair Value
Jasper, Inc.	600	$ 9,000	$10,500
Parker Corp.	900	21,000	23,400
Smithfield Corp.	1,800	32,500	31,900
Total		$62,500	$65,800

On May 10, 2013, Arnott purchased 900 shares of Violet Inc. at $42 per share plus a $125 brokerage fee.

a. Provide the journal entries to record the following:

1. The adjustment of the available-for-sale security portfolio to fair value on December 31, 2012.

2. The May 10, 2013, purchase of Violet Inc. stock.

b. How are unrealized gains and losses treated differently for available-for-sale securities than for trading securities?

OBJ. 3, 4

EX 15-22 Fair value journal entries, available-for-sale investments

Cumberland, Inc., purchased the following available-for-sale securities during 2012, its first year of operations:

Name	Number of Shares	Cost
Abbotford Electronics, Inc.	1,500	$ 42,500
Ryan Co.	400	28,200
Sharon Co.	2,200	66,100
Total		$136,800

The market price per share for the available-for-sale security portfolio on December 31, 2012, was as follows:

	Market Price per Share Dec. 31, 2012
Abbotford Electronics, Inc.	$22
Ryan Co.	65
Sharon Co.	32

a. Provide the journal entry to adjust the available-for-sale security portfolio to fair value on December 31, 2012.

b. Describe the income statement impact from the December 31, 2012, journal entry.

OBJ. 4

EX 15-23 Balance sheet presentation of available-for-sale investments

During 2012, its first year of operations, Newton Company purchased two available-for-sale investments as follows:

Security	Shares Purchased	Cost
Starlight Products, Inc.	700	$31,000
Reynolds Co.	1,900	41,000

Assume that as of December 31, 2012, the Starlight Products, Inc., stock had a market value of $55 per share and the Reynolds Co. stock had a market value of $18 per share. Newton Company had net income of $250,000, and paid no dividends for the year ending December 31, 2012.

a. Prepare the Current Assets section of the balance sheet presentation for the available-for-sale investments.

b. Prepare the Stockholders' Equity section of the balance sheet to reflect the earnings and unrealized gain (loss) for the available-for-sale investments.

OBJ. 4

EX 15-24   Balance sheet presentation of available-for-sale investments

During 2012, Norcross Corporation held a portfolio of available-for-sale securities having a cost of $175,000. There were no purchases or sales of investments during the year. The market values at the beginning and end of the year were $215,000 and $150,000, respectively. The net income for 2012 was $110,000, and no dividends were paid during the year. The Stockholders' Equity section of the balance sheet was as follows on December 31, 2011:

Norcross Corporation
Stockholders' Equity
December 31, 2011

Common stock	$ 50,000
Paid-in capital in excess of par value	350,000
Retained earnings	265,000
Unrealized gain (loss) on available-for- sale investments	40,000
Total	$705,000

Prepare the Stockholders' Equity section of the balance sheet for December 31, 2012.

Appendix
EX 15-25   Comprehensive income

On April 23, 2012, Frost Co. purchased 1,500 shares of Apex, Inc., for $88 per share including the brokerage commission. The Apex investment was classified as an available-for-sale security. On December 31, 2012, the fair value of Apex, Inc., was $101 per share. The net income of Frost Co. was $60,000 for 2012.

Compute the comprehensive income for Frost Co. for the year ended December 31, 2012.

Appendix
EX 15-26   Comprehensive income

On December 31, 2011, Memphis Co. had the following available-for-sale investment disclosure within the Current Assets section of the balance sheet:

Available-for-sale investments (at cost)	$105,000
Plus valuation allowance for available-for-sale investments	15,000
Available-for-sale investments (at fair value)	$120,000

There were no purchases or sales of available-for-sale investments during 2012. On December 31, 2012, the fair value of the available-for-sale investment portfolio was $94,000. The net income of Memphis Co. was $150,000 for 2012.

Compute the comprehensive income for Memphis Co. for the year ended December 31, 2012.

OBJ. 6

FAI

EX 15-27   Dividend yield

At the market close on February 19, 2010, McDonald's Corporation had a closing stock price of $64.74. In addition, McDonald's Corporation had a dividend per share of $2.05 over the previous year.

Determine McDonald's Corporation's dividend yield. (Round to one decimal place.)

OBJ. 6

✔ a. Dec. 31, 2008, 2.37%

EX 15-28 Dividend yield

The market price for Microsoft Corporation closed at $19.40 and $30.48 on December 31, 2008, and 2009, respectively. The dividends per share were $0.46 for 2008 and $0.52 for 2009.

a. Determine the dividend yield for Microsoft on December 31, 2008, and 2009. (Round percentages to two decimal places.)

b. Interpret these measures.

OBJ. 6

EX 15-29 Dividend yield

eBay Inc. developed a Web-based marketplace at **http://www.ebay.com**, in which individuals can buy and sell a variety of items. eBay also acquired PayPal, an online payments system that allows businesses and individuals to send and receive online payments securely. In a recent annual report, eBay published the following dividend policy:

We have never paid cash dividends on our stock and currently anticipate that we will continue to retain any future earnings for the foreseeable future.

Given eBay's dividend policy, why would an investor be attracted to its stock?

Problems Series A

OBJ. 2, 4

PR 15-1A Debt investment transactions, available-for-sale valuation

Fleet Inc. is an athletic footware company that began operations on January 1, 2012. The following transactions relate to debt investments acquired by Fleet Inc., which has a fiscal year ending on December 31:

2012

Mar. 1. Purchased $36,000 of Madison Co. 5%, 10-year bonds at face value plus accrued interest of $150. The bonds pay interest semiannually on February 1 and August 1.

Apr. 16. Purchased $45,000 of Westville 4%, 15-year bonds at face value plus accrued interest of $75. The bonds pay interest semiannually on April 1 and October 1.

Aug. 1. Received semiannual interest on the Madison Co. bonds.

Sept. 1. Sold $12,000 of Madison Co. bonds at 98 plus accrued interest of $50.

Oct. 1. Received semiannual interest on Westville bonds.

Dec. 31. Accrued $500 interest on Madison Co. bonds.

31. Accrued $450 interest on Westville bonds.

2013

Feb. 1. Received semiannual interest on the Madison Co. bonds.

Apr. 1. Received semiannual interest on the Westville bonds.

Instructions

1. Journalize the entries to record these transactions.

2. If the bond portfolio was classified as available-for-sale, what impact would this have on financial statement disclosure?

OBJ. 3, 4

PR 15-2A Stock investment transactions, trading securities

Heritage Insurance Co. is a regional insurance company that began operations on January 1, 2012. The following transactions relate to trading securities acquired by Heritage Insurance Co., which has a fiscal year ending on December 31:

2012

Feb. 21. Purchased 4,000 shares of Astor Inc. as a trading security at $30 per share plus a brokerage commission of $600.

Mar. 9. Purchased 800 shares of Millsaps Inc. as a trading security at $41 per share plus a brokerage commission of $160.

May 3. Sold 600 shares of Astor Inc. for $27.50 per share less an $80 brokerage commission.

June 8. Received an annual dividend of $0.22 per share on Astor Inc. stock.

Dec. 31. The portfolio of trading securities was adjusted to fair values of $32 and $30 per share for Astor Inc. and Millsaps Inc., respectively.

2013

May 21. Purchased 2,000 shares of Essex Inc. as a trading security at $21 per share plus a $200 brokerage commission.

June 11. Received an annual dividend of $0.25 per share on Astor Inc. stock.

Aug. 16. Sold 400 shares of Essex Inc. for $25 per share less an $80 brokerage commission.

Dec. 31. The portfolio of trading securities had a cost of $169,230 and fair value of $170,560, requiring a debit balance in Valuation Allowance for Trading Investments of $1,330 ($170,560 − $169,230). Thus, the credit balance from December 31, 2012, is to be adjusted to the new balance.

Instructions

1. Journalize the entries to record these transactions.

2. Prepare the investment-related current asset balance sheet disclosures for Heritage Insurance Co. on December 31, 2013.

3. How are unrealized gains or losses on trading investments disclosed on the financial statements of Heritage Insurance Co.?

OBJ. 3, 4

PR 15-3A   Stock investment transactions, equity method and available-for-sale securities

White Way Inc. produces and sells theater set designs and costumes. The company began operations on January 1, 2012. The following transactions relate to securities acquired by White Way Inc., which has a fiscal year ending on December 31:

2012

Jan. 10. Purchased 8,000 shares of Lott Inc. as an available-for-sale security at $14 per share, including the brokerage commission.

Mar. 10. Received the regular cash dividend of $0.12 per share on Lott Inc. stock.

Sept. 9. Lott Inc. stock was split two for one. The regular cash dividend of $0.06 per share was received on the stock after the stock split.

Oct. 16. Sold 2,000 shares of Lott Inc. stock at $5 per share, less a brokerage commission of $100.

Dec. 31. Lott Inc. is classified as an available-for-sale investment and is adjusted to a fair value of $8.50 per share. Use the valuation allowance for available-for-sale investments account in making the adjustment.

2013

Jan. 5. Purchased an influential interest in Stage Hand Inc. for $235,000 by purchasing 50,000 shares directly from the estate of the founder of Stage Hand Inc. There are 200,000 shares of Stage Hand Inc. stock outstanding.

Mar. 9. Received the regular cash divided of $0.07 per share on Lott Inc. stock.

Sept. 10. Received the regular cash dividend of $0.07 per share plus an extra dividend of $0.03 per share on Lott Inc. stock.

Dec. 31.   Received $21,500 of cash dividends on Stage Hand Inc. stock. Stage Hand Inc. reported net income of $136,000 in 2013. White Way Inc. uses the equity method of accounting for its investment in Stage Hand Inc.

31.   Lott Inc. is classified as an available-for-sale investment and is adjusted to a fair value of $8 per share. Use the valuation allowance for available-for-sale investments account in making the adjustment for the decrease in fair value from $8.50 to $8.00 per share.

Instructions

1. Journalize the entries to record these transactions.

2. Prepare the investment-related asset and stockholders' equity balance sheet disclosures for White Way Inc. on December 31, 2013, assuming the Retained Earnings balance on December 31, 2013, is $310,000.

OBJ. 2, 3, 4

✔ h. $(4,500)

PR 15-4A   Investment reporting

Luminous Publishing, Inc., is a book publisher. The comparative unclassified balance sheets for December 31, 2013 and 2012 are provided below. Selected missing balances are shown by letters.

Luminous Publishing, Inc.
Balance Sheet
December 31, 2013 and 2012

	Dec. 31, 2013	Dec. 31, 2012
Cash	$178,000	$157,000
Accounts receivable (net)	106,000	98,000
Available-for-sale investments (at cost)—Note 1	a.	53,400
Less valuation allowance for available-for-sale investments	b.	3,900
Available-for-sale investments (fair value)	$ c.	$ 49,500
Interest receivable	$ d.	—
Investment in Quest Co. stock—Note 2	e.	$ 55,000
Office equipment (net)	90,000	95,000
Total assets	$ f.	$454,500
Accounts payable	$ 56,900	$ 51,400
Common stock	50,000	50,000
Excess of issue price over par	160,000	160,000
Retained earnings	g.	197,000
Less unrealized gain (loss) on available-for-sale investments	h.	3,900
Total liabilities and stockholders' equity	$ i.	$454,500

Note 1. Investments are classified as available for sale. The investments at cost and fair value on December 31, 2012, are as follows:

	No. of Shares	Cost per Share	Total Cost	Total Fair Value
Barns Co. Stock	1,600	$12	$19,200	$17,500
Dynasty Co. Stock	900	38	34,200	32,000
			$53,400	$49,500

Note 2. The investment in Quest Co. stock is an equity method investment representing 32% of the outstanding shares of Quest Co.

The following selected investment transactions occurred during 2013:

May   5.   Purchased 2,200 shares of Gypsy, Inc., at $22 per share including brokerage commission. Gypsy, Inc., is classified as an available-for-sale security.

Sept.   1.   Purchased $30,000 of Norton Co. 5%, 10-year bonds at 100. The bonds are classified as available for sale. The bonds pay interest on September 1 and March 1.

9.   Dividends of $9,000 are received on the Quest Co. investment.

Dec. 31. Quest Co. reported a total net income of $80,000 for 2013. Luminous recorded equity earnings for its share of Quest Co. net income.

31. Accrued four months of interest on the Norton bonds.

31. Adjusted the available-for-sale investment portfolio to fair value using the following fair value per-share amounts:

Available-for-Sale Investments	Fair Value
Barns Co. stock	$11 per share
Dynasty Co. stock	$33 per share
Gypsy Inc. stock	$23 per share
Norton Co. bonds	98 per $100 of face value

Dec. 31. Closed the Luminous Publishing Inc. net income of $114,000 for 2013. Luminous paid no dividends during 2013.

Instructions

Determine the missing letters in the unclassified balance sheet. Provide appropriate supporting calculations.

Problems Series B

OBJ. 2, 4

PR 15-1B   Debt investment transactions, available-for-sale valuation

Savers Mart Inc. is a general merchandise retail company that began operations on January 1, 2012. The following transactions relate to debt investments acquired by Savers Mart Inc., which has a fiscal year ending on December 31:

2012

May   1.   Purchased $80,000 of Northridge City 4.5%, 10-year bonds at face value plus accrued interest of $600. The bonds pay interest semiannually on March 1 and September 1.

June 16.   Purchased $38,000 of Hancock Co. 6%, 12-year bonds at face value plus accrued interest of $95. The bonds pay interest semiannually on June 1 and December 1.

Sept.   1.   Received semiannual interest on the Northridge City bonds.

Oct.   1.   Sold $24,000 of Northridge City bonds at 102 plus accrued interest of $90.

Dec.   1.   Received semiannual interest on Hancock Co. bonds.

31.   Accrued $840 interest on Northridge City bonds.

31.   Accrued $190 interest on Hancock Co. bonds.

2013

Mar.   1.   Received semiannual interest on the Northridge City bonds.

June   1.   Received semiannual interest on the Hancock Co. bonds.

Instructions

1. Journalize the entries to record these transactions.

2. If the bond portfolio was classified as available-for-sale, what impact would this have on financial statement disclosure?

OBJ. 3, 4

PR 15-2B   Stock investment transactions, trading securities

Ophir Investments Inc. is a regional investment company that began operations on January 1, 2012. The following transactions relate to trading securities acquired by Ophir Investments Inc., which has a fiscal year ending on December 31:

2012

Feb.   3.   Purchased 2,000 shares of Mapco Inc. as a trading security at $42 per share plus a brokerage commission of $500.

Mar. 23. Purchased 1,400 shares of Swift Inc. as a trading security at $23 per share plus a brokerage commission of $210.

May 19. Sold 500 shares of Mapco Inc. for $46 per share less an $80 brokerage commission.

June 12. Received an annual dividend of $0.14 per share on Mapco stock.

Dec. 31. The portfolio of trading securities was adjusted to fair values of $40 and $29 per share for Mapco Inc. and Swift Inc., respectively.

2013

Apr. 9. Purchased 900 shares of Corvair Inc. as a trading security at $62 per share plus a $90 brokerage commission.

June 15. Received an annual dividend of $0.16 per share on Mapco Inc. stock.

Aug. 30. Sold 200 shares of Corvair Inc. for $51 per share less a $60 brokerage commission.

Dec. 31. The portfolio of trading securities had a cost of $139,255 and fair value of $133,470, requiring a credit balance in Valuation Allowance for Trading Investments of $5,785 ($139,255 − $133,470). Thus, the debit balance from December 31, 2012, is to be adjusted to the new balance.

Instructions

1. Journalize the entries to record these transactions.

2. Prepare the investment-related current asset balance sheet disclosures for Ophir Investments Inc. on December 31, 2013.

3. How are unrealized gains or losses on trading investments disclosed on the financial statements of Ophir Investments Inc.?

OBJ. 3, 4

PR 15-3B Stock investment transactions, equity method and available-for-sale securities

Samson Products, Inc., is a wholesaler of men's hair products. The company began operations on January 1, 2012. The following transactions relate to securities acquired by Samson Products, Inc., which has a fiscal year ending on December 31:

2012

Jan. 3. Purchased 5,000 shares of Merlin Inc. as an available-for-sale investment at $22 per share, including the brokerage commission.

July 8. Merlin Inc. stock was split two for one. The regular cash dividend of $0.40 per share was received on the stock after the stock split.

Oct. 19. Sold 1,200 shares of Merlin Inc. stock at $13 per share, less a brokerage commission of $50.

Dec. 12. Received the regular cash dividend of $0.40 per share.

31. Merlin Inc. is classified as an available-for-sale investment and is adjusted to a fair value of $9.50 per share. Use the valuation allowance for available-for-sale investments account in making the adjustment.

2013

Jan. 5. Purchased an influential interest in Juarez Co. for $540,000 by purchasing 60,000 shares directly from the estate of the founder of Juarez. There are 150,000 shares of Juarez Co. stock outstanding.

July 9. Received the regular cash divided of $0.50 per share on Merlin Inc. stock.

Dec. 8. Received the regular cash dividend of $0.50 per share plus an extra dividend of $0.05 per share on Merlin Inc. stock.

Dec. 31. Received $21,000 of cash dividends on Juarez Co. stock. Juarez Co. reported net income of $96,000 in 2013. Samson Products uses the equity method of accounting for its investment in Juarez Co.

31. Merlin Inc. is classified as an available-for-sale investment and is adjusted to a fair value of $10 per share. Use the valuation allowance for available-for-sale investments account in making the adjustment for the increase in fair value from $9.50 to $10 per share.

Instructions

1. Journalize the entries to record the preceding transactions.

2. Prepare the investment-related asset and stockholders' equity balance sheet disclosures for Samson Products, Inc., on December 31, 2013, assuming the Retained Earnings balance on December 31, 2013, is $395,000.

OBJ. 2, 3, 4

✔ b. $250

PR 15-4B Investment reporting

Guardian Devices, Inc., manufactures and sells commercial and residential security equipment. The comparative unclassified balance sheets for December 31, 2013 and 2012 are provided below. Selected missing balances are shown by letters.

Guardian Devices, Inc.
Balance Sheet
December 31, 2013 and 2012

	Dec. 31, 2013	Dec. 31, 2012
Cash	$104,000	$ 98,000
Accounts receivable (net)	71,000	67,500
Available-for-sale investments (at cost)—Note 1	a.	36,000
Plus valuation allowance for available-for-sale investments	b.	6,000
Available-for-sale investments (fair value)	$ c.	$ 42,000
Interest receivable	$ d.	—
Investment in Omaha Co. stock—Note 2	e.	$ 62,000
Office equipment (net)	60,000	65,000
Total assets	$ f.	$334,500
Accounts payable	$ 56,900	$ 45,100
Common stock	50,000	50,000
Excess of issue price over par	160,000	160,000
Retained earnings	g.	73,400
Plus unrealized gain (loss) on available-for-sale investments	h.	6,000
Total liabilities and stockholders' equity	$ i.	$334,500

Note 1. Investments are classified as available for sale. The investments at cost and fair value on December 31, 2012, are as follows:

	No. of Shares	Cost per Share	Total Cost	Total Fair Value
Tyndale Inc. Stock	600	$24	$14,400	$17,000
UR-Smart Inc. Stock	1,200	18	21,600	25,000
			$36,000	$42,000

Note 2. The Investment in Omaha Co. stock is an equity method investment representing 32% of the outstanding shares of Omaha Co.

The following selected investment transactions occurred during 2013:

Apr. 21. Purchased 500 shares of Walton Winery, Inc., at $25 including brokerage commission. Walton Winery is classified as an available-for-sale security.

Sept. 9. Dividends of $7,500 are received on the Omaha Co. investment.

Oct. 1. Purchased $15,000 of Yokohama Co. 6%, 10-year bonds at 100. The bonds are classified as available for sale. The bonds pay interest on October 1 and April 1.

Dec. 31. Omaha Co. reported a total net income of $50,000 for 2013. Guardian recorded equity earnings for its share of Omaha Co. net income.

Dec. 31. Accrued interest for three months on Yokohama bonds purchased on October 1.

31. Adjusted the available-for-sale investment portfolio to fair value using the following fair value per-share amounts:

Available-for-Sale Investments	Fair Value
Tyndale Inc. stock	$26 per share
UR-Smart, Inc., stock	$15 per share
Walton Winery, Inc., stock	$30 per share
Yokohama Co. bonds	101 per $100 of face value

31. Closed the Guardian Devices, Inc., net income of $28,925 for 2013. Guardian paid no dividends during 2013.

Instructions
Determine the missing letters in the unclassified balance sheet. Provide appropriate supporting calculations.

Comprehensive Problem 4

Selected transactions completed by Everyday Products Inc. during the fiscal year ending December 31, 2012, were as follows:

a. Issued 12,500 shares of $25 par common stock at $32, receiving cash.

b. Issued 2,000 shares of $100 par preferred 5% stock at $105, receiving cash.

c. Issued $400,000 of 10-year, 6% bonds at 105, with interest payable semiannually.

d. Declared a quarterly dividend of $0.45 per share on common stock and $1.25 per share on preferred stock. On the date of record, 85,000 shares of common stock were outstanding, no treasury shares were held, and 17,000 shares of preferred stock were outstanding.

e. Paid the cash dividends declared in (d).

f. Purchased 5,500 shares of Kress Corp. at $22 per share, plus a $275 brokerage commission. The investment is classified as an available-for-sale investment.

g. Purchased 6,500 shares of treasury common stock at $35 per share.

h. Purchased 36,000 shares of Lifecare Co. stock directly from the founders for $18 per share. Lifecare has 112,500 shares issued and outstanding. Everyday Products Inc. treated the investment as an equity method investment.

i. Declared a 2% stock dividend on common stock and a $1.25 quarterly cash dividend per share on preferred stock. On the date of declaration, the market value of the common stock was $40 per share. On the date of record, 85,000 shares of common stock had been issued, 6,500 shares of treasury common stock were held, and 17,000 shares of preferred stock had been issued.

j. Issued the stock certificates for the stock dividends declared in (h) and paid the cash dividends to the preferred stockholders.

k. Received $24,500 dividend from Lifecare Co. investment in (h).

l. Purchased $62,000 of Nordic Wear Inc. 10-year, 6% bonds, directly from the issuing company at par value, plus accrued interest of $550. The bonds are classifed as a held-to-maturity long-term investment.

m. Sold, at $42 per share, 2,600 shares of treasury common stock purchased in (g).

n. Received a dividend of $0.65 per share from the Kress Corp. investment in (f).

o. Sold 500 shares of Kress Corp. at $26.50, including commission.

p. Recorded the payment of semiannual interest on the bonds issued in (c) and the amortization of the premium for six months. The amortization was determined using the straight-line method.

q. Accrued interest for three months on the Nordic Wear Inc. bonds purchased in (l).

r. Lifecare Co. recorded total earnings of $205,000. Everyday Products recorded equity earnings for its share of Lifecare Co. net income.

s. The fair value for Kress Corp. stock was $18.50 per share on December 31, 2012. The investment is adjusted to fair value using a valuation allowance account. Assume Valuation Allowance for Available-for-Sale Investments had a beginning balance of zero.

Instructions

1. Journalize the selected transactions.

2. After all of the transactions for the year ended December 31, 2012, had been posted [including the transactions recorded in part (1) and all adjusting entries], the data below and on the following page were taken from the records of Everyday Products Inc.

   a. Prepare a multiple-step income statement for the year ended December 31, 2012, concluding with earnings per share. In computing earnings per share, assume that the average number of common shares outstanding was 84,000 and preferred dividends were $85,000. (Round earnings per share to the nearest cent.)

   b. Prepare a retained earnings statement for the year ended December 31, 2012.

   c. Prepare a balance sheet in report form as of December 31, 2012.

Income statement data:	
Advertising expense	$ 125,000
Cost of merchandise sold	3,650,000
Delivery expense	29,000
Depreciation expense—office buildings and equipment	26,000
Depreciation expense—store buildings and equipment	95,000
Dividend revenue	3,575
Gain on sale of investment	2,225
Income from Lifecare Co. investment	65,600
Income tax expense	128,500
Interest expense	19,000
Interest revenue	1,800
Miscellaneous administrative expense	7,500
Miscellaneous selling expense	13,750
Office rent expense	50,000
Office salaries expense	165,000
Office supplies expense	10,000
Sales	5,145,000
Sales commissions	182,000
Sales salaries expense	365,000
Store supplies expense	22,000

Retained earnings and balance sheet data:	
Accounts payable	$ 195,000
Accounts receivable	543,000
Accumulated depreciation—office buildings and equipment	1,580,000
Accumulated depreciation—store buildings and equipment	4,126,000
Allowance for doubtful accounts	8,150
Available-for-sale investments (at cost)	110,250
Bonds payable, 6%, due 2022	400,000
Cash	240,000
Common stock, $25 par (400,000 shares authorized; 86,570 shares issued, 82,670 outstanding)	2,164,250
Dividends:	
Cash dividends for common stock	155,120
Cash dividends for preferred stock	85,000
Stock dividends for common stock	62,800
Goodwill	510,000
Income tax payable	40,000
Interest receivable	930
Investment in Lifecare Co. stock (equity method)	689,100
Investment in Nordic Wear Inc. bonds (long term)	62,000

Merchandise inventory (December 31, 2012), at lower of cost (FIFO) or market	$ 780,000
Office buildings and equipment	4,320,000
Paid-in capital from sale of treasury stock	18,200
Paid-in capital in excess of par—common stock	842,000
Paid-in capital in excess of par—preferred stock	150,000
Preferred 5% stock, $100 par (30,000 shares authorized; 17,000 shares issued)	1,700,000
Premium on bonds payable	19,000
Prepaid expenses	26,500
Retained earnings, January 1, 2012	8,708,150
Store buildings and equipment	12,560,000
Treasury stock (3,900 shares of common stock at cost of $35 per share)	136,500
Unrealized gain (loss) on available-for-sale investments	(17,750)
Valuation allowance for available-for-sale investments	(17,750)

Cases & Projects

CP 15-1 Benefits of fair value

On August 16, 1997, Parson Corp. purchased 20 acres of land for $500,000. The land has been held for a future plant site until the current date, December 31, 2012. On December 5, 2012, Overland, Inc., purchased 20 acres of land for $3,000,000 to be used for a distribution center. The Overland land is located next to the Parson Corp. land. Thus, both Parson Corp. and Overland, Inc., own nearly identical pieces of land.

1. What are the valuations of land on the balance sheets of Parson Corp. and Overland, Inc., using generally accepted accounting principles?

2. How might fair value accounting aid comparability when evaluating these two companies?

CP 15-2 International fair value accounting

International Accounting Standard No. 16 provides companies the option of valuing property, plant, and equipment at either historical cost or fair value. If fair value is selected, then the property, plant, and equipment must be revalued periodically to fair value. Under fair value, if there is an increase in the value of the property, plant, and equipment over the reporting period, then the increase is credited to stockholders' equity. However, if there is a decrease in fair value, then the decrease is reported as an expense for the period.

1. Why do International Accounting Standards influence U.S. GAAP?

2. What would be some of the disadvantages of using fair value accounting for property, plant, and equipment?

3. How is the international accounting treatment for changes in fair value for property, plant, and equipment similar to investments?

CP 15-3 Ethics and fair value measurement

Financial assets include stocks and bonds. These are fairly simple securities that can often be valued using quoted market prices. However, Wall Street has created many complex and exotic securities that do not have quoted market prices. These complex securities must still be valued on the balance sheet at fair value. Generally accepted accounting principles require that the reporting entity use assumptions in valuing investments when market prices or critical valuation inputs are unobservable.

What are the ethical considerations in making subjective valuations of complex and exotic investments?

CP 15-4   Warren Buffett and "look-through" earnings

Berkshire Hathaway, the investment holding company of Warren Buffett, reports its "less than 20% ownership" investments according to generally accepted accounting principles. However, it also provides additional disclosures that it terms "look-through" earnings.

Warren Buffett states,

Many of these companies (in the less than 20% owned category) pay out relatively small proportions of their earnings in dividends. This means that only a small proportion of their earning power is recorded in our own current operating earnings. But, while our reported operating earnings reflect only the dividends received from such companies, our economic well-being is determined by their earnings, not their dividends.

The value to Berkshire Hathaway of retained earnings (of our investees) is not determined by whether we own 100%, 50%, 20%, or 1% of the businesses in which they reside.... Our perspective on such "forgotten-but-not-gone" earnings is simple: the way they are accounted for is of no importance, but their ownership and subsequent utilization is all-important. We care not whether the auditors hear a tree fall in the forest; we do care who owns the tree and what's next done with it.

I believe the best way to think about our earnings is in terms of "look-through" results, calculated as follows: Take $250 million, which is roughly our share of the operating earnings retained by our investees (<20% ownership holdings); subtract... incremental taxes we would have owed had that $250 million been paid to us in dividends; then add the remainder, $220 million, to our reported earnings of $371 million. Thus our, "look-through" earnings were about $590 million.

Source: Warren Buffett, *The Essays of Warren Buffett: Lessons for Corporate America,* edited by Lawrence A. Cunningham, pp. 180–183 (excerpted).

1. What are "look-through" earnings?

2. Why does Warren Buffett favor "look-through" earnings?

CP 15-5   Reporting investments

Group Project

In groups of three or four, find the latest annual report for Microsoft Corporation. The annual report can be found on the company's Web site at **http://www.microsoft.com/ msft/default.mspx.**

The notes to the financial statements include details of Microsoft's investments. Find the notes that provide details of its investments (Note 4) and the income from its investments (Note 3).

From these disclosures, answer the following questions:

1. What is the total cost of investments?

2. What is the fair value (recorded value) of investments?

3. What is the total unrealized gain from investments?

4. What is the total unrealized loss from investments?

5. What percent of total investments (at fair value) are:

    a. Cash and equivalents

    b. Short-term investments

    c. Equity and other investments (long term)

6. What was the total combined dividend and interest revenue?

7. What was the recognized net gain or loss from sale of investments?

Internet Project

Financial Statements for Mornin' Joe

The financial statements of Mornin' Joe are provided in the following pages. Mornin' Joe is a fictitious coffeehouse chain featuring drip and espresso coffee in a café setting. The financial statements of Mornin' Joe are provided to illustrate the complete financial statements of a corporation using the terms, formats, and reporting illustrated throughout this text. In addition, excerpts of the Mornin' Joe financial statements are used to illustrate the financial reporting presentation for the topics discussed in Chapters 7–15. Thus, you can refer to the complete financial statements shown here or the excerpts in Chapters 7–15. A set of real world financial statements by Nike, Inc., is provided in Appendix C.

Mornin' Joe
Income Statement
For the Year Ended December 31, 2012

Revenue from sales:			
Sales		$5,450,000	
Less: Sales returns and allowances	$ 26,500		
Sales discounts	21,400	47,900	
Net sales			$5,402,100
Cost of merchandise sold			2,160,000
Gross profit			$3,242,100
Operating expenses			
Selling expenses:			
Wages expense	$825,000		
Advertising expense	678,900		
Depreciation expense—buildings	124,300		
Miscellaneous selling expense	26,500		
Total selling expenses		$1,654,700	
Administrative expenses:			
Office salaries expense	$325,000		
Rent expense	425,600		
Payroll tax expense	110,000		
Depreciation expense—office equipment	68,900		
Bad debt expense	14,000		
Amortization expense	10,500		
Total administrative expenses		954,000	
Total operating expenses			2,608,700
Income from operations			$ 633,400
Other income and expense:			
Interest revenue		$ 18,000	
Interest expense		(136,000)	
Loss on disposal of fixed asset		(23,000)	
Unrealized gain on trading investments		5,000	
Equity income in AM Coffee		57,000	(79,000)
Income before income taxes			$ 554,400
Income tax expense			132,800
Net income			$ 421,600
Basic earnings per share [($421,600 − $30,000)/44,000 shares issued and outstanding]			$ 8.90

Mornin' Joe
Balance Sheet
December 31, 2012

Assets

Current assets:

Cash and cash equivalents		$ 235,000
Trading investments (at cost)	$ 420,000	
Plus valuation allowance for trading investments	45,000	465,000
Accounts receivable	$ 305,000	
Less allowance for doubtful accounts	12,300	292,700
Merchandise inventory—at lower of cost		
(first-in, first-out method) or market		120,000
Prepaid insurance		24,000
Total current assets		$1,136,700

Investments:

Investment in AM Coffee (equity method)		565,000

Property, plant, and equipment:

Land	$1,850,000	
Buildings	$2,650,000	
Less accumulated depreciation	420,000	2,230,000
Office equipment	$ 350,000	
Less accumulated depreciation	102,000	248,000
Total property, plant, and equipment		4,328,000

Intangible assets:

Patents		140,000
Total assets		$6,169,700

Liabilities

Current liabilities:

Accounts payable		$ 133,000
Notes payable (current portion)		200,000
Salaries and wages payable		42,000
Payroll taxes payable		16,400
Interest payable		40,000
Total current liabilities		$ 431,400

Long-term liabilities:

Bonds payable, 8%, due December 31, 2030	$ 500,000	
Less unamortized discount	16,000	$ 484,000
Notes payable		1,400,000
Total long-term liabilities		$1,884,000
Total liabilities		$2,315,400

Stockholders' Equity

Paid-in capital:

Preferred 10% stock, $50 par (6,000 shares		
authorized and issued)	$ 300,000	
Excess of issue price over par	50,000	$ 350,000
Common stock, $20 par (50,000 shares		
authorized, 45,000 shares issued)	$ 900,000	
Excess of issue price over par	1,450,000	2,350,000
Total paid-in capital		$2,700,000
Retained earnings		1,200,300
Total		$3,900,300
Deduct treasury stock (1,000 shares at cost)		46,000
Total stockholders' equity		$3,854,300
Total liabilities and stockholders' equity		$6,169,700

Mornin' Joe
Retained Earnings Statement
For the Year Ended December 31, 2012

Retained earnings, January 1, 2012			$ 852,700
Net income		$421,600	
Less dividends:			
Preferred stock	$30,000		
Common stock	44,000	74,000	
Increase in retained earnings			347,600
Retained earnings, December 31, 2012			$1,200,300

Mornin' Joe
Statement of Stockholders' Equity
For the Year Ended December 31, 2012

	Preferred Stock	Common Stock	Additional Paid-In Capital	Retained Earnings	Treasury Stock	Total
Balance, January 1, 2012	$300,000	$800,000	$1,325,000	$ 852,700	$(36,000)	$3,241,700
Net income				421,600		421,600
Dividends on preferred stock				(30,000)		(30,000)
Dividends on common stock				(44,000)		(44,000)
Issuance of additional common stock. . .		100,000	175,000			275,000
Purchase of treasury stock.					(10,000)	(10,000)
Balance, December 31, 2012	$300,000	$900,000	$1,500,000	$1,200,300	$(46,000)	$3,854,300

Mornin' Joe International

Mornin' Joe is planning to expand operations to various places around the world. Financing for this expansion will come from foreign banks. While financial statements prepared under U.S. GAAP may be appropriate for U.S. operations, financial statements prepared for foreign bankers should be prepared using international accounting standards.

The European Union (EU) has developed accounting standards similar in structure to U.S. standards. Its accounting standards board is called the International Accounting Standards Board (IASB). The IASB issues accounting standards that are termed *International Financial Reporting Standards* (IFRS). The intent of the IASB is to create a set of financial standards that can be used by public companies worldwide, not just in the EU.

Currently, the EU countries and over 100 other countries around the world have adopted or are planning to adopt IFRS. As a result, there are efforts under way to converge U.S. GAAP with IFRS so as to harmonize accounting standards around the world.

The following pages illustrate the financial statements of Mornin' Joe International using IFRS. This illustration highlights reporting and terminology differences between IFRS and U.S. GAAP. Differences in recording transactions under IFRS and U.S. GAAP are discussed in Appendix D and in various International Connection boxes throughout the text.

The following Mornin' Joe International financial statements are simplified and illustrate only portions of IFRS that are appropriate for introductory accounting. The financial statements are presented in euros (€) for demonstration purposes only. The euro is the standard currency of the European Union. The euro is translated at a 1:1 ratio from the dollar to simplify comparisons. Throughout the illustration, call-outs and end notes to each statement are used to highlight the differences between financial statements prepared under IFRS and under U.S. GAAP.

Title includes the word "Comprehensive."

This is a common term for an equity method investment.

The term "Finance costs" is used, rather than "Interest expense."

The term "Profit for the year" is used, rather than "Net income."

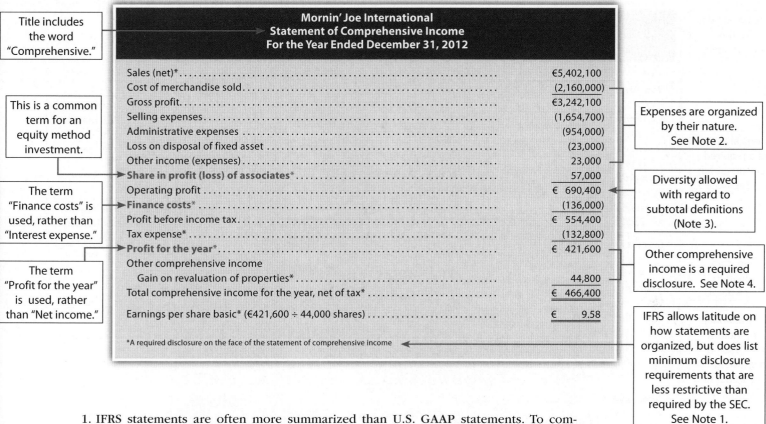

Mornin' Joe International
Statement of Comprehensive Income
For the Year Ended December 31, 2012

Sales (net)*	€5,402,100
Cost of merchandise sold	(2,160,000)
Gross profit	€3,242,100
Selling expenses	(1,654,700)
Administrative expenses	(954,000)
Loss on disposal of fixed asset	(23,000)
Other income (expenses)	23,000
Share in profit (loss) of associates*	57,000
Operating profit	€ 690,400
Finance costs*	(136,000)
Profit before income tax	€ 554,400
Tax expense*	(132,800)
Profit for the year*	€ 421,600
Other comprehensive income	
Gain on revaluation of properties*	44,800
Total comprehensive income for the year, net of tax*	€ 466,400
Earnings per share basic* (€421,600 ÷ 44,000 shares)	€ 9.58

*A required disclosure on the face of the statement of comprehensive income

Expenses are organized by their nature. See Note 2.

Diversity allowed with regard to subtotal definitions (Note 3).

Other comprehensive income is a required disclosure. See Note 4.

IFRS allows latitude on how statements are organized, but does list minimum disclosure requirements that are less restrictive than required by the SEC. See Note 1.

1. IFRS statements are often more summarized than U.S. GAAP statements. To compensate, IFRS requires specific disclosures on the face of the financial statements (denoted *) and additional disclosures in the footnotes to the financial statements. Since additions and subtractions are grouped together in sections of IFRS statements, parentheses are used to indicate subtractions.

2. Expenses in an IFRS income statement are classified by either their nature or function. The nature of an expense is how the expense would naturally be recorded in a journal entry reflecting the economic benefit received for that expense. Examples include salaries, depreciation, advertising, and utilities. The function of an expense identifies the purpose of the expense, such as a selling expense or an administrative expense.

   IFRS does not permit the natural and functional classifications to be mixed together on the same statement. That is, all expenses must be classified by either nature or function. However, if a functional classification of expenses is used, a footnote to the income statement must show the natural classification of expenses. To illustrate, because Mornin' Joe International uses the functional classification of expenses in its income statement, it must also show the following natural classification of expenses in a footnote:

Cost of product	€2,100,000	The cost of product purchased for resale
Employee benefits expense	1,260,000	Required natural disclosure
Depreciation and amortization expense	203,700	Required natural disclosure
Rent expense	425,600	
Advertising expense	678,900	
Other expenses	58,500	
Total natural expenses	€4,726,700	

3. IFRS provides flexibility with regard to line items, headings, and subtotals on the income statement. There is less flexibility under U.S. GAAP for public companies.

4. IFRS requires the reporting of other comprehensive income (see appendix to Chapter 15) either on the income statement (illustrated) or in a separate statement. In contrast, other comprehensive income is often disclosed on the statement of changes in stockholders' equity under U.S. GAAP. For Mornin' Joe International, other comprehensive income consists of the restatement of café locations to fair value (see Note 6 for more details).

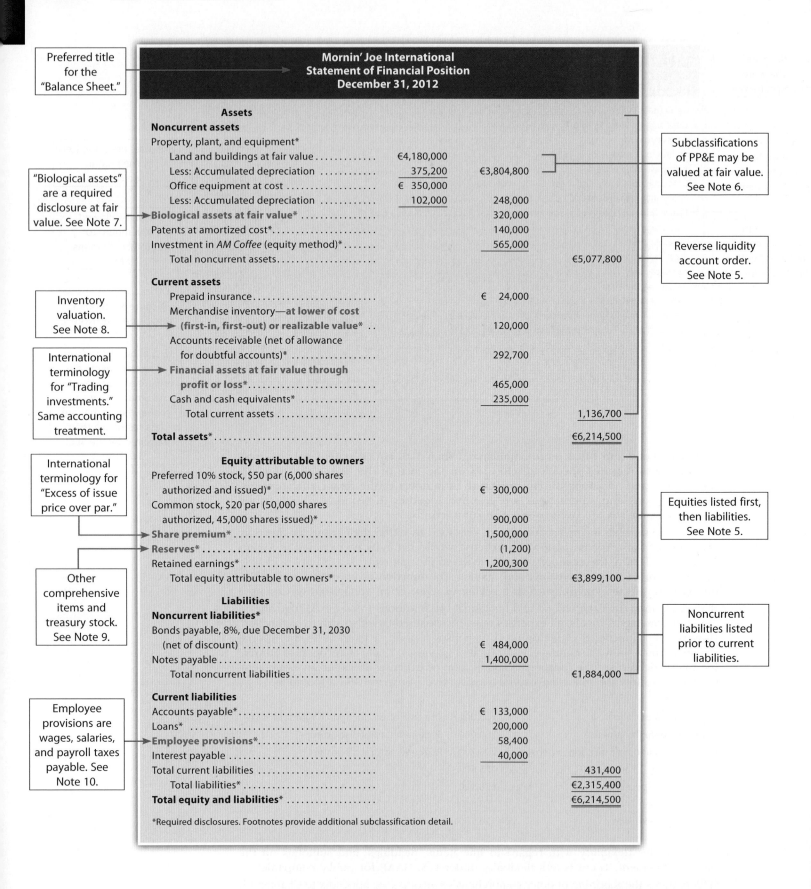

Preferred title for the "Balance Sheet."

Mornin' Joe International
Statement of Financial Position
December 31, 2012

Assets

Noncurrent assets

Property, plant, and equipment*

Land and buildings at fair value............	€4,180,000	
Less: Accumulated depreciation	375,200	€3,804,800
Office equipment at cost	€ 350,000	
Less: Accumulated depreciation	102,000	248,000
Biological assets at fair value*		320,000
Patents at amortized cost*....................		140,000
Investment in *AM Coffee* (equity method)*.......		565,000
Total noncurrent assets...................		€5,077,800

Current assets

Prepaid insurance.........................	€ 24,000	
Merchandise inventory—at lower of cost (first-in, first-out) or realizable value* ..	120,000	
Accounts receivable (net of allowance for doubtful accounts)*	292,700	
Financial assets at fair value through profit or loss*.........................	465,000	
Cash and cash equivalents*	235,000	
Total current assets		1,136,700
Total assets*.................................		€6,214,500

Equity attributable to owners

Preferred 10% stock, $50 par (6,000 shares authorized and issued)*	€ 300,000	
Common stock, $20 par (50,000 shares authorized, 45,000 shares issued)*	900,000	
Share premium*.............................	1,500,000	
Reserves*	(1,200)	
Retained earnings*	1,200,300	
Total equity attributable to owners*........		€3,899,100

Liabilities

Noncurrent liabilities*

Bonds payable, 8%, due December 31, 2030 (net of discount)	€ 484,000	
Notes payable..................................	1,400,000	
Total noncurrent liabilities...................		€1,884,000

Current liabilities

Accounts payable*...........................	€ 133,000	
Loans*	200,000	
Employee provisions*........................	58,400	
Interest payable	40,000	
Total current liabilities		431,400
Total liabilities*...........................		€2,315,400
Total equity and liabilities*		€6,214,500

*Required disclosures. Footnotes provide additional subclassification detail.

Callout boxes:

- "Biological assets" are a required disclosure at fair value. See Note 7.
- Inventory valuation. See Note 8.
- International terminology for "Trading investments." Same accounting treatment.
- International terminology for "Excess of issue price over par."
- Other comprehensive items and treasury stock. See Note 9.
- Employee provisions are wages, salaries, and payroll taxes payable. See Note 10.
- Subclassifications of PP&E may be valued at fair value. See Note 6.
- Reverse liquidity account order. See Note 5.
- Equities listed first, then liabilities. See Note 5.
- Noncurrent liabilities listed prior to current liabilities.

5. Under IFRS, there is no standard format for the balance sheet (statement of financial position). A typical format for European Union companies is to begin the asset section of the balance sheet with noncurrent assets. This is followed by current assets listed in reverse order of liquidity. That is, the asset side of the balance sheet is reported

in reverse order of liquidity from least liquid to most liquid. Listing noncurrent assets first emphasizes the going concern nature of the entity.

The liability and owners' equity side of the balance sheet is also reported differently than under U.S. GAAP. Specifically, owners' equity is reported first followed by noncurrent liabilities and current liabilities. Listing equity first emphasizes the going concern nature of the entity and the long-term financial interest of the owners in the business.

6. Under IFRS, property, plant, and equipment (PP&E) may be measured at historical cost or fair value. If fair value is used, the revaluation must be for similar classifications of PP&E, but need not be for all PP&E. This departs from U.S. GAAP which requires PP&E to be measured at historical cost. Mornin' Joe International restated its Land and Buildings to fair value since the café sites have readily available real estate market prices. Land and buildings are included together because their fair values are not separable. The office equipment remains at historical cost since its does not have a readily available market price. The increase in fair value is recorded by reducing accumulated depreciation and recognizing the gain as other comprehensive income. This element of other comprehensive income is accumulated in stockholders' equity under the heading Property revaluation reserve.* This treatment is similar (with different titles) to the U.S. GAAP treatment of unrealized gains (losses) from available-for-sale securities. For Mornin' Joe International, there is an increase in the property revaluation reserve of €44,800. This amount is the only difference between Mornin' Joe's U.S. GAAP net income, total assets, and total stockholders' equity and Mornin' Joe International's IFRS total comprehensive income, total assets, and total stockholders' equity.

7. Mornin' Joe International recently acquired a coffee plantation. This is an example of a biological asset. IFRS requires separate reporting of biological assets (principally agricultural assets) at fair value.

8. Inventories are valued at lower of cost or market; however, "market" is defined as net realizable value under IFRS. U.S. GAAP defines "market" as replacement cost under most conditions. In addition, IFRS prohibits LIFO cost valuation.

9. Under IFRS, some elements of other comprehensive income and owner's equity are often aggregated under the term "reserves." In contrast, under U.S. GAAP "reserve" is used to identify a liability. IFRS also does not require separate disclosure of treasury stock as does U.S. GAAP. Specifically, treasury stock may be reported as a reduction of a reserve, a reduction of a stock premium, or as a separate item.

10. The term "provision" is used to denote a liability under IFRS, whereas this term often indicates an expense under U.S. GAAP. For example, "Provision for income taxes" means "Income tax expense" under U.S. GAAP, whereas it would mean "Income taxes payable" under IFRS.

---

* The term "property revaluation surplus" is also used.

Mornin' Joe International
Statement of Changes in Equity
For the Year Ended December 31, 2012

	Preferred Stock	Common Stock	Share Premium	Property Revaluation Reserve	Reserve for Own Shares	Retained Earnings	Total Equity Attributable to Owners
				Reserves			
Balance, January 1, 2012........	€300,000	€800,000	€1,325,000	€ 0	(€36,000)	€ 852,700	€3,241,700
Profit for the year................						421,600	421,600
Other comprehensive income							
Property revaluation (gain).......				44,800			44,800
Total comprehensive income ...				€44,800		€ 421,600	€ 466,400
Contributions by and distributions to owners							
Dividends on preferred stock.....						(30,000)	(30,000)
Dividends on common stock......						(44,000)	(44,000)
Issuance of additional common stock		100,000	175,000				275,000
Purchase of own shares					(10,000)		(10,000)
Total contributions and distributions to owners.......	€ 0	€100,000	€ 175,000	€ 0	(€10,000)	(€ 74,000)	€ 191,000
Balance, December 31, 2012	€300,000	€900,000	€1,500,000	€44,800	(€46,000)	€1,200,300	€3,899,100

"Reserves", see Notes 9 and 11.

11. The statement of changes in equity under IFRS is similar to U.S. GAAP. For example, both IFRS and GAAP include other comprehensive income items and total comprehensive income disclosures in the statement of changes in equity. In this illustration, treasury stock is included as part a reserve (Reserve for Own Shares). As discussed in Note 9, under U.S. GAAP the term "reserve" denotes a liability.

DiscussionQuestions

1. Contrast U.S. GAAP income statement terms with their differing IFRS terms, starting with the name of the statement.

2. What is the difference between classifying an expense by nature or function?

3. If a functional expense classification is used for the statement of comprehensive income, what must also be disclosed?

4. What is an example of "Other comprehensive income"? How would it be reported on the statement of comprehensive income?

5. How is the term "provision" used differently under IFRS than under U.S. GAAP?

6. What are two main differences in inventory valuation under IFRS compared to U.S. GAAP?

7. What is a "biological asset"?

8. What is the most significant IFRS departure from U.S. GAAP for valuing property, plant, and equipment?

9. What is a "share premium"?

10. How is the term "reserve" used under IFRS, and how does it differ from its meaning under U.S. GAAP?

11. How is treasury stock reported under IFRS? How does this differ from its treatment under U.S. GAAP?

IFRS Activity 1

Unilever Group is a global company that markets a wide variety of products, including Lever® soap, Breyer's® ice cream, and Hellman's® mayonnaise. The income statement and statement of comprehensive income for the Dutch company, Unilever Group is shown below.

Unilever Group Consolidated Income Statement For the Year Ended December 31, 2009 (in millions of euros)	
Turnover	€39,823
Operating profit	5,020
After (charging)/crediting:	
Restructuring	(897)
Business disposals, impairments, other	29
Net finance costs	(593)
Finance income	75
Finance costs	(504)
Pensions and similar obligations	(164)
Share of net profit/(loss) of joint ventures	111
Share of net profit/(loss) of associates	4
Other income from non-current investments	374
Profit before taxation	€ 4,916
Taxation	(1,257)
Net profit	€ 3,659
Earnings per share—basic	€ 1.21
Earnings per share—diluted	€ 1.17

Consolidated Statement of Comprehensive Income For the Year Ended December 31, 2009	
Fair value gains (losses), net of tax	€ 65
Actuarial gains (losses) on pensions, net of tax	18
Currency retranslation gains (losses), net of tax	396
Net income (expense) recognized directly into equity	€ 519
Net profit	3,659
Total comprehensive income	€4,178

a. What do you think is meant by "turnover"?

b. How does Unilever's income statement presentation differ significantly from that of Mornin' Joe?

c. How is the total for net finance costs presented differently than would be typically found under U.S. GAAP?

d. What are two ways in which other comprehensive income items can be disclosed under IFRS, and how does this differ from U.S. GAAP?

IFRS Activity 2

The following is the consolidated statement of financial position for LVMH, a French company that markets the Louis Vuitton® and Moët Hennessy® brands.

LVMH Statement of Financial Position December 31, 2009 (in millions of euros)	
Assets	
Brands and other intangible assets—net	€ 8,697
Goodwill—net	4,270
Property, plant, and equipment—net	6,140
Investment in associates	213
Non-current available for sale financial assets	540
Other non-current assets	750
Deferred tax	521
Non-current assets	€21,131
Inventories	€ 5,644
Trade accounts receivable	1,455
Income taxes receivable	217
Other current assets	1,213
Cash and cash equivalents	2,446
Current assets	€10,975
TOTAL ASSETS	€32,106
Liabilities and Equity	
Share capital	€ 147
Share premium	1,763
Treasury shares	(929)
Revaluation reserves	871
Other reserves	10,684
Net profit, group share	1,755
Equity, group share	€13,796
Minority interests	989
Total equity	€14,785
Long-term borrowings	€ 4,077
Provisions	990
Deferred tax	3,117
Other non-current liabilities	3,089
Total non-current liabilities	€11,273
Short-term borrowings	1,708
Trade accounts payable	1,911
Income taxes payable	221
Provisions	334
Other current liabilities	1,874
Total current liabilities	€ 6,048
TOTAL LIABILITIES AND EQUITY	€32,106

a. Identify presentation differences between the balance sheet of LVMH and a balance sheet prepared under U.S. GAAP. Use the Mornin' Joe balance sheet on page 714 as an example of a U.S. GAAP balance sheet. (Ignore minority interests.)

b. Compare the terms used in this balance sheet with the terms used by Mornin' Joe (page 714), using the table below.

LVMH Term	U.S. GAAP Term as Used by Mornin' Joe
Statement of financial position	
Share capital	
Share premium	
Other reserves	
Provisions	

c. What does the "Revaluation reserves" in the equity section of the balance sheet represent?

IFRS Activity 3

Under U.S. GAAP, LIFO is an acceptable inventory method. Listed below is financial statement information for three companies that use LIFO. All table numbers are in millions of dollars.

	LIFO Inventory	FIFO Inventory (from footnotes)	Impact on Net Income from Using LIFO Rather than FIFO (from footnotes)	Total Current Assets	Net Income as Reported
ExxonMobil	$11,553	$28,653	$207	$55,235	$19,280
Kroger	4,902	5,705	(49)	7,450	70
Ford Motor*	5,450	6,248	33	40,560	1,212

*Autos and trucks only

Assume these companies adopted IFRS, and thus were required to use FIFO, rather than LIFO. Prepare a table with the following columns as shown below.

(1) Difference between FIFO and LIFO inventory valuation.

(2) Revised IFRS net income using FIFO.

(3) Difference between FIFO and LIFO inventory valuation as a percent of total current assets.

(4) Revised IFRS net income as a percent of the reported net income.

(1)	(2)	(3)	(4)
FIFO less LIFO	IFRS Net Income	$\dfrac{\text{(FIFO less LIFO)}}{\text{Total Current Assets}}$	$\dfrac{\text{IFRS Net Income Col. (2)}}{\text{Reported Net Income}}$

a. Complete the table.

b. For which company would a change to IFRS for inventory valuation have the largest percentage impact on total current assets (Col. 3)?

c. For which company would a change to IFRS for inventory valuation have the largest percentage impact on net income (Col. 4)?

d. Why might Kroger have a negative impact on net income from using LIFO, while the other two companies have a positive impact on net income from using LIFO?

© AP Photo/Elaine Thompson

Statement of Cash Flows

Jones Soda Co.

Suppose you were to receive $100 from an event. Would it make a difference what the event was? Yes, it would! If you received $100 for your birthday, then it's a gift. If you received $100 as a result of working part time for a week, then it's the result of your effort. If you received $100 as a loan, then it's money that you will have to pay back in the future. If you received $100 as a result of selling your iPod, then it's the result of giving up something tangible. Thus, $100 received can be associated with different types of events, and these events have different meanings to you, and different implications for your future. You would much rather receive a $100 gift than take out a $100 loan. Likewise, company stakeholders view inflows and outflows of cash differently depending on their source.

Companies are required to report information about the events causing a change in cash over a period of time. This information is reported in the statement of cash flows. One such company

is Jones Soda Co. Jones began in the late 1980s as an alternative beverage company, known for its customer-provided labels, unique flavors, and support for extreme sports. You have probably seen Jones Soda at Barnes & Noble, Panera Bread, or Starbucks, or maybe sampled some of its unique flavors, such as Fufu Berry®, Blue Bubblegum®, or Lemon Drop®. As with any company, cash is important to Jones Soda. Without cash, Jones would be unable to expand its brands, distribute its product, support extreme sports, or provide a return for its owners. Thus, its managers are concerned about the sources and uses of cash.

In previous chapters, we have used the income statement, balance sheet, statement of retained earnings, and other information to analyze the effects of management decisions on a business's financial position and operating performance. In this chapter, we focus on the events causing a change in cash by presenting the preparation and use of the statement of cash flows.

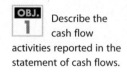

OBJ. 1 Describe the cash flow activities reported in the statement of cash flows.

Reporting Cash Flows

The **statement of cash flows** reports a company's cash inflows and outflows for a period.[1] The statement of cash flows provides useful information about a company's ability to do the following:

1. Generate cash from operations
2. Maintain and expand its operating capacity
3. Meet its financial obligations
4. Pay dividends

The statement of cash flows is used by managers in evaluating past operations and in planning future investing and financing activities. It is also used by external users such as investors and creditors to assess a company's profit potential and ability to pay its debt and pay dividends.

The statement of cash flows reports three types of cash flow activities as follows:

Cash flows from operating activities are cash flows from transactions that affect the net income of the company.

    Example: Purchase and sale of merchandise by a retailer.

Cash flows from investing activities are cash flows from transactions that affect investments in the noncurrent assets of the company.

    Example: Purchase and sale of fixed assets, such as equipment and buildings.

---

1 As used in this chapter, *cash* refers to cash and cash equivalents. Examples of cash equivalents include short-term, highly liquid investments, such as money market accounts, bank certificates of deposit, and U.S. Treasury bills.

Cash flows from financing activities are cash flows from transactions that affect the debt and equity of the company.

Example: Issuing or retiring equity and debt securities.

The cash flows are reported in the statement of cash flows as follows:

Cash flows from operating activities	$XXX
Cash flows from investing activities	XXX
Cash flows from financing activities	XXX
Net increase or decrease in cash for the period	$XXX
Cash at the beginning of the period	XXX
Cash at the end of the period	$XXX

The ending cash on the statement of cash flows equals the cash reported on the company's balance sheet at the end of the year.

Exhibit 1 illustrates the sources (increases) and uses (decreases) of cash by each of the three cash flow activities. A *source* of cash causes the cash flow to increase and is called a *cash inflow*. A *use* of cash causes cash flow to decrease and is called *cash outflow*.

Note:
The statement of cash flows reports cash flows from operating, investing, and financing activities.

EXHIBIT 1

Cash Flows

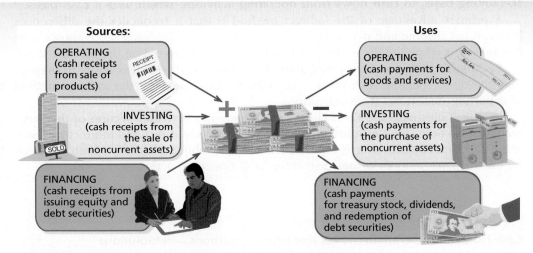

Cash Flows from Operating Activities

Cash flows from operating activities is the cash inflow or outflow from a company's day-to-day operations. Companies may select one of two alternative methods for reporting cash flows from operating activities in the statement of cash flows:

1. The direct method
2. The indirect method

Both methods result in the same amount of cash flows from operating activities. They differ in the way they report cash flow from operating activities as discussed below.

The **direct method** reports operating cash inflows (receipts) and cash outflows (payments) as follows:

Cash flows from operating activities:		
Cash received from customers		$XXX
Less: Cash payments for merchandise	$XXX	
Cash payments for operating expenses	XXX	
Cash payments for interest	XXX	
Cash payments for income taxes	XXX	XXX
Net cash flows from operating activities		$XXX

The primary operating cash inflow is cash received from customers. The primary operating cash outflows are cash payments for merchandise, operating expenses, interest, and income tax payments. The cash received from operating activities less the cash payments for operating activities is the net cash flow from operating activities.

The primary advantage of the direct method is that it *directly* reports cash receipts and cash payments in the statement of cash flows. Its primary disadvantage is that these data may not be readily available in the accounting records. Thus, the direct method is normally more costly to prepare and, as a result, is used by less than 1% of companies.[2]

The **indirect method** reports cash flows from operating activities by beginning with net income and adjusting it for revenues and expenses that do not involve the receipt or payment of cash as follows:

Cash flows from operating activities:		
Net income	$XXX	
Adjustments to reconcile net income to net cash flow from operating activities	XXX	
Net cash flow from operating activities		$XXX

The adjustments to reconcile net income to net cash flow from operating activities include such items as depreciation and gains or losses on fixed assets. Changes in current operating assets and liabilities such as accounts receivable or accounts payable are also added or deducted depending on their effect on cash flows. In effect, these additions and deductions adjust net income, which is reported on an accrual accounting basis, to cash flows from operating activities, which uses a cash basis.

A primary advantage of the indirect method is that it reconciles the differences between net income and net cash flows from operations. In doing so, it shows how net income is related to the ending cash balance that is reported on the balance sheet.

Because the data are readily available, the indirect method is less costly to prepare than the direct method. As a result, over 99% of companies use the indirect method of reporting cash flows from operations.

Exhibit 2 illustrates the Cash Flows from Operating Activities section of the statement of cash flows for **NetSolutions**. Exhibit 2 shows the direct and indirect methods using the NetSolutions data from Chapter 1. As Exhibit 2 illustrates, both methods report the same amount of net cash flow from operating activities, $2,900.

EXHIBIT 2   **Cash Flow from Operations: Direct and Indirect Methods—NetSolutions**

Direct Method

Cash flows from operating activities:	
Cash received from customers	$7,500
Deduct cash payments for expenses and payments to creditors	4,600
Net cash flow from operating activities	$2,900

Indirect Method

Cash flows from operating activities:	
Net income	$3,050
Add increase in accounts payable	400
	$3,450
Deduct increase in supplies	550
Net cash flow from operating activities	$2,900

the same

Cash Flows from Investing Activities

Cash flows from investing activities show the cash inflows and outflows related to changes in a company's long-term assets. Cash flows from investing activities are reported on the statement of cash flows as follows:

Cash flows from investing activities:		
Cash inflows from investing activities	$XXX	
Less cash used for investing activities	XXX	
Net cash flows from investing activities		$XXX

In October 2008, the U.S. government invested $250 billion of cash into U.S. banks to help stabilize the financial system.

2 *Accounting Trends & Techniques*, AICPA, 2008 edition.

Cash inflows from investing activities normally arise from selling fixed assets, investments, and intangible assets. Cash outflows normally include payments to purchase fixed assets, investments, and intangible assets.

Cash Flows from Financing Activities

Cash flows from financing activities show the cash inflows and outflows related to changes in a company's long-term liabilities and stockholders' equity. Cash flows from financing activities are reported on the statement of cash flows as follows:

Cash flows from financing activities:		
Cash inflows from financing activities	$XXX	
Less cash used for financing activities	XXX	
Net cash flows from financing activities		$XXX

Cash inflows from financing activities normally arise from issuing long-term debt or equity securities. For example, issuing bonds, notes payable, preferred stock, and common stock creates cash inflows from financing activities. Cash outflows from financing activities include paying cash dividends, repaying long-term debt, and acquiring treasury stock.

Noncash Investing and Financing Activities

A company may enter into transactions involving investing and financing activities that do not *directly* affect cash. For example, a company may issue common stock to retire long-term debt. Although this transaction does not directly affect cash, it does eliminate future cash payments for interest and for paying the bonds when they mature. Because such transactions *indirectly* affect cash flows, they are reported in a separate section of the statement of cash flows. This section usually appears at the bottom of the statement of cash flows.

In fiscal 2009, Apple, Inc., generated $10.1 billion in cash flow from operating activities.

Example Exercise 16-1 Classifying Cash Flows   OBJ. 1

Identify whether each of the following would be reported as an operating, investing, or financing activity in the statement of cash flows.

a. Purchase of patent
b. Payment of cash dividend
c. Disposal of equipment

d. Cash sales
e. Purchase of treasury stock
f. Payment of wages expense

Follow My Example 16-1

a. Investing
b. Financing
c. Investing

d. Operating
e. Financing
f. Operating

Practice Exercises: **PE 16-1A, PE 16-1B**

No Cash Flow per Share

Cash flow per share is sometimes reported in the financial press. As reported, cash flow per share is normally computed as *cash flow from operations per share*. However, such reporting may be misleading because of the following:

1. Users may misinterpret cash flow per share as the per-share amount available for dividends. This would not be the case if the cash generated by operations is required for repaying loans or for reinvesting in the business.

2. Users may misinterpret cash flow per share as equivalent to (or better than) earnings per share.

For these reasons, the financial statements, including the statement of cash flows, should not report cash flow per share.

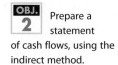

Prepare a statement of cash flows, using the indirect method.

Statement of Cash Flows— The Indirect Method

The indirect method of reporting cash flows from operating activities uses the logic that a change in any balance sheet account (including cash) can be analyzed in terms of changes in the other balance sheet accounts. Thus, by analyzing changes in noncash balance sheet accounts, any change in the cash account can be *indirectly* determined.

To illustrate, the accounting equation can be solved for cash as shown below.

Assets = Liabilities + Stockholders' Equity

Cash + Noncash Assets = Liabilities + Stockholders' Equity

Cash = Liabilities + Stockholders' Equity − Noncash Assets

Therefore, any change in the cash account can be determined by analyzing changes in the liability, stockholders' equity, and noncash asset accounts as shown below.

Change in Cash = *Change* in Liabilities + *Change* in Stockholders' Equity
− *Change* in Noncash Assets

Under the indirect method, there is no order in which the balance sheet accounts must be analyzed. However, net income (or net loss) is the first amount reported on the statement of cash flows. Since net income (or net loss) is a component of any change in Retained Earnings, the first account normally analyzed is Retained Earnings.

To illustrate the indirect method, the income statement and comparative balance sheets for Rundell Inc. shown in Exhibit 3 are used. Ledger accounts and other data supporting the income statement and balance sheet are presented as needed.[3]

EXHIBIT 3   **Income Statement and Comparative Balance Sheet**

Rundell Inc.
Income Statement
For the Year Ended December 31, 2012

Sales		$1,180,000
Cost of merchandise sold		790,000
Gross profit		$ 390,000
Operating expenses:		
Depreciation expense	$ 7,000	
Other operating expenses	196,000	
Total operating expenses		203,000
Income from operations		$ 187,000
Other income:		
Gain on sale of land	$ 12,000	
Other expense:		
Interest expense	8,000	4,000
Income before income tax		$ 191,000
Income tax expense		83,000
Net income		$ 108,000

---

3 An appendix that discusses using a spreadsheet (work sheet) as an aid in assembling data for the statement of cash flows is presented at the end of this chapter. This appendix illustrates the use of this spreadsheet in reporting cash flows from operating activities using the indirect method.

EXHIBIT 3   **Income Statement and Comparative Balance Sheet** *(concluded)*

Rundell Inc.
Comparative Balance Sheet
December 31, 2012 and 2011

	2012	2011	Increase Decrease*
Assets			
Cash	$ 97,500	$ 26,000	$ 71,500
Accounts receivable (net)	74,000	65,000	9,000
Inventories	172,000	180,000	8,000*
Land	80,000	125,000	45,000*
Building	260,000	200,000	60,000
Accumulated depreciation—building.................	(65,300)	(58,300)	7,000**
Total assets	$618,200	$537,700	$ 80,500
Liabilities			
Accounts payable (merchandise creditors)	$ 43,500	$ 46,700	$ 3,200*
Accrued expenses payable (operating expenses)	26,500	24,300	2,200
Income taxes payable	7,900	8,400	500*
Dividends payable	14,000	10,000	4,000
Bonds payable	100,000	150,000	50,000*
Total liabilities	$191,900	$239,400	$ 47,500*
Stockholders' Equity			
Common stock ($2 par)	$ 24,000	$ 16,000	$ 8,000
Paid-in capital in excess of par......................	120,000	80,000	40,000
Retained earnings...................................	282,300	202,300	80,000
Total stockholders' equity............................	$426,300	$298,300	$128,000
Total liabilities and stockholders' equity...............	$618,200	$537,700	$ 80,500

**There is a $7,000 increase to Accumulated Depreciation—Building, which is a contra asset account. As a result, the $7,000 increase in this account must be subtracted in summing to the increase in Total assets of $80,500.

Retained Earnings

The comparative balance sheet for Rundell Inc. shows that retained earnings increased $80,000 during the year. The retained earnings account shown below indicates how this change occurred.

Account *Retained Earnings*					**Account No.**	
					Balance	
Date		Item	Debit	Credit	Debit	Credit
2012 Jan.	1	Balance				202,300
Dec.	31	Net income		108,000		310,300
	31	Cash dividends	28,000			282,300

The retained earnings account indicates that the $80,000 ($108,000 − $28,000) change resulted from net income of $108,000 and cash dividends of $28,000. The net income of $108,000 is the first amount reported in the Cash Flows from Operating Activities section.

Adjustments to Net Income

The net income of $108,000 reported by Rundell Inc. does not equal the cash flows from operating activities for the period. This is because net income is determined using the accrual method of accounting.

Under the accrual method of accounting, revenues and expenses are recorded at different times from when cash is received or paid. For example, merchandise may be sold on account and the cash received at a later date. Likewise, insurance premiums may be paid in the current period, but expensed in a following period.

Thus, under the indirect method, adjustments to net income must be made to determine cash flows from operating activities. The typical adjustments to net income are shown in Exhibit 4.[4]

Net income is normally adjusted to cash flows from operating activities using the following steps:

Step 1.   Expenses that do not affect cash are added. Such expenses decrease net income but do not involve cash payments and, thus, are added to net income.

Examples: *Depreciation* of fixed assets and *amortization* of intangible assets are added to net income.

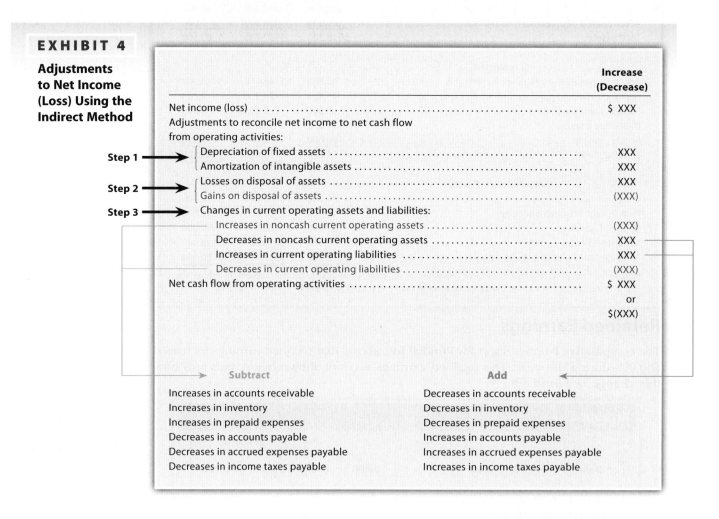

EXHIBIT 4

Adjustments to Net Income (Loss) Using the Indirect Method

	Increase (Decrease)
Net income (loss)	$ XXX
Adjustments to reconcile net income to net cash flow from operating activities:	
Step 1 → Depreciation of fixed assets	XXX
Amortization of intangible assets	XXX
Step 2 → Losses on disposal of assets	XXX
Gains on disposal of assets	(XXX)
Step 3 → Changes in current operating assets and liabilities:	
Increases in noncash current operating assets	(XXX)
Decreases in noncash current operating assets	XXX
Increases in current operating liabilities	XXX
Decreases in current operating liabilities	(XXX)
Net cash flow from operating activities	$ XXX
	or
	$(XXX)

Subtract	Add
Increases in accounts receivable	Decreases in accounts receivable
Increases in inventory	Decreases in inventory
Increases in prepaid expenses	Decreases in prepaid expenses
Decreases in accounts payable	Increases in accounts payable
Decreases in accrued expenses payable	Increases in accrued expenses payable
Decreases in income taxes payable	Increases in income taxes payable

Step 2.   Losses and gains on disposal of assets are added or deducted. The disposal (sale) of assets is an investing activity rather than an operating activity. However, such losses and gains are reported as part of net income. As a result, any *losses* on disposal of assets are *added* back to net income. Likewise, any *gains* on disposal of assets are *deducted* from net income.

Example: Land costing $100,000 is sold for $90,000. The loss of $10,000 is added back to net income.

4 Other items that also require adjustments to net income to obtain cash flows from operating activities include amortization of bonds payable discounts (add), losses on debt retirement (add), amortization of bonds payable premiums (deduct), and gains on retirement of debt (deduct).

Step 3.   Changes in current operating assets and liabilities are added or deducted as follows:

> Increases in noncash current operating assets are deducted.
> Decreases in noncash current operating assets are added.
> Increases in current operating liabilities are added.
> Decreases in current operating liabilities are deducted.

Example: A sale of $10,000 on account increases sales, accounts receivable, and net income by $10,000. However, cash is not affected. Thus, an increase in accounts receivable of $10,000 is deducted. Similar adjustments are required for the changes in the other current asset and liability accounts such as inventory, prepaid expenses, accounts payable, accrued expenses payable, and income taxes payable as shown in Exhibit 4.

Example Exercise 16-2   Adjustments to Net Income—Indirect Method   **OBJ. 2**

Omni Corporation's accumulated depreciation increased by $12,000, while $3,400 of patents were amortized between balance sheet dates. There were no purchases or sales of depreciable or intangible assets during the year. In addition, the income statement showed a gain of $4,100 from the sale of land. Reconcile Omni's net income of $50,000 to net cash flow from operating activities.

Follow My Example 16-2

Net income	$50,000
Adjustments to reconcile net income to net cash flow from operating activities:	
Depreciation	12,000
Amortization of patents	3,400
Gain from sale of land	(4,100)
Net cash flow from operating activities	$61,300

Practice Exercises: **PE 16-2A, PE 16-2B**

To illustrate, the Cash Flows from Operating Activities section of Rundell's statement of cash flows is shown in Exhibit 5. Rundell's net income of $108,000 is converted to cash flows from operating activities of $100,500 as follows:

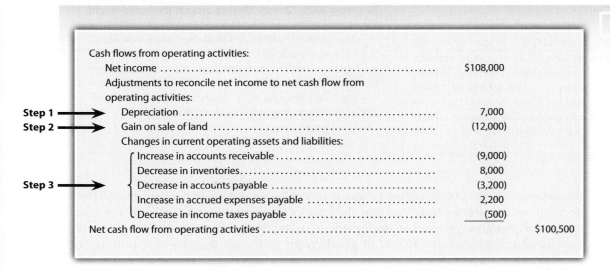

Step 1 →
Step 2 →
Step 3 →

Cash flows from operating activities:	
Net income	$108,000
Adjustments to reconcile net income to net cash flow from operating activities:	
Depreciation	7,000
Gain on sale of land	(12,000)
Changes in current operating assets and liabilities:	
Increase in accounts receivable	(9,000)
Decrease in inventories...........................	8,000
Decrease in accounts payable	(3,200)
Increase in accrued expenses payable	2,200
Decrease in income taxes payable	(500)
Net cash flow from operating activities	$100,500

EXHIBIT 5

Cash Flows from Operating Activities— Indirect Method

Step 1.   Add depreciation of $7,000.

> Analysis: The comparative balance sheet in Exhibit 3 indicates that Accumulated Depreciation—Building increased by $7,000. The account, shown on the following page, indicates that depreciation for the year was $7,000 for the building.

Account Accumulated Depreciation—Building					Account No.	
					Balance	
Date		**Item**	**Debit**	**Credit**	**Debit**	**Credit**
2012 Jan.	1	Balance				58,300
Dec.	31	Depreciation for year		7,000		65,300

Step 2. Deduct the gain on the sale of land of $12,000.

Analysis: The income statement in Exhibit 3 reports a gain from the sale of land of $12,000. The proceeds, which include the gain, are reported in the Investing section of the statement of cash flows.[5] Thus, the gain of $12,000 is deducted from net income in determining cash flows from operating activities.

Step 3. Add and deduct changes in current operating assets and liabilities.

Analysis: The increases and decreases in the current operating asset and current liability accounts are shown below.

	December 31		**Increase**
Accounts	**2012**	**2011**	**Decrease***
Accounts Receivable (net)	$ 74,000	$ 65,000	$9,000
Inventories	172,000	180,000	8,000*
Accounts Payable (merchandise creditors)	43,500	46,700	3,200*
Accrued Expenses Payable (operating expenses)	26,500	24,300	2,200
Income Taxes Payable	7,900	8,400	500*

Accounts receivable (net): The $9,000 increase is deducted from net income. This is because the $9,000 increase in accounts receivable indicates that sales on account were $9,000 more than the cash received from customers. Thus, sales (and net income) includes $9,000 that was not received in cash during the year.

BusinessConnection

CASH CRUNCH!

Automobile manufacturers such as Chrysler Group LLC sell their cars and trucks through a network of independently owned and operated dealerships. The vehicles are sold to the dealerships on credit by issuing a trade receivable, which is repaid to Chrysler Group LLC after the vehicles are sold by the dealership. The economic crisis of 2008 created a slump in car sales that lasted well into 2009.

By spring 2009, Chrysler dealers around the world found themselves with large inventories of unsold cars and trucks, resulting in their inability to repay their trade receivables from Chrysler Group LLC. This led to a significant decline in Chrysler's cash flow from operating activities that forced the company into a financial restructuring. Ultimately, the company was rescued by a significant investment (cash inflow from financing activities) from Fiat and the U.S. and Canadian governments.

Source: "Chrysler Restructuring Plan for Long-Term Viability," Chrysler Group LLC, February 17, 2009.

Inventories: The $8,000 decrease is added to net income. This is because the $8,000 decrease in inventories indicates that the cost of merchandise *sold* exceeds the cost of the merchandise *purchased* during the year by $8,000. In other words, cost of merchandise sold includes $8,000 of goods from inventory that was not purchased (used cash) during the year.

Accounts payable (merchandise creditors): The $3,200 decrease is deducted from net income. This is because a decrease in accounts payable indicates that the cash *payments* to merchandise creditors exceed the merchandise *purchased on account*

---

5 The reporting of the proceeds (cash flows) from the sale of land as part of investing activities is discussed later in this chapter.

by $3,200. Therefore, cost of merchandise sold is $3,200 less than the cash paid to merchandise creditors during the year.

Accrued expenses payable (operating expenses): The $2,200 increase is added to net income. This is because an increase in accrued expenses payable indicates that operating expenses exceed the cash payments for operating expenses by $2,200. In other words, operating expenses reported on the income statement include $2,200 that did not require a cash outflow during the year.

Income taxes payable: The $500 decrease is deducted from net income. This is because a decrease in income taxes payable indicates that taxes paid exceed the amount of taxes incurred during the year by $500. In other words, the amount reported on the income statement for income tax expense is less than the amount paid by $500.

Example Exercise 16-3 — Changes in Current Operating Assets and Liabilities—Indirect Method

OBJ. 2

Victor Corporation's current operating assets and liabilities from the company's comparative balance sheet were as follows:

	Dec. 31, 2013	Dec. 31, 2012
Accounts receivable	$ 6,500	$ 4,900
Inventory	12,300	15,000
Accounts payable	4,800	5,200
Dividends payable	5,000	4,000

Adjust Victor's net income of $70,000 for changes in operating assets and liabilities to arrive at cash flows from operating activities.

Follow My Example 16-3

Net income	$70,000
Adjustments to reconcile net income to net cash flow from operating activities:	
Changes in current operating assets and liabilities:	
Increase in accounts receivable	(1,600)
Decrease in inventory	2,700
Decrease in accounts payable	(400)
Net cash flow from operating activities	$70,700

Note: The change in dividends payable impacts the cash paid for dividends, which is disclosed under financing activities.

Practice Exercises: **PE 16-3A, PE 16-3B**

Using the preceding analyses, Rundell's net income of $108,000 is converted to cash flows from operating activities of $100,500 as shown in Exhibit 5, on page 725.

Integrity, Objectivity, and Ethics in Business

CREDIT POLICY AND CASH FLOW

One would expect customers to pay for products and services sold on account. Unfortunately, that is not always the case. Collecting accounts receivable efficiently is the key to turning a current asset into positive cash flow. Most entrepreneurs would rather think about the exciting aspects of their business—such as product development, marketing, sales, and advertising—than credit collection. This can be a mistake. Hugh McHugh of Overhill Flowers, Inc., decided that he would have no more trade accounts after dealing with Christmas orders that weren't paid for until late February, or sometimes not paid at all. As stated by one collection service, "One thing business owners always tell me is that they never thought about [collections] when they started their own business." To the small business owner, the collection of accounts receivable may mean the difference between succeeding and failing.

Source: Paulette Thomas, "Making Them Pay: The Last Thing Most Entrepreneurs Want to Think About Is Bill Collection; It Should Be One of the First Things," *The Wall Street Journal*, September 19, 2005, p. R6.

Example Exercise 16-4 **Cash Flows from Operating Activities—Indirect Method**

Omicron Inc. reported the following data:

Net income	$120,000
Depreciation expense	12,000
Loss on disposal of equipment	15,000
Increase in accounts receivable	5,000
Decrease in accounts payable	2,000

Prepare the Cash Flows from Operating Activities section of the statement of cash flows using the indirect method.

Follow My Example 16-4

Cash flows from operating activities:

Net income		$120,000
Adjustments to reconcile net income to net cash flow from operating activities:		
Depreciation expense		12,000
Loss on disposal of equipment		15,000
Changes in current operating assets and liabilities:		
Increase in accounts receivable		(5,000)
Decrease in accounts payable		(2,000)
Net cash flow from operating activities		$140,000

Practice Exercises: **PE 16-4A, PE 16-4B**

Dividends

The retained earnings account of Rundell Inc., shown on page 723, indicates cash dividends of $28,000 declared during the year. However, the dividends payable account, shown below, indicates that only $24,000 of dividends were paid during the year.

Account Dividends Payable					Account No.	
					Balance	
Date		**Item**	**Debit**	**Credit**	**Debit**	**Credit**
2012 Jan.	1	Balance				10,000
	10	Cash paid	10,000		—	—
June	20	Dividends declared		14,000		14,000
July	10	Cash paid	14,000		—	—
Dec.	20	Dividends declared		14,000		14,000

Since dividend payments are a financing activity, the dividend payment of $24,000 is reported in the Financing Activities section of the statement of cash flows, as shown below.

Cash flows from financing activities:	
Cash paid for dividends	$24,000

Common Stock

The common stock account increased by $8,000, and the paid-in capital in excess of par—common stock account increased by $40,000, as shown below. These increases were from issuing 4,000 shares of common stock for $12 per share.

Account *Common Stock*					Account No.	
					Balance	
Date		**Item**	**Debit**	**Credit**	**Debit**	**Credit**
2012 Jan.	1	Balance				16,000
Nov.	1	4,000 shares issued for cash		8,000		24,000

Account *Paid-In Capital in Excess of Par—Common Stock*					Account No.	
					Balance	
Date		**Item**	**Debit**	**Credit**	**Debit**	**Credit**
2012 Jan.	1	Balance				80,000
Nov.	1	4,000 shares issued for cash		40,000		120,000

This cash inflow is reported in the Financing Activities section as follows:

Cash flows from financing activities:
  Cash received from sale of common stock $48,000

Bonds Payable

The bonds payable account decreased by $50,000, as shown below. This decrease is from retiring the bonds by a cash payment for their face amount.

Account *Bonds Payable*					Account No.	
					Balance	
Date		**Item**	**Debit**	**Credit**	**Debit**	**Credit**
2012 Jan.	1	Balance				150,000
June	1	Retired by payment of cash at face amount	50,000			100,000

This cash outflow is reported in the Financing Activities section as follows:

Cash flows from financing activities:
  Cash paid to retire bonds payable $50,000

Building

The building account increased by $60,000, and the accumulated depreciation—building account increased by $7,000, as shown below.

Account Building						Account No.	
						Balance	
Date		**Item**	**Debit**	**Credit**	**Debit**	**Credit**	
2012 Jan.	1	Balance			200,000		
Dec.	27	Purchased for cash	60,000		260,000		

Account Accumulated Depreciation—Building						Account No.	
						Balance	
Date		**Item**	**Debit**	**Credit**	**Debit**	**Credit**	
2012 Jan.	1	Balance				58,300	
Dec.	31	Depreciation for the year		7,000		65,300	

The purchase of a building for cash of $60,000 is reported as an outflow of cash in the Investing Activities section as follows:

Cash flows from investing activities:
Cash paid for purchase of building $60,000

The credit in the accumulated depreciation—building account represents depreciation expense for the year. This depreciation expense of $7,000 on the building was added to net income in determining cash flows from operating activities, as reported in Exhibit 5, on page 725.

Land

The $45,000 decline in the land account was from two transactions, as shown below.

Account Land						Account No.	
						Balance	
Date		**Item**	**Debit**	**Credit**	**Debit**	**Credit**	
2012 Jan.	1	Balance			125,000		
June	8	Sold for $72,000 cash		60,000	65,000		
Oct.	12	Purchased for $15,000 cash	15,000		80,000		

The June 8 transaction is the sale of land with a cost of $60,000 for $72,000 in cash. The $72,000 proceeds from the sale are reported in the Investing Activities section, as follows:

Cash flows from investing activities:
Cash received from sale of land $72,000

The proceeds of $72,000 include the $12,000 gain on the sale of land and the $60,000 cost (book value) of the land. As shown in Exhibit 5, on page 725, the $12,000 gain is deducted from net income in the Cash Flows from Operating Activities section. This is so that the $12,000 cash inflow related to the gain is not included twice as a cash inflow.

The October 12 transaction is the purchase of land for cash of $15,000. This transaction is reported as an outflow of cash in the Investing Activities section, as follows:

Cash flows from investing activities:
    Cash paid for purchase of land $15,000

Example Exercise 16-5   Land Transactions on the Statement of Cash Flows   **OBJ. 2**

Alpha Corporation purchased land for $125,000. Later in the year, the company sold a different piece of land with a book value of $165,000 for $200,000. How are the effects of these transactions reported on the statement of cash flows?

Follow My Example 16-5

The gain on sale of land is deducted from net income as shown below.

Gain on sale of land . . . . $ (35,000)

The purchase and sale of land is reported as part of cash flows from investing activities as shown below.

Cash received from sale of land   200,000
Cash paid for purchase of land . . . .   (125,000)

Practice Exercises: **PE 16-5A, PE 16-5B**

Preparing the Statement of Cash Flows

The statement of cash flows for Rundell Inc. using the indirect method is shown in Exhibit 6. The statement of cash flows indicates that cash increased by $71,500 during the year. The most significant increase in net cash flows ($100,500) was from operating activities. The most significant use of cash ($26,000) was for financing activities. The ending balance of cash on December 31, 2012, is $97,500. This ending cash balance is also reported on the December 31, 2012, balance sheet shown in Exhibit 3 on page 723.

EXHIBIT 6

Statement of Cash Flows— Indirect Method

Rundell Inc.
Statement of Cash Flows
For the Year Ended December 31, 2012

Cash flows from operating activities:			
Net income.		$108,000	
Adjustments to reconcile net income to net cash flow from operating activities:			
Depreciation		7,000	
Gain on sale of land.		(12,000)	
Changes in current operating assets and liabilities:			
Increase in accounts receivable.		(9,000)	
Decrease in inventories..		8,000	
Decrease in accounts payable		(3,200)	
Increase in accrued expenses payable.		2,200	
Decrease in income taxes payable		(500)	
Net cash flow from operating activities			$100,500
Cash flows from investing activities:			
Cash from sale of land.		$ 72,000	
Less: Cash paid to purchase land	$15,000		
Cash paid for purchase of building	60,000	75,000	
Net cash flow used for investing activities.			(3,000)
Cash flows from financing activities:			
Cash received from sale of common stock.		$ 48,000	
Less: Cash paid to retire bonds payable	$50,000		
Cash paid for dividends.	24,000	74,000	
Net cash flow used for financing activities		(26,000)	
Increase in cash		$ 71,500	
Cash at the beginning of the year.		26,000	
Cash at the end of the year.		$ 97,500	

Statement of Cash Flows—The Direct Method

The direct method reports cash flows from operating activities as follows:

Cash flows from operating activities:		
Cash received from customers		$ XXX
Less: Cash payments for merchandise	$ XXX	
Cash payments for operating expenses............................	XXX	
Cash payments for interest	XXX	
Cash payments for income taxes	XXX	XXX
Net cash flows from operating activities		$ XXX

The Cash Flows from Investing and Financing Activities sections of the statement of cash flows are exactly the same under both the direct and indirect methods. The amount of cash flows from operating activities is also the same, but the manner in which it is reported is different.

Under the direct method, the income statement is adjusted to cash flows from operating activities as follows:

Income Statement	Adjusted to	Cash Flows from Operating Activities
Sales	→	Cash received from customers
Cost of merchandise sold	→	Cash payments for merchandise
Operating expenses:		
Depreciation expense	N/A	N/A
Other operating expenses	→	Cash payments for operating expenses
Gain on sale of land	N/A	N/A
Interest expense	→	Cash payments for interest
Income tax expense	→	Cash payments for income taxes
Net income	→	Cash flows from operating activities

N/A—Not applicable

As shown above, depreciation expense is not adjusted or reported as part of cash flows from operating activities. This is because deprecation expense does not involve a cash outflow. The gain on sale of land is also not adjusted and is not reported as part of cash flows from operating activities. This is because the cash flow from operating activities is determined directly, rather than by reconciling net income. The cash proceeds from the sale of land are reported as an investing activity.

To illustrate the direct method, the income statement and comparative balance sheet for Rundell Inc. shown in Exhibit 3, on pages 722–723, are used.

Cash Received from Customers

The income statement (shown in Exhibit 3) of Rundell Inc. reports sales of $1,180,000. To determine the *cash received from customers*, the $1,180,000 is adjusted for any increase or decrease in accounts receivable. The adjustment is summarized below.

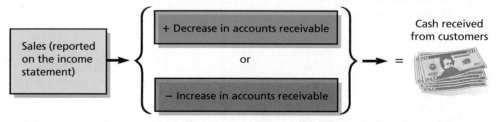

The cash received from customers is $1,171,000, computed as follows:

Sales	$ 1,180,000
Less increase in accounts receivable	9,000
Cash received from customers	$1,171,000

The increase of $9,000 in accounts receivable (shown in Exhibit 3) during 2012 indicates that sales on account exceeded cash received from customers by $9,000. In other words, sales include $9,000 that did not result in a cash inflow during the year. Thus, $9,000 is deducted from sales to determine the *cash received from customers*.

Example Exercise 16-6 Cash Received from Customers—Direct Method

OBJ. 3

Sales reported on the income statement were $350,000. The accounts receivable balance declined $8,000 over the year. Determine the amount of cash received from customers.

Follow My Example 16-6

Sales...	$350,000
Add decrease in accounts receivable	8,000
Cash received from customers......................................	$358,000

Practice Exercises: **PE 16-6A, PE 16-6B**

Cash Payments for Merchandise

The income statement (shown in Exhibit 3) for Rundell Inc. reports cost of merchandise sold of $790,000. To determine the *cash payments for merchandise*, the $790,000 is adjusted for any increases or decreases in inventories and accounts payable. Assuming the accounts payable are owed to merchandise suppliers, the adjustment is summarized below.

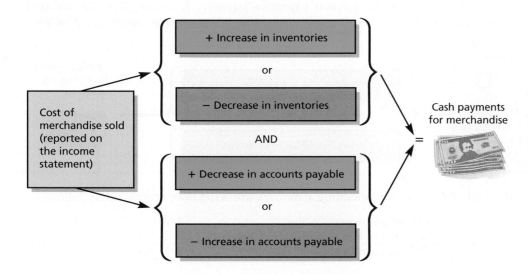

The cash payments for merchandise are $785,200, computed as follows:

Cost of merchandise sold	$790,000
Deduct decrease in inventories	(8,000)
Add decrease in accounts payable	3,200
Cash payments for merchandise	$785,200

The $8,000 decrease in inventories (from Exhibit 3) indicates that the merchandise sold exceeded the cost of the merchandise purchased by $8,000. In other words, cost of merchandise sold includes $8,000 of goods sold from inventory that did not require a cash outflow during the year. Thus, $8,000 is deducted from the cost of merchandise sold in determining the *cash payments for merchandise*.

The $3,200 decrease in accounts payable (from Exhibit 3) indicates that cash payments for merchandise were $3,200 more than the purchases on account during 2012. Therefore, $3,200 is added to the cost of merchandise sold in determining the *cash payments for merchandise*.

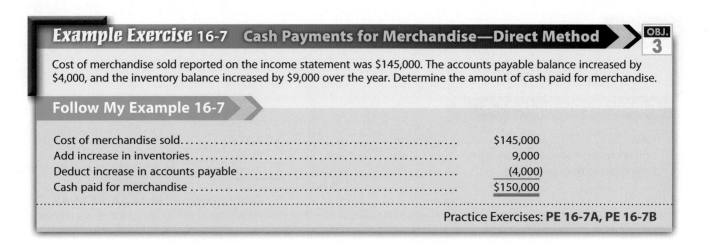

Example Exercise 16-7 Cash Payments for Merchandise—Direct Method OBJ. 3

Cost of merchandise sold reported on the income statement was $145,000. The accounts payable balance increased by $4,000, and the inventory balance increased by $9,000 over the year. Determine the amount of cash paid for merchandise.

Follow My Example 16-7

Cost of merchandise sold..	$145,000
Add increase in inventories...	9,000
Deduct increase in accounts payable	(4,000)
Cash paid for merchandise	$150,000

Practice Exercises: **PE 16-7A, PE 16-7B**

Cash Payments for Operating Expenses

The income statement (from Exhibit 3) for Rundell Inc. reports total operating expenses of $203,000, which includes depreciation expense of $7,000. Since depreciation expense does not require a cash outflow, it is omitted from *cash payments for operating expenses.*

To determine the *cash payments for operating expenses*, the other operating expenses (excluding depreciation) of $196,000 ($203,000 − $7,000) are adjusted for any increase or decrease in accrued expenses payable. Assuming that the accrued expenses payable are all operating expenses, this adjustment is summarized below.

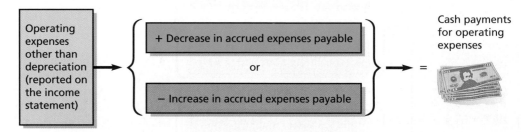

The cash payments for operating expenses are $193,800, computed as follows:

Operating expenses other than depreciation	$196,000
Deduct increase in accrued expenses payable	(2,200)
Cash payments for operating expenses	$193,800

The increase in accrued expenses payable (from Exhibit 3) indicates that the cash payments for operating expenses were $2,200 less than the amount reported for operating expenses during the year. Thus, $2,200 is deducted from the operating expenses in determining the *cash payments for operating expenses.*

Gain on Sale of Land

The income statement for Rundell Inc. (from Exhibit 3) reports a gain of $12,000 on the sale of land. The sale of land is an investing activity. Thus, the proceeds from the sale, which include the gain, are reported as part of the cash flows from investing activities.

Interest Expense

The income statement (from Exhibit 3) for Rundell Inc. reports interest expense of $8,000. To determine the *cash payments for interest*, the $8,000 is adjusted for any increases or decreases in interest payable. The adjustment is summarized as follows:

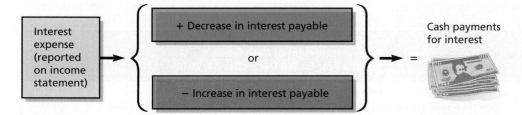

The comparative balance sheet of Rundell Inc. in Exhibit 3 indicates no interest payable. This is because the interest expense on the bonds payable is paid on June 1 and December 31. Since there is no interest payable, no adjustment of the interest expense of $8,000 is necessary.

Cash Payments for Income Taxes

The income statement (from Exhibit 3) for Rundell Inc. reports income tax expense of $83,000. To determine the *cash payments for income taxes*, the $83,000 is adjusted for any increases or decreases in income taxes payable. The adjustment is summarized below.

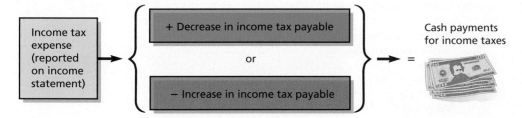

The cash payments for income taxes are $83,500, computed as follows:

Income tax expense	$83,000
Add decrease in income taxes payable	500
Cash payments for income taxes	$83,500

The $500 decrease in income taxes payable (from Exhibit 3) indicates that the cash payments for income taxes were $500 more than the amount reported for income tax expense during 2012. Thus, $500 is added to the income tax expense in determining the *cash payments for income taxes*.

Reporting Cash Flows from Operating Activities—Direct Method

The statement of cash flows for Rundell Inc. using the direct method for reporting cash flows from operating activities is shown in Exhibit 7. The portions of the statement that differ from those prepared under the indirect method are highlighted in color.

EXHIBIT 7

Statement of Cash Flows— Direct Method

Rundell Inc.
Statement of Cash Flows
For the Year Ended December 31, 2012

Cash flows from operating activities:			
Cash received from customers		$1,171,000	
Deduct: Cash payments for merchandise...............	$785,200		
Cash payments for operating expenses........	193,800		
Cash payments for interest	8,000		
Cash payments for income taxes	83,500	1,070,500	
Net cash flow from operating activities		$100,500	

(Continued)

EXHIBIT 7

Statement of Cash Flows— Direct Method (concluded)

Rundell Inc.
Statement of Cash Flows
For the Year Ended December 31, 2012

Cash flows from investing activities:			
Cash from sale of land		$ 72,000	
Less: Cash paid to purchase land	$ 15,000		
Cash paid for purchase of building	60,000	75,000	
Net cash flow used for investing activities			(3,000)
Cash flows from financing activities:			
Cash received from sale of common stock		$ 48,000	
Less: Cash paid to retire bonds payable	$ 50,000		
Cash paid for dividends	24,000	74,000	
Net cash flow used for financing activities			(26,000)
Increase in cash			$ 71,500
Cash at the beginning of the year			26,000
Cash at the end of the year			$ 97,500

Schedule Reconciling Net Income with Cash Flows from Operating Activities:

Cash flows from operating activities:	
Net income	$108,000
Adjustments to reconcile net income to net cash flow from operating activities:	
Depreciation	7,000
Gain on sale of land	(12,000)
Changes in current operating assets and liabilities:	
Increase in accounts receivable	(9,000)
Decrease in inventory	8,000
Decrease in accounts payable	(3,200)
Increase in accrued expenses payable	2,200
Decrease in income taxes payable	(500)
Net cash flow from operating activities	$100,500

Exhibit 7 also includes the separate schedule reconciling net income and net cash flow from operating activities. This schedule is included in the statement of cash flows when the direct method is used. This schedule is similar to the Cash Flows from Operating Activities section prepared under the indirect method.

International Connection

IFRS FOR STATEMENT OF CASH FLOWS

The statement of cash flows is required under International Financial Reporting Standards (IFRS). The statement of cash flows under IFRS is similar to that reported under U.S. GAAP in that the statement has separate sections for operating, investing, and financing activities. Like U.S. GAAP, IFRS also allow the use of either the indirect or direct method of reporting cash flows from operating activities. IFRS differ from U.S. GAAP in some minor areas, including:

- Interest paid can be reported as either an operating or a financing activity, while interest received can be reported as either an operating or an investing activity. In contrast, U.S. GAAP reports interest paid or received as an operating activity.
- Dividends paid can be reported as either an operating or a financing activity, while dividends received can be reported as either an operating or an investing activity. In contrast, U.S. GAAP reports dividends paid as a financing activity and dividends received as an operating activity.
- Cash flows to pay taxes are reported as a separate line in the operating activities, in contrast to U.S. GAAP, which does not require a separate line disclosure.

* IFRS are further discussed and illustrated on pages 716-716G and in Appendix D.

Financial Analysis and Interpretation: Free Cash Flow

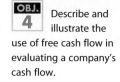

OBJ. 4

Describe and illustrate the use of free cash flow in evaluating a company's cash flow.

A valuable tool for evaluating the cash flows of a business is free cash flow. **Free cash flow** measures the operating cash flow available to a company to use after purchasing the property, plant, and equipment (PP&E) necessary to maintain current productive capacity.[6] It is computed as follows:

Cash flow from operating activities	$XXX
Less: Investments in PP&E needed to maintain current production	XXX
Free cash flow	$XXX

Analysts often use free cash flow, rather than cash flows from operating activities, to measure the financial strength of a business. Industries such as airlines, railroads, and telecommunications companies must invest heavily in new equipment to remain competitive. Such investments can significantly reduce free cash flow. For example, Verizon Communications Inc.'s free cash flow is less than 35% of the cash flow from operating activities. In contrast, The Coca-Cola Company's free cash flow is approximately 74% of the cash flow from operating activities.

To illustrate, the cash flow from operating activities for Research in Motion, Inc., maker of BlackBerry® smartphones, was $1,452 million in a recent fiscal year. The statement of cash flows indicated that the cash invested in property, plant, and equipment was $834 million. Assuming that the amount invested in property, plant, and equipment is necessary to maintain productive capacity, free cash flow would be computed as follows (in millions):

Cash flow from operating activities	$1,452
Less: Investments in PP&E needed to maintain current production	834
Free cash flow	$ 618

Research in Motion's free cash flow was 43% of cash flow from operations and over 5% of sales. Compare this to the calculation of free cash flows for Apple, Inc. (a computer company), The Coca-Cola Company (a beverage company), and Verizon Communications, Inc. (a telecommunications company) shown below (in millions):

	Apple, Inc.	The Coca-Cola Company	Verizon Communications, Inc.
Sales	$36,537	$31,944	$97,354
Cash flow from operating activities	$10,159	$ 7,571	$26,620
Less: Investments in PP&E needed to maintain current production	1,144	1,968	17,238
Free cash flow	$ 9,015	$ 5,603	$ 9,382
Free cash flow as a percentage of cash flow from operations	89%	74%	35%
Free cash flow as a percentage of sales	25%	18%	10%

Positive free cash flow is considered favorable. A company that has free cash flow is able to fund internal growth, retire debt, pay dividends, and benefit from financial flexibility. A company with no free cash flow is unable to maintain current productive capacity. Lack of free cash flow can be an early indicator of liquidity problems. As one analyst notes, "Free cash flow gives the company firepower to reduce debt and ultimately generate consistent, actual income."[7]

---

6 Productive capacity is the number of goods the company is currently producing and selling.

7 Jill Krutick, *Fortune*, March 30, 1998, p. 106.

Example Exercise 16-8 Free Cash Flow

OBJ. 4

Omnicron Inc. reported the following on the company's cash flow statement in 2012 and 2011:

	2012	2011
Net cash flow from operating activities	$140,000	$120,000
Net cash flow used for investing activities	(120,000)	(80,000)
Net cash flow used for financing activities	(20,000)	(32,000)

Seventy-five percent of the cash flow used for investing activities was used to replace existing capacity.

a. Determine Omnicron's free cash flow.

b. Has Omnicron's free cash flow improved or declined from 2011 to 2012?

Follow My Example 16-8

a.

	2012	2011
Cash flow from operating activities	$140,000	$120,000
Less: Investments in fixed assets to maintain current production	90,000[1]	60,000[2]
Free cash flow	$ 50,000	$ 60,000

[1] $120,000 × 75%
[2] $80,000 × 75%

b. The change from $60,000 to $50,000 indicates an unfavorable trend.

Practice Exercises: **PE 16-8A, PE 16-8B**

A P P E N D I X

Spreadsheet (Work Sheet) for Statement of Cash Flows—The Indirect Method

A spreadsheet (work sheet) may used in preparing the statement of cash flows. However, whether or not a spreadsheet (work sheet) is used, the concepts presented in this chapter are not affected.

The data for Rundell Inc., presented in Exhibit 3 on pages 722–723, are used as a basis for illustrating the spreadsheet (work sheet) for the indirect method. The steps in preparing this spreadsheet (work sheet), shown in Exhibit 8, are as follows:

Step 1. List the title of each balance sheet account in the Accounts column.

Step 2. For each balance sheet account, enter its balance as of December 31, 2011, in the first column and its balance as of December 31, 2012, in the last column. Place the credit balances in parentheses.

Step 3. Add the December 31, 2011 and 2012 column totals, which should total to zero.

Step 4. Analyze the change during the year in each noncash account to determine its net increase (decrease) and classify the change as affecting cash flows from operating activities, investing activities, financing activities, or noncash investing and financing activities.

EXHIBIT 8   **End-of-Period Spreadsheet (Work Sheet) for Statement of Cash Flows—Indirect Method**

Step 2

	A	B	C	D	E	F	G
1			Rundell Inc.				
2		End-of-Period Spreadsheet (Work Sheet) for Statement of Cash Flows					
3		For the Year Ended December 31, 2012					
4	Accounts	Balance,	Transactions				Balance,
5		Dec. 31, 2011	Debit			Credit	Dec. 31, 2012
6	Cash	26,000	(o)	71,500			97,500
7	Accounts receivable (net)	65,000	(n)	9,000			74,000
8	Inventories	180,000			(m)	8,000	172,000
9	Land	125,000	(k)	15,000	(l)	60,000	80,000
10	Building	200,000	(j)	60,000			260,000
11	Accumulated depreciation—building	(58,300)			(i)	7,000	(65,300)
12	Accounts payable (merchandise creditors)	(46,700)	(h)	3,200			(43,500)
13	Accrued expenses payable (operating expenses)	(24,300)			(g)	2,200	(26,500)
14	Income taxes payable	(8,400)	(f)	500			(7,900)
15	Dividends payable	(10,000)			(e)	4,000	(14,000)
16	Bonds payable	(150,000)	(d)	50,000			(100,000)
17	Common stock	(16,000)			(c)	8,000	(24,000)
18	Paid-in capital in excess of par	(80,000)			(c)	40,000	(120,000)
19	Retained earnings	(202,300)	(b)	28,000	(a)	108,000	(282,300)
20	Totals	0		237,200		237,200	0
21	Operating activities:						
22	Net income		(a)	108,000			
23	Depreciation of building		(i)	7,000			
24	Gain on sale of land				(l)	12,000	
25	Increase in accounts receivable				(n)	9,000	
26	Decrease in inventories		(m)	8,000			
27	Decrease in accounts payable				(h)	3,200	
28	Increase in accrued expenses payable		(g)	2,200			
29	Decrease in income taxes payable				(f)	500	
30	Investing activities:						
31	Sale of land		(l)	72,000			
32	Purchase of land				(k)	15,000	
33	Purchase of building				(j)	60,000	
34	Financing activities:						
35	Issued common stock		(c)	48,000			
36	Retired bonds payable				(d)	50,000	
37	Declared cash dividends				(b)	28,000	
38	Increase in dividends payable		(e)	4,000			
39	Net increase in cash				(o)	71,500	
40	Totals			249,200		249,200	

Step 1 (rows 6–20); Step 3 → Totals row 20

Steps 4–7

Step 5. Indicate the effect of the change on cash flows by making entries in the Transactions columns.

Step 6. After all noncash accounts have been analyzed, enter the net increase (decrease) in cash during the period.

Step 7. Add the Debit and Credit Transactions columns. The totals should be equal.

Analyzing Accounts

In analyzing the noncash accounts (Step 4), try to determine the type of cash flow activity (operating, investing, or financing) that led to the change in account. As each noncash account is analyzed, an entry (Step 5) is made on the spreadsheet (work sheet) for the type of cash flow activity that caused the change. After all noncash accounts have been analyzed, an entry (Step 6) is made for the increase (decrease) in cash during the period.

The entries made on the spreadsheet are not posted to the ledger. They are only used in preparing and summarizing the data on the spreadsheet.

The order in which the accounts are analyzed is not important. However, it is more efficient to begin with Retained Earnings and proceed upward in the account listing.

Retained Earnings

The spreadsheet (work sheet) shows a Retained Earnings balance of $202,300 at December 31, 2011, and $282,300 at December 31, 2012. Thus, Retained Earnings increased $80,000 during the year. This increase is from the following:

1. Net income of $108,000
2. Declaring cash dividends of $28,000

To identify the cash flows from these activities, two entries are made on the spreadsheet.

The $108,000 is reported on the statement of cash flows as part of "cash flows from operating activities." Thus, an entry is made in the Transactions columns on the spreadsheet as follows:

(a)	Operating Activities—Net Income..............................	108,000	
	Retained Earnings...		108,000

The preceding entry accounts for the net income portion of the change to Retained Earnings. It also identifies the cash flow in the bottom portion of the spreadsheet as related to operating activities.

The $28,000 of dividends is reported as a financing activity on the statement of cash flows. Thus, an entry is made in the Transactions columns on the spreadsheet as follows:

(b)	Retained Earnings...	28,000	
	Financing Activities—Declared Cash Dividends		28,000

The preceding entry accounts for the dividends portion of the change to Retained Earnings. It also identifies the cash flow in the bottom portion of the spreadsheet as related to financing activities. The $28,000 of declared dividends will be adjusted later for the actual amount of cash dividends paid during the year.

Other Accounts

The entries for the other noncash accounts are made in the spreadsheet in a manner similar to entries (a) and (b). A summary of these entries is as follows:

(c)	Financing Activities—Issued Common Stock........................	48,000	
	Common Stock		8,000
	Paid-In Capital in Excess of Par—Common Stock		40,000
(d)	Bonds Payable	50,000	
	Financing Activities—Retired Bonds Payable....................		50,000
(e)	Financing Activities—Increase in Dividends Payable...............	4,000	
	Dividends Payable		4,000
(f)	Income Taxes Payable	500	
	Operating Activities—Decrease in Income Taxes Payable		500
(g)	Operating Activities—Increase in Accrued Expenses Payable	2,200	
	Accrued Expenses Payable		2,200

(h)	Accounts Payable	3,200	
	Operating Activities—Decrease in Accounts Payable		3,200
(i)	Operating Activities—Depreciation of Building	7,000	
	Accumulated Depreciation—Building		7,000
(j)	Building	60,000	
	Investing Activities—Purchase of Building		60,000
(k)	Land..	15,000	
	Investing Activities—Purchase of Land........................		15,000
(l)	Investing Activities—Sale of Land..............................	72,000	
	Operating Activities—Gain on Sale of Land		12,000
	Land..		60,000
(m)	Operating Activities—Decrease in Inventories...................	8,000	
	Inventories..		8,000
(n)	Accounts Receivable	9,000	
	Operating Activities—Increase in Accounts Receivable		9,000
(o)	Cash..	71,500	
	Net Increase in Cash..		71,500

After all the balance sheet accounts are analyzed and the entries made on the spreadsheet (work sheet), all the operating, investing, and financing activities are identified in the bottom portion of the spreadsheet. The accuracy of the entries is verified by totaling the Debit and Credit Transactions columns. The totals of the columns should be equal.

Preparing the Statement of Cash Flows

The statement of cash flows prepared from the spreadsheet is identical to the statement in Exhibit 6 on page 731. The data for the three sections of the statement are obtained from the bottom portion of the spreadsheet.

At a Glance 16

OBJ. 1 Describe the cash flow activities reported in the statement of cash flows.

Key Points   The statement of cash flows reports cash receipts and cash payments by three types of activities: operating activities, investing activities, and financing activities. Cash flows from operating activities are the cash inflow or outflow from a company's day-to-day operations. Cash flows from investing activities show the cash inflows and outflows related to changes in a company's long-term assets. Cash flows from financing activities show the cash inflows and outflows related to changes in a company's long-term liabilities and stockholders' equity. Investing and financing for a business may be affected by transactions that do not involve cash. The effect of such transactions should be reported in a separate schedule accompanying the statement of cash flows.

Learning Outcomes	Example Exercises	Practice Exercises
• Classify transactions that either provide or use cash into either operating, investing, or financing activities.	EE16-1	PE16-1A, 16-1B

OBJ. 2

Prepare a statement of cash flows, using the indirect method.

Key Points The indirect method reports cash flow from operating activities by adjusting net income for revenues and expenses that do not involve the receipt or payment of cash. Noncash expenses such as depreciation are added back to net income. Gains and losses on the disposal of assets are added to or deducted from net income. Changes in current operating assets and liabilities are added to or subtracted from net income depending on their effect on cash. Cash flow from investing activities and cash flow from financing activities are reported below cash flow from operating activities in the statement of cash flows.

Learning Outcomes	Example Exercises	Practice Exercises
• Determine cash flow from operating activities under the indirect method by adjusting net income for noncash expenses and gains and losses from asset disposals.	EE16-2	PE16-2A, 16-2B
• Determine cash flow from operating activities under the indirect method by adjusting net income for changes in current operating assets and liabilities.	EE16-3	PE16-3A, 16-3B
• Prepare the Cash Flows from Operating Activities section of the statement of cash flows using the indirect method.	EE16-4	PE16-4A, 16-4B
• Prepare the Cash Flows from Investing Activities and Cash Flows from Financing Activities sections of the statement of cash flows.	EE16-5	PE16-5A, 16-5B

OBJ. 3

Prepare a statement of cash flows, using the direct method.

Key Points The amount of cash flows from operating activities is the same under both the direct and indirect methods, but the manner in which cash flow from operating activities is reported is different. The direct method reports cash flows from operating activities by major classes of operating cash receipts and cash payments. The difference between the major classes of total operating cash receipts and total operating cash payments is the net cash flow from operating activities. The Cash Flows from Investing and Financing Activities sections of the statement are the same under both the direct and indirect methods.

Learning Outcomes	Example Exercises	Practice Exercises
• Prepare the cash flows from operating activities and the remainder of the statement of cash flows under the direct method.	EE16-6 EE16-7	PE16-6A, 16-6B PE16-7A, 16-7B

OBJ. 4

Describe and illustrate the use of free cash flow in evaluating a company's cash flow.

Key Points Free cash flow measures the operating cash flow available for company use after purchasing the fixed assets that are necessary to maintain current productive capacity. It is calculated by subtracting these fixed asset purchases from cash flow from operating activities. A company with strong free cash flow is able to fund internal growth, retire debt, pay dividends, and enjoy financial flexibility. A company with weak free cash flow has much less financial flexibility for such activities.

Learning Outcomes	Example Exercises	Practice Exercises
• Describe free cash flow.		
• Calculate and evaluate free cash flow.	EE16-8	PE16-8A, 16-8B

Key Terms

cash flow per share (721)

cash flows from financing activities (719)

cash flows from investing activities (718)

cash flows from operating activities (718)

direct method (719)

free cash flow (737)

indirect method (720)

statement of cash flows (718)

Illustrative Problem

The comparative balance sheet of Dowling Company for December 31, 2012 and 2011, is as follows:

Dowling Company
Comparative Balance Sheet
December 31, 2012 and 2011

	2012	2011
Assets		
Cash	$ 140,350	$ 95,900
Accounts receivable (net)	95,300	102,300
Inventories	165,200	157,900
Prepaid expenses	6,240	5,860
Investments (long-term)	35,700	84,700
Land	75,000	90,000
Buildings	375,000	260,000
Accumulated depreciation—buildings	(71,300)	(58,300)
Machinery and equipment	428,300	428,300
Accumulated depreciation—machinery and equipment	(148,500)	(138,000)
Patents	58,000	65,000
Total assets	$1,159,290	$1,093,660
Liabilities and Stockholders' Equity		
Accounts payable (merchandise creditors)	$ 43,500	$ 46,700
Accrued expenses payable (operating expenses)	14,000	12,500
Income taxes payable	7,900	8,400
Dividends payable	14,000	10,000
Mortgage note payable, due 2023	40,000	0
Bonds payable	150,000	250,000
Common stock, $30 par	450,000	375,000
Excess of issue price over par—common stock	66,250	41,250
Retained earnings	373,640	349,810
Total liabilities and stockholders' equity	$1,159,290	$1,093,660

The income statement for Dowling Company is shown here.

Dowling Company
Income Statement
For the Year Ended December 31, 2012

Sales		$1,100,000
Cost of merchandise sold		710,000
Gross profit		$ 390,000
Operating expenses:		
Depreciation expense	$ 23,500	
Patent amortization	7,000	
Other operating expenses	196,000	
Total operating expenses		226,500
Income from operations		$ 163,500
Other income:		
Gain on sale of investments	$ 11,000	
Other expense:		
Interest expense	26,000	(15,000)
Income before income tax		$ 148,500
Income tax expense		50,000
Net income		$ 98,500

An examination of the accounting records revealed the following additional information applicable to 2012:

a. Land costing $15,000 was sold for $15,000.

b. A mortgage note was issued for $40,000.

c. A building costing $115,000 was constructed.

d. 2,500 shares of common stock were issued at $40 in exchange for the bonds payable.

e. Cash dividends declared were $74,670.

Instructions

1. Prepare a statement of cash flows, using the indirect method of reporting cash flows from operating activities.

2. Prepare a statement of cash flows, using the direct method of reporting cash flows from operating activities.

Solution

1.

Dowling Company **Statement of Cash Flows—Indirect Method** **For the Year Ended December 31, 2012**		
Cash flows from operating activities:		
Net income...		$ 98,500
Adjustments to reconcile net income to net		
cash flow from operating activities:		
Depreciation...................................		23,500
Amortization of patents........................		7,000
Gain on sale of investments		(11,000)
Changes in current operating assets and		
liabilities:		
Decrease in accounts receivable		7,000
Increase in inventories		(7,300)
Increase in prepaid expenses		(380)
Decrease in accounts payable............		(3,200)
Increase in accrued expenses payable		1,500
Decrease in income taxes payable........		(500)
Net cash flow from operating activities		$115,120
Cash flows from investing activities:		
Cash received from sale of:		
Investments...................................	$60,000[1]	
Land...	15,000	$ 75,000
Less: Cash paid for construction of building		115,000
Net cash flow used for investing activities.............		(40,000)
Cash flows from financing activities:		
Cash received from issuing mortgage note payable.....		$ 40,000
Less: Cash paid for dividends.........................		70,670[2]
Net cash flow used for financing activities		(30,670)
Increase in cash		$ 44,450
Cash at the beginning of the year........................		95,900
Cash at the end of the year..............................		$140,350
Schedule of Noncash Investing and Financing Activities:		
Issued common stock to retire bonds payable..........		$100,000

[1] $60,000 = $11,000 gain + $49,000 (decrease in investments)

[2] $70,670 = $74,670 − $4,000 (increase in dividends)

2.

Dowling Company Statement of Cash Flows—Direct Method For the Year Ended December 31, 2012			
Cash flows from operating activities:			
Cash received from customers[1].......................		$1,107,000	
Deduct: Cash paid for merchandise[2]...................	$720,500		
Cash paid for operating expenses[3].............	194,880		
Cash paid for interest expense	26,000		
Cash paid for income tax[4]....................	50,500	991,880	
Net cash flow from operating activities			$115,120
Cash flows from investing activities:			
Cash received from sale of:			
Investments......................................	$ 60,000[5]		
Land...	15,000	$ 75,000	
Less: Cash paid for construction of building		115,000	
Net cash flow used for investing activities..............			(40,000)
Cash flows from financing activities:			
Cash received from issuing mortgage note payable......		$ 40,000	
Less: Cash paid for dividends[6].........................		70,670	
Net cash flow used for financing activities			(30,670)
Increase in cash			$ 44,450
Cash at the beginning of the year.........................			95,900
Cash at the end of the year................................			$140,350
Schedule of Noncash Investing and			
Financing Activities:			
Issued common stock to retire bonds payable..........			$100,000
Schedule Reconciling Net Income with Cash Flows			
from Operating Activities[7]			

Computations:

[1]$1,100,000 + $7,000 = $1,107,000

[2]$710,000 + $3,200 + $7,300 = $720,500

[3]$196,000 + $380 − $1,500 = $194,880

[4]$50,000 + $500 = $50,500

[5]$60,000 = $11,000 gain + $49,000 (decrease in investments)

[6]$74,670 + $10,000 − $14,000 = $70,670

[7]The content of this schedule is the same as the Operating Activities section of part (1) of this solution and is not reproduced here for the sake of brevity.

Discussion Questions

1. What is the principal disadvantage of the direct method of reporting cash flows from operating activities?

2. What are the major advantages of the indirect method of reporting cash flows from operating activities?

3. A corporation issued $1,000,000 of common stock in exchange for $1,000,000 of fixed assets. Where would this transaction be reported on the statement of cash flows?

4. A retail business, using the accrual method of accounting, owed merchandise creditors (accounts payable) $240,000 at the beginning of the year and $265,000 at the end of the year. How would the $25,000 increase be used to adjust net income in determining the amount of cash flows from operating activities by the indirect method? Explain.

5. If salaries payable was $75,000 at the beginning of the year and $40,000 at the end of the year, should $35,000 be added to or deducted from income to determine the amount of cash flows from operating activities by the indirect method? Explain.

6. A long-term investment in bonds with a cost of $800,000 was sold for $910,000 cash. (a) What was

the gain or loss on the sale? (b) What was the effect of the transaction on cash flows? (c) How should the transaction be reported in the statement of cash flows if cash flows from operating activities are reported by the indirect method?

7. A corporation issued $10,000,000 of 20-year bonds for cash at 102. How would the transaction be reported on the statement of cash flows?

8. Fully depreciated equipment costing $25,000 was discarded. What was the effect of the transaction on cash flows if (a) $10,000 cash is received, (b) no cash is received?

9. For the current year, Bearings Company decided to switch from the indirect method to the direct method for reporting cash flows from operating activities on the statement of cash flows. Will the change cause the amount of net cash flow from operating activities to be (a) larger, (b) smaller, or (c) the same as if the indirect method had been used? Explain.

10. Name five common major classes of operating cash receipts or operating cash payments presented on the statement of cash flows when the cash flows from operating activities are reported by the direct method.

Practice Exercises

Example
Exercises

PE 16-1A   Classifying cash flows

Identify whether each of the following would be reported as an operating, investing, or financing activity in the statement of cash flows.

a. Retirement of bonds payable

b. Payment of accounts payable

c. Issuance of common stock

d. Payment for administrative expenses

e. Cash received from customers

f. Purchase of land

PE 16-1B   Classifying cash flows

Identify whether each of the following would be reported as an operating, investing, or financing activity in the statement of cash flows.

a. Issuance of bonds payable

b. Cash sales

c. Collection of accounts receivable

d. Payment for selling expenses

e. Disposal of equipment

f. Purchase of investments

PE 16-2A   Adjustments to net income—indirect method

Martin Corporation's accumulated depreciation—furniture increased by $10,500, while $3,850 of patents were amortized between balance sheet dates. There were no purchases or sales of depreciable or intangible assets during the year. In addition, the income statement showed a loss of $5,600 from the sale of land. Reconcile a net income of $150,500 to net cash flow from operating activities.

PE 16-2B   Adjustments to net income—indirect method

Chu Corporation's accumulated depreciation—equipment increased by $5,600, while $2,080 of patents were amortized between balance sheet dates. There were no purchases or sales of depreciable or intangible assets during the year. In addition, the income statement showed a gain of $12,000 from the sale of investments. Reconcile a net income of $112,000 to net cash flow from operating activities.

PE 16-3A   Changes in current operating assets and liabilities—indirect method

Phelps Corporation's comparative balance sheet for current assets and liabilities was as follows:

	Dec. 31, 2013	Dec. 31, 2012
Accounts receivable	$22,500	$27,000
Inventory	15,000	12,900
Accounts payable	13,500	11,850
Dividends payable	41,250	44,250

Adjust net income of $138,000 for changes in operating assets and liabilities to arrive at net cash flow from operating activities.

OBJ. 2   EE 16-3 *p. 727*   **PE 16-3B   Changes in current operating assets and liabilities—indirect method**

Dali Corporation's comparative balance sheet for current assets and liabilities was as follows:

	Dec. 31, 2013	Dec. 31, 2012
Accounts receivable	$25,500	$20,400
Inventory	49,300	42,075
Accounts payable	39,100	29,325
Dividends payable	11,900	15,300

Adjust net income of $240,000 for changes in operating assets and liabilities to arrive at net cash flow from operating activities.

OBJ. 2   EE 16-4 *p. 728*   **PE 16-4A   Cash flows from operating activities—indirect method**

Salem Inc. reported the following data:

Net income	$168,750
Depreciation expense	18,750
Gain on disposal of equipment	15,375
Decrease in accounts receivable	10,500
Decrease in accounts payable	2,700

Prepare the Cash Flows from Operating Activities section of the statement of cash flows using the indirect method.

OBJ. 2   EE 16-4 *p. 728*   **PE 16-4B   Cash flows from operating activities—indirect method**

Malibu Inc. reported the following data:

Net income	$393,750
Depreciation expense	67,500
Loss on disposal of equipment	27,450
Increase in accounts receivable	24,300
Increase in accounts payable	12,600

Prepare the Cash Flows from Operating Activities section of the statement of cash flows using the indirect method.

OBJ. 2   EE 16-5 *p. 731*   **PE 16-5A   Land transactions on the statement of cash flows**

Seeing Double Corporation purchased land for $510,000. Later in the year, the company sold land with a book value of $217,500 for $165,000. How are the effects of these transactions reported on the statement of cash flows?

OBJ. 2   EE 16-5 *p. 731*   **PE 16-5B   Land transactions on the statement of cash flows**

Pilot Corporation purchased land for $480,000. Later in the year, the company sold land with a book value of $288,000 for $328,000. How are the effects of these transactions reported on the statement of cash flows?

OBJ. 3   EE 16-6 *p. 733*   **PE 16-6A   Cash received from customers—direct method**

Sales reported on the income statement were $450,000. The accounts receivable balance increased $47,000 over the year. Determine the amount of cash received from customers.

OBJ. 3   EE 16-6 *p. 733*   **PE 16-6B   Cash received from customers—direct method**

Sales reported on the income statement were $85,600. The accounts receivable balance decreased $7,400 over the year. Determine the amount of cash received from customers.

Learning Objectives	Example Exercises	

OBJ. 3 EE 16-7 p. 734

PE 16-7A Cash payments for merchandise—direct method

Cost of merchandise sold reported on the income statement was $360,000. The accounts payable balance decreased $17,800, and the inventory balance decreased by $28,000 over the year. Determine the amount of cash paid for merchandise.

OBJ. 3 EE 16-7 p. 734

PE 16-7B Cash payments for merchandise—direct method

Cost of merchandise sold reported on the income statement was $210,000. The accounts payable balance increased $8,600, and the inventory balance increased by $16,900 over the year. Determine the amount of cash paid for merchandise.

OBJ. 4 EE 16-8 p. 738

PE 16-8A Free cash flow

Totson Inc. reported the following on the company's statement of cash flows in 2012 and 2011:

	2012	2011
Net cash flow from operating activities	$ 210,000	$ 200,000
Net cash flow used for investing activities	(160,000)	(180,000)
Net cash flow used for financing activities	(45,000)	(30,000)

Eighty percent of the cash flow used for investing activities was used to replace existing capacity.

a. Determine Totson's free cash flow.

b. Has Totson's free cash flow improved or declined from 2011 to 2012?

OBJ. 4 EE 16-8 p. 738

PE 16-8B Free cash flow

Burkenfelt Inc. reported the following on the company's statement of cash flows in 2012 and 2011:

	2012	2011
Net cash flow from operating activities	$ 340,000	$ 325,000
Net cash flow used for investing activities	(305,000)	(270,000)
Net cash flow used for financing activities	(30,000)	(42,000)

Seventy percent of the cash flow used for investing activities was used to replace existing capacity.

a. Determine Burkenfelt's free cash flow.

b. Has Burkenfelt's free cash flow improved or declined from 2011 to 2012?

Exercises

OBJ. 1

EX 16-1 Cash flows from operating activities—net loss

On its income statement for a recent year, Continental Airlines, Inc. reported a net *loss* of $68 million from operations. On its statement of cash flows, it reported $457 million of cash flows from operating activities.

➤ Explain this apparent contradiction between the loss and the positive cash flows.

OBJ. 1

✔ c. Cash payment, $560,000

EX 16-2 Effect of transactions on cash flows

State the effect (cash receipt or payment and amount) of each of the following transactions, considered individually, on cash flows:

a. Sold equipment with a book value of $65,000 for $83,000.

b. Sold a new issue of $400,000 of bonds at 98.

c. Retired $550,000 of bonds, on which there was $5,000 of unamortized discount, for $560,000.

d. Purchased 2,000 shares of $25 par common stock as treasury stock at $50 per share.

e. Sold 5,000 shares of $20 par common stock for $100 per share.

f. Paid dividends of $1.00 per share. There were 50,000 shares issued and 6,000 shares of treasury stock.

g. Purchased land for $320,000 cash.

h. Purchased a building by paying $40,000 cash and issuing a $60,000 mortgage note payable.

OBJ. 1

EX 16-3   Classifying cash flows

Identify the type of cash flow activity for each of the following events (operating, investing, or financing):

a. Sold equipment.

b. Issued bonds.

c. Issued common stock.

d. Paid cash dividends.

e. Purchased treasury stock.

f. Redeemed bonds.

g. Purchased patents.

h. Purchased buildings.

i. Sold long-term investments.

j. Issued preferred stock.

k. Net income.

OBJ. 2

EX 16-4   Cash flows from operating activities—indirect method

Indicate whether each of the following would be added to or deducted from net income in determining net cash flow from operating activities by the indirect method:

a. Decrease in accounts payable

b. Increase in notes receivable due in 90 days from customers

c. Decrease in accounts receivable

d. Loss on disposal of fixed assets

e. Increase in notes payable due in 90 days to vendors

f. Amortization of patent

g. Depreciation of fixed assets

h. Gain on retirement of long-term debt

i. Decrease in salaries payable

j. Increase in merchandise inventory

k. Decrease in prepaid expenses

OBJ. 2

✔ Net cash flow from operating activities, $752,880

EX 16-5   Cash flows from operating activities—indirect method

The net income reported on the income statement for the current year was $720,000. Depreciation recorded on store equipment for the year amounted to $32,700. Balances of the current asset and current liability accounts at the beginning and end of the year are as follows:

	End of Year	Beginning of Year
Cash	$78,450	$72,300
Accounts receivable (net)	56,250	53,400
Merchandise inventory	76,800	81,330
Prepaid expenses	9,000	6,900
Accounts payable (merchandise creditors)	73,500	68,400
Wages payable	40,200	44,700

a. Prepare the Cash Flows from Operating Activities section of the statement of cash flows, using the indirect method.

b. ➤ Briefly explain why cash flows from operating activities is different than net income.

OBJ. 1, 2

✔ Net cash flow from operating activities, $466,110

EX 16-6   Cash flows from operating activities—indirect method

The net income reported on the income statement for the current year was $378,000. Depreciation recorded on equipment and a building amounted to $112,500 for the year. Balances of the current asset and current liability accounts at the beginning and end of the year are as follows:

	End of Year	Beginning of Year
Cash	$100,800	$107,100
Accounts receivable (net)	127,800	132,120
Inventories	252,000	227,700
Prepaid expenses	14,040	15,120
Accounts payable (merchandise creditors)	112,680	119,520
Salaries payable	16,200	14,850

a. Prepare the Cash Flows from Operating Activities section of the statement of cash flows, using the indirect method.

b. ━━━━▶ If the direct method had been used, would the net cash flow from operating activities have been the same? Explain.

OBJ. 1, 2

✔ Net cash flow from operating activities, $197,220

EX 16-7 Cash flows from operating activities—indirect method

The income statement disclosed the following items for 2013:

Depreciation expense	$ 21,600
Gain on disposal of equipment	12,600
Net income	190,500

Balances of the current assets and current liability accounts changed between December 31, 2012, and December 31, 2013, as follows:

Accounts receivable	$3,360
Inventory	1,920*
Prepaid insurance	720*
Accounts payable	2,280*
Income taxes payable	720
Dividends payable	510

*Decrease

a. Prepare the Cash Flows from Operating Activities section of the statement of cash flows, using the indirect method.

b. Briefly explain why cash flows from operating activities is different than net income.

OBJ. 2

EX 16-8 Determining cash payments to stockholders

The board of directors declared cash dividends totaling $260,000 during the current year. The comparative balance sheet indicates dividends payable of $74,500 at the beginning of the year and $65,000 at the end of the year. What was the amount of cash payments to stockholders during the year?

OBJ. 2

EX 16-9 Reporting changes in equipment on statement of cash flows

An analysis of the general ledger accounts indicates that office equipment, which cost $89,000 and on which accumulated depreciation totaled $36,000 on the date of sale, was sold for $43,500 during the year. Using this information, indicate the items to be reported on the statement of cash flows.

OBJ. 2

EX 16-10 Reporting changes in equipment on statement of cash flows

An analysis of the general ledger accounts indicates that delivery equipment, which cost $246,000 and on which accumulated depreciation totaled $124,500 on the date of sale, was sold for $110,500 during the year. Using this information, indicate the items to be reported on the statement of cash flows.

OBJ. 2

EX 16-11 Reporting land transactions on statement of cash flows

On the basis of the details of the following fixed asset account, indicate the items to be reported on the statement of cash flows:

ACCOUNT *Land*   ACCOUNT NO.

Date		Item	Debit	Credit	Balance Debit	Balance Credit
2012						
Jan.	1	Balance			620,000	
Apr.	6	Purchased for cash	74,500		694,500	
Nov.	23	Sold for $68,250		45,600	648,900	

OBJ. 2

EX 16-12 Reporting stockholders' equity items on statement of cash flows

On the basis of the following stockholders' equity accounts, indicate the items, exclusive of net income, to be reported on the statement of cash flows. There were no unpaid dividends at either the beginning or the end of the year.

ACCOUNT *Common Stock, $30 par*   ACCOUNT NO.

Date		Item	Debit	Credit	Balance Debit	Balance Credit
2012						
Jan.	1	Balance, 90,000 shares				2,700,000
Mar.	7	22,500 shares issued for cash		675,000		3,375,000
June	30	3,300-share stock dividend		99,000		3,474,000

ACCOUNT *Paid-In Capital in Excess of Par—Common Stock*   ACCOUNT NO.

Date		Item	Debit	Credit	Balance Debit	Balance Credit
2012						
Jan.	1	Balance				300,000
Mar.	7	22,500 shares issued for cash		1,080,000		1,380,000
June	30	Stock dividend		178,200		1,558,200

ACCOUNT *Retained Earnings*   ACCOUNT NO.

Date		Item	Debit	Credit	Balance Debit	Balance Credit
2012						
Jan.	1	Balance				1,500,000
June	30	Stock dividend	277,200			1,222,800
Dec.	30	Cash dividend	260,550			962,250
	31	Net income		1,080,000		2,042,250

OBJ. 2

EX 16-13 Reporting land acquisition for cash and mortgage note on statement of cash flows

On the basis of the details of the following fixed asset account, indicate the items to be reported on the statement of cash flows:

ACCOUNT *Land*   ACCOUNT NO.

Date		Item	Debit	Credit	Balance Debit	Balance Credit
2012						
Jan.	1	Balance			195,000	
Feb.	10	Purchased for cash	307,500		502,500	
Nov.	20	Purchased with long-term mortgage note	405,000		907,500	

EX 16-14 **Reporting issuance and retirement of long-term debt**

On the basis of the details of the following bonds payable and related discount accounts, indicate the items to be reported in the Financing section of the statement of cash flows, assuming no gain or loss on retiring the bonds:

ACCOUNT *Bonds Payable*   **ACCOUNT NO.**

Date		Item	Debit	Credit	Balance Debit	Balance Credit
2012						
Jan.	1	Balance				800,000
	2	Retire bonds	160,000			640,000
June	30	Issue bonds		480,000		1,120,000

ACCOUNT *Discount on Bond Payable*   **ACCOUNT NO.**

Date		Item	Debit	Credit	Balance Debit	Balance Credit
2012						
Jan.	1	Balance			36,000	
	2	Retire bonds		12,800	23,200	
June	30	Issue bonds	32,000		55,200	
Dec.	31	Amortize discount		2,800	52,400	

EX 16-15 **Determining net income from net cash flow from operating activities**

Shinlund, Inc., reported a net cash flow from operating activities of $243,750 on its statement of cash flows for the year ended December 31, 2012. The following information was reported in the Cash Flows from Operating Activities section of the statement of cash flows, using the indirect method:

Decrease in income taxes payable	$ 5,250
Decrease in inventories	13,050
Depreciation	20,100
Gain on sale of investments	9,000
Increase in accounts payable	3,600
Increase in prepaid expenses	2,025
Increase in accounts receivable	9,750

a. Determine the net income reported by Shinlund, Inc., for the year ended December 31, 2012.

b. Briefly explain why Shinlund's net income is different than cash flows from operating activities.

EX 16-16 **Cash flows from operating activities—indirect method**

Selected data derived from the income statement and balance sheet of Jones Soda Co. for a recent year are as follows:

Income statement data (in thousands):	
Net earnings	$(10,547)
Losses on inventory write-down and fixed assets	2,248
Depreciation expense	811
Stock based compensation expense (noncash)	727
Balance sheet data (in thousands):	
Decrease in accounts receivable	364
Decrease in inventory	210
Decrease in prepaid expenses	206
Decrease in accounts payable	(165)
Decrease in accrued liabilities	(1,117)

a. Prepare the Cash Flows from Operating Activities section of the statement of cash flows using the indirect method for Jones Soda Co. for the year.

b. ➡ Interpret your results in part (a).

OBJ. 2

✔ Net cash flow from operating activities, $90

EX 16-17   Statement of cash flows—indirect method

The comparative balance sheet of Hobson Medical Equipment Inc. for December 31, 2013 and 2012, is as follows:

	Dec. 31, 2013	Dec. 31, 2012
Assets		
Cash	$294	$ 96
Accounts receivable (net)	168	120
Inventories	105	66
Land	240	270
Equipment	135	105
Accumulated depreciation—equipment	(36)	(18)
Total	$906	$639
Liabilities and Stockholders' Equity		
Accounts payable (merchandise creditors)	$105	$ 96
Dividends payable	18	—
Common stock, $10 par	60	30
Paid-in capital in excess of par—common stock	150	75
Retained earnings	573	438
Total	$906	$639

The following additional information is taken from the records:

 a. Land was sold for $75.

 b. Equipment was acquired for cash.

 c. There were no disposals of equipment during the year.

 d. The common stock was issued for cash.

 e. There was a $195 credit to Retained Earnings for net income.

 f. There was a $60 debit to Retained Earnings for cash dividends declared.

Respond to the following:

a. Prepare a statement of cash flows, using the indirect method of presenting cash flows from operating activities.

b. Was Hobson Medical Equipment's cash flow from operations more or less than net income? What is the source of this difference?

OBJ. 2

EX 16-18   Statement of cash flows—indirect method

List the errors you find in the following statement of cash flows. The cash balance at the beginning of the year was $180,576. All other amounts are correct, except the cash balance at the end of the year.

Hough Inc.
Statement of Cash Flows
For the Year Ended December 31, 2012

Cash flows from operating activities:		
Net income	$266,544	
Adjustments to reconcile net income to net cash flow from operating activities:		
Depreciation	75,600	
Gain on sale of investements	12,960	
Changes in current operating assets and liabilities:		
Increase in accounts receivable	20,520	
Increase in inventories	(26,568)	
Increase in accounts payable	(7,992)	
Decrease in accrued expenses payable	(1,944)	
Net cash flow from operating activities		$339,120

(Continued)

Cash flows from investing activities:

Cash received from sale of investments		$183,600	
Less: Cash paid for purchase of land	$194,400		
Cash paid for purchase of equipment.	324,360	518,760	
Net cash flow used for investing activities.			(335,160)

Cash flows from financing activities:

Cash received from sale of common stock.		$231,120	
Cash paid for dividends.		97,200	
Net cash flow provided by financing activities.			133,920
Increase in cash			$ 86,904
Cash at the end of the year.			180,576
Cash at the beginning of the year.			$267,480

OBJ. 3

✔ a. $546,375

EX 16-19 Cash flows from operating activities—direct method

The cash flows from operating activities are reported by the direct method on the statement of cash flows. Determine the following:

a. If sales for the current year were $513,750 and accounts receivable decreased by $32,625 during the year, what was the amount of cash received from customers?

b. If income tax expense for the current year was $34,500 and income tax payable decreased by $3,900 during the year, what was the amount of cash payments for income tax?

c. Briefly explain why the cash received from customers in (a) is different than sales.

OBJ. 3

EX 16-20 Cash paid for merchandise purchases

The cost of merchandise sold for Kohl's Corporation for a recent year was $10,680 million. The balance sheet showed the following current account balances (in millions):

	Balance, End of Year	Balance, Beginning of Year
Merchandise inventories	$2,923	$2,799
Accounts payable	2,374	1,827

Determine the amount of cash payments for merchandise.

OBJ. 3

✔ a. $624,442

EX 16-21 Determining selected amounts for cash flows from operating activities—direct method

Selected data taken from the accounting records of Bentson Inc. for the current year ended December 31 are as follows:

	Balance, December 31	Balance, January 1
Accrued expenses payable (operating expenses)	$ 7,826	$ 8,554
Accounts payable (merchandise creditors)	58,422	64,428
Inventories	108,290	117,754
Prepaid expenses	4,550	5,460

During the current year, the cost of merchandise sold was $627,900, and the operating expenses other than depreciation were $109,200. The direct method is used for presenting the cash flows from operating activities on the statement of cash flows.

Determine the amount reported on the statement of cash flows for (a) cash payments for merchandise and (b) cash payments for operating expenses.

OBJ. 3

✔ Net cash flow from operating activities, $52,320

EX 16-22   Cash flows from operating activities—direct method

The income statement of Goliath Industries Inc. for the current year ended June 30 is as follows:

Sales	$273,600
Cost of merchandise sold	155,400
Gross profit	$118,200
Operating expenses:	
Depreciation expense $21,000	
Other operating expenses 55,440	
Total operating expenses	76,440
Income before income tax	$ 41,760
Income tax expense	11,580
Net income	$ 30,180

Changes in the balances of selected accounts from the beginning to the end of the current year are as follows:

	Increase Decrease*
Accounts receivable (net)	$6,300*
Inventories	2,100
Prepaid expenses	2,040*
Accounts payable (merchandise creditors)	4,320*
Accrued expenses payable (operating expenses)	660
Income tax payable	1,440*

a. Prepare the Cash Flows from Operating Activities section of the statement of cash flows, using the direct method.

b. What does the direct method show about a company's cash flow from operating activities that is not shown using the indirect method?

OBJ. 3

✔ Net cash flow from operating activities, $183,430

EX 16-23   Cash flows from operating activities—direct method

The income statement for Kipitz Company for the current year ended June 30 and balances of selected accounts at the beginning and the end of the year are as follows:

Sales	$657,800
Cost of merchandise sold	227,500
Gross profit	$430,300
Operating expenses:	
Depreciation expense .... $ 56,875	
Other operating expenses 170,300	
Total operating expenses	227,175
Income before income tax	$203,125
Income tax expense	58,500
Net income	$144,625

	End of Year	Beginning of Year
Accounts receivable (net)	$ 52,975	$ 46,085
Inventories	136,500	118,625
Prepaid expenses	21,450	23,595
Accounts payable (merchandise creditors)	99,775	92,625
Accrued expenses payable (operating expenses)	28,275	30,875
Income tax payable	6,500	6,500

Prepare the Cash Flows from Operating Activities section of the statement of cash flows, using the direct method.

OBJ. 4

EX 16-24 Free cash flow

Iglesias Enterprises, Inc. has cash flows from operating activities of $385,000. Cash flows used for investments in property, plant, and equipment totaled $145,000, of which 80% of this investment was used to replace existing capacity.

a. Determine the free cash flow for Iglesias Enterprises, Inc.

b. How might a lender use free cash flow to determine whether or not to give Iglesias Enterprises, Inc. a loan?

OBJ. 4

EX 16-25 Free cash flow

The financial statements for Nike, Inc., are provided in Appendix C at the end of the text.

a. Determine the free cash flow for the year ended May 31, 2010. Assume that 90% of additions to property, plant and equipment were used to maintain productive capacity.

b. How might a lender use free cash flow to determine whether or not to give Nike, Inc. a loan?

c. Would you feel comfortable giving Nike a loan based on the free cash flow calculated in (a)?

OBJ. 4

EX 16-26 Free cash flow

Matthias Motors, Inc. has cash flows from operating activities of $900,000. Cash flows used for investments in property, plant, and equipment totaled $550,000, of which 75% of this investment was used to replace existing capacity.

Determine the free cash flow for Matthias Motors, Inc.

Problems Series A

OBJ. 2

✔ Net cash flow from operating activities, $37,140

PR 16-1A Statement of cash flows—indirect method

The comparative balance sheet of Flack Inc. for December 31, 2013 and 2012, is shown as follows:

	Dec. 31, 2013	Dec. 31, 2012
Assets		
Cash	$234,660	$219,720
Accounts receivable (net)	85,440	78,360
Inventories	240,660	231,420
Investments	0	90,000
Land	123,000	0
Equipment	264,420	207,420
Accumulated depreciation—equipment	(62,400)	(55,500)
	$885,780	$771,420
Liabilities and Stockholders' Equity		
Accounts payable (merchandise creditors)	$159,180	$151,860
Accrued expenses payable (operating expenses)	15,840	19,740
Dividends payable	9,000	7,200
Common stock, $1 par	48,000	36,000
Paid-in capital in excess of par—common stock	180,000	105,000
Retained earnings	473,760	451,620
	$885,780	$771,420

The following additional information was taken from the records:

a. The investments were sold for $105,000 cash.

b. Equipment and land were acquired for cash.

c. There were no disposals of equipment during the year.

d. The common stock was issued for cash.

e. There was a $58,140 credit to Retained Earnings for net income.

f. There was a $36,000 debit to Retained Earnings for cash dividends declared.

Instructions

Prepare a statement of cash flows, using the indirect method of presenting cash flows from operating activities.

OBJ. 2

✔ Net cash flow from operating activities, $296,800

PR 16-2A Statement of cash flows—indirect method

The comparative balance sheet of Hinson Enterprises, Inc. at December 31, 2013 and 2012, is as follows:

	Dec. 31, 2013	Dec. 31, 2012
Assets		
Cash	$ 128,275	$ 157,325
Accounts receivable (net)	196,525	211,750
Merchandise inventory	281,400	261,800
Prepaid expenses	11,725	8,400
Equipment..	573,125	469,875
Accumulated depreciation—equipment	(149,450)	(115,675)
	$1,041,600	$ 993,475
Liabilities and Stockholders' Equity		
Accounts payable (merchandise creditors)	$ 218,925	$ 207,900
Mortgage note payable..	0	294,000
Common stock, $1 par...	91,000	21,000
Paid-in capital in excess of par—common stock	455,000	280,000
Retained earnings...	276,675	190,575
	$1,041,600	$ 993,475

Additional data obtained from the income statement and from an examination of the accounts in the ledger for 2012 are as follows:

a. Net income, $220,500.

b. Depreciation reported on the income statement, $72,975.

c. Equipment was purchased at a cost of $142,450, and fully depreciated equipment costing $39,200 was discarded, with no salvage realized.

d. The mortgage note payable was not due until 2014, but the terms permitted earlier payment without penalty.

e. 7,000 shares of common stock were issued at $35 for cash.

f. Cash dividends declared and paid, $134,400.

Instructions

Prepare a statement of cash flows, using the indirect method of presenting cash flows from operating activities.

OBJ. 2

✔ Net cash flow from operating activities, $(128,800)

PR 16-3A Statement of cash flows—indirect method

The comparative balance sheet of Mills Engine Co. at December 31, 2013 and 2012, is as follows:

	Dec. 31, 2013	Dec. 31, 2012
Assets		
Cash	$ 714,000	$ 750,400
Accounts receivable (net)	644,700	592,620
Inventories	986,580	904,540
Prepaid expenses	22,820	27,300
Land	245,700	373,100
Buildings	1,137,500	700,700
Accumulated depreciation—buildings..........................	(317,800)	(297,360)
Equipment...	398,440	353,640
Accumulated depreciation—equipment	(109,900)	(123,480)
	$3,722,040	$3,281,460

(Continued)

Liabilities and Stockholders' Equity

Accounts payable (merchandise creditors)	$ 717,500	$ 745,360
Bonds payable	210,000	0
Common stock, $20 par.......................................	245,000	91,000
Paid-in capital in excess of par—common stock	588,000	434,000
Retained earnings...	1,961,540	2,011,100
	$3,722,040	$3,281,460

The noncurrent asset, noncurrent liability, and stockholders' equity accounts for 2010 are as follows:

ACCOUNT *Land*   **ACCOUNT NO.**

Date		Item	Debit	Credit	Balance Debit	Balance Credit
2013						
Jan.	1	Balance			373,100	
Apr.	20	Realized $117,600 cash				
		from sale		127,400	245,700	

ACCOUNT *Buildings*   **ACCOUNT NO.**

Date		Item	Debit	Credit	Balance Debit	Balance Credit
2013						
Jan.	1	Balance			700,700	
Apr.	20	Acquired for cash	436,800		1,137,500	

ACCOUNT *Accumulated Depreciation—Buildings*   **ACCOUNT NO.**

Date		Item	Debit	Credit	Balance Debit	Balance Credit
2013						
Jan.	1	Balance				297,360
Dec.	31	Depreciation for year		20,440		317,800

ACCOUNT *Equipment*   **ACCOUNT NO.**

Date		Item	Debit	Credit	Balance Debit	Balance Credit
2013						
Jan.	1	Balance			353,640	
	26	Discarded, no salvage		36,400	317,240	
Aug.	11	Purchased for cash	81,200		398,440	

ACCOUNT *Accumulated Depreciation—Equipment*   **ACCOUNT NO.**

Date		Item	Debit	Credit	Balance Debit	Balance Credit
2013						
Jan.	1	Balance				123,480
	26	Equipment discarded	36,400			87,080
Dec.	31	Depreciation for year		22,820		109,900

ACCOUNT *Bonds Payable*   **ACCOUNT NO.**

Date		Item	Debit	Credit	Balance Debit	Balance Credit
2013						
May	1	Issued 20-year bonds		210,000		210,000

ACCOUNT *Common Stock, $20 par*   **ACCOUNT NO.**

Date		Item	Debit	Credit	Balance Debit	Balance Credit
2013						
Jan.	1	Balance				91,000
Dec.	7	Issued 7,700 shares of common stock for $40 per share		154,000		245,000

ACCOUNT *Paid-In Capital in Excess of Par—Common Stock*   **ACCOUNT NO.**

Date		Item	Debit	Credit	Balance Debit	Balance Credit
2013						
Jan.	1	Balance				434,000
Dec.	7	Issued 7,700 shares of common stock for $40 per share		154,000		588,000

ACCOUNT *Retained Earnings*   **ACCOUNT NO.**

Date		Item	Debit	Credit	Balance Debit	Balance Credit
2013						
Jan.	1	Balance				2,011,100
Dec.	31	Net loss	24,360			1,986,740
	31	Cash dividends	25,200			1,961,540

Instructions

Prepare a statement of cash flows, using the indirect method of presenting cash flows from operating activities.

OBJ. 3

✔ Net cash flow from operating activities, $352,320

PR 16-4A   Statement of cash flows—direct method

The comparative balance sheet of Rowe Products Inc. for December 31, 2013 and 2012, is as follows:

	Dec. 31, 2013	Dec. 31, 2012
Assets		
Cash	$ 772,080	$ 815,280
Accounts receivable (net)	680,160	656,880
Inventories	1,213,200	1,179,360
Investments	0	288,000
Land	624,000	0
Equipment..	1,056,000	816,000
Accumulated depreciation	(293,280)	(240,480)
	$4,052,160	$3,515,040

(Continued)

Liabilities and Stockholders' Equity

Accounts payable (merchandise creditors)	$ 926,160	$ 898,080
Accrued expenses payable (operating expenses)	76,080	84,960
Dividends payable...	10,560	7,680
Common stock, $10 par......................................	177,600	38,400
Paid-in capital in excess of par—common stock	369,600	230,400
Retained earnings..	2,492,160	2,255,520
	$4,052,160	$3,515,040

The income statement for the year ended December 31, 2012, is as follows:

Sales		$7,176,000
Cost of merchandise sold		2,942,400
Gross profit		$4,233,600
Operating expenses:		
Depreciation expense	$ 52,800	
Other operating expenses	3,720,000	
Total operating expenses		3,772,800
Operating income..		$ 460,800
Other expense:		
Loss on sale of investments		(76,800)
Income before income tax		$ 384,000
Income tax expense		123,360
Net income		$ 260,640

The following additional information was taken from the records:

a. Equipment and land were acquired for cash.

b. There were no disposals of equipment during the year.

c. The investments were sold for $211,200 cash.

d. The common stock was issued for cash.

e. There was a $24,000 debit to Retained Earnings for cash dividends declared.

Instructions

Prepare a statement of cash flows, using the direct method of presenting cash flows from operating activities.

OBJ. 3

✔ Net cash flow from operating activities, $37,140

PR 16-5A Statement of cash flows—direct method applied to PR 16-1A

The comparative balance sheet of Flack Inc. for December 31, 2013 and 2012, is as follows:

	Dec. 31, 2013	Dec. 31, 2012
Assets		
Cash	$234,660	$219,720
Accounts receivable (net)	85,440	78,360
Inventories	240,660	231,420
Investments	0	90,000
Land	123,000	0
Equipment..	264,420	207,420
Accumulated depreciation—equipment	(62,400)	(55,500)
	$885,780	$771,420
Liabilities and Stockholders' Equity		
Accounts payable (merchandise creditors)	$159,180	$151,860
Accrued expenses payable (operating expenses)	15,840	19,740
Dividends payable...	9,000	7,200
Common stock, $1 par.....................................	48,000	36,000
Paid-in capital in excess of par—common stock	180,000	105,000
Retained earnings...	473,760	451,620
	$885,780	$771,420

The income statement for the year ended December 31, 2013, is as follows:

Sales		$1,508,520
Cost of merchandise sold		928,320
Gross profit		$ 580,200
Operating expenses:		
Depreciation expense	$ 6,900	
Other operating expenses	491,400	
Total operating expenses		498,300
Operating income		$ 81,900
Other income:		
Gain on sale of investments		15,000
Income before income tax		$ 96,900
Income tax expense		38,760
Net income		$ 58,140

The following additional information was taken from the records:

a. The investments were sold for $105,000 cash.

b. Equipment and land were acquired for cash.

c. There were no disposals of equipment during the year.

d. The common stock was issued for cash.

e. There was a $36,000 debit to Retained Earnings for cash dividends declared.

Instructions

Prepare a statement of cash flows, using the direct method of presenting cash flows from operating activities.

Problems Series B

OBJ. 2

✔ Net cash flow from operating activities, $246,720

PR 16-1B   Statement of cash flows—indirect method

The comparative balance sheet of Juras Equipment Co. for December 31, 2013 and 2012, is as follows:

	Dec. 31, 2013	Dec. 31, 2012
Assets		
Cash	$ 99,840	$ 67,680
Accounts receivable (net)	292,560	265,680
Inventories	421,440	409,200
Investments	0	144,000
Land	417,600	0
Equipment	619,200	505,440
Accumulated depreciation	(139,920)	(119,040)
	$1,710,720	$1,272,960
Liabilities and Stockholders' Equity		
Accounts payable (merchandise creditors)	$ 290,400	$ 274,080
Accrued expenses payable (operating expenses)	43,200	37,920
Dividends payable	36,000	28,800
Common stock, $1 par	162,000	144,000
Paid-in capital in excess of par—common stock	594,000	288,000
Retained earnings	585,120	500,160
	$1,710,720	$1,272,960

The following additional information was taken from the records of Juras Equipment:

a. Equipment and land were acquired for cash.

b. There were no disposals of equipment during the year.

c. The investments were sold for $129,600 cash.

d. The common stock was issued for cash.

e. There was a $228,960 credit to Retained Earnings for net income.

f. There was a $144,000 debit to Retained Earnings for cash dividends declared.

Instructions

Prepare a statement of cash flows, using the indirect method of presenting cash flows from operating activities.

OBJ. 2

✔ Net cash flow from operating activities, $481,200

PR 16-2B   Statement of cash flows—indirect method

The comparative balance sheet of Beets Industries, Inc. at December 31, 2013 and 2012, is as follows:

	Dec. 31, 2013	Dec. 31, 2012
Assets		
Cash	$ 379,920	$ 309,360
Accounts receivable (net)	570,240	507,600
Inventories	761,040	876,480
Prepaid expenses	27,120	21,600
Land	259,200	259,200
Buildings	1,468,800	972,000
Accumulated depreciation—buildings....................	(399,600)	(355,320)
Machinery and equipment.............................	669,600	669,600
Accumulated depreciation—machinery and equipment.....	(183,600)	(164,160)
Patents	91,680	103,680
	$3,644,400	$3,200,040
Liabilities and Stockholders' Equity		
Accounts payable (merchandise creditors)	$ 717,840	$ 794,640
Dividends payable.....................................	28,080	21,600
Salaries payable......................................	67,680	74,640
Mortgage note payable, due 2017	192,000	0
Bonds payable	0	336,000
Common stock, $2 par.................................	99,200	43,200
Paid-in capital in excess of par—common stock	388,000	108,000
Retained earnings.....................................	2,151,600	1,821,960
	$3,644,400	$3,200,040

An examination of the income statement and the accounting records revealed the following additional information applicable to 2013:

a. Net income, $441,960.

b. Depreciation expense reported on the income statement: buildings, $44,280; machinery and equipment, $19,440.

c. Patent amortization reported on the income statement, $12,000.

d. A building was constructed for $496,800.

e. A mortgage note for $192,000 was issued for cash.

f. 28,000 shares of common stock were issued at $12 in exchange for the bonds payable.

g. Cash dividends declared, $112,320.

Instructions

Prepare a statement of cash flows, using the indirect method of presenting cash flows from operating activities.

OBJ. 2

✔ Net cash flow from operating activities, $70,200

PR 16-3B   Statement of cash flows—indirect method

The comparative balance sheet of Wen Technology, Inc. at December 31, 2013 and 2012, is as follows:

	Dec. 31, 2013	Dec. 31, 2012
Assets		
Cash	$ 450,900	$ 506,700
Accounts receivable (net)	1,056,600	914,400
Inventories	1,377,900	1,298,700
Prepaid expenses	27,900	39,600
Land	1,485,000	2,079,000
Buildings	2,970,000	1,485,000
Accumulated depreciation—buildings.....................	(595,800)	(549,000)
Equipment	990,900	794,700
Accumulated depreciation—equipment	(199,800)	(243,000)
	$7,563,600	$6,326,100
Liabilities and Stockholders' Equity		
Accounts payable (merchandise creditors)	$ 891,000	$ 946,800
Income tax payable	39,600	32,400
Bonds payable	495,000	0
Common stock, $10 par.....................................	378,000	270,000
Paid-in capital in excess of par—common stock	1,701,000	1,215,000
Retained earnings...	4,059,000	3,861,900
	$7,563,600	$6,326,100

The noncurrent asset, noncurrent liability, and stockholders' equity accounts for 2013 are as follows:

ACCOUNT *Land* **ACCOUNT NO.**

Date		Item	Debit	Credit	Balance Debit	Balance Credit
2013						
Jan.	1	Balance			2,079,000	
Apr.	20	Realized $684,000 cash from sale		594,000	1,485,000	

ACCOUNT *Buildings* **ACCOUNT NO.**

Date		Item	Debit	Credit	Balance Debit	Balance Credit
2013						
Jan.	1	Balance			1,485,000	
Apr.	20	Acquired for cash	1,485,000		2,970,000	

ACCOUNT *Accumulated Depreciation—Buildings* **ACCOUNT NO.**

Date		Item	Debit	Credit	Balance Debit	Balance Credit
2013						
Jan.	1	Balance				549,000
Dec.	31	Depreciation for year		46,800		595,800

ACCOUNT *Equipment*   ACCOUNT NO.

Date		Item	Debit	Credit	Balance Debit	Balance Credit
2013						
Jan.	1	Balance			794,700	
	26	Discarded, no salvage		99,000	695,700	
Aug.	11	Purchased for cash	295,200		990,900	

ACCOUNT *Accumulated Depreciation—Equipment*   ACCOUNT NO.

Date		Item	Debit	Credit	Balance Debit	Balance Credit
2013						
Jan.	1	Balance				243,000
	26	Equipment discarded	99,000			144,000
Dec.	31	Depreciation for year		55,800		199,800

ACCOUNT *Bonds Payable*   ACCOUNT NO.

Date		Item	Debit	Credit	Balance Debit	Balance Credit
2013						
May	1	Issued 20-year bonds		495,000		495,000

ACCOUNT *Common Stock, $10 par*   ACCOUNT NO.

Date		Item	Debit	Credit	Balance Debit	Balance Credit
2013						
Jan.	1	Balance				270,000
Dec.	7	Issued 10,800 shares of common stock for $10 per share		108,000		378,000

ACCOUNT *Paid-In Capital in Excess of Par—Common Stock*   ACCOUNT NO.

Date		Item	Debit	Credit	Balance Debit	Balance Credit
2013						
Jan.	1	Balance				1,215,000
Dec.	7	Issued 10,800 shares of common stock for $10 per share		486,000		1,701,000

ACCOUNT *Retained Earnings*   ACCOUNT NO.

Date		Item	Debit	Credit	Balance Debit	Balance Credit
2013						
Jan.	1	Balance				3,861,900
Dec.	31	Net income		315,900		4,177,800
	31	Cash dividends	118,800			4,059,000

Instructions

Prepare a statement of cash flows, using the indirect method of presenting cash flows from operating activities.

OBJ. 3

✔ Net cash flow from operating activities, $254,610

PR 16-4B   Statement of cash flows—direct method

The comparative balance sheet of Middaugh Restaurant Supplies Inc. for December 31, 2013 and 2012, is as follows:

	Dec. 31, 2013	Dec. 31, 2012
Assets		
Cash	$ 330,960	$ 341,550
Accounts receivable (net)	496,320	457,200
Inventories	697,200	681,900
Investments	0	216,000
Land	480,000	0
Equipment..	612,000	492,000
Accumulated depreciation	(240,750)	(184,200)
	$2,375,730	$2,004,450
Liabilities and Stockholders' Equity		
Accounts payable (merchandise creditors)	$ 540,000	$ 483,300
Accrued expenses payable (operating expenses)	33,900	39,600
Dividends payable...	50,400	45,600
Common stock, $10 par	108,000	15,000
Paid-in capital in excess of par—common stock	364,500	225,000
Retained earnings..	1,278,930	1,195,950
	$2,375,730	$2,004,450

The income statement for the year ended December 31, 2012, is as follows:

Sales		$2,256,000
Cost of merchandise sold		1,176,000
Gross profit		$1,080,000
Operating expenses:		
Depreciation expense	$ 56,550	
Other operating expenses	672,420	
Total operating expenses		728,970
Operating income...		$ 351,030
Other income:		
Gain on sale of investments............................		78,000
Income before income tax		$ 429,030
Income tax expense		149,550
Net income		$ 279,480

The following additional information was taken from the records:

a. Equipment and land were acquired for cash.

b. There were no disposals of equipment during the year.

c. The investments were sold for $294,000 cash.

d. The common stock was issued for cash.

e. There was a $196,500 debit to Retained Earnings for cash dividends declared.

Instructions

Prepare a statement of cash flows, using the direct method of presenting cash flows from operating activities.

OBJ. 3

✔ Net cash flow from operating activities, $246,720

PR 16-5B   Statement of cash flows—direct method applied to PR 16-1B

The comparative balance sheet of Juras Equipment Co. for Dec. 31, 2013 and 2012, is:

	Dec. 31, 2013	Dec. 31, 2012
Assets		
Cash	$ 99,840	$ 67,680
Accounts receivable (net)	292,560	265,680
Inventories	421,440	409,200
Investments	0	144,000
Land	417,600	0
Equipment	619,200	505,440
Accumulated depreciation	(139,920)	(119,040)
	$1,710,720	$1,272,960
Liabilities and Stockholders' Equity		
Accounts payable (merchandise creditors)	$ 290,400	$ 274,080
Accrued expenses payable (operating expenses)	43,200	37,920
Dividends payable	36,000	28,800
Common stock, $1 par	162,000	144,000
Paid-in capital in excess of par—common stock	594,000	288,000
Retained earnings	585,120	500,160
	$1,710,720	$1,272,960

The income statement for the year ended December 31, 2013, is as follows:

Sales		$3,246,048
Cost of merchandise sold		1,997,568
Gross profit		$1,248,480
Operating expenses:		
Depreciation expense	$ 20,880	
Other operating expenses	831,600	
Total operating expenses		852,480
Operating income		$ 396,000
Other expenses:		
Loss on sale of investments		(14,400)
Income before income tax		$ 381,600
Income tax expense		152,640
Net income		$ 228,960

The following additional information was taken from the records:

a. Equipment and land were acquired for cash.

b. There were no disposals of equipment during the year.

c. The investments were sold for $129,600 cash.

d. The common stock was issued for cash.

e. There was a $144,000 debit to Retained Earnings for cash dividends declared.

Instructions

Prepare a statement of cash flows, using the direct method of presenting cash flows from operating activities.

Cases & Projects

CP 16-1   Ethics and professional conduct in business

Chris Ruth, president of Fairazon Industries Inc., believes that reporting operating cash flow per share on the income statement would be a useful addition to the company's just completed financial statements. The following discussion took place between Chris Ruth and Fairazon controller, Phil Tungsten, in January, after the close of the fiscal year.

Chris: I've been reviewing our financial statements for the last year. I am disappointed that our net income per share has dropped by 10% from last year. This won't look good to our shareholders. Is there anything we can do about this?

Phil: What do you mean? The past is the past, and the numbers are in. There isn't much that can be done about it. Our financial statements were prepared according to generally accepted accounting principles, and I don't see much leeway for significant change at this point.

Chris: No, no. I'm not suggesting that we "cook the books." But look at the cash flow from operating activities on the statement of cash flows. The cash flow from operating activities has increased by 20%. This is very good news—and, I might add, useful information. The higher cash flow from operating activities will give our creditors comfort.

Phil: Well, the cash flow from operating activities is on the statement of cash flows, so I guess users will be able to see the improved cash flow figures there.

Chris: This is true, but somehow I feel that this information should be given a much higher profile. I don't like this information being "buried" in the statement of cash flows. You know as well as I do that many users will focus on the income statement. Therefore, I think we ought to include an operating cash flow per share number on the face of the income statement—someplace under the earnings per share number. In this way, users will get the complete picture of our operating performance. Yes, our earnings per share dropped this year, but our cash flow from operating activities improved! And all the information is in one place where users can see and compare the figures. What do you think?

Phil: I've never really thought about it like that before. I guess we could put the operating cash flow per share on the income statement, under the earnings per share. Users would really benefit from this disclosure. Thanks for the idea—I'll start working on it.

Chris: Glad to be of service.

▶ How would you interpret this situation? Is Phil behaving in an ethical and professional manner?

CP 16-2   Using the statement of cash flows

You are considering an investment in a new start-up company, Over Armour Inc., an Internet service provider. A review of the company's financial statements reveals a negative retained earnings. In addition, it appears as though the company has been running a negative cash flow from operating activities since the company's inception.

▶ How is the company staying in business under these circumstances? Could this be a good investment?

CP 16-3   Analysis of statement of cash flows

Dave Chuck is the president and majority shareholder of Xenon Inc., a small retail store chain. Recently, Dave submitted a loan application for Xenon Inc. to Chemistry Bank. It called for a $450,000, 9%, 10-year loan to help finance the construction of a building and the purchase of store equipment, costing a total of $562,500, to enable Xenon Inc. to open a store in Chemistry. Land for this purpose was acquired last year. The bank's loan officer requested a statement of cash flows in addition to the most recent income statement, balance sheet, and retained earnings statement that Dave had submitted with the loan application.

As a close family friend, Dave asked you to prepare a statement of cash flows. From the records provided, you prepared the following statement:

Xenon Inc.
Statement of Cash Flows
For the Year Ended December 31, 2012

Cash flows from operating activities:	
Net income	$225,000
Adjustments to reconcile net income to net cash flow from operating activities:	
Depreciation.	63,000
Gain on sale of investments	(22,500)
Changes in current operating assets and liabilities:	
Decrease in accounts receivable	15,750
Increase in inventories	(31,500)
Increase in accounts payable	22,500
Decrease in accrued expenses payable	(4,500)

(Continued)

Net cash flow from operating activities		$267,750
Cash flows from investing activities:		
Cash received from investments sold	$135,000	
Less cash paid for purchase of store equipment	(90,000)	
Net cash flow provided by investing activities		45,000
Cash flows from financing activities:		
Cash paid for dividends.......................................	$(94,500)	
Net cash flow used for financing activities......................		(94,500)
Increase in cash		$218,250
Cash at the beginning of the year...............................		81,000
Cash at the end of the year....................................		$299,250

Schedule of Noncash Financing and Investing Activities:

Issued common stock for land	$180,000

After reviewing the statement, Dave telephoned you and commented, "Are you sure this statement is right?" Dave then raised the following questions:

1. "How can depreciation be a cash flow?"

2. "Issuing common stock for the land is listed in a separate schedule. This transaction has nothing to do with cash! Shouldn't this transaction be eliminated from the statement?"

3. "How can the gain on sale of investments be a deduction from net income in determining the cash flow from operating activities?"

4. "Why does the bank need this statement anyway? They can compute the increase in cash from the balance sheets for the last two years."

After jotting down Dave's questions, you assured him that this statement was "right." But to alleviate Dave's concern, you arranged a meeting for the following day.

a. ➤ How would you respond to each of Dave's questions?

b. ➤ Do you think that the statement of cash flows enhances the chances of Xenon Inc. receiving the loan? Discuss.

CP 16-4 Analysis of cash flow from operations

The Retailing Division of Argon Clothing Inc. provided the following information on its cash flow from operations:

Net income	$ 675,000
Increase in accounts receivable	(810,000)
Increase in inventory	(900,000)
Decrease in accounts payable	(135,000)
Depreciation	150,000
Cash flow from operating activities	$(1,020,000)

The manager of the Retailing Division provided the accompanying memo with this report:

From: Senior Vice President, Retailing Division

I am pleased to report that we had earnings of $675,000 over the last period. This resulted in a return on invested capital of 10%, which is near our targets for this division. I have been aggressive in building the revenue volume in the division. As a result, I am happy to report that we have increased the number of new credit card customers as a result of an aggressive marketing campaign. In addition, we have found some excellent merchandise opportunities. Some of our suppliers have made some of their apparel merchandise available at a deep discount. We have purchased as much of these goods as possible in order to improve profitability. I'm also happy to report that our vendor payment problems have improved. We are nearly caught up on our overdue payables balances.

➤ Comment on the senior vice president's memo in light of the cash flow information.

CP 16-5 Statement of cash flows

Group Project

This activity will require two teams to retrieve cash flow statement information from the Internet. One team is to obtain the most recent year's statement of cash flows for Johnson & Johnson, and the other team the most recent year's statement of cash flows for AMR Corp.

The statement of cash flows is included as part of the annual report information that is a required disclosure to the Securities and Exchange Commission (SEC). SEC documents can be retrieved using the EdgarScan™ service at **http://www.sec.gov/edgar/searchedgar/webusers.htm.**

To obtain annual report information, type in a company name in the appropriate space. EdgarScan will list the reports available to you for the company you've selected. Select the most recent annual report filing, identified as a 10-K or 10-K405. EdgarScan provides an outline of the report, including the separate financial statements. You can double-click the income statement and balance sheet for the selected company into an Excel™ spreadsheet for further analysis.

As a group, compare the two statements of cash flows.

a. How are Johnson & Johnson and AMR Corp. similar or different regarding cash flows?

b. Compute and compare the free cash flow for each company, assuming additions to property, plant, and equipment replace current capacity.

© AP Photo/Matt York

Financial Statement Analysis

Nike, Inc.

"**J**ust do it." These three words identify one of the most recognizable brands in the world, **Nike**. While this phrase inspires athletes to "compete and achieve their potential," it also defines the company.

Nike began in 1964 as a partnership between University of Oregon track coach Bill Bowerman and one of his former student-athletes, Phil Knight. The two began by selling shoes imported from Japan out of the back of Knight's car to athletes at track and field events. As sales grew, the company opened retail outlets, calling itself **Blue Ribbon Sports**. The company also began to develop its own shoes. In 1971, the company commissioned a graphic design student at Portland State University to develop the swoosh logo for a fee of $35. In 1978, the company changed its name to Nike, and in 1980, it sold its first shares of stock to the public.

Nike would have been a great company to invest in at the time. If you had invested in Nike's

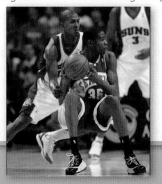

common stock back in 1990, you would have paid $5.00 per share. As of July 2010, Nike's stock was worth $70.15 per share. Unfortunately, you can't invest using hindsight.

How can you select companies in which to invest? Like any significant purchase, you should do some research to guide your investment decision. If you were buying a car, for example, you might go to **Edmunds.com** to obtain reviews, ratings, prices, specifications, options, and fuel economies to evaluate different vehicles. In selecting companies to invest in, you can use financial analysis to gain insight into a company's past performance and future prospects. This chapter describes and illustrates common financial data that can be analyzed to assist you in making investment decisions such as whether or not to invest in Nike's stock.

Source: http://www.nikebiz.com/.

OBJ. 1 Describe basic financial statement analytical methods.

Basic Analytical Methods

Users analyze a company's financial statements using a variety of analytical methods. Three such methods are as follows:

1. Horizontal analysis
2. Vertical analysis
3. Common-sized statements

Horizontal Analysis

The percentage analysis of increases and decreases in related items in comparative financial statements is called **horizontal analysis**. Each item on the most recent statement is compared with the same item on one or more earlier statements in terms of the following:

1. *Amount* of increase or decrease
2. *Percent* of increase or decrease

When comparing statements, the earlier statement is normally used as the base year for computing increases and decreases.

Exhibit 1 illustrates horizontal analysis for the December 31, 2012 and 2011, balance sheets of Lincoln Company. In Exhibit 1, the December 31, 2011, balance sheet (the earliest year presented) is used as the base year.

Exhibit 1 indicates that total assets decreased by $91,000 (7.4%), liabilities decreased by $133,000 (30.0%), and stockholders' equity increased by $42,000 (5.3%).

EXHIBIT 1

Comparative
Balance Sheet—
Horizontal
Analysis

Lincoln Company
Comparative Balance Sheet
December 31, 2012 and 2011

	Dec. 31, 2012	Dec. 31, 2011	Increase (Decrease) Amount	Percent
Assets				
Current assets..	$ 550,000	$ 533,000	$ 17,000	3.2%
Long-term investments...........................	95,000	177,500	(82,500)	(46.5%)
Property, plant, and equipment (net)	444,500	470,000	(25,500)	(5.4%)
Intangible assets	50,000	50,000	—	—
Total assets	$1,139,500	$1,230,500	$ (91,000)	(7.4%)
Liabilities				
Current liabilities................................	$ 210,000	$ 243,000	$ (33,000)	(13.6%)
Long-term liabilities............................	100,000	200,000	(100,000)	(50.0%)
Total liabilities	$ 310,000	$ 443,000	$(133,000)	(30.0%)
Stockholders' Equity				
Preferred 6% stock, $100 par	$ 150,000	$ 150,000	—	—
Common stock, $10 par..........................	500,000	500,000	—	—
Retained earnings...............................	179,500	137,500	$ 42,000	30.5%
Total stockholders' equity........................	$ 829,500	$ 787,500	$ 42,000	5.3%
Total liabilities and stockholders' equity............	$1,139,500	$1,230,500	$ (91,000)	(7.4%)

Since the long-term investments account decreased by $82,500, it appears that most of the decrease in long-term liabilities of $100,000 was achieved through the sale of long-term investments.

The balance sheets in Exhibit 1 may be expanded or supported by a separate schedule that includes the individual asset and liability accounts. For example, Exhibit 2 is a supporting schedule of Lincoln's current asset accounts.

Exhibit 2 indicates that while cash and temporary investments increased, accounts receivable and inventories decreased. The decrease in accounts receivable could be caused by improved collection policies, which would increase cash. The decrease in inventories could be caused by increased sales.

EXHIBIT 2

Comparative
Schedule of
Current Assets—
Horizontal
Analysis

Lincoln Company
Comparative Schedule of Current Assets
December 31, 2012 and 2011

	Dec. 31, 2012	Dec. 31, 2011	Increase (Decrease) Amount	Percent
Cash	$ 90,500	$ 64,700	$ 25,800	39.9%
Temporary investments...........................	75,000	60,000	15,000	25.0%
Accounts receivable (net)	115,000	120,000	(5,000)	(4.2%)
Inventories	264,000	283,000	(19,000)	(6.7%)
Prepaid expenses	5,500	5,300	200	3.8%
Total current assets..............................	$550,000	$533,000	$ 17,000	3.2%

Exhibit 3 illustrates horizontal analysis for the 2012 and 2011 income statements of Lincoln Company. Exhibit 3 indicates an increase in sales of $296,500, or 24.0%. However, the percentage increase in sales of 24.0% was accompanied by an even greater percentage increase in the cost of goods (merchandise) sold of 27.2%.[1] Thus, gross profit increased by only 19.7% rather than by the 24.0% increase in sales.

1 The term *cost of goods sold* is often used in practice in place of *cost of merchandise sold*. Such usage is followed in this chapter.

EXHIBIT 3

Comparative
Income
Statement—
Horizontal
Analysis

			Increase (Decrease)	
Lincoln Company				
Comparative Income Statement				
For the Years Ended December 31, 2012 and 2011				
	2012	2011	Amount	Percent
Sales	$1,530,500	$1,234,000	$296,500	24.0%
Sales returns and allowances	32,500	34,000	(1,500)	(4.4%)
Net sales	$1,498,000	$1,200,000	$298,000	24.8%
Cost of goods sold	1,043,000	820,000	223,000	27.2%
Gross profit	$ 455,000	$ 380,000	$ 75,000	19.7%
Selling expenses	$ 191,000	$ 147,000	$ 44,000	29.9%
Administrative expenses	104,000	97,400	6,600	6.8%
Total operating expenses	$ 295,000	$ 244,400	$ 50,600	20.7%
Income from operations	$ 160,000	$ 135,600	$ 24,400	18.0%
Other income	8,500	11,000	(2,500)	(22.7%)
	$ 168,500	$ 146,600	$ 21,900	14.9%
Other expense (interest)	6,000	12,000	(6,000)	(50.0%)
Income before income tax	$ 162,500	$ 134,600	$ 27,900	20.7%
Income tax expense	71,500	58,100	13,400	23.1%
Net income	$ 91,000	$ 76,500	$ 14,500	19.0%

Exhibit 3 also indicates that selling expenses increased by 29.9%. Thus, the 24.0% increases in sales could have been caused by an advertising campaign, which increased selling expenses. Administrative expenses increased by only 6.8%, total operating expenses increased by 20.7%, and income from operations increased by 18.0%. Interest expense decreased by 50.0%. This decrease was probably caused by the 50.0% decrease in long-term liabilities (Exhibit 1). Overall, net income increased by 19.0%, a favorable result.

Exhibit 4 illustrates horizontal analysis for the 2012 and 2011 retained earnings statements of Lincoln Company. Exhibit 4 indicates that retained earnings increased by 30.5% for the year. The increase is due to net income of $91,000 for the year, less dividends of $49,000.

EXHIBIT 4

Comparative
Retained
Earnings
Statement—
Horizontal
Analysis

			Increase (Decrease)	
Lincoln Company				
Comparative Retained Earnings Statement				
For the Years Ended December 31, 2012 and 2011				
	2012	2011	Amount	Percent
Retained earnings, January 1	$137,500	$100,000	$37,500	37.5%
Net income for the year	91,000	76,500	14,500	19.0%
Total	$228,500	$176,500	$52,000	29.5%
Dividends:				
On preferred stock	$ 9,000	$ 9,000	—	—
On common stock	40,000	30,000	$10,000	33.3%
Total	$ 49,000	$ 39,000	$10,000	25.6%
Retained earnings, December 31	$179,500	$137,500	$42,000	30.5%

Example Exercise 17-1 Horizontal Analysis

OBJ.
1

The comparative cash and accounts receivable balances for a company are provided below.

	Dec. 31, 2012	Dec. 31, 2011
Cash	$62,500	$50,000
Accounts receivable (net)	74,400	80,000

Based on this information, what is the amount and percentage of increase or decrease that would be shown on a balance sheet with horizontal analysis?

Follow My Example 17-1

Cash $12,500 increase ($62,500 – $50,000), or 25%
Accounts receivable $5,600 decrease ($74,400 – $80,000), or (7%)

Practice Exercises: **PE 17-1A, PE 17-1B**

Vertical Analysis

The percentage analysis of the relationship of each component in a financial statement to a total within the statement is called **vertical analysis**. Although vertical analysis is applied to a single statement, it may be applied on the same statement over time. This enhances the analysis by showing how the percentages of each item have changed over time.

In vertical analysis of the balance sheet, the percentages are computed as follows:

1. Each asset item is stated as a percent of the total assets.
2. Each liability and stockholders' equity item is stated as a percent of the total liabilities and stockholders' equity.

Exhibit 5 illustrates the vertical analysis of the December 31, 2012 and 2011, balance sheets of Lincoln Company. Exhibit 5 indicates that current assets have increased from 43.3% to 48.3% of total assets. Long-term investments decreased from 14.4% to 8.3% of total assets. Stockholders' equity increased from 64.0% to 72.8% with a comparable decrease in liabilities.

EXHIBIT 5

Comparative Balance Sheet— Vertical Analysis

Lincoln Company
Comparative Balance Sheet
December 31, 2012 and 2011

	Dec. 31, 2012		Dec. 31, 2011	
	Amount	Percent	Amount	Percent
Assets				
Current assets..............................	$ 550,000	48.3%	$ 533,000	43.3%
Long-term investments.....................	95,000	8.3	177,500	14.4
Property, plant, and equipment (net)	444,500	39.0	470,000	38.2
Intangible assets	50,000	4.4	50,000	4.1
Total assets	$1,139,500	100.0%	$1,230,500	100.0%
Liabilities				
Current liabilities...........................	$ 210,000	18.4%	$ 243,000	19.7%
Long-term liabilities........................	100,000	8.8	200,000	16.3
Total liabilities	$ 310,000	27.2%	$ 443,000	36.0%
Stockholders' Equity				
Preferred 6% stock, $100 par	$ 150,000	13.2%	$ 150,000	12.2%
Common stock, $10 par.....................	500,000	43.9	500,000	40.6
Retained earnings..........................	179,500	15.7	137,500	11.2
Total stockholders' equity...................	$ 829,500	72.8%	$ 787,500	64.0%
Total liabilities and stockholders' equity.......	$1,139,500	100.0%	$1,230,500	100.0%

In a vertical analysis of the income statement, each item is stated as a percent of net sales. Exhibit 6 illustrates the vertical analysis of the 2012 and 2011 income statements of Lincoln Company.

Exhibit 6 indicates a decrease in the gross profit rate from 31.7% in 2011 to 30.4% in 2012. Although this is only a 1.3 percentage point (31.7% − 30.4%) decrease, in dollars of potential gross profit, it represents a decrease of about $19,500 (1.3% × $1,498,000). Thus, a small percentage decrease can have a large dollar effect.

EXHIBIT 6

Comparative
Income
Statement—
Vertical Analysis

Lincoln Company
Comparative Income Statement
For the Years Ended December 31, 2012 and 2011

	2012		2011	
	Amount	Percent	Amount	Percent
Sales	$1,530,500	102.2%	$1,234,000	102.8%
Sales returns and allowances	32,500	2.2	34,000	2.8
Net sales	$1,498,000	100.0%	$1,200,000	100.0%
Cost of goods sold	1,043,000	69.6	820,000	68.3
Gross profit	$ 455,000	30.4%	$ 380,000	31.7%
Selling expenses	$ 191,000	12.8%	$ 147,000	12.3%
Administrative expenses	104,000	6.9	97,400	8.1
Total operating expenses	$ 295,000	19.7%	$ 244,400	20.4%
Income from operations	$ 160,000	10.7%	$ 135,600	11.3%
Other income	8,500	0.6	11,000	0.9
	$ 168,500	11.3%	$ 146,600	12.2%
Other expense (interest)	6,000	0.4	12,000	1.0
Income before income tax	$ 162,500	10.9%	$ 134,600	11.2%
Income tax expense	71,500	4.8	58,100	4.8
Net income	$ 91,000	6.1%	$ 76,500	6.4%

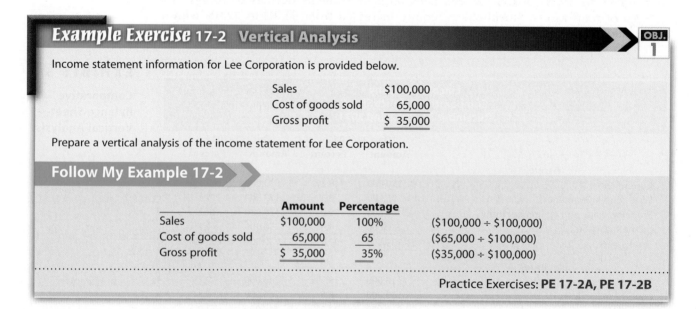

Example Exercise 17-2 **Vertical Analysis**

OBJ.
1

Income statement information for Lee Corporation is provided below.

Sales	$100,000
Cost of goods sold	65,000
Gross profit	$ 35,000

Prepare a vertical analysis of the income statement for Lee Corporation.

Follow My Example 17-2

	Amount	Percentage	
Sales	$100,000	100%	($100,000 ÷ $100,000)
Cost of goods sold	65,000	65	($65,000 ÷ $100,000)
Gross profit	$ 35,000	35%	($35,000 ÷ $100,000)

Practice Exercises: **PE 17-2A, PE 17-2B**

Common-Sized Statements

In a **common-sized statement**, all items are expressed as percentages with no dollar amounts shown. Common-sized statements are often useful for comparing one company with another or for comparing a company with industry averages.

Exhibit 7 illustrates common-sized income statements for Lincoln Company and Madison Corporation. Exhibit 7 indicates that Lincoln Company has a slightly higher

	Lincoln Company	Madison Corporation
Sales	102.2%	102.3%
Sales returns and allowances	2.2	2.3
Net sales	100.0%	100.0%
Cost of goods sold	69.6	70.0
Gross profit	30.4%	30.0%
Selling expenses	12.8%	11.5%
Administrative expenses	6.9	4.1
Total operating expenses	19.7%	15.6%
Income from operations	10.7%	14.4%
Other income	0.6	0.6
	11.3%	15.0%
Other expense (interest)	0.4	0.5
Income before income tax	10.9%	14.5%
Income tax expense	4.8	5.5
Net income	6.1%	9.0%

EXHIBIT 7

Common-Sized Income Statement

rate of gross profit (30.4%) than Madison Corporation (30.0%). However, Lincoln has a higher percentage of selling expenses (12.8%) and administrative expenses (6.9%) than does Madison (11.5% and 4.1%). As a result, the income from operations of Lincoln (10.7%) is less than that of Madison (14.4%).

The unfavorable difference of 3.7 (14.4% − 10.7%) percentage points in income from operations would concern the managers and other stakeholders of Lincoln. The underlying causes of the difference should be investigated and possibly corrected. For example, Lincoln Company may decide to outsource some of its administrative duties so that its administrative expenses are more comparative to that of Madison Corporation.

Other Analytical Measures

Other relationships may be expressed in ratios and percentages. Often, these relationships are compared within the same statement and, thus, are a type of vertical analysis. Comparing these items with items from earlier periods is a type of horizontal analysis.

Analytical measures are not a definitive conclusion. They are only guides in evaluating financial and operating data. Many other factors, such as trends in the industry and general economic conditions, should also be considered when analyzing a company.

Solvency Analysis

 OBJ. 2 Use financial statement analysis to assess the solvency of a business.

All users of financial statements are interested in the ability of a company to do the following:

1. Meet its financial obligations (debts), called **solvency**
2. Earn income, called **profitability**

Solvency and profitability are interrelated. For example, a company that cannot pay its debts will have difficulty obtaining credit. A lack of credit will, in turn, limit the company's ability to purchase merchandise or expand operations, which decreases its profitability.

Solvency analysis focuses on the ability of a company to pay its liabilities. It is normally assessed using the following:

1. Current position analysis
   Working capital
   Current ratio
   Quick ratio

Note:
Solvency analysis focuses on the ability of a business to pay its current and noncurrent liabilities.

One popular printed source for industry ratios is *Annual Statement Studies* from Risk Management Association. Online analysis is available from Zacks Investment Research site, which is linked to the text's Web site at **www.cengage .com/accounting/ warren.**

2. Accounts receivable analysis
      Accounts receivable turnover
      Number of days' sales in receivables

3. Inventory analysis
      Inventory turnover
      Number of days' sales in inventory

4. The ratio of fixed assets to long-term liabilities
5. The ratio of liabilities to stockholders' equity
6. The number of times interest charges are earned

The Lincoln Company financial statements presented earlier are used to illustrate the preceding analyses.

Current Position Analysis

A company's ability to pay its current liabilities is called **current position analysis**. It is of special interest to short-term creditors and includes the computation and analysis of the following:

1. Working capital
2. Current ratio
3. Quick ratio

Working Capital A company's **working capital** is computed as follows:

$$\text{Working Capital} = \text{Current Assets} - \text{Current Liabilities}$$

To illustrate, the working capital for Lincoln Company for 2012 and 2011 is computed below.

	2012	2011
Current assets	$550,000	$533,000
Less current liabilities	210,000	243,000
Working capital	$340,000	$290,000

The working capital is used to evaluate a company's ability to pay current liabilities. A company's working capital is often monitored monthly, quarterly, or yearly by creditors and other debtors. However, it is difficult to use working capital to compare companies of different sizes. For example, working capital of $250,000 may be adequate for a local hardware store, but it would be inadequate for The Home Depot.

Current Ratio The **current ratio**, sometimes called the *working capital ratio* is computed as follows:

$$\text{Current Ratio} = \frac{\text{Current Assets}}{\text{Current Liabilities}}$$

To illustrate, the current ratio for Lincoln Company is computed below.

	2012	2011
Current assets	$550,000	$533,000
Current liabilities	$210,000	$243,000
Current ratio	2.6 ($550,000/$210,000)	2.2 ($533,000/$243,000)

The current ratio is a more reliable indicator of a company's ability to pay its current liabilities than is working capital, and it is much easier to compare across companies. To illustrate, assume that as of December 31, 2012, the working capital of a competitor is much greater than $340,000, but its current ratio is only 1.3. Considering these facts alone, Lincoln Company, with its current ratio of 2.6, is in a more favorable position to obtain short-term credit than the competitor, which has the greater amount of working capital.

Quick Ratio One limitation of working capital and the current ratio is that they do not consider the types of current assets a company has and how easily they can be turned in to cash. Because of this, two companies may have the same working capital and current ratios, but differ significantly in their ability to pay their current liabilities.

To illustrate, the current assets and liabilities for Lincoln Company and Jefferson Corporation as of December 31, 2012, are as follows:

	Lincoln Company	Jefferson Corporation
Current assets:		
Cash	$ 90,500	$ 45,500
Temporary investments	75,000	25,000
Accounts receivable (net)	115,000	90,000
Inventories	264,000	380,000
Prepaid expenses	5,500	9,500
Total current assets	$550,000	$550,000
Total current assets	$550,000	$550,000
Less current liabilities	210,000	210,000
Working capital	$340,000	$340,000
Current ratio ($550,000/$210,000)	2.6	2.6

Lincoln and Jefferson both have a working capital of $340,000 and current ratios of 2.6. Jefferson, however, has more of its current assets in inventories. These inventories must be sold and the receivables collected before all the current liabilities can be paid. This takes time. In addition, if the market for its product declines, Jefferson may have difficulty selling its inventory. This, in turn, could impair its ability to pay its current liabilities.

In contrast, Lincoln's current assets contain more cash, temporary investments, and accounts receivable, which can easily be converted to cash. Thus, Lincoln is in a stronger current position than Jefferson to pay its current liabilities.

A ratio that measures the "instant" debt-paying ability of a company is the **quick ratio**, sometimes called the *acid-test ratio*. The quick ratio is computed as follows:

$$\text{Quick Ratio} = \frac{\text{Quick Assets}}{\text{Current Liabilities}}$$

Quick assets are cash and other current assets that can be easily converted to cash. Quick assets normally include cash, temporary investments, and receivables but exclude inventories and prepaid assets.

To illustrate, the quick ratio for Lincoln Company is computed below.

	2012	2011
Quick assets:		
Cash	$ 90,500	$ 64,700
Temporary investments	75,000	60,000
Accounts receivable (net)	115,000	120,000
Total quick assets	$280,500	$244,700
Current liabilities	$210,000	$243,000
Quick ratio	1.3 ($280,500 ÷ $210,000)	1.0 ($244,700 ÷ $243,000)

Example Exercise 17-3 Current Position Analysis

OBJ. 2

The following items are reported on a company's balance sheet:

Cash	$300,000
Temporary investments	100,000
Accounts receivable (net)	200,000
Inventory	200,000
Accounts payable	400,000

Determine (a) the current ratio and (b) the quick ratio.

Follow My Example 17-3

a. Current Ratio = Current Assets ÷ Current Liabilities
    Current Ratio = ($300,000 + $100,000 + $200,000 + $200,000) ÷ $400,000
    Current Ratio = 2.0

b. Quick Ratio = Quick Assets ÷ Current Liabilities
    Quick Ratio = ($300,000 + $100,000 + $200,000) ÷ $400,000
    Quick Ratio = 1.5

Practice Exercises: **PE 17-3A, PE 17-3B**

Accounts Receivable Analysis

A company's ability to collect its accounts receivable is called **accounts receivable analysis**. It includes the computation and analysis of the following:

1. Accounts receivable turnover
2. Number of days' sales in receivables

Collecting accounts receivable as quickly as possible improves a company's solvency. In addition, the cash collected from receivables may be used to improve or expand operations. Quick collection of receivables also reduces the risk of uncollectible accounts.

Accounts Receivable Turnover The **accounts receivable turnover** is computed as follows:

$$\text{Accounts Receivable Turnover} = \frac{\text{Net Sales}^2}{\text{Average Accounts Receivable}}$$

To illustrate, the accounts receivable turnover for Lincoln Company for 2012 and 2011 is computed below. Lincoln's accounts receivable balance at the beginning of 2011 is $140,000.

	2012	2011
Net sales	$1,498,000	$1,200,000
Accounts receivable (net):		
Beginning of year	$ 120,000	$ 140,000
End of year	115,000	120,000
Total	$ 235,000	$ 260,000
Average accounts receivable	$117,500 ($235,000 ÷ 2)	$130,000 ($260,000 ÷ 2)
Accounts receivable turnover	12.7 ($1,498,000 ÷ $117,500)	9.2 ($1,200,000 ÷ $130,000)

The increase in Lincoln's accounts receivable turnover from 9.2 to 12.7 indicates that the collection of receivables has improved during 2012. This may be due to a change in how credit is granted, collection practices, or both.

For Lincoln Company, the average accounts receivable was computed using the accounts receivable balance at the beginning and the end of the year. When

---

2 If known, *credit* sales should be used in the numerator. Because credit sales are not normally known by external users, we use net sales in the numerator.

sales are seasonal and, thus, vary throughout the year, monthly balances of receivables are often used. Also, if sales on account include notes receivable as well as accounts receivable, notes and accounts receivables are normally combined for analysis.

Number of Days' Sales in Receivables   The **number of days' sales in receivables** is computed as follows:

$$\text{Number of Days' Sales in Receivables} = \frac{\text{Average Accounts Receivable}}{\text{Average Daily Sales}}$$

where

$$\text{Average Daily Sales} = \frac{\text{Net Sales}}{365 \text{ days}}$$

To illustrate, the number of days' sales in receivables for Lincoln Company is computed below.

	2012	**2011**
Average accounts receivable	$117,500 ($235,000 ÷ 2)	$130,000 ($260,000 ÷ 2)
Average daily sales	$4,104 ($1,498,000 ÷ 365)	$3,288 ($1,200,000 ÷ 365)
Number of days' sales in receivables	28.6 ($117,500 ÷ $4,104)	39.5 ($130,000 ÷ $3,288)

The number of days' sales in receivables is an estimate of the time (in days) that the accounts receivable have been outstanding. The number of days' sales in receivables is often compared with a company's credit terms to evaluate the efficiency of the collection of receivables.

To illustrate, if Lincoln's credit terms are 2/10, n/30, then Lincoln was very *inefficient* in collecting receivables in 2011. In other words, receivables should have been collected in 30 days or less, but were being collected in 39.5 days. Although collections improved during 2012 to 28.6 days, there is probably still room for improvement. On the other hand, if Lincoln's credit terms are n/45, then there is probably little room for improving collections.

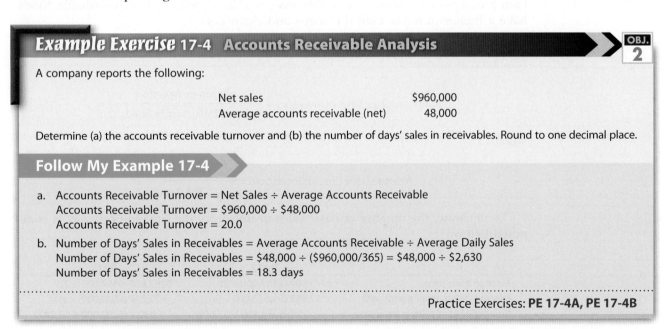

Example Exercise 17-4   Accounts Receivable Analysis   OBJ. 2

A company reports the following:

Net sales	$960,000
Average accounts receivable (net)	48,000

Determine (a) the accounts receivable turnover and (b) the number of days' sales in receivables. Round to one decimal place.

Follow My Example 17-4

a.   Accounts Receivable Turnover = Net Sales ÷ Average Accounts Receivable
     Accounts Receivable Turnover = $960,000 ÷ $48,000
     Accounts Receivable Turnover = 20.0

b.   Number of Days' Sales in Receivables = Average Accounts Receivable ÷ Average Daily Sales
     Number of Days' Sales in Receivables = $48,000 ÷ ($960,000/365) = $48,000 ÷ $2,630
     Number of Days' Sales in Receivables = 18.3 days

Practice Exercises: **PE 17-4A, PE 17-4B**

Inventory Analysis

A company's ability to manage its inventory effectively is evaluated using **inventory analysis**. It includes the computation and analysis of the following:

1. Inventory turnover
2. Number of days' sales in inventory

Excess inventory decreases solvency by tying up funds (cash) in inventory. In addition, excess inventory increases insurance expense, property taxes, storage costs, and other related expenses. These expenses further reduce funds that could be used elsewhere to improve or expand operations.

Excess inventory also increases the risk of losses because of price declines or obsolescence of the inventory. On the other hand, a company should keep enough inventory in stock so that it doesn't lose sales because of lack of inventory.

Inventory Turnover The **inventory turnover** is computed as follows:

$$\text{Inventory Turnover} = \frac{\text{Cost of Goods Sold}}{\text{Average Inventory}}$$

To illustrate, the inventory turnover for Lincoln Company for 2012 and 2011 is computed below. Lincoln's inventory balance at the beginning of 2011 is $311,000.

	2012	2011
Cost of goods sold	$1,043,000	$820,000
Inventories:		
Beginning of year	$ 283,000	$311,000
End of year	264,000	283,000
Total	$ 547,000	$594,000
Average inventory	$273,500 ($547,000 ÷ 2)	$297,000 ($594,000 ÷ 2)
Inventory turnover	3.8 ($1,043,000 ÷ $273,500)	2.8 ($820,000 ÷ $297,000)

The increase in Lincoln's inventory turnover from 2.8 to 3.8 indicates that the management of inventory has improved in 2012. The inventory turnover improved because of an increase in the cost of goods sold, which indicates more sales, and a decrease in the average inventories.

What is considered a good inventory turnover varies by type of inventory, companies, and industries. For example, grocery stores have a higher inventory turnover than jewelers or furniture stores. Likewise, within a grocery store, perishable foods have a higher turnover than the soaps and cleansers.

Number of Days' Sales in Inventory The **number of days' sales in inventory** is computed as follows:

$$\text{Number of Days' Sales in Inventory} = \frac{\text{Average Inventory}}{\text{Average Daily Cost of Goods Sold}}$$

where

$$\text{Average Daily Cost of Goods Sold} = \frac{\text{Cost of Goods Sold}}{365 \text{ days}}$$

To illustrate, the number of days' sales in inventory for Lincoln Company is computed below.

	2012	2011
Average inventory	$273,500 ($547,000 ÷ 2)	$297,000 ($594,000 ÷ 2)
Average daily cost of goods sold	$2,858 ($1,043,000 ÷ 365)	$2,247 ($820,000 ÷ 365)
Number of days' sales in inventory	95.7 ($273,500 ÷ $2,858)	132.2 ($297,000 ÷ $2,247)

The number of days' sales in inventory is a rough measure of the length of time it takes to purchase, sell, and replace the inventory. Lincoln's number of days' sales in inventory improved from 132.2 days to 95.7 days during 2012. This is a major improvement in managing inventory.

Example Exercise 17-5   Inventory Analysis   **OBJ. 2**

A company reports the following:

Cost of goods sold	$560,000
Average inventory	112,000

Determine (a) the inventory turnover and (b) the number of days' sales in inventory. Round to one decimal place.

Follow My Example 17-5

a. Inventory Turnover = Cost of Goods Sold ÷ Average Inventory
    Inventory Turnover = $560,000 ÷ $112,000
    Inventory Turnover = 5.0

b. Number of Days' Sales in Inventory = Average Inventory ÷ Average Daily Cost of Goods Sold
    Number of Days' Sales in Inventory = $112,000 ÷ ($560,000/365) = $112,000 ÷ $1,534
    Number of Days' Sales in Inventory = 73.0 days

Practice Exercises: **PE 17-5A, PE 17-5B**

Ratio of Fixed Assets to Long-Term Liabilities

The **ratio of fixed assets to long-term liabilities** provides a measure of whether note-holders or bondholders will be paid. Since fixed assets are often pledged as security for long-term notes and bonds, it is computed as follows:

$$\text{Ratio of Fixed Assets to Long-Term Liabilities} = \frac{\text{Fixed Assets (net)}}{\text{Long-Term Liabilities}}$$

To illustrate, the ratio of fixed assets to long-term liabilities for Lincoln Company is computed below.

	2012	2011
Fixed assets (net)	$444,500	$470,000
Long-term liabilities	$100,000	$200,000
Ratio of fixed assets to long-term liabilities	4.4 ($444,500 ÷ $100,000)	2.4 ($470,000 ÷ $200,000)

During 2012, Lincoln's ratio of fixed assets to long-term liabilities increased from 2.4 to 4.4. This increase was due primarily to Lincoln paying off one-half of its long-term liabilities in 2012.

Ratio of Liabilities to Stockholders' Equity

The **ratio of liabilities to stockholders' equity** measures how much of the company is financed by debt and equity. It is computed as follows:

$$\text{Ratio of Liabilities to Stockholders' Equity} = \frac{\text{Total Liabilities}}{\text{Total Stockholders' Equity}}$$

To illustrate, the ratio of liabilities to stockholders' equity for Lincoln Company is computed below.

	2012	2011
Total liabilities	$310,000	$443,000
Total stockholders' equity	$829,500	$787,500
Ratio of liabilities to stockholders' equity	0.4 ($310,000 ÷ $829,500)	0.6 ($443,000 ÷ $787,500)

Lincoln's ratio of liabilities to stockholders' equity decreased from 0.6 to 0.4 during 2012. This is an improvement and indicates that Lincoln's creditors have an adequate margin of safety.

Example Exercise 17-6 Long-Term Solvency Analysis

OBJ.
2

The following information was taken from Acme Company's balance sheet:

Fixed assets (net)	$1,400,000
Long-term liabilities	400,000
Total liabilities	560,000
Total stockholders' equity	1,400,000

Determine the company's (a) ratio of fixed assets to long-term liabilities and (b) ratio of liabilities to total stockholders' equity.

Follow My Example 17-6

a. Ratio of Fixed Assets to Long-Term Liabilities = Fixed Assets ÷ Long-Term Liabilities
   Ratio of Fixed Assets to Long-Term Liabilities = $1,400,000 ÷ $400,000
   Ratio of Fixed Assets to Long-Term Liabilities = 3.5

b. Ratio of Liabilities to Total Stockholders' Equity = Total Liabilities ÷ Total Stockholders' Equity
   Ratio of Liabilities to Total Stockholders' Equity = $560,000 ÷ $1,400,000
   Ratio of Liabilities to Total Stockholders' Equity = 0.4

Practice Exercises: **PE 17-6A, PE 17-6B**

Number of Times Interest Charges Earned

The **number of times interest charges are earned**, sometimes called the *fixed charge coverage ratio*, measures the risk that interest payments will not be made if earnings decrease. It is computed as follows:

$$\text{Number of Times Interest Charges Are Earned} = \frac{\text{Income Before Income Tax} + \text{Interest Expense}}{\text{Interest Expense}}$$

Interest expense is paid before income taxes. In other words, interest expense is deducted in determining taxable income and, thus, income tax. For this reason, income *before taxes* is used in computing the number of times interest charges are earned.

The *higher* the ratio the more likely interest payments will be paid if earnings decrease. To illustrate, the number of times interest charges are earned for Lincoln Company is computed below.

	2012	2011
Income before income tax	$162,500	$134,600
Add interest expense	6,000	12,000
Amount available to pay interest	$168,500	$146,600
Number of times interest charges earned	28.1 ($168,500 ÷ $6,000)	12.2 ($146,600 ÷ $12,000)

The number of times interest charges are earned improved from 12.2 to 28.1 during 2012. This indicates that Lincoln Company has sufficient earnings to pay interest expense.

The number of times interest charges are earned can be adapted for use with dividends on preferred stock. In this case, the *number of times preferred dividends are earned* is computed as follows:

$$\text{Number of Times Preferred Dividends Are Earned} = \frac{\text{Net Income}}{\text{Preferred Dividends}}$$

Since dividends are paid after taxes, net income is used in computing the number of times preferred dividends are earned. The *higher* the ratio, the more likely preferred dividends payments will be paid if earnings decrease.

Example Exercise 17-7   Times Interest Charges Are Earned   OBJ. 2

A company reports the following:

Income before income tax	$250,000
Interest expense	100,000

Determine the number of times interest charges are earned.

Follow My Example 17-7

Number of Times Interest Charges Are Earned = (Income Before Income Tax + Interest Expense) ÷ Interest Expense
Number of Times Interest Charges Are Earned = ($250,000 + $100,000) ÷ $100,000
Number of Times Interest Charges Are Earned = 3.5

Practice Exercises: **PE 17-7A, PE 17-7B**

Profitability Analysis

OBJ. 3   Use financial statement analysis to assess the profitability of a business.

Profitability analysis focuses on the ability of a company to earn profits. This ability is reflected in the company's operating results, as reported in its income statement. The ability to earn profits also depends on the assets the company has available for use in its operations, as reported in its balance sheet. Thus, income statement and balance sheet relationships are often used in evaluating profitability.

Common profitability analyses include the following:

1. Ratio of net sales to assets
2. Rate earned on total assets
3. Rate earned on stockholders' equity
4. Rate earned on common stockholders' equity
5. Earnings per share on common stock
6. Price-earnings ratio
7. Dividends per share
8. Dividend yield

Note:
Profitability analysis focuses on the relationship between operating results and the resources available to a business.

Ratio of Net Sales to Assets

The **ratio of net sales to assets** measures how effectively a company uses its assets. It is computed as follows:

$$\text{Ratio of Net Sales to Assets} = \frac{\text{Net Sales}}{\substack{\text{Average Total Assets} \\ \text{(excluding long-term investments)}}}$$

As shown above, any long-term investments are excluded in computing the ratio of net sales to assets. This is because long-term investments are unrelated to normal operations and net sales.

To illustrate, the ratio of net sales to assets for Lincoln Company is computed below. Total assets (excluding long-term investments) are $1,010,000 at the beginning of 2011.

	2012	2011
Net sales	$1,498,000	$1,200,000
Total assets (excluding long-term investments):		
Beginning of year	$1,053,000*	$1,010,000
End of year	1,044,500**	1,053,000***
Total	$2,097,500	$2,063,000
Average total assets	$1,048,750 ($2,097,500 ÷ 2)	$1,031,500 ($2,063,000 ÷ 2)
Ratio of net sales to assets	1.4 ($1,498,000 ÷ $1,048,750)	1.2 ($1,200,000 ÷ $1,031,500)

  *($1,230,500 − $177,500)
  **($1,139,500 − $95,000)
  ***($1,230,500 − $177,500)

For Lincoln Company, the average total assets was computed using total assets (excluding long-term investments) at the beginning and the end of the year. The average total assets could also be based on monthly or quarterly averages.

The ratio of net sales to assets indicates that Lincoln's use of its operating assets has improved in 2012. This was primarily due to the increase in net sales in 2012.

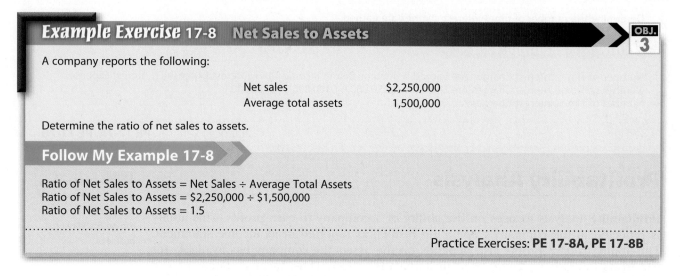

Example Exercise 17-8   Net Sales to Assets

OBJ. 3

A company reports the following:

Net sales	$2,250,000
Average total assets	1,500,000

Determine the ratio of net sales to assets.

Follow My Example 17-8

Ratio of Net Sales to Assets = Net Sales ÷ Average Total Assets
Ratio of Net Sales to Assets = $2,250,000 ÷ $1,500,000
Ratio of Net Sales to Assets = 1.5

Practice Exercises: **PE 17-8A, PE 17-8B**

Rate Earned on Total Assets

The **rate earned on total assets** measures the profitability of total assets, without considering how the assets are financed. In other words, this rate is not affected by the portion of assets financed by creditors or stockholders. It is computed as follows:

$$\text{Rate Earned on Total Assets} = \frac{\text{Net Income} + \text{Interest Expense}}{\text{Average Total Assets}}$$

The rate earned on total assets is computed by adding interest expense to net income. By adding interest expense to net income, the effect of whether the assets are financed by creditors (debt) or stockholders (equity) is eliminated. Because net income includes any income earned from long-term investments, the average total assets includes long-term investments as well as the net operating assets.

To illustrate, the rate earned on total assets by Lincoln Company is computed below. Total assets are $1,187,500 at the beginning of 2011.

	2012	2011
Net income	$ 91,000	$ 76,500
Plus interest expense	6,000	12,000
Total	$ 97,000	$ 88,500
Total assets:		
Beginning of year	$1,230,500	$1,187,500
End of year	1,139,500	1,230,500
Total	$2,370,000	$2,418,000
Average total assets	$1,185,000 ($2,370,000 ÷ 2)	$1,209,000 ($2,418,000 ÷ 2)
Rate earned on total assets	8.2% ($97,000 ÷ $1,185,000)	7.3% ($88,500 ÷ $1,209,000)

The rate earned on total assets improved from 7.3% to 8.2% during 2012.

The *rate earned on operating assets* is sometimes computed when there are large amounts of nonoperating income and expense. It is computed as follows:

$$\text{Rate Earned on Operating Assets} = \frac{\text{Income from Operations}}{\text{Average Operating Assets}}$$

Since Lincoln Company does not have a significant amount of nonoperating income and expense, the rate earned on operating assets is not illustrated.

Example Exercise 17-9 **Rate Earned on Total Assets** **OBJ. 3**

A company reports the following income statement and balance sheet information for the current year:

Net income	$ 125,000
Interest expense	25,000
Average total assets	2,000,000

Determine the rate earned on total assets.

Follow My Example 17-9

Rate Earned on Total Assets = (Net Income + Interest Expense) ÷ Average Total Assets
Rate Earned on Total Assets = ($125,000 + $25,000) ÷ $2,000,000
Rate Earned on Total Assets = $150,000 ÷ $2,000,000
Rate Earned on Total Assets = 7.5%

Practice Exercises: **PE 17-9A, PE 17-9B**

Rate Earned on Stockholders' Equity

The **rate earned on stockholders' equity** measures the rate of income earned on the amount invested by the stockholders. It is computed as follows:

$$\text{Rate Earned on Stockholders' Equity} = \frac{\text{Net Income}}{\text{Average Total Stockholders' Equity}}$$

To illustrate, the rate earned on stockholders' equity for Lincoln Company is computed below. Total stockholders' equity is $750,000 at the beginning of 2011.

	2012	2011
Net income	$ 91,000	$ 76,500
Stockholders' equity:		
Beginning of year	$ 787,500	$ 750,000
End of year	829,500	787,500
Total	$1,617,000	$1,537,500
Average stockholders' equity	$808,500 ($1,617,000 ÷ 2)	$768,750 ($1,537,500 ÷ 2)
Rate earned on stockholders' equity	11.3% ($91,000 ÷ $808,500)	10.0% ($76,500 ÷ $768,750)

The rate earned on stockholders' equity improved from 10.0% to 11.3% during 2012.

Leverage involves using debt to increase the return on an investment. The rate earned on stockholders' equity is normally higher than the rate earned on total assets. This is because of the effect of leverage.

For Lincoln Company, the effect of leverage for 2012 is 3.1% and for 2011 is 2.7% computed as follows:

	2012	2011
Rate earned on stockholders' equity	11.3%	10.0%
Less rate earned on total assets	8.2	7.3
Effect of leverage	3.1%	2.7%

Exhibit 8 shows the 2012 and 2011 effects of leverage for Lincoln Company.

Rate Earned on Common Stockholders' Equity

The **rate earned on common stockholders' equity** measures the rate of profits earned on the amount invested by the common stockholders. It is computed as follows:

$$\text{Rate Earned on Common Stockholders' Equity} = \frac{\text{Net Income} - \text{Preferred Dividends}}{\text{Average Common Stockholders' Equity}}$$

EXHIBIT 8

Effect of
Leverage

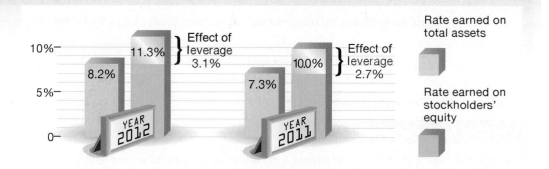

Because preferred stockholders rank ahead of the common stockholders in their claim on earnings, any preferred dividends are subtracted from net income in computing the rate earned on common stockholders' equity.

Lincoln Company had $150,000 of 6% preferred stock outstanding on December 31, 2012 and 2011. Thus, preferred dividends of $9,000 ($150,000 × 6%) are deducted from net income. Lincoln's common stockholders' equity is determined as follows:

	December 31		
	2012	**2011**	**2010**
Common stock, $10 par	$500,000	$500,000	$500,000
Retained earnings	179,500	137,500	100,000
Common stockholders' equity	$679,500	$637,500	$600,000

The retained earnings on December 31, 2010, of $100,000 is the same as the retained earnings on January 1, 2011, as shown in Lincoln's retained earnings statement in Exhibit 4.

Using this information, the rate earned on common stockholders' equity for Lincoln Company is computed below.

	2012	**2011**
Net income	$ 91,000	$ 76,500
Less preferred dividends	9,000	9,000
Total	$ 82,000	$ 67,500
Common stockholders' equity:		
Beginning of year	$ 637,500	$ 600,000
End of year	679,500*	637,500**
Total	$1,317,000	$1,237,500
Average common stockholders' equity	$ 658,500 ($1,317,000 ÷ 2)	$618,750 ($1,237,500 ÷ 2)
Rate earned on common stockholders' equity	12.5% ($82,000 ÷ $658,500)	10.9% ($67,500 ÷ $618,750)

*($829,500 – $150,000)
**($787,500 – $150,000)

Lincoln Company's rate earned on common stockholders' equity improved from 10.9% to 12.5% in 2012. This rate differs from the rates earned by Lincoln Company on total assets and stockholders' equity as shown below.

	2012	2011
Rate earned on total assets	8.2%	7.3%
Rate earned on stockholders' equity	11.3%	10.0%
Rate earned on common stockholders' equity	12.5%	10.9%

These rates differ because of leverage, as discussed in the preceding section.

Example Exercise 17-10 **Common Stockholders' Profitability Analysis** **OBJ. 3**

A company reports the following:

Net income	$ 125,000
Preferred dividends	5,000
Average stockholders' equity	1,000,000
Average common stockholders' equity	800,000

Determine (a) the rate earned on stockholders' equity and (b) the rate earned on common stockholders' equity.

Follow My Example 17-10

Rate Earned on Stockholders' Equity = Net Income ÷ Average Stockholders' Equity
Rate Earned on Stockholders' Equity = $125,000 ÷ $1,000,000
Rate Earned on Stockholders' Equity = 12.5%

Rate Earned on Common Stockholders' Equity = (Net Income – Preferred Dividends) ÷ Average
Common Stockholders' Equity
Rate Earned on Common Stockholders' Equity = ($125,000 – $5,000) ÷ $800,000
Rate Earned on Common Stockholders' Equity = 15%

Practice Exercises: **PE 17-10A, PE 17-10B**

Earnings per Share on Common Stock

Earnings per share (EPS) on common stock measures the share of profits that are earned by a share of common stock. Earnings per share must be reported in the income statement. As a result, earnings per share (EPS) is often reported in the financial press. It is computed as follows:

$$\text{Earnings per Share (EPS) on Common Stock} = \frac{\text{Net Income} - \text{Preferred Dividends}}{\text{Shares of Common Stock Outstanding}}$$

When preferred and common stock are outstanding, preferred dividends are subtracted from net income to determine the income related to the common shares.

To illustrate, the earnings per share (EPS) of common stock for Lincoln Company is computed below.

	2012	2011
Net income	$91,000	$76,500
Preferred dividends	9,000	9,000
Total	$82,000	$67,500
Shares of common stock outstanding	50,000	50,000
Earnings per share on common stock	$1.64 ($82,000 ÷ 50,000)	$1.35 ($67,500 ÷ 50,000)

Lincoln Company had $150,000 of 6% preferred stock outstanding on December 31, 2012 and 2011. Thus, preferred dividends of $9,000 ($150,000 × 6%) are deducted from net income in computing earnings per share on common stock.

Lincoln did not issue any additional shares of common stock in 2012. If Lincoln had issued additional shares in 2012, a weighted average of common shares outstanding during the year would have been used.

Lincoln's earnings per share (EPS) on common stock improved from $1.35 to $1.64 during 2012.

Lincoln Company has a simple capital structure with only common stock and preferred stock outstanding. Many corporations, however, have complex capital structures with various types of equity securities outstanding, such as convertible preferred stock,

stock options, and stock warrants. In such cases, the possible effects of such securities on the shares of common stock outstanding are considered in reporting earnings per share. These possible effects are reported separately as *earnings per common share assuming dilution* or *diluted earnings per share*. This topic is described and illustrated in advanced accounting courses and textbooks.

Price-Earnings Ratio

The **price-earnings (P/E) ratio** on common stock measures a company's future earnings prospects. It is often quoted in the financial press and is computed as follows:

$$\text{Price-Earnings (P/E) Ratio} = \frac{\text{Market Price per Share of Common Stock}}{\text{Earnings per Share on Common Stock}}$$

To illustrate, the price-earnings (P/E) ratio for Lincoln Company is computed below.

	2012	2011
Market price per share of common stock	$41.00	$27.00
Earnings per share on common stock	$1.64	$1.35
Price-earnings ratio on common stock	25 ($41 ÷ $1.64)	20 ($27 ÷ $1.35)

The price-earnings ratio improved from 20 to 25 during 2012. In other words, a share of common stock of Lincoln Company was selling for 20 times earnings per share at the end of 2011. At the end of 2012, the common stock was selling for 25 times earnings per share. This indicates that the market expects Lincoln to experience favorable earnings in the future.

Example Exercise 17-11   Earnings per Share and Price-Earnings Ratio   OBJ. 3

A company reports the following:

Net income	$250,000
Preferred dividends	$15,000
Shares of common stock outstanding	20,000
Market price per share of common stock	$35.00

a. Determine the company's earnings per share on common stock.
b. Determine the company's price-earnings ratio. Round to one decimal place.

Follow My Example 17-11

a. Earnings per Share on Common Stock = (Net Income – Preferred Dividends) ÷ Shares of Common Stock Outstanding
   Earnings per Share = ($250,000 – $15,000) ÷ 20,000
   Earnings per Share = $11.75

b. Price-Earnings Ratio = Market Price per Share of Common Stock ÷ Earnings per Share on Common Stock
   Price-Earnings Ratio = $35.00 ÷ $11.75
   Price-Earnings Ratio = 3.0

Practice Exercises: **PE 17-11A, PE 17-11B**

Dividends per Share

Dividends per share measures the extent to which earnings are being distributed to common shareholders. It is computed as follows:

$$\text{Dividends per Share} = \frac{\text{Dividends on Common Stock}}{\text{Shares of Common Stock Outstanding}}$$

To illustrate, the dividends per share for Lincoln Company are computed below.

	2012	2011
Dividends on common stock	$40,000	$30,000
Shares of common stock outstanding	50,000	50,000
Dividends per share of common stock	$0.80 ($40,000 ÷ 50,000)	$0.60 ($30,000 ÷ 50,000)

The dividends per share of common stock increased from $0.60 to $0.80 during 2012.

Dividends per share are often reported with earnings per share. Comparing the two per-share amounts indicates the extent to which earnings are being retained for use in operations. To illustrate, the dividends and earnings per share for Lincoln Company are shown in Exhibit 9.

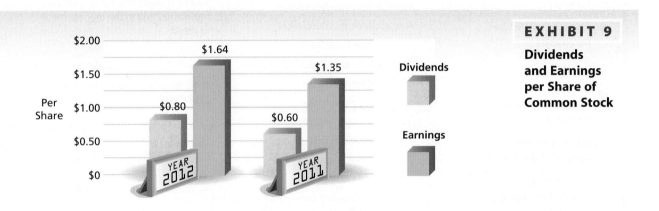

Dividend Yield

The **dividend yield** on common stock measures the rate of return to common stockholders from cash dividends. It is of special interest to investors whose objective is to earn revenue (dividends) from their investment. It is computed as follows:

$$\text{Dividend Yield} = \frac{\text{Dividends per Share of Common Stock}}{\text{Market Price per Share of Common Stock}}$$

To illustrate, the dividend yield for Lincoln Company is computed below.

	2012	2011
Dividends per share of common stock	$0.80	$0.60
Market price per share of common stock	$41.00	$27.00
Dividend yield on common stock	2.0% ($0.80 ÷ $41)	2.2% ($0.60 ÷ $27)

The dividends per share, dividend yield, and P/E ratio of a common stock are normally quoted on the daily listing of stock prices in *The Wall Street Journal* and on Yahoo!'s finance Web site.

The dividend yield declined slightly from 2.2% to 2.0% in 2012. This decline was primarily due to the increase in the market price of Lincoln's common stock.

Summary of Analytical Measures

Exhibit 10 shows a summary of the solvency and profitability measures discussed in this chapter. The type of industry and the company's operations usually affect which measures are used. In many cases, additional measures are used for a specific industry. For example, airlines use *revenue per passenger mile* and *cost per available seat* as profitability measures. Likewise, hotels use *occupancy rates* as a profitability measure.

The analytical measures shown in Exhibit 10 are a useful starting point for analyzing a company's solvency and profitability. However, they are not a substitute for sound judgment. For example, the general economic and business environment should always be considered in analyzing a company's future prospects. In addition, any trends and interrelationships among the measures should be carefully studied.

EXHIBIT 10   Summary of Analytical Measures

Solvency measures:	Method of Computation	Use
Working Capital	Current Assets – Current Liabilities	To indicate the ability to meet currently maturing obligations
Current Ratio	$\dfrac{\text{Current Assets}}{\text{Current Liabilities}}$	
Quick Ratio	$\dfrac{\text{Quick Assets}}{\text{Current Liabilities}}$	To indicate instant debt-paying ability
Accounts Receivable Turnover	$\dfrac{\text{Net Sales}}{\text{Average Accounts Receivable}}$	To assess the efficiency in collecting receivables and in the management of credit
Numbers of Days' Sales in Receivables	$\dfrac{\text{Average Accounts Receivable}}{\text{Average Daily Sales}}$	
Inventory Turnover	$\dfrac{\text{Cost of Goods Sold}}{\text{Average Inventory}}$	To assess the efficiency in the management of inventory
Number of Days' Sales in Inventory	$\dfrac{\text{Average Inventory}}{\text{Average Daily Cost of Goods Sold}}$	
Ratio of Fixed Assets to Long-Term Liabilities	$\dfrac{\text{Fixed Assets (net)}}{\text{Long-Term Liabilities}}$	To indicate the margin of safety to long-term creditors
Ratio of Liabilities to Stockholders' Equity	$\dfrac{\text{Total Liabilities}}{\text{Total Stockholders' Equity}}$	To indicate the margin of safety to creditors
Number of Times Interest Charges Are Earned	$\dfrac{\text{Income Before Income Tax} + \text{Interest Expense}}{\text{Interest Expense}}$	To assess the risk to debtholders in terms of number of times interest charges were earned
Profitability measures:		
Ratio of Net Sales to Assets	$\dfrac{\text{Net Sales}}{\text{Average Total Assets (excluding long-term investments)}}$	To assess the effectiveness in the use of assets
Rate Earned on Total Assets	$\dfrac{\text{Net Income} + \text{Interest Expense}}{\text{Average Total Assets}}$	To assess the profitability of the assets
Rate Earned on Stockholders' Equity	$\dfrac{\text{Net Income}}{\text{Average Total Stockholders' Equity}}$	To assess the profitability of the investment by stockholders
Rate Earned on Common Stockholders' Equity	$\dfrac{\text{Net Income} - \text{Preferred Dividends}}{\text{Average Common Stockholders' Equity}}$	To assess the profitability of the investment by common stockholders
Earnings per Share (EPS) on Common Stock	$\dfrac{\text{Net Income} - \text{Preferred Dividends}}{\text{Shares of Common Stock Outstanding}}$	
Price-Earnings (P/E) Ratio	$\dfrac{\text{Market Price per Share of Common Stock}}{\text{Earnings per Share on Common Stock}}$	To indicate future earnings prospects, based on the relationship between market value of common stock and earnings
Dividends per Share	$\dfrac{\text{Dividends on Common Stock}}{\text{Shares of Common Stock Outstanding}}$	To indicate the extent to which earnings are being distributed to common stockholders
Dividend Yield	$\dfrac{\text{Dividends per Share of Common Stock}}{\text{Market Price per Share of Common Stock}}$	To indicate the rate of return to common stockholders in terms of dividends

Integrity, Objectivity, and Ethics in Business

CHIEF FINANCIAL OFFICER BONUSES

A recent study by compensation experts at Temple University found that chief financial officer salaries are correlated with the complexity of a company's operations, but chief financial officer bonuses are correlated with the company's ability to meet analysts' earnings forecasts. These results suggest that financial bonuses may provide chief financial officers with an incentive to use questionable accounting practices to improve earnings. While the study doesn't conclude that bonuses lead to accounting fraud, it does suggest that bonuses give chief financial officers a reason to find ways to use accounting to increase apparent earnings.

Source: E. Jelesiewicz, "Today's CFO: More Challenge but Higher Compensation," *News Communications* (Temple University, August 2009).

Corporate Annual Reports

OBJ. 4 Describe the contents of corporate annual reports.

Public corporations issue annual reports summarizing their operating activities for the past year and plans for the future. Such annual reports include the financial statements and the accompanying notes. In addition, annual reports normally include the following sections:

See Appendix D for more information

- Management discussion and analysis
- Report on internal control
- Report on fairness of the financial statements

Management Discussion and Analysis

Management's Discussion and Analysis (MD&A) is required in annual reports filed with the Securities and Exchange Commission. It includes management's analysis of current operations and its plans for the future. Typical items included in the MD&A are as follows:

- Management's analysis and explanations of any significant changes between the current and prior years' financial statements.
- Important accounting principles or policies that could affect interpretation of the financial statements, including the effect of changes in accounting principles or the adoption of new accounting principles.
- Management's assessment of the company's liquidity and the availability of capital to the company.
- Significant risk exposures that might affect the company.
- Any "off-balance-sheet" arrangements such as leases not included directly in the financial statements. Such arrangements are discussed in advanced accounting courses and textbooks.

Report on Internal Control

The Sarbanes-Oxley Act of 2002 requires a report on internal control by management. The report states management's responsibility for establishing and maintaining internal control. In addition, management's assessment of the effectiveness of internal controls over financial reporting is included in the report.

Sarbanes-Oxley also requires a public accounting firm to verify management's conclusions on internal control. Thus, two reports on internal control, one by management and one by a public accounting firm, are included in the annual report. In some situations, these may be combined into a single report on internal control.

Report on Fairness of the Financial Statements

All publicly held corporations are required to have an independent audit (examination) of their financial statements. The Certified Public Accounting (CPA) firm that conducts the audit renders an opinion, called the *Report of Independent Registered Public Accounting Firm*, on the fairness of the statements.

An opinion stating that the financial statements present fairly the financial position, results of operations, and cash flows of the company is said to be an *unqualified opinion*, sometimes called a *clean opinion*. Any report other than an unqualified opinion raises a "red flag" for financial statement users and requires further investigation as to its cause.

The annual report of Nike Inc. is shown in Appendix C. The Nike report includes the financial statements as well as the MD&A Report on Internal Control, and Report on Fairness of the Financial Statements.

Integrity, Objectivity, and Ethics in Business

BUY LOW, SELL HIGH

Research analysts work for banks, brokerages, or other financial institutions. Their job is to estimate the value of a company's common stock by reviewing and evaluating the company's business model, strategic plan, and financial performance. Based on this analysis, the analyst develops an estimate of a stock's value, which is called its *fundamental value*. Analysts then advise their clients to "buy" or "sell" a company's stock based on the following guidelines:

Current market price is greater than
   fundamental value   Sell
Current market price is lower than
   fundamental value   Buy

If analysts are doing their job well, their clients will enjoy large returns by buying stocks at low prices and selling them at high prices.

A P P E N D I X

Unusual Items on the Income Statement

Generally accepted accounting principles require that unusual items be reported separately on the income statement. This is because such items do not occur frequently and are typically unrelated to current operations. Without separate reporting of these items, users of the financial statements might be misled about current and future operations.

Unusual items on the income statement are classified as one of the following:

1. Affecting the *current period* income statement
2. Affecting a *prior period* income statement

Unusual Items Affecting the Current Period's Income Statement

Unusual items affecting the current period's income statement include the following:

1. Discontinued operations
2. Extraordinary items

These items are reported separately on the income statement for any period in which they occur.

Discontinued Operations A company may discontinue a segment of its operations by selling or abandoning the segment's operations. For example, a retailer might decide to sell its product only online and, thus, discontinue selling its merchandise at its retail outlets (stores).

Any gain or loss on discontinued operations is reported on the income statement as a *Gain (or loss) from discontinued operations*. It is reported immediately following *Income from continuing operations*.

To illustrate, assume that Jones Corporation produces and sells electrical products, hardware supplies, and lawn equipment. Because of lack of profits, Jones discontinues its electrical products operation and sells the remaining inventory and other assets at a loss of $100,000. Exhibit 11 illustrates the reporting of the loss on discontinued operations.[3]

EXHIBIT 11

Unusual Items in the Income Statement

Jones Corporation Income Statement For the Year Ended December 31, 2012	
Net sales..	$12,350,000
Cost of merchandise sold	5,800,000
Gross profit..	$ 6,550,000
Selling and administrative expenses.................................	5,240,000
Income from continuing operations before income tax.............	$ 1,310,000
Income tax expense	620,000
Income from continuing operations	$ 690,000
Loss on discontinued operations	100,000
Income before extraordinary items	$ 590,000
Extraordinary items:	
Gain on condemnation of land	150,000
Net income..	$ 740,000

In addition, a note accompanying the income statement should describe the operations sold including such details as the date operations were discontinued, the assets sold, and the effect (if any) on current and future operations.

Extraordinary Items An **extraordinary item** is defined as an event or a transaction that has both of the following characteristics:

1. Unusual in nature
2. Infrequent in occurrence

Gains and losses from natural disasters such as floods, earthquakes, and fires are normally reported as extraordinary items, provided that they occur infrequently. Gains or losses from land or buildings taken (condemned) for public use are also reported as extraordinary items.

Any gain or loss from extraordinary items is reported on the income statement as *Gain (or loss) from extraordinary item.* It is reported immediately following *Income from continuing operations* and any *Gain (or loss) on discontinued operations.*

To illustrate, assume that land owned by Jones Corporation was taken for public use (condemned) by the local government. The condemnation of the land resulted in a gain of $150,000. Exhibit 11 illustrates the reporting of the extraordinary gain.[4]

Reporting Earnings per Share Earnings per common share should be reported separately for discontinued operations and extraordinary items. To illustrate, a partial income statement for Jones Corporation is shown in Exhibit 12.

Exhibit 12 reports earnings per common share for income from continuing operations, discontinued operations, and extraordinary items. However, only earnings per share for income from continuing operations and net income are required by generally accepted accounting principles. The other per-share amounts may be presented in the notes to the financial statements.

3 The gain or loss on discontinued operations is reported net of any tax effects. To simplify, the tax effects are not specifically identified in Exhibit 11.

4 The gain or loss on extraordinary operations is reported net of any tax effects.

EXHIBIT 12

Income Statement with Earnings per Share

Jones Corporation Income Statement For the Year Ended December 31, 2012	
Earnings per common share:	
Income from continuing operations...	$3.45
Loss on discontinued operations	0.50
Income before extraordinary items	$2.95
Extraordinary items:	
Gain on condemnation of land	0.75
Net income	$3.70

Unusual Items Affecting the Prior Period's Income Statement

An unusual item may occur that affects a prior period's income statement. Two such items are as follows:

1. Errors in applying generally accepted accounting principles
2. Changes from one generally accepted accounting principle to another

If an error is discovered in a prior period's financial statement, the prior-period statement and all following statements are restated and thus corrected.

A company may change from one generally accepted accounting principle to another. In this case, the prior-period financial statements are restated as if the new accounting principle had always been used.[5]

For both of the preceding items, the current-period earnings are not affected. That is, only the earnings reported in prior periods are restated. However, because the prior earnings are restated, the beginning balance of Retained Earnings may also have to be restated. This, in turn, may cause the restatement of other balance sheet accounts. Illustrations of these types of adjustments and restatements are provided in advanced accounting courses.

---

5 Changes from one acceptable depreciation method to another acceptable depreciation method are an exception to this general rule and are to be treated prospectively as a change in estimate, as discussed in Chapter 10.

At a Glance 17

OBJ. 1

Describe basic financial statement analytical methods.

Key Points   The basic financial statements provide much of the information users need to make economic decisions. Analytical procedures are used to compare items on a current financial statement with related items on earlier statements, or to examine relationships within a financial statement.

Learning Outcomes	Example Exercises	Practice Exercises
• Prepare a vertical analysis from a company's financial statements.	EE17-1	PE17-1A, 17-1B
• Prepare a horizontal analysis from a company's financial statements.	EE17-2	PE17-2A, 17-2B
• Prepare common-sized financial statements.		

Key Points   All users of financial statements are interested in the ability of a business to pay its debts (solvency) and earn income (profitability). Solvency and profitability are interrelated. Solvency analysis is normally assessed by examining the following: current position analysis, accounts receivable analysis, inventory analysis, the ratio of fixed assets to long-term liabilities, the ratio of liabilities to stockholders' equity, and the number of times interest charges are earned.

Learning Outcomes	Example Exercises	Practice Exercises
• Determine working capital.		
• Compute and interpret the current ratio.	EE17-3	PE17-3A, 17-3B
• Compute and interpret the quick ratio.	EE17-3	PE17-3A, 17-3B
• Compute and interpret accounts receivable turnover.	EE17-4	PE17-4A, 17-4B
• Compute and interpret number of days' sales in receivables.	EE17-4	PE17-4A, 17-4B
• Compute and interpret inventory turnover.	EE17-5	PE17-5A, 17-5B
• Compute and interpret number of days' sales in inventory.	EE17-5	PE17-5A, 17-5B
• Compute and interpret the ratio of fixed assets to long-term liabilities.	EE17-6	PE17-6A, 17-6B
• Compute and interpret the ratio of liabilities to stockholders' equity.	EE17-6	PE17-6A, 17-6B
• Compute and interpret the number of times interest charges are earned.	EE17-7	PE17-7A, 17-7B

OBJ.
3   Use financial statement analysis to assess the profitability of a business.

Key Points   Profitability analysis focuses on the ability of a company to earn profits. This ability is reflected in the company's operating results as reported on the income statement and resources available as reported on the balance sheet. Major analyses include the ratio of net sales to assets, the rate earned on total assets, the rate earned on stockholders' equity, the rate earned on common stockholders' equity, earnings per share on common stock, the price-earnings ratio, dividends per share, and dividend yield.

Learning Outcomes	Example Exercises	Practice Exercises
• Compute and interpret the ratio of net sales to assets.	EE17-8	PE17-8A, 17-8B
• Compute and interpret the rate earned on total assets.	EE17-9	PE17-9A, 17-9B
• Compute and interpret the rate earned on stockholders' equity.	EE17-10	PE17-10A, 17-10B
• Compute and interpret the rate earned on common stockholders' equity.	EE17-10	PE17-10A, 17-10B
• Compute and interpret the earnings per share on common stock.	EE17-11	PE17-11A, 17-11B
• Compute and interpret the price-earnings ratio.	EE17-11	PE17-11A, 17-11B
• Compute and interpret the dividends per share and dividend yield.		
• Describe the uses and limitations of analytical measures.		

OBJ.
4   Describe the contents of corporate annual reports.

Key Points   Corporations normally issue annual reports to their stockholders and other interested parties. Such reports summarize the corporation's operating activities for the past year and plans for the future.

Learning Outcomes	Example Exercises	Practice Exercises
• Describe the elements of a corporate annual report.		

Key Terms

accounts receivable
  analysis (782)

accounts receivable turnover (782)

common-sized statement (778)

current position analysis (780)

current ratio (780)

dividend yield (793)

dividends per share (792)

earnings per share (EPS)
  on common stock (791)

extraordinary item (797)

horizontal analysis (774)

inventory analysis (783)

inventory turnover (784)

Management's Discussion and
  Analysis (MD&A) (795)

number of days' sales in
  inventory (784)

number of days' sales in
  receivables (783)

number of times interest
  charges are earned (786)

price-earnings (P/E) ratio (792)

profitability (779)

quick assets (781)

quick ratio (781)

rate earned on common
  stockholders' equity (789)

rate earned on stockholders'
  equity (789)

rate earned on total assets (788)

ratio of fixed assets to long-term
  liabilities (785)

ratio of liabilities to
  stockholders' equity (785)

ratio of net sales to assets (787)

solvency (779)

vertical analysis (777)

working capital (780)

Illustrative Problem

Rainbow Paint Co.'s comparative financial statements for the years ending December 31, 2012 and 2011, are as follows. The market price of Rainbow Paint Co.'s common stock was $25 on December 31, 2012, and $30 on December 31, 2011.

Rainbow Paint Co.
Comparative Income Statement
For the Years Ended December 31, 2012 and 2011

	2012	2011
Sales	$5,125,000	$3,257,600
Sales returns and allowances	125,000	57,600
Net sales	$5,000,000	$3,200,000
Cost of goods sold	3,400,000	2,080,000
Gross profit	$1,600,000	$1,120,000
Selling expenses	$ 650,000	$ 464,000
Administrative expenses	325,000	224,000
Total operating expenses	$ 975,000	$ 688,000
Income from operations	$ 625,000	$ 432,000
Other income	25,000	19,200
	$ 650,000	$ 451,200
Other expense (interest)	105,000	64,000
Income before income tax	$ 545,000	$ 387,200
Income tax expense	300,000	176,000
Net income	$ 245,000	$ 211,200

Rainbow Paint Co.
Comparative Retained Earnings Statement
For the Years Ended December 31, 2012 and 2011

	2012	2011
Retained earnings, January 1	$723,000	$581,800
Add net income for year	245,000	211,200
Total	$968,000	$793,000
Deduct dividends:		
On preferred stock	$ 40,000	$ 40,000
On common stock	45,000	30,000
Total	$ 85,000	$ 70,000
Retained earnings, December 31	$883,000	$723,000

Rainbow Paint Co.
Comparative Balance Sheet
December 31, 2012 and 2011

	Dec. 31, 2012	Dec. 31, 2011
Assets		
Current assets:		
Cash	$ 175,000	$ 125,000
Temporary investments	150,000	50,000
Accounts receivable (net)	425,000	325,000
Inventories	720,000	480,000
Prepaid expenses	30,000	20,000
Total current assets	$1,500,000	$1,000,000
Long-term investments	250,000	225,000
Property, plant, and equipment (net)	2,093,000	1,948,000
Total assets	$3,843,000	$3,173,000
Liabilities		
Current liabilities	$ 750,000	$ 650,000
Long-term liabilities:		
Mortgage note payable, 10%, due 2015	$ 410,000	—
Bonds payable, 8%, due 2018	800,000	$ 800,000
Total long-term liabilities	$1,210,000	$ 800,000
Total liabilities	$1,960,000	$1,450,000
Stockholders' Equity		
Preferred 8% stock, $100 par	$ 500,000	$ 500,000
Common stock, $10 par	500,000	500,000
Retained earnings	883,000	723,000
Total stockholders' equity	$1,883,000	$1,723,000
Total liabilities and stockholders' equity	$3,843,000	$3,173,000

Instructions

Determine the following measures for 2012:

1. Working capital

2. Current ratio

3. Quick ratio

4. Accounts receivable turnover

5. Number of days' sales in receivables

6. Inventory turnover

7. Number of days' sales in inventory

8. Ratio of fixed assets to long-term liabilities

9. Ratio of liabilities to stockholders' equity

10. Number of times interest charges are earned

11. Number of times preferred dividends earned

12. Ratio of net sales to assets

13. Rate earned on total assets

14. Rate earned on stockholders' equity

15. Rate earned on common stockholders' equity

16. Earnings per share on common stock

17. Price-earnings ratio

18. Dividends per share

19. Dividend yield

Solution

(Ratios are rounded to the nearest single digit after the decimal point.)

1. Working capital: $750,000
   $1,500,000 − $750,000

2. Current ratio: 2.0
   $1,500,000 ÷ $750,000

3. Quick ratio: 1.0
   $750,000 ÷ $750,000

4. Accounts receivable turnover: 13.3
   $5,000,000 ÷ [($425,000 + $325,000) ÷ 2]

5. Number of days' sales in receivables: 27.4 days
   $5,000,000 ÷ 365 days = $13,699
   $375,000 ÷ $13,699

6. Inventory turnover: 5.7
   $3,400,000 ÷ [($720,000 + $480,000) ÷ 2]

7. Number of days' sales in inventory: 64.4 days
   $3,400,000 ÷ 365 days = $9,315
   $600,000 ÷ $9,315

8. Ratio of fixed assets to long-term liabilities: 1.7
   $2,093,000 ÷ $1,210,000

9. Ratio of liabilities to stockholders' equity: 1.0
   $1,960,000 ÷ $1,883,000

10. Number of times interest charges are earned: 6.2
    ($545,000 + $105,000) ÷ $105,000

11. Number of times preferred dividends earned: 6.1
    $245,000 ÷ $40,000

12. Ratio of net sales to assets: 1.5
    $5,000,000 ÷ [($3,593,000 + $2,948,000) ÷ 2]

13. Rate earned on total assets: 10.0%
    ($245,000 + $105,000) ÷ [($3,843,000 + $3,173,000) ÷ 2]

14. Rate earned on stockholders' equity: 13.6%
    $245,000 ÷ [($1,883,000 + $1,723,000) ÷ 2]

15. Rate earned on common stockholders' equity: 15.7%
    ($245,000 − $40,000) ÷ [($1,383,000 + $1,223,000) ÷ 2]

16. Earnings per share on common stock: $4.10
($245,000 − $40,000) ÷ 50,000 shares

17. Price-earnings ratio: 6.1
$25 ÷ $4.10

18. Dividends per share: $0.90
$45,000 ÷ 50,000 shares

19. Dividend yield: 3.6%
$0.90 ÷ $25

Discussion Questions

1. What is the difference between horizontal and vertical analysis of financial statements?

2. What is the advantage of using comparative statements for financial analysis rather than statements for a single date or period?

3. The current year's amount of net income (after income tax) is 20% larger than that of the preceding year. Does this indicate an improved operating performance? Discuss.

4. How would the current and quick ratios of a service business compare?

5. a. Why is it advantageous to have a high inventory turnover?
   b. Is it possible for the inventory turnover to be too high? Discuss.
   c. Is it possible to have a high inventory turnover and a high number of days' sales in inventory? Discuss.

6. What do the following data taken from a comparative balance sheet indicate about the company's ability to borrow additional funds on a long-term basis in the current year as compared to the preceding year?

	Current Year	Preceding Year
Fixed assets (net)	$600,000	$720,000
Total long-term liabilities	120,000	180,000

7. a. How does the rate earned on total assets differ from the rate earned on stockholders' equity?
   b. Which ratio is normally higher? Explain.

8. a. Why is the rate earned on stockholders' equity by a thriving business ordinarily higher than the rate earned on total assets?
   b. Should the rate earned on common stockholders' equity normally be higher or lower than the rate earned on total stockholders' equity? Explain.

9. The net income (after income tax) of McCants Inc. was $40 per common share in the latest year and $100 per common share for the preceding year. At the beginning of the latest year, the number of shares outstanding was doubled by a stock split. There were no other changes in the amount of stock outstanding. What were the earnings per share in the preceding year, adjusted for comparison with the latest year?

10. Describe two reports provided by independent auditors in the annual report to shareholders.

Practice Exercises

OBJ. 1   EE 17-1 *p. 777*

PE 17-1A   Horizontal analysis

The comparative accounts payable and long-term debt balances of a company are provided below.

	2012	2011
Accounts payable	$114,000	$100,000
Long-term debt	143,000	130,000

Based on this information, what is the amount and percentage of increase or decrease that would be shown in a balance sheet with horizontal analysis?

OBJ. 1   EE 17-1 *p. 777*

PE 17-1B   Horizontal analysis

The comparative temporary investments and inventory balances for a company are provided below.

	2012	2011
Temporary investments	$218,400	$240,000
Inventory	269,800	284,000

Based on this information, what is the amount and percentage of increase or decrease that would be shown in a balance sheet with horizontal analysis?

OBJ. 1   EE 17-2 *p. 778*

PE 17-2A   Vertical analysis

Income statement information for Battus Corporation is provided below.

Sales	$680,000
Gross profit	231,200
Net income	74,800

Prepare a vertical analysis of the income statement for Battus Corporation.

OBJ. 1   EE 17-2 *p. 778*

PE 17-2B   Vertical analysis

Income statement information for Canace Corporation is provided below.

Sales	$1,400,000
Cost of goods sold	910,000
Gross profit	490,000

Prepare a vertical analysis of the income statement for Canace Corporation.

OBJ. 2   EE 17-3 *p. 782*

PE 17-3A   Current position analysis

The following items are reported on a company's balance sheet:

Cash	$200,000
Temporary investments	100,000
Accounts receivable (net)	60,000
Inventory	100,000
Accounts payable	200,000

Determine (a) the current ratio and (b) the quick ratio. Round to one decimal place.

PE 17-3B   Current position analysis

The following items are reported on a company's balance sheet:

Cash	$250,000
Temporary investments	180,000
Accounts receivable (net)	220,000
Inventory	200,000
Accounts payable	500,000

Determine (a) the current ratio and (b) the quick ratio. Round to one decimal place.

PE 17-4A   Accounts receivable analysis

A company reports the following:

Net sales	$1,600,000
Average accounts receivable (net)	100,000

Determine (a) the accounts receivable turnover and (b) the number of days' sales in receivables. Round to one decimal place.

PE 17-4B   Accounts receivable analysis

A company reports the following:

Net sales	$700,000
Average accounts receivable (net)	50,000

Determine (a) the accounts receivable turnover and (b) the number of days' sales in receivables. Round to one decimal place.

PE 17-5A   Inventory analysis

A company reports the following:

Cost of goods sold	$880,000
Average inventory	110,000

Determine (a) the inventory turnover and (b) the number of days' sales in inventory. Round to one decimal place.

PE 17-5B   Inventory analysis

A company reports the following:

Cost of goods sold	$360,000
Average inventory	50,000

Determine (a) the inventory turnover and (b) the number of days' sales in inventory. Round to one decimal place.

PE 17-6A   Long-term solvency analysis

The following information was taken from Wheat Company's balance sheet:

Fixed assets (net)	$836,000
Long-term liabilities	380,000
Total liabilities	550,000
Total stockholders' equity	500,000

Determine the company's (a) ratio of fixed assets to long-term liabilities and (b) ratio of liabilities to stockholders' equity.

PE 17-6B   Long-term solvency analysis

The following information was taken from Chaff Company's balance sheet:

Fixed assets (net)	$1,000,000
Long-term liabilities	625,000
Total liabilities	840,000
Total stockholders' equity	600,000

Determine the company's (a) ratio of fixed assets to long-term liabilities and (b) ratio of liabilities to stockholders' equity.

PE 17-7A   Times interest charges are earned

A company reports the following:

Income before income tax	$4,000,000
Interest expense	500,000

Determine the number of times interest charges are earned.

PE 17-7B   Times interest charges are earned

A company reports the following:

Income before income tax	$10,000,000
Interest expense	800,000

Determine the number of times interest charges are earned.

PE 17-8A   Net sales to assets

A company reports the following:

Net sales	$1,200,000
Average total assets	750,000

Determine the ratio of net sales to assets.

PE 17-8B   Net sales to assets

A company reports the following:

Net sales	$3,500,000
Average total assets	2,500,000

Determine the ratio of net sales to assets.

PE 17-9A   Rate earned on total assets

A company reports the following income statement and balance sheet information for the current year:

Net income	$ 820,000
Interest expense	80,000
Average total assets	5,000,000

Determine the rate earned on total assets.

PE 17-9B   Rate earned on total assets

A company reports the following income statement and balance sheet information for the current year:

Net income	$ 700,000
Interest expense	50,000
Average total assets	4,687,500

Determine the rate earned on total assets.

Learning Objectives	Example Exercises	
OBJ. 3	EE 17-10 *p. 791*	

PE 17-10A   Common stockholders' profitability analysis

A company reports the following:

Net income	$ 210,000
Preferred dividends	30,000
Average stockholders' equity	1,750,000
Average common stockholders' equity	1,000,000

Determine (a) the rate earned on stockholders' equity and (b) the rate earned on common stockholders' equity. Round to one decimal place.

OBJ. 3   EE 17-10 *p. 791*

PE 17-10B   Common stockholders' profitability analysis

A company reports the following:

Net income	$ 600,000
Preferred dividends	50,000
Average stockholders' equity	6,000,000
Average common stockholders' equity	5,000,000

Determine (a) the rate earned on stockholders' equity and (b) the rate earned on common stockholders' equity. Round to one decimal place.

OBJ. 3   EE 17-11 *p. 792*

PE 17-11A   Earnings per share and price-earnings

A company reports the following:

Net income	$440,000
Preferred dividends	$40,000
Shares of common stock outstanding	50,000
Market price per share of common stock	$100

a. Determine the company's earnings per share on common stock.

b. Determine the company's price-earnings ratio.

OBJ. 3   EE 17-11 *p. 792*

PE 17-11B   Earnings per share and price-earnings

A company reports the following:

Net income	$650,000
Preferred dividends	$50,000
Shares of common stock outstanding	120,000
Market price per share of common stock	$75

a. Determine the company's earnings per share on common stock.

b. Determine the company's price-earnings ratio.

Exercises

OBJ. 1

✔ a. 2012 net income: $4,000; 0.5% of sales

EX 17-1   Vertical analysis of income statement

Revenue and expense data for Mandell Technologies Co. are as follows:

	2012	2011
Sales	$800,000	$740,000
Cost of goods sold	504,000	407,000
Selling expenses	120,000	140,600
Administrative expenses	128,000	125,800
Income tax expense	33,600	48,100

a. Prepare an income statement in comparative form, stating each item for both 2012 and 2011 as a percent of sales. Round to one decimal place.

b. ━━━━ Comment on the significant changes disclosed by the comparative income statement.

OBJ. 1

✔ a. Fiscal year 2008 income from continuing operations, 29.2% of revenues

EX 17-2 Vertical analysis of income statement

The following comparative income statement (in thousands of dollars) for the fiscal years 2008 and 2007 was adapted from the annual report of Speedway Motorsports, Inc., owner and operator of several major motor speedways, such as the Atlanta, Texas, and Las Vegas Motor Speedways.

	Fiscal Year 2008	Fiscal Year 2007
Revenues:		
Admissions	$188,036	$179,765
Event-related revenue	211,630	197,321
NASCAR broadcasting revenue	168,159	142,517
Other operating revenue	43,168	42,030
Total revenue	$610,993	$561,633
Expenses and other:		
Direct expense of events	$113,477	$100,414
NASCAR purse and sanction fees	118,766	100,608
Other direct expenses	116,376	163,222
General and administrative	84,029	80,913
Total expenses and other	$432,648	$445,157
Income from continuing operations	$178,345	$116,476

a. Prepare a comparative income statement for fiscal years 2007 and 2008 in vertical form, stating each item as a percent of revenues. Round to one decimal place.

b. ━━━━ Comment on the significant changes.

OBJ. 1

✔ a. Shoesmith net income: $144,000; 3.6% of sales

EX 17-3 Common-sized income statement

Revenue and expense data for the current calendar year for Shoesmith Electronics Company and for the electronics industry are as follows. The Shoesmith Electronics Company data are expressed in dollars. The electronics industry averages are expressed in percentages.

	Shoesmith Electronics Company	Electronics Industry Average
Sales	$4,200,000	105.0%
Sales returns and allowances	200,000	5.0
Net sales	$4,000,000	100.0%
Cost of goods sold	2,120,000	59.0
Gross profit	$1,880,000	41.0%
Selling expenses	$1,160,000	24.0%
Administrative expenses	480,000	10.5
Total operating expenses	$1,640,000	34.5%
Operating income	$ 240,000	6.5%
Other income	84,000	2.1
	$ 324,000	8.6%
Other expense	60,000	1.5
Income before income tax	$ 264,000	7.1%
Income tax	120,000	6.0
Net income	$ 144,000	1.1%

a. Prepare a common-sized income statement comparing the results of operations for Shoesmith Electronics Company with the industry average. Round to one decimal place.

b. ━━━━ As far as the data permit, comment on significant relationships revealed by the comparisons.

OBJ. 1

✔ Retained earnings,
Dec. 31, 2012, 33.0%

EX 17-4   Vertical analysis of balance sheet

Balance sheet data for Bryant Company on December 31, the end of the fiscal year, are shown below.

	2012	2011
Current assets	$ 775,000	$ 585,000
Property, plant, and equipment	1,425,000	1,597,500
Intangible assets	300,000	67,500
Current liabilities	525,000	360,000
Long-term liabilities	900,000	855,000
Common stock	250,000	270,000
Retained earnings	825,000	765,000

Prepare a comparative balance sheet for 2012 and 2011, stating each asset as a percent of total assets and each liability and stockholders' equity item as a percent of the total liabilities and stockholders' equity. Round to one decimal place.

OBJ. 1

✔ a. Net income
increase, 105.0%

EX 17-5   Horizontal analysis of the income statement

Income statement data for Boone Company for the years ended December 31, 2012 and 2011, are as follows:

	2012	2011
Sales	$446,400	$360,000
Cost of goods sold	387,450	315,000
Gross profit	$ 58,950	$ 45,000
Selling expenses	$ 27,900	$ 22,500
Administrative expenses	21,960	18,000
Total operating expenses	$ 49,860	$ 40,500
Income before income tax	$ 9,090	$ 4,500
Income tax expenses	5,400	2,700
Net income	$ 3,690	$ 1,800

a. Prepare a comparative income statement with horizontal analysis, indicating the increase (decrease) for 2012 when compared with 2011. Round to one decimal place.

b. ➤ What conclusions can be drawn from the horizontal analysis?

OBJ. 2

✔ a. 2012 working
capital, $1,342,000

EX 17-6   Current position analysis

The following data were taken from the balance sheet of Beatty Company:

	Dec. 31, 2012	Dec. 31, 2011
Cash	$ 330,000	$ 238,000
Temporary investments	465,000	385,000
Accounts and notes receivable (net)	425,000	295,000
Inventories	420,000	291,000
Prepaid expenses	312,000	141,000
Total current assets	$1,952,000	$1,350,000
Accounts and notes payable (short-term)	$ 420,000	$ 400,000
Accrued liabilities	190,000	140,000
Total current liabilities	$ 610,000	$ 540,000

a. Determine for each year (1) the working capital, (2) the current ratio, and (3) the quick ratio. Round ratios to one decimal place.

b. ➤ What conclusions can be drawn from these data as to the company's ability to meet its currently maturing debts?

OBJ. 2

✔ a. (1) Dec. 27, 2008
current ratio, 1.2

EX 17-7 Current position analysis

PepsiCo, Inc., the parent company of Frito-Lay snack foods and Pepsi beverages, had the following current assets and current liabilities at the end of two recent years:

	Dec. 26, 2009 (in millions)	Dec. 27, 2008 (in millions)
Cash and cash equivalents	$3,943	$2,064
Short-term investments, at cost	192	213
Accounts and notes receivable, net	4,624	4,683
Inventories	2,618	2,522
Prepaid expenses and other current assets	1,194	1,324
Short-term obligations	464	369
Accounts payable	8,292	6,494
Other current liabilities	0	1,924

a. Determine the (1) current ratio and (2) quick ratio for both years. Round to one decimal place.

b. ➤ What conclusions can you draw from these data?

OBJ. 2

EX 17-8 Current position analysis

The bond indenture for the 10-year, 10% debenture bonds dated January 2, 2011, required working capital of $700,000, a current ratio of 1.7, and a quick ratio of 1.2 at the end of each calendar year until the bonds mature. At December 31, 2012, the three measures were computed as follows:

1. Current assets:

Cash......................................	$302,400	
Temporary investments	144,000	
Accounts and notes receivable (net)..........	353,600	
Inventories.................................	114,400	
Prepaid expenses...........................	45,600	
Intangible assets	388,000	
Property, plant, and equipment..............	172,000	
Total current assets (net)		$1,520,000
Current liabilities:		
Accounts and short-term notes payable	$256,000	
Accrued liabilities...........................	544,000	
Total current liabilities		800,000
Working capital		$ 720,000
2. Current ratio	1.9	$1,520,000 ÷ $800,000
3. Quick ratio......................................	1.3	$ 332,000 ÷ $256,000

a. List the errors in the determination of the three measures of current position analysis.

b. ➤ Is the company satisfying the terms of the bond indenture?

OBJ. 2

✔ a. Accounts
receivable turnover,
2012, 6.6

EX 17-9 Accounts receivable analysis

The following data are taken from the financial statements of Saladin Inc. Terms of all sales are 2/10, n/60.

	2012	2011	2010
Accounts receivable, end of year	$ 221,250	$ 237,000	$247,500
Net sales on account	1,512,225	1,380,825	

a. Determine for each year (1) the accounts receivable turnover and (2) the number of days' sales in receivables. Round to nearest dollar and one decimal place.

b. ➤ What conclusions can be drawn from these data concerning accounts receivable and credit policies?

OBJ. 2

EX 17-10 Accounts receivable analysis

Klick Company and Klack Inc., are large retail department stores. Both companies offer credit to their customers through their own credit card operations. Information from the financial statements for both companies for two recent years is as follows (all numbers are in millions):

	Klick	Klack
Merchandise sales	$18,000	$70,980
Credit card receivables—beginning	3,300	9,000
Credit card receviables—ending	2,700	6,600

a. Determine the (1) accounts receivable turnover and (2) the number of days' sales in receivables for both companies. Round to one decimal place.

b. ▬▬▬▶ Compare the two companies with regard to their credit card policies.

OBJ. 2

✔ a. Inventory turnover, current year, 8.2

EX 17-11 Inventory analysis

The following data were extracted from the income statement of Hestia Systems Inc.:

	Current Year	Preceding Year
Sales	$2,443,600	$2,592,000
Beginning inventories	158,000	130,000
Cost of goods sold	1,221,800	1,440,000
Ending inventories	140,000	158,000

a. Determine for each year (1) the inventory turnover and (2) the number of days' sales in inventory. Round to the nearest dollar and one decimal place.

b. ▬▬▬▶ What conclusions can be drawn from these data concerning the inventories?

OBJ. 2

✔ a. Dell inventory turnover, 49.0

EX 17-12 Inventory analysis

Dell Inc. and Hewlett-Packard Company (HP) compete with each other in the personal computer market. Dell's primary strategy is to assemble computers to customer orders, rather than for inventory. Thus, for example, Dell will build and deliver a computer within four days of a customer entering an order on a Web page. Hewlett-Packard, on the other hand, builds some computers prior to receiving an order, then sells from this inventory once an order is received. Below is selected financial information for both companies from a recent year's financial statements (in millions):

	Dell Inc.	Hewlett-Packard Company
Sales	$61,101	$74,051
Cost of goods sold	50,144	56,503
Inventory, beginning of period	1,180	7,879
Inventory, end of period	867	6,128

a. Determine for both companies (1) the inventory turnover and (2) the number of days' sales in inventory. Round to one decimal place.

b. ▬▬▬▶ Interpret the inventory ratios by considering Dell's and Hewlett-Packard's operating strategies.

OBJ. 2

✔ a. Ratio of liabilities to stockholders' equity, Dec. 31, 2012, 0.7

EX 17-13 Ratio of liabilities to stockholders' equity and number of times interest charges earned

The following data were taken from the financial statements of Hermes Inc. for December 31, 2012 and 2011:

	Dec. 31, 2012	Dec. 31, 2011
Accounts payable	$ 473,960	$ 325,000
Current maturities of serial bonds payable	500,000	500,000
Serial bonds payable, 9%, issued 2007, due 2017	2,500,000	3,000,000
Common stock, $1 par value	100,000	100,000
Paid-in capital in excess of par	1,200,000	1,200,000
Retained earnings	3,662,800	2,950,000

The income before income tax was $891,000 and $787,500 for the years 2012 and 2011, respectively.

a. Determine the ratio of liabilities to stockholders' equity at the end of each year. Round to one decimal place.

b. Determine the number of times the bond interest charges are earned during the year for both years. Round to one decimal place.

c. ➤ What conclusions can be drawn from these data as to the company's ability to meet its currently maturing debts?

OBJ. 2

✔ a. Hasbro, 1.3

EX 17-14 Ratio of liabilities to stockholders' equity and number of times interest charges earned

Hasbro and Mattel, Inc., are the two largest toy companies in North America. Condensed liabilities and stockholders' equity from a recent balance sheet are shown for each company as follows (in thousands):

	Hasbro	Mattel
Current liabilities	$ 799,892	$ 1,259,974
Long-term debt	709,723	750,000
Other liabilities	268,396	547,930
Total liabilities	$ 1,778,011	$ 2,557,904
Shareholders' equity:		
Common stock	$ 104,847	$ 441,369
Additional paid in capital	450,155	1,642,092
Retained earnings	2,456,650	2,085,573
Accumulated other comprehensive loss and other equity items	62,256	(430,635)
Treasury stock, at cost	(1,683,122)	(1,621,264)
Total stockholders' equity	$ 1,390,786	$ 2,117,135
Total liabilities and stockholders' equity	$ 3,168,797	$ 4,675,039

The income from operations and interest expense from the income statement for both companies were as follows (in thousands):

	Hasbro	Mattel
Income from operations	$494,296	$541,792
Interest expense	47,143	81,944

a. Determine the ratio of liabilities to stockholders' equity for both companies. Round to one decimal place.

b. Determine the number of times interest charges are earned for both companies. Round to one decimal place.

c. ➤ Interpret the ratio differences between the two companies.

OBJ. 2

✔ a. H.J. Heinz, 6.9

EX 17-15 Ratio of liabilities to stockholders' equity and ratio of fixed assets to long-term liabilities

Recent balance sheet information for two companies in the food industry, H.J. Heinz Company and The Hershey Company, is as follows (in thousands of dollars):

	H.J. Heinz	Hershey
Net property, plant, and equipment	$1,978,302	$1,458,949
Current liabilities	2,062,846	1,270,212
Long-term debt	5,076,186	1,505,954
Other long-term liabilities	1,305,214	540,354
Stockholders' equity	1,219,938	318,199

a. Determine the ratio of liabilities to stockholders' equity for both companies. Round to one decimal place.

b. Determine the ratio of fixed assets to long-term liabilities for both companies. Round to one decimal place.

c. ➤ Interpret the ratio differences between the two companies.

EX 17-16 Ratio of net sales to assets

Three major segments of the transportation industry are motor carriers, such as YRC Worldwide; railroads, such as Union Pacific; and transportation arrangement services, such as C.H. Robinson Worldwide Inc. Recent financial statement information for these three companies is shown as follows (in thousands of dollars):

	YRC Worldwide	Union Pacific	C.H. Robinson Worldwide Inc.
Net sales	$8,940,401	$17,970,000	$8,578,614
Average total assets	4,514,368	38,877,500	1,813,514

a. Determine the ratio of net sales to assets for all three companies. Round to one decimal place.

b. ➡ Assume that the ratio of net sales to assets for each company represents their respective industry segment. Interpret the differences in the ratio of net sales to assets in terms of the operating characteristics of each of the respective segments.

EX 17-17 Profitability ratios

The following selected data were taken from the financial statements of Preslar Inc. for December 31, 2012, 2011, and 2010:

	December 31		
	2012	2011	2010
Total assets	$4,500,000	$4,050,000	$3,600,000
Notes payable (8% interest)	1,500,000	1,500,000	1,500,000
Common stock	600,000	600,000	600,000
Preferred 4% stock, $100 par (no change during year)	300,000	300,000	300,000
Retained earnings	1,765,500	1,341,750	900,000

The 2012 net income was $435,750, and the 2011 net income was $453,750. No dividends on common stock were declared between 2010 and 2012.

a. Determine the rate earned on total assets, the rate earned on stockholders' equity, and the rate earned on common stockholders' equity for the years 2011 and 2012. Round to one decimal place.

b. ➡ What conclusions can be drawn from these data as to the company's profitability?

EX 17-18 Profitability ratios

Ann Taylor Retail, Inc., sells professional women's apparel through company-owned retail stores. Recent financial information for Ann Taylor is provided below (all numbers in thousands).

	Fiscal Year Ended	
	February 2, 2008	February 3, 2007
Net income	$97,235	$142,982
Interest expense	2,172	2,230

	February 2, 2008	February 3, 2007	January 28, 2006
Total assets	$1,393,755	$1,568,503	$1,492,906
Total stockholders' equity	839,484	1,049,911	1,034,482

Assume the apparel industry average rate earned on total assets is 5.0%, and the average rate earned on stockholders' equity is 8.0% for the year ended February 2, 2008 (fiscal year 2007).

a. Determine the rate earned on total assets for Ann Taylor for the fiscal years ended February 2, 2008, and February 3, 2007. Round to one digit after the decimal place.

b. Determine the rate earned on stockholders' equity for Ann Taylor for the fiscal years ended February 2, 2008, and February 3, 2007. Round to one decimal place.

c. ➡ Evaluate the two-year trend for the profitability ratios determined in (a) and (b).

d. ➡ Evaluate Ann Taylor's profit performance relative to the industry.

EX 17-19   Six measures of solvency or profitability

The following data were taken from the financial statements of Ares Inc. for the current fiscal year. Assuming that long-term investments totaled $3,000,000 throughout the year and that total assets were $6,250,000 at the beginning of the current fiscal year, determine the following: (a) ratio of fixed assets to long-term liabilities, (b) ratio of liabilities to stockholders' equity, (c) ratio of net sales to assets, (d) rate earned on total assets, (e) rate earned on stockholders' equity, and (f) rate earned on common stockholders' equity. Round to one decimal place.

Property, plant, and equipment (net)			$ 2,700,000
Liabilities:			
Current liabilities.....................................		$ 666,500	
Mortgage note payable, 8%, issued 2001, due 2017......		1,800,000	
Total liabilities			$ 2,466,500
Stockholders' equity:			
Preferred $10 stock, $100 par (no change during year) ...			$ 1,200,000
Common stock, $10 par (no change during year)			1,000,000
Retained earnings:			
Balance, beginning of year............................	$2,203,000		
Net income	750,000	$2,953,000	
Preferred dividends	$ 120,000		
Common dividends	100,000	220,000	
Balance, end of year			2,733,000
Total stockholders' equity			$ 4,933,000
Net sales..			$17,211,375
Interest expense			$ 144,000

EX 17-20   Six measures of solvency or profitability

The balance sheet for Kronos Inc. at the end of the current fiscal year indicated the following:

Bonds payable, 10% (issued in 2002, due in 2022)	$3,750,000
Preferred $4 stock, $40 par	2,000,000
Common stock, $10 par	3,600,000

Income before income tax was $2,400,000, and income taxes were $400,000, for the current year. Cash dividends paid on common stock during the current year totaled $720,000. The common stock was selling for $72 per share at the end of the year. Determine each of the following: (a) number of times bond interest charges are earned, (b) number of times preferred dividends are earned, (c) earnings per share on common stock, (d) price-earnings ratio, (e) dividends per share of common stock, and (f) dividend yield. Round to one decimal place except earnings per share, which should be rounded to two decimal places.

EX 17-21   Earnings per share, price-earnings ratio, dividend yield

The following information was taken from the financial statements of Bailey Inc. for December 31 of the current fiscal year:

Common stock, $10 par value (no change during the year)	$4,000,000
Preferred $5 stock, $25 par (no change during the year)	1,250,000

The net income was $1,250,000 and the declared dividends on the common stock were $800,000 for the current year. The market price of the common stock is $40 per share.

For the common stock, determine (a) the earnings per share, (b) the price-earnings ratio, (c) the dividends per share, and (d) the dividend yield. Round to one decimal place except earnings per share, which should be rounded to two decimal places.

OBJ. 3

EX 17-22   Price-earnings ratio; dividend yield

The table below shows the stock price, earnings per share, and dividends per share for three companies as of May 2010:

	Price	Earnings per Share	Dividends per Share
The Home Depot	$ 33.43	$ 1.57	$0.95
Google	493.14	21.99	0.00
The Coca-Cola Company	52.67	3.04	1.76

a. Determine the price-earnings ratio and dividend yield for the three companies. Round to one decimal place.

b. ➡ Explain the differences in these ratios across the three companies.

Appendix

✔ b. Earnings per
share on common
stock, $11.80

EX 17-23   Earnings per share, extraordinary item

The net income reported on the income statement of Styx Co. was $3,200,000. There were 250,000 shares of $5 par common stock and 250,000 shares of $1 preferred stock outstanding throughout the current year. The income statement included two extraordinary items: a $700,000 gain from condemnation of land and a $350,000 loss arising from flood damage, both after applicable income tax. Determine the per-share figures for common stock for (a) income before extraordinary items and (b) net income.

Appendix

EX 17-24   Extraordinary item

Assume that the amount of each of the following items is material to the financial statements. Classify each item as either normally recurring (NR) or extraordinary (E).

a. Gain on sale of land condemned by the local government for a public works project.

b. Uninsured flood loss. (Flood insurance is unavailable because of periodic flooding in the area.)

c. Loss on the disposal of equipment considered to be obsolete because of the development of new technology.

d. Uncollectible accounts expense.

e. Loss on sale of investments in stocks and bonds.

f. Uninsured loss on building due to hurricane damage. The building was purchased by the company in 1910 and had not previously incurred hurricane damage.

g. Interest revenue on notes receivable.

Appendix

EX 17-25   Income statement and earnings per share for extraordinary items and discontinued operations

Eris, Inc., reports the following for 2012:

Income from continuing operations before income tax	$800,000
Extraordinary property loss from hurricane	$100,000*
Loss from discontinued operations	$120,000*
Weighted average number of shares outstanding	50,000
Applicable tax rate	40%
*Net of any tax effect.	

a. Prepare a partial income statement for Eris, Inc., beginning with income from continuing operations before income tax.

b. Calculate the earnings per common share for Eris, Inc., including per-share amounts for unusual items.

Appendix

EX 17-26 Unusual items

Discuss whether Daphne Company correctly reported the following items in the financial statements:

a. In 2012, the company discovered a clerical error in the prior year's accounting records. As a result, the reported net income for 2011 was overstated by $30,000. The company corrected this error by restating the prior-year financial statements.

b. In 2012, the company voluntarily changed its method of accounting for long-term construction contracts from the percentage of completion method to the completed contract method. Both methods are acceptable under generally acceptable accounting principles. The cumulative effect of this change was reported as a separate component of income in the 2012 income statement.

Problems Series A

OBJ. 1

✔ 1. Net sales, 14.4% increase

PR 17-1A Horizontal analysis for income statement

For 2012, Eurie Company reported its most significant decline in net income in years. At the end of the year, H. Finn, the president, is presented with the following condensed comparative income statement:

Eurie Company
Comparative Income Statement
For the Years Ended December 31, 2012 and 2011

	2012	2011
Sales	$928,000	$800,000
Sales returns and allowances	70,000	50,000
Net sales	$858,000	$750,000
Cost of goods sold	640,000	500,000
Gross profit	$218,000	$250,000
Selling expenses	$ 85,800	$ 65,000
Administrative expenses	43,400	35,000
Total operating expenses	$129,200	$100,000
Income from operations	$ 88,800	$150,000
Other income	16,000	10,000
Income before income tax	$104,800	$160,000
Income tax expense	9,200	8,000
Net income	$ 95,600	$152,000

Instructions

1. Prepare a comparative income statement with horizontal analysis for the two-year period, using 2011 as the base year. Round to one decimal place.

2. ➤ To the extent the data permit, comment on the significant relationships revealed by the horizontal analysis prepared in (1).

OBJ. 1

✔ 1. Net income, 2012, 14.0%

PR 17-2A Vertical analysis for income statement

For 2012, Selene Company initiated a sales promotion campaign that included the expenditure of an additional $25,000 for advertising. At the end of the year, Scott Brown, the president, is presented with the following condensed comparative income statement:

Selene Company
Comparative Income Statement
For the Years Ended December 31, 2012 and 2011

	2012	2011
Sales	$999,600	$867,000
Sales returns and allowances..	19,600	17,000
Net sales..	$980,000	$850,000
Cost of goods sold..	460,600	433,500
Gross profit	$519,400	$416,500
Selling expenses	$225,400	$178,500
Administrative expenses..	107,800	102,000
Total operating expenses	$333,200	$280,500
Income from operations	$186,200	$136,000
Other income..	49,000	42,500
Income before income tax	$235,200	$178,500
Income tax expense	98,000	85,000
Net income	$137,200	$ 93,500

Instructions

1. Prepare a comparative income statement for the two-year period, presenting an analysis of each item in relationship to net sales for each of the years. Round to one decimal place.

2. ➤ To the extent the data permit, comment on the significant relationships revealed by the vertical analysis prepared in (1).

OBJ. 2

✔ 2. c. Current ratio, 2.2

PR 17-3A   Effect of transactions on current position analysis

Data pertaining to the current position of Brin Company are as follows:

Cash	$520,000
Temporary investments	380,000
Accounts and notes receivable (net)	700,000
Inventories	720,000
Prepaid expenses	80,000
Accounts payable	300,000
Notes payable (short-term)	360,000
Accrued expenses	340,000

Instructions

1. Compute (a) the working capital, (b) the current ratio, and (c) the quick ratio. Round to one decimal place.

2. List the following captions on a sheet of paper:

Transaction	Working Capital	Current Ratio	Quick Ratio

Compute the working capital, the current ratio, and the quick ratio after each of the following transactions, and record the results in the appropriate columns. *Consider each transaction separately* and assume that only that transaction affects the data given above. Round to one decimal place.

a. Sold temporary investments at no gain or loss, $90,000.

b. Paid accounts payable, $175,000.

c. Purchased goods on account, $125,000.

d. Paid notes payable, $200,000.

e. Declared a cash dividend, $160,000.

f. Declared a common stock dividend on common stock, $45,000.

g. Borrowed cash from bank on a long-term note, $300,000.

h. Received cash on account, $140,000.

i. Issued additional shares of stock for cash, $700,000.

j. Paid cash for prepaid expenses, $80,000.

OBJ. 2, 3

✔ 5. Number of days' sales in receivables, 68.4

PR 17-4A Nineteen measures of solvency and profitability

The comparative financial statements of Blige Inc. are as follows. The market price of Blige Inc. common stock was $60 on December 31, 2012.

Blige Inc.
Comparative Retained Earnings Statement
For the Years Ended December 31, 2012 and 2011

	2012	2011
Retained earnings, January 1	$1,810,000	$1,526,000
Add net income for year	410,750	322,000
Total	$2,220,750	$1,848,000
Deduct dividends:		
On preferred stock	$ 16,000	$ 16,000
On common stock	22,000	22,000
Total	$ 38,000	$ 38,000
Retained earnings, December 31	$2,182,750	$1,810,000

Blige Inc.
Comparative Income Statement
For the Years Ended December 31, 2012 and 2011

	2012	2011
Sales	$2,211,000	$2,037,200
Sales returns and allowances	11,000	7,200
Net sales	$2,200,000	$2,030,000
Cost of goods sold	825,000	811,200
Gross profit	$1,375,000	$1,218,800
Selling expenses	$ 445,500	$ 484,000
Administrative expenses	321,750	290,400
Total operating expenses	$ 767,250	$ 774,400
Income from operations	$ 607,750	$ 444,400
Other income	33,000	26,400
	$ 640,750	$ 470,800
Other expense (interest)	176,000	96,000
Income before income tax	$ 464,750	$ 374,800
Income tax expense	54,000	52,800
Net income	$ 410,750	$ 322,000

Blige Inc.
Comparative Balance Sheet
December 31, 2012 and 2011

	Dec. 31, 2012	Dec. 31, 2011
Assets		
Current assets:		
Cash	$ 528,000	$ 410,000
Temporary investments	800,000	725,000
Accounts receivable (net)	425,000	400,000
Inventories	310,000	240,000
Prepaid expenses	100,000	75,000
Total current assets	$2,163,000	$1,850,000
Long-term investments	633,000	560,000
Property, plant, and equipment (net)	3,146,750	2,150,000
Total assets	$5,942,750	$4,560,000
Liabilities		
Current liabilities	$ 720,000	$ 710,000
Long-term liabilities:		
Mortgage note payable, 8%, due 2017	$1,000,000	$ 0
Bonds payable, 8%, due 2021	1,200,000	1,200,000
Total long-term liabilities	$2,200,000	$1,200,000
Total liabilities	$2,920,000	$1,910,000
Stockholders' Equity		
Preferred $0.80 stock, $20 par	$ 400,000	$ 400,000
Common stock, $10 par	440,000	440,000
Retained earnings	2,182,750	1,810,000
Total stockholders' equity	$3,022,750	$2,650,000
Total liabilities and stockholders' equity	$5,942,750	$4,560,000

Instructions

Determine the following measures for 2012, rounding to one decimal place:

1. Working capital
2. Current ratio
3. Quick ratio
4. Accounts receivable turnover
5. Number of days' sales in receivables
6. Inventory turnover
7. Number of days' sales in inventory
8. Ratio of fixed assets to long-term liabilities
9. Ratio of liabilities to stockholders' equity
10. Number of times interest charges earned
11. Number of times preferred dividends earned
12. Ratio of net sales to assets
13. Rate earned on total assets
14. Rate earned on stockholders' equity
15. Rate earned on common stockholders' equity
16. Earnings per share on common stock
17. Price-earnings ratio
18. Dividends per share of common stock
19. Dividend yield

OBJ. 2, 3

PR 17-5A   Solvency and profitability trend analysis

Itzkoff Company has provided the following comparative information:

	2012	2011	2010	2009	2008
Net income	$ 170,879	$ 229,985	$ 394,485	$ 552,500	$ 500,000
Interest expense	350,027	325,002	300,094	281,250	250,000
Income tax expense	49,492	83,179	166,358	124,800	156,000
Total assets (ending balance)	6,023,425	5,624,113	5,089,695	4,552,500	3,750,000
Total stockholders' equity (ending balance)	2,647,848	2,476,970	2,246,985	1,852,500	1,300,000
Average total assets	5,823,769	5,356,904	4,821,098	4,151,250	3,375,000
Average stockholders' equity	2,562,409	2,361,977	2,049,743	1,576,250	1,050,000

You have been asked to evaluate the historical performance of the company over the last five years.

Selected industry ratios have remained relatively steady at the following levels for the last five years:

	2008–2012
Rate earned on total assets	11%
Rate earned on stockholders' equity	16%
Number of times interest charges earned	3.1
Ratio of liabilities to stockholders' equity	1.5

Instructions

1. Prepare four line graphs with the ratio on the vertical axis and the years on the horizontal axis for the following four ratios (rounded to one decimal place):

   a. Rate earned on total assets

   b. Rate earned on stockholders' equity

   c. Number of times interest charges earned

   d. Ratio of liabilities to stockholders' equity

Display both the company ratio and the industry benchmark on each graph. That is, each graph should have two lines.

2. ➤ Prepare an analysis of the graphs in (1).

Problems Series B

PR 17-1B Horizontal analysis for income statement

For 2012, McFadden Inc. reported its most significant increase in net income in years. At the end of the year, John Mayer, the president, is presented with the following condensed comparative income statement:

McFadden Inc.
Comparative Income Statement
For the Years Ended December 31, 2012 and 2011

	2012	2011
Sales	$516,600	$410,000
Sales returns and allowances	12,200	10,000
Net sales	$504,400	$400,000
Cost of goods sold	240,000	200,000
Gross profit	$264,400	$200,000
Selling expenses	$ 69,600	$ 60,000
Administrative expenses	44,800	40,000
Total operating expenses	$114,400	$100,000
Income from operations	$150,000	$100,000
Other income	12,600	10,000
Income before income tax	$162,600	$110,000
Income tax expense	9,000	5,000
Net income	$153,600	$105,000

Instructions

1. Prepare a comparative income statement with horizontal analysis for the two-year period, using 2011 as the base year. Round to one decimal place.

2. ➤ To the extent the data permit, comment on the significant relationships revealed by the horizontal analysis prepared in (1).

PR 17-2B Vertical analysis for income statement

For 2012, Avatar Industries Inc. initiated a sales promotion campaign that included the expenditure of an additional $35,000 for advertising. At the end of the year, Leif Grando, the president, is presented with the following condensed comparative income statement:

Avatar Industries Inc.
Comparative Income Statement
For the Years Ended December 31, 2012 and 2011

	2012	2011
Sales	$630,000	$504,000
Sales returns and allowances	30,000	24,000
Net sales	$600,000	$480,000
Cost of goods sold	330,000	259,200
Gross profit	$270,000	$220,800
Selling expenses	$144,000	$ 86,400
Adminstrative expenses	72,000	62,400
Total operating expenses	$216,000	$148,800
Income from operations	$ 54,000	$ 72,000
Other income	24,000	19,200
Income before income tax	$ 78,000	$ 91,200
Income tax expense (benefit)	48,000	38,400
Net income (loss)	$ 30,000	$ 52,800

Instructions

1. Prepare a comparative income statement for the two-year period, presenting an analysis of each item in relationship to net sales for each of the years. Round to one decimal place.

2. ➤ To the extent the data permit, comment on the significant relationships revealed by the vertical analysis prepared in (1).

PR 17-3B   Effect of transactions on current position analysis

Data pertaining to the current position of Diaz Industries, Inc., are as follows:

Cash	$560,000
Temporary investments	520,000
Accounts and notes receivable (net)	800,000
Inventories	900,000
Prepaid expenses	100,000
Accounts payable	800,000
Notes payable (short-term)	700,000
Accrued expenses	300,000

Instructions

1. Compute (a) the working capital, (b) the current ratio, and (c) the quick ratio. Round to one decimal place.

2. List the following captions on a sheet of paper:

Transaction	Working Capital	Current Ratio	Quick Ratio

Compute the working capital, the current ratio, and the quick ratio after each of the following transactions, and record the results in the appropriate columns. *Consider each transaction separately* and assume that only that transaction affects the data given above. Round to one decimal place.

a. Sold temporary investments at no gain or loss, $200,000.

b. Paid accounts payable, $400,000.

c. Purchased goods on account, $150,000.

d. Paid notes payable, $380,000.

e. Declared a cash dividend, $220,000.

f. Declared a common stock dividend on common stock, $200,000.

g. Borrowed cash from bank on a long-term note, $680,000.

h. Received cash on account, $110,000.

i. Issued additional shares of stock for cash, $1,400,000.

j. Paid cash for prepaid expenses, $50,000.

PR 17-4B   Nineteen measures of solvency and profitability

The comparative financial statements of Chattah Inc. are as follows. The market price of Chattah Inc. common stock was $25 on December 31, 2012.

Chattah Inc.
Comparative Retained Earnings Statement
For the Years Ended December 31, 2012 and 2011

	2012	2011
Retained earnings, January 1	$1,646,120	$ 976,120
Add net income for year	847,000	850,000
Total	$2,493,120	$1,826,120
Deduct dividends:		
On preferred stock	$ 30,000	$ 30,000
On common stock	150,000	150,000
Total	$ 180,000	$ 180,000
Retained earnings, December 31	$2,313,120	$1,646,120

Chattah Inc.
Comparative Income Statement
For the Years Ended December 31, 2012 and 2011

	2012	2011
Sales (all on account)	$9,056,000	$7,840,000
Sales returns and allowances	56,000	40,000
Net sales	$9,000,000	$7,800,000
Cost of goods sold	4,500,000	3,680,000
Gross profit	$4,500,000	$4,120,000
Selling expenses	$1,936,000	$1,840,000
Administrative expenses	1,296,000	1,216,000
Total operating expenses	$3,232,000	$3,056,000
Income from operations	$1,268,000	$1,064,000
Other income	128,000	96,000
	$1,396,000	$1,160,000
Other expense (interest)	309,000	110,000
Income before income tax	$1,087,000	$1,050,000
Income tax expense	240,000	200,000
Net income	$ 847,000	$ 850,000

Chattah Inc.
Comparative Balance Sheet
December 31, 2012 and 2011

	Dec. 31, 2012	Dec. 31, 2011
Assets		
Current assets:		
Cash	$ 420,000	$ 306,000
Temporary investments	760,000	408,000
Accounts receivable (net)	663,000	482,120
Inventories	1,072,700	850,000
Prepaid expenses	92,400	89,250
Total current assets	$ 3,008,100	$2,135,370
Long-term investments	825,000	637,500
Property, plant, and equipment (net)	6,450,020	5,100,000
Total assets	$10,283,120	$7,872,870
Liabilities		
Current liabilities	$ 770,000	$ 726,750
Long-term liabilities:		
Mortgage note payable, 12%, due 2017	$ 1,200,000	$ 0
Bonds payable, 11%, due 2021	1,500,000	1,000,000
Total long-term liabilities	$ 2,700,000	$1,000,000
Total liabilities	$ 3,470,000	$1,726,750
Stockholders' Equity		
Preferred $2.00 stock, $100 par	$ 1,500,000	$1,500,000
Common stock, $5 par	3,000,000	3,000,000
Retained earnings	2,313,120	1,646,120
Total stockholders' equity	$ 6,813,120	$6,146,120
Total liabilities and stockholders' equity	$10,283,120	$7,872,870

Instructions

Determine the following measures for 2012, rounding to one decimal place:

1. Working capital
2. Current ratio
3. Quick ratio
4. Accounts receivable turnover
5. Number of days' sales in receivables
6. Inventory turnover
7. Number of days' sales in inventory
8. Ratio of fixed assets to long-term liabilities

 9. Ratio of liabilities to stockholders' equity

10. Number of times interest charges earned

11. Number of times preferred dividends earned

12. Ratio of net sales to assets

13. Rate earned on total assets

14. Rate earned on stockholders' equity

15. Rate earned on common stockholders' equity

16. Earnings per share on common stock

17. Price-earnings ratio

18. Dividends per share of common stock

19. Dividend yield

OBJ. 2, 3

PR 17-5B   Solvency and profitability trend analysis

Haviland Company has provided the following comparative information:

	2012	2011	2010	2009	2008
Net income	$ 2,785,860	$ 1,857,240	$1,386,000	$ 924,000	$ 700,000
Interest expense	736,442	624,103	538,020	427,000	350,000
Income tax expense	612,786	422,611	320,160	220,800	160,000
Total assets (ending balance)	16,321,384	12,554,911	9,511,296	6,993,600	5,640,000
Total stockholders' equity (ending balance)	9,653,100	6,867,240	5,010,000	3,624,000	2,700,000
Average total assets	14,438,147	11,033,103	8,252,448	6,316,800	4,820,000
Average stockholders' equity	8,260,170	5,938,620	4,317,000	3,162,000	2,350,000

You have been asked to evaluate the historical performance of the company over the last five years.

Selected industry ratios have remained relatively steady at the following levels for the last five years:

	2008–2012
Rate earned on total assets	18%
Rate earned on stockholders' equity	22%
Number of times interest charges earned	3.0
Ratio of liabilities to stockholders' equity	1.5

Instructions

1. Prepare four line graphs with the ratio on the vertical axis and the years on the horizontal axis for the following four ratios (rounded to one decimal place):

    a. Rate earned on total assets

    b. Rate earned on stockholders' equity

    c. Number of times interest charges earned

    d. Ratio of liabilities to stockholders' equity

    Display both the company ratio and the industry benchmark on each graph. That is, each graph should have two lines.

2. ➤ Prepare an analysis of the graphs in (1).

Nike, Inc., Problem

Financial Statement Analysis

The financial statements for Nike, Inc., are presented in Appendix C at the end of the text. The following additional information (in thousands) is available:

Accounts receivable at May 31, 2007	$ 2,795.3
Inventories at May 31, 2007	2,438.4
Total assets at May 31, 2007	12,442.7
Stockholders' equity at May 31, 2007	7,825.3

Instructions

1. Determine the following measures for the fiscal years ended May 31, 2010, and May 31, 2009, rounding to one decimal place.

   a. Working capital

   b. Current ratio

   c. Quick ratio

   d. Accounts receivable turnover

   e. Number of days' sales in receivables

   f. Inventory turnover

   g. Number of days' sales in inventory

   h. Ratio of liabilities to stockholders' equity

   i. Ratio of net sales to average total assets

   j. Rate earned on average total assets, assuming interest expense is $36.4 million for the year ending May 31, 2010, and $40.2 million for the year ending May 31, 2009

   k. Rate earned on average common stockholders' equity

   l. Price-earnings ratio, assuming that the market price was $57.05 per share on May 31, 2010, and $68.37 per share on May 31, 2009

   m. Percentage relationship of net income to net sales

2. ➤ What conclusions can be drawn from these analyses?

Cases & Projects

CP 17-1   Analysis of financing corporate growth

Assume that the president of Smokey Mountain Brewery made the following statement in the Annual Report to Shareholders:

"The founding family and majority shareholders of the company do not believe in using debt to finance future growth. The founding family learned from hard experience during Prohibition and the Great Depression that debt can cause loss of flexibility and eventual loss of corporate control. The company will not place itself at such risk. As such, all future growth will be financed either by stock sales to the public or by internally generated resources."

➤ As a public shareholder of this company, how would you respond to this policy?

CP 17-2   Receivables and inventory turnover

Lewis Industries, Inc., has completed its fiscal year on December 31, 2012. The auditor, Bill Brewer, has approached the CFO, Rob Beets, regarding the year-end receivables and inventory levels of Lewis Industries. The following conversation takes place:

Bill: We are beginning our audit of Lewis Industries and have prepared ratio analyses to determine if there have been significant changes in operations or financial position. This helps us guide the audit process. This analysis indicates that the inventory turnover has decreased from 5.1 to 2.7, while the accounts receivable turnover has decreased from 11 to 7. I was wondering if you could explain this change in operations.

Rob: There is little need for concern. The inventory represents computers that we were unable to sell during the holiday buying season. We are confident, however, that we will be able to sell these computers as we move into the next fiscal year.

Bill: What gives you this confidence?

Rob: We will increase our advertising and provide some very attractive price concessions to move these machines. We have no choice. Newer technology is already out there, and we have to unload this inventory.

Bill: ... and the receivables?

Rob: As you may be aware, the company is under tremendous pressure to expand sales and profits. As a result, we lowered our credit standards to our commercial customers so that we would be able to sell products to a broader customer base. As a result of this policy change, we have been able to expand sales by 35%.

Bill: Your responses have not been reassuring to me.

Rob: I'm a little confused. Assets are good, right? Why don't you look at our current ratio? It has improved, hasn't it? I would think that you would view that very favorably.

━━━━━▶ Why is Bill concerned about the inventory and accounts receivable turnover ratios and Rob's responses to them? What action may Bill need to take? How would you respond to Rob's last comment?

CP 17-3 Vertical analysis

The condensed income statements through income from operations for Dell Inc. and Apple Computer, Inc., are reproduced below for recent fiscal years (numbers in millions of dollars).

	Dell Inc.	Apple Computer, Inc.
Sales (net)	$61,101	$36,537
Cost of sales	50,144	23,397
Gross profit	$10,957	$13,140
Selling, general, and administrative expenses	$ 7,104	$ 4,149
Research and development	663	1,333
Operating expenses	$ 7,767	$ 5,482
Income from operations	$ 3,190	$ 7,658

━━━━━▶ Prepare comparative common-sized statements, rounding percents to one decimal place. Interpret the analyses.

CP 17-4 Profitability and stockholder ratios

Harley-Davidson, Inc., is a leading motorcycle manufacturer in the United States. The company manufactures and sells a number of different types of motorcycles, a complete line of motorcycle parts, and brand-related accessories, clothing, and collectibles. In recent years, Harley-Davidson has attempted to expand its dealer network and product lines internationally.

The following information is available for three recent years (in millions except per-share amounts):

	2008	2007	2006
Net income (loss)	$655	$934	$1,043
Preferred dividends	$0.00	$0.00	$0.00
Interest expense	$4.50	$0.00	$0.00
Shares outstanding for computing earnings per share	233	238	258
Cash dividend per share	$1.29	$1.06	$0.81
Average total assets	$6,743	$5,595	$5,394
Average stockholders' equity	$2,246	$2,566	$2,921
Average stock price per share	$31.29	$58.44	$60.98

1. Calculate the following ratios for each year:
   a. Rate earned on total assets
   b. Rate earned on stockholders' equity
   c. Earnings per share
   d. Dividend yield
   e. Price-earnings ratio

2. What is the ratio of average liabilities to average stockholders' equity for 2008?

3. ━━━━━▶ Explain the direction of the dividend yield and price-earnings ratio in light of Harley-Davidson's profitability trend.

4. Based on these data, evaluate Harley-Davidson's strategy to expand to international markets.

CP 17-5 Comprehensive profitability and solvency analysis

Marriott International, Inc., and Starwood Hotels and Resorts Worldwide, Inc. are two major owners and managers of lodging and resort properties in the United States. Abstracted income statement information for the two companies is as follows for a recent year:

	Marriott (in millions)	Starwood (in millions)
Operating profit before other expenses and interest	$ 815	$ 635
Other income (expenses)	57	(95)
Interest expense	(163)	(210)
Income before income taxes	$ 709	$ 330
Income tax expense	350	76
Net income	$ 359	$ 254

Balance sheet information is as follows:

	Marriott (in millions)	Starwood (in millions)
Total liabilities	$7,523	$8,082
Total stockholders' equity	1,380	1,621
Total liabilities and stockholders' equity	$8,903	$9,703

The average liabilities, stockholders' equity, and total assets were as follows:

	Marriott (in millions)	Starwood (in millions)
Average total liabilities	$7,518	$7,814
Average total stockholders' equity	1,405	1,849
Average total assets	7,494	9,663

1. Determine the following ratios for both companies (round to one decimal place after the whole percent):

   a. Rate earned on total assets

   b. Rate earned on total stockholders' equity

   c. Number of times interest charges are earned

   d. Ratio of liabilities to stockholders' equity

2. ➡ Analyze and compare the two companies, using the information in (1).

Appendices

Appendix A

Interest Tables

Present Value of $1 at Compound Interest Due in _n_ Periods

Periods	5%	5.5%	6%	6.5%	7%	8%
1	0.95238	0.94787	0.94334	0.93897	0.93458	0.92593
2	0.90703	0.89845	0.89000	0.88166	0.87344	0.85734
3	0.86384	0.85161	0.83962	0.82785	0.81630	0.79383
4	0.82270	0.80722	0.79209	0.77732	0.76290	0.73503
5	0.78353	0.76513	0.74726	0.72988	0.71290	0.68058
6	0.74622	0.72525	0.70496	0.68533	0.66634	0.63017
7	0.71068	0.68744	0.66506	0.64351	0.62275	0.58349
8	0.67684	0.65160	0.62741	0.60423	0.58201	0.54027
9	0.64461	0.61763	0.59190	0.56735	0.54393	0.50025
10	0.61391	0.58543	0.55840	0.53273	0.50835	0.46319
11	0.58468	0.55491	0.52679	0.50021	0.47509	0.42888
12	0.55684	0.52598	0.49697	0.46968	0.44401	0.39711
13	0.53032	0.49856	0.46884	0.44102	0.41496	0.36770
14	0.50507	0.47257	0.44230	0.41410	0.38782	0.34046
15	0.48102	0.44793	0.41726	0.38883	0.36245	0.31524
16	0.45811	0.42458	0.39365	0.36510	0.33874	0.29189
17	0.43630	0.40245	0.37136	0.34281	0.31657	0.27027
18	0.41552	0.38147	0.35034	0.32189	0.29586	0.25025
19	0.39573	0.36158	0.33051	0.30224	0.27651	0.23171
20	0.37689	0.34273	0.31180	0.28380	0.25842	0.21455
21	0.35894	0.32486	0.29416	0.26648	0.24151	0.19866
22	0.34185	0.30793	0.27750	0.25021	0.22571	0.18394
23	0.32557	0.29187	0.26180	0.23494	0.21095	0.17032
24	0.31007	0.27666	0.24698	0.22060	0.19715	0.15770
25	0.29530	0.26223	0.23300	0.20714	0.18425	0.14602
26	0.28124	0.24856	0.21981	0.19450	0.17211	0.13520
27	0.26785	0.23560	0.20737	0.18263	0.16093	0.12519
28	0.25509	0.22332	0.19563	0.17148	0.15040	0.11591
29	0.24295	0.21168	0.18456	0.16101	0.14056	0.10733
30	0.23138	0.20064	0.17411	0.15119	0.13137	0.09938
31	0.22036	0.19018	0.16426	0.14196	0.12277	0.09202
32	0.20987	0.18027	0.15496	0.13329	0.11474	0.08520
33	0.19987	0.17087	0.14619	0.12516	0.10724	0.07889
34	0.19036	0.16196	0.13791	0.11752	0.10022	0.07304
35	0.18129	0.15352	0.13010	0.11035	0.09366	0.06764
40	0.14205	0.11746	0.09722	0.08054	0.06678	0.04603
45	0.11130	0.08988	0.07265	0.05879	0.04761	0.03133
50	0.08720	0.06877	0.05429	0.04291	0.03395	0.02132

Present Value of $1 at Compound Interest Due in *n* Periods

Periods	9%	10%	11%	12%	13%	14%
1	0.91743	0.90909	0.90090	0.89286	0.88496	0.87719
2	0.84168	0.82645	0.81162	0.79719	0.78315	0.76947
3	0.77218	0.75132	0.73119	0.71178	0.69305	0.67497
4	0.70842	0.68301	0.65873	0.63552	0.61332	0.59208
5	0.64993	0.62092	0.59345	0.56743	0.54276	0.51937
6	0.59627	0.56447	0.53464	0.50663	0.48032	0.45559
7	0.54703	0.51316	0.48166	0.45235	0.42506	0.39964
8	0.50187	0.46651	0.43393	0.40388	0.37616	0.35056
9	0.46043	0.42410	0.39092	0.36061	0.33288	0.30751
10	0.42241	0.38554	0.35218	0.32197	0.29459	0.26974
11	0.38753	0.35049	0.31728	0.28748	0.26070	0.23662
12	0.35554	0.31863	0.28584	0.25668	0.23071	0.20756
13	0.32618	0.28966	0.25751	0.22917	0.20416	0.18207
14	0.29925	0.26333	0.23199	0.20462	0.18068	0.15971
15	0.27454	0.23939	0.20900	0.18270	0.15989	0.14010
16	0.25187	0.21763	0.18829	0.16312	0.14150	0.12289
17	0.23107	0.19784	0.16963	0.14564	0.12522	0.10780
18	0.21199	0.17986	0.15282	0.13004	0.11081	0.09456
19	0.19449	0.16351	0.13768	0.11611	0.09806	0.08295
20	0.17843	0.14864	0.12403	0.10367	0.08678	0.07276
21	0.16370	0.13513	0.11174	0.09256	0.07680	0.06383
22	0.15018	0.12285	0.10067	0.08264	0.06796	0.05599
23	0.13778	0.11168	0.09069	0.07379	0.06014	0.04911
24	0.12640	0.10153	0.08170	0.06588	0.05323	0.04308
25	0.11597	0.09230	0.07361	0.05882	0.04710	0.03779
26	0.10639	0.08390	0.06631	0.05252	0.04168	0.03315
27	0.09761	0.07628	0.05974	0.04689	0.03689	0.02908
28	0.08955	0.06934	0.05382	0.04187	0.03264	0.02551
29	0.08216	0.06304	0.04849	0.03738	0.02889	0.02237
30	0.07537	0.05731	0.04368	0.03338	0.02557	0.01963
31	0.06915	0.05210	0.03935	0.02980	0.02262	0.01722
32	0.06344	0.04736	0.03545	0.02661	0.02002	0.01510
33	0.05820	0.04306	0.03194	0.02376	0.01772	0.01325
34	0.05331	0.03914	0.02878	0.02121	0.01568	0.01162
35	0.04899	0.03558	0.02592	0.01894	0.01388	0.01019
40	0.03184	0.02210	0.01538	0.01075	0.00753	0.00529
45	0.02069	0.01372	0.00913	0.00610	0.00409	0.00275
50	0.01345	0.00852	0.00542	0.00346	0.00222	0.00143

Present Value of Ordinary Annuity of $1 per Period

Periods	5%	5.5%	6%	6.5%	7%	8%
1	0.95238	0.94787	0.94340	0.93897	0.93458	0.92593
2	1.85941	1.84632	1.83339	1.82063	1.80802	1.78326
3	2.72325	2.69793	2.67301	2.64848	2.62432	2.57710
4	3.54595	3.50515	3.46511	3.42580	3.38721	3.31213
5	4.32948	4.27028	4.21236	4.15568	4.10020	3.99271
6	5.07569	4.99553	4.91732	4.84101	4.76654	4.62288
7	5.78637	5.68297	5.58238	5.48452	5.38923	5.20637
8	6.46321	6.33457	6.20979	6.08875	5.97130	5.74664
9	7.10782	6.95220	6.80169	6.65610	6.51523	6.24689
10	7.72174	7.53763	7.36009	7.18883	7.02358	6.71008
11	8.30641	8.09254	7.88688	7.68904	7.49867	7.13896
12	8.86325	8.61852	8.38384	8.15873	7.94269	7.53608
13	9.39357	9.11708	8.85268	8.59974	8.35765	7.90378
14	9.89864	9.58965	9.29498	9.01384	8.74547	8.22424
15	10.37966	10.03758	9.71225	9.40267	9.10791	8.55948
16	10.83777	10.46216	10.10590	9.76776	9.44665	8.85137
17	11.27407	10.86461	10.47726	10.11058	9.76322	9.12164
18	11.68959	11.24607	10.82760	10.43247	10.05909	9.37189
19	12.08532	11.60765	11.15812	10.73471	10.33560	9.60360
20	12.46221	11.95038	11.46992	11.01851	10.59401	9.81815
21	12.82115	12.27524	11.76408	11.28498	10.83553	10.01680
22	13.16300	12.58317	12.04158	11.53520	11.06124	10.20074
23	13.48857	12.87504	12.30338	11.77014	11.27219	10.37106
24	13.79864	13.15170	12.55036	11.99074	11.46933	10.52876
25	14.09394	13.41393	12.78336	12.19788	11.65358	10.67478
26	14.37518	13.66250	13.00317	12.39237	11.82578	10.80998
27	14.64303	13.89810	13.21053	12.57500	11.98671	10.93516
28	14.89813	14.12142	13.40616	12.74648	12.13711	11.05108
29	15.14107	14.33310	13.59072	12.90749	12.27767	11.15841
30	15.37245	14.53375	13.76483	13.05868	12.40904	11.25778
31	15.59281	14.72393	13.92909	13.20063	12.53181	11.34980
32	15.80268	14.90420	14.08404	13.33393	12.64656	11.43500
33	16.00255	15.07507	14.23023	13.45909	12.75379	11.51389
34	16.19290	15.23703	14.36814	13.57661	12.85401	11.58693
35	16.37420	15.39055	14.49825	13.68696	12.94767	11.65457
40	17.15909	16.04612	15.04630	14.14553	13.33171	11.92461
45	17.77407	16.54773	15.45583	14.48023	13.60552	12.10840
50	18.25592	16.93152	15.76186	14.72452	13.80075	12.23348

Present Value of Ordinary Annuity of $1 per Period

Periods	9%	10%	11%	12%	13%	14%
1	0.91743	0.90909	0.90090	0.89286	0.88496	0.87719
2	1.75911	1.73554	1.71252	1.69005	1.66810	1.64666
3	2.53130	2.48685	2.44371	2.40183	2.36115	2.32163
4	3.23972	3.16986	3.10245	3.03735	2.97447	2.91371
5	3.88965	3.79079	3.69590	3.60478	3.51723	3.43308
6	4.48592	4.35526	4.23054	4.11141	3.99755	3.88867
7	5.03295	4.86842	4.71220	4.56376	4.42261	4.28830
8	5.53482	5.33493	5.14612	4.96764	4.79677	4.63886
9	5.99525	5.75902	5.53705	5.32825	5.13166	4.94637
10	6.41766	6.14457	5.88923	5.65022	5.42624	5.21612
11	6.80519	6.49506	6.20652	5.93770	5.68694	5.45273
12	7.16072	6.81369	6.49236	6.19437	5.91765	5.66029
13	7.48690	7.10336	6.74987	6.42355	6.12181	5.84236
14	7.78615	7.36669	6.96187	6.62817	6.30249	6.00207
15	8.06069	7.60608	7.19087	6.81086	6.46238	6.14217
16	8.31256	7.82371	7.37916	6.97399	6.60388	6.26506
17	8.54363	8.02155	7.54879	7.11963	6.72909	6.37286
18	8.75562	8.20141	7.70162	7.24967	6.83991	6.46742
19	8.95012	8.36492	7.83929	7.36578	6.93797	6.55037
20	9.12855	8.51356	7.96333	7.46944	7.02475	6.62313
21	9.29224	8.64869	8.07507	7.56200	7.10155	6.68696
22	9.44242	8.77154	8.17574	7.64465	7.16951	6.74294
23	9.58021	8.88322	8.26643	7.71843	7.22966	6.79206
24	9.70661	8.98474	8.34814	7.78432	7.28288	6.83514
25	9.82258	9.07704	8.42174	7.84314	7.32998	6.87293
26	9.92897	9.16094	8.48806	7.89566	7.37167	6.90608
27	10.02658	9.23722	8.54780	7.94255	7.40856	6.93515
28	10.11613	9.30657	8.60162	7.98442	7.44120	6.96066
29	10.19828	9.36961	8.65011	8.02181	7.47009	6.98304
30	10.27365	9.42691	8.69379	8.05518	7.49565	7.00266
31	10.34280	9.47901	8.73315	8.08499	7.51828	7.01988
32	10.40624	9.52638	8.76860	8.11159	7.53830	7.03498
33	10.46444	9.56943	8.80054	8.13535	7.55602	7.04823
34	10.51784	9.60858	8.82932	8.15656	7.57170	7.05985
35	10.56682	9.64416	8.85524	8.17550	7.58557	7.07005
40	10.75736	9.77905	8.95105	8.24378	7.63438	7.10504
45	10.88118	9.86281	9.00791	8.28252	7.66086	7.12322
50	10.96168	9.91481	9.04165	8.30450	7.67524	7.13266

Appendix B

Reversing Entries

Some of the adjusting entries recorded at the end of the accounting period affect transactions that occur in the next period. In such cases, a reversing entry may be used to simplify the recording of the next period's transactions.

To illustrate, an adjusting entry for accrued wages expense affects the first payment of wages in the next period. Without using a reversing entry, Wages Payable must be debited for the accrued wages at the end of the preceding period. In addition, Wages Expense must also be debited for only that portion of the payroll that is an expense of the current period.

Using a reversing entry, however, simplifies the analysis and recording of the first wages payment in the next period. As the term implies, a *reversing entry* is the exact opposite of the related adjusting entry. The amounts and accounts are the same as the adjusting entry, but the debits and credits are reversed.

Reversing entries are illustrated by using the accrued wages for **NetSolutions** presented in Chapter 3. These data are summarized in Exhibit 1.

EXHIBIT 1

Accrued Wages

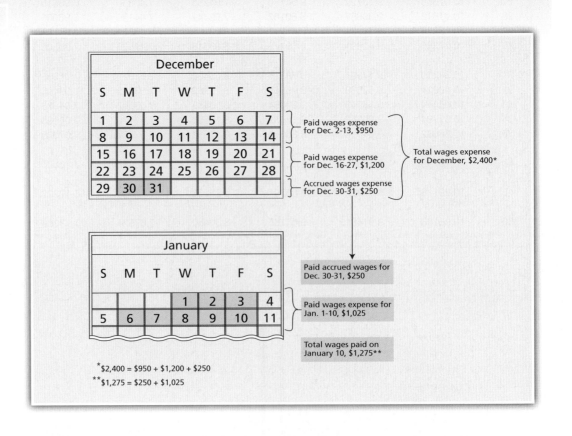

*$2,400 = $950 + $1,200 + $250

**$1,275 = $250 + $1,025

The adjusting entry for the accrued wages of December 30 and 31 is as follows:

2011						
Dec.	31	Wages Expense	51	250	
		Wages Payable	22		250
		Accrued wages.			

After the adjusting entry is recorded, Wages Expense will have a debit balance of $4,525 ($4,275 + $250), as shown on the top of page B-3. Wages Payable will have a credit balance of $250, as shown on page B-3.

After the closing entries are recorded, Wages Expense will have a zero balance. However, since Wages Payable is a liability account, it is not closed. Thus, Wages Payable will have a credit balance of $250 as of January 1, 2012.

Without recording a reversing entry, the payment of the $1,275 payroll on January 10 would be recorded as follows:

2012						
Jan.	10	Wages Payable	22	250	
		Wages Expense	51	1,025	
		Cash	11		1,275

As shown above, to record the January 10 payroll correctly Wages Payable must be debited for $250. This means that the employee who records the January 10 payroll must refer to the December 31, 2011, adjusting entry or to the ledger to determine the amount to debit Wages Payable.

Because the January 10 payroll is not recorded in the normal manner, there is a greater chance that an error may occur. This chance of error is reduced by recording a reversing entry as of the first day of the next period. For example, the reversing entry for the accrued wages expense would be recorded on January 1, 2012, as follows:

2012						
Jan.	1	Wages Payable	22	250	
		Wages Expense	51		250
		Reversing entry.			

The preceding reversing entry transfers the $250 liability from Wages Payable to the credit side of Wages Expense. The nature of the $250 is unchanged—it is still a liability. However, because of its unusual nature, an explanation is written under the reversing entry.

When the payroll is paid on January 10, the following entry is recorded:

Jan.	10	Wages Expense	51	1,275	
		Cash	11		1,275

After the January 10 payroll is recorded, Wages Expense has a debit balance of $1,025. This is the wages expense for the period January 1–10, 2012.

Wages Payable and Wages Expense after posting the adjusting, closing, and reversing entries are shown on the next page.

Account *Wages Payable*   Account No. *22*

Date		Item	Post. Ref.	Debit	Credit	Balance Debit	Balance Credit
2011							
Dec.	31	Adjusting	5		250		250
2012							
Jan.	1	Reversing	7	250		—	—

Account *Wages Expense*   Account No. *51*

Date		Item	Post. Ref.	Debit	Credit	Balance Debit	Balance Credit
2011							
Nov.	30		1	2,125		2,125	
Dec.	13		3	950		3,075	
	27		3	1,200		4,275	
	31	Adjusting	5	250		4,525	
	31	Closing	6		4,525	—	—
2012							
Jan.	1	Reversing	7		250		250
	10		7	1,275		1,025	

In addition to accrued expenses (accrued liabilities), reversing entries are also used for accrued revenues (accrued assets). To illustrate, the reversing entry for NetSolutions' accrued fees earned as of December 31, 2011, is as follows:

Jan.	1	Fees Earned	41	500	
		Accounts Receivable	12		500
		Reversing entry.			

The use of reversing entries is optional. However, in computerized accounting systems, data entry employees often input routine accounting entries. In such cases, reversing entries may be useful in avoiding errors.

EX B-1 Adjusting and reversing entries

On the basis of the following data, (a) journalize the adjusting entries at December 31, the end of the current fiscal year, and (b) journalize the reversing entries on January 1, the first day of the following year.

1. Sales salaries are uniformly $21,000 for a five-day workweek, ending on Friday. The last payday of the year was Friday, December 26.

2. Accrued fees earned but not recorded at December 31, $33,750.

EX B-2 Adjusting and reversing entries

On the basis of the following data, (a) journalize the adjusting entries at June 30, the end of the current fiscal year, and (b) journalize the reversing entries on July 1, the first day of the following year.

1. Wages are uniformly $48,000 for a five-day workweek, ending on Friday. The last payday of the year was Friday, June 27.

2. Accrued fees earned but not recorded at June 30, $23,900.

EX B-3 Entries posted to the wages expense account

Portions of the wages expense account of a business are shown below.

a. Indicate the nature of the entry (payment, adjusting, closing, reversing) from which each numbered posting was made.

b. Journalize the complete entry from which each numbered posting was made.

Account	Wages Expense				Account No. 53	
Date	Item	Post. Ref.	Dr.	Cr.	Balance Dr.	Balance Cr.
2011						
Dec. 26	(1)	125	32,000		1,600,000	
31	(2)	126	19,200		1,619,200	
31	(3)	127		1,619,200	—	—
2012						
Jan. 1	(4)	128		19,200		19,200
2	(5)	129	32,000		12,800	

EX B-4 Entries posted to the salaries expense account

Portions of the salaries expense account of a business are shown below.

Account	Salaries Expense				Account No. 53	
Date	Item	Post. Ref.	Dr.	Cr.	Balance Dr.	Balance Cr.
2011						
Dec. 27	(1)	29	18,500		897,800	
31	(2)	30	7,400		905,200	
31	(3)	31		905,200	—	—
2012						
Jan. 1	(4)	32		7,400		7,400
2	(5)	33	18,500		11,100	

a. Indicate the nature of the entry (payment, adjusting, closing, reversing) from which each numbered posting was made.

b. Journalize the complete entry from which each numbered posting was made.

NIKE INC (NKE)

ONE BOWERMAN DR
BEAVERTON, OR, 97005–6453
503–671–3173
www.nikebiz.com

10–K

Annual report pursuant to section 13 and 15(d)
Filed on 7/20/2010
Filed Period 5/31/2010

 THOMSON REUTERS

An Internal Audit department reviews the results of its work with the Audit Committee of the Board of Directors, presently consisting of three outside directors. The Audit Committee is responsible for the appointment of the independent registered public accounting firm and reviews with the independent registered public accounting firm, management and the internal audit staff, the scope and the results of the annual examination, the effectiveness of the accounting control system and other matters relating to the financial affairs of NIKE as they deem appropriate. The independent registered public accounting firm and the internal auditors have full access to the Committee, with and without the presence of management, to discuss any appropriate matters.

Management's Annual Report on Internal Control Over Financial Reporting

Management is responsible for establishing and maintaining adequate internal control over financial reporting, as such term is defined in Rule 13a–15(f) and Rule 15d–15(f) of the Securities Exchange Act of 1934, as amended. Internal control over financial reporting is a process designed to provide reasonable assurance regarding the reliability of financial reporting and the preparation of the financial statements for external purposes in accordance with generally accepted accounting principles in the United States of America. Internal control over financial reporting includes those policies and procedures that: (i) pertain to the maintenance of records that, in reasonable detail, accurately and fairly reflect the transactions and dispositions of assets of the company; (ii) provide reasonable assurance that transactions are recorded as necessary to permit preparation of financial statements in accordance with generally accepted accounting principles, and that receipts and expenditures of the company are being made only in accordance with authorizations of our management and directors; and (iii) provide reasonable assurance regarding prevention or timely detection of unauthorized acquisition, use or disposition of assets of the company that could have a material effect on the financial statements.

While "reasonable assurance" is a high level of assurance, it does not mean absolute assurance. Because of its inherent limitations, internal control over financial reporting may not prevent or detect every misstatement and instance of fraud. Controls are susceptible to manipulation, especially in instances of fraud caused by the collusion of two or more people, including our senior management. Also, projections of any evaluation of effectiveness to future periods are subject to the risk that controls may become inadequate because of changes in conditions, or that the degree of compliance with the policies or procedures may deteriorate.

Under the supervision and with the participation of our Chief Executive Officer and Chief Financial Officer, our management conducted an evaluation of the effectiveness of our internal control over financial reporting based upon the framework in *Internal Control — Integrated Framework* issued by the Committee of Sponsoring Organizations of the Treadway Commission (COSO). Based on the results of our evaluation, our management concluded that our internal control over financial reporting was effective as of May 31, 2010.

PricewaterhouseCoopers LLP, an independent registered public accounting firm, has audited (1) the consolidated financial statements and (2) the effectiveness of our internal control over financial reporting as of May 31, 2010, as stated in their report herein.

Mark G. Parker
Chief Executive Officer and President

Donald W. Blair
Chief Financial Officer

54

REPORT OF INDEPENDENT REGISTERED PUBLIC ACCOUNTING FIRM

To the Board of Directors and
Shareholders of NIKE, Inc.:

In our opinion, the consolidated financial statements listed in the index appearing under Item 15(a)(1) present fairly, in all material respects, the financial position of NIKE, Inc. and its subsidiaries at May 31, 2010 and 2009, and the results of their operations and their cash flows for each of the three years in the period ended May 31, 2010 in conformity with accounting principles generally accepted in the United States of America. In addition, in our opinion, the financial statement schedule listed in the appendix appearing under Item 15(a)(2) presents fairly, in all material respects, the information set forth therein when read in conjunction with the related consolidated financial statements. Also in our opinion, the Company maintained, in all material respects, effective internal control over financial reporting as of May 31, 2010, based on criteria established in *Internal Control — Integrated Framework* issued by the Committee of Sponsoring Organizations of the Treadway Commission (COSO). The Company's management is responsible for these financial statements and financial statement schedule, for maintaining effective internal control over financial reporting and for its assessment of the effectiveness of internal control over financial reporting, included in Management's Annual Report on Internal Control Over Financial Reporting appearing under Item 8. Our responsibility is to express opinions on these financial statements, on the financial statement schedule, and on the Company's internal control over financial reporting based on our integrated audits. We conducted our audits in accordance with the standards of the Public Company Accounting Oversight Board (United States). Those standards require that we plan and perform the audits to obtain reasonable assurance about whether the financial statements are free of material misstatement and whether effective internal control over financial reporting was maintained in all material respects. Our audits of the financial statements included examining, on a test basis, evidence supporting the amounts and disclosures in the financial statements, assessing the accounting principles used and significant estimates made by management, and evaluating the overall financial statement presentation. Our audit of internal control over financial reporting included obtaining an understanding of internal control over financial reporting, assessing the risk that a material weakness exists, and testing and evaluating the design and operating effectiveness of internal control based on the assessed risk. Our audits also included performing such other procedures as we considered necessary in the circumstances. We believe that our audits provide a reasonable basis for our opinions.

A company's internal control over financial reporting is a process designed to provide reasonable assurance regarding the reliability of financial reporting and the preparation of financial statements for external purposes in accordance with generally accepted accounting principles. A company's internal control over financial reporting includes those policies and procedures that (i) pertain to the maintenance of records that, in reasonable detail, accurately and fairly reflect the transactions and dispositions of the assets of the company; (ii) provide reasonable assurance that transactions are recorded as necessary to permit preparation of financial statements in accordance with generally accepted accounting principles, and that receipts and expenditures of the company are being made only in accordance with authorizations of management and directors of the company; and (iii) provide reasonable assurance regarding prevention or timely detection of unauthorized acquisition, use, or disposition of the company's assets that could have a material effect on the financial statements.

Because of its inherent limitations, internal control over financial reporting may not prevent or detect misstatements. Also, projections of any evaluation of effectiveness to future periods are subject to the risk that controls may become inadequate because of changes in conditions, or that the degree of compliance with the policies or procedures may deteriorate.

/s/   PRICEWATERHOUSECOOPERS LLP

Portland, Oregon
July 20, 2010

55

NIKE, INC.
CONSOLIDATED STATEMENTS OF INCOME

	Year Ended May 31,		
	2010	**2009**	**2008**
	(In millions, except per share data)		
Revenues	$19,014.0	$19,176.1	$18,627.0
Cost of sales	10,213.6	10,571.7	10,239.6
Gross margin	8,800.4	8,604.4	8,387.4
Selling and administrative expense	6,326.4	6,149.6	5,953.7
Restructuring charges (Note 16)	—	195.0	—
Goodwill impairment (Note 4)	—	199.3	—
Intangible and other asset impairment (Note 4)	—	202.0	—
Interest expense (income), net (Notes 6, 7 and 8)	6.3	(9.5)	(77.1)
Other (income) expense, net (Notes 17 and 18)	(49.2)	(88.5)	7.9
Income before income taxes	2,516.9	1,956.5	2,502.9
Income taxes (Note 9)	610.2	469.8	619.5
Net income	$ 1,906.7	$ 1,486.7	$ 1,883.4
Basic earnings per common share (Notes 1 and 12)	$ 3.93	$ 3.07	$ 3.80
Diluted earnings per common share (Notes 1 and 12)	$ 3.86	$ 3.03	$ 3.74
Dividends declared per common share	$ 1.06	$ 0.98	$ 0.875

The accompanying notes to consolidated financial statements are an integral part of this statement.

56

NIKE, INC.
CONSOLIDATED BALANCE SHEETS

	May 31,	
	2010	2009
	(In millions)	
ASSETS		
Current assets:		
Cash and equivalents	$ 3,079.1	$ 2,291.1
Short–term investments (Note 6)	2,066.8	1,164.0
Accounts receivable, net (Note 1)	2,649.8	2,883.9
Inventories (Notes 1 and 2)	2,040.8	2,357.0
Deferred income taxes (Note 9)	248.8	272.4
Prepaid expenses and other current assets	873.9	765.6
Total current assets	10,959.2	9,734.0
Property, plant and equipment, net (Note 3)	1,931.9	1,957.7
Identifiable intangible assets, net (Note 4)	467.0	467.4
Goodwill (Note 4)	187.6	193.5
Deferred income taxes and other assets (Notes 9 and 18)	873.6	897.0
Total assets	$ 14,419.3	$ 13,249.6
LIABILITIES AND SHAREHOLDERS' EQUITY		
Current liabilities:		
Current portion of long–term debt (Note 8)	$ 7.4	$ 32.0
Notes payable (Note 7)	138.6	342.9
Accounts payable (Note 7)	1,254.5	1,031.9
Accrued liabilities (Notes 5 and 18)	1,904.4	1,783.9
Income taxes payable (Note 9)	59.3	86.3
Total current liabilities	3,364.2	3,277.0
Long–term debt (Note 8)	445.8	437.2
Deferred income taxes and other liabilities (Notes 9 and 18)	855.3	842.0
Commitments and contingencies (Note 15)	—	—
Redeemable Preferred Stock (Note 10)	0.3	0.3
Shareholders' equity:		
Common stock at stated value (Note 11):		
Class A convertible — 90.0 and 95.3 shares outstanding	0.1	0.1
Class B — 394.0 and 390.2 shares outstanding	2.7	2.7
Capital in excess of stated value	3,440.6	2,871.4
Accumulated other comprehensive income (Note 14)	214.8	367.5
Retained earnings	6,095.5	5,451.4
Total shareholders' equity	9,753.7	8,693.1
Total liabilities and shareholders' equity	$ 14,419.3	$ 13,249.6

The accompanying notes to consolidated financial statements are an integral part of this statement.

57

NIKE, INC.

CONSOLIDATED STATEMENTS OF CASH FLOWS

	Year Ended May 31,		
	2010	2009	2008
		(In millions)	
Cash provided by operations:			
Net income	$ 1,906.7	$ 1,486.7	$ 1,883.4
Income charges (credits) not affecting cash:			
Depreciation	323.7	335.0	303.6
Deferred income taxes	8.3	(294.1)	(300.6)
Stock–based compensation (Note 11)	159.0	170.6	141.0
Impairment of goodwill, intangibles and other assets (Note 4)	—	401.3	—
Gain on divestitures (Note 17)	—	—	(60.6)
Amortization and other	71.8	48.3	17.9
Changes in certain working capital components and other assets and liabilities excluding the impact of acquisition and divestitures:			
Decrease (increase) in accounts receivable	181.7	(238.0)	(118.3)
Decrease (increase) in inventories	284.6	32.2	(249.8)
(Increase) decrease in prepaid expenses and other current assets	(69.6)	14.1	(11.2)
Increase (decrease) in accounts payable, accrued liabilities and income taxes payable	298.0	(220.0)	330.9
Cash provided by operations	3,164.2	1,736.1	1,936.3
Cash used by investing activities:			
Purchases of short–term investments	(3,724.4)	(2,908.7)	(1,865.6)
Maturities and sales of short–term investments	2,787.6	2,390.0	2,246.0
Additions to property, plant and equipment	(335.1)	(455.7)	(449.2)
Disposals of property, plant and equipment	10.1	32.0	1.9
Increase in other assets, net of other liabilities	(11.2)	(47.0)	(21.8)
Settlement of net investment hedges	5.5	191.3	(76.0)
Acquisition of subsidiary, net of cash acquired (Note 4)	—	—	(571.1)
Proceeds from divestitures (Note 17)	—	—	246.0
Cash used by investing activities	(1,267.5)	(798.1)	(489.8)
Cash used by financing activities:			
Reductions in long–term debt, including current portion	(32.2)	(6.8)	(35.2)
(Decrease) increase in notes payable	(205.4)	177.1	63.7
Proceeds from exercise of stock options and other stock issuances	364.5	186.6	343.3
Excess tax benefits from share–based payment arrangements	58.5	25.1	63.0
Repurchase of common stock	(741.2)	(649.2)	(1,248.0)
Dividends — common and preferred	(505.4)	(466.7)	(412.9)
Cash used by financing activities	(1,061.2)	(733.9)	(1,226.1)
Effect of exchange rate changes	(47.5)	(46.9)	56.8
Net increase in cash and equivalents	788.0	157.2	277.2
Cash and equivalents, beginning of year	2,291.1	2,133.9	1,856.7
Cash and equivalents, end of year	$ 3,079.1	$ 2,291.1	$ 2,133.9
Supplemental disclosure of cash flow information:			
Cash paid during the year for:			
Interest, net of capitalized interest	$ 48.4	$ 46.7	$ 44.1
Income taxes	537.2	765.2	717.5
Dividends declared and not paid	130.7	121.4	112.9

The accompanying notes to consolidated financial statements are an integral part of this statement.

NIKE, INC.
CONSOLIDATED STATEMENTS OF SHAREHOLDERS' EQUITY

	Common Stock				Capital in Excess of Stated Value	Accumulated Other Comprehensive Income	Retained Earnings	Total
	Class A		Class B					
	Shares	Amount	Shares	Amount				
				(In millions, except per share data)				
Balance at May 31, 2007	117.6	$ 0.1	384.1	$ 2.7	$ 1,960.0	$ 177.4	$ 4,885.2	$ 7,025.4
Stock options exercised			9.1		372.2			372.2
Conversion to Class B Common Stock	(20.8)		20.8					—
Repurchase of Class B Common Stock			(20.6)		(12.3)		(1,235.7)	(1,248.0)
Dividends on Common stock ($0.875 per share)							(432.8)	(432.8)
Issuance of shares to employees			1.0		39.2			39.2
Stock–based compensation (Note 11):					141.0			141.0
Forfeiture of shares from employees			(0.1)		(2.3)		(1.1)	(3.4)
Comprehensive income (Note 14):								
Net income							1,883.4	1,883.4
Other comprehensive income:								
Foreign currency translation and other (net of tax expense of $101.6)						211.9		211.9
Realized foreign currency translation gain due to divestiture (Note 17)						(46.3)		(46.3)
Net loss on cash flow hedges (net of tax benefit of $67.7)						(175.8)		(175.8)
Net loss on net investment hedges (net of tax benefit of $25.1)						(43.5)		(43.5)
Reclassification to net income of previously deferred losses related to hedge derivatives (net of tax benefit of $49.6)						127.7		127.7
Total Comprehensive income						74.0	1,883.4	1,957.4
Adoption of FIN 48 (Note 1 and 9)							(15.6)	(15.6)
Adoption of EITF 06–2 Sabbaticals (net of tax benefit of $6.2)							(10.1)	(10.1)
Balance at May 31, 2008	96.8	$ 0.1	394.3	$ 2.7	$ 2,497.8	$ 251.4	$ 5,073.3	$ 7,825.3
Stock options exercised			4.0		167.2			167.2
Conversion to Class B Common Stock	(1.5)		1.5					—
Repurchase of Class B Common Stock			(10.6)		(6.3)		(632.7)	(639.0)
Dividends on Common stock ($0.98 per share)							(475.2)	(475.2)
Issuance of shares to employees			1.1		45.4			45.4
Stock–based compensation (Note 11):					170.6			170.6
Forfeiture of shares from employees			(0.1)		(3.3)		(0.7)	(4.0)
Comprehensive income (Note 14):								
Net income							1,486.7	1,486.7
Other comprehensive income:								
Foreign currency translation and other (net of tax benefit of $177.5)						(335.3)		(335.3)
Net gain on cash flow hedges (net of tax expense of $167.5)						453.6		453.6
Net gain on net investment hedges (net of tax expense of $55.4)						106.0		106.0
Reclassification to net income of previously deferred net gains related to hedge derivatives (net of tax expense of $39.6)						(108.2)		(108.2)
Total Comprehensive income						116.1	1,486.7	1,602.8
Balance at May 31, 2009	95.3	$ 0.1	390.2	$ 2.7	$ 2,871.4	$ 367.5	$ 5,451.4	$ 8,693.1
Stock options exercised			8.6		379.6			379.6
Conversion to Class B Common Stock	(5.3)		5.3					—
Repurchase of Class B Common Stock			(11.3)		(6.8)		(747.5)	(754.3)
Dividends on Common stock ($1.06 per share)							(514.8)	(514.8)
Issuance of shares to employees			1.3		40.0			40.0
Stock–based compensation (Note 11):					159.0			159.0
Forfeiture of shares from employees			(0.1)		(2.6)		(0.3)	(2.9)
Comprehensive income (Note 14):								
Net income							1,906.7	1,906.7
Other comprehensive income:								
Foreign currency translation and other (net of tax benefit of $71.8)						(159.2)		(159.2)
Net gain on cash flow hedges (net of tax expense of $27.8)						87.1		87.1
Net gain on net investment hedges (net of tax expense of $21.2)						44.8		44.8
Reclassification to net income of previously deferred net gains related to hedge derivatives (net of tax expense of $41.7)						(121.6)		(121.6)
Reclassification of ineffective hedge gains to net income (net of tax expense of $1.4)						(3.8)		(3.8)
Total Comprehensive income						(152.7)	1,906.7	1,754.0
Balance at May 31, 2010	90.0	$ 0.1	394.0	$ 2.7	$ 3,440.6	$ 214.8	$ 6,095.5	$ 9,753.7

The accompanying notes to consolidated financial statements are an integral part of this statement.

NIKE, INC.

NOTES TO CONSOLIDATED FINANCIAL STATEMENTS

Note 1 — Summary of Significant Accounting Policies

Description of Business

NIKE, Inc. is a worldwide leader in the design, marketing and distribution of athletic and sports–inspired footwear, apparel, equipment and accessories. Wholly–owned NIKE subsidiaries include Cole Haan, which designs, markets and distributes dress and casual shoes, handbags, accessories and coats; Converse Inc., which designs, markets and distributes athletic and causal footwear, apparel and accessories; Hurley International LLC, which designs, markets and distributes action sports and youth lifestyle footwear, apparel and accessories; and Umbro Ltd., which designs, distributes and licenses athletic and casual footwear, apparel and equipment, primarily for the sport of soccer.

Basis of Consolidation

The consolidated financial statements include the accounts of NIKE, Inc. and its subsidiaries (the "Company"). All significant intercompany transactions and balances have been eliminated.

Recognition of Revenues

Wholesale revenues are recognized when title passes and the risks and rewards of ownership have passed to the customer, based on the terms of sale. This occurs upon shipment or upon receipt by the customer depending on the country of the sale and the agreement with the customer. Retail store revenues are recorded at the time of sale. Provisions for sales discounts, returns and miscellaneous claims from customers are made at the time of sale. As of May 31, 2010 and 2009, the Company's reserve balances for sales discounts, returns and miscellaneous claims were $370.6 million and $363.6 million, respectively.

Shipping and Handling Costs

Shipping and handling costs are expensed as incurred and included in cost of sales.

Advertising and Promotion

Advertising production costs are expensed the first time the advertisement is run. Media (TV and print) placement costs are expensed in the month the advertising appears.

A significant amount of the Company's promotional expenses result from payments under endorsement contracts. Accounting for endorsement payments is based upon specific contract provisions. Generally, endorsement payments are expensed on a straight–line basis over the term of the contract after giving recognition to periodic performance compliance provisions of the contracts. Prepayments made under contracts are included in prepaid expenses or other assets depending on the period to which the prepayment applies.

Through cooperative advertising programs, the Company reimburses retail customers for certain costs of advertising the Company's products. The Company records these costs in selling and administrative expense at the point in time when it is obligated to its customers for the costs, which is when the related revenues are recognized. This obligation may arise prior to the related advertisement being run.

Total advertising and promotion expenses were $2,356.4 million, $2,351.3 million, and $2,308.3 million for the years ended May 31, 2010, 2009 and 2008, respectively. Prepaid advertising and promotion expenses recorded in prepaid expenses and other assets totaled $260.7 million and $280.0 million at May 31, 2010 and 2009, respectively.

60

Table of Contents

NIKE, INC.
NOTES TO CONSOLIDATED FINANCIAL STATEMENTS — (Continued)

Cash and Equivalents

Cash and equivalents represent cash and short–term, highly liquid investments with maturities of three months or less at date of purchase. The carrying amounts reflected in the consolidated balance sheet for cash and equivalents approximate fair value.

Short–term Investments

Short–term investments consist of highly liquid investments, primarily commercial paper, U.S. treasury, U.S. agency, and corporate debt securities, with maturities over three months from the date of purchase. Debt securities that the Company has the ability and positive intent to hold to maturity are carried at amortized cost. At May 31, 2010 and 2009, the Company did not hold any short–term investments that were classified as held–to–maturity.

At May 31, 2010 and 2009, short–term investments consisted of available–for–sale securities. Available–for–sale securities are recorded at fair value with unrealized gains and losses reported, net of tax, in other comprehensive income, unless unrealized losses are determined to be other than temporary. The Company considers all available–for–sale securities, including those with maturity dates beyond 12 months, as available to support current operational liquidity needs and therefore classifies all securities with maturity dates beyond three months as current assets within short–term investments on the consolidated balance sheet.

See Note 6 — Fair Value Measurements for more information on the Company's short term investments.

Allowance for Uncollectible Accounts Receivable

Accounts receivable consists primarily of amounts receivable from customers. We make ongoing estimates relating to the collectability of our accounts receivable and maintain an allowance for estimated losses resulting from the inability of our customers to make required payments. In determining the amount of the allowance, we consider our historical level of credit losses and make judgments about the creditworthiness of significant customers based on ongoing credit evaluations. Accounts receivable with anticipated collection dates greater than 12 months from the balance sheet date and related allowances are considered non–current and recorded in other assets. The allowance for uncollectible accounts receivable was $116.7 million and $110.8 million at May 31, 2010 and 2009, respectively, of which $43.1 million and $36.9 million was classified as long–term and recorded in other assets.

Inventory Valuation

Inventories are stated at lower of cost or market and valued on a first–in, first–out ("FIFO") or moving average cost basis.

Property, Plant and Equipment and Depreciation

Property, plant and equipment are recorded at cost. Depreciation for financial reporting purposes is determined on a straight–line basis for buildings and leasehold improvements over 2 to 40 years and for machinery and equipment over 2 to 15 years. Computer software (including, in some cases, the cost of internal labor) is depreciated on a straight–line basis over 3 to 10 years.

Impairment of Long–Lived Assets

The Company reviews the carrying value of long–lived assets or asset groups to be used in operations whenever events or changes in circumstances indicate that the carrying amount of the assets might not be

61

NIKE, INC.

NOTES TO CONSOLIDATED FINANCIAL STATEMENTS — (Continued)

recoverable. Factors that would necessitate an impairment assessment include a significant adverse change in the extent or manner in which an asset is used, a significant adverse change in legal factors or the business climate that could affect the value of the asset, or a significant decline in the observable market value of an asset, among others. If such facts indicate a potential impairment, the Company would assess the recoverability of an asset group by determining if the carrying value of the asset group exceeds the sum of the projected undiscounted cash flows expected to result from the use and eventual disposition of the assets over the remaining economic life of the primary asset in the asset group. If the recoverability test indicates that the carrying value of the asset group is not recoverable, the Company will estimate the fair value of the asset group using appropriate valuation methodologies which would typically include an estimate of discounted cash flows. Any impairment would be measured as the difference between the asset groups carrying amount and its estimated fair value.

Identifiable Intangible Assets and Goodwill

The Company performs annual impairment tests on goodwill and intangible assets with indefinite lives in the fourth quarter of each fiscal year, or when events occur or circumstances change that would, more likely than not, reduce the fair value of a reporting unit or an intangible asset with an indefinite life below its carrying value. Events or changes in circumstances that may trigger interim impairment reviews include significant changes in business climate, operating results, planned investments in the reporting unit, or an expectation that the carrying amount may not be recoverable, among other factors. The impairment test requires the Company to estimate the fair value of its reporting units. If the carrying value of a reporting unit exceeds its fair value, the goodwill of that reporting unit is potentially impaired and the Company proceeds to step two of the impairment analysis. In step two of the analysis, the Company measures and records an impairment loss equal to the excess of the carrying value of the reporting unit's goodwill over its implied fair value should such a circumstance arise.

The Company generally bases its measurement of fair value of a reporting unit on a blended analysis of the present value of future discounted cash flows and the market valuation approach. The discounted cash flows model indicates the fair value of the reporting unit based on the present value of the cash flows that the Company expects the reporting unit to generate in the future. The Company's significant estimates in the discounted cash flows model include: its weighted average cost of capital; long-term rate of growth and profitability of the reporting unit's business; and working capital effects. The market valuation approach indicates the fair value of the business based on a comparison of the reporting unit to comparable publicly traded companies in similar lines of business. Significant estimates in the market valuation approach model include identifying similar companies with comparable business factors such as size, growth, profitability, risk and return on investment, and assessing comparable revenue and operating income multiples in estimating the fair value of the reporting unit.

The Company believes the weighted use of discounted cash flows and the market valuation approach is the best method for determining the fair value of its reporting units because these are the most common valuation methodologies used within its industry; and the blended use of both models compensates for the inherent risks associated with either model if used on a stand-alone basis.

Indefinite-lived intangible assets primarily consist of acquired trade names and trademarks. In measuring the fair value for these intangible assets, the Company utilizes the relief-from-royalty method. This method assumes that trade names and trademarks have value to the extent that their owner is relieved of the obligation to pay royalties for the benefits received from them. This method requires the Company to estimate the future revenue for the related brands, the appropriate royalty rate and the weighted average cost of capital.

62

Table of Contents

NIKE, INC.

NOTES TO CONSOLIDATED FINANCIAL STATEMENTS — (Continued)

Foreign Currency Translation and Foreign Currency Transactions

Adjustments resulting from translating foreign functional currency financial statements into U.S. dollars are included in the foreign currency translation adjustment, a component of accumulated other comprehensive income in shareholders' equity.

The Company's global subsidiaries have various assets and liabilities, primarily receivables and payables, that are denominated in currencies other than their functional currency. These balance sheet items are subject to remeasurement, the impact of which is recorded in other (income) expense, net, within our consolidated statement of income.

Accounting for Derivatives and Hedging Activities

The Company uses derivative financial instruments to limit exposure to changes in foreign currency exchange rates and interest rates. All derivatives are recorded at fair value on the balance sheet and changes in the fair value of derivative financial instruments are either recognized in other comprehensive income (a component of shareholders' equity), debt or net income depending on the nature of the underlying exposure, whether the derivative is formally designated as a hedge, and, if designated, the extent to which the hedge is effective. The Company classifies the cash flows at settlement from derivatives in the same category as the cash flows from the related hedged items. For undesignated hedges and designated cash flow hedges, this is within the cash provided by operations component of the consolidated statement of cash flows. For designated net investment hedges, this is generally within the cash used by investing activities component of the cash flow statement. As our fair value hedges are receive–fixed, pay–variable interest rate swaps, the cash flows associated with these derivative instruments are periodic interest payments while the swaps are outstanding, which are reflected in net income within the cash provided by operations component of the cash flow statement.

See Note 18 — Risk Management and Derivatives for more information on the Company's risk management program and derivatives.

Stock–Based Compensation

The Company estimates the fair value of options granted under the NIKE, Inc. 1990 Stock Incentive Plan (the "1990 Plan") and employees' purchase rights under the Employee Stock Purchase Plans ("ESPPs") using the Black–Scholes option pricing model. The Company recognizes this fair value, net of estimated forfeitures, as selling and administrative expense in the consolidated statements of income over the vesting period using the straight–line method.

See Note 11 — Common Stock and Stock–Based Compensation for more information on the Company's stock programs.

Income Taxes

The Company accounts for income taxes using the asset and liability method. This approach requires the recognition of deferred tax assets and liabilities for the expected future tax consequences of temporary differences between the carrying amounts and the tax basis of assets and liabilities. United States income taxes are provided currently on financial statement earnings of non–U.S. subsidiaries that are expected to be repatriated. The Company determines annually the amount of undistributed non–U.S. earnings to invest indefinitely in its non–U.S. operations. The Company recognizes interest and penalties related to income tax matters in income tax expense.

63

Table of Contents

NIKE, INC.
NOTES TO CONSOLIDATED FINANCIAL STATEMENTS — (Continued)

See Note 9 — Income Taxes for further discussion.

Earnings Per Share

Basic earnings per common share is calculated by dividing net income by the weighted average number of common shares outstanding during the year. Diluted earnings per common share is calculated by adjusting weighted average outstanding shares, assuming conversion of all potentially dilutive stock options and awards.

See Note 12 — Earnings Per Share for further discussion.

Management Estimates

The preparation of financial statements in conformity with generally accepted accounting principles requires management to make estimates, including estimates relating to assumptions that affect the reported amounts of assets and liabilities and disclosure of contingent assets and liabilities at the date of financial statements and the reported amounts of revenues and expenses during the reporting period. Actual results could differ from these estimates.

Reclassifications

Certain prior year amounts have been reclassified to conform to fiscal year 2010 presentation, including a reclassification to investing activities for the settlement of net investment hedges in the consolidated statement of cash flows for the year ended May 31, 2008. These reclassifications had no impact on previously reported results of operations or shareholders' equity and do not affect previously reported cash flows from operations, financing activities or net change in cash and equivalents.

Recently Adopted Accounting Standards:

In January 2010, the Financial Accounting Standards Board ("FASB") issued guidance to amend the disclosure requirements related to recurring and nonrecurring fair value measurements. The guidance requires additional disclosures about the different classes of assets and liabilities measured at fair value, the valuation techniques and inputs used, the activity in Level 3 fair value measurements, and the transfers between Levels 1, 2, and 3 of the fair value measurement hierarchy. This guidance became effective for the Company beginning March 1, 2010, except for disclosures relating to purchases, sales, issuances and settlements of Level 3 assets and liabilities, which will be effective for the Company beginning June 1, 2011. As this guidance only requires expanded disclosures, the adoption did not and will not impact the Company's consolidated financial position or results of operations. See Note 6 — Fair Value Measurements for disclosure required under this guidance.

In February 2010, the FASB issued amended guidance on subsequent events. Under this amended guidance, SEC filers are no longer required to disclose the date through which subsequent events have been evaluated in originally issued and revised financial statements. This guidance was effective immediately and the Company adopted these new requirements since the third quarter of fiscal 2010.

In June 2009, the FASB established the FASB Accounting Standards Codification (the "Codification") as the single source of authoritative U.S. GAAP for all non-governmental entities. The Codification, which launched July 1, 2009, changes the referencing and organization of accounting guidance. The Codification became effective for the Company beginning September 1, 2009. The issuance of the FASB Codification did not change GAAP and therefore the adoption has only affected how specific references to GAAP literature are disclosed in the notes to the Company's consolidated financial statements.

Table of Contents

NIKE, INC.

NOTES TO CONSOLIDATED FINANCIAL STATEMENTS — (Continued)

In April 2009, the FASB updated guidance related to fair value measurements to clarify the guidance related to measuring fair value in inactive markets, to modify the recognition and measurement of other–than–temporary impairments of debt securities, and to require public companies to disclose the fair values of financial instruments in interim periods. This updated guidance became effective for the Company beginning June 1, 2009. The adoption of this guidance did not have an impact on the Company's consolidated financial position or results of operations. See Note 6 — Fair Value Measurements for disclosure required under the updated guidance.

In June 2008, the FASB issued new accounting guidance applicable when determining whether instruments granted in share–based payment transactions are participating securities. This guidance clarifies that share–based payment awards that entitle their holders to receive non–forfeitable dividends before vesting should be considered participating securities and included in the computation of earnings per share pursuant to the two–class method. This guidance became effective for the Company beginning June 1, 2009. The adoption of this guidance did not have a material impact on the Company's consolidated financial position or results of operations.

In April 2008, the FASB issued amended guidance regarding the determination of the useful life of intangible assets. This guidance amends the factors that should be considered in developing renewal or extension assumptions used to determine the useful life of a recognized intangible asset. The intent of the position is to improve the consistency between the useful life of a recognized intangible asset and the period of expected cash flows used to measure the fair value of the asset. This guidance became effective for the Company beginning June 1, 2009. The adoption of this guidance did not have a material impact on the Company's consolidated financial position or results of operations.

In December 2007, the FASB issued amended guidance regarding business combinations, establishing principles and requirements for how an acquirer recognizes and measures identifiable assets acquired, liabilities assumed, any resulting goodwill, and any non–controlling interest in an acquiree in its financial statements. This guidance also provides for disclosures to enable users of the financial statements to evaluate the nature and financial effects of a business combination. This amended guidance became effective for the Company beginning June 1, 2009. The adoption of this amended guidance did not have an impact on the Company's consolidated financial statements, but could impact the accounting for future business combinations.

In December 2007, the FASB issued new guidance regarding the accounting and reporting for non–controlling interests in subsidiaries. This guidance clarifies that non–controlling interests in subsidiaries should be accounted for as a component of equity separate from the parent's equity. This guidance became effective for the Company beginning June 1, 2009. The adoption of this guidance did not have an impact on the Company's consolidated financial position or results of operations.

Recently Issued Accounting Standards:

In October 2009, the FASB issued new standards that revised the guidance for revenue recognition with multiple deliverables. These new standards impact the determination of when the individual deliverables included in a multiple–element arrangement may be treated as separate units of accounting. Additionally, these new standards modify the manner in which the transaction consideration is allocated across the separately identified deliverables by no longer permitting the residual method of allocating arrangement consideration. These new standards are effective for the Company beginning June 1, 2011. The Company does not expect the adoption will have a material impact on its consolidated financial positions or results of operations.

In June 2009, the FASB issued a new accounting standard that revised the guidance for the consolidation of variable interest entities ("VIE"). This new guidance requires a qualitative approach to identifying a controlling financial interest in a VIE, and requires an ongoing assessment of whether an entity is a VIE and whether an

65

NIKE, INC.

NOTES TO CONSOLIDATED FINANCIAL STATEMENTS — (Continued)

interest in a VIE makes the holder the primary beneficiary of the VIE. This guidance is effective for the Company beginning June 1, 2010. The Company is currently evaluating the impact of the provisions of this new standard.

Note 2 — Inventories

Inventory balances of $2,040.8 million and $2,357.0 million at May 31, 2010 and 2009, respectively, were substantially all finished goods.

Note 3 — Property, Plant and Equipment

Property, plant and equipment included the following:

	As of May 31,	
	2010	**2009**
	(In millions)	
Land	$ 222.8	$ 221.6
Buildings	951.9	974.0
Machinery and equipment	2,217.5	2,094.3
Leasehold improvements	820.6	802.0
Construction in process	177.0	163.8
	4,389.8	4,255.7
Less accumulated depreciation	2,457.9	2,298.0
	$ 1,931.9	$ 1,957.7

Capitalized interest was not material for the years ended May 31, 2010, 2009 and 2008.

Note 4 — Acquisition, Identifiable Intangible Assets, Goodwill and Umbro Impairment

Acquisition

On March 3, 2008, the Company completed its acquisition of 100% of the outstanding shares of Umbro, a leading United Kingdom–based global soccer brand, for a purchase price of 290.5 million British Pounds Sterling in cash (approximately $576.4 million), inclusive of direct transaction costs. This acquisition is intended to strengthen the Company's market position in the United Kingdom and expand NIKE's global leadership in soccer, a key area of growth for the Company. This acquisition also provides positions in emerging soccer markets such as China, Russia and Brazil. The results of Umbro's operations have been included in the Company's consolidated financial statements since the date of acquisition as part of the Company's "Other" operating segment.

The acquisition of Umbro was accounted for as a purchase business combination. The purchase price was allocated to tangible and identifiable intangible assets acquired and liabilities assumed based on their respective estimated fair values on the date of acquisition, with the remaining purchase price recorded as goodwill.

Based on our preliminary purchase price allocation at May 31, 2008, identifiable intangible assets and goodwill relating to the purchase approximated $419.5 million and $319.2 million, respectively. Goodwill recognized in this transaction is deductible for tax purposes. Identifiable intangible assets include $378.4 million for trademarks that have an indefinite life, and $41.1 million for other intangible assets consisting of Umbro's

66

NIKE, INC.

NOTES TO CONSOLIDATED FINANCIAL STATEMENTS — (Continued)

sourcing network, established customer relationships, and the United Soccer League Franchise. These intangible assets are amortized on a straight–line basis over estimated lives of 12 to 20 years.

During fiscal 2009, the Company finalized the purchase–price accounting for Umbro and made revisions to preliminary estimates, including valuations of tangible and intangible assets and certain contingencies, as further evaluations were completed and information was received from third parties subsequent to the acquisition date. These revisions to preliminary estimates resulted in a $12.4 million decrease in the value of identified intangible assets, primarily Umbro's sourcing network, and an $11.2 million increase in non–current liabilities, primarily related to liabilities assumed for certain contingencies and adjustments made to deferred taxes related to the fair value of assets acquired. These changes in assets acquired and liabilities assumed affected the amount of goodwill recorded.

The following table summarizes the allocation of the purchase price, including transaction costs of the acquisition, to the assets acquired and liabilities assumed at the date of acquisition based on their estimated fair values, including final purchase accounting adjustments (in millions):

	May 31, 2008 Preliminary	Adjustments	May 31, 2009 Final
Current assets	$ 87.2	$ —	$ 87.2
Non–current assets	90.2	—	90.2
Identified intangible assets	419.5	(12.4)	407.1
Goodwill	319.2	23.6	342.8
Current liabilities	(60.3)	—	(60.3)
Non–current liabilities	(279.4)	(11.2)	(290.6)
Net assets acquired	$ 576.4	$ —	$ 576.4

The pro forma effect of the acquisition on the combined results of operations for fiscal 2008 was not material.

Umbro Impairment in Fiscal 2009

The Company performs annual impairment tests on goodwill and intangible assets with indefinite lives in the fourth quarter of each fiscal year, or when events occur or circumstances change that would, more likely than not, reduce the fair value of a reporting unit or intangible assets with an indefinite life below its carrying value. As a result of a significant decline in global consumer demand and continued weakness in the macroeconomic environment, as well as decisions by Company management to adjust planned investment in the Umbro brand, the Company concluded sufficient indicators of impairment existed to require the performance of an interim assessment of Umbro's goodwill and indefinite lived intangible assets as of February 1, 2009. Accordingly, the Company performed the first step of the goodwill impairment assessment for Umbro by comparing the estimated fair value of Umbro to its carrying amount, and determined there was a potential impairment of goodwill as the carrying amount exceeded the estimated fair value. Therefore, the Company performed the second step of the assessment which compared the implied fair value of Umbro's goodwill to the book value of goodwill. The implied fair value of goodwill is determined by allocating the estimated fair value of Umbro to all of its assets and liabilities, including both recognized and unrecognized intangibles, in the same manner as goodwill was determined in the original business combination.

The Company measured the fair value of Umbro by using an equal weighting of the fair value implied by a discounted cash flow analysis and by comparisons with the market values of similar publicly traded companies. The Company believes the blended use of both models compensates for the inherent risk associated with either

67

NIKE, INC.

NOTES TO CONSOLIDATED FINANCIAL STATEMENTS — (Continued)

model if used on a stand–alone basis, and this combination is indicative of the factors a market participant would consider when performing a similar valuation. The fair value of Umbro's indefinite–lived trademark was estimated using the relief from royalty method, which assumes that the trademark has value to the extent that Umbro is relieved of the obligation to pay royalties for the benefits received from the trademark. The assessments of the Company resulted in the recognition of impairment charges of $199.3 million and $181.3 million related to Umbro's goodwill and trademark, respectively, for the year ended May 31, 2009. A tax benefit of $54.5 million was recognized as a result of the trademark impairment charge. In addition to the above impairment analysis, the Company determined an equity investment held by Umbro was impaired, and recognized a charge of $20.7 million related to the impairment of this investment. These charges are included in the Company's "Other" category for segment reporting purposes.

The discounted cash flow analysis calculated the fair value of Umbro using management's business plans and projections as the basis for expected cash flows for the next 12 years and a 3% residual growth rate thereafter. The Company used a weighted average discount rate of 14% in its analysis, which was derived primarily from published sources as well as our adjustment for increased market risk given current market conditions. Other significant estimates used in the discounted cash flow analysis include the rates of projected growth and profitability of Umbro's business and working capital effects. The market valuation approach indicates the fair value of Umbro based on a comparison of Umbro to publicly traded companies in similar lines of business. Significant estimates in the market valuation approach include identifying similar companies with comparable business factors such as size, growth, profitability, mix of revenue generated from licensed and direct distribution, and risk of return on investment.

Holding all other assumptions constant at the test date, a 100 basis point increase in the discount rate would reduce the adjusted carrying value of Umbro's net assets by an additional 12%.

Identified Intangible Assets and Goodwill

All goodwill balances are included in the Company's "Other" category for segment reporting purposes. The following table summarizes the Company's goodwill balance as of May 31, 2010 and 2009 (in millions):

	Goodwill	Accumulated Impairment	Goodwill, net
May 31, 2008	$ 448.8	$ —	$ 448.8
Purchase price adjustments	23.6	—	23.6
Impairment charge	—	(199.3)	(199.3)
Other	(79.6)	—	(79.6)
May 31, 2009	392.8	(199.3)	193.5
Other	(5.9)	—	(5.9)
May 31, 2010	$ 386.9	$ (199.3)	$ 187.6

_____

(1)   Other consists of foreign currency translation adjustments on Umbro goodwill.

68

Table of Contents

NIKE, INC.

NOTES TO CONSOLIDATED FINANCIAL STATEMENTS — (Continued)

The following table summarizes the Company's identifiable intangible asset balances as of May 31, 2010 and 2009.

	May 31, 2010			May 31, 2009		
	Gross Carrying Amount	Accumulated Amortization	Net Carrying Amount	Gross Carrying Amount	Accumulated Amortization	Net Carrying Amount
	(In millions)					
Amortized intangible assets:						
Patents	$ 68.5	$ (20.8)	$ 47.7	$ 56.6	$ (17.2)	$ 39.4
Trademarks	40.2	(17.8)	22.4	37.5	(10.9)	26.6
Other	32.7	(18.8)	13.9	40.0	(19.6)	20.4
Total	$ 141.4	$ (57.4)	$ 84.0	$ 134.1	$ (47.7)	$ 86.4
Unamortized intangible assets — Trademarks			$ 383.0			$ 381.0
Identifiable intangible assets, net			$ 467.0			$ 467.4

The effect of foreign exchange fluctuations for the year ended May 31, 2010 increased unamortized intangible assets by approximately $2 million.

Amortization expense, which is included in selling and administrative expense, was $13.5 million, $11.9 million and $9.2 million for the years ended May 31, 2010, 2009 and 2008, respectively. The estimated amortization expense for intangible assets subject to amortization for each of the years ending May 31, 2011 through May 31, 2015 are as follows: 2011: $13.4 million; 2012: $12.7 million; 2013: $10.8 million; 2014: $8.7 million; 2015: $5.1 million.

Note 5 — Accrued Liabilities

Accrued liabilities included the following:

	May 31,	
	2010	2009
	(In millions)	
Compensation and benefits, excluding taxes	$ 598.8	$ 491.9
Endorser compensation	266.9	237.1
Fair value of derivatives	163.6	68.9
Taxes other than income taxes	157.9	161.9
Dividends payable	130.7	121.4
Advertising and marketing	124.9	97.6
Import and logistics costs	80.0	59.4
Restructuring charges[(2)]	8.2	149.6
Other	373.4	396.1
	$ 1,904.4	$ 1,783.9

<hr>

[(1)] Accrued restructuring charges primarily consist of severance costs relating to the Company's restructuring activities that took place during the year ended May 31, 2009. See Note 16 — Restructuring Charges for more information.

[(2)] Other consists of various accrued expenses and no individual item accounted for more than 5% of the balance at May 31, 2010 and 2009.

NIKE, INC.
NOTES TO CONSOLIDATED FINANCIAL STATEMENTS — (Continued)

Note 6 — Fair Value Measurements

The Company measures certain financial assets and liabilities at fair value on a recurring basis, including derivatives and available–for–sale securities. Fair value is a market–based measurement that should be determined based on the assumptions that market participants would use in pricing an asset or liability. As a basis for considering such assumptions, the Company uses a three–level hierarchy established by the FASB which prioritizes fair value measurements based on the types of inputs used for the various valuation techniques (market approach, income approach, and cost approach).

The levels of hierarchy are described below:

- Level 1: Observable inputs such as quoted prices in active markets for identical assets or liabilities.

- Level 2: Inputs other than quoted prices that are observable for the asset or liability, either directly or indirectly; these include quoted prices for similar assets or liabilities in active markets and quoted prices for identical or similar assets or liabilities in markets that are not active.

- Level 3: Unobservable inputs in which there is little or no market data available, which require the reporting entity to develop its own assumptions.

The Company's assessment of the significance of a particular input to the fair value measurement in its entirety requires judgment and considers factors specific to the asset or liability. Financial assets and liabilities are classified in their entirety based on the most stringent level of input that is significant to the fair value measurement.

70

NIKE, INC.

NOTES TO CONSOLIDATED FINANCIAL STATEMENTS — (Continued)

The following table presents information about the Company's financial assets and liabilities measured at fair value on a recurring basis as of May 31, 2010 and 2009 and indicates the fair value hierarchy of the valuation techniques utilized by the Company to determine such fair value.

	May 31, 2010				
	Fair Value Measurements Using			Assets / Liabilities at Fair Value	Balance Sheet Classification
	Level 1	Level 2	Level 3		
		(In millions)			
Assets					
Derivatives:					
Foreign exchange forwards and options	$ —	$ 420.2	$ —	$ 420.2	Other current assets and other long–term assets
Interest rate swap contracts	—	14.6		14.6	Other current assets and other long–term assets
Total derivatives	—	434.8	—	434.8	
Available–for–sale securities:					
U.S. Treasury securities	1,231.7	—	—	1,231.7	Cash and equivalents
Commercial paper and bonds	—	461.9	—	461.9	Cash and equivalents
Money market funds	—	684.5	—	684.5	Cash and equivalents
U.S. Treasury securities	1,084.0	—	—	1,084.0	Short–term investments
U.S. Agency securities	—	298.5	—	298.5	Short–term investments
Commercial paper and bonds	—	684.3	—	684.3	Short–term investments
Total available–for–sale securities	2,315.7	2,129.2	—	4,444.9	
Total Assets	$ 2,315.7	$ 2,564.0	$ —	$ 4,879.7	
Liabilities					
Derivatives:					
Foreign exchange forwards and options	$ —	$ 165.1	$ —	$ 165.1	Accrued liabilities and other long–term liabilities
Total Liabilities	$ —	$ 165.1	$ —	$ 165.1	

71

NIKE, INC.

NOTES TO CONSOLIDATED FINANCIAL STATEMENTS — (Continued)

May 31, 2009

	Fair Value Measurements Using			Assets / Liabilities at Fair Value	Balance Sheet Classification
	Level 1	Level 2	Level 3		
		(In millions)			
Assets					
Derivatives:					
Foreign exchange forwards and options	$ —	$ 364.9	$ —	$ 364.9	Other current assets and other long–term assets
Interest rate swap contracts	—	13.8	—	13.8	Other current assets and other long–term assets
Total derivatives	—	378.7	—	378.7	
Available–for–sale securities:					
U.S. Treasury securities	240.0	—	—	240.0	Cash and equivalents
Commercial paper and bonds	—	235.3	—	235.3	Cash and equivalents
Money market funds	—	1,079.5	—	1,079.5	Cash and equivalents
U.S. Treasury securities	467.9	—	—	467.9	Short–term investments
U.S. Agency securities	—	304.9	—	304.9	Short–term investments
Commercial paper and bonds	—	391.2	—	391.2	Short–term investments
Total available–for–sale securities	707.9	2,010.9	—	2,718.8	
Total Assets	$ 707.9	$ 2,389.6	$ —	$ 3,097.5	
Liabilities					
Derivatives:					
Foreign exchange forwards and options	$ —	$ 68.9	$ —	$ 68.9	Accrued liabilities and other long–term liabilities
Total Liabilities	$ —	$ 68.9	$ —	68.9	

Derivative financial instruments include foreign currency forwards, option contracts and interest rate swaps. The fair value of these derivatives contracts is determined using observable market inputs such as the forward pricing curve, currency volatilities, currency correlations and interest rates, and considers nonperformance risk of the Company and that of its counterparties. Adjustments relating to these risks were not material for the years ended May 31, 2010 and 2009.

Available–for–sale securities are primarily comprised of investments in U.S. Treasury and agency securities, commercial paper, bonds and money market funds. These securities are valued using market prices on both active markets (level 1) and less active markets (level 2). Level 1 instrument valuations are obtained from real–time quotes for transactions in active exchange markets involving identical assets. Level 2 instrument valuations are obtained from readily–available pricing sources for comparable instruments.

As of May 31, 2010 and 2009, the Company had no material Level 3 measurements and no assets or liabilities measured at fair value on a non–recurring basis.

72

Table of Contents

NIKE, INC.

NOTES TO CONSOLIDATED FINANCIAL STATEMENTS — (Continued)

Short–term Investments

As of May 31, 2010 and 2009, short–term investments consisted of available–for–sale securities. As of May 31, 2010, the Company held $1,900.4 million of available–for–sale securities with maturity dates within one year and $166.4 million with maturity dates over one year and less than five years within short–term investments. As of May 31, 2009, the Company held $1,005.0 million of available–for–sale securities with maturity dates within one year and $159.0 million with maturity dates over one year and less than five years within short–term investments.

Short–term investments classified as available–for–sale consist of the following at fair value:

	As of May 31,	
	2010	2009
	(In millions)	
Available–for–sale investments:		
U.S. treasury and agencies	$ 1,382.5	$ 772.8
Commercial paper and bonds	684.3	391.2
Total available–for–sale investments	$ 2,066.8	$ 1,164.0

Included in interest expense (income), net for the years ended May 31, 2010, 2009 and 2008 was interest income of $30.1 million, $49.7 million, and $115.8 million, respectively, related to cash and equivalents and short–term investments.

For fair value information regarding notes payable and long–term debt, refer to Note 7 — Short–Term Borrowings and Credit Lines and Note 8 — Long–Term Debt.

Note 7 — Short–Term Borrowings and Credit Lines

Notes payable to banks and interest–bearing accounts payable to Sojitz Corporation of America ("Sojitz America") as of May 31, 2010 and 2009, are summarized below:

	May 31,			
	2010		2009	
	Borrowings	Interest Rate	Borrowings	Interest Rate
	(In millions)			
Notes payable:				
Commercial paper	$ —	—	$ 100.0	0.40%
U.S. operations	18.0	—[1]	31.2	1.81%[1]
Non–U.S. operations	120.6	6.35%[1]	211.7	4.15%[1]
	$ 138.6		$ 342.9	
Sojitz America	$ 88.2	1.07%	$ 78.5	1.57%

[1]   Weighted average interest rate includes non–interest bearing overdrafts.

The carrying amounts reflected in the consolidated balance sheet for notes payable approximate fair value.

The Company purchases through Sojitz America certain athletic footwear, apparel and equipment it acquires from non–U.S. suppliers. These purchases are for the Company's operations outside of the United States, Europe and Japan. Accounts payable to Sojitz America are generally due up to 60 days after shipment of goods from the foreign port. The interest rate on such accounts payable is the 60–day London Interbank Offered Rate ("LIBOR") as of the beginning of the month of the invoice date, plus 0.75%.

73

NIKE, INC.

NOTES TO CONSOLIDATED FINANCIAL STATEMENTS — (Continued)

As of May 31, 2010, the Company had no amounts outstanding under its commercial paper program. As of May 31, 2009, the Company had $100.0 million outstanding at a weighted average interest rate of 0.40%.

In December 2006, the Company entered into a $1 billion revolving credit facility with a group of banks. The facility matures in December 2012. Based on the Company's current long–term senior unsecured debt ratings of A+ and A1 from Standard and Poor's Corporation and Moody's Investor Services, respectively, the interest rate charged on any outstanding borrowings would be the prevailing LIBOR plus 0.15%. The facility fee is 0.05% of the total commitment. Under this agreement, the Company must maintain, among other things, certain minimum specified financial ratios with which the Company was in compliance at May 31, 2010. No amounts were outstanding under this facility as of May 31, 2010 and 2009.

Note 8 — Long–Term Debt

Long–term debt, net of unamortized premiums and discounts and swap fair value adjustments, is comprised of the following:

	May 31,	
	2010	2009
	(In millions)	
5.375% Corporate bond, payable July 8, 2009	$ —	$ 25.1
5.66% Corporate bond, payable July 23, 2012	27.0	27.4
5.4% Corporate bond, payable August 7, 2012	16.1	16.2
4.7% Corporate bond, payable October 1, 2013	50.0	50.0
5.15% Corporate bond, payable October 15, 2015	112.4	111.1
4.3% Japanese Yen note, payable June 26, 2011	115.7	108.5
1.52125% Japanese Yen note, payable February 14, 2012	55.1	51.7
2.6% Japanese Yen note, maturing August 20, 2001 through November 20, 2020	53.1	54.7
2.0% Japanese Yen note, maturing August 20, 2001 through November 20, 2020	23.8	24.5
Total	453.2	469.2
Less current maturities	7.4	32.0
	$445.8	$437.2

The scheduled maturity of long–term debt in each of the years ending May 31, 2011 through 2015 are $7.4 million, $178.1 million, $47.4 million, $57.4 million and $7.4 million, at face value, respectively.

The Company's long–term debt is recorded at adjusted cost, net of amortized premiums and discounts and interest rate swap fair value adjustments. The fair value of long–term debt is estimated based upon quoted prices for similar instruments. The fair value of the Company's long–term debt, including the current portion, was approximately $453 million at May 31, 2010 and $456 million at May 31, 2009.

In fiscal years 2003 and 2004, the Company issued a total of $240 million in medium–term notes of which $190 million, at face value, were outstanding at May 31, 2010. The outstanding notes have coupon rates that range from 4.70% to 5.66% and maturity dates ranging from July 2012 to October 2015. For each of these notes, except the $50 million note maturing in October 2013, the Company has entered into interest rate swap agreements whereby the Company receives fixed interest payments at the same rate as the notes and pays variable interest payments based on the six–month LIBOR plus a spread. Each swap has the same notional amount and maturity date as the corresponding note. At May 31, 2010, the interest rates payable on these swap agreements ranged from approximately 0.3% to 1.1%.

NIKE, INC.

NOTES TO CONSOLIDATED FINANCIAL STATEMENTS — (Continued)

In June 1996, one of the Company's Japanese subsidiaries, NIKE Logistics YK, borrowed ¥10.5 billion (approximately $115.7 million as of May 31, 2010) in a private placement with a maturity of June 26, 2011. Interest is paid semi–annually. The agreement provides for early retirement of the borrowing.

In July 1999, NIKE Logistics YK assumed a total of ¥13.0 billion in loans as part of its agreement to purchase a distribution center in Japan, which serves as collateral for the loans. These loans mature in equal quarterly installments during the period August 20, 2001 through November 20, 2020. Interest is also paid quarterly. As of May 31, 2010, ¥7.0 billion (approximately $76.9 million) in loans remain outstanding.

In February 2007, NIKE Logistics YK entered into a ¥5.0 billion (approximately $55.1 million as of May 31, 2010) term loan that replaced certain intercompany borrowings and matures on February 14, 2012. The interest rate on the loan is approximately 1.5% and interest is paid semi–annually.

Note 9 — Income Taxes

Income before income taxes is as follows:

| | Year Ended May 31, | | |
	2010	2009	2008
		(In millions)	
Income before income taxes:			
United States	$ 698.6	$ 845.7	$ 713.0
Foreign	1,818.3	1,110.8	1,789.9
	$ 2,516.9	$ 1,956.5	$ 2,502.9

The provision for income taxes is as follows:

| | Year Ended May 31, | | |
	2010	2009	2008
		(In millions)	
Current:			
United States			
Federal	$200.2	$ 410.1	$ 469.9
State	50.0	46.1	58.4
Foreign	348.5	307.7	391.8
	598.7	763.9	920.1
Deferred:			
United States			
Federal	17.7	(251.4)	(273.0)
State	(1.1)	(7.9)	(5.0)
Foreign	(5.1)	(34.8)	(22.6)
	11.5	(294.1)	(300.6)
	$610.2	$ 469.8	$ 619.5

75

NIKE, INC.
NOTES TO CONSOLIDATED FINANCIAL STATEMENTS — (Continued)

A reconciliation from the U.S. statutory federal income tax rate to the effective income tax rate follows:

	Year Ended May 31,		
	2010	2009	2008
Federal income tax rate	35.0%	35.0%	35.0%
State taxes, net of federal benefit	1.3%	1.2%	1.4%
Foreign earnings	−13.6%	−14.9%	−12.9%
Other, net	1.5%	2.7%	1.3%
Effective income tax rate	24.2%	24.0%	24.8%

The effective tax rate for the year ended May 31, 2010 of 24.2% increased from the fiscal 2009 effective rate of 24.0%. The effective tax rate for the year ended May 31, 2009 was favorably impacted by a tax benefit associated with the impairment of goodwill, intangible, and other assets of Umbro (See Note 4 — Acquisition, Identifiable Intangible Assets, Goodwill and Umbro Impairment), and the retroactive reinstatement of the research and development tax credit. The Tax Extenders and Alternative Minimum Tax Relief Act of 2008, which was signed into law during the second quarter of fiscal 2009, reinstated the U.S. federal research and development tax credit retroactive to January 1, 2008. Also reflected in the effective tax rate for the years ended May 31, 2010, 2009 and 2008 is a reduction in our on−going effective tax rate resulting from our operations outside of the United States, as our tax rates on those operations are generally lower than the U.S. statutory rate.

Deferred tax assets and (liabilities) are comprised of the following:

	May 31,	
	2010	2009
	(In millions)	
Deferred tax assets:		
Allowance for doubtful accounts	$ 16.7	$ 17.9
Inventories	47.3	52.8
Sales return reserves	52.0	52.8
Deferred compensation	143.7	127.3
Stock−based compensation	145.0	127.3
Reserves and accrued liabilities	85.8	66.7
Foreign loss carry−forwards	26.2	31.9
Foreign tax credit carry−forwards	148.3	32.7
Hedges	0.4	1.1
Undistributed earnings of foreign subsidiaries	128.4	272.9
Other	37.0	46.2
Total deferred tax assets	830.8	829.6
Valuation allowance	(36.2)	(26.0)
Total deferred tax assets after valuation allowance	794.6	803.6
Deferred tax liabilities:		
Property, plant and equipment	(99.3)	(92.2)
Intangibles	(98.6)	(100.7)
Hedges	(71.5)	(86.6)
Other	(8.1)	(4.2)
Total deferred tax liability	(277.5)	(283.7)
Net deferred tax asset	$ 517.1	$ 519.9

76

NIKE, INC.

NOTES TO CONSOLIDATED FINANCIAL STATEMENTS — (Continued)

The following is a reconciliation of the changes in the gross balance of unrecognized tax benefits:

	May 31,		
	2010	2009	2008
		(In millions)	
Unrecognized tax benefits, as of the beginning of the period	$ 273.9	$251.1	$122.5
Gross increases related to prior period tax positions	86.7	53.2	71.6
Gross decreases related to prior period tax positions	(121.6)	(61.7)	(23.1)
Gross increases related to current period tax positions	52.5	71.5	87.7
Settlements	(3.3)	(29.3)	(13.4)
Lapse of statute of limitations	(9.3)	(4.1)	(0.7)
Changes due to currency translation	3.2	(6.8)	6.5
Unrecognized tax benefits, as of the end of the period	$ 282.1	$273.9	$251.1

As of May 31, 2010, the total gross unrecognized tax benefits, excluding related interest and penalties, were $282.1 million, $158.4 million of which would affect the Company's effective tax rate if recognized in future periods. Total gross unrecognized tax benefits, excluding interest and penalties, as of May 31, 2009 was $273.9 million, $110.6 million of which would affect the Company's effective tax rate if recognized in future periods.

The Company recognizes interest and penalties related to income tax matters in income tax expense. The liability for payment of interest and penalties increased $6.0 million, $2.2 million and $41.2 million during the years ended May 31, 2010, 2009 and 2008, respectively. As of May 31, 2010 and 2009, accrued interest and penalties related to uncertain tax positions was $81.4 million and $75.4 million, respectively (excluding federal benefit).

The Company is subject to taxation primarily in the U.S., China and the Netherlands as well as various state and other foreign jurisdictions. The Company has concluded substantially all U.S. federal income tax matters through fiscal year 2006. The Company is currently under audit by the Internal Revenue Service for the 2007, 2008, 2009 and 2010 tax years. The Company's major foreign jurisdictions, China and the Netherlands, have concluded substantially all income tax matters through calendar 1999 and fiscal 2003, respectively. It is reasonably possible that the Internal Revenue Service audits for the 2007, 2008 and 2009 tax years will be completed during the next 12 months, which could result in a decrease in our balance of unrecognized tax benefits. An estimate of the range cannot be made at this time; however, we do not anticipate that total gross unrecognized tax benefits will change significantly as a result of full or partial settlement of audits within the next 12 months.

The Company has indefinitely reinvested approximately $3.6 billion of the cumulative undistributed earnings of certain foreign subsidiaries. Such earnings would be subject to U.S. taxation if repatriated to the U.S. Determination of the amount of unrecognized deferred tax liability associated with the permanently reinvested cumulative undistributed earnings is not practicable.

During the year ended May 31, 2009, a portion of the Company's foreign operations was granted a tax holiday that will phase out in 2019. The decrease in income tax expense for the year ended May 31, 2010 as a result of this arrangement was approximately $30.1 million ($0.06 per diluted share). The effect on income tax expense for the year ended May 31, 2009 was not material.

Deferred tax assets at May 31, 2010 and 2009 were reduced by a valuation allowance relating to tax benefits of certain subsidiaries with operating losses where it is more likely than not that the deferred tax assets will not be realized. The net change in the valuation allowance was an increase of $10.2 million for the year ended May 31, 2010 and a decrease of $14.7 million and $1.6 million for the years ended May 31, 2009 and 2008, respectively.

77

NIKE, INC.
NOTES TO CONSOLIDATED FINANCIAL STATEMENTS — (Continued)

The Company does not anticipate that any foreign tax credit carry–forwards will expire. The Company has available domestic and foreign loss carry–forwards of $89.8 million at May 31, 2010. Such losses will expire as follows:

| | Year Ending May 31, | | | | | | | |
	2011	2012	2013	2014	2015	2016–2028	Indefinite	Total
					(In millions)			
Net Operating Losses	$2.0	$1.9	$3.6	$8.9	$11.1	$25.7	$ 36.6	$89.8

During the years ended May 31, 2010, 2009, and 2008, income tax benefits attributable to employee stock–based compensation transactions of $56.8 million, $25.4 million, and $68.9 million, respectively, were allocated to shareholders' equity.

Note 10 — Redeemable Preferred Stock

Sojitz America is the sole owner of the Company's authorized Redeemable Preferred Stock, $1 par value, which is redeemable at the option of Sojitz America or the Company at par value aggregating $0.3 million. A cumulative dividend of $0.10 per share is payable annually on May 31 and no dividends may be declared or paid on the common stock of the Company unless dividends on the Redeemable Preferred Stock have been declared and paid in full. There have been no changes in the Redeemable Preferred Stock in the three years ended May 31, 2010, 2009 and 2008. As the holder of the Redeemable Preferred Stock, Sojitz America does not have general voting rights but does have the right to vote as a separate class on the sale of all or substantially all of the assets of the Company and its subsidiaries, on merger, consolidation, liquidation or dissolution of the Company or on the sale or assignment of the NIKE trademark for athletic footwear sold in the United States.

Note 11 — Common Stock and Stock–Based Compensation

The authorized number of shares of Class A Common Stock, no par value, and Class B Common Stock, no par value, are 175 million and 750 million, respectively. Each share of Class A Common Stock is convertible into one share of Class B Common Stock. Voting rights of Class B Common Stock are limited in certain circumstances with respect to the election of directors.

In 1990, the Board of Directors adopted, and the shareholders approved, the NIKE, Inc. 1990 Stock Incentive Plan (the "1990 Plan"). The 1990 Plan provides for the issuance of up to 132 million previously unissued shares of Class B Common Stock in connection with stock options and other awards granted under the plan. The 1990 Plan authorizes the grant of non–statutory stock options, incentive stock options, stock appreciation rights, stock bonuses, and the issuance and sale of restricted stock. The exercise price for non–statutory stock options, stock appreciation rights and the grant price of restricted stock may not be less than 75% of the fair market value of the underlying shares on the date of grant. The exercise price for incentive stock options may not be less than the fair market value of the underlying shares on the date of grant. A committee of the Board of Directors administers the 1990 Plan. The committee has the authority to determine the employees to whom awards will be made, the amount of the awards, and the other terms and conditions of the awards. The committee has granted substantially all stock options at 100% of the market price on the date of grant. Substantially all stock option grants outstanding under the 1990 Plan were granted in the first quarter of each fiscal year, vest ratably over four years, and expire 10 years from the date of grant. In June 2010, the Board of Directors amended the 1990 Plan to require, among other things, that the exercise price for non–statutory stock options and stock appreciation rights may not be less than 100% of the fair market value of the underlying shares on the date of grant.

78

NIKE, INC.

NOTES TO CONSOLIDATED FINANCIAL STATEMENTS — (Continued)

The following table summarizes the Company's total stock–based compensation expense recognized in selling and administrative expense:

	Year Ended May 31,		
	2010	2009	2008
		(In millions)	
Stock options[1]	$134.6	$128.8	$127.0
ESPPs	13.7	14.4	7.2
Restricted stock	10.7	7.9	6.8
Subtotal	159.0	151.1	141.0
Stock options and restricted stock expense — restructuring[2]	—	19.5	—
Total stock–based compensation expense	$159.0	$170.6	$141.0

[1] Accelerated stock option expense is recorded for employees eligible for accelerated stock option vesting upon retirement. Accelerated stock option expense reported during the years ended May 31, 2010, 2009 and 2008 was $74.4 million, $58.7 million and $40.7 million, respectively.

[2] In connection with the restructuring activities that took place during fiscal 2009, the Company recognized stock–based compensation expense relating to the modification of stock option agreements, allowing for an extended post–termination exercise period, and accelerated vesting of restricted stock as part of severance packages. See Note 16 — Restructuring Charges for further details.

As of May 31, 2010, the Company had $86.8 million of unrecognized compensation costs from stock options, net of estimated forfeitures, to be recognized as selling and administrative expense over a weighted average period of 2.2 years.

The weighted average fair value per share of the options granted during the years ended May 31, 2010, 2009 and 2008, as computed using the Black–Scholes pricing model, was $23.43, $17.13 and $13.87, respectively. The weighted average assumptions used to estimate these fair values are as follows:

	Year Ended May 31,		
	2010	2009	2008
Dividend yield	1.9%	1.5%	1.4%
Expected volatility	57.6%	32.5%	20.0%
Weighted average expected life (in years)	5.0	5.0	5.0
Risk–free interest rate	2.5%	3.4%	4.8%

The Company estimates the expected volatility based on the implied volatility in market traded options on the Company's common stock with a term greater than one year, along with other factors. The weighted average expected life of options is based on an analysis of historical and expected future exercise patterns. The interest rate is based on the U.S. Treasury (constant maturity) risk–free rate in effect at the date of grant for periods corresponding with the expected term of the options.

79

NIKE, INC.

NOTES TO CONSOLIDATED FINANCIAL STATEMENTS — (Continued)

The following summarizes the stock option transactions under the plan discussed above:

	Shares (In millions)	Weighted Average Option Price
Options outstanding May 31, 2007	39.7	$ 35.50
Exercised	(9.1)	33.45
Forfeited	(0.9)	44.44
Granted	6.9	58.50
Options outstanding May 31, 2008	36.6	$ 40.14
Exercised	(4.0)	35.70
Forfeited	(1.3)	51.19
Granted	7.5	58.17
Options outstanding May 31, 2009	38.8	$ 43.69
Exercised	(8.6)	37.64
Forfeited	(0.6)	51.92
Granted	6.4	52.79
Options outstanding May 31, 2010	36.0	$ 46.60
Options exercisable at May 31,		
2008	16.2	$ 32.35
2009	21.4	36.91
2010	20.4	41.16

The weighted average contractual life remaining for options outstanding and options exercisable at May 31, 2010 was 6.2 years and 4.8 years, respectively. The aggregate intrinsic value for options outstanding and exercisable at May 31, 2010 was $926.8 million and $636.0 million, respectively. The aggregate intrinsic value was the amount by which the market value of the underlying stock exceeded the exercise price of the options. The total intrinsic value of the options exercised during the years ended May 31, 2010, 2009 and 2008 was $239.3 million, $108.4 million and $259.4 million, respectively.

In addition to the 1990 Plan, the Company gives employees the right to purchase shares at a discount to the market price under employee stock purchase plans ("ESPPs"). Employees are eligible to participate through payroll deductions up to 10% of their compensation. At the end of each six-month offering period, shares are purchased by the participants at 85% of the lower of the fair market value at the beginning or the end of the offering period. Employees purchased 0.8 million shares, 1.0 million shares and 0.8 million shares during the years ended May 31, 2010, 2009 and 2008, respectively.

From time to time, the Company grants restricted stock and unrestricted stock to key employees under the 1990 Plan. The number of shares granted to employees during the years ended May 31, 2010, 2009 and 2008 were 499,000, 75,000 and 110,000 with weighted average values per share of $53.16, $56.97 and $59.50, respectively. Recipients of restricted shares are entitled to cash dividends and to vote their respective shares throughout the period of restriction. The value of all of the granted shares was established by the market price on the date of grant. During the years ended May 31, 2010, 2009 and 2008, the fair value of restricted shares vested was $8.0 million, $9.9 million and $9.0 million, respectively, determined as of the date of vesting.

NIKE, INC.

NOTES TO CONSOLIDATED FINANCIAL STATEMENTS — (Continued)

Note 12 — Earnings Per Share

The following is a reconciliation from basic earnings per share to diluted earnings per share. Options to purchase an additional 0.2 million, 13.2 million and 6.6 million shares of common stock were outstanding at May 31, 2010, 2009 and 2008, respectively, but were not included in the computation of diluted earnings per share because the options were anti–dilutive.

| | Year Ended May 31, | | |
	2010	2009	2008
	(In millions, except per share data)		
Determination of shares:			
Weighted average common shares outstanding	485.5	484.9	495.6
Assumed conversion of dilutive stock options and awards	8.4	5.8	8.5
Diluted weighted average common shares outstanding	493.9	490.7	504.1
Basic earnings per common share	$ 3.93	$ 3.07	$ 3.80
Diluted earnings per common share	$ 3.86	$ 3.03	$ 3.74

Note 13 — Benefit Plans

The Company has a profit sharing plan available to most U.S.–based employees. The terms of the plan call for annual contributions by the Company as determined by the Board of Directors. A subsidiary of the Company also has a profit sharing plan available to its U.S.–based employees. The terms of the plan call for annual contributions as determined by the subsidiary's executive management. Contributions of $34.9 million, $27.6 million and $37.3 million were made to the plans and are included in selling and administrative expense for the years ended May 31, 2010, 2009 and 2008, respectively. The Company has various 401(k) employee savings plans available to U.S.–based employees. The Company matches a portion of employee contributions with common stock or cash. Company contributions to the savings plans were $34.2 million, $37.6 million and $33.9 million for the years ended May 31, 2010, 2009 and 2008, respectively, and are included in selling and administrative expense.

The Company also has a Long–Term Incentive Plan ("LTIP") that was adopted by the Board of Directors and approved by shareholders in September 1997 and later amended in fiscal 2007. The Company recognized $24.1 million, $17.6 million and $35.9 million of selling and administrative expense related to cash awards under the LTIP during the years ended May 31, 2010, 2009 and 2008, respectively.

The Company has pension plans in various countries worldwide. The pension plans are only available to local employees and are generally government mandated. The liability related to the unfunded pension liabilities of the plans was $113.0 million and $82.8 million at May 31, 2010 and 2009, respectively.

81

Table of Contents

NIKE, INC.

NOTES TO CONSOLIDATED FINANCIAL STATEMENTS — (Continued)

Note 14 — Accumulated Other Comprehensive Income

The components of accumulated other comprehensive income, net of tax, are as follows:

	May 31, 2010	May 31, 2009
	(In millions)	
Cumulative translation adjustment and other	$ (94.6)	$ 64.6
Net deferred gain on net investment hedge derivatives	107.3	62.5
Net deferred gain on cash flow hedge derivatives	202.1	240.4
	$214.8	$367.5

Note 15 — Commitments and Contingencies

The Company leases space for certain of its offices, warehouses and retail stores under leases expiring from 1 to 25 years after May 31, 2010. Rent expense was $416.1 million, $397.0 million and $344.2 million for the years ended May 31, 2010, 2009 and 2008, respectively. Amounts of minimum future annual rental commitments under non–cancelable operating leases in each of the five years ending May 31, 2011 through 2015 are $334.4 million, $264.0 million, $219.9 million, $177.2 million, $148.0 million, respectively, and $465.8 million in later years.

As of May 31, 2010 and 2009, the Company had letters of credit outstanding totaling $101.1 million and $154.8 million, respectively. These letters of credit were generally issued for the purchase of inventory.

In connection with various contracts and agreements, the Company provides routine indemnifications relating to the enforceability of intellectual property rights, coverage for legal issues that arise and other items where the Company is acting as the guarantor. Currently, the Company has several such agreements in place. However, based on the Company's historical experience and the estimated probability of future loss, the Company has determined that the fair value of such indemnifications is not material to the Company's financial position or results of operations.

In the ordinary course of its business, the Company is involved in various legal proceedings involving contractual and employment relationships, product liability claims, trademark rights, and a variety of other matters. The Company does not believe there are any pending legal proceedings that will have a material impact on the Company's financial position or results of operations.

Note 16 — Restructuring Charges

During fiscal 2009, the Company took necessary steps to streamline its management structure, enhance consumer focus, drive innovation more quickly to market and establish a more scalable, long–term cost structure. As a result, the Company reduced its global workforce by approximately 5% and incurred pre–tax restructuring charges of $195 million, primarily consisting of severance costs related to the workforce reduction. As nearly all of the restructuring activities were completed in fiscal 2009, the Company does not expect to recognize additional costs in future periods relating to these actions. The restructuring charge is reflected in the corporate expense line in the segment presentation of earnings before interest and taxes in Note 19 — Operating Segments and Related Information.

NIKE, INC.

NOTES TO CONSOLIDATED FINANCIAL STATEMENTS — (Continued)

The activity in the restructuring accrual for the years ended May 31, 2010 and 2009 is as follows (in millions):

Restructuring accrual — June 1, 2008	$ —
Severance and related costs	195.0
Cash payments	(29.4)
Non–cash stock option and restricted stock expense	(19.5)
Foreign currency translation and other	3.5
Restructuring accrual — May 31, 2009	149.6
Cash payments	(142.6)
Foreign currency translation and other	1.2
Restructuring accrual — May 31, 2010	$ 8.2

The accrual balance as of May 31, 2010 will be relieved throughout the first half of fiscal year 2011, as final severance payments are completed. The restructuring accrual is included in Accrued liabilities in the Consolidated Balance Sheet.

Note 17 — Divestitures

On December 17, 2007, the Company completed the sale of the Starter brand business to Iconix Brand Group, Inc. for $60.0 million in cash. This transaction resulted in a gain of $28.6 million during the year ended May 31, 2008.

On April 17, 2008, the Company completed the sale of NIKE Bauer Hockey for $189.2 million in cash to a group of private investors ("the Buyer"). The sale resulted in a net gain of $32.0 million recorded in the fourth quarter of the year ended May 31, 2008. This gain included the recognition of a $46.3 million cumulative foreign currency translation adjustment previously included in accumulated other comprehensive income. As part of the terms of the sale agreement, the Company granted the Buyer a royalty free limited license for the use of certain NIKE trademarks for a transitional period of approximately two years. The Company deferred $41.0 million of the sale proceeds related to this license agreement, to be recognized over the license period.

The gains resulting from these divestitures are reflected in other (income) expense, net and in the corporate expense line in the segment presentation of earnings before interest and taxes in Note 19 — Operating Segments and Related Information.

Note 18 — Risk Management and Derivatives

The Company is exposed to global market risks, including the effect of changes in foreign currency exchange rates and interest rates, and uses derivatives to manage financial exposures that occur in the normal course of business. The Company does not hold or issue derivatives for speculative trading purposes.

The Company formally documents all relationships between hedging instruments and hedged items, as well as its risk management objective and strategy for undertaking hedge transactions. This process includes linking all derivatives to either specific firm commitments or forecasted transactions. The Company also enters into foreign exchange forwards to mitigate the change in fair value of specific assets and liabilities on the balance sheet, which are not designated as hedging instruments under the accounting standards for derivatives and hedging. Accordingly, changes in the fair value of hedges of recorded balance sheet positions are recognized

83

NIKE, INC.
NOTES TO CONSOLIDATED FINANCIAL STATEMENTS — (Continued)

immediately in other (income) expense, net, on the income statement together with the transaction gain or loss from the hedged balance sheet position. The Company classifies the cash flows at settlement from these undesignated hedges in the same category as the cash flows from the related hedged items, generally within the cash provided by operations component of the cash flow statement.

The majority of derivatives outstanding as of May 31, 2010 are designated as either cash flow, fair value or net investment hedges under the accounting standards for derivatives and hedging. All derivatives are recognized on the balance sheet at their fair value and classified based on the instrument's maturity date. The total notional amount of outstanding derivatives as of May 31, 2010 was $6.2 billion, which was primarily comprised of cash flow hedges denominated in Euros, Japanese Yen and British Pounds.

The following table presents the fair values of derivative instruments included within the consolidated balance sheet as of May 31, 2010 and 2009:

	Asset Derivatives			Liability Derivatives		
	Balance Sheet Classification	May 31, 2010	May 31, 2009	Balance Sheet Classification	May 31, 2010	May 31, 2009
		(In millions)				
Derivatives formally designated as hedging instruments:						
Foreign exchange forwards and options	Prepaid expenses and other current assets	$ 315.9	$ 270.4	Accrued liabilities	$ 24.7	$ 34.6
Interest rate swap contracts	Prepaid expenses and other current assets	—	0.1	Accrued liabilities	—	—
Foreign exchange forwards and options	Deferred income taxes and other assets	0.4	81.3	Deferred income taxes and other liabilities	0.1	—
Interest rate swap contracts	Deferred income taxes and other assets	14.6	13.7	Deferred income taxes and other liabilities	—	—
Total derivatives formally designated as hedging instruments		330.9	365.5		24.8	34.6
Derivatives not designated as hedging instruments:						
Foreign exchange forwards and options	Prepaid expenses and other current assets	$ 103.9	$ 12.8	Accrued liabilities	$ 138.9	$ 34.3
Foreign exchange forwards and options	Deferred income taxes and other assets	—	0.4	Deferred income taxes and other liabilities	1.4	—
Total derivatives not designated as hedging instruments		103.9	13.2		140.3	34.3
Total derivatives		$ 434.8	$ 378.7		$ 165.1	$ 68.9

84

NIKE, INC.

NOTES TO CONSOLIDATED FINANCIAL STATEMENTS — (Continued)

The following tables present the amounts affecting the consolidated statements of income for years ended May 31, 2010 and 2009:

| | Amount of Gain (Loss) Recognized in Other Comprehensive Income on Derivatives[1] | | Amount of Gain (Loss) Reclassified From Accumulated Other Comprehensive Income into Income[1] | | |
	Year Ended May 31, 2010	Year Ended May 31, 2009	Location of Gain (Loss) Reclassified From Accumulated Other Comprehensive Income Into Income[1] (In millions)	Year Ended May 31, 2010	Year Ended May 31, 2009
Derivatives formally designated					
Derivatives designated as cash flow hedges:					
Foreign exchange forwards and options	$ (29.9)	$ 106.3	Revenue	$ 51.4	$ 92.7
Foreign exchange forwards and options	89.0	350.1	Cost of sales	60.0	(13.5)
Foreign exchange forwards and options	4.7	(0.4)	Selling and administrative expense	1.0	0.8
Foreign exchange forwards and options	51.1	165.1	Other (income) expense, net	56.1	67.8
Total designated cash flow hedges	$ 114.9	$ 621.1		$ 168.5	$ 147.8
Derivatives designated as net investment hedges:					
Foreign exchange forwards and options	$ 66.0	$ 161.4	Other (income) expense, net	$ —	$ —

[1] For the year ended May 31, 2010, $5.2 million of income was recorded to other (income) expense, net as a result of cash flow hedge ineffectiveness. For the year ended May 31, 2009, an immaterial amount of ineffectiveness from cash flow hedges was recorded in other (income) expense, net.

| | Amount of Gain (Loss) recognized in Income on Derivatives | | Location of Gain (Loss) Recognized in Income on Derivatives |
	Year Ended May 31, 2010	Year Ended May 31, 2009 (In millions)	
Derivatives designated as fair value hedges:			
Interest rate swaps[1]	$ 7.4	$ 1.5	Interest expense (income), net
Derivatives not designated as hedging instruments:			
Foreign exchange forwards and options	$ (91.1)	$ (83.0)	Other (income) expense, net

[1] All interest rate swap agreements meet the shortcut method requirements under the accounting standards for derivatives and hedging. Accordingly, changes in the fair values of the interest rate swap agreements are exactly offset by changes in the fair value of the underlying long-term debt. Refer to section "Fair Value Hedges" for additional detail.

Refer to Note 5 — Accrued Liabilities for derivative instruments recorded in accrued liabilities, Note 6 —Fair Value Measurements for a description of how the above financial instruments are valued, Note 14 — Accumulated Other Comprehensive Income and the Consolidated Statement of Shareholders' Equity for additional information on changes in other comprehensive income for the years ended May 31, 2010 and 2009.

NIKE, INC.
NOTES TO CONSOLIDATED FINANCIAL STATEMENTS — (Continued)

Cash Flow Hedges

The purpose of the Company's foreign currency hedging activities is to protect the Company from the risk that the eventual cash flows resulting from transactions in foreign currencies, including revenues, product costs, selling and administrative expenses, investments in U.S. dollar–denominated available–for–sale debt securities and intercompany transactions, including intercompany borrowings, will be adversely affected by changes in exchange rates. It is the Company's policy to utilize derivatives to reduce foreign exchange risks where internal netting strategies cannot be effectively employed. Hedged transactions are denominated primarily in Euros, British Pounds and Japanese Yen. The Company hedges up to 100% of anticipated exposures typically 12 months in advance, but has hedged as much as 34 months in advance.

All changes in fair values of outstanding cash flow hedge derivatives, except the ineffective portion, are recorded in other comprehensive income until net income is affected by the variability of cash flows of the hedged transaction. In most cases, amounts recorded in other comprehensive income will be released to net income some time after the maturity of the related derivative. The consolidated statement of income classification of effective hedge results is the same as that of the underlying exposure. Results of hedges of revenue and product costs are recorded in revenue and cost of sales, respectively, when the underlying hedged transaction affects net income. Results of hedges of selling and administrative expense are recorded together with those costs when the related expense is recorded. Results of hedges of anticipated purchases and sales of U.S. dollar–denominated available–for–sale securities are recorded in other (income) expense, net when the securities are sold. Results of hedges of anticipated intercompany transactions are recorded in other (income) expense, net when the transaction occurs. The Company classifies the cash flows at settlement from these designated cash flow hedge derivatives in the same category as the cash flows from the related hedged items, generally within the cash provided by operations component of the cash flow statement.

Premiums paid on options are initially recorded as deferred charges. The Company assesses the effectiveness of options based on the total cash flows method and records total changes in the options' fair value to other comprehensive income to the degree they are effective.

As of May 31, 2010, $187.2 million of deferred net gains (net of tax) on both outstanding and matured derivatives accumulated in other comprehensive income are expected to be reclassified to net income during the next 12 months as a result of underlying hedged transactions also being recorded in net income. Actual amounts ultimately reclassified to net income are dependent on the exchange rates in effect when derivative contracts that are currently outstanding mature. As of May 31, 2010, the maximum term over which the Company is hedging exposures to the variability of cash flows for its forecasted and recorded transactions is 18 months.

The Company formally assesses both at a hedge's inception and on an ongoing basis, whether the derivatives that are used in the hedging transaction have been highly effective in offsetting changes in the cash flows of hedged items and whether those derivatives may be expected to remain highly effective in future periods. Effectiveness for cash flow hedges is assessed based on forward rates. When it is determined that a derivative is not, or has ceased to be, highly effective as a hedge, the Company discontinues hedge accounting prospectively.

The Company discontinues hedge accounting prospectively when (1) it determines that the derivative is no longer highly effective in offsetting changes in the cash flows of a hedged item (including hedged items such as firm commitments or forecasted transactions); (2) the derivative expires or is sold, terminated, or exercised; (3) it is no longer probable that the forecasted transaction will occur; or (4) management determines that designating the derivative as a hedging instrument is no longer appropriate.

86

NIKE, INC.

NOTES TO CONSOLIDATED FINANCIAL STATEMENTS — (Continued)

When the Company discontinues hedge accounting because it is no longer probable that the forecasted transaction will occur in the originally expected period, or within an additional two–month period of time thereafter, the gain or loss on the derivative remains in accumulated other comprehensive income and is reclassified to net income when the forecasted transaction affects net income. However, if it is probable that a forecasted transaction will not occur by the end of the originally specified time period or within an additional two–month period of time thereafter, the gains and losses that were accumulated in other comprehensive income will be recognized immediately in net income. In all situations in which hedge accounting is discontinued and the derivative remains outstanding, the Company will carry the derivative at its fair value on the balance sheet, recognizing future changes in the fair value in other (income) expense, net. For the year ended May 31, 2010, $5.2 million of income was recorded to other (income) expense, net as a result of cash flow hedge ineffectiveness. For the years ended 2009 and 2008, the Company recorded in other (income) expense an immaterial amount of ineffectiveness from cash flow hedges.

Fair Value Hedges

The Company is also exposed to the risk of changes in the fair value of certain fixed–rate debt attributable to changes in interest rates. Derivatives currently used by the Company to hedge this risk are receive–fixed, pay–variable interest rate swaps. As of May 31, 2010, all interest rate swap agreements are designated as fair value hedges of the related long–term debt and meet the shortcut method requirements under the accounting standards for derivatives and hedging. Accordingly, changes in the fair values of the interest rate swap agreements are exactly offset by changes in the fair value of the underlying long–term debt. The cash flows associated with the Company's fair value hedges are periodic interest payments while the swaps are outstanding, which are reflected in net income within the cash provided by operations component of the cash flow statement. No ineffectiveness has been recorded to net income related to interest rate swaps designated as fair value hedges for the years ended May 31, 2010, 2009 and 2008.

In fiscal 2003, the Company entered into a receive–floating, pay–fixed interest rate swap agreement related to a Japanese Yen denominated intercompany loan with one of the Company's Japanese subsidiaries. This interest rate swap was not designated as a hedge under the accounting standards for derivatives and hedging. Accordingly, changes in the fair value of the swap were recorded to net income each period through maturity as a component of interest expense (income), net. Both the intercompany loan and the related interest rate swap matured during the year ended May 31, 2009.

Net Investment Hedges

The Company also hedges the risk of variability in foreign–currency–denominated net investments in wholly–owned international operations. All changes in fair value of the derivatives designated as net investment hedges, except ineffective portions, are reported in the cumulative translation adjustment component of other comprehensive income along with the foreign currency translation adjustments on those investments. The Company classifies the cash flows at settlement of its net investment hedges within the cash used by investing component of the cash flow statement. The Company assesses hedge effectiveness based on changes in forward rates. The Company recorded no ineffectiveness from its net investment hedges for the years ended May 31, 2010, 2009, and 2008.

Credit Risk

The Company is exposed to credit–related losses in the event of non–performance by counterparties to hedging instruments. The counterparties to all derivative transactions are major financial institutions with investment grade credit ratings. However, this does not eliminate the Company's exposure to credit risk with

87

NIKE, INC.

NOTES TO CONSOLIDATED FINANCIAL STATEMENTS — (Continued)

these institutions. This credit risk is limited to the unrealized gains in such contracts should any of these counterparties fail to perform as contracted. To manage this risk, the Company has established strict counterparty credit guidelines that are continually monitored and reported to senior management according to prescribed guidelines. The Company utilizes a portfolio of financial institutions either headquartered or operating in the same countries the Company conducts its business. As a result of the above considerations, the Company considers the impact of the risk of counterparty default to be immaterial.

Certain of the Company's derivative instruments contain credit risk related contingent features. As of May 31, 2010, the Company was in compliance with all such credit risk related contingent features. The aggregate fair value of derivative instruments with credit risk related contingent features that are in a net liability position at May 31, 2010 was $18.3 million. The Company was not required to post any collateral as a result of these contingent features.

Note 19 — Operating Segments and Related Information

Operating Segments.   The Company's operating segments are evidence of the structure of the Company's internal organization. The major segments are defined by geographic regions for operations participating in NIKE Brand sales activity excluding NIKE Golf. Each NIKE Brand geographic segment operates predominantly in one industry: the design, production, marketing and selling of sports and fitness footwear, apparel, and equipment. In fiscal 2009, the Company initiated a reorganization of the NIKE Brand into a new model consisting of six geographies. Effective June 1, 2009, the Company's new reportable operating segments for the NIKE Brand are: North America, Western Europe, Central and Eastern Europe, Greater China, Japan, and Emerging Markets. Previously, NIKE Brand operations were organized into the following four geographic regions: U.S., Europe, Middle East and Africa (collectively, "EMEA"), Asia Pacific, and Americas.

The Company's "Other" category is broken into two components for presentation purposes to align with the way management views the Company. The "Global Brand Divisions" category primarily represents NIKE Brand licensing businesses that are not part of a geographic operating segment, selling, general and administrative expenses that are centrally managed for the NIKE Brand and costs associated with product development and supply chain operations. The "Other Businesses" category primarily consists of the activities of Cole Haan, Converse Inc., Hurley International LLC, NIKE Golf and Umbro Ltd. Activities represented in the "Other" category are considered immaterial for individual disclosure. Prior period amounts have been reclassified to conform to the Company's new operating structure described above.

Revenues as shown below represent sales to external customers for each segment. Intercompany revenues have been eliminated and are immaterial for separate disclosure.

Corporate consists of unallocated general and administrative expenses, which includes expenses associated with centrally managed departments, depreciation and amortization related to the Company's headquarters, unallocated insurance and benefit programs, including stock-based compensation, certain foreign currency gains and losses, including hedge gains and losses, certain corporate eliminations and other items.

Effective June 1, 2009, the primary financial measure used by the Company to evaluate performance of individual operating segments is Earnings Before Interest and Taxes (commonly referred to as "EBIT") which represents net income before interest expense (income), net and income taxes in the Consolidated Statements of Income. Reconciling items for EBIT represent corporate expense items that are not allocated to the operating segments for management reporting. Previously, the Company evaluated performance of individual operating segments based on pre-tax income or income before income taxes.

88

NIKE, INC.

NOTES TO CONSOLIDATED FINANCIAL STATEMENTS — (Continued)

As part of the Company's centrally managed foreign exchange risk management program, standard foreign currency rates are assigned to each NIKE Brand entity in our geographic operating segments and are used to record any non–functional currency revenues or product purchases into the entity's functional currency. Geographic operating segment revenues and cost of sales reflect use of these standard rates. For all NIKE Brand operating segments, differences between assigned standard foreign currency rates and actual market rates are included in Corporate together with foreign currency hedge gains and losses generated from the centrally managed foreign exchange risk management program and other conversion gains and losses. For the years ended May 31, 2009 and 2008, foreign currency hedge results along with other conversion gains and losses generated by the Western Europe and Central and Eastern Europe geographies were recorded in their respective results.

Additions to long–lived assets as presented in the following table represent capital expenditures.

Accounts receivable, inventories and property, plant and equipment for operating segments are regularly reviewed by management and are therefore provided below.

Certain prior year amounts have been reclassified to conform to fiscal 2010 presentation.

89

NIKE, INC.
NOTES TO CONSOLIDATED FINANCIAL STATEMENTS — (Continued)

	Year Ended May 31,		
	2010	2009	2008
		(In millions)	
Revenue			
North America	$ 6,696.0	$ 6,778.3	$ 6,660.5
Western Europe	3,892.0	4,139.1	4,320.0
Central and Eastern Europe	1,149.9	1,373.2	1,309.2
Greater China	1,741.8	1,743.3	1,353.6
Japan	882.0	925.9	822.4
Emerging Markets	2,041.6	1,702.0	1,630.3
Global Brand Divisions	105.3	95.3	117.9
Total NIKE Brand	16,508.6	16,757.1	16,213.9
Other Businesses	2,529.5	2,419.0	2,413.1
Corporate	(24.1)	—	—
Total NIKE Consolidated Revenues	$19,014.0	$19,176.1	$18,627.0
Earnings Before Interest and Taxes			
North America	$ 1,538.1	$ 1,429.3	$ 1,460.4
Western Europe	855.7	939.1	922.5
Central and Eastern Europe	281.2	415.1	358.4
Greater China	637.1	575.2	430.7
Japan	180.3	205.4	178.9
Emerging Markets	492.6	342.6	306.6
Global Brand Divisions	(866.8)	(811.5)	(736.8)
Total NIKE Brand	3,118.2	3,095.2	2,920.7
Other Businesses[1]	299.4	(192.6)	358.6
Corporate	(894.4)	(955.6)	(853.5)
Total NIKE Consolidated Earnings Before Interest and Taxes	2,523.2	1,947.0	2,425.8
Interest expense (income), net	6.3	(9.5)	(77.1)
Total NIKE Consolidated Earnings Before Taxes	$ 2,516.9	$ 1,956.5	$ 2,502.9
Additions to Long–lived Assets			
North America	$ 45.3	$ 99.2	$ 141.9
Western Europe	58.9	69.6	63.5
Central and Eastern Europe	4.3	8.1	5.5
Greater China	80.4	58.5	13.1
Japan	11.6	10.0	21.9
Emerging Markets	10.5	10.9	12.4
Global Brand Divisions	29.9	37.8	22.6
Total NIKE Brand	240.9	294.1	280.9
Other Businesses	52.1	89.6	61.5
Corporate	42.1	72.0	106.8
Total Additions to Long–lived Assets	$ 335.1	$ 455.7	$ 449.2
Depreciation			
North America	$ 64.7	$ 64.3	$ 52.4
Western Europe	57.1	51.4	61.1
Central and Eastern Europe	4.6	4.0	3.7
Greater China	11.0	7.2	3.8
Japan	26.2	29.9	20.4
Emerging Markets	11.0	10.2	10.8
Global Brand Divisions	33.8	42.3	34.3
Total NIKE Brand	208.4	209.3	186.5
Other Businesses	45.7	37.5	28.1
Corporate	69.6	88.2	89.0
Total Depreciation	$ 323.7	$ 335.0	$ 303.6

NIKE, INC.

NOTES TO CONSOLIDATED FINANCIAL STATEMENTS — (Continued)

(1) During the year ended May 31, 2009, the Other category included a pre−tax charge of $401.3 million for the impairment of goodwill, intangible and other assets of Umbro, which was recorded in the third quarter of fiscal 2009. See Note 4 — Acquisition, Identifiable Intangible Assets, Goodwill and Umbro Impairment for more information.

(2) During the year ended May 31, 2009, Corporate expense included pre−tax charges of $195.0 million for the Company's restructuring activities, which were completed in the fourth quarter of fiscal 2009. See Note 16 — Restructuring Charges for more information.

	Year Ended May 31,	
	2010	2009
	(In millions)	
Accounts Receivable, net		
North America	$ 848.0	$ 897.7
Western Europe	401.8	508.8
Central and Eastern Europe	293.6	368.3
Greater China	128.9	122.3
Japan	166.8	207.2
Emerging Markets	327.2	268.2
Global Brand Divisions	22.8	53.3
Total NIKE Brand	2,189.1	2,425.8
Other Businesses	442.1	439.7
Corporate	18.6	18.4
Total Accounts Receivable, net	$ 2,649.8	$ 2,883.9
Inventories		
North America	$ 767.5	$ 868.8
Western Europe	347.2	341.6
Central and Eastern Europe	124.8	278.1
Greater China	103.5	110.4
Japan	68.3	95.7
Emerging Markets	262.2	258.2
Global Brand Divisions	20.6	32.4
Total NIKE Brand	1,694.1	1,985.2
Other Businesses	346.7	371.8
Corporate	—	—
Total Inventories	$ 2,040.8	$ 2,357.0
Property, Plant and Equipment, net		
North America	$ 324.7	$ 354.3
Western Europe	282.1	326.5
Central and Eastern Europe	12.3	15.0
Greater China	145.5	78.2
Japan	332.6	318.5
Emerging Markets	47.0	47.3
Global Brand Divisions	99.6	103.1
Total NIKE Brand	1,243.8	1,242.9
Other Businesses	167.4	163.7
Corporate	520.7	551.1
Total Property, Plant and Equipment, net	$ 1,931.9	$ 1,957.7

91

Table of Contents

NIKE, INC.

NOTES TO CONSOLIDATED FINANCIAL STATEMENTS — (Continued)

Revenues by Major Product Lines.   Revenues to external customers for NIKE Brand products are attributable to sales of footwear, apparel and equipment. Other revenues to external customers primarily include external sales by Cole Haan, Converse, Exeter (whose primary business was the Starter brand business which was sold December 17, 2007), Hurley, NIKE Bauer Hockey (through April 16, 2008), NIKE Golf, and Umbro (beginning March 3, 2008).

	2010	Year Ended May 31, 2009 (In millions)	2008
Footwear	$ 10,333.1	$ 10,306.7	$ 9,731.6
Apparel	5,036.6	5,244.7	5,234.0
Equipment	1,033.6	1,110.4	1,130.4
Other	2,610.7	2,514.3	2,531.0
	$ 19,014.0	$ 19,176.1	$ 18,627.0

Revenues and Long–Lived Assets by Geographic Area.   Geographical area information is similar to what was shown previously under operating segments with the exception of the Other activity, which has been allocated to the geographical areas based on the location where the sales originated. Revenues derived in the United States were $7,913.9 million, $8,019.8 million and $7,938.5 million, for the years ended May 31, 2010, 2009 and 2008, respectively. The Company's largest concentrations of long–lived assets primarily consist of the Company's world headquarters and distribution facilities in the United States and distribution facilities in Japan and Belgium. Long–lived assets attributable to operations in the United States, which are comprised of net property, plant & equipment, were $1,070.1 million, $1,142.6 million and $1,109.9 million at May 31, 2010, 2009 and 2008, respectively. Long–lived assets attributable to operations in Japan were $335.6 million, $322.3 million and $303.8 million at May 31, 2010, 2009 and 2008, respectively. Long–lived assets attributable to operations in Belgium were $163.7 million, $191.0 million and $219.1 million at May 31, 2010, 2009 and 2008, respectively.

Major Customers.   Revenues derived from Foot Locker, Inc. represented 8% of the Company's consolidated revenues for the year ended May 31, 2010 and 9% for the years ended May 31, 2009 and 2008. Sales to this customer are included in all segments of the Company.

International Financial Reporting Standards (IFRS)

The Need for Global Accounting Standards

As discussed in Chapter 1, the Financial Accounting Standards Board (FASB) establishes generally accepted accounting principles (GAAP) for public companies in the United States. Of course, there is a world beyond the borders of the United States. In recent years, the removal of trade barriers and the growth in cross-border equity and debt issuances have led to a dramatic increase in international commerce. As a result, companies are often reporting financial results to users outside of the United States.

Historically, accounting standards have varied considerably across countries. These variances have been driven by cultural, legal, and political differences, and resulted in financial statements that were not easily comparable and difficult to interpret. These differences caused problems for companies in Europe and Asia, where local economies have become increasingly tied to international commerce.

During the last decade, however, a common set of International Financial Reporting Standards (IFRS) has emerged to reduce cross-country differences in accounting standards, primarily in countries outside of North America. While much of the world has migrated to IFRS, the United States has not. Because of the size of the United States and its significant role in world commerce, however, U.S. GAAP still has a global impact. As a result, there are currently two major accounting standard-setting efforts in the world, U.S. GAAP and IFRS. These two sets of accounting standards add cost and complexity for companies doing business and obtaining financing internationally.

Overview of IFRS

International Financial Reporting Standards (IFRS) have emerged during the last 10 years to meet the financial reporting needs of an increasingly global business environment.

What Is IFRS? International Financial Reporting Standards are a set of global accounting standards developed by an international standard-setting body called the International Accounting Standards Board (IASB). Like the Financial Accounting Standards Board (FASB), the IASB is an independent entity that establishes accounting rules. Unlike the FASB, the IASB does not establish accounting rules for any specific country. Rather, it develops accounting rules that can be used by a variety of countries, with the goal of developing a single set of global accounting standards.

Who Uses IFRS? IFRS applies to companies that issue publicly traded debt or equity securities, called **public companies**, in countries that have adopted IFRS as their accounting standards. Since 2005, all 27 countries in the European Union (EU) have been required to prepare financial statements using IFRS. In addition, over

100 other countries have adopted or are planning to adopt IFRS for public companies (see Exhibit 1). Canada will adopt IFRS by 2011, with Mexico following in 2012. Japan will consider mandatory use of IFRS in 2012. In addition, the G20 (Group of 20) leadership has called for uniform global accounting standards by June 2011.

EXHIBIT 1

IFRS Adopters

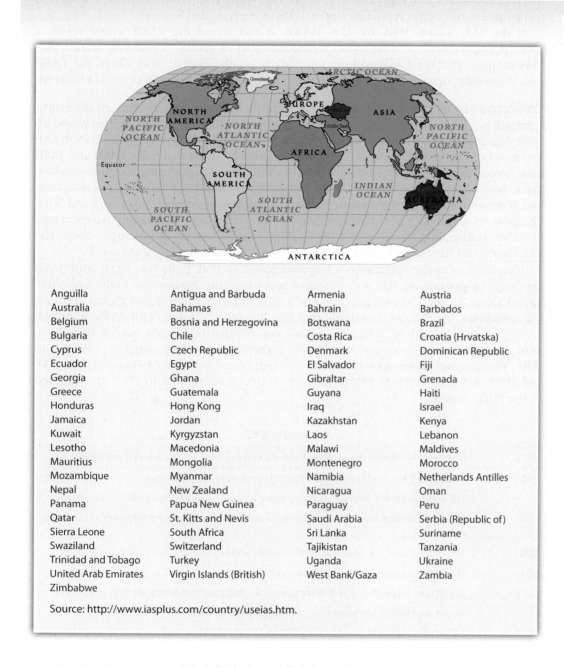

Anguilla	Antigua and Barbuda	Armenia	Austria
Australia	Bahamas	Bahrain	Barbados
Belgium	Bosnia and Herzegovina	Botswana	Brazil
Bulgaria	Chile	Costa Rica	Croatia (Hrvatska)
Cyprus	Czech Republic	Denmark	Dominican Republic
Ecuador	Egypt	El Salvador	Fiji
Georgia	Ghana	Gibraltar	Grenada
Greece	Guatemala	Guyana	Haiti
Honduras	Hong Kong	Iraq	Israel
Jamaica	Jordan	Kazakhstan	Kenya
Kuwait	Kyrgyzstan	Laos	Lebanon
Lesotho	Macedonia	Malawi	Maldives
Mauritius	Mongolia	Montenegro	Morocco
Mozambique	Myanmar	Namibia	Netherlands Antilles
Nepal	New Zealand	Nicaragua	Oman
Panama	Papua New Guinea	Paraguay	Peru
Qatar	St. Kitts and Nevis	Saudi Arabia	Serbia (Republic of)
Sierra Leone	South Africa	Sri Lanka	Suriname
Swaziland	Switzerland	Tajikistan	Tanzania
Trinidad and Tobago	Turkey	Uganda	Ukraine
United Arab Emirates	Virgin Islands (British)	West Bank/Gaza	Zambia
Zimbabwe			

Source: http://www.iasplus.com/country/useias.htm.

U.S. GAAP and IFRS: The Road Forward

The United States has not formally adopted IFRS for U.S. companies. The wide acceptance being gained by IFRS around the world, however, has placed considerable pressure on the United States to align U.S. GAAP with IFRS. There are two possible paths that the United States could take to achieve this: (1) adoption of IFRS by the U.S. Securities and Exchange Commission and (2) convergence of U.S. GAAP and IFRS. These two options are briefly discussed below.

Adoption of IFRS by the SEC The U.S. Securities and Exchange Commission (SEC) is the U.S. governmental agency that has authority over the accounting and financial disclosures for U.S. public companies. Only the SEC has the authority to adopt IFRS for U.S. public companies. In 2008, the SEC presented a "roadmap" to adopting IFRS, which outlined a timetable along with a set of "milestones" that needed to be met before the SEC would be willing to adopt IFRS. In 2010, the SEC reiterated the milestones outlined in the roadmap. According to the work plan, the SEC plans on deciding whether to incorporate IFRS into U.S. GAAP for public companies by 2011. If adopted, companies could begin reporting under IFRS as early as 2015.

If the SEC adopts IFRS for U.S. GAAP, it has stated the FASB would retain a "critical and substantive role in achieving the goal of global accounting standards." This suggests that the FASB will not necessarily be eliminated. More likely, the FASB would provide input to the IASB so that U.S. accounting perspectives are considered.

Convergence of U.S. GAAP and IFRS If the SEC does not adopt IFRS, an alternative approach would be for the FASB and IASB to converge U.S. GAAP and IFRS. This would involve aligning IFRS and U.S. GAAP one topic at a time, slowly merging IFRS and U.S. GAAP into two broadly uniform sets of accounting standards. To this end, the FASB and IASB have agreed to work together on a number of difficult and high-profile accounting issues. These issues frame a large portion of the disagreement between the two sets of standards and, if accomplished, will significantly reduce the differences between U.S. GAAP and IFRS. The projects selected for the convergence effort represent some of the more technical topics in accounting, and are covered in intermediate and advanced accounting courses. The FASB and IASB have set mid-2011 as the deadline for establishing final standards.

One of the major limitations of convergence is that both the FASB and IASB continue to operate as the accounting standard-setting bodies for their respective jurisdictions. As such, convergence would not result in a single set of global accounting standards. Only those standards that go through the joint FASB–IASB standard-setting process would be released as uniform. Standards that do not go through a joint standard-setting process may create inconsistencies between U.S. GAAP and IFRS. Thus, convergence does not guarantee complete uniformity between U.S. GAAP and IFRS. A brief summary of the major U.S. decisions related to IFRS are outlined in the table below.

The Road to IFRS	
2002	IASB and FASB jointly agree to work toward making IFRS and U.S. GAAP compatible.
2005	EU adopts IFRS for all companies engaged in international markets.
	SEC and European Commission jointly agree to work toward a "Roadmap for Convergence."
2007	SEC allows foreign (non-U.S.) companies to use IFRS financial statements to meet U.S. filing requirements.
2008	SEC issues proposed "Roadmap" with timeline and key milestones for adopting IFRS.
2010	SEC reiterates milestones in the proposed "Roadmap."
2011	Target date for FASB and IASB convergence on major standard-setting projects.
	Target date for SEC's tentative decision regarding IFRS adoption.
2015	Earliest date the SEC would require IFRS for U.S. public companies.

Differences Between U.S. GAAP and IFRS

U.S. GAAP and IFRS differ both in their approach to standard setting, as well as their financial statement presentation and recording of transactions.

Rules-Based vs. Principles Approach to Standard Setting U.S. GAAP is considered to be a "rules-based" approach to accounting standard setting. The accounting standards provide detailed and specific rules on the accounting for business transactions. There are few exceptions or varying interpretations of the accounting for a business event. This structure is consistent with the U.S. legal and regulatory system, reflecting the social and economic values of the United States.

In contrast, IFRS is designed to meet the needs of many countries. Differences in legal, political, and economic systems create different needs for and uses of financial information in different countries. For example, Germany needs a financial reporting system that reflects the central role of banks in its financial system, while the Netherlands needs a financial reporting system that reflects the significant role of outside equity in its financial system.

To accommodate economic, legal, and social diversity, IFRS must be broad enough to capture these differences, while still presenting comparable financial statements. Under IFRS, there is greater opportunity for different interpretations of the accounting treatment of a business event across different business entities. To support this, IFRS often has more extensive disclosures that support alternative assumptions. Thus, IFRS provides more latitude for professional judgment than typically found in comparable U.S. GAAP. Many countries find this feature attractive in reducing regulatory costs associated with using and auditing financial reports. This "principles-based" approach presents one of the most significant challenges to adopting IFRS in the United States.

Technical Differences Between IFRS and U.S. GAAP Although U.S. GAAP is similar to IFRS, differences arise in the presentation format, balance sheet valuations, and technical accounting procedures. The Mornin' Joe International financial statements presented on pages 716–716G highlight the financial statement format, presentation, and recording differences between U.S. GAAP and IFRS. In addition, the International Connection boxes in Chapters 1, 4, 7, 10, 13, and 16 discuss some of the significant differences between U.S. GAAP and IFRS. A more comprehensive summary of the key differences between U.S. GAAP and IFRS that are relevant to an introductory accounting course is summarized in the table on the following pages.

DiscussionQuestions

1. Briefly discuss why global accounting standards are needed in today's business environment.

2. What are International Financial Reporting Standards? Who uses these accounting standards?

3. What body is responsible for setting International Financial Reporting Standards?

4. Briefly discuss the differences between (a) convergence of U.S. GAAP with IFRS and (b) adoption of IFRS by the U.S. Securities and Exchange Commission.

5. Briefly discuss the difference between (a) a "rules-based" approach to accounting standard setting and (b) a "principles-based" approach to accounting standard setting.

6. How is property, plant, and equipment measured on the balance sheet under IFRS? How does this differ from the way property, plant, and equipment is measured on the balance sheet under U.S. GAAP?

7. What inventory costing methods are allowed under IFRS? How does this differ from the treatment under U.S. GAAP?

Comparison of Accounting for Selected Items Under U.S. GAAP and IFRS

	U.S. GAAP	IFRS	Text Reference
General:			
Financial statement titles	Balance Sheet Income Statement Statement of Stockholders' Equity Statement of Cash Flows	Statement of Financial Position Statement of Comprehensive Income Statement of Changes in Equity Statement of Cash Flows	General
Financial periods presented	Public companies must present two years of comparative information for income statement, statement of stockholders' equity, and statement of cash flows	One year of comparative information must be presented	General
Conceptual basis for standard setting	"Rules-based" approach	"Principles-based" approach	General
Internal control requirements	Sarbanes-Oxley Act (SOX) Section 404		Ch 8; LO 1
Balance Sheet:			
Terminology differences	"Payable" "Stockholders' Equity" "Net Income (Loss)"	**Statement of Financial Position** "Provision" "Capital and Reserves" "Profit or (Loss)"	Ch 11 Ch 13 General
Inventory—LIFO	LIFO allowed	LIFO prohibited	Ch 7; LO 3, 4, 5
Inventory—valuation	Market is defined as "replacement value" Reversal of lower-of-cost-or-market write-downs not allowed	Market is defined as "fair value" Reversal of write-downs allowed	Ch 7; LO 6 Ch 7; LO 6
Long-lived assets	May NOT be revalued to fair value	May be revalued to fair value on a regular basis	Ch 10; LO 1

(Continued)

Comparison of Accounting for Selected Items Under U.S. GAAP and IFRS (Continued)

	U.S. GAAP	IFRS	Text Reference
Land held for investment	Treated as held for use or sale, and recorded at historical cost	May be accounted for on a historical cost basis or on a fair value basis with changes in fair value recognized through profit and loss	Ch 10; LO 1
Property, plant, & equipment—valuation	Historical cost	May select between historical cost or revalued amount (a form of fair value)	Ch 10; LO 1
	If impaired, impairment loss may NOT be reversed in future periods	If impaired, impairment loss may be reversed in future periods	
Cost of major overhaul (Capital and revenue expenditures)	Different treatment for ordinary repairs and maintenance, asset improvement, extraordinary repairs	Typically included as part of the cost of the asset if future economic benefit is probable and can be reliably measured	Ch 10; LO 1
Intangible assets—valuation	Acquisition cost, unless impaired	Fair value permitted if the intangible asset trades in an active market	Ch 10; LO 5
Intangible assets—impairment loss reversal	Prohibited	Prohibited for goodwill, but allowed for other intangible assets	Ch 10; LO 5
Deferred tax liability	The amount due within one year classified as current	Always noncurrent	Appendix D
Income Statement:	**Income Statement**	**Statement of Comprehensive Income**	
Revenue recognition	Detailed guidance depending on the transaction	Broad guidance	Ch 3; LO 1
Classification of expenses on income statement	Public companies must present expenses on the income statement by function (e.g., cost of goods sold, selling, administrative)	Expenses may be presented based either by function (e.g., cost of goods sold, selling) or by the nature of expense (e.g., wages expense, interest expense)	Ch 6; LO 1
Research and development costs	Expensed as incurred	Research costs expensed	Ch 10; LO 5
		Development costs capitalized once technical and economic feasibility attained	
Extraordinary items	Allowed for items that are both unusual in nature and infrequent in occurrence	Prohibited	Ch 17; Appendix

(Continued)

Comparison of Accounting for Selected Items Under U.S. GAAP and IFRS *(Concluded)*

	U.S. GAAP	IFRS	Text Reference
Statement of Cash Flows:	**Statement of Cash Flows**	**Statement of Cash Flows**	
Classification of interest paid or received	Treated as an operating activity	Interest paid may be treated as either an operating or a financing activity, interest received may be treated as an operating or investing activity	Ch 16; LO 3
Classification of dividend paid or received	Dividend paid treated as a financing activity, Dividend received treated as an operating activity	Dividend paid may be treated as either an operating or a financing activity, dividend received may be treated as an operating or investing activity	Ch 16; LO 3

Glossary

A

accelerated depreciation method A depreciation method that provides for a higher depreciation amount in the first year of the asset's use, followed by a gradually declining amount of depreciation. (455)

account An accounting form that is used to record the increases and decreases in each financial statement item. (52)

account form The form of balance sheet that resembles the basic format of the accounting equation, with assets on the left side and Liabilities and Owner's Equity sections on the right side. (18, 258)

account payable The liability created by a purchase on account. (11)

account receivable A claim against the customer created by selling merchandise or services on credit. (12, 65, 402)

accounting An information system that provides reports to stakeholders about the economic activities and condition of a business. (3)

accounting cycle The process that begins with analyzing and journalizing transactions and ends with the post-closing trial balance. (162)

accounting equation Assets = Liabilities + Owner's Equity. (9)

accounting period concept The accounting concept that assumes that the economic life of the business can be divided into time periods. (104)

accounting system The methods and procedures used by a business to collect, classify, summarize, and report financial data for use by management and external users. (206)

accounts payable subsidiary ledger The subsidiary ledger containing the individual accounts with suppliers (creditors). (207)

accounts receivable analysis A company's ability to collect its accounts receivable. (782)

accounts receivable subsidiary ledger The subsidiary ledger containing the individual accounts with customers. (207)

accounts receivable turnover The relationship between net sales and accounts receivable, computed by dividing the net sales by the average net accounts receivable; measures how frequently during the year the accounts receivable are being converted to cash. (417, 782)

accrual basis of accounting Under this basis of accounting, revenues and expenses are reported in the income statement in the period in which they are earned or incurred. (104)

accrued expenses Expenses that have been incurred but not recorded in the accounts. (108)

accrued revenues Revenues that have been earned but not recorded in the accounts. (107)

accumulated depreciation The contra asset account credited when recording the depreciation of a fixed asset. (117)

accumulated other comprehensive income The cumulative effects of other comprehensive income items reported separately in the Stockholders' Equity section of the balance sheet. (687)

adjusted trial balance The trial balance prepared after all the adjusting entries have been posted. (123)

adjusting entries The journal entries that bring the accounts up to date at the end of the accounting period. (105)

adjusting process An analysis and updating of the accounts when financial statements are prepared. (105)

administrative expenses (general expenses) Expenses incurred in the administration or general operations of the business. (257)

aging the receivables The process of analyzing the accounts receivable and classifying them according to various age groupings, with the due date being the base point for determining age. (409)

Allowance for Doubtful Accounts The contra asset account for accounts receivable. (405)

allowance method The method of accounting for uncollectible accounts that provides an expense for uncollectible receivables in advance of their write-off. (403)

amortization The periodic transfer of the cost of an intangible asset to expense. (462)

assets The resources owned by a business. (9, 54)

available-for-sale securities Securities that management expects to sell in the future but which are not actively traded for profit. (679)

average inventory cost flow method The method of inventory costing that is based on the assumption that costs should be charged against revenue by using the weighted average unit cost of the items sold. (314)

B

Bad Debt Expense The operating expense incurred because of the failure to collect receivables. (403)

balance of the account The amount of the difference between the debits and the credits that have been entered into an account. (53)

balance sheet A list of the assets, liabilities, and owner's equity as of a specific date, usually at the close of the last day of a month or a year. (15)

bank reconciliation The analysis that details the items responsible for the difference between the cash balance reported in the bank statement and the balance of the cash account in the ledger. (369)

bank statement A summary of all transactions mailed to the depositor or made available online by the bank each month. (366)

bond A form of an interest-bearing note used by corporations to borrow on a long-term basis. (626)

bond indenture The contract between a corporation issuing bonds and the bondholders. (628)

book value The cost of a fixed asset minus accumulated depreciation on the asset. (455)

book value of the asset (or net book value) The difference between the cost of a fixed asset and its accumulated depreciation. (118)

boot The amount a buyer owes a seller when a fixed asset is traded in on a similar asset. (468)

business An organization in which basic resources (inputs), such as materials and labor, are assembled and processed to provide goods or services (outputs) to customers. (2)

business combination A business making an investment in another business by acquiring a controlling share, often greater than 50%, of the outstanding voting stock of another corporation by paying cash or exchanging stock. (676)

business entity concept A concept of accounting that limits the economic data in the accounting system to data related directly to the activities of the business. (7)

business transaction An economic event or condition that directly changes an entity's financial condition or directly affects its results of operations. (9)

C

capital account An account used for a proprietorship that represents the owner's equity. (54)

capital expenditures The costs of acquiring fixed assets, adding to a fixed asset, improving a fixed asset, or extending a fixed asset's useful life. (449)

capital leases Leases that include one or more provisions that result in treating the leased assets as purchased assets in the accounts. (450)

carrying amount The balance of the bonds payable account (face amount of the bonds) less any unamortized discount or plus any unamortized premium. (635)

cash Coins, currency (paper money), checks, money orders, and money on deposit that is available for unrestricted withdrawal from banks and other financial institutions. (363)

cash basis of accounting Under this basis of accounting, revenues and expenses are reported in the income statement in the period in which cash is received or paid. (104)

cash dividend A cash distribution of earnings by a corporation to its shareholders. (590)

cash equivalents Highly liquid investments that are usually reported with cash on the balance sheet. (374)

cash flow per share Normally computed as cash flow from operations per share. (721)

cash flows from financing activities The section of the statement of cash flows that reports cash flows from transactions affecting the equity and debt of the business. (719)

cash flows from investing activities The section of the statement of cash flows that reports cash flows from transactions affecting investments in noncurrent assets. (718)

cash flows from operating activities The section of the statement of cash flows that reports the cash transactions affecting the determination of net income. (718)

cash payments journal The special journal in which all cash payments are recorded. (217)

cash receipts journal The special journal in which all cash receipts are recorded. (212)

cash short and over account An account which has recorded errors in cash sales or errors in making change causing the amount of actual cash on hand to differ from the beginning amount of cash plus the cash sales for the day. (364)

Certified Public Accountant (CPA) Public accountants who have met a state's education, experience, and examination requirements. (6)

chart of accounts A list of the accounts in the ledger. (54)

clearing account Another name for the income summary account because it has the effect of clearing the revenue and expense accounts of their balances. (157)

closing entries The entries that transfer the balances of the revenue, expense, and drawing accounts to the owner's capital account. (156)

closing process The transfer process of converting temporary account balances to zero by transferring the revenue and expense account balances to Income Summary, transferring the income summary account balance to the owner's capital account, and transferring the owner's drawing account to the owner's capital account. (156)

closing the books The process of transferring temporary accounts balances to permanent accounts at the end of the accounting period. (156)

common stock The stock outstanding when a corporation has issued only one class of stock. (585)

common-sized statement A financial statement in which all items are expressed only in relative terms. (778)

compensating balance A requirement by some banks requiring depositors to maintain minimum cash balances in their bank accounts. (375)

comprehensive income All changes in stockholders' equity during a period, except those resulting from dividends and stockholders' investments. (686)

consigned inventory Merchandise that is shipped by manufacturers to retailers who act as the manufacturer's selling agent. (327)

consignee The name for the retailer in a consigned inventory arrangement. (327)

consignor The name for the manufacturer in a consigned inventory arrangement. (327)

consolidated financial statements Financial statements resulting from combining parent and subsidiary statements. (676)

contingent liabilities Liabilities that may arise from past transactions if certain events occur in the future. (507)

contra account (or contra asset account) An account offset against another account. (117)

contract rate The periodic interest to be paid on the bonds that is identified in the bond indenture; expressed as a percentage of the face amount of the bond. (629)

control environment The overall attitude of management and employees about the importance of controls. (359)

controlling account The account in the general ledger that summarizes the balances of the accounts in a subsidiary ledger. (207)

copyright An exclusive right to publish and sell a literary, artistic, or musical composition. (463)

corporation A business organized under state or federal statutes as a separate legal entity. (8)

correcting journal entry An entry that is prepared when an error has already been journalized and posted. (72)

cost concept A concept of accounting that determines the amount initially entered into the accounting records for purchases. (8)

cost method A method of accounting for equity investments representing less than 20% of the outstanding shares of the investee. The purchase is at original cost, and any gains or losses upon sale are recognized by the difference between the sale proceeds and the original cost. (673)

cost of merchandise sold The cost that is reported as an expense when merchandise is sold. (254)

credit memorandum (credit memo) A form used by a seller to inform the buyer of the amount the seller proposes to credit to the account receivable due from the buyer. (263)

credit period The amount of time the buyer is allowed in which to pay the seller. (262)

credit terms Terms for payment on account by the buyer to the seller. (262)

credits Amounts entered on the right side of an account. (53)

cumulative preferred stock Stock that has a right to receive regular dividends that were not declared (paid) in prior years. (586)

current assets Cash and other assets that are expected to be converted to cash or sold or used up, usually within one year or less, through the normal operations of the business. (155)

current liabilities Liabilities that will be due within a short time (usually one year or less) and that are to be paid out of current assets. (155)

current position analysis A company's ability to pay its current liabilities. (509, 780)

current ratio A financial ratio that is computed by dividing current assets by current liabilities. (175, 780)

D

debit memorandum (debit memo) A form used by a buyer to inform the seller of the amount the buyer proposes to debit to the account payable due the seller. (267)

debits Amounts entered on the left side of an account. (53)

debt securities Notes and bond investments that provide interest revenue over a fixed maturity. (669)

deficiency The debit balance in the owner's equity account of a partner. (555)

deficit A debit balance in the retained earnings account. (585)

defined benefit plan A pension plan that promises employees a fixed annual pension benefit at retirement, based on years of service and compensation levels. (505)

defined contribution plan A pension plan that requires a fixed amount of money to be invested on the employee's behalf during the employee's working years. (505)

depletion The process of transferring the cost of natural resources to an expense account. (461)

depreciate To lose usefulness as all fixed assets except land do. (117)

depreciation The systematic periodic transfer of the cost of a fixed asset to an expense account during its expected useful life. (117, 451)

depreciation expense The portion of the cost of a fixed asset that is recorded as an expense each year of its useful life. (117)

direct method A method of reporting the cash flows from operating activities as the difference between the operating cash receipts and the operating cash payments. (719)

direct write-off method The method of accounting for uncollectible accounts that recognizes the expense only when accounts are judged to be worthless. (403)

discount The interest deducted from the maturity value of a note or the excess of the face amount of bonds over their issue price. (587, 629)

dishonored note receivable A note that the maker fails to pay on the due date. (415)

dividend yield A ratio, computed by dividing the annual dividends paid per share of common stock by the market price per share at a specific date, that indicates the rate of return to stockholders in terms of cash dividend distributions. (685, 793)

dividends Distribution of a corporation's earnings to stockholders. (584)

dividends per share Measures the extent to which earnings are being distributed to common shareholders. (792)

double-declining-balance method A method of depreciation that provides periodic depreciation expense based on the declining book value of a fixed asset over its estimated life. (455)

double-entry accounting system A system of accounting for recording transactions, based on recording increases and decreases in accounts so that debits equal credits. (55)

drawing The account used to record amounts withdrawn by an owner of a proprietorship. (54)

E

earnings per common share (EPS) Net income per share of common stock outstanding during a period. (600, 627)

earnings per share (EPS) on common stock The profitability ratio of net income available to common shareholders to the number of common shares outstanding. (627, 791)

e-commerce The use of the Internet for performing business transactions. (223)

effective interest rate method The method of amortizing discounts and premiums that provides for a constant rate of interest on the carrying amount of the bonds at the beginning of each period; often called simply the "interest method." (632)

effective rate of interest The market rate of interest at the time bonds are issued. (629)

electronic funds transfer (EFT) A system in which computers rather than paper (money, checks, etc.) are used to effect cash transactions. (365)

elements of internal control The control environment, risk assessment, control activities, information and communication, and monitoring. (358)

employee fraud The intentional act of deceiving an employer for personal gain. (358)

employee's earnings record A detailed record of each employee's earnings. (500)

equity method A method of accounting for an investment in common stock by which the investment account is adjusted for the investor's share of periodic net income and cash dividends of the investee. (674)

equity securities The common and preferred stock of a firm. (669)

ethics Moral principles that guide the conduct of individuals. (4)

expenses Assets used up or services consumed in the process of generating revenues. (12, 55)

F

fair value The price that would be received for selling an asset or paying off a liability, often the market price for an equity or debt security. (677)

fees earned Revenue from providing services. (12)

FICA tax Federal Insurance Contributions Act tax used to finance federal programs for old-age and disability benefits (social security) and health insurance for the aged (Medicare). (496)

financial accounting The branch of accounting that is concerned with recording transactions using generally accepted accounting principles (GAAP) for a business or other economic unit and with a periodic preparation of various statements from such records. (3)

Financial Accounting Standards Board (FASB) The authoritative body that has the primary responsibility for developing accounting principles. (7)

financial statements Financial reports that summarize the effects of events on a business. (15)

first-in, first-out (FIFO) inventory cost flow method The method of inventory costing based on the assumption that the costs of merchandise sold should be charged against revenue in the order in which the costs were incurred. (314)

fiscal year The annual accounting period adopted by a business. (173)

fixed asset turnover ratio The number of dollars of sales that are generated from each dollar of average fixed assets during the year, computed by dividing the net sales by the average net fixed assets. (466)

fixed assets (or plant assets) Long-term or relatively permanent tangible assets such as equipment, machinery, and buildings that are used in the normal business operations and that depreciate over time. (116, 155, 446)

FOB (free on board) destination Freight terms in which the seller pays the transportation costs from the shipping point to the final destination. (269)

FOB (free on board) shipping point Freight terms in which the buyer pays the transportation costs from the shipping point to the final destination. (269)

free cash flow The amount of operating cash flow remaining after replacing current productive capacity and maintaining current dividends. (737)

freight in Costs of transportation. (255)

fringe benefits Benefits provided to employees in addition to wages and salaries. (504)

G

general journal The two-column form used for entries that do not "fit" in any of the special journals. (208)

general ledger The primary ledger, when used in conjunction with subsidiary ledgers, that contains all of the balance sheet and income statement accounts. (207)

general-purpose financial statements A type of financial accounting report that is distributed to external users. The term "general purpose" refers to the wide range of decision-making needs that the reports are designed to serve. (4)

generally accepted accounting principles (GAAP) Generally accepted guidelines for the preparation of financial statements. (7)

goodwill An intangible asset that is created from such favorable factors as location, product quality, reputation, and managerial skill. (463)

gross pay The total earnings of an employee for a payroll period. (494)

gross profit Sales minus the cost of merchandise sold. (254)

gross profit method A method of estimating inventory cost that is based on the relationship of gross profit to sales. (333)

H

held-to-maturity securities Investments in bonds or other debt securities that management intends to hold to their maturity. (681)

horizontal analysis Financial analysis that compares an item in a current statement with the same item in prior statements. (73, 774)

I

in arrears Cumulative preferred stock dividends that have not been paid in prior years are said to be in arrears. (586)

income from operations (operating income) Revenues less operating expenses and service department charges for a profit or an investment center. (257)

income statement A summary of the revenue and expenses for a specific period of time, such as a month or a year. (15)

Income Summary An account to which the revenue and expense account balances are transferred at the end of a period. (157)

indirect method A method of reporting the cash flows from operating activities as the net income from operations adjusted for all deferrals of past cash receipts and payments and all accruals of expected future cash receipts and payments. (720)

installment note A debt that requires the borrower to make equal periodic payments to the lender for the term of the note. (636)

intangible assets Long-term assets that are useful in the operations of a business, are not held for sale, and are without physical qualities. (462)

interest revenue Money received for interest. (12)

internal controls The policies and procedures used to safeguard assets, ensure accurate business information, and ensure compliance with laws and regulations. (207, 356)

International Accounting Standards Board (IASB) An organization that issues International Financial Reporting Standards for many countries outside the United States. (7)

inventory analysis A company's ability to manage its inventory effectively. (783)

inventory shrinkage (inventory shortage) The amount by which the merchandise for sale, as indicated by the balance of the merchandise inventory account, is larger than the total amount of merchandise counted during the physical inventory. (274)

inventory turnover The relationship between the volume of goods sold and inventory, computed by dividing the cost of goods sold by the average inventory. (330, 784)

investee The company whose stock is purchased by the investor. (672)

investments The balance sheet caption used to report long-term investments in stocks not intended as a source of cash in the normal operations of the business. (669)

investor The company investing in another company's stock. (672)

invoice The bill that the seller sends to the buyer. (209, 262)

J

journal The initial record in which the effects of a transaction are recorded. (57)

journal entry The form of recording a transaction in a journal. (58)

journalizing The process of recording a transaction in the journal. (58)

L

last-in, first-out (LIFO) inventory cost flow method A method of inventory costing based on the assumption that the most recent merchandise inventory costs should be charged against revenue. (314)

ledger A group of accounts for a business. (54)

liabilities The rights of creditors that represent debts of the business. (9, 54)

limited liability company (LLC) A business form consisting of one or more persons or entities filing an operating agreement with a state to conduct business with limited liability to the owners, yet treated as a partnership for tax purposes. (8, 540)

liquidation The winding-up process when a partnership goes out of business. (550)

liquidity The ability to convert assets into cash. (174)

long-term liabilities Liabilities that usually will not be due for more than one year. (155)

lower-of-cost-or-market (LCM) method A method of valuing inventory that reports the inventory at the lower of its cost or current market value (replacement cost). (324)

M

management (or managerial) accounting The branch of accounting that uses both historical and estimated data in providing information that management uses in conducting daily operations, in planning future operations, and in developing overall business strategies. (3)

Management's Discussion and Analysis (MD&A) An annual report disclosure that provides management's analysis of the results of operations and financial condition. (795)

manufacturing business A type of business that changes basic inputs into products that are sold to individual customers. (2)

market rate of interest The rate determined from sales and purchases of similar bonds. (629)

matching concept (or matching principle) A concept of accounting in which expenses are matched with the revenue generated during a period by those expenses. (15, 104)

maturity value The amount that is due at the maturity or due date of a note. (414)

merchandise available for sale The cost of merchandise available for sale to customers calculated by adding the beginning merchandise inventory to net purchases. (255)

merchandise inventory Merchandise on hand (not sold) at the end of an accounting period. (254)

merchandising business A type of business that purchases products from other businesses and sells them to customers. (2)

mortgage notes An installment note that may be secured by a pledge of the borrower's assets. (636)

multiple-step income statement A form of income statement that contains several sections, subsections, and subtotals. (255)

N

natural business year A fiscal year that ends when business activities have reached the lowest point in an annual operating cycle. (174)

net income or net profit The amount by which revenues exceed expenses. (15)

net loss The amount by which expenses exceed revenues. (15)

net pay Gross pay less payroll deductions; the amount the employer is obligated to pay the employee. (494)

net realizable value The estimated selling price of an item of inventory less any direct costs of disposal, such as sales commissions. (325, 405)

net sales Revenue received for merchandise sold to customers less any sales returns and allowances and sales discounts. (257)

normal balance of an account The normal balance of an account can be either a debit or a credit depending on whether increases in the account are recorded as debits or credits. (56)

notes receivable A customer's written promise to pay an amount and possibly interest at an agreed-upon rate. (155, 402)

number of days' sales in inventory The relationship between the volume of sales and inventory, computed by dividing the inventory at the end of the year by the average daily cost of goods sold. (330, 784)

number of days' sales in receivables The relationship between sales and accounts receivable, computed by dividing the net accounts receivable at the end of the year by the average daily sales. (417, 783)

number of times interest charges are earned A ratio that measures creditor margin of safety for interest payments, calculated as income before interest and taxes divided by interest expense. (639, 786)

O

objectivity concept A concept of accounting that requires accounting records and the data reported in financial statements to be based on objective evidence. (8)

operating leases Leases that do not meet the criteria for capital leases and thus are accounted for as operating expenses. (451)

other comprehensive income Specified items that are reported separately from net income, including foreign currency items, pension liability adjustments, and unrealized gains and losses on investments. (686)

other expense Expenses that cannot be traced directly to operations. (258)

other income Revenue from sources other than the primary operating activity of a business. (258)

outstanding stock The stock in the hands of stockholders. (585)

owner's equity The owner's right to the assets of the business. (9, 54)

P

paid-in capital Capital contributed to a corporation by the stockholders and others. (584)

par The monetary amount printed on a stock certificate. (585)

parent company The corporation owning all or a majority of the voting stock of the other corporation. (676)

partnership An unincorporated business form consisting of two or more persons conducting business as co-owners for profit. (7, 539)

partnership agreement The formal written contract creating a partnership. (539)

patents Exclusive rights to produce and sell goods with one or more unique features. (462)

payroll The total amount paid to employees for a certain period. (493)

payroll register A multicolumn report used to assemble and summarize payroll data at the end of each payroll period. (498)

pension A cash payment to retired employees. (505)

periodic inventory system The inventory system in which the inventory records do not show the amount available for sale or sold during the period. (257)

perpetual inventory system The inventory system in which each purchase and sale of merchandise is recorded in an inventory account. (257)

petty cash fund A special cash fund to pay relatively small amounts. (373)

physical inventory A detailed listing of merchandise on hand. (313)

posting The process of transferring the debits and credits from the journal entries to the accounts. (61)

preferred stock A class of stock with preferential rights over common stock. (586)

premium The excess of the issue price of a stock over its par value or the excess of the issue price of bonds over their face amount. (587, 629)

prepaid expenses Items such as supplies that will be used in the business in the future. (11, 105)

price-earnings (P/E) ratio The ratio of the market price per share of common stock, at a specific date, to the annual earnings per share. (792)

prior period adjustments Corrections of material errors related to a prior period or periods, excluded from the determination of net income. (597)

private accounting The field of accounting whereby accountants are employed by a business firm or a not-for-profit organization. (3)

profit The difference between the amounts received from customers for goods or services provided and the amounts paid for the inputs used to provide the goods or services. (2)

profitability The ability of a firm to earn income. (779)

proprietorship A business owned by one individual. (7)

public accounting The field of accounting where accountants and their staff provide services on a fee basis. (6)

public companies Companies that issue publicly traded debt or equity securities. (D-1)

purchase order The purchase order authorizes the purchase of the inventory from an approved vendor. (312)

purchase return or allowance From the buyer's perspective, returned merchandise or an adjustment for defective merchandise. (267)

purchases discounts Discounts taken by the buyer for early payment of an invoice. (266)

purchases journal The journal in which all items purchased on account are recorded. (214)

Q

quick assets Cash and other current assets that can be quickly converted to cash, such as marketable securities and receivables. (510, 781)

quick ratio A financial ratio that measures the ability to pay current liabilities with quick assets (cash, marketable securities, accounts receivable). (510, 781)

R

rate earned on common stockholders' equity A measure of profitability computed by dividing net income, reduced by preferred dividend requirements, by common stockholders' equity. (789)

rate earned on stockholders' equity A measure of profitability computed by dividing net income by total stockholders' equity. (789)

rate earned on total assets A measure of the profitability of assets, without regard to the equity of creditors and stockholders in the assets. (788)

ratio of cash to monthly cash expenses Ratio that helps assess how long a company can continue to operate without additional financing or generating positive cash flows from operations. (375)

ratio of fixed assets to long-term liabilities A leverage ratio that measures the margin of safety of long-term creditors, calculated as the net fixed assets divided by the long-term liabilities. (785)

ratio of liabilities to stockholders' equity A comprehensive leverage ratio that measures the relationship of the claims of creditors to stockholders' equity. (21, 785)

ratio of net sales to assets Ratio that measures how effectively a company uses its assets, computed as net sales divided by average total assets. (276, 787)

real (permanent) accounts Term for balance sheet accounts because they are relatively permanent and carried forward from year to year. (156)

realization The sale of assets when a partnership is being liquidated. (550)

receivables All money claims against other entities, including people, business firms, and other organizations. (402)

receiving report The form or electronic transmission used by the receiving personnel to indicate that materials have been received and inspected. (312)

rent revenue Money received for rent. (12)

report form The form of balance sheet with the Liabilities and Owner's Equity sections presented below the Assets section. (259)

residual value The estimated value of a fixed asset at the end of its useful life. (451)

restrictions Amounts of retained earnings that have been limited for use as dividends. (597)

retail inventory method A method of estimating inventory cost that is based on the relationship of gross profit to sales. (332)

retained earnings Net income retained in a corporation. (584)

retained earnings statement A summary of the changes in the retained earnings in a corporation for a specific period of time, such as a month or a year. (596)

revenue expenditures Costs that benefit only the current period or costs incurred for normal maintenance and repairs of fixed assets. (449)

revenue journal The journal in which all sales and services on account are recorded. (209)

revenue recognition concept The accounting concept that supports reporting revenues when the services are provided to customers. (104)

revenues Increases in owner's equity as a result of selling services or products to customers. (11, 54)

rules of debit and credit In the double-entry accounting system, specific rules for recording debits and credits based on the type of account. (55)

S

sales The total amount charged customers for merchandise sold, including cash sales and sales on account. (12, 256)

sales discounts From the seller's perspective, discounts that a seller may offer the buyer for early payment. (256)

sales returns and allowances From the seller's perspective, returned merchandise or an adjustment for defective merchandise. (256)

Sarbanes-Oxley Act of 2002 An act passed by Congress to restore public confidence and trust in the financial statements of companies. (356)

Securities and Exchange Commission (SEC) An agency of the U.S. government that has authority over the accounting and financial disclosures for companies whose shares of ownership (stock) are traded and sold to the public. (7)

selling expenses Expenses that are incurred directly in the selling of merchandise. (257)

service business A business providing services rather than products to customers. (2)

single-step income statement A form of income statement in which the total of all expenses is deducted from the total of all revenues. (258)

slide An error in which the entire number is moved one or more spaces to the right or the left, such as writing $542.00 as $54.20 or $5,420.00. (71)

solvency The ability of a firm to pay its debts as they come due. (174, 779)

special journals Journals designed to be used for recording a single type of transaction. (207)

special-purpose fund A cash fund used for a special business need. (374)

specific identification inventory cost flow method Inventory method in which the unit sold is identified with a specific purchase. (314)

statement of cash flows A summary of the cash receipts and cash payments for a specific period of time, such as a month or a year. (15, 718)

statement of members' equity A summary of the changes in each member's equity in a limited liability corporation that have occurred during a specific period of time. (557)

statement of owner's equity A summary of the changes in owner's equity that have occurred during a specific period of time, such as a month or a year. (15)

statement of partnership equity A summary of the changes in each partner's capital in a partnership that have occurred during a specific period of time. (557)

statement of partnership liquidation A summary of the liquidation process whereby cash is distributed to the partners based on the balances in their capital accounts. (552)

statement of stockholders' equity A summary of the changes in the stockholders' equity in a corporation that have occurred during a specific period of time. (598)

stock Shares of ownership of a corporation. (582)

stock dividend A distribution of shares of stock to its stockholders. (592)

stock split A reduction in the par or stated value of a common stock and the issuance of a proportionate number of additional shares. (599)

stockholders The owners of a corporation. (582)

stockholders' equity The owners' equity in a corporation. (584)

straight-line method A method of depreciation that provides for equal periodic depreciation expense over the estimated life of a fixed asset. (453)

subsidiary company The corporation that is controlled by a parent company. (676)

subsidiary inventory ledger The subsidiary ledger containing individual accounts for items of inventory. (313)

subsidiary ledger A ledger containing individual accounts with a common characteristic. (207)

T

T account The simplest form of an account. (52)

temporary (nominal) accounts Accounts that report amounts for only one period. (156)

trade discounts Discounts from the list prices in published catalogs or special discounts offered to certain classes of buyers. (272)

trade-in allowance The amount a seller allows a buyer for a fixed asset that is traded in for a similar asset. (468)

trademark A name, term, or symbol used to identify a business and its products. (463)

trading securities Securities that management intends to actively trade for profit. (677)

transposition An error in which the order of the digits is changed, such as writing $542 as $452 or $524. (71)

treasury stock Stock that a corporation has once issued and then reacquires. (593)

trial balance A summary listing of the titles and balances of accounts in the ledger. (70)

U

unadjusted trial balance A summary listing of the titles and balances of accounts in the ledger prior to the posting of adjusting entries. (71)

unearned revenue The liability created by receiving revenue in advance. (63, 106)

unit of measure concept A concept of accounting requiring that economic data be recorded in dollars. (8)

units-of-production method A method of depreciation that provides for depreciation expense based on the expected productive capacity of a fixed asset. (453)

unrealized gain or loss Changes in the fair value of equity or debt securities for a period. (677)

V

vertical analysis An analysis that compares each item in a current statement with a total amount within the same statement. (125, 777)

voucher A special form for recording relevant data about a liability and the details of its payment. (366)

voucher system A set of procedures for authorizing and recording liabilities and cash payments. (366)

W

working capital The excess of the current assets of a business over its current liabilities. (174, 780)

Subject Index

Company Index

Abbreviations and Acronyms Commonly Used in Business and Accounting

AAA	American Accounting Association
ABC	Activity-based costing
AICPA	American Institute of Certified Public Accountants
CIA	Certified Internal Auditor
CIM	Computer-integrated manufacturing
CMA	Certified Management Accountant
CPA	Certified Public Accountant
Cr.	Credit
Dr.	Debit
EFT	Electronic funds transfer
EPS	Earnings per share
FAF	Financial Accounting Foundation
FASB	Financial Accounting Standards Board
FEI	Financial Executives International
FICA tax	Federal Insurance Contributions Act tax
FIFO	First-in, first-out
FOB	Free on board
GAAP	Generally accepted accounting principles
GASB	Governmental Accounting Standards Board
GNP	Gross National Product
IMA	Institute of Management Accountants
IRC	Internal Revenue Code
IRS	Internal Revenue Service
JIT	Just-in-time
LIFO	Last-in, first-out
Lower of C or M	Lower of cost or market
MACRS	Modified Accelerated Cost Recovery System
n/30	Net 30
n/eom	Net, end-of-month
P/E Ratio	Price-earnings ratio
POS	Point of sale
ROI	Return on investment
SEC	Securities and Exchange Commission
TQC	Total quality control

Classification of Accounts

Account Title	Account Classification	Normal Balance	Financial Statement
Accounts Payable	Current liability	Credit	Balance sheet
Accounts Receivable	Current asset	Debit	Balance sheet
Accumulated Depletion	Contra fixed asset	Credit	Balance sheet
Accumulated Depreciation	Contra fixed asset	Credit	Balance sheet
Advertising Expense	Operating expense	Debit	Income statement
Allowance for Doubtful Accounts	Contra current asset	Credit	Balance sheet
Amortization Expense	Operating expense	Debit	Income statement
Bonds Payable	ZLong-term liability	Credit	Balance sheet
Building	Fixed asset	Debit	Balance sheet
_____ Capital	Owner's equity	Credit	Statement of owner's equity/ Balance sheet
Capital Stock	Stockholders' equity	Credit	Balance sheet
Cash	Current asset	Debit	Balance sheet
Cash Dividends	Stockholders' equity	Debit	Retained earnings statement
Cash Dividends Payable	Current liability	Credit	Balance sheet
Common Stock	Stockholders' equity	Credit	Balance sheet
Cost of Merchandise (Goods) Sold	Cost of merchandise (goods sold)	Debit	Income statement
Deferred Income Tax Payable	Current liability/Long-term liability	Credit	Balance sheet
Delivery Expense	Operating expense	Debit	Income statement
Depletion Expense	Operating expense	Debit	Income statement
Discount on Bonds Payable	Long-term liability	Debit	Balance sheet
Dividend Revenue	Other income	Credit	Income statement
Dividends	Stockholders' equity	Debit	Retained earnings statement
_____ Drawing	Owner's equity	Debit	Statement of owner's equity
Employees Federal Income Tax Payable	Current liability	Credit	Balance sheet
Equipment	Fixed asset	Debit	Balance sheet
Exchange Gain	Other income	Credit	Income statement
Exchange Loss	Other expense	Debit	Income statement
Factory Overhead (Overapplied)	Deferred credit	Credit	Balance sheet (interim)
Factory Overhead (Underapplied)	Deferred debit	Debit	Balance sheet (interim)
Federal Income Tax Payable	Current liability	Credit	Balance sheet
Federal Unemployment Tax Payable	Current liability	Credit	Balance sheet
Finished Goods	Current asset	Debit	Balance sheet
Freight In	Cost of merchandise sold	Debit	Income statement
Freight Out	Operating expense	Debit	Income statement
Gain on Disposal of Fixed Assets	Other income	Credit	Income statement
Gain on Redemption of Bonds	Other income	Credit	Income statement
Gain on Sale of Investments	Other income	Credit	Income statement
Goodwill	Intangible asset	Debit	Balance sheet
Income Tax Expense	Income tax	Debit	Income statement
Income Tax Payable	Current liability	Credit	Balance sheet
Insurance Expense	Operating expense	Debit	Income statement
Interest Expense	Other expense	Debit	Income statement
Interest Receivable	Current asset	Debit	Balance sheet
Interest Revenue	Other income	Credit	Income statement
Investment in Bonds	Investment	Debit	Balance sheet
Investment in Stocks	Investment	Debit	Balance sheet
Investment in Subsidiary	Investment	Debit	Balance sheet
Land	Fixed asset	Debit	Balance sheet
Loss on Disposal of Fixed Assets	Other expense	Debit	Income statement
Loss on Redemption of Bonds	Other expense	Debit	Income statement